CŪḶAVAṂSA

CŪḶAVAMSA

Being the More Recent Part of the

MAHĀVAMSA

[*Two Parts Bound in One*]

Translated by

WILHELM GEIGER

And From the German into English by

MRS. C. MABEL RICKMERS (NÉE DUFF)

Author of "The Chronology of India"

MOTILAL BANARSIDASS PUBLISHERS
PRIVATE LIMITED • DELHI

First Indian Edition: Delhi, 1996

ISBN: 81-208-1300-6

Also available at:
MOTILAL BANARSIDASS
41 U.A. Bungalow Road, Jawahar Nagar, Delhi 110 007
120 Royapettah High Road, Mylapore, Madras 600 004
16 St. Mark's Road, Bangalore 560 001
8 Camac Street, Calcutta 700 017
Ashok Rajpath, Patna 800 004
Chowk, Varanasi 221 001

PRINTED IN INDIA

BY JAINENDRA PRAKASH JAIN AT SHRI JAINENDRA PRESS,
A-45 NARAINA, PHASE I, NEW DELHI 110 028
AND PUBLISHED BY NARENDRA PRAKASH JAIN FOR
MOTILAL BANARSIDASS PUBLISHERS PRIVATE LIMITED,
BUNGALOW ROAD, DELHI 110 007

To

Mrs. C. A. F. Rhys Davids

in sincere veneration
and friendship

W. G.

PART I

FOREWORD

On completing the first volume of my translation of the Cūlavaṃsa, I feel it to be my duty above all to tender my most hearty thanks to the Government of Ceylon for the opportunity it gave me of visiting the Island before beginning my work. In Colombo Mr. M. A. Young, at that time First Assistant Colonial Secretary, arranged matters for me in the kindest manner.

My thanks are no less due to my esteemed colleagues in England whose friendly advocacy and recommendation did so much towards furthering affairs.

Without the journey which took me into all parts of the Island, I should have been without that vivid idea of the country and the people which is necessary for the understanding of their history. Without it too, I should have lost that mass of information and the stimulating intercourse which met me in Ceylon from the most varied quarters.

I mention in the first place with special pleasure and sincere gratitude the present Archaeological Commissioner, Mr. A. M. Hocart, whose lively and intelligent interest in my aims and tasks I shall always remember, as well as that of his temporary representative, Mr. Sudbury. In their company I was able to visit a series of important ruins partly in very out of the way places, and so familiarize myself with some of the most pressing questions connected with ancient Sinhalese architecture.

In the same way I owe warm thanks to Mr. H. W. Codrington. Himself the greatest authority on the history and mediaeval topography of Ceylon, he gave me much help and ready encouragement, as a glance at the notes to my translation will show.

Mr. P. E. Pieris also smoothed many a path for me and to his good offices I owe many a valuable connection. Of my old friends I may mention lastly in this place the indefatigable Mudaliyar A. M. Gunasekara. I must add however, that wherever I came, new Sinhalese friends — amongst others I may mention Ratemahatmaya Bibile — gave me willing and active support.

My principle in working has been to make my translation approach as closely as possible to the original. We must as far as is practicable, know exactly what the chroniclers say. The aesthetic value of the Cūlavaṃsa as a literary work is small. The carrying out of this principle has been made more difficult by the fact that the German text has had to be re-translated into English. I am however greatly indebted to my co-worker, Mrs. C. Mabel Rickmers, for most kindly making my principle her own, in doing which I believe her to have achieved full success.

One difficulty met with by every translator of an Indian text lies in the multitude of the synonyms. It is impossible for us to imitate them. Consider for a moment the many terms for "King". In order to be as fair as possible to the conditions of the original, we have reserved, though with occasional exceptions, the translation "King" for *rājan.* Combinations with *pati* (like *dharaṇīpati* etc.) we have rendered by "ruler", those with *pa* or *pāla* (like *bhūmipa* etc.) by "monarch", other terms by "sovereign". That proper names with variants such as *Parakkamabāhu* and *-bhuja* have been unified will probably meet with approval.

The second volume will contain a detailed chronological introduction with a list of the kings, as well as a full index. As the German text is almost finished and the English rendering already in progress, we should not now have to wait long for the completion of the whole work.

The last ten chapters it is true, are not an unmixed joy for the translator. The language is faulty, the style clumsy, often very stilted. Instead of the long-winded, stereotyped descriptions of festivals and bounties, one would like to hear more of those outward events which just in the 16 th, 17 th and 18 th centuries shook the old Sinhalese kingdom to its foundations. To make good the omissions of the Chronicle here would mean writing a new history of Ceylon. This has already been done by more competent scholars and where it seemed desirable, I have referred to their works in my notes.

Lastly I would ask the reader before using the book, to be kind enough to consult the appendices and to take note of corrections and also of emendations in the original text.

Munich-Neubiberg
November 1928

WILH. GEIGER.

INTRODUCTION

I

As to the credibility of the Cūlavaṃsa: the history of Parakkamabāhu's youth

The question of the credibility of the Cūlavaṃsa cannot be answered with a simple yes or no. It is somewhat more complicated than that of the more ancient Mahāvaṃsa whose author kept more closely and I might say, more naively to his source. One thing is certain: the compiler of the first part of the Cūlavaṃsa (chaps. 37–79) with which I am at present dealing, did not consciously relate what was false. What he tells us is drawn from his own knowledge, as derived from his. sources and his personal conviction. That much valuable material is contained therein is shown by the way in which various statements are confirmed by inscriptions. In the notes to my translation I have repeatedly referred to these corroborations of the Cūlavaṃsa. Moreover statements in one part of the work are frequently confirmed by passages in another part. How remarkably for instance, do the geographical data in chaps. 65–67 regarding the flight of Prince Parakkamabāhu from Saṅkhatthalī in Dakkhiṇadesa correspond with those in chaps. 70 and 72 in the description of the campaign against Rājaraṭṭha. Codrington has shown that plainly enough.

But two points must be borne in mind. The compiler — let us call him Dhammakitti — was after all a bhikkhu and the sources of which he made use were written by bhikkhus, the records forming the foundation were written down in the spirit and in the interests of the Buddhist Church. They were in the main apparently *puññapotthakāni* (cf. Mhvs. 32. 25) that is registers of meritorious works by which the prince had furthered the Church (*sāsana*) and the laity (*loka*). About such things therefore we are particularly well informed. We hear of the vihāras built by the king, of the repairs he had had undertaken on the more ancient buildings, of his bounty to the needy, the poor and the sick and above all to the priesthood. Of much however, equally interesting if not more interesting to the historian we hear nothing at all. It is these gaps of which one has a growing consciousness without being able to lay one's finger with certainty on them, which constitute the chief lack in the narrative of the Cūlavaṃsa. Not what is said but what is left unsaid is the besetting difficulty of Sinhalese history.

To take but one example — how explain the fact that of so mighty a work as the fortress of Sīgiri not a single detail is described? Even the name is only mentioned in four places. And yet this is perhaps the most magnificent building of which Ceylon can boast. It is not impossible that the personality of Kassapa I. might appear in a different light if a layman and not a priest had been the author of the chronicle.

I must repeat here that not the least doubt is thrown on Dhammakitti's good faith by such criticisms. They merely point out the range of ideas by which his work was conditioned and restricted.

It is of course clear that it was not solely of such *puññāni* that Dhammakitti's sources and tradition had to tell. We hear also of secular proceedings[1] with which often enough the "meritorious works" of the princes were connected. But it is indisputable that what the Cūlavaṃsa had above all in mind was the relation of the king to the church. This relation fills so large a space in the narrative that if we follow it

---

[1] That the Sinhalese kings had records kept of the events of their reigns is clear from 59. 7-9.

alone the history of Ceylon takes on a hue not quite in keeping with fact. Unfortunately we are not in a position to fill up satisfactorily the gaps in the historical tradition. Later Sinhalese writings are not essentially different in character and the inscriptions which would undoubtedly be our best source, are unfortunately occupied almost entirely with ecclesiastical matters. Nevertheless certain of these give much desired confirmation of purely secular events mentioned in the Cūlavaṃsa. Their importance for its chronology will be dealt with later.

A further point. Already Mahānāma the author of the older Mahāvaṃsa, was fain to create a *kāvya*, an artificial poem, and he was no stranger to the rules of *alaṃkāra*. But this is true in a still higher degree of Dhammakitti. He was a man of literary culture. I believe I have proved in the notes to my translation of 66. 129 ff. that he must have been acquainted with Indian Nīti literature, perhaps with its chief work, the Arthaśāstra of Kauṭalya. These literary reminiscences were of course not without influence on his attitude towards historical events and persons.

Above all is this true of the personality of Parakkamabāhu. I should like to elaborate this point further. For Bishop Copleston is perfectly right in regarding the history of Parakkama as the real kernel, the main subject of the Cūlavaṃsa, especially of the first part which was the work of Dhammakitti, and in speaking of a Parakkama epic[1].

Now if we look closely at the figure of Parakkamabāhu as it meets us in the Cūlavaṃsa, especially at the period before he achieved universal sovereignty, we find ourselves faced by a series of contradictions and improbabilities. We are convinced that things did not happen historically in that way. Nor is it possible to form a harmonious and credible picture of the single acts attributed to the youthful Parakkama.

The explanation lies in Dhammakitti's conception of the way in which his task was to be achieved. From literary

[1] JRAS. C. B. nr. 44, 1893, p. 60 ff.

sources, from what he had read he drew an ideal picture of an Indian king. The man whose glorification was his aim must correspond to this picture. He must have all the qualities belonging to an Indian king and employ all the methods of statecraft which political science prescribes or recommends. All these individual traits the compiler combines with the data furnished by tradition, without question as to probability or improbability of these.

According to the Cūlavaṃsa the youth of Parakkama was passed somewhat as follows:

Parakkamabāhu is the son of the eldest of the three brothers Mānābharaṇa, Kittisirimegha and Sirivallabha who rule over Dakkhiṇadesa and Rohaṇa in opposition to Vikkamabāhu who holds the royal dignity in virtue of his possession of Rājaraṭṭha with its capital Pulatthinagara. Parakkama's father Mānābharaṇa has retained as his share the important province of Dakkhiṇadesa, Rohaṇa is divided between the two younger brothers.

The birth of the prince is accompanied by all kinds of miraculous phenomena. Vikkamabāhu is informed of it and wishes to bring the boy up at his court in order to make him his heir instead of his own son. Mānābharaṇa, however, refuses and dies soon after of a disease. Thereupon his next brother, Kittisirimegha takes over Dakkhiṇadesa and leaves the whole of Rohaṇa to the youngest, Sirivallabha who brings Mānābharaṇa's widow Ratanāvalī, her two daughters Mittā and Pabhāvatī and the youthful Parakkama to take up their abode in his capital of Mahānāgahula. Meanwhile Vikkamabāhu also dies and is succeeded in Rājaraṭṭha by his son Gajabāhu who maintains himself against Kittisirimegha and Sirivallabha.

The youthful Parakkama finds no scope in Rohaṇa, so he betakes himself to his uncle in Dakkhiṇadesa who receives him joyfully. He lives with him in the chief locality of the country Saṅkhatthalī. He finishes his education and his coming of age is celebrated with festivities. The Senāpati Saṅkha who was stationed in Badalatthalī, is entrusted with the preparations for the festival. Sirivallabha dies in Rohaṇa and is succeeded by his son, the younger Māṇābharaṇa.

Parakkama's ambition finds no satisfaction in Dakkhiṇadesa. He hankers after the royal dignity in Rājaraṭṭha and determines to go thither and discover conditions for himself. Of dissensions between the prince and his uncle there is never any word. On the contrary, the fiction is constantly upheld that Kittisirimegha is tenderly attached to his nephew, and that it is only fear of the dangers involved which makes him discourage the visit to Rājaraṭṭha.

So the prince leaves Saṅkhatthalī secretly and comes first to Badalatthalī where he has the Senāpati Saṅkha killed because he had informed[1]. the king of Parakkama's flight. He then goes northwards to Buddhagāma not far from the borders of Rājaraṭṭha. The inhabitants of the country make repeated efforts to check the prince's advance but he repulses all such attempts by force of arms.

Parakkama's uncle meanwhile, alarmed at his nephew's disappearance, consults with his ministers (66. 57 ff.) and sends a strong force to fetch him back. But it is ambushed by the prince and completely routed. He even pursues the pursuers (66. 82 ff.) and surprises them by a night assault in Khīravāpi. After repulsing a countre attack he proceeds to cross the frontiers of Rājaraṭṭha.

Gajabāhu is apparently greatly alarmed but puts a good face on the matter and greets the guest through messengers with gifts, marches to meet him in person and fetch him to the capital.

During his sojourn in Pulatthinagara Parakkamabāhu enmeshes the town and its surroundings in a net of espionage

---

[1] The compiler is obviously at a loss to account for Parakkama's action. In 65. 35 ff. the affair is so described as if circumstances had driven the prince to it, but he had already (v. 21 ff.) declared his intention of committing an extraordinary deed — the allusion can only be to the removal of Saṅkha — by which his courage and determination would be proved. Thus even Dhammakitti admits that the action was deliberately planned.

(66. 129 ff.). He goes the length of wedding his sister Bhaddavatī to King Gajabāhu in order to lull his suspicions. He himself keeps her dowry, or at least the greater part of it, in his own hands.

Eventually however, the prince has fears that Gajabāhu may see through his intentions and he leaves the town secretly at night to return to Dakkhiṇadesa (67. 32 ff.). During this flight he meets with all kinds of adventures in which his personal courage is put to the test. Kittisirimegha is delighted at the return of his nephew and sends messengers to Saraggāma to meet him. The prince however, hesitates — the reason is not given — to enter the capital Saṅkhatthalī. His mother comes from Rohaṇa and persuades him to do so. He is joyfully received by Kittisirimegha who dies shortly afterwards when Parakkamabāhu takes over the sovereignty of the province.

What then is the character of Parakkamabāhu if we follow tradition? Here I go beyond the chapter whose contents I have just sketched, the question is what kind of personality had Dhammakitti in mind when he gave a poetical picture of his hero. Of course he is extraordinarily fearless and courageous. High-sounding words are put into his mouth. With his weapon alone for which he calls, will he strike terror into the foe (66. 31). He is capable alone of facing all his enemies, as the lion needs no allies when he tears elephants in pieces (72. 88). No one, not even the king of the gods can cross the frontiers of his realm, so long as he is in life (72. 154). Were he fain to seize the sovereignty in Pulatthinagara, the wrinkling of his brows were sufficient thereto (67. 12).

What then of the deeds? An action reminiscent of a feat of Alexander the Great is described 66. 87 ff. during the attack on Khīravāpi. Parakkamabāhu's people are unable to break through the barricade of thorns which surrounds the place. Thereupon he pierces it alone and announces his name with resounding voice. That suffices to scatter the enemy in all directions. The scene described 66. 104 may also be mentioned here. But the narratives of the courage displayed by the prince against a she-bear that attacked him in the wilderness (67. 41) and against a boar (67. 44), savour rather of an invention of the author for elaborating the events and adorning the poem. In contrast to these we have in the miraculous story of the male elk (70. 33 ff.) which attacks Parakkamabāhu during the chase and shedding his antlers directly in front of him, falls to the ground, possibly a piece of ancient tradition. Are we not told that the antlers with an inscription describing the occurrence "are even now" preserved in the royal treasury?

In the great military engagements against Gajabāhu and still later against the revolt in Rohaṇa Parakkamabāhu keeps completely in the background. It is his generals who carry out his plans. Without doubt this tallies with the actual conditions of the time. The heroic age of a Duṭṭhagāmaṇī belongs to the past and where Parakkamabāhu is depicted as a hero of this stamp we have, at least as a rule, to do with the creations of poetic imagination, with literary ornamentation. Highly characteristic is the episode described 72. 95 ff. where it looks as if Parakkamabāhu at a critical moment intended to save the situation. He calls for his Sīhala sword. But it is not he who wields it but two of his officers whose efforts at saving the position were only partially successful.

To place Parakkamabāhu's courage in the best possible light Dhammakitti makes use of two purely literary devices. In his youth he is a harmless, almost childlike nature. He takes pleasure in music, games and dancing (70. 30–31), even on serious occasions where it seems to us almost inappropriate. When he is attacked in Nāvāgirisa by the pursuers sent by his uncle, he is playing a game to which he had been accustomed from childhood (66. 101), and when he has crossed the frontiers of the "King's Province", Rājaraṭṭha, he devotes himself for days to the local games (66. 111). When his position is apparently most critical and his attendants take flight he proudly conscious of his personal worth, has nothing but a cheerful smile (66. 30, 72. 99) even when as after the death of the Adhikārin Rakkha (72. 87), it seems to us hardly appropriate.

Again, what a brilliant contrast is Parakkamabāhu's heroism to the almost grotesque cowardice of his own people as also of the enemy. When the inhabitants of Buddhagāma prepare to attack the prince, his own people flee in all directions (66. 28). At the mere sound of his voice Kittisirimegha's soldiers in Khīravāpi take flight leaving behind their clothes and weapons (66. 90). When attacked in Nāvāgirisa his own people flee to the wilderness without striking a blow (66. 105) and only meet again when they hear their ruler's voice. Before the she-bear and the elk the people take to their heels leaving their prince in the lurch[1].

Here Dhammakitti manifestly does his countrymen an injustice. The Sinhalese are perhaps not naturally a warlike race, but they can hardly be so cowardly, so senselessly cowardly a they are here depicted. Against the Portuguese they at times gave proof of a death-despising courage. In Parakkamabāhu's times they were certainly not mere cravens. If the poet paints them as such he does it so that the figure of his hero should stand forth the more brilliantly against such a background. The methods employed by Dhammakitti for attaining this end, seem naive and clumsy enough, but we must remember that he himself as a bhikkhu would have but little idea or understanding of military matters.

The following is typical of Dhammakitti's standpoint. During all the events described in 64 and the following paricchedas it is deliberately stated that the relation between Parakkamabāhu and his uncle Kittisirimegha was always one of fatherly love on the one side and of deep gratitude on the other. The prince himself stresses this with zeal 66. 12 ff. And according to 67. 56 ff., 84 ff. the uncle welcomes the return of his nephew from Pulatthinagara with heartfelt joy.

[1] For us the description in 66. 47 ff. of how the Nagaragiri Gokaṇṇa was seized with terror as the result of a dream sounds comical, almost ludicrous. Dreams however, had at that time for the Sinhalese a quite peculiar significance, as indeed they still have.

The reason why the compiler holds so firmly to this fiction is clear. The ideal figure of Parakkama must be protected against the possible reproach of ingratitude. The facts however, will not tally with the fiction. Already the words put into the uncle's mouth 66. 58 ff. throw a different light on their relations. Then comes the brutal murder of the Senāpati Sena who was obviously a particularly loyal vassal of Kittisirimegha to whom his death must have been a painful loss. Further the fact that the prince had to fight his way through the various provinces whose inhabitants obviously looked upon him as somewhat of a rebel and traitor. Kittisirimegha himself sends troops after the fugitive who scatters them in a series of skirmishes. Without doubt the description of these fights is accompanied by a great many exaggerations. Parakkamabāhu cannot possibly come to Pulatthinagara at the head of a whole army. But the spirit in which the accounts of these conflicts are conceived is irreconcilable with the fiction of untroubled relations between uncle and nephew.

Then finally the return of the prince to Dakkhiṇadesa after Pulatthinagara had obviously become too hot to hold him. We are forced to ask what made him delay so long at the frontier (67. 59 ff.). The reason must have been his uncertainty as to the reception he was likely to get from the monarch. This explains too the part played here by Parakkamabāhu's mother. She feels it to be her task to reconcile the two or rather to induce the uncle to give his nephew a favorable reception. She plays the part of mediator.

If now we consider dispassionately the facts as set forth by he chronicle, leaving aside all the inaccuracies due to the character and tendencies of the author, we get I believe a quite intelligible picture of the youthful Parakkamabāhu.

The most striking characteristic of the prince is his ambition and his activity. In Mahānāgahula life with his mother and sisters is too restricted. He dreams of great enterprises. The union of the whole of Ceylon in his hand is the ideal before him at this period. It is possible that his mother, the proud Ratanāvalī (cf. 63. 11 ff.) inspired him with these plans and fed them. At any rate it is the idea of greater possibilities for his own activity which makes him leave Mahānāgahula and betake himself to Dakkhiṇadesa to the court of his uncle Kittisirimegha. That this province was politically of more consequence than that of Rohaṇa is clear from the way in which the provinces were divided among the three brothers, as I have shown above p. VII. Kittisirimegha has no eligible son as his successor, he receives the young prince therefore with open arms and the relation between uncle and nephew was plainly for some time a friendly one. But it changed. Owing to the bias of the chronicle, we have neither knowledge nor means of judging of the details. The main cause at any rate lay in the restless activity of the young prince. It may be that Kittisirimegha himself felt uncertain of him or that he feared being drawn by him into difficulties with Gajabāhu II., the king of Rājaraṭṭha. Parakkamabāhu will have realised himself that his position at the court of Saṅkhatthalī had become untenable. Accompanied by his devoted attendants he flees from the town at night to betake himself to King Gajabāhu. Now we see that Parakkamabāhu is by no means the innocent youth described in the chronicle. He shrinks from no deed of blood if it is in the interests of his plans and of his own safety.

The murder of the Senāpati Saṅkha seems hardly intelligible if we accept the motive alleged for it by the chronicle. The reality was certainly otherwise. We may assume that at first the prince hoped to bring Kittisirimegha's powerful vassal over to his own side. But Saṅkha remained true to his master. The prince has now reason to fear that Saṅkha may seize and deliver him up to the monarch. The danger for him is great, for Kittisirimegha would doubtless look upon him as a rebel and punish him as such. Thus he determines on extremes and has Saṅkha slain. What was thought of this deed is proved by the way it again and again later on throws its shadow on the actions of Parakkamabāhu.

Gajabāhu seems (cf. 66. 112) to have received the news of Parakkamabāhu's approach with decidedly mixed feelings. He knew of course enough of his dangerous temperament. On the other hand it is certain that even then the prince was looked upon as an exceptional personality gifted with extraordinary qualities. The king must have regarded Kittisirimegha as his most serious rival. He may have hoped to gain the prince as ally against this rival. In any case however, it was politically short-sighted to receive him with such honour and to place more trust in him than prudence warranted.

Parakkamabāhu probably employed his sojourn in Pulatthinagara to find out the conditions obtaining in Rājaraṭṭha. We may be sure however, that this was not done in the way described 66. 129 ff. Here Dhammakitti as I hope I have shown in my notes to the whole passage, conforms to the whole scheme of the Indian Nīti Literature, exhibiting his knowledge of it with great complacency. At any rate the prince by his whole conduct arouses more and more the suspicions of Gajabāhu and his counsellors so that in the same way as he fled from Saṅkhatthalī, he leaves the capital at night convinced that he has been detected. But there is one remarkable difference. Gajabāhu seemingly sends no armed messengers out to fetch back the fugitive. He was probably glad to be rid of a guest who was becoming so dangerous.

Parakkamabāhu's mother, as I assume, reconciles him with his uncle whose death shortly afterwards solves all difficulties.

My remarks are an attempt to remove the facts of a circumscribed period of Sinhalese history from the light in which the compiler of the Cūlavaṃsa saw and was forced by his mentality to see them and to place them in the light of historical consideration. I repeat that this is merely an attempt. But the employment of this or similar methods may possibly prove fruitful in the interpretation of native tradition.

II

Kingship and the Law of Succession in mediaeval Ceylon

The form of government in mediaeval Ceylon was to all appearance of course despotic. The king is head and crown of the state. The state does not exist for itself but for the king. All attributes of power and greatness are heaped on the king. Yet in his decisions and actions he is by no means so free as one might imagine. In these he is strongly influenced and also restricted by custom which has assumed the force of law, by the *pubbacārittaṃ* — use and wont. Again and again it is said in praise of the best princes that in their actions they followed former kings, that they did not stray from the path of tradition. This conservative trait forms without doubt a strong counterbalance to the ideas of unlimited power which the popular mind associates with the idea of sovereignty.

There exist a number of names and titles for "king". With no term is the Indian love of synonyms so marked as with this one. It is unnecessary to enumerate the many and varied terms for "king". They are the crux of every translator. The expression "king" I have reserved for *rājan*. Then there come in addition *mahārāja*, *rājādhirāja*, used 75. 203 of Parakkamabāhu I. which last however is an ancient title. It is used already in the Taittirīya āraṇyaka 1. 31. 6. For the ruler of a small island like Ceylon the titles strike us at times as somewhat grandiose: *mahīpati*, *mahīpāla*, *dharaṇīpati*, *bhūpati*, *bhūpāla*, *jagatīpati*, *narapati*, *narādhipa*, *narādhinātha* etc. One must bear in mind that these titles have by frequent and arbitrary use — very often it is the metre that decides the matter — become worn down and defaced. It would not be in keeping with the mentality of the compiler of the Cūlavaṃsa if we were to translate these expressions always by "ruler of the earth" and the like.

Next to the king comes the queen, the *mahesī*, his chief consort in contrast to the unrestricted number of concubines, the harem (*orodha*, *antepura*). In the case of the mahesī equality of birth is strictly enforced and only her sons have a right to the succession. Herr Hocart expressed to me the opinion that there were two mahesīs and pointed out the mention of the queens Anulādevī and Somadevī in Mhvs. 33. 45–46. He is certainly right. It is also expressly stated of Vijayabāhu I. (59. 25 and 30) that he raised two princesses to the dignity of mahesī, first Līlāvatī and then Tilokasundarī (*mahesitte abhisecayi*, *-siñci*) and a *dutiyā devī* of Mānābharaṇa of Rohaṇa is mentioned in 64. 24. The mention of the title *aggamahesī* (54. 10; 70. 33) inclines us to believe that there was a difference in rank between the two mahesīs. This assumption however receives no support from the inscription of Potgul-vehera in Polonnaruva in which Queen Candavatī is described as *dutiyaṃ aggataṃ gatā*, that she was the second *aggamahesī* of Parakkamabāhu together with the first, Līlāvatī[1].

Special titles also exist for the sons and daughters of the reigning king, for the princes and princesses (*rājaputta*, *rājaputtī*), for the sons the title *ādipāda*, for the daughters that of *rājinī*. The fact that *rājinī* is not merely a general term for "queen", but also a particular title with a particular rank corresponding to the title *ādipāda* for princes is clear from 49. 3. Udaya I. makes his eldest son yuvarāja, the other sons ādipādas, the daughters rājinīs. In the same way Sena I. according to 50. 58 raises his daughters to the rank of rājinīs (*rājinīṭhāne*) and Mahinda IV. according to 54. 11 makes his sons ādipādas and his daughter rājinī[2].

---

[1] See now A. M. Hocart, Duplication of Office in Indian State, A: The Two Queens (CJSc. G, I, p. 207 ff.). I may add, that Nissaṅka Malla in the Galpota Inscription (B, line 2; EZ. II. 106) also mentions two mahesīs, Subhadrā and Kalyāṇa.

[2] The correction of *copirājiniṃ* into *cāpi rājiniṃ* is doubtless preferable to the *coparājiniṃ* of S. and B. An *uparājinī* certainly never existed. The reading *rājinīkatā* too in 60. 84 which I have adopted in the text, shows that Vijayabāhu I raised his daughter Yasodharā to the

As to the title *ādipāda*, we first meet with it in 41. 34. Here it is stated that Silākāla bestowed it on his eldest son Moggallāna (later King M. II). Two passages dealing with the granting of the title by the king to his sons are just quoted (49. 3; 54. 11). Dappula II. does not make the son of his eldest brother Mahinda ādipāda, because, contrary to the existing law (see below), he wishes to leave the crown to his own sons. Thus it seems that with the title is bound up the acknowledgment of the right of succession. Thus it is legally borne (50. 8 and 25) by Udaya and Kassapa as younger brothers and presumptive heirs of Sena I. Likewise by Dappula (afterwards D. IV.) 53. 1 as brother of Dappula III., and 53. 4 by Udaya (afterwards U. III.) as nephew and heir of Dappula IV. Vijayabāhu I. grants his youngest brother Jayabāhu the rank of ādipāda (*ādipādapadaṃ* 59. 12), while his brother next in age Vīrabāhu receives the dignity of an uparāja. Later on after the death of Vīrabāhu (60. 86–88) Jayabāhu becomes uparāja and Vikkamabāhu, Vijayabāhu's son, becomes ādipāda.

It is self understood that with the ascent of the throne or more strictly speaking with the *abhiseka*, the consecration of the king, the title of ādipāda lapses. Mahinda I. who repudiates this ceremony is called ādipāda throughout the whole of his reign (48. 31, 68).

The granting of the title seems to have some connection with the coming of age. It is said at least of Kitti afterwards Vijayabāhu I. in 57. 61, that he attained the "rank of an ādipāda" in his fifteenth year. Here the political conditions of the time preclude the idea of an act on the part of the reigning king. At first sight it may strike one as strange that the title of *ādipāda* should be ascribed to Dappula, the sister's son of Aggabodhi VI. 48. 90, 93 and also to his two nephews 48. 116 who were otherwise (48. 110) designated simply as "princes". According to the prevailing law Dappula

---

dignity of a rājinī and that she then had the building erected which is mentioned in the verse.

has no claim to the succession, but as we shall see, he was an ardent champion of another law. Thus he must have claimed the title advisedly, as did his two relatives who on their side declared themselves his legitimate heirs.

The eldest ādipāda, the one nearest the throne bears the title of *mahāādipada, mahādipāda* "grand ādipāda". Mahinda as the eldest of the three younger brothers of Sena I. is so named 50. 10, the two others, Udaya and Kassapa (see above), are ādipādas. Thus the title of *mahādipāda* is closely allied with the term *yuvaraja.* It is expressly said of this Mahinda (50. 6) that he was yuvarāja. Udaya II. confers the dignity of a mahādipāda (*mahādipādaṭhānamhi ṭhapi* 51. 91) on his brother Kassapa who in the sequel becomes his successor (52. 1). For lack of an heir male Aggabodhi I. appoints his sister's son of the same name *mahādipāda* (42. 38), and is eventually succeeded by him on the throne. Kitti-Vijayabāhu I. is in Rohaṇa after the subjugation of his foes. But henceforth he has the position of yuvarāja (*yuvarājapade* 58. 1) until his consecration as king and bears the title of a mahādipāda (58. 7). The mahādipāda of the usurper Dāṭhopatissa was according to 44. 136, his nephew Ratanadāṭha. But at the same time Kassapa (afterwards K. II.) is described as yuvarāja (44. 137) since as younger brother of the legitimate king Aggabodhi III. Sirisaṃghabodhi he had the right to the succession. The granting of the title mahādipāda seems from 67. 91 to have been a festive act, the prince receiving a fillet which was obviously his special badge.

It may be mentioned that the two titles *ādipāda* and *mahādipāda* frequently occur[1] in inscriptions in the forms *āpa* and *mahapa.*

---

[1] See Wickremasinghe, EZ. I, Index s. vv. That *mahayā* also (see l. c. p. 26, n. 4; p. 98, n. 5; p. 187, n. 6; p. 225, n. 3) should stand for *mahādipāda* raises doubts. The disappearance of *p* in the joint of the compound is surprising. In favour of the identification, meanwhile, is the fact that the frequently occurring phrase *äpa mahayā siri vindä* (EZ. I. 25, 91, 221) is replaced in the inscription of the Jetavanārāma (EZ. I. 234) by *ayipaya mahapaya siri vindä.* Codrington has every

The heir to the throne has as we have seen, the title *yuvarāja*. This brings us to the question of the right of succession obtaining in mediaeval Ceylon. But first a remark on the relation of the term yuvarāja to that of uparāja.

In the first place I must point out that the investiture of the uparāja was a solemn ceremony. The uparāja is "consecrated" like the king or the mahesī (*Mānaṃ oparajje 'bhisiñciya* 44. 84; *oparajje kumāraṃ ca abhisiñcittha* 48. 42, cf. 48. 69; *Mahindaṃ . . . oparajje 'bhisecayi* 51. 7; cf. 51. 12). So far as I can see, the expression "consecrate" is never used of the yuvarāja. One is yuvarāja either in virtue of the right of succession or if necessary or desirable, the position of yuvarāja is conferred like an office or a title (*adāsi yuvarājattaṃ* 49. 3; *yuvarājapadaṃ adā* 52. 42, 53. 4, 54. 1 and 58); one is nominated yuvarāja (*yuvarājaṃ akā* 53. 28), appointed to the position (*ṭhapetvā yuvarājatte* 45. 23). It is self understood that these expressions of a more general kind are also used for the appointment of an uparāja (ex. 41. 93, 42. 6, 48. 32). The main point is that where a "consecration" is spoken of (*abhi-sic*) this has never reference to a yuvarāja but always and without exception to an uparāja.

A yuvarāja is found in every reign along with the king. Of a more limited number of rulers it is related that they appointed an uparāja. Frequently the yuvarāja is invested with this dignity. We can almost say that this was the rule, so that the announcement of the appointment of an uparāja contains the information that the individual in question was at the same time the heir to the throne. Aggabodhi III. consecrates his younger brother Māna (44. 84) uparāja, his heir to the throne according to the law, and described later (44. 123) as yuvarāja. After Māna's premature death his next youngest brother Kassapa becomes uparāja and yuvarāja (44. 124, 137). In the same way Mahinda is the uparāja of his father Aggabodhi VII. and is called in the sequel yuvarāja

---

right to point to this passage when he explains *Māyāraṭṭha* as *Mahādipāda-raṭṭha*.

(48. 69, 75). The same is the case with an unnamed son of Mahinda II. who however dies before him. It is related of Vijayabāhu I. that he first made his next youngest brother uparāja (59. 11), thus acknowledging him as his heir, his yuvarāja. On his death he transfers the dignity of uparāja to the youngest brother Jayabāhu (60. 86, 87), who is then (61. 3) called yuvarāja.

In view of these instances the appointment of another individual than the yuvarāja to be uparāja would seem to be a rare exception due to very special circumstances. Aggabodhi I. for instance, appoints as uparāja his maternal uncle, but the yuvarāja is his younger brother (42. 6) who is not even named and presumably died before the king. Sena II. consecrates as uparāja his younger brother Mahinda who was also yuvarāja (51. 7, 13). After his quarrel with Mahinda he transfers the dignity of uparāja to his own son Kassapa (51. 12). In his disappointment at his experiences he probably wished to exclude his brothers altogether from the succession but this he fails to do. Mahinda remains nevertheless yuvarāja and at his death his place is taken by the next youngest brother of the king, Udaya (51. 63).

The matter, I think, is clear and just what one has from the first expected. Yuvarāja is the legitimate heir to the throne. The dignity of uparāja on the other hand, is a position of trust carrying with is certain rights, apparently a share in the business of government. It seems to have been a matter of the king's pleasure whether to have such a support in his royal office or not.

As to the right of succession, the rule was that the next youngest brother of the king succeeded him on the throne. Only when no other brother existed did the crown pass to the next generation, and here again to the eldest son of the eldest brother of the preceding generation. There are frequent instances of such a sequence.

Aggabodhi V. is succeeded by his younger brother Kassapa III. he being followed by the third brother Mahinda I. Then the succession passes to the next generation and as Aggabodhi apparently left no son of equal rank, to Kassapa's son Aggabodhi VI. If he had had brothers capable of succeeding him, they would have been his heirs. As this was not the case, Aggabodhi VII. the son of Mahinda becomes king after him (48. 1, 20, 26, 42, 68).

Sena II. has three brothers. Mahinda the eldest of them is yuvarāja (51. 13). He dies however, before the king Hereupon the next brother Udaya II. becomes heir and successor of Sena II. (51. 63, 90) and after him the youngest brother Kassapa IV. (51, 91; 52. 1). Hereupon it is the turn of the next generation and in the first instance the sons of Sena II. — Kassapa V., Dappula III. and Dappula IV., then those of Mahinda — Udaya III., Sena III. and Udaya IV. Of Kassapa V. it is expressly stated that he came to the throne in regular succession, that is according to the existing law (*kamāgato* 52. 37). Udaya II. and Kassapa IV. seem to have left no legitimate heirs. Thus after the death of Mahinda's youngest son the sons of Kassapa V., Sena IV. (53. 39; *Laṅkābhisekaṃ kamāgataṃ* 54. 1) and Mahinda IV. (54. 1, 7) come to the throne.

After the three brothers — Mahinda III., Aggabodhi VIII. and Dappula II. — had reigned in regular succession (49. 38, 43, 65) the crown went by rights to the like-named son of the eldest of them. But Dappula desires to reserve it for his own son. Hence he does not make the younger Mahinda (8) ādipāda. That this was a breach of the law is clear from 49. 84. Mahinda betakes himself full of resentment to India.

An important point is the custom of bestowing on the yuvarāja, the Southern Province — Dakkhinadesa — that is the region west of the central mountains as far as the seacoast (45. 23; 50. 49; 51. 19; 52. 1). This was after Rājaraṭṭha economically and politically the most important province in the kingdom, even more so than Rohaṇa which always maintained a more independent and special position. Dakkhiṇadesa is in consequence directly described as *yuvarājaraṭṭha* 67. 26 and 79. 60. According to Codrington, as already mentioned above (p. XVIII note), the name of Māyāraṭṭha which appears later (81. 15, 18, 62; 87. 24) would mean the same, being derived, as he explains, from *Mahādipādaraṭṭha*.

Without doubt the Sinhalese right of succession rests on patriarchy. Nevertheless in Ceylon as elsewhere in India, remnants of an older matriarchy have been preserved. This is particularly noticeable in the part played by the sister's son, the *bhāgineyya*. The fact of this relationship being designated by a special term is in itself significant (Skr. *bhāgineya*). For a brother's sons no such term exists. They are merely called *sūnavo*. Thus Parakkamabāhu is called (63. 51) the son (*sūnu*) of his uncle Kittisirimegha who again is called his father (*pitā* 63. 53). Their relationship to one another is always described as that between father and son. The three brothers Mānābharaṇa, Kittisirimegha and Sirivallabha are even described as the "three fathers" of the youthful Parakkamabāhu (64. 33, 55). One is reminded of the conditions of ancient polyandry.

If a distinction is to be made between the uncle who is the father's elder brother, and between the father's younger brother, the first is called the *mahāpitā* and the second the *cullapitā*. Thus Sena I. is the *mahāpitā* of Sena II. (51. 24). The cousins who are the sons of two brothers call themselves quite consistently brothers, as for instance, Aggabodhi VI. and Aggabodhi VII. (48. 61), the sons of the brothers Kassapa III. and Mahinda I. Thus Buddhaghosa calls Ānanda the brother of the Buddha because he was the son of his uncle (*Tathāgatassa bhātā cullapitu-putto* DCo. I. 4).

It is undoubtedly the case that the sister's son enjoyed a certain preference: the last remnant of that special position accorded to him under matriarchy. Dhātusena's sister's son holds the important office of senāpati and receives the king's daughter in marriage (38. 81). In the same way Dappula II marries his daughter Devā to his sister's son Kittaggabodhi (49. 71).

This remnant of an earlier matriarchy can at times be a furthering or a disturbing factor in the right of succession. Aggabodhi I. makes his brother *yuvarāja* and appoints his sister's son *malayarāja*. Later on he gives him his daughter in marriage and confers on him the dignity of *mahādipāda*. This sister's son afterwards ascends the throne as successor of his uncle under the name of Aggabodhi II. (42. 6, 10, 38, 40). It is not necessary to assume a breach of the law here. We may suppose that the younger brother of Aggabodhi I., the original yuvarāja, had died before him. As no male heir existed, the crown might legally go to the relative in the female line[1].

The matter is somewhat different in the case of Kassapa II. He had it is true, no younger brother but he had sons of whom the eldest Mānaka was his legal successor. As these sons however were minors, he summons his sister's son Māna from Rohaṇa and entrusts him with his sons and with the kingdom. Here we have a regency carried on however, after Kassapa's death, not by Māna but by his father Dappula, Kassapa's brother-in-law. The whole affair causes serious disturbances in the kingdom (45. 6 ff.).

A zealous champion of matriarchy and of his claims to the throne based on it was Dappula, the *bhāgineyya* of King Aggabodhi VI. Silāmegha. He waged a long and obstinate fight with Mahinda II., Aggabodhi's son who was the legal heir, no younger brother existing. He was supported in his struggle by two sister's sons in Rohaṇa who in their turn hoped to become his heirs (48. 90, 98 ff.). Here we have obviously matriarchy against patriarchy.

Of special interest is what is related as to the settlement of the succession after the death of Vijayabāhu I. (61. 1 ff.). The yuvarāja is his youngest brother Jayabāhu. If he ascended the throne then Vijayabāhu's son Vikkamabāhu who is sojourning in Rohaṇa, would be his heir and successor. But now begin the intrigues of Mittā, the sister of Vijayabāhu and Jayabāhu, who taking her stand on matriarchy seeks to divert the crown to her line. In agreement with the highest court officials she decides that Jayabāhu shall indeed be con-

[1] Parakkamabāhu I. is also succeeded by his *bhāgineyya* Vijayabāhu (80. 1), since the male line is extinct.

secrated king over Laṅkā, but that the dignity of uparāja and therewith the succession (see above p. XIX f.) shall be conferred on her eldest son Mānābharaṇa to the exclusion of Vikkamabāhu. That was a coup d'Etat and the chronicle too says expressly that here was a distinct breach with old established custom (*pubbacārittamagga*).

By way of supplement a brief remark on the dignity of the *malayarāja*. It is not clear whether this was conferred only on members of the royal family. Malaya is the name of the central mountain region of Ceylon which however, according to the testimony of the Cūlavaṃsa (70. 3 ff.) was in Parakkamabāhu's time, that is in the 12 th century, still a wilderness. Nevertheless the title "Malaya King" must have denoted some kind of dominion, if only a nominal one, over that province.

Silākāla makes his second son Dāṭhāpabbuti malayarāja (41. 35). The yuvarāja according to law was his elder son Moggallāna (afterwards Moggallana II.). But it was not he but the malayarāja who got the province of Dakkhiṇadesa. Perhaps the custom of bestowing Dakkhiṇadesa on the yuvarāja had not at that time taken root, or else Dāṭhāpabhuti was to be specially favoured. After his father's death he seized the government by force from Moggallāna.

Under Kassapa V. his younger son Siddhattha is malayarāja (52. 68), and this would seem to be the normal condition as against the granting of Dakkhiṇadesa to the eldest son. Under Aggabodhi IV. there is mention of a Malayarāja Bodhitissa (46. 29), but nothing is said as to the relation in which he stood to the king. The dignity is conferred by Moggallana III. on the traitorous senāpati of his predecessor Saṃghatissa (44. 43, 53). No conclusion can however be drawn from this. Moggallana III. was apparently himself a usurper. He was commander-in-chief of Aggabodhi II. (44, 2), as Saṃghatissa before him had been *asiggāha*. Here it was the case of founding a new dynasty.

A later form of the title showing Dravidian influence, is *malayarāyaro* (70. 62, 155).

III

Offices, Dignities and Titles in mediaeval Ceylon

It is interesting to note how the organisation of officialdom and the system of titles became more and more complex, reaching a climax in the middle ages about the time of Parakkamabāhu. The difference between the Cūlavaṃsa and the older Mahāvaṃsa is here a very considerable one. In the first we meet with an imposing array of expressions and designations which are absent from the other.

Nor is it easy at times to determine whether a word is merely a general term for an official or whether it is associated with a strictly defined sphere of action, This is the case for instance with *adhikārin* and *adhināyaka* (*adhinātha*)[1]. These terms almost certainly represent a difference in degree; for according to 70. 278 Parakkamabāhu conferred on the Adhinātha Māyāgeha as a reward for his military services, the dignity of an adhikārin (*adhikāripadaṃ*). The title Damiḷādhikārin may be mentioned here. It is borne by one of the two Rakkhas, the generals of Parakkamabāhu (75. 20, 69 ff.), further by a *gaṇakāmacca* named Ādicca (76. 39 ff.).

The word *amacca* (Skr. *amātya*) is certainly one of general meaning. It is used alike of civil and military officials. To translate it always by "minister" I believe is wrong. By comparison with what we now understand by that word it gets a shade of meaning foreign to it. *Sāmanta* I believe to be a purely military title. It has the same meaning as our word "officer", corpscommanders of various ranks subject to the commander-in-chief (cf. for ex. 69. 16; 70. 57, 67, 173, 314-6, 319). Even when it stands next to *maṇḍalika* it pro-

---

[1] Cf. notes to 70. 278 and 72. 10. The word *adhikāra* has also in the Kauṭalīya the meaning "sphere of action", proper authority, office. Cf. J. J. Meyer, Das altindische Buch vom Welt- und Staatsleben, das Arthaçāstra des Kauṭilya, p. 291, n. 1; p. 480, n. 2.

bably means a military official alongside of the civilian, the governor of a *maṇḍala*, of a larger or of a smaller district (46. 31; 69. 5, 15) by which is apparently meant the smallest division within a province, a *raṭṭha*.

Nāyaka would also seem to be a general term. It about corresponds to the English "Colonel". Sirināga the uncle of Jeṭṭhatissa III., bears this title 44. 70. Vajiragga is the nāyaka of Udaya II. (51. 105, 118) and Rukkha that of Kassapa IV. (52. 31). Not infrequently *nāyaka* is found in compounds thus in *kañcukināyaka* (see note to 72. 58) "Head or chief of the chamberlains", or in *saṅkhanāyaka* (70. 278; 72. 31, 41; 75. 75), or in *saṃvaccharikanāyaka* "chief of the astrologers" (57. 48). *Kesadhātunāyaka* (see below) also perhaps denotes a higher rank among the members of the Order of the Kesadhātus. The function of the *kammanāyaka* or *kammanātha* (72. 58, 206; 74. 168) is not clear nor the meaning of the title *disāvijayanāyaka*.

On the other hand it is probably certain that *daṇḍanāyaka* (*daṇḍanātha*) denotes an officer of high rank[1]. Our rendering of it by "General" probably meets the case. Amongst the commanders of Parakkamabāhu the two brothers Kitti and Saṃkhadhātu bear the title (70. 279 ff.) as also the Nagaragiri Gokaṇṇa (70. 68) and others (see note to 70. 5).

Head of the whole army is however the *senāpati*[2]. His position was without doubt one of extreme importance and the king only granted it to a man in whom he had the fullest confidence. Dhātusena appoints his sister's son senāpati (38. 81). In the same way Parakkamabāhu II. in the war against the

---

[1] *Daṇḍa* must be taken in the meaning of "army". According to J. J. Meyer (loc. cit. p. 398, n. 3; cf. also p. 834) the expression *daṇḍanāyī* should also be inserted in the Kauṭalīya, the same as the *netā daṇḍasya* of Kāmandaka. Here also a corps-commander is meant.

[2] In *dhajinīpati* we have nothing but a synonym for *senāpati*. In the translation I have always therefore inserted "senāpati". In the Kauṭalīya (10. 6) the senāpati has not a commanding position. He is here commander of 10 *padikas* (?) and there are 10 senāpatis under one nāyaka. Cf. J. J. Meyer, l. c. p. 586. Shamasastry differs somewhat, Kauṭilya's Arthaśāstra, p. 452.

Jāvakas, entrusts the highest command in the army[1] to his sister's son Vīrabāhu (83. 41). I do not think however, that the conclusion is warranted that this position was reserved for the *bhāgineyya*. He could indeed become senāpati if he had the necessary qualifications and if he possessed the confidence of the monarch, but the king was not bound in his choice by conditions of relationship. Udaya who had distinguished himself by his courage, was made senāpati by his father Mahinda II. (48. 154), just as Mahinda, afterwards Mahinda II., was made senāpati by his father Aggabodhi VI. Our chronicle mentions a whole series of senāpatis by name without saying whether and how they were related to the king (48. 78). Migāra is the senāpati of Kassapa I. (39. 6), Uttara that of Moggallāna I. (39. 58), Vajira of Dappula II. (49. 80), Bhadda of Sena I. (50. 82), Kuṭṭhaka of Sena II. (51. 88), Rakkhaka Ilaṅga of Dappula IV. (53. 11); the nāyaka Viduragga of Udaya IV. (53. 46), Sena of Mahinda IV. (54. 13), Deva of Parakkamabāhu I. (70. 123), Mitta of Vijayabāhu IV. (90. 2). Of Sena Ilaṅga, the senāpati of Kassapa IV. it is merely said that he belonged to the royal family (52. 16). It would be very remarkable if in all these cases or even in the majority of them the *bhāgineyya* should be meant and the chronicler not mention the fact.

A special title is that of *sakkasenāpati*[2]. Kassapa V. appoints as such his own son (*sakkasenāpatiṭṭhānaṃ datvā* 52. 52; cf. 52. 61, 64, 72, 74). After his death the dignity is transferred to his son, thus to Kassapa's grandson (52. 79). I believe we have the same title in the *saksenevi* of the Bilibeva inscription (EZ. II. 40 ff.). A synonym of *sakkasenāpati* is *sakkasenānī* (54. 53). Difficult of explanation is the term *andhasenāpati* which occurs but once (41. 87). I am inclined to think that Andha here is the Skr. *andhra*, the name of a people which occurs along with such as *pulinda* and *sabara*.

---

[1] The title *senāpati* is, however, not used here.

[2] The word means "senāpati of Sakka" (the King of the gods), denotes therefore very high rank. We may infer from its meaning that it was merely a title and not the name of an office with special functions.

Like these two names *Andha* might then have reference to the Väddās and *andhasenāpati* would be a title with its counterpart in *damiḷādhikārin*. This last title is borne by one of the generals Rakkha (75. 20, 69, 74 &c), as well as by the Gaṇakāmacca Ādicca (76. 39, 63, 64).

Amongst the officials in personal contact with the king are the umbrella-bearer (*chattagāhaka*) and the sword-bearer (*asiggāhaka*). The umbrella is the symbol of the royal dignity. Saṃghā, the daughter of Mahānāma is married to the king's umbrella-bearer — a proof of the high rank held by this official — and obtains for him the crown by murdering her brother of inferior rank (38. 1-3). Under Vijayabāhu I. three brothers revolt against the king, one of whom is the "chief of the umbrella-bearers" (*chattagāhakanātha*), the second *dhammagehakanāyaka*, the third *seṭṭhinātha* (59. 16). These two last names of offices do not occur elsewhere in the Cūlavaṃsa. The first of the two (lit. "chief of the House of the Law") is probably the highest judicial official, the second the "President of the Guild of Merchants".

The title *asiggāha* was like that of the umbrella-bearer without doubt one of high rank. Moggallana I. gives his sister in marriage to his sword-bearer Silākāla and entrusts him with the guardianship of the Hair Relic (*kesadhātu* 39. 54, 55). Perhaps we have here the beginnings of the Order of the Kesadhātu. Aggabodhi II. appoints a relative of his mahesī as asiggāha (42. 42). Moggallāna III. appoints as sword-bearer the son of the senāpati of his predecessor Saṃghatissa to whom he feels under obligations for helping him to obtain the sovereignty (44. 43), Later on this same sword-bearer himself gains the crown and reigns under the name of Silāmeghavaṇṇa (44. 64-65), just as Samghatissa had been *asiggāha* before his ascent of the throne (44. 1).

Of great importance was the office of the Government Scribe (*mahālekha*). We may assume in Ceylon the same or similar conditions as the Kauṭalīya describes[1] them for the

[1] Arthaśāstra 2. 10 (28th subject); J. J. Meyer, p. 100 ff., in Shamasastry's translation p. 80 ff.

India of the period of which it writes. The Government Scribe is called here likewise *lekhaka.* His task is the drafting of the royal edicts (*śāsana*) to whose content and form the greatest importance is attached. The rules laid down by the Kauṭalīya are extraordinarily minute. The mahālekha of Kassapa IV. was called Sena and I have pointed out (note to 52. 33) that this official is also mentioned in inscriptions. The Government Scribe of the younger Mānābharaṇa was Mahinda (72. 1, 4, 166). He had it seems at the same time military rank. The same holds good of Rakkha the mahālekha of Parakkamabāhu I. (72. 161, 170, 182).

Several official titles are formed with the word *potthakin*, namely: *bhaṇḍāra-*, *ādi-*, *mūla-* and *jīvita-potthakin.* We shall see that it is probably a case here of various synonymous designations for one and the same office. According to its origin *potthakin* has reference to an official who in some sphere or other has to do with book-keeping, the making of lists and inventories. Now *bhaṇḍārapotthakin* is of itself intelligible. It probably corresponds[1] to *koṣṭhāgārādhyakṣa* "overseer of the provision house" in the Kauṭalīya. The title is borne (72. 182) by an officer of Parakkamabāhu I., Kitti[2] by name. But the same Kitti is also described (72. 27, 207) as *ādipotthakin.* This therefore is probably a synonym of *bhaṇḍārapotthakin* and means simply "first or highest potthakin". But the same meaning is also attached to *mūlapotthakin* which is the title of Māna (75. 139, 140) another officer of Parakkama. I may point to *mūlaṭṭhāna* (57. 38) "the first, the highest and most influential position", the foremost office in the state. My impression is that *jīvitapotthakin* has the same meaning. This title is also applied to Kitti (74. 90) as well as to another official of Parakkamabāhu's Mandin by name (70. 318; 72. 161). It should be remembered that the Skr. *jīvita* means "livelihood, food". By *bhaṇḍāra* was meant the necessary food-stuffs which were under the supervision and control of the potthakin.

---

[1] Arthaśāstra 2. 15 (33rd subject). In J. J. Meyer p. 138 ff. In Shamasastry, p. 112 ff.

[2] Besides Kitti also Bhūta in 72. 196, another officer of Parakkama.

Only once is mention made of a *gaṇakāmacca* (76. 39). This as the etymology shows, was apparently an official whose business was finance or accounts. In the Mahābhārata the *gaṇaka* (BR. s. v.) is placed side by side with the *lekhaka*. It is difficult to say what *sabhāpati*[1] (67. 64, 70) or *sabhānāyaka* (thus 67. 61, 80) stands for. The context shows almost certainly that it denoted an officer of very high rank.

In conclusion I mention some terms which are manifestly nothing but honorary titles, bestowed by the king for public services such as those in war. In the first rank of these is the title *kesadhātu*. I have noticed it in the note to 57. 65. It is a distinction corresponding to our orders. It may have originated in the members of the Order being entrusted with the care of the Hair Relic. See above p. XXVI. Later on this became a mere formality. It is doubtful whether *kesadhātu* in the meaning of "member of the K. Order" is an abbreviation for *kesadhātunāyaka* or whether this last term denotes a higher rank within the Order.

Several of the titles are joined with the word *giri* (Skr. *giri*) or *galla* (Sinh. *gala*). It is not impossible that in such titles names of localities are meant as in the family names of our nobility. Very frequent is the title *nagaragiri* or *nagaragalla* (see note to 66. 35). Again we have *māragiri* (note to 72. 11), *laṅkāgiri* (note to 72. 27), *nīlagiri* (note to 70. 137), *lokagalla* (note to 72. 222) and the uncertain *jitagiri*. All these are verifiable as place names: Nagaragalla (48. 36), Māragalla (55. 26) or Mārapabbata (48. 129), Laṅkāgiri (70. 88) or -pabbata (66. 80), Nīlagiri (70. 20; 72. 12) or -galla (70. 14, 16, 83) and Lokagalla (74. 79, 81, 83, 166).

In addition *laṅkāpura* seems to have been a title (see note to 70. 218) and such are most certainly the terms *laṅkānātha*, *laṅkādhinātha*, *laṅkādhināyaka* (see note to 70. 24), as also *laṅkādhikārin* (see note to 70. 278). The last, it is worth noting, denotes a higher degree in rank.

---

[1] P. *sabhā* means "hall, assembly room". In Sanskrit the word is also used for a "law court". Sabhāpati might therefore denote a high legal official.

Contents of Chapters 37–72

Chap. 37

Sirimeghavaṇṇa atones for the wrongs done to the bhikkhus of the Mahāvihāra by his father Mahāsena (51-63). — Buildings erected by the king (64-5). — Erection of a golden image of Mahinda (66-86). — Further works (87-91). — The Tooth Relic comes to Ceylon (92-7). — Further meritorious works of the king (98-9). — King Jeṭṭhatissa I., a skilled carver in ivory (100-4). — Buddhadāsa's meritorious works (105-11). — Marvellous healing of men and animals (112-44). — Further meritorious works, propitiation of one who had been his foe in a former life (145-74). — The thera Mahādhammakathin (175). — Eighty sons of the king named after the disciples of the Buddha (176-8). — Upatissa I. His meritorious works (179-88). — Saves the land from drought (189-98). — Clemency of the king, also towards criminals (199-208). — Mahānāma and his architectural works (209-14). — History of Buddhaghosa (215-48).

Chap. 38

Sotthisena murdered by his sister who places her husband, the king's umbrella-bearer, on the throne in his stead (1-3). — Mittasena (4-10). — The Damiḷa Paṇḍu (11-3). — History of Dhātusena's youth (14-28). — Successors of Paṇḍu: Parinda, Khuddapārinda, Tīritara, Dāṭhiya, Pīṭhiya (29-34). — Dhātusena, his architectural works, construction of the Kālavāpi and other meritorious deeds (35-79). — His sons Kassapa and Moggallāna, flight of Moggallāna to Jambudīpa (80-6). — Dhātusena dethroned and slain by Kassapa; his fate the consequence of a wrong done to a bhikkhu (87-115).

Chap. 39

Kassapa I. founds Sīhagiri; he seeks to expiate his parrocide by pious actions (1-19). — Moggallāna comes from Jambudīpa; Kassapa defeated in battle dies by his own hand (20-8). — Moggallāna I. performs meritorious works, punishes the adherents of Kassapa, builds vihāras (29-43). — History of Silākāla; he brings the Hair Relic to Ceylon (44-56). — End of Moggallāna (57-9).

Chap. 41

Kumāradhātusena, Kittisena, Sīva reign meritoriously (1-5). — Upatissa II. makes Silākāla his son-in-law; his son is Kassapa (6-9). — Revolt of Silākāla; Kassapa losing the battle commits suicide. Death of Upatissa (10-25). — Silākāla; his meritorious works (26-32). — His three sons (33-6). — The Dhammadhātu comes to Ceylon (37-41). — Silākāla's second son Dāṭhāpabhuti seizes the sovereignty; murders his younger brother and is attacked by his elder brother Moggallāna. Duel of the brothers. Dāṭhāpabhuti takes his own life (42-53). — Moggallāna II.; his reverence for the teaching of the Buddha, his meritorious works (54-63). — His son Kittisirimegha. Disturbances in the kingdom (64-8). — History of Mahānāga (69-90). — Mahānāga slays the king and seizes the throne (91-3). — Meritorious works of Mahānāga (94-103).

Chap. 42

Aggabodhi I.; his character and his meritorious works (1-34). — The thera Jotipāla and the ādipāda Dāṭhāpabhuti (35-9). — Aggabodhi II. The Kaliṅga King comes with his consort to Ceylon and is received into the Order by Jotipāla (40-50). — The Thūpārāma damaged; the king erects a temple for the Collar bone Relic (51-60). — Further meritorious works (61-69).

Chap. 44

Saṃghatissa becomes king. Moggallāna the senāpati of Aggabodhi II. revolts against him and gains the upper hand through the treachery of Saṃghatissa's general (1-21). — Moggallāna III. as king has a young son of Saṃghatissa's mutilated (22-7). — Another son Jeṭṭhatissa escapes to Malaya. Saṃghatissa himself with a third son and his minister are caught during flight and beheaded (28-43). — Meritorious works of Moggallāna III. (44-52). — The king quarrels with the treacherous general and has him mutilated. The general's son joins Jeṭṭhatissa, defeats Moggallāna and while Jeṭṭhatissa remains in Malaya, ascends the throne under the name of Silāmeghavaṇṇa (53-64). — His meritorious works (65-9). — Sirināga an uncle of Jeṭṭhatissa comes with a Damiḷa army but is defeated (70-3). — Divisions in the Abhayagiri-vihāra, purification of the Church (74-81). — The king's death (82). — Succeeded by his son Aggabodhi III. Sirisaṃghabodhi. Revolt of Jeṭṭhatissa; Aggabodhi flees to Jambudīpa (83-94). — Reign of Jeṭṭhatissa II. (95-102). — Aggabodhi comes from Jambudīpa, Jeṭṭhatissa is defeated and takes his life (103-12). — His minister does likewise; the queen also dies (113-7). — Second reign of Aggabodhi III.; his meritorious works (118-22). — After the murder of Māna the king's younger brother Kassapa is appointed yuvarāja (123-4). — Dāṭhopatissa I. revolts and drives out the king (125-9). — The wars of the two kings damage the country; violent actions of Dāṭhopatissa and Kassapa; death of Aggabodhi III. (130-44). — Kassapa II. becomes king after defeating Dāṭhopatissa and makes good his former misdeeds (145-51). — Last attempt of Dāṭhopatissa to regain the throne and his death (152-5).

Chap. 45

Meritorious works of Kassapa II; the thera Mahādhammakathin (1-5). — The king entrusts kingdom and sons to his nephew Māna and dies (6-10). — Revolt of the Damiḷas. While Māna raises his father Dappula I. to the throne,

Hatthadāṭha a nephew of Dāṭhopatissa I. comes from Jambudīpa and seizes the sovereignty (11-21). — He reigns as Dāṭhopatissa II. His conflict with the bhikkhus of the Mahāvihāra; his death (22-37). — Early history of Dappula I.; his meritorious works in Rohaṇa (38-82).

Chap. 46

Aggabodhi IV. Sirisaṃghabodhi becomes king; his character; meritorious works of himself and his officials (1-33). — His death (34-8). — The Damiḷa Potthakuṭṭha raises at first Datta and later Hatthadāṭha to the throne while carrying on the government himself (39-47).

Chap. 47

History of Mānavamma. He goes to Jambudīpa, enters the service of Narasīha and becomes his friend (1-14). — He supports him in his war with Vallabha (15-27). — Out of gratitude Narasīha gives him an army with which to gain the sovereignty in Ceylon. The army however leaves him in the lurch and he has again to seek refuge in Jambudīpa (28-41). — He returns with a freshly equipped army to Ceylon and gains the victory. Hatthadāṭha is slain by the populace, Potthakuṭṭha kills himself (42-61). — Mānavamma as king (62-66).

Chap. 48

Aggabodhi V. and his works (1-19). — Reign of Kassapa III. (20-5). — Mahinda I. rules as ādipāda without adopting the royal title (26-38). — Aggabodhi VI. Silāmegha. he quarrels with a cousin of the same name; war and reconciliation of the two (39-54). — Conflict with a third Aggabodhi (55-63). — Meritorious works of the king (64-7). — Aggabodhi VII. and his deeds (68-75). — Mahinda II. reigns at first in the name of the widowed queen (76-89). — He twice defeats Dappula the sister's son of his father (90-112). — The king marries the queen dowager and begets with her a son whom he makes uparāja (113-5). — A renewed struggle with Dappula ends with a treaty (116-32). — Meritorious works of the king (133-48). — After the death of the uparāja the king transfers the dignity to an elder son of the period of his regency (149-60).

Chap. 49

The uparāja, probably Udaya I. becomes king; he crushes a rebellion; weds his daughter Devā to a prince Mahinda of Rohaṇa (1-13). — Meritorious works of the king and his consort (14-37). — His son Mahinda III. becomes king (38-42). — Aggabodhi VIII.; his meritorious works (43-50). — His reverence for his mother (51-61). — Further proofs of his noble character (62-4). — Dappula II. supports Kittaggabodhi in gaining possession of Rohaṇa (65-73). — Meritorious works of the king and of the Senāpati Vajira (74-82). — Aggabodhi IX.; Mahinda, son of Mahinda III. who would have been the rightful successor flees to Jambudīpa (83-6). — Meritorious works of the king (87-93).

Chap. 50

Sena I. His meritorious works. Removal of Mahinda. Younger brothers of the king (1-7). — Revolt of Udaya and reconciliation (8-11). — Incursion of the Paṇḍu king. Is successful in battle. Sena flees to Malaya. The Yuvarāja Mahinda kills himself, his brother Kassapa wins through. The capital occupied and plundered by the Damiḷas (12-37). — After making a treaty with Sena the Paṇḍu king retires with great booty. Sena returns to the capital and settles the succession (38-49). — Dynastic strife in Rohaṇa, intermarriage with the Rohaṇa line (50-60). — Meritorious works of the royal couple and of their minister (61-87).

Chap. 51

Sena II., his character, his family (1-21). — Conceives the plan of a war of retaliation against the Damiḷas (22-6). — Supporting a Paṇḍu prince in his claims to the throne, he sends his senāpati with an army to the Continent. Madhurā is taken and plundered and the captured treasures brought back to Ceylon (27-51). — The Paṃsukūlika bhikkhus of the Abhayagiri found a special sect (52). — Meritorious works of the Yuvarāja Mahinda; his death (53-62). — Meritorious works of the king, of his consort and of his senāpati (63-89). — Udaya II. Intermarriages in the royal family (90-3). — Kittaggabodhi revolts and seizes Rohaṇa. The king sends a great nephew against him. Conquest of Rohaṇa (94-125). — Punishment of the rebels; meritorious works of the king (126-36).

Chap. 52

Kassapa IV. and his family (1-3). — Revolt of Prince Mahinda in Rohaṇa and reconciliation with him (4-9). — Purification of the Church (10). — Meritorious works of the king and of his dignitaries (11-36). — Kassapa V. Meritorious works of the king, honouring of the sacred scriptures. Meritorious works of relatives of the royal family (37-69). — Kassapa supports the Paṇḍu king in war against the Coḷa king; his army obliged to return in consequence of a pestilence (70-82).

Chap. 53

Dappula III. dies after a short reign (1-3). — Dappula IV. harbours the Paṇḍu king who flees to him; meritorious works of the king and of his senāpati (4-12). — Udaya III. The Uparāja Sena abuses the right of asylum of the Tapovana; the bhikkhus betake themselves to Rohaṇa (13-5). — The Uparāja with his friend forced to flee thither from the enraged populace. Reconciliation with the priests and return to the capital (16-27). — Sena III. Meritorious works (28-38). — Udaya IV. Invasion of the Coḷas, flight of the king to Rohaṇa. Retreat of the Coḷas after an unsuccessful attack on Rohaṇa (39-45). — The senāpati of the king, Viduragga undertakes a campaign in the Coḷa country (46-7). — Meritorious works of Udaya (48-52).

Chap. 54

Sena IV. His character and his works (1-6). — Mahinda IV. marries a Kalinga princess. His war with the Coḷa prince Vallabha ended by a treaty (7-16). — Honour shown by him to distinguished theras and many other meritorious works of the king, as of the Queen Kitti and of her son and of the Sakkasenāpati (17-56). — Sena V. Conflict with the senāpati Sena because the king makes Udaya senāpati instead of him (57-61). — The king forced to flee to Rohaṇa. Sena favours the Damiḷas on whose support he relies. The king dismisses Udaya, makes friends with Sena and returns to the capital (62-9). — Drinks himself to death (70-3).

Chap. 55

Mahinda V. reigns in Anurādhapura. Mutiny of the Keraḷa mercenaries. The king flees to Rohaṇa. The other provinces ravaged by the licentious soldiery (1-12). — The Coḷa king exploits these disturbances. He invades the country, plunders it and seizes the king, his consort and all valuables (13-22). — The generals Kitti and Buddha organize successful resistance in Rohaṇa in favour of Prince Kassapa (23-32). — Mahinda dies after a twelve years' captivity in the Coḷa country (33-4).

Chap. 56

Kassapa VI. Vikkamabāhu prepares a campaign against the Coḷas, but dies before accomplishing it (1-6). — He is succeeded by the usurpers Kitti, Mahālānakitti, Vikkamapaṇḍu, Jagatīpāla and Parakkama. They are restricted to Rohaṇa, the Coḷas are masters of the country (7-17).

Chap. 57

General Loka prince in Rohaṇa (1-2). — Early history of Kitti, the later Vijayabāhu: Kassapa and his sons Mānavamma and Māna (3-26). — Kassapa husband of Lokitā, father of Moggallāna and Loka (27-30). — A grandson of Dāṭhopatissa becomes a bhikkhu and gains a high reputation (31-9). — Kitti, son of Moggallāna and Lokitā, the daughter of Bodhi gives early proofs of his heroism. Becomes chief opponent of Loka (40-64). — After Loka's death he conquers and slays Kassapa who was about to seize the sovereignty and becomes himself lord of Rohaṇa (65-76).

Chap. 58

Kitti rules in Rohaṇa under the name of Vijayabāhu. Evades an attack by the Coḷas (1-6). — Prepares for war (7-10). — Defeats a second Coḷa army sent against him. Advances on Pulatthinagara but has again to abandon it (11-32). — After suppressing a revolt in Rohaṇa he fights a decisive action (33-39). — Ably supported by his generals he takes Anurādhapura and Pulatthinagara, the Coḷas give up the fight (40-59).

Chap. 59

The kingdom made secure, preparations for the coronation, suppression of the revolt of Ādimalaya (1-6). — After his consecration as king in Anurādhapura Vijayabāhu returns to Pulatthinagara. Adopts the name of Sirisaṃghabodhi (7-10). — Granting of titles to his brothers and of offices to his followers (11-4). — Suppression of a rebellion in Rohaṇa, Malaya and Dakkhiṇadesa (15-22). — Wives and children of the king (23—33). — Perceives signs in his daughter Ratanāvalī that she will become the mother of a famous son (34-9). — Marries his daughters, Ratanāvalī and Lokanāthā, to the sons of his sister. Further marriages of a dynastic character (40-51).

Chap. 60

Vijayabāhu's architectural works. Cares for the Church by fetching bhikkhus from Rāmañña. Further meritorious works (1-23). — The Coḷa king ill-treats envoys of King Vijayabāhu. The latter arms for war. A revolt of the Velakkāras is bloodily suppressed (24-44). — At the coast he awaits in vain the arrival of the Coḷas (45-7). — Tanks repaired by the king, ecclesiastical buildings erected, condign punishment of the mahesī who had disturbed the peace of the vihāras (48-62). — The road to Samantakūṭa rendered safe, meritorious works for the good of the priesthood, encouragement of the art of poetry, support of the poor (63-82) — Works of the king's followers (83-5). — Death of Vijayabāhu after settling the succession (86-91).

Chap. 61

Mānābharaṇa and his two brothers make Jayabāhu king to the exclusion of Vikkamabāhu. Vikkamabāhu conquers them and seized Pulatthinagara (1-20). — The brothers divide Rohaṇa and Dakkhiṇadesa between them, renew the war but are again beaten (21-35). — Invasion of Vīradeva who advances as far as Pulatthinagara but is finally defeated by Vikkamabāhu (36-47). — Anarchy in the country, many bhikkhus taking with them the tooth and alms-bowl relics seek refuge along with members of noble houses in Rohaṇa (48-73).

Chap. 62

Jayabāhu's death, children of Vallabha and Mānābharaṇa (1). — Dreams of Mānābharaṇa and his consort presage the birth of a distinguished son (2-29). — Good works of Mānābharaṇa; pregnancy of Ratanāvalī; birth of a boy who receives the name of Parakkamabāhu (30-52). — At the news of this Vikkamabāhu desires to bring up the child at his court; refusal of the father (53-66). — Death of Mānābharaṇa Vīrabāhu (67).

Chap. 63

Kittisirimegha, the second brother takes over the province ruled by Mānābharaṇa, Dakkhiṇadesa; the third, Sirivallabha takes over Rohaṇa with the capital Mahānāgahula together with the upbringing of Parakkama. Marries Mānābharaṇa's daughters to his son (1-17). — In Pulatthinagara Gajabāhu ascends the throne; successfully repulses attacks by Kittisirimegha and Sirivallabha (18-37). — Parakkamabāhu's youth. The prince leaves the court of Sirivallabha and betakes himself to his uncle Kittisirimegha in Saṅkhanāyakatthalī (38-53).

Chap. 64

Kittisirimegha and his nephew Parakkamabāhu visit the general Saṅkha in Badalatthalī; celebration of the upanayana festival for the prince (1-17). — Death of Sirivallabha. Is succeeded in Rohaṇa by his son, the younger Mānābharaṇa. Each of M.'s two wives bears him a son (18-24). — Parakkamabāhu's ambition aroused by the history of the heroes of antiquity. To gather information as to the political conditions in Rājaraṭṭha he decides to go thither in person and leaves the town by night (25-64).

Chap. 65

The prince meets his followers at the appointed trysting-place and comes to Badalatthalī (1-26). — General Saṅkha is surprised, receives the prince nevertheless with due honours. As Parakkama however fears betrayal by him he has him slain (27-37). — Great consternation at the deed. A soldier desirous of avenging Saṅkha is hewn down (37-44).

Chap. 66

Parakkama proceeds farther to Buddhagāma (1-19). — Subdues the resistance of the inhabitants (20-34). — The commander of Kālavāpi, Gokaṇṇa, visits the prince. Frightened however, by a dream he flees by night to Kālavāpi. His people follow him (35-56). — Kittisirimegha determines to fetch the Prince back by force but Parakkama ambushes the troops sent to seize him and cuts them up (57-77). — There follows a series of further skirmishes until the Prince at Janapada reaches the territory of Gajabāhu (78-111). — Gajabāhu receives him with honour. Parakkama now seeks by systematic espionage to discover the temper of the king's subjects and does the same in the society in which he moves (112-45). — He fetches his sister Bhaddavatī from Rohaṇa. Marries her to the king thus gaining his confidence and makes himself everywhere popular (146-58).

Chap. 67

By his determination the prince subdues a mad buffalo. His courage universally admired (1-8). — He decides to return to Dakkhiṇadesa in order to seize the kingdom from there.

Gajabāhu has no inkling of his plans (9-31). — Flight from Pulatthinagara. All kinds of adventures on the way give the prince the opportunity of showing his courage (32-54). — Kittisirimegha sends people to receive him, his mother Ratanāvalī fetches him in person (55-82). — Death of Kittisirimegha; Parakkamabāhu in the dignity of the mahādipāda (83-96).

Chap. 68

Parakkama furthers culture in Dakkhiṇadesa; builds dams on the Jajjara river and widens the Paṇḍavāpi tank (1-42). — Erection of further dams and constructions for increasing the productive power of the country (43-59).

Chap. 69

Military preparations in particular by organisation of recruiting in the various districts of the country (1-38).

Chap. 70

Parakkama through his generals extends his dominion over Malaya. First encounter with Gajabāhu (1-29). — Adventure with an elk during the chase (30-52). — Parakkamabāhu opens the campaign against Rājaraṭṭha. His generals fight those of Gajabāhu along the frontier from the pearl districts in the west as far as Āḷisāra in the east (53-172). — Parakkama determines to attack Pulatthinagara. Mānābharaṇa of Rohaṇa supports him. The town taken after severe fighting, the king captured and generously treated (173-250). — Embittered at the looting of their town the inhabitants summon Mānābharaṇa. He comes, seizes all Gajabāhu's powers, takes him prisoner and plans to remove him. Gajabāhu begs for Parakkama's protection, whose generals take Pulatthinagara a second time and set Gajabāhu free. Mānābharaṇa escapes to Rohaṇa (251-310). — Gajabāhu tries once more to recover the sovereignty. Once more vanquished, he seeks the bhikkhus as mediators (311-36).

Chap. 71

Death of Gajabāhu, Parakkamabāhu king (1-5). — Gajabāhu's followers summon Mānābharaṇa to their support; Parakkama secures the frontier along the Mahāvālukagaṅgā against him (6-18). — Parakkama undergoes consecration at the express wish of his ministers (19-32).

Chap. 72

Combats at the different fords of the Mahāvālukagaṅgā (1-54). — Parakkama sends his generals against Rohaṇa also from the Pañcayojana province (55-64). — Revolt of Nārāyaṇa in Anurādhapura quickly crushed by Parakkama (65-9). — Mānābharaṇa succeeds in crossing the Mahāvālukagaṅgā and there follows a series of chequered combats. Parakkama forced eventually to give up Pulatthinagara (70-147). — Forced back to the frontiers of Dakkhiṇadesa, Parakkama opens a new attack on the capital. His generals fight numerous battles (148-204). — Mānābharaṇa at bay. Decisive action at Mihiraṇabibbila; a fortification erected by General Rakkha. Mānābharaṇa flees secretly to Rohaṇa, triumphant entry of Parakkamabāhu into Pulatthinagara (205-300). — Death of Mānābharaṇa. Before dying he advises his relatives to give up the resistance to Parakkama (301-10). — Parakkamabāhu celebrates his second coronation (311-29).

TO THE EXALTED ONE, THE PERFECT ONE THE FULLY ENLIGHTENED ONE REVERENCE!

CHAPTER XXXVII

(Continuation)

THE SIX KINGS

So after the Ruler Mahāsena[1] had in consequence of his 51
association with impious people, done good and evil all his
life, he went according to his doing[2]. Therefore should the 52
wise man shunning from afar as a poisonous serpent, the
company of the impious, do speedily that which tends to his
own salvation. Thereupon his son Sirimeghavaṇṇa[3] be- 53

[1] There is not the slightest doubt that with v. 51 the work of the continuator of the old Mahāvaṃsa begins. We must assume that originally an ornate strophe followed 37. 50 as conclusion of Mahānāma's work. The continuator like his successors (cf. 79. 84; 90. 102), veiled the gap. The content of the lost strophe is apparent from v. 51—52, as also from the last verse of the Dīpavaṃsa (22. 76), which Dhammakitti seems to have taken as his starting-point.

[2] P. *gato yathākammaṃ* "he went according to his kamma" a frequent expression (cf. JāCo. I 109[11], 153[13], 178[6]; II. 313[11] etc.) with reference to the five *gati* or forms of rebirth ... 1. in Hell, 2. as animal, 3. as *peta* "ghost", 4. as man, 5. as *deva* „god". Here one must bear in mind that *kamma* "doing" is for Buddhist readers or hearers a technical term, the conception for the sum of all our good and evil deeds in the latest as in the former existences. Our rebirth, our whole fate is determined by *kamma* which is distinctly held to be something concrete.

[3] King Siri Mekavana Aba is mentioned in the inscription of Debel-gala (20 miles E. N. E. of Anurādhapura) which is dated in the first year of his reign. Ed. Müller (AIC., p. 30) attributes the inscrip-

came king, bestowing like Mandhātar[1] all kinds of blessings
54 on the world. In the Mahāvihāra which Mahāsena fallen under the influence of evil people, had destroyed, he gathered
55 together the whole of the bhikkhus, went thither himself, greeted them respectfully, seated himself and asked them full of reverence: "What then has been destroyed by my father
56 in company with Saṃghamitta?" The bhikkhus answered the Lord of men: "Although thy father strove to bring about the
57 removal of the boundary[2], he was unable to do so, as there were still bhikkhus within the boundary. Seven bhikkhus
58 namely, were hidden here in an underground room. The minister Soṇa and the still worse Saṃghamitta[3] influenced the

tion to the king Goṭhābhaya (Mhvs. 36. 98). There are however, not far from Debel-gala at Timbiriveva two further inscriptions in which our Sirimeghavaṇṇa is undoubtedly mentioned. Bell, ASC. VIIth Rep. 1891 = SP. XIII. 1896, p. 50. Sirimeghavaṇṇa is further mentioned in a Chinese source, in the Hing-Tchoan of Wang Hiuen-tse under the name of Chi-mi-kia-po-mo ("cloud of merit"). He is said to have sent two Bhikkhus to India to the King San-maon-to-lo-kiu-to, that is Samudragupta (who reigned according to V. A. Smith approximately between 345 and 380 A. D.), asking him to provide shelter there for the Sinhalese monks who were on a pilgrimage to the sacred tree at Bōgayā. Cf. Sylvain Lévi, JAs. 1900, p. 316 sqq.; J. M. Senaveratne, JRAS. C. B. XXIV, Nr. 68, 1, p. 75; H. W. Codrington, Short History of Ceylon, p. 29.

[1] A legendary king of the dynasty of Mahāsammata, son of Uposatha. His story is told in the Mandhātu-Jātaka (Nr. 258 = JāCo. II. 310 ff.), which is again quoted in DhCo. III. 240^5. The name Mandhātar occurs already in the Rigveda. In the Aṅguttara-Nikāya (A. II. 17) Mandhātar is described as *aggo kāmabhogīnaṃ*.

[2] P. *sīmāy' ugghāṭanaṃ*. What is meant here is the boundary of the enclosure of the Mahāvihāra. The verb *ugghāṭeti* means "to put on one side, to set aside", as for instance, *ghaṭikaṃ*, the door bolt, Vin. II. 207^{10}, III. 119^{24}; then "to open, to undo", for instance, *kavāṭakaṃ* Mhvs. 35. 25; *sīhapañjaraṃ* JāCo. I. 124^{17}, II. 31^{15}; *thūpaṃ* Thvs. 39^{18}; lastly "to make known, to reveal", eg. *atītabhave* DhCo. IV. 51^2. The removal of the boundaries would only have been legal, if the bhikkhus themselves had given up the vihāra.

[3] The Thera Saṃghamitta belonged to the Vetulla sect and worked together with his lay disciple Soṇa for the advantage of the Abhayagirivihāra against the bhikkhus of the Mahāvihāra. See Mhvs. 36. 110 ff., 37. 1 ff.

king and determined him to do evil. They destroyed the splen- 59
did seven-storeyed Lohapāsāda[1] as well as various other buil-
dings and carried off (the material) to the Abhayagiri (-vihāra)[2].
In the court of the Cetiya[3] where four Buddhas had sojourned, 60
the deluded ones had mungo beans planted; behold (in its
consequences) the intercourse with fools." When the King 61
heard of these doings of his father, he being averse himself
from all association with fools, had everything which his father
had destroyed, restored in its original form. To begin with, 62
he set up the Lohapāsāda, making visible as it were, the
magnificent palace of Mahāpanāda[4] on (the island of) Sīhala.

[1] The *Lohapāsāda* was laid out by King Devānampiyatissa as dwelling for the inmates of the Mahāvihāra (Mhvs. 27. 4 ff.). There are 1600 monolithic stone columns still standing which formed the framework of the lowest storey. As the inmost pillars are the strongest, and had thus evidently the heaviest weight to bear, we may suppose the building to have been a stepped pyramid. The upper storeys were apparently of wood and were covered with plates of copper. Hence the name "Brazen Palace". The word *pāsāda* is applied to all larger buildings of several storeys. The meaning "palace" though not always appropriate, is of course so whenever, as below v. 62, the *pāsāda* of a prince is meant. That the Lohapāsāda was in the main built of perishable material is proved by the fact that under Saddhātissa (77—59 B. C.) it was destroyed by fire and had to be rebuilt.

[2] *Abhayagiri* is without doubt the northern of the three large thūpas in Anurādhapura, Jetavana the eastern, not conversly. The question was admirably treated recently by A. M. HOCART (Mem. ASC. I. 10 ff.). A reference might still be made to Mhvs. 37. 33 where it reads: *Mahāvihārasīmante uyyāne Jotināmake Jetavanavihāram so vāriyanto pi kārayi.* This of course is applicable only to the eastern not to the northern thūpa.

[3] Regarding the untranslated *termini* (here *cetiya*) see Mhvs. trsl., Appendix D, p. 292 ff. *Cetiya* and *thūpa* are used synonymously for the bell-shaped structures designed to hold relics. The fundamental form was without doubt the burial mound.

[4] A legendary king of the Mahāsammata dynasty (Mhvs. 2. 4). An account of his splendid palace (*yūpa*) is given in the verses Thag. 163-4 = Jā. II. 334 (Mahāpanādajātaka). It was sunk in the Ganges at Payāga. A legend relates of the Thera Bhaddaji that to prove his miraculous strength, he raised the palace with his toes out of the bed of the stream and showed it to the astonished people. (Jā. II. 333; Mhvs. 31. 7 ff.)

63 He built up all the demolished pariveṇas[1] and fixed the re-
64 venues of the helpers of the monastery[2] as heretofore. The
wise (Sirimeghavaṇṇa) refilled the vihāra which had become
sparsely inhabited through his unwise father having stinted it
65 of necessaries. In the vihāra begun by his father in Jotivana[3]
66 the monarch had all unfinished work completed. Now when
the Ruler of men had heard from the beginning the whole
history of the Thera Mahinda, the (spiritual) son of the Ruler
67 of the Samaṇas (Buddha), he felt a believing joy in his merit
in having brought the island to the faith and thought: "Of
68 a truth the Thera is lord over the island". He then had an
image of gold made corresponding with the size of Mahinda
69 and brought it to the Ambatthala-cetiya[4], so called after the
mango tree of the Thera[5]. There he left it on the eighth
70 day. But on the ninth day he took a great host like to an
army of the gods, as also the women of the harem and the
71 inhabitants of the town, save the watchmen, gathered together
also all the bhikkhus in Laṅkādīpa, and freed the people who

[1] *Pariveṇa* (Sinh. *piriveṇa*) denotes now a building intended for the instruction of the bhikkhus. That *pariveṇa* originally, or at any rate in early times, must have denoted more than the single cell inhabited by a bhikkhu is clear from 37. 172.

[2] P. *ārāmikānaṃ*. The *ārāmikā* had to do work for the monastery and to keep it in order. See Vin. I. 206 ff. — Cf. Vin. II. 211[23] ff. the grades *bhikkhu—sāmaṇera—ārāmikā*.

[3] What is meant here is the Jetavana-vihāra which was built according to Mhvs. 37. 33, by Mahāsena in the Jotivana which lies outside the southern gate of the town of Anurādhapura (Mhvs. 15. 202. See the note on 37. 59.) A special Jotivana-vihāra did not exist. Cf. also below 52. 59 with note.

[4] *Cetiyambathale* (so also v. 69, 74). Probably a mere inversion for *Ambatthalacetiye* metri causa. The Ambatthalacetiya stands on a terrace of the Missaka hill, now Mihintale (8 miles east of Anurādhapura) below the highest summit, on the spot where according to the legend, the emissary Mahinda converted King Devānampiyatissa to the doctrine of the Buddha.

[5] By the riddle of the mango tree (Mhvs. 14, 17 ff.) the Thera Mahinda put the King's discernment to the proof. Even now there are mango trees planted near the Ambatthalacetiya in memory of the event.

were in prison in the town. Then he instituted a great alms- 72
giving for all living beings, and celebrating with all offerings
a matchless sacrifice, he went forth to greet the master of 73
the island, the best son of the Master (Buddha), as the King
of the gods (Sakka) had aforetime (greeted) the Master[1]. He 74
had the street from the Ambatthala-cetiya to the town put in
order even as the road from Vesālī to the town Sāvatthī, and 75
by the spending of a whole fortune on this occasion, as the
King (Asoka), the father of the Thera (had done) on the arri-
val of the Thera Moggaliputta[2], he satisfied the poor, travellers 76
and beggars by instituting a great almsgiving and the bhik-
khus by (the gift of) the four necessaries[3]. Then the Illustrious 77
One with the wish: the people shall see the arrival of the
Thera, lifted up the image amid great reverence, descended 78
from the mountain (Missaka), (and) while he placed himself
at the head (of the procession), made the bhikkhus surround
it on all sides — the golden image of the Thera shone as 79
the golden Mount Meru[4] rising out of the milky sea (shines)
when irradiated by the evening glow — and showed it to 80
the people with the thought: Even thus the Leader of the
World went forth to Vesālī to preach the Sutta[5]. Thus paying 81

[1] On the occasion of Buddha's visit to the Tāvatiṃsa-hea en. Cf. Divyāvadāna, ed. E. B. Cowell and R. A. Neil, 401; Rockhill, Life of the Buddha, p. 80 f.; Bigandet, Life or Legend of Gaudama the Buddha, I, p. 225 ff.; Th. Kern, Manual of Indian Buddhism, p. 33.

[2] The fetching of the Mahinda image by Sirimeghavaṇṇa is compared with that of Moggaliputtatissa by King Asoka, as it is described in Mhvs. 5. 245 ff. The Thera dwells in a hermitage on the upper Ganges. He is wanted to settle the disputes which have arisen in the Buddha Order. Only after many vain attempts does Asoka's emissary succeed in persuading him to take the journey to Pāṭaliputta where the King receives him with the highest honours. There follows the holding of the Third Council.

[3] P. *paccayehi catūhi*, namely: clothing (*cīvara*), food (*piṇḍapāta*), dwelling (*senāsana*) and medicine (*bhesajja*).

[4] Meru or Sumeru is the mythical world mountain which rises in the centre of the earth, on whose summit lies the heaven of the Tāvatiṃsā, of the 33 Gods. S. Kirfel, Kosmographie der Inder, p, 16, 187 etc.

[5] Verses 66—80 form one sentence. The subj. is *manujindo* in 66

reverence and homage (to the image) the Lord of men set out
in the evening for the vihāra Sotthiyākara[1] which he had him-
82 self erected near the eastern gate, and there also he let the
image of the (spiritual) son of the Conqueror (Buddha) tarry
83 three days. Then after he had on the 12th day put the town
well in order, even as the town of Rājagaha at the first entry
84 of the Master[2], he fetched the image from the Sotthiyākara-
vihāra and brought it, while the town had the semblance of
85 the ocean by reason of the great festival, to the Mahāvihāra,

taken up again by *rājā* in 67, *so* in 70 and *ayaṃ* in 72, verb. fin. *dassesi* in 80, obj. *paṭibimbaṃ* in 68 (taken up again by *taṃ* in 77). The construction of the sentence is disturbed by the verb. fin. *sobhatha* in 79. I believe either that the whole of verse 79 was inserted later or perhaps better still that it is to be regarded as a parenthesis. The Sutta preached by the Buddha in Vesālī is the Ratanasutta (No. 6 of the Khuddakapāṭha = v. 222 ff. or Cūlavagga 1 in the Suttanipāta). Its previous history is related by Buddhaghosa (Kh. A. p. 158 ff.), appears also in the Mahāvastu (I. 253 ff.) In Vesālī, the capital of the Licchavi clan (T. W. Rhys Davids, Buddhist India, p. 25 f.) bad plagues caused by evil spirits are rife. The terrified inhabitants appeal to the Buddha who is sojourning in Rājagaha. He comes, drives off the evil spirits and pronounces over Vesālī the verses of blessing (*Svastyayanagāthā* in the Mahāvastu) of the Ratanasutta. It is now expressly insisted on that the street from Rājagaha to the Ganges and again on the territory of the Licchavi from Vesālī to the Ganges was put in the most perfect order and decorated. I should therefore refer v. 74 also to the journey of the Buddha to Vesālī, though in that case Sāvatthī would be erroneously substituted for Rājagaha. That there was a tendency to make Sāvatthī a dwelling place of the Buddha is shown by Mrs. Rhys Davids's acute observations on the Saṃyutta-Nikāya. (The Book of the Kindred Sayings trsl. by F. C. Woodward, III, p. XI f.)

[1] From the description of the position the name would best fit that collection of buildings east of Anurādhapura now called Puliyankulam. The foundation of this vihāra would then have to be placed in the 4th century A. D., as Sirimeghavaṇṇa built it himself (*sayaṃkataṃ*). The fact of the present ruins belonging in style to a later period is no argument against the identification, as all these monasteries were repeatedly enlarged and renewed.

[2] On the Buddha's first visit to Rājagaha on which occasion King Bimbisāra presented him with the Veḷuvana park see Vin. I. 35 ff.; JāCo. I. 82^{28} ff.; Rockhill, Life of the Buddha, p. 48.

left it three months in the court of the Bodhi tree, brought it
then in the same (solemn) manner to the inner town and had 86
a handsome shelter built for the image near the royal palace
at its south-eastern corner. The wise, discerning (King) had 87
images of Iṭṭhiya and of the others[1] made and put them in
the same spot. He set a watch there and spent a sum of money 88
as an offering and gave orders to proceed year by year in
like manner. In obedience to his order the kings of his race 89
keep up the custom here (in Ceylon) to this day and do not
neglect it. On the day of Pavāraṇā[2] he brought the image 90
from the town to the vihāra and ordered that every year an
offering be made on the 13th day. Beside the Bodhi tree 91
Tissavasabha in the Abhaya-vihāra[3] he had a stone terrace
and a handsome wall built.

In the ninth year of this (King) a Brahman woman brought 92
hither (to Anurādhapura[4]) from the Kaliṅga country the Tooth

[1] The theras Iṭṭhiya, Uttiya, Sambala and Bhaddasāla (Mhvs. 12. 7), the sāmaṇera Sumana and the lay-brother Bhaṇḍuka (Mhvs. 13. 18, 14. 33) were companions of Mahinda on his flight to Ceylon.

[2] *Pavāraṇā* is the ceremony observed by the bhikkhus at the close of the three months' *vassa*, that is the rainy season spent in the vihāra. The *vassa* begins according to the directions of the Vinaya (I. 137[26]; cf. with this Vin.-A. III. 293[4] the commentary of Buddhaghosa) on the day after the day of full moon of the month Āsāḷha (May-June) or a month later and lasts three months. As the Pavāraṇā festival takes place on the 14th and 15th days of the final month, the 13th day mentioned in v. 90 is the day immediately preceding it for which the King ordains a yearly festival of offering. (See Th. Kern, Manual of Indian Buddhism, p. 100.)

[3] Differently rendered by Turnour-Wijesiṃha: "and he built stone cornices and beautiful walls also at the Abhaya and Tissa-Vasabha vihāras, as well as at the bodhi tree." I think, however, that *silāvediṃ* can only belong to *bodhipādape*. The sacred fig trees (*Ficus religiosa*) are as a rule sourrounded by a stone terrace. *Vihāre Abhaye* refers without doubt the Abhayagiri-vihāra in the north of the town. I am inclined to look upon Tissavasabha as the name of the Bodhi tree, named perhaps after the name of the man who planted it and who came from the village of Vasabha. There was a village of this name near Anurādhapura its revenues (see 41. 97) being later made over to the Jetavana by Mahānāga.

[4] A more detailed account of this event by which the most famous

93 Relic of the great Sage (Buddha). In the manner set forth in
the Chronicle of the Tooth Relic the Ruler received it with
94 reverence, paid it the highest honours, laid it in an urn of pure
95 crystal, and brought it to the building called Dhammacakka
built by Devānampiyatissa on the royal territory. Henceforth
96 this building was the Temple of the Tooth Relic[1]. The King
his heart swelling with joy, spent 900000 (kahāpaṇas) and ar-
97 ranged therewith a great festival for the Tooth Relic. He de-
creed that it should be brought every year to the Abhayuttara-
vihāra[2], and that the same sacrificial ceremonial should be ob-
98 served. The Ruler had eighteen vihāras built and (he con-
structed) tanks which always contained water, because of his
99 pity for all living creatures. After performing innumerably
many meritorious works such as offerings for the Bodhi Tree
and the like, he went in the 28th year (of his reign) thither
whither his merit took him[3].

relic of the Buddha came to Ceylon, is to be found in the Rājāvaliya (see p. 53 of B. Guṇasekara's translation); in the Rājaratnākaraya (ed. Saddhānanda, Colombo, 1887, p. 29) and in the Pūjāvaliya (Contribution to the History of Ceylon, extracted from the Pújávaliya, ed. B. Guṇasekara, p. 23-4). The country of Kaliṅga corresponds roughly to the present Orissa on the mainland of India. V. 93 refers to the Dāṭhādhātuvaṃsa written in 1211 by Dhammakitti, an older namesake of the author of the first part of the Cūlavaṃsa, or to the copy of it written in the Sinhalese tongue. The Pāli Dāṭhādhātuvaṃsa has been edited by T. W. Rhys Davids, JPTS. 1884, p. 108 ff.

[1] One must look for the remains of the building in the so-called Daḷadā-Māligāva in the south-eastern part of the city of Anurādhapura, not in the ruin of the same name at the Thūpārāma. See E. R. Ayrton, Ceylon Notes and Queries III, Apr. 1914, p. XII ff.

[2] „The Northern Vihāra of Abhaya", the same as the Abhayagiri-vihāra. We often meet with the name *Uttara-Mahā-Ceta* in inscriptions. Thus in that of King Malu-Tissa, Wickremasinghe, EZ. I, p. 256, cf. also ib. p. 221, 236; as well as A. M. Hocart, Mem. ASC. I, p. 12. In the older Mahāvaṃsa (35. 119) we also find the name *Abhayuttaramāhāthūpa*.

[3] Literally: "he went there where was the way to rebirth (*gati*)". Means the same as *yathākammaṃ gato* (see above note 2 to v. 51), here of course in a good sense. According to Pūjāvaliya and Rājāvaliya the king reigned fully 28 years.

The youthful **Jeṭṭhatissa**, the youngest son of his brother[1], 100
then raised the umbrella of dominion in Laṅkā, (he being) ex-
perienced in the art of ivory carving. Extraordinarily skilful, 101
he carried out many[2] difficult works and taught the practice of
his art to many people. At his father's[3] request he made a 102
beautiful, charming figure representing the Bodhisatta, as beau-
tiful as if it had been produced by miraculous power, as well 103
as a chair of state with a back, an umbrella, a maṇḍapa[4] with
jewels: Here and there[5] (were) all kinds of work by him in
splendid ivory. After ruling the island of Laṅkā for nine years[6] 104
and doing numerous meritorious works, he passed away in ac-
cordance with his deeds.

Thereupon his son **Buddhadāsa**[7] became king, a mine of 105
virtues, as the sea (is such) of all jewels. Creating happiness 106
by every means for the inhabitants of the island, protecting the
town[8], as the wealthy Vessavaṇa protects the town of Ālaka-
mandā[9], gifted with wisdom and virtue, a refuge of pure pity 107

[1] According to the reading *bhātu tassa kaniṭṭhako* as against *bhātā t. k.* cf. Cūlavs. ed., Introd. p. XVII. Nevertheless I have scruples in adopting this reading, since in the historical literature of Ceylon Jeṭṭhatissa is distinctly called the brother, not the nephew of his predecessor.

[2] P. *citrāni*. I do not believe that this word refers to painting. It is always a question of Jeṭṭhatissa's ivory carving only.

[3] The „father" may be king Sirimeghavaṇṇa, the paternal uncle being always called *pitar*.

[4] By *maṇḍapa* is understood a light, open, arbour-like structure whose roof is supported on pillars, often put up for merely temporary purposes.

[5] The construction of the sentence is not quite clear. I think v. 103 c d is a summary of what has gone before.

[6] Pūjāvaliya has the same; but according to the Rājāvaliya, 10 years.

[7] The Sinhalese sources (Pūjāv., Rājāv., Rājaratn.) call him Bujasraja. Also Nikāya-saṃgraha ed. Wickremasinghe, 16^{8}.

[8] *Rakkhaṃ* is to be supplemented from d by the object *puraṃ*, while on the other hand *puraṃ* must be supplemented by the participle *rakkhaṃ* from c.

[9] *Vessavaṇa* — Skr. *Vaiśravaṇa*, patronymic of Kuvera the god of wealth. His capital is called in Skr. *Alakā* (E. W. Hopkins, Epic Mythology, p. 142 ff.). In D. II. 147^{6}, 170^{7} Ālakamandā is called the capital of the Devas.

108 and endowed with the ten qualities of kings[1], while avoiding the
four wrong paths[2], practising justice, he won over his subjects
109 by the four heart-winning qualities[3]. The Ruler lived openly
before the people the life that bodhisattas lead and had pity
110 for (all) beings as a father (has pity for) his children. He ful-
filled the wishes of the poor by gifts of money, those of the
111 rich by protecting their property and their life. Great in dis-
cernment he treated the good with winning friendliness, the
wicked with sternness. the sick with remedies.

112 Now one day as the King riding on the back of his ele-
phant was on his way, in the principal street, to bathe in the
113 Tissa-tank, he beheld a large snake smitten with belly disease,
lying not far from the Puttabhāga-vihāra outstretched on its
114 back on a white ant -heap to display its disease of the belly,
115 called a tumour. He thought: the snake is certainly ill[4]. There-
upon he got down from the great elephant and approaching the
great snake, thus spake the hero, the Spotless One, to the great
116 snake[5]: "I understand, great Snake, the reason of thy coming.
117 But ye (snakes) are very fiery[6] and easily fly into a rage[7]. There-

[1] On the *dasa rājadhammā* see M. and W. Geiger, Pali Dhamma, p. 17. They are enumerated J. III. 274[1]: *dāna* "giving of alms", *sīla* "leading a moral life", *pariccāga* "liberality", *ajjava* "fair dealing", *maddava* "gentleness", *tapas* "self-discipline", *akkodha* "without wrath", *avihiṃsā* "not wounding", *khanti* "patience", *avirodhana* "peaceableness".

[2] P. *catasso agatī hitvā*. The four *agati* are *chanda* "desire", *dosa* "hate", *moha* "illusion", *bhaya* "fear".

[3] The *cattāri saṃgahavatthūni* are *dāna* "the giving of alms, liberality", *peyyavajja* "friendly, winning speech", *atthacariyā* "beneficent action", *samānattatā* "sociability". Cf. 41. 56.

[4] One must read "*nāgo rogī ti nicchayaṃ*", The *ti* is, as often, placed in the *oratio recta*. Cf. 44, 16; 45, 20; 48, 30.

[5] The verse contains a play upon words impossible for us to render, *nāga* being used in the threefold meaning of "snake" especially cobra, "elephant" and "great man, hero". Add to this the similarity in sound with *anāgavā* (Skr. *āgas* "guilt, sin").

[6] P. *mahāteja*. Turnour's translation "highly gifted" is wrong.

[7] Literally: "You are quickly such who bear the character of being wrathful". See Cūlavs. ed., vol. II, Index 2, s. v. *kuppana*.

fore it is impossible for me to touch thee and so to accomplish
my work; but without touching thee it is also not possible.
What then is to be done?" At these words the prince of the 118
snakes stuck his whole neck[1] into the cavity (of the white ant-
heap) and remained lying motionless. He stepped up to it, took 119
the knife that he wore at his side and slit open the belly of the
snake. After he had taken out the diseased parts and applied 120
an excellent remedy, he at once cured the reptile. Then he 121
gloried thus: "Even the beasts have known my great charity;
in the right way have I ruled." When the snake saw that it 122
was cured, it gave the Monarch as a mark of esteem, its own
precious jewel[2]. The King placed the jewel as eye in the stone 123
image of the Perfectly Enlightened One in the Abhayuttara-
vihāra.

A bhikkhu on his mendicant round in the village of Thusa- 124
vaṭṭhika had been given only dry mendicant's food. When then
he went begging for milk he got milk with worms in it which 125
he drank. In his belly the worms multiplied and fed on his
bowels. Then he went and told the King. The King asked: 126
"At what meal did this pain arise and of what kind is it?"
The other answered: "At the meal that I took with milk in 127
the village of Thusavaṭṭhi". The King recognised that it had
been milk with worms in it. Now just at that time a horse 128
had to be cured by bleeding. The King himself bled it, took
the blood, gave it tho the samaṇa to drink and spake, waiting 129
a moment[3]: "That was horse's blood." When the samaṇa[4]
heard that he vomited. The worms came up with the blood, 130
the bhikkhu was cured, but the King showed his joy: "By a 131

[1] P. *phaṇa*, the hood of the cobra which it inflates when irritated. Pun with *phaṇinda* "prince of the hooded snakes".

[2] In allusion to the widespread popular belief that snakes or particular snakes have a jewel in their head. Cf. for instance, Chakesadhātu-vaṃsa, JPTS. 1885, p. 14[16].

[3] I now prefer to read *vitināmayaṃ* with the MSS. S 3 or., 6, or *vitināmiya* with the Colombo edition.

[4] On the term *samaṇa* cf. R. O. Franke, D. trsl. p. 304 ff. In the Mahāvaṃsa the word is used in the same sense as *bhikkhu*.

single stroke of the knife worms, samaṇa and horse have been
cured: excellent of a truth are my activities as healer."
132 A man in drinking water swallowed the egg of a water
133 snake[1]; out of it there came a water snake. It sucked itself
fast[2] in his inside. Tortured by the pain caused by this he
134 sought the King. The latter asked him as to the cause[3]. He
recognised that a reptile was within him, made him fast a
week and had him, after being bathed and rubbed with oil,
135 laid on a well prepared bed. Now as he lay there in deep
136 slumber with open mouth, he placed before his mouth a piece
of meat with a string attached. (Lured) by the smell the rep-
tile came out of him, bit fast at it and wanted to crawl in
137 (again). Thereupon the King held it fast by means of the
string, drew it out, threw it in a jug into water and spake
138 these words: "As is well known the physician of the Perfectly
Enlightened One was Jīvaka[4]. Can the world show a work of
139 his harder (than this)? Certainly he also would accomplish a
work like this — of that there can be no doubt — if he
did it[5] with the utmost care. Behold the consequences of my
good deeds![6]"

[1] *deḍḍubha.* Cf. *udakadeḍḍubha* J. I. 361^{6}, III. 16^{19}. In J. VI. 194^{16} the Comm. explains the word *d.* by *udakasappa.* In Sinh. also *deḍuba* means a water snake. The closely allied skr. word *duṇḍubha* is a kind of lizard without feet living in the water (Böhtlingk-Roth, s. v.).

[2] P. *anto tudittha tuṇḍaṃ*, lit. "it stuck (or bored) its mouth in".

[3] P. *nidāna* is like skr. *nidāna* a medical term: "the theory of the causes of diseases and of their nature: Aetiology, Pathology" PTSPD. s. v. Cf. Milp. 272^{13}: *roguppattiṃ ca nidānaṃ* ca.

[4] For this famous physician, Jīvaka Komārabhacca, see namely Vin. I. 268 ff.

[5] Turnour has misunderstood the passage. W. has got nearer to the sense, but he has misinterpreted *sabbādarena kubbanto* ("in all loving-kindness"). The meaning is this: Buddhadāsa has no intention of placing himself above Jīvaka, but his achievements are equal to the highest of those of Jīvaka. The latter also had to use all his skill to achieve such cures as Buddhadāsa can boast of having accomplished.

[6] P. *puññodaya*, lit. "ascent of acquired merit", a technical expression denoting the moment, in which the effects of former good deeds make themselves felt. See 53. 23.

In the same way in Helloligāma he saved a Caṇḍāla woman 140
the fruit of whose womb had taken a wrong position[1], seven
times with the child. A bhikkhu was disturbed[2] in his exer- 141
cises by the writhing disease[3]; as he had become (bent) like
a roof-tree[4] the wise (King) freed him from his ailment. A 142
young man was drinking a little water in which were frog's
eggs. An egg penetrating by the nostril entered his skull. It 143
opened and was a frog; it grew and dwelt[5] there. At the
approach of the rainy season the young man was greatly tor-
tured by it. The King split the skull, took out the frog, put 144
the parts of the skull together again and cured the young man
at once[6]. For the good of the inhabitants of the Island the 145
ruler had refuges for the sick set up in every village and placed
physicians in them. He made a summary of the essential con- 146
tent of all the medical text-books and charged one physician
with (the care of) twice five villages[7] and gave the physicians 147
the produce of ten fields as livelihood. He also appointed phy-
sicians for elephants, horses and soldiers. For cripples[8] and 148

[1] One must join *mūḷhagabbhiniṃ jātaṃ*. On *mūḍhagarbha* cf. Jolly, Medizin (der Inder), p. 64 f. *Satta vāresu* belongs to *mūḷhagabbhiniṃ* as well as to *sukhitaṃ akā* "cured, saved".

[2] P. *vuṭṭhāpito*. The verb *(v)uṭṭhā* is the term for awaking from the state of absorption in meditation (*samādhi*). Thus Vin. I. 2[29], 3[12] etc. D. II. 156[5] ff.; M. I. 302[8–10] etc. Also the substantive *(v)uṭṭhāna* M. I. 296[4] etc. Manifestly our passage means that the pain awakened the bhikkhu out of his sleep of meditation.

[3] P. *vātābādhena*. See Jolly loc. cit. p. 118 f. The disease consists in contraction of the joints, cramp, paralysis etc.

[4] P. *gopānasī* a roof beam in gable form ∧. The expression *gopānasivaṅka* "bent like a *g.*" is used of people bent by age.

[5] P. *tattha gacchati* in the more general meaning "was there" (cf. skr. *tatragata*), the present expressing the permanent condition.

[6] Lit. made him (as he had been) originally.

[7] I do not take *sāratthasaṃgahaṃ* as does Turnour, for the title of a medical work. In this case the construction of the preceding genitive *sabbesaṃ vejjasatthānaṃ* would be quite unintelligible. Cf. also the note to v. 171.

[8] P. *pīṭhasappīnaṃ*, who moved about with the help of a chair-like frame. PTSPD. s. v.

for the blind he built refuges in various places and refuges
149 with maintenance in the principal street[1]. He hearkened con-
stantly to the good doctrine, showing reverence to the preachers
of the doctrine[2]. He also fixed the salaries of the preachers
150 in different places. Of his great pity he had a pocket for his
knife[3] made in the inside of his mantle and whereever he met
them he freed the afflicted from their pains.
151 Now one day the King royally adorned came forth with his
152 army like Vāsava[4] with the Gods. Now when a leper who in
a former existence had been his enemy, beheld the Ruler at
the very summit of his glory and good fortune[5] shining in royal
153 splendour, he was filled with fury; he struck the earth with
his hand and smiting the ground again and again with his staff,
154 he reviled him with many abusive words. As the discerning
(King) witnessed this curious behaviour[6] from afar, he thought:
155 "I cannot remember having done evil to any being; he is cer-
tainly my enemy from former times. I will appease this (his

[1] Evidently for travellers: *bhoga* means here "feeding". In TURNOUR's translation the double *sālāyo* is disregarded.

[2] P. *dhammabhāṇaka* (below in v. 173 the synonym *dhammaghosaka*). The word *dhamma* means here the teaching of Buddha as formulated in the sacred texts. Recitations from such texts (Suttas) by the bhikkhus are even now frequent in Ceylon. They often last the whole night through and pious laymen listen with intense devotion, although they understand not a single word of the recital (Sinh. *baṇa*). P. TUXEN is undoubtedly right in regarding this as "in the first place a kind of spiritual adjustment", thus "a sort of Yoga", facilitated by the musical effect of the recital, by the rhythm which is peculiar to the Pāli texts. The feeling for rhythm is as I have frequently noticed, extraordinarily developed amongst the Sinhalese. P. TUXEN, Einige Bemerkungen über die Konstruktion der Pālitexte, Festschrift Hermann Jacobi, p. 98 ff.

[3] P. *satthavaṭṭim.* The word *sattha* is used here for the surgical knife. So already above v. 119. For the expression "cover" "receptacle" for *vaṭṭi* cf. *maricavaṭṭi* = pepper pod.

[4] A name for the King of the Gods, Sakka or Indra.

[5] Here we must either regard the *m* in *sirisobhagga-m-aggappattaṃ* as neutralising the hiatus, or we must separate *sirisobhaggaṃ aggappattaṃ* so that the first word is dependent as acc. on the second.

[6] P. *vippakāraṃ*, lit. change, demeanour deviating from the normal.

enmity)," and he said to a man who stood near: "Go and find 156
out the feelings of the leper yonder." He went. Like a good 157
friend he seated himself by the leper and asked him why he
was so angry. The leper told him everything: "This Buddhadāsa 158
here was (once upon a time) my slave; for his meritorious deeds
he has become monarch. To slight me he rides past me there
on his elephant. He shall learn to know me in a few days![1] 159
If he puts himself in my power (again), I shall make him par-
take of the full chastisement of slaves. If he does not fall into 160
my hands, I shall slay him and drink his throat's blood. Of
that there is no doubt. Thou shalt see it shortly." The man 161
went and related the matter to the prince. The discerning
(King) (now) felt certain that that (leper) was his enemy of
old. He thought: "It is meet to put an end by (some) means 162
(or other) to the enmity of a foe", and (thus) directed the man:
"win him in the right way." He went to the leper and spoke 163
to him like a good friend: "For a long time I have harboured
the thought of destroying the King; but as I found no accom- 164
plices for his murder, I could not (carry it out). But now that
I have found thee, I can fulfil my wish. Come to my house, 165
dwell with me and be my helper, in a few days I shall destroy
his life." After these words he took the leper to his house 166
and having had him bathed and oiled, clad with a choice gar-
ment, well fed with dainty food and served by youthful women, 167
he had him laid on a splendid, well-prepared bed. In the same 168
fashion he sheltered him for several days and when he saw
that he had grown trustful and that he was happy and con-
tented, he gave him food and drink with the words: "This is 169
a gift from the King." Twice and thrice he refused it, then
begged (by the other) he took it. Gradually he learned to put 170
full trust in the Monarch and when he heard (later) that the
Monarch was dead his heart broke in twain.

[1] Lit. "I will make him know myself". Erroneous by W. "I will make him know himself". The acc. *attānaṃ* can only be related reflectively to the subject contained in *jānāpessāmi*. The gerund *kāretvā* in v. 159 belongs to *jānāpessāmi*, the ger. *māretvā* in v. 160 to *pivissāmi*. The sense is: if he voluntarily becomes again my slave (*hatthaṃ me eti—āyāti*) I shall chastise him as such, if he does it not, I will slay him.

171 Thus the King healed physical and spiritual disease and he installed physicians in the island to provide for the cure (of the sick) in the future[1].
172 In the Mahāvihāra the King had the Moraparivena[2] built which was beautified by a pāsāda five and twenty cubits[3] high.
173 He made over to it the two villages of Samaṇa(gāma) and Goḷapānu(gāma) and to the bhikkhus who held forth on the
174 doctrine (he assigned) revenues and servants[4]. He built vihāras and pariveṇas which were fitted up with the four necessaries,
175 and (he built) tanks and alms-halls, and (erected) images. In the reign of the same king the ascetic Mahādhammakathin[5]
176 translated the Suttas into the Sīhala tongue. The King possessed eighty heroic, vigorously grown sons of winning mien who bore the names of the eighty disciples (of the Buddha[6]).

[1] The Col. ed. takes out the second half of this verse "and he installed" etc. which all MSS. known to me have in this place, and adds it above to v. 146 (= v. 96 of the ed.) after "summary of the essential content of the medical books". On grounds of method I cannot accept this. Besides which the verse is quite appropriate here. The compiler summarizes what the king had done for the furtherance of medical lore not only in his own day but also for the future.

[2] P. *Moraparivena* or *Mayūraparivena* means "Peacock-P." The traditional name Mayūra-Pirivena is applied even to-day to a very ruinous building lying not far from the south-west corner of the present Mahāvihāra on the road leading to Kurunegala. H. C. P. Bell ASC., Ann. Rep. 1894 (= SP. XXXIX, 1904), p. 5.

[3] P. *hattha*. As the *hattha* according to Fleet, JRAS. 1906, p. 1011 was not smaller than 17. 75 inches (= 45. 08 cm.) and certainly not larger than 18. 25 inches (= 46. 35 cm.), the height of the pāsāda of the Moraparivena must have been roughly 37 to 38 ft. (= 11. 28 to 11. 58 m.)

[4] P. *bhoge kappiyakārake*. By *bhogā* is meant the produce taxes of certain lands. The *kappiyakārakā* (lit. who do what is meet) are probably no other than the *ārāmikā* (note to 37, 63).

[5] Without doubt the same as the one named as his contemporary by the Chinese pilgrim Fa-hian, *Ta-mo-kiu-ti* (Beal, Buddhist Records of the Western World I, p. XXVI. As Fa-hian stayed in Ceylon about 411-12 we have here a valuable confirmation of Buddhadāsa's time. E. R. Ayrton, JRAS. 1911, p. 1142.

[6] The *asītisāvakā* are mentioned for instance in the Chakesadhātuvaṃsa, JPTS. 1885 p. 16[5]; the *asītimahātherā* DhCo. I. 14[3], 19[16]. Cf. below 85. 102.

Sorrounded by these (his) sons who were named Sāriputta and 177
so forth, Buddhadāsa shone like the Perfectly Enlightened One.
After he had thus wrought blessings for the dwellers in the 178
Island the Lord of men, Buddhadāsa, went to the world of the
gods[1] in the twenty-ninth year[2] (of his reign).

Hereupon his eldest son Upatissa became king: endowed 179
with all royal virtues, ever leading a moral life, great in pity.
Shunning the ten sinful actions, he practised the ten merito- 180
rious works; the King fulfilled the ten royal duties and the
ten pāramitās[3]. By the four heart-winning qualities[4] he won 181
over the four regions of the world. In the Mahāpāli Hall[5] he
had the remains of the royal table[6] distributed. For cripples, 182

[1] P. *tidiva* = *sagga* (Skr. *tridiva* = *svarga*) designation of the Tāvatiṃsa-heaven, the heaven of the 33 gods at the head of whom stands Sakka (Indra).

[2] The Pūjāvaliya gives Buddhadāsa a reign of full 29 years, the Rājāvaliya one of eighty years!

[3] The ten "meritorious works" (*puññakiriyā*) are *dāna* "giving of alms", *sīla* "leading a moral life", *bhāvanā* "spiritual discipline", *apaciti* "reverence", *veyyāvacca* "diligence", *pattianuppadāna* "transference of one's own merits to another", *abbhanumodanā* "gratitude", *desanā* "instruction", *savana* "hearkening (to sermons)", *diṭṭhujukakamma* "right views" (see PTSPD. s. v. *puñña*). — On the *dasa rājadhammā* see above note to v. 107. — The ten *pāramitā* ("perfections") which must be attained by each future Buddha (*bodhisatta*) are *dāna*, *sīla*, *nekkhamma* "renunciation", *paññā* "knowledge", *viriya* "manliness", *khanti* "patience", *sacca* "uprightness", *adhiṭṭhāna* "will power", *mettā* "love", *upekkhā* "serenity".

[4] See above note to v. 108.

[5] Most probably the building whose remains lie S. E. of the Mahāthūpa (Ruvanveli-Dagoba) close to the present post-office. That this building served for the distribution of alms is proved by the stone canoe 44 ft. long (= 13.4 m.) lying near. This was obviously a receptacle for gifts of rice which were then portioned out. According to **42. 67** this stone canoe was presented by King Aggabodhi II. The erection of the hall is ascribed, Mhvs. 20. 23, to Devānampiyatissa, 247-207 B. C. Cf. on the building H. C. P. Bell ASC., Ann. Rep. 1902 (= SP. LXVII, 1907), p. 1-3.

[6] The reading of the MSS. *rājānubhojanaṃ* is certainly right. Cf. Cūlavs. II, Index 2, List of Words, s. v. *anubhojana*.

women in travail, for the blind and the sick he erected great
183 nursing shelters and alms-halls. In a northerly direction from
the Maṅgalacetiya he erected a thūpa, an image house[1] and
184 an image. In carrying this out he with the thought: my sub-
jects must not be estranged[2] (from me) had (the work) done
185 by boys to whom he distributed sugar and rice. He had built
at various places innumerable and meritorious works, (such
as) the Rājuppala (tank), the Gijjhakūṭa, Pokkharapāsaya, Valā-
186 hassa and Ambuṭṭhi (tanks) and the tank of Goṇḍigāma, the
Khaṇḍarāja-vihāra and (further) tanks always filled with water[3].
187 (Once) when rain poured (into the house) he passed the night
nevertheless lying on his bed, thinking: it would be a trouble
188 to the people (if I were to call anyone). When the Minister
noticed this he took him into the garden and had the house
(meantime) covered in[4]. Thus never for his own sake did he
cause trouble to living beings.

189 In the time of this (King) the Island was vexed by the ills
of a famine and a plague. The benevolent (King) who was as
190 a light for the darkness of sin, asked the bhikkhus: "Did not
the great Sage (Buddha) when the world was visited by such
evils as famine and the like, provide some kind of help for
191 the world?" They pointed to the origin of the Gaṅgārohana-

[1] The *paṭimāgeha* is an essential part of every monastic establishment. It is known by its having besides the main entrance on the east side, an extra entrance from the north.

[2] The ingenious correction *khijjantu* "shall (not) be wearied" (instead of *bhijjantu*) of the Colombo edition is tempting. Nevertheless I feel unable to accept it. It will be argued that if the work is wearisome for adults it must be so in a far greater degree for boys. The idea is rather this: the King will not make enemies of his subjects by giving them tasks which keep them from more important work. Boys have free time and consider such work when rewarded by sweetmeats, as play.

[3] The construction of vv. 185-6 is difficult, the translation uncertain. It is worth noting that in the Pūjāvaliya and the Rājāvaliya the construction of the Tōpāveva, the lake of Polonnaruva, is ascribed to Upatissa.

[4] Here too the construction is brief and obscure. But W. has grasped the meaning properly.

Sutta[1] on such an occasion. When he heard this he made an
image wholly of gold of the departed Buddha[2], laid the stone 192
alms bowl of the Master[3] (filled) with water in the hollow of
its hands and placed this his figure on a great chariot. He 193
took upon himself the duties of a moral life and made the
people also take them on themselves, he instituted a great
almsgiving and established security (of life) for all living crea-
tures. Then after he had adorned the town (so that it was) 194
comely as the world of the gods, he descended surrounded by
all the bhikkhus dwelling in the Island, to the principal street[4]. 195
Then the bhikkhus who had gathered there reciting the Ratana-
Sutta and pouring out water[5], walked about the street, not far 196
from the royal palace, near the wall, round which they walked
with their right side towards it[6] in the three watches of the
night. When morning dawned a great cloud poured rain on 197
the earth and all who had suffered from disease, held refreshed
high festival. But the Lord of men decreed: "When there 198
shall be on the Island an evil such as famine, plague or the
like, thus shall it be done."

[1] Must be a name for the Ratana-Sutta mentioned in v. 195. On this see above note to v. 80.

[2] P. *sambuddhadhātuno*, lit: of the relic of the Perfectly Enlightened One. As Buddha himself has entered Nirvana, an image of his outward appearance as he was in life, can only be a "relic" of him. TURNOUR's translation: "for the tooth relic" is wrong.

[3] The bowl relic (*pattadhātu*) was next to the sacred tooth the relic most revered on the Island. See below 61. 61, 74. 100 ff. It was originally kept in Pāṭaliputta by King Asoka (Mhvs. 17. 20). The Sāmaṇera Sumana, one of Mahinda's companions, brought it so Ceylon, and King Devānampiyatissa deposited it in his palace (Mhvs. 20. 13).

[4] What is meant here is the sacred street which starting from the city of Anurādhapura in the N., runs southwards to the Mahāvihāra.

[5] A fine example of popular rain magic adopted by the official religion. For the filled water vessels and the pouring out of water in Indian rain magic see OLDENBERG, die Religion des Veda[2], p. 505. Further analogies in L. von SCHRÖDER, Arische Religion II, p. 253 ff.

[6] P. *kurumānā padakkhiṇam*. The walking round a sacred object or a holy person with the right side towards it or him, thus *to the left* is a ceremony of reverence. As we were informed in the Subhadrārāma

199 When he having ascended to the Cetiya, perceived ants and
other (insects) he with the words: walk slowly in the forest,
200 was wont to sweep the earth with a peacock's feather and to
use for the cleaning of a seat a shell filled with water[1]. In
201 the south-west corner of the royal palace he had a house built
for the Uposatha festival[2], and a house with an image of Bud-
202 dha as well as a pleasant garden surrounded by a wall. On the
fourteenth, on the fifteenth, as well as on the eighth day of
the half of the month and on extraordinary festivals[3] he stayed
203 there accessible to instruction[4], taking upon himself the eight-
fold Uposatha vow. His whole life long he ate of the food
204 (served) in the Mahāpāli Hali[5]. When he took a walk in the

in Balapitiya the person showing reverence must *go to the right*. A young bhikkhu performed the ceremony in our presence before the thūpa of the monastery. This however must be an innovation. This we learn from the Borobudur in Java. In the case of the reliefs of the first terrace, the pilgrim can only follow the single events in the life of the Buddha in their proper order if ascending the terrace from the east side, he walks round it *to the left*.

1 The passage is difficult. A tolerable construction is only possible if we regard *ādāya carati* as a periphrastic formation. As a rule certainly *car* is joined with the pres. part. But already in Skr. when similarly used, it is found occasionally also joined with the gerund. S. BR. s. v.

2 Uposatha is the Buddhist sabbath which is kept four times in the lunar month, on the day of the new moon (*cātuddasī*), on that of the full moon (*pañcadasī*), and on the 8th day (*aṭṭhamī*) of each half of the month. On the first two days the confession festival (*pāṭimokkhuddesa*) of the bhikkhus took place. Special buildings or halls were erected for this ceremony. Mhvs. trsl., p. 296, nr. 29; SPENCE HARDY, Eastern Monachism p. 237 ff.; TH. KERN, Indian Buddhism p. 99 f.

3 P. *pāṭihāriyapakkha* "an extra holiday, an ancient festival, not now kept" (PTSPD. s. v.) Cf. Sn. 402. The two lines of verse 202 are also found with slight variation S. I. 208^{26}, Vv. 15. 6, 19. 9; DhCo. IV, p. 21. With the help of these parallel passages we should read *cātuddasiṃ pañcadasiṃ yā ca pakkhassa aṭṭhamī*.

4 P. *sāpadānaṃ* is an adverb, = *sa-ap*. The word *apadāna* means "instruction". Thus Th 1, 47 where the Co. renders it by *ovāda*. The opposite of *sāpadāna* is *anapadāna* "accessible to no instruction" which in Vin. II. 4^{20} stands next to *bāla*, *avyatta* and *āpattibahula*. What is meant is of course instruction by the sermon.

5 He lived thus as simply, as the poor who are dependent on charity.

garden, having set up a feeding-place for the Kalanda birds[1],
he had his own food served to them, and this is a custom to
this day. (Once) seeing a criminal who was to be executed being 205
led forth, he was deeply moved and had a corpse fetched from
the burying ground and thrown into a copper barrel. He then 206
gave the criminal money and let him escape by night, but after
sunrise, full of wrath, he had the corpse burnt as if it had
been the criminal. He instituted a great festival for all the 207
cetiyas in the Island and (presented) a gold casing for the
crowning ornament on the Thūpa in the Thūpārāma[2]. After 208
he had for forty and two years[3] performed meritorious works
without leaving even a moment unemployed, he entered into
the company of the King of the gods.

The queen-consort of this King who had an intrigue[4] with 209
his younger brother Mahānāma, murdered him by stabbing
him in a lonely spot. This younger brother who during his 210
brother's lifetime had undergone[5] the ceremony of renunciation
of the world, returned after the murder of the King, to the

[1] According to the northern tradition the Skr. *kalanta(ka)* denotes a bird. Cf. Rockhill, The Life of the Buddha, p. 43, the legend of the Veṇuvana park (P. *veḷuvana*) and of the Kalantakanivāpa (P. *kalandaka-nivāpa*). In my opinion we must assume the same meaning for P. *kalanda(ka)*, although Sinh. *kalada* is said to stand for "squirrel". That we have to do with a kind of bird seems clear from Milp. 368[13]. Here the expression *naṅguṭṭhaṃ papphoṭetvā* is used of the *kalandaka*; JāCo. II. 153[22] we have *pakkhe papphoṭetvā*, said also of a bird.

[2] The Thūpārāma lies near the southern gate of the city of Anurādhapura on the west side of the sacred street (see note to 37. 194). It was built by Devānampiyatissa (247-207 B.C.) See Mhvs. trsl., Note to 17. 50. Cf. now with my translation of 17. 41 A. M. Hocart, Ceylon Journal of Science, Sect. G, I. 2, p. 44, note 4. The relic preserved in the Cetiya of the Thūpārāma was the right collar-bone of the Buddha (see 42. 53). Its history is related Mhvs. 17. 9 ff.

[3] Pūjāvaliya and Rājāvaliya give the same length of reign.

[4] Also W: "His consort who was intimate with his younger brother Mahānāma . . ." Nevertheless the union of *vallabhā* with the instr. is surprising, as also the use of the word to denote a criminal relationship.

[5] The *pabbajjā*, while the actual admission into the Order is carried out by the *upasampadā* which follows later. See Mhvs. trsl. p. 294, nr. 15 and p. 296, nr. 28.

211 lower life[1] and became monarch. He took as his Mahesī the
Mahesī[2] who had murdered his brother. He built refuges for
212 the sick and enlarged the Mahāpāli Hall. He erected three
vihāras, Lohadvāra, Ralaggāma and Koṭipassāvana[3] and pre-
213 sented them to the bhikkhus of the Abhayuttara-vihāra. After
having built a vihāra on the Dhūmarakkha mountain[4], he besto-
wed it at the Mahesī's instigation, on the bhikkhus of the
214 Theravāda School[5]. He had renovations made in ruined vihāras.
He was always one who rejoiced in the almsgiving and in the
leading of a moral life and one who reverenced the (three
sacred) objects[6].

215 A young Brāhmaṇa born near Bodhimaṇḍa[7], who understood
science, the arts and accomplishments and was perfectly versed
216 in the three Vedas, who knew the (various) systems of doctrine
thoroughly, who was skilled in disputation and also fond of con-
troversy, wandering about Jambudīpa[8], sought out the various
217 masters of controversy. Thus he came (once) to a vihāra and

[1] The lay life is regarded as inferior (*hīna*) to the monkish.

[2] *Mahesī* (skr. *mahiṣī*) is the title of the first wife of the King. See the Introduction II.

[3] A Koṭipassāva-vihāra is mentioned 38. 46, but here as founded by Dhātusena. The two other names do not occur otherwise, neither are they, as far as I know, to be found in Siṅhalese historical literature.

[4] The mountain is mentioned, Mhvs. 10. 46 ff., in the history of Paṇḍukābhaya. It lies on the left bank of the Mahaveliganga by the Kacchaka ford (now Mahagantota), E. of Polonnaruva.

[5] That is to the bhikkhus of the Mahāvihāra in which the Theravādins had their seat.

[6] P. *vatthupūjaka*. These are the *tīṇi vatthūni*, the *vatthuttayaṃ* (Buddha, the Doctrine and the Order) TURNOUR's translation is too general.

[7] *Bodhimaṇḍa* "Place of Enlightenment", the spot not far from the present Bō-Gayā in Southern Bihār where, according to tradition, the Bodhisatta meditating under a *Ficus religiosa*, by attainment of the highest knowledge became the Buddha. For the history of Buddhaghosa cf. BIMALA CHARAN LAW, The Life and Work of Buddhaghosa, Calcutta and Simla 1923.

[8] Name for the continental India.

elucidated during the night the ideas of Patañjali[1] word for
word and quite exhaustively[2]. Hereupon the Grand Thera[3] (of 218
the vihāra) named Revata realised: "This is a being of the
highest wisdom; he must be won over," and he said: "Who 219
then is he who cries there with the cry of an ass?" The
(Brāhmaṇa) said to him: "Dost thou then understand (at
all) the meaning of the cry of asses?" and on the reply: "I 220
understand it" he expounded his ideas. Revata answered each
single thesis and pointed out the (logical) contradictions. On 221
the request: "Explain then thy own system of doctrine," he
held forth to him on the text and content of the Abhidhamma.
The (Brāhmaṇa) did not understand it. He asked: "Whose 222
sayings[4] are these?" "These are the sayings of the Buddha,"
answered the other. To the request (of the Brāhmaṇa): "make
them known to me," Revata answered: "Thou shalt receive
them when thou hast undergone the ceremony of world-renun-
ciation." As the Brāhmaṇa craved for the sayings he under- 223
went the ceremony of world-renunciation and learnt the Tipi-
ṭaka[5]. He recognised: this path leads alone to the goal[6], and
accepted it thereafter[7]. As his speech was profound like that 224

[1] The author of the Yogasūtrāṇi (Strauss, Indische Philosophie, p. 178 ff.) who must accordingly, if our notice is credible, have lived before middle of the 5th century A. D.

[2] Lit.: with comprehensive words and well rounded off.

[3] P. *thera* (= Skr. *sthavira*) and *mahāthera* are titles of older bhikkhus in leading positions, something like presbyter.

[4] P. *manta*, skr. *mantra*. What is meant by this word are the sayings of the Veda. Here the word has a wider meaning, something like "sacred text".

[5] That is the whole of the canonical books consisting of the three parts Vinaya-, Sutta-, Abhidhammapiṭaka. See Mhvs. trsl. p. 296, nr. 27.

[6] The sentence *ekāyano ayaṃ maggo* is an allusion to a passage in the Saṃyutta. Here (S. V. 167[8] ff.) the Buddha says: *ekāyano 'yaṃ* (sic!) *maggo sattānaṃ visuddhiyā . . . nibbāṇassa sacchikiriyāya yad idaṃ cattāro satipaṭṭhānā.* We see at once from the passage that *ekāyana* is an adjective something like "alone accessible". In the Chāndogya-Upanishad 7. 1. 2 the word is used substantively to denote a branch of science. Śaṅkara explains it by *nītiśāstra.*

[7] That is: he now entered the Order with the ceremony of the *upasampadā*, making its duties and principles his own.

of the Buddha he was called Buddhaghosa; for his speech (re-
225 sounded) through the earth like (that of the) Buddha[1]. After
he had written a book Ñāṇodaya yonder (in Jambudīpa), he
also wrote the Atthasālinī[2], an interpretation of the Dhamma-
226 saṅgaṇī. The sage (Buddhaghosa) also began to compose a
commentary to the Paritta[3]. When the Thera Revata saw that,
227 he spake the following words: "The text alone has been handed
down here (in Jambudīpa), there is no commentary here. Nei-
228 ther have we the deviating systems of the teachers[4]. The com-
mentary in the Sīhala tongue[5] is faultless. The wise Mahinda
who tested the tradition[6] laid before the three Councils[7] as it
229 was preached by the Perfectly Enlightened one and taught by
Sāriputta and the others, wrote it in the Sīhala tongue and it
230 is spread among the Sīhalas. Go thither, learn it[8] and render
it into the tongue of the Māgadhas[9]. It will bring blessing
231 to the whole world." Thus addressed, the wise (Buddhaghosa)
sallied forth joyful in the faith and entered the Island just in
232 the time of this King (Mahānāma). He came to the Mahā-
vihāra, the abode of all pious (people), went into the great
233 practising-house[10], learned from Saṃghapāla the commentary

[1] "Speech" in P. *ghosa*. The second time TURNOUR translates it by "fame", scarcely right. In this case the motivation with *hi* would not apply. TURNOUR avoids the difficulty by translating "and throughout etc."

[2] The Dhammasaṅgaṇī is one of the books of the Abhidhamma (cf. note to 44. 109). It and its commentary the Atthasālinī were published by E. MÜLLER (PTS. 1885, and 1897). On *kaccha* "elucidation" see Cūlavs. ed. II, Index 2 s. v.

[3] For the Paritta see GEIGER, Pali, p. 16 f. Cf. note to 46. 5.

[4] P. *ācariyavādā*. In the Mhvs. (5. 2) all these later schools are placed in opposition to *theravāda*, the original school represented in the Pāli Canon.

[5] P. *sīhalaṭṭhakathā*. For this see GEIGER, Pali, p. 17.

[6] P. *kathāmagga*, concrete: the traditional text as handed down to-day, just as in JāCo. I. $2^{7, 9}$ the word means "traditional history".

[7] For the history of the three Councils (*saṃgīti*) see Mhvs. 3, 4, 5.

[8] Lit. "hearken to it", all teaching being oral.

[9] That is from the Old Sinhalese into the Pāli tongue.

[10] P. *mahāpadhānaghara*. By *padhāna* is meant the practices in which the zealous bhikkhu engages in order to attain through the

in the Sīhala tongue and the doctrinal system of the Theras
perfectly, reached the conclusion: it is just this system which
interprets the intentions of the Master of Truth; gathered 234
together there the community[1] and said: "give me all the
books that I may compose a commentary". To test him the 235
community gave him two verses with the words: "Show here
thy qualification! Once we have seen it, whe shall give thee
all the books." Briefly summing up the three Piṭakas[2] together 236
with the commentary he wrote the work called Visuddhi-
magga[3]. Then calling together the community who was versed 237
in the thoughts of the Enlightened One, he began to read the
work in the vicinity of the great Bodhi Tree. But the devatās[4] 238
to convince the people of his greatness, caused the book to
vanish; but twice and thrice he reproduced it. When the book 239
was brought forth a third time to be read the gods then pro-
duced the two other books. Then the bhikkhus read out all 240
the three books together. Neither in composition and content,
nor also as regards the sequence (of the subjects[5]), in the 241
teaching of the Theras, in the quotations[6], in words and sen-

various grades of ecstatic meditation to the dignity of the Arahant, of the "perfected".

[1] The *saṃgha*, that is the totality of the bhikkhus belonging to the vihāra.

[2] See Note to 37. 223.

[3] Visuddhimagga (ed. by Mrs. Rhys Davids, 2 vols. PTS. 1920—21) alludes to the verse:

> *sīle patiṭṭhāya naro sapañño cittaṃ paññaṃ ca bhāvayaṃ*
> *ātāpī nipako bhikkhu, so imaṃ vijaṭaye jaṭaṃ*

which Warren (Buddhism in Translations, Harvard Oriental Series vol. III, p. 285) has rendered thus:

> "What man his conduct guardeth, and hath wisdom,
> And thoughts and wisdom traineth well,
> The strenuous and the able priest,
> He disentangles all this snarl."

[4] On those spiritual beings common to the popular belief called *devatā* see Zeitschr. für Buddhismus VII, p. 28. In the following verse they are called *Marū* "gods".

[5] Lit: regarding the earlier and the later.

[6] P. *pālīhi* refers to passages quoted from the canonical texts, the

242 tences was there any kind of deviation in all three books. Then
the community satisfied and exceedingly well pleased, cried
243 again and again: "without doubt this is Metteyya![1]" and handed
over to him the books of the three Piṭakas together with the
commentary. Then dwelling in the Ganthākara-vihāra[2] which
244 lies far from all unquiet intercourse, he rendered the whole
of the Sīhala commentaries into the tongue of the Māgadhas,
245 the original speech of all. For beings of all tongues this
(rendering) became a blessing and all the teachers of the Thera-
246 vāda[3] accepted it as the original text. Then having accom-
plished what he had to do, he set out for Jambudīpa to adore
the sacred Bodhi Tree[4].

247 When Mahānāma had enjoyed the (dominion of the) earth twenty and two years[5] and done many meritorious works, he passed away in accordance with his doing.

248 For all the power they had amassed and for all the glorious splendours they had enjoyed all the rulers of the earth were at the end unable to escape death. With the thought: thus all beings are subject to the law of decay, the wise man should forever entirely forsake the desire for wealth and even for life.

Here ends the thirty-seventh chapter, called 'The Six Kings', in the Mahāvaṃsa, compiled for the serene joy and emotion of the pious.

foregoing *theravādehi*, on the other hand, means quotations from the commentaries.

[1] The next expected Buddha. He is now living as a Bodhisatta in the Tusita heaven according to Mhvs. 32. 73. Cf. Th. Kern, Manual of Indian Buddhism, p. 64, 65, 95.

[2] Cf. 52. 57 with note.

[3] See note to 37. 227.

[4] The sacred tree of Bō-Gayā (see note to 37. 215), of which according to the legend, the Bodhi Tree in the Mahāvihāra at Anurādhapura is a cutting.

[5] So also the Pūjāvaliya; only 20 years according to the Rājāvaliya. According to Chinese sources the King Mo-ho-nan (= Mahānāma) sent a letter to the court of the Chinese emperor in the year which corresponds to 428 A. D. This however does not agree with the Sinhalese chronology as it is generally accepted. See JRAS. C. Br. xxiv, nr. 68, p. 83.

CHAPTER XXXVIII

THE TEN KINGS

Mahānāma's son **Sotthisena**[1] was sprung from the womb 1
of a Damiḷa woman, but his daughter Saṃghā was the (daugh-
ter) of the Mahesī. Now after Sotthisena had begun to reign 2
he was killed by Saṃghā. The selfsame day she had the drum
beaten[2] and ceded (the sovereignty) to her husband, the um- 3
brella bearer[3] (of the king). The latter built the Chattaggā-
haka-tank and died in the course of the year.

Now a wise minister, a friend of this (umbrella bearer) 4
had the dead (prince) burnt in the (royal) demesne and secretly
made **Mittasena** a powerful rice thief, king in the belief 5
that he was suited for the sovereignty. He kept him in the
interior (of the palace) and under the pretext that the King
was ill, he himself wielded the sceptre. Now (on one occasion) 6
when there was a feast the people cried: "If a king is there,
let him come with us." When the Lord of men heard that, 7
he, arrayed in all his ornaments, said to those who led forth
the royal elephant: "this befits me not", and indicated the 8

[1] Pūjāvaliya, Rājāvaliya and Rājaratnākaraya call this prince Sengot. The two first sources agree that he was murdered in the afternoon of the day he succeeded to the throne.

[2] Government decrees were made public by beat of drum.

[3] P. *chattaggāhakajantuno.* The "umbrella bearer" who has to hold the umbrella, the symbol of sovereignty, over the prince is a high court official. We have all erred however (Turnour, Wijesiṇha and I myself in my edition of the Cūlavs.) in regarding *jantu* as the *name* of the official. The word means simply "individual, person" and stands almost pleonastically at the end of the compound, similarly to *putta.* In none of the other sources is the name Jantu met with. Rājāvaliya takes Chattaggāhaka (Sinh. *Satgāhaka*) itself for a proper name. In the Pūjā-

elephant made of stucco at the temple of the Tooth Relic[1].
At the words: "it is the King's command", the elephant began
9 to move. The (King) mounted it, rode round the town with
his right side towards it and when he reached the eastern gate
by the Paṭhamacetiya[2], he restored it to the Relic Temple[3].
10 At the elephant wall[4] of the three great cetiyas[5] he had a
gateway[6] constructed. After doing many meritorious works
Mittasena died in a year[7].
11 The Damiḷa named Paṇḍu had slain Mittasena in battle
and now having come over from the opposite coast[8], held sway
12 in Laṅkā. All the kinsmen of the noble families betook them-

valiya and the Rājaratnākaraya the King is called Lämäni-Tis (Lambakaṇṇa-Tissa). They agree in giving the duration of his reign as one year.

[1] Turnour and W. have misunderstood the passage, translating *sudhānāgaṃ* as "the white elephant", as if the text had *suddhanāgaṃ*. The miraculous story as related here, thus differs in no way from the version found in the Pūjāvaliya (Rājāvaliya and Rājaratnākaraya).

[2] On this cetiya see Mhvs. 14. 44 f.; Geiger, Mhvs. trsl., p. 95, n. 2; Parker, Ancient Ceylon, p. 275. Remains of the thūpa have been discovered, as is shown by the newest plan of Anurādhapura.

[3] The reading of the MSS. *kātuṃ nagaram appayi* is certainly wrong. I have not, however, ventured to alter it. My translation gives the more likely sense. This would be in Pāli something like *dhātughare tam appayi*. The edition has *dhātunāgaṃ samappayi*. Accordingly W. taking *paṭhamacetiyaṭṭhāne* as the more distant object of *samappayi*, translates "and commanded that he should (in future) be stationed at the Paṭhama Cetiya outside the eastern gate." This is certainly wrong both as to sense and construction.

[4] The *hatthipākāra* is the supporting wall of the terrace on which the stūpa stands. It takes its name from the row of brick and stucco elephants which project from it and appear to bear the platform. See below 39. 30 and 41. 95, as also Dīpavs. 20. 6.

[5] Where three large cetiyas or thūpas are named together, Ruvanveli (*mahāthūpa*), Jetavana (Eastern Stūpa) and Abhayagiri (Northern Stūpa) are meant.

[6] P. *toraṇa*, probably at the stairs which lead at the four sides to the terrace.

[7] Pūjāvaliya also gives Mittasena one year (*havuruddak*).

[8] That is from Southern India.

selves to Rohaṇa, on this side of the stream[1] the Damiḷas ruled.
Those of the Moriya[2] clan who had fled through fear of the 13
door-keeper Subha[3] dwelt here and there (scattered about
the country). Amongst these was a house-owner in Nandivā- 14
pigāma[4] named Dhātusena. His son Dāṭhānāma who lived in 15
the village Ambilayāgu, had two sons, Dhātusena and Silā-
tissabodhi, (both) by (a mother of) the same caste. Their mother's 16
brother had in faith undergone the ceremony of renunciation
of the world and lived in the dwelling built by Dīghasanda[5].
The young Dhātusena underwent with him likewise the cere- 17
mony of world-renunciation. Now once as the latter was reciting
(sacred texts) at the foot of a tree a cloud began to rain. A
snake seeing this, encircled him in her folds and covered the 18
book and the boy with her hood. The uncle saw that. Another
time another penitent in his wrath threw dung at his head 19
but failed therewith to disturb[6] his spirit. The uncle beheld

[1] On the left bank of the Mahaveliganga which was always regarded as the boundary between North Ceylon with Anurādhapura and later Polonnaruva as centre and the south-eastern province Rohaṇa.

[2] The organisation of society was throughout totemistic. Five clan names known to me: Taracchā, Lambakaṇṇā, Balibhojakā, Moriyā, Kuliṅgā (and probably Gokaṇṇā), are one and all names of beasts (hyenas, tigers or hares, crows, peacocks, fork-tailed shrikes). A sixth name Monasīhakā (90. 7) contains in its second part a beast name. To these must be added the name of the Sīhalā themselves, the "Lion-men" so-called after Vijaya who belonged to the Lion clan. His father was Sīhabāhu, his grandfather a lion. Fables according to which the members of a clan are descended from the animal whose name they bear are very frequent. Tylor, Anfänge der Cultur, II, 235; Frazer, Totemism, p. 3 ff.

[3] Mhvs. 35. 51 ff. Subha reigned 118-124 A. D.

[4] A Nandigāma-vihāra was built by that same Subha *gaṅgante*, that is on the bank, near the Mahāvālukagaṅgā (Mhvs. 35. 58). Nandigāma was not far from Kacchakatittha. See 37. 213, note.

[5] Dīghasandana was the senāpati of King Devānampiyatissa. He built (Mhvs. 15. 212 f.) a pariveṇa in the Mahāvihāra which was called after him.

[6] We have to imagine that Dhātusena was sunk in meditation which even the inconsiderate conduct of the penitent could not disturb. He

20 that too and thinking: "that is in very truth a most excellent
being, without doubt he will become king, he must be pro-
21 tected", he went along with him into a vihāra and in-
structed him in the Gonisa-vihāra with the object: "he must
22 be made a master in state-craft[1]". Paṇḍuka heard this and
sent people to seize him. In the night the Thera had a dream
23 about it and fetched the boy away. Scarcely had he departed
when the people surrounded (the house) but did not find him
in the pariveṇa. The twain (uncle and nephew) departed thence
24 and when, farther south[2], they reached the great river called
Goṇa[3] then just in flood, they were obliged to halt, much
25 as they wished to press forward. The Thera spake: "even as
this river holds us back, so do thou (in future time) hold back
26 its course by collecting its waters in a tank,"[4] and he descended
with the boy into the stream. A snake king saw the twain
27 and offered its back. With its aid he reached the bank and
brought the boy to the frontier, and (once) while staying there

was not moved to indignation by it. It must be noted that the same breach of conduct as that of the penitent is ascribed (38. 113 f.) to Dhātusena himself and that his fearful end was regarded as expiation of it.

[1] The passage is somewhat dubious. In the first place I believe that the words *ādāya tam vihāraṃ upāgato* mean: he fetched him out of the Dīghasanda-pariveṇa. As that lay in Anurādhapura the youthful Dhātusena was here not safe enough from possible machinations of the king. His uncle took him to the Gonisa monastery (*gonisādivihāra* means the monastery whose name begins with *gonisa*). We do not know where this monastery was as it is not otherwise mentioned — possibly in the south of the capital. For the rest I follow the conjectural *nītimā* of M. Geiger which makes the sense far more pregnant. As his uncle regards Dhātusena as the future king, his task is to acquaint him with *nīti*, i. e. statecraft. W. turns Gonisādivihāra into the *oratio recta*: "I must render this youth accomplished at the Gonisáda (sic!) vihára" — a meaning to my mind less probable.

[2] Or perhaps "near the Dakkhiṇadesa". See 41. 35, note.

[3] Now the Kala-oya flowing into Dutch Bay.

[4] An allusion to the Kālavāpi afterwards constructed by King Dhātusena. See 38. 42.

he got milk broth (as alms); he ate thereof and put what was
over into the alms-bowl[1] of his nephew. The latter out of 28
reverence for the Thera poured the rice on the ground. Then
the Thera perceived that he would enjoy the earth[2].

After reigning, King Paṇḍu died in the fifth year, likewise 29
his son Parinda in the third year[3]. Parinda's youngest brother, 30
Khuddapārinda, then ruled the wide earth and persecuted all
those who attached themselves to Dhātusena. Dhātusena won 31
over the people for himself and fought against the King. The
latter after accomplishing works both meritorious and evil,
died at the end of sixteen years. Hereupon Tīritara became 32
King; two months later he was destroyed by Dhātusena who
fought a great battle with him. After this prince had been 33
killed, the Damiḷa Dāṭhiya became king, but was slain at
the end of three years by Dhātusena. Hereupon there followed 34
the Damiḷa Pīṭhiya who after seven months went to his de-
struction. The race of the Damiḷas was annihilated in battle
with Dhātusena.

Now the Lord of men Dhātusena became king in Laṅkā. 35
Together with his brother he waged on the Island by every
means unceasing warfare with the ravagers of the Island, the 36
Damiḷas, building[4] fortresses, twenty-one in number. And having
thus thoroughly cleared the country and made its inhabitants 37

[1] P. *pattena*. Not "*with* the refection dish", as translated by Turnour.

[2] P. *bhuñjate mahiṃ* is a figurative expression for "ruling".

[3] I should now prefer the reading *putto Parindo pi tatiye, tassa bhātuko* etc. (with the Colombo edition and Wijesiṇha). Rājaratnākaraya namely, speaks of six Damiḷa princes who had reigned together 27 years before Dhātusena ascended the throne. The same number is found in the Rājāvaliya and the sum of the single numbers in the Cūlavaṃsa gives the same figure, in so far as we allot Parinda a reign of not quite three years.

[4] Turnour's translation "he entirely extirpated the Damiḷas" etc. is inexact. That is not there. The acc. *Damiḷe* in 35 can only be governed by *katvā yuddhaṃ* in 36, which is treated (see also 76. 100) as a transitive verb: after he building fortresses had fought the Damiḷas, and after he had cleared the country and had made . . ., he restored . . .

happy, he restored to its former place the Order[1] which
38 had been destroyed by the foe. But wroth with those belonging to noble clans or to kinship villages[2] who had attached themselves to the Damiḷas and protected neither himself
39 nor the sacred doctrine, he deprived them of their villages and left their villages defenceless. But to all the people of noble
40 clans who had come to Rohana and supported him he showed fitting honour and (gave) marks of esteem, and to his ministers, the companions of his misfortunes, he brought contentment.
41 By damming up the great stream[3] he created fields which were permanently watered. In the Mahāpāli Hall he distributed rice
42 fare to the bhikkhus. As dwelling-place for cripples and for such as suffered from a disease the wise (prince) built asylums. By building the Kālavāpi[4] he dammed up the mighty Goṇa river.
43 After he had provided the peaceful Mahāvihāra with bands of ornament[5] he had a house, worthy to behold, erected for
44 the Bodhi Tree[6]. He provided the bhikkhus plentifully with

[1] P. *sāsanaṃ* "the doctrine" is used in exactly the same sense as we speak of "church". He restored the Buddhist church.

[2] The contrast is between single individuals (*kulīnā*) and clan unions (*kulagāmā* with shortening of the final vowel metri causa). W.'s translation "nobles and landlords" is inexact.

[3] The Mahāvālukagaṅgā (Mahaveliganga).

[4] Now Kala-veva, 25 miles (= 40 km.) S. S. E. of Anurādhapura.

[5] W. translates the passage thus: "he improved the mahāvihāra by adding regular walks thereto". It is quite right that here as one might expect, *pantiyuttaṃ* and *anākulaṃ* are closely associated, but I do not know how *panti* can be made to mean "walk". In the Mhvs. the word is chiefly used of the decorative pictures done in relief or painted on the walls of the buildings: See 27. 37; 30. 65; 32. 4 etc. I should be inclined to use the word in this sense in our passage and in v. 69.

[6] P. *bodhighara*. Mr. Hocart writes (18-9-26) that by *bōgē* (P. *bodhigeha*) is understood now, in Dambadeniya for instance, a small chapel erected *beside* the bodhi tree. At the same time he points out that the picture of a tree with a superstructure occurs in the Sānchi reliefs. I believe in fact that in the first instance *bodhighara* or *-geha* denotes a building or a wooden roof, erected *over* the bodhi tree, of course only over the trunk which in the case of the *Ficus religiosa* is always very short, while the straggling branches spread away over it. Cf. with this

the four necessaries and like Dhammāsoka[1] he brought about
a redaction of the three Piṭakas. He had eighteen vihāras built 45
and provided with revenues for the adherents of the Thera
School and (he erected) eighteen tanks on the Island[2]. Kāla- 46
vāpi-vihāra, the (vihāra) called Koṭipassāva, the (vihāra) called
Dakkhiṇāgiri and the vihāra called Vaḍḍha; the Paṇṇavalla- 47
kabhūta and the (vihāra) called Bhallātaka and in the district
Pāsāṇasinna the vihāra Dhātusenapabbata; the Maṅgana(-vihā- 48
ra), the Thūpaviṭṭhi(-vihāra) and the Dhātusena(-vihāra) in the
north, the Pācīnakambaviṭṭhi(-vihāra) and the Antaramegiri
(-vihāra); the (vihāras) Attāḷhidhātusena and Kassipiṭṭhika- 49
dhātusena, in Rohaṇa the (vihāras) Dāyagāma, Sālavāna, Vibhī-
sana and the vihāra Bhillivāna: these eighteen vihāras are 50
mentioned[3]. This best of men built the tanks Pādūlaka, Ham-
baṭṭhī, Mahādatta and others[4], and also eighteen smaller vihāras 51

51. 54. I had the impression on the spot in the Mahāvihāra, that it would have been an easy matter to shut off the terrace built round the sacred tree by means of a roof. For the analogous *thūpaghara* see note to 48. 66.

[1] Alluding to the Third Council at Pāṭaliputta under Asoka (269-227 B. C.) See Mhvs. trsl. p. LVI ff.

[2] The same is related of Dhātusena by the Pūjāvaliya, the Rājāvaliya and the Rājaratnākaraya. In these later sources the form of the name is Dāsenkāliya.

[3] Of these eighteen vihāras only four are also mentioned in other parts of the Cūlavaṃsa, namely Kālavāpi, Dakkhiṇāgiri, Bhallātaka and Sālavāna. The Kālavāpi-vihāra is perhaps the monastery which now bears the name of Aukuna-vihāra. If the Koṭipassāva-vihāra is the same as the Koṭipassāvana mentioned 37. 212, then it was not founded by Dhātusena but merely restored. The same is the case with the Dakkhiṇāgiri-vihāra which according to Mhvs. 33. 7, was founded by Saddhātissa, the brother of Duṭṭhagāmaṇī. I am inclined (see D. Ferguson, JRAS. C. B. 1911, XXII, Nr. 64, p. 197 ff.) to identify this with the Mulkirigala-vihāra N. E. from Mātara. Instead of *vihāro vaḍḍhanāmako* the Col. ed. reads contrary to the MSS. v. *vaḍḍhamānako,* probably because a bodhi tree of this name occurs twice (48. 5 and 49. 15).

[4] Pūjāvaliya names the following tanks as Dhātusena's work: Kaḷā, Balalu, Keḷavasā, Badulu, Kaḷunnaru, Danavallā, Uḍanviṭi, Pāṇagamu, Mānāmatu, Kitmiṇi, Mahaḍabarā, Saṃgamu, Surulu, Malāsu, Mahamidel, Mahaeli. The two first are the Kala- and Balaluveva which are connected

and likewise (many small) tanks which he made over to them.
52 He removed the Mayūra-pariveṇa[1] which was five and twenty
cubits high, and replaced it by a pāsāda twenty-one cubits in
53 height. To Kumārasena (his brother) he made over his former
revenues and fixed them exactly[2]: (namely) one half to the
54 Kālavāpi and two hundred fields. He renovated the ruined
Lohapāsāda and he restored the dilapidated umbrellas[3] on the
55 three great thūpas. For the Bodhi Tree of him (the Buddha)
to whom was vouchsafed the highest enlightenment, he insti-
tuted a bathing festival like the Bodhi Tree festival instituted
56 by Devānaṃpiyatissa. He set up there sixteen bath maidens
of bronze[4] and arranged for the adornment and consecration
57 of the Prince of the wise[5]. Since the planting of the great
Bodhi Tree[6] the rulers of Laṅkā have instituted in every twelfth
58 year (of their reign) a festival for the Bodhi Tree. After having
an image made of the great Thera Mahinda he brought it to
the spot where the Thera's body had been burnt[7], to organise

with each other. The Rājaratnākaraya mentions Kalahallu (Kala-Balalu?) and Badulu.

[1] The same as Mora-pariveṇa 37. 172. See note to the passage. The new building was 6 ft. (roughly 1.80 metres) lower than the former pāsāda.

[2] P. *appetvā visodhayi*. Cf. Skr. *viśodhayati* meaning "to make clear, to determine, to fix" (BR. the word *śudh* with *vi*).

[3] *Chatta* in P. denotes the sharp cone forming the top of a thūpa. It is a conventionalized umbrella as symbol of dominion, of the spiritual world dominion of the Buddha. For the three thūpas see note to 38. 10.

[4] All MSS. have *dhāvanālohakaññāyo*. In spite of 42. 33 I do not venture to alter the traditional text into *-nārāyo*. What the "bath maidens" were, whether perhaps bronze figures with water vessels, we do not know.

[5] We must imagine a ceremony in which the image of the Buddha is clad in royal garments and solemnly consecrated just as a king at his coronation.

[6] By Devānaṃpiyatissa in the Mahāvihāra according to Mhv. 18. 1 ff. The Bō tree here was according to the legend, a cutting of the tree at Bō-Gayā.

[7] Local tradition regards the remains on the north side of the Thūpārāma as those of the cetiya built for Mahinda. To the east of the Thūpārāma lies the grave of his sister Saṃghamittā. For the death and burial of the two see Mhvs. 20. 30 ff.

there at great cost a sacrificial festival. He gave orders with 59
the outlay of a thousand gold pieces[1], for the interpretation of
the Dīpavaṃsa[2] and commanded sugar to be distributed among
the bhikkhus dwelling there. Remembering how once a bhikkhu 60
had thrown dung at his head, he gave to the pariveṇa where he
himself had dwelt no gifts of any kind[3]. He undertook buildings 61
for the enlargement of the Abhayuttara-vihāra and for the
stone image of the Master (Buddha)[4] he had a shrine erected
with a maṇḍapa[5]. As the eye[6] placed by Buddhadāsa (in the 62
image) had been lost, he made a pair of costly jewels into eyes
for the Master. Further he wrought a gleaming diadem of 63
rays and out of dark blue gems a shining coil of hair, like-
wise a bandolier of gold and a tuft of down (between the brows)
and a golden garment, a mandorla of gold, a lotus flower and 64
a magnificent lamp. There also he presented countless robes of
divers colours[7]. In the image house of the Bahumaṅgala-ceti- 65

[1] Where only figures are given in the mention of values the uniform currency, the *kahāpaṇa* should be added. On this see Rhys Davids, Buddhist India p. 101 f.

[2] P. *dīpetuṃ Dīpavaṃsaṃ*. Fleet has translated this ingeniously as: "to write a dīpikā on the Dīpavaṃsa" (JRAS. 1909, p. 5, n. 1). In this *dīpikā* he recognises the (older) Mahāvaṃsa for whose composition an approximate date might thus be found. I was myself (Mhvs. trsl. p. XI f.) inclined to follow him. But I have since had scruples. Verses 58—59 belong in construction most closely together. Consequently *dīpetuṃ Dīpavaṃsaṃ* must refer to an action which took place within the framework of a festival. That however, can only have been a reading of the Dīpavaṃsa, perhaps with historical and legendary explanations, but not the composition of so voluminous a work as the Mahāvaṃsa.

[3] See above 38. 19. I believe we must read *attanā* instead of *-no*: "the pariveṇa inhabited by Dhātusena himself", an instrumental case being absolutely necessary in connection with the Partic. Praet. *vutthassa*.

[4] This stone image was a celebrated statue of the Buddha manifestly held peculiarly sacred and which is repeatedly mentioned under various names: here *Silāsatthar*, 39. 7 *Silāsambuddha*, 51. 77, 87 *Silāmayamunin-da*, probably also 38. 65 *kālaselasatthar* (see note to the passage).

[5] See note to 37. 103. [6] See above 37. 123.

[7] Verses 62-64 show us how people were accustomed to adorn the

ya[1] he erected Bodhisatta figures and in the same (image house)
66 he had a diadem of rays made for the image of the Master
in black stone[2] and for the world teacher named Upasumbha.
67 Also he had the ornament described above made for the Buddha
image known as Abhiseka and a Bodhisatta temple on the left
68 side of the Bodhi Tree. For the (Bodhisatta) Metteyya[3] he had
the complete equipment of a king prepared and ordained a
69 guard for him within the radius of a yojana[4]. He had the
vihāras adorned with bands of ornament called dhāturāji and

Buddha statues and decorate them with jewels. The *raṃsicūḷāmaṇi* (often only *cūḷāmaṇi*) seems to be the bundle of rays or flames above the head which distinguishes the figures of the Buddha from those of his disciples (cf. also below v. 66 and Mhvs. 52. 65; 53. 49). By *kesāvaṭṭaṃsu* we must understand the knot or tuft of hair on the top of the head, so often found in Buddha images. To imitate the blue-black colour of the hair it is here made of dark sapphires. The *hemavaḍḍha* (cf. *aṃsavaḍḍhaka* Vin. I. 204[10]) is probably the carrying band for the alms bowl. On a bronze figure of the Buddha in my possession there is a band over the left shoulder. The tuft of hair obove the nose (*uṇṇaloma*) is a well known physical feature of the Mahāvīra. The golden garment (*sovaṇṇacīvara*) is the yellow robe of the Order of Buddha and of his disciples, the lotus flower (*paduma*) the throne on which the figure sits or stands. The *pādajāla* (cf. also Mhv. 52. 65, 53. 50, as well as the inscriptional *pādadāla*, Wickremasinghe, EZ. I 221[15]) is the mandorla behind the figure as is frequently seen in bronzes and in the Buddha pictures of Central Asia (cf. A. von Le Coq, Die Buddhistische Spätantike Mittelasiens V, plate 7, 18). Amongst the votive gifts there must of course be a lamp (*dīpa*). The robes of divers colours are probably draped about the image at various festivals, according to the character of these.

[1] Probably the Maṅgala-cetiya mentioned 37. 183.

[2] I suggest reading: *bodhisatte ca tatthāpi Kālaselassa satthuno* with slight alteration of *tatthāsi* which is certainly corrupt. What follows shows that the different Buddha images had their special names. The Kālasela was obviously so called because the statue was made of black stone (amphibolic gneiss?). It is very likely the same as the *Silāsambuddha, -satthar* (see above v. 61, note). The Abhiseka is named again 39. 6, 40.

[3] See 37. 212, note.

[4] Fleet (JRAS. 1906 p. 1011 f.) calculates the Buddhist *yojana* as being 4.54 miles = roughly 8 km.

(he erected) for a hundred thousand (gold pieces) a large and
splendid house for the Bodhi Tree. In the Thūpārāma (he in- 70
stituted) as offering to the thūpa a restoration of what was
ruined (in the thūpa). Likewise in the Temple of the Tooth
Relic he repaired what was dilapidated, and to the Tooth Relic 71
he dedicated a casket for the tooth relic, a halo made of clo-
sely fitting mosaic thickly set with precious stones[1] and golden 72
lotus flowers, and he instituted offerings without number. To
the bhikkhus dwelling on the Island he distributed robes and
other (gifts). Having undertaken renovations in the vihāras 73
here and there, he had some fine stucco work executed for the
wall of the (Relic) house. (In the same way) he had valuable 74
stucco work made for the three big cetiyas and put up a golden
umbrella[2] as well as a ring for protection against lightning[3].
Dhammarucika bhikkhus[4] dwelt (at that time) in the Mahā- 75
vihāra which had been destroyed by the ruthless Mahāsena.
After Dhātusena had built the Ambatthala-vihāra on the Cetiya- 76
pabbata[5] he wished to hand it over to the adherents of the
Thera School. But being entreated by the Dhammarucikas the
monarch accordingly made it also over to them. For the pro- 77

[1] W. here mistakenly connects *mahagghamaṇisaṃkiṇṇaṃ* with *padmāni* instead of with *raṃsiṃ ghanakuṭṭimaṃ*. For *ghanakuṭṭima* cf. Cūlavs. ed. II, List of Words s. v. *kuṭṭima*; further Mhvs. 51. 69.

[2] Cf. above note to 38. 54. The cones of the thūpas were gilded. Cf. with verses 74 and 75 also 41. 95.

[3] P. *vajiracumbaṭaṃ*. It is related Mhvs. 36. 66 of Saṃghatissa that he placed a *vajiracumbaṭaṃ* on the top of the Mahāthūpa. On this the Ṭikā has the following interesting notice (p. 487, 19): *tatheva Mahāthūpassa muddhani satasahassagghanakaṃ mahāmaṇiñca patiṭṭhāpetvā tassa heṭṭhā asaniuppaddavaviddhaṃsanatthaṃ ādhāravalayañca katvā anagghaṃ vajiracumbaṭakañca pūjesīti attho.* It is thus a case of an appliance against lightning placed at the top of the cone of the thūpa. What is doubtful is whether *vajira* means here "diamond" or "lightning".

[4] A sect which according to Mhvs. 5. 13, branched off in Ceylon. For the history of this sect see A. M. Hocart, ASC. Mem. I. 15 ff.

[5] Name of the Missaka mountain (now Mihintale). Cf. above note to 37. 69. The Dhammarucikas, therefore, got possession of both vihāras, the Mahāvihāra and the Ambatthala-vihāra.

cession of the Relic he had a boat[1] made of copper and instituted a regular alms with the produce of twice five ammaṇas
78 (field)[2]. Within and without the city this incomparable (prince) like Dhammāsoka[3] built temples to the Victor (Buddha) and
79 raised images. What man would be capable of enumerating one after another his meritorious works? Thus these have been but superficially noted.

80 Dhātusena had two sons: Kassapa by a mother of unequal birth and the mighty Moggallāna by a mother of equal caste,
81 also a charming daughter who was dear to him as his life. On his sister's son he bestowed the dignity of senāpati[4] and
82 gave him his daughter (to wife). Without blame (on her part) he struck her with his whip on the thigh. When the King
83 saw the blood-stained garment of his daughter and heard (of the affair) he in his wrath had his nephew's mother[5] burnt naked. From that time onward (his nephew) nursed hatred
84 (against the king), joined Kassapa, awoke in him the desire for the royal dignity, estranged him from his father, won over his subjects and took the ruler (Dhātusena) prisoner alive.
85 Thereupon Kassapa raised the umbrella of dominion and destroyed the people who sided with his father, having every
86 scoundrel as his comrade. Moggallāna whose intention it was to fight him, betook himself, as he could raise no forces, to
87 Jambudīpa to find troops there. Now to torment still farther the Lord of men (Dhātusena) sorely smitten as he already was

[1] The use of barks or boats for carrying the images or symbols of the Deity (here the relics) in festive processions is widespread. Germany offers numerous examples (MANNHARDT, Wald- und Feldkulte, I. 593 ff., v. SCHRÖDER, Arische Religion II. 661 Anm.); but we meet with the custom also among the Egyptians (TIELE, Religion im Altertum I. 67) and among other peoples.

[2] P. *ammaṇa* is a dry measure for measuring corn, then also the measure for a field, as much as one can sow with an *ammaṇa*. In Sinh. an *amuṇu* (see CLOUGH, Sinhalese Dictionary) represents as field measure about 2 to 2½ acres (roughly o. 8 to 1 hectar).

[3] Cf. above 38. 44 with note.

[4] P. *senāpacca*, the dignity of commander-in-chief of the army (*senāpati*).

[5] Thus his own sister.

by loss of his kingdom, separation from his son (Moggallāna)
and by life in a dungeon, the deluded (Senāpati) spake thus 88
to King Kassapa: "There are treasures lying in the King's
palace, O King, has thy father told it to thee?" On the answer 89
"no" he said: "Knowest thou not his intention, O Monarch?
for Moggallāna he keeps his wealth". When he heard that, 90
this most wicked of men grew furious and sent messengers
to his father with the command to make known the place
where the treasure lay. The latter thought: this is a pretext 91
of the villain to kill us, and he kept silence. The messengers
went and told the King. He became very wroth and sent 92
(messengers) again and again. Dhātusena thought: it is well,
I will visit my friend[1], bathe in the Kālavāpi and then die, 93
and (he) spake to the messengers: "if he lets me go to the
Kālavāpi he shall learn it." The messengers went and told 94
the King and the King joyful in his thirst for gold, sent mes-
sengers to whom he gave a chariot with a damaged axle[2]. As 95
the Monarch drove thither, the driver who guided the chariot,
ate roasted corn and gave him also a little of it. He ate of 96
it, had joy over the man and gave him a leaf for Moggallāna
asking him to make him gate-keeper as a reward[3]. Thus is 97
good fortune fleeting as the lightning. How then can the sen-
sible man be intoxicated by it? When the Thera heard: the 98
King comes, he put aside the bean soup and chicken[4] he had
received remembering: the King likes that, and took his seat 99

[1] He means the Thera who had been his teacher. Cf. 38. 16 ff.

[2] P. *jiṇṇena-m-akkhinā*. W. translates "with his eyes sunk in grief", but *akkhi* is here not "eye", but „axle". The word for "axle" is otherwise *akkha* = Skr. *akṣa*. The form *akkhi* which is borne out by our passage, is important as it is nearer to the Latin *axis*, lit. *ašis*. In *jiṇṇenamakkhiṇā* the consonant *m* is as often used to remove a hiatus. See Geiger, Pāli § 73. 2. It would also be possible to read *jiṇṇena c'akkhinā*.

[3] The inf. *kātuṃ* is in a sense to be taken twice, first with the obj. *saṃgahaṃ*, then with the obj. *dvāranāyakaṃ*.

[4] P. *maṃsaṃ sākunaṃ* for *sākulaṃ* according to the perfectly correct conjecture of Sumangala and Batuwantudawa, primarily "flesh of birds".

(awaiting the guest). The King came, greeted him respectfully
100 and took a place at his side. Thus the twain sat side by side
(joyful) as if they had gained a kingdom, and their mutual
101 converse chased their cares away. After the Thera had enter-
tained the King, he admonished him in many ways and en-
couraged him to strive ceaselessly, showing him how the world
102 is subject to the law (of impermanency). Then Dhātusena betook
himself to the tank, plunged as he liked therein, bathed and
103 drank and spake to the King's henchmen: "This here, my friends,
is my whole wealth[1]". When the King's henchmen heard that
they took him with them to the town and informed the King.
104 The Lord of men thought: he is keeping his treasure for his
son and as long as he lives he will estrange the people of
the Island from me. He was filled with fury and commanded
105 the Senāpati thus: "Slay my father." He (the Senāpati) rejoiced
(saying): now I have seen the back of my foe[2]. Full of bitter-
106 ness, adorned with all his ornaments, he betook himself to the
King (Dhātusena) and strutted up and down before him. When
107 the King saw that he thought: this villain wants to ruin my
soul even as my body and bring it to hell. Shall I fulfil his
108 wish by letting anger rise within me? Awaking loving thoughts
within himself, he spake to the Senāpati: "I have the same
109 feelings for thee as for Moggallāna.". The other laughing shook
his head. When the ruler saw this he realised: to-day even
110 he will slay me. Thereupon the brutal (Senāpati) stripped the
king naked, bound him with chains and fetters in a niche in
111 the wall[3] with his face outwards[4] and closed it up with clay.
What wise man seeing this would still hanker after pleasures

[1] With these words Dhātusena points at the Kālavāpi constructed by him.

[2] That is: I am the victor, I have won the game.

[3] Lit: in the inside of the wall.

[4] P. *puratthābhimukhaṃ*. W. translates this "with the face to the east". This is of course possible, but one sees no particular reason why he should face the east. According to my conception of the passage, the idea is that Dhātusena's torture should be increased by his being a witness of the whole process of being immured.

or life or fame? The Lord of men Dhātusena went thus after 112
18 years[1], murdered by his son, to the King of the gods. When
this king was building the Kālavāpi tank he saw a bhikkhu 113
sunk in meditation and as he could not rouse him out of his
absorption, he had a clod of earth flung at the bhikkhu's head. 114
The consequence of this deed experienced in his lifetime has
been described (in the story of his violent death).

These ten excellent kings also with all their treasures have 115
fallen into the jaws of death, robbed of their treasures. Can
a wise man when he sees the fleeting nature of the rich and
of wealth[2] crave for earthly joys[3]?'

Here ends the thirty-eighth chapter, called 'The Ten Kings', in the Mahāvaṃsa, compiled for the serene joy and emotion of the pious.

[1] Pūjāv. Rājāv. and Rājaratn. all give the same number.

[2] P. *bhogavato dhane ca*. The loc. *dhane* stands, as frequently, for the genitive *dhanassa*.

[3] W. does not translate this indispensable strophe. It occurs in all the MSS. known to me.

CHAPTER XXXIX

THE HISTORY OF THE TWO KINGS

1 Thereupon the wicked ruler called Kassapa sent forth his
2 groom and his cook. But as he was unable (through these)
to slay his brother, he betook himself through fear to Sīha-
3 giri[1] which is difficult of ascent for human beings. He cleared
(the land) round about, surrounded it with a wall and built
a staircase[2] in the form of a lion. Thence it took its name
4 (of Sīhāgiri). He collected treasures and kept them there
well protected and for the (riches) kept by him he set guards
5 in different places. Then he built there a fine palace, worthy

[1] Now Sigiri, about 38 miles S. E. of Anurādhapura and ten miles N. E. of Dambulla in the Central Province.

[2] P. *nissenigehāni*. The word cannot refer, as W. assumes, to the galleries which partly cut into the rock, lead halfway up the face of the Sigiri rock, as *sīhākārena* is inapplicable to these. It is far more likely that what is meant is the staircase built on the north terrace of the rock at the end of the galleries where the second half of the ascent begins. This structure had in fact the form of a recumbent lion, perhaps of the fore part of the body. It was made of brick. The claws of the outstretched right paw of the lion still exist. Their dimensions — they reach to the breast of a man standing upright — give some idea of the gigantic proportions of the lion's figure. It appears there was a door between the two paws into the breast of the lion whence steps led through its body to the beginning of the staircase leading to the heights of the Sigiri rock. I am inclined to think that this staircase was of wood. There were no galleries on this part of the rock on its northern side. The ascent is made now by means of a steep iron ladder. The use of the plural *nissenigehāni* is due to the fact that the structure consists of a series of separate parts.

to behold, like another Ālakamandā[1] and dwelt there like (the
god) Kuvera. The Senāpati by name Migāra, built a pari- 6
veṇa called after himself and a house for the victor Abhiseka[2].
He sought (permission to hold) a consecration festival[3] for it 7
even greater than that for the stone image of the Buddha[4].
As leave was not granted him, he refrained with the resolve:
I shall seek for it (again) under the sovereignty of the rightful ruler.

Kassapa began to rue the deed he had done and with the 8
thought: how can I be saved? he performed many meritorious
works. He planted gardens about the gates of the city and 9
mango groves over the Island at a yojana's distance from each
other. He restored the Issarasamaṇārāma[5] so that it was 10
larger than the former ground[6], bought villages for its support and granted them to it. He had two daughters, Bodhī 11
and Uppalavaṇṇā; he gave their names and his own to this
vihāra[7]. When he handed it over to the samaṇas of the 12

[1] See above note to 37. 106.

[2] As to this and other images of the Buddha see 38. 65-67 with note.

[3] W. (note to the passage): "The *abhiseka* of an image is the setting or painting of its eyes, a ceremony generally performed with great splendour. It is the *Netra-pinkama* of the Sinhalese Buddhists". The name of the Abhiseka festival suggests however, that it had a still more comprehensive meaning.

[4] The festival instituted by Dhātusena for the Silā-Buddha is described 38. 62 ff. See the notes.

[5] Now the Isurumuni-vihāra, in the south of Anurādhapura situated not far from the Tissaveva tank. It is first mentioned under Devānaṃpiyatissa (Mhvs. 20. 14).

[6] I join *adhikaṃ* directly with *kāretvā* "he made . . . larger than . . . See the following note.

[7] Our chronicle here gets valuable confirmation from inscriptions. In an inscription of Mahinda IV. found in Vessagiri, it is stated that the King had taken care that the Isurameṇu-Bo-Upulvan-Kasubgiri-vihāra should be constantly supplied with water from the Tissaveva (Wickremasinghe, EZ. I, p. 31 ff.). The Vessagiri-vihāra lies only about $^1/_2$ a mile south of the Issarasamaṇa-vihāra at the south-east corner of the Tissaveva. From the agreement of the inscription and the expression *kāretvā pubbavatthuto adhikaṃ* in v. 10 it is clear that Kassapa I. made a great

Thera School they were loth to take it, fearing the reproach
13 of the people[1], because it was the work of a parricide. As
however, the King wished to give it to them, he presented it
to the image of the Supreme Buddha. Then the bhikkhus
14 agreed, thinking: it belongs to the Master[2]. In the same way
he built a vihāra in the Niyyanti-garden near the mountain,
15 which then bore their name[3]. He granted this vihāra equip-
ped with the four necessaries, to the Dhammarucis[4] and in
16 addition a garden lying to the north of it. Now once when
eating a tasty dish of rice prepared with sannīra[5] fruit, cooked
with butter and exquisite spices which a woman had offered
17 him, he thought: this is delicious, I will treat the brethren[6]
to it, and he had the like dish of rice given to the bhikkhus
18 along with a robe. He kept the Uposatha festival[7] and culti-
vated the appamaññā[8], he took on himself the pious du-

monastic establishment out of the Vessagiri and Issarasamaṇa vihāras and that this enlarged monastery was named after his two daughters and after Kassapa himself. Wickremasinghe's assumption loc. cit. is thus confirmed. Vessagiri is first mentioned Mhvs. 20. 15 in close connection with Issarasamaṇa.

[1] Lit. "somewhat fearing what the world finds blamable".

[2] P. *bhogo no satthuno*, thus something that benefits not the monastery or its inmates, but the Buddha himself.

[3] Uncertain. I take *Niyyanti* for the name of the garden. The mountain near which it lies is very likely the Sīhagiri. *Tesaṃnāmo* means the names of the King and of his daughters.

[4] See above note to 38. 75.

[5] P. *sannīra* occurs besides here three times: 74. 204 as tree along with *kadalī, pūga, nālikera*; as fruit along with many other fruits 100. 5, and as blossom 100. 26. It is pretty certain that what is meant is the royal coco-nut.

[6] P. *ayyānaṃ* according to the happy conjecture of S. and B. *Ayyā* used of the bhikkhus in general is found for instance Vin. I. 101[16], it is frequently used with a proper name as *ayyo Ānando* Vin. II. 290[28], *ayyo Mahākassapo* S. II. 215[31] etc.

[7] That is he kept on the Uposatha days the five or eight Buddhist moral commands (*sīlāni*, see Childers s. v.)

[8] By *appamaññā* certain virtues are understood which the believing Buddhist practises and which regulate his relations with the outside world. There are four of these, D. III. 223 f: *mettā* "a loving spirit", *karuṇā* "pity"; *muditā* "joyous sympathy", *upekhā* "serenity".

ties[1] and had books copied. He made images, built alms-halls 19
and the like in great numbers: always he lived in fear of the
other world and of Moggallāna.
Now in the eighteenth year the royal hero Moggallāna 20
came hither at the information of the Nigaṇṭhas[2] with twelve
distinguished friends from Jambudīpa and collected troops at 21
the Kuṭhāri-vihāra in the Ambaṭṭhakola district. When the 22
King heard of it he thought: I will seize and devour[3] him,
and though the soothsayer declared it to be impossible, he
went forth with an array of forces. Moggallāna likewise (set 23
forth) with an army ready for battle, accompanied by his
heroic friends, like to the god Sujampati[4] who fares forth[5]
to fight with the demons. When the two hosts fell on each 24
other like two seas that have burst their bounds, they fought
a mighty battle. Kassapa espying a great stretch of swamp 25
in front of him, turned his elephant to seek another road.
When his troops seeing that, with the cry: Friends, our com- 26
mander here flees! broke up in disorder, the troops of Mog-
gallāna cried: "We see their backs"[6]! But the King with his 27
dagger cut his throat, raised the knife on high and stuck it

[1] The *dhutaṅgā* are certain ascetic observances of an outward kind thirteen in number. It is not expected that these should be kept simultaneously, but it is meritorious to observe one or other of them. They are meant primarily for the bhikkhus not for laymen.

[2] Name for the adherents of the Jaina sect.

[3] As a ferocious beast seizes his prey and devours it.

[4] According to the Abhidhānappadīpikā 18 name of the god Sakka or Indra "consort of Sujā".

[5] *Moggallāno pi* must be supplemented by the verb *nikkhami* from the preceding verse. The part. *gacchanto* belongs to Sujampati. It must not be regarded as representing a finite verb, as we have to deal here not with the description of a condition but with the narration of a fact.

[6] Cf. for this phrase 38. 105 with the note. The construction of the sentence is difficult. The Col. Ed. changes *balakāyā* into *balakāyo* and reads with the inferior MSS. *pabhijjittha*. It is possible to retain the reading of the better MSS. if we assume for this passage the freer use of the gerund in the sense of an absolute participle, as it frequently occurs in the later chapters. See Cūlavs. ed., Introd. p. XVI; as also 48. 78—79.

28 in the sheath[1]. Moggallāna carried out the ceremonies of
burning, glad at his brother's deed[2]. He took the whole of
29 the (royal) treasure[3] and came to the capital[4]. When the
bhikkhus heard of this event, decently clad in their upper
and nether robes, and having cleansed the vihāra, they ran-
30 ged themselves according to rank. When Moggallāna came
to the Mahāmeghavana[5], as the King of the gods to the
Nandana (grove), he made his great army turn back outside
31 the elephant wall[6]. He approached the community, greeted
it respectfully and pleased with this community, he as a mark
of distinction, presented it with his umbrella[7]. The community
32 returned it to him. They called the spot the Chattavaḍḍhi[8],

[1] W. has discussed the passage and the parallel passages 41. 24 f., 41. 52 f., 44. 112 and 116, 50. 23 in detail p. 6 ff. All objections vanish if one takes *churikaṃ* as the object of *ukkhipiya* and not *sīsaṃ*. It is also the object of *hatthimhi appetvā* in 44. 112. In 44. 116 we have only *khipitvā churikaṃ* and in 41. 24 instead of it *katvā kosiyaṃ asiputtakaṃ*. As to *sīsaṃ chindati* W. himself has seen that it must not be translated too literally by "he cuts his head", but by "he cuts his throat". This clearly follows from 41. 52 f. where we first have *chinditum sīsaṃ attano* and then *chindi kandharaṃ*. The meaning of our passage (39. 27) is: Kassapa dying swings his dagger in the air to call his brother's attention to his own suicide. — Kassapa's date is approximately fixed by Chinese sources where we are told that a letter of the king was received at the Chinese court in the year 527 A. D. See JRAS. C. Br. xxiv, Nr. 68, p. 85; H. W. Codrington, H. C., p. 30.

[2] Because he had thereby spared him the necessity of meting out justice himself.

[3] P. *sādhana* denotes the Regalia. Cf. *rājasādhana* 41. 20.

[4] Thus I translate *nagaraṃ varaṃ*.

[5] The park in the south of Anurādhapura in which the Mahāvihāra lay.

[6] The *hatthipākāra* is by no means the town wall as W. thinks (the elephant rampart of the city) but the wall supporting the terrace of the Mahāthūpa. The passage deals not with the march into the town, but with the entry into the domain of the monastery. The bhikkhus are assembled on the terrace. Moggallāna lets his troops turn back and goes up alone to greet them. Cf. above 38. 10 with note.

[7] "In token of submission to the Church" (W.). The umbrella is the symbol of the ruler.

[8] That is: "increase, flourishing of the umbrella". Its value has

and a pariveṇa built there received this name. After he had
entered the city he visited the two other vihāras[1], honoured 33
also the community there and having attained to the great
kingdom, he protected the world in justice. But at the thought: 34
high dignitaries have attached themselves to my father's
murderer, he gnashed his teeth[2] with rage — therefore he
received the name Rakkhasa[3] — and had more than a thou- 35
sand of these dignitaries put to death. He cut off their ears
and their noses and sent many into banishment. When he 36
heard the (sermon about) the pious doctrine he became peace-
ful in spirit and well minded and instituted a great almsgiving,
as a rain-cloud (pours a shower of rain) over the earth. On 37
the day of the full moon of the month Phussa[4] he ordained
a yearly alms and since then this alms is customary in the
Island to this day. And the charioteer[5] who had given his 38
father roasted corn, brought his father's letter and showed
it to Moggallāna. When the latter saw it he wept, praised 39
the love he had borne to his father and he, the powerful one,
appointed him to the office of gate-keeper. And the Senāpati 40
Migāra who had sent him reports in a fitting manner, instituted
a dedication festival for the Abhiseka-Buddha according to his
desire[6]. The vihāras Daḷha and Dāṭhākondañña by name on 41
the Sīhagiri Moggallāna granted to the adherents of the
Dhammaruci and Sāgali Schools[7]. The Pabbata-vihāra which 42

been increased by the King receiving it again out of the hand of the bhikkhus.

[1] Namely Jetavana and Abhayagiri.

[2] P. *vithari dāṭhaṃ*, lit. he revealed his eye-tooth, let it be seen, bared it. The alteration into *dāyaṃ* in the Col. Ed. is certainly wrong. It deprives the following *rakkhasanāmavā* of all sense.

[3] That is "devil". Characteristic of all representations of Rakkhasas (Skr. *rākṣasa*) are the powerful eye-teeth protruding from the mouth like the tusks of a boar.

[4] December to January. See calendar Mhvs. trsl. p. 2, n. 3.

[5] Cf. above 38. 95 f. [6] See 39. 6 f.

[7] The Sāgalikas are like the Dhammarucikas a sect only found in Ceylon. Mhv. 5. 13; 38. 75. The Dhammarucikas had their seat in the Abhayagiri-vihāra. See also 52. 17.

he had built he granted to the Thera called Mahānāma in
43 the Dīghāsana vihāra[1]. Having built a shelter for bhikkhunīs[2]
called Rājinī, the wise (king) made it over to the bhikkhunīs
of the Sāgalika School.

44 A man of the clan of the Lambakaṇṇas[3] named Dāṭhā-
pabhuti, who had been in the service of Kassapa, had in ill-
45 humour betaken himself to the Mereliya district and dwelt
46 there. He had a son known by the name of Silākāla. He too
out of fear of Kassapa had betaken himself with his kinsman
47 Moggallāna from here[4] to Jambudīpa and had undergone the
ceremony of world-renunciation in the Bodhimaṇḍa-vihāra[5].
Fulfilling his duties to the community with zeal and great
48 skill he had (once) presented a mango fruit to the community.
The community pleased thereat, gave him the name of Am-
49 basāmaṇera[6]. Therefore he bore that name. Later on as
described in the Kesadhātuvaṃsa[7], he got possession of the
50 Hair Relic and brought it hither from that land. Moggallāna
honoured him, accepted the Hair Relic, preserved it in a pre-
51 cious casket of crystal, housed it in a beautiful building with
a picture of Dīpaṃkara's[8] city and instituted with pomp a

[1] It is very probable that what is meant here is the vihāra built by Dīghasanda (see 38. 16). But whether with the Col. Ed. we are at liberty to alter the name seems to me doubtful. Mahānāma is the author of the older Mahāvaṃsa.

[2] P. *bhikkhunupassayaṃ*. This is the usual name for vihāras intended for female members of the order

[3] One of the most famous clans in Ceylon from which sprang a whole series of Sinhalese kings.

[4] The author lives in Ceylon and Anurādhapura. The former is for him *ayaṃ dīpo*, "this our island", Anurādhapura *idaṃ nagaraṃ* "this our capital"; "here, hither, from here" means "in, to, from Ceylon (or also: Anurādhapura)" etc.

[5] Cf. 37. 215 with note.

[6] That means: the novice with the mango fruit. After the *pabbajjā* and until the *upasampadā* one is not *bhikkhu*, but *sāmaṇera* that is a future samaṇa, one in the making.

[7] The work is unknown to us. Neither as regards period or content has it anything to do with the Chakesadhātuvaṃsa published by MINAYEFF, JPTS. 1885, p. 5 ff.

[8] Dīpaṃkara is the first of the 24 legendary forerunners of the hi-

great sacrificial festival. He had statues made of his maternal 52
uncle and of his wife and placed them there, as well as the
beautiful figure of a horse[1]. Further he had constructed a 53
casket for the Hair Relic, an umbrella, a maṇḍapa studded with
jewels, portraits of the two eminent disciples and a fan of
hair[2]. The King also made provision for the relic greater 54
than his own, and the Ruler entrusted Silākāla with the
keeping of the relic appointing him sword-bearer[3] — hence 55
he was known by the name of Asiggāhasilākāla — and gave
him his sister (to wife) together with (the necessary) revenues.
Here we give but a short extract; an intelligent man can find 56
a full account in every respect in the Kesadhātuvaṃsa. By 57
instituting a guard for the sea-coast he freed the island from
danger[4]. By a regulative act[5] he purified the good doctrine,

storical Buddha He worked in the town of Rammavatī or Rammanagara, Buddhavaṃsa 2. 207 ff.; JāCo I. 11⁹ ff. The conjecture *Dīpaṃkarassa nāthassa* of the Col. Ed. instead of *Dīpaṃkaranagarassa* is tempting. I have however, not accepted it, because it is difficult to see how the first perfectly clear and simple reading could be turned into the second. It seems to me that we have to deal here with a picture with which the house was decorated.

[1] W. has not properly understood the construction of the sentence. There can be no question of its being "other images also". The literal translation would be as follows: "having fashioned his uncle and his wife of gold, he placed the images there and a beautiful image of a horse" These two individuals had obviously played an important part in the bringing over of the relic, the horse too, very likely. It is impossible to say more in the absence of the quoted text (Kesadhātuvaṃsa).

[2] The assortment seems at first curious. We have to imagine the reliquary resting under a pillar-supported canopy, the *ratanamaṇḍapa*, on a royal throne. Umbrella and fan made of a yak's tail (*vālavījanī*), are attributes of the royal dignity. The portraits of the two *aggasāvakā* — Sāriputta and Moggallāna — stand at the side of the relic, as the highest dignitaries at the side of the throne.

[3] The *asiggāha* is like the *chattaggāha* (see 38. 3 with note), a high court official. Cf. 42. 42; 44. 43 ff. See the Introduction III.

[4] Of a hostile attack from India.

[5] P. *dhammakammena*. This is an act which the priesthood carries out according to the formalities laid down in the Vinaya. The King orders its carrying out. Cf. with this especially 44. 76, 52. 44. It is

58 the Order of the Victor (Buddha). The Senāpati Uttara founded a practising-house[1] which was called after him. After Moggallāna had carried out meritorious works he went to his death in the eighteenth year (of his reign[2]).

59 Thus even he though better far than the ferocious Kassapa[3], was not able once his merit was exhausted, to conquer approaching death as if he were but its slave. Therefore the wise when they have conquered the fear of death, will be happy. Nirvana the highest eternal state of bliss is attainable (only) by him who knows the (nature of the) ego.

Here ends the thirty-ninth chapter, called "The History of The Two Kings", in the Mahāvaṃsa, compiled for the serene joy and emotion of the pious.

always concerned with the removal of abuses which have crept into the Order and with the punishment of guilty bhikkhus.

[1] See 37. 232 with note.

[2] Pūjāv. and Rājāv. also give him 18 years.

[3] *Kassapakopino* is a transposition of *kopikassapassa*. Cf. 37. 69, n. The whole strophe is very corrupt in the MSS. I have attempted to reconstruct it in less arbitrary fashion than has been done in the Col. Ed.

CHAPTER XLI

THE NINE KINGS

After his death his vigourous son of god-like form, called 1
Kumāradhātusena[1] became king. In the vihāra built by 2
his father he had repairs carried out, he had a revision made
of the sacred texts and he reformed the Order. He supplied 3
the great community abundantly with the four necessaries and
after accomplishing many meritorious works, he passed away
in the ninth year[2] (of his reign). Hereupon his son Kitti- 4
sena became king. After he had in divers ways done meri-
torious works he was forced to quit the throne in the ninth
month[3]. His mother's brother, Sīva killed him and became 5
(himself) king; he did several meritorious deeds and was slain[4]
on the five-and-twentieth day by Upatissa.

[1] Pūjāv. and Rājāv. — in the first of these the King is called *Kumāradāsa* — tell of his friendship with Kālidāsa. Kumāradāsa flung himself into the flames of the pyre on which his dead friend was burnt and died with him. Popular tradition places this event in Mātara. Here as we observed for ourselves on the spot, the people are well acquainted with the names of the two friends and their tragic fate. Tradition makes Kālidāsa the son of the first minister of Kumāradāsa's father and the youthful comrade of Kumāradāsa. The grave of the latter in Mātara is still pointed out.

[2] Pūjāv. also gives him 9 years. Likewise Rājāv. (the translation gives erroneously 18 years).

[3] Rājāv. gives the length of reign as 9 years, Pūjāv. in accordance with Mhvs. as 9 months.

[4] Pūjāv., Rājāv., Rājaratn. and Nik.-s. call the prince Mādisivraja. He reigned according to the Pūjāv. 25 days, Rājāv. has erroneously 25 years.

6 Then Upatissa[1], husband of the sister of Moggallāna and
7 his general, having slain Sīva, became king. After the king
by granting offices and the like, had won over the people for
himself, he gave his daughter (in marriage) to Silākāla to-
8 gether with (the necessary) revenues. King Upatissa had a
son, Kassapa. He was a hero associated with sixteen heroic
9 comrades of the same breed. He lived by his manliness in
pious fashion, showing reverence to the aged[2].
10 Silākāla whose heart was deluded by lust for power,
hereupon betook himself to southern Malaya[3], collected a
11 mighty force and plundering the frontier, arrived near the city
(Anurādhapura). When Kassapa the eldest (son of the King)
12 heard that, he mounted his favourite elephant, comforted his
father, took his companions with him and fared forth to meet
13 Silākāla. After the latter had been routed seven or eight times
and his courage had ebbed, he brought the districts east and
14 west by a ruse into his power and advanced to the Pācīna-
tissapabbata[4] to renew the combat. Kassapa with his comrades
15 mounted his elephant, came thither, sent the rebels flying and
drove his elephant to the summit of the mountain. Hence they
16 called him Girikassapa. Silākāla remaining obdurate, made
the kingdom still more rebellious and brought it entirely into
17 his power. He advanced with an invincible army and train
of followers upon the town and besieged it. For seven days

[1] Sinhalese sources call this king Lämäṇiupatissa. He sprang thus from the Lambakaṇṇa clan.

[2] P. *jeṭṭhāpacāyaka* does not mean "honoured his parents greatly". the term is found in *kule jeṭṭhāpacāyika* Pv. 2. 7. 18 beside *matteyya* and *petteyya*. Cf. further *kulajyeṣṭhāpacāyaka* Mahāvastu I. 198[6]. It is a matter of the reverence shown to the oldest and noblest members of the clan.

[3] Name of the Central Province, the mountain country of Ceylon.

[4] One of the mountains east of Anurādhapura. King Jeṭṭhatissa I. (beginning of 4th century A. D.) had founded a monastery there and had brought the stone image of the Buddha from the Thūpārāma to the new vihāra (Mhvs. 36. 127 ff). His successor Mahāsena then transferred it to the Abhayagiri-vihāra (37. 14). It was at the Pācīnatissapabbata that according to 44. 14 ff., the decisive battle was fought between Saṅghatissa and Moggallāna III.

the King's people fought, then they weakened. Thereupon 18
Kassapa thought: "All living creatures here are perishing because of the siege of the town, the troops are enfeebled, the
King is old and blind. I will take my father and mother 19
(for safety) to Merukandara[1], collect the troops and then
punish the rebels[2]." In the night he took his comrades and 20
the royal treasure[3] and set off for Malaya. But as the guides 21
did not know the way, they lost themselves and wandered
hither and thither near the town. Hearing of this Silākāla 22
hastened out and surrounded them. A terrible fight ensued.
As the battle went off like the battle of the gods and the 23
demons, when his comrades had fallen and the royal elephant
had succumbed, Kassapa handed him over to his driver, cut 24
his throat, wiped the blood from his dagger and stuck it in
the sheath. Then supporting both hands on the temples of 25
the elephant he sank down. Upatissa when he heard this,
died also, pierced by the arrow of grief.

When after a year and a half[4] (of his reign) Upatissa had en- 26
tered Heaven Silākāla became king. Together with his former
name he was called Ambasāmaṇerasilākāla[5]. Living for thir- 27
teen years (longer) he protected the Island in justice[6]. He had 28
delicious meats (prepared in the same way as) for the King,
distributed in the Mahāpāli hall and concerned for the wel-

[1] A district in Malaya which often served as place of refuge (cf. 44. 28, 47. 58 &c.).

[2] Here *me* stands for *mayā* and belongs to *niggaṇhiya* "by me is ... to be punished". The gerunds *katvā* and *saṃgahetvā* are then to be taken in conjunction with *me*.

[3] For *rājasādhana* see note to 39. 28. Cf. also 48. 89.

[4] Pūjāv. the same, Rājāv. however, one year and ten months.

[5] See above 39. 48–50.

[6] Pūjāv. and Nik.-s. call the King Lämäṇi-Ambaheraṇa-Salamevan (= Silāmeghavaṇṇa), likewise Rājaratn.; In Rājāv. he is called Lämäṇi-Akbō (= Aggobodhi). Pūjāv. and Rājāv. give him in agreement with our chronicle, a reign of 13 years. Rājaratn. contains a chronological statement. It says that his reign began 1088 years after Buddha's Nirvana and 852 years after the introduction of the Buddhist doctrine into Ceylon.

fare of his people, he increased the revenues of the hospitals.
29 Daily he sacrificed to the Bodhi Tree, he had images made and
to all bhikkhus dwelling on the Island he distributed the three
30 garments[1]. He decreed throughout the Island preservation of
life for all creatures. In most fitting manner he sacrificed to
31 the Hair Relic brought (hither) by himself. The Rahera canal
he made over to the Abhayuttara-vihāra. Here beside the
32 Monarch of trees[2] he set up the throne called Kunta which
he had fetched away from the eastern vihāra of the adherents
of the Thera School. All his life long he performed meritorious deeds without number.

33 The King had three sons: Moggallāna, Dāṭhāpabhuti and
Upatissa. To the eldest (Moggallāna) he handed over the
34 Eastern Province and after conferring on him the dignity of
the title of Ādipāda, he dismissed him with the words: "Go
35 and dwell there". He went and took up his abode there. On
the second son (Dāṭhāpabhuti) he conferred the post of Malayarāja[3] and the province of Dakkhiṇadesa and entrusted him
36 with the care of the sea-coast[4]. But Upatissa, a young man

[1] Namely robe (*saṃghāṭi*), under-garment (*uttarāsaṅga*) and shirt (*antaravāsaka*).

[2] That is, beside the Bodhi Tree in the Abhayagiri-vihāra (*tattha*!)

[3] I believe that *ṭhānaṃ Malayarājaggaṃ* means the same as *ṭh. Malayarājādiṃ* or in composition *Malayarājādiṭṭhānaṃ*. But this is a circumlocution for *Malayarājaṭṭhānaṃ*, as so often happens, for instance *Kumārādidhātusena* (= *Kumāradhātusena*) 41. 1. See following note for the title *Malayarāja*.

[4] Here appears for the first time the title *ādipāda* which in course of time becomes the title for the princes of the royal house. The heir to the throne is Mahādipāda. The title *Malayarāja*, so frequent later, is here mentioned for the first time. Apparently the owner of it was entrusted with the administration of the province Malaya, the central mountain country. I regard the province called *desa Puratthima* as the one otherwise called *Pācīnadesa* "Eastern Province". *Dakkhiṇadesa* as H. W. Codrington (Notes on Ceylon Topography in the twelfth century, JRAS. C. B. XXIX, Nr. 75, 1922, p. 62 ff.) rightly saw, is not a general term for the south of the island (Rohana) but a special province, the territory in the west of the mountains up to the sea. The two provinces get their names from their position in relation to Anurādha-

of good looks he took to live with himself for he was particularly fond of him.

In the twelfth year (of his reign) a young merchant who 37
had betaken himself from here to Kāsipura[1] brought hither
from there the (book) Dhammadhātu[2]. The King as incapable 38
of distinguishing truth from falsehood as the moth which
flies to the lamp it takes for gold, when he saw it, believing 39
it to be the true doctrine of the Buddha received it with
ceremony. He showed it reverence and honour and placed
it in a house not far from the royal palace. Every year he 40
was wont to take it over to the Jetavana-vihāra and there to
arrange a festival which he made into a permanent institution[3],
regarding this as a blessing for all beings. After Silākāla had 41
thus performed numerous meritorious deeds he passed away
on reaching the thirteenth year of his reign, according to
his deeds.

After Dāṭhāpabhuti had seized the throne the deluded 42
one had his brother (Upatissa) murdered, because he sought
to hinder him, it not being his turn. When Moggallāna heard 43
that, he spake full of fierce wrath: "He hath usurped the
government though he had no right to it, without cause he

pura. It is worthy of note here that Dakkhiṇadesa is not yet, as regularly later, the province of the heir to the Throne, but is handed over to the second son, being apparently united with Malaya. Or does Silākāla wish for some reason or other that Dāṭhāpabhuti and not Moggallāna should be his successor?

[1] The town (in the land) of the Kāsis, that is Bārāṇasī i. e. Benares.

[2] According to the wording of the Pāli text, one is inclined to assume that *dhammadhātu* is meant for some relic of the Buddha, perhaps his *dhammakaraka*, his water vessel, and that this relic turned out to be a fake. The Nikāyasaṃgraha however, which treats the subject in greater detail (p. 16^{21}—17^{6}), says distinctly that it is a book containing the heretical doctrines of the Vaitulya School (see note to 42. 35). The King was not able to distinguish these teachings from the true Buddha doctrine. We must therefore assume that *Dhammadhātu* was the title of the book. The Nik.-s. gives the name of the merchant's son (*relaṅdaputrayā*) who brought the book as Punna.

[3] P. *kāresi cārittaṃ*; the infin. *kātuṃ* governs the acc. *mahaṃ*.

44 hath slain my youngest brother who spake the truth. I will
see that he has a merry reign[1]." He took a strong army
45 and advanced to the Rahera mountain. When the King heard
it, he erected an armed camp with troops ready for battle on
46 the Karinda mountain. Hearing of this Moggallāna sent the
King this message: "The people living on the Island have
never failed in their duty to thee or me and if one (of us) is
47 dead, the government need not be divided between us[2]. Others
shall not fight therefore, we two alone will fight a combat
48 here on elephants". The other declared that he was willing
and armed with the five weapons[3], he mounted his elephant
and prepared at once[4] for battle, like Māra[5] against the Sage
49 (Buddha). Moggallāna also mounted his favourite elephant
and took his place. The huge elephants rammed each other.
50 A crash was heard at their onslaught like the roar of thunder
and sparks like lightning flew at the striking of their tusks.
51 The blood-stained elephants were as evening clouds. Wounded
by Moggallāna's elephant the King's elephant began to give
52 way. When the King saw that he made as if to cut his
throat. But Moggallāna greeting him with reverence, besought
53 him: "Forbear to do that!" Despite the request, he persisted
in his defiance and cut his neck. Thus after six months and
(six) days[6] he lost the kingdom.

[1] P. *kārāpessāmi majjarajjaṃ*, lit. "I shall see that his reign is an intoxicating draught". That means either a reign the pleasure of which is as short as that of an intoxicating drink, or in scorn a reign that will make as merry as an intoxicating drink.

[2] This seems to me the sense of this not quite easy passage: the people who are loyal to us both are then not obliged to choose between us.

[3] According to Clough, Sinhalese Dictionary, *s. v.* the weapons were: sword, spear, bow, battle-axe and shield.

[4] P. *otthari* "descended (into the arena, to the place of combat)".

[5] Māra, the tempter, who with his army of demons fights against Buddha in the night of enlightenment and is routed by him, is a favourite subject for artistic representation. Thus at Borobudur, relief nr. 94 (l. gallery, main wall, upper row). Cf. N. J. Krom, the Life of Buddha on the Stūpa of Barabuḍur, p. 102 ff.

[6] According to Pūjāv. and Rājāv. he reigned six months.

Hereupon the mighty Moggallāna became king on the 54
Island. On account of his mother's brother[1] they called him
Cūla(moggallāna). He had poetic gifts without equal, as 55
highest (good) he held the three (sacred) objects[2], He was an
abode of virtues like generosity, self-control, purity, goodness.
By largess, friendly speech, by working for the good (of others) 56
and by his natural feelings for others[3], he won over the mass
of his subjects. By almsgiving and the (founding of) vihāras, 57
by (gifts of) medicine and garments he won the community
of the bhikkhus and by just protection. While distinguishing 58
the preachers of the doctrine by abundant gifts of honour, he
had the three Piṭakas together with the Aṭṭhakathā[4] recited.
Boys he lured with sweetmeats which delighted them and had 59
them constantly instructed in the good doctrine, he, the sage
who was a shining light of the good doctrine. He also com- 60
posed a poem in praise of the good doctrine which he, the
best of men, from the height of his elephant[5], recited at the
close of the sermon, in the town. He dammed up the Ka- 61
damba river[6] among the mountains forming thereby the
Pattapāsāṇavāpi, Dhanavāpi and Garītara tanks. With the 62
thought: this is a work that ensures long life, he, full of zeal,
had the sacred texts written down and a solemn festival held
for the (three sacred) objects. While full of pity for the world 63
as a mother for the son of her womb, he died, having given
and enjoyed according to desire, in the twentieth year (of
his reign)[7].

[1] P. *ayyakaṃ* = Moggallāna I. who was his *mātula*, since according to 39. 55, his father Silākāla had married Moggallāna's I. sister.

[2] The *vatthuttaya* are the Buddha, his doctrine (*dhamma*) and his Order (*saṃgha*).

[3] P. *samānattassabhāvena*. By this the *cattāri saṃgahavatthūni* are meant. See note to 37. 108.

[4] That is the sacred texts together with the commentaries.

[5] P. *kuñjarasekhare nisā*. Here *nisā* stands for *nissā* metri causa and the latter for *nissāya* as expressing a local relation.

[6] The river flowing past the east side of Anurādhapura, now called Malvatu-oya.

[7] Pūjāv. and Rājāv.: 20 years. In both works and in the Rājaratn. the king is called Daḷa-Mogalan. See below note to 44. 63.

64 His Mahesī had killed his kindred with poison. She then
made her son king and carried on the government herself.
65 Lord of men Kittisirimegha thus made king, at once had
the house of the Monarch of trees[1] covered with tin plates.
66 For the poor, for travellers and beggars he instituted a great
almsgiving. As protector of the road in such manner he could
67 be useful to all[2]. But in all enterprises the Mahesī took the
lead, thus everything in his kingdom was turned upside down.
68 The royal officials and the high dignitaries thought only of
bribery, and the powerful in the land terrorized the weak.

69 At the time of Silākāla there lived in a village called
Saṅgilla, a man called Bhayasīva, a scion of the Moriya clan.
70 Sīva had a son by name Aggabodhi and also a sister's son
71 known by the name of Mahānāga. His sister's son was of
tall stature, Aggabodhi was handsome[3]. On account of his
72 high-soaring plans, the vigorous Mahānāga gave up field la-
bour and led a robber's life in the forest. Once when he
73 caught an iguana[4] he sent it to his aunt[5]. When she saw

[1] The Bodhi Tree in the Mahāvihāra.

[2] The conjectural *maggamālo* "road-hall" (perhaps = rest-house) of the Col. Ed. for-*pālo* is without doubt tempting. According to it W. translates as follows: "Yes, he was like unto a public hall of charity wherein all men were able to partake freely of according to their necessities." I have however, scruples about taking such liberties with the MS. reading, more especially as it gives tolerable sense. In the foregoing travellers and wandering beggars have been mentioned. Here the compiler of our chronicle adds the remark: the king would have been a signpost and a guide to all these (*sabbopabhogiyo*, lit. = one who must or can be enjoyed by all), had not the queen prevented him. She interfered everywhere and thereby brought the kingdom to chaos.

[3] An alteration of the text is certainly necessary if the MSS. have *bhāgineyyo mahānāgo aggabodhi ca sundaro*. The writer of S. 6 has felt that, when he has changed *sundaro* into *-rā*. But it seems to me that in this verse a contrast, not a resemblance, between the two cousins has to be emphasized, to make the future conduct of Mahānāga intelligible. I should incline therefore, to read *mahākāyo* instead of *Mahānāgo*, and refer the reader to the critical note in my edition.

[4] P. *godhā*, Sinh. *goyā*. Two species are distinguished: *talagoyā* "land-iguana" (*Varanus dracaena*) and *kabaragoyā* "speckled iguana" (*Hydrosaurus salvator*). The flesh of iguanas is eaten.

[5] P. *mātulānī*, the wife of the mother's brother, hence the wife of Bhayasīva.

the iguana she understood (what he wanted) and ordered to
send him a basket of corn[1]. He also sent to the blacksmith
a hare and he did the same (as the aunt). From his sister[2] 74
he begged seed corn and a bringer of the seed corn[3]; she
handed him over a slave and provided him secretly with food
and drink.

Now during a famine a certain man, skilled in magic spells, 75
in order to get alms, was wont to beg food from everybody
clad in the robe of a bhikkhu. He had betaken himself to 76
the village (of Saṅgilla) but as he got no food, overcome
with hunger, he sat down trembling. When the merciful 77
Mahānāga saw him, he had pity on him, took the alms-bowl,
but although he traversed the village in all directions, he got 78
not even rice soup. But when he gave up his upper-garment,
he got food. The other ate, was content and thought: I will 79
make him worthy of the kingdom on the Island. He took him
with him and came in a moment to the Gokaṇṇa[4] sea. Sea- 80
ting himself there and murmuring in the usual way the for-
mula of incantation, he conjured up the Nāga King in the 81
night of the full moon of the month Phussa[5]. "Touch the
great Nāga[6]", he commanded Mahānāga. In the first watch

[1] P. *pasaṃsayi* must not be corrected. The root *saṃs* is intimately connected with *sās*, just as in Skr. *śaṃs* and *śās* merge in each other; *pasaṃs* means here "to determine, to direct". The aunt understands that by sending the iguana her nephew wishes to indicate that while he has the flesh of game in abundance, he lacks bread.

[2] The son of this sister is (42. 1) the future king Aggabodhi I.

[3] P. *bījagāha*, purposely formed like *asigāha*, *chattagāha*.

[4] *Gokaṇṇa(ka)* is also 57. 5 the theatre of a similar scene of magic as the one here described. In 71. 18 it is the farthest spot down the Mahaveliganga ("from Sarogāmatittha as far as Gokaṇṇa"), which must be protected from the enemy in Rohaṇa. As in our passage it is described as *mahaṇṇava* "ocean", it can be no other than the mouth of the Mahaveliganga, the Koddiyar Bay, the Bay of Trincomalee.

[5] December to January.

[6] The Nāgas are semi-divine beings in the form of snakes. They are always held to be zealous worshippers of the Buddha and of his teaching. They are represented in human form with a snake's head growing from between the shoulder blades over the head.

of the night, through fear, he did not touch the Nāga who
82 had appeared. It was even so in the middle watch of the
night. But in the last watch he caught him by the tail and
(immediately) let go of him. (Only) with three fingers had
83 he touched him[1]. When the magician saw that he foretold:
"My effort succeeds: After thou hast had war with three kings
84 and slain the fourth, thou shalt be king in thy old age and
live yet three years; and three people out of thy clan will be
85 kings (after thee). Go thither, serve the King; later thou
shalt witness my power." With these words he sent him forth.
86 Mahānāga went, sought the monarch[2] and entered his service.
The King made him collector of revenue in Rohaṇa and he
87 collected many goods which were produced there. The King
was pleased with him and gave him the rank of an andhasenā-
pati[3] and commanded him to betake himself thither (to Rohaṇa)
88 again. He took the son of Bhayasīva and his sister's son[4]
with him, went thither and raised rebellion in the whole pro-
89 vince. He made of Rohaṇa a territory whose products fell
exclusively to himself and took up his abode there[5]. In order
to wage war with Dāṭhāpabhuti he advanced with a great
90 array of forces, but from fear of Moggallāna[6], he returned to

[1] W. translates: "he raised it by the tail with three of his fingers and dropped it", but *khip* does not mean "to raise" nor *chup* "to drop". In my edition the punctuation of the text is also wrong. One must place the semi-colon after *khipi* and take *tīh' evaṃ angulīhi sa taṃ chupi* as a connected sentence.

[2] The event takes place, as is apparent from v. 69 and from what follows, in the time of King Silākāla.

[3] This title only occurs here. See Introd. III.

[4] The former was called Aggabodhi (41. 70). By *bhāgineyya* we have probably to understand the nephew of Mahānāga who according to v. 93 died prematurely.

[5] The present part. *vasaṃ* is used here instead of a finite verb to express a permanent state.

[6] Before it came to a fight, the reign of Dāṭhāpabhuti had come to an end, after lasting six months.

Rohaṇa. While he dwelt there he heard of the confusion[1] in
King Kittsirimegha's kingdom. Mahānāga thought it was 91
now time to seize the government, set out hastily from Ro-
haṇa, slew the Ruler on the nineteenth day[2], took over the 92
government himself and reestablished order. Then he sent a
letter to his sister's son bidding him come. The latter coming 93
turned back because of an (unlucky) omen and died. There-
upon Mahānāga out of gratitude, made the son of his mother's
brother (Aggabodhi) Uparāja[3]. After building an irrigation 94
trench round the Monarch of trees he had a roof put over
its golden house and set up images of the King of Sages. He 95
decorated the three great cetiyas with stucco work and (put
up) a protecting ring (against lightning). He also repaired
the elephant terrace and the paintings[4]. The weavers' village 96
Jambelambaya[5] he affiliated to the Uttara-vihāra[6] and the
village called Tintiṇika to the Mahāvihāra. The village of 97
Vasabha in Uddhagāma he granted to the Jetavana, he also
instituted a giving of garments for the three fraternities[7].
After granting three hundred fields to the Jeta(vana)- 98
vihāra he instituted there a permanent (gift of) rice soup for

[1] P. *asamañjasa*, lit. "uneven road" a figurative expression for the idea of disorder and confusion.

[2] Pūjāv., Rājāv., Nik.-s., Rājaratn. call the king Kuḍākitsirimevan to distinguish him from Sirimeghavaṇṇa, the first prince of the Cūlavaṃsa line. The two first chronicles attribute to him a reign of 19 years.

[3] For the Uparāja, the co-regent of the reigning king and his relation to the Yuvarāja, the heir-apparent, see Introduction II.

[4] Cf. for the works mentioned here 38. 10 and 74 with the notes. The stucco work is of course the masonry of the thūpa; *cumbaṭa* is short for *vajiracumbaṭa*; *hatthivedī* is the same as *hatthipākāra*.

[5] Or "the weavers' village called Jambela" according to the reading *jambelachayaṃ* preferred by S. and B.

[6] P. *Uttare*. This doubtless stands here for *Abhayuttare*, is therefore the Abhayagiri-vihāra. Cf. note to 37. 97.

[7] The *tayo nikāyā* are the communities of the Mahā-, Jetavana- and Abhayagiri-vihāras. But in a Sinhalese work, quoted by WICKREMASINGHE, EZ. II. 275, note 1, it is pointed out that they are the three sects of the Dhammarucis, Sāgalikas, and Vetullas. Sometimes, as 46. 15 f. "two fraternities" are mentioned along with the three.

99 the bhikkhus. He handed over to the Ascetics[1] a thousand
fields (watered by the tank) called Dūratissa. For the inmates
of the Mahāvihāra he instituted a permanent (dole of) rice
100 soup. The Cīramātikavāra (canal) he granted thither, rejoicing
at virtuous dealing. In the Mayūra-pariveṇa[2] he undertook
101 renovations and in the Mahādevarattakurava-vihāra in (the di-
strict of) Kāsikhaṇḍa he restored the dilapidated Anurārāma.
102 After he had performed in this and in other ways works which
lead to Heaven he joined after three years[3] the company of
the gods.

103 These eight kings who were all contented in spirit[4], whose
wealth was endless as that of the King of Kings[5], who gloried
in their troops, their elephants, their chargers and in the
chariots of their heroic army[6], they had finally to surrender
all and forsaken by their followers, mount the pyre. The wise

[1] I do not think that we can connect *tapassinaṃ* directly with *Mahāvihāravāsinaṃ*. The former belongs to the first, the latter to the second half of the verse. The ascetics do not live in the vihāra but in the *arañña*. Probably the ascetics of the Tapovana 52. 22, 53. 14, 54. 20 are meant, the settlement in the wilderness west of Anurādhapura, recently more accurately investigated by AYRTON and HOCART. See Memoirs Archaeol. Survey Ceylon I. 1924, p. 18 ff.

[2] See 37. 172 and 38. 52 with the notes.

[3] Pūjāv. and Rājāv. call the prince Senevi or Senevi-Mānā. The duration of his reign is given as 3 years. In Rājaratn. and Nik.-s. he is also called Senevi. After him all four chronicles insert a king whose name is missing in the Cūlavaṃsa. Pūjāv.: Lämāṇi-Siṅgān-Saladaḷabōnā (9 years), Rājāv.: Lämāṇi-Siṃha-Saladaḷabōnā (9 years), Rājaratn. and Nik.-s.: Lämāṇi-Siṅgānāya.

[4] Because they had attained the highest human goal, the dignity of kingship.

[5] The word *rājarāja* denotes also in Skr. Kuvera, the god of wealth.

[6] The two first lines of the strophe offend repeatedly against the law of style. They can only be translated according to their sense. *Rājarājena rūpā* and *narakarituragā sūrasenārathehi* are disintegrated compounds. They stand instead of *rājarājarūpā* (°*rūpa* = "like", as in *bhagavantarūpa*, D. I. 51[28]) and *narakarituragasūrasenārathehi*.

man when he remembers this should, if he seeks his salvation, harbour the wish to fling away from him the happiness of existence.

Here ends the forty-first chapter, called 'The Nine Kings'[1] in the Mahāvaṃsa, compiled for the serene joy and emotion of the pious.

[1] The MSS. have it is true, *aṭṭharājako* "the eight kings". Cf. the note to the signature of the following pariccheda.

CHAPTER XLII

THE TWO KINGS

1 **Aggabodhi** the highly favoured of fortune, sister's son
of King Mahānāga[1], now became king whose aspiration was
2 the attainment of the highest enlightenment. In splendour
imitating the sun, in charm the moon with full disk, in stead-
3 fastness the Sumeru mountain[2], in depth the ocean, in firm-
ness the earth, in impartiality[3] the wind, in insight the ma-
4 gician among the gods[4], in purity the autumn heavens, in the
enjoyment of wishes fulfilled the King of the gods, in wealth

[1] Here S. and B., and W. obviously dependent on their rendering, translate *ikbiti Mahānāga-naraniñduhu mayilpit*, W: "the son of Mahānāga's mother's brother." In itself that would be quite simple. Aggabodhi would then be the son of Bhayasīva mentioned 41. 70 whom Mahānāga according to 41. 93, appointed uparāja. But there is one difficulty about the matter It absolutely contradicts the text. Aggabodhi is here perfectly plainly described as *bhāgineyya* of Mahānāga. The Pūjāv. also calls him *Mānaraja-bāna* and likewise the Rājāv. We must stick to this if we wish to keep firm ground under our feet. We must thus assume that the Cūlavaṃsa says nothing about the after fate of Bhayasīva's son, just as it is so often silent where we should like to hear more, and that the Aggabodhi named in 42. 1 has nothing but the name in common with him. Still's genealogical tree (in his very valuable Index to the Mahawansa) which rests on the translations, needs correction accordingly.

[2] Sumeru is the same as Meru or Hemameru. Cf. 37. 79 with note.

[3] P. *samavutti* refers to the impartial demeanour towards others, none being favoured, none being disadvantaged, as the wind blows equally for all beings without distinction. It is interesting to find quite similar phrases as those in v. 2 and 3 in an inscription of Mahinda IV. (Wickremasinghe, EZ. I. 225).

[4] That is Bṛhaspati.

the commander of treasures[1], in justice the upright Vāseṭṭha[2],
in courage the king of beasts, in royal virtues a ruler of the 5
world, in generosity a Vessantara[3], it was thus his people
knew him. On his mother's brother he conferred the dignity 6
of uparāja, on his brother that of yuvarāja, on his sister's son
that of king of Malaya[4]. To the most distinguished officials 7
also he gave positions according to their merits. He won over
his subjects by the heartwinning qualities and by the royal
virtues[5]. The province of Dakkhiṇadesa with the appropriate 8
retinue[6] he made over to the Yuvarāja. The latter while he
dwelt there, built the Sirivaḍḍhamāna tank. After the wise 9
(prince) had erected the Giri-vihāra intended for the community (of the bhikkhus) he granted it two hundred fields
for the support of the community. To the Malayarāja he gave 10
his daughter Dāṭhā by name (to wife); he also built the pariveṇa which bears the name Sirisaṃghabodhi. For Mahāsiva 11
he built a pariveṇa[7] which was called after him. His companions also were chiefly intent on meritorious works. Thus 12
by a pious mode of life[8] he followed the good old custom

[1] The term *amaramantar* applied to Bṛhaspati here bears out his close association with the Atharvaveda given him in the Indian epics. Hopkins, Epic Mythology, p. 181. — The King of the Gods is Indra, the Lord of treasure Kuvera.

[2] A ṛṣi, a primeval sage (Skr. *Vasiṣṭha*).

[3] Vessantara was the last human incarnation of the Buddha. His history is told in the Jātaka bearing his name (Nr. 547) Fausböll's edition, VI. p. 479 ff.

[4] Cf. for these titles the notes to **41. 33-35**.

[5] See notes to **37. 107** and **108**.

[6] P. *sayoggaṃ*. the adj. *yogga* is made into a substantive by supplementing it with a nominal term like "accessories, equipment, retinue". *Sayoggabalavāhana* in **44. 84** is used in the same connection. Here for the first time we have the Southern Province, the *dakkhiṇadesa* as territory reserved for the heir to the throne, as is thenceforward the rule. Cf. also the note to **41. 35**.

[7] Note to **37. 63**.

[8] P. *-sādhūpacārena*. W. translates this: "by continually keeping the company of good men", which is also possible.

and to remove hindrances, he restored[1] it where it had fallen
13 into decay. During his reign poets wrote numerous poems
in the Sīhala tongue which were distinguished by various
14 useful doctrines[2]. In the Dakkhiṇa-vihāra[3] he erected a splen-
did pāsāda[4] and in the course of nine years he cleared the
15 island of all briers[5]. After building the vihāra called Ku-
ruṇda destined for the whole Order (of bhikkhus) and a tank of
the same name[6] and (after planting) a cocopalm garden three yo-

[1] Refers directly to "the good old custom" (*porāṇaṃ dhammiyaṃ vidhiṃ*) which is figuratively likened to a building that has fallen into decay and must be restored. The "hindrances" are things, actions, circumstances which obstruct the path to delivrance.

[2] So I translate *naya* which is chiefly used of prudent policy. The names of the twelve poets said to have flourished under Aggabodhi I. are enumerated in the Pūjāv., the Rājāv., and the Nik.-s.

Pūjāv:		Rājāv:		Nik.-s.:	
	1. Dähämi		Dahanet		Dämīya
	2. Temal		Pusu		Suriyabāhuya
	3. Bäbiri		Bäri		Bābiriya
	4. Bisodaḷa		Miyo		Daḷabisōya
	5. Anurut		Kuma		Anurutkumaruya
	6. Daḷagot		Dalagot		Daḷagotkumaruya
	7. Puravaḍu		Puravā		Puravaḍukumaruya
	8. Daḷasalakumaru		Dasalā		Daḷasalakumaruya
	9. Kitsiri		Kitsiri		Kitsirikumaruya
	10. Kasub		Käsubu		Kasupkotaäpāya
	11. Koṭa		Kota		Sakdāmalaya (? = 2)
	12. Äpā		Äpaya		Asakdāmalaya

In addition it is stated in the Pūjāv. and Rājāv. that the Thera Dhammakitti (sinh. Dämi, Dähämikit) held office under King Aggabodhi.

[3] That is: the "Southern Monastery". According to Mhvs. 33. 88 its builder was Uttiya, one of the warriors of Vaṭṭagāmaṇi. It lay *nagaramhā dakkhiṇato.* In the latest plan of Anurādhapura the Dakkhiṇa-vihāra is identified with the cetiya known in local tradition as "Eḷāra's tomb" (Cf. Mhvs. 25. 72-73). As regards this monument, I should prefer keeping to the local tradition. The Dakkhiṇa-vihāra has thus still to be identified.

[4] See note to 37. 59.

[5] Said figuratively; *kaṇṭaka* "thorn" is used of all enemies of the throne and the church, of all pests of the organism of the State.

[6] The building of the Kurunda tank is also narrated in Pūjāv. Rājāv. and Rājaratn. H. W. Codrington (H. C., p. 35) identifies it with the Giant's tank near Mannar.

janas in length, he granted it to Mahāsiva as his dwelling[1] 16
and in addition to it revenues, honours and distinctions and
a hundred monastery attendants[2]. Near to it he built the 17
Ambilapassava-vihāra and granted the village of this name to
the Ascetics of the Thera School[3]. To the Unnavalli-vihāra 18
he granted the far-famed village of Ratana[4] and placed (in
the vihāra) a stone image of the Master. In Kelivāta he built 19
the (vihāra) called Sumanapabbata and beside the Bodhi temple
a stone terrace with a large oil pit[5]. After he had restored 20
the Lohapāsāda, he distributed at the dedication festival of
the pāsāda to six and thirty thousand bhikkhus the three gar-
ments[6]. He assigned to it a village and ordered that it should 21
be guarded. In the Hatthikucchi-vihāra[7] the enlightened
(prince) likewise erected a pāsāda which bore the name of his
daughter. He kept piously to the instruction of the bhikkhu 22
Dāṭhāsiva and living according to the law, he looked after
him heedfully[8]. Further he built the great vihāra Mūgasenā- 23

[1] The Col. Ed. differs greatly here from the MSS. It reads *mahāsīmadvayañceva sassaṃ kārayituṃ adā*, but it is just the first syllables *mahāsiva* which are well preserved in all the MSS. It seems to me very doubtful for the rest, that *mahāsīmadvayaṃ* should mean "two large tracts of defined land" as translated by W. For *sīmā* I know only the meaning "boundary", but not "defined territory".

[2] See note to 37. 63.

[3] See notes to 41. 99 and 37. 227.

[4] Is Ratanagāma not the present Ratnapura? The epithet *dīghavaṇṇita* would then point to its having been famous then as a mine of precious stones. Here attention may also be called to the district Ratanākara-raṭṭha (69. 31) which lies in the Southern Province.

[5] The Bodhi temple in the Mahāvihāra is meant here (note to 38. 43). The "oil pit" was probably a cup-like hollow intended for the reception of the oil presented for festive illumination.

[6] See note to 41. 29.

[7] Is also mentioned 48. 65 in the reign of Aggabodhi VI and 49. 76 in that of Dappula II.

[8] Apparently Dāṭhāsiva took a post at court corresponding to that of the *purohita* in the Indian courts. This is the beginning of the political influence of the bhikkhus. Cf. 57. 38 f. and note.

pati and assigned it[1] the village Lajjika for the (necessary)
24 maintenance of the slaves. For the merit of King Mahānāga
King Aggabodhi built a (vihāra) called by his name[2] and as-
signed it to the Grand Thera who was versed in the three
25 Piṭakas[3]. But he who no longer possessed wishes, handed
over the vihāra to sixty-four bhikkhus of his kind who practis-
26 ed yoga[4]. After building the Bhinnorudīpa(-vihāra) for the
same (thera) who dwelt in the Mahāpariveṇa[5], and granting[6]
27 it (revenues) from Vaṭṭākārapiṭṭhi, he erected halls for the
Uposatha festival[7] in the vihāra called Dakkhiṇāgiridaḷha, in
28 Mahānāgapabbata and in the Kālavāpi-vihāra. In the Abhaya
(giri)-vihāra he constructed a large bathing tank and on the
Cetiyapabbata he provided a permanent water supply for the
29 Nāgasoṇḍi tank[8]. After having the Mahindataṭa tank[9] con-
structed in the proper way, he decided to set up (the image

[1] The reading *ekassa* which W. accepts, is certainly wrong. It can only be a question of a foundation for the benefit of the vihāra mentioned in the first half of the verse and which is alluded to by *etassa*.

[2] *Vihāraṃ* must be inserted from v. 23. We might translate "he gave it (i. e. the Mūgasenāpati-vihāra) the name Mahānāga-vihāra". The building of this vihāra by Aggabodhi (*Mānāradapiriveṇa*) is also mentioned in Pūjāv. and Rājaratn.

[3] See note to 37. 223. Who the Grand Thera was is not said, probably Dāṭhāsiva.

[4] I. e. who gave themselves to ascetic and meditative practices. H. Beckh, Buddhismus II, 9 ff., was the first to show the significance of Yoga in Buddhism in its true light.

[5] According to 50. 67 a building in the Jetavana-vihāra. Mentioned again 48. 65.

[6] The translation is not quite certain on account of the brevity of the original. W. has, however, disregarded the gerund *katvā* in his rendering.

[7] See note to 37. 201.

[8] I think what is meant here is the bathing tank now called Nāgapokuṇa, situated just under the summit of the Mihintale mountain (see 38. 75 note) where hewn in the rock face the heads of a cobra (*nāga*) seem to rise out of the water. Not "Elephant's Pool" as W. translates. See Mhvs. trsl. p. 94, note 1.

[9] The tank at the foot of the Missaka mountain by which the present fields of the village Mihintale are irrigated.

of) the Thera (Mahinda) on its dike and he decreed that when 30
the Grand Thera Mahinda should be brought to the place,
people from the Taraccha[1] clan should carry him. He plac- 31
ed a golden umbrella[2] on the (thūpas of the) three fra-
ternities, seven- eight- and nine-fold[3] and (set) with pre-
cious stones. He presented the Mahāthūpa with a golden 32
umbrella weighing four and twenty bhāras[4] and here and there
(he offered) a superb jewel of great value. Having decorated 33
the temple of the Tooth Relic with brightly gleaming precious
stones he made a golden reliquary (for the relic) and in the
Pāli Hall a canoe of bronze[5]. He built the Mahāmekhala 34
bund and conducted a great canal from the Maṇihīra tank[6].

At that time a Grand Thera called Jotipāla had beaten in 35
controversy the adherents of the Vetulla School[7] on the Is-
land. The Ādipāda called Dāṭhāpabhuti, ashamed (at the 36
defeat), raised his hand to strike him (the thera). At the self-
same moment an ulcer appeared (on his hand). But the King 37
who was pleased with Jotipāla, assigned him a dwelling in
that very vihāra[8]. In his pride Dāṭhāpabhuti went not to

[1] P. *taracchā*. See note to 38. 13. W. is not at all clear about this passage. The Taracchā are already mentioned Mhvs. 19. 2 along with the Kuliṅgā.

[2] See note to 38. 54, as also to 41. 97.

[3] Has reference to the single storeys of the chatta which apparently differed in the three thūpas (Mahāthūpa, Jetavana and Abhayagiri) in the way indicated.

[4] A *bhāra* (= 20 Tulā = 2000 Pala) is according to BR. (Sanskrit Wtb. *s. v.*), equal to about 140 lbs. That would give a total weight of 33 to 34 cwt. According to the Sinhalese weight (1 *pala* = 4 *karṣa* = a little more than 72. 5 gr.) we should get double that quantity. The umbrella was of course of stone and gilded.

[5] See note to 37. 181.

[6] Now Minneri-veva, N. W. of Polonnaruva.

[7] The Mahāvaṃsa regards the Vetulla School as a heretical sect They were the representatives of the Mahāyāna in Ceylon and are first mentioned Mhvs. 36. 41 in the reign of Vohāraka-Tissa (2nd half of the 3rd c. A. D.). They had their seat in the Abhayagiri-vihāra according to Mhvs. 36. 111. Cf. Mhvs. trsl., p. 259. n. 2.

[8] Presumably in the vihāra where the controversy had taken place. (Abhayagiri ?)

38 him[1] and so died. The King conferred the dignity of ma-
hādipāda[2] on his sister's son Aggabodhi and charged him to
39 take the Thera under his protection, which he did. After
building the Nīlageha cell[3] the King gave it to that same
Thera. Thus he wrought many meritorious works and died
in the thirty-fourth year (of his reign)[4].
40 Hereupon Aggabodhi became king. As the former king
was the elder he was distinguished by the name Khudda[5].
41 Versed in the former customs he protected the Island and he
made Saṃghabhaddā the daughter of his mother's brother
42 mahesī[6]. As sword-bearer he appointed a kinsman of the
Mahesī. He distributed posts according to worth, without
43 preference[7]. The Veḷuvana(-vihāra) which the king had built he
made over to the adherents of the Sāgali School[8]. He also built
the Jamburantaragalla(-vihāra) and the Mātikapiṭṭhi(-vihāra).
44 During the reign of this (king) the prince of the Kālinga
country whose mind was disturbed when he saw the death of
45 living beings in war, came hither to our Island with the re-
solve of world renunciation[9]. He underwent the ceremony of
world renunciation under Jotipāla and the King maintained
46 him honourably for a long time. He built him a prac-

[1] He was too proud to go to Jotipāla and ask his forgiveness.

[2] The title mahādipāda is usually borne by the heir to the throne.

[3] What a *pariccheda* was in a monastic establishment is difficult to say. I suppose it to have been single cells for the inmates. Cf. 48. 2, 50. 77.

[4] Pūjāv: 34 years, Rājāv: 30 years.

[5] I. e. the little, the younger. In the Sinhalese sources he is also called *Kuḍa-Akbō*.

[6] See note to 37. 211.

[7] W.'s translation of *anālayo* by "as he envied not to give power into the hands of others" is certainly not right. *Ālaya* means "wish, affection". What is meant is merely that the king was not influenced by personal wishes but by objective considerations. Cf. also 46. 4.

[8] See note to 39. 41. The Sāgaliyā had their seat in Jetavana, as the Dhammarucikā in Abhayagiri (A. M. Hocart, Memoirs ASC. I, p. 15 ff.). For the Veḷuvana-vihāra see note to 44. 29.

[9] It seems that he was driven from his country by Pulakeśin I., the founder of the Chalukya dynasty who conquered the Kaliṅga kingdom. According to Jouveau-Dubreuil this took place 609 A. D. See H. W. Codrington, H. C., p. 35, 51.

tising-house[1] in the Mattapabbata-vihāra. The Kāliṅga
prince's minister and his Mahesī betook themselves to the same
(Jotipāla) and under him they (likewise) underwent the cere-
mony of world renunciation. When the Mahesī of the King 47
(Aggabodhi) heard of her splendid renunciation of the world,
she supported her honourably and had the Ratana(-vihāra)
built (for her). To the minister the King granted the Vetta- 48
vāsa-vihāra in Pācīnakaṇḍarāji[2], but the ascetic handed it over
to the community[3]. The royal Thera died; the King (Agga- 49
bodhi) mourned for him and wept for him and after that
built a practising-house in the Cūlagalla-vihāra[4] as well as
one in the Palaṃnagara-vihāra[5]. Thus in his place and for 50
him[6] the ruler performed many meritorious works.

Once while the Thera Jotipāla was performing his devo- 51
tions in front of the cetiya in the Thūpārāma a piece of
(masonry) got loosened and fell in front of him. The troubled 52
Thera called the King and showed it to him. When the King
saw it he was horrified and had the work at once taken in
hand. He housed the Relic of the Right Collar-bone[7], care- 53
fully guarded, in an inner room of the Lohapāsāda and
honoured it day and night. As the repairs in the Thūpārāma 54
were delayed, the devatās[8] dwelling there appeared to the

[1] See notes to 37. 232.

[2] The name occurs in what is probably the right form Pācīnakhaṇḍarāji also in Mhvs. 23. 4. I believe it to be the name of a village near the Citta mountain.

[3] I. e. he refused personal possession and handed over the vihāra to the community of the bhikkhus.

[4] Mentioned also Mhvs. 35. 13. The vihāra was built by Cūlābhaya at the end of the 1st c. A. D. on the bank of the Goṇanadī (Kala-oya), south of Anurādhapura.

[5] In *Palaṃnagaraya* the *-ga* means "found in". It is thus not part of the name, as W. supposes.

[6] This is a *patti*, that is an action whose merits are transferred to another person who has died. The reward for the pious foundations made by Aggabodhi are to fall to the royal thera from Kālinga.

[7] See above note to 37. 207.

[8] *Thūpārāmamhi* belongs to *navakamme* as well as to *devatā*. According to popular belief devatās are everywhere, in every field, every tree, every building, even in the single parts of a house.

55 King in a dream as attendants of the monastery. "If the King
hesitates to rebuild the shrine of the relic we shall take the
relic and go where it pleaseth us", said they. At that mo-
56 ment the King awoke and greatly perturbed, he had the work
on the shrine finished in a short time, including the paintings
57 and the like. Further (he had) four images and thrones of
stone, a golden umbrella and work in stone and ivory (made)
58 for the shrine. His dignitaries and others (of high rank) made
nine hundred reliquaries and renewed[1] the whole work of
59 Devānampiyatissa[2]. When with immense pains he had got
together the offering in fitting manner he with the greatest
60 reverence, brought the relic from the Lohapāsāda hither. He
had the relic surrounded by the Grand Thera Jotipāla together
with the community, carried in festive procession[3] in a reli-
61 quary. To the relic-shrine he dedicated the island of Laṅkā
together with his own person[4] and handed over to its guar-
dians the village the proceeds of which had belonged to the
62 Mahesī. In Nāgadīpa (he presented) the Uṇṇalomaghara temple
to the Rājāyatanadhātu(-vihāra), as well as an umbrella for
63 the Āmalacetiya[5]. He granted to the vihāra there a village
for the provision of rice soup. To the Abhaya(giri)-vihāra
64 he granted the village of Aṅgaṇasālaka. Giving it his own
name and that of the Mahesī, he erected in the Abhayuttara[6]
65 the Dāṭhāggabodhi house. The Queen piously built the
Kapālanāga-vihāra and handed it over provided with the four

[1] In v. 57 the v. *kārayi* must be supplemented to the accusatives from v. 56. *Navaṃ kammaṃ* in v. 58 d must have the v. *akāsuṃ* added from 58 a.

[2] He is the builder of the Thūpārāma-cetiya according to Mhvs. 17. 1 ff., 62.

[3] P. *parihārena*. The word has obviously here already the meaning of its Sinhalese equivalent *perahara* "procession".

[4] See above 39. 31 for a case of similar homage to the Church.

[5] The verb is missing in the sentence. We must probably supplement it with an *adā* from the foregoing. My interpretation differs greatly from that of W. I take Rājāyatanadhātu for the name of a vihāra. Nāgadīpa means the most northerly part of Ceylon.

[6] See note to 37. 97.

necessaries, to the same monastery. In the Jetavana the King 66
erected a building with a glittering crowning ornament[1] and
near the house of the Bodhi Tree he had a well dug. He also 67
built the Gaṅgātaṭa, Valāhassa and Giritaṭa tanks[2]. He enlarged
the Mahāpāli Hall and set up a canoe for the gifts of rice[3].
For the bhikkhunīs the Mahesī ordered permanent gifts of rice[4]. 68
Thus after King Aggabodhi had performed meritorious works,
he went to Heaven in the tenth year (of his reign)[5].

Thus (both) these Lords of men, who rejoiced in meritorious 69
works, who were blessed with riches, fell into the clutches of death. Then should the wise man when he beholds rightly the course of existence, shunning according to precept, all connection with existence, (his face) turned towards Nirvana, live discerningly, surrendering himself to the renunciation of the world.

Here ends the forty-second chapter, called "The Two Kings[6]", in the Mahāvaṃsa, compiled for the serene joy and emotion of the pious.

[1] There is no reason to change the reading of the MSS. *rājānacumbaṭaṃ* into *rājatacumbaṭam* as do S. and B. There is nothing strange in the archaic participial form in *-āna* in the eclectic style of the Cūlavaṃsa.

[2] Rājāv. and Pūjāv. relate that in all he built 13 tanks. The Gangatala, Giritalā, Hovaṭu, Neraḷu, Māṭombu, Siravalāskāṭiya, Eṇḍerahaḷu, Kaḷunnaru, Mahaudalu, Kāngomu, Mādāta and Kalamvāvu are named in the Pūjāv. In addition both chronicles ascribe to him the building of the Velunnā-vehera.

[3] P. *bhattanāvaṃ*. Cf. note to 37. 181.

[4] P. *bhattavaṃsaṃ*. The regular recurrence of the gifts is compared with the succession of the generations in a family.

[5] Rājāv. and Pūjāv. likewise give the duration of the reign as ten years.

[6] The MSS. have *Tirājako* "the three kings" and having regard to the signature of the foregoing pariccheda, it would have been more consistent to have retained this reading. As in our signature one king more, in the foregoing one less is given than actually occurs in the pariccheda, we may perhaps assume that the difference is traceable to a copy in which the last king of the series of the 41st chapter, Mahānāga, is treated not with his predecessors but with his successors, the two Aggabodhis.

CHAPTER XLIV

THE SIX KINGS

1 Hereupon the Sword-bearer Saṃghatissa[1] became ruler.
With the wish to further religion as well as the kingdom he
2 rejoiced in righteous action. Bestowing office according to
merit, he won his subjects for himself. But when the general
3 of the younger king (Aggabodhi), Moggallāna, who dwelt in
Rohaṇa, learnt that Saṃghatissa had become king, in order
to begin war he occupied a fortified camp in Mahāgalla[2].
4 When Saṃghatissa heard this he sent troops to fight him,
5 but the mighty Moggallāna routed them. Thereupon he be-
took himself with elephants and horses to Rattivihāra, collec-
6 ted his troops there and took up a position. At news of this
the King returned, gave him battle at Kadalīnivāta[3] and

[1] Pūjāv. and Rājāv. describe him as younger brother (*mal*) of Aggabodhi II. But is seems to be more probable that he is the asiggāha mentioned in 42. 42 as a kinsman of Aggabodhi's II. mahesī.

[2] Mahāgalla is mentioned in three places. According to 58. 42—43 (q. v.) it was situated in Dakkhiṇadesa. The sequence Tilagulla, Mahāgalla, Maṇḍagalla, Anurādhapura, Mahātittha in a successful campaign of Vijayabāhu I. allows of our determining the situation. It is evidently the present *Magallegama* N. W. of Kurunegala halfway on the road to Puttalam not far from Nikaveratiya (Census of Ceylon 1921, II. 282-3, nr. 62). So also H. W. Codrington in a letter dated 19. X. 26. Mahāgallakavāpi is likewise mentioned three times, namely 68. 34 and 43 among the water works built by Parakkamabāhu I. to further cultivation in Dakkhiṇadesa. The passage 79. 66 is either a repetition of what is related in Chap. 68 or it refers to the restoration of the tank.

[3] Not Kadallādi-Nivāta. The *ādi* serves only, as so frequently, for paraphrase "beginning with Kaḍalī". Cf. Kadalyādinivāta 48. 50; Mahāpānādidīpa 44. 122; Sirisaṃghādibodhiko 46. 1.

defeated him. Then he sent his troops (after him), but re- 7
turned himself to the town. Moggallāna restored his van-
quished army[1] to its former state and marched to Rahera[2].
The King's Senāpati sent his son against the rebels, he him- 8
self feigned (sickness) as if suffering and distressed like one 9
very sick, he kept his bed. When the King heard of it he
at once sought him out and admonished him: "Be not troubled. 10
Only set the Prince[3] his tasks here (in Anurādhapura) and
protect the city; it is impossible for thee to accompany me 11
to the seat of war as thou art sick". Because all the people
had left[4] the city and the King's food was thereby curtailed,
they placed before the King food that had been prepared in 12
the Mahāpāli Hall. When the King saw that, he was much
perturbed and thinking: (it must be) before he becomes weaker 13
than (he is[5]) now, he went forth in haste to war. With his
son he mounted his elephant at the head of an army in figh-
ting trim and marched with a small force to Pācīnatissapabbata[6]. 14
When both sides[7] were engaged in battle the treacherous 15
Senāpati opened the attack from behind. When the Ruler's

[1] It is unnecessary to change *savāhanaṃ* into *savāhiniṃ*. *Vāhana* (primarily: baggagetrain, camp-followers) is several times used in just this section as "army". Thus vv. 13 and 22.

[2] The Rahera mountain is already mentioned 41. 44 on the occasion of the battles between Dāṭhāpabhuti I. and his brother Moggallāna. The Col. Ed. reads, it is true, *Kareheram upāgami*.

[3] Jeṭṭhatissa is presumably meant by the "Prince". According to v. 28 he had remained in the town, probably as Regent under the Minister's guidance, while his father was in the field.

[4] P. *ubbāsite*, lit. "caused to depart". The people had left the town from fear of the enemy. It does not mean that they were in the field. The loc. *sabbe* is one of the incorrest forms peculiar to the language of the Cūlavaṃsa. Cf similarly *sabbe-Jambudīpe* 75. 26 and also *Laṅkātale sabbe* 44. 44.

[5] The idea is this: The King feels that he cannot do without the advice and help of his Senāpati in the city while he himself is absent. He wants therefore to hasten the decision in the field so that the sick man does not die before it. *Yāva na* means "until — before"; *mando* stands for the comparative and the ablative *etto* belongs to this.

[6] See note to 41. 14. [7] I. e. Saṃghatissa and Moggallāna.

16 son saw that, he said: "I will slay him". But the King re-
strained him: "Think not of such a thing; our army is unable
17 to stand this, it is certainly[1] much too weak." The King was
in the centre between the two hostile armies, therefore his
forces had to be divided against the rebel (Moggallāna) and
18 the Senāpati. The King's elephant sought the shade of a
madhūka tree[2] whereupon the umbrella fell to the ground
19 because it knocked against a branch. The rebel's army saw
that, took possession of it and handed it over to their com-
mander. He raised the umbrella, standing on the summit of
20 the mountain. Thereupon the King's troops thinking he was
now king, came and surrounded him. But King Saṃghatissa
21 was alone. He dismounted from the back of his elephant and
fled with his son and a faithful minister[3] to the Merumajjara
forest near by.

22 The victorious Moggallāna[4] took the host, the treacherous
23 Senāpati and his ruthless son, came to the capital and was
king as sovereign of the Laṅkā country. Then he thought:
24 "As long as the foe is in life there is no good luck." When
he heard that a son of the former king was here (in Anurādha-
pura) he was wroth and at once commanded that his hands
25 and feet be cut off. The man charged by the King, went
thither immediately to cut off his hands and feet. The boy
26 wept in distress: "If my hands which I have for eating cake,
are cut off with what shall I then eat the cakes?" When the

[1] P. *hessati*. The future in the sense of a mitigated statement where otherwise the potential is used. The *ti*, as so frequently, is inserted in the oratio recta. Cf. note to 37. 114; further 48. 116; 77. 99.

[2] Bassia latifolia. Skr. *madhūka*, BR. s. v. This is the *mī-gaha* of the Sinhalese which Clough defines as Bassia longifolia.

[3] The governing verb of *puttaṃ 'maccaṃ ca sohadaṃ* is wanting. Hence the writer of MS. S. 6 recorred the text to *puttam ādāya sohadaṃ*. It seems to me probable that *sohadaṃ* was a gloss to distinguish the *amacca* from the faithless Senāpati and that this gloss displaced an *ādiya* in the text. The gerund *ādiya* which is found already in Mbvs. 1. 74 is found again in v. 22.

[4] Pūjāv. calls him Lāmāni-Bō-nā-Mugalan, Rājāv. Mādi-Bō-Mugalan, Nik.-s. and Rājaratn. Lāmāni-Bō-nāya.

King's servant heard that he wept and wailed, sorely grieved 27
at the King's command. Nevertheless he cut off his left hand
and his left foot, the wretch. Jeṭṭhatissa another son of the 28
King, fled and betook himself unrecognised to Malaya in the
Merukandara[1] district. Meanwhile the King (Saṃghatissa) 29
with his son and his minister had secretly reached Veḷuvana[2].
At the instigation of the bhikkhus there he donned the yellow
robe. He had the intention of betaking himself in the dis- 30
guise of a bhikkhu to Rohaṇa and got as far as Maṇihīra[3].
Here the servants of the King who were there, recognised 31
the three, put fetters on their feet and told Moggallāna. When
the King heard that, he rejoiced exceedingly and gave the 32
command: "Go with all haste, take the three to the secure
and safe Sīhagiri[4]. There cut the King's head off and that 33
of his son, but bring the minister to me alive". Thus charged, 34
the people took the three, brought them to Sīhagiri and set
about to do what had been commanded them. Then spake 35
the King's son to the people who carried out the deed: "Do
me the boon of cutting my head off first." The King's men 36
did so, then they struck off the head of King (Saṃghatissa).
Behold ye who know well what righteous action is, the action
of fools! So transitory are (worldly) delights, so uncertain 37
and unstable: how could ye setting your hearts on these,
neglect to seek your eternal salvation?

They informed the minister of the King's command, as 38
they had his good at heart[5]. When he heard that he laughed

[1] See note to 41. 19.

[2] See above 42. 43. The Veḷuvana-vihāra must hence be looked for somewhere on a line between Anurādhapura and Maṇihīra.

[3] Now Minneriya-veva, one of the largest and most beautiful tanks in the island, about 10 miles W.N.W. of Polonnaruva.

[4] Sigiri lies about 10 miles W.S.W. from the Minneri lake.

[5] W. refers *hitesino* to *amacassa* "unto the faithful minister". I believe though, that it is a nom. plu. belonging to the subject contained in *āhaṃsu*. From what follows it seems that Moggallāna's henchmen wished to save the minister's life by offering him the prospect of service with the new King.

39 and spake these words: "While I was still in life I saw my
master beheaded; shall I alas! serve another master besides
40 him? After ye have slain him here will ye also take from
him his shadow? Alas! ignorant are ye, I trow, and deluded."
41 After he had spoken thus he took hold of his master's feet
and lay thus there. The henchmen (of Moggallāna) seeing
42 no means of bringing him away, willy-nilly struck his head
off too. Then they took the three (heads) and showed them
to the King. He struck at them and rejoiced, being rid of
43 his fear. To the treacherous Senāpati he granted the dignity
of Malayarāja and gave his son the office of sword-bearer.
44 Moggallāna covered the three thūpas with new material
and instituted a great thūpa festival[1] throughout the territory
45 of Laṅkā. With a great offering he celebrated with reverence
the Hair Relic of the Master, likewise the Tooth Relic and the
46 great Bodhi Tree. In accordance with ancient custom he held
the entire Vesākha[2] festival and the like. By a regulative
47 act[3] he reformed the Order of the Perfected One. With a great
festival he instituted a recitation of the (three) Piṭakas and
he honoured the learned priests by giving them specially high
48 revenues. To all the bhikkhus dwelling on the Island he pre-
sented a robe and in all their dwellings he had kaṭhina[4] robes

[1] The covering over of the thūpas with white linen cloths was a token of festive homage. Cf. 52. 67 and 54. 37. The word *sabbe* belongs most likely to *Laṅkātale* (see note to 44. 11) and *thūpe mahussavaṃ* is the same as *thūpassa m°* and takes the place of the compound *thūpamahussavaṃ*.

[2] The month Vesākha corresponds to April-May. The birthday of the Buddha was celebrated on the day of the full moon of this month.

[3] See note to 39. 57.

[4] By *kaṭhina* we are to understand a gift of clothing to the community carried out in a specially solemn form at the end of the Pavāraṇā festival (see note to 37. 90). It is considered highly meritorious. The term is *atthatakaṭhino* (lit. "outspread raw cotton"), *kaṭhinatthāra*, in our passage *kaṭhinaṃ attharāpati*. The ceremony consists in the uninterrupted making of the garments in the course of a day and a night from raw cotton. The cotton is spun by women, the stuff woven, dyed and finally made up into garments. Cf. Vinaya I. 253 ff. (= Mahāvagga VII. 1 ff.).

made. He made images and repaired what was decayed. He 49
made over to the community more than 300 salt-pans. In 50
Kārapiṭṭhi he built the Moggallāna-vihāra, further the Piṭṭhi-
gāma-vihāra and Vaṭagāma together with a village (assigned
to it). He also built a cetiya temple in the Rakkha-vihāra[1] 51
and he granted villages to many vihāras for their maintenance.
Thus the Monarch performed countless meritorious works in 52
remembreance of the fleeting nature of the fortunes of the
preceding king.

Now it happened that for some offence or other he became 53
displeased with the Malayarāja[2]. He remembered his shame-
ful conduct towards the former king. He got him into his 54
power by craft and had his hands and feet cut off. When
the Sword-bearer[3] heard that he betook himself with his son
to Rohaṇa. Dwelling there he soon brought the land into 55
his power. He sought out Jeṭṭhatissa who kept himself hidden
in Malaya. In league with him he conquered in a short time 56
the province of Janapada. He then betook himself to the
Dohaḷapabbata and took up his position in an armed camp[4].
When the King heard all that he (likewise) took up his 57
position near him with an army and a train ready for
battle. Now at that time many of the King's people suf- 58
fered from fever and died. When the Sword-bearer heard
that he took up the fight with vehemence. The King's army 59
was too weak, it was scattered and fled. The King fled be-

[1] I read *Rakkhavihārake* as against *-kaṃ* of the MSS.

[2] See 44. 43. [3] The Malayarāja's son (44. 43).

[4] I believe that we must read *raṭṭhaṃ Janapadaṃ* and that with this is meant the country often mentioned later (66. 110 etc.), situated in northern Malaya towards Dakkhiṇadesa. The verb *ghātento* is curious. The Dohaḷa mountain is most likely to be sought in the district of Janapada. The form of the name agrees in all MSS. The alteration to *Doḷhapabbata* in the Col. Ed. is arbitrary. It cannot be the mountain Dolagalvela. That lies on the right bank of the Mahaveliganga and occurs in the Mahāvaṃsa (10. 44) under the name *Doḷapabbata*. The scenes described in our verses took place without doubt somewhere in the neighbourhood of the present Dambul. In v. 60 Sigiri (*Sīhapabbata*) is also mentioned in connection with the battle.

60 hind it. When the Sword-bearer met him alone near Sīhagiri
61 he slew the Great King together with his attendants. In order
to kill Jeṭṭhatissa also whom he had left behind, he sent him
62 a message: "Come and be King, come." Jeṭṭhatissa saw through
the plan, turned and fled to Malaya (for he said to himself:)
"Would he really hand over to me the royal dignity gained
with so much trouble?"

63 When after six years[1] he had slain the Prince Moggallāna
64 surnamed Dalla[2], the Sword-bearer with army and train entered
splendid Anurādhapura, became king and rolled the wheel of
65 dominion over the earth's circle. He was called Silā-
meghavaṇṇa[3], reverenced the Order and the Bodhi Tree,
sacrificed to the three thūpas and enlarged the Mahāpāli Hall.
66 During a bad famine he dispensed milk rice made with butter
and syrup to the community and (presented it) also with filters.
67 Through sheer generosity he won the hearts of the poor,
of travellers and beggars. To boys the bountiful (Prince) gave
68 money to buy cakes. In the Abhayagiri-vihāra he honoured
the stone image of the Buddha by an offering. He had its
ruined temple (restored and) brightly decorated with divers
69 precious stones. He dedicated (unto it) the Kolavāpi tank
to protect[4] the Victor and he continually instituted sacrificial
festivals at the greatest cost.

70 While the Monarch thus lived as a vessel[5] for meritorious
action, a general named Sirināga, mother's brother of Jeṭṭha-
71 tissa, had betaken himself to the opposite shore[6]. He returned

[1] The same number in Pūjāv. and Rājāv.

[2] The Sinhalese chronicles give this Surname to Moggallāna II. See note to 41. 63.

[3] The Sinhalese chronicles do not mention the name of this king. They merely call him *asiggāhaka*.

[4] That is, as wages for the guarding of the image and its temple he allotted the proceeds of the tank. The words *ārakkhatthaṃ jinassa* belong to *datvāna*, not to the following.

[5] The word *bhājana* is used in Skr. with the same figurative sense. See BR. s. v., nr. 4.

[6] I. e. to the mainland of India.

with many Damiḷas and began to take possession of (the northern province) Uttaradesa. At the tidings of this, the King 72
advanced, offered battle at the village of Rājamittaka, beat
the Damiḷas who had accompanied him, captured those who 73
remained over from the slaughter, subjected them to all kinds
of humiliation and distributed them here and there as slaves
to the vihāras.

When the Monarch had thus gained the victory, he return- 74
ed to the city and while he, after he had cleared the whole
kingdom and was menaced from no side, dwelt there, a bhikkhu 75
called Bodhi who had seen many undisciplined bhikkhus in
the Abhayuttara-vihāra, though reckoned by the ceremony of
world renunciation, he was still young, came to the King and 76
begged him to proclaim a regulative act[1]. The King had the
regulative act carried out by him himself in the vihāra. Then 77
all the undisciplined bhikkhus who had been expelled from
the Order, took counsel together, murdered Bodhi secretly
and annulled the act. When the King heard that, he was 78
wroth, seized them all together and made them, their hands
cut off and in fetters, guardians of the bathing tanks; another 79
hundred bhikkhus there he expelled to Jambudīpa. In remem-
brance of Bodhi's efforts he thus cleansed the Order. When 80
then he invited the bhikkhus of the Thera School with the
others[2] to celebrate together the Uposatha festival, he was
refused. He flew into a rage and offending all respect, he 81
abused and reviled them with harsh words. Then he betook
himself without demanding pardon of the bhikkhus, to
Dakkhiṇadesa. There he was attacked by a fell disease and 82
died suddenly. Thus after nine years[3] he left the earth.

[1] See note to 39. 57.

[2] The other bhikkhus meant here are those of the Abhayagiri-vihāra. As the King has expelled the unworthy members of the Order, he thinks the time come for a common celebration with the bhikkhus of the Mahāvihāra, which they however reject.

[3] The same length of reign is assigned to Asiggāhaka in the Pūjāv. and Rājāv.

83 His son the young prince, Aggabodhi by name, then
84 became king, known by the name of Sirisaṃghabodhi[1]. He
invested his youngest brother Māna with the dignity of uparāja
and granted him (the province of) Dakkhiṇadesa with fitting
85 army and train. The King who did no discredit to the con-
duct of former kings, protected the kingdom in justice and
86 deeply reverenced the Order. Jeṭṭhatissa who heard all this
in Malaya, betook himself to the Ariṭṭha mountain[2] and brought
87 the population over to his side. After he had brought the
southern and eastern districts into his power and made them
his friends[3], he began gradually to march with strong forces
88 on the capital. He sent his minister Dāṭhāsiva to occupy the
territory in the west[4] and took up a position himself in the
89 village Siripiṭṭhi. When the King heard all that he sent the
Uparāja[5] (Māna) with a force into the western territory. He
90 went up and put Dāṭhāsiva to flight. The King thought: one
can kill the fellow like a young bird in the nest[6] and took

[1] For the first time Sirisaṃghabodhi occurs as royal *biruda*. Wickremasinghe has made the happy observation that in the sequel this epithet is used alternately with that of Silāmeghavaṇṇa, so that when a king bears the *biruda* Sirisaṃghabodhi, his successor calls himself Silāmeghavaṇṇa and conversely. EZ. II, p. 9. As name Sirisaṃghabodhi is first met with Mhvs. 36. 73 ff. (300 A. D.). The title was obviously chosen in honour of this pious king of the Lambakaṇṇa clan. The Sinhalese chronicles only know King Aggabodhi III. under the name Sirisangabō.

[2] Now *Ritigala*, the isolated massif halfway between Anurādhapura and Polonnaruva.

[3] P. *susamānase*, not *-so* as in the Col. Ed. Jeṭṭhatissa not only brings the districts into his power, but also wins over the inhabitants as adherents (*samānasa* "being like-minded").

[4] It seems to me that *pacchimaṃ disaṃ* in v. 88 as also *pacchimaṃ desaṃ* in v. 89 are not to be taken as proper names of a district, as little as *pubbadakkhiṇe* in v. 87, but merely as a general geographical designation.

[5] See v. 84.

[6] *Dārakaṃ* is probably to be taken in the oratio recta as S. and B. have it in their Sinhalese translation. The word is used contemptuously of the inexperienced *amacca* of prince Jeṭṭhatissa.

prisoner the prince's minister (Dāṭhāsiva) who had marched to
Māyetti. Then he thought: I will catch Jeṭṭhatissa in the 91
same way, and with a few troops the fearless one marched
recklessly against him. But Jeṭṭhatissa on the news thereof, 92
fell with a skilled army and train on the King's army like
a sea that has burst its bounds. The army of the King was 93
scattered; the King mounted his elephant and fled at once
alone and in disguise. In the sixth month after his accession 94
he hastily took ship and betook himself to Jambudīpa, deserting wealth, country and kinsfolk.

Jeṭṭhatissa now became king in the city; he fulfilled 95
all duties as was formerly customary and protected the Order.
Mahādāragiri he granted to the Abhayuttara-vihāra, to the 96
Mahāvihāra he made over the Bodhi Tree called Mahāmetta.
To the Jetavana the King granted Goṇḍigāma. To the prac- 97
tising-house in the Mahānāga(-vihāra)[1] he assigned the villages
Mātulaṅgaṇa and Odumbaraṅgaṇa and to the Kassapagiri[2] 98
(-vihāra) (the village of) Ambilāpika for the (supply of) food.
The village of Kakkhalaviṭṭhi he gave to the Veḷuvaṇa(-vi- 99
hāra[3]) and to the Gangāmāti-vihāra the village of Keheta; to 100
the (vihāra) called Antarāgaṅga he gave the village of Cullamātika and to the (vihāra) Mayettikassapāvāsa (the village of)
Sahannanagara. To the Kālavāpi-vihāra he assigned the vil- 101
lage called Lada. This and other (vihāras) he provided
abundantly with maintenance villages. What was ruinous he 102
restored (at a cost of) three hundred thousand (kahāpaṇas);
to the bhikkhus dwelling in the Island he presented the three garments.

The King (Aggabodhi) who had betaken himself to Jam- 103
budīpa had brothers in blood. These hidden here and there,
sought to make the land rebellious. When Jeṭṭhatissa heard 104
this, he betook himself to Kālavāpi, made war on them and

[1] For this vihāra see 42. 24. For *padhānaghara* cf. 37. 232.

[2] Inscriptional mention is made of this monastery under the name Kasubgiri on a tablet of Mahinda IV. See Wickremasinghe EZ. I, p. 216. It is mentioned again in Cūlavs. 48. 24 under Kassapa III.

[3] See note to 44. 29.

105 took up a position with his army on the spot. The King
(Aggabodhi) who had gone to the other coast and there hired
Damiḷa troops, came to Kālavāpi and began the combat. Jeṭṭha-
tissa ready for war with a well equiped force, first letting his mi-
106 nister Dāṭhāsiva escape[1] to Jambudīpa, mounted his armoured
107 elephant, but seeing his troops fall back in the battle, he spake
108 thus to the high dignitary who rode with him on the elephant:
"Take my message to the Mahesī, then mayest thou do what thou
109 wilt: forsake O great Queen, the world, recite the sacred texts,
learn the Abhidhamma[2] and transfer the merit to the King[3]."
110 After he had given this order, he hewed down the Damiḷas
as many of them as met him in the course of the battle. But
111 when his strength was failing[4] he saw a Damiḷa called Veluppa
coming to fight with him. Then as he was wont to keep a
112 knife in the betel-nut bag in his hand, he quickly drew his
dagger out of that and cut his throat. Then leaning upon the
113 elephant, he stuck the knife back in the sheath. The great
army cried aloud. The high dignitary set off, thinking ever
114 and only of how the King had cut his throat, and gave the
Queen the message. Together with her he underwent in the
Order the ceremony of world renunciation and after he had
115 mastered the Abhidhamma together with the commentary, he

[1] P. *palāpetvā*. The translation "he sent" does not give the full sense of the original. According to v. 90, Dāṭhāsiva had become the prisoner of Aggabodhi. But as it is expressly stated, v. 93, that Aggabodhi escaped alone (*eko*) in disguise to Jambudīpa, Dāṭhāsiva can no longer be in his power. It is thus not a case of freeing Dāṭhāsiva from captivity, the latter must be again in Jeṭṭhatissa's service. The idea is rather the following: Jeṭṭhatissa sends Dāṭhāsiva to Southern India, to cut off Aggabodhi's rearward communications, thereby unconsciously letting his minister escape the disaster overtaking himself.

[2] The Abhidhamma is the third part of the Buddhist Canon, in which its philosophical content is systematically summarized — the third *piṭaka*. See 37. 221.

[3] P. *pattiṃ dehi rājino*. For the term *patti* see note to 42. 50.

[4] P. *āyumhi khayam āgate* perhaps "when his lifetime came to an end" according to his kamma.

came down (once) from the teacher's chair[1] and seated himself on the ground. At the Queen's request: come and show me
how the King died, he seated himself in front of her, cut his 116
throat, stuck the knife (in the sheath) and spake: "Thus died
his Majesty". When she saw that her heart broke through 117
heavy sorrow and she died. Thus after five months King Jeṭṭhatissa went to Heaven[2].

After Aggabodhi had thus victoriously subdued the foe 118
in battle, he restored his royal dominion and resided in the
capital. To the practising-house[3] called Mahallarāja which had 119
been erected[4] by himself in company with the Uparāja (Māna),
he granted the two villages of Haṅkāra and Sāmugāma as 120
well as the royal share in (the revenues) of Kehella, and the
whole of the (necessary) staff. To the Jetavana(-vihāra) he 121
gave (the village) Mahāmaṇikagāma and he honoured the
Mayettikassapāvāsa(-vihāra) by the grant of Sālaggāma. To 122
the Cetiya mountain[5] he granted Ambillapadara and in Pulatthinagara he built the Mahāpānadīpa (-vihāra)[6].

The court officials of the King slew the Yuvarāja Māna 123
who had committed an offence in the women's apartments,

[1] *Dhammāsana* is a raised seat in the centre of the assembly-hall of the bhikkhus on which the priest, who recites the sacred text, takes his place, his face turned towards the east. It differs from the *therāsana* on which the head of the Chapter has his seat, facing north. See Mhvs. 3. 21–22, 32, 35.

[2] Pūjāv. and Rājāv. give Lämäni-Kaṭusara-Deṭatis — so the King is called in these chronicles — likewise a reign of five months.

[3] See 37. 232; 39. 58.

[4] In the Col. Ed the text of the MSS. has been arbitrarily altered. There is nothing surprising in the use of the loc. *kārite* instead of the genitive *kāritassa* used with *padhānagharakassa*. Cf. Cūlavs. ed., Introd. p. XVIII.

[5] *Cetiyagiri* = *Cetiyapabbata* here of the monastery erected on the Mihintale mountain. See notes to 38 75 and 42. 28.

[6] For the form of the name see note to 44. 6. The name of the later capital of the kingdom, Pulatthinagara (now Polonnaruva) is here mentioned for the first time in the Cūlavamsa. It does not occur at all in the older Mahāvaṃsa.

124 although they had promised him absolute safety[1]. Therefore
the King wishful of securing the succession (for his family),
invested his youngest brother Kassapa by name with the
125 dignity of Uparāja. Now when Dāṭhāsiva heard of the death
of Māna he came in haste with Damiḷa troops to the village
126 called Tintiṇi[2]. At the tidings of his advance Aggabodhi
marched out with his army, gave battle and was forced in
127 the twelfth year (of his reign) to flee to Jambudīpa. At his
flight he left everything behind. He took with him only the
pearl chain of one string[3] by which to make himself known,
128 and departed quite alone. Even without the chain of one
string of pearls Dāṭhāsiva became king, according to custom,
known over the circle of the earth under the name of
129 Dāṭhopatissa. The other (Aggabodhi) seized the op-
portunity and got hold of the government again by fighting.
130 So each drove out the other in turn. But the whole people
suffering under the wars of these two kings, fell into
131 great misery and lost money and field produce. Dāṭhopatissa
exhausted the whole property of former kings and seized all
objects of value in the three fraternities[4] and in the relic
132 temples. He broke in pieces the golden images and took the
gold for himself and plundered all the golden wreaths and
133 other offerings. In the Thūpārāma likewise he took away
the golden crowning ornament on the temple and smashed
the umbrella on the cetiya which was studded with costly
134 precious stones. The canoes in the Mahāpāli Hall he left to

[1] I now believe that the conjecture *aparajjhitvā* of S. and B. instead of *aparujjhitvā* must be accepted with regard to 51. 8. The construction of the sentence is certainly irregular. The gerund *aparajjhitvā* is used like a Loc. absol. The court officials killed the Yuvarāja because an offence in the women's apartments had been committed by him.

[2] As the yield from taxation of this village according to 41. 96 was assigned to the Mahāvihāra, it cannot be situated very far from Anurādhapura. Thus Dāṭhāsiva advances from the coast direct on the capital.

[3] Obviously a peculiarly valuable part of the regalia, of the *rāja-sādhana*. Cf. Skr. *ekāvalī*, as well as 46. 17.

[4] See note to 41. 97.

the Damiḷas; (and) they burned down the royal palace together
with the Relic Temple[1]. Later he repented and to acknow- 135
ledge his wrong he founded the Sākavatthu-vihāra with the
(necessary) revenues. His sister's son also, the Mahādipāda, 136
known among the people by the name Ratanadāṭha, supported
the King with his income. (Once) when Aggabodhi had by 137
military superiority got hold of the kingdom, the Yuvarāja,
Kassapa[2], the deluded one, to provide for his army led by 138
evil-natured villains, broke open by force the cetiya of the
Thūpārāma and plundered the valuable treasures given by 139
Devānaṃpiyatissa, the younger Aggabodhi[3] and (other) former
kings. He also broke open the cetiya of the Dakkhiṇa-vihāra 140
and seized the valuable treasures and he had yet other (cetiyas)
broken open. When he acted thus led away by evil-natured 141
people, the King was powerless to prevent him — alas!
evil-doers will not be hindered (in their action) — and as 142
he could not hinder him he by the organisation of a festival,
restored the cetiya of the Thūpārāma shattered by him, at
the cost of a thousand (kahāpaṇas).

Now the Lord of men Aggabodhi was defeated by Dāṭhopa- 143
tissa and betook himself to Rohaṇa to restore his army and
train. While he sojourned there he fell ill and died in the 144
sixteenth year[4] (of his reign). Thereupon his youngest brother
the Yuvarāja Kassapa, sent King Dāṭhopatissa flying to 145
Jambudīpa and united the country under one dominion; but
the crown he did not wear[5]. Through intercourse with pious 146
people he repented and with the thought: I will make an end

[1] See note to 37. 95.

[2] Younger brother of Aggabodhi III.

[3] By Aggabodhi II. Cf. with this, 42. 51 ff.

[4] The calculation evidently starts from the beginning of the reign of Aggabodhi III. Thus the 15-16 years include the first period of Aggabodhi (6 months), the interregnum of Jeṭṭhatissa II, as well as the reign of Dāṭhopatissa who, according to v. 126, seized the sovereignty in the twelfth year of Aggabodhi. Pūjāv. and Rājāv. simply say that Jeṭṭhatissa reigned 5 months, Dāṭhopatissa (Lāmāni Dalupatis) 12 years and Aggabodhi (Sirisaṅgabō) 16 years.

[5] Evidently Dāṭhopatissa had secured the Regalia.

147 of my evil doings[1], he laid out flower gardens, fruit gardens
and tanks and he honoured the three great cetiyas by large
148 offerings. To the Thūpārāma also he brought an offering
and granted it a village and he had the sacred texts recited
149 by all the foreign bhikkhus[2]. In the Maricavaṭṭi(-vihāra) he
erected a very massive pāsāda and let the Grand Thera live
150 there who had his seat in Nāgasālā. While he sojourned there,
he provided him with the four necessaries and had the
151 Abhidhamma with the commentary recited by him. Then after
he had had the Nāgasālā dwelling put in order[3] he made it
over to him also, and granted him the village of Mahāniṭṭhila
for the supply of the (four) necessaries.

152 Now Dāṭhopatissa came hither from Jambudīpa with a
153 great force; but when he offered battle to Kassapa he was
defeated by the latter who had a well equipped army, and
was slain. Twelve years had passed since he became king[4].
154 A sister's son of Dāthopatissa named Hatthadāṭha fled full of
fear from the great battle to Jambudīpa[5].

155 Thus in truth all joys are fleeting, hard to attain is their
delight and lasts but a moment. Therefore he who seeks his
salvation will give up his joy in these and will turn to the truth.

Here ends the forty-fourth chapter, called "The Six Kings", in the Mahāvaṃsa, compiled for the serene joy and emotion of the pious.

[1] Lit: I will bring about the destruction of my evil kamma.

[2] The *āgāmiyabhikkhavo* are the opposite of the *bhikkhavo dīpavāsino*, the bhikkhus settled in the Island. Those are bhikkhus who come from outside, on a pilgrimage to Ceylon, for instance. When W. translates: "holy monks who lived not among the habitations of men", he was probably thinking of *āraññakā bhikkhavo.*

[3] We must take *katvā* in the sense of "to restore", in which the verb *kar* is often used. It would also be possible to translate *Nāgasālakaṃ āvāsaṃ katvā* by "after he had made a habitable dwelling out of N." In any case the meaning is that the former dwelling of the Mahāthera, Nāgasālā, had become dilapidated and that until its restoration the King assigned him as dwelling the newly built pāsāda in the Maricavaṭṭi-vihāra.

[4] If we compare this with the calculation in the note to 44. 144, we find that Dāṭhopatissa's death falls in the eighth year of Kassapa's reign.

[5] See for this passage my edition of the Cūlavaṃsa, Introd. p. XIX.

CHAPTER XLV

THE FOUR KINGS

Hereupon Kassapa, the victor in the fight, whose aspiration 1
was fulfilled, gave a most excellent repast in the Mahāpāli
Hall to the community. He honoured the ascetic Mahā- 2
dhammakathin who lived in the Nāgasālā by a great offering
and induced him to recite the true doctrine. In honour of 3
the Thera who was a native of Kaṭandhakāra, who lived in
the building erected by his brother, he had the sacred text
written down with a short summary[1]. What was delapidated 4
he restored and had new works undertaken on the cetiyas and
provided sundry revenues for the community in several places.
He had three diadem jewels[2] wrought which glittered with 5
different precious stones, and he gladdened a hundred Paṇḍu-
palāsas[3] by an offering of garments.

Kassapa had many sons, the eldest of them was Mānaka. 6
They were not yet in riper years, children without much sense.

[1] *Kaṭandhakāravāsin* probably refers to the home of the thera whose name is not mentioned, just as to-day when a bhikkhu enters the Order the name of his native place is prefixed to his adopted one. His abode was evidently the *padhānaghara* called Mahallarāja built according to 44. 119 by Kassapa's brother Aggabodhi III. in company with the Yuvarāja Māna. With "summary" (*saṃgaha*) of the sacred text one should compare titles like Abhidhammatthasaṃgaha, Dhammasaṃgaha, Saddhammasaṃgaha, Sārasaṃgaha.

[2] Evidently as crowning ornaments for the three great cetiyas — Mahāthūpa, Jetavana- and Abhayagiri-Thūpa. Does the epithet *nānāmaṇisamujjotaṃ* indicate that each cetiya had its own particular colour?

[3] W. (p. 32, note); "A *paṇḍupalāsa* is a lay candidate for holy orders living in the vihāra until he could get his robes and alms-bowl made."

7 Now once when he was seized by a bad illness, he thought:
8 my sons are all still children, incapable of reigning, and he
sent for his very clever sister's son (Māna) who lived in the
province of Rohaṇa and transferred to him the whole govern-
9 ment, together with the care of his sons. After he had
honoured the cetiyas with perfumes, flowers and other offerings
he made his peace with the bhikkhu community by supplying
10 them with the four necessaries. Thus the Lord of men practis-
ed justice towards friends, officials and subjects and went
after nine years[1] according to his doing.

11 Māna having piously fulfilled the prescribed duties towards
his uncle, won over the people and had the Damiḷas[2] expelled.
12 But the Damiḷas banded themselves together with the resolve:
we will drive him out, and just while he was away they seized
13 the town. To Hatthadāṭha who was in Jambudīpa, they sent
the message: "It is time for thee to come and take over the
14 government." Māna also sent a message in haste to his father
to Rohaṇa. When his father heard it he came hither from
15 Rohaṇa without delay. The two took counsel together and
made a mock treaty with the Damiḷas. Thereupon they were
16 all in accord. Māna now crowned his father (Dappula[3])
king. He when he was consecrated, presented the (three)
17 fraternities with three thousand (kahāpaṇas). Having thus
won over the Order and the kingdom, for himself, he sent all
provisions found in the palace to Rohaṇa to secure them from
18 the enemy. When Hatthadāṭha heard the news of the Damiḷas
19 he came immediately to this Island with a Damiḷa force. All
the despised Damiḷas who dwelt here, arose and joined him
20 on the way as he approached. And Māna thought when he
heard all that: it is no time to fight now, and sent his father,

[1] The same number in Pūjāv. and Rājāv. where the king has the name Päsuḷu-Kasubu. Likewise in Rājaratn. and Nik.-s.

[2] The mercenaries whom Dāṭhopatissa had brought with him from Southern India and who according to 44. 134 f. had become an undisciplined rabble.

[3] The King's name is first mentioned in v. 36. The Sinhalese chronicles agree in calling the successor of Päsuḷu Kasubu Dappulu.

the King, with the valuable property to Rohaṇa. He betook 21
himself to the Eastern Province and bringing the people round
to his side, took up his abode there. But Hatthadāṭha who
had won over the party of the Damiḷas for himself, occupied
the royal city and publicly took the name of Dāṭhopatissa. 22
After his mother's brother the people called him by this name.
Having fetched his father's brother's son, Aggabodhi by name, 23
he placed him in the position of Yuvarāja and granted him
the province of Dakkhiṇadesa. Upon his supporters he bestow- 24
ed honourable office according to merit and towards the Order
and the people he fulfilled every duty. In the Mahāpāli Hall 25
he had besides clothing, rice with sour milk, milk and milk
rice distributed and keeping the Uposatha day, he hearkened
to the sermon. As he made all offerings and had sermons 26
preached, he by these and other merits made himself happy.
To the Kassapa-vihāra[1] he granted the village of Senāmagāma 27
and Mahāgalla[2] he gave to the practising-house. To the Mora- 28
pariveṇa[3] he granted (the village of) Kasagāma and the cetiya
of the Thūpārāma he honoured by the grant of Puṇṇeli. In 29
the Abhayuttara(-vihāra) he built the Kappūra-pariveṇa[4] and
he built the vihāra called Tiputthulla and added it to the
same (vihāra). As he was about to do this, the bhikkhus of 30
the Thera School wanted to prevent him, because the vihāra
was situated within their boundary[5]. But he treated them
without consideration and carried the thing through by force.

[1] What is meant is probably the Kassapagiri-vihāra mentioned 44. 98 (see the note) and again 48. 24.

[2] Cf. note to 44. 3. The "practising-house" is probably the padhānaghara Mahallarāja mentioned 44. 119 and which is probably meant in 45. 3.

[3] See note to 37. 172.

[4] This pariveṇa is mentioned again twice. Aggabodhi IV. built a *pāsāda* there according to 46. 21 and Sena I. according to 50. 77 a *pariccheda* (s. note to 42. 39).

[5] The passage is surprising. As the Abhayuttara (Abhayagiri) is without doubt the northern thūpa it is difficult to understand how a boundary dispute can arise between it and the Mahāvihāra, the seat of the Thera Bhikkhus.

31 Then the bhikkhus of the Thera School were bitter against
the King, saw in him an unbeliever and applied to him the
32 turning down of the alms-bowl[1]. For the wise Master hath
33 said: "If an unbelieving layman thinks to lessen the income
of the bhikkhus or taunts them, the turning down of the
alms-bowl is to be applied." Hence they carried out this
34 action against him — the laity thought otherwise — and they
made the agreement that when a bhikkhu goes on the mendi-
cant's round bearing the alms-bowl upright, he shall turn it
35 down at the gate of his house. Now at that time the King
was smitten with a fell disease and died in the ninth year
(of his reign[2]), since the end of his lifetime had come.

36 King Dappula had meanwhile betaken himself to his Rohaṇa
and took up his abode there, heaping up a store of meri-
37 torious works. Now we will relate the history of his house
in due order, because if it is related now it will cause no
disturbance[3].

38 There was once a man of the lineage of Okkāka[4], known
by the name of Mahātissa, rich in merit, a mine of heaped-up
39 virtues. He had a wife known by the name of Saṃghasivā
gifted with wealth and virtue, the daughter of the ruler of

[1] The meaning of *pattanikkujjana* is clear from this passage. If the bhikkhus wish a layman to be regarded as expelled from the society, they make this known by refusing to take alms from him, turning down the bowl as it were. V. 33 d is a parenthesis: Though the laymen did not approve it, the bhikkhus carried out the action.

[2] Pūjāv. and Rājāv. say also that Lāmāṇi-Daḷupatissa reigned 9 years. They make him the successor of Dāpulu. Nik.-s. mentions two successors of Dāpulu: Lāmāṇi-Daḷupatissa and Pāsulu-Daḷupatissa.

[3] To judge by the form of the introduction to the following passage appearing so disconnectedly in the context, it seems to me beyond a doubt that the author has here made use of another source, apparently a chronicle of Rohaṇa and its dynasty. It must be the same source which is employed in 57. 3 ff., where just as abruptly as here, a section from the history of Rohaṇa is inserted. Cf. also note to 47. 1.

[4] A mythical king (Skr. Ikṣvāku, Hopkins, Epic Mythology, p. 201), through whom (Mhvs. 2. 1 ff.) the Sākya family from which the Buddha sprang, is derived from Mahāsammata. See also Rockhill, the Life of the Buddha, p. 9 ff.

Rohaṇa. She had three sons: the first was called Aggabodhi, 40
the second Dappula, the third Maṇiakkhika. She also had 41
a daughter who came to the court of the King. The eldest
son was the independent ruler[1] of the province called Rohaṇa.
Rich as he was, he had the Mahāpāli Hall built in Mahāgāma[2] 42
and there also the pariveṇa called Dāṭhaggabodhi. In Kāṇa- 43
gāma[3] (he built) hospitals for the blind and the sick and a
large image house in the Paṭimā-vihāra. There the wise (prince) 44
set up a stone image of the Buddha which he had made and
which received the name of "the great", produced as by a
miracle. Further he built the Sālavāṇa-vihāra which bore his 45
name and the Pariveṇa-vihāra as well as that of Kājara-
gāma[4]. He erected new buildings in the Dhammasāla-vihāra 46
and the discerning (prince) himself cleaned out the privies
therein. Once having enjoyed the food left over by the 47
bhikkhu community he (being) pleased, granted the village
of Maṇḍagāma[5] to the community. When he after performing 48
these and other meritorious works, had gone to Heaven, his
next brother Dappula by name, became ruler (in the land).
He carried on the government after subduing his enemies, 49
instituted a great almsgiving, (and) made Rohaṇa secure. His 50
subjects were contented with him and said: he is our great
lord and since then the people called him "Great Lord".

[1] This passage shows that Rohaṇa about 600 A. D. was not yet incorporated with the kingdom with the capital Anurādhapura, but that it held or at any rate claimed an independent position beside it.

[2] The name is contained in that of the present Magama (Census of Ceylon, 1921, II, 194, on the left bank of the Kirinda-oya not far from its mouth in the Hambantoṭa district) whose cultivated land is watered by the Magam-Ela diverted from the Yoda-veva in Tissamahārāma. Mahāgāma is first mentioned Mhvs. 22. 8 as the residence of Devānampiyatissa's younger brother, Mahānāga.

[3] The name means "village of the blind".

[4] Now *Kataragam* north of Tissamahārāma, on the Menikganga, on the old road from Mahāgāma to Guttasālā (now Buttala). It is known by a much visited shrine of Skanda. According to the Census of Ceylon (II. 464) the village had 103 inhabitants in 1921.

[5] A Madugama in the Mahavedirata Korale of the Badulla District (N. E. of Buttala) is mentioned in the Census of Ceylon II. 460.

51 When the Ruler of men Silādāṭha[1] heard of that he gave
him his daughter (to wife) and delighted at his many good
52 qualities, he granted him the office of Yuvarāja, indicating by
that that he was fitted for the royal dignity. Mānavamma and
53 other men of high repute were his sons. When he was with the
Mahāthera who dwelt in the Pāsāṇadīpa (-vihāra) and had
heard the sermon of the sacred texts, he experienced believing
54 trust in him and to honour him he built the Rohaṇa-vihāra[2]
and gave it to him. But the Thera made it over for the use
55 of the community in the four quarters of the earth. Dappula
built the Ambamālā-vihāra and many other vihāras; he also
56 erected the Khadirāḷi-vihāra and offered to the god[3]. The
discerning (prince) repaired the Anurārāma-pāsāda, the badly
decayed Muttolamba(-pāsāda)[4], the Sirivaḍḍha-pāsāda and a
57 further one (called) Takkambila, and housed thirty-two bhikkhus
therein whom he gladdened by the gift of the four necessaries.
58 The village of Kevaṭṭagambhīra he granted to the Nāga-
vihāra[5], to the Rāja-vihāra he assigned the village of Gonna-
59 gāma. In the same way he gave to the Tissa-vihāra (the

[1] The name as name of a king does not occur in this form in the Cūlavaṃsa — another proof of the separate character of the Rohaṇa Chronicle. King Silāmeghavaṇṇa is meant; for in 45. 8, 11 Māna, the son of Dappula, is described as sister's son (*bhāgineyya*) of Kassapa II., the son of Silāmeghavaṇṇa. Thus Dappula was married to the sister of Kassapa II, a daughter of Silāmeghavaṇṇa.

[2] The Col. Ed. has *vihāraṃ Rohaṇe* and W. accordingly translates "a vihāra in Rohaṇa". The MSS. reading meanwhile, is *vihāraṃ Rohaṇaṃ* and it is quite correct, for in the Pūjāv. and Rājāv. also the building of the Ruhuṇuvehera is ascribed to Dāpulu. Cf. Cūlavs. ed., Introd. p. XIX.

[3] Presumably there was at this spot a local Hindu cult, probably of Skanda, the God of Kājaragāma, a kind of patron saint of Rohaṇa; and the King did not neglect to reverence the deity.

[4] I take *Muttolambaṃ* for the name of a pāsāda. At any rate W.'s translation "ornamented it with festoons of pearls" is impossible to reconcile with the text. The finite verb would be wanting.

[5] One of the oldest vihāras in Rohaṇa, built by the founder of the dynasty, Mahānāga, the brother of Devānampiyatissa. Mhvs. 22. 9.

village of) Kattikapabbata and to the Cittalapabbata(-vihāra)[1]
the village of Gonnaviṭṭhi. Having granted to the Ariyākari 60
(-vihāra) the village of Mālavatthu, he built in that place a
superb image house. For the (image of) the Victor (Buddha) 61
there he had a valuable tuft of hair (between the brows) made
and a bandolier[2] of gold and brought it every kind of offering.
Decayed cetiyas he adorned with a new coating of stucco and 62
further he had a statue fifteen cubits[3] high made of the saviour Metteyya[4]. These and other meritorious works without 63
number the Prince performed himself and had them also performed in pious fashion by his retinue. Amongst the people 64
surrounding him were many men of meritorious action; numerous vihāras furnished with (all) necessaries were built by them.

Once when Dappula was on the march in a pathless wil- 65
derness, he after finding quarters for his army, pitched his
camp at night. As he lay there, well bathed and oiled and 66
well fed, outstretched on a splendid couch and in a comfortable tent, he tried to sleep. Nevertheless he found no sleep 67
and although with the thought, what then could be the cause,
he pondered over all that he had experienced during the day,
he found no cause in himself[5]. Thus he thought it must lie 68
outside (of his person) and entrusted people with the task of
seeking it. He spake thus: "Without doubt worthy friends[6] 69
of mine have tarried during the night at the foot of a tree

[1] The Tissa-vihāra, now the Tissamahārāma near Hambantoṭa, and the Cittalapabbata-vihāra were founded by Kākavaṇṇatissa (Mhvs. 22. 23). The ruins of the latter, now called Situlpav-vehera (Nik.-s. 15. 17) lie fifteen miles N. E. of Tissamahārāma not far from Katagamuva. See JAYAVARDANA, Ceylon National Review II, p. 23. For an inscription in the Situlpav-vehera see E. MÜLLER, Anc. Inscr. Ceylon, Nr. 16, p. 29, 74, 110; WICKREMASINGHE, EZ. I, p. 60, 67.

[2] For the *uṇṇaloma* and the *hemapaṭṭa* (or *hemavaḍḍha*) on the Buddha images s. note to 38. 64.

[3] About 22½ ft. (= 6.86 m). See note to 37. 172.

[4] Note to 37. 242.

[5] The word *anto* which refers to the person of the King, stands in opposition to *bahi*.

[6] The word *ayyakā* refers to bhikkhus.

70 and have become wet. Bring them hither!" Numbers of
people with torches in their hands set forth to the search
and found[1] bhikkhus who came from Mahāgāma, under a tree.
71 They returned and told the tidings to the King. He hastened
thither, and when he saw the bhikkhus brought them full
72 of joy to his own tent, gave them red garments which he
kept ready for constantly renewed gifts to the bhikkhus, took
73 the wet garments himself and had them dried, practised the
custom of feet-washing and the like, made them all sit on a
74 well covered couch, offered them medicine, handed it to them
himself, did for them also in the morning everything that
75 had to be done, such as feeding and the like, gave them servants and let them go when they liked. Thus was the beginning of the day[2] spent by him who had his pleasure in doing meritorious works.

76 While thus this most excellent of men directed his life
and also the kingdom, thinking only of meritorious works,
77 keeping all his subjects to meritorious action, Māna tarried
in the Eastern Province and collected troops. Then he
78 brought together his father's army and resources and marched
to Tīsucullasagāma[3] to begin war. Dāṭhopatissa also marched
on hearing the tidings of this, with strong forces to Tambala.
79 When they met they fought a great battle. Dāṭhopatissa's
80 warriors sent Māna to Heaven. When Dappula heard that,
he died also, pierced with the arrow of grief. Seven days long dwelling in Anurādhapura he had wielded the sceptre[4];

[1] *Gavesantā* has the meaning of seeking as well as finding. The verb governs the acc. *bhikkhū* "when during their search they found bhikkhus . . . they returned . . ."

[2] The reading of the MSS. *tassādidivasaṃ gataṃ* (as emendation instead of *gato*) is very good and must not be altered as in the Col. Ed., into *tassāsi divasaṃ gataṃ*. The point lies just in this, that already in the early morning the King could satisfy his desire for *puñña*, how much more in the course of the day.

[3] The greater number of my MSS. have this reading. Only in one of them is it corrected into *Tipullaheyagāmakaṃ*. The Col. Ed. reads *Tipucullasagāmakam*.

[4] Namely immediately after the death of Kassapa II. Then he re-

in Rohaṇa he wielded it three years: therefore we have spoken 81
of him in Rohaṇa as well as here[1].

Thus were the joys which a man won toilsomely only by 82
killing his foes in fight, effulgent but for a moment, like the
lightning. What wise man would find his pleasure in them?

Here ends the forty-fifth chapter, called "The Four Kings", in the Mahāvaṃsa, compiled for the serene joy and emotion of the pious.

tired to Rohaṇa, his son Māna to the Eastern Province. The events described in v. 78 ff. took place three years later, thus still in the first half of the reign of Dāṭhopatissa. According to Pūjāv. Dappula reigned 3 years and 3 months. According to Rājāv. 10 years. Both sources have in mind the reign in Rohaṇa.

[1] Namely in Anurādhapura.

CHAPTER XLVI

THE THREE KINGS

1 After Hatthadāṭha's death the younger brother of the king,
the prince Aggabodhi became (king) under the name of Siri-
2 saṃghabodhi[1]. He was a just monarch, gifted with right
views; therefore he performed meritorious works without number.
3 He took care of the eating-houses of the inmates of the three
fraternities, enlarged the Mahāpāli Hall and decreed the kee-
4 ping of the command not to slay. He bestowed office accor-
ding to worth without preference[2], and by showing favour in
accordance with rank, clans and so forth he won over these
5 to himself. Wherever the discerning (prince) saw bhikkhus he
honoured them and made them recite the Paritta[3] which is
6 contained in the doctrine (of the Buddha). (Once) when he
visited the Thera Dāṭhāsiva who dwelt in Nāgasālā, rich in
7 knowledge, virtuous, highly learned, he paid him reverence,
heard from him the doctrine of the Perfectly Enlightened One,

[1] From *rājino* we must supply the predicative substantive *rājā*.

[2] P. *anālayo*. Cf. note to 42. 42.

[3] Ceremonies at which a Paritta Text is recited are observed on the most divers occasions, joyful and sad, at the inauguration of a new house, on a journey or at similar undertakings, for warding off sickness, after cases of death, etc. For such a ceremony at which I was present see Journ. PTS. 1924—27, p. 227. The epithet *sāsanogadha* stresses the canonical character of the Paritta. The texts of the Paritta are taken from the canonical writings and the Khuddaka-Pāṭha itself is a kind of Paritta (s. Seidenstücker, Khuddaka Pāṭho, trsl. p. 2 ff.) I am inclined to believe that it is this book which is meant by the Paritta mentioned 37. 226. The Paritta ceremonies are derived from popular magic. This is clearly seen in the narrative 51. 80, 52. 80.

rejoiced fervently over the doctrine since it offers absolute
peace. When then he heard of the many injuries done to the 8
bhikkhus of the Thera School by evil-minded villains, former
relatives of his own kinsfolk, he restored the ruined vihāras 9
and pariveṇas as they had been originally and granted them
here and there maintenance villages with abundant revenues.
Where the necessaries had been curtailed he brought them now 10
as it were to new growth. Slaves he placed at the disposal of
the community where they were wanted. For the above named 11
Thera he built a practising-house which bore his name; the discerning (Thera) accepted it and made it over to the community. As maintenance villages the King granted it[1] Bharattāla, 12
Kihimbila, Kataka, Tulādhāra and Andhanāraka, Andhakāra, 13
Antureḷi, Bālava, Dvāranāyaka, as well as Mahānikkaḍḍhika
and further Peḷahāla. Having granted these and other main- 14
tenance villages, the Ruler of men placed at its disposal helpers
for the monastery who were even of his own kindred. Having 15
further seen and heard that necessaries flowed sparingly to the
vihāras of the two fraternities[2], he granted them also many
maintenance villages. What need (is there) of many words? 16
Also to the three fraternities he gave a thousand villages
with large and assured revenues. Bearing in mind the splendid 17
qualities of the three Jewels[3], he took the pearl chain[4] of
one string and made of it a rosary[5]. Thus he was in all 18
his dealings one to whom the teaching of the Buddha was the
highest (good), and vying with him all the people also fulfilled
the (commands of that) doctrine. The Damiḷa by name Pottha- 19
kuṭṭha, who was in his service, erected the wonderful practising-

[1] P. *tassa; padhānagharassa* must be supplied. All the foundations enumerated in vv. 12—14 had to do evidently with the "practising-house" mentioned in v. 11. For the monastery helpers (*ārāmikā* v. 14) see note to 37. 63.

[2] Perhaps the Thūpārāma and the Maricavaṭṭi-vihāra. See note to 41. 97.

[3] Buddha, Dhamma and Saṃgha, the Buddha, his doctrine and his Order are thus called.

[4] See note to 44. 127.

[5] P. *akkhamālā* = skr. *akṣamālā* with the same meaning.

20 house, called Māṭambiya[1] and assigned it the Ambavāpi (tank)
at Būkakalla, the village of Tantavāyikacāṭikā, as well as the
21 village of Niṭṭhilaveṭṭhi together with slaves. In the Kappūra-
pariveṇa[2], as well as in the Kurundapillaka (-vihāra) and (in
the vihāra of) Mahārājaghara the same (Potthakuṭṭha) erected
22 pāsādas. In addition he granted, wealthy as he was, three
villages to the vihāras. The wise Senāpati, Potthasāta by
23 name, finished in the vihāra called Jeta a pariveṇa that bore
the King's name. The Damiḷa Mahākanda built the pariveṇa
24 called after him, another (built) the Cullapantha (-pariveṇa)
and Saṃghatissa, the Uparāja of the King, (built) the Sehā-
25 la-uparājaka. Many people besides erected these and other vi-
hāras, emulating the King; for it is the rule with living crea-
26 tures: what he who is master does, evil or good, the same
is done by his subjects; let the wise man take heed of that.
27 The highly virtuous Mahesī of the King, Jeṭṭhā by name, built
28 the Jeṭṭhārāma as abode for the bhikkhunīs and granted it
two villages in the Pattapāsāṇa domain and the village of
Buddhabhelagāma, as well as a hundred monastery helpers.
29 The wealthy Malayarāja gave a costly relic-house for the cetiya
30 in the Maṇḍalagiri-vihāra[3] and on the Lohapāsāda he covered
the central pinnacle. The Bodhitissa-vihāra was erected by the
31 highly respected Bodhitissa. All the heads of districts in the
Island built here and there according to their means, numerous
32 vihāras and pariveṇas. The time of this Ruler of men con-
sisted as it were, in nothing but meritorious works; for fear
33 of prolixity they have not been fully enumerated[4]. Even
the foregoing form of the narrative which gives but a sur-

[1] Wickremasinghe (EZ. II, p. 10, note 5) identifies with this building the *Mādbiyan piriveṇa* mentioned in the Timbiriveva pillar inscription.

[2] A building in the Abhayagiri-vihāra according to 45. 29.

[3] Mentioned as *Mädiligiri* in the Medirigiri inscription (Wickremasinghe, EZ. II. p. 28), about 46 m. E. S. E. of Anurādhapura in Tamankaduva, N. E. of the Minneri lake. The ruins are described in the ASC., Ann. Rep. for 1897 (= XLII. 1904), p. 7.

[4] P. *vicāritaṃ*. One must start from the meaning "explained singly (*vi-*), analyzed".

vey of the most important matters[1], seems to me too long-winded[2].

At another time he had taken up his abode in Pulatthi- 34
nagara[3] whither he had betaken himself, amassing a store of
meritorious works. He was attacked by an incurable disease 35
and as he saw that the time for his death had come, he called
his subjects, exhorted them to piety and went to his death. 36
When he was dead his subjects mourned all in deep grief,
performed for him on his pyre all ceremonies without fail, 37
made for themselves medicine[4] from the ashes of the pyre,
then they took carefully all the royal treasures and the whole 38
army and train under their protection and betook themselves
to the town (Anurādhapura).

Thus the King went in the sixteenth year (of his reign[5]) 39
to Heaven, the Damiḷa Potthakuṭṭha administered his kingdom.
He seized the person of the Uparāja Dāṭhāsiva, had him 40
thrown into prison and ordered him to be strictly guarded[6].
But as he thought: without a king it is impossible to rule the 41
earth, he fetched hither the chief of Dhanapiṭṭhi[7] Datta by

[1] Lit.: A general view (*upalakkhaṇaṃ*) of the cases (or examples, *hetūnaṃ*, cf. the meaning of latin *causa*) according to the degree of their importance (*yathāpadhānaṃ* is used exactly like skr. *yathāpradhānam*). W.'s translation: "inasmuch as it has been mixed up with remarks on the nature and condition of things which lead men to good and evil" — a free rendering rather than a translation — misses the point.

[2] Figurative in the original, the comparison with a road (*magga*) which is overcrowded with people (*ākula*).

[3] For the first time here Polonnaruva (cf. 44. 122 with note) is mentioned as a royal residence, though only temporarily.

[4] A very characteristic trait of primitive mentality.

[5] The Sinhalese chronicles call the king only by his epithet *Sirisangbō*. Pūjāv. and Rājāv. give him a reign of 16 years. Both chronicles as also Rājaratn. ascribe to him the building of the Piyagal-piriveṇa and of the Devnuvara(-vihāra). This is Devanagara, now Dondra at the southern point of Ceylon.

[6] The guard (*rakkhāvaraṇa*) refers not as W. thinks, to the country, but to the prisoner, Dāṭhāsiva.

[7] A now uninhabited village, Danpitigama, lies to the north of Ku-

42 name, who belonged to the royal family, and consecrated him
43 king; and in his name[1] he administered the whole. Datta
erected in Dhanapiṭṭhi a vihāra which was called after him
44 and heaped up other meritorious works. After living exactly
two years[2], he died. But Potthakuṭṭha after his death, sum-
45 moned another young man, Hatthadāṭha who was a native
of Uṇhānagara. Him also he consecrated king and acted as
46 before. Having built the practising-house of Kāladīghāvika and
performed other meritorious works, Hatthadāṭha fell after six
months into the power of death[3].

47 When the wise have once realised how baleful are treasures, wealth and power[4] they will surely give up the desire for royal dignity and find their whole joy solely in meritorious works.

Here ends the forty-sixth chapter, called "The Three Kings", in the Mahāvaṃsa, compiled for the serene joy and emotion of the pious.

runegala in the Korale Katuvana, Ambagasse-Palata (Census of Ceylon, II. p. 288).

[1] Lit.: putting forth his (Datta's) name.

[2] In the Sinhalese sources the king is called *Valpiṭivāsi-dat*. Pūjāv. gives him a reign of 2, Rājāv. one of 10 years. The place name *Valpita* is often met with in Ceylon.

[3] In Sinhalese sources he is called *Huṇannaruriyan-Daḷa* or the like. The length of reign given him in Pūjāv. and Rājāv. is the same as in the Cūlavs. 6 months.

[4] P. *vāhanāni* "chariot" as emblem of the military power of princes.

[CHAPTER XLVII]

After the death of this king, Mānavamma[1] became king. 1
Of what clan was he? Whose son was he? How came he to
reign[2]?

Now there was belonging to the line of Mahāsammata and 2
bringing with him (as inheritance) the good qualities of his
clan, a son of Kassapa, the depredator of the Thūpārāma and
(there was also) a daughter of the Malayarāja King Saṃgha- 3
māna[3]. He wedded her and lived with her in retirement in
Uttaradesa (the Northern Province). When this affair had 4
been spied out by the prince Hatthadāṭha, he betook himself
to Jambudīpa and sought out the ruler Narasīha, told him his 5
name and entered his service. He satisfied the Lord of men in
every way. When he felt assured of his friendly feeling, he 6
let his wife come and took up his abode there, serving (the
King) day and night. But the ruler of Kaṇḍuveṭhi[4] who 7

[1] Sinhalese documents call the king Mahalä-pānō.

[2] Here it is again probable that the author has taken a new source for his narrative. Cf. note to 45. 37.

[3] I consider the alterations of the text in the Col. Ed. *bhedino* for *bhojino* in v. 2 and *Saṃghā nām'assa rājinī* instead of *Saṃghamānassa rājino* as inadmissible in view of the complete agreement of the MSS. They are also unnecessary. The word *bhojin* has also in Skr. the meaning of "exploiting" in an unfavourable sense, as we have to take it here. The verses 2 and 3 a. b. are evidently a kind of title, hence the absence of the finite verb. The name of the wife Saṃghā is first mentioned in v. 8.

[4] Namely Narasīha. W. says erroneously "another king, Kaṇḍuveṭhi". The name of the territory *Kaṇḍuveṭhi* over which Narasīha ruled, reminds one of Kaṇḍuveṭṭi in 77. 79 used as the name of a vassal prince

governed the whole kingdom, well pleased with him, granted
8 him a large income. In wedlock with him his wife, Saṃghā
by name, bore four daughters and four sons.
9 Now once as the King was taking an airing for pleasure
on the back of his elephant, together with Mānavamma, being
10 thirsty, he drank without dismounting[1], a young coconut, and
passed it then to Mānavamma whom he did not regard as his
11 equal[2]. Mānavamma took it and thought: "My friend is mo-
narch here. Is there for such beings such a thing as leavings
12 in the strict sense of the word? It is right therefore if I
drink thereof". Thus he thought and drank thereof. Such
13 great efforts[3] are made by those who wish for success. The
King saw that, was alarmed, and in his turn drank what the
other had left over. This is ever the way of acting of the
14 honourable. From that time onward he made him his equal in
food and dwelling, in equipment and means of conveyance.
15 While the two so lived (together), the Vallabha King[4]
16 came to make war on Narasīha. Narasīha reflected: "This
(my friend) serves me untiringly night and day in the ex-
pectation that through my service he will gain the royal
17 dignity which belongs to him by right of descent. If he were

in Southern India. It is probably a case of writing the same name in two ways. Hultzsch, JRAS. 1913, p. 527 has shown that Kaṇḍuveṭṭi or -veṭhi is synonymous with Kāḍavāṇ, a designation of the Pallava kings. Thus Narasīha was a Pallava.

[1] Lit.: being there (namely on the back of his elephant).

[2] It is contrary to custom to offer an equal the remains of one's own meal. The word *añña* "not his equal" stands in opposition to *saka* in v. 14. Narasīha realises his error and makes it good by taking the coconut from Mānavamma and drinking what he has left.

[3] In this case the effort of self-restraint.

[4] The *Vallabhas* are a South Indian tribe. Their ruler is simply described (as also in 54. 12 ff.) as the Vallabha. Vallabha as the name of a people occurs also in Skr. Bahadur Venkayya EI. III. 277; Hultzsch (JRAS. 1913, p. 528) has proved that Narasīha is identical with the Pallava king Narasiṃhavarman I and his enemy the Vallabha with Pulakeśin II. whose capital Vātāpi was taken by Narasīha. Fleet (Hultzsch l. c., p. 529) has calculated the date as A. D. 642. Cf. H. W. Codrington, H. C., p. 35–6.

now to march out with me and found his death in battle,
then all that he and I have planned together would be without
result." Pondering thus, the King let Mānavamma return to 18
his town (and) he himself began the war against the Vallabha
king. Mānavamma thought likewise: "If this king, while I 19
am in life, falls in this war, of what value would my life
then be to me? His trust in me would have been an error 20
if I were to behave so. Why by making me his equal did
he favour me?[1] Is is therefore meet that I go forth with him 21
to the battle-field; for it is happiness for me to live or die
with him here." Thus pondering, armed he mounted his fa- 22
vourite elephant, went forth and appeared before the King on
he battle-field. When Narasīha saw him he cried out full of 23
joy: "Truly I have shown him friendship[2] as I was bound
to show it." Thereupon the army of Māna(vamma) and the 24
army of the King scattered the army of the Vallabha king
at their encounter. Mānavamma showed his heroism, distin- 25
guishing himself by his courage like Nārāyaṇa[3] in the battle
of the gods. But Narasīha rejoiced over Mānavamma's bravery 26
and embraced him lovingly with the words: "It is thou who
hast brought me the victory." He returned to his town, held 27
a festival of victory and showed all (honour) that was due to
Mānavamma's army. Now the King thought thus: "My friend 28
has done all that was due on his part; from to-day he is
without obligation towards me. I will now also discharge my 29
debt by doing on my part what is due; for grateful people
who remember what has been done for them are very hard
to find." He assembled the dignitaries and spake these words: 30
"Ye are witnesses of the deeds of this my friend. I also must 31

[1] He has favoured me in the expectation that I might help him in his difficulties.

[2] The acc. *saṃthavaṃ* is governed by *aho.* I now see that he was worthy of what I have done him.

[3] As Indra-Sakka is otherwise always considered as the protagonist of the Gods in the battle against the asuras or demons, we must take *Nārāyaṇa* here to be one of his names. In a passage of the Saṃyutta commentary (ed. Cal. p. 279[22]) the strength of the chaddanta elephants, elephants with 6 tusks, is described as *Nārāyaṇa-balaṃ.*

now show him all the love and happiness which are his due.
A return service for him who has earlier rendered us a ser-
32 vice is the duty of the pious." At these words the dignitaries
answered the Ruler: "Whatsoever the King wishes finds favour
33 with us." Thereupon the Sovereign gave Mānavamma an army
with the attendant train and the whole equipment and all the
34 necessary servants and spake to him: go forth then, and as
he gazed after him as he marched forth with the army, he wept
35 as for a son that goes to a far country. Mānavamma embarked in
the vessels at the sea-coast and arrived quickly, after he had
36 with speedy voyage crossed the sea[1] and penetrated into
Laṅkādīpa with his army laying waste. At tidings of this
37 King Dāṭhopatissa fled. Mānavamma came into the town
(Anurādhapura) and without taking over the sovereignty[2], he
38 arose and pursued closely the fugitive (Dāṭhopatissa). Then
the Damiḷa army heard that its Lord (Narasīha) was smitten
39 with a fell disease. On these tidings it departed. When
Dāṭhopatissa heard that, he marched with a strong force
40 against Mānavamma and began the fight. Mānavamma thought:
"My whole army has gone; if I fall[3] then the wish of my
41 foe is fulfilled; I shall betake myself therefore to Jambudīpa
to fetch troops there and recover the dominion." Therefore
42 he did so. He departed, sought again his friend Narasīha,
43 and cleverly satisfying him, he served him heedfully. During
the reigns of four kings[4] Mānavamma stayed there. Then
Narasīha thought: "With pride unbroken, finding in honour
44 his wealth, my friend serves me for the sake of the royal

[1] The *tam* in 35 d must be supplemented by *jaladhiṃ* from *jaladhītaṭe* in b.

[2] P. *ahutvā va narāḍhipo.* What is meant is that he wasted no time in performing the ceremonies of *abhiseka* connected with the solemn ascent of the throne. Cf. 48. 26.

[3] P. *mate mama.* Here the gen. *mama* takes the place of the loc. *mayi.* See Cūlavs. ed. I, Introd. p. XVI.

[4] These were the kings Dāṭhopatissa II., his enemy in his unsuccessful attempt to seize the throne, as described v. 35—41, further Aggabodhi IV., Datta and Hatthadāṭha.

dignity and will become old and grey-headed thereby. How
can I when I see this, exercise dominion? If I cannot at 45
this time by sending forth my troops, gain the kingdom[1] for
him of what use is my life to me? Having so pondered, he 46
collected his army, equipped it with what was needful, gave
it (the pay) it demanded, marched himself at its head to the 47
sea-coast, had numerous strong ships of different shape built
here and spake to the dignitaries: "Go ye with this man 48
here." But all the people there refused to go on board. Then 49
Narasīha reflected, hid himself, but gave his own armour,
known everywhere as badge of the King, and all his own 50
ornaments to Mānavamma, told him to embark and said: "Go
thou and when thou art at sea have this drum called Koṭṭha 51
sounded." He did all this. But the people in the belief it
was their king who was going forth, went on board and left 52
the Ruler of men alone behind. Māna(vamma) began the
voyage with the army. The whole ocean was as a (floating) 53
town. Having reached the port he landed with his army,
remained there a few days that his troops might rest, took 54
Uttaradesa (the North Province), brought the inhabitants into
his power and began with his invincible great army to march 55
on the town. When Potthakuṭṭha[2] heard this he advanced
against him with a large force. The two armies clashed with 56
each other like seas that have burst their bounds. Mānavamma
who fully armed had mounted his elephant, separated Pottha- 57
kuṭṭha and the King and put them to flight. When the people
in the country saw Hatthadāṭha fleeing, they seized his head 58
and showed it to Mānavamma. Potthakuṭṭha fleeing reached
Merukandara[3]. When the chief (of the district) saw him there 59
he thought: "He has been for long my friend; therefore when

[1] The words *imasmiṃ pana vārasmiṃ* as far as *na gahessāmi* form a conditional introductory sentence without a conjunction. Such conditional sentences occur also in Skr. See Speyer, Vedische und Sanskrit-Syntax, § 283. W.'s translation goes to pieces on the negative *na*.

[2] He carried on the government for Hatthadāṭha who was nominally king, according to 46. 44 ff.

[3] See note to 41. 19.

he, in his need, takes refuge with me I must not desert him.
60 But how can I towards these two, my master and my friend,
remain free from blame?" and he ate poisoned cake and died.
61 Poṭṭhakuṭṭha ate of the cake with him and died likewise.
Thus for Mānavamma the Island was freed of the briers (of
enemies).

62 From that time Mānavamma set up in the Island the um-
brella (of his dominion) warding off therewith as it were, all
63 harm from the inhabitants of the Island. He performed many
inestimable meritorious works; what man would be able to
64 enumerate these in their order? After founding two villages,
he the excellent one erected in the Padhānarakkha(-vihāra)
65 (of the one) the pāsāda called Sepaṇṇi and in the Sirisaṃgha-
bodhi(-vihāra) (of the other) the blissgiving (pāsāda) Sirī. He
roofed over the Lohapāsāda as well as the temple in the Thū-
66 pārāma. After he had built a pāsāda in the Thūpārāma, he
made it over to the Paṃsukūlins[1]. . . . .
. . . .

[1] P. *paṃsukūlin* denotes ascetic bhikkhus who only wore garments made of rags (*paṃsukūla*) patched together. In Ceylon the word has without doubt come to designate a particular sect whose members were pledged to the observance described above. According to 51. 52 the Paṃsukūlins belonged up to the time of Sena II. to the congregation of the Abhayagiri-vihāra, when however, they seceded and formed a special group of their own.

The MSS. are here all badly mutilated. Only the MS. of the Colombo Museum tested by me on the spot, gives a text at all capable of translation (Cf. Cūlavs. ed., vol. II. Introd. p. II): "After building a pāsāda in the Thūpārāma, he made it over to the Paṃsukūlins. What was decayed he restored, after providing that the vihāra could be easily supplied with (the four) necessaries. He even restored the umbrella on the decayed temple and he also granted to the adherents of the Dhammaruci (sect) the Rājinīdīpa-vihāra." It seems to me beyond a doubt that we have here an attempt at emendation on the part of the copyist. The Col. Ed. also tries to restore at least v. 66. The text should be translated thus: "After he had built a pāsāda in the Thūpārāma, he handed it over to the Paṃsukūlins. He repaired the decayed umbrella on the top of the cetiya; and he also restored numerous shrines which had fallen into decay."

Then too the Sinhalese sources name as successor of Mānavamma (Mahalāpānō) an Aggabodhi (Akbō). According to Pūjāv. and Rājāv. he was the son of Mānavamma to whom, it is true, they ascribe the reign of 35 years, including no doubt the time of his sejourn in India, while Akbō is said to have reigned 6 years. Also in Mhvs. 57. 25 an Aggabodhi is named as eldest son of Mānavamma.

Now as the signature of our chapter describes it as the 48th, a 47th would therefore be entirely absent. Thus S. and B. have assumed that there is a gap in our MSS. The missing part should have contained as conclusion of chapter 47, the end of the reign of Mānavamma and in the new chapter 48 the beginning of the reign of Aggabodhi V, the further course of which is described in the 19 verses which have been preserved. A gap might be explained by the loss of a leaf out of the archetype.

I have adopted this assumption in my edition and translation, must insist however, that the arguments taken singly are not compelling. That the Sinhalese chronicles insert a king who does not occur in the Cūlavaṃsa we have already seen (s. note to 41. 102). Yet on the other hand, the mention of Aggabodhi in 57. 25 must be taken into account. The absence of the chapter number 47 is also not decisive. Numbers 40 and 43 are also wanting without any gap being noticeable in the account of events. It is therefore not impossible that it is merely a case of the mutilation of single verses. The assumption of the loss of a leaf would in the first instance only explain a gap, it would not explain the mutilation of the text after v. 66. It is however, the combination of the two first arguments which make the assumption of a gap probable and the probability is perhaps strengthened by the fact that just at the place where the gap might have to be assumed, the text of the MSS. is in disorder.

CHAPTER XLVIII

THE SIX KINGS

1 . . . . . After he had made thereof a mansion for which the
necessaries could easily be provided, he also presented the
Rājinidīpika(-vihāra) to the bhikkhus of the Dhammaruci
2 School. After building the Mahānettapādika cells (for dwel-
ling in), he granted to the same (Dhammarucis) the village
3 of Devatissa in (the district of) Koṭṭhavāta. In Mahāthala he
built (the vihāra) called Kadambagona, further in Devapāli
4 the (vihāra) called Girinagara, in Antarasobbha the Deva-vihāra,
further he built the Rājamātika monastery and gave it [1] to
5 the Paṃsukūlins [2]. In the Gokaṇṇaka-vihāra [3] he erected a
practising-house and the ruined temple of the Vaḍḍhamāna
6 Bodhi Tree [4] he had restored. In the vihāra called Saṃghamitta
and elsewhere he, the highly-famed, had here and there new
7 works undertaken on the vihāras. At a cost of six and twenty
thousand gold pieces [5] he restored whatever had fallen into
8 decay on the Cetiyapabbata. Having restored the Tālavatthu-

[1] It is possible that besides *Rājamātikaṃ ārāmaṃ* as object *adā* should receive the names of all the vihāras mentioned in v. 3 and 4.

[2] Of the localities mentioned in v. 2-4 Antarasobbha alone is mentioned in Mhvs. 25. 11 as a district. Instead of Koṭṭhavāta Col. ed. reads Kokavāta which occurs 37. 42 and 47 as the name of a village and of a tank built by Mahāsena (4th c. A. D.). The MSS. however, give no authority for this reading. Mahāthala is probably the present Matale (north of Kandy) (Thus W. in Index s. v.). For the Paṃsukūlins s. note to 47. 66.

[3] Built by Mahāsena according to Mhvs. 37. 41.

[4] Cf. below 49. 15. Like the images of the Buddha, the Bodhi trees had their special names.

[5] P. *suvaṇṇa*. In Skr. *suvarṇa* is a weight = *karṣa*. This is according to BR. = 11.375 gr. This would give an expenditure of over £ 40,000 according to the present value of gold.

vihāra he granted (the village of) Paṇṇabhatta to the vihāra
called after the Ruler of men Mahāsena[1]. The Goṇḍigāmika 9
tank which had burst he dammed up as before and to all
living beings he gave as a gift whatever they needed. The 10
Uposatha day he observed with fasting together with the in-
habitants of the Island, and preached to them the doctrine
in order to procure them spiritual happiness. Everyone in his 11
kingdom cultivated action which leads to Heaven, for as the
monarch acts so do also his subjects. Therefore should a wise 12
king ever practise piety; in every place where men dwell[2]
he will become renowned and finally, surrounded by his com- 13
panions, he enters Nirvana. Therefore the prudent man should
contemplate that which is for his good and for that of others.
For if all the subjects attain good discipline through an in- 14
dividual who himself has good discipline, how could a discerning
man let such an one come to harm?[3] No means for bringing 15
to beings happiness in both worlds was left untried by him
who was unflagging day and night. The fine garments worn 16
by himself he gave to the Paṃsukūlin bhikkhus as raiment.
The employment (of officials) in wrong places, undeserved fa- 17
vour or unlawful seizure (of property) was unknown with him.
To all creatures he gave the nourishment by which each of 18
them live, and whatever makes them happy with that he
blessed them. Thus after the Ruler of men had performed 19
meritorious works for six years[4] he, the peace-maker went
(to the Heaven of) the King of the gods[5].

[1] As neither Tālavatthu nor Paṇṇabhatta are otherwise mentioned it is difficult to understand rightly the sense of this passage. It seems to me that Tālavatthu was an older monastery which Aggabodhi restored and to which he granted a village, afterwards giving it the name of Mahāsena by whom perhaps the older structure had been built. A Buddha image in the Mahāsena monastery is mentioned in 51. 76.

[2] P. *nivutthanivutthamhi ṭhāne*, lit. "in each inhabited place" applied by W. to the King "wheresoever he may dwell", which is also possible.

[3] The meaning seems to be this: it lies in his own interest to educate his people to piety by his own example, as this assures his own safety. He will have all the right-minded on his side.

[4] The same length of reign in Pūjāv. and Rājāv.

[5] That is to the heaven of the Tāvatiṃsā gods at whose head stands the King of the gods, Sakka-Indra.

20 Now his brother next in age, the prince Kassapa, became
king, well qualified for the royal burden[1], for taking it over
21 according to ancient custom. As a father (wins) his son, so
he won his people by generosity, by friendly speech and by
22 care for their welfare. Offices he bestowed on various people
according to merit and he himself enjoyed the pleasures of
23 life, free from all sorrow. For laymen, bhikkhus and brāh-
maṇas the prince encouraged the way of life fitting for each
24 and carried out the command to kill no living creature. The
25 two Macchatitthas[2], the mansion Heligāma, the monastery
Vāṇijagāma, as well as Kassapagiri; further the superb prac-
tising-house called Ambavana, maintenance village[3] . . . .
. . . .
26 Amongst them all the youngest was the prince called
Mahinda. When the royal dignity came to him he was yet
27 not king[4], although he bore the burden of the kingdom. He
had a friend by name Nīla, with whom he had for long had
intimate intercourse. But he had died beforehand. In memory
28 of him he would not have it[5]. Alas! even the dominion over
the Island he deemed not blissful, since his friend was wan-
29 ting. Friends are so hard to get. Hence the Sage (Buddha)

[1] I believe that *rājabhārassa* (or *rajja°*) is directly governed by *samattho.* In Skr. in the same way with *samartha* the thing for which one is qualified may stand in the loc. or the dative. *Bhārassa* would correspond to both. Instead of *pubbavuttino* I should prefer to read *pubbavuttito,* adverbial ablative.

[2] Inscriptional *Mastoṭa* in an inscription of Mahinda IV. WICKREMASINGHE, EZ. I. 216, 221, 227.

[3] Here again there is a gap in the recorded text. Of the MSS. with which I am acquainted one, at least, indicates this by leaving a space free for about $4^{1}/_{2}$ ślokas. The finite verb is missing for the objects in vv. 24, 25. The missing verses must have contained the end of the reign of Kassapa III. According to Pūjāv. and Rājāv. he reigned 7 years. Both sources as well as Rājaratn. mention the building of the Helagampariveṇa. Of the other names which are mentioned above, Kassapagiri alone occurs again (44. 98).

[4] P. *nāhosi rājā,* see note to 47. 37.

[5] Namely the festivities connected with the *abhiseka.*

hath said[1]: "All worldly things and all spiritual things which
lead to Nirvana, these all are the lot of beings who have asso- 30
ciated with a staunch friend; therefore must one ever strive after
(gaining) staunch friends." Only as Ādipāda[2] he administered 31
the kingdom to protect as it were, during his life, living
beings on the Island. On Aggabodhi, the son of his brother 32
Kassapa he conferred the dignity of Uparāja and gave him
abundant revenues. He assigned him (the Eastern Province) Pā- 33
cīnadesa and sent him forth to take up his abode therein. (The
province of) Dakkhiṇadesa the King gave to his own son[3].
To the Mahāpāli Hall he gave an offering of ten cart-loads 34
and beggars he provided with luxuries like his own. He ate 35
nothing without first having given to the beggars, and if
without thinking of it, he had eaten, he used to give them
double of what he had himself enjoyed. For the bhikkhunīs 36
he built an abode which was called after himself and granted
them as convent boundary[4] (the village of) Nagaragalla. He 37
built the Mahindataṭa monastery[5], provided it with the four
necessaries and performed many another meritorious work,
rejoicing at the worth of such works. After the discerning 38
(prince) had reigned in this way for three years[6], he seeking
his friend, entered into the world of the gods.

[1] The *kalyāṇamittā* are often praised in the Canon. It seems to me that this passage is an allusion to Saṃyutta 3. 18 (= I, p. 88) where the Buddha after a eulogy of the *kalyāṇamittatā*, says of himself: *mamaṃ hi, Ananda, kalyāṇamittaṃ āgamma* (cf. v. 30 a!) *jātidhammā sattā jātiyā parimuccanti* etc. The passage occurs once again Saṃy. 45. 2 (= V, p. 3). [2] See note to 41. 35.

[3] Who likewise bore the name *Aggabodhi*, (See v. 39). W.'s "the southern country (only)" gives a wrong shade of meaning to the context. The bestowal of Dakkhiṇadesa was in no sense a slight. It was just this province which was reserved for the heir apparent.

[4] W. takes *ārāmamariyādaka* as the name of another village.

[5] The *Mahindataṭa* tank had already been built by Aggabodhi I and given this name in honour of the Thera Mahinda who converted the Island to Buddhism. See **42. 29.**

[6] The Sinhalese sources call this king Midelpanā or Midel only. The name is missing in the Nik.-s.; Pūjāv. and Rājāv. give him a reign of three years like the Cūlavs.

39 Now Prince Aggabodhi (son of Mahinda) who dwelt in
Dakkhiṇadesa, had for some reason or other come to the ca-
40 pital. While he sojourned there the Ādipāda Mahinda died;
41 thus the kingly power came into his hands. After taking
possession of it and securing it he sent a message[1] to Agga-
42 bodhi, the Governor of Pācīnadesa. He came hither and be-
came king under the name of Silāmegha[2]. The dignity of
Uparāja the monarch conferred on the Prince (Aggabodhi of
43 Dakkhiṇadesa). The latter entreated the King thus: free
thyself from the burden of cares and enjoy life's pleasures,
44 and administered the government himself. As was meet, he
treated his subjects with severity and clemency and all un-
disciplined people on the Island the discerning one brought
45 on to the right path. While the twain lived thus, the evil-
minded found no opportunity for interfering, and they thought:
46 the twain must be estranged. They went to the King and
spake slanderously to him in secret: "Thou art King in name,
47 in reality the other is king; the Uparāja will take the royal
dignity for himself; the people he has already won over; in
a short time he will be king, of that there can be no doubt."
48 When the Monarch heard that he fell out with the Prince
and the Prince when he noticed that, became a rebel against
49 the King. He fled to his province, won over the inhabitants
50 and with mighty forces began the war. At Kadalīnivāta[3] a

[1] A message to the effect that everything is ready for him to take over the government. As Aggabodhi of Pācīnadesa is a son of the elder brother Kassapa, he is according to Sinhalese law, the legal successor of Mahinda. Mahinda's son Aggabodhi willingly recognises this.

[2] Sylvain Lévi (Journ. Asiatique, May-June, 1900, p. 418; cf. JRAS. Ceyl. Br. XXIV, Nr. 68, 1915-16, p. 87 ff.) communicates a Chinese account according to which an Indian monk, Vajrabodhi, on the way to India touches at Ceylon where he is invited by the king Chi-li-Chi-lo (i. e. Siri-Sīla). S. Lévi identifies this king with Mānavamma (see 47. 1 ff.), but E. R. Ayrton (Ceylon Notes and Queries II. Jan. 1914, p. XXVII ff.) probably more correctly, with Aggabodhi VI. Silāmegha.

[3] Must be situated according to 44. 6, on the line of march from Dakkhiṇadesa, (more exactly from Mahāgalla, not far from the present Nikaveratiya) to Anurādhapura.

bitter fight took place. The Prince suffered a defeat and be-
took himself to Malaya. Later the King thought gratefully 51
of his cousin's support[1], of the transference of the royal dignity
and the rest and grieved quite openly. The Prince too on 52
hearing this, became conciliatory. So they let each other
know how they loved one another. The King betook himself 53
quite alone to Malaya, took the prince with him and returned
to his capital . . . . . .[2] he married him to his daughter 54
Saṃghā by name. While he lived with her in intimate inter- 55
course with the King, he (once) angered at some fault or
other, struck her a blow. She went to her father and wept 56
before him bitterly. "Without reason the husband thou
gavest me kills me." Scarcely had the King heard this than 57
he thought: of a truth I have done wrong, sent her at once
to a home for bhikkhunīs and made her undergo the ceremony
of world renunciation. Now the son of her maternal uncle, 58
Aggabodhi by name, whose heart had been long filled with
love for her, thought this was a favourable time to flee with 59
her, seized her secretly and betook himself alone (with her)
to Rohaṇa. The Ruler of men Aggabodhi took (his cousin) 60
Aggabodhi with him and betook himself with him to Rohaṇa
to slay (the seducer) Aggabodhi. (The Uparāja) Aggabodhi 61
made his cousin (the King) Aggabodhi halt[3], and went him-
self to the western mountains[4] so slay (the seducer) Aggabodhi.
When at the head of a great army he had brought the whole 62
of Rohaṇa into his power, he delivered battle and seized him
and his own wife Saṃghā. From that time onward the three 63

[1] Lit. "of his brother". As the father's brother is called father, so the sons of brothers are brothers.

[2] The line a b of v. 54 is defective in all the MSS. I propose to complete it thus: *hoti nissaṃsayaṃ dhīro iti tuṭṭho atīva so* "with the thought; he is no doubt firm, he, being highly pleased, gave him &c. &c.

[3] The verb *nisīditvā* stands here in a causative sense instead of *nisīdāpetvā*. Cf. Cūlavs. ed. Introd. p. XIV.

[4] The western mountains of Rohaṇa are probably the not inconsiderable mountain range rising south-east of Ratnapura which reaches its greatest height (over 3000 ft.) to the south of Rakvana where it is crossed by the Bulutota Pass.

lived happily and in harmony in mutual intimate intercourse
64 at their ease. The King built the Vāpārani monastery and
the Mānaggabodhi monastery, further the Sabhattudesabhoga
65 in the Abhayuttara-vihāra as well as pāsādas in the vihāras
Hatthikucchi[1] and Punapiṭṭhi, in the Mahāpariveṇa[2] and in
66 Vāhadīpa[3]. In the Thūpārāma he restored the damaged doors
of the temple as they were before and transposed the pillars[4]
67 therein. After performing these and other meritorious works
according to his power, he passed away in the fortieth year
of his reign according to his doing[5].

68 Thereupon the Uparāja Aggabodhi, the fortunate, became
69 king, son of the wise Ādipāda Mahinda. To the Order and
to the laity he showed favour according to merit. With the
70 dignity of Uparāja he invested his own son Mahinda. The
ruined temple of the great Bodhi Tree he built anew and solidly; he also built two monasteries: Kalanda and Mallavāta.
71 By legal acts he carefully reformed the Order of the Conqueror
(Buddha) and judging according to justice, he rooted out un-
72 just judges. He himself studied the medicinal plants over

[1] See note to 42. 21. [2] See note to 42. 26.

[3] Mentioned again 49. 33 under Udaya I and 49. 76, along with the Hatthikucchi-vihāra, under Dappula II.

[4] It seems to me that what is meant by the temple (*geha*) of the Thūpārāma is the superstructure of the cetiya. What makes this likely is the mention of the pillars which were re-arranged by the King. The pillars which surround the thūpa in four rows are in the Thūpārāma (as also in the Laṅkārāma cetiya) still partially preserved. They were intended to support the roof which was of wood. Cf. for plan Smither Architectural Remains, Anurádhapura, p. 4 ff. Such superstructures are described as *cetiya-* or *thūpa-gharāni* or *-gehāni* analogous to the *bodhi-gharāni* or *-gehāni*. Smither doubts it is true, whether the pillars at the Thūpārāma cetiya could have borne such a structure, while Parker (Ancient Ceylon p. 270) quite admits the possibility. The custom of building over a cetiya is even to-day not unknown. I myself saw an interesting example in the Budumutava monastery at Nikaveratiya which I visited on the 20th April 1926 in the company of the Archaeological Commissioner Mr. A. M. Hocart. The term *thūpaghara* is inseparable from that of *bodhighara* (s. note to 38. 43).

[5] Pūjāv. and Rājāv. also give King Akbō a reign of 40 years.

the whole island of Laṅkā (to find out) whether they were
wholesome or harmful[1] for the sick. He had rice by allot- 73
ment[2] distributed to the inmates of the three fraternities
and delicious foods fitting for himself, to the Paṃsukūlins.
The King, having thus with unrestricted royal power, per- 74
formed these and other meritorious works, died after six years
just as he was sojourning in Pulatthinagara[3].

Formerly Aggabodhi had a son; he had died as Yuvarāja. 75
Since then no son existed as heir to the throne[4]. There was 76
however a son of the King Silāmegha[5] by name **Mahinda**,
fitted for the royal dignity, rich in merit, capable of winning
the people for himself. On the day of his birth the King 77
(Silāmegha) consulted the astrologers and when he heard their
answer that the boy was fitted for the royal dignity, he gave 78
them plenty of money and kept the matter a secret. But when
he grew up he made him his senāpati. He gave the entire 79
government into his hands[6] and as independent ruler the
discerning (prince) fulfilled the royal duties in a just way[7].

[1] W. gives an entirely different rendering. He separates *maṅgalaṃ cāvamaṅgalaṃ* from *bhesajjaṃ* and translates: "ordained the form and manner of holding festivities and funerals". There is no verb in the text corresponding to "ordained". All the accusatives are governed by *vicārayi*. But if *maṅgalaṃ cāvamaṅgalaṃ* meant what W. assumes, the objects to be tested by the King would still have been very heterogeneous and the combination of *m. cāvam.* with *bhesajjaṃ* very amazing.

[2] S. Childers, Pali Dict. s. v. *salākā*: "Food belonging to the collective saṅgha of a monastery was sometimes distributed to the monks by tickets called *salākā*, and consisting of slips of wood, bark, bamboo, talipot leaf or other similar material. Food so distributed was called *salākabhattaṃ* "ticket-food" . . . Similar tickets seem to have been issued by private persons, like our soup-tickets".

[3] The same number in Pūjāv. and Rājāv. Pulatthinagara is here again a temporary royal residence as in 46. 34.

[4] Lit.: The kingdom was sonless. *Yuvarāja* is here used of Mahinda as *uparāja* above in v. 69.

[5] I. e. Aggabodhi VI. Cf. above v. 42.

[6] This happened evidently at the time when Aggabodhi VI. was in conflict with his Uparāja, afterwards King Aggabodhi VII. Cf. above v. 48 ff.

[7] We have here one of these cases where in the course of a sentence the subject changes the gerund being used in the sense of a Loc. abs.

80 Therefore when (King Silāmegha) died, he as clever statesman[1]
took not the dignity of senāpati from the hand of his suc-
81 cessor Aggabodhi (VII). (On the contrary) at that time he
betook himself with some kind of commission from the King
to the sea-coast and took up his abode in the seaport of
82 Mahātittha[2]. When he heard here of the death of his uncle[3]
he came hither in haste (fearing) rebels might seize the king-
dom and destroy it.

83 Then in (the Northern Province) Uttaradesa the chiefs of
districts together with the dwellers in the province seized the
84 land by force and refused tribute to the King[4]. At the ti-
dings of this Mahinda advanced with a great army to Uttara-
desa, crushed all the chiefs of districts together with the
85 dwellers in the province, betook himself then to the spot
where the King had died, sought out the Queen, wept (with
her), comforted her according to the circumstances of the time,
86 and spake the following words: "Grieve not, Great Queen, that
thy husband is dead. I will shelter the Island, thou mayest
87 keep the royal dignity." By her silence she seemed to assent;
in secret the crafty one took measures to slay him, as she
88 wanted to live in her own way. When the Senāpati (Mahinda)
found this out, he had her watched and put her adherents,
89 a great number of people, to flight in combat. Then he had
the Queen put into fetters and brought in a chariot, took her

(See note to 39. 26). Aggabodhi is subject of *katvā* in 78 b and *katvāna* in 79 a. With *so* in 79 c Mahinda is meant. W. gets out of the difficulty by apparently separating *sayaṃvasī* into *sayaṃ vasi* and translating "he lived (without care and anxiety)". But for this interpretation there are no corresponding words in the text for those which the translator has put in brackets.

[1] P. *nayaññu*. One can perhaps see in such expressions the influence of the Indian Nīti-literature. Cf. *yathānayaṃ* below in v. 96.

[2] Now *Mantai* or *Mantota* not far from Mannar. It is already mentioned in Vijaya's time (Mhvs. 7. 58) as the place where settlers from the Indian mainland land.

[3] P. *cūlapituno*, lit.: of his little father. His grand-father and the father of Aggabodhi VII. were brothers. Cf. note to 51. 24.

[4] Lit.: they made the country into one where the King's taxes were cut off.

with him to the capital and seized the royal power together
with the (royal) treasure[1].

Now there was also a sister's son of King Silāmegha called 90
Dappula, an ādipāda who had at his disposal a large army
and considerable means. He sojourning in Kālavāpi, collected 91
his army and advanced to the neighbourhood of Saṅgagāma
to begin the war[2]. At the tidings of these events the Senā- 92
pati marched in haste thither, at the head of his army, taking
the Queen with him. A terrible battle took place there be- 93
tween the two. When the Ādipāda saw his army falling back
he took flight and escaped with his army into the mountains[3]. 94
After the Senāpati had put him to flight there, he lived
happily.

When the district chiefs of Uttaradesa heard that the ca- 95
pital was unoccupied they all came together and took the
town. But the Senāpati, a hero of indomitable courage, chased 96
them away again, entered the town himself and administered
the government according to the rules of statecraft[4]. For the 97
bhikkhu community, for the laity, for fishes, game and birds,
for his kinsfolk and for the troops he did everything that was
meet for them. Later on Dappula who was in Malaya, brought 98
together a reserve army. He summoned his two sister's sons
from Rohaṇa and taking all the inhabitants of the province 99
with him, he reached the town with a great army at night
time and broke over it like the ocean. The troops encom- 100

[1] See 39. 28; 41. 20.

[2] As *bhāgineyya* of Aggabodhi VI. he held that he was the legal heir before Aggabodhi's son Mahinda. The same view is taken by Dappula's brothers (see v. 116) who believe themselves entitled to the crown after him.

[3] According to the Col. Ed. one should translate: "he climbed with his train the Acchasela mountain". This name does not occur in any of the MSS. with which I am acquainted. The majority have simply *palāyitvānamāruhittha savāhano.* Two MSS. insert *saseno* before *savāhano,* evidently a gloss to this word. The object of *āruhittha* is everywhere missing. I have supplied it according to the sense. Perhaps one should read *Malayaṃ so savāhano.*

[4] See note to 48. 80.

passed the town with clangour on all sides. With the neighing
101 of the steeds, the trumpeting of the elephants, the rattle of
the drums with their rhythmic sound[1] and the battle cries of
the warriors the firmament was at that time near to bursting.
102 When the Senāpati saw the great army he was light-hearted
and informed his own troops of the matter with the words:
103 "Three king's sons have shut in our town with a great force:
104 what must ye then do?" Thus addressed, these warlike heroes
answered: "On a day when they have not served their king
105 there is for his servants no life[2]. If at such a time as this
we were from love of life to flinch, for what then had our
master maintained us for so long a time for our well-being?"
106 At these words Mahinda full of confidence, placed his army
in readiness at night and at daybreak mounted his tried ele-
107 phant, broke through a gate like a downrushing thunderbolt,
and began with his thousand warriors the irresistible combat.
108 After scattering the troops of the Ādipāda in all directions,
he gathered (his people) together at one spot and proclaimed
109 a truce[3]. The Ādipāda Dappula already vanquished at early
morning, fled with those who had escaped the slaughter to

[1] *Tālāvacarasaddānaṃ* is adjective attribute to *kāhalānaṃ*.

[2] The manuscript reading *devāsevādine* (= *deva-asevā-dine*) alone gives the right sense: only when their whole life is absorbed in service of their king do his servants wholly fulfil their duty. W.'s translation "from the day that your servants entered your service, their lives have they given unto you" is impossible. It is made so by the loc. *dine* and by the negation in *sevakānaṃ na jīvitaṃ* which was simply not taken into account. In any case one would have to translate "their life belongs to his servants no longer". Even then the difficulty with *dine* remains, it cannot possibly mean "from the day".

[3] P. *niyattiṃ sampavedayi.* The word *niyatti* is otherwise unknown. It is derived from the root *yat* with *ni*, which probably means "to unyoke (the horses), to rest". Also in the single passage in the Rigveda (I. 186. 11), where the verb occurs, it seems to me to have this meaning. I should be inclined to translate *ní yā devéṣu yátate vasūyúr* by "that (namely our supplication) which prays for good enters into (the abode of) the Gods". GELDNER, Rigveda I. 241: "that . . . . . aspires to the Gods". The idea is that Mahinda to prevent further bloodshed, forbids the pursuit of the enemy.

Rohaṇa. But the two princes who had some time before come 110
from Rohaṇa, Mahinda captured alive and took with him to
the capital. The hero who had thus gained the victory, now 111
that the Island was at peace, sent his army forth to subdue
(the East Province) Pācīnadesa. They marched into the pro- 112
vince and also into (the North Province) Uttaradesa, subdued
them in a short time and brought over a large force to their
side. The King[1] however, made the Great Queen his consort, 113
as he thought she could neither be set free nor slain[2]. In 114
consequence of their intercourse she became with child and
brought forth a splendid son who bore[3] on him the signs of
(former) merit. After that she was very dear to the King 115
who granted his son the dignity of uparāja with the (cor-
responding) revenues.

When the two Ādipādas who were in Pācīnadesa heard 116
of this they said to each other: that is our undoing. They
raised an army from both their provinces and large sums of 117
money, then summoned their brother (Dappula) from Rohaṇa,
made with him a treaty and took up a position with large 118
forces on the bank of the (Mahāvāluka-)Gaṅgā. When the King
heard all that he brought the district chiefs here and there 119
(by kindly speech) over to his side, imprisoned the obdurate
and also had a few executed. He appointed a guard in the
town, decreed exactly what was to be done and with a large 120
army and taking the Mahesī with him, he occupied an armed

[1] It is not by chance that the royal title is here for the first time awarded to Mahinda. At the beginning of the campaign against Dappula (v. 102) he was still called Senāpati. Probably he only underwent the ceremony of consecration (*abhiseka*) after his marriage with the widow of his predecessor, as a queen must also take part therein.

[2] By her marriage with the King this woman who was inclined to intrigue (v. 87) is kept under his supervision and influence, without the necessity of force being used against her. That distrust of the Queen still existed is shown by v. 120.

[3] P. *puññalakkhaṇasaṃyutaṃ*. The marks on the boy established by the soothsayers point to a favourable *kamma*, to the boy having accumulated abundant merit in former existences, so that he is called to greatness in this new existence.

121 camp at the village of Mahummāra. When the three Ādipādas
had knowledge of his advance they began a great battle at
122 Koviḷāragāma. But the King with his strong army destroyed
their forces. Dappula fled, the two Ādipādas fell.

123 Here also again victorious, the Monarch returned to the
capital; he practised the royal duties and instituted a great
124 almsgiving. For the great Bodhi Tree, that prince of trees,
for the three great cetiyas and for the relics he, full of re-
125 verence, instituted a great offering. Dappula who had betaken
himself to Rohaṇa, arriving there, raised troops to fight anew
126 against the King. The King (wishing) to bring order into
the land for his children and his children's children assembled
127 in the Thūpārāma all the bhikkhus and other wise persons
who knew what is seemly and what is unseemly — he who
was versed in all the duties of a king, they who were learned
128 in statecraft. He informed them of the events, and after de-
creeing everywhere what was to be done throughout the Is-
129 land and in the capital, he with their consent set out with
a great army consisting of the four members[1], and provided
with all resources, and came within a short time to the Māra
130 mountains[2]. He laid waste the country and immediately there-
after ascended the mountains. When they saw that in Rohaṇa
131 they yielded themselves through fear. Hereupon the haughty[3]
one made a treaty with Dappula. He received from his hands
132 elephants, steeds and jewels, decreed the Gāḷhagaṅgā[4] as the

[1] The four *aṅgāni* of an army are the elephants, the chariot fighters, the riders and the infantry.

[2] A Maragala (probably = Māragallaka in 55. 26) is situated east of Madampe in the Atakalan Korale of the province of Ratnapura, Medapattu. If we can associate our Mārapabbata with this, Mahinda II must have pushed against Rohaṇa from the N. W. (Ratnapura—Pelmadulla—Madampe). The mountains he ascended would be the range to the South of Rakvana with the Bulutota Pass.

[3] P. *sadappaka* contains a pun on Dappula's name.

[4] The MSS. undoubtedly point to this reading. The name Gāḷhagaṅgā is however, otherwise unknown. One might take it for a name of the Mahaveliganga since *oragaṅga* "land on this side of the Gaṅgā" is always used of the territory on the left bank of this stream. In this

boundary of the rulers of Rohaṇa and kept the land on this side of the river for himself, making thereof royal property.

Thus had the powerful (prince) freed the Island from all 133
briers[1], as sole monarch he entered the capital and lived
therein happily. The mighty King founded the Dāmavihāra- 134
pariveṇa and the Sannīratittha(-vihāra) in Pulatthinagara. In 135
the Abhayagiri he erected the Mahālekha-pariveṇa. Then the
wealthy (prince) having built at a cost of three hundred thou-
sand (kahāpaṇas) the superb, many-storeyed Ratanapāsāda[2], 136
like a second Vejayanta[3], and having at a cost of sixty thou-
sand (kahāpaṇas) had made of pure gold an image of the 137
Master, furnished with a costly diadem of jewels, he held
with all pomp a magnificent dedicatory festival for the 138
consecration of the Pāsāda, and dedicated (to the Buddha)
thereby his whole kingdom[4]. He also had a splendid Bodhi- 139
satta[5] made of silver and placed the beautiful (statue) in the
Silāmegha[6] home for bhikkhunīs. In the Thūpārāma he made 140
a gold casing of the thūpa and for the sake of diversity he

treaty the Mahaveliganga would then be fixed for the first time as the boundary between Rohana and the territory immediately belonging to the king, being always held as such later on. The Col. Ed. reads *Gālhabhogaṃ*.

[1] See note to 42. 14.

[2] A. M. Hocart supposes the Ratanapāsāda to be the very considerable building known by tradition as the "Elephant Stables" whose ruins lie to the west, not far from the Abhayagiri Thūpa (Northern Thūpa), Memoirs ASC. I (1924), p. 1 ff. According to the Mahāvs. it was built by Kaniṭṭhatissa (223—241 A. D.) for the Thera Mahānāga who lived in the Bhūtārāma. It is, however, interesting that in the building which according to Hocart's discovery, lay below the later structure, there was an inscription belonging to Gajabāhu I. (171—193 A. D.) Mahinda II. evidently rebuilt the pāsāda of Kaniṭṭhatissa. A *Ruvan-Mahapahā* is mentioned in an inscription of Mahinda IV. Wickremasinghe, EZ. I. 215, 218, 226.

[3] Skr. *Vaijayanta*, name of Indra's palace.

[4] For this custom cf. 39. 31 (with note).

[5] Probably the Bodhisatta *Metteyya*, the only future Buddha whom the Southern Schools mention by name.

[6] The same convent for nuns is mentioned 49. 25 under the successor of Mahinda II.

141 had strips of silver introduced at regular intervals[1]. There
too he repaired the decayed pāsāda. Instituting a great festi-
142 val, the discerning (prince) had the Abhidhamma recited by
the Grand Thera dwelling in the Hemasāli(-vihāra) and
143 built a bathing tank there for his use. He restored many
decayed temples of the gods[2] here and there and had costly
144 images of the gods fashioned. He gave the brāhmaṇas de-
licious foods such as the King receives and gave them milk
145 with sugar to drink in golden goblets. To the lame he gave
bulls as well as the needful maintenance, and to the Damiḷas
146 he gave horses, as they would not take cattle. The poor who
were ashamed to beg he supported in secret, and there were
none on the Island who were not supported by him according
147 to their deserts. Pondering how food could be provided for
cattle, he gave them young corn full of milky juice from a
148 thousand fields. He also strengthened the weir[3] of the
Kālavāpi tank. Such like meritorious works of his were
boundless.

149 His son, the Yuvarāja, was then already dead, but there
was still another son, born to him at the time when he was
150 Senāpati[4]. The King fearing that the (other) princes might
kill him, thinking he was fitted for the royal dignity, let him
151 grow up without care, just as chance might determine. When

[1] P. *thūpassa 'kāsi sovaṇṇakañcukaṃ.* When a thūpa became dilapitated one used to build round it a new casing of brick. Such a casing was called *kañcuka.* Mahinda places a casing of gold and silver plates on the cetiya of the Thūpārāma. In 49. 81 we are told that king Dappula II. also covered the thūpaghara in the same vihāra with golden bricks, and in 50. 35 that the gold plates of the Thūpārāma cetiya were plundered by the Paṇḍu King.

[2] The Brahmanical religion, Hinduism, had always a place in Ceylon along with Buddhism and was recognised by the reigning princes.

[3] P. *vārisampāta.* Cf. 68. 35, 37.

[4] Hence in the time before his marriage with the Queen Dowager who bore him the son (see v. 115) who was appointed Uparāja and who had in the meantime died. Note that neither of the princes is named. Cf. below note to 49. 1.

the town was surrounded by foes, this prince came to his
father and begged from him a fighting elephant. The King 152
gave him his big elephant, terrible as the elephant of Māra[1],
and in addition a trained force versed in the use of arms.
He spake: now it is time, girt his sword, mounted the mighty 153
elephant, went forth from the town, scattered the whole al- 154
most invincible army and won the victory[2]. When the King
saw that he rejoiced and granted him the dignity of senāpati.
He (then) betook himself with his forces to (the North Pro- 155
vince) Uttaradesa[3] and put to flight the Ādipāda Dappula
together with his army. Therefore was Dappula filled with 156
a great hatred towards him. When he met him face to face
in the battle of Mahāummāra[4] he grew furious and hastily 157
spurred on his elephant to kill him. But the other rammed
with his own elephant (that of Dappula) and put him to flight.
When the King saw that he was highly pleased and as other- 158
wise none was there (suitable) to claim the royal dignity, he
conferred on him the office of his Uparāja.

After Mahinda had thus for twenty years[5] enjoyed the full 159
(dominion over the) Island he entered Heaven to enjoy the
fruits of his meritorious actions.

Thus all the delights of fortune won by all kinds of means 160
through bitter suffering disappear in a moment. Truly only
fools can find delight therein.

Here ends the forty-eighth chapter, called "The Six Kings", in the Mahāvaṃsa, compiled for the serene joy and emotion of the pious.

[1] See note to 41. 48.

[2] This episode took place in the sortie (described in v. 106 ff.) from Anurādhapura when it was besieged by Dappula.

[3] Refers to what is described in v. 112.

[4] See above v. 120.

[5] The same number in Pūjāv. and Rājāv.

CHAPTER XLIX

THE FIVE KINGS

1 After his father's death the Uparāja (Udaya) became king[1], apt to mete out punishment and favour to foes and friends.
2 As Mahesī the King had the clever Senā by name and little children (had he) who were very dear to the king and charming

[1] There is no doubt that the Uparāja meant here is the one mentioned in 48. 158, as the son of Mahinda by a former mariage (48. 149). The name of this prince is, however, nowhere directly mentioned in the Cūlavamsa. The four Sinhalese sources have Udā = Udaya as successor of Mahinda II, and the accuracy of their statement is indirectly confirmed by the Cūlavaṃsa: The successor of the unnamed king is his son Mahinda (III.). After him comes an Aggabodhi (VIII.) whose relationship with his predecessor is not mentioned. As however, there is mention (49. 44) of his grandfather in a way which clearly points to Mahinda II., he must have been the brother of Mahinda III and like him, the son of the unnamed king. Now it is said of this Aggabodhi VIII. in 49. 45, that he built a pariveṇa and called it *Udayaggabodhi* by joining his father's name with his own. Hence the son of Mahinda II. and father of Mahinda III. and Aggabodhi VIII. was called Udaya. In the Sinhalese translation of Sumangala and Batuwantudawa, also in Wijesinha's English translation and in all following publications, as far as I can see, this king gets the name of Dappula. I suppose on the ground of the following consideration: According to 49. 30, the unnamed King built a *Dappulapabbata* and in 50. 80, it is said that King Sena I. finished the *Dappulapabbata* begun in the time of King Dappula. Thus the unnamed king was called Dappula. This in no way upsets the absolutely conclusive argument for the name Udaya; the more so, since the two notices about the Dappulapabbata do not in the least agree. According to 49. 30, it was an *āvāsa* erected (not: begun) by the King himself in the Ambuyyāna-vihāra and granted to the bhikkhus. In 50. 80, it was a structure (vihāra?) commenced by one Mahādeva under King Dappula and finished by King Sena I. This

to look at[1]. The dignity of yuvarāja he bestowed on his 3
eldest son, the others he made ādipādas; of his daughters he
made queens[2]. Offices the King bestowed on these and those 4
persons according to their deserts, and his subjects he won
by the four heart-winning qualities. Now the King had for 5
some reason or other betaken himself to Maṇihīra[3], and while
he sojourned there he heard that the border-land was in re-
bellion. Thereupon he sent with all haste the Senāpati and 6
his son with the order to go thither and bring the district
under his sway. When these had betaken themselves there, 7
slanderers who were planning strife, by all kinds of idle talk
estranged the twain from the Ruler of men. Now the twain 8
began as foes (of the King) to get possession of the country
for themselves. On tidings of this the King betook himself
at once to Dūratissa[4]. He slew the twain, took possession 9
of everything they had, slaughtered all their accomplices, and
betook himself to Pulatthinagara[5].

Dappula can very well be Dappula II. (49. 65 ff.), the second predecessor of Sena I. It is a question therefore, whether the two Dappulapabbatas had anything at all to do with each other. If we assume that they had, then the building in 49. 30, is wrongly ascribed to Udaya I. or at least its name is due to a mistake. It was erected, as we are told by the more exact and therefore more trustworthy notice in 50. 80, under Dappula II. (W: D. III.). Sena finished the building and it probably only then got its name.

1 The Col. Ed. alters the reading *khuddā puttā* in which all MSS. agree, to *khuddaputtā*. W. translates: "(she) had a little son." I merely point out that in the very next verse several sons and daughters are mentioned.

2 W.'s translation "and gave his daughters away to the other governor of the Rohaṇa to be his queens" is quite wrong. We have to do with the granting of titles and honours (*rājinī* acc. pl.). Cf. below 50. 58 and 54. 11.

3 See 42. 34 with note.

4 A Dūratissa tank is mentioned 79. 32, among the tanks restored by Parakkamabāhu. The events described evidently take place in the North Province.

5 W.'s translation: "returned again to the city of Pulatthi" is inexact; for the text has *gami* not *paccāgami*. It also gives a wrong picture; for Udaya was not in Pulatthinagara before, but in Maṇihīra.

10 At that time there lived in the province of Rohaṇa a
nobleman Mahinda by name, a son of the Ādipāda Dāṭhāsiva
11 who administered the revenues of the country. He fell
out with his father and betook himself to the King. When
the King beheld him he was much pleased and showed him
12 grace according to his deserts. To strengthen the friendship
with him he gave him his daughter, by name Devā, and sent
13 troops to Rohaṇa. Mahinda set out, laid Rohaṇa waste with
the help of the royal army, drove out his father to Jambudīpa
and took possession of Rohaṇa.

14 In the Mahāvihāra Udaya[1] built a fine, solid house for
the distribution of food by allotment[2]. To the Kholakkhiya
image of the Lord of Sages (Buddha) he granted, for the
15 outlay on festivals, the village of Mahāmaga, having himself
offered (to the image) according to his capacity. For the prince
16 of trees, Vaḍḍhamāna[3], he restored the broken down temple
and granted for its guardianship the wealthy village of Koṭṭhā-
17 gāma. To the Nīlārāma (monastery) he gave the village of Kāḷussa
and to the bronze image (of the Buddha) he gave the village of
18 Ārāmassa. What was broken down he restored and he had
images fashioned as well as a great many pāsādas, cetiyas and
19 vihāras erected[4]. In Pulatthinagara[5] he built of his great
pity a large hall for the sick, and likewise in Paḍāvi, each
20 provided with a maintenance village, also halls for cripples[6]
and the blind in different places. Judgments which were just
21 he had entered in books and (these) kept in the royal palace
because of the danger of violation of justice. To the vihāra
called Nāgavaḍḍhana he made over several maintenance villages

[1] In the original the name is n o t mentioned, it simply says h e built.

[2] P. *salākagga*; for *salākā* cf. note to 48. 73.

[3] See note to 48. 5.

[4] I now prefer to add the accusatives *pāsāde* etc. in v. 18 a b to the preceding verse so that they are governed by *kārayi* in 17 d. The new sentence begins then with *Pulatthinagare*.

[5] Note how Pulatthinagara gains more and more in importance (cf. also 48. 134).

[6] P. *pīṭhasappin*, lit.: who moves with aid of a chair (*pīṭha*), i. e. a support that one pushes in front of one.

and without annulling ancient charters[1], and observing former
decrees, he maintained permanently the great almsgiving[2] in- 22
stituted by his father and all the other meritorious works
which he carried out without curtailment. The Mahesī, too, 23
of the great King performed many meritorious works. The
Queen built on the Cetiya mountain the Katthaka-cetiya[3], and 24
having built the Jayasenapabbata(-vihāra), she granted it to
the Damiḷa bhikkhu community[4]. She also made over to them
the village of Mahummāra. Then she built a home for bhikkhunīs 25
called Silāmegha, and gave it to the (former) home for
bhikkhunīs called Silāmegha[5]. Villages which had been sold 26
she redeemed, by giving the (necessary) money to the vihāra
and granting the villages to the vihāra in question. Having 27
had all the great trees on the Cetiya mountain clipped[6], the

[1] P. *lekhe*. We have to do here with deeds of gift, so-called *sannas*, engraven on copperplates, occasionally on silver or gold, or written on palm leaves such as are still preserved in considerable numbers. H. C. P. BELL, Report on the Kegalla-District, p. 91. This passage is probably the oldest confirmation of the custom.

[2] See above 48. 123-4.

[3] In contradiction to all the MSS. the Col. Ed. alters the name into *Kaṇṭakaṃ cetiyaṃ*, apparently merely for the sake of getting hold of a familiar Pāli word (*kaṇṭaka* "thorn").

[4] Very doubtful. The MSS. are all corrupt. They read *dāmissadā*, have thus a syllable too little. If my restoration *dāmiḷassadā* is right — it is at any rate nearer the MSS. than the *gāmikassadā* of the Col. Ed. — it would mean that also Damiḷas in Ceylon were Buddhists, but that the bhikkhus of this nationality formed a special group.

[5] We must assume that the old convent of this name mentioned 48. 139, had fallen into decay. The Queen built a new convent, gave it the same name and granted it to the bhikkhunīs who lived in the former one, as their home.

[6] That *chedayitvāna* here means "after he had felled" is not plausible to me. But the clipping of the branches to facilitate the putting on of the flags and to enable them to be seen is quite intelligible. This makes the trees into votive "rag-trees". For analogies s. R. ANDRÉE, Ethnographische Parallelen und Vergleiche (1878), p. 58 ff.; MANNHARDT, Wald- und Feldkulte[2] (1904), I. p. 219 ff. and passim; v. SCHRÖDER, Arische Religion (1916), II. p. 282.

King[1] gave brightly coloured flags and streamers as offerings.
28 In the domain of the Pucchārāma[2](-vihāra) he restored the
pāsāda and for it he made out of the poor maintenance vil-
29 lage of Ussānaviṭṭhi a rich one. The vihāra Giribhaṇḍa[3]
which had gone to rack and ruin he restored as it had been
formerly, and granted maintenance villages to the bhikkhus
30 dwelling there. In the Ambuyyāna(-vihāra) he built the dwel-
ling house Dappulapabbata[4] and made it over, provided with
31 the four necessaries to three hundred bhikkhus. Having built
the beautiful monastery Nīlagalla, he had a canal laid out
which made fruitful much country and granted it (to the
32 monastery). In the Arikāri-vihāra he renewed what was broken
down and built (there) a house for the distribution of food
by allotment, and a pāsāda which was formerly missing.
33 In Vāhadīpa[5] he built the Senaggabodhipabbata(-pāsāda) and
in the three fraternities he, the deeply learned, had the sa-
34 cred texts recited. To those among the bhikkhus who were
engaged in the hardest studies[6] he presented[7] bronze alms-
bowls and he left undone nothing of that which one calls a
35 meritorious work. To widowed women of good family he gave
ornaments and when they wanted food he handed them food

[1] It is uncertain whether the works enumerated in 27-30 are to be ascribed to the Queen or the King. In 26 we have *sā* as subject, but in 31 *so*. I prefer to assume the King as author, the services of the Queen being usually devoted to the bhikkhunīs.

[2] The Col. Ed. changes the name, against the MSS., into Pubbārāma. See note to 50. 69.

[3] Mhvs. 34. 81 speaks of a great festivity instituted by King Mahādāṭhikamahānāga (66-78 A. D.) on the Cetiya mountain (Mihintale), which received the name *Giribhaṇḍa-mahāpūjā*. This name is probably connected with that of the vihāra.

[4] See below 50. 80 and above note to 49. 1. [5] See note to 48. 65.

[6] P. *suganthike* from *gantha*, skr. *grantha*. Cf. *ganthika-bhikkhu*, Dhammapadaṭṭhakathā ed. H. C. Norman, I. 156[2]. See Rhys Davids and Stede, PTS. P. D. s. v. *ganthika*. W.'s translation "compelled the priests to accept his offering of alms-bowls" is impossible. For that it would have to be *bhikkhū* instead of the genitive *bhikkhūnaṃ* of the text.

[7] Lit.: he let them receive (*gaṇhāpesi*).

at night. To the cattle he gave young corn, to the crows 36
and other birds rice, and to the children grain with honey
and syrup. Thus the King with his attendants performed 37
meritorious works, and after enjoying the earth, he had to
leave it after five years[1].

Hereupon his son Mahinda by name became sovereign 38
of the Sīhalas, a nobleman, equipped with excellence of every
kind. Known all the earth round by the name of Dhammi- 39
kasilāmegha[2], he was a light of the true doctrine[3], a banner
of the doctrine[3], to whom the true doctrine[3] was the highest,
and he performed without fail every work that followed the 40
right[3] path and which had been done by former kings, but
he avoided wrong. To allow of repairs being made at all 41
times on the Ratanapāsāda[4] he granted it the Geṭṭhumba
canal[5]. What was ruined he rebuilt, and performed (other) 42
meritorious works. After reigning for four years[6] he went
to his death.

Aggabodhi then raised the umbrella of dominion in the 43
capital, preparing unremittingly welfare and happiness for all
creatures. He instituted a sacrificial festival for the relics, 44
worthy of all the virtues of the Master, and a great festival
for the image of the Sambuddha set up by his grandfather[7].
He, the Ruler of men, built the Udayaggabodhi-pariveṇa, 45

[1] Pūjāv. and Rājāv. the same.

[2] In Pūjāv. and Rājāv. the king is called Häligāravil Iskābō Mihindu, in Rājaratn. and Nik.-s. Sōmihindu.

[3] Three times here the ambiguous word *dhamma* occurs in the text; for "wrong" *adhamma*. The compiler paraphrases the adjunct *dhammika* in Mahinda's biruda.

[4] See note to 48. 135.

[5] Whose waters could only be employed for tillage by payment of a tax, otherwise accruing to the king, to the inmates of the Ratanapāsāda.

[6] Pūjāv. the same; Rājāv. 7 years.

[7] Without doubt what is meant here is the golden statue mentioned 48. 137 as having been made by Mahinda II. This proves that Aggabodhi VIII., whose relationship to his predecessor is not mentioned in any of our sources, was a grandson of Mahinda II., a son of Udaya I. and brother of his predecessor Mahinda III.

46 choosing for it his father's name[1] and his own. Further, he
built the pariveṇa[2] called Bhūta, furnished with (the needful)
revenues and granted it to his own teacher and three hundred
47 bhikkhus. To the Rājasāla(-vihāra)[3] he granted the village
of Cūlavāpiyagāma and two villages to the Kālūla and Malla-
48 vāta[4] vihāras. On the Uposatha days he forbade the bringing
in of fish, meat and intoxicating drinks into the centre of the
49 town. When he had done reverence to the bhikkhus or the
cetiyas, he used, when leaving, to clean his feet thoroughly,
50 that no sand might be lost. All actions leading to Heaven
and to delivrance, all those actions he performed with faith
in the three (sacred) objects[5].

51 The King found pleasure in the serving of his mother day
and night. He went to wait on her already early in the
52 morning, rubbed her head with oil, perfumed the parts moist
53 with sweat[6], cleaned her nails and bathed her carefully. He
clad her himself in a new garment, pleasant to the touch,
54 and the cast-off raiment he took and cleaned it himself. With
the water therefrom he sprinkled his own head together with
the diadem, and worshipped her perfectly with fragrant flo-
55 wers as a cetiya. After making obeisance before her three
times, and walking, with right side facing, round her and

[1] The name Udaya. See note to 49. 1. The vihāra Udā-Agbō is mentioned in an inscription of Mahinda IV. Wickremasinghe EZ. I. p. 216, 221, 227.

[2] A Bhūtārāma is mentioned already under Kaniṭṭhatissa (223-241 A. D.). Here we have probably to do with a new building in this monastery.

[3] According to my conjecture, *Rājasālāya* instead of *rājā sālāya*. The word *sālā* alone says too little.

[4] Mallavāta-vihāra, built according to 48. 70, by Aggabodhi VII.

[5] See note to 37. 214 and 41. 55.

[6] W.'s translation "cleanse her body" is too general. The verb *ubbaṭṭeti* is used of rubbing in with some kind of perfumed substance. To the passages cited by Rhys Davids and Stede, I may add Dīghanik. II. $324^{14, 16}$; Vinaya ed. Oldenberg III. 329^{9}; Thūpavaṃsa ed. Col. p. 39^{11}; Mahāv. Tīkā, ed. Col. p. 132^{9}. The word *jallikā* means "sweat drops" just as the more frequent *rajojalla* must be translated by "dirt and sweat". Cf. *sedajallikā* Sn. 198 (Rh. D. and St.).

giving her attendants raiment and the like to their heart's
content; he offered her delicious food with his own hand, 56
partook himself of what she left and strewed thereof on his
head. To her attendants he gave the best food such as was 57
meant for the king, and when he had put in order her
chamber, fragrant with sweet odours, he carefully prepared 58
there with his own hand her couch, washed her feet, rubbed
her gently with fragrant oil, sat by her rubbing her limbs
and sought to make her sleep[1]. Then with right side facing, 59
he walked round her bed, did reverence three times in the
right way, ordered slaves or servants as guard and without 60
turning his back on her, went out. At a spot where she
could no longer see him, he halted and three times again did
reverence. Then happy at his action, and ever thinking of 61
her, he went home[2]. As long as she lived he served her in
this way.

Once he addressed one of his slaves with the word "slave"; 62
to make up to him for it, he let him use[3] the same word
towards himself. The wise (prince) made his mother offer 63
his own person as a gift to the bhikkhu community, then
paid down a sum equal to his own value and was thus again
a free man. Thus holding meritorious works as the highest, 64
he did good to the Island and went after (a reign of) eleven
years[4] to the world of the gods.

[1] P. *katvā niddaṃ upecca taṃ*, a highly curious construction. *niddaṃ upecca* would mean "after she had fallen asleep". By the addition of *katvā taṃ* the causative meaning is given "after he had brought about that she fell asleep". See Cūlavs. ed., Introd. p. XV.

[2] In the original this whole section from v. 55 to 61 forms one sentence. The fin. verb *yāti* is in the pres. to express continued repetition. All the preceding verbs are gerunds.

[3] W.'s translation "it grieved him so that he himself sought to obtain his servant's forgiveness" is too vague and overlooks the point, namely, that he permits his servant to call him by the same contemptuous epithet which he himself had used to him.

[4] Pūjāv. and Rājāv. have the same. In Rājaratn. and Nik.-s. the king is called Mădī-Akbō.

65 His younger brother Dappula[1] now became king after
his death. He kept closely to the conduct of the earlier kings.
66 At that time the sons of the ruler of Rohaṇa, Mahinda by
name, driven out by their father, came to the King, their
67 maternal uncle[2]. He beholding them and hearing their story,
gave them a strong force and sent them away to fight with
68 their father, concerned for the welfare of his kinsmen. But
when the ruler of Rohaṇa, Mahinda, recognised the situation,
he began on his part to make war on them with strong forces.
69 The twain had to retreat and after appointing a commander
over the army, they returned to the King and abode there
70 (in Anurādhapura) serving him. Their father was content
therewith, but in combat with another kinsman he was slain
71 and this kinsman too lost his life. Hereupon the King gave
his sister's son Kittaggabodhi his daughter Devā to wife, gifted
72 with all virtues. He (Kittaggabodhi) appointed (his brother)
Dappula to the king's service and betook himself at the head
73 of an army division to Rohaṇa. He became sovereign of Ro-
haṇa and favoured by every kind of good fortune, took up
his abode there increasing in sons and daughters.
74 The King had the ruined temple of the Prince of Trees
newly and durably built and gilded[3]. At the festival of his
75 consecration he instituted a sacrificial feast which he so

[1] In accordance with the old Sinhalese law of inheritance three sons of Udaya I. reign one after the other. According to this law Dappula's legitimate successor would have been the son of his eldest brother Mahinda III. But cf. below 49. 84 and 50. 4.

[2] Their father Mahinda according to 49. 10—12, was married to Devā the daughter of Udaya I., a sister of Dappula II. The quarrels in Rohaṇa about the succession described there, of the details of which we are ignorant, thus continue. It was the policy of the Sinhalese kings to exploit these to strengthen their position in Rohaṇa. Note the similarity of the events, as described in 49. 10 ff. and in 49. 66 ff., especially the repetition of the name Devā.

[3] The construction of the sentence is not quite simple. W. translates it "the king rebuilt the old house of the Bodhi-tree, so that it may last, and ornamented it with works inlaid with gold".

arranged that it was fully worthy of his own royal dignity
and the perfection of the Master (Buddha). He rebuilt the ruined 76
pāsāda in the Hatthikucchi-vihāra, the Vāhadīpa monastery and
the Lāvarāvapabbata(-vihāra)[1]. For the vihāra called Jeta he 77
made a golden image of the Master and on its delivery to
the Bodhi temple[2] he held a sacrificial festival of unimaginable
splendour. Every year he instituted in the Island a gift of 78
raiment. He enlarged the Mahāpāli Hall, and eager for the
good of the refectory he dispensed as much (rice) as tallied 79
with the weight of his body[3]. Ruined buildings he restored,
he kept to the conduct of former kings without neglecting
anything. He had a discerning senāpati by name Vajira. This 80
(Vajira) built the Kacchavāla monastery for the Paṃsukūlins.
In the Thūpārāma the King covered the temple of the thūpa 81
with golden bricks in the right way and put in doors of gold[4].
After the Ruler of men had thus reigned sixteen years[5], he 82
went to that land whither all beings must go.

This King having gone to the world of the gods, Aggabodhi 83
(by name) had the drums of dominion beaten the selfsame day[6]. His father (Dappula) to safeguard the succession 84

[1] Very doubtful, as all our MSS. are corrupt. For the first two names mentioned here, cf. 48. 65 with the notes.

[2] We must assume that it was a figure seated in the attitude of meditation, and that it was placed at the foot of the Bodhi tree, just as the Buddha sitting under such a tree, received the highest enlightenment.

[3] I am inclined now to assume that the words *bhattaggaṃ avalokiya* in 78 belong to the following and not to the preceding.

[4] *Chādayi* is here probably wrong, as also *kārayi* in the Col. Ed. It will perhaps be best to retain the reading of the MSS. *pādayi* (*padeti* = skr. *pra-dā* treated after the analogy of the causative, like *kāreti*).

[5] So Pūjāv.; Rājāv.: 12 years. According to Rājāv. and Rājaratn. an incursion of the Damiḷas took place in this reign. They plundered Anurādhapura and carried away much valuable booty.

[6] The original has *tadā ahū*. This seems to give no sense, so in the edition (of the text) I have remarked at this passage: "we expect something like *tadatrajo*." I am inclined now to think that we have here an etymological puerility, and that for the sake of the metre, *tadahū* has been split up into *tadā ahū*.

for his sons, had not made[1] his brother's son, Mahinda by
85 name, ādipāda. As the latter could not bring himself to show
reverence to his younger kinsman, he fled in his confusion to
86 the other coast[2] . . . . When he (the King) heard of their
arrival he sent out a strong force gave them battle and seized
their heads[3].

87 In the monastic fraternities he ordered everything that
had to be done and throughout the Island he caused the pre-
88 vention of evil action. The bhikkhus in the smaller vihāras[4]
used to receive rice gruel as medicine in the Mahāvihāra.
89 When the King heard of it he was dipleased; he granted (the
small vihāras) the important village of Kaṇṭhapiṭṭhi, (the village
90 of) Yābālagāma, (the village of) Telagāma and a well-filled canal
and gave orders that the bhikkhus should receive their rice
gruel in (their own) vihāra. After that they all received the
91 gruel gratefully (in their vihāra). On the Island he had the
drums beaten and summoned the beggars, distributing to them
gold as much as they wanted, for three days.

92 Having performed these and other meritorious works, the
King went after three years[5] to behold the reward for his
faith in the three (sacred) objects, driving, as it were, in a
heavenly chariot to death.

[1] Against the law of succession. See above note to v. 65.

[2] Hence to southern India. The word refers to Mahinda's inner conflict. He sees no way of escape except by flight to the mainland.

[3] The *tesaṃ* at the beginning of the verse is surprising, since only one Mahinda was mentioned before. W. seeks to make the plural intelligible by supplementing (v. 85) "with all his brethren". But that is not in the text. Besides, according to 50. 4, it is the succeeding king, Sena I. who kills Mahinda. I think we must assume a gap in our text. The missing part (perhaps only a single verse) dealt with friends and adherents of Mahinda who fought at first for his rights and were defeated by Aggabodhi.

[4] What is meant are the smaller vihāras of Anurādhapura in contrast to the three great nikāyas.

[5] So Pūjāv. In Rājāv. and Rājaratn. Aggabodhi IX. is not named. His successor Sena is also omitted. Nik.-s. calls him Pāsulu-Akbō.

Thus all corporeal beings are impermanent. Even the all- 93
wise Buddhas are doomed to die. Hence a prudent man giving up (everything) that proceeds from the lust of being, will keep his thoughts fixed on nirvana[1].

Here ends the forty-ninth chapter, called The Five Kings, in the Mahāvaṃsa, compiled for the serene joy and emotion of the pious.

[1] P. *buddho vibhave bhaveyya.* Cf. skr. *budh* with acc. or gen. "to direct the mind to something". In P. the loc. is used instead of the gen.

CHAPTER L

THE ONE KING

1 Hereupon his younger brother Sena[1] raised the umbrella
(of dominion) in the town, abounding in riches, who looked
2 on all creatures as on a dear son. He adhered to the con-
duct of former kings in accordance with tradition, and he per-
3 formed also pious actions before unheard of. Towards bhikkhus,
bhikkhunīs, his kinsfolk and (the other) islanders, towards
fishes, four-footed beasts and the birds he fulfilled every duty.
4 He had Mahinda who had betaken himself to the opposite
shore[2], slain by agents. In such wise he cleared his path of
5 all who could dispute with him the royal dignity. He in-
stituted a great almsgiving for needy beggars, to bhikkhus
and brāhmaṇas (he dispensed) delicious food such as the king
6 receives. He had three younger brothers: Mahinda, Kassapa
7 and Udaya. Of these Mahinda was the Yuvarāja who, obedient
to him, served him in fitting manner. The Queen, Saṃghā
by name, was the queen-consort of the King.

8 Once when the King had betaken himself for pleasure to
a port on the sea, the Ādipāda Udaya who had remained be-
9 hind in the town, took to wife the daughter of the wife of
his maternal uncle by name Nālā who was under the King's
10 protection[3], and took her with him to Pulatthinagara. Without

[1] Sena I. is called *Matvaḷasen* in the Nik.-s.

[2] See above 49. 85-86 with the notes.

[3] P. *rakkhantīm* is to be understood as pres. part. of the passive *rakkhati* = skr. *rakṣyate*. The name Nālā is contained in that of the monastery Nālārāma which according to the inscription of Mahakalatteva (E. Müller AIC. nr. 110; p. 77, 112) the Grand Scribe Sena (cf. 52. 33) built in honour of his mother and named after her. This Nālā however, cannot well be as Wickremasinghe assumes (EZ. I. 154, n. 7), the daughter of Mahinda of Rohaṇa and of Devā; since Devā was not the *mātulānī*, but the *pitucchā* of Udaya.

being wroth with him the King made with him an inviolable treaty, sent the Mahādipāda (Mahinda) to him, quieted him
and brought him hither again[1]. Thus the princes were again 11
at one and lived sheltering the Order (of the Buddha) and the laity, in perfect peace.

Once later came the Paṇḍu King[2] with a great force from 12
Jambudīpa and began to take possession of the Island. When 13
the King heard thereof he sent a strong army against him, but owing to the discord among the high dignitaries, the prince, the Paṇḍu king, found opportunity to get a firm
footing; he laid waste the whole of Uttaradesa (the North 14
Province) and occupied an armed camp in Mahātālitagāma.
The many Damiḷas who dwelt (scattered) here and there, went 15
over to his side. Thereby he gained great power. The great 16
army which had gathered there (in Mahātālitagāma) began war with the King; the Paṇḍu King went into the field riding
on the back of his elephant. The Damiḷa army who beheld 17
the face of its leader, was full of vigour and determination,
and ready to lay down its life for him. But the Island army 18
as its leaders were absent, was without zeal; it scattered in
fight and fled in all directions. The great army of the Paṇḍu 19
King broke in at the same moment crushing in onset the
people, like the hosts of Māra. When the King heard of the 20
dispersion of his army, he took all his valuable property, left
the town and turned towards Malaya. Thereupon the Yuvarāja, 21
Mahinda, mounted his elephant; but when he saw in battle
the flight of his army, he thought: "Alone it is impossible 22
for me to kill all these; but death at the hands of these base
people is not beautiful; therefore is death by my own hand 23
to be preferred" and sitting on the back of his elephant, he
cut his throat. When his men saw that, many of them like- 24

[1] From the standpoint of the author: to Anurādhapura.

[2] The Paṇḍus or Pāṇḍiyas were a Dravidian people inhabiting the southernmost part of the Indian peninsula. Their capital was at first Korkai, later Madhurā. Cf. V. A. Smith, Early History of India, p. 335 ff. For the name of the Pāṇḍiya king who invaded Ceylon, cf. H. W. Codrington, HC., p. 52.

wise cut their throats and when the Damiḷa army beheld this
25 it rejoiced with exceeding joy. When the Ādipāda Kassapa
surveyed all that, just at it was, he mounted his favourite
26 horse, armed, weapon in hand, and came alone as far as the
27 Abhaya-vihāra[1]. Even as a supaṇṇa when it catches a snake
breaks through[2] her watery abode, so he broke through this
great army by storm. He forced the whole (army) to retreat
28 and remained himself unscathed[3]. His one horse looked as if
it were a line of steeds. When he saw none following him
29 he thought: "What would it avail if I alone (by my death)
were to fulfil the wish of the foe? meanwhile I shall, if I
30 remain in life, be able to fulfil my own wish. Therefore it
is right if I retreat". Therewith the great hero broke fear-
31 lessly through the great army and escaped to Koṇḍivāta. The
great army of the Paṇḍu King thereupon took the town.
32 They showed the Yuvarāja's head to the Paṇḍu King. When
he saw it he had (the corpse) burned and gave orders for the
observance at the pyre of all the ceremonies prescribed by
the Paṇḍus for their kings.

33 The Paṇḍu King took away all valuables in the treasure
house of the King and plundered what there was to plunder
34 in vihāra and town. In the Ratanapāsāda the golden image
of the Master (Buddha)[4] the two jewels which had been set

[1] Abhayagiri-vihāra. The pursuing enemy had thus already approached the northern gate of the town.

[2] The words *ogāhitvā vidārayi* belong to both objects *mahāsenaṃ* and *salilālayaṃ*. In W.'s translation the simile is not rightly grasped or at least blurred. For Kassapa's breaking through the hostile army the expression *o-gāh* "to dive" has been chosen with reference to the simile. The Supaṇṇas are mythical birds griffinlike. They are considered the deadly enemies of the Nāgas. In this passage these are described as *bhujaṅgā*, snake-like dwellers in the sea.

[3] Lit.: preserved (or protected) himself well. Note in *sugopayi* the rarer association of *su* with a finite verb, as shortly before, in v. 4 *suvisodhesi*.

[4] W. has not understood the passage aright, nor I myself in my edition (but cf. the corrections and additions in vol. II). It deals with the golden image set up by Mahinda II (48. 135 ff.) in the Ratanapāsāda which he had built in the Abhayagiri-vihāra. See also 51. 22 ff. We must therefore read *Pāsāde Ratane sabbasovaṇṇaṃ satthubimbakaṃ*.

as eyes in the stone (image of the) Prince of Sages, likewise 35
the gold plates on the cetiya[1] in the Thūpārāma, and the
golden images here and there in the vihāras — all these he 36
took and made the Island of Laṅkā deprived of her valuables
leaving the splendid town in a state as if it had been plundered
by yakkhas[2].

The King (Sena) had posted guards at various places along 37
the highway and in great alarm had taken up his abode at
the confluence of the two rivers[3]. In order to make a treaty 38
with the Sīhala ruler, the Paṇḍu King now sent dignitaries
thither. When the Sīhala sovereign saw them and heard 39
their message, he agreed to everything, bestowed favours on
the ambassadors to their hearts' content, presented them with 40
a couple of elephants as well as with all his jewels and sent
messengers to the Paṇḍu King, thinking of his own advantage.
When the Paṇḍu King saw all this he was highly pleased, 41
handed over the capital on the same day to the messengers,
evacuated the town and betook himself at once to the seaport. 42
There he embarked and returned to his country.

Thereupon the Ruler Silāmegha (Sena)[4] entered the town, 43
brought the Island again to its former condition and lived in
peace. His second brother[5], the nobleman Udaya by name, 44

[1] Cf. on this 48. 140, as well as 49. 81.

[2] By *yakkha* are meant the prehistoric inhabitants of Ceylon whom Vijaya found when he migrated to the island. They were believed to have magic powers, hence the word means superhuman, demoniacal beings generally. Ethnologists consider the Vāddās as remnants of these aborigines. Cf. the monograph of A. K. Coomaraswamy, Yakṣas, Smithsonian Miscellaneous Collections, vol. 80, Nr. 4. Washington 1928.

[3] The *mahāmagga* is probably the highway which led from Anurādhapura to Pulatthinagara and from here to Rohaṇa. *Malayābhimukho gato* above in v. 20 evidently gives merely the general direction in which Sena retreated. The "confluence of the two rivers" where he took up a waiting position must be the point of junction of the Mahaveliganga and Ambanganga where he commanded the two fords: Dastota (Sahassatittha) and Mahagantota (Kacchakatittha).

[4] Silāmegha is the surname of Sena. Cf. note to 44. 83.

[5] After Mahinda's death (v. 23) his brother Kassapa became heir to the throne. But as he was slain by the Paṇḍu King according to v. 46 the youngest brother of Sena I., Udaya by name, took up his position, but he died very soon so that the succession passed to Kassapa's eldest son.

he appointed mahādipāda and assigned him for his revenues
45 (the Southern Province) Dakkhiṇadesa. But he, after per-
forming meritorious works as was meet, was seized after a
short time with illness and fell into the jaws of death[1].

46 The Ādipāda Kassapa while he sojourned in Pulatthi-
nagara, was slain by the Paṇḍu King who had ordered it.
47 Now this Ādipāda Kassapa by name, had four able sons
48 endowed with the marks (of future) power. Of these the first
was the prince Sena by name, a hero, a man of great energy,
capable of bearing the burden of the royal dignity, an eminent
49 man. To him the King assigned in accordance with the custom
the dignity of mahādipāda and assigned him for his revenues
Dakkhiṇadesa together with the (needful) troops.

50 The ruler of Rohaṇa, Kittaggabodhi, had four sons and
51 three attractive, charming daughters. His eldest son, the
nobleman by name Mahinda, was murdered by his father's
sister who took the country with the royal treasure for her-
52 self. The three brothers enraged at the murder of their
brother[2] took their three sisters and betook themselves to the
53 King (Sena). When the King who greatly loved them, in
deepest pity[3] beheld them, he brought them all up full of
love in the best way possible as if they were royal princes[4].
54 Then the Ruler of men sent the eldest of them, Kassapa by
55 name, with forces: "Take possession of thy country, go!". He

[1] According to the inscription mentioned above (note to 50. 9) the marriage of Udaya with Nālā produced a son. He is there called Mahalā-Sen. That is the Sena of 52. 33, who under his cousin Kassapa IV., evidently at an advanced age, enjoyed the dignity of Mahālekhaka. But as according to v. 6, Kassapa was older than Udaya, his sons succeeded before those of Udaya.

[2] The MSS. point to the reading *bhātughātake*. But since the word refers to a female, S. and B. in conjunction with one MS. read *-ghātane*. The MS. S 6 originally had this reading, but it is corrected to *-ghātake*.

[3] P. *dayāmukho*. At the end of a compound *mukha* is used in the sense of *padhāna*.

[4] Not as W. has it "as if they were the offspring of the gods." The children of the house of Rohaṇa are treated as if they belonged to the family of the reigning king (*deva*).

set forth, slew her, brought the whole of Rohaṇa into his
power and took up his abode there without mishap. Then 56
he fetched his two brothers Sena and Udaya, shared with
them the country and dwelt with them. But King Sena 57
brought up the maidens in a most excellent way and when
the three princesses were grown up, gifted and beautiful as
divine nymphs, he gave the one called Saṃghā to whom he 58
assigned the rank of queen[1], to the Uparāja Sena to wife, with
large revenues worthy[2] of the royal dignity. The younger 59
brother of the Uparāja, Mahinda by name, was endowed with
all virtues, practised in all sciences. To him the King gave 60
the two princesses, called Tissā and Kitti, with revenues which
he deemed fitting. Thus the King showed favour to his kindred 61
according to (their) deserts. By favours such as almsgiving
and the like he won the people for himself. Endowed with 62
the ten qualities of kings[3], he enjoyed (while) performing
meritorious works, the earth. For the Paṃsukūlika bhikkhus[4] 63
he built a monastery on the Ariṭṭha mountain[5], erected as if
by magic, and endowed it with large revenues. He granted 64
it also an equipment without flaw, worthy of a king, many
helpers of the monastery and slaves as work people. In the 65
Jetavana-vihāra the Sovereign whose aspiration was directed to
the Buddha step, erected[6] a pāsāda of several storeys. After 66

[1] It is possible to refer *ṭhapetvā rājiniṭhāne* to all three princesses. In 49. 3, we already had a case of the king granting the title of *rājinī* to princesses in the same way as that of *ādipāda* to princes. Cf. further 54. 11, as also 60. 84.

[2] The alteration of *sarikkhakaṃ* which all the MSS. have, into *parikkhakaṃ* is unnecessary. The skr. *sadṛśa* can also mean "suited to, worthy of". The context demands an adjectival attribute to *mahābhogaṃ*.

[3] See note to 37. 107.

[4] Cf. above note to 47. 66.

[5] The Ritigala (see 44. 86 with note) is extremely rich in ruins. Cf. ASC. 1893 (= XXXVIII, 1904, p. 8 ff.). Then Plans and Plates for Annual Report 1893 (Colombo 1914). A. M. Hocart identifies the monastery built by Sena with the ruins of Banda Pokuna. See Memoirs ASC. I. 44.

[6] A pun in the original on *bhūmi* in its three meanings of earth, platform or step and storey. Note the Mahāyānistic idea of striving after the attainment of future Buddhahood. It occurs here for the first time in the Mahāvamsa.

bringing thither[1] a wholly golden image of the Victor (Buddha)
that he had had made and having fixed large revenues for the
67 pāsāda, he let bhikkhus take up their abode there. In the same
vihāra he had the splendid pāsāda in the Mahāpariveṇa re-
68 built, which had been destroyed by fire. In the Abhayuttara-
vihāra he built the Vīraṅkurārāma[2] and granted it to the
69 bhikkhus of the Mahāsaṃgha[3] and of the Thera School. The
Pubbārāma[4] also furnished with the four necessaries, he built
70 together with his royal consort Saṃghā. Likewise together
with her the discerning Monarch built in the Mahāvihāra, the
71 dwelling-house Saṃghasena[5] with large revenues. Having had
made of pure gold a reliquary for the hair relic[6] he instituted
a great sacrificial festival. The sublime (prince) dedicated to
72 it the kingly dignity. To the Cetiya mountain he assigned
the productive Kāṇavāpi tank, and to the bhikkhus dwelling
73 on the Island he had the three garments[7] distributed. In Pu-
latthinagara he built at the Thusavāpi[8] tank the Senaggabodhi
74 shrine, endowed with villages and monastery helpers, and here

[1] Thus I understand *vaḍḍhetvā*. Cf. for the meaning Cūlavs. ed. II, Index of Words, s. v. *vaḍḍheti*.

[2] Is mentioned in a Vessagiri inscription of King Dappula IV. (V.) Wickremasinghe, EZ. I. 23 ff.

[3] For the Mahāsaṃghikā who branched off from the Theravādins (Mhvs. 5. 4-5), at the first Council, s. M. Walleser, Die Sekten des alten Buddhismus, p. 24 ff.

[4] If above in 49. 28, one reads with the Col. Ed. Pubbārāma instead of Pucchārāma, which however, is contrary to the MSS., then in our passage it is only a question of rebuilding the monastery. Cf. EZ. I. 183.

[5] This is probably the *Saṅgsen-aram* mentioned in the inscription of Kassapa V. which was restored by this king together with the Maricavaṭṭi-thūpa. Wickremasinghe, EZ. I. 41 ff.

[6] The relic was brought to Ceylon by Silākāla. See Mhvs. 39. 49 ff.

[7] See note to 41. 29.

[8] W. follows the reading *vāpiyo* of the Col. Ed. and translates accordingly: "with the help of the great tank Thusavāpi he built several smaller tanks . . . and he also built" etc. In this case however, a *ca* in the second line of the verse would be indispensable.

beside this building[1], he built a large eating-hall where good
food was distributed, as well as for all (the bhikkhus) an
eating-hall in the Mahānettapabbata(-vihāra). He also had a 75
hall for the sick built in the west of the town and for the
destitute he made an offering of rice soup with the solid food
(belonging thereto). For the Paṃsukūlika-bhikkhus the sublime 76
(prince) built a separate kitchen and dutifully gave them per-
manent support. When he was (still) Mahādipāda he built 77
in the Kappūra-pariveṇa and in the Uttarāḷha(-pariveṇa)[2]
single cells which bore his name. Three times the wealthy 78
prince dispensed alms equal in weight to his body and yet
other meritorious works of divers kinds were performed by
the King. His royal consort, Saṃghā by name, had built 79
in the Uttara-vihāra[3] a dwelling-house called Mahindasena
and let bhikkhus take up their abode there. The charming 80
Dappulapabbata-vihāra[4] was begun in the time of the wise
King Dappula by Mahādeva, and the Kassaparājaka(-vihāra) 81
by the young prince called Kassapa — both these unfinished
(buildings) the same King (Sena) completed[5]. His Senāpati 82
Bhadda built the pariveṇa, called Bhaddasenāpati, endowed
with slaves and revenues. The dignitary Uttara built in the 83
Abhayuttara-vihāra the dwelling house, called Uttarasena,
excellently provided[6] with the (four) necessaries. In the same 84
place Vajira (by name) built the dwelling house Vajirasenaka,
and Rakkhasa (by name) built the dwelling-house, called
Rakkhasa.

[1] I supplement *tasmiṃ yeva* not with *nagare*, as does W., but with *āvāse* from 73 c to get the antithesis to *sabbesaṃ* in 74 c. The first Mahāpāli hall belonged specially to the Senaggabodhi house, the second was for general use.

[2] Of the first we know from 45. 29 that it belonged to the Abhayagiri-vihāra; the second pariveṇa is mentioned again 51. 75.

[3] I. e. Abhayuttara-vihāra = Abhayagiri-vihāra.

[4] Cf. with the verse the note to 49. 1.

[5] By Dārukassapa is probably meant the younger brother of the king whose death is announced in v. 46. W. takes it for the name of a minister. For Kassaparājaka s. note to 52. 45.

[6] Pun on the word *uttara*. occurring 4 times in the verse.

85 Thereupon after twenty years[1] the King who had ever fixed his gaze on the highest, while sojourning in Pulatthinagara, pondering over the misdeeds of the Paṇḍu King,
86 and in sense making way[2] for the hero Sena, had to leave the Island and depart as a lamp (goes out) which the storm has quenched.
87 Riches are fleeting together with life, how much more so are even kindred and friends. Behold the King who forsaken fell into the terrible jaws of death.

Here ends the fiftieth chapter, called ‹The One King›, in the Mahāvaṃsa, compiled for the serene joy and emotion of the pious.

[1] So also Pūjāv.

[2] P. *dadanto viya Senassa sūrassāvasaraṃ.* He leaves to his successor the possibility and the opportunity to take vengeance on the Paṇḍus.

CHAPTER LI

THE HISTORY OF THE TWO KINGS

After Sena had thus died the Mahādipāda Sena by name 1
performed all that there was to do[1] for him in pious manner,
then with army and train he entered the town and was king over 2
the earth's circle. Showing conduct like that of the kings of
the first age of the world, pious, wealthy, heroic, generous, 3
impartial, succouring the needy, equipped with large revenues,
with army and train, he represented in his spotless fame and 4
his splendid ability, as it were, a union of the sun and the
moon: richly gifted with unblemished qualities, practising every 5
kind of virtue, devoid of all sin, weary of the cycle of births,
his gaze fixed on the highest. Saṃghā who was his consort, 6
he consecrated Mahesī and gave her a dowry according to the
custom. His younger brother, the able Mahinda by name, he 7
made uparāja, assigning him (the Southern Province) Dakkhiṇa-
desa. As however, he had committed an offence in the wo- 8
men's apartments, he disappeared on being discovered by the
King, and betook himself with wife and child unrecognised
to Malaya.

At that time time the King's consort Saṃghā bore him a 9
son who embodied[2], as it were, in himself the princely form

[1] Namely the prescribed funeral ceremonies. Sena II. is called in Pūjāv., Rājāv., Rājaratn. and Nik.-s. Mugayin-Sen. In Pūjāv. he is erroneously called brother (*mal*) of his predecessor.

[2] For Panāda or Mahāpanāda see note to 37. 62. It cannot be a question here of son of Panāda, as such does not otherwise occur, but of Panāda himself when he was prince. We must thus read *kumāra-rūpaṃ* and this belongs to *Panādassa* as well as to *attano*. For Mahāpanāda as prince see Jātaka IV, p. 323 ff. Suruci-Jātaka.

10 of Panāda. When the King beheld the newly-born he was
overjoyed, as Suddhodana over Siddhattha born in the Lumbinī
11 garden, (thinking): my son endowed with the qualities of
power and virtue, is worthy of the royal dignity not alone
12 in this single island but in all Jambudīpa, and already on the
day of name-giving he consecrated him uparāja[1] in the most
solemn manner and granted him (the Southern Province)
13 Dakkhiṇadesa. The Yuvarāja (Mahinda) who was sojourning
in Malaya, understood by prudent conduct[2] to appease the
14 sovereign, and with his brother's consent, he came accompanied
by the bhikkhus dwelling in the three fraternities, sought
out the King, and made here at once an inviolable treaty
with him.

15 The consort of the Yuvarāja[3], Tissā by name, the Queen,
16 bore a daughter, named Saṃghā, and his other consort Kitti
17 bore likewise four sons and a daughter. Then the King
thought: under these circumstances[4] my younger brother will
18 be reliable for me, and he took careful counsel with his
ministers and prudently married the beautiful daughter of the
19 Yuvarāja, Saṃghā by name, to his own son Kassapa. Dakkhiṇa-
desa (the South Province) he granted in like manner to his
younger brother, but to the Prince (Kassapa) he made over
20 a special share of his own revenues and assigned him all the

[1] The son of Sena II. was Kassapa, later King Kassapa V. In an inscription of Anurādhapura he expressly says of himself: *dunū säṇähi me yuva-raj bisev-siri pämäṇā* "who at the same time that he was born (P. *janita*), received the consecration as yuvarāja". Wickremasinghe, EZ. I. 42 ff. As to the difference between the Cūlavs. and the inscription regarding the title *uparāja* and *yuvarāja* see note to v. 15.

[2] P. *upāyena*. W.: cunningly.

[3] As the reconciliation between Sena and Mahinda has taken place the latter regains his rights as heir apparent, Dakkhiṇadesa (v. 19) being assigned him for the same reason. The more formal dignity of uparāja which is generally associated with that of yuvarāja, remained apparently with the son of King Sena.

[4] P. *evaṃ sati*: if he (the king) so acts as he intends, and as he acts subsequently, after holding counsel with his ministers: by kinship through marriage.

extraordinary revenues in the kingdom[1]. But the administration of the whole island he looked after (himself), concerned
for the welfare of the Island. In consequence of the living 21
together of the twain (Kassapa and Saṃghā) who performed meritorious works, sons and daughters were born, endowed with the qualities of power and virtue.

Once when the Ruler with all pomp was holding high 22
festival for the Tooth Relic, he ascended the splendid Ratana-
pāsāda and when he beheld the pedestal of the golden Buddha 23
empty whereon formerly the image stood[2], he asked why that
was so. Thereupon his councillors replied: "Knowest thou 24
not O Ruler! that in the time of the great King thy
uncle[3], O Sovereign! the Paṇḍu king came hither, ravaged this 25
Island and departed with whatever belonged to the treasures
of the Island?" When the King heard that, he was ashamed, 26
as if he himself had suffered the defeat, and gave orders the selfsame day to his councillors to collect troops[4].

[1] According to the reading of the Col. Ed. *rajjaṃ pi sabbaṃ tass' eva paribhogāya dāpayi* one would have to translate: "also he assigned him the whole kingdom for the drawing of his income". *Rajja* might mean that part of the Island that was later called *Rājaraṭṭha* and still later *Patiṭṭhāraṭṭha*, but that would have been monstrous, since Sena would thereby have deprived himself of all rights and of nearly all his revenues. It would be difficult too to see how what is said in 19 c d could be distinguished from what is contained in v. 20 a b. The point here lies I believe, in the little word *pari* in *paribhoga*. It implies the idea of "more" of "acquisition" "addition to something" (Cf. BR., Wtb. s. v. *pari* 2 a ε), thus *paribhoga* stands in contrast to the simple *bhoga* of the preceding line.

[2] Without doubt the passage must be so translated, although the construction is not without difficulty. Cf. 50. 34 with the note.

[3] The uncle of Sena II., his predecessor Sena I. is here described as "great father" (*mahāpitā*). The elder brothers of the father are thus described, the younger brothers being called "little father" (*cūlapitā*). See note to 63. 51.

[4] The successful war of Sena II. against the Paṇḍus is mentioned in several inscriptions. The King is called *Siri Sangbo* (so in the inscr. of Bilibeva, of Etaviragolleva and Elleveva, WICKREMASINGHE, EZ. II. 39, 44 ff.; BELL, ASC., VII th Progress Rep. = XIII. 1896, p. 45). The four Sinhalese sources also relate the victory over the Paṇḍus and the regaining of the drum of victory and the jewelled goblet which they had captured.

27 Now at that time there arrived a son of the Paṇḍu King
who ill-treated by the king, had made the resolve to gain
28 the kingship for himself. When the King (Sena) saw him he
rejoiced greatly, treated him as was meet[1], betook himself
then to the seaport Mahātittha[2] and while he sojourned there,
29 collected a great force as well as all the appliances of war
30 completely[3], like to a war-equipped army of the gods. Then
the glorious (Prince) commanded his Senāpati together with
the son of the Paṇḍu King thus: "Arise, slay the Paṇḍu King,
31 bring hither all the jewels formerly carried away from here,
transfer to him the royal dignity and come hither again
32 at once". The Senāpati declared himself ready to do so, bade
farewell to the Ruler, took the army and set sail on the
33 spot. He came then to the opposite coast with his whole
army and train and laying waste the neighbouring country,
34 surrounded the town of Madhurā. He blockaded the gates,
cut off all traffic and set fire to towers, bastions and gates[4].
35 When thus the Sīhala army had penetrated his town, pillaging
36 the whole (town) and slaughtering the garrison, then the
Paṇḍu King at the news, collected his army, came on in haste
37 and opened fight. But as his troops were not complete the
Ruler who riding on the back of an elephant was himself
38 wounded by a spear, left the town to its fate, took flight and
lost his life at the place whither he had betaken himself. His
consort who had come with him also found (her) death.
39 Thereupon the Sīhala army which had fearlessly entered the

[1] I. e. he fulfilled all the duties due to a guest of royal blood.

[2] Now Mantai (Mantota) in the Mannar District.

[3] P. *anūnaṃ* is adverb.

[4] S. *gopuraṭṭālakoṭṭhake*. According to the description of the plan of an Indian fortress given in Kauṭalya's Arthaśāstra, 2. 3. 21, *gopura* means a bastion-like structure above the gates, while *aṭṭāla* is a tower built on the wall. Cf. *aṭṭālauddāmaparikhādīni* DhCo. III. 488[16] and *pākāraparikhaaṭṭālakādīni* JāCo. VI. 341[31], with which is meant the whole fortification of a town; also *pākāro gopuraṭṭālako* JāCo. VI. 433[1]. *Dvāraṭṭāla* also occurs in P. (Dīpavs. 13. 21; 22. 10 and 19); JāCo. VI. 390[2] distinguishes this last from *antaraṭṭālaka*. Thus *dvāraṭṭāla* is almost synonymous with *gopura*.

town, plundered it completely, as the gods the town of the
asuras[1]. The Senāpati thereupon inspected the treasures in 40
the royal palace; and all the valuables which had been carried
away from our island, as well as that found in the town and 41
in the country, he took for himself and carried on the administra-
tion which he had seized. Hereupon he consecrated the son of 42
the Paṇḍu King and transferred the country to him with cele-
bration of the (customary) festivities. He took elephants and 43
horses and men also, as he pleased, and stayed here and there
at his pleasure, from no side threatened. Then he betook 44
himself to the sea-coast, sojourned there so long as he chose,
embarked with unruffled calm, as if for amusement, came to 45
Mahātittha, greeted the Ruler respectfully, gave a report and
showed him the treasures he had brought along. "Good", 46
said the King, showed him favour and entered the capital
with his joyful army. He held a victory banquet and cele- 47
brated a festival of victory and instituted a great offering for
beggars according to their hearts' desire. He restored all 48
valuable property in the Island as it was heretofore, without
partiality, and the golden images he set up in the places
where they belonged. The empty pedestal (of the statue) of 49
the Master in the Ratanapāsāda he filled again[2] and he made
the country secure by setting up guards against every danger.
From that time onward he made the Island hard to subdue 50
by the foe and made it increase in wealth like the land of
the Uttarakurus[3]. Living beings on the Island who in the 51
time of the former king had been in distress, felt themselves
delivered in that they came to peace as from heat into the
shade of clouds.

1 The Indian epics speak of three towns of the asuras. They are built by the demon Maya of gold, silver and stone, in Heaven, in the firmament and on the earth. Śiva destroys them with fire and is therefore named *tripuraghna, tripuradahana, tripurahan* etc. See BR. s. v. *tripura*; Hopkins, Epic Mythology, p. 50.

2 By setting up the recaptured image.

3 A mythical people of sages and seers who live beyond the Himālaya. Their country is often held to be the land of bliss. Hopkins, Epic Mythology, p. 186.

52 In the twentieth year of his reign, in the Abhayuttara-
vihāra the Paṃsukūlika bhikkhus separated and formed special
53 groups[1]. The Yuvarāja Mahinda had built for the Prince of
54 trees of the Master a beautiful, wonderful, graceful temple. The
carpenters who were building the Bodhi house[2], noticed that
a branch of the sacred Bodhi Tree by striking on a beam,
55 threatened to break[3]. They considered what should be done,
and informed the Yuvarāja (of the matter). He came hither,
reverenced (the tree) with a great sacrificial offering (and said):
56 "If the Master is born for the salvation of all living beings,
as one that accepts the priceless merit which lies in the buil-
57 ding of the temple[4], then let the branch bend upwards so
that it is possible to build the temple." Having thus favorably
58 influenced it and done it reverence he went home. Then the
branch on the Prince of trees during the night bent upwards
59 and all the workmen made it known to their master. The
Yuvarāja was highly delighted, told his brother, the King,
and reverenced (the tree) with a great sacrificial offering for
60 which he spent much money. Having built the pariveṇa called
Mahindasena he made it over to the community together with

[1] See note to 47. 66. Here we must keep strictly to the MSS. reading *gaṇāhesuṃ* (for which *ganāhesuṃ* in some MSS. is merely a frequently recurring inaccurate spelling). The alteration into *gatāhesuṃ* of the Col. Ed. is poor. *Gaṇa* means a group of persons closely assotiated for the pursuit of common aims, a corporation, here an independent branch of bhikkhus, a sect. Wilson, Dict. in Skr. and Engl., gives for *gaṇa* etc. also the meaning "a sect in philosophy or religion". Cf. also *gaṇassa satthā* Saṃyutta I. 66[24, 31].

[2] See note to 38. 43.

[3] For *bhindantaṃ* cf. Cūlavs. ed. I. p. XV.

[4] Here we have a *saccakiriyā* (Mhvs. trsl. p. 125, note 3) of which the formula is: as certainly as this or that is the case, so certainly will this or that occur. W. changes the subject between 1 and 2. In line 2 he takes "I" as subject: "and if by the building of this house... I shall gain merit." That is impossible. In such a case *ahaṃ* would not be absent. The idea is rather this: The building of the temple is an offering, a *pūjā* which the Master — *satthā* remains the subject — shall graciously accept. In it there lies at the same time great merit, of course for the builder. Hence the work is described as *puñña*.

the (needful) revenues and accumulated still further merit. He 61
dispensed raiment, umbrellas, shoes which had come to him-
self[1], further rice for wayfaring (bhikkhus)[2] and baths with
cheer. After the mighty Prince had thus carried out all kinds 62
of works of inferior merit, he passed away in the thirty-third
year of the King's reign in accordance with his doing.

He being dead, the King set his younger brother Udaya 63
in his place and assigned him all that had belonged to the
other. With an offering equal to the weight of his body he 64
comforted the poor and the helpless and by a regulative act
he, at the same time, reformed the three fraternities. He had 65
a thousand jars of gold filled with pearls and on the top of
each he placed a costly jewel and presented (it) to a thousand 66
brāhmaṇas whom he had fed with milk rice in pure jewelled
goblets, as well as golden threads[3]. He clothed them also, 67
as a friend of meritorious works, with new garments at their
hearts' desire, and gladdened them with festive pomp. To the 68
bhikkhus dwelling on the Island he dispensed the three gar-
ments, and presented all the women with quite exquisite rai-
ment. Having restored the Lohapāsāda so that it resembled 69
the Vejayanta palace[4] he brought thither[5] an image of the
Buddha of closely jointed gold mosaic[6]. When he heard that 70
the pāsāda had been an Uposatha house for all the great
sages, he made it into a dwelling for the community with the
wish that it should never stand empty. He assigned it main- 71
tenance villages, placed guards and ordered that thirty-two
bhikkhus should dwell there. On the (Mahāvāluka-)gaṅgā he 72

1 Cf. with *sapaṭisambhattaṃ vatthaṃ* the phrase *savatthaṃ paṭisambhattaṃ* in 52. 14.

2 Vin. I. 292 has *āgantukabhatta* "rice food for newly arrived bhikhhus" and *gamikabhatta* beside *gilānabhatta*. These are the monks who are unable to live by *piṇḍapāta*, that is the almsfood collected on the regular mendicant round.

3 The idea here is of the cotton thread which, according to brahmanical rite, the three highest castes wear over the shoulder. In this case these were evidently interwoven with gold thread.

4 See note to 48. 136.

5 See note to 50. 66.

6 P. *suvaṇṇaghanakoṭṭimaṃ*; cf. DhCo. iv. 135[16]; Mhvs. 30. 97.

had the Maṇimekhala dam built and on the Maṇihīra tank he
73 built an outlet for the water. At Kaṭṭhantanagara he dammed
up the Kāṇavāpi[1] (tank) and on the Cetiya mountain he built
74 a hospital[2]. The Buddhagāma-vihāra, the Mahiyaṅgaṇa-vihāra[3]
and the Kūṭatissa-vihāra[4] he enriched with a maintenance
75 village. To the Maṇḍalagiri-vihāra[5] he made over villages
which belonged to himself and in the Uttarāḷha-pariveṇa[6] he
76 built a pāsāda. To the Mahāsena[7] Buddha he granted a vil-
lage and gave it watchmen, in the Sobbha-vihāra he built an
77 image house. He brought figures of Bodhisattas into the
Maṇimekhala-pāsāda and the ruined temple of the stone statue
78 of the Prince of Sages[8] he restored. The King united there-

[1] Here it is a case of restoring the dam, as the tank itself existed already at the time of Sena I. Cf. 50. 72.

[2] P. *vejjasālā*, lit. hall of physicians. The sick there found medical assistance.

[3] Now Alutnuvara on the right bank of the Mahaveliganga in the Bintenne district. Evidently an ancient place of worship, probably already in pre-Aryan times, if the tale related in Mhvs. 1. 14—43 rests on any kind of tradition. The thūpa in Alutnuvara is held to be the oldest in the Island. The Dutchman Spilberg saw it in the year 1602 in good condition, white as marble and crowned by a gilded pyramid (See Tennent, Ceylon II. 421). This was certainly not its original form. In Tennent's time it lay in a ruinous condition "a huge semicircular mound of brickwork three hundred and sixty feet in circumference, and still one hundred feet high, but so much decayed at the top, that its original outline is no longer ascertainable". Later the thūpa was apparently repaired in the usual way by a casing. When we visited Mahiyaṅgaṇa it lay again in ruins. The year before the southern half had been pulled down and the relic chamber also destroyed. What it contained in the way of votive gifts, as far as I saw these, belonged to more modern times.

[4] Mentioned as Kuṭutisa-rad-mahaveher in the pillar inscription of Mahinda IV. in Polonnaruva, Rāja-Māligāva, EZ. II. 50, the reading of the name is however, not quite certain.

[5] For this see note to 46. 29.

[6] See 50. 77.

[7] This means most likely the Buddha image in the Mahāsena-vihāra. For this cf. note to 48. 8.

[8] See note to 38. 61.

with the Bodhisatta with the temple[1]. Having dammed up[2] (anew) the irrigation trench of the Prince of trees he held
a great festival. He had the whole of the Ratanasutta[3] written 79
down upon a golden plate and held for it a great sacrificial
festival. He had the Abhidhamma recited. The image of 80
Ānanda[4] he brought into the town, walked round it facing to the right[5] and made the community of the bhikkhus recite
the Paritta[6] in the usual way. By sprinkling with the Paritta 81
water the King charmed people against illness and so removed
the danger of plague from his country. After receiving the 82
consecration at the Hemavāluka-cetiya[7] he decreed in writing
that this action should be performed every year. On the four 83
Uposatha days in the month he dispensed to four thousand
(persons) a gift of garments and rice food to boot. The Ve- 84
sākha festival he celebrated[8] in common with the poor, giving
them food and drink and clothing as they desired. For the 85

[1] The passage is not clear. It seems to deal with the affiliation of the Maṇimekhalapāsāda to the shrine of the Silāmayabuddha. It is curious that in v. 77 Bodhisattas are mentioned, whereas in v. 78 only one Bodhisatta is spoken of. According to an inscription in Jetavana the Miṇimevulā-maha-pahā was built by the grandfather of Mahinda IV. (EZ. I. 214).

[2] Such a trench had already been dug by Mahānāga according to 41. 94.

[3] Sutta I in the Cūlavagga of the Suttanipāta (v. 222 ff.) This Sutta exists also in "Sanskrit" in the Mahāvastu (ed. Senart I. 290 ff.).

[4] Ānanda was the Buddha's favourite disciple and his constant companion. What portrait of him is meant, and where it used to be formerly we do not know.

[5] W. translates: "and carried it in procession round about the city" But it is impossible to get this meaning out of *katvā padakkhiṇaṃ*.

[6] See. note to 46. 5.

[7] The same as the Mahāthūpa (in Anurādhapura), now Ruvanväli Dāgoba.

[8] Tradition places the parinibbāna of the Buddha on the day of full moon of Vesākha (April-May). See Mhvs. 3. 2; Fleet, JRAS. 1909, p. 6 ff. The Vesākhapūjā is often mentioned in the Mhvs., thus 32. 35, 35. 100. It was a favourite day for specially solemn actions such as the crowning of King Devānampiyatissa (Mhvs. 11. 42), the laying of the foundation stone of the Mahāthūpa (Mhvs. 29. 1) etc.

bhikkhu community of the Island he instituted a permanent offering and the poor, travellers and beggars he comforted by
86 gifts. The Mahesī of the King, Saṃghā by name, built in the Abhayuttara(-vihāra) the building called Saṃghasena-
87 pabbata[1] together with the (necessary) revenues. She placed a dark blue jewel diadem on the stone image of the Prince of Sages and instituted at great cost a sacrificial festival
88 for the Master (Buddha). His Senāpati, the hero Kuṭṭhaka[2] by name, built the pariveṇa called Senasenāpati with great
89 revenues. Thus the glorious (prince) with his court performed many meritorious works and entered in the thirty-fifth year of his reign[3] into the world of the gods.

90 Thereupon his next youngest brother, the nobleman Udaya[4] by name, became king, concerned in every way for the wel-

[1] Different from the Saṃghasenārāma named 50. 70 (see note here) which belonged to the Mahāvihāra. Cf. also note to 52. 45.

[2] Here again inscriptions offer a valuable confirmation of our Chronicle. The Senevirad Kuṭṭhā = Senāpati Kuṭṭhaka and the Senevirad Pirivena = Senasenāpati-pariveṇa are mentioned in the Rambeva inscription as well as in the Iripinniyeva inscription (WICKREMASINGHE, EZ. I. 164, 175). In my edition I have given the name of the Senāpati in the form Tuṭṭhaka, as all my MSS. read thus. Now however, I am more inclined to regard the difference as being due, less to varying tradition, than to a slip of the pen, as BELL has already done, ASC. VII th Progress Rep. 1891 = XIII. 1896 p. 59 n. 2. Cf. Errata et Corrigenda, Cūlavs. ed. II. We may thus change *Tuṭṭhakanāmako* into *Kuṭṭhakanāmako* which is also the reading according to WICKREMASINGHE, of a MS. in the Indian Institute at Oxford.

[3] Pūjāv. 35 years, also Rājāv.

[4] Without doubt the inscriptions of Iripinniyeva and Rambeva (EZ. I. 163 ff., 172 ff.) belong to this king, Udaya II. (as I have, otherwise Udaya I.). In these the king calls himself Salamevan = Silāmeghavaṇṇa, which would not fit Kassapa IV., as his biruda was Sirisaṃghabodhi. The king in the Kirigalleva and Noccipotana inscriptions (EZ. II. 1 ff. 5 ff.) of the 2 nd and 9 th years of his reign has the same name. He is mentioned as a brother of Kassapa (IV.) in the Moragoda and the Timbiriveva inscriptions. See note to 52. 1. The Negama inscr. (EZ. II. 14 ff.) dates from the time before Udaya's (II.) ascent of the throne, as he still calls himself there Udā Mahāpā i. e. Udaya Mahādipāda. This Udā Mahāpā cannot be Udaya III. who reigned later (Udā

fare of the islanders. While himself king, he raised his 91
youngest brother Kassapa to the rank of Mahādipāda. The 92
King considered that one should show favour to his kindred
and gave his brother's son (likewise) called Kassapa, the 93
daughter of the Yuvarāja (Kassapa), Senā by name, to wife.
The King himself took the other (daughter) called Tissā[1].

The son of the (former) Uparāja, Mahinda, and of the 94
princess Kitti, the Ādipāda Kittaggabodhi, the deluded one,
rebelled against the great King, escaped by night and came 95
alone in undiscovered disguise to Rohaṇa. He brought all the 96
people into his power, laid waste the whole province and had his
maternal uncle[2] who dwelt there murdered. When the Monarch 97
heard this he was filled with rage and sought a means of
bringing him hither. He summoned the son of his brother, 98
the Yuvarāja Kassapa[3], and spake to him thus: "Most ex-
cellent One, thou must be my helper". Said the other: "What 99
shall I do?" The Ruler replied: "Thy son, the powerful
Mahinda, has become a man. He has from his father and 100
his mother a claim on the province of Rohaṇa[4]. He is brave,

Mahayā, note to 53. 13), because apart from palaeographical reasons, the reigning king in the Negama inscr. has the biruda Sirisangbo. This fits Sena II. whose yuvarāja was Udaya II. but not Dappula IV. Silāmeghavaṇṇa the predecessor of Udaya III.

1 The Mahādipāda or Yuvarāja Kassapa is the king who reigns later as Kassapa IV.; the son of Udaya's brother (Sena II.) is the later Kassapa V.

2 The brothers of Kitti, the mother of Kittaggabodhi, were according to 50. 50 ff. Kassapa, Sena and Udaya. It is the first of these probably who is meant here.

3 With the reading *yuvarājassa* which is accepted in the Col. Ed. nothing can be done. We must decide therefore for the reading *yuvarājaṃ sa*. Still the designation of the brother's son (*bhātuputta*) of Udaya II. as yuvarāja is curious. In the verse 93 not this Kassapa is called yuvarāja, but on the contrary, the youngest brother of the King, who is likewise called Kassapa. Nevertheless according to the Sinhalese law of succession, the nephew Kassapa was heir to the throne after the brother, and probably for that reason he is here, in anticipation, called yuvarāja.

4 On the father's side, because Mahinda's father Kassapa (later Kassapa V.) was the son of Saṃghā, the daughter of the Rohaṇa prince Kittaggabodhi, and on the mother's side because his mother, the younger Saṃghā, was a daughter of Tissā and thus granddaughter of the same Aggabodhi.

able, a hero, adroit, skilful in the management of the bow,
101 warlike, discerning, prudent and experienced in statecraft. We
will send him to bring the villain hither who slew his uncle."
102 When Kassapa heard the King's words he spake full of re-
verence: "O King, summoned by the King, I would myself
103 go, how much more so my son. My line is safe and thy good
graces[1], O Monarch; do therefore, that time be not lost, what
104 thou desirest." When the Ruler of men heard his words he
rejoiced greatly, had a great force completely equipped and
105 gave orders to the general Vajiragga[2] to take the young
106 prince Mahinda with great care under his protection. Having
thereby made the town empty as it were, he gave the whole
army and train with all the appliances of war to Mahinda.
107 The Ruler of men himself accompanied him on foot and en-
joined him: "O excellent One, go hence and defend the king-
108 dom." Mahinda shone glorious as great Indra[3] when he set
forth at the head of the army of the gods for the great battle
109 between gods and demons. He arose and speedily came to
Guttasāla[4]. All the inhabitants, the chiefs of districts, as well
110 as those of the provinces who had been oppressed by the
murderer of his uncle, came hither and joined him thinking:
111 our (lawful) lord has arrived. The rebel who was in Giri-

[1] The sense is: so long as I enjoy thy favour the continuance of my family is assured. Therefore I shall always fulfil thy desires.

[2] A descendant of a Ṃekāppar Vädārum Vijuragu is mentioned in the Buddhannehela inscription. As this inscription (see Wickremasinghe, EZ. I. 191 ff.) belongs in all probability to the time of Kassapa V., the Vijuragu named there may well be our Vajiragga. In the same inscription there is mention of a Viduragu and in the Moragoda inscription of Kassapa V. of a Vadurā in the same connection, possibly variants of the same name. Bell, ASC., VIIth Progress Rep. (= XIII. 1896), p. 60.

[3] Punning comparison of the name Mahinda with Mahinda, Skr. *Mahendra* "the great Indra".

[4] Now Buttala in the Korale of the same name in the Badulla District, Province Uva. Guttasāla or -hāla is already mentioned at the time of Duṭṭhagāmaṇi. The importance of Guttasāla was due to its lying on a main road which led from Mahāgāma to Mahiyaṅgaṇa and from there along the Mahāvālukagaṅgā to Pulatthinagara. The older form for the name Buttala is *Guttala*. It occurs for instance, in the Sinhalese Thūpavaṃsa (ed. W. Dhammaratana, 1889, p. 133).

maṇḍala[1], lost courage; he seized all valuable royal property 112
and withdrew with elephants and steeds to Malaya. Mahinda's
army defeated his army at different places pursued it on foot, 113
and when it caught sight of the elephants and the horses,
seized them before Malaya, and convinced that he was there, 114
entered Malaya, hewing down the whole wilderness of forest
of Malaya and making rivers and tanks (look) like roads.
When the fool saw the people (advance), he overcome by fury, 115
flung all his treasures into rivers, bogs, chasms and the like
and hid himself alone in the forest in a rock cave. People who 116
sought him found the ruthless one and captured him. Full of
joy the people took him with them, came with haste and show- 117
ed him to Mahinda who had halted in Guttasāla. When the latter 118
saw him he asked him laughing: "Well hast thou enjoyed
Rohaṇa?" and gave him in charge to Vajiragga the King's
general. He himself took the army and betook himself to 119
Mahāgāma[2]. He became ruler of Rohaṇa, showing kindness
to the people. He saw to it that the people who had been 120
oppressed by the fool recovered, and he restored the Buddha
Order which had been injured by him, to the place (befitting
it). He laid out gardens of fruit and flowers at divers places, 121
enclosed tanks and dammed up the Mahānadī[3]. Everywhere 122
he brought the four necessaries within reach of the (bhikkhu)
community. By keeping down the evil-minded district chiefs and
the chiefs of the provinces, and by rooting out the rebels and 123
making (the country) free from briers, he made the whole people
content, exercising generosity and giving himself up to enjoy-
ment. As one who must be honoured by prudent men and served 124
by those who wish for their own advantage, he was like to a
wishing tree[4], a dispenser of blessings for all the needy. He 125

[1] Corresponds perhaps to the modern Kandapalla-Korale embracing the hill country to the west of Buttala, south of the Koslanda-Haldumulla road.

[2] At that time the capital of Rohaṇa. Cf. note to 45. 42.

[3] Perhaps name of the Menik-ganga?

[4] P. *kapparukkha* = skr. *kalpavṛkṣa*. For the Indian tales about heavenly trees which fulfil wishes and offer mankind all that it needs and desires, see Hopkins, Epic Mythology, 7.

abandoned the evil conduct practised by former rulers, and took up his abode there, cherishing justice.

126 The General (Vajiragga) took the Ādipāda (Kittaggabodhi) with him and betook himself to Anurādhapura and showed
127 him to the King. When the King saw him he was furious, had him at once thrown into prison, appointed a secure guard
128 for him and ill-used him in all kinds of ways. Three times he the glorious one gave an offering (of rice) equal to his body weight and he had the thūpa in the Thūpārāma covered
129 with golden plates. There too he built a pāsāda and caused a bhikkhu community to dwell there. In vihāra and town he
130 restored what was ruined. On the Kadamba-river[1] he provided an overflow of water with a strong weir, and he enlarged
131 the dam of the Mayettī-tank. There too the Monarch built an overflow of water and every year[2] he had distributed beautiful, specially fine stuffs for (the making of) the robes.
132 During a famine he had alms-halls built for all living beings and instituted a great alms-giving; he also enlarged the Mahā-
133 pāli(-hall). Amongst the inmates of the three fraternities he had rice with sour milk distributed, as well as rice continuously for the destitute and rice soup with solid food.
134 Having thus performed these and other meritorious works which lead to Heaven, he entered after reigning eleven years[3],
135 into the company of the gods. The gold that he had spent in these eleven years was estimated at thirteen hundred thousand (kahāpaṇas).

136 Thus after these two Rulers of men had brought into their power the one the formidable Paṇḍu King, the other Rohaṇa with its terrible wildernesses, they themselves fell into the power of death.

Here ends the fifty-first chapter, called "The History of the Two Kings", in the Mahāvaṃsa, compiled for the serene joy and emotion of the pious.

[1] See note to 41. 61.

[2] *Anuvassaṃ* belongs to *dāpayi*, not to *akā* as W. has it.

[3] The same number of years in Pūjāv. In Rājāv. on the other hand, 40 years. Both sources, as well as Rājaratn. ascribe to King Udaya the building of the Mahatumburuppē-vihāra in Rohaṇa. Udaya II. is mentioned under the name of **Udā Abhay** in the Moragoda inscription where he is credited with having subdued Rohaṇa and Malaya. Bell, ASC. VIIth Progress Rep. 1891 (= XIII. 1896), p. 60 ff. Wickremasinghe, EZ. I. 200 ff. See also note to 51. 90.

CHAPTER LII

THE TWO KINGS

Thereupon Kassapa[1] took over the government and as- 1
signed to the discerning Yuvarāja called Kassapa[2] (the Southern Province) Dakkhiṇadesa. The consecration as chief 2
queen[3] he conferred on the daughter of the Yuvarāja, the princess Tissā who was his consort. For mendicant artists[4] 3
who came from different regions the King dispensed permanently an offering which was called Daṇḍissara.

The Ādipāda Mahinda who sojourned at that time in Ro- 4
haṇa, advanced with forces to seize the Royal Province[5]. At 5
the tidings thereof the indignant King sent his own army against him, but Mahinda, a great warrior, defeated it in battle. Thereupon the King to prevail upon him to turn back, 6

[1] Several inscriptions date from the time of Kassapa IV. as for instance, the Moragoda inscription just mentioned (note to 51. 134) where Kasub Sirisaṅgbo is described as brother (*sohovur*) of Udā Abhay (= Udaya II.) Also in the inscription of Timbiriveva (EZ. II. 9 ff.). In the inscription of the Kiribat-vehera (EZ. I. 153 ff.) the King calls himself merely Sirisangbo, as also in the Mahakalatteva, Koṅgolleva and Inginimitiya inscriptions (E. Müller, AIC. nr. 110, 112, 113), also in the Negama inscr. (EZ. II. 14 ff.), in that of Kukurumahandamana (ib. II. 21ff. as also in that of Alutveva which Wickremasinghe (ib. II. 230) ascribes for palaeographic reasons to Kassapa IV.

[2] The son of Sena II. See note to 51. 98.

[3] P. *aggābhiseka* means the same as *abhiseka* as *aggamahesī*.

[4] *Yācakānaṃ sippīnaṃ* belong together, the first being in apposition to the last, *ca* joins the sentence with the preceding one. Cf. 53. 30; 60. 22.

[5] P. *rājino raṭṭhaṃ*. Here for the first time the name *Rājaraṭṭha* occurs in a less conventional form. It means in the sequel northern Ceylon with Anurādhapura and Pulatthinagara as capitals as distinguished from Rohana and from Dakkhiṇadesa, the province of the Yuvarāja.

7 sent forth his father, the Yuvarāja Kassapa. The latter be-
took himself to his son, made all kinds of prudent remon-
strances accompanied by various instructive tales, induced the
8 son to give up the fight and then returned. But later the
Ādipāda (Mahinda) had (several) chiefs of districts executed,
and when he saw that the people rose in rebellion, he approach-
9 ed the capital. The bhikkhu community brought him to
the King and presented him to him. The King gave him his
daughter to wife and sent him back to Rohaṇa.
10 When the King had expelled those bhikkhus in the three
fraternities whose discipline was bad, he let new bhikkhus
11 take up their abode here and there. Through his nephew[1]
who was born of the twice consecrated queen[2] he had
amid celebration of a sacrifice the soil about the Bodhi
12 Tree in the Mahāvihāra increased. In the three frater-
nities he put up three stone images, thereto boards of gold
13 with rays and umbrellas, as well as diadems jewels[3]. Having
built in the Abhayagiri-vihāra a pāsāda with his name[4], he

[1] P. *sūnunā.* The brother's son is called "son", just as the father's brother is called "father". See note to 51. 24.

[2] The title p. *dvayābhisekajāta* or *dvayābhisekasaṃjāta* (v. 37) is applied to Kassapa (afterwards K. V.), the son of Sena II. by Saṃghā, a daughter of Kittagabodhi (1) and of Devā. Kassapa V. has the same title in the Sinhalese form *debiseväjā* in an inscription of Anurādhapura (Wickremasinghe EZ. I. 50, note 17), as well as in the Medirigiriya inscr. (EZ. II. 30: *debisevhudā*) and in that of Bilibeva (EZ. II. 41: *debisevädā*). According to W. (Mhvs. trsl., p. 78, n. 11) the epithet *debisavajā* also occours in the signature to the Dampiyā-aṭuvā-gäṭapada.

[3] The passage is certainly difficult, but the emendations of the Col. Ed. are much too arbitrary. In the first place *tīṇi bimbe silāmaye* is quite unobjectionable. We have in the same way Mhvs. 41. 58 *piṭake tīṇi.* Even *raṃsiphalaka* needs no alteration. We have merely to realise that behind the images, as one often sees in the case of bronze statuettes, boards were fastened on which the rays emanating from the Buddha (the mandorla) were painted. *Suvaṇṇaye* is more difficult to place. It probably belongs to the following dvandva-compound and is put in the plural because one is dealing here with two different objects . . Perhaps one should read *tathā* rather than *tadā.*

[4] Wickremasinghe (EZ. I. 216) identifies with this the Kasub-vad-mahapahā mentioned in an inscr. of Mahinda IV. in the Jetavanārāma.

made bhikkhus dwell there and assigned them a village. To 14
the cetiya in the Mahiyaṅgaṇa-vihāra[1] he granted a village;
and to all the bhikkhus he distributed his own garments as
they had come to him[2]. To all creatures on land and water 15
he granted safety and observed in all respects the conduct of
the ancient kings. His Senāpati, Sena Ilaṅga, who was of 16
royal lineage, built for the bhikkhus of the Thera School a
dwelling in the west of the Thūpārāma. For the Dhamma- 17
rucika bhikkhus he founded the Dhammārāma and for the
Sāgalikas[3] the (monastery) called Kassapasena[4]. On the Cetiya 18
mountain he built the pariveṇa called Hadayuṇha and made
it over to the Dhammarucika bhikkhus. For grove-dwelling 19
bhikkhus[5] the General built in the groves here a hut and
there a hut and gave them to them. On the Rattamāla moun- 20
tain he built a pleasing, agreeable, charming hut and handed
it over to the ascetics, the Masters of the Order[6]. In the 21
Mahāvihāra he had the splendid pariveṇa called Samuddagiri
built and made it over to the Paṃsukūlika bhikkhus[7]. Having 22
made a dwelling in the wilderness[8] called after his family, he
granted it to the bhikkhus in the Mahāvihāra who dwelt in
the forests. In ruined vihāras he had renovations undertaken 23
and to all bhikkhus he gave patches for their worn out gar-

[1] See note to 51. 74.

[2] See 51. 61 with note.

[3] The two sects are also mentioned together in 39. 41.

[4] Mentioned as Kasub-senevirad-pirivena in the Bilibeva inscr. of Kassapa V. (EZ. II. 40).

[5] The *ārāmikā bhikkhavo* must not be confounded with the monastery servants which are called *ārāmikā* (see note to 37. 63). The term coincides with *āraññakā bhikkhavo* or is at any rate closely allied to it. Cf. 52. 22 and 64.

[6] P. *sāsanassa sāmikānaṃ* reminds one of the honorific title *vathimiyā* occurring not infrequently in inscriptions. (cf. EZ. I. 33, l. 12; 48, l. 29 etc.) or *bik-sang-h.* (EZ. I. 91, l. 18; 92, l. 17 etc.) or merely *himiyā* (EZ. I. 94, B, l. 1).

[7] See note 47. 66.

[8] By *arañña* is meant the *tapovana* (see 53. 14 ff.), the forest district to the west of Anurādhapura in which the group of the so-called Western Monasteries lies. On these ruins see A. M. Hocart, ASC. Mem. I. 18 ff.

24 ments. The Tissārāma[1] he built as a home for bhikkhunīs and
entrusted these with the care of the sacred Bodhi Tree in the
25 Maricavaṭṭi(-vihāra). In Anurādhapura and also in Pulatthina-
gara he had hospitals built for combating the upasagga disease[2].
26 To the dwellings that he had built (for priests[3]) he granted
maintenance villages and villages which were bound to provide
helpers for the monastery[4], and ornaments for the images.
27 He built houses where medicine was to be had in different
parts of the town and to the mothers of the Paṃsukūlika
28 (-bhikkhus) he dispensed rice and clothing. Many quadrupeds
were freed by the Senāpati from their captivity, and to the
29 poor he had large offerings dispensed. Having brought together
spices, rice, broth, and all kinds of solid nourishment, he
30 distributed sugar to the bhikkhus in the form of pigs[5]. In
performing these and other meritorious works Sena, the gene-
ral of the army, illumined the land with the moonlight beams
31 of his glory. A kinsman of his, the general Rukkha by name[6],
built in the village of Savāraka a very charming vihāra and
32 handed it over to the inmates of the Mahāvihāra, laying down
as the best (requisite) for the attainment of the degrees
33 of salvation the strictest fulfilment of duty[7]. The Grand

[1] Mentioned in the Ayitigeveva inscription of Kassapa V. (EZ. II. 34).

[2] Cf. also 52.77. What disease was meant by *upasagga* is impossible to determine. According to Jolly, Medizin, p. 48, 87, the Skr. word *upasarga* means: "sequelae" or "complication". According to BR. it denotes "possession". Perhaps *upasagga* is just any kind of epidemic, as "influenza" with us.

[3] W. connects *attanā katāvāsānaṃ* with the *vejjasālā* mentioned in the preceding verse and translates: "to these buildings". That this is wrong is proved by the mention of the helpers of the monastery and of the images. [4] P. *ārāmikagāme*. See note to 37. 63.

[5] It will be as well on the whole to keep to the reading of the MSS.: *sūkararūpaṃ*. *Guḷa* always means sugar kneaded into a shape. We have to do here with some kind of form (cf. our sugar*loaf*) which may have had very little likeness to a pig.

[6] I see no reason for altering the traditional MS. rendering *rukkhasavhayaṃ* into *rakkhasavhayaṃ*. Rukkha reminds one of the Skr. *rukṣa* meaning "rough".

[7] A difficult passage. I take *sāra* in a concrete sense, meaning "the essential, the highest", here in the plural: the various stages on the

Scribe[1], Sena by name, built in the Mahāvihāra the Mahā-
lekhakapabbata house, an excellent abode for the bhikkhus.
A minister of the King called Colarāja, repaired the charming 34
parivena that had been destroyed, so that it had again solidity.
In the three fraternities the King (himself) had maṇḍapas 35
built, resembling Vejayanta, painted in different colours, in
a fashion (rendered) charming by figure ornaments. And after
he had instituted relic festivals to the delight of the people 36
he passed away in accordance with his deeds after a reign
lasting seventeen years[2].

Hereupon the Yuvarāja, Kassapa[3] born of the twice 37
consecrated queen[4], attained the royal consecration in the
kingdom of Laṅkā to which he came in order of succession.
He was pious, had reached the path of salvation, wise as one 38
who possesses supernatural powers[5], eloquent as the teacher

road to salvation. For the combination *sāranaṃ paṭipatti* cf. *paṭipatti-sāro* JaCo. I. 418^{7}. *Sādhu* "the good, the right, the best" is the predicative object of *ṭhapetvā*. It was evidently Rukkha's intention that the vihāra built by him should serve as a *padhānaghara* (note to 37. 232). W.'s translation is too general and vague. The word "daily" inserted by him is not in the text.

[1] He is mentioned as *Mahalā Sen* (= *Seno mahālekho*) in the Mahakalatteva inscr. in which the building of the Nālārāma is ascribed to him. See note to 50. 9.

[2] Pūjāv. the same. Rājāv. does not mention Kassapa IV., the only Kassapa mentioned there is Kassapa V.

[3] There is an excellently preserved inscription belonging to this king in Anurādhapura (Wickremasinghe, EZ. I. 42 ff.) which confirms a number of statements made by the Mahāvaṃsa. The Medirigiriya and the Budannehela inscriptions of the same king are dated in the 3rd year of his reign, that of Ayitigeveva in the 5th year and that of Bilibeva in the 7th year (EZ. II. 27, 35, 39). In all inscriptions he has the name Abhā Salamevan = Abhaya Silāmeghavaṇṇa. For the literary work ascribed to king Kassapa V. cf. H. W. Codrington, H. C., p. 38.

[4] Cf. note to 52. 11.

[5] P. *sābhiñño.* The five *abhiññā* are: 1) magic power, 2) the heavenly ear, 3) knowledge of the thoughts of others, 4) the memory of former births, 5) the heavenly eye. They are often described in the canonical works. (Cf. amongst others, SN. trsl. by Geiger, II. 165 ff.). Heiler, Die buddhistische Versenkung, p. 26 ff.

39 of the gods (Bṛhaspati), generous as the dispenser of treasure
(Kubera), deeply learned, a preacher of the true doctrine,
practised in all the arts, adroit in proving what is right and
40 what is not right, versed in statecraft, immovable as the pillar
of a gate, standing firmly in the teaching of the Leader on
the path to delivrance, not to be shaken by all the storms of
41 other opinions, keeping himself free from all evil such as guile,
hypocrisy, pride, a mine of virtues as the ocean (is one) of
42 all jewels. The King who was a moon for the earth, granted
to the Ādipāda Dappula[1], a scion of his house, the rank of
43 yuvarāja. Carrying on the government with the ten (royal)
virtues and with the five means of winning hearts, he pro-
44 tected the world as an only (son)[2] of his own. He reformed
the whole Order of the Master by regulative acts, took in
young bhikkhus and thus provided for the filling of the
45 dwellings. The Maricavaṭṭi-vihāra built by King Duṭṭhagāmaṇi,
which had been destroyed, he restored[3], adorned with various
46 dwellings, made it over at the celebration of a festival to the
bhikkhus sprung from the Thera School and granted them,
who were five hundred[4] (in number), maintenance villages.
47 There the Ruler of Laṅkā revealed, as it were, to the world
that Master of the worlds Metteya who in the delectable Tu-
sita Heaven, at the head of the assembly of the gods, preaches

[1] See below note to 53. 1.

[2] P. *ekaṃ va attano*, thus all the MSS. The Col. Ed. alters the text arbitrarily into *nettaṃ va attano*. But the text gives perfectly good sense, as a comparison with 54. 6 shows. *Ekaṃ* must be supplemented by *puttaṃ*. See also notes to 37. 107 and 108.

[3] The restoration of the Maricavaṭṭi-vihāra by Kassapa V. is also mentioned in the inscription at Anurādhapura (l. 6) cited above (note to v. 37). Along with Mirisiviṭi Sangsen-aram and Kasubraj-vehera are also mentioned there. The former was built, according to 51. 86, by the mother of the King, the latter according to 50. 81, was finished by Sena I. There is no contradiction between the Cūlavaṃsa and the inscription. As the association with the Maricavaṭṭi shows, it was a case of renovation with the latter. Wickremasinghe also translates the verb *karay* (ger.) by "(re)built".

[4] *Tesaṃ* is not as W. thinks (to five hundred of them) gen. part., but obj. to *dāpayi* and *pañcasatānaṃ* attrib. to *tesaṃ*.

the glorious doctrine of the truth, in that he himself in the 48
perfectly equipped vihāra, sitting in a maṇḍapa decorated with
all kinds of jewels, surrounded by all the bhikkhus[1] of the 49
town, recited the Abhidhamma with the grace of a Buddha.
He had the Abhidhamma-piṭaka written on tablets of gold, the 50
book Dhammasaṅgaṇī[2], adorned with all kinds of jewels, and
having built a splendid temple in the midst of the town he 51
placed the book in it and caused festival processions to be held for
it. The position of Sakkasenāpati he granted to his own son[3] and 52
entrusted him with the care of this sacred book[4]. Every year 53
the King had the town festively decorated as the town of the
gods, and surrounded by his decked-out army, resplendent as 54
the King of the gods in all his royal robes, riding on the
back of his elephant, he marched through the streets of the
town and brought with great pomp (that book containing) the 55
summary of the true doctrine to the vihāra built by himself,
delectable, perfectly equipped. There, in the relic temple, 56
under a graceful jewel-studded maṇḍapa, he placed it on the
relic cushion and held a sacrificial festival. He restored the 57
Ganthākara-pariveṇa[5] in the Mahāmeghavana, built a hospital
in the town and assigned it villages. In the Abhayagiri(-vi- 58
hāra) he built the Bhaṇḍikā-pariveṇa[6] and the Silāmegha-

[1] I regard *nāgarehi* not as subst. with W., but as adjective attribute to *bhikkhūhi*. The *ca* joins *nisinno* with *parivārito*.

[2] See notes to 37. 225 and 44. 109. I believe that *dhammasaṃgaṇikaṃ potthaṃ* is in apposition to *abhidhammapiṭakaṃ*.

[3] Unfortunately we do not learn the name of this son. It cannot however, be the Mahinda mentioned 51. 99 ff., as this M. was apparently a son of Saṃghā, not of Devā. (Cf. v. 64 and note to 54. 48.)

[4] P. *dhammapotthaka* "a work belonging to the dhamma", the collection of the sacred books.

[5] The Ganthākara-vihāra is already mentioned in 37. 243 as the place of Buddhaghosa's sojourn. It belonged to the Mahāvihāra which was situated in the grove called Mahāmeghavana. We must assume therefore, that *akā* in our verse is used in a double sense: "restored" and "built", or we must translate *Ganthākara-pariveṇa* by "a pariveṇa belonging to the Ganthākara (vihāra)".

[6] Evidently called so in honour of his mother Saṃghā who has the name of *Saṅg Baṇḍay* in the Anurādhapura inscription (l. 3). EZ. I. 23, n. 6.

59 pabbata[1] and granted them villages. In the vihāra of the
Jotivana the King, the Sovereign of Laṅkā, granted to the
eating-house a village, and the same to the one in the Abhaya-
60 giri[2]. To the vihāra called Dakkhiṇāgiri[3] the King who was
filled with the deepest piety, granted out of gratitude a vil-
61 lage. The Sakkasenāpati[4] had a graceful pariveṇa that received
his name, built in a charming fashion and handed it over to-
gether with villages to the adherents of the Thera School.
62 His wife Vajirā handed over to the same (bhikkhus) a pari-
veṇa bearing her name which she had built, together with a
63 village. Further she had a home built in Padalañchana[5]
and granted it to the bhikkhunīs of the universally reverenced
64 Thera School. Devā, the mother of the Sakkasenāpati, built
for the bhikkhus who lived in the wilderness[6] and who were
the light of the Thera stock, a dwelling which received her
65 name. Further she made for the image of the Master in the
Maricavaṭṭi a diadem jewel, a net of rays[7], an umbrella and
a garment.

66 On the king's demesne the King built a royal dwelling
named after himself, (and) the delightful pāsāda bearing the
67 name of Pālika[8]. Another consort of the King, called Rājinī,
honoured the Hemamālika-cetiya by the dedication of a co-
68 vering of cloth[9]. She had a son by name Siddhattha who

[1] Again confirmed by the Anurādhapura inscr., l. 13 (Salameyvanpavu). The word *pabbata* "mountain" often appears at the end of the names of monastery buildings.

[2] The vihāra of the Jotivana (see note to 37. 65) is again the Jetavana-vihāra situated in the Jotivana. This is shown also by the combination with the Abhayagiri.

[3] See note to 38. 50, also 42. 27.

[4] The son of the King according to v. 52. [5] Cf. 54. 44.

[6] P. *araññakabhikkhūnaṃ*. See notes to 52. 19 and 22.

[7] For *cūḷāmaṇi* and *pādajāla* see note to 38. 64.

[8] The wording of the text makes it likely that v. 66 deals only with one building. This was called, therefore, either Kassapapālika or originally Kassapāvāsa and later, at the time of the author of the passage, Pālikapāsāda.

[9] See note to 44. 44. Hemamālika or Ratanavāluka (now Ruvanvāli) is the name for the Mahāthūpa in Anurādhapura.

being placed over the government here[1], was known by the title of Malayarāja; he was beauteous as the God of Love. After his death the King built a splendid hall for the bhikkhus 69
and instituted an offering of alms, transferring to him the merit[2] thereof.

While thus the Sovereign of Laṅkā held sway in justice, 70
the Paṇḍu King was vanquished in battle by the Coḷa King.
To gain military aid he sent numerous gifts. The King, the 71
Ruler of Laṅkā, took counsel with his officials, equipped mili- 72
tary forces, appointed his Sakkasenāpati as leader of the troops
and betook himself to Mahātittha. Standing at the edge of 73
the coast he spake of the triumph of former kings and having
thus aroused their enthusiasm, he made his troops embark.
With his army the Sakkasenāpati thereupon safely crossed 74
the sea and reached the Paṇḍu country. When the Paṇḍu 75
King saw the troops and him he spake full of cheer: "I will join
all Jambudīpa under one umbrella". The King took the two 76
armies; but as he could not vanquish him (the King) of the
Coḷa line, he gave up the fight and retired. The Sakkasenā- 77
pati set forth once more, with the purpose of fighting further,
made halt, and died of the upasagga plague[3] to the undoing
of the Paṇḍu (king). When the Ruler of Laṅkā heard that 78
the troops were also perishing of the same disease, out of pity
he had the army brought back[4]. He then granted the position 79
of Sakkasenāpati to the son of the dead (man). He honoured

[1] I. e. over the government of the Malaya province.

[2] P. *pattiṃ*. For this term see note to 42. 50.

[3] See note to 52. 25.

[4] Therefore the campaign was unsuccessful. The Coḷaking who vanquished in battle the Pāṇḍya king, was no doubt Parāntaka I. who ascended the throne in A. D. 907. In the Udayēndiram plates he actually boasts of having defeated the Pāṇḍya king Rājasiṃha and of having routed an army of the king of Ceylon. This inscription is dated in the 15th year of Parāntaka's reign (= 921-2). In another inscription of his 12th year, noticed by R. B. Venkayya, the king "refers incidentally to an invasion of the Pāṇḍya and the king of Ceylon". See Hultzsch, JRAS. 1913, p. 525 f.; H. W. Codrington, H. C. p. 38, 52.

80 the latter by making his son leader of the army[1]. By the inmates of the three fraternities he had a Paritta ceremony[2] observed in the town and thus warded off from
81 his people the danger of plague and bad harvest. Having thus secured for the Order and for his people by all manner of means peace, the King in the tenth year (of his reign)[3] entered happily into Heaven.

82 Even as this ruler of kings, Kassapa, who so long as he held sway in Laṅkā, was a reader of the Tipiṭaka, a light of all knowledge, a ready speaker, a monarch among poets, a shining light in presence of mind and determination, a teacher, a saviour, gifted with wisdom, faith and pity, rejoicing in the welfare of others, wise in knowledge of the world, loyal (to his people) — even thus, rich in spotless virtue, should the whole world be.

Here ends the fifty-second chapter, called "The Two Kings", in the Mahāvaṃsa, compiled for the serene joy and emotion of the pious.

[1] W. translates the passage thus: "And then he gave the office of Sakkasenāpati to his (the late general's) son, and made him the chief of the army and brought him up in the father's name."

[2] On *paritta* see note to 46. 5.

[3] According to Pūjāv. and Rājāv. (here only one Kassapa is named) the king reigned six years. Both sources relate that under him the Queen Saṅgā (Pūjāv. calls her the mother of the King) enriched the Lohamahāpāsāda by providing it with a crowning ornament.

CHAPTER LIII

THE FIVE KINGS

Thereupon the Yuvarāja by name Dappula[1], became king. 1
To the dignity of uparāja he appointed the Ādipāda of his
own name. To the Maricavaṭṭi-vihāra he granted a village. 2
And then the King who in the town maintained the pious
ways of former kings, unable on account of former deeds[2] to 3
enjoy this kingdom for a longer time, fell in the seventh
month (of his reign) into the jaws of death.
The Uparāja Dappula[3] then became king after him. He 4
granted the position of yuvarāja to the Ādipāda Udaya. At 5

[1] The nomination by Kassapa V. of Dappula III. (otnerwise D. IV.) as yuvarāja is related in 52. 42. Neither Pūjāv. nor Rājāv., nor any other Sinhalese source explains in what relationship he stood to his predecessor. Mhvs. 52. 42 says of him merely *vaṃse jātassa attano.*

[2] P. *pubbkammena attano.* What is meant are his actions in a former existence. His short reign is thus attributed to his unfavourable kamma. Pūjāv. and Rājāv. also give him a 7 months' reign.

[3] In Pūjāv., Rājāv., Rājaratn. and Nik.-s. Dappula IV. (V) is called Kuḍā-Dāpuḷu to distinguish him from his predecessor. The three first call him brother (*mal*) of the latter. The Vessagiri inscription (Wickremasinghe, EZ. I. 28 ff.) which must be placed palaeographically in the 10th cent. belongs to this King. He calls himself here Buddas Abhay Salamevan Dāpuḷu, son of Buddas Sirisaṅgboy Abahay and of Devā Rājna. The name Sirisaṃghabodhi can only apply to Senā II. or Kassapa IV. The latter is ruled out since according to the Sinhalese right of succession, sons of Kassapa IV. could not possibly come to the throne before Udaya III., the son of Mahinda, the younger brother of Sena II. Thus Dappula IV. (and of course his predecessor D. III.) was a brother of Kassapa V., but by another mother (Devā) who is however not mentioned in the Mhvs. The Etaviragolleva inscription AIC. nr. 117; EZ. II. 44 ff.) might be attributed either to Kassapa V. or to Dappula IV. The latter is the more likely, as Kassapa V. has as a rule, the special

that time the Paṇḍu King through fear of the Coḷa (king)
6 left his country, took ship and came to Mahātittha. The King
had him brought to him, rejoiced greatly when he saw him,
gave him an abundant income and granted him a dwelling
7 outside the town. When the King of Laṅkā had armed (with
the purpose): "I will make war on the Coḷa King, take from
8 him his two thrones[1] and give them to the Paṇḍu King", the
nobles dwelling on the Island for some reason or other stirred
9 up a sorry strife to the undoing of the Paṇḍu King[2]. The
Paṇḍu King thought his sojourn here was of no use to him.
He left his diadem and other valuables behind and betook
10 himself to the Keraḷas[3]. When the strife was ended the King
granted a village near the town to the temple of the great
11 Bodhi Tree in the Mahāvihāra. His Senāpati Rakkhaka Ilaṅga
built a dwelling house not far from the Thūpārāma, that was
12 called after the King. The King kept to all that former kings
had done and on reaching the twelfth year[4] (of his reign) he
passed away in accordance with his doing.

13 The Yuvarāja Udaya[5] now became monarch over the
dwellers in Laṅkā. He invested the Ādipāda Sena by name,

title *de-bisevā-dā* (see notes to 52. 11 and 37) which is not the case with the king Abhā Salamevan mentioned in that inscription. Further we have the Elleveva inscription of Dappula IV. (AIC. nr. 116) in which he calls himself Abhā Salamevan Dāpuḷu. Lastly, the Mahādipāda Udaya (afterwards U. III.) issued the Puliyankulam inscription (EZ. II. 44 ff.) in the last (12 th) year of the King's reign.

[1] P. *sayanadvayaṃ*. Thus in all MSS. with which I am acquainted. The Col. Ed. alters the word arbitrarily into *paṭṭanadvayaṃ*.

[2] Cf. with *pāpakammena Paṇḍuno* the phrase *pāpena Paṇḍuno* 52. 77. The two passages cannot be separated from one another.

[3] A people settled on the Malabar coast of southern India where Malayālam is now spoken. The fact that a Paṇḍu king left his crown in Ceylon is confirmed by a south Indian inscription of King Rājendra Coḷa who boasts of having brought it back (Hultzsch, JRAS. 1913 p. 522).

[4] Pūjāv. and Rājāv. also give Kuḍā Dāpuḷu a twelve years' reign. They tell of a victorious fight with the Damilas who came from the Soḷi land. Rājaratn. the same.

[5] The Puliyankulam inscription (EZ. I. 182 ff., cf. note to v. 4) belongs to the time just before his ascent of the throne. It is dated in the

with the dignity of uparāja. At that time officials of the 14
Court fled for fear of the King to the Grove of the Penitents[1].
The King and the Uparāja went thither and had their heads
cut off. Being indignant at this deed, the ascetics dwelling 15
there left the King's land and betook themselves to Rohaṇa.
Thereupon the people in town and country and the troops 16
became rebellious like the ocean stirred by wild storm. They 17
climbed the Ratanapāsāda[2] in the Abhayuttara(-vihāra), terri-
fied the King by threats[3], struck off the heads of the officials 18
who had helped the strife in the Penitent's Grove and flung
them out of the window. When the Yuvarāja and his friend, 19
the Ādipāda[4], saw that, they sprang over the wall and fled
in haste to Rohaṇa. A division of troops pursued them to 20
the banks of the Kaṇha-nadī[5], but as they could get no boats

twelfth year of Dappula IV. Udaya III. (II.) still calls himself here U d ā M a h a y ā, son of Mihind Maḥayā and of Kitā. The title *mahayā* must actually be *mahādipāda*. Linguistically there are difficulties. According to the example of *äpā* = *ādipāda*, we should expect the *p* to be retained in the joint of the compound. In the Galpota inscription at Polonnaruva (C, l. 19; AIC. p. 99; EZ. II. p. 114) we have the combination *äpā mahapā* which Wickremasinghe (EZ. I. 187, n. 7) has pointed out. We meet also repeatedly in inscriptions with the phrase *äpā mahayā siri vindä* (EZ. I. 25, 91, 221) for which curiously enough, *ayipaya mahapaya siri vindä* stands in the Jetavanārāma inscription of Mahinda IV. (l. 4, EZ. I. 234). From this it looks almost as if *mahayā* were a specially worn down form of *mahādipāda* or *mahāpāda*. As regards the parents of Udā Mahayā, there is no doubt that the father was Mahinda, a younger brother of Sena II. According to 51. 7 he enjoyed the dignity of uparāja, was therefore Mahādipāda, and he was married to Kitti or Kittā (50. 60). He quarreled with the King, was reconciled with him and bore from that time the title of yuvarāja (for ex. 51. 15). But he never became king, since he died according to 51. 63 before Sena II. He remained therefore as the inscription says *mahayā* all his life.

[1] P. *tapovana.* See note to 52. 22. [2] See note to 48. 135.

[3] Lit. "by showing him a horror". Cf. 53. 47.

[4] The Yuvarāja is Sena (v. 13), his friend (v. 25) is Udaya, later King Udaya IV.

[5] P. *yāva Kaṇhanadītaṭaṃ.* The *Kaṇhanadī* seems to be the same as *Kālanadī* (86. 40, 44), the river forming the boundary of Rohaṇa.

21 and the two were already across, they returned. The princes
who in the Penitents' Grove had broken (the precept of) in-
violability betook themselves to the ascetics, threw themselves
22 to the ground at their feet, with their damp garments and
hair, wailed much, lamented and whined and sought to con-
23 ciliate the penitents. Through the influence of the peaceability
and benevolence of the Masters of the Order[1] the good deeds
24 of the Island princes told in their favour[2]. When the army
had calmed down, the inmates of the three fraternities
25 went to pacify[3] the troops of the Yuvarāja. The two
princes who were cultured and well-instructed people turned
imploringly to the Paṃsukūlin(-bhikkhus)[4], and returned with
26 them to their town. At the head of the bhikkhus[5] the King
advanced towards them, obtained their pardon, took them
with him, brought them back to their grove and betook him-
27 self to the royal palace. From that time onwards the King
observed the conduct of former kings and passed away in the
third year[6] (of his reign) in accordance with his deeds.

The princes were pursued up to this point. When they arrived in Rohaṇa their garments and hair were still damp from crossing that river (v. 22).

[1] P. *sāsanasāminaṃ*. The word *sāmin* as title of honour of the bhikkhus corresponds to the *himiyā* so often used in inscriptions. Cf. also *mahāsāmin* 86. 38; 89. 64. See 52. 20 with note.

[2] P. *puññodayo ahu*. Cf. with this note to 37. 139. W.'s translation "the great kindness and longsuffering of these lords of religion moved the king towards the two offenders" is something quite different to what stands in the Text.

[3] The alteration of the Text by the Col. Ed. into *te samānetuṃ* is quite unnecessary. The reading of the MSS. *tosam ānetuṃ* gives excellent sense.

[4] The Ascetics are meant who had left the Penitents' Grove and gone to Rohaṇa. As the King was implicated in the wrong that had been committed in the Penitents' Grove, he had also to get their pardon (v. 26).

[5] That is of those inmates of the three fraternities who were working for conciliation. At their head the king advances towards the ascetics coming from Rohaṇa in company of the princes.

[6] Pūjāv. 3 years; Rājāv. 8 years.

After receiving consecration as king in Laṅkā, the discern- 28
ing Sena[1] made his friend, the Ādipāda Udaya, yuvarāja.
A thousand kahāpaṇas the Ruler of men was wont to give 29
away to the poor on the Uposatha day, being all his life
long one who kept the Uposatha vow. To the bhikkhus the 30
Ruler gave food and raiment for the images[2] and to mendi-
cant artists the Daṇḍissara offering[3]. Having had built in 31
various places for the bhikkhus graceful pāsādas, the Ruler
granted them maintenance villages. At a cost of a thousand 32
or five hundred kahāpaṇas he had ruined dwellings in Laṅkā
restored. Forty thousand kahāpaṇas did the Ruler lay out 33
for a stone paving[4] of the Abhayuttara-cetiya. On the great 34
tanks in Laṅkā he had the decayed outflow canals renewed
and the dams made firm with stones and earth. In the royal 35
palace he built a beautiful, costly house for flowers and he
retained in full the almsgiving instituted by former kings.
Once when visiting the Nāgasālā-pariveṇa built by the Ma- 36
layarāja, the minister Aggabodhi, he granted it a village. In 37
the four vihāras[5] he set up in pious fashion sculptured figures,
built beautiful maṇḍapas and held constantly sacrificial festi-
vals for the relics. After performing these and even many 38
other meritorious works of divers kind, he passed away in
the ninth year[6] (of his reign) in accordance with his deeds.
Hereupon the Yuvarāja Udaya[7] received the consecration 39
as King in Laṅkā and ordained as uparāja the Ādipāda Sena

[1] He was according to Pūjāv., Rājāv. and Rājaratn., the brother of his predecessor.

[2] So I understand the compound *paṭimābhattavatthāni.* This would mean that a certain cult was accorded the images whereby food was placed before them and garments swathed about them.

[3] Cf. note to 52. 3; 60. 22.

[4] P. *silāpattharaṇatthāya.* It probably means the paving of the square terrace on which the thūpa stands.

[5] Probably the four large monasteries Mahāvihāra, Jetavana, Abhayagiri with the Maricavaṭṭi-vihāra.

[6] Pūjāv.: 9 years, Rājāv.: 3 years (mistake for Sena IV. see note to 54. 1).

[7] None of our sources contain any information as so the relationship

40 by name. The King was slothful and a friend of spirituous drinks to the undoing of his subjects[1]. The Coḷa (king) hear-
41 ing of his sloth was greatly pleased, and as he wished to achieve consecration as king in the Paṇḍu kingdom, he sent (messengers) about the diadem and the other (things) which
42 the Paṇḍu (king) had left behind[2] (in Laṅkā). The King did not give them up, so the mighty Coḷa equipped an army and
43 sent it forth to fetch them by force. Now at that time the Senāpati here[3] was absent in a rebellious border province. The King had him fetched and sent him forth to begin the
44 war. The Senāpati set forth, delivered battle and fell in the fight. Thereupon the King (Udaya[4]) took the crown and the
45 rest and betook himself to Rohaṇa. The Coḷa troops marched thither, but finding no way of entering Rohaṇa they turned and betook themselves through fear from here to their own
46 country. Thereupon the Ruler of Laṅkā appointed the general Viduragga[5], a man of great energy and discernment, to the
47 position of the Senāpati. The Senāpati laid waste the border-land of the Coḷa King and forced him with threats[6] to restore[7]

of Udaya IV. (III. in W.'s list) to his predecessor. Wickremasinghe (EZ. II. 59, Genealogical Tables) supposes him to have been a younger brother of Udaya III. (II.) and of Sena III. This makes it possible for him to insert Mahinda IV. in the genealogical tree. (See note to 54. 48).

[1] P. *pāpena jantunaṃ*. Cf. 52. 77 and 53. 8 with note.

[2] See 53. 9.

[3] I. e. in Ceylon, of course, or, as in v. 45 and 47, from Ceylon.

[4] It is inexplicable why W. should have added to *rājā so* the words (of Coḷa). What could the Coḷa King then have done in Rohaṇa? On the other hand Rohaṇa has forever been the refuge of the Sinhalese kings after being worsted in fight with the Damiḷas. The meaning of the passage is accordingly (as Hultzsch, JRAS. 1913, p. 525 rightly saw): the Coḷa King wins the battle, it is true, but King Udaya flees with the valuables which the former wants to get back — *makuṭādīni* in v. 44 must be the same as *makuṭādinaṃ* in v. 41 — to Rohaṇa. The Coḷa troops pursue him, but as they cannot penetrate into Rohaṇa, they are obliged to return empty-handed. The Coḷa King therefore, did not get hold of the Crown jewels. Hultzsch supposes the Coḷa King might have been Parāntaka I. who calls himself in his latest inscription (943/4—947/8) "conqueror of Ceylon". Cf. H. W. Codrington, H. C. p. 39 f.

[5] For the name *Viduragu* or *Vijuragu* see note to 51. 105.

[6] See note to 53. 17.

[7] P. *ānāpesi*: lit. "he had brought hither".

all that he had carried away from here (as booty). Thereupon 48
the King had distributed to all the Paṃsukūlika-bhikkhus
dwelling on the Island articles of equipment in costly fashion.
For the image of the Master in the Mahāvihāra the Monarch 49
of Laṅkā fashioned a diadem of jewels which sparkled with
the rays of precious stones. One of the ladies of the harem, 50
Vidurā, honoured his stone image with a network of rays[1]
which glittered with jewels. When he had begun to rebuild 51
the so-called Maṇipāsāda which the troops of the Coḷa King
had burned down, he died in the eighth year (of his reign)[2].

These five rulers of the earth who ruled over an earth united 52
under one umbrella and who had governed the whole world
with severity and clemency, (they all) with wives and children, ministers, women and henchmen fell into the power of death. Hence should the wise ever be minded to give up sloth and pride.

Here ends the fifty-third chapter, called "The Five Kings", in the Mahāvaṃsa, compiled for the serene joy and emotion of the pious.

[1] For *pādajāla* (mandorla) see note to 38. 64, as well as 52. 65.

[2] Pūjāv.: 8 years, Rājāv.: 3 years. But cf. note to 54. 6.

CHAPTER LIV

THE THREE KINGS

1 When thereupon Sena[1] had by inheritance attained con-
secration as king in Laṅkā he made over the dignity of yu-
2 varāja to the Ādipāda Mahinda[2]. The King was wise, an ex-
cellent poet, learned, impartial towards friend and foe, ever
3 full of pity and goodwill. Without letting the right season
pass, the god at that time sent showers of rain streaming in
the right way, the people who dwelt in the land were ever
4 happy and without fear. The King was wont sitting in the
Lohapāsāda, surrounded by the inmates of the three frater-
5 nities, to explain the Suttantas. He fashioned a casket for
the Tooth Relic ornamented with various precious stones and

[1] In the Sinhalese sources the order of the kings after Dappula IV. (V) = Kuḍā Dāpuḷu is a follows:

Pūjāv.:	Rājāv.:	Rājar.:	Nik.-s.:
Udā (3)	Udā (8)	Udā	Udā
Sen (9)	Sen (3)	Sen	Sen
Udā (8)	Udā (3)	Udā	Udā
Sen (9)	Sen (9)	Sen	Päsuḷu-Sen
Sen (3)	Sen (3)	Sen	Mädi-Sen

Mhvs. Udaya (2—3), Sena (8—9), Udaya (7—8), Sena (3). The figures in brackets denote the number of years reigned. The main difference is that the Sinhalese sources insert two Senas after Udaya IV. (III.) and before Mahinda IV. (see note to 54. 7) whereas Mhvs. has only one. We shall probably have to keep to the older source. It should be noted that Pūjāv. and Rājāv. call the last Sena of the above list the son of his predecessor.

[2] Wickremasinghe considers this Mahinda to be the later Mahinda IV., a younger brother of Sena IV., because in an inscription in the Jetavanārāma (EZ. I. 214) Mahinda IV. says of the Huligam-piriven, that his brother, the Great King, had begun it while he himself had finished it. This pariveṇa might be the one mentioned in v. 6. But cf. note to 54. 7.

in the four vihāras[1] he instituted, in divers ways, sacrificial
festivals for the relics. After turning Sitthagāma where he 6
had himself dwelt, into a pariveṇa and after protecting the
world like a son he entered into Heaven after a three years'
reign.

The Yuvarāja Mahinda[2] became king after him, rich in 7
merit, rich in splendour, rich in military power, rich in fame.
He united Laṅkā under one umbrella after overcoming the 8
peril (threatened) by rebels. The chiefs of districts always
upheld him. Although there was also in Laṅkā a race of 9
nobles[3], the Ruler of men had a princess of the line of the
ruler of Kāliṅga fetched and made her his first mahesī. Of 10

[1] See note to 53. 37.

[2] P. Goldschmidt, E. Müller and Wickremasinghe ascribe to King Mahinda IV. a series of inscriptions in which the author calls himself Sirisangboi-Abahay (Sirisaṃghabodhi Abhaya). These are: 1) a slab inscription in Vessagiri (EZ. I. 29); 2) the two well-known inscriptions halfway up the Mihintale mountain (EZ. I. 75); 3) the pillar inscription of Rāja-maligāva in Polonnaruva (EZ. II. 49); 4) two slab inscriptions in the Jetavanārāma (EZ. I. 213); 5) a slab inscription in Vevelketiya (EZ. I. 241), with a parallel inscription in Kahata-gasdigiliya, Bell ASC., 7 th Prog. Rep. 1891 = XIII. 1896, p. 51; 6) a slab inscription in Rambeva (EZ. II. 64). In addition there in 7) the pillar inscription of Mayilagastota in which the author merely calls himself *äpā Mihindu*, that is Ādipāda, not king. No. 1 is the most certain because the author in addition to his biruda SSB. calls himself Mihindu, and because in it the Senāpati Sena is mentioned with an allusion to the successful campaign against the Damiḷas, which is mentioned in Mhvs. 54. 12. For the rest there are certain difficulties. The author of inscrs. 2 and 3 names as his parents Salamevan (Silāmeghavaṇṇa) — which fits Kassapa V. father of Mahinda IV. — and Dev Gon. Inscr. 7 however, speaks of these as Salamevan and Sang Gon. Again they are called in inscrs. 4 and 6 Sirisangbo and Dev Gon. In nr. 5 the father is likewise called Sirisangbo while no mother is mentioned. Wickremasinghe (EZ. I. 213) explains the difference in the father's name by assuming that Kassapa V. used both birudas SSB. and SMV., a way out of the difficulty which I adopt very unwillingly, being more inclined to believe in a regular alternation of the two epithets. The difficulty with Dev Gon and Sang Gon has not been got rid of. Cf. below note to 54. 48.

[3] *Vijjamāne* must be supplemented by *vaṃse* from pāda d.

11 her were born two sons and a charming daughter. He made his sons ādipādas and his daughter a queen: thus the Ruler founded the royal house of the Sīhalas.

12 The Vallabha King[1] sent a force to Nāgadīpa to subdue
13 this our country. The Ruler hearing this, the King sent thither the Senāpati Sena by name, to whom he had made over an army, to fight with the troops of the Vallabha King.
14 The Senāpati betook himself thither, fought with the troops of this (Vallabha) King, defeated them and remained master
15 of the battlefield. As the kings with the Vallabha (king) at their head, were unable to vanquish our King, they made a
16 friendly treaty with the ruler of Laṅkā. In this way the fame of the King penetrated to Jambudīpa, spreading over Laṅkā and crossing the Ocean.

17 The priests who preached the true doctrine the King treated with the most marked distinction. He hearkened to the doc-
18 trine and believed in the Order of the Buddha. The King assembled the Paṃsukūlin bhikkhus, invited them in a friendly
19 manner and had them brought into his house. He had seats prepared for them, made them sit down and had pure[2] food abundantly set before them, and this always as on the one
20 day[3]. To the ascetics living in the wilderness[4] the King sent continually food pure, costly and abundant, with all kinds of
21 seasoning. To sick ascetics the King who was a fount of pity, sent physicians and sought continually to heal them.
22 Pieces of sugar baked in melted butter, juice of garlic, and betel as sweet odour for the mouth, he gave them always as
23 dessert. He had the alms-bowls of the Paṃsukūlika bhikkhus filled with garlic, black pepper[5], long pepper[6] and ginger,

[1] For Vallabha, which is not a personal name as W. thinks, see note 47. 15. On Sena's campaign see note to v. 7.

[2] P. *suddha* pure in a ritual sense. What is meant are foods of which ascetics may also eat.

[3] W.'s translation: "thus did he always, as if it seemed to him the work of one day" is certainly wrong.

[4] See notes to 41. 99, 52. 22, 53. 14.

[5] P. *marica*, Piper nigrum. [6] P. *pipphali*, Piper longum.

sugar and the three kinds of myrobalans[1] and to evary single 24
(bhikkhu) he distributed continually melted butter, oil and
honey. as also cloaks and blankets[2]. All necessaries such as 25
clothing and the like the Ruler had made and distributed
among the Paṃsukūlin bhikkhus. In the Mahāvihāra the King 26
had new cloth to make robes therewith provided for every
single bhikkhu. To the Lābhavāsin bhikkhus[3] dwelling in 27
the three fraternities the Ruler twice dispensed (rice) equal
in weight to that of his body. The decree "Kings shall in 28
future take no revenues for themselves out of the revenues
of the Order" the King had engraved in stone and set (the
stone) up[4]. He made poor people recite the formula of the 29
(threefold) refuge[5] and the nine qualities[6] of the Buddha and
then gave them food and clothing. He built an alms-hall on 30
the grounds of the Elephant House and gave to beggars alms
and couches. In all the hospitals he distributed medicine and 31
beds, and he had food given regularly to criminals in prison.
To apes, the wild boar, the gazelle and to dogs he, a fount 32
of pity, had rice and cakes distributed as much as they would.
In the four vihāras the King had raw rice laid down in heaps 33
with the injunction that the poor should take of it as much
as they wanted. While holding various sacrificial festivals 34
and while instituting a great feast he had the Vinaya re-
cited by learned bhikkhus. Having made presents to him he 35

[1] P. *tiphala* = skr. *triphala*, the fruit of the Terminalia chebula, Terminalia bellerica and Phyllanthus emblica (P. *harītaka, vibhītaka, āmalaka*).

[2] P. *pāpurattharaṇāni* is an abbreviation of *pāpuraṇa-attharaṇāni*.

[3] It is clear from 60. 68, 72, that the Lābhavāsins like the Paṃsukūlins formed a group of ascetics within the great community.

[4] It is of course, impossible to determine to what inscription of the King this alludes. The Mihintale plates as far as I can see, have no injunction identical with the above.

[5] P. *saraṇāni*. What is meant is the formula *buddhaṃ saraṇaṃ gacchāmi, dhammaṃ s. g., saṃghaṃ s. g.* which is usually repeated three times.

[6] P. *guṇe nava*. Cf. on the navaguṇa formula *iti pi so bhagavā* etc. Childers, PD. s. v.

had a commentary to the Abhidhamma written by the Thera
Dhammamitta[1] who dwelt in the Sitthagāma(-pariveṇa)[2].
36 By the Thera called Dāṭhānāga, dwelling in the wilderness,
an ornament of Laṅkā, he had the Abhidhamma recited.
37 He paid honour to the Hemamālika-cetiya by the gift of a
covering of stuff, by dance and song, by parfumes and flowers
38 of divers kinds, by garlands of lamps and incense of many
kinds, and he presented the bhikkhus there with raiment which
39 he himself distributed among them. Continually from the
gardens[3] here and there in his kingdom he had flowers brought
40 and paid honour therewith to the three Jewels. He began to
build the pāsāda called Candana in the Maricavaṭṭi(-vihāra)
41 and granted the bhikkhus maintenance villages. There the
Ruler had the Hair Relic preserved, had fashioned (for it) a
reliquary of jewels and (this) set up as a dedicatory gift.
42 The Ruler had the cetiya in the Thūpārāma covered with
stripes of gold and silver and instituted for it a sacrificial
43 festival in accordance with his royal dignity. In the relic
temple there the King had a golden door put up like to
44 Mount Sineru[4] gleaming in the beams of the sun. He restored
the beautiful temple of the four cetiyas in Padalañchana[5]
which had been burnt down by the troops of the Coḷa King.
45 (In like manner) he restored the burnt temple of the Tooth
Relic[6] in the centre of the town, the Dhammasaṅgaṇi
46 house[7] and the Mahāpāli Hall. The Ruler having had a
betel-maṇḍapa[8] built, made over the earnings from it to the

[1] Wickremasinghe (EZ. I. 215) supposes that this thera might be the thera mentioned in an inscription of Mahinda's in the Jetavana as *Mahadämi* (P. *mahādhammika*).

[2] See above v. 6.

[3] The loc. *uyyānesu* stands here instead of the abl.

[4] Name of the mythical mountain Meru (Sumeru, Hemameru). See 37. 79.

[5] See 52. 63.

[6] Evidently the temple mentioned 37. 93-95 which was situated near the palace, thus *nagaramajjhamhi*.

[7] See 52. 50-51. This building also was situated *nagaramajjhamhi*.

[8] I. e. a pavilion where betel was sold.

bhikkhus of the Thera School[1] for (the purchase of) medi-
cines. He built a home called Mahāmallaka and made it over 47
to the bhikkhunīs proceeding from the Thera School. Now 48
too the Monarch completed the so-called Maṇipāsāda, begun
by his mother's brother, the pious King Udaya[2]. Four officials 49
of the King thereupon had four pariveṇas built in the Jeta-
vana. The gracious consort of the King Kitti by name, his 50
equal in fame, built a beautiful pariveṇa west of the Thūpā-
rama and in this pariveṇa, in Kappāsagāma and in the Cīvara- 51
cetiya she laid down three pure bathing tanks. To the Hema- 52
mālika-cetiya she dedicated, rich in meritorious works, a golden
banner twelve cubits long. For the laity her son built a ho- 53
spital in the town, and the able Sakkasenānī[3] one for bhikkhus
outside of the town. In the four vihāras the King had maṇ- 54
ḍapas erected, like to heavenly palaces and by holding sacri-
ficial festivals in divers ways for the relics for longer than 55

[1] P. *theravaṃse* (loc. instead of gen. *-sassa*). W. remarks about this passage that the Thera bhikkhus "traced their line of succession from the great apostle Mahinda". The term *theriyā* however, goes back (Mhvs. 3. 40) to the First Council. The expression *vaṃsa* is used here as in 52. 63, figuratively for "School", likewise again in v. 47.

[2] The drawing up of the family tree of Mahinda IV. is beset with difficulties. Wickremasinghe (plate to EZ. II. 59) has tried very ingeniously to remove them. He assumes that Udaya IV. was the younger brother of Sena III., and Sena IV. (cf. note to 54. 1) the elder brother of Mahinda IV. In this way as Saṃghā the wife of Kassapa V. (see 51. 18) was a sister of Udaya IV., the latter could be called the *mātula* of Mahinda IV. Two objections remain. Udaya IV. is twice (53. 19 and 28) called the "friend" of Sena III. This term used of a younger brother is surprising. Further, the mother of Mahinda IV. was, if the Mihintale plates are really his, not Saṃghā, but the Devā mentioned 52. 64. — Possibly the following hypothesis may help to clear up the matter. Kassapa V. had two sons called Mahinda, one by Saṃghā, and one by Devā. The first is the Mahinda mentioned in 51. 99 ff., the author of the Mayilagastota inscription (Nr. 7 in note to 54. 7). He never became king but died earlier, of which however we have no account. The second Mahinda is the later king Mahinda IV. Let us assume further that Devā, the second wife of Kassapa V. as to whose origin we know nothing, was a half-sister of Saṃghā, then Udaya IV. would be the *mātula* of Mahinda IV. I must point out that my Udaya IV. is W.'s U. III.

[3] The same as *sakkasenāpati*. See 52. 52. This is probably the son of the Sakkasenāpati (the son of Kassapa V.), who (52. 79) after his father's death, inherited his dignity.

56 a year, he kept to the pious ways of former kings. Having thus performed these and other eminent, meritorious works in sundry ways the King entered in the sixteenth year (of his reign) into the heaven of the gods[1].

57 Sena, the twelve years old son of the King[2] by the Kālinga
58 princess now came to the throne. The position of yuvarāja he conferred on his younger brother Udaya. Sena, his father's
59 senāpati, was also his senāpati. Once when the Senāpati was away with the army in the border country he had his younger
60 brother Mahāmalla[3] who had committed an offence[4] with his mother, slain and made a court official Udaya by name, who
61 was loyal to him, senāpati. When the Senāpati Sena heard this he was wroth and came with his army, intending to take
62 his foes captive. Hearing the tidings thereof the Monarch thought: I shall bring herewith my court official who has (always) carried out my decrees, into safety, left (the town)
63 and betook himself to Rohaṇa[5]. But his mother turned back, took the Yuvarāja (Udaya) and the Queen with her, and wroth with him (the King), summoned the Senāpati (Sena)
64 to her[6]. Supported therein by her, he collected Damiḷas, gave over the country to them and took up his abode in Pulatthi-
65 nagara. To fight him the King sent troops from Rohaṇa, but the Senāpati annihilated the whole army of the King.

[1] Pūjāv., Rājāv. and Nik.-s. call the King Kuḍā-Midel, Rājar. Midel-Salā. Pūjāv. gives him a reign of 16, Rājāv. one of 12 years.

[2] Thus according to the reading *rājaṃ* of the Col. Ed. which I now prefer to *rājā* of the MSS. *Jāto paṭicca taṃ rājaṃ*, lit.: born to the king.

[3] W. connects *Mahāmallaṃ* wrongly with *Udayaṃ*, whereas it belongs to *bhātaraṃ* in 59 d.

[4] W.'s translation: "who dwelt in his mother's house" says nothing and misses the point. As regards the meaning I have adopted for *vattantaṃ*, I refer the reader to skr. *vart* (BR. s. v., 7) which is likewise used in the sense of forbidden sexual intercourse with a woman.

[5] The reading of the text and the translation are very doubtful. W.'s rendering: "And when the King heard thereof, he departed and fled to Rohaṇa taking with him the minister who had been as a slave unto him, and whom he regarded as his saviour" can scarcely be reconciled with the text as contained in the Col. Ed.

[6] The Queen-mother is angry with her son because he has done away with her lover, so takes the part of the Senāpati Sena, the elder brother of the murdered man.

The Damiḷas now plundered the whole country like devils 66
and pillaging, seized the property of its inhabitants. In their 67
distress the people betook themselves to Rohaṇa to the King
and told him of the matter. He took counsel with his ministers
and to protect the Order of the Buddha, he sent his Senāpati 68
(Udaya) forth from the kingdom[1], made a treaty with (the
Senāpati) Sena and came to Pulatthinagara. He made the 69
daughter of the latter his mahesī, to continue his line. With
her he begot an excellent son, called Kassapa. But while now 70
the Ruler of Laṅkā had his abode there[2] his low class[3] favou-
rites who obtained no leave from their teacher to drink
surā, praised in his presence[4] the advantages of drinking in- 71
toxicating liquors and induced the Ruler to drink. After
taking intoxicating drinks he was like a wild beast gone mad.
As he could no longer digest food the Ruler had to surrender 72
the dearly-won place and died in the tenth year (of his reign),
still youthful in years[5].

When they see from this that the yielding to evil friends 73
leads to destruction, let those who seek their highest good here or hereafter, avoid such (evil friends) as a snake full of deadly poison.

Here ends the fifty-fourth chapter, called "The Three Kings", in the Mahāvaṃsa, compiled for the serene joy and emotion of the pious.

[1] The Col. Ed. changes the *raṭṭhā* of the MSS. into *raṭṭhaṃ* which then stands next to *sāsanaṃ*. We miss *ca*. W. translates after the Col. Ed. text, "to save the religion and his country".

[2] Namely in Pulatthinagara.

[3] P. *hīnajā*. W.'s translation "who cared not for him" is wrong.

[4] Thus, if my conjecture *tassa santike* instead of *tassa sattavo* is right. If one keeps to *sattavo*, then the passage would have to be translated thus: "his low-class favourites who otherwise found no opportunity of drinking surā, being his teachers (and at the same time) his foes, praised the advantages etc.".

[5] The Sinhalese sources call the King Salamevan after his biruda (Silāmeghavaṇṇa). His predecessor had the surname Sirisaṃghabodhi. Pūjāv. and Rājāv. give Salamevan a reign of 10 years. They tell of his initial successes against the Damiḷas and of his conflict with the Senāpati who then brought an army of 95000 Damiḷas into the country.

CHAPTER LV

THE PILLAGE OF LAṄKĀ

1 The Prince **Mahinda**[1], his younger brother, who after
his death raised the white umbrella in splendid Anurādhapura
2 which was full of strangers brought hither by the Senāpati Sena,
3 abode there ten years amid difficult circumstances[2]. As he wan-
dered from the path of statecraft and was of very weak cha-
racter, the peasants did not deliver him his share of;the produce.
4 As the Prince in his tenth year had entirely lost his fortune,
he was unable to satisfy his troops by giving them their pay.
5 All the Keraḷas[3] who got no pay planted themselves one
with another at the door of the royal palace, determined on
6 force, bow in hand, armed with swords and (other) weapons,
(with the cry) "So long as there is no pay he shall not eat."
7 But te King duped them. Taking with him all his moveable
goods he escaped by an underground passage[4] and betook
8 himself in haste to Rohaṇa. In Sīdupabbatagāma he set up
an armed camp and took up his abode there, after making
9 his brother's wife mahesī. When she died shortly after, he
10 raised his brother's daughter to the rank of mahesī. When
of this Queen a son was born who received the name of
11 Kassapa, the Ruler gave up the stronghold inhabited by him

1 We hear nothing of the reasons why Udaya who according to 54. 58, was appointed yuvarāja, did not come to the throne.

2 P. *kicchena* ("with trouble") *dasavacchare*. W. has "twelve years".

3 See note to 53. 9. The Keraḷas were enlisted as mercenaries by the Sīhala king.

4 The Kauṭalīya speaks I. 20. 1 ff. of secret exits, underground tunnels which have to be made in the royal palace (*antaḥpura*). Cf. Kauṭilya's Arthaśāstra, trsl. by R. Shamasastry, p. 45 ff., J. J. Meyer, Das Altind. Buch vom Welt- und Staatsleben, p. 49. The skr. expression in the Kauṭalīya is *suruṅgā*. See O. Stein, ZII. 3. 313.

and founded a town at the village of Kappagallaka and dwelt, carrying on the government, for long time among the people of Rohaṇa. But in the remaining parts of the country Keraḷas, 12
Sīhalas and Kaṇṇāṭas[1] carried on the government as they pleased. But a horse-dealer who had come hither from the 13
opposite coast, told the Coḷa King on his return about the conditions in Laṅkā. On hearing this, the powerful (prince), 14
with the purpose of taking possession of Laṅkā, sent off a strong body of troops. They landed speedily in Laṅkā. From 15
the spot where they disembarked, oppressing the mass of the inhabitants, the Coḷa army advanced on Rohaṇa. In the six 16
and thirtieth year of the King's reign the Coḷas seized the Mahesī[2], the jewels, the diadem, that he had inherited, the whole of the (royal) ornaments, the priceless diamond bracelet, 17
a gift of the gods, the unbreakable sword and the relic of the torn strip of cloth[3]. But the Ruler himself who had fled 18

[1] *Karṇāṭa* embraced the territory of the present Mysore and adjoining strips of country. The name is preserved in that of the Kanarese language. LSI. IV. 362.

[2] For the acc. *mahesiṃ* etc., the governing verb *agaṇhiṃsu* must be taken from v. 18. To the articles of the regalia (*rājasādhana* or *rājabhaṇḍa*) belong also the umbrella (*chatta*) and the so-called *ekāvali*, a chain consisting of one row of pearls. Their possession means at the same time that of the royal dignity. In times of danger, therefore, the first thing the king does is to secure the insignia (41. 20). A new king takes care to get hold of them in order to legalize therewith his possession of the throne. Thus Moggallāna I. after the suicide of Kassapa I. (39. 28), so also in Rohaṇa the aunt of Mahinda after his murder (*desaṃ gaṇhi sasādhanaṃ*, 50. 51; cf. also 48. 89). After the death of Aggabodhi IV. as there is no heir, the people take charge of the *rājabhaṇḍaṃ* (46. 38). After the death of Mahālānakitti the Coḷas take possession of the diadem and the other valuables (*kirīṭādidhanaṃ* 56. 10). The Coḷa king claims therewith symbolically the dominion over Laṅkā. When Aggabodhi III. flees, he takes the string of pearls *ekāvalī* with him. It is expressly said of Dāṭhopatissa, that he became king without the *ekāvali* (44. 127-8), thus something of his dignity is wanting. It is significant too, that when Saṃghatissa's royal umbrella by a mere accident falls into the hands of the rebel Moggallāna the army at once recognises him as the legitimate king (44. 18—20).

[3] W. translates: "and the sacred forehead band" and adds in a note

in fear to the jungle, they captured alive, with the pretence
19 of making a treaty. Thereupon they sent the Monarch and all
the treasures which had fallen into their hands at once to
20 the Coḷa Monarch. In the thre fraternities and in all Laṅkā
(breaking open) the relic chambers, (they carried away) many
21 costly images of gold[1] etc., and while they violently
destroyed here and there all the monasteries, like blood-
sucking yakkhas[2] they took all the treasures of Laṅkā for
22 themselves. With Pulatthinagara as base, the Coḷas held sway
over Rājaraṭṭha[3] as far as the locality known as Rakkha-
23 pāsāṇakaṇṭha. People in the kingdom took the young prince
Kassapa and brought him up, carefully protecting him through
24 fear of the Coḷas. When the Coḷa King heard that the boy had
reached his twelfth year, he sent high officials with a large
25 force to seize him. They brought with them warriors a hundred
thousend less five thousand (in number) and they ransacked

"the term is of doubtful meaning, but it evidently refers to the fillet worn round the forehead". This translation of *chinnapaṭṭikādhātuka* is perhaps not impossible. Apparently a piece of stuff is meant of the Buddha's dress which belonged as highly prized relic to the regalia of the Sinhalese kings.

[1] For the acc. *dhātugabbhe* in v. 20 we must take as governing verb the gerund *bhinditvā* from v. 21 and from the same verse *aggahuṃ* for governing *paṭibimbe* in v. 20.

[2] The *ojohārino yakkhā* correspond to the vampires of Slav popular belief. F. S. Krauss, Slavische Volkforschungen, p. 124 ff.

[3] The designation so frequently used later of *Rājaraṭṭha* "King's Province" for northern Ceylon is used in contrast to Rohaṇa (cf. for ex. 70. 184 f.) as well as to Dakkhiṇadesa (for ex., 72. 176-79). Later the name Patiṭṭhāraṭṭha is substituted for it (s. note to 82. 26). The Coḷa king who conquered Ceylon was, according to Hultzsch, JRAS. 1913, p. 522 ff.) Parakesarivarman alias Rājendra-Coḷa I. who in the Tirumalai Rock Inscription (EI. IX, p. 229 ff.) boasts of having seized the crown of the king of Ceylon, the crowns of the queens of that king, as well as the "crown and the necklace of Indra" which the king of the South (i. e. the Pāṇḍya king) hat previously deposited with the king of Ceylon. The conquest of Ceylon is first recorded in inscriptions of Rājendra's 6 th year = 1017-8 A. D., but not mentioned in those of the 5 th year, and consequently it must have taken place in A. D. 1017. See also H. W. Codrington, H. C., p. 40, 53.

the whole province of Rohaṇa in every direction. A court 26
official called Kitti, who dwelt in Makkhakudrūsa, and a minister
named Buddha, a native of Māragallaka[1], these two vali- 27
ant men, well versed in the ways of war, made the resolve
to destroy the Coḷa army completely. At a place called Pa- 28
luṭṭhagiri[2] they took up fortified positions, carried on war
for six months and killed a great number of Damiḷas. The 29
Coḷas who had survived the slaughter in this fight, seized
with fear, fled and took up their abode as before ir Pulatthi-
nagara. When thereupon the Prince saw the two victorious 30
officials, he was highly pleased and spake to them (thus):
"Choose a wish my friends". Buddha asked as wish for the 31
village in which his family dwelt; Kitti chose as wish that
the part of his revenues which the bhikkhu community had
appropriated might be remitted. After the most excellent of 32
officials had their wishes fulfilled by the most excellent of
princes, these brave men, fearless, and full of humility, wor-
shipped his feet.

King Mahinda dwelt twelve years in Coḷa land and entered 33
into heaven in the forty-eighth year[3] (from his ascent of the
throne).

Thus fortune's goods if they were gained by one smitten 34
with indolence, are not abiding. Therefore should the prudent
man, who strives after his salvation, ever display ceaseless
endeavour.

Here ends the fifty-fifth chapter, called "The Pillage of Laṅkā", in the Mahāvaṃsa, compiled for the serene joy and emotion of the pious.

[1] For Māragallaka, now Maragala see note to 48. 129.

[2] Cf. 58. 18 with note.

[3] Cf. v. 16. Pūjāv. and Rājāv. ascribe a reign of 48 years to Mahinda, without a word about anything that happened during it. According to them the arrival of the 95000 Damilas took place in the time of his predecessor.

CHAPTER LVI

THE SIX KINGS

1 After they had given the name of Vikkamabāhu to the Monarch's son, all the Sīhalas acted full of humility according
2 to his command. The King collected by every means, money for defeating the Damiḷas, showing, as was meet, favour to
3 his adherents. At the request of his court officials he had ornament and diadem, umbrella and throne made ready for
4 the festival of the King's consecration, but he refused (the festival with the words): "What boots me the ceremony of the raising of the umbrella so long as the possession of Rā-
5 jaraṭṭha[1] is not achieved?" Then the mighty (Prince) assembled a hundred thousand men. But as at the time when the campaign should have begun, he was suffering from the wind
6 disease[2], he thought it not the time to carry on war and entered suddenly in the twelfth year (of his reign) into the city of gods and came into the company of the gods[3].

7 A court official called Kitti, who was invested with the dignity of senāpati, aspired to the kingship and maintained his authority for eight days.

8 He was slain by the mighty Mahālānakitti, who attained consecration as king, and holding sway over the province called
9 Rohaṇa, was vanquished in his third year in battle against

[1] Vikkamabāhu is still restricted to Rohaṇa. See note to 55. 22.

[2] P. *vātaroga*. For the various diseases which Indian medicine groups under this term (*vātavyādhi*) see Jolly, Medicin, p. 118 f.

[3] The same length of reign (12 years) is ascribed to Vikkamabāhu by Pūjāv. and Rājāv. They say of him, though certainly wrongly, that he drove out the Damiḷas who had entered the country under his father. Rājar. and Nik.-s. merely mention his name.

the Coḷas and with his own hand he cut his throat and so
died a sudden death[1].

Thereupon the Damiḷas took the chief treasures, such as 10
the diadem and the like and sent them to the Monarch of the
Coḷa land. The only son of the Prince (Mahālānakitti) known 11
by the name of Vikkamapaṇḍu, had through fear left his
kingdom and was sojourning in the Duḷu country. But when 12
he had tidings of the events in Laṅkā, he betook himself to
the province of Rohaṇa, and dwelling in Kālalittha[2], carried
on the government there for a year[3].

Then a powerful prince of the line of Rāma, known by 13
the name of Jagatīpāla, a Sovereign's son who had come
from the town Ayojjha[4], slew Vikkamapaṇḍu in battle and 14
ruled as a mighty man in Rohaṇa four years[5]. Him also the 15
Coḷas slew in battle and sent the Mahesī with her daughter
and all the valuable property to the Coḷa kingdom.

Then King Parakkama, son of the Paṇḍu King, reigned[6] 16
two years[7]. The Coḷas slew him also when fighting with him.

These (princes) who were too much swayed by the power 17
of desire, went without exception, helplessly to destruction.
Wen the wise man has recognised this, he will doubtless ever
be bent on the annihilation of desire.

Here ends the fifty-sixth chapter, called "The Six Kings"; in the Mahāvaṃsa, compiled for the serene joy and emotion of the pious.

[1] The Sinhalese sources pass over Kitti entirely. They call his successor Mahālānakitti Mahalō. He reigned according to Pūjāv. and Rājāv. 3 years.

[2] Now Kalutara at the mouth of the Kaluganga.

[3] According to Pūjāv. and Rājāv. Vikramapaṇḍi had reigned 3 years.

[4] Skr. *Ayodhya*, the present Oudh in India, situated on the river Gogra.

[5] Pūjāv. the same; Rājāv. 1 year.

[6] *Akā* must be supplemented by *rajjaṃ* from v. 14. Vikkamapaṇḍu is probably meant by the Paṇḍu King.

[7] Pūjāv. 1 year; Rājāv. 6 years. In Rājar. the name is missing. In Pūjāv. he is called Parākramapaṇḍi, in Rājāv. Parākramabāhu-pāṇḍi, in Nik.-s. Parākramapāṇḍiya.

CHAPTER LVII

THE SUBJUGATION OF THE ENEMIES OF ROHANA

1 An army leader called Loka[1], who dwelt in Makkhakudrūsa, a trustworthy, determined man, capable of breaking
2 the arrogance of the Coḷas, after bringing the people over to his side, took possession of the government in the district of Rohaṇa and dwelt in Kājaragāma[2], versed in the conduct determined by custom.

3 Ad that time there lived a powerful prince of the name of Kitti. The history of his lineage will now be told in the sequel[3].

[1] In the Sinhalese sources he is called Lokesvara. Pūjāv. gives him a reign of six years. The end of Loka's reign is related 57. 45-64. For the following period of Sinhalese history it is very difficult to bring the statements of South Indian inscriptions into accordance with those of the Cūlavaṃsa. I refer to Hultzsch, JRAS. 1913, p. 519—21; H. W. Codrington, H. C., p. 55 ff. [2] See note to 45. 45.

[3] From the way it is introduced, the following section seems to be taken from a new source, possibly (see note to 45. 37) from what I have called the "Chronicle of Rohaṇa". There are however certain differences between its statements and the rest of the contents of the Cūlavaṃsa. That the Kassapa in v. 4 is meant for Kassapa II. (44. 144, 45. 1 ff.) seems certain. But there is a confusion about the names Māna and Mānavamma. Māna is called the eldest son of Kassapa II. in 45. 6. The question is whether he is identical with the Mānavamma who later (47. 2, 62) ascends the throne. In the Rohaṇa Chronicle (57. 5) the elder son of Kassapa is called Mānavamma, the younger who comes to the throne, 57. 14, Māna, but in 57. 25 Mānavamma. Of all the difficulties which according to the Cūlavaṃsa (47. 2 ff.) preceded Mānavamma's ascent of the throne, the Rohaṇa Chronicle apparently says nothing. A similar difference exists as regards the names of the sons of Dappula I. According to the Rohaṇa Chronicle the eldest of these is Mānavamma; the Cūlavamsa speaks of the sister's son of Kassapa II. only as Māna.

King Kassapa had a son known by the name of Māṇa. 4
He was ādipāda, a brave man and distinguished by his good
conduct. His elder brother the wise Mānavamma had at one 5
time seated himself on the bank of the river in the neigh-
bourhood of Gokaṇṇaka[1] and had made full preparations ac- 6
cording to custom for an incantation. He began after taking
the rosary[2] in his hand, to murmur the magic verse. To him 7
there appeared Kumāra on his riding bird[3]. The peacock pecked
with its beak at the plate with the offerings[4], but finding no 8
drink in the old coconut shell with its holes, out of which
the water had run[5], he flew at the magician's face[6]. The latter 9
thinking[7] (only) of future success, offered it his eye. The
peacock slit it open and drank thereout violently. Kumāra 10
was pleased, he granted the Prince his prayed-for wish and
departed brightly gleaming through the air[8]. When his 11
court officials beheld Mānavamma with his destroyed eye, they
grieved, but he comforted the people by telling them of the

[1] See note to 41. 79.

[2] See note to 46. 17.

[3] The God Skanda, who is worshipped in Kājaragāma, riding on the peacock which is sacred to him. Hopkins, Epic Mythology p. 227.

[4] P. *balipaṭṭaṃ*. W. has a note to this: "The tray or bowl in which food, flowers, etc. are presented to spirits at the performances of magical rites". P. *paṭṭa* may mean "tray", but for "bowl" we should expect *patta* = skr. *pātra*.

[5] W.: "Water is generally placed in a coconut shell on the altar for the benefit of the evil spirit".

[6] P. *japantassa mukhaṃ gato*. W. translates this by: "He went up and stood in the presence of the wizard". That is misleading.

[7] P. *bhāviniṃ siddhiṃ apekkhaṃ*. W. interprets the passage quite differently. He translates: "The wizard remembered the Bháviní siddhi" and remarks thereto in the note: "A course of action under certain emergencies, prescribed in magical rites".

[8] Popular tradition places the legend of the incantation described in v. 5 ff. in the Vākirigala-vihāra in the Kegalla District. The magician is mentioned only by his later monk's name of Mayūrapāda. The Vākirigala-vihāra is said to have been called in former times Mayūrapāda-pāya after him. Bell, Report on the Kégalla District, p. 45.

12 fulfilment of his wish. Thereupon his companions were con-
tent and urged him to come to Anurādhapura and carry out
13 his consecration as king. "What boots me the royal dignity
now that I have a maimed body? I will practise asceticism
as soon as I have undergone the ceremony of world-renun-
14 ciation. Let my younger brother, Māna by name, preserve
the inherited reign of Laṅkā." With that he rejected the royal
15 dignity which had come to him. Having thoroughly grasped his
purpose, his court officials sent people to tell that his younger
16 brother. At the tidings thereof, the brother came speedily
hither, sought out his brother, fell at his feet, wept and grieved
17 sore and betook himself along with the elder brother, to
Anurādhapura where in accordance with the purposes of the
18 elder (brother), he took over the crown. Hereupon he betook
himself to Abhayagiri and doing reverence, besought the as-
cetics for admission for his brother to the ceremony of world-
19 renunciation. Thereupon the ascetics carried out with the
cripple the ceremonies of world-renunciation and of admission
20 into the Order without regard to the regulations[1]. The Ruler
built for him the superb pariveṇa Uttaromūla and made him
21 head of the pariveṇa. He placed under him there six hundred
bhikkhus, gave him the seven supervisory officials[2] and the
22 five groups of servitors[3]. He gave him further assistants who

[1] According to the Vinaya (Mahāvagga I. 71 = Vin. ed. Oldenberg I. p. 91) cripples are not admitted to the Order.

[2] P. *paṭihāre satta.* According to Abhp. 1018, *paṭihāra* is equivalent to *dvārapālaka.* That is too narrow an interpretation if it is a case here of "seven *paṭihārā*". The word probably means in general a monastery official. In fact the Mihintale tablet A (line 20-21) enumerates seven of these: 1) *veher-pirivahanuvā,* 2) *niyam-jeṭu,* 3) *ā-kämiyā,* 4) *pasak-kämiyā,* 5) *veher-leyā,* 6) *karaṇḍ-leyā,* 7) *karaṇḍu-atsamu.* For attempts at explaining these difficult terms see Wickremasinghe, EZ. I. 101. In slab B, line 5 an eighth is added, *särāyin-gannak.* The *mangul-jeṭak* mentioned here in line 6 corresponds probably to the *niyam-jeṭu* in A.

[3] Cf. 67. 58, as well as 84. 5. In the last passage, in addition to the five groups of servants, ten others are also distinguished. W. says in a note to our passage that the five mean "carpenters, weavers, dyers, barbers and workers in leather". I believe rather that what is meant

were versed in various handicrafts and placed under him the
guardians of the Tooth Relic. His (the King's) counsellors were 23
the bhikkhus of the Abhayagiri(-vihāra) and the King pro-
tected the people wholly according to his (brother's) advice.
But certain people who were of his lineage, but had no de- 24
sire for world-renunciation, dwelt as they liked and were
addressed by the title of "Great Lord"[1]. From the pure race 25
of this King Mānavamma versed in the law and in statecraft,
that was propagated in sons and grandsons with Aggabodhi[2] 26
at the head, that was first among princely dynasties, there went
forth sixteen (sovereigns) of equal birth who held legitimate
sway in Laṅkā.

The monarch Mahinda had two (cousins) daughters of his 27
mother's brother. These fair (maidens) were known by the
names of Devalā und Lokitā. Of these two daughters, Lokitā 28
conceived by the son of her father's sister[3], the handsome 29
prince Kassapa by name, two sons called Moggallāna and
Loka[4]. The elder of these, versed in all the ways of the
world and the Order, known by the title "Great Lord"[5], 30

are workmen as enumerated in the Mihintale tablet B, line 7 ff. We have no idea it is true, of the principle on which the division of these servants into five or ten groups was made.

1 P. *mahāsāmipadaṃsita* = Skr. *mahāsvāmipradarśita*. On the title *himiyā* = P. *sāmi* used of bhikkhus see note to 52. 10.

2 Aggabodhi. V. It is true he is not mentioned by name in the list of kings in the Cūlavaṃsa, perhaps owing to a gap in the text. See above 48. 1 ff. It should be noted that here the King, father of Aggabodhi, is not called Māna as in v. 14, but Mānavamma. Cf. note to 57. 3.

3 P. *mātulattajaṃ*. I am inclined to assume that *mātulā* here is used in the sense "father's sister". This would bring us back to the family tree as Still has drawn it up in the Index to the Mhvs. Kassapa the husband of Lokitā, would then be the son of Mahinda V. (55. 10), later King Vikkamabāhu I. (56. 1).

4 I take *Moggallānaṃ ca Lokavhe* for a disintegrated compound. The change into *Moggallānalokavhe* of the Col. Ed. is suggestive, but gets no support from the MSS.

5 This title apparently customary in Rohaṇa is derived according to 45. 50 from Dappula I.

zealous in the service of the community, a habitation of many choice virtues, took up his abode in Rohaṇa.

31 A grandson of King Dāṭhopatissa[1] who had undergone the
ceremony of world-renunciation in the Order of the Holy Buddha,
32 dwelt full of faith, practising asceticism, controlled by discipline,
selfcontrolled in spirit, as hermit in a solitary spot. The
gods who had pleasure in him, praised everywhere his virtue.
33 When the Ruler of Laṅkā heard of his excellence, the fame
of which had spread everywhere, he sought him out, bowed
34 before him and sought to gain him as his counsellor[2]. But as
he would not, he besought him again and again, had him
fetched and made him take up his abode in a finely built
35 pāsāda. The King who prized highly the excellence of the
Master of the ascetics, as long as he dwelt there, ruled the
people in justice, walking in the way marked out by his ad-
36 vice. But because the Master among ascetics in consequence
of the invitation given him in honourable fashion by the
Master of Laṅkā, had of his pity forsaken the mountain world[3],
37 and having gathered bhikkhus round him, had taken up his
abode there, (the pāsāda) got the name of Selantara-
38 samūha. Since that time the sovereigns of Laṅkā make a
bhikkhu spend the night in a small temple[4] of the gods and

[1] It is impossible to determine whether Dāṭhopatissa I. or II. is meant here.

[2] The inf. *kātuṃ attānusāsanaṃ*, "to give him counsel" is governed by *ārādhayaṃ* in 34 a. Which King of Laṅkā is meant we do not know. Perhaps Mānavamma? The fragment vv. 31—39 has evidently only the object of leading from Mahinda from whom Kitti is descended on his father's side, to Dāṭhopatissa from whom he is descended on his mother's side through Lokitā (v. 41).

[3] P. *selantara* lit. "rock interior" (perhaps = "rock cave") with reference to the name *Selantarasamūha*. Cf. *samūhetvā* in v. 37 a.

[4] P. *devapalli*. Cf. skr. *palli* "hut". The whole passage is very curious. We are told here of a *mūlaṭṭhāna*, that is (according to v. 39) of the position of a premier and highest counsellor (cf. *mūlāmacca*, 69. 34; 70. 151). It is held by a bhikkhu who must be confirmed in it by a kind of oracle. This confirmation again is granted by the devatās, another proof of the way in which Buddhism is interwoven with popular ideas.

place him, if he has found favour with the deity, in the
leading position and when they protect Order and people, they 39
act according to the counsel of the ascetics who hold the
leading position.

By Prince Bodhi of the line of Dāṭhopatissa te Princess 40
Buddhā of like lineage conceived a daughter, Lokitā by name, 41
distinguished by most excellent marks. Afterwards she was
wedded to the able Moggallāna. She conceived by him four 42
children, Kitti, the princess Mittā, Mahinda and Rakkhita.
The eldest son (Kitti) was (already) in his thirteenth year a 43
plucky hero, and extremely skilled in the use of the bow.
Swayed by one thought alone: how shall I become possessed 44
of Laṅkā once I have rid it of the briers of the foe? he dwelt
in the village called Mūlasālā.

A powerful man known by the name of Buddharāja, quar- 45
relled at that time with the general Loka[1]. He fled in haste 46
to the district called Cuṇṇasālā and having there by every
means made subject to himself many people, such as Kitti and
others, he dwelt together with numerous warlike kindred at 47
the foot of the Malaya mountains where he was difficult to
reach. To him there came a distinguished astrologer[2] Saṃgha 48
by name, and portrayed the character of the prince (Kitti)
in favourable fashion. "The eldest son of the Great Lord 49
(Moggallāna), who bears the name of Kitti, carries on him
the marks of power and is gifted with insight and courage.
Even in Jambudīpa he would, I believe, be capable of uniting 50
the whole realm under one umbrella, how much more so in
the Island of Laṅkā!" When the other heard that, he made 51
the resolve to support the Prince and sent people to the
Prince. When the illustrious hero heard their message, he 52
for fear that they might hold him back, left the house without

[1] The Loka described in 57. 1 as *camūnātha*. W. inserts here the words: "who ruled Rohaṇa". That is not in the text, but it is correct as far as Loka resided in Kājaragāma. It is also not said that Buddharāja was a "prince".

[2] P. *saṃvaccharikanāyako*, lit. a chief of the *s*. Cf. skr. *sāṃvatsarika* BR., s. v. nr. 2.

53 his parents' knowledge, with nothing but his bow and seeing
all kinds of favourable signs, he prudently betook himself in
54 haste to the village of Sarīvaggapiṭṭhi. While sojourning there,
the hero sent away his servants and captured the village
55 of Bodhivāla then in possession of the opposite party[1]. There-
upon the arrogant general (Loka) sent his army thither; it sur-
56 rounded the village and opened fight[2]. The prince who full
of impetuous courage, fought with his soldiers against them,
scattered them in all directions, as a stormy wind (scatters)
57 cotton. He then betook himself, knowing the opportunity, to
the Cuṇṇasālā district and during his sojourn there brought
58 the whole region of Malaya into his power. Even now the
general[3] sent off his army over and over again, but as he
59 could not gain the upper hand, he became furious. A son of
the henchman Kitti[4] dwelling in Makkhakudrūsa, a powerful
60 man known by the name of Devamalla, now came hither, ac-
companied by kinsmen and friends, at the head of many people
dwelling in Rohaṇa, and with reverence sought out the Prince
61 (Kitti). He able and farfamed, at the age of fifteen girt on
62 his sword and demanded the dignity of ādipāda. Thereupon
he betook himself with a mighty force to Hiraññamalaya and
63 built there on the Remuṇa rock a stronghold. Thither too the
general[5] sent his army, but as he did not stay victorious in
64 battle, he gave up the idea of renewing the war. The ruler
Loka[6], the army's commander, now forsook this his world,

[1] Namely of the general Loka.

[2] The dat. *saṃgāmāya* with *samārabhi* (instead of the acc.) is irregular.

[3] P. *seninda* is like *senanī* a synonym of *senāpati*. The title of "King" is never accorded to Loka.

[4] See above 55. 26, 31.

[5] P. *camūpati* stands in the text and v. 64 *camūnātha*, both synonyms for *senāpati* (Loka).

[6] In their list of Errata S. and B. correct *lokanātho* into *lokanāmo*. That is certainly wrong. Without doubt a pun is intended with *camūnātho*, and the form *Lokanātha* corresponds to the *Lokesvara* of the Sinhalese sources. Another pun is that with *loka*. The word is contained in the name, in *lokaṃ sakaṃ* "his world" or "his people" and in *paraloka*.

and in the sixth year of his reign his goal was the other world.

Now a Chief of the Kesadhātus[1], Kassapa by name, got 65
the upper hand of the people and carried on the government
in Rohaṇa. At the tidings of this the Coḷa general, armed 66
for war, set out from Pulatthinagara and marched against
Kājaragāma. But the Kesadhātu scattered the forces of the 67
Damiḷas in a battle, set up guards at the frontier of Rakkha-
pāsāṇa[2], and then the hero proud of his victory, returned 68
with his great army and entered Kājaragāma. When the vi- 69
gorous[3] Ādipāda (Kitti) heard all this, he quickly equipped
an army, to overwhelm the Kesadhātu. When the latter had 70
tidings of this he advanced full of pride with befitting troops
from Kājaragāma to Sippatthalaka[4]. But when the invincible 71
Prince (Kitti) at the head of many of the inhabitants of
Pañcayojana[5] and other districts drew near, he betook him- 72
self, perceiving that many of the dwellers in his own district
were averse from war, (and) believing that a battle here
would be difficult, to Khadiraṅgaṇi[6]. With a great army 73
the royal youth (Kitti) aged sixteen years, entered at once
free from all fear, into Kājaragāma. Having ruled Rohaṇa 74
six months, the Chief of the Kesadhātus full of bitterness,

[1] Here we meet for the first time with the remarkable expression so frequently used later of *kesadhātu*. W. translates *kesadhātunāyaka* by "the Chief of the Hair Relic". But *nāyaka* is used here in the same way as in *saṃvaccharikanāyaka*, v. 48, for in the sequel *kesadhātu* is used alone. Cf. on this title the "Introduction" III.

[2] W. suggests doubtfully Rakvāna.

[3] P. *sutthiradhātuko*. The word *dhātu* at the end of a bahuvrīhi compound often means "kind, nature, peculiarity, character" and is much, almost exclusively, used periphrastically. Thus in *samadhātuka* "of similar kind". JaCo. II. 31[22]; *kiliṭṭhadhātuka* "defiled" JaCo. I. 438[20]; *badhiradhātuka* "hard of hearing" JaCo. II. 63[13].

[4] See also 58. 7.

[5] Now Pasdun-Korale, east of Kalutara, in the province Sabaragamuva. The P. word *raṭṭha* is frequently used quite in the sense of the Sinh. *kōralē*.

[6] See also 58. 36.

75 marched thither to battle. But the army of the royal youth (Kitti) engaged him in hard battle and the mighty one captured the head of the Chief of the Kesadhātus.

76 Having reached the age of seventeen years, the Prince the glory of whose great fame had spread on every side, who was extraordinarily skilled in the use of the many expedients such as kindness and the like had freed the whole of Rohaṇa from the briers of the foe.

Here ends the fifty-seventh chapter, called "The Subjugation of the Enemies of Rohaṇa", in the Mahāvaṃsa, compiled for the serene joy and emotion of the pious.

CHAPTER LVIII

THE ADVANCE TO ANURĀDHAPURA

The name Vijayabāhu[1] of the Prince wise in statecraft, 1
who now found himself in the position of yuvarāja, was known
everywhere. Gifted with abundant knowledge, he had the 2
drums beaten for his entering on the government and placing
numbers of his followers in befitting positions and applying 3
the four methods[2] of warriors for the destruction of the Coḷas
who were ravaging Rājaraṭṭha, he took up his abode there
(in Rohaṇa). When the Coḷa King heard of that, he sent off 4
his Senāpati who was then in Pulatthinagara, with army and
train. As Vijayabāhu recognised that the (Coḷa) general who 5

[1] Kitti adopts this name when he wins his claim to the throne. In the rock inscription of Ambagamuva (Bell, ASC. Ann. Rep. 1910—11 = III. 1915, p. 121, no. 196; Wickremasinghe, EZ. II. 202 ff.) the king calls himself Sirisangbo Vijayabāhu. He names as his parents Abhā Salamevan and Dev Gon, names which seem to have been taken over mechanically from the Rāja-māligāva inscription of Polonnaruva on the introduction to which that of the Ambagamuva inscription rests (See note to 54. 7). Important for the history of the reign of Vijayabāhu I. is the Tamil inscription of Polonnaruva dealt with by C. Rásanáyagam Mudaliyar in JRAS. C. Br. xxix, no. 77, 1924, p. 266 ff., and recently also by Wickremasinghe, EZ. II. 242 ff.

[2] According to Abhp. 348 the *caturo upāyā* the four means of success are *bheda* "division (of the enemy)", *daṇḍa* "open war, offensive", *sāma* "friendly negotiations, treaty" and *dānāni* "gifts, bribes". The doctrine of the four *upāya* is also well known in Sanskrit literature. It is found in the Mahābhārata, in the Amarakośa, in Hemacandra's Abhidhānacintāmaṇi, in the Yājñavalkyasmṛti, in Manu, 7. 109 (BR. s. v. *daṇḍa* 11). Finally they are enumerated in Kauṭalya's Arthaśāstra 2. 10, 28: *upāyāḥ sāmopapradānabhedadaṇḍāḥ* as a method of royal policy. See J. J. Meyer, Das altind. Buch vom Welt- und Staatsleben, p. 105.

had advanced close to Kājaragāma, could scarcely be defeated,
6 he withdrew into the mountain jungle. The (Coḷa) general
plundered Kājaragāma in haste, but as he could not stay
7 there, he betook himself again to his province. Thereupon
the Mahādipāda[1] came hastily from Malaya and besieged
8 Sippatthalaka[2] with strong forces. The King (Vijayabāhu) sent
to the King in the Rāmañña[3] country numbers of people and
9 much costly treasure[4]. Then arrived in the harbour many
ships laden with various stuffs, camphor, sandelwood and other
10 goods. By all kinds of valuable gifts he inclined the soldiers
to him and with large forces at his command, he took up
his abode in Tambalagāma[5].

11 All the inhabitants of Rājaraṭṭha grew hostile to one
12 another and paid no further tribute. The adversaries of the
Coḷa King full of arrogance, left his commands unheeded, ill-
treated the appointed officials and did what they pleased.
13 When the Coḷa Monarch heard this, he was filled with rage
14 and he sent off one of his henchmen with a great army. The
latter landed in Mahātittha, slew many people here and there
15 and subdued the inhabitants of Rājaraṭṭha. Later on he came
then, cruel in his commands, to Rohaṇa and fell upon it with

[1] The title mahādipāda belongs to Vijayabāhu in his position of yuvarāja.

[2] See 57. 70.

[3] Name for Burma. Note that Vijayabāhu from now onwards is called *rājā*.

[4] P. *sāraṃ dhanajātaṃ*. The word *sāra* is here (as also in v. 21) used as an adjective (see skr. *sāra*, BR. s. v., 4); *dhanajāta* which is also used in v. 10, is nearly always a mere paraphrase for *dhana*.

[5] A Tambalagama lies (Census of Ceylon 1921, II., p. 152) in the Hinidum-Pattuva of the Galle District not far from Batuvangala on the upper Gin-ganga. If this is our Tambalagāma that would mean that the centre of gravity of Vijayabāhu's influence was in the west of Rohaṇa, on the borders of Dakkhiṇadesa. The fact that the troops which Kitti led against the Kesadhātu Kassapa came according to 57. 71 chiefly from the Pañcayojana-raṭṭha supports this. It is supported too by the further development of events. The Tambala mentioned 45. 78 cannot be identified with the Tambalagāma of our passage.

his army like the ocean which has burst its bounds[1]. Two 16
mighty men, Ravideva and Cala by name, became opponents
of the King (Vijayabāhu) and went over both of them, to the
Damiḷa commander. When the general saw them accompanied 17
by a great troop of adherents, he believed Rohaṇa would
shortly be in his power.

In the twelfth year (of his reign) the King (Vijayabāhu) 18
put up an entrenchment for the conquest of the Coḷas, on the
Paluṭṭha mountain[2] and took up his abode there. The Coḷa 19
army surrounded the rocks on all sides and a terrible fight
between the two armies took place. The King's soldiers 20
annihilated the Damiḷa army, pursued the fleeing general of
the Coḷa Sovereign and got possession of his head at the vil- 21
lage of Tambaviṭṭhi[3]. Taking with them all the captured
implements of war, together with draught animals and chariots 22
and all valuable treasures, they showed it (the head) to the

[1] I feel bound to keep to the text *ajjhottharittha senāya saṃbhinna-velo va sāgaro* as adopted by me in my edition. The fact of the second pāda having a syllable too much is of no account. See Cūlavs. ed., Introd. p. XII. If one compares the MSS. it is almost certain in the first place, that *ajjhottharittha* and *saṃbhinna* are right, since they have been preserved in all groups of the MSS. The only question is as to what came between the two words. The Col. Ed. with *ajjhotthari saseno sa bhinna°* follows closely the MS. S 3. But what is remarkable is that this MS. is here quite isolated and differs also from S 7. This looks as if we had to do with an arbitrary alteration on the part of the copyist. And how is *tato* or *nato* in all the other MSS. to be explained? I think thus: In the archetype a *tato* was added by mistake to *senāya*, intended originally for *gantvāna* in pāda a. In group S 1, 2, 4 the word is inserted besides *senāya*, in S 6, 7 it has ousted this entirely.

[2] P. *Paluṭṭhapabbata*, identical with the Paluṭṭhagiri mentioned 55. 28. As this occurs here in association with Māragallaka (see Note to 48. 129), the mention of the Paluṭṭha mountain would take us to the west of Rohaṇa, to the borders of Dakkhiṇadesa. Mr. Hocart however is inclined to identify it with Palatupana, 8 miles East of Tissamahārāma. ASC. 1928, p. 17.

[3] If this is the Tambavita in the Paranakuru Korale of the Kegalla-District, the pursuit must have extended far to the north, into Dakkhiṇadesa. That is also not unlikely, for up to his occupation of Pulatthinagara Vijayabāhu evidently meets with no further resistance.

King and spake to him (thus): "It is time to march to Pu-
23 latthinagara." When the Monarch heard these words of his
followers he betook himself now with large forces to Pulatthi-
24 nagara. When the Coḷa Sovereign heard of all these events
he was overcome with fury, and as he desired to capture the
25 Monarch (Vijayabāhu), the hero went in all haste himself to
the harbour on the sea-coast and sent a still larger army to
26 the Island of Laṅkā. When the Ruler (Vijayabāhu) heard
that he sent off his general with a great force to fight with
27 the Coḷa army. The general marched to the neighbourhood
of Anurādhapura and gave the Damiḷa host a fiery battle.
28 There fell in this fight many warriors of the Monarch and
still more of the inhabitants of his kingdom came into the
29 power of the Damiḷas. Thereupon the Monarch abandoned
Pulatthinagara and betook himself in haste to the district
30 called Villikābā. Having removed the two officials who were
placed over this district, he took up his abode there, gathering
31 his soldiers. On the tidings that the Coḷa general was pur-
suing him, he betook himself, aware of the right time[1], to
32 the rocky hill of Vātagiri[2]. At the foot of this mountain he
built a stronghold and fighting, kept the Damiḷas three months
at bay.

33 The younger brother of the Chief of the Kesadhātus[3] who
had been slain earlier in battle, had meanwhile gathered to-
34 gether a large troop of adherents and nursing wrath in his
heart at the slaying of his brother, he raised the whole di-
35 strict of Guttasālā[4] in rebellion. Thereupon the Sovereign of

[1] That is, he knew well that the time for open resistance to the Coḷas had not yet come.

[2] From 60. 39 it is clear that Vātagiri was situated in the province of Dakkhiṇadesa. Thus Vijayabāhu retires not as one might expect, eastwards or south-eastwards over the Mahaveliganga but to the south-west. Evidently he seeks to regain the base in the borders of Rohaṇa and Dakkhiṇadesa from which he started. Vātagiri is no doubt the mountain Vakirigala in the Galboda Korale of the Kegalla District. Bell, Rep. on the Kégalla District = ASC., xix, 1892, p. 45.

[3] See above 57. 65 ff.

[4] See note to 51. 109.

Laṅkā marched thither in haste with a large force and set
up an armed camp at the place called Maccutthala. Then when 36
he had driven his foe in fight out of the stronghold Khadiraṅ-
gaṇi[1], he chased him, still fighting, from Kubūlagalla. He 37
left his ample possessions together with wife and child as well
as his troops in the lurch and fled in haste to the province
occupied by the Coḷas. Thereupon the Lord of men (Vijaya- 38
bāhu) took to himself the whole of his possessions and betook
himself to Tambalagāma[2] where he erected a new stronghold.
In the course of time he went to the town called Mahānā- 39
gahula[3] and sojourned there arming his troops to fight with
the Coḷas. Thereupon the King summoned two of his hench- 40
men and sent them with large forces to Dakkhiṇadesa[4] to
subdue the inhabitants there. Another pair of able[5] officials 41
the Sovereign sent to the coast highroad[6] to destroy the arrog-

[1] See above 57. 72.

[2] After Vijayabāhu had protected his rear by subduing the rebellion in Guttasālā, he returns at first to the position which is to serve him as basis for his future operations (see note to 58. 10) and strengthens it by fortifications. He next betakes himself to the place which may now be looked upon as the capital of Rohaṇa, to make further preparations for the Coḷa war.

[3] According to native tradition we must look for *Mahānāgahula* on the lower Valave-ganga, N. W. of Ambalantota where to-day there are extensive rice-fields similar to those of Tissamahārāma (H. W. Codrington, Notes on Ceylon Topography in the twelfth Century II, from a proof-slip which I owe to the courtesy of the author). In agreement with this is the statement in v. 10 of the Mānāvulu-sandeśa that the river on which the town stood was the *Vanavāhinī*. Mr. Jayaratana of the Colombo Museum drew my attention to this passage. The Commentary explains the name of the river by *vala-hoya*, which is the Valave-ganga.

[4] H. W. Codrington (Notes on Ceylon Topography in the Twelfth Century, JRAS. C. B. Nr. 75, 1922, p. 64) rightly stresses the fact that *dakkhiṇaṃ passaṃ* does not mean "southward" as translated by W. but is the same as *dakkhiṇaṃ desaṃ*.

[5] P. *kakkhaḷa* "hard" in a good sense, as much as firm, enduring, energetic.

[6] Vijayabāhu's strategy is clear. He attacks the position of the Coḷas from two sides: from Dakkhiṇadesa in the direction of Anurādhapura and eastwards from the mountains in the direction of Polonnaruva. The

42 ance of the Coḷas. The officials sent with large forces to Dakkhiṇadesa, took the stronghold at the village of Muhunnaru,
43 further Badalatthala, the stronghold at Vāpinagara, Buddha-
44 gāma, Tilagulla, Mahāgalla and Maṇḍagalla[1]. When later

"coast highroad" I would identify with the old road which avoiding the hill country, led from Mahāgāma to Dastoṭa or Mahagantota on the Mahaveliganga not far from Polonnaruva. I am inclined to look upon the embankment called Kalugalbämma which is crossed between Ekiriyankumbura and Mahaoya by the Passara-Batticaloa road as the remains of this road. The road does not run along the sea, it is true, but it runs from coast to coast, from Mahāgāma to Mahātittha. It is doubtful whether the southern part of this road led over Buttala. The Ratemahatmaya Bibile informed me that one can recognize the southern continuation of the Kalugalbämma further east at Kadiyangoda and that the road runs from here beside an old beaten elephant track direct to Mahāgāma. At any rate the northern continuation of the Kalugalbämma does not lead to Mahiyaṅgaṇa, but leaving this to the left, it seems to lead by Dolagalvela direct to the Mahaveliganga. Thus this highroad must be distinguished from that which runs from Mahāgāma by way of Kataragama, Buttala, Medagama, Bibile to Mahiyaṅgaṇa and from there along the Mahaveliganga towards the north. I myself found remains of this road in Bibile, other remains might perhaps come to light at Alut-nuvara (Mahiyaṅgaṇa) behind the hospital. Vijayabāhu apparently took advantage of a civil war raging at that time in the Coḷa country. It ended with the accession to the throne of Kulōttunga Coḷa I. in A. D. 1069—70. H. W. Codrington, H. C., p. 56.

[1] The topographical identification of the greater part of these localities we owe H. W. Codrington in the treatise cited above (note to 58. 39). Of the names occurring here the following are mentioned elsewhere 1) Badalatthala, 2) Buddhagāma, 3) Tilagulla and 4) Mahāgalla. Muhunnaru and Vāpinagara are doubtful. Badalatthala has been identified by Codrington (following Parker) with Batalagoda in the Ihalavisideke Korale West of the Kurunegala District. Storey on the strength of the mention in an inscription of the Budgam-vehera (ASC. 1908 = S. P. VI. 1913, p. 14-15) considers Buddhagāma to be Menikdena (see ASC. 1908 = VI. 1913, p. 13 ff.) in the Vagapanaha Udasiya Pattu of the District Matale North, where the two roads leading from Kurunegala and from Nalanda to Dambul approach one another, and Codrington supports this assumption. As to Tilagulla, Mr. Codrington refers me by letter to Talagalle Ela in the Katuvanna Korale of the Kurunegala District. According to 68. 44 it is at least certain that it was situated in Dakkhiṇadesa. For Mahāgalla see note to 44. 3.

they had also taken Anurādhapura, they brought the whole
kingdom into their power and pushed forward to Mahātittha.
The two generals sent out to the coast highroad, plundered 45
Chagāma[1] and other armed camps here and there, and when 46
later they had got near to Pulatthinagara, they sent mes-
sengers to the King that he should speedily come hither.
When the Ruler heard of the extraordinary deeds of heroism 47
accomplished by the generals whom he had sent in two
directions, he aware of the time being propitious, equipped 48
his whole army and experienced in methods of war, he left
the town (Mahānāgahula) to exterminate the Colas. During 49
the march the Sovereign set up a camp on the (Mahāvāluka)-
gaṅgā not far from the Mahiyaṅgaṇa-thūpa[2] and took up his
abode there for a time. Afterwards the great hero aware of 50
the opportunity, betook himself to the neighbourhood of
Pulatthinagara and set up here an extremely strong forti-
fication. But all the warlike, valiant Colas who were to be 51
found here and there, gathered together in Pulatthinagara to
make war. The Colas came forth from the town and engaged 52
outside in a great battle, but they were beaten and returned
to the town. Then having secured all the gates of the town, 53
they carried on with great strenuousness a terrifying fight
from bastions and towers. For a month and a half the great 54
army of the Monarch kept the town surrounded but could
not subdue it. The great heros, the great fighters, the great 55
warriors of the Great King, the mighty ones with great pride,
Ravideva, Cala[3] and the others scaled the walls, broke furi- 56

Finally Maṇḍagalla is according to Mr. C. = Mahamadagalla in Hiriyala Hatpattu N. E. of Kurunegala. A Madagala is also marked on sheet F. 9 of the map (scale one mile to the inch) 5 miles S. S. W. of Anurādhapura as name of a mountain. All the evidence points, at any rate, to the progress of the operations against Anurādhapura from South to North through Dakkhiṇadesa.

[1] Chagāma or Chaggāma, it seems to me, has not been identified with certainty. That it was situated in eastern Rohaṇa is clear from 75. 3.

[2] See note to 51. 74.

[3] It was stated in v. 16 that these two generals had gone over to

ously into the town and at once exterminated all the Damiḷas
57 root and branch[1]. After King Vijayabāhu had thus achieved the victory, he the discerning one, had the drums of his
58 dominion beaten[2] in the town. But when the Ruler of the Coḷas heard of this destruction of his army, he thought: the Sīhalas are (too) strong, and sent out no further army.
59 When the hero the discerning one, who had utterly destroyed the best of the proud Coḷas, had placed the whole of Rājaraṭṭha on a sure foundation[3], he the best of kings, greatly rejoicing, advanced in the fifteenth year (of his reign) to the greatly longed for, the best (town of) Anurādhapura[4].

Here ends the fifty-eighth chapter, called "The Advance to Anurādhapura", in the Mahāvaṃsa, compiled for the serene joy and emotion of the pious.

the Coḷas. It would seem that later they again acknowledged the sovereignty of Vijayabāhu. Or we have to do with a mistake of the compiler.

[1] P. *mūlaghaccaṃ aghātayuṃ*. I think we have to take *mūlaghaccaṃ* as adverb. Cf. Dh. 250 *m. samūhataṃ* "radically removed", as also *m. kar* D. III. 67[12] ff., 68[1]. Of the overthrow of the Damiḷas by Vijayabāhu the Ambagamuva inscription (see note to 58. 1) says: "through his own courage he drove away the whole darkness of the Damiḷa forces and brought the whole of the Island of Laṅkā under his umbrella" (line 23).

[2] I. e. he made known by beat of drum that he had ascended the throne.

[3] P. *susādhu* (adv.) *ṭhapitākhilarājaraṭṭho*. We have here no doubt in *Rājaraṭṭha* the name of the province freed from the Damiḷas. See note to 55. 22.

[4] The fact that the King entered Anurādhapura is mentioned in the Tamil inscription of Polonnaruva line 7—8; cf. note to 58. 1.

CHAPTER LIX

THE BESTOWAL OF FAVOURS

With the protection of Laṅkā in the vicinity of the sea 1
the King charged powerful followers, acknowledged warriors,
in regular turn[1]. Since for the festival of the royal conse- 2
cration[2] a pāsāda and many other things had to be prepared,
he (likewise) charged one of his followers with this and after 3
he had there[3] done reverence to the various places deserving
of honour, he returned, after a sojourn of three months, to
Pulatthinagara.

A troop leader known by the name of Ādimalaya rebelled 4
quite openly against the Monarch and came, the deluded one,
hither with all his troops to fight, as far as the village known 5
by the name of Andu, in the vicinity of the town. The Ruler 6
of Laṅkā marched thither, destroyed the haughty one[4] and
returned to Pulatthinagara after bringing his troops into
his power.

From the time that he was yuvarāja, the wise Prince, 7
that best of men, had seventeen years chronicled in writing[5].

[1] I read *paṭipāṭiṃ* and take the accus. in an adverbial sense. His followers had to take over alternately the protection of the coast. The Col. Ed. has *paṭipattiṃ* and W. accordingly translates: "having (before) instructed them in their duties".

[2] I should prefer now to put *abhisekamaṅgalatthaṃ* in the oratio recta.

[3] Namely in Anurādhapura.

[4] Pun on *uddharitvā, uddhataṃ*. For the meaning of "annihilate" cf. skr. *har + ud*, BR., 8.

[5] The passage is important, since it shows that annals were kept at court of the events during each year of the reign. The narrative of Vijayabāhu's reign bears in particular a strongly annalistic character.

8 Having betaken himself hereupon to Anurādhapura and well
versed in custom, had enjoyed the high festival of the coro-
9 nation after the manner of tradition, keeping not to evil but
keeping firmly to pious action, he, secure[1] (in the royal
10 dignity), had the eighteenth year chronicled. Thereupon he
betook himself to splendid Pulatthinagara and dwelt there,
11 known by the name of Sirisaṃghabodhi. He invested his next
youngest brother Vīrabāhu with the dignity of uparāja and
distinguished him in the customary way, by making over to
12 him the province of Dakkhiṇadesa. On his youngest brother
Jayabāhu the Prince[2] conferred the dignity of an ādipāda and
13 bestowed on him the province of Rohaṇa. But on all his
ministers he bestowed office according to merit and directed
them to collect the dues in the kingdom in fitting manner.
14 The administration of justice which had long lain low, the
Sovereign a fount of pity, carried out himself, keeping to
the law, with justice.

15 While now the Ruler of men having rooted out the heaped
up briers of numerous foes, ruled his realm of Laṅkā ever in
16 most excellent fashion, three brothers, the Head of the umbrella
bearers, the President of the Court of Justice and the Chief
17 of the merchants[3] became hostile to the King and betook
themselves, in flight, to Jambudīpa. In the nineteenth year
18 they landed again in Laṅkā. Together they soon roused re-
volt in the province of Rohaṇa, the district of Malaya and
19 the whole of Dakkhiṇadesa. The prudent (Prince) marched to
Rohaṇa and the Malaya district, slew here and there many
20 enemies and when he had thoroughly pacified the country[4],

Cf. 57. 43, 61, 73, 76; 58. 18, 59; 59. 9, 17; 60. 36, 45, as also the chronological summary of Wickremasinghe, EZ. II. 207-8. It is noteworthy too that the King's coronation is celebreated in the anciently sacred town of Anurādhapura although Pulatthinagara is the capital.

[1] Pun on *aṭṭhito, suṭṭhito, susaṃṭhito.*

[2] P. *bāhujā*, the same as *khattiya*, because the caste of the Khattiya issued from the arms of God Brahman.

[3] P. *chattagāhakanātha, dhammagehakanāyaka, seṭṭhinātha.*

[4] P. *taṃ*, namely *Rohaṇaṃ tathā Malayamaṇḍalaṃ.*

and appointed officials there, he, the able one, advanced him-
self with great forces to Dakkhiṇadesa. The hero there sent 21
on a general of the lineage of the brother of Samaṇi[1], cap-
tured his foes in bitter fight, had them impaled and after 22
freeing Laṅkā from the briers (of the rebels) he returned to
Pulatthinagara which was now devoid of all fear[2].

At that time the royal consort of Jagatīpāla[3] who dwelt 23
in the Coḷa Kingdom, had escaped with her youthful daughter
Līlāvatī by name, from the power of the Coḷas, had embarked 24
in haste, landed in the Island of Laṅkā and sought out the
Sovereign of Laṅkā. When the King heard the story of her 25
lineage and saw from that that she was of irreproachable
descent, he had Līlāvatī consecrated as his mahesī. The Ma- 26
hesī conceived by the King a daughter and the Ruler gave
her the name of Yasodharā. Together with the province of 27
Merukandara the King gave his daughter to Vīravamma. She
conceived two daughters. The elder received the same name 28
as her grandmother[4], Sugalā by name was the younger of the
two. The King wishful for the continuance of his line, fetch- 29
ed from the Kālinga country the charming young princess
of the royal family of Kalinga, Tilokasundarī by name, and 30
had her consecrated as his mahesī[5]. She conceived five 31
daughters: Subhaddā, Sumittā, Lokanāthā, Ratanāvalī and
Rūpavatī and a son Vikkamabāhu, furnished with the marks 32

[1] I believe that by *Samaṇī* the foster mother of the Buddha, Mahāpajāpatī, is meant. As she was according to the Cullavagga X. 1 (= Vin. II. 253 ff.), the first woman to receive the *upasampadā* she can be described as "the Nun" pure and simple. The general (*saciva*) belonged thus to the family of Gotama.

[2] Or with the Col. Ed. *nirātaṅkaṃ* "free of harm". The MSS. vary. W. refers the word as predicative object, like *vigatakaṇṭakaṃ* to *Laṅkaṃ*. From the position of the words it seems to me more correct to combine *nirāsaṅkaṃ* with the following *Pulatthinagaraṃ*.

[3] See 56. 16.

[4] Like her *mātāmahī*, the mother of her mother. She was called therefore, Līlāvatī.

[5] Vijayabāhu had, therefore, two mahesīs, Līlāvatī (v. 25) and Tilokasundarī.

of future power. Now that he had obtained increase of off-
33 spring, his wives won the King's heart[1]. Of the other women
of the court, except the wives of equal birth[2], none concei-
ved by the Monarch a fruit of the womb.
34 Now one day as the King surrounded by the throng of
his courtiers, gazed on each of his daughters standing there
35 and, versed in signs, perceived on none of his other daughters
except on Ratanāvalī the sign indicative of the birth of a son
36 (himself) furnished with the signs of power; seized by loving
emotion, he called Ratanāvalī to him, kissed her on the head,
37 and with tender joy spake to her thus: "This thy body shall
be the place for the birth of a son[3] who will surpass all
38 former and future monarchs in glorious qualities, generosity,
wisdom and heroism, who will be able to keep Laṅkā ever in
39 safety[4] and united under one umbrella, who will be in perfect
wise a patron of the Order, and who will display an abundant
40 and fine activity". Though repeatedly entreated by the Coḷa
Monarch, the King proud of his family, would not give him
41 his younger sister. On the contrary, he fetched the Paṇḍu
King who came of an unblemished line[5], and wedded to him
his royal sister Mittā by name who had been born after him.
42 She bore three sons, Mānābharaṇa, Kittisirimegha by name,
43 and him who was called Sirivallabha. (His daughter) Subhaddā
the Ruler gave with ample dowry to Vīrabāhu and Sumittā
44 to Jayabāhu[6]. To Mānābharaṇa he gave his daughter Ratanā-

[1] I believe that *harantā* which all MSS. have, should be separated into *haran tā*. By *tā* are meant the two queens Līlāvatī and Tilokasundarī who have borne children to the King. There is no need to change the text.

[2] That is of course the two Mahesīs. The word *itthāgāra*, lit. "women's house" = Harem women, is used for the inmates, like the German "Frauenzimmer".

[3] A prophecy concerning Parakkamabāhu the Great, the future son of Ratanāvalī.

[4] The Col. Ed. has here *nirāsaṅkaṃ* contrary to all the MSS. while in v. 22 it has *nirātaṅkaṃ*.

[5] See below note to 63. 15.

[6] Vīrabāhu and Jayabāhu were younger brothers of Vijayabāhu.

valī, the one with the name Lokanāthā to Kittisirimegha (to
wife). As the one called Rūpavatī had died, he gave to Siri- 45
vallabha the princess called Sugalā. When he beheld the 46
princes Madhukaṇṇava, Bhīmarāja and Balakkāra, kinsmen of
the Mahesī (Tilokasundarī), who had come from Sīhapura[1],
the Monarch found pleasure in them and granted each of them 47
befitting maintenance. All of them having enjoyed such honour 48
and distinction, dwelt ever loyal to the Ruler, where they
pleased. The younger sister of these princes, Sundarī by name[2], 49
he, concerned for the continuance of his house, gave to
Vikkamabāhu (to wife). Further he also gave Vikkamabāhu 50
the excellent Līlāvatī together with (befitting) income, taking
pleasure in the welfare of his kindred.

Thus caring for those belonging to him, full of riches, 51
above all bent on kindness, he did what served the good of
his kindred and what at the same time was politically wise.

Here ends the fifty-ninth chapter, called "The Bestowal of Favours", in the Mahāvaṃsa, compiled for the serene joy and emotion of the pious.

[1] Sīhapura is the town which according to the legend (cf. Mhvs. 6. 35) was founded in Lāḷa by Vijaya's father Sīhabāhu. Lāḷa borders in the north on the Kaliṅga kingdom, the home of Tilokasundarī, as must be inferred from Mhvs. 6. 1-5. The south-eastern district of Chutiā Nāgpur to the west of Bengal, is still called Singhbhūm.

[2] All the MSS. have the form *Sunārī* with the single exception of S 7, which has *Sundarī*. The latter is confirmed by an inscription. In the rock inscription of Dimbulagala (EZ. II. 184 ff., 194 ff.) the Queen calls herself Sundaramahadevī, consort of the King Vikumbā (i. e. Vikkamabāhu) and mother of Gaja-bāhu-deva. In the course of the inscription she refers to a meritorious work which she had performed in the reign of her husband's predecessor Jayabāhu.

CHAPTER LX

CARE FOR THE LAITY AND FOR THE ORDER.

1 The Ruler chose people of good family whom he had all
around him[1] and, as was customary, charged them with his
2 protection[2]. In Pulatthinagara he had a high and strong
wall built, provided with many bastions, well faced with stucco,
3 defended round about with a long, broad and deep trench and
equipped with high parapets[3] difficult for the foe to reduce.
4 As the number of the bhikkhus was not sufficient to make the
chapter full for the (holding of the) ceremony of admission into
5 the Order and other acts, the Ruler of men who had at heart the
continuance of the Order, sent to his friend, the Prince Anuruddha[4]
6 in the Rāmañña country messengers with gifts and had fetch-
ed thence bhikkhus who had thoroughly studied the three

[1] P. *sabbe samādiya*, overlooked in W.'s translation.

[2] They were his permanent bodyguard. P. *yathācāraṃ* "as was customary" like the skr. *yathācāram*, with the same meaning. BR., s. v.

[3] P. *patthaṇḍila*. The word occurs again M. II. 155 as the designation of a part of a hermitage and in the combination *-ḍile caṅkamāno*. The skr. *sthaṇḍila* = *pa-tthaṇḍila* means "a level floor, bare floor". What *patthaṇḍila* is in a fortification cannot be determined. Unfortunately the descriptions which Kauṭalya's Arthaśāstra 2. 3, 21, gives of the construction of a fortress, are so obscure and difficult that they do not help us further.

[4] King Anuruddha of Burma, the national hero of the Burmese, was crowned in the year 1010 (PHAYRE, Hist. of Burma, p. 22). There are chronological difficulties about Anuruddha's being the contemporary of Vijayabāhu I. The assumption is probably an arbitrary one on the part of the author of our part of the Mahāvaṃsa or of his source. That Vijayabāhu fetched bhikkhus from Burma is confirmed by the Tamil inscription of Polonnaruva mentioned above (note to 58, 1). The fact is also related in Pūjāv. Rājāv. and Nik.-s.

Piṭakas, who were a fount of moral discipline and other vir-
tues, (and) acknowledged as theras. After distinguishing them 7
by costly gifts, the King had the ceremonies of world-re-
nunciation and of admission into the Order repeatedly per-
formed by them and the three Piṭakas together with the com- 8
mentary frequently recited and saw to it that the Order of
the Victor which had declined in Laṅkā again shone brightly.
Within Pulatthinagara he had many charming vihāras built 9
at different places[1], made bhikkhus who belonged to the 10
three fraternities[2], take up their abode there and gladdened
them by abundant (gifts of the) four necessaries. After buil- 11
ding a vihāra beautiful by reason of its threshold pillar[3],
provided with wall and trench, beautified by a splendid five-
storeyed pāsāda, well equipped with charming rows of dwel- 12
lings round about, filled with people[4], provided with a roomy,
superb, sumptuous gateway[5], he, holding precious above all 13
things the three (sacred) objects, made it over to the bhikkhus
dwelling in the three fraternities. For their support with 14
food he granted to the community the whole district of Āḷi-
sāra[6] together with the canal diggers[7] dwelling there. To 15
several hundred bhikkhus he assigned dwellings there, sup-
plying them regularly with the four necessaries in ample

[1] P. *padesasmiṃ tahiṃ tahiṃ*, equivalent to *tasmiṃ tasmiṃ padese.*

[2] See below note to 60. 56.

[3] It is doubtful whether *eḷakatthambha* is to be understood as a dvandva or as a tatpuruṣa compound. At any rate what is meant is the whole frame of the entrance gate on which great care was expended in the buildings of Ceylon.

[4] What is meant probably are the monastery servants who were present in great numbers.

[5] P. *gopura* here probably the main gateway of the whole establishment.

[6] Now Elahera in the Matale District, N. E. of Nalanda on the Ambanganga. Bell, ASC. 1910-11 = X. 1914, p. 42; ASC. 1911-12 = III. 1915, p. 66.

[7] P. *nettika* "one who makes conduits for irrigating rice-fields" (Childers). Cf. *udakaṃ hi nayanti nettikā* Dh. 80, 145; Therag. 19; M. II. 105[5]. These people had to keep in order the rice fields granted to the monastery. W.'s translation "the chiefs of the people who dwelt there" is wrong.

16 measure. After building for the Tooth Relic a beautiful and
costly temple[1] he instituted permanently for the Tooth Relic a
17 great festival. Holding himself aloof from intercourse with a
large circle[2], he translated the Dhammasaṅgaṇi every morning
18 in the beautiful preaching-hall[3]. While instituting many offerings
of sweet-smelling savours, flowers and the like with dance
and so forth, he was wont, joined with him in faith, to wor-
19 ship the Enlightened One with bowed head. The many scho-
lars[4] who came from Jambudīpa and who were worthy of a
gift, the mighty Monarch who was a hero in giving, gladdened
20 with gifts of money. For the preachers of the true doctrine
he instituted offerings of divers kinds, and rejoicing ever at
the merits of the doctrine, made them teach the true doc-
21 trine. Thrice he dispensed alms to the poor of a weight
equal to that of his body[5] and on the Uposatha day he kept
22 the Uposatha vow in blameless fashion. Every year the So-
vereign instituted a Daṇḍissara offering[6]; he had the Tipiṭaka
23 copied and presented it to the bhikkhu community. By the
sending of costly pearls, precious stones and other jewels,
he reverenced, sacrificing many times over, the sacred Bodhi
Tree in Jambudīpa.

24 Envoys sent by the Kaṇṇāta Monarch[7] and by the Coḷa
25 King came hither with rich presents. They sought out the
Monarch. He was greatly pleased thereat and after rendering
26 both embassies what was their due, he sent at first[8] with the

[1] Confirmed by the Tamil inscription cited above 58. 1.

[2] P. *gaṇasaṃgaṇikā*, the same meaning as DhCo. 4. 143[13], here a pun on *dhammasaṅgaṇi*.

[3] P. *dhammamandira*, synonym for *dhammasālā*.

[4] P. *sūri*, plur. *sūrayo*. At the end of a compound, Mhvs. 85. 44 with the meaning "skilful in" etc. I. Sg. *sūriṇā* Mhvs. 26. 23.

[5] Confirmed again by the Tamil inscription of Polonnaruva l. 11.

[6] The origin of the name is unknown. All we know from parallel passages (52. 3; 53. 30) is that it was alms dispensed to wandering beggars and artists.

[7] See note to 55. 12.

[8] P. *tesu* (i. e. of the two embassies) *ādo* (at first). The envoys of the Coḷa king were thus at first retained.

Kaṇṇāta messengers his own envoys to Kaṇṇāta with choice
gifts. But the Colas maimed the noses and ears of the Sīhala 27
messengers horribly when they entered their country[1]. Thus 28
disfigured they returned hither and told the King everything
that had been done to them by the Coḷa King. In flaming 29
fury Vijayabāhu in the midst of all his courtiers had the
Damiḷa envoys summoned and gave them the following message
for the Coḷa king. "Beyond ear-shot[2], on a lonely island in 30
the midst of the ocean shall a trial of the strength of our
arms take place in single combat, or, after arming the whole 31
forces of thy kingdom and of mine a battle shall be fought
at a spot to be determined by thee: exactly in the manner I 32
have said it shall ye report to your master". After these
words he dismissed the envoys clad in women's apparel in 33
haste to the Cola King, then he betook himself with his army
to Anurādhapura. To the seaports Mattikāvāṭatittha[3] and 34
Mahātittha he sent two generals to betake themselves to the
Coḷa kingdom and begin the war[4]. While the generals were 35
procuring ships and provisions in order to send the troops to
the Cola kingdom, then, in the thirtieth year (of the King's
reign), the division of the troops called Velakkāra[5] revolted as 36

[1] On the way into the Kaṇṇāta-country.

[2] Some MSS. have *sonaṃ vinā*, some *sotaṃ vinā* which comes to the same thing *n* and *t* being constantly mistaken for each other. I keep to *sotaṃ vinā* which gives excellent sense, but believe that we must derive *sota* from the Skr. *śrotra* rather than from *śrotas*. The alteration of the Col. Ed. into *senaṃ vinā* would merely be tautological.

[3] The name means "clay-pit landing-place". The place is otherwise never mentioned.

[4] Nothing is said about any answer of the Coḷa King to Vijayabāhu's challenge.

[5] In the Tamil inscription of Polonnaruva the Veḷaikkāra are mentioned as the troops which had taken over the guarding of the Tooth Relic. They were a group of soldiers or a military clan and accompanied, as we learn from inscriptions of Southern India (Wickremasinghe, EZ. II. 247), King Rājendra Coḷa I to Ceylon. Since that time they had great influence in the Island, serving as mercenaries to the king. According to Rásanáyagam Mudaliyar (JRAS. C. Br. xxix, nr. 77, 1924, p. 268 f.) they took the vow to kill themselves if any evil befalls

37 they did not want to go thither. They slew the two generals
and like rutting elephants in their unbridledness, they plun-
38 dered the country round Pulatthinagara. They captured the
younger sister of the King with her three sons[1] and burned
39 down with violence the King's palace. The King left the
town and betook himself in haste to Dakkhiṇadesa and having
40 hidden all his valuable possessions on the Vātagiri[2] rook, he
advanced together with the Uparāja Vīrabahu, of lion-like
41 courage, and surrounded by a great force, to Pulatthinagara
where after a sharp fight he shortly put the assembled troops
42 to flight. Placing them around the pyre on which were
laid the remains of the murdered generals, he had the recreant
43 leaders of the troops, their hands bound fast to their backs,
chained to a stake and burnt in the midst of the flames bla-
44 zing up around them. The Ruler having (thus) executed there
the ringleaders of the rebels[3], freed the soil of Laṅkā every-
where from the briers (of the rebels).

45 The King did not lose sight of the aim he had set him-
self of fighting with the Coḷa (King), and in the forty-fifth
46 year (of his reign) he marched with war-equipped troops to
the port on the sea and stayed there some time awaiting his
47 arrival. But as the Coḷa (King) did not appear, the King
dismissed his envoys, returned to Pulatthinagara and resided
there a considerable time.

48 The tanks Mahāheli, Sareheru and Mahādattika by name,
49 Kaṭunnarū, Paṇḍavāpi and Kalalahallika by name, the tank

the king. Although their disloyalty was punished by Vijayabāhu with bloody severity, rebellions of the Velakkāras took place even at the time of Gajabāhu (63. 24 ff.) and Parakkamabāhu I. (74. 44 ff.).

[1] The Princess Mittā with her sons Mānābharaṇa, Kittisirimegha and Sirivallabha. See 59. 41-2.

[2] See 58. 31 with note.

[3] In *mānīnaṃ gāmaṇi* the latter must be taken as acc. pl., the former as gen. pl. *Mānin* "proud, arrogant" is evidently the same as "unbridled, rebellious", as noun "rebel". W. translates: "moreover, the king laid waste the lands of the haughty nobles who dwelt there". But v. 44 still evidently refers to the execution of the rebel leaders.

Eraṇḍegalla and the Dīghavatthuka tank, the tanks Maṇḍavā-
ṭaka and that of Kittaggabodhipabbata; the tanks Valāhassa, 50
Mahādāragalla and Kumbhīlasobbhaka, the Pattapāsāṇa tank
and the tank called Kāṇa[1]: these and many other tanks whose 51
dams had burst, he had (newly) dammed up, since his efforts
were ever directed to the welfare of the distressed. By build- 52
ing dams here and there on brooks, rivers and streams the
Sovereign made his kingdom fruitful. While damming up 53
(anew) the damaged Tilavatthuka canal he filled the Maṇihīra
tank with water. His own Mahesī who disturbed the peaceful 54
life of the vihāras, he deprived of her revenues and had her
led out into the town with an iron collar[2], conciliated the 55
community and thus testified to the world his reverence for
the Order. In the three fraternities in Mahāgāma he restored 56
the relic shrines[3] destroyed by the Coḷas[4] and likewise the

[1] Of these lakes several have been already mentioned, others are mentioned later. The Mahādattika is mentioned 38. 50 under Dhātusena, the Valāhassa 37. 185 under Upatissa II., as well as 42. 67 under Aggabodhi II. The Pattapāsāṇa was built according to 41. 61 by Moggallāna by the damming-up of the Kadambanadī which flows past Anurādhapura. The Kāṇa which is mentioned under Sena I. and II., 50. 72 and 51. 73, must probably be looked for in the vicinity of the Mihintale mountain. Amongst the many tanks restored by Parakkamabāhu I. which are enumerated 79. 31 ff. the Mahādatta, the Valāhassa, the Kumbhīlasobbhaka, the Mahādāragalla, the Pattapāsāṇa and the Kāṇa recur. Lastly, among the lakes made or restored by Parakkamabāhu in Dakkhiṇadesa before his ascent of the throne (68. 43 ff.) are the Kaṭunnarū and the Kalalahallika (cf. also 70. 73, 163). The Paṇḍavāpi according to 68. 39 was enlarged by him. This must surely be the Paṇḍāvāva in the North-West Province, about 16 miles N. W. of Kurunegala, notwithstanding Parker's opinion against it. See Codrington I. 70.

[2] Lit.: "by having her caught by the neck". It would seem that the Queen had infringed the right of asylum (*abhaya*) of the vihāra.

[3] P. *dhātugabbha*, equivalent to Sinh. *dāgaba, dāgoba, dāgäba*. The word occurs already in the Mhvs. 31. 94. Note that Pulatthinagara (60. 10) and Mahāgāma had each its three monastic fraternities (*tayo nikāyā*, note to 41. 97) just as Anurādhapura.

[4] Refers probably to the plundering of Rohaṇa by the Damiḷas under Mahinda V. See 55. 15 ff.

57 two Thūpārāmas[1]. At the place of his mother's fire-burial as
also at that of his father in Budalaviṭṭhi he erected five large
58 dwelling houses (for bhikkhus). The vihāras Paṇḍavāpi, Pāṭhīna,
Rakkhacetiyapabbata, likewise Maṇḍalagiri, and the Madhutthala-
59 vihāra, the vihāra called Uruvela and the vihāra in Devanagara,
the vihāra Mahiyaṅgaṇa and the cave temple Sītalaggāma,
60 the Jambukola-vihāra and Girikaṇḍaka, the Kuruindiya-vihāra
61 and the cave temple of Jambukola, the Bhallātaka-vihāra and
Paragāmaka, the vihāra called Kāsagalla and the vihāra called
62 Candagiri, the Velagāmi-vihāra and that in the village Mahā-
sena by name, the vihāra in Anurādhapura and the temple
63 of the Bodhi Tree (there): these and many other vihāras[2]
which had fallen into decay, the Sovereign restored and granted
64 villages to every single one of them. With the wish that all

[1] That the Thuparāma of Anurādhapura and that of Pulatthinagara are meant is not at all certain. According to the wording of the text — Mahāgāma stands at the beginning of the whole verse — one would expect the Thūpārāmadvayaṃ to be in Mahāgāma.

[2] Of these vihāras that of Paṇḍavāpi lies without doubt near the lake mentioned 60. 48. Whether the Rakkhacetiyapabbata is identical with the Rakkha-vihāra of 44. 51 remains doubtful. Cf. note 46. 29 for Maṇḍalagiri. Madhutthala is mentioned 75. 147 as a fortified place (*dugga*), and this is identified by Codrington (Notes on Ceylon Topography in the twelfth century, II.) with Migoda, a hamlet not far from Urubokka (Moravak Korale, Matara District). The Census of 1921 (II. 142) mentions a Migoda (and also a Madugoda) in the Talpe Pattuva of the Galle District. That sinh. *goḍa* is the equivalent of *thala* in the Pali form of place names in the Mhvs. is a discovery whose credit belongs to Codrington. Devanagara is the present Dondra. One could also translate v. 59 as follows: "the vihāra called Uruvela in Devanagara". Jambukolavihāra and Jambukolalena are the Dambul monastery 26 miles N. of Matale, and its celebrated rock temple. The Bhallātaka-vihāra was built according to 38. 47 by Dhātusena. Kuruindiya might be identical with the Kurunda mentioned in 42. 15 as a foundation of Aggabodhi I. I believe the Candagiri-vihāra to be the monastery belonging to the Sandagiri Tope in Tissamahārāma. A Mahāsena-vihāra is mentioned 48. 8 and 51. 76, a village Mahāsenāgāma 75. 109. Mahiyaṅgaṇa is known, see 51. 74, note. The other vihāras are only named in our passage. The reading Kāsagalla is doubtful.

the people who trod the difficult road to worship the foot-
print of the Sage on the Samantakūṭa[1] mountain might not 65
become weary, he granted for the dispensing of gifts, the
village called Gilīmalaya[2] where there were rice fields and
the like, and had rest-houses built on the road past Kadalīgāma 66
and on the path from the province of Hūva[3] hither, granting
villages to each of these (for providing maintenance) and after 67
having the words "In future kings shall not take possession
of these" engraved on a stone pillar the Monarch set this up.
The villages of Antaraviṭṭhi, Saṃghātagāma and Sirimaṇḍagala- 68
gāma he granted to the Lābhavasin (bhikkhus)[4]. To the 69
Vantajīvaka bhikkhus[5] he gave the four necessaries and to
their kindred he granted maintenance villages. In the cool 70
season he gave to the bhikkhus abundantly of rugs and char-
coal pans[6], as well as of all kinds of medicine. He dispensed, 71
the discerning (Prince), to the bhikkhu community in careful
fashion over and over again all articles of necessity and of

[1] The old Mahāvaṃsa has only Sumanakūṭa as name for Adam's Peak. In the second part Samantakūṭa is the form used. From chapter 86 onwards the old name appears with it and is used by preference.

[2] Gilīmalaya situated in the Kuruviti Korale of the Ratnapura District (Census of C. 1921, II. 476), is an example of resumption of a royal grant in Ceylon. Under the Kandyan government it was a royal village. H. W. Codrington, H. C., p. 54.

[3] Kadalīgāma is without doubt the present Kehelgamuva (Codrington) north of Adam's Peak, situated on the small river that joins the Maskeliya a little farther down. The river then joins the Kelaniganga at Yatiyantota. The sacred mountain was climbed from the North by way of Kadalīgāma. From the East the path of approach led through the province *Hūva*, i. e. now Uva. The inscription of Ambagamuva (note to 58. 1) describes minutely all that the King did for the famous place of pilgrimage and so confirms the content of our passage.

[4] See note to 54. 27. Of the three villages mentioned Antaraviṭṭhi occurs also in 61. 46 and 70. 322. It was situated in Rājaraṭṭha apparently not far from Pulatthinagara.

[5] Evidently an ascetic sect similar to the Lābhavāsins just mentioned. The name means "one who has thrown away his life".

[6] P. *aggikapalla* JaCo. VI. 8^{18} (D. Andersen and H. Smith).

72 the necessaries he gave eight-fold[1]. The many villages in
Rohaṇa granted by former kings, for the feeding of the com-
73 munity, to the Lābhavāsin bhikkhus and to those who made
it their duty to sacrifice to the cetiyas and other sacred ob-
jects, did he further without exception decree for the
74 same purpose. To cripples the strong one gave strong oxen
(for work) and to crows, dogs and other animals he dispensed
75 food, great in pity. To many authors of poems he gave, him-
self an eminent poet, great possessions with heritable villages[2].
76 Did he hear verses composed by the sons of royal officials
and by others, this prince of poets gave them befitting gifts
77 of money. To the blind and the lame he granted villages
separately and of that which was formerly spent for the shrines
78 of the gods[3] he took nothing away. To women of good
family who were unprotected or widowed, the Sovereign gave
79 according to their deserts, villages, food and clothing. The
highly gifted King stood in the composition of Sīhala poems
80 at the head of the Sīhala poets. The Uparāja (Vīrabāhu)[4] who
hung with reverence on the beautiful Baddhaguṇa-vihāra, had
the cetiya here that had been destroyed by the Coḷas restored.
81 Generous as he was[5], he then made over to this superb vihāra
82 fine villages and instituted regular sacrificial festivals. Near
to the forest[6] which lay close to this vihāra, he had a tank
83 built which was solid and held abundant water. In the
Kappūramūlāyatana[7] the King's daughter Yasodharā built

[1] The *aṭṭha parikkhārā* of the bhikkhu are the alms-bowl, the three garments, girdle, razor, needle and water sieve. For the *catupaccayā*, on the other hand, see 37. 76 note.

[2] P. *paveṇigāma* is a village that remains in possession of the family. The word is formed like *paveṇirajja* DhCo. I. 169[8].

[3] The temples of the Hindu deities are meant.

[4] See 59. 11; 60. 40.

[5] P. *muttacāgī* as otherwise *muttacāgo* (Skr. *muktatyāga*) S. I. 228[20]; A. I. 226[12]; DhCo. I. 421[19]; Mhvs. 51. 3.

[6] P. *upacāravana*. Cf. PTS. P. D. s. v. *upacāra* 4: entrance, access, i. e. immediate vicinity or neighbourhood.

[7] As *āyatana* at the end of names is used occasionally as *vihāra*

a massive, charming and large image house, and in the Se- 84
lantarasamūha(-vihāra)[1] she, created Queen[2] by the King,
erected a beautiful, lofty pāsāda which received the name of
Pasāda[3]. In the same way many courtiers and women of his 85
harem amassed many merits in many ways.

While thus the Sovereign of Laṅkā reigned over Laṅkā, 86
the Uparāja (Vīrabāhu), a man of excellent character, was
brought by cruel death into his power. After performing all 87
the funeral rites for him, he granted the dignity of uparāja,
at the counsel of the bhikkhus, to Jayabāhu[4]. The rank of 88
ādipāda he bestowed on Vikkamabāhu, and when later a son
was born to Vikkamabāhu, known by the name of Gajabāhu,
the King having taken counsel with his ministers, made over to 89
him, desirous of the welfare of his son, the whole of Rohaṇa
as dwelling-place. He (Vikkamabāhu) betook himself thither, 90
made the town of Mahānāgahula[5] the capital and took up
his abode in it.

After this Ruler of men, Vijayabāhu, had thus for five 91
and fifty years rolled the wheel of dominion[6] without its

(cf. Selantarāyatana, 78. 10) Kappūramūlāyatana may be meant for the Kappūra-pariveṇa (45. 29; 46. 21; 50. 77) belonging to the Abhayagiri.

[1] Cf. 57. 37.

[2] I retain the reading *rājinīkatā* to which the MSS. point. We know from 49. 3; 50. 58; 54. 11 that *rājinī* is a title bestowed by the King on his female kinswomen. It is thus clear from our passage that the King raised his daughter Yasodharā to the rank of rājinī and that she then built the structure described in the verse.

[3] The name was thus probably Pasādapāsāda, so called because of the satisfaction (*pasāda*) felt by Yasodharā at the distinction conferred on her.

[4] This is quite in keeping with the Sinhalese law of succession according to which before the son, in this case Vikkamabāhu, the younger brother, has claim to the throne.

[5] See note to 58. 39.

[6] In the Tamil inscription of Polonnaruva (note to 58. 1) it is said that the King Sirisaṃghabodhivarman Sirivijayabāhudēvar reigned 55 years and celebrated 73 birthdays. According to Pūjāv. he reigned over 50, according to Rājāv. even 80 years.

wavering, and had served the Order as also the people sore vexed by fear of the wicked Damiḷas, he ascended to the heavenly world to behold the rich reward that had sprung from his meritorious works.

Here ends the sixtieth chapter, called "Care for the Laity and for the Order", in the Mahāvaṃsa, compiled for the serene joy and emotion of the pious.

CHAPTER LXI

HISTORY OF THE LIVES OF THE FOUR KINGS

Thereupon Mittā, the younger sister of the King, her three 1
sons, the highest dignitaries and the ascetics dwelling in the
district met together and without sending news of the Monarch's 2
death to the Ādipāda (Vikkamabāhu) dwelling in Rohaṇa, they
took counsel together and when they had become of one mind 3
they bestowed the consecration as king of Laṅkā on the Yuva-
rāja (Jayabāhu). But to the dignity of uparāja they appoint- 4
ed the prince called Mānābharaṇa, all thereby quitting the
path of former custom[1]. And all three brothers with Mānā- 5
bharaṇa at the head, in company with Jayabāhu, took for-
cible possession of all valuables regarded as specially costly, 6
such as pearls, jewels and the like, as well as of the vehicl-
es, and of the elephants and so on, and left Pulatthinagara 7
with the whole army (with the intention): we will speedily
seize (the person of) Vikkamabāhu. At the tidings of all these 8
events Vikkamabāhu thought: "Unhappily I had no chance of
paying my father the last honours, I will now betake myself 9
in haste to Pulatthinagara and by gazing on my father's
funeral pyre, assuage the heavy grief which weighs on my 10
soul." With this firm resolve the Ādipāda left his town

[1] Jayabāhu's ascent of the throne is lawful (see note to 60. 87), unlawful on the other hand, is the appointment of Mānābharaṇa as uparāja, which at once makes him heir to the throne. After Jayabāhu, Vikkamabāhu is heir, as son of Vijayabāhu. Evidently descent in the female line has to do with this, the *bhāgineyya* the son of the sister, having an exceptional position, a circumstance utilized by Mittā in furtherance of her ambitious plans. Jayabāhu is, as will appear, a puppet king. The whole influence is now already in Mānābharaṇa's hand.

11 (Mahānāgahula) and full of high courage, accompanied by a
force seven to eight hundred strong, set out for Pūlatthina-
12 gara. While still on the way, in the district of Guttasālā at
the village of Panasabukka, he caught sight of the great
13 army approaching in battle array, but he wholly a hero[1],
free of all fear, opened fight and at once scattered the foe
14 in all directions. Having suffered this defeat, the three bro-
thers, stubborn-minded, armed troops and train anew, and
15 gave battle in the district called by the name of Ādipāda-
jambu, but Vikkamabāhu routed the three (brothers) still more
16 severely in the battle. For the third time he fought them at
Kaṭagāma, for the fourth time at Kālavāpi, for the fifth time
17 at Uddhanadvāra, for the sixth time at Paṅkavelaka[2] and
ever he was victorious, and reached Pulatthinagara accompa-
18 nied by his ministers and attendants. In the intended way
he visited his father's place of burial and freed of his great
19 grief, and comforted he took up his abode in the town. On
his ministers who had been his friends in need he bestowed
20 according to merit, full maintenance by means of office; and
to all the soldiers also who had come with him, he gave fit-
ting reward mindful thereof that they had stood by him in
his need.

21 The Monarch Mānābharaṇa with the other brothers seized

[1] P. *ekavīro*, wrongly translated by W. "being the only brave man in his company". *Eka* here has rather the sense of "only, purely, nothing but" as in *sakalanivesanaṃ ekaravaṃ katvā* JaCo. I 486^{9}, *aggiṃ ekajālasamāhitaṃ* Ja. VI. 495^{28} etc.

[2] It can be proved that all these skirmishes took place in a comparatively narrow space to the north and north-east of Buttala. This is proved by the mention in the last place but one of Uddhanadvāra (= sinh. Udundora). The position of this place which is mentioned several times in chapters 74 and 75, has been in the main determined by Codrington in his second article on the Topography of Ceylon in the 12th century. According to a notice in the Daḷadā-Pūjāvalī Udundora was situated at the mountain Amaragiri and this, as the Rate Mahatmaya Bibile was able to prove, is the older name for Monaragala N. E. of Buttala. Kālavāpi, if the reading is right, has at any rate nothing to do with Kalaveva.

Dakkhiṇadesa and Rohaṇa[1], and thereupon conferred on Kit- 22
tisirimegha the province of Dvādasasahassaka[2] and ordered
him to take up his abode there. Charged by his brother, the 23
Ruler of men Kittisirimegha betook himself thither and dwelt
in the town called Mahānāgahula[3]. To the Prince Sirivallabha 24
by name he granted the region called Aṭṭhasahassa[4] and com-
manded him to dwell there. So the latter betook himself thi- 25
ther, made of the village of Uddhanadvāra by name, the
royal capital and dwelling there, ruled the land. He himself 26
(Mānābharaṇa) advanced with the army to Dakkhiṇadesa and
dwelt, under the name of Vīrabahu, in Puṅkhagāma[5]. The 27
mother of the three brothers and the Monarch Jayabāhu so-
journed at that time with Kittisirimegha (in Mahānāgahula).

A year having passed, Mānābharaṇa and the others remem- 28
bering all the shameful[6], severe defeats inflicted on them in
battle by Vikkamabāhu, egged on ever and again by their 29

[1] A complete change of front has taken place. Vikkamabāhu has lost the province of Rohaṇa and in addition Dakkhiṇadesa to his enemies. On the other hand, he is now master of Rājaraṭṭha which was formerly in the hands of Jayabāhu and the sons of Mittā.

[2] The name means "Province of the twelve thousand (villages)". The Sinhalese Dolosdas corresponds to this (CODRINGTON I. p. 63. 73). This name is even now, as I was able to verify in Matara, used as designation of the Giruva-Pattu of the Southern Province on the right bank of the lower Valaveganga. Cf. also note to v. 24.

[3] In our passage the form Mahānāgasula is used.

[4] Whether the name Aṭṭhasahassaka "the province of the eight thousand (villages)" may be compared with that of the Atakalan Korale in the Ratnapura District is doubtful. At any rate, another district was meant at the time to which our passage refers. This is already proved by the fact that Uddhanadvāra (note above to v. 16) was according to v. 25, made the capital of Aṭṭhasahassaka. It seems that the whole of Rohaṇa at that time was split in two. The region west of the Valaveganga was called Dvādasasahassaka, that east of the river Aṭṭhasahassaka. CODRINGTON l. c.

[5] We do not know where Puṅkhagāma is situated, although according to 79. 61 Parakkamabāhu I. erected a tope there 120 cubits high of which there ought still to be traces.

[6] P. *durussaha*, lit. "difficult to endure".

30 stubborn pride, thought thus: "How in Rājaraṭṭha of the
Kings of consecrated head dare this single man hold sway
31 without the royal consecration?" Their envy reached its highest point and with still more[1] followers (than the first time)
32 they set forth united to begin the war. When Vikkamabāhu
learned of this matter from messengers he advanced at the
33 head of a large army thither where they were[2]. In Dakkhiṇadesa by the village of Bodhisenapabbata Vikkamabāhu de-
34 feated in battle the three (brothers). With the intention to
root out now all his enemies he pursued the fugitives at
35 their heels. They withdrew into a stronghold in the province
of Pañcayojana, but he in order to capture them, advanced
to Kalyāṇī[3].

36 A warrior, lord of the Ariya country[4], Vīradeva by name,
37 sole sovereign of Palandīpa, a most foolhardy man, landed at
that time with brave warriors in Mahātittha in the belief he
would be able to bring the whole of Laṅkā into his power.
38 Now when the Sovereign Vikkamabāhu heard of the matter,
he thought: so long as he has not yet gained a firm footing
39 in Laṅkā he must be rooted out. So he marched from Ka-
lyāṇi and betook himself to the village called Mannāra[5] near
40 Mahātittha. Vīradeva offered the King[6] battle. Two princes,
41 brothers, Anīkaṅga and the other, as well as the Commander-
in-chief, known by the name of Kitti, he killed by violence
42 as well as many people, acknowledged warriors. The Senāpati

[1] I connect *bhūyo* with *saṃgayha sāvake*. To change the MSS. reading *bhūyo* into *bhīyo* is unnecessary. The compilers of the later Mahāvaṃsa were strongly influenced by Sanskrit.

[2] P. *tesaṃ visayaṃ*, lit. "to their domain or district".

[3] If Mānābharaṇa and his brothers retire as far as Pañcayojana (see note to 57. 71) then they must surrender the greater part of Dakkhiṇadesa. In the pursuit Vikkamabāhu penetrates to Kalyāṇi that is to the district on the lower Kälani-ganga (Colombo and its hinterland).

[4] We have probably to read *Ariyadesīso* = *Ariya-desa-īso*.

[5] The present Mannar in the district of the same name in the Northern Province.

[6] I prefer to read *tena rājinā* with the Col. Ed. against the *rājino* of the MSS.

Rakkhaka he captured alive, and after defeating Vikkamabāhu
and his army, he followed him at his heels. Fleeing in ter- 43
ror Vikkamabāhu reached his capital, took all his movable
property and betook himself in haste to Koṭṭhasāra[1]. Vīra- 44
deva who was ever hard at his heels, reached the capital and
took up his abode there for some days, then he set off in 45
haste thither to capture Vikkamabāhu. But the latter sent
off his whole large army, forced Vīradeva to fight in a great 46
swampy wilderness near the village of Antaraviṭṭhika[2], slew
him and dwelling then with might in Pulatthinagara, without 47
the royal consecration it is true, he held sway as monarch
in Rājaraṭṭha.

The three brothers now gave up their lust for war and 48
dwelt each in his province to which he had betaken himself.
But despite their efforts, the four princes[3], were quite 49
unable to unite this country under one umbrella. In their heed- 50
less way of acting they slighted people of good family and
placed ambitious[4] men of the lower classes in leading posi-
tions. The deluded ones injured the Order and the laity who 51
had variously been furthered in the best possible way by
Vijayabāhu. From people of good family even in the absence 52
of an equivalent offence, they would seize forcibly their pos-
sessions. In their insatiability[5] and money lust they squeezed 53
out the whole people as sugar cane in a sugar mill, by

[1] This passage together with 70. 305 and 71. 6 makes it certain that Koṭṭhasāra was situated in the east (south or north-east) of Pulatthinagara. Codrington II. says also: "This place, therefore, probably was not far from Kantalai and was in the King's Country".

[2] Antaraviṭṭhi must thus have been situated about halfway between Koṭṭhasāra and Pulatthinagara. The name occurs also in 60. 68, and again in 70. 322 in an account of battles which apparently took place in the neighbourhood of Pulatthinagara.

[3] The three brothers and Vikkamabāhu.

[4] I take *sābhimata* to mean the same as *sābhimāna* (skr. the same) "proud". The p. part. *abhimata* stands as so frequently, instead of the abstract substantive (cf. for ex. *mata* "dying, the death" = *maraṇa* Therag. 194 etc.).

[5] Most likely we have to read *te 'khīṇatosā*.

54 levying excessive taxes. King Vikkamabāhu took the main-
tenance villages which belonged to the Buddha and so forth
55 and gave them to his attendants. In Pulatthinagara he gave
over several vihāras distinguished by (the possession of) relics,
56 to foreign soldiers to live in. Precious stones, pearls and the
like, presented by the pious as offerings for the Relic of the
57 Alms-bowl, and for the sacred Tooth Relic, the sandelwood,
the aloes, the camphor, the many images of gold and the
58 like which he took forcibly, he used as it pleased him. Be-
holding this manifold evil committed against the Order and
59 the laity, the ascetics in the eight chief vihāras[1], looked up
to as people worthy of honour, and the Paṃsukūlin bhikkhus
60 belonging to the two divisions[2], were wroth at the matter
and thinking it were better to remove themselves from the
vicinity of people who like those erring from the faith,
61 wrought in this way so much evil against the Order, they
took the sacred Tooth Relic and the Alms-bowl Relic, betook
themselves to Rohaṇa and settled themselves here and there
62 in places where it pleased them. In the same way people of
good family, scattered here and there, kept themselves hid-
den in places which seemed good to them and made their
abode there.

63 The officers belonging to the retinue of the monarchs on
both sides who were established on the frontiers, fought with
64 each other continually. By setting fire to many flourishing
villages and market towns, by piercing tanks filled with water,
65 by destroying everywhere the weirs on all the canals and
by hewing down all useful trees like the coconut palm and
66 others, they in fighting each other, so devastated the king-
dom that it was impossible to trace even the sites of the old
67 villages. And even the rulers did evil to the people letting
their retainers plunder the towns and commit highway rob-

[1] P. *aṭṭhamūlavihāresu* in Pulatthinagara. Later (84. 4, 18) *aṭṭhā-yatanāni* are mentioned in Jambuddoṇi = Dambadeniya.

[2] We hear nothing further of this organisation of the Paṃsukūlins. It is worth noting that the sect now wholly vanishes. It is never mentioned again.

bery. The slaves too and the workmen of people of good 68
family despised their masters without respect and void of
all fear. They became mercenaries to the kings and worming 69
themselves into their confidence, they, by means of offices
conferred on them, attained ever greater power. The people 70
dwelling in places difficult of access like the Samantakūṭa
and so forth, no longer paid to the monarch the taxes formerly levied on them. They despised the king, became rene- 71
gades[1] and dwelt independent, each in his own region. "What 72
is based on wrong speedily changes," this proverb was by no
means true of the land of Laṅkā at that time[2].

Like (greedy) tenants of villages wholly and ever void of 73
all dignity, their mind bent on destruction without end, wholly lacking in royal pride, false to their own or to others' welfare, without any restraint in their efforts: thus lived all these rulers forsaking the path of (good and ancient) custom.

Here ends the sixty-first chapter, called "History of the Lives of the Four Kings", in the Mahāvaṃsa, compiled for the serene joy and emotion of the pious.

[1] Here we meet for the first time a word frequently occurring in chapters 74-76 *dāmarika,* in the abstract form *dāmarikattana* (suff. *-ttana* = skr. *-tvana*, cf. WHITNEY, Sanskrit Grammar, § 1240). I find *dāmarika* for the first time in Buddhaghosa, in the Samantapāsādikā, OLDENBERG, Vinaya III. 320[30]. In Skr. we have *ḍāmarika* with cerebral initial sound, for ex. Kauṭ. 4. 9 (84) near the end.

[2] Lit.: "The land Laṅkā never came at that time to such a condition that one could say: "What is based on wrong etc." One should compare with this *iti vattabbataṃ nāpajjati* DhCo. IV. 44. We have to do evidently with the quotation of a popular proverb equivalent to the English saying: "Ill gotten good seldom thrives". But this proverb could not be applied to Laṅkā at that time, had no bearing on Laṅkā (the *n'eva* of the MSS. must not be altered to *yeva*), since the evil, the wrong was just in full bloom.

CHAPTER LXII

THE BIRTH OF THE PRINCE

1 The Ruler Jayabāhu[1] and the Queen Mittā by name who
2 had sojourned in Rohaṇa, departed now by death. The con-
sort of Sirivallabha, Sugalā, bore two children, a son Mā-
3 nābharaṇa and a daughter Līlāvatī. The royal consort of
Prince Mānābharaṇa also bore two daughters, Mittā and Pa-
4 bhāvatī. When the Mahādipāda Vīrabāhu[2] beheld these his
two daughters, he was struck by the following consideration:
5 "We are sprung from the pure dynasty of the Moon[3], highly
6 esteemed in the world, at the head of all royal houses. In
outward appearance (we are) enviable, distinguished by every
aptitude, experienced in the various sciences, skilful in the
7 managing of elephants, horses and the like. And yet we
three have over and over again suffered severe defeat in fight
8 by the single Vikkamabāhu and there is no prospect of the
birth of a son who would be capable of wiping out this stain.
9 Ah, how small is our merit! What avails me a royal dig-
nity which is defiled by the evil tattle of the people? I must
10 now give up my bent to worldly things and spend[4] my days

[1] The length of the reign is not given. According to Pūjāv. it was 13 years. Rājāv. where we have the name Vijayabāhu, not Jayabāhu, says 3 years. In Rājaratn. a Vijayabāhu is inserted after Jayabāhu. Here it is evident that the name of the father of Vikkamabāhu which is expressly given in the two other sources, has crept into the text as the name of a new king.

[2] I. e. Mānābharaṇa, who according to 61. 26 had assumed this name. He bore the title Mahādipāda being considered by his brothers the lawful successor of Jayabāhu.

[3] P. *somavaṃsa*, skr. *somavaṃśa*. Soma is the Moon deity.

[4] *Netabbā* instead of the meaningless *te tayo* is apparently a conjectural reading by S. and B. At any rate it is so convincing that I adopt it without scruple.

unweariedly in pious works." He made over the whole ad-
ministration of the kingdom to his ministers[1] and while he 11
himself sojourned there seven or eight months, he camped
one night in the temple of the King of the gods[2], observing
the precepts of moral discipline. Now about dawn the Ruler 12
saw in a dream a wondrous god with glittering raiment and
ornaments, adorned with fragrant flower wreaths, illuminating 13
with his sublime beauty and the glory of his presence the
whole heavens[3] like to the sun when it has risen on the 14
firmament and he heard him speak thus: "Be content, O great-
ly blessed! be joyful, O King! A splendid son, furnished 15
with the tokens of power, who shall be able to carry out his
designs, well instructed, of a courage whose splendour shall
spread through the world, glorious in might and strength, 16
honour and fame, a fount of excellent qualities, a furtherer of
the Order and of the laity shall be attained by thee ere long, 17
O mighty King! Now go at once to the town where dwell
wife and child." As at daybreak he awoke full of joyful ex- 18
citement, the best of men betook himself to Puṅkhagāma.
Even as he had seen it so the Ruler related the beautiful 19
dream to his ministers in the presence of the Mahesī. He 20
then in company with the Mahesī, with the wish for a
distinguished son, amassed all kinds of good deeds, such
as almsgiving, the observing of the moral prescripts and
the like. And one day at morn he saw himself in a dream 21
entering the sleeping chamber of the Mahesī holding gently
by the ear a beautiful, pure white elephant calf endowed 22
with all auspicious marks. When he awoke he rose from his 23
splendid couch and his heart merry with joy and rapture, he
betook himself at this time to the sleeping chamber of the 24
Mahesī and told her the dream, as he had seen it. "I also 25

[1] Here we must supplement "and withdrew into solitude".

[2] Name of Indra = Sakka.

[3] *Asesāsā* (= *asesa-āsā*, skr. *āśā*) Another excellent emendation by S. and B. instead of *asesāyo*. Perhaps *asesāsāyo* would be even better in spite of the metrical irregularity. It might then be assumed that it was just this which led to the corruption of the text.

in a dream have embraced such a young elephant. It walked
round my bed its right side turned towards it, then stood still.
26 Drawing it by the trunk to me and raising it up to my
couch (I tenderly embraced it.)" Thus the Queen told him.
27 The twain having thus made known to each other what
they had seen, awaited joyfully and without slumbering, the
28 break of day. In the morning they inquired of the house
priest[1] who had come to pay his respects, and the sooth-
sayers. When these heard this they announced full of joy:
29 "Within a short time, without doubt, the birth will take
place of a son who shall bear on him the marks of (future)
30 power". When they heard that, then all of them – ministers,
citizens and the Ruler of men had the feeling of a great
31 festival of joy. From that moment onward the Prince who
wished above all a happy issue, had the Paritta recited over
32 and over again by the community of the bhikkhus. To count-
less beggars he distributed daily as alms costly gifts — jewels,
33 pearls and the like. Rites like the Homa[2] sacrifice and others
held to be salutary, he had performed by the house priest
and other brāhmaṇas versed in the Veda and the Vedaṅgas[3].
34 Ruined vihāras and relic shrines and destroyed tanks he or-
35 dered the royal workmen to rebuild. While the Lord of men
thus spent the day in pious action there grew shortly in the
36 womb of the Queen a splendid fruit. When the Lord of men
heard this, full of joy, he had an ample pregnancy gift[4]

[1] P. *purohita*. He was a Brahman. Cf. below v. 33 and specially v. 45 ff. The court life was organised according to Brahmanical rules.

[2] Skr. *homa* (from *hu* "to pour into the fire") is the general term for "sacrifice". *Āhuti* is older. An enumeration of the different *homā* with a terminology differing in part from that of Sanskrit ritual literature, is given D. I. 9 (= I. 1. 21). This passage has already been alluded to by HILLEBRANDT, Ritual-Litteratur, Vedische Opfer und Zauber, p. 18.

[3] The *vedāṅgāni*, the ancillary sciences of the Veda, include *sikṣā* "phonetics", *chandas* "metre", *nirukta* "etymology", *vyākaraṇa* "grammar", *kalpa* "ritual" and *jyotiṣa* "astronomy". A. A. MACDONELL, Hist. of Sanskrit Literature, p. 264 ff. M. WINTERNITZ, Gesch. der indischen Litteratur, I, p. 229 ff.

[4] P. *gabbhaparihāra*. By *parihāra* is meant every extraordinary grant

bestowed on the Queen. When in course of time the fruit 37
of her body grew ripe, the Queen bore a son at a moment
marked by a lucky constellation. Clear at this moment were 38
all the quarters of the heavens and cool, fragrant, gentle
breezes blew. With the trumpeting of the elephants and the 39
neighing[1] of the horses the royal courtyard was filled with
resounding din. When the Ruler Mānābharaṇa full of as- 40
tonishment beheld the extraordinary signs and wonders mani-
fested in such divers ways, and when he then heard the news 41
of the birth of his son, he was filled with joy at the fulfil-
ment of his wish, as if anointed with ambrosia. He set many 42
free who lay bound in fetters in prison and gave a splendid
alms to the samaṇas and the brāhmaṇas. And the people 43
who dwelt in the town, with the ministers at the head,
adorned the whole of the royal capital in divers ways, with
arches of banana leaves and the like and trimmed and beauti- 44
fully clad, they held for several days a great and joyous feast.
According to the rules laid down in the Veda, the Monarch 45
had the birth rites[2] and the other ceremonies performed for
the boy. He then summoned the house priest and the other 46
brāhmaṇas versed in the lore of body marks and having shown
them the customary reverence and distinction, he charged 47

given for a special occasion. *Gäbaperahära* in Sinhalese means a particular ceremony to be performed when pregnancy has taken place (the Kusajātaka v. 150, ed. by A. M. Gunasekara has *gäbapeḷahära*); but the verb *adāpayi* does not agree with this meaning.

[1] Amongst the ancient Germans the neighing of a horse was also regarded as a propitious sign. Grimm, Deutsche Mythologie, 3. 442; cf. Hillebrandt, Ritual-Litteratur, S. 183. We are familiar with the tale of Herodotus 3. 84, 85, according to which Darius gained his crown through the neighing of his horse. The Slaves on the other hand, consider the restlessness and neighing of horses as an ill omen. Thus in the Serbian folk song of Ibrāhim Nukić, F. S. Krauss, Slavische Volksforschungen, p. 397.

[2] P. *jātakamma* = skr. *jātakarman* in which four ceremonies are to be distinguished: 1) *āyuṣya* "giving of life", 2) *medhājanana* "the giving of understanding" 3) *stanapratidhāna* "the giving of the breast" and 4) *nāmakaraṇa* "the giving of the name". Hillebrandt, l. c. p. 45. Speijer, Jātakarman, Leiden 1872.

them with the determination of the body marks of the boy. After carefully observing all the marks on his hands and feet
48 they announced joyfully to the King who stood amid the
49 throng of his courtiers and to the Queen thus: "Apart from the island of Laṅkā he is able to unite under one umbrella
50 and to rule even the whole of Jambudīpa." The King gladdened them with gifts and asked further courteously: "Is
51 there any unfavourable sign to be seen or not?" "The boy will have a long life but there is an unfavourable constella-
52 tion for the father," they answered the Ruler. Having regard to the heroic strength of his foe-crushing arms, he received
53 the significant name of Parakkamabāhu[1]. Versed in the ritual, his father had the ceremony of the piercing of the ears[2] and the ceremony of the first rice food[3] performed
54 exactly according to custom. He then sent his messengers to Pulatthinagara to bring Vikkamabāhu[4] the news of the
55 birth of his son. When Vikkamabāhu heard from them of the splendour promising qualities of his sister's son but also of the inauspicious constellation for the father he thought:
56 "A splendid nephew, gleaming like a jewel that is the centre stone[5] in the chain of kings beginning with King Vijaya

[1] The ceremony of the *nāmakaraṇa* is performed according to most of the Gṛhyasūtras on the 10th day. According to others even later, after a hundred nights or after a year. Hillebrandt, l. c., p. 46 f.

[2] P. *kaṇṇavedha* = skr. *karṇavedha*, a ceremony mentioned only in one MS. of Pāraskara's Gṛhyasūtra, performed in the third or the fifth year. Speijer, l. c., p. 21; Hillebrandt, l. c., p. 50.

[3] P. *annapāsana* = skr. *annaprāśana*. According to the rule common to all the Gṛhyasūtras the ceremony is performed in the 6th month. Hillebrandt, l. c., p. 48. There is no mention here of the ceremony of the taking out of the child for the first time that he may see the sun *ādityadarśanārthaṃ*. It takes place according to Manu I. 34 *caturthe māsi*.

[4] One may assume from this passage that after their unsuccessful wars against Vikkamabāhu the princes of Rohaṇa recognised him as king.

[5] P., skr. *nāyaka*. For the meaning of "central gem" see BR. s. v., 3. The fundamental meaning is "leader, chief".

hath he begotten me. That no harm may at any time befall 57
him, the boy shall grow up here in my immediate neighbourhood. To win unachieved and to keep achieved advantage 58
this my son Gajabāhu will in no case be able. And my other 59
son Mahinda, though gifted with heroic courage and other excellent qualities, stands lower owing to his mother's origin and is unworthy of the crown. My sister's son shall one day 60
enjoy to his heart's desire the dominion which is prosperous through the treasures I have amassed in many ways." He 61
then sent messengers to fetch the boy and gave them ornaments for the boy and other valuables as gift. When the 62
Ruler Vīrabāhu heard all this out of the mouth of the messengers he said to himself: "These prudent words he hath spoken in thought for my good. Nevertheless it is not meet 63
to send away such a jewel of a son of one's own body for the warding off of evil which threatens me. Moreover, if the 64
boy is taken thither, the party of Vikkamabāhu like fire 65
joined with the strength of the storm, will gleam[1] with mighty, up-shooting flames, but our misfortune, alas so great, will become still worse!" So he gave not his son to the mes- 66
sengers who had arrived in his dominions but dismissed them after satisfying them with a gift of money.

The Lord of men who leading there with wife and child 67
a harmonious life, was attacked by an evil disease and was forced to give up his life at the same moment with the royal dignity.

Here ends the sixty-second chapter, called "The Birth of the Prince", in the Mahāvaṃsa, compiled for the serene joy and emotion of the pious.

[1] The translation rests on the conjectural reading of the Col. Ed. *saṃjalissati* in place of the *saṃkilissati* of the MSS.

CHAPTER LXIII

THE ARRIVAL IN THE CITY OF SANKHATTHALĪ

1 When the two other brothers heard of the death of the
eldest, they came hither in haste and had the last rites per-
2 formed for him. Kittisirimegha hereupon took possession of
the province of his elder brother. He then summoned the
3 youngest brother (Sirivallabha), made over to him the two
other provinces and ordered him to live there. The latter
4 obeyed the orders of his elder brother, took the boy (Parak-
kamabāhu) and the Queen Ratanāvalī and her two daughters[1]
5 and betook himself to the town of Mahānāgahula. While he
dwelt there in harmony (with them) he had the ceremony of
the first dressing of the hair[2] performed on the boy and
6 brought him up with great pomp. Thereupon he wished to
marry the eldest daughter of the Queen, Mittā by name, to
his son (Mānābharaṇa) and took counsel thereupon with his
7 ministers: „Princes of the dynasty of Kāliṅga have many
times and oft attained to dominion in this island of Laṅkā.
8 If now this Queen were to send her daughter away secretly
to wed her to Gajabāhu[3] who is sprung from the Kālinga
9 stock, he would in connection with the marriage become
mightier, but my son here would be without any support at
10 all. Hence it is advisable to give the princess to my son:
11 as the matter lies this will be for our advantage." When

[1] Mittā and Pabhāvatī, 62. 3.

[2] P. *sikhāmaha*. This corresponds to the *cūḍākaraṇa* of the Gṛhya-sūtras. According to Sāṅkhāyana this ceremony should be performed on a Kshatriya in the fifth year, otherwise the third year is generally given. HILLEBRANDT l. c., p. 49.

[3] He was the grandson of Vijayabāhu I. and of Tilokasundarī who came from the Kaliṅga country.

the Queen who was an ornament of the Sun dynasty, heard all this, as she by no means wished the affair, she spake to
the Ruler thus: "After the Prince named Vijaya had slain 12
all the yakkhas and made this island of Laṅkā habitable for
men, since then one has allied the family of Vijaya with 13
ours by unions above all with scions of the Kaliṅga line.
Union with other princes was also hitherto unknown with 14
us save with kings of the Moon dynasty. How then, just 15
because he is your son, could there be for us a union with
that prince who has sprung from the Ariya dynasty[1]? Al- 16
though the Queen in this wise protested over and over again,
he nevertheless forcing (the matter) wedded the princess to
his son. This (prince) accompanied by his consort, distin- 17
guished by many virtues, winning all people for himself,
dwelt with his father.

Vikkamabāhu having enjoyed the royal dignity one and 18
twenty years[2], death ensuing, he passed to the other world.
Hereupon Gajabāhu[3] took possession of the flourishing king- 19
dom endowed with army and train, and dwelt in Pulatthina-
gara. When however the Monarchs (of Rohaṇa) Kittisirimegha 20
and Sirivallabha heard of the event, they reflected thus: "As 21
Vikkamabāhu was the elder, his dominion in the chief king-
dom could in no wise be a reproach to us, but that his son 22

[1] What is meant is the Aryan dynasty of the Pāṇḍya (called Paṇḍu in the Mahāvaṃsa) in Southern India. The mother of Sirivallabha and grandmother of the young prince Mānābharana, Mittā, was according to 59. 41, married to the Paṇḍurāja. Ratanāvalī evidently denies to Mittā's offspring the connection with the Moon dynasty of which they boast in 62. 5.

[2] According to Pūjāv. and Rājāv. Vikkamabāhu reigned 28 years.

[3] It is worthy of note that of the four Sinhalese sources which I have consulted for comparison, only Nik.-s. mentions Gajabāhu. Pūjāv. Rājāv. and Rājaratn. pass from Vikkamabāhu at once to Parakkamabāhu, whom the two first, in addition, describe as the son of Kittisirimegha. It was mentioned above (note to 59. 49) that Gajabāhu is named in the Dimbulagala inscription as son of Sundarī and Vikkamabāhu. An inscription of Gajabāhu at Kapuru-vedu-oya (Matale District) was published by H. W. Codrington, JRAS. C. B. xxvi, Nr. 71, 1919, p. 53 ff.

who is not of age should now rule in the main realm — it is
23 in truth not meet for us to permit that. So long as he has
not taken root in his province, we must take forcible pos-
24 session of this province." The whole of the Velakkāra[1] troops
they suborned by gifts of money. Save for a few retainers
25 of his immediate retinue, all the inhabitants of the kingdom
soon fell away from their ruler Gajabāhu and sent messengers
26 over and over again to the two kings: "With one accord we
will seize the kingdom and give it over to you, but ye must
27 give us support." Thereupon the two brothers equipped in
haste their army and advanced from two sides to the centre
28 of the kingdom[2]. They sent off envoys[3]. The Monarch Ga-
jabāhu assembled thereupon his ministers and took counsel
29 with them: "The whole of the Velakkāra troops are in open
revolt; the two kings have advanced to fight against our realm.
30 If we first can deal the mightier part of them a decisive
31 blow[4], then it will be easy to get rid of the others." Having
thus resolved, he took his whole army and marched against
32 King Sirivallabha to fight him. King Sirivallabha fought an
33 extraordinarily bitter action from morning till evening. But
being unable to defeat the other he beat a retreat and betook
34 himself in haste to his own province again. The Ruler Kitti-
sirimegha also, vanquished by Gokaṇṇa[5], an officer of Gaja-
35 bāhu, returned to his province. The Ruler of men, Gaja-
bāhu, who had suffered no harm in this war, also be-
36 took himself again to the neighbourhood of his capital. After
the powerful (Gajabāhu) had punished many generals who

[1] See note to 60. 36.

[2] The centre of the kingdom is the capital Pulatthinagara. Kittisirimegha must have marched against it from Dakkhiṇadesa that is from the South-West, Sirivallabha from the South-East.

[3] Evidently to Gajabāhu, demanding that he should voluntarily surrender the kingdom.

[4] P. *mukhabhaṅga* lit. a "smashing of the face or the mouth", an expression evidently borrowed from the terminology of the prize fighter. It occurs again 75. 75.

[5] For this general who had his headquarters in Kālavāpi, see further below 66. 35 ff., 70. 68 ff.

had offended against him, and having pacified the kingdom,
he entered his town. After that the (three) Monarchs each 37
in his province, lived in amity with one another. But the 38
Monarch's son[1] Parakkamabāhu, the discerning one, who was
well schooled in all the arts, with his intelligence, capable 39
of distinguishing amid the multitude of things what should
and what should not be done, with his soaring plans and his
extraordinary greatness, cared not at heart for the comfort 40
of a life lived together with his mother and sisters, nor for
the delight of the many childish games. He thought: "Prin- 41
ces like myself, gifted with heroism and other such like qua-
lities—how can they live in such a secluded district? I will 42
betake myself now to the land of my birth which as Yu-
varāja I may enjoy", and he left his place of abode, accom-
panied by his retinue. In course of time he came near to 43
the village which bore the name Saṅkhanāyakatthalī[2]. When
Kittisirimegha heard of it the heartache he felt at being 44
so alone, because he lacked a son fit to inherit the royal
dignity, was assuaged and he thought: "My great, enduring 45
merit is rewarded in that I now can behold in him who is
his living image, as it were my elder brother". Swayed by 46
joyful excitement, the Ruler of men had the charming town
decked out abundantly with triumphal arches and the like
and on a day and under a special constellation held to be 47
propitious, he, surrounded by his hosts, went forth to meet
him. And when he beheld the Prince gifted with qualities 48
with which those of others could not compare, and with all

[1] P. *nandana*, here "son" like skr. *nandana*. Cf. v. 51, note.

[2] The situation of this place, called also *Saṅkhanāthatthalī* (66. 9; 67. 78, 82) or *Saṅkhatthalī* (64. 22), is unknown. According to 65. 4 ff. it was about 5 *gāvuta* (about 10 miles) distant from Badalatthalī. It is clear too from 67. 81-82, that the two places were not far from each other. Badalatthalī must indeed have lain on the borders of Dakkhiṇadesa. As Badalatthalī or-la (see note to 58. 43) is probably the present Batalagoda, N. E. of Kurunegala, Saṅkhatthalī would have to be looked for somewhere in the region of Polgahawela or Kegalla. At any rate under Kittisirimegha it was the capital of Dakkhiṇadesa.

49 favourable marks, then full of joy he embraced him tenderly,
drawing him to his breast and kissing him again and again on
50 the head, whereby in face of the great multitude he shed con-
51 tinuously from his eyes floods of joyful tears. Thereupon he
mounted with his son[1] a beautiful chariot and filling the ten
52 regions of the firmament[2] round about with the clanging of the
drums, he entered the town and showing his son all the beau-
tiful decorations there, he entered the royal palace (with him).
53 When then a numerous retinue such as crowds of chamber-
lains, cooks and the like had been bestowed on him, he lived
happily with his father whose heart was contented by his
manifold excellences.

Here ends the sixty-third chapter, called "The Arrival in the City of Saṅkhatthalī", in the Mahāvaṃsa, compiled for the serene joy and emotion of the pious.

[1] The brother's son is called "son" just as on the other hand, the nephew calls the brother of his father simply "father" (v. 53, cf. note to 51. 24). Cousins who are sons of brothers, call each other brothers, thus 48. 51, 61. Aggabodhi VI. and VII. Buddhaghosa calls Ānanda the "brother of the Buddha" because he was *cullapitu putto* (Sumaṅgalavilāsinī ed. Rhys Davids and J. E. Carpenter I. p. 4[29]) The position of the sister's son (*bhāgineyya*) is thereby the more marked.

[2] Namely the four chief regions of the heavens, the four intermediary regions, zenith (skr. *ūrdhvaṃ*) and nadir (skr. *tiryak* or *adhaḥ*). Cf. skr. *daśa diśaḥ*.

CHAPTER LXIV

THE DEPARTURE FOR THE OTHER COUNTRY

After the arrival in his beloved native land, his heart's 1
desire was fulfilled and all anxious yearning left him. And 2
now with the help of his lightning-like intelligence he learned
easily and quickly from his teachers the various accomplish-
ments. In the numerous books of the Victor (Buddha), in 3
the works on politics, as in that of Koṭalla[1] and others, in
grammar and poetry together with the knowledge of voca-
bulary and ritual[2], in dance and song, in the art of driving 4
the elephant and so forth, above all in the lore of the mani-
pulation of the bow, the sword and other weapons he was
past master. Admirably trained, he did everything that ac- 5
corded with the King's, his father's wishes and was never
lacking in reverence.

[1] Conjectural reading for the *kosalla*, *komulla* or *kocalla* of the MSS. Cf. 70. 56. I believe that Kauṭalya i. e. Cāṇakya, the famous minister of Candragupta is meant. He is alleged to be the author of a text book on politics, Artha-śāstra, which has been recently discovered. What is important is that the Cūlavaṃsa seems to confirm the name *Kauṭalya* as against *Kauṭilya*. It is handed down by Hemacandra, Abhidhānacintāmaṇi 853 (see BR. s. v., Hillebrandt, Ueber das Kauṭilīyaśāstra und Verwandtes, p. 1) and seems to be the reading of the best MSS. so that in Ganapati's new edition it appears throughout. I regard it as the original form for the following simple reason. The fact that the forms Kauṭalya and Kauṭilya have been handed down together is indisputable. Now *kauṭilya* as a variant of the original *kauṭalya*, in allusion to the content and character of the Artha-śāstra (skr. *kuṭila* "crooked, cunning") is quite intelligible. On the other hand, it is not easy to explain why a word so distinct and of such definite meaning as *kauṭilya* should be changed into *kauṭalya*. See however J. Jolly, Zeitschr. für Indologie und Iranistik V. 216 ff.

[2] P. *sanighaṇḍukakeṭubhe*. See PTS. P. D. s. vv. *nighaṇḍu* and *keṭubha*.

6 The Ruler (Kittisirimegha) at heart ever well pleased
with the virtue (practised by the Prince) of reverent demean-
7 our, enjoyed with him as with a good friend various pas-
times, such as sport in the garden and in the water and
while he was travelling here and there about the country
8 with him, he came one day near the village called Ba-
9 dalatthalī which served as the abode of the loyal, powerful
Senāpati Saṅkha who was entrusted with the defence of the
10 frontier. When the Senāpati heard that, he had the village
at once made ready, went forth to meet the Monarch and his
son and remained, after he had bowed himself, standing before
11 them. The twain, father and son, addressed him with friendly
words and being satisfied by him in various ways, they visited
12 the village. When the Monarch had sojourned there some
days he summoned the Senāpati to him and spake the follo-
13 wing words: "My son is now grown to manhood and is ripe
for admission[1]. To perform the ceremony of admission great
14 preparations are necessary". When the Senāpati heard that,
he made at once the best of preparations for the festival.
15 After instituting with sweet savours, lamps, flowers and other
things of the kind for three days an abundant offering[2] for
16 the three jewels and after he had the ceremony performed, in
a manner befitting his high rank, by Brahmans versed in
17 the ritual of the Veda, the Ruler together with the Prince
Parakkama in the midst of his courtiers set about enjoying a
great spring festival[3].

[1] P. skr. *upanayana*. This is the ceremony of taking the son to the Brahman teacher. With the Kshatriya it takes place between the 11 th and the 22 nd year. With this is associated at the same time the admission to the religious community as fully qualified member. BR. s. v.; Hillebrandt, Ritual-Litteratur, p. 50 ff.

[2] P. *pubbakāra*. The expression is found also in A. iv. $25^{16, 25}$, where among things harmful for the lay brother is mentioned the choosing by him outside of the Order, (*ito bahiddhā*) of a person who seems worthy of reverence, a *dakkhiṇeyya, tattha ca pubbakāraṃ karoti*.

[3] Cf. skr. *vasantotsava*, *vasantamahotsava* or *vasantasamayotsava* as below in v. 21 *vasantasamayussava*.

Now King Kittisirimegha learned through messengers who 18
came from Rohaṇa that his brother named Sirivallabha who
dwelt in Rohaṇa, was dead and that Sirivallabha's son Mā- 19
nābharaṇa by name, had taken over the government and had
made Mittā his queen[1]. He overcame the grief heavy to be 20
borne caused by his brother's death through hearing the 21
news of the birth of a son to Mittā. But he gave up the
spring festival and returned, leaving the Senāpati named 22
Saṅkha behind on the spot, with his son to the town of
Saṅkhatthalī[2]. While the Monarch lived there happily with 23
Prince Parakkama a year passed. The second queen of the 24
Monarch Mānābharaṇa, Pabhāvatī[3], likewise bore a son, named
Kittisirimegha. When Kittisirimegha heard that he thought: 25
our line has become great, and felt still happier.

The Prince (Parakkamabāhu) urged by his great, incom- 26
parable merit by whose virtue alone he was destined for the
dominion over Laṅkā, valued not so much as grass the love 27
shown him by his father as by a good friend, and his great
tenderness, as well as the services of his many retainers per- 28
formed for him from fear and devotion[4]. And in his zeal 29
to (unite and thereby) make Laṅkā happy under one um-
brella as speedily as possible, he thought to himself thus:
"Since it has ever been the home of the hair, collar-bone, 30
neck-bone, tooth and alms-bowl relics[5] as well as of the

[1] See 63. 6 ff. *Deviyā Mittāya paṭilābhaṃ Sirivallabhasūnuno* does not mean, as translated by W. "a birth of a son, Siri Vallabha, to the Queen Mittā".

[2] See note to 63. 43. *Nivattitvāna* must be understood as gerund of the caus. *nivatteti*, one MS. even reading *-ttetvāna*. Parakkama's Upanayana festival had taken place in Badalatthalī. There Kittisirimegha receives the various news from Rohaṇa. He leaves the general Saṅkha, who had to prepare the festival, behind in that place (*tatth'eva*) and betakes himself with his nephew to the capital, Saṅkhatthalī.

[3] We see from this that Sirivallabha's son had married both the sisters of Parakkamabāhu, Mittā and Pabhāvatī.

[4] Lit.: whereby fear and devotion went before, i. e. were the motive. W's translation is inexact.

[5] The hair relic (*kesadhātu*) was (Mhvs. 39. 49) brought to Ceylon by

token of the footprint of the Master and of his sacred Bodhi
31 Tree branch, further of the eighty-four thousand sections of
the doctrine which give a picture of the Perfectly Enlighte-
32 ned one, and as it is a mine of gems, pearls and many other
treasures, this island although not so large, has always coun-
33 ted for something special. My three fathers, the Monarchs,
and also my mother's brother[1] were not able to unite it
34 under one umbrella. They divided it therefore and with the
thought: if we only rule it to this extent we have done our
duty, each in his province renouncing the desire customary
35 in our family for the royal consecration, carried on the go-
vernment like village chiefs whose one aim is their farming
36 and the like. Of these save my father's brother, Kittisiri-
megha, the three remaining monarchs have passed away in
37 accordance with their deeds. Man's longest span of life is
now alas, but meagre; boy, youth, greybeard, all these living
38 beings will one after another suffer death, so fixed a rule as
39 this there is otherwise nowhere else in this world. Therefore
must sons of kings such as I am, take no heed of this
frail, worthless body which is despised by all whose eyes
40 are fixed on what is precious, and must ever pay heed to
that which is worthy of aspiration and is abiding, namely
41 fame[2]. (I hear[3]) in tales as in the Ummaggajātaka[4] and

Silākāla under Moggallāna I. The relic of the neck bone (*gīvaṭṭhi*) was according to the legend, brought by Sarabhu to Mahiyaṅgaṇa immediately after the death of the Buddha (Mhvs. 1. 37), the alms-bowl (*patta*) by Sumana from Pāṭaliputta (Pupphapura) to Anurādhapura in the reign of Devānaṃpiyatissa. Sumana is also said to have fetched the relic of the (right) collar bone (*akkhaka*) from Indra's Heaven (Mhvs. 17. 14 ff., 20). For the tooth relic (*dāthādhātu*) see above 37. 92 ff.

[1] The three fathers are the father Mānābharaṇa and his two brothers. The brother of his mother (Ratanāvalī) is Vikkamabāhu II.

[2] Lit.: "to that body of fame which is worthy of aspiration" (*pihaniyye yasodehe*).

[3] Verses 41-47 form one sentence. The accus. *caritaṃ* in 41, *vikkamaṃ* in 42 etc. up to *suladdhaṃ jīvitaṃ* in 47 are all governed by *sutvā* in v. 45. The verse 46 is a parenthesis.

[4] Mahāummaggajātaka, no. 546 in Fausböll's edition of the Jātakas (VI. 329 ff.).

others, of deeds done by the Bodhisatta in the different
stages of his development[1], the outcome of his heroic nature
and of other qualities. (I hear) in secular stories, in the 42
Rāmāyaṇa, the Bhārata and the like of the courage of Rāma
who slew Rāvana and of the extraordinary deeds of heroism 43
performed in battle by the five sons of Paṇḍu, how they
slew Duyyodhana[2] and the other kings. (I hear) in the 44
Itihāsa[3] tales of the wonders worked from of old by princes
like Dussanta[4] and others in combat with gods and demons. —
(I hear) of the great wisdom of Cāṇakka[5], that best of Brāh- 45
maṇas who uprooted the kings of the Nanda dynasty. — All 46
these deeds though they belong not to our time, have attained
among the people up to the present day, the highest renown.
— When I hear such a happy and incomparable life of those 47
who are able on earth to accomplish extraordinary deeds,
then if I, sprung of a noble stock, do not that which befits 48
the best among noble heroes, my birth will be useless. These 49
were aided alone by favourable conditions of the time, but
were they superior to me in insight and other qualities?"
After he had thus reflected he thought further: "My father, 50
the King, is now on the last stage of life; if now this my
father's kingdom comes to me, but in consequence of the 51
enervation of my spirit under the influence of royal pleasures,
I am not so successful as I wish, my harm will be the greater.
But if I now staying here on the spot, send out my scouts 52

[1] P. *bhūmisu*. For the ten "stages" or "steps" of the Bodhisatta see Senart, Le Mahāvastu I., p. 77 ff., 436.

[2] *Duyyodhana*, skr. *Duryodhana*, the eldest son of Dhṛtarāṣṭra, the chief of the Kurus who was vanquished and slain in the great battle on the Kuru field by the five Paṇḍu brothers Yudhiṣṭhira etc. Duryodhana fell on the last day of the battle by the hand of Bhīma.

[3] *Itihāsa* is the collective name for all the literature of historical narrative based on tradition. Knowledge of the Itihāsa is part of Brahmanical education. Cf. D. I, p. 88 (= III. 1. 3), M. II, p. 133 (= 91).

[4] Skr. *Duṣyanta*, the husband of Śakuntalā, a king of the Moon dynasty.

[5] Skr. *Cāṇakya*. See note to 64. 3, as also Lassen, Indische Altertumskunde[2] II, p. 212 ff.

and let them find out how conditions really are in the other
53 country, — my scouts might be in a position to discover a
weakness among my enemies favourable to my plans, or not[1] —
54 all the people here will describe[2] the strength of the foe to
55 me in all possible ways. (They will say:) 'For the three
Monarchs, thy fathers, of whom each was lord of a province,
56 although united they undertook war seven times, it was difficult to conquer the kingdom. How then shall a solitary
youth who merely rules a small province, take possession
57 of it? But it is easy to govern over the original province:
58 therefore thou must give up thy baneful project'. With such
words — boring glowing rods into my ears — they will
describe again and again, in every possible way, the great-
59 ness of the other country. But one should really refuse to
believe all this tattle of fools who speak without knowing
60 the real state of affairs. So under some kind of pretext I
shall myself go to the other country and find out its con-
61 ditions. But my father the Monarch, if he hears of these
plans, through fear that some evil may befall his noble son,
62 the light of his line, if he betakes himself into the country
of the foe, will, tender-hearted as he is, hinder my departure.
63 There will then be no fulfilment of my designs. It is therefore best if I go in disguise".

64 When the clever Prince who knew well what (right) occasions are, one day at night-time found such an occasion, he who was certainly not lacking in resources, left the house in such wise that his father knew nought of his departure.

Here ends the sixty-fourth chapter, called "The Departure for the other Country", in the Mahāvaṃsa, compiled for the serene joy and emotion of the pious.

[1] If we regard v. 53 as a parenthesis, we get rid of all difficulties of language and content. The sense is: nothing is to be gained by spying from here, for whatever the result, the people here will always exaggerate the dangers and in consequence will not join me. They must be encouraged by my lead.

[2] The pres. *kathayanti* is remarkable. One expects *kathessanti*.

CHAPTER LXV

THE KILLING OF THE SENĀPATI

As the Prince set forth accompanied only by his weapons, 1
there sounded at the same moment in front of him the peal
of a shell trumpet. Hearing it he versed in the divers omens, 2
knew that his plan would shortly succeed and was full of joy. 3
Without the watchmen placed at different points noticing it, he
got out of the town free from fear, lion-hearted. In haste he 4
covered a distance of five gāvutas[1] and reached in a region
not far from Badalatthalagāma[2] a village called Pilimvatthu. 5
It had been fixed as goal for the meeting together of his
people, to halt here before his own arrival, awaiting 6
him on the way. Now when he saw that of those who
had received orders only some had appeared on the spot, the 7
Prince asked why so few had come. But they answered:
„Why doth our Lord speak so, though he knows the whole 8
demeanour of the people. With whom is there no fear of
death? Our Lord is at an age immediately following that of 9
boyhood, even to-day the odour of milk plays about his lips.
There is no separate fortune acquired by thee, nor is there 10
any other accumulation of resources save these present. Ex- 11
cept for ourselves whose character has long been tested and
whose devotion is firmly rooted, who otherwise would follow
thee? And what thy father the Sovereign, will do with us 12
who have come hither, no man knows. In our path there is 13
still the Senāpati Saṅkha by name, a great and mighty hero
who has his abode on the frontier, apart from other foes, 14

[1] A *gāvuta* (skr. *gavyūti*) is a quarter of a yojana (DhCo. II. 13[4]), thus about two miles. PTS. P. D. s. v.

[2] See note to 58. 43; 64. 43.

and we few people are made one by the other ever more
15 terror-stricken. And the time of daybreak is now close at
hand". Thus each for himself made known the fear that
16 dwelt in their hearts. When the Prince heard their words
he smiled kindly, looked them fearlessly in the face and spake:
17 "Although all these people here who have such fear, have
lived together with me a long time, yet have they not
18 learnt to know me", and to chase away the fear that had
risen in them, the lion-hearted let sound[1] a mighty lion's
19 roar. "Leave all men aside; when I have my weapons in my
hand, what can Sakka, the King of the gods, do even if he
20 is enraged? Because ye thought I am a boy these foolish
thoughts have come to you. Have ye not heard that one
21 looks up to splendid might, not to age? But if ye fear my
father's army will pursue me, then will I — by a single deed
22 that I have devised to carry out and in such a way that the
people in my own and in the other country shall offer me
23 fear and devotion and ye shall rid yourselves of this your
terror — at once, as soon as this night is past, manifest my
24 pre-eminent insight, determination and courage. Go forward!"
With these words the hero seized his weapons, left that vil-
25 lage full of determination and like to a second image of the
sun risen in the western heavens to surpass the sun disk
26 standing on the summit of the eastern mountain, he lighted
up the lotus thicket of the eyes of his attendants and came
at early morn to Badalatthalī.

[1] It is interesting here to note the fundamental difference between the narrative of the Cūlavaṃsa and that of the older Mahāvaṃsa and between the ideas of their authors as shown particularly in the comparison of the personalities of Duṭṭhagāmaṇi and Parakkamabāhu. In the one case deeds of true heroism, culminating in the dauntless duel with Eḷāra, in the other big, high-sounding words as prelude to an action of very doubtful courage and of still more doubtful moral justification. It is therefore significant that in Ceylon, more especially in Rohaṇa, one meets again and again with traditions connected with Duṭṭhagāmaṇi. He is the real national hero of the Sinhalese and his name still lives in the popular memory. Parakkamabāhu is almost forgotten though he is nearer by more than a thousand years to the present than the other.

By the peal of the victorious trumpets the Senāpati (Saṅkha) 27
awoke. With consternation[1] he perceived that the Prince had
come. Accompanied by a great host he went forth to meet 28
him and full of reverence, bowed himself to the earth to offer
the customary homage. When with the thought: what may 29
not this man do to us if he remains alive? he must be slain
on the spot, the soldiers looked at their leader, but he checked 30
them with a sign, for he thought: it is unworthy of a man to
kill anyone against whom no guilt can be proven, only in
case of hostile demeanour is the death penalty permitted.
The lion-like (Prince) took the hand of the Senāpati, spake 31
friendly words to him and entered his abode. The Senāpati 32
thought: "The Prince's departure must have taken place
without the King's knowing of it. Until I learn the state of
affairs these people who have come with him, must be each 33
separately housed so that they may not remain in communi-
cation with him, the Prince however, must dwell in my house".
He did so, and in order to dupe the discerning (prince), he 34
paid him the honours due to a guest and sent messengers to
the King. Now when the Prince perceived the deception 35
practised by Saṅkha he thought: "If now without doing what
must be done, I remain inactive, of a truth my plan will 36
come to nought: this man must needs now be slain". He gave 37
one of his attendants the order to strike down[2] the Senāpati.
A great tumult arose: the Senāpati is slain. A soldier of the 38
Senāpati hearing that the general had been murdered, cried:
For what reason did the murder of my Lord take place? and 39
sword in hand, risking his own life for his Lord, he rushed
at the Prince standing there alone. But when he glanced at 40
the Prince's countenance, trembling with fear, he could not
stand upright and flung himself at his feet. Before the Prince 41
could say the words: "Seize him", one of the soldier's com-

[1] P. *saṃjātasaṃbhamo.* Not translated by W.

[2] As it is described here, the murder of Saṅkha who was a loyal and devoted adherent of the royal house, is an act as brutal as it is senseless. Probably the whole episode is in this form unhistorical. See Introduction I.

42 panions himself struck him down. "The deed he has done
without my orders is unseemly", with these words the Prince
43 had him punished accordingly. But the terrible excitement
which had arisen at the same time, the Prince stilled by the
mere wrinkling of the brows.

44 The hero whose greatest wealth was fame, the Prince of firm character, who well understood the rewarding of his heroes, whose most precious treasure was his famous name, left his soldiers to take all what they would of the abundant property amassed by the Senāpati.

Here ends the sixty-fifth chapter, called "The Slaying of the Senāpati", in the Mahāvaṃsa, compiled for the serene joy and emotion of the pious.

CHAPTER LXVI

THE SPYING OUT OF THE CONDITIONS IN THE OTHER COUNTRY

"If I were to set forth to-day to carry out my plan, 1
these people would think: the Prince has left through fear.
I will stay here and see what my father does as long as he has not 2
heard that I am staying here after the slaying of the Senāpati".
With such reflections the hero, the best of all far-seeing men, 3
sojourned a few days on the spot. The soldiers of the Senā- 4
pati and many people who dwelt in the province, who in con-
sequence of the slaying of the Senāpati, were seized with 5
terror were not able to remain each in his place, but sought
out the Prince, streaming together from all sides. "Acting in 6
opposition to his father the Prince has slain the Senāpati",
thought the inhabitants of the province. "If powerful people 7
like ourselves, whose devotion is deep-rooted, are his slaves[1]
what then is impossible for our Lord? If the (lawful) Lord 8
is in life, how dare thy uncle under the pretext, the prince
is still a boy, hold sway in the kingdom belonging to thy
father? We will join together, march on the town of Saṅ- 9
khaṭthalī and fetch hither by force the king together with
his treasure and his harem". With this firm resolve and bent 10
solely on the gaining of the dominion, they betook themselves
to the place Padavārasuññakaṇḍa by name. The Prince sent 11
some of his people thither, summoned the leaders of the sol-
diers to him (and spake to them): "Ye must not think that 12

[1] I read with the MSS. *dāsesu.* S 2 alone differs, for *daṃsesu* in S 3, 7 is only a variant in the writing. The *dakkhesu* adopted by S. and B. is an unnecessary alteration.

the slaying of the Senāpati by me took place out of enmity
13 to my father; away then with your agitation[1]! I have in no
wise come hither in enmity to my royal father, nor do I mean
14 to bring this part of the province into my power. For sons
such as I am is there not but one thing to do — to cause little
15 sorrow themselves to their aged fathers and to ward off the
evil which may be done them by another and so ever to serve
16 them with devotion. Why have ye such thoughts?" Therewith
the prudent one removed their scruples and reflecting on his
17 further course, came to this decision: "If I sojourn here some
days, illmeaning people will try to sow discord between us
18 twain, father and son. Without lingering here I must arise
and busy myself with the carrying out of my former plans".
19 Therewith the Prince left the village of Badalatthalī to
betake himself to Buddhagāma near the Siridevī mountain.
20 Before he reached the village of Siriyāla[2] the inhabitants[3]
21 who had banded together, fled on every side. Accompanied
alone by his own followers, the heroic prince now advanced
22 well armed along the highway. "Now if we quietly suffer
the prince to escape after his having slain the Senāpati, what

[1] W. translates "ill-will towards me". That is, I believe, wrong. The context is rather this: the people have taken the killing of Saṅkha as a sign that the prince is in open rebellion against his uncle. They take his side and civil war threatens. To hinder this, Parakkamabāhu explains to the people that there is no enmity between himself and his uncle, and exhorts them to keep quiet.

[2] The topographical problems have been most satisfactorily solved by Codrington (I. 66). Following Mr. Storey, he identifies Buddhagāma (see note 58. 43) with Menikdena, S. S. W. of Dambul, since an inscription was found there in which a Budgam-vehera is mentioned (ASC. 1908 = VI. 1913, p. 14 f.). Near there is a mountain Nikula which, according to Forbes, was formerly called "Heereedevatai", that is, Siridevī. Before Parakkamabāhu got there he passed Siriyāla. That is without doubt the present Hiriyalgama in the Gantihe Korale, which gives its name to the Hiriyala district north of Kurunegala.

[3] While the inhabitants of the Badalatthalī district were not disinclined to support the Prince against his uncle, those of Siriyāla and later, to a greater extent, those of Buddhagāma showed themselves hostile, even inclined to capture him and give him up to the King.

kind of loyalty would that be on our part to the King who
gives us our daily bread?" So thought certain traitors, con- 23
ceived the plan of capturing him and pursued him from be-
hind while he was on the march. Without being in the least 24
afraid of them, the Prince fought them sword in hand and
scattered them in flight. Together with his followers among 25
whom no falling off was noticeable[1], the discerning Prince,
free of all danger, reached Buddhagāma. When a few days 26
of his sojourn there had passed, the inhabitants assembled
together to capture the Prince. Raining a furious, uninter- 27
rupted shower of arrows, they surrounded the village full of
zeal to begin the fight. "We must give up our lives if he 28
benefits thereby" thought the soldiers who had come with
him and, flurried by fear all, save the umbrella-bearer and 29
the sword-bearer of the Prince, fled on every side before
the Prince's eyes. When he saw his soldiers fleeing, he smil- 30
ed a little and having now found an opportunity of showing
his extraordinary courage, the Prince thought: „With my 31
weapon even will I strike terror into the foe and scatter
him in flight", and cried with vehemence: "Give me my
sword!" When the soldiers who had at first fled, heard along 32
with these loud and resoundingly spoken words, the blare of
the victorious trumpets penetrating the circle of the firmament, 33
and when they saw the struck off heads of the foe, falling
to the ground, they turned and fighting, scattered the troops 34
some thousands in number in flight, surrounded the Prince
and praised his courage.

While now the Prince sojourned there he desired to have 35
the nagaragiri[2] of King Gajabāhu, Gokaṇṇa[3], who had the
control of Kālavāpi, in his presence, to find out his views. 36

[1] P. *adiṭṭhaparihānike*, quite ignored in W's translation. It must hewever be emphasised that not one of the original followers of the Prince had deserted him.

[2] The title *nagaragiri* is met with here for the first time (cf. also 66. 62 and 70. 68). See Introduction III.

[3] *Gokaṇṇa* is probably a clan name (see above 38. 13, note); skr. *gokarṇa*, P. *gokaṇṇa* denotes a species of stag, an elk.

He sent therefore, one of his henchmen to him with a letter.
37 When the latter saw the missive he nodded consent, read it
38 and learned from it of all that had taken place. Believing
that the superiority of the Prince's forces made disobedience
39 to his commands an impossibility and without waiting for
news as to the opinion[1] of his own Monarch, he came to
40 Buddhagāma and sought out the Prince with reverence. "Thou
hast heard how I have come hither away from my father the
King, how I have caused the violent death of the mighty
41 Senāpati, and how I have performed marvellous deeds of he-
42 roism against the foe following in my rear. Without even
a thought that thou shouldst learn the opinion of thine own
king, while before the sending of my messenger no connec-
43 tion (between us) existed, thou (nevertheless) settest out to
see me the moment thou didst see my letter; thou hast done
44 well," with these words the Prince full of joy, presented him
with all the ornaments he had himself worn, consisting of divers
45 precious stones, along with an excellent elephant. To the
leaders among his soldiers he gave valuable ornaments of
46 divers kinds, such as costly earrings and the like. Hereupon
he dismissed the chief (Gokaṇṇa) with his soldiers that they
might rest, having shown himself friendly to them by the
assigning of dwellings, food and the like.

47 Arrived in his quarters for the night, Gokaṇṇa beheld
himself in a dream in the form[2] of the Senāpati who had
48 been murdered at the Prince's command, surrounded on all
sides by robbers with swords in their hands to kill him. In
49 mortal terror he gave a shriek and fell from his bed to the
50 ground, and without heed for the people who bore his sword, his
umbrella and the like, he left the whole of the force which
had come with him in the lurch. But as he could not even
51 find his way by the heavens, he got into a great forest and
losing the path, wandered about in it. Only at daybreak did

[1] P. *bhāva* (the same in v. 42) in reality "kind, character", then "attitude towards something, conception".

[2] Thus I explain the *viya*: he saw himself (*attānaṃ*) as the Senāpati.

he find the road leading to Kālavāpi, followed it in haste 52
and reached his village. His men too, when they heard of
the flight of their lord, seeing no other escape, smitten with 53
the greatest terror, left each of them his[1] weapons behind and
wandered like their master bewildered about the forest, reaching 54
Kālavāpi in haste at break of day. When the Prince heard 55
the story of the flight he smiled and remained there (in
Buddhagāma) a few days longer. And from that time this 56
story was for him who appreciated humorous tales[2], a means
in moments when he was downhearted, of chasing away his
depression.

When Kittisirimegha heard of all these events he sum- 57
moned his great dignitaries together and took counsel with
them: "The Prince has escaped in disguise from our well 58
protected town, looked after by officials and filled with soldiers.
Thereupon together with certain villainous and undutiful people 59
who went with him from here[3], he has fled, has slain the 60
mightiest vassal in my kingdom, the Senāpati, has seized the
whole of the costly property accumulated by him, has then in
his flight slain here and there many soldiers among the country 61
folk who pursued him, has summoned to him the nagaragiri 62
Gokaṇṇa of King Gajabāhu[4] and has brought him under his
influence and now sojourns in Buddhagāma[5]. This is no time 63
to look on inactively. If the foe in this threatening situation[6]

[1] Note the free treatment of the gender in *āyudhāni . . . sake sake.*

[2] P. *nānābhassarasa*, lit. "for the many kinds of tastes in narratives". One might read *nānāhassarasa*: *hassa* = skr. *hāsya* is the cheerful laughter-rousing fundamental character (*rasa*) of a literary work.

[3] The MS. reading *te tato* in 59 b is disturbing. It is difficult to place *te* in the construction of the sentence and *tato* stands already at the beginning of the verse. I propose reading *ten' ato*: *tena* is comitative "with him" and *ato* means "from here" that is from Saṅkhatthalī.

[4] The same wording as in v. 35 c b.

[5] The present part. *vasaṃ* stands here again instead of a finite verb to express a permanent state. Cf. note to 41. 89.

[6] P. *asmiṃ chiddamhi*, lit. "at this break" (= weakness, want), or possibly in the original meaning "at this moment where a division (an estrangement between me and my nephew) has taken place"

64 make a treacherous treaty with the Prince who is favoured
by fortune and gifted with insight and courage, and think
65 to begin war, that will be for us a great misfortune. Before
he can think out other worse plans he must be seized during
66 his stay in that village". Thus resolved, he summoned the two
Adhikārins[1], Sena and Mahinda bỳ name, further Maṅgalāna,
67 the son of a royal servant[2], as well as other retainers and
sent them forth with the words: "Take with you all people
68 in my kingdom who live by soldiering, go forth in haste
69 and bring the Prince hither by force". These took each his
great army and with powerful forces divided into ten columns
70 they approached Siriyāḷa. When the Prince heard thereof
he thought: "I will take up my position at a spot difficult
to pass[3], in such a way as to force the troops which are
marching separately in ten columns, to join each other and then
71 I shall immediately destroy them". The hero betook himself
in haste from Buddhagāma to Saraggāma[4] in the district of
72 Mahātila. The officers (of Kittisirimegha) thought however:
„if the Prince flees from Buddhagāma and withdraws into an
73 impassible region surrounded by mountains, his capture will
be difficult, whatever means one uses", and marched united
74 thither. When the Prince heard that he rejoiced at the success
of his plan. In front he left space for the advancing army,
75 placed his numerous men on both sides of the road, hidden, well

[1] From 70. 278 it is clear that *adhikārin* denotes a certain office or a certain rank. See Introduction III.

[2] W. seems here to adopt the reading *mahālānaṃ* of the Col. Ed. which however has no support from the MSS. and translates "the mahálána" — with the note "chief secretary" (?) — Devapádamúla Dáraka". The word *pādamūlaka* or *-lika* with the meaning of "servant" occurs frequently in the Jātakas (PTS. P. D. s. v., also DhCo. I. 183[4]).

[3] Not "at such a stronghold" as W. translates. It is a case of a narrow pass in the mountains.

[4] Saraggāma has certainly nothing to do with Sarogāmatittha on the Mahāvālukagaṅgā (71. 18; 72. 1, 31). Codrington identifies it, following Storey, with Selagama in the District Matale, Asgiri Pallesiya Pattuva (Census of C., 1921, II., p. 94). Instead of "from Buddhagāma" the text has simply *tato* "from there", the same in v. 72.

armed, such as were deemed especially brave. Then when 76
the mighty one saw that the whole of the hostile force had
advanced to the centre, he experienced in the art of war,
had numbers of soldiers cut down. Those who remained over 77
from the slaughter threw their weapons away as the case
might be and fled, with no thought of renewing the fight,
on all sides. The victorious Prince left the place thereupon 78
and betook himself to Bodhigāmavara[1] there to await his father's
decisions[2]. Sojourning there the hero spent several days and 79
after scattering in that same place a (further) army which
came forth to fight at the command of his father the King, 80
he retired from thence and betook himself to the village of
Ranambura in the region of the Laṅkā mountains[3]. To 81
remove the footsoreness of his soldiers the intrepid one
spent several days sojourning there. Then he reflected thus: 82
"Although my foes have all been repeatedly crushed by me
in battle, they will not retire out of fear of my father, gi-
ving up the hope (of success) in fight. Because their evil 83
counsellors have wrongly thought: this Prince falls not into
our power only because he is in inaccessible country, there- 84
fore I shall now betake myself to the spot where they are
sojourning and drive away their evil thoughts". He advanced 85

[1] W. translates "returned to the village Bodhigāma. He thus obviously considers Bodhigāmavara to be the same as Buddhagāma. But the text has not *paccagā* "he returned", but *agā* "he went". Codrington (I. 69) regards Bodhigāmavara as the present Bogambara in the Matale Pallesiya Pattuva (N. E. of Matale). The prince thus stayed near the battlefield to await the development of events.

[2] P. *pitucittānurakkhatthaṃ*. W's translation "that he might calm the anxiety of his father" is wrong. All Parakkamabāhu's actions have the character of open enmity and are opposed to the fiction of the compiler that no conflict had taken place between uncle and nephew.

[3] The Prince withdrew from Bodhigāmavara further E. or N. E. There is no doubt that the name Laṅkāpabbata or Laṅkāgiri (thus 70. 88, mentioned again in connection with Bodhigāmavara) is preserved in the present Laggala, the name of a district between Matale Pallesiya Pattuva and the Mahaveliganga. It is also advisable to read instead of the *Ratamburaṃ* of the Col. Ed., *Ranamburaṃ* in which Codrington recognises the present Ranamure in Laggala Udasiya Pattuva.

to the village of Khīravāpi occupied by their army and
86 reached the district called Ambavana[1]. He occupied it and
having found out himself from the people there the exact
route to march against the foe[2], he set out in the evening
87 and reached the village at night. When his soldiers reached
the enclosure consisting of terrible briers full of prickles from
top to bottom[3], they stayed without, being unable to pene-
88 trate it. The hero placed himself at the head, broke fearlessly
through the fence, and standing in the middle of the village
89 called out his name. The enemy who had already witnessed
the marvellous courage of the Prince, were seized with terror
90 when they heard his resounding voice and all (of them)
without even thinking of clothes or weapons, fled on all
91 sides, like gazelles that have caught sight of a lion. His
soldiers who had entered by the way he had forced, slew
whomsoever they caught sight of, and set fire to the village.
92 The Prince immediately marched to the village of Nāvāgirisa
and resting there awaited the dawn.

93 The dignitaries of his father, the King, now assembled
and spoke with each other of the great energy (of the Prince)
94 in the various battles: "With our plan of capturing the Prince
quickly with our forces of so many thousand men, we have
95 brought ruin on our own army, and since they have everywhere
fled in fight, we have only caused the Prince's fame to become
96 more widely known. But if we disregard the terrible com-
mand sent us repeatedly by the King, then the life of our
97 kinsfolk is at stake[4]. It is not meet that we spend our time
here without taking pains to carry out the King's command
98 by every possible means. Even at the cost of our lives we

[1] The name is preserved in that of the Ambanganga (Codrington) which flows through the valley of Matale and turns eastward at Nalanda towards the Mahaveliganga.

[2] P. *etehi* refers to the inhabitants of Ambavana, *tesaṃ* to the enemy; *saṃcāra* means the possibility of approaching the enemy.

[3] So I understand *tikkhaggapada* "where the top part (*agga*) and the foot end (*pada*) are sharp".

[4] They are hostages in the hands of the king.

must satisfy the Lord who gives us our living, and thereby ensure the protection of our kindred". Therewith full of 99
defiant courage, with large, well armed forces, they set forth like the army of Māra on a road shown them by scouts.
From four sides they forced their way into the village and 100
surrounded the Prince's house. As the hilly region was cool, 101
the latter had donned a red woollen shawl and sat there playing a game to which he was accustomed from his childhood. From the noise he noticed that the foe was quite 102
near, but since he saw not one of his own followers, he at once bound his topknot fast, wrapped himself tightly in the 103
woollen shawl he had been wearing, and terrible, sword in hand, he plunged like a savage lion into the middle of the 104
fight and in a moment chased the whole of the enemy to the world's end[1]. Then after raising his voice and calling 105
together his own people who had come with him and who terrorized by the clamour, had fled into the wilderness, he reflected: "The fear which must beset the King of the hostile 106
party[2] when he thinks what may be the cause of my leaving the King my father and coming hithor — all that I have hitherto 107
done, beginning with the slaying of the Senāpati[3], suffices to remove it. I must now betake myself to the other country".
Therewith he set forth thence and at the place Porogāhāli- 108
khaṇḍa[4] he cleansed by the pouring over with water the blood stains[5] from sword and hand[6], laid aside the blood- 109

[1] Lit.: "he made the enemy (*dise*) into such as turned themselves to the end of the firmament (*disānta*)".

[2] I. e. Gajabāhu.

[3] The train of thought is this: It is intelligible that Gajabāhu should regard my coming with distrust. He may fear that I intend evil towards him. But all my actions so far have been directed not against him but against my father. This should allay his fears so that I can now enter his country without danger.

[4] I prefer to read °*gāhāli*° (instead of °*gāhāli*°) because the name seems to me to contain the word *āli* "canal" (Sinh. *ǟla*). *Khaṇḍa* means "district", a narrower area than *raṭṭha* or *maṇḍala*.

[5] Lit. "the union with the red blood".

[6] Or perhaps "from the sword hand", from the hand which had wielded the sword.

soiled mantle that he had worn and enjoyed after a change
110 of garment a comfortable rest. He then crossed the frontier
of the province of his royal father and reached in the realm
111 of Gajabāhu the small place called Janapada[1]. With all kinds
of sportive games, such as were customary in the country,
he spent several days, sojourning there.
112 Now when Gajabāhu heard from the mouth of his watch-
men of the gradual approach of the Prince he was seized
113 with great alarm. He spoke with his councillors and after
determining what was to be done, he sent him a gift of
114 raiment, ornaments and the like. To his envoys he gave this
message[2]: "Since hearing of thy leaving my uncle[3], the King,
and of the wonderful deeds of courage which thou hast
115 performed on the way and that thou instead of applying
elsewhere[4], hast entered my realm, my heart has become
116 narrow through expanding joy. Besides myself what kindred
hast thou who would be ready to serve thee[5]. A coronation
117 festival truly is thy visit for me. Since my uncle, the King, in
his old age does not hold such a jewel of a son as his most
118 precious possession and by some imprudent attitude has let
him come into my hands, that means for me the reward in
119 full for a highly meritorious action. If we twain are now for
120 ever united, what foe will dare to make war on us? My splendour
will now in every respect become great, even as that of the
121 fire when it has gained the storm wind as its ally. Once we

[1] Janapada is often mentioned as borderland of Rājaraṭṭha towards Dakkhiṇadesa. Cf. 67. 22; 70. 87. It is probably to be looked for in the neighbourhood of the present Vagapanaha, Udasiya Pattuva, east of Dambul.

[2] Cf. v. 122: *iti vatvāna* etc.

[3] Kittisirimegha was married to Lokanāthā, the sister of Gajabāhu's father Vikkamabāhu, according to 59. 44.

[4] With the majority of the MSS. we must read here *āgantvā 'ññattha*. If with the Col. Ed. we read *āgantvā* (thus only in MS. S 6) *aññattha* remains unintelligible, for the meaning is not "somewhere or other" (W. "into a place"), but "somewhere else".

[5] P. *vassabandhave*. I take *vassa* = Skr. *vaśya* as "tractable, obedient" W. has "kinsfolk . . . on your mother's side".

have met each other, I shall have no difficulty in conferring on the prince the royal dignity which belonged to his father.
Meanwhile thou must without loss of time carry out thy visit 122
to me". With this message he dismissed his envoys. When 123
the Prince whose intelligence was well capable of discrimination (between the true and the false) heard this news from the envoys, he thought: "It is ever very hard to see through
the craftiness of princes; I will test him and then set off", 124
and he sent together with the envoys, a warrior Nimmala by
name, versed in all expedients. After learning (through him) 125
the true character of the king as well as that of all his advisers, the Prince advanced further towards Pulatthinagara.

Thereupon King Gajabāhu advanced to meet him at the 126
head of a great army, showed him in joyful zeal many fa-
vours, let the Prince mount the elephant on which he him- 127
self was riding, showed him the beauty of the town and
betook himself (with him) to the royal palace. The Prince 128
made known his joy called forth by the seeing Gajabāhu and
after spending some days there he in order to become ac- 129
quainted with those of the King's people dwelling in the
outlying districts who were for him and against him[1], sought 130
out such as understood all kinds of tricks and knew the dialect of the various regions and who were distinguished by
devotion to their Lord. Of these he being versed in the 131
methods to be applied, made those who understood the mixing
of poisons[2], adopt the garb of the snake charmer. Others 132
skilled in telling of the lines of the hand and other marks

[1] The work of espionage now begins. That the compiler was influenced by the reading of text books on *nīti*, as for instance, Kauṭalya's Arthaśāstra (I. 11, 7 ff.) is unmistakable. The *sānurāgā* and *sāparāgā* of our passage correspond to the *akṛtyā* and *kṛtyā* of K. I. 13-15, the faithful who cannot be influenced and the unfaithful whom one can win over to oneself. Cf. Arthaśāstra of Kauṭilya, ed. R. Shama Sastri, p. 22 ff.; Kauṭilya's Arthaśāstra trsl. by R. Shamasastry p. 26 ff.; Das altindische Buch vom Welt- und Staatsleben, das Arthaçāstra des Kauṭilya, übers. von J. J. Meyer, p. 24 ff.

[2] P. *visavijjāsu kovide* corresponding to the *rasadāḥ* of Kauṭalya I. 11. Cf. also with this the *rasakriyābhiñña* below in v. 138.

on the body[1] he had disguised as wandering musicians, as
133 caṇḍālas and as brāhmaṇas. Amongst the many Damiḷas and
others he made such as were practised in dance and song[2],
appear as people who played with leather dolls and the like.
134 Others again after they had laid aside their own garb, he ordered
to go round[3] selling goods such as rings and bracelets of glass and
135 the like. Others again he sent forth with the command that they
should go in the garb of ascetics[4], with the equipment of such,
136 the umbrella, the beggar's staff and the like, wandering like
unto pious pilgrims from village to village and thereby
137 performing their devotions in front of the cetiyas. People
versed in the art of healing he commanded to seek out villages and market towns and there to practise the healing
138 art[5]. Such as understood the instruction of boys in the art
of writing and in the handling of weapons, who were skilled
in the preparation of magic potions and versed in spirit in-
139 cantation as well as craftsmen possessed of skill in the working of gold and the like he ordered to move from place to
140 place, practising their profession. In order to find out himself the actual conditions as these existed amongst the inhabitants of the inner district (of the town), he by showing a
141 great innocence founded on his youth, learned amongst the
people who came to him under the pretext of entertainment
142 and who dwelt on the weakness of the King, to distinguish
amongst the highest officials, officers and soldiers those who were
ambitious, those who nursed a grudge, those who were afraid

[1] According to the Kauṭalīya I. 12, the knowledge of the *lakṣaṇa* and of the *aṅgavidyā* belongs to the equipment of a particular kind of spy. These are the so-called *sattriṇaḥ saṃsargavidyāḥ*.

[2] The *naṭa-nartaka-gāyana-vādaka-vāgjīvana-kuśīlavāḥ* of the Kauṭalīya (I. 12).

[3] In the Kauṭalīya (I. 11) the *vaidehakavyañjanaḥ*, the spy disguised as trader. Peddling with bracelets of glass and similar trinkets is common in the villages of Ceylon at the present day.

[4] Kauṭalīya I. 11 deals with the *tāpasa* as spy (*muṇḍo vā jaṭilo vā vṛittikāmastāpasavyañjanaḥ*).

[5] The strolling quack is missing in the Kauṭalīya, as well as the strolling schoolmaster and the strolling craftsman.

and those who were avaricious[1]. He took care[2] too, that 143
spies who were versed in the divers rites and ceremonies[3] in
use in the various schools and who knew the tales from the
Itihāsas, Purāṇas and many other books, should visit the dif- 144
ferent houses in the assumed garb of samaṇas. As soon then
as confidence in them had been established, and when they
had found trust and reverence, they came forward as (spi- 145
ritual) advisers, estranged the people and brought them under
their influence. Believing that if the King were made un- 146
suspicious, he could then move about as he would, and easily
learn the actual conditions in the interior of the country, he 147
sent a letter to his mother who was dwelling in Rohaṇa,
fetched thence his younger sister, the charming Princess
Bhaddavatī, as well as abundant money, under the pretext that 148
it was her property. The money he took to himself but the 149
Princess he wedded to the Lord of men Gajabāhu and so ma-
naged matters that the Ruler completely trusted him even as 150
also the royal family[4]. He used also under the pretence of
sport, to go about the streets with a rutting elephant that

[1] The *Kauṭalīya* I. 14 distinguishes in exactly the same way, four groups amongst those who can be manipulated and won over for one's own schemes. The close relation of our passage to the Arthaśāstra and the allied literature is shown by the fact that the terms are the same in Sanskrit and in Pāli: 1) the *kruddhavargaḥ* = P. *saṃkuddhā*, the group of the indignant, 2) the *bhītavargaḥ* = P. *bhītā*, the group of the fearful, 3) the *lubdhavargaḥ* = P. *luddhā*, the group of the avaricious and, 4) the *mānivargaḥ* = P. *abhimānino*, the group of the ambitious. The last group is placed first by the Cūlavaṃsa. For the whole subject cf. W. Geiger, Kenntnis der Indischen Nītiliteratur in Ceylon, Festschrift für H. Jacobi (Beiträge zur Literaturwissenschaft und Geistesgeschichte Indiens), p. 418 ff.

[2] P. *vidhānaṃ tathā kari yathā* . . . in v. 145: "he acted in the way, arranged it so that . . ."

[3] P. *upāya-vidhāna*, not "folklore" as translated by W. The Kauṭalīya I. 9 uses *upāya* along with *atharvan* in the meaning of "rite, sorcery".

[4] W's translation is wrong. He has not realised that *tato rājakulaṃ* belongs still to the preceding. The Sinhalese translators S. and B. have also overlooked it.

151 had rut discharge, and when he was pursued by it would quickly flee under the pretext that refuge was difficult to find, into the house of people who were to be brought under his in-
152 fluence. He then gave them fitting money reward, costly ornaments and the like and brought them thus imperceptibly
153 under his influence. All the people down to the lowest grades, and the soldiers who dwelt in the town, thought, each for
154 himself that this courtesy was paid to him. Thereupon he ordered his skilled scribes to make an estimate of the King's revenues, of his stocks of grain, of his troops, of his various
155 war material and so on, with the charge: record these by stealing into the various departments of the administration[1].
156 Others he appointed to find out the inmost thoughts of the people entrusted with the guarding of the town and (of those)
157 of the leaders of the army. He himself under the pretext of youthful pastimes, roamed about everywhere and thus, avoiding every peril, explored the conditions in both spheres[2].
158 When the wise man realises how all enterprises undertaken by beings equipped with a great fulness of meritorious deeds accumulated in previous existences, have a successful issue, not meeting with any hindering cause, he will certainly do good.

Here ends the sixty-sixth chapter, called "The Spying out of the Conditions in the other Country", in the Mahāvaṃsa, compiled for the serene joy and emotion of the pious.

[1] Lit. "groups of scribes (*lekhaka*)".

[2] What is meant is *antomaṇḍalaṃ* the territory inside the town, and *bahimaṇḍalaṃ* that outside of the town. Cf. above v. 129, 140.

CHAPTER LXVII

THE FESTIVAL OF THE MAHĀDIPĀDA

Now one day the Prince mounted his chariot and drove, 1
accompanied by his retainers, along the King's highway. Then 2
a terrible buffalo broken loose, that killed everyone it saw,
with rolling bloodshot eyes sprang upon him. When the 3
charioteer and the people of the retinue saw it dashing on-
wards, seized with fear they fled in haste. Then the Prince 4
thought: it is not meet for me to flee like those there, and
fearless and without excitement, the hero swiftly went for him 5
and called to him suddenly with loud resounding voice. When 6
the buffalo heard this, like to a lion's roar, it turned in terror
and ran away, killing or trampling down everyone it met.
All who had seen the miracle with their own eyes or had 7
heard of it broke, full of astonishment, into words of admira-
tion: "Behold the heroism, behold the courage, behold the 8
determination, behold his steadfastness, behold the effect of
his meritorious deeds!"

When the Ruler of men Gajabāhu heard how the people 9
praised his bravery and his other qualities, he thought: that 10
is a great man, of terrible courage whose extraordinary might
cannot be compared with that of others, and he began to be
afraid of him. Now when the Prince perceived the suspicious 11
thoughts which had arisen in the King Gajabāhu he reflected
thus: "If I wish while sojourning here, to achieve the so- 12
vereignty, I shall without doubt succeed by the mere wrinkling
of my brows. But in this case my dignity, and my extra- 13
ordinary courage and the strength of my arms will have no
renown in the world. And the incessant twitching in my arms 14
will nevermore cease without the pastime of a war game.

15 Therefore I will return to the land of my birth, overwhelm
this king by war and capture him and his retainers alive.
16 Then when I bring my father Kittisirimegha into this town
and by the water of the royal coronation which will be poured
17 on his head, I efface the shame of the defeat of my three
fathers — then will my fame spread itself also over Jambudīpa."
18 Hereupon he found out through hunters a way of approach
for the army in making an assault on the town and a way
19 for its retirement, if there should be cause for retreat, as well
as a way suitable for his own spies, well understanding how
20 to discriminate between the different ways, while he himself
under the pretext of the chase, wandered about the forest
near the town, and distinguished the main roads from the
bypaths by particular signs.
21 Mindful of the words of the Buddha: if one lets time slip
away, time drinks up the best[1], he with the intention of be-
22 taking himself to his own country, then sent away first of
all his followers having fixed the goal where one should meet,
23 in the locality of Janapada[2]. But as he thought, that after
having stayed there so long it was not in keeping with his
24 manliness, to leave without giving notice thereof, he paid a
visit in the evening in richly decorated attire, to the King
25 Gajabāhu. Then when twilight had come when people were
wont to amuse themselves with divers games, he smiling, with
26 cheerful mien, spake thus: "I must start even to-day to be-
take myself to the province of the Yuvarāja, and having paid
27 a visit to my father, then return hither in haste." When
the King heard this, thanks to his naturally defective under-
28 standing, he thought he had said this with reference to his

[1] Lit.: "In the passing of time time drinks away the sap (*rasa*) thereof." That is: a work loses its value if it is not carried out without hesitation. This is held to be a *buddhavaco*, like many ancient sayings of wisdom. S. and B. have changed the word evidently because it is not to be found in the Canon, into *vuddhavaco* "ancient saying" (thus W.) I think however, that *vuddha* is only used of age in respect of human life.

[2] Thus already near the frontier of Dakkhiṇadesa. See note to 66. 110.

intention to betake himself to his house[1], and said to him
with cheerful smile the favourable words: "May what you 29
have in mind be swiftly fulfilled!"[2] The chief Brāhmaṇa
who stood near the King likewise at the same moment spake
a favourable word of happy augury of which it is acknow- 30
ledged that it aims at the abundant accumulation (of means)
for the attainment of an object, for peace and victory and
for the destruction of the hostile party. When the Prince 31
heard that, he thought with joy: the present constellation is
favourable to my course, and betook himself to his home.

Thereupon the Prince great in virtue and insight, hearing 32
and seeing favourable omens of many kinds, left the house.
Running as if in fun after his elephant called Rāmakula, he 33
roamed from street to street and left the town at night. By 34
moonlight wandering thence, he met a man resting at the
foot of a tree and asked him who he was. When he heard 35
that he was a wayfarer he spake quickly with raised voice:
"Dost thou know me?" The other stood silent from fear.
"Ādipāda Parakkamabāhu, so they call me; fear not". With 36
these words he quickly quieted him and won him for himself.
He spake to him: "That I met thee here was in truth for me 37
a great gain. Betake thee now in all haste to the camp and 38
tell there thou hast seen Prince Parakkamabāhu on the way
into his own country". With that he sent him off hurriedly.
Near the Khajjūrakavaḍḍhamāna tank he kept a lookout 39
whether a force were in pursuit of him. As the Prince 40
saw no troop pursuing him, he set out to betake himself to
(the place) called Kāṇapaddāuda. A dreadful, savage she-bear, 41
with great sharp claws[3], sprang at him in the vast wilder-

[1] Lit.: "with reference to the going to his own house". Thus Gajabāhu takes *yuvarājaraṭṭha* as a joking expression of Parakkamabāhu's for his house, as he is of course playing the part of *yuvarāja*. The King does not for a moment think that Dakkhiṇadesa is meant. Even the words *vidhāya pitudassanaṃ* he refers to himself not to Kittisirimegha.

[2] These are words of favourable augury, *vacanaṃ maṅgalasaṃhitaṃ*, which the Prince at once applies to his high-soaring plans.

[3] The jungle bear (*melursus labiatus*) native to Ceylon, is distinguished by its enormous claws.

42 ness with her cubs, with a fearful howl. Forcing her down
with the edge of his shield, he split her with his sword in
two halves, but with the back of his foot he quickly cast off
43 the cubs. He then called together his comrades who had
fled in fear into the forest. While hereupon still free from
44 fear, he passed over rocky country[1], he brought down a boar
terrible beyond all measure, who had attacked him as if it
were a whole herd[2], and who gave vent to a terrible grunt.
45 Then when marching further at the village of Demeliyagama[3]
at daybreak, he beheld the peasants who were named after
46 it[4], setting forth sword in hand on some kind of enterprise,
he thinking they came at the head of the (pursuing) army[5],
47 smote vehemently with his sword on his shield and with a
48 savage cry: "I will slay the villains" sprang into the midst
of them like a lion among gazelles. They fled frightened into
49 the big forest, throwing away their weapons. Thereupon the
Prince looked thither on every side and when he saw a man
50 who had fallen into a chasm, he drew him out of the abyss
and asked him who they were. When he had heard out of
his mouth the state of affairs in accordance with the truth,
51 he spake full of pity: "Leave off fearing everyone and take
up your weapons", and declared to them openly his own
52 purpose. Near Maṅgalabegāma he saw for the first time sol-

[1] P. *silākhaṇḍaṃ*. W. takes the word for a proper name.

[2] The Col. Ed. changes the MSS. reading *yathā yūthābhiyantaṃ* unnecessarily into *tathā y°* W. accordingly translates "leading a herd".

[3] The form of the name is quite uncertain. The MSS. waver. The Col. Ed. has *Demeliyanaga* but it is just the *m* which is present in all the MSS.

[4] The passage is very difficult. W. takes *vopanāmike* as a place name, but the locality is already given in *Demeliyagamavhaye gāme*. I think that *vopanāmike* belongs to the immediately preceding *gāmike* and that the word corresponds to a Skr. **aupanāmika* (**upanāman* "surname, nickname"). *Gāmike vopanāmike* thus means the same as *Demeliyagamagāmike*.

[5] We must connect *puretaraṃ* with *yānā* (abl.); *yāna* has the meaning of the Latin *agmen*. Lit.: here they come in advance of the army (oratio recta).

diers of his retinue[1] who had come according to the agreement, and accompanied by them, he betook himself to the 53
locality called Janapada and joined his retinue who had arrived there beforehand[2]. The Prince tarried there with his 54
people two or three days, giving himself up to the pleasures of the chase and various other entertainments.

When King Kittisirimegha now learned from a letter sent 55
him by his watchmen, that his son had betaken himself thither, he rejoiced in the thought that after the Prince had 56
sojourned so long with the enemy, he had now without taking any harm, happily escaped out of the power of the foe. With the command: "Ye must, my friends, without delay bring 57
hither to me the son who chases away my grief, and before a hindrance arises, show him to me", he sent to him people 58
from the five groups of menials, who were known to be courageous[3], together with an autograph letter and gifts.

[1] P. *bhaṭe sahavaḍḍhite*. Cf. with this *sahavaḍḍhitānaṃ amaccānaṃ* 68. 5, *sahavaḍḍhitayodhehi* 70. 189, as well as *saddhiṃvaḍḍhitaposesu* 70. 277. The meaning of *sahavaḍḍhita* is apparently the same as that of *sahāgata* "come along with", and then "belonging to the immediate retinue". Is there perhaps a connection between *vaḍḍhita* and the Sinh. *vaḍinavā*?

[2] The localities, *Khajjūravaḍḍhamāna, Kāṇapaddāuda, Demeliyagama* and *Maṅgalabegāma* all lie on a line running from Polonnaruva to east of Dambul. See note to 66. 110. The Prince had covered the distance — about 20—25 miles as the crow flies — in a night and part of the following day, reaching Demeliyagama at daybreak. His retinue expect him according to agreement (see 67. 22) at Janapada, and from here according to orders, some people have come to Maṅgalabegāma to meet him. Of this place Codrington says (I. 70): "Maṅgalaba seems to represent some such name as Magul-ebé; a Makul-ebé is said locally to be between Konduraveva and Puvakgaha Ulpota in Matale District."

[3] The Col. Ed. has *nāyaka*° and W. accordingly translates: "reputed heads of the five trades". But the MSS. have all *nāsaka*° which points rather to *nāsaṅka*° (after *jane* = *anāsaṅka*°). Kittisirimegha entrusts with the commission people whose hearts are in the right place, bearing in mind the violent death suffered by the Senāpati Saṅkha. According to W. *pessiyā* were artisans, such as carpenters, weavers, washermen, barbers and shoemakers (note to the passage). In 84. 5 in addition to

59 The Prince was glad when he saw the people and the presents
they had brought, and betook himself thence to Saraggāma[1]
60 desirous of meeting again with his father. Now when Kit-
61 tisirimegha heard that his son was there, he sent thither the
head of the Kuṭhārasabhā[2] as well as Abhaya, the chief of
the ascetics, who dwelt in the Pañcapariveṇamūla monastery
with the order to fetch him hither without loss of time.
62 When the Prince had learned the circumstances of his royal
father as narrated by them, he spake: if the stars are fa-
63 vourable, I will depart and ye must go with me, and for yet
a few days he passed the time with games at waterfalls and
other pleasant places.

64 When the Prince's companions saw the soldiers who came
from every side, to seek the officials with the chief of the
65 Sabhā at their head, they remembering the wrong they had
themselves formerly done[3] the King by their adherence to
66 the Prince, became agitated through fear. And they spake
to one another: "Many soldiers are gathering here from
divers places. Hard to see through are the intentions of these
67 officials. They are all united here, surround us on every side
and taking us in the centre, have occupied the various places".
68 And being perturbed, they told the matter also to the King's son.
69 He was wroth. "Never and nowhere do all these cowards look
at things as they really are, and therefore they see nothing
70 but danger where no danger is. At the sight of the village
guard who have come to see the head of the Sabhā they

the five, ten *pessiyavaggā* are distinguished. They are *rājakulāyattā*, belong to the royal household.

[1] See note to 66. 71.

[2] *Kuṭhārādisabhā* is, as so often, nothing but a paraphrase for *Kuṭhārasabhā* (see note to 44. 6). It is a case of some kind of council chamber (*sabhā*). The word *kuṭhāra* means "axe". Instead of °*vāsi 'bhaya*° the Col. Ed. reads °*vāsiñca*; thus the name of the priest is missing here.

[3] The following translation is also possible: "remembering the wanton deed which they themselves in common with the Prince, had committed against the King." The sentence would then contain an allusion to the murder of the Senāpati Saṅkha.

talk contemptible nonsense to me" — and he spake to them 71
words to this effect. But they melted away gradually hither and
thither. When the Prince heard of it he spake: "Although 72
they have witnessed my courage on divers occasions and their
own rescue over and over again by me from evil situations, 73
their inborn cowardice doth not forsake these cravens. What
boots it me whether they stay here or run away, and what 74
man can plot anything and what (can he plot) so long as
I live?" And he spent yet some time tarrying there.

When Queen Ratanāvalī heard that her son was there, 75
but that he was not coming with the (envoys) sent out by
his father, she thought: "It is not meet that grief should 76
be caused to the King by my son passing the time without
coming; I will myself at once bring my son to the Monarch and 77
present him, to him". Thereupon she came in haste from
Rohaṇa hither, betook herself to Saṅkhanāthatthalī, sought 78
out the Ruler, exchanged with him many friendly words and,
asked by the Monarch, she informed him of the reason for her 79
coming. Then she went thence to Saraggāma, sought out her 80
son, the Thera, the chief of the ascetics, and the head of the
Sabhā and took close counsel with them as to what was to
be done. And as (in her opinion) it was not at all seemly 81
to linger far (from the capital), she took the Prince along
with her and betook herself to Badalatthalī. Together with 82
the Senāpati Deva[1] stationed there she went to Saṅkhanā-
thatthalī and presented (the Prince) to his father, the King.
When then Kittisirimegha beheld his son, he spake in his 83
love to the highest officials thus: "To-day the arrow of 84
anxiety as to who here might look after me in my old age
and show me the last honours, is taken out of my soul. But 85
think not that it is for me only a blessing, is it not also for
you a reward brought forth by former merits? From now 86
onwards ye must all yield obedience to the Prince". With
these words the King commended to them his son. While 87

[1] Deva who is here called *senādhipati*, was apparently the successor of the murdered Saṅkha. Like the latter he lived at Badalatthalī.

the officials full of zeal, did according to his command, King Kittisirimegha departed this life.

88 The steadfast Prince who knew the writings of the Master (Buddha)[1], was not mastered by the agitation called forth by
89 the grief at his father's death. He comforted the inhabitants of the kingdom beginning with the high dignitaries, carried out the fire burial of his father in a manner worthy of him,
90 appointed here and there in the country and on the frontiers of the realm loyally devoted officials amongst his immediate
91 followers[2]. Then versed in the laws valid for the nobility, at a favourable constellation, during the festival of the bind-
92 ing on of the frontlet denoting the rank of mahādipāda he held a solemn procession — he the ornament of Laṅkā, adorned with all ornaments, around the town adorned with every or-
93 nament in every way — he the mighty round the troop-filled (town), he the most dexterous riding on his elephant — even
94 as the King of the gods round the city of the gods[3]. By the rain of an abundant gift of money to the samaṇas and the brāhmaṇas and others he stilled then the persistence of the
95 glow of their poverty. To the King Gajabāhu and to the King Mānābharaṇa he sent hereupon his envoys to inform them of the affair[4].

[1] P. *ñātasatthāgama*. It is doubtful whether *sattha* contains the Skr. *śāstra* or *śāstṛ* (P. *satthar*). W. seems to assume the former, since he translates: "versed in all knowledge and religion". I think the latter and take *satthāgama* as a synonym of *buddhāgama*. The Buddha teaches in the sacred scriptures, absolute quiet of soul, indifference towards joy and sorrow.

[2] W. translates "officers whom he had trained". That is in itself unobjectionable. *Nijaraḍḍhita* would correspond then to skr. *nija-vardhita* = *svavardhita* (BR. s. v. *nija*, near the end). I find it difficult however, to separate *nijavaḍḍhita* from the *sahavaḍḍhita* so often used in the same context. See note to 67. 52.

[3] The whole section is full of puns. Notice in v. 91 *nakhatte* and *khatta*, in v. 92 *alaṃkāra* and *alaṃkata*, *nekehi* and *nekadhā*, in v. 93 *pabala* and *bala*, *dakkhiṇagga* and *padakkhiṇa* (which I have rendered by "solemn procession"), as well as *akari* and *kariṃ*, *surindo* and *surālayaṃ*.

[4] Thus he observes diplomatic courtesy in notifying the change of

He (Parakkamabāhu) who had won[1] the hearts of his many officers through the fulness of his excellent qualities, who had reduced all hostility to nothing[2], who had won lustrous glory, whose wealth consisted in his renown which filled the whole universe, dwelt in that town doing much good. 96

Here ends the sixty-seventh chapter, called "The Festival of the Mahādipāda", in the Mahāvaṃsa, compiled for the serene joy and emotion of the pious.

reign. But it is to be noted that he assumes the title of *mahādipāda*. This looks like modesty, but it includes as against Gajabāhu, for future time the claim to the crown in the whole of the kingdom.

[1] *nīta*, lit. "directed, led" is to be taken in the sense of *vasaṃ nīta* "brought under his influence, won over for himself".

[2] For *vidhunita* cf. skr. *dhū* with *vi*, in BR. 2.

CHAPTER LXVIII

THE IMPROVEMENT OF HIS OWN KINGDOM

1 With his high-soaring plans and with his exact knowledge
of the other country, though now in possession of the royal
dignity, he did not give way to empty boasting[1] (such as):
2 "the reward of my royal dignity, after the subjugation of all
my foes, consists (now already) in the gain of prosperity and
3 welfare for the laity and the Order", but he thought: "It
is true, I have by my extraordinary insight brought my king-
dom although it is small, so far that much in it has pro-
4 spered, but I will now within a short time further it so
greatly that it will surpass the greatness of other kingdoms".
5 With this reflection the Prince granted to all the dignitaries
amongst his followers[2], to each according to his merit, posts

[1] A difficult passage. The alteration of pāda c in the Col. Ed. into *tattha mantanam-āpajja* (W. "he took counsel with . . .") is unnecessary. I believe that *katthamattam anāpajja* which some of the MSS. have, while the writing of others suggests it, gives quite good sense. That would be the skr. **katthāmātram* (**katthā* "boasting" from the root *katth*). At most a quite slight alteration might be made — *katthanattaṃ*: *katthana* (skr. the same) and suff. *-tta* (skr. *-tva*) "condition of boasting". *Neyuttaka* in d I regard on account of the *e* in the first syllable, as a secondary derivative of *niyutta* (skr. *niyukta*) and as a substantive at that, formed like *rāmaṇīyaka* "loveliness". Pāṇini's rule 5. 1. 132, it is true, allows this formation only with adjectives in *-ya*. Strophe 2 gives then the content of the boasting from which Parakkamabāhu refrains, being conscious of the great tasks which still await him. He is not satisfied by what he has achieved till now and by a quiet and pious life in his present realm, but he aspires after the sovereignty over whole Ceylon.

[2] See above notes to 67. 52 and 90. W. translates here and also in

and inclined them to himself by gifts of money. From the 6
Samantakūṭa[1] mountain to the port at the sea he divided his
army along the frontier of the kingdom into various camps,
and reflecting that in the first place, in every possible way 7
grain must be stored in mass, he spake thus to his hench-
men: "In the realm that is subject to me there are, apart 8
from many strips of country where the harvest flourishes
mainly by rain water, but few fields which are dependent on 9
rivers with permanent flow or on great reservoirs. Also by 10
many mountains, by thick jungle, and by widespread swamps
my kingdom is much straitened. Truly in such a country 11
not even a little water that comes from the rain must flow
into the ocean without being made useful to man. Except at 12
the mines where there are precious stones, gold and the like,
in all other places the laying out of fields must be taken in
hand. For a life of enjoyment of what one possesses, without 13
having cared for the welfare of the people, in no wise befits
one like myself. And when it is the case of a difficult task, 14
ye also all with untiring energy must not regard it as hard;
without neglecting the command given by me, ye must fully 15
carry out the work as ordered". The highly renowned gave 16
the order to rebuild on the river Jajjarā[2] the great causeway
known as Koṭṭhabaddha which had since long been in ruins,
so that the name alone remained, and which had caused the 17
kings of former times the greatest difficulties. The officials 18
all described in every way the difficulties of the work and its
lack of permanence even if it were carried out. The King 19
Parakkamabāhu[3] repudiated the word: "What is there in the
world that cannot be carried out by people of energy? That 20

70. 189 and 277 "officers that had been brought up with him", but in 67. 52 "his fellow soldiers".

[1] See note to 60. 64.

[2] Now the Deduru-oya. The river rises southwest of Kurunegala, flows at first in a northwesterly and northerly direction, turns west below its junction with the Kimbulvana-oya, flows at no great distance past Nikaveratiya and falls into the sea to the north of Chilav.

[3] Note that from now onwards Parakkamabāhu has the title of King.

even Rāma had a great causeway built by the monkey hosts
over the ocean — this tale lives among the people to this day.
21 If my extraordinary power should be the cause of the fur-
thering of the laity and the Order by the union of Laṅkā
22 under one umbrella, then even at the beginning of the enter-
prise one sees (in anticipation) its fulfilment". By such words
23 the energetic one fired their energy. From the causeway as
starting-point to the district called Rattakara[1] the discerning
24 ruler before building the causeway, laid down a large canal,
in depth many times the length of a man, very broad and
25 exceedingly solid. As in this district there was a lack of
stone masons[2], the far-famed (King) called together in great
26 number coppersmiths, blacksmiths and goldsmiths and made
over to them the business of masonry and made them lay
down a dam in which the joints of the stones were scarcely
27 to be seen, very firm, quite massive, like to a solid rock[3]

[1] W. is thinking of the Ratkerauva (?) in the Atakalan Korale of Sabaragamuva; that is of course geographically quite impossible. Codrington (I. 70) refers us to Ratkaravva, about $4^1/_2$ miles N. W. of Kurunegala in the Kuda Galboda Korale. If this is right, then the small river that flows immediately past Kurunegala and joins the Deduru-oya further north, would be included in the irrigation system. The great reservoir must then be sought not far from the spot where the road from Kurunegala to Dambul crosses the Deduru-oya. But I believe that the form of the name is Rattakara, and *-avhaya* the word *-avha* occuring so frequently at the end of names with the meaning "called so and so". The large map of Ceylon too has not the form Ratkaravva but Ratkara-veva.

[2] I believe that my emendation of the MSS. *silākoṭṭakānammahāpālohakārake* into °*kānam abhāvā loha*° is simpler than that of the Col. Ed. °*kānaṃ nivahaṃ loha*°; *bha* is very easily confused with *ha* and *va* with *pa*. The familiar *mahā* led to a doubling of the *m*. The sense is now even more pregnant. If a number (*nivaha*) of stone masons had been available, one would not have needed the various smiths for the building of the reservoir and the canal. For they are only employed for *silākoṭṭanakamma*.

[3] P. *piṭṭhipāsāṇa*, according to PTS. P. D. s. v. "a flat stone or rock, plateau, ridge". The idea is: the whole causeway looks like a single immense slab of stone, like a monolith.

and provided with a complete coating of stucco. As a be- 28
liever he placed on the height of the causeway a bodhi tree,
an image house and a relic shrine[1]. And expert as he was, 29
he so arranged matters that the whole quantity of water was
borne through the canal to the sea. On both sides of the 30
canal he had the great wildernesses cleared and many thou-
sands of day's work[2] fields laid out, and because the land 31
was thickly studded with granaries full of untrussed rice[3] he
caused it to be called by the fitting name of Koṭṭhabaddha.

Hereupon at the place of union of the two rivers Saṅkha- 32
vaḍḍhamānaka and Kumbhīlavāna[4] the Sovereign had the place 33
Sūkaranijjhara dammed up in the aforesaid way and likewise
a canal laid down. He had the water from there carried to 34
the Mahāgallaka tank[5] and after he had dammed up every-
thing there that was decayed and ruined, having first cleared 35
out the drainage canals, he built a weir[6] of larger propor-
tions than before. From this place as far as Sūkaranijjhara 36
he had fields made and collected in this way stocks of grain.
In the middle of the Jajjarā river at the place Dorādattika 37
he built a dam and a large canal and also from there as far 38
as Sūkaranijjhara he had fields made and brought together a

[1] P. *dhātugabbhaṃ*. Here, as already in 60. 56 and below in 79. 14, the word appears with the meaning of the Sinhalese *dāgäba* or *dāgoba*, not as originally for the relic chamber built into the stūpa, but for the stūpa itself (*dhātugabbha* = *thūpa*).

[2] P. *vāha*, a land measure, as much ground as one can cultivate with a "load" of seed corn.

[3] The reading *abaddhavīhi* of the MSS. which has been arbitrarily altered in the Col. Ed. into *akhaṇḍavīhi*, is necessary, in order to explain the second part of the name *Koṭṭhabaddha*.

[4] These are the rivers Hakvaṭunu-oya and Kimbulvana-oya (Codrington I. 70). The former joins the latter from the right about 4 miles above its junction with the Deduru-oya. Cf. above note to v. 16.

[5] As the Mahāgallakavāpi is in all probability the Magalle-veva reservoir in the Magul Otota Korale near Nikaveratiya, the canal must have followed the right bank of the Deduru-oya for a length of about 16 miles. Cf. note to 44. 3.

[6] P. *vāripāta*, lit. "waterfall". Cf. 48. 148 and 79. 66, 67 with the notes.

39 large quantity of corn[1]. The Paṇḍavāpi[2] tank which was former-
ly quite small he provided with a solid dam whose height,
length and breadth were enlarged (as compared with former
40 dimensions), and (also) with an immense, high[3] weir and with
overflow canals and gave it the name Parakkamasamudda.
41 On the island in the middle of the tank he built on the
summit of a rock a cetiya that showed forth the beauty of
42 the Kelāsa mountain[4]. In its centre he built a royal pleasure
house three storeys high and very beautiful, which was a
43 habitation for a fulness of worldly joys. The reservois Mahā-
galla, Seṭṭhivāpi and Chattunnata, Tabbāvāpi, as well as
44 Ambavāsāvāpi, Giribāvāpi, Pāṭala, Maṇḍika, Moravāpi, Sādiya-
45 ggāmavāpi and also Tilagullaka; Mālavalli and Kāli as well as
Kittakaṇḍaka, Kaṇṇikāragallavāpi and Buddhagāmakanijjhara;
46 Sūkaraggāmavāpi and Mahākirāḷavāpi, Giriyāvāpi, Rakkhamāna,
47 Ambāla and Kaṭunnaru; Jallibāva, Uttarāla and Tintiṇigāma,
48 Dhavalaviṭṭhikagāma, Kirāvāpi, Naḷannaru; Karaviṭṭhavilatta,
as well as Udumbaragāma, Munaru and Kasālla and Kalala-
49 hallika; Mūlavārikavāpi and Girisigāmuka, Polonnarutala and
50 also Visirātthala[5] — these many tanks and sixteen others in

[1] The statement *majjhe Jajjaranajjāya* is too vague, to allow of fixing the position of Dorādattika with certainty. I think, however, that it must be looked for above the mouth of the Kumbhīlayāna-nadī. If it were below, the canal described in vv. 32 ff. would stand in the way of a diversion from the right bank. With a diversion from the left bank however the junction with Sūkaranijjhara would cross the Deduru-oya itself.

[2] See note to 60. 50.

[3] P. *abbhunnata*. It is difficult to say what the special meaning of the word is here.

[4] By the brilliant white of the coating which reminds one of the summit of the Kailāsa wrapped in eternal snow. This is a mountain group of over 20000 ft. in height, belonging to the trans-Himalayan system. The Tibetans call the mountain Kang-rinpotsche and, like the Hindus, they hold it sacred. Cf. Sven Hedin, Transhimalaya II. 91 ff., 164 ff., III. 170 ff.

[5] Mr. Codrington had the kindness to send me by letter (19. 10. 1926) a series of identifications established by him for vv. 43-49: 1. Mahāgalla = Magalleveva (see notes to 44. 3 and 68. 34); 2. Vāsāvāpi =

which the weirs were destroyed[1] he whose heart was chained
to pity[2], had restored in his realm. In the Pañcayojana 51
District where there were great swamp ponds, he took the
water from there and conducted it to rivers, laid out fields 52
and collected a large quantity of grain. In the wildernesses
there and at very many other places he determined every- 53
where what was to remain as wilderness[3], and assembling all
the village chiefs, he entrusted the inhabitants with the
cultivation (of the remaining country). The discerning (Prince) 54
thereby brought it about that the new fields yielded a tax
which was greater than the old taxes produced in the king-
dom, and at the same time brought it to pass that the in- 55
habitants of the country never more knew fear of famine.
Versed in administration he thought: in my kingdom wherever 56
it may be, there shall not be even a small courtyard without
its roofing of leafage, and had therefore here and there charm- 57

Vasiyava in the Magul Otota Korale (near Nikaveratiya); 3. Giribāvāpi = Giribava in Mi-oyen Egoda Korale (on the left bank of the Kala-oya); 4. Maṇḍika = Mediyava in the Pahala Visideke Korale (north of Maho); 5. Tilagullaka = Talagalle Ela (see note to 58. 43), in the Katuvana Korale (east of Magul Otota K.); 6. Kāli? = Kaliyavaḍana, a large irrigation work in Pitigal Korale (at Chilav); 7. Buddhagāmakanijjhara? = Butgomu-oya, Yatikaha Korale (20 miles west of Kurunegala); 8. Sūkaraggāmavāpi? = Urapotta, Kiniyama Korale (left bank of the lower Deduru-oya); 9. Mahākirālavāpi = Mahagirilla, Magul Medagandahaye Korale East (north of the Magul Otota K.); 10. Giriyāvāpi = Galgiriyāva, Nikavagampahe Korale (north-east of Maho); 11. Ambāla = Ambale, Magul Medagandahaye Korale East (see under 9); 12. Tintiṇigāmaka = Siyambalangomuva, Hatalispaha Korale (between Nikavagampahe K. and Mi-oyen Egoda K., a large now abandoned tank north-east of Galgamuva); 13. Kirāvāpi = Kiraveva, Yagam Pattu Korale (10 miles E. of Chilav); 14. Karaviṭṭhavilatta = Karavita and Vilattava, Pitigal Korale North (at Chilav), and Yagam Pattu Korale (see under 13). — For *Moravāpi* see notes to 69. 9, 70. 67.

[1] I think we must read *naṭṭhanijjharavāpiyo* instead of *naṭṭhā nijjh°*.

[2] Pun on *dayābaddhamano* and *bandhāpesi*.

[3] Lit.: "determining the wilderness places"; *vavatthā* is a gerund and stands for *-tthāya* with a causative meaning. Thus he separated the cultivable land from that which was incapable of cultivation.

58 ing parks laid out, filled full with numerous species of creepers and trees which bore fruits and which bore blossoms, and which offered many delights[1] and which were beautified by all kinds of garden beds[2].

59 Aware of the right method, the Prince so acted that in consequence of his extraordinary insight his own kingdom though small, (now) brought to such prosperity, surpassed another, even a great kingdom.

Here ends the sixty-eighth chapter, called "The Improvement of his own Kingdom", in the Mahāvaṃsa, compiled for the serene joy and emotion of the pious.

[1] P. *aneka-anubhava-ādhāre* "the foundations of many delights". For the meaning of *anubhava* cf. those of the kindred verb. *anu-bhū*.

[2] P. *nānānuyyānasundare*, which I split up into *nānā anuyyāna s°*; *anuyyāna* corresponds to *uyyāna* as *anudhamma* to *dhamma* and is used of the smaller secondary garden-like beds in the *ārāmā*.

CHAPTER LXIX

THE COLLECTION OF MILITARY FORCES AND MONEY

When Parakkamabāhu had thus set his whole kingdom in 1
order in the best possible way, he pondered over what was
now to be done: "Former foolish kings to whom good direc- 2
tion of affairs of state was unknown, for long injured at
their pleasure people and Order. The ascetics made the 3
Order abandon the teaching and discipline of the Master;
they neglected religious duties and lived according to their
own pleasure. If now I soon unite Laṅkā under one umbrella, 4
I shall perchance be able to raise up again Order and people."
After these reflections he gave orders to officers and district 5
chiefs to put troops and war material in readiness. First of 6
all the Prince summoned to him the official with the title
of King of Malaya who was leader of the Damiḷa army in
the district called Rattakara[1], and after he had placed in 7
readiness many thousands of men, as well as armaments and
weapons, he sent him away to take up his abode there. From 8
the Tabbā district, from the Giribā district, from Moravāpi,
from the Mahīpāla district, and from the Pilaviṭṭhika district;
from the Buddhagāma district and from the district called 9
Ambavana, from the Bodhigāmavara district and from the 10
Kaṇṭakapeṭaka[2] district he summoned the officials of the

[1] See note to 68. 23.

[2] Of the names mentioned here the following are already known: 1) Tabbā in Tabbāvāpi 68. 43; 2) Giribā in Giribāvāpi, cf. note to 68. 49, nr. 3; 3) Moravāpi 68. 44; 4) Buddhagāma, cf. note to 58. 48; 5) Ambavana, cf. note to 66. 85; 6) Bodhigāmavara, cf. note to 66. 78. It is clear that here we have the enumeration of the frontier districts of Dakkhiṇadesa towards Rājaraṭṭha from N.W. to S.E.

frontier guard singly, placed at their disposal many thousands
11 of men, strong mails and divers weapons, such as swords,
javelins, lances and the like and sent each of them to his
12 place to dwell there. At that time Laṅkāmahālāna, Sikhānā-
13 yaka, Jayamahālāna, Seṭṭhināyaka and Mahinda by name —
these five highly respected men belonging to the Lambakaṇṇas[1]
14 dwelt in the Moriya[2] district. He made each one of them
supply a thousand warriors and ordered them to get ready
15 the (necessary) war equipment. In the interior of the country
the King set up twelve district chiefs and allotted to each
16 of them two thousand men. Further he appointed eighty four
officers, men tested by victory, and entrusted to each of them
17 a force of a thousand men. He also raised several thousand
soldiers armed with clubs, tall men and strong, and the (need-
18 ful) war appliances. Of the foreign soldiers, such as the
Keraḷas and others, who were in his service, he raised several
19 thousand. Of one thousand he made moonlight archers, versed
in night-fighting, and gave them leathern doublets and the like.
20 Many thousand Vyādhas[3] too he brought together, (men) who
understood their task and gave them what was fitting for
21 them: spears, drums[4] and the like. Of the many work people

The Tabbā district accordingly lies in the extreme northwest on the left bank of the lower Kala-oya probably in Rajavanni-Pattuva. I find a Mahatabbova marked on the 12-sheet-map. Moravāpi, Mahīpāla and Pilaviṭṭhika must be looked for in this order between Giriba and Menikdena. It is clear from 72. 163, 170 that Pilaviṭṭhi or Pillaviṭṭhi (the two are certainly identical) lay not far from Kālavāpi. Possibly Kaṇṭakapeṭaka lay east or northeast of Matale.

[1] Cf. note to 39. 44.

[2] Moriya is otherwise (38. 13, 41. 69) a clan name.

[3] That *vyādha* here is a rendering of the Sinh. *vädda* seems to me certain, though this does not prove that the etymological derivation of the latter from the former is correct.

[4] W. separates *sattikāḷambara* into *satti-kāḷa-ambara* and translates "swords, black clothes". That is certainly wrong. We must separate into *sattikā-āḷambara*. *Sattikā* is the deminutive of *satti* "spear" = skr. *śakti*. One might also derive it from *satti* "knife" = skr. *śastrī*, but I consider that less likely. *Āḷambara* is the skr. *āḍambara* "drum".

the King then ordered each thousand to perform the work
appropriate to them[1]. With the wish that people skilled in 22
the art of riding elephants or horses and of handling the
sword, in the use of foreign tongues, in dance and song, in
court service should increase in number, the Sovereign brought 23
up many of the sons, brothers and grandchildren of distin-
guished families in his own palace. Of the many groups such 24
as the Churikaggāhaka, the Kappūravaḍḍhaka, the Khuddase-
vaka, the Sīhalagandhabba, the Santikāvacara and so on[2] he 25
supported several thousand of each of them at the royal
court. To the young people among the chamberlains, bar- 26
bers and the like he gave weapons and commanded them
always to acknowledge the eldest among them as their leaders.
Having established through the people who had been the 27
treasurers of his father the King, the state of the finances,
he came to the decision, that with such means it would be 28
impossible to establish a universal dominion in Laṅkā, and
collected without oppressing the people (further) money in
the following way: The monarch separated finance admini- 29
stration and the army from each other and made them over
to two officials who were the chief officials[3]. The whole 30
realm ruled by him the King divided equally (into two halves)
and appointed a couple of auditors who came in regular ad-

[1] Parakkama thus supplies the demand for workers for the army by recruiting from the castes.

[2] It is not possible to determine what various groups (*vaggabhedā*), castes or guilds are meant. Taken in order the names singly denote: 1) knife bearers, dagger bearers, 2) camphor producers (cf. *cīvaravaḍḍhaka* "makers of clothing"), 3) little servants, 4) Sīhalā musicians, 5) comrades of the immediate entourage.

[3] Parakkama must thus have created two chief ministries, a ministry of War and one for the internal administration, each with a highest official at the head. For simplification the latter was locally divided into two parts (v. 30) to which a third was added which embraced in particular the administration of the mines (? *sāraṭṭhāna*, v. 32). It is clear that the compiler is here describing the system of administration set up in certain works of the Nīti literature. It is of course possible that Parakkama himself adopted this system.

31 vancement[1] (to the office). From the district on the sea coast[2],
from the district Ratanākara[3], from the great Malaya country
32 and from other districts the Ruler separated all land of
extraordinary value and placed it under an official for whom
33 he created the so-called "Office of the Interior"[4]. By ship he
sent off many precious stones, traded with these and so increased
34 the money resources. In charge of the two chief officials he
caused to supply war material and troops of many thousand
35 men, and in that of the three (other) officials also, him of
the office of the Interior and the two heads of provinces, he
36 raised very many troops. To test the military fitness of the
soldiers[5] he arranged fights on the street, sifted out the most
37 skilled and granted them high distinction. Those unfitted for
fight he dismissed out of pity: they were to till the fields
and perform other work and live in peace.

38 Thus versed in right method, he placed in readiness mails and weapons and skilled troops and without oppressing the people, he collected with ease large resources in money.

Here ends the sixty-ninth chapter, called "The Collection of military Forces and Money", in the Mahāvaṃsa, compiled for the serene joy and emotion of the pious.

[1] P. *kamāgate*. I believe that what is meant is that these officials, in order to have the necessary expert knowledge, had to work their way up through the various grades of service.

[2] Here it is probably a case of the strips of coast where pearl fishing was carried on.

[3] I have no doubt that the district meant is that in which the present Ratnapura lies (cf. W., note to the passage), and which was ever and again the "mine of precious stones" (*ratanākara*).

[4] P. *antaraṅgadhura*. See skr. *antaraṅga*.

[5] By *bhaṭa* are meant all people of an age to bear arms.

CHAPTER LXX

THE SURRENDER OF THE ROYAL DIGNITY

Hereupon, after Parakkamabāhu had surveyed his great 1
army and the abundant stocks in money and corn and his
whole war material, he thought: quite apart from the island 2
of Sīhala it would not be difficult to conquer even Jambudīpa,
and he set about getting the royal dominion into his power.
Into the great Malaya country[1] which was difficult to pene- 3
trate owing to the inaccessibility of the many mountains and
on account of the danger from wild animals, shut off from
intercourse with other men, passable only on footpaths, offer- 4
ing all kinds of perils and dangerous by reason of deep
waters with man-eating crocodiles, in Yaṭṭhikaṇḍa and Dum- 5
bara[2], he summoned Rakkha the daṇḍādhināyaka[3] of King 6
Gajabāhu, and graciously showed him great distinction. He then
gave him the order to take possession of the Malaya country
and make it over to him. When the inhabitants heard of the 7
affair, they agreed that they would kill the general when he
came to them. At these tidings the general came hither in 8
haste, fought, scattered the enemy in flight and occupied the
district of Dumbara. Thereupon he continued the fight in 9

[1] Parakkamabāhu goes to work with great deliberation. Before undertaking the attack on Rājaraṭṭha, he secures his right flank by occupying the mountain country of Malaya. This is called, as in 69. 31, *Mahāmalayadesa*.

[2] Probably the province of Dumbara (Pata D. and Uda D.) which stretches N. E. of Kandy, though possibly its scope was more restricted in ancient times than now. See below note to v. 14.

[3] The title occurs in different forms; also *daṇḍanātha* (so v. 7, 8), *daṇḍanāyaka* (70. 279 etc.). It seems to be of a military character; *daṇḍa* is probably to be understood as "army".

Yaṭṭhikaṇḍa and seized the head of the chief there, after he
10 had beaten the foe. At the village of Tālakkhetta he twice
offered battle and he likewise fought two combats at Nāga-
11 pabbata[1]. Also at the village Suvaṇṇadoṇi[2] by name, at
Rāmucchuvallika and at Demaṭṭhapādatthalī he delivered at
12 each in turn an action, and after all the enemy inhabiting
the different places were subjugated he took possession of the
13 Yaṭṭhikaṇḍa district with strong forces. After leaving there his
younger brother behind with the army, he betook himself to
14 the King to consider what was to be done. The soldiers at
the head of whom was his brother, now marched forth and
after a fight with the enemy, seized the district called Nī-
15 lagallaka[3]. The general returned and after he had successi-
vely delivered battle at Sayakhettaka, at Rattabeduma and at
16 Dhanuvillika[4] and had slain the foe, he made the conquered
17 district Nīlagallaka into a safe possession. Hereupon he twice
offered action against the powerful Otturāmallaka the chief
18 of Dhanumaṇḍala, and after conquering the Nisseṇikkhettaka
district and clearing it of the briers (of the foe), he brought
19 Otturāmallaka and his people into his power. Thereupon the
King summoned the general Rakkha to him and conferred
on him the dignity of a Kesadhātu[5] and great distinction.

[1] The place mentioned here has nothing to do with the Nakapawata vihāra mentioned in the Tammanakanda inscription (E. Müller AIC., No. 55).

[2] Corresponds probably to a modern Randeniya. The Census of 1921 mentions five localities of this name; but the position of none of them fits our Suvaṇṇadoṇi.

[3] A Nilgala lies in Udasiya Pattu North in Dumbara (thus Codrington), that is in the mountains north of Teldeniya. If the indentification is right, then the engagements described in vv. 8 ff. must have taken place in a comparatively restricted area in the region N. E. of Kandy. The names in vv. 8 and 9 do not occur again. Rāmucchuvallika (v. 11) might be meant for Rambukvela in Gampaha Korale West, 7 miles east of Teldeniya (cf. W. note to passage).

[4] A Dunuvila lies about five miles S. E. of Teldeniya, only just over two miles south of the spot where the last king of Ceylon was captured. Thus also Codrington.

[5] Cf. the note to 57. 65. The Order of the Kesadhātu was not founded for the first time now, as one might assume from the note in W's translation. It existed already at the time of Vijayabāhu I.

The King sent him forth to take the district of Majjhima- 20
vagga[1]. He betook himself to Nīlagiri[2] and after he had
armed his troops there, the mighty one fought in the pro- 21
vince Vāpivāṭaka by name and in Majjhimavagga and won
the victory. When the Lord of men Gajabāhu heard of these 22
events, he sent out a great army to fight him. At news of 23
this the Kesadhātu, who had with him a correspondingly
strong army and train, scattered the enemy forces and oc-
cupied Majjhimavagga. Lokajitvāṇa by name and the Laṅ- 24
kādhināyaka Rakkha[3], the lion-hearted ones, armed a division,
marched forth and fought the Laṅkānātha Hukitti; they de- 25
feated him and brought the district called Rerupallika into
their power. In Kosavagga the King brought Samantamalla 26
by name by amicable means under his influence and showed
him great honour; he then sent him war material and a big 27
army and charged him to seize Kosavagga. Samantamallaka 28
by name, Otturāmallaka and his people fought with the
hostile army and slew many in the battle. After they had 29
fought a great battle at the place called Sīsacchinnakabodhi,
the mighty ones got hold of the Kosavagga district[4].

When he had thus made peaceful the province of Malaya 30
where owing to its inhabitants there had been no peace, he
dwelt at ease in his town and passed the time with games 31

[1] Contrary to all the MSS. the Col. Ed. reads *rājaraṭṭhaṃ* instead of *rājā raṭṭhaṃ.* Accordingly W. translates "sent him to the king's country to take the district of Majjhima-vaggaka". That is wrong. The scene is not yet Rājaraṭṭha but Malaya. Majjhimavagga is identified by Codrington with Medivaka in Gampaha Korale, Dumbara.

[2] Nīlagiri is probably identical with the Nīlagallaka mentioned above. It is now the base for further operations.

[3] *Laṅkādhināyaka* (variants *laṅkānātha*, ex. 70. 25, or *laṅkādhinātha*, ex. 70. 232) is again a title which occurs frequently in just this pariccheda. The Laṅkādhināyaka Rakkha is of course different from the Daṇḍādhināyaka ("general") Rakkha, now Kesadhātu Rakkha. The two are mentioned together 70. 282, 283. Cf. also note to 70. 278.

[4] We must very likely assume that the military engagements described from v. 20 onwards, took place north of the Dumbara district, so that Parakkama's troops worked their way gradually to the frontier of Rājaraṭṭha.

in the garden and in the water, with dance and song and
32 the like, fulfilling the duties of a king, and for the sake of
the exertions[1] for the subjugation of hostile kings and for
defeat of rebels, the Ruler was wont to follow the chase.
33 Now one day the King together with the chief Mahesī, with
34 ministers and retainers went hunting. When then the Sovereign beheld a big forest that had signs of being inhabited
by game, he made the Mahesī take her stand on the one
35 side and then had the whole forest surrounded by hunters
with spears in their hands and nets and caused them to make
36 a noise here and there. Now when an elk bull[2] large as an
elephant calf, heard the frightful noise, he broke out of the
37 forest thicket. Glancing in all sides, he roused by fear came
running thence, plunging down the mountain slopes, leaping
38 mountain gorges, cracking the tree branches, dragging creepers after it like a net, trampling down the brushwood in
39 the forest, tearing asunder the outspread net, killing everyone
he met or putting them to flight — thus he dashed straight
at the Mahesī with the fury and the swiftness of the storm.
40 Everybody who beheld him rushing onwards fled on all sides,
overcome by fright, and left the Mahesī and the King in the
41 lurch. When the King beheld the fearful stag approaching he
ran towards him with terrible courage and hit him with hurled
42 spear. Wounded by him, the stag lowered its head[3] to slay
the King, but shedding both its antlers, flung itself at his
43 feet. The ministers, the hunters, the chamberlains, the barbers and the others hearing the cry that the animal gave
44 forth after receiving its severe wound[4], turning back, came

[1] In order to be capable of those exertions. I do not think that *vāyāmattham* is in a parallel position to the two *nisedhattham* as W. assumes, but that these latter are dependent on the former.

[2] P. *gokaṇṇamigo*, Sinh. *gōnā*, Rusa Aristotelis, the Sambar, living in India and Ceylon.

[3] Lit.: When by him (the stag), that had received the (spear) wound the head was lowered to kill him (the King), he fell . . ."

[4] The MSS. have *laddhā pahāraṃ karaṇaṃ*. I have changed only the last word into *karuṇaṃ* "plaintive, pitiful". The gerund is subject to the part. *ravato*. The Col. Ed. has *laddhā pahārakaraṇā*, which gives neither clear construction nor clear sense.

together from all sides. When they beheld the two antlers
and the lion-hearted Ruler they were full of astonishment 45
and overjoyed and happy, they filled the whole forest with
the clamour of their loud praises. Ever and anon praising 46
the extraordinary bravery of the King, his great good for-
tune, his heroism and his manly courage, they took the 47
antlers and surrounding the King, entered the town which
was adorned like the city of the gods, told the great digni- 48
taries of the astonishing events and showed all of them the
two antlers. When the high officials heard of the miracle, they 49
came together and spake with one another with astonishment
about the extraordinary occurrence: "Were this man with his 50
majesty born in Jambudīpa, he would become without doubt
a world-ruling king". With these and words of like praise 51
they lauded his inflexible courage hard to surpass, and placed 52
the two antlers, having had an inscription put on them, in
the treasure house where they are to this day.

When hereupon the Lord of men (Parakkamabāhu) heard 53
that the Ruler Gajabāhu had fetched nobles of heretical faith
from abroad and had thus filled Rājaraṭṭha with the briers 54
(of heresy), wrath seized his soul and he thought: though people
of my kind are there, possessing insight, virtue, miraculous power 55
and extraordinary courage, he has nevertheless acted thus — and
he commanded his generals to take possession also of Rājaraṭṭha[1].
With careful consideration of the works profitable for the 56
carrying on of war, such as the text book of Koṭalla[2], the
Yuddhaṇṇava[3] and others he, versed in the procedure of war, 57
worked out with ingenuity in a way according with the
locality and the time, the plan of campaign[4], wrote it down,
had it handed out to the officers and gave the order: "Doubt 58
not that ye do a thing of great moment, if ye do but swerve

[1] In the same way as they had already conquered Malaya.

[2] For Koṭalla = skr. Kauṭalya see note to 64. 3.

[3] I do not know a work with this title. Chapters 123—125 of the Agnipurāṇa are however called *Yuddhajayārṇava*. Aufrecht, Catalogus Catalogorum, p. 219.

[4] P. *yuddhopāyaṃ*. For *upāya* cf. note to 58. 3.

59 by a hair's breadth from this my instruction". They all received the words of the King with bowed head and went forth with large forces to open the campaign.

60 The Lord of men Gajabāhu had as chief of the umbrella bearers Komba, equipped with an army and experienced in
61 war. The latter had built a very strong fortress at the village of Mallavāḷāna[1] for defence against the foe and had long
62 had his dwelling there. The Malayarāyara who held the stronghold Vālikākhetta[2], fought with him, put him to flight
63 and took his fortress. Then the hero marched thence at the head of a strong force and came by ship on the water to
64 Muttākara[3]. The mighty one fought a great battle in the middle of the sea against the general there, in which the
65 enemy troops were scattered. He then fought even a second bitter action at the selfsame spot and sent many thousands
66 (of the foe) to (the god of death) Yama. The forces also of the Chief of the Kesadhātus, called Tamba, and other troops
67 destroyed the foe at (the place) Mālavalliya by name, and the officer in Moravāpi, Nīlagallaka by name, came to Kaṭiyāgāma and slew great numbers of the enemy[4].

68 In the village of Kālavāpi Gajabāhu had the general known
69 by the name of Nagaragiri Gokaṇṇa[5] stationed. He was

[1] The operations begin on the extreme left wing of Parakkamabāhu who evidently intends to cut off Rājaraṭṭha from the sea. Mallavālāna should therefore be looked for not far from the coast, somewhere about the mouth of the Kala-oya.

[2] Malayarāyara is a variant of Malayarāja (cf. note to 41. 35). Vālikākhetta is identified by Codrington (I. 71) with "Vellavela in Anaivilundan Pattuva near Battulu Oya". There is no Vellavela in the list of places in the Census of 1921.

[3] "Pearl mine". What is meant are probably the pearl banks stretching from the south of Mannar to near Portugal Bay.

[4] These fights take place, since Kālavāpi is mentioned in the sequel, west of this lake, about the Mi Oyen Egoda Korale. But the Moragasveva situated here can scarcely be identified with the Moravāpi named in v. 67. Moravāpi is also mentioned in 69. 8 and 70. 67, 72. 177 (see the note).

[5] For Gokaṇṇa see above note to 66. 35.

gifted with high heroic virtues, in possession of a fitting army and train, skilled in war, a loyal and devoted adviser
of his Lord. The general Rakkhadīvāna of the Lord of men 70
Parakkama vanquished him in battle at the place Goṇagāmuka.
The officer Gokaṇṇa grown lax through his defeat, after equipping 71
an army again suffered defeats at the fortress of Pilaviṭṭhika
and at the fortress called Kasāllaka, at Taṭavāpika, at Jambukola, 72
at Vajiravāpi, at Nandivāpi, at Pallikāvāpi and at Kalalahallika, 73
after he had on each occasion offered battle[1]. Then he thought:
"My army that was formerly victorious even in battle with 74
the King[2], has now when it is double as strong, fighting
with two or three officers of Parakkamabāhu at the border 75
of the kingdom, each time suffered defeat, and the leaders
of the troops have fallen: now it is no longer capable of 76
fighting", and he sent a report of all that had happened to
Gajabāhu. When the Ruler Gajabāhu heard all this, he took 77
counsel with his ministers and spake as follows: "Never for- 78
merly have we heard that we were defeated; now we have
suffered a defeat and that was a great injury for us. Even 79
he who among my dignitaries was of special power and
courage, has been vanquished several times in battle. Were 80
another misfortune to overtake him that would not be good
for me". Having thus taken counsel with his ministers, he
made ready abundant money, troops and troop leaders, as 81
also divers weapons and impenetrable armour and sent these
off to Gokanna. The general Gokaṇṇa now made the army 82
sent by the king, his own former army as well as the army
of the inhabitants of the country[3] in all haste ready for 83

[1] The localities named in 70 to 73 must all be situated southwest or south of the Kalaveva, Goṇagāmuka probably farthest away (? Gonagama in the Gantihe Korale south of Galgamuva). For Pilaviṭṭhika see note to 69. 10). Jambukola is probably Dambul, though CODRINGTON inclines to identify it with Dambagolla in Gangala Palesiya Pattuva, west of Elahera. The names Kasālla and Kalalahallika are met with also in 68. 48 amongst the tanks restored by Parakkamabāhu in Dakkhiṇadesa.

[2] Cf. the defeat of Kittisirimegha by Gokaṇṇa in 63. 34.

[3] The militia in contrast to the regular, standing army.

battle, advanced again to Nīlagala[1] and fought a great battle
84 with the general Māyāgeha. In this action many of his
people fell or flung away their weapons and fled into the
85 wilderness. It went so far that one was forced to say that
nobody had escaped[2]. He himself also left chariot and um-
86 brella in the lurch and fled into the forest. From now he
gave up the idea of fighting and stayed in Kālavāpi after
building a strong fortification there.

87 Thereupon the officers stationed in the Sūraambavana[3]
district pressed forward to Janapada and cut down the ho-
88 stile army. The troop leaders who had been sent to the pro-
vince of Bodhigāmavara entered Laṅkāgiri[4] and destroyed
the foe there.

89 The troop leaders at the head of whom stood the Na-
garagiri Mahinda, were sent again by Parakkama to the
90 district of Mallavāḷāna to fight[5]. He marched thither, drove
back the mighty enemy, penetrated the province, conquered

[1] This is very probably the Nīlagallakā mentioned earlier (70. 14 with note) or Nīlagiri (70. 20) in Dumbara. Thus Gokaṇṇa, successful perhaps at the outset, had penetrated far to the south into the districts of Malaya which Parakkama's soldiers had already occupied (hence *puna!*), before he suffered his decisive defeat.

[2] Lit.: "there were none of such (*n'atthi*) who had gone after they had freed themselves". *Muccitvāna gatā* is a periphrastic formation akin to analogous Sinhalese expressions. Cf. Sinh. *palā-yanavā*, prt. *palāgiyā*.

[3] Sūraambavana is manifestly a part of Ambavana, name of the region of the Ambanganga (see above note to 66. 85). Parakkama's officers thus press forward, pursuing the beaten enemy northwards through Ambavana Korale to Vagapanaha Udasiya Pattuva (= Janapada, note to 66. 110).

[4] For Bodhigāmavara see note to 66. 78, for Laṅkāgiri now Laggala, east of Vagapanaha, note to 66. 80, Codrington, I. 71.

[5] According to 70. 60 ff. Mallavāḷāna had already been taken earlier by the Malayarāyara. There must have been a reverse in the interval in which the territory gained was again lost. As to this failure the chronicle is silent. Now after the victorious advance of the right wing the operations on the extreme left wing are begun again in the former way (see note to 70. 61).

it and brought it into safe possession. From there they all 91
started off, gave battle at sea with many hundreds of ships
and after seizing the general stationed there and (the Nor- 92
thern Province) Uttararaṭṭha[1], they sent the pearls found
there to their Lord. Thereupon the Monarch had a fortress 93
built at the place called Pilavasu and made the troops take
up their abode there.

When the Lord of men Gajabāhu heard of these events, 94
he took counsel with his ministers and set about sending out
troops. When Parakkamabāhu who well understood the (right) 95
method, learned thereof, he sent the Laṅkānātha (Rakkha)[2]
to the district called Janapada. At the tidings of this action 96
the Lord of men Gajabāhu gathered his army together,
divided his forces and sent in two directions an army equipp- 97
ed with armour and weapons — to the locality Janapada and
to the fortress called Pilavasu. The Laṅkādhinātha Rakkha 98
advanced thereupon at the head of a strong force for the
destruction of the hostile army, to Ambavana[3] and after cut- 99
ting up in battle many foes at the village called Bubbula[4],
he put the army of the enemy to flight. The inhabitants of 100
the country now made the roads difficult of access by hewn

[1] The MSS. are without doubt corrupt. But I cannot accept the reading of the Col. Ed. *tatraṭṭhaṃ daṇḍanāthaṃ taṃ muttā raṭṭhaṃ balam pi ca.* It is too violent and arbitrary. I would far rather read with slight alteration, *tatraṭṭhaṃ daṇḍanāthaṃ ca* (– *thañca,* which differs slightly from the *-thaba-* of the MSS.) *raṭṭhaṃ taṃ Uttaraṃ pi ca.* Parakkama wants above all to get hold of Uttararaṭṭha, the province north of Anurādhapura, in order to cut off Rājaraṭṭha completely. Still better perhaps would be the emendation *raṭṭhaṃ Muttākaraṃ pi ca* especially in consideration of 70. 63. The translation would then run: "and after they had seized the general stationed there and the province of Muttākara".

[2] See 70. 24 with the note.

[3] As according to 70. 87 Ambavana lies further south than Janapada, it must be assumed that Parakkama's troops who had already advanced to Janapada, had at first retired southwards, till Rakkha restored the balance.

[4] Evidently Bibila in Vagapanaha Udasiya Pattuva, Matale North (Census of C. 1921, II, p. 102; H. W. Codrington L. 71).

101 down and felled trees and by thorny creepers and posted in
ambush on the road, continued the fight. The Laṅkānātha
102 determined to annihilate the foe, pursued them in every
direction, broke even through the stockades and pushed for-
ward delivering big engagements at divers places, to Janapada.
103 After taking Janapada he following instructions of Parakkama-
bāhu, built an entrenchment and took up his abode there.
104 Thereupon King Gajabāhu sent the Laṅkādhināyaka Deva and
105 Dāṭhābhāra by name to withstand him. The Laṅkādhinātha
(Rakkha) thereupon delivered a great battle, defeated them
106 and took Yagālla. The Lord of men Gajabāhu sent to the
Āḷisāra[1] district the so-called four companies[2] to renew the
107 combat. The Laṅkānātha (Rakkha) likewise marched forth,
fought with them, captured several alive and occupied Ta-
108 ḷātthala[3]. King Gajabāhu sought now by a kindly gift to
bring him under his influence and sent him abundant pre-
109 sents, such as costly ornaments of jewels and divers garments
110 of linen, silk and other stuffs as an offering. The general
accepted the gifts, mutilated the envoys and sent presents
111 and messengers to his Lord. When the King (Parakkama)
saw that, he rejoiced greatly and sent him back the whole
112 treasure and costly gifts (in addition). The general now left
the fortress of Taḷātthala and took up a position in the
113 stronghold of Āḷigāma[4] at the side of the river. Thereupon
Gajabāhu sent the general Sīka and other skilful warriors
114 with great forces to fight once more with him. They all set
forth equipped with troops and train, surrounded the fortress

[1] The name is preserved in the modern Elahera on the left bank of the Ambanganga in Gangala Pallesiya Pattuva (Census of C. 1921, II. 102).

[2] P. *catasso parisā*, evidently the name of a particular troop which perhaps had its headquarters in the Āḷisāra district or was recruited from the able-bodied inhabitants of this district.

[3] Now Talagoda (Codrington), somewhat above Elahera and also situated on the left bank of the Ambanganga.

[4] H. W. Codrington compares this with the modern Elagamuva which lies slightly above Talagoda but on the right bank of the Ambanganga. The Census of 1921 names both villages together in Gangala Pallesiya Pattuva.

(Āḷigāma) and rained down a hail of arrows. Several warriors 115
of the Laṅkādhinātha well armed, took up their position at
the gate and began a terrific fight. The archers and other 116
combatants standing on the turrets of the gate, slew numbers
of the foe with arrows, spears and javelins. In this way they 117
all carried on without interruption for three days a violent
combat with great endurance and great strength. The troops 118
of King Gajabāhu determined above everything on the de-
struction of the foe, set about blowing up the main gates of
the fortress. Thereupon the Laṅkādhinātha and his warriors 119
burst forth and cut down the enemy in combat as far as
the opposite bank of the river[1]. They made the water of 120
the river muddy with the blood of the foe and captured
many troop leaders alive. After gaining the victory in the 121
battle, the Laṅkādhinātha Rakkha celebrated a great festival
of victory in the castle, but the heads of the hostile officers, 122
the umbrellas, chariots and weapons and the captives caught
alive he sent to his Lord.

Hereupon the Sovereign (Parakkamabāhu) summoned to 123
him the Senāpati Deva, told him all that the Laṅkādhinātha
Rakkha had accomplished, and with the reflection that Ga- 124
jabāhu at the tidings of the defeat of his troops, would cer-
tainly send forth a great force to seize the general (Rakkha),
he sent the far-famed army leader to the Giribā district[2] to 125
cut off the great force of the Lord of men Gajabāhu. The 126
shrewd (Deva) set out, having put his whole army into
fighting trim and while occupying an entrenchment which
he had raised on the bank of the Kālavāpi river[3], he at the 127

[1] The Ambanganga flows at Elagamuva from S.W. to N. E. It must be assumed that Rakkha had abandoned Taḷātthalī and that the enemy are advancing by Taḷātthalī = Talagoda to their new position at Elagamuva. To do this they must cross the river and are now driven back over it. Cf. below vv. 173 ff.

[2] Cf. note to 68. 49 (nr. 3) and 69. 8. Thus the expected pressure on the right wing is to be relieved by an attack on the left flank.

[3] This is the Kala-oya, since the Kālavāpi tank is formed by the damming up of this river.

instruction of the King, threw a long, very fine, and very
solid bridge across the river of the Kālavāpi tank, passable
128 by files of elephants, horses and chariots[1], held together with
iron bands and nails, made of beams of timber and twenty
129 cubits[2] broad. After leaving certain officers there, the Se-
nāpati marched off and while delivering here and there heavy
130 engagements in which he remained victorious, he reached a
place named Aṅgamu[3], built an entrenchment for fighting
131 with the hostile army, and took up a position there. At the
tidings thereof the opposing army erected an impregnable for-
tification at Senāgāma to ward off the Senāpati and took up
132 a position there. The illustrious Senāpati now marched thither,
fought with the hostile army and captured the fortification
133 in Senāgāma. After the enemy had fought twice over and
suffered defeat, they built a fortification in Manyāgāma and
134 took up a position there. Thereupon the Senāpati marched
thither and took the fortress of Manyā; likewise a stronghold
135 in Mita and the fortress Sūkaragāma. He had new earth-
works laid down in all these fortifications and leaving none
136 of them unoccupied, he placed commanders (in them). The
Senāpati having built a stronghold at Terigāma, made of-
ficers known as capable warriors take up their position there
137 with troops. King Gajabāhu now sent his officer, the Nīlagiri

[1] The Col. Ed. has *hatthassarathapattīhi* and W. translates therefore: "by elephants, and horses and chariots, and footmen". According to my MSS. I have felt obliged to read *-pantīhi*.

[2] The MSS. have in pāda b c *dārūhi āyataṃ vīsatīhatthavitthataṃ*. Thus three syllables are missing. I have added a *kāritaṃ* to *dārūhi*, for *kāresi* seemed to me too far away to be joined with the instr. The Col. Ed. puts *āyataṃ* in pāda b and gives as length *dvisataṃ* in c. Here again one would have to supplement a *hattha* from the following compound. Twenty cubits are nearly = 30 feet.

[3] The name is preserved in that of the Ambagomuva tank which lies a little over $2^{1}/_{2}$ miles to the north of the Kala-oya. The distance of Giribā from the southern bank is the same. The river is particularly narrow at the part between the two places and therefore probably easy to cross.

Rāma[1] and numerous troop leaders[2] to destroy him. They 138
set forth all well armed with army and train and occupied
an armed camp not far from Terigāma. From early morning 139
the two armies began the battle with vehemence and con-
tinued it until evening. Now when the Nīlagiri and his 140
warriors, who were acknowledged to be brave, saw their troops
yielding, they armed with their weapons, striking down the best 141
soldiers, spreading panic amongst the foe, flung themselves
into the midst of the army like lions amid a herd of elephants.
But the warriors of the Senāpati (Deva) did not flinch in fight, 142
but surrounding the Nīlagiri Rāma and the many troop leaders
on all sides, they slew them on the battlefield and captured 143
the chief warrior Kaḍakkuḍa and other fighters alive. The 144
Senāpati who had gained the victory in this battle, sent those
captured alive to his Lord.

Parakkamabāhu who was staying[3] quietly in the neigh- 145
bourhood of the scene of heroic deeds now summoned in his
shrewd way, the Nagaragiri Mahinda who was in his vicinity 146
and told him of the extraordinary courage of those digni-
taries[4]. When the latter heard that, his ambition awoke 147
within him and with the words: I will set forth and take it,
he pledged himself to take Anurādhapura shortly. With strong 148
forces the foe-crusher set forth and delivered a great battle

[1] Here we must probably take *nīlagiri* as a title similar to *nagaragiri* (see note to 66. 85), *laṅkāgiri* (see note to 72. 27) and *lokagalla* (see note to 72. 222). The word hewever, occurs only in connection with Rāma and specially noticeable is the *Rāmanāmo Nīlagiriṭṭhito* in 72. 12. Cf. the note to this passage.

[2] P. *balapāmokkhe*. These are the *yodhā* of v. 140 and 143 c d, the *balanātha* of v. 143 a. It seems to me that the leaders of the local militia troops are meant.

[3] The Col. Ed. quite unnecessarily alters *nivasanto* into *nivāsattham*. Then 145 a b would have to be joined to the preceding, and W. translates accordingly "sent the man whom he had taken alive to live in comfort with his master (Parakkama)". Now that is as regards content in the highest degree unlikely. S. and B. have not recognised that *parakkammanikaṭamhi* in a b contains a pun on *parakkamabhujo* in c.

[4] Of Rakkha and Deva.

149 at the place called Badarībhātikamāna. Then when the illustrious one had fought a great action at the village of the
150 name of Siyāmahantakuddāla and near the Tissavāpi reservoir not far from Anurādhapura, he surrounded by the multitude
151 of his troops, entered Anurādhapura[1]. When the Lord of men Gajabāhu heard of these events, he sent off several troop
152 leaders accompanied by the highest dignitaries. They all armed for combat, raised a barricade round the town and cut off
153 access to the road. Now when the Senāpati Deva heard of these events, in order to relieve the general besieged in the
154 town, he set off in haste, delivered battle again at the village of Siyāmahantakuddāla and fought on the way three terrible
155 battles. The Malayarāyara at the tidings thereof left his stronghold[2] and came hither after twice fighting a battle on
156 the way. At the instruction of the Senāpati, he marched in the same direction[3] and fought with the hostile army not far
157 from Anurādhapura. The Senāpati also fought here and there a sharp action, pressed forward to the vicinity of Anurādha-
158 pura and opened the combat here. At news of this the general Mahinda with strong forces suddenly made a sortie out of
159 glorious Anurādhapura and overthrowing the foe and storming many barricades on the way, he quickly reached the Senāpati.
160 United the army of the Senāpati and the army of Mahinda fought with the hostile army and once more put it to flight.
161 The Senāpati returned to Siyāmahantakuddāla, set up a strong, entrenched camp and took up a position here[4].

[1] Anurādhapura was probably also the objective of Deva's advance from the S.W. As Parakkamabāhu's headquarters must have been nearer to the centre of the whole theatre of operations it may be assumed that Mahinda was advancing on the town from the south, more or less on the line Galgamuva-Talava.

[2] He was stationed according to 70. 62—65, in the north-west, in Muttākara, at the extreme left wing.

[3] P. *ekamukhena* (for the meaning of *mukha* in such a connection see 70. 217), i. e. with the same goal as the Senāpati.

[4] For judging the military situation it is of importance that though Gajabāhu has won back Anurādhapura, the threat to this town and therefore to his right flank from the Senāpati Deva continues.

Parakkamabāhu now summoned the chief Māyāgeha to 162
him and ordered him to carry on the war in Āḷisāra. Full 163
of joy the latter marched, accompanied by skilled warriors,
built a fortification in Kalalahallika and took up a position
there. At the stronghold of Nandāmūlakagāma he fought 164
three actions and brought this castle into his power. Marching
on Āḷisāra, he captured the entrencament at Kaddūragāma 165
and after fighting once again, he then took also the fortification
at the place called Kirāṭi[1]. The army of the Lord of men 166
Gajabāhu came hither to fight, and after throwing up an
entrenchment at a place named Vilāṇa, it halted here. Now 167
when Parakkamabāhu of valour hard to overcome, after
occupying an entrenched camp at Nālandā[2], during his sojourn
there, heard of this, he sent off secretly two or three hundred 168
thieves practised in house-breaking[3] and directed them to steal 169
up to the entrenchment with sharp antelope horns in the
middle of the night and to undermine it and so to take it.
The chief Māyāgeha following this instruction, had the eṇ- 170
trenchment broken into and the enemy there seized. At the 171
village of Mattikāvāpi he again captured an entrenchment,
and at Uddhakuraṃgāma and Adhokuraṃgāma he likewise cap-
tured two fortifications. After breaking through and taking 172
an entrenchment at the village called Nāsinna, he brought
the district of Āḷisāra into his power.

[1] As the situation of Kalalahallika cannot be exactly determined, it can only be said generally of Māyāgeha's advance against Āḷisāra = Elahera, that it apparently took place from the west, while Rakkha threatened it from the south. The mention of Nālandā in v. 167 agrees with this. H. W. CODRINGTON (I. 72) is inclined to see in Kirāṭi a slip of the pen for Sirāṭi = Hīraṭi, the name of a small river that flows from the left into the Ambanganga at Maluveyaya below Talagoda. The place Sirāṭi would then probably have to be looked for far up that river.

[2] Halfway between Matale and Dambul.

[3] P. *saṃdhibheda.* The phrase *saṃdhiṃ chindati* means "to carry out a burglary". D.I. 52^{24}; M.I. 516^{6}, II. 88^{7}; *saṃdhicchedana* DhCo. IV. 84^{5}. Likewise in Pkr., JACOBI, Erzählungen in Mâhârâshtrî, p. $67^{9,33}$, 74^{35} ff.

173 Now about this time the King (Parakkama), acquainted with the right method, gave his officers the order to take
174 Pulatthinagara at once. The Laṅkādhinātha Rakkha and the Jīvitapotthakin[1] Sukha marched in haste from the Taḷākatthalī[2]
175 entrenchment, fought actions at several places on the way with the hostile army and fought a battle at the place Ra-
176 jakamatasambādha. Then after fighting in the region of Milānakkhetta and setting forth from there, fighting in the
177 open field and slaying many of the enemy, they in pursuit of the foe, reached Daraaga, delivered there also an action
178 in which they remained victorious, advanced then thence to Maṅgalabegāma[3], broke through the entrenchment here by force and after annihilating the enemy, halted at this entrenchment.

179 The ruler of Rohaṇa, the Prince Mānābharaṇa[4], who had on several occasions fought with the officers of the Lord of
180 men Gajabāhu and suffered defeats and losses, had at that time given up the idea of war and discouraged in heart, kept
181 quiet. He had appeared in company with the bhikkhu order which dwelt in the three fraternities[5], and entered into
182 an alliance[6] with Gajabāhu. But now when he heard that the officers of the Monarch Parakkama had waged war

[1] The title occurs again 70. 318 and 72. 161 (Mandin) and 74. 90 (Kitti). In our passage all MSS. (and also Col. Ed.) have °*putthikī*, likewise 70. 318.

[2] Rakkha had evidently after his victory at Āḷigāma (see above vv. 112 ff.) again occupied Taḷātthalī (= Talagoda) and had halted here to await the operations of Māyāgeha. Their successful issue has safeguarded Rakkha's left flank and made possible the main thrust against Pulatthinagara.

[3] For this place which is mentioned as the first station in the description of Parakkamabāhu's withdrawal from Pulatthinagara see note to 67. 53. Rakkha is now only about 10 or 15 miles from the capital.

[4] Son of Sirivallabha and cousin of Parakkamabāhu.

[5] See note to 60. 56.

[6] P. *vasī karitasaṃdhāno*, lit.: "he lived with G. as one who had concluded a friendly treaty with him".

with great forces against the Lord of men Gajabāhu and had 183
in every battle cut down the enemy and carried off the victory,
the Prince Mānābharaṇa reflected thus: "Assuredly King 184
Parakkamabāhu who has vast resources at his disposal, will
shortly take Rājaraṭṭha; but once Rājaraṭṭha is taken possession 185
of by the Monarch, it will be impossible to remain in the
province of Rohaṇa." He therefore gave up his treaty with 186
King Gajabāhu and joined Parakkamabāhu with whom he concluded an alliance. The mighty one armed the able-bodied men 187
amongst the inhabitants of his two provinces and occupied an
entrenched camp at the village called Sobara.

At this time the King Parakkamabāhu, who wished to 188
perform a deed of exceeding prowess, thought thus: "Without 189
my officers who are stationed at divers places, learning of it,
I shall betake myself with warriors of my immediate retinue[1],
to Pulatthinagara, storm in combat gateway, turrets and bas- 190
tions, force my way into the town and — hurrah — capture
Gajabāhu." The clever one summoned to him the chief Māyā- 191
geha who was stationed in Ambavana and told him what he
had planned. Now in order to come to Ambavana under the 192
pretext of another object and to reach Pulatthinagara from
there, he spake secretly to him thus: "Send me a message to 193
this effect: I intend celebrating a specially splendid festival
for the Buddha. For making offerings unto the Buddha let
Their Lordships send me the sacrificial objects, the shells, 194
the five loud-sounding musical instruments, the fly whisks,
the white umbrella and the flag streamers, and come thither 195
and behold my festival." Māyāgeha betook himself to Amba- 196
vana and after he had prepared for the festival, sent back the
message in obedience to these words. When the glorious 197
King beheld it, he rejoiced and after having had the message
read aloud to the circle of his dignitaries, he sent off the 198
sacrificial implements with all speed to Māyāgeha and gave his
dignitaries to understand in every way that he himself meant
to go. The highest (of the officials) who saw through the 199

[1] For *sahavaḍḍhita* see note to 67. 52.

King's intention, sent word to his brother, the Nagaragiri
200 (Mahinda). When the latter heard of the affair, he left Moravāpi[1] and appeared in haste with his troops before the Ruler.
201 To the question why he had come, he made reply that he had come because he had seen through the intention of his
202 Lord, and he spake further: "For slaves such as I am, if they are in existence, the aim is solely the conquest of the hostile
203 king. Therefore have I arisen and shall capture Gajabāhu
204 with army and train and deliver him up to the Lord." With these words the King's officer craved permission to depart.
205 When the ambitious chief Māyāgeha, the Laṅkādhinātha Kitti and many other powerful officers saw this they (likewise)
206 besought leave and cried: I first, I first. Thereupon the Monarch who was skilled in plans of war, explained his plan of
207 action and sent off his officers to begin the campaign. They all began to march with adequate[2] army and train and occu-
208 pied an entrenched camp not far from Nālandā. Heavy clouds[3] formed and began to rain, cleaving the earth, as it were, on
209 every side with the floods of water. When the Sovereign saw the clouds, he who loved the power of truth, fearing the army might become wet through, made the solemn declaration[4] with
210 this determination: "If the winning of the royal dominion is to serve only for the welfare of the people and of the Order, then shall the god not let it rain." And even so it happened
211 there. Thereupon he sent food prepared in vinegar, bananas, crushed rice and the like and all kinds of cakes in great
212 quantities (to the troops). In order that many people could

[1] Mahinda had thus taken up his position here after being relieved by Deva. For the situation of the lake see notes to 70. 67, 72. 177.

[2] I take *yogga* to be the adjective "fitting, corresponding". W. on the other hand, regards it as substantive with the meaning "conveyance, carriage", since he translates "with their chariots and men and waggons". But in this case it seems to me that *yogga* and *vāhana* would form a barely tolerable tautology. See also above v. 23, 69 &c.

[3] In my edition I have kept more closely to the MSS. Now I should prefer to adopt the emendation of the Col. Ed. *mahāmegho*, as otherwise there is no suitable subject to *vasitum ārabhi*.

[4] P. *saccakiriyā*. For this term see Mhvs. trsl. p. 125, n. 3.

drink water at the same time, he sent several thousand bamboo
staves in which holes had been made, which were hollow[1] 213
throughout and in which one, after filling them with water,
had closed the holes[2]. The dignitary Mahinda now marched 214
with strong forces and took the stronghold at the place called
Lahulla, after slaying the enemy. At the news of this the 215
Laṅkānātha (Kitti[3]) also started in haste, took the fort at the
place called Hattanna and cut down the foe. When the chief 216
Māyāgeha heard that he marched in haste with large forces
and pushed forward as far as Khaṇḍigāma. The four-membered 217
army[4] of the Lord of men Gajabāhu was hemmed in on three
sides in the narrow pass of Khaṇḍigāma. The son of the 218
Laṅkādhinātha (Kitti), Laṅkāpura[5] by name, a great war hero,
came to the Khaṇdigāma pass[6]. He brought the whole of 219
the forces which had come from three directions into one
direction and pursued them, the great war hero, as a lion a
herd of elephants. Thereupon the troop leaders with the 220
Laṅkādhinātha (Kitti) at the head, after killing a great mass
of troops of the Lord of men Gajabāhu, advanced to the place 221
called Koddhaṅgulikakedāra. The troops of Gajabāhu reached
Pulatthinagara in disorder.

When the Lord of men Gajabāhu saw his great army 222
enter, he thought, since pride had awakened mightily in him,

[1] P. *ekarandhaṃ*. For the meaning cf. skr. *randhravaṃśa* "hollow bamboo." (BR. s. v.)

[2] Not only the openings above and below, but for the transport of the water, also the holes bored lengthwise for drinking.

[3] It is clear from v. 205, that the Laṅkādhinātha mentioned here is Kitti.

[4] The four members (*aṅgāni*) or elements of the army are: elephants, cavalry, chariot warriors and infantry.

[5] This must be the Daṇḍanātha Laṅkāpura mentioned so often later, (76. 82 ff.). But otherwise *laṅkāpura* is a title. Thus Kaḍakkuḍa l., 72. 39, Rakkha l., 75. 70, Deva l., 75. 130.

[6] A Kandegama lies in the Negampaha Korale, northwest of Dambul-Jambukola. If this is our Khaṇdigāma, it must be assumed that Gajabāhu in order to hold up the advance of Kitti and the other generals, undertook an attack on the left flank. The assault is parried by Kitti's son.

223 thus: "When my father, the Monarch, entered into the com-
pany of the gods and when as yet no stability had been
224 attained in my father's realm, then came Kittisirimegha and
Sirivallabha, advancing from two sides with the intention of
225 making war on me, but they were unable to behold my
victorious banner and fled, since then they have their whole
226 life long given up the idea of war. Now I have achieved
stability in Rājaraṭṭha and I possess a complete, four-membered
227 army. If now, equipping army and train, I advance to fight,
228 what king will be able to hearken to my war drum?" Thus
swollen with pride, King Gajabāhu ordered the dignitaries of
229 his immediate retinue to put the army in battle trim. After
they had placed in readiness well armoured elephants and
horses proved in battle and large masses of troops of capable
230 warriors, armed with the five weapons, further also the
mercenaries of the Keraḷas, Kaṇṇātas, Damiḷas, and the like,
231 the dignitaries at once informed the King. With a strong
force the latter left glorious Pulatthinagara and reached the
232 place called Sīkaviyala. The troop leaders with the Laṅkā-
dhinātha Rakkha[1] at the head offered battle there to the Lord
233 of men Gajabāhu. The great heroes broke through the (ranks
of the) elephants and horses, unhorsed their riders and put
234 to flight the Ruler of men together with his army. The King
withdrew in haste to his town, had the gates locked and hid
235 himself in a sewer[2]. In pursuit of the King the soldiers (of
Rakkha) arrived, surrounded Pulatthinagara on all sides and
236 began to break through walls, turrets and bastions, and the
237 spies who were stationed in the town opened the gate. They
entered with ease, captured the Monarch Gajabāhu alive and
238 brought him to the palace. The Princes Coḷagaṅgakumāra
and Vikkantabāhu they fettered and threw into prison.

[1] According to v. 177-8 of our pariccheda, Rakkha was stationed at Maṅgalabegāma.

[2] The translation is only guess-work. The idea seems to be to express something derogatory to Gajabāhu. The word *manurā* is otherwise unknown. W. has Anurā, but this is no doubt wrong. It might of course have also been *āmanurā*.

Thereupon the dignitaries informed their master of what had 239
taken place. When the Monarch (Parakkamabāhu) heard that,
with the insight which grasps the right method, he sent with 240
the message: until we see one another under an auspicious
star thou shalt live free of all fear of me — costly garments 241
and perfumes and ornaments, articles of his own use, to Gaja-
bāhu. The officers and the heads of districts hereupon took 242
counsel together and sent the following message to the Mo-
narch (Parakkamabāhu): "So long as the King (Gajabāhu) is 243
alive, the people dwelling in the kingdom will not submit to
thy sovereignty: he must therefore be put to death." When 244
the Monarch heard that, his heart was moved with pity, and
he thought: the king must in no case be put to death. He 245
fetched the clever Senāpati Deva who was stationed in Senā-
gāma[1], and spake to him as follows: "If the heads of districts 246
and the officers, grown insolent by their victory in fight, slay
the King (Gajabāhu) whom they have captured, that is not
right. And if they plunder the town and ill-treat the people 247
and become unbridled, that is likewise not right. The gaining 248
of the royal dignity takes place for the welfare of the Order
and the people alone, but not for the purpose of slaying the
Monarch does it happen. Therefore thou must go there, hold 249
the unbridled in check, take the King under thy protection
and make the town secure." Thus with this charge the King 250
sent away the Senāpati[2]; the latter marched with the army
and betook himself to Pulatthinagara.

Meanwhile already before the departure of the Senāpati, 251
unbridled, low-minded people disregarding the commands of
the Lord of men, had broken open the house doors in 252
Pulatthinagara, plundered goods and stolen raiment and
ornaments of the people. Splendid Pulatthinagara afflicted 253

[1] The place is mentioned above in v. 131 and 132 in connection with the operations of Deva. But according to v. 161 Deva had finally taken up a position at Siyāmahantakuddāla. Thus he must in the meantime have altered his position.

[2] P. *rājindo senindaṃ* with pun: "the lord among kings (sends) the lord over the army."

by the soldiers was at that time (in wild agitation) like the
sea, when at the end of a world age it is lashed by the storm.
254 Enraged at such action, all the people who dwelt in the town,
the officials and the councillors, the townsmen and the troops
255 gathered together, betook themselves to Mānābharaṇa, told
256 him of the events and spake as follows: "Ye must come with
us, we shall take to ourselves the royal dominion and make
257 it over to you. Only help must be brought so us." Also the
officer Gokaṇṇa, who was stationed in Kālavāpi, sent a mes-
258 senger to him (with the request) to come speedily. When the
Monarch Mānābharaṇa heard the whole tale the imprudent
259 one took counsel with his foolish ministers. He thought: under
the pretext of setting free the King, I will arise, slay the
260 enemy and get hold of the whole of Rājaraṭṭha. He equipped
in haste the able-bodied men among the inhabitants of his
two provinces and marched together with the officials and the
261 forces hailing from Rājaraṭṭha, to the town, delivered there
a bitter action and cut down the whole army large as it was,
262 without remnant. Then the Monarch went up to the palace
and visited the Ruler of men Gajabāhu, showing him the
263 customary reverence. Hereupon in order to remove the fears of
this Lord of men and of the dwellers in his realm, he let some
264 days pass, then he slew the whole of the officers of the Mo-
narch Gajabāhu, took the King captive and threw him into a
265 dungeon. Then when he had seized everything, all the ele-
phants and horses and the wealth in the treasure house, in
266 the belief that his dominion was now assured, he fetched the
sacred Tooth Relic, the Relic of the Alms-bowl, his mother[1] and
267 all his wives from Rohaṇa, and himself void of all pity, the
foolish Prince, took counsel secretly with his mother and his
268 officers thus: "The troops in Rājaraṭṭha, so long as this King
269 is in life, will never submit; therefore he must be slain. If
we were to kill him openly, there would be a great tumult,

[1] Sugalā, the granddaughter of Vijayabāhu I. who also later on plays a leading part in the wars between Rohaṇa and Parakkamabāhu. The tooth relic (*dāṭhādhātu*) and the alms-bowl relic (*pattadhātu*) have already become the palladium of the kingdom.

therefore this Monarch must be slain in secret." He had the 270
King ill-treated with bad food and a bad couch and set about
putting him to death by poison. King Gajabāhu could not 271
stand the ill-treatment he received from the Prince Mānābharaṇa.
He sent secretly to Parakkamabāhu and let him know: "I see 272
no other help for me save through thee. Therefore without 273
delay revive thou me who am tortured with the fiery torment
of pain, by the rain shower of pity." When the King (Pa- 274
rakkamabāhu) had rightly heard all these words of the King
(Gajabāhu) he who was a fount of pity, was filled with the
greatest distress. He thought: it is fitting that I, since he 275
has suffered on my account this great wrong through Mānā-
bharaṇa, should free him from his misfortune, and although 276
his forces and his implements of war had been lost, he being
of the breed of great men, let not his courage sink, but chose 277
from among the people of his retinue capable men, granted
them offices and showed them great distinction. To the chief 278
Māyāgeha he granted the office of adhikārin and that of a
laṅkādhikārin[1] to the Saṅkhanāyaka[2] Kitti. Of the two brothers, 279
the generals[3], the prudent Monarch conferred on the elder the
rank of a chief of the Kesadhātus[4], on the younger that of 280
a nagaragalla[5]. He granted to both great distinction and
numerous troops and thus won them for himself.

After the prudent (Prince) had in this way, in a short 281
time equipped a large and strong force he sent it in divers
directions. To the place with the name of Vacāvāṭaka in the 282
Merukandara district he sent Rakkha, the Chief of the Kesadhātus 283
with his troops, to Maṅgalabegāma the Laṅkādhikārin Rakkha,

[1] The title *laṅkādhikārin* seems to denote a higher rank than *laṅkādhināyaka* etc. (see note to 70. 24); for Kitti on whom the former title has just been conferred as a distinction, was up till now (cf. 70. 205) Laṅkādhinātha.

[2] The title *saṅkhanāyaka* (here *saṅkhaka*°) occurs again in conjunction with Nātha (72. 31, 75. 75) and Rakkha (72. 41).

[3] The *daṇḍanāyakabhātaro* who are mentioned several times, are called according to 72. 162, Kitti and Saṅkhadhātu.

[4] See note to 57. 65.

[5] The same as *nagaragiri*. See note to 66. 35.

the Laṅkādhikārin Kitti to the locality called Kyānagāma,
284 but the two brothers, the generals, the Ruler sent with
285 large forces to the village of Tīṇimakkula[1]. To the Senā-
pati Deva shut up in Pulatthinagara, the Monarch then sent
286 his house-breakers, fetched him hither[2], gave him a great
army, like to the army of the gods, and sent him, aware of
287 the right method, to Gangātaṭāka[3]. All of them as they were
appointed for the various districts, marched forth with their
troops, plundered here and there on the road leading to the
288 town, struck off the heads of the foe, spread great panic, cut
off the grain supplies and thus harassed the people in the
289 town. Within and without Pulatthinagara the soldiers[4] sta-
tioned for that (purpose) slew (the enemy) and put him to
290 flight. No people now left the town for wood or leaves
291 through fear of the wholesale pillage[5]. By blocking at va-
rious points the road leading from Rohaṇa, they also stopped
292 the traffic for the people dwelling there. All the people shut
up in the town with King Mānābharaṇa were like weakened
293 birds in a cage[6]. The two brothers, the generals, hereupon

[1] Of the localities here named besides Maṅgalabegāma (see above notes to 67. 53 and 70. 178) Merukandara (41. 19, 44. 28 etc.) occurs as a safe refuge in Malaya for the pursued and Kyānagāma (72. 207, 264) in another connection. They all lay probably at no great distance southwest and south of Pulatthinagara.

[2] But cf. the note below to v. 289. As to the "burglars" (*corā*) see 70. 168.

[3] The modern Kantalai, the name of a big reservoir on the road from Dambul to Trincomalee (cf. W. note to the passage). Deva had thus the task of attacking the capital from the north.

[4] From this verse it must be assumed that Deva's whole force had not left the town, but that at least a part had remained behind, perhaps in the citadel, in order to work with the troops coming from outside. How W's translation can be brought into harmony with the traditional text I fail to see.

[5] The acc. *sabbaṃ* is governed by the first part — *vilumpana* — of the following compound, a construction not rare in the Cūlavaṃsa.

[6] The Col. Ed. reads *khittā pakkhino viya pañjare*; the MSS. all have as far as I can see, *khinnā* or *khiṇṇā*. Cf. 72. 209.

engaged in action with the chief Kontadisāvijaya[1] and after 294
fighting with the force under the command of the Laṅkā-
dhinātha Bodhi, they pursued (the foe) to Pulatthinagara.
The Chief of the Kesadhātus (Rakkha) who was stationed at 295
the village of Vacāvāṭaka, fought an action with the general
called Uttama; he gained the victory, advanced to the village 296
called Nāla, fought here with the general of the name of
Buddhanāyaka[2] and was victorious. The Adhikārin[3] Rakkha 297
who was stationed at Maṅgalabegāma, then fought with the
enemy and took the place called Hattanna[4]. The same fought 298
at Khaṇḍigāma[5] full of bitterness, with the Adhikārin Nātha
and put him and his army gloriously to flight. When the 299
Sovereign Mānābharaṇa heard that, he marched with his war-
riors to Māsīviyala to fight with him. At the same time the 300
Adhikārin Kitti who stood in Kyānagāma, and the Senāpati
Deva in Gaṅgātaṭāka, and the two brothers, the generals, who 301
stood in the village of Tīṇimakkula, also went forth to fight
with large forces. Slaying or routing all the foes who faced 302
them, they pressed forward in a short time from various
sides to Pulatthinagara, drove away the soldiers who were 303
stationed round the town to protect it, set free the Ruler
Gajabāhu and brought the wives, the children and the mother, 304
as well as the whole fortune of King Mānābharaṇa into their
power. The Lord of men Gajabāhu set free from these, fled 305
at once and betook himself in haste to Koṭṭhasāra[6]. When 306
the Monarch Mānābharaṇa who was fighting with the Laṅ-
kādhikārin Rakkha, heard of all these events, he was struck 307

[1] It is possible that the name is Konta and disāvijayanāyaka a title. The man is not otherwise mentioned.

[2] I assume that here *nāyaka* or *nātha* is not the title "chief" or "general", but belongs to the name. Cf. 72. 266 *Buddhanāyakanāmena*. See also 72. 171, 270.

[3] An abbreviation of laṅkhādhikārin; See 70. 283, 72. 37 etc.

[4] Cf. 70. 215.

[5] Cf. 70. 216-218. Thus all the places formerly taken which had been lost in the interval, are now recaptured.

[6] See note to 61. 43.

by the arrow of pain which comes from the separation from
the loved ones, and no longer caring for his life, he came
308 again equipped with armour and weapons with large forces
at night into the town and fought a great battle, thinking
309 of naught else but the destruction of the foe. But when the
Laṅkādhinātha Bodhi[1] fell fighting in the battle, he was
310 unable to hold out longer in Pulatthinagara. He took the
sacred Tooth Relic and the Alms-bowl Relic, his mother and
his wives and betook himself to Rohaṇa.

311 Now at this time Parakkamabāhu left Buddhagāma[2], to
set free the King, came to the neighbourhood of the town
312 and after having a fine two-storeyed palace built, he sojourned
313 with his army and train in the village of Giritaṭāka[3]. Now
at that time some warriors of the Monarch (Parakkamabāhu)
had betaken themselves, to recover from the hardships of the
314 war, to the village of the name of Tannaru. Treacherous
officers of the Ruler Gajabāhu without troubling[4] themselves
315 about the King, began suddenly a squabble with them. When
King Parakkamabāhu heard that, he was wroth and sent his
316 own officers to take Gajabāhu captive. The Laṅkādhikārin Kitti
and the Senāpati Deva hereupon marched with large forces to
317 the village of Tannaru. Fighting three times with the officers
of the Monarch Gajabāhu a great battle, they destroyed nu-
318 merous foes. The Nagaragiri Nātha and the Jīvitapotthakin

[1] See above v. 294.

[2] Thus his headquarters were here between Nalanda and Dambul. See note to 58. 43.

[3] Now Giritala beside the road leading from the Minneri lake (Maṇihīra) to Polonnaruva, distant from the latter about six miles as the crow flies. Cf. Bell, ASC. 1905 (= SP. XX, 1909) p. 20.

[4] P. *rājānaṃ piṭṭhito katvā*. Cf. for the meaning skr. *pṛṣṭhataḥ kṛ* "to leave someone or something unnoticed, disregarded". BR. s. v. *pṛṣṭha*. The King is Parakkamabāhu: His nearness does not disturb their pugnacity. Or the King may be Gajabāhu: The officers are "treacherous", because they attack the soldiers of Parakkamabāhu who at that time was Gajabāhu's ally and tried to rescue him. Parakkama considered, of course, Gajabāhu the culprit and held him responsible for the treachery of his officers.

Mandin[1], put the hostile army to flight at the village of Vā-
lukapatta. And also at the village of Tannaru the officers 319
with their large force destroyed a hostile army that faced
them, then marched farther, fought an action once more at 320
Kohombagāma and after slaying many, they broke down the
fortification and captured it. Numerous well-armed foes sta- 321
tioned[2] at Ambagāma they put to flight and brought the
fortress into their power. Thence they set off and after again 322
winning a victory at Tannitittha, they marched to Antara-
viṭṭhi and beat the enemy here. At this time some officers 323
of Parakkamabāhu were in Pulatthinagara at the head of a
large force. To fight with them there came officers of Gaja- 324
bāhu under the command of the Adhikārin Deva, but (they)
suffered a defeat. In the same way they[3] defeated numerous 325
foes at the place named Kālapilla and after cutting down the
enemy, took up their position at Madhukavanagaṇṭhi. They 326
all started in haste and marched further dispersing themselves
in different directions with the intention of seizing the King.
When the Ruler (Gajabāhu) heard that the enemy widespread 327
on all sides, was approaching, he saw no other step that he
could take; so the King sent to the congregation of bhikkhus 328
belonging to the three fraternities, settled in Pulatthinagara,
the message: "I see for myself no protection save with the 329
venerable brethren; let them out of pity free me from my
sorrow". When the bhikkhus heard these words, they started 330
off, their hearts moved with pity, for Giritaṭāka, sought out
the Ruler (Parakkamabāhu), and after exchanging greetings, 331
they asked by the King the reason for their coming, spake
the following conciliatory words: "The Exalted One to whom 332
pity was the highest, expounded many times in many dis-
courses the misery of discord and the blessings of concord.

[1] These two officers have so far not been mentioned. For the titles see notes to 66. 35 and 70. 174.

[2] The gerund *saṃnayhitvā* is subordinate to the part. past *ṭhite*, as in v. 327 *avattharitvāna* to the part. pres. *āyantiṃ*.

[3] I. e. the troops of Parakkamabāhu.

333 Now the Ruler of men (Gajabāhu) has neither a son nor
334 brothers, but he himself, being old, is near death. Thy pledged word that the gaining of the royal dominion has as object only the furtherance of the laity and of the Order will thus
335 shortly be fulfilled. Therefore shalt thou give up the strife and return to thine own province, hearkening to the word of the bhikkhu congregation".

336 Thus the King (Parakkamabāhu), hearkening to the words of the Order, gave up the kingdom gained with great trouble to King (Gajabāhu) and betook himself to his own province. Ha, how great was his mercy!

Here ends the seventieth chapter, called "The Surrender of the Royal Dignity", in the Mahāvaṃsa, compiled for the serene joy and emotion of the pious.

CHAPTER LXXI

— — — — — —[1]

The Ruler Gajabāhu betook himself to Gaṅgātaṭāka, made it 1
his residence and dwelt there happily. But the Monarch Mānā- 2
bharaṇa sent gifts to him in order to remain allied with him
after the conclusion of a treaty. But the Ruler of men Gajabāhu 3
who desired no treaty with him, betook himself to the vihāra
by name Maṇḍalīgiri[2]. Here he had the words: "I have made 4
over Rājaraṭṭha to the King Parakkama" graven on a stone 5
tablet, returned then to Gaṅgātaṭāka and died during his so-
journ there, visited by a disease after reigning two and twenty
years. Thereupon the foolish ministers of Gajabāhu met to- 6
gether, betook themselves to Kotthasāra, whither they had
the body brought, and after sending messengers to Mānābharaṇa 7
to come hither in all haste, they took up their abode there.
When the Lord of men Parakkama heard the news of the 8
King's death he equipped his army and came to Pulatthina-
gara.

The Monarch Mānābharaṇa in the province of Rohaṇa 9
listened to the words of evil-minded people who had come
with large forces from Rājaraṭṭha and thought: "If I make 10
these people my allies[3], I shall certainly get possession of
Rājarattha." With a host of troops he left Rohaṇa and came 11
to Kotthasāra swayed by wishes impossible of fulfilment. When 12

[1] Cf. below note to v. 32.

[2] See note to 46. 29.

[3] The pronoun *ime* shows that these words are still part of the oratio recta. W. includes them erroneously in the principal sentence.

the mighty Parakkamabāhu whose valour transcending the limits of thought was scarcely to be surpassed, heard of these
13 events, he thought: "The gossip of worthless people from Rājaraṭṭha who have forsaken the Lord of men Gajabāhu, the dispenser of great favours, and his officers, and have given
14 up the desire to fight, and not even master of the clothes
15 they wear, fleeing from fear have come to him, the Ruler Mānābharaṇa has believed as if it were pure truth and has
16 come forth to fight[1]. My dignitaries will give him a defeat twofold as heavy even as that which the Lord of men Gaja-
17 bāhu had to suffer. I shall not permit him to come to this
18 bank of the Mahāvālukagaṅgā." And versed in preparations for war, the prudent one made his four-membered army with the officers take up their position at the different fords from Sarogāmatittha as far as Gokaṇṇa[2].

19 Now the great dignitaries who were of great wisdom, came together and with clasped hands begged of the Monarch the
20 (holding of the) king's consecration. "Former kings, O Great King, have when they were victorious, in order to increase

[1] W. has neither understood the construction of the sentence nor its meaning. Verses 13-15 belong together. The subject is *Mānābharaṇabhūpati*. The principal verb is *āgañchi*. Subordinate to this is the gerund *saddahitvā palāpaṃ*. The gen. *dujjanānaṃ paviṭṭhānaṃ* is governed by *palāpaṃ*. Subordinate to this participle again are the gerunds *cajitvā, patvā, palāyitvā*. The four missing syllables in 13 c I have supplied in a similar way to the Col. Ed.

[2] The Mahaveliganga is evidently regarded here in its whole course from the mountains up to its mouth as the frontier between Rohaṇa and Rājaraṭṭha. A happy discovery of H. W. Codrington's I. 68 was the indentification of Sarogāma with the modern *Vilgamuva* (Sinh. *vil* "pond, lake" = P. *saro*) in Laggala Pallesiya Pattuva (Census II, p. 100) at a short distance from the left bank of the stream. Here evidently the Hembarave crossing was to be safeguarded. It seems to me curious that the Veragantota crossing at Alut-nuvara is not mentioned. It lies 13 miles higher up and is much used now. The bed of the Mahaveliganga is however subject to great changes. *Gokaṇṇa* I regard as the Bay of Trincomalee (Koddiyar Bay), or the spot where the Mahaveliganga flows into it. This explains the mention in 41. 79 of a *Gokaṇṇakamahaṇṇava*.

by every means the fear and affection of their subjects and 21
to show forth everywhere their own abundance of glory, performed the king's consecration, even while they were still
at the seat of war. A ruler fully equipped with political 22
wisdom and self-discipline, must ever pay heed to the keeping up of good ancient custom. Thine age, your majesty, is 23
youthful, but thy glory is irresistible and scarce to be surpassed the fulness of the courage of thine arms. Thy blossom- 24
ing fortune[1] would be capable of wielding sovereign power[2]
over the whole of Jambudīpa, let alone the island of Laṅkā.
From the first age of the world to the present day thy line 25
was pure as milk poured into a white shell: hence on a 26
favourable day must be performed the king's consecration
which must of necessity bring happiness to the whole world."
King Parakkamabāhu who overcame evil by the wrinkling of 27
his brows, granted the request, he the best of the wise[3], and 28
on a day proved auspicious by a favourable constellation he
placed the crown on his head, arrayed in all his jewels. And, 29
though he received the tidings that the Ruler Mānābharaṇa
had come to this bank of the stream, he heeded that as little
as grass, and laid his armour and his weapons near at hand 30
in a jewel maṇḍapa which he himself ascended. Then in 31
gorgeous procession he left his palace, marched round the
town with his right side towards it, like a fearless lion,
stunned with amazement by his splendour the thronging people, 32
and returned to the royal palace which was an abode of
bliss[4].

[1] So I translate *kusalodaya*. It is very nearly the same as the favourite *puññodaya*. See 37. 139.

[2] P. *vibhutta* = skr. *vibhutva*.

[3] P. *pavivekin* from *paviveka*, a term suggestive of the Sāṅkhya System, in which *viveka* is the expression for the discerning knowledge through which delivrance is attained. Garbe, die Sâṃkhya-Philosophie, p. 137.

[4] S. and B. have assumed that here we have the end of pariccheda 71 and at the same time a gap of unknown extent. The signature at the close of the whole chapter describes it as the 72nd, thus number 71

is missing completely. In my edition I have adopted this view and have begun the verses of the new section with the number 1. I must point out however, that as far as the contents go, a gap is scarcely to be noticed. The coronation festival is evidently at an end with the return to the palace. Perhaps it was hastened by Mānābharaṇa's advance. On the other hand Parakkamabāhu had already made preparations for the war according to v. 17-18, by occupying the various fords, and now the attack begins at the first of these places, at Sarogāma. W. thinks that all that is missing is the artificial strophe (together with the signature) which is customary at the close of a pariccheda.

CHAPTER LXXII

DESCRIPTION OF THE FESTIVAL OF THE CONSECRATION

Now the Mahālekha[1] Mahinda approached with a great 1
army and fought a great battle with the mighty Kesadhātu 2
Rakkha who was stationed at Sarogāmatittha. The Kesadhātu
Rakkha by name, the mighty one, slew like a lion that has 3
broken into an elephant herd, many of his men in combat
and drove the Mahālekha before him as a fierce storm wind
blows cotton, he the mighty him together with his army and 4
train. When then the latter crossing by the ford of Talanī-
gāma, was fain to renew the fight, the Kesadhātu Rakkha 5
put him again to flight after a sharp encounter with him.

In like manner the Kesadhātu named Buddha[2], having fought 6
with the (enemy's) many officers a terrible battle and having 7
slain many warriors, defeated and put to flight the Ruler
Mānābharaṇa who offering battle had crossed the river at the 8
Pūnagāma ford. He also took care that he (Mānābharaṇa)
gave up the idea of ever approaching this ford again.

The chief Māyāgeha[3] who was appointed to guard the 9
ford called Samīrukkha[4] alone at the head of his officers in
the same way crushed Gajabhuja who with his army had 10
crossed that ford with the object of fighting.

With the Māragiri[5] Mattatāla by name, who with his 11
army came with the intention of crossing the Mahārukkha

[1] See note to 52. 33.

[2] This officer of Parakkamabāhu's is not otherwise mentioned.

[3] In 70. 83, 162 etc. described as *Māyāgehādhinātha* or °*adhināyaka* here simply *Māyāgehanāyaka*.

[4] Name of a tree = skr. *śamī*, acacia suma. Corresponds to *sāma-gas* in modern Sinh.

[5] The title *māragiri* occurs again 72. 164, 174 (Nigrodha m.)

12 ford[1], Rāma[2] by name who was stationed in Nīlagiri which
was his own district, in his extraordinary courage, fought a
13 bitter engagement and after capturing the best soldiers whom
he could get alive, he put the rest of the army to flight so
that it no longer dared to go into action.
14 Another officer who guarded the Nālikeravatthu[3] ford
fought then a battle against a hostile army who had ap-
15 proached to fight, cut down many soldiers and scattered the
rest of the army without remnant on all sides.
16 Another distinguished officer who was appointed to the
ford called Anantarabhaṇḍaka for the guarding of it, drove
with a large force a strong army of the hostile king that had
17 advanced to fight, together with its officers to the last man,
to the four winds of heaven, whereby the hero turned the
18 battlefield into a mass of flesh, just as the storm wind
(scatters) a mountain of cloud so that its violence is scattered
flutteringly on all sides[4].
19 Again another high officer appointed to guard the Kāṇa-
tālavana[5] ford, saw to it that the hostile army that had come
20 forward to battle, gave up all thought of resuming (the
enterprise) after he had fought a great battle with his whole
army and train.
21 The Adhikārin, Kitti[6] by name, who was stationed at the

[1] "Ford of the great tree" or "ford of the euphorbia" (skr. *mahāvṛkṣa*, as borrowed word in Sinh. with the same meaning). The corresponding Sinh. word *māruk* means however, coco-nut palm. W. H. Codrington recognises the locality in Marake situated five miles below Hembarave on the left bank of the Mahaveliganga.

[2] Cf. note to 70. 137 where *nīlagiri* seems to be used as a title. When in our passage Rāma is described as *saraṭṭhavāsiko* that seems to point to the fact that the ford protected by Rāma was situated in the district which was controlled by him or which was his birth-place and that the name of this district was Nīlagiri. The title which is applied exclusively to Rāma would then in this case be borrowed from the name of his home (*nīlagiriṭṭhita*).

[3] "Coco-nut palm plantation."

[4] P. *samantā-ābaddha-saṃrambhaṃ*. For *saṃrambha* "violence" cf. PTS. PD. s. v.

[5] "Palmyra palm wood of the blind."

[6] See 70. 278, where the advancement of Kitti to the rank of *laṅkādhikārin* (here in short *adhikārin*) is mentioned.

Yakkhasūkara[1] ford after destroying many soldiers in a bitter
fight[2], defeated there a hostile body of troops that had ap- 22
proached for combat. Now while he stood at the same ford
he had in consequence of a scarcely to be evaded command 23
of the Great King Parakkama, to betake himself to him while
he entrusted (another) high dignitary there with the guarding
of the ford. This man also three times crushed a hostile 24
force that came hither and took care that it lost all courage
to fight once more.

The Jitagiri[3] Santa stationed at the Vihāravejjasāla ford, 25
completely annihilated a great army that was about to cross,
the army, namely, of the hostile king, fighting with him a 26
terrific battle with mighty army and train.

The Ādipotthakin[4] by name Kitti, stationed at the Assa- 27
maṇḍala[5] ford with a large force, the Laṅkāgiri Mahī[6] by
name, with a strong army, and yet another large army cut 28
up a hostile army that had approached, and returned then
with speed each to his appointed place[7].

[1] H. W. Codrington is certainly right in identifying this name with the present *Yakkure* (Census 1921, II, p. 438). It lies on the right bank of the river and at the entrance of the Sabassatittha crossing mentioned so frequently later, now Dastota, south of Polonnaruva.

[2] P. *katvā kathāsese*, lit.: "after making them so that only the tidings (of them) remained."

[3] The title, if it is such, which I think probable, only occurs in this place.

[4] The title which is only borne by Kitti (also 72. 160, 207) alternates 72. 182 with *bhaṇḍārapotthakin*. It therefore designates the superintendent of the royal store-rooms.

[5] If the name preserves the memory of the legend related Mhvs. 10. 53 ff., then we must look for Assamaṇḍalatittha at Kacchakatittha now Mahagantota, east of Polonnaruva.

[6] W. takes Mahīnāma for the name of the officer, which is quite possible. The title *laṅkāgiri* occurs again 72. 124 f., and 76. 250 in conjunction with the names Nātha and Sora.

[7] The verse is incomplete in the MSS. Nine syllables are missing in cd. The Col. Ed. supplies these rather differently to what I do, so that to translate with W. it would be "and returned to the king". The meaning seems to me to be that the three divisions of the troops were

29 (Other) warriors crossed the bridge of the Sakkharālaya-
30 gaṅgā[1], at once penetrated the grove called Sākkuṇḍa, and having there in fight deprived numerous warriors of life, they took from the foe the desire to attack once more from this quarter.

31 Hereupon the Saṅkhanāyaka by name Nātha, stationed at the Sarogāma[2] ford, after he had shattered an army of the
32 hostile king come hither for battle, crossed the stream himself at the village of Vātīyamaṇḍapa, cut up a strong hostile force and returned again to his post.

33 In the same way a large army stationed at the Samī ford cut up a strong hostile force which had marched for battle
34 in this direction and chased away its desire to come again. A strong royal army that had its stand at the ford called
35 Cullanāga annihilated in like manner the whole large force of the hostile king, that equipped with armour and weapons,
36 marched in this direction. At Burudatthalī the two brothers, the generals, scattered a hostile army that had advanced in this direction.

37 The Adhikārin[3] Rakkha by name, who guarded the ford
38 Niguṇḍivālukā, the great hero, free from all fear, destroyed a strong hostile force fain to cross, by carrying on the ever
39 renewed war for two months. In the same way the Laṅkā-
pura[4] known by the name of Kaḍakkuḍa, a great hero, fight-

posted at different places on the river, and that they only united in order to carry out the attack on the advancing hostile army, which was probably superior to the single divisions. Cf. v. 32.

[1] D. Jayaratna has compared Sakkharālaya with the present Akurala on the S. W. coast of Ceylon, midway between Ambalangoda and Hikkaduva. If this is correct then the above passage gives us a very different theatre of war. Mānābharaṇa would not merely have attacked along the Mahaveliganga, but also in the extreme southwest. This does not seem to be very probable.

[2] According to v. 1 and v. 9 fighting had already taken place at the two crossings mentioned in v. 31 and 33. The generals of Parakkamabāhu now seem to take the offensive at these two fords.

[3] As above in v. 21 *adhikārin* stands here for *laṅkādhikārin*.

[4] See note to 70. 218.

ing a severe action at Yācitagāma, scattered the raging army 40
of the foe, destroying it root and branch, the courageous
(scattered) the discouraged (army), the mighty the hostile
might.

The Saṅkhanāyaka Rakkhaka stationed at Hillapattakakhaṇḍa 41
crushed a hostile army that came to fight there. Another 42
great dignitary entrusted with the care of Titthagāma, after
undertaking a great battle[1] and fighting a bitter action, put 43
to flight with his great army a royal army that had advanced
to fight, so that it lost the courage to renew the fight.
Another powerful (officer), stationed at Nandigāma, fought a 44
great battle and scattered the raging army that had advanc-
ed thither.

At the place Hedillakhaṇḍagāma the Senāpati Deva when 45
Prince Mahinda came on with strong forces in order to fight, 46
delivered battle against him four times with army and train 47
in fighting trim. He covered the battlefield with the skeletons
of the hostile warriors and robbed the Prince of his troops
without loss to his (own) army and train, followed him at 48
his heels as he took flight with his army and pushed on at
once as far as the ford called Billagāma. There for two months 49
terrible combats were waged. Even in his position there the
Senāpati put the army of the enemy to flight.

A high officer stationed at the ford called Mālāgāma[2], 50
undertaking five times[3] the festival of a great battle, scattered 51
a mighty hostile army that had come there to cross over, as
the rising sun (disperses) the mass of the darkness. Another 52
high officer appointed to watch the Goḷabāha ford, a man of

[1] P. *samāraddhamahāyuddhakaccho.* The translation is very difficult. W. translates thus "began the strife with the enemy with great vigour when he essayed to make his way through is". But I think one must judge the passage in connection with v. 50 *āraddhamahāhavasamussavo.* Possibly *kaccha* here is not skr. *kakṣā*, but *kathya.*

[2] A *Malayomuva-veva* lies midway between Ambanganga and Mahaveliganga, 12 miles N. E. of Elahera. A ford named after it would have to be looked for not far from Yakkhasūkara.

[3] P. *dasaddhavāraṃ*, thus not "ten times" as W. translates.

53 great strength and courage, routed in action a hostile force
with its officers who advanced to fight, as a lion a herd of
54 gazelles. Another officer stationed at the ford called Dīpāla,
dispersed with his troops in combat the forces which had
advanced there.
55 The course of the war[1] being such, the Great King
Parakkamabāhu who in his terrible courage was like King
56 Duṭṭhagāmaṇī thought: "Not even in Rohaṇa will I permit
King Mānābharaṇa who is here crushed in war, so find a hold."
57 And the energetic (Prince) ordered the two Kesadhātus, Devila
and Loka, who were stationed in the district of Mahāniyyāma[2]
58 and in Pañcayojana[3], the Kammanātha Ārakkha[4] and the Kañ-
59 cukināyaka[5], utterly warlike men, to enter Rohaṇa. And at
his command these doughty men fared forth thence even as the
four great kings[6] at the (command) of the King Sakka.
60 Hereupon having reached the district called Navayojana[7] and
61 having celebrated with the strong hostile army there twenty
times the main festival of a main battle and having cut up
62 the great army, they captured Navayojanā. They then marched

[1] By the successful combats at the fords along the Mahaveliganga the defence seemed safeguarded. Parakkamabāhu now on his side takes the offensive in the southwest, from Dakkhiṇadesa, thus with the clear intention of outflanking the enemy's left wing. The success is at once seen in the relief of the pressure on the line of the Mahavèliganga. Mānābharaṇa is forced to withdraw a part of his troops from there. It is true, a reverse soon takes place, on the one hand through the revolt of Nārāyaṇa in Anurādhapura and on the other by the enemy succeeding in crossing the river at an unguarded spot.

[2] Only mentioned here. A Maniyangama lies in the Panaval Korale not far from Avisavella. So also CODRINGTON (II).

[3] Now Pasdun Korale, the territory to the east of Kalutara.

[4] A Kammanāyaka Añjana is mentioned 72. 206, 74. 168. I think therefore that the first part of *ārakkhakammanātha* contains the name.

[5] "Chief of the chamberlains". The Kañcukināyaka mentioned here is the Rakkha named so often 75. 20 ff.

[6] The four mahārājas are the four protectors of the world, the *lokapālā*: Yama, Varuṇa, Indra, Kubera.

[7] Now Navadun Korale, the territory S. and S. E. of Ratnapura.

thence and came to Kālagiribhaṇḍa[1]. After fighting with the
army there twenty battles, they brought it likewise into their 63
power, advanced thence farther and took likewise Dīghālika-
mahākhetta[2]. When the Ruler Mānābharaṇa received tidings 64
of these events he divided his own army and sent a part
thither.

Now at one time a great dignitary who had the care of 65
Anurādhapura, the general Nārāyaṇa, in his delusion reflected
thus: "I will bring this province into my power, build a 66
fortress and remain there independent of the kings." When 67
the Lord of men Parakkama heard of the matter he thought:
"I will destroy him without letting him take root." In all 68
haste the hero sent forth the Chief of the umbrella bearers.
As a lion of incomparable courage (falls) upon small gazelles 69
or even on elephants, so the great dignitary set forth, gave
battle to Nārāyaṇa, slew him along with his army and set
the province free from the briers (of the rebels).

As the known fords at that time were everywhere guarded 70
by the high dignitaries of the great King, as if they were
under the dominion of rakkhasas, Mānābharaṇa was not able 71
to cross them, but he passed over at an unknown ford which 72
was made known to him by dwellers in Rājaraṭṭha who had
come under his influence[3]. Now when King Parakkama-

[1] Identified by Codrington (II) with the Kalugalboḍa-raṭa of the Kaḍaimpota by which is understood the mountain country of the present Korales Kukulu, Atakalan, Kolonna and Moravak.

[2] As in 75. 60 and 75. 50 *Dīghāli* and *Mahākhetta* are mentioned separately we have to do in this passage with the coalescence of the names of two apparently adjoining localities, just as with Sūkarālibheripāsāṇa in 75. 98, 146. Codrington (II) looks for Mahākhetta at Paraduva, 11 miles N. N. W. of Matara, since here there are extensive rice fields on the right bank of the Nilvalaganga. Mahākhetta means "large field". On the opposite or left bank there is said to be a long canal. This might be the *Dighāli* = Sinh. *dik-äla*. I should however expect both these localities to be farther east. Ayrton has in fact compared Dīghāli with Dikvela, east of Matara situated on the coast.

[3] W's translation *gatehi vasam attano* "who were faithful to him" is inexact.

73 bāhu heard of this event he thought to destroy him along
with his whole army at the crossing of the river, occupied
74 a stronghold at the place Mayūrapāsāṇa and sent off the
Adhikārin Rakkha, surrounded by many soldiers, a man of
75 extraordinary bravery, with a strong army and train. But
this man in his great envy could not bear the great favour
76 which the pleased and grateful King Parakkama showed to
his enemy, the Senāpati Deva, after the great battle fought
77 by him. He bore resentment to the great King and was not
zealous in the war. Groaning in the fever of his jealousy he
78 was careless and developed no energy. Now an officer of the
Lord of men Gajabāhu, a crafty man who had obtained from
79 the Monarch Parakkamabāhu freedom from punishment, had
gone with Rakkha. He rightly guessed his mood and as he
80 had formerly given counsel to King Mānābharaṇa, so now
he sent quickly to King Mānābharaṇa the message to come
81 in all haste before the fortifications were begun[1]. When the
Monarch Mānābharaṇa heard these tidings, he entrusted his
82 army with warlike enterprises at different places[2]. The Prince
Mahinda marched to Vallitittha and fought with the officers
83 of the Senāpati Deva. These killed there many warriors in
bitter fight and vanquished in one moment the Prince, the
84 powerful the powerless. The King himself fought a great
battle with the Adhikārin Rakkha in which sparks flew from
85 the clash of swords. Many doughty warriors perished there
on both sides, finally the followers of the Adhikārin Rakkha
86 were scattered. Thereupon this man with his own hand alone

[1] All MSS. have *sāsanaṃ* twice over, first in pāda a then in c. The Col. Ed. has altered the second into *āsannaṃ*. I could not adopt this emendation. It is not impossible that it is a case of carelessness on the part of the compiler. But if there is to be an alteration, I should suggest reading instead of *sāsanaṃ* in c *sampataṃ* "now" = skr. *sāṃprataṃ* (in contrast to *pageva* in 79 d). The unusual form — one says generally *sampati* = skr. *saṃprati* — in conjunction with the preceding *pesesi* may have occasioned the erroneous *sāsanaṃ*.

[2] He wants in this way to conceal his action against Rakkha and make it impossible for Parakkamabāhu's other generals to come to his aid.

continued the combat and fell himself after slaying many a
good soldier. When King Parakkamabāhu, that man of ter- 87
rible courage, heard of this event he thought with smiling
lotus face: "As long as I am there what matters it whether 88
they are alive or dead? The lion seeks not allies when he
tears elephants in pieces. Even to-day I shall fulfil in combat 89
the long awakened wish of my two arms which are filled
with lust of battle. This earth ravished by intercourse with 90
many kings who plotted only evil, will I bathe in the water
of the blood of the limbs of my foes and then make her at 91
once my spouse purchased by combat[1]. For heroes such as
I am she forms in her whole expanse but a hall[2]. How 92
can any other power aid me, perhaps as a firebrand the sun
in extinguishing the mass of hostile darkness?" After reflect- 93
ing thus he came to the battlefield comparable to the fifth
sun[3] in the great ocean that was for him the army of the
hostile king. Arrived he tarried there hearkening to the sing- 94
ing given forth by numerous songstresses, feeling out the
underlying motif, as one who is first[4] among those versed in
the knowledge of moods.

[1] There is no need to depart from the reading of the MSS. *paṇikataṃ*. The word belongs to skr. *paṇa* "trade, purchase", *paṇi* "trader". The allusion is to the old custom of purchasing the bride.

[2] The meaning seems to be this: It is to me a matter of indifference at what place I celebrate my marriage with the earth — this is of course a symbol for its dominion. In what place so ever I begin the combat there is a fitting chamber (*sālā*) for the festival. He then goes on to show why he can at once perform the ceremony. He needs not to wait for outside aid, for in comparison to him it would be as a firebrand to the sun.

[3] W: "alluding to the seven suns that are said to rise in succession at the destruction of the world, the fifth drying up the waters of the deep" (note).

[4] The compiler shows here his knowledge of the Indian Rasa doctrine. Every work of art, poetry like music, must have its special *rasa*, its underlying motif. Theory distinguishes eight, nine or ten of these. The most important are: *śṛṅgāra* "love", *vīra* "heroic mood", *bhayānaka* "horror engendering" and *hāsya* "merriment arousing motif".

95 Against the hostile army[1] with which was the Monarch
(Mānābharaṇa) approaching in pursuit of the scattered great
96 army, the great dignitaries of the Great King Parakkama hasten-
ed forth and fought with it a terrible battle near the village
97 Badaravallī. Although the victorious army (Mānābharaṇa's)
was scattered, they nevertheless after themselves fighting the
great battle and suffering heavy losses in combat, but having
98 also slain many soldiers — beat a retreat exhausted, and wended
their way to their own country. Now the great army of the
99 foe displayed redoubled energy. Parakkamabāhu left those
who had received wounds, to the care of physicians. He
100 gazed smiling merrily at the fleeing army. The dignitaries
who had bidden their bearers[2] turn, he forced with stern glance
101 and wrinkled brow to go back. The bearers he sent himself
against the hostile army, and in order to hold high festival
102 for the meeting with Lakkhī i. e. the foe[3], and to send a clever
maiden herald, his sword liane[4], to the field of battle, he,
wishing to begin the feast of war, called to the bearer of his
103 hand weapons: Give me the Sīhala sword! Now when this
man out of ignorance brought as Sīhala sword the weapon

[1] W. has not rightly understood the context. The gerund *anubandhiya* does not belong to the subj. *mahāmaccā* but is subordinate to the part. past *āgatāya* in 95 c. Mānābharaṇa is pursuing the defeated troops of the Adhikārin Rakkha. His army is therefore called *jayasenā* in 97. Then he is met by Parakkamabāhu's generals. On account of the great losses they suffer, they have to retire. Parakkama tries to prevent an absolute collapse. His generals Rakkha Kesadhātu and Nātha (v. 107) restore the balance for the time being. There follows finally however, the general retreat to Pulatthinagara.

[2] Their palanquin bearers. For the high officers the palanquin was the method of transport also in the field.

[3] The alteration of *veri°* into *vīra°* in the Col. Ed. is wrong. The image is again borrowed from a wedding (cf. v. 90-91). As in wedlock the man becomes master of the woman, in this case Lakkhī, the goddess of fortune and victory, so in battle the victor of the foe. The picture here is quite different to that of 72. 112 according to which the corrections of S. and B. have evidently been made.

[4] In Skr. literature also the sword or the blade is compared with a liane. The combination *khaḍgalatā* (as here P. *khaggalatā*) occurs frequently in the Kathāsaritsāgara (BR. s. v. *latā* 1 c).

called the Jambudīpa blade[1], he spake: "That is not the 104
Sīhala blade. Leave this (sword) that could put an end to
all the lines of hostile kings in Jambudīpa and bring me
quickly the Sīhala blade[2]". Now when, after these words, 105
they handed him the terrible Sīhala blade the King thought
again, full of pride, he who was an elephant for the binding
of elephants[3], namely the foe: In Sīhaladīpa I am unable to 106
grasp the weapon with my arm, and looked significantly[4] at 107
the face of the Kesadhātu named Rakkha standing near him
and in that of the Nagaragiri Nātha. And these twain car- 108
ried out the hint of the King and flung themselves with the
courage of lions into the midst of the great (hostile) army.
The twain seemed in consequence of their incomparable bra- 109

[1] P. *Jambudīpapāṭava.* We may take for *pāṭava* without scruple the meaning "sharpness, edge, blade". Skr. *paṭu* means "sharp, cutting" and *pāṭava* is the abstract noun, derived from *paṭu.*

[2] We have here in the MSS. a śloka of 6 pādas and what follows becomes badly confused if we do not accept it. In the present case it is certainly possible that it arose through a later interpolation of the line *Jambudīpamhi nissesaverirājakulantakaṃ.*

[3] What is thought of here is the capture of wild elephants. When the herd has been surrounded and enclosed in the corral tame elephants are brought in with whose aid the wild elephants are chained.

[4] I have interpreted the passage wrongly in my edition where I have tried to put *sāvadhāraṇaṃ* in the oratio recta with the meaning "with the exception (of my arm)". That is too forced. W's translation "that there was not a man who could even place in his hand a (proper) weapon" is also quite impossible. The text has literally: "in Sīhaladīpa with my arm unable to take the weapon, so thinking . . ." Thus the subject to *asamattho* is missing. It can only be *ahaṃ* "I". With the oratio indirecta this can be clearly seen: *he* thought *he* was incapable etc. The idea is this: At sight of the sword the King has scruples whether he should use the Sīhala sword on the island of Sīhala, that is in civil war against Sīhalas. He looks therefore *sāvadhāraṇaṃ* at his ablest generals, handing over the task to them. With undoubted skill Dhammakitti manages the transition from the heroic pose which he has ascribed to the King, to the real state of affairs and the later conditions in which the King is no longer the first among his soldiers, the leader of the army, as in the heroic age of Duṭṭhagāmaṇī, but makes his generals carry out warlike enterprises according to his instructions.

very like thousands in number appearing in the midst of
110 the battlefield. From morning until far into the night they
fought a great battle terrible by reason of the bodies of
111 hostile soldiers hewn in pieces by sword strokes. With folded
hands the great dignitaries then informed the King: "Shattered
112 is the whole great army, we few people alone are left. But
even in our small number, O Lord of men, fighting a great
battle, we have not let the luck of heroes (away from us)
113 turn to the other side. As if from fear of the sight of the
combat the sun has hidden himself behind the western mount.
We will return[1] to Pulatthinagara and take up to-morrow
the destruction of the foe. Now is not the right time[2]."
114 When the King heard that, such action found no favour in
his sight, as he desired to spend the night on the spot and
115 renew the combat in the morning. Now the King void of
all fear, gave himself up to slumber for a moment during
116 which the dignitaries brought him to Pulatthinagara. Now
when at midnight they came to Pañcavihāra, the King awoke
117 and asked what name the place had. When the Lord of men
heard from the people that it was Pañcavihāra, he flew into a
rage: "That ye brought me hither while I slept was wrong of
118 you". But as he wished to take every single one of his
119 retinue without exception with him, he remained there. He
filled the village with the din of the five loud clanging shell
trumpets[3] and after he had himself (awaited) his retinue that
120 had not yet appeared, (and) surveyed (them), he sent his
train on in front, kept behind them himself and came when
morning time was near to Pulatthinagara.

121 When then the sun, the ancestor of his race, had risen,
Parakkamabāhu who by his singular courage had the whole

[1] Important, as we see from this, as also from what follows, that the scene of these fights lay in the immediate vicinity of the capital.

[2] Again a śloka with 6 pādas in all the MSS. Here also there is the possibility of a later interpolation of the line *raṇadassanabhīto va līno atthacale ravi.*

[3] These are the five musical instruments, of which one, the shell trumpet, is named as the most warlike.

world in his power[1], heard that at the ford called[2] Billa- 122
(gāma) the Senāpati Deva and the Adhikārin, named Kitti,
at the head of a great army had poured an uninterrupted 123
rain of arrows on the Adhikāriṇ of the name of Nātha[3], on
the Prince Mahinda, the Senāpati Sukha, the Laṅkāgiri 124
Nātha and on others who had approached in that direction
and who came with their army to fight; that they had rob- 125
bed of life the Senāpati Sukha and the Laṅkāgiri Nātha
along with many warriors and had pursued the Adhikārin 126
Nātha and the Prince Mahinda who had fled with their troop
divisions; that when they had penetrated far into the pro- 127
vince, the whole army of the foe together with the troops
belonging to the country had made the road impassable and 128
hiding themselves on all sides had captured them[4]. At these
tidings the foe-tamer (Parakkamabāhu) who took ever the
greatest pleasure in doughty deeds, marched forth to relieve
the generals. But here in order to persuade the Monarch in 129

[1] Verses 122 up to the beginning of 128 *tirokatvā gahesi* form one sentence (cf. however, note on 128), the content of the news which Parakkamabāhu receives next day and which must lead to an alteration of his decisions. W. has understood that. In my edition this is not made sufficiently clear (but cf. the emendations in vol. II). Because of the new tidings the King determines in the first place to relieve his surrounded generals. The action planned against Mānābharaṇa is deferred.

[2] There had been fighting before at this ford (see 72. 48) under the Senāpati Deva who had pushed forward there from Hedillabhaṇḍagāma in pursuit of the defeated Mahinda.

[3] Mentioned above in 70. 298.

[4] The construction of the whole sentence is not correct in the original. The subject is changed as happens in the latest parts of the Cūlavs., chiefly in sentences with many gerunds: in the first place *Devasenādhināyako Kittināmādhikarī ca* is the subject, then *sakalā arātivāhinī*. The construction would be right if it ran: *Devasenādhināyake Kittināmādhikārini ca ... vattetvā ... pāpetvā ... anubandiya ... paviṭṭhesu, sakalā arātivāhinī ... gahesi*. Here the gerunds *vattetvā* &c. would be subordinate to the past part. *paviṭṭhesu*. The word *gahesi* refers only to the encirclement by which Deva and Kitti have lost their freedom of action.

whom had awakened the resolve for combat, to return, the
130 great dignitaries with folded hands spake to him: "Save thy
exceeding great ability, scarce to be surpassed, O Lord of
131 men, we have no further might left; and the inhabitants of
the country are all under hostile influence. We must betake
ourselves from here to Nandamūla and from there begin the
132 fight". With these and like representations they induced the
Lord of men to turn back; they started from there and set
133 out with the King on their way. When the retainers native
to the country stationed in Nandamūla, beheld the Monarch
134 approaching with few followers they began to rain from
all sides a hail of arrows. The Ruler who had halted at
135 the place called Karavāḷagiri[1] sent thence certain dignitaries
acknowledged to be excellent warriors and brought it to pass
136 that that division of the army gave up its desire to fight. While
thus the great hero, the Ruler, sent on his retinue in advance
and followed after on the march, he came to Jambukola.
137 Starting thence to relieve the Senāpati Deva, he came on the
march to a place named Navagāmapura.

138 At that time the Senāpati Deva and the Adhikārin Kitti,
because they had not obeyed the instructions given them by
139 the Great King, lay exhausted there with their army. They
had given up the fight and had fallen[2] into the power of
140 the enemy at the village named Surulla. In order to persuade
the Ruler (Parakkama) — who was advancing[3] with the

[1] The Census 1921 (II. 296) has a Karavalagala in the Tittaveligandahe Korale, thus in the mountains east of Hiripitiya, 13 miles north of Kurunegala. But there are difficulties about identifying the two names. We expect rather a position between Polonnaruva and Dambul. Cf. note to 72. 147.

[2] They are probably still surrounded by the enemy but have not yet capitulated. All we learn further is that Parakkama had to give up the plan of relieving them, as apparently their capitulation could no longer be prevented. Of their later fate we hear nothing. It seems however that they were freed or ransomed. The Adhikārin Kitti appears again 74. 90 ff. and the Laṅkāpura Deva mentioned 75. 130, 76. 250 ff., might be identical with the Senāpati Deva.

[3] P. *vibhajitvā nijārakkhāya.* The verb *vibhajati* seems to be used

strong intention of rescuing his generals — to turn back,
they sent him the following message: "We have fallen here 141
in the midst of Mahāraṭṭha[1] into the power of the enemy;
but our Lord has no other means of power than his extra-
ordinary courage. Even the country folk have turned away 142
from us and are on the side of the foe. But if there
are Lords of exceeding ability, then there is no doubt that 143
by uniting the ocean-girt earth under one umbrella they are
heedful of the furtherance of the laity and of the Order. We 144
to whom this boon belongs, in consequence of which we shall
have the comfort of again beholding the lotus flowers of thy 145
feet, shall be set free by the protector of the castes and of the
hermitages[2]. But (now) thou must give up thy resolve to come
hither." When the Great King heard that, the far-seeing one 146
perceived that even before his march thither ruin would ensue.
Entreated by all his dignitaries with folded hands the discern- 147
ing one turned and betook himself to Vikkamapura[3].

here in a quite peculiar meaning "to be intent upon something". The literal translation of v. 140 would be "they, wishing to cause to return the Ruler who advanced, being intent upon their own protection, sent the message . ." The meaning of the message in this: Give up the plan of rescuing us now. We know that a great king like you will finally gain the victory, and then we will be set free and again join your retinue.

[1] Cf. note to 72. 147.

[2] P. *vaṇṇānaṃ assamānaṃ ca* is here synonymous with the usual *lokasāsana*.

[3] The actions described vv. 121-147 are not easy to understand. The reason probably lies in the fact that the narrator gives as short an account as possible of a series of catastrophes which overtook Parakkamabāhu and which led to complete reversal of the situation. As regards the encirclement of Deva and Kitti in the first place, one would have expected it from the account to have taken place somewhere in hostile territory, in Rohaṇa. What does not agree with this is that the starting-point of the relief should be Jambukola, whether we understand by this Dambul, which I think the more likely, or Dambagolla (note to 70. 72) west of Elahera. The generals themselves speak in v. 141 of Mahāraṭṭha. But that is according to v. 163, a district bordering (eastwards) on the Kālavāpi, if indeed the *mahāraṭṭha-majjhe* in v. 141 altogether contains a proper name, and not an appella-

148 Now when the high dignitaries learned that the Monarch
Mānābharaṇa had come with his whole army to Pulatthina-
149 gara and again marching thence had reached the place called
Giritaṭāka[1] and other matters, they informed the King truth-
150 fully according to the facts, as they had heard them, and
also that the army had been here and there destroyed in
151 fight. They reported further it would be best to march to
Parakkamapura[2] or even to the village called Kalyāṇī[3] to
gather together the army there and then begin the war
152 again. But when the lion-king heard that he answered in
the fire of his wrath, discernible in the fume of his wrinkled
153 brow[4]: "For the fearful I have no use, they may go where
they like. Men like myself possess a great army in the
154 courage of their arms. From the King of the gods down-
wards I know none in the three worlds capable so long as I
155 am in life, of crossing the frontier of my realm. A hostile

tive "in the midst of the great province" (i. e. Rohaṇa). The final result of all the military events is clear. Parakkamabāhu is forced to give up Pulatthinagara and Rājaraṭṭha and to retire to Dakkhiṇadesa. The first halt is at Vikkamapura. The position of the town can be pretty well fixed. It is mentioned v. 263 in connection with Kyānagāma which in its turn occurs next to Maṅgalabegāma, thus not far distant from Pulatthinagara. Vikkamapura must thus have been situated in Janapada. Is it perhaps the name for the town belonging to Sīhagiri?

[1] As Giritaṭāka (now Giritala), lies about 7 miles W. N. W. of Pulatthinagara, Mānābharaṇa has thus occupied the capital advancing from E. or S. and now advances without delay against the hostile front at Vikkamapura.

[2] The building of Parakkamapura is first described later 74. 15. It was probably a case of rebuilding on an older site. Should the town be looked for at the Parakkamasamudda, the reservoir Paṇḍavāpi? See 68. 40 and note to 60. 50.

[3] Now Kelaniya at the mouth of the Kelaniganga not far from Colombo. The officers thus advise giving up the fight entirely for the time being and retiring to Dakkhiṇadesa.

[4] The reading of the MSS. gives no sense. In my edition I have followed the Col. Ed. But I should like now to suggest: the reading *bhūbhaṅgadhūmaviññeyyakopaggi paccabhās' ato.* This keeps more closely to the text of the MSS., assumes merely the change of a single letter (*v* into *s*) and gives the expected sense.

prince can force his way into the realm ruled by me as little
as a king of elephants into a lion-guarded den. Who would 156
not become a hero when my glance falls on him? If I so
will, boys who still drink milk will fight. In two or three 157
months I shall no longer permit the Ruler Mānābharaṇa to
establish himself in his own province, let alone in Rājaraṭṭha.
It is just for such an occasion which is quite hopeless that 158
the worth of the courage of the arms of heroes of my breed
holds good." In this way he made the discouraged courageous 159
by speaking a self-confident word filled with heroic spirit[1].
Then experienced in warcraft, he sent the Adhikārin Rakkha 160
and the officer (Kitti) the Ādipotthakin[2], forth to take up a
position[3] at the village of Maṅgalabegāma. Hereupon after 161
distributing dignities to people who deserved dignities, the
illustrious one, versed in the right expedients, entrusted the
Mahālekha called Rakkha and the Jīvitapotthakin Mandin, as 162
well as the two brothers, the generals, Saṅkhadhātu and Kitti,
with a great army and he, the mighty one, sent it to Pillaviṭṭhi 163
in Mahāraṭṭha which borders on the Kālavāpi tank to take
possession of it[4]. Likewise the exceeding brave (Prince) placed 164
the Māragiri Nigrodha[5] in Uddhavāpi with an army. In order 165
to carry on the war in this way in different directions he
placed a strong army with officers at various places.

Now the troops stationed in Janapada, skilled in the game 166
of war, offered battle and put to flight at the locality called
Janapada, the Mahālekha called Mahinda who had come hither 167
to fight at the command of Mānābharaṇa, so that his courage
for a renewal of the conflict was broken. To the Lord of 168
men, Parakkama, who while ever bringing forth all kinds of

[1] P. *vīrarasa*, see note to 72. 94.

[2] Cf. 72. 27 together with note.

[3] The theatre of the war is very much the same as in the operations against Gajabāhu described 70. 281 ff.

[4] For Mahāraṭṭha see note to 72. 147. The district is mentioned again twice (v. 190, 199). Pillaviṭṭhi is certainly identical with the Pilaviṭṭhika mentioned 69. 8 (see note to the passage).

[5] See note to 72. 11.

meritorious works in profusion and, like to the King of the
169 gods, enjoying diversion in divers games, sojourned in Nālandā[1], the army sent a report of the events in accord with the truth.

170 Thereupon the officers stationed in Pillaviṭṭhi with the Mahālekha Rakkha at the head[2] fought for eight days an
171 embittered battle with Buddhanāyaka[3] and the general Mahā-
172 māladeva stationed at Kālavāpi, slew many warriors, put the enemy to flight, brought Kālavāpi into their power and freed
173 it shortly from the briers (of the foe). Then carrying out the instructions of the Lord of men Parakkama, they threw up an entrenchment and remained with the army on the spot.

174 The Māragiri Nigrodha stationed at Uddhavāpi, fought
175 three times, scattered the hostile army and having fortified the monastery grove at the village called Tannaru, he took up a position there at the command of the Great King.

176 The Monarch Mānābharaṇa now granted to the Prince Mahinda a post of honour and a province of considerable
177 extent and spake to him: "Take up, marching in the direction of Moravāpi, in order to conquer Dakkhiṇadesa, thy position
178 with strong forces in Anurādhapura[4]. I will betake myself to Pallavavāla, to march in the direction of Buddhagāma[5]."
179 Thus having sent him in advance with a strong army to fair Anurādhapura, he himself took up a position again at the same place[6] in Rājaraṭṭha.

180 When the great councillors of the Great King who were stationed in Kālavāpi, learned that Prince Mahinda had betaken

[1] Nālandā was thus again Parakkama's headquarters as in the campaigns against Gajabāhu (see 70. 167, 207).

[2] See above v. 161 ff. [3] See note to 70. 296.

[4] For Moravāpi see notes to 69. 9, 70. 67. From all the passages in which it is mentioned it is clear that it was situated south of Anurādhapura and west of Kālavāpi. Mānābharaṇa's plan is evidently to turn Parakkamabāhu's left flank in order to force him to withdraw his front which threatened Pulatthinagara.

[5] See notes to 58. 43 and 66. 19.

[6] It is only later that Mānābharaṇa goes to Pallavavāla (see v. 220); thus *tatth' eva* here probably means *Giritaṭāke* (s. v. 149).

himself with large forces to Anurādhapura, they at once, in 181
order to destroy him before he had taken root, entrusted the 182
Mahālekha Rakkha and the Bhaṇḍārapotthakin Kitti[1] with
the charge there and marched themselves with army and train
to the locality called Kāṇamūla, threw up an entrenchment 183
here and took up their position here after they themselves
had left Kālavāpi. When the Great King Parakkama who 184
was skilled in expedients not to be thwarted, heard of this
undertaking and had as expert examined it, (he told the officers): "As people who do not know the country, ye should 185
not without my order, penetrate into the innermost part of
the district to take up the fight. Such a command he whose 186
commands were like those of Pākasāsana[2], far-seeing and
discerning, issued repeatedly (to the officers). But they hastened 187
thither, neglecting the command of the King and believed in
their folly that they would immediately seize Anurādhapura.
The unhappy ones who themselves discovered not the object 188
and left the King's command unheeded[3], came to the locality
named Kaṭuvandu, ignorant of the localities and without the 189
right precautions, as if desirous of tasting the effects of their
disobedience to the King's command. When they, carrying 190
out their ill-starred undertaking, had penetrated there, their
followers dispersed themselves over the various places in
Mahāraṭṭha. When the Prince Mahinda heard of the affair, 191
he held a council, surrounded them and began the combat,
and owing to the faulty concentration of the army, the Prince 192
Mahinda scattered the whole of the forces on the battlefield.
Completely beaten in this battle, the officers returned to 193
Kālavāpi remembering the neglected royal command. But the 194

[1] See note to 72. 27, as well as to 72. 196.

[2] P. *pākasāsana* = skr. *pākaśāsana* is an epithet of the god Indra. The meaning attached to the word here is probably "whose commands become ripe, i. e. are fulfilled or carried out".

[3] Verse 188 is mutilated in the MSS. as four syllables are missing. The text of the Col. Ed. differs from mine. W. translates thus: "and those among them who were not fortunate would not be advised by the king's message".

Prince (Mahinda) returned to Anurādhapura, collected in haste
195 the division of the army belonging to his province and sent
it off, as he intended taking Kālavāpi with large forces.
When the discerning Ruler (Parakkama) received tidings of
196 this, he sent in haste the Bhaṇḍārapotthakin Bhūta[1] thither
to whom he gave a considerable army consisting only of
197 skilled warriors. They all met there together and three months
198 long the valiant heroes fought bitter battles day by day. Not
neglecting the royal instructions the doughty ones fought a
hard fight and (finally) shattered the four-membered army of
199 Mahinda. They took Mahāraṭṭha which bordered on Kālavāpi
and remained at the spot awaiting the command of the King.
200 The Prince (Mahinda) made exultant by his afore mentioned
crafty fight with the people who had transgressed the King's
201 command, came on[2] himself in full armour. An officer who
was stationed at Moravāpi not neglecting the instructions of
202 the far-seeing King, distributed his followers on both sides of
the road and as soon as the hostile army were completely
203 inside (the ambush) he surrounded it on all sides, slew while
204 delivering a terrific action, numerous high officers, vanquished
the Prince and sent many heads of enemies slain on the battle-
field to the King.

205 Hereupon King Parakkamabāhu, a man of terrible courage,
gathered together[3] his army which was distributed in divers
206 places, and in order to drive the Ruler Mānābharaṇa out of
Rājaraṭṭha, he placed the Mahālekha called Rakkha, the
207 Kammanāyaka Añjana[4] and the Ādipotthakin Kitti at Kyāna-
gāma and sent the Adhikārin Rakkha to Maṅgalabegāma.

[1] The title *bhaṇḍārapotthakin* is also borne by Kitti. See 72. 182 together with the note to 72. 27.

[2] As the mention of Moravāpi shows, we have to do here with Mahinda's main thrust against Dakkhiṇadesa announced in v. 177.

[3] By the victory at Moravāpi Parakkamabāhu has done away with the pressure on his left wing (cf. note to v. 177) and can now undertake his action against Pulatthinagara. As to the localities see 70. 281 ff.

[4] See note to 72. 58.

Then he sent his train of hunters, robbers[1] and the like who 208
were skilled in wandering by night in the wildernesses of
forest and mountain, and had many people in divers places 209
slain[2] by them by night and day. Like birds shut up in a
cage[3] the dwellers in Pulatthinagara for long dared not even 210
by day leave their houses and go outside of the gate when
they wanted supplies of water and wood. For the work for 211
which they needed wood each robbed his house completely of
its roof[4] and so destroyed it. In the shops here and there 212
on the outskirts of the town the various businesses were
completely given up. As circulation in all the approaches to 213
the town had been stopped by the King, the whole town
trembled with excitement. Great harassment he caused to the 214
King Mānābharaṇa in that he vexed the town even to the
royal castle. In his great distress the Ruler Mānābharaṇa 215
whose heart was sore weighted with cares, reflected thus:
"If I would betake myself to my province of Rohaṇa the 216
inhabitants of Rājaraṭṭha who are there would not permit me
to go thither, to show their affection for the Sovereign 217
Parakkama, if by my taking flight they discover my weakness.
But if I think it is right for me to stay here, that too for 218
me is hard, since day and night I must suffer such hardships.
The best thing for me is to fight a decisive battle with the 219
foe and to suffer the fortune or misfortune that issues from
it." After putting his large four-membered army in fighting 220
trim, he betook himself, his loins girt for combat, to Pallava-
vāla[5]. When thereupon King Parakkamabāhu, who possessed 221

[1] These were probably Vāddas who were in the king's retinue. *Kirāta* "hunter" is also used in Skr. to describe savage mountain tribes.

[2] Verses 205-214 form a single sentence which I have split up in the translation into its component parts. The principal verb is *akāsi pīḷaṃ* in 214 which governs directly three "that" sentences with *yathā* 1) v. 209 c-211, 2) v. 212, 3) v. 213. Then to *akāsi* belongs *ghātayanto* in v. 209 a and subordinate are the various gerunds in vv. 205-208.

[3] The same simile in 70. 292.

[4] Lit.: "they made it grassless", i. e. they turned the grass which served as roof into fuel and so ruined the whole house.

[5] See above v. 178.

the courage of a lion, and (yet) was wont to act with reflec-
222 tion, heard of all these events, he sent off the Laṅkāpura,
the two brothers, the generals, and the Lokagalla[1], after
223 instructing them in divers plans of war, in three directions,
as he, the prudent one, intended to separate[2] the hostile army
224 that was marching hither from that direction. They betook
themselves with large forces thither and spent a month de-
225 livering day by day a sharp action. In his double distress
the Ruler Mānābharaṇa reflected thus: "I have left my
entrenched camp and have come hither, desirous of fighting.
226 There is no breathing freely for me; my misfortune is deep-
227 rooted and grows at its pleasure day and night. Since I have
come hither without tasting the good and the evil that were
my lot in that wilderness[3], I deserve this misfortune hard to
228 be borne. And an attempt to come thither[4] again? That is
also hard to carry out, since hostile forces are posted at dif-
229 ferent places on the main road. Here in this place where
we are so confined, I may not tarry, since the hostile army
230 is marching from every side towards the centre. I will in-
quire of people well acquainted with this part and will march
231 forth by some little known way which they tell me of." Thus
having asked the inhabitants be betook himself by a way
232 told him by them to the village of Konduruva[5]. Thereupon
the Adhikārin Rakkha who, carrying out the command of the
Great King, had taken up a position at the village named
233 Mihiraṇabibbila, had stakes made like spearpoints and had
them bound together driven into the ground in such a way
234 that they were not even to be shaken by elephants. Then

[1] The Laṅkāpura is Kaḍakkuḍa (72. 39). Who is meant by the Lokagalla we do not know, but the word occurs also as title in 75. 138.

[2] P. *vimukhaṃ kātukāmo.* I take *vimukha* here in the meaning of "turned in different directions".

[3] By the "wilderness" (*vana*) he means his former country, Rohaṇa with which he ought to have been satisfied.

[4] Namely to Rohaṇa.

[5] There is a Koṇduruveva S. W. of Giritale, W. S. W. of Pulatthinagara.

outside (of these) he had strong stakes of still greater size
driven in, so that there was no gap and had them interwoven
with wattle-work of branches. Then in the middle (between 235
the two rows of stakes) he had a trench dug twenty to thirty
cubits broad for a distance of a hundred lengths of a man[1].
There he placed sharpened stakes and[2] thorns and also in 236
the ground lying outside he had sharpened sticks driven in
and a hedge of thorns put up, tightly closed and unbroken 237
and between these a trench dug as before. There also he 238
placed sharpened sticks and thorns and outside of the hedge
he had a trench dug which reached to the underground
water[3]. There also he again placed pointed stakes and thorns 239
and outside of the trench he had the big forest felled at a
blow over a tract two or three bowshots in extent, as well 240
as great pits dug beyond this tract on the robber paths[4].
Here again he placed everywhere sharp thorns, had them 241
covered on all sides with sand and withered leaves, and pre- 242
pared (everything) in such a way that at first glance it
looked like a passable road. Then in order to destroy without
remnant the hostile army when it approached this way, he 243
had robber paths made in every direction and posted sharp
shooting archers on them. In the middle of the stockade he 244
built a structure[5] of four storeys and distributed archers about
it at divers places. But in order to entice hither the hostile 245
army (from where it was marching), he sent out two or three
thousand archers who understood shooting by the flash of

[1] The "cubit" (*ratana*) equals 17. 82 inches. Thus the breadth was about 30 to 45 ft. a "man's length" (*porisa*) is about five cubits, that is 89. 10 in. So the length of the trench measured 740 to 745 ft.

[2] I should now prefer the reading *ca* instead of *va*. Also in what follows the stakes always appear a l o n g w i t h the thorns. It often happens in the Cūlavs. that *ca* is not enclitic, but stands between the objects which it connects. Cf. v. 238 b.

[3] Thus I interpret *odakantika*. We must assume that it is derived from a skr. *udakānta*, *audakāntika*. W's view is probably the same.

[4] What is meant are the footpaths leading through the wilderness.

[5] P. *pāsāda*. The passage is characteristic of the general meaning of "structure" given to the word *pāsāda*.

246 lightning[1]. Now when amid a rain of arrows pouring from
all sides the irresistible, terrible hostile army approached,
247 they cunningly feigned as if they had been routed by it and
turned back. When then the others approached in pursuit
248 of them, then suddenly skilled warriors, doughty soldiers,
experienced in the war game, a thousand in number like
249 singly marching elephants[2], made a dash at them and fought
an action, appearing in front of the hostile forces like the
250 army of King Yama[3]. A hail of arrows began to rain on
all sides and the people who stood on the structure began
251 to shoot at those who were on the ground. There followed
a hail[4] of stones which hurled from engines, flew[5] here and
252 there vast in size. From the burning, sharp-pointed[6] bamboo

[1] P. *akkhanavedhino.* Cf. also JāCo. III. 322[22], V. 129[17]. I accept the explanation in JāCo. II. 91[11]. H. Kern, Toevoegselen op't Woordenboek van Childers I. 69, compares skr. *ākhaṇa* "target". This seems to me too colourless. Moreover Mhvs. 23. 86 distinguishes the *saddavedhī*, "who shoots according to the sound" (without seeing the mark), the *vālavedhī* "who hits a hair" and the *vijjuvedhī* "who shoots by the gleam of the lightning". To these three categories JāCo. V. 129[17] adds that of the *saravedhino* who can shoot a second arrow on to the first one already sticking in the target. The art is still practised in India. I know a young Indian who claims to be both a *vālavedhī* and a *saddavedhī*.

[2] I read *paccekahatthino.* What is meant are the solitary or rogue elephants who are known for attacking furiously and are therefore much dreaded. The word is formed on the *paccekabuddha* model.

[3] The god of death. In the whole section from v. 232 to v. 249 *vattesuṃ (samaraṃ)* in 249 is the first and only finite verb. We have thus to do with a single sentence. The construction meanwhile is not correct. The subject changes *Rakkhādhikārī* in 232 and *vīrā subhaṭā* in 248. An alteration of *pesetvā* (246) into *pesesi* would get over the difficulty. I dare not suggest it however, as I believe that irregular sentences with accumulated gerunds are typical of the compiler's style. Cf. note to 72. 128.

[4] Lit. "a spreading out" (a broad throwing).

[5] P. *pharantānaṃ.* The verb *phar* is a favourite one for expressing the flashing of the lightning.

[6] Indian dictionaries give *tikṣṇa* "sharp", "pointed" as the meaning of *caṇḍa.*

rods which cut into single pieces were hurled[1] down there
spread an unbearable heat. With many glowing iron rods 253
which were tied to strings and which they drew up again,
they performed seven days long their terrible deeds. Thus 254
the discerning great dignitaries of the Great King carried on
the combat in accordance with the instruction of their King.
Seized by fear the army of the foe dispersed at once like the 255
wave-crowned flood[2] when it breaks on the ocean's shore.
Thus the army with the Monarch were wiped out on the battle- 256
field as the stars with the moon at the rising of the dawn.

Then at Rajatakedāra day by day for six months in bitter 257
fight they weakened the forces of the foe. The Monarch 258
Mānābharaṇa set about building a stronghold for his sojourn[3]
by making a stockade of thorns. When King Parakkamabāhu, 259
the energetic, the exceeding wise, the lotus-eyed, in his vigi-
lance heard of this proceeding, he thought in his heart: 260
"This plan is clever. If he now sets about building a strong-
hold he must, methinks, as his army is weakened, be about 261
to retire. Now is the right moment to get Mānābharaṇa
entirely into one's power. I also must march thither and it 262
is well if I march, to march in such manner that he notices
nothing, else he will take flight." With this resolve he left 263
Vikkamapura[4] and while feigning that he was going to the
chase, he betook himself to Kyānagāma accompanied by many 264
skilful musicians, who made music on the lute and the flute.
While now the wise Ruler versed in moods, sojourned like 265
Vāsava[5] in that village, he sent a message to the Adhikārin
Rakkha to put his division of the army with all speed in 266
fighting trim and to hold a war festival with the officer of

[1] P. *pavīta*; cf. skr. *pravīta*.

[2] To supplement *kallolamālinī* "bearing waves as wreaths" one must take *vāhinī* as a substantive of more general meaning "flood". *Vāhinī* it should be remembered, generally denotes "river".

[3] I take *sa* in *sasaṃnivesaṃ* as equivalent to the skr. *sva*. W. translates "with an encampment".

[4] The headquarters of Parakkamabāhu, see 72. 147 and note.

[5] A name of the god Indra.

267 King Māṇābharaṇa, Buddhanāyaka by name[1]. When the
discerning Adhikārin had hearkened carefully to all of the
message sent, he at once carrying out the order of the Great
268 King put his army in readiness, and sent the war-practised
(host) forth, which was like to a whirlwind when it scatters
269 cotton, namely the enemy. The four-membered army marched
to Rajatakedāra, delivered there till sunset a bitter action,
270 slew Buddhanāyaka and the other officers, put the rest of the
271 army to flight and stayed the night on the spot. When the
Sovereign Parakkamabāhu heard of this event the prudent
272 one betook himself to the village called Mihiraṇabibbila[2]. He
had fetched the Laṅkāpura Kaḍakkuḍa who was endowed
with extraordinary courage, and the two brothers, the generals:
273 "King Māṇābharaṇa will certainly to-day in the night take
274 flight, his heart swayed by great fear; betake yourselves to
him on his way and cut off his flight", such was the order
275 given them by the discerning (king). While the heavens
without ceasing drizzled and rained, while thickest darkness
276 held sway, these marched in black night, but were not able
to overtake the Monarch Māṇābharaṇa on the way who was
fleeing tortured by dread.

277 The Monarch Māṇābharaṇa had at that time thought thus:
278 "In the stronghold occupied to-day by the hostile army, a
terrible noise can be heard like the raging of the vast ocean.
279 The hostile king has, methinks, entered the fort. If instead
of fleeing, I remain here during the night, to-morrow I shall
280 certainly be delivered helplessly into his hands. Without lett-
ing any single one of all my companions know it, I must
281 leave this place." Racked by fear, with such thoughts he
left his own children in the lurch and while heavy rain
282 streamed down and thick darkness reigned, he hastened hither
and thither, every now and again falling into a deep pit,
stumbling amid the undergrowth of the forest, ever and anon
283 starting with fear his heart filled with terror, to the Mahā-

[1] See note to 70. 296, as well as below v. 270.

[2] Cf. above v. 232.

vālukagaṅgā. But fearing that if he fled by a well known
ford, the foe pursuing might take him alive, he crossed the 284
river with difficulty at some unknown ford and regained 285
courage for a moment. But as he had exceeding fear of the
able-bodied inhabitants of the country, he wandered in dis- 286
guise full of terror from village to village and so fleeing came
to his own province stripped of everything[1].

When the warriors of the Great King Parakkamabāhu 287
who were posted at divers places, noticed that King Mānābharaṇa
had departed, then thousands of them joyfully waved their 288
garments[2], they lit around hundreds of thousands of torches,
and while taking the lives of many thousands of warriors, 289
they clapped their hands, shouted with joy, jumped about,
and broke at one swoop from all sides into the great entrench- 290
ment which King Mānābharaṇa had occupied, captured alive 291
the Prince called Sirivallabha who had been left behind and
other great dignitaries, seized the rich treasures scattered here 292
and there of the hostile king, elephants and horses, equipment
and an array of weapons. Having made the necessary ar- 293
rangements for their custody, they all set off in pursuit of the
Ruler Mānābharaṇa, reached in the shortest (possible) time the 294
Mahāvālukagaṅgā, cut to pieces there also a hostile army
down to the last man[3], and having seen to it that the whole 295
river carried[4] along with it naught but flesh and blood, they
were fain to press on farther, resolved not to turn back before
they had captured the Ruler Mānābharaṇa even if they had 296
to march to the ocean[5]. But Parakkamabāhu of the strength-

[1] P. *gativivajjito*. For the meaning of skr. *gati* "resource" s. BR. s. v. nr. 6. W's translation "undisguised" (in contrast to *aññātavesena* in pāda a) is certainly wrong.

[2] Lit. "they instituted thousands of wavings of garments". *Celukkhepa* signifies expression of approval. See JāCo. II. 90[1]; III. 292[12]; Mhvs. 15, App. B, 7.

[3] P. *aparicchinaṃ*, lit. unlimited, unrestricted, complete.

[4] Pun on *vāhinī* with threefold meaning 1) army (294 d), 2) river (295 a), 3) adj. for "carrying with it" (295 b).

[5] The past part. *nikkhantā* takes the place of a finite verb.

297 defying arms, whose commands were scarce to be evaded, gave
them the order not to cross to the other bank of the stream,
298 and thus made them turn back. Thereupon King Parakkama-
bāhu, the unvanquished sovereign, put on all his ornaments
299 and surrounded by his army, with Prince Sirivallabha in front,
he filling the heavens with great rejoicings of victory, enter-
300 ed the fair city of Pulatthinagara, even as the King of the
gods (entered) the city of the gods after his victory in the
battle with the asuras[1].

301 Now the Monarch Mānābharaṇa by reason of a disease
caused by his fear of Prince Parakkama had come to the end
302 of his life force. As he lay there on his bed, near to death,
enmeshed in misery amongst his wives who wailed with out-
303 spread arms, he had Prince Kittisirimegha and yet other high
304 dignitaries fetched and spake these words: "Rich treasures,
that sacrificed to the venerable Tooth Relic and to the sacred
305 Alms-bowl by believing sons of good family, and besides these
divers villages belonging to the bhikkhu order have I seized
306 and destroyed, swayed by the lust for kingly power. Now I
lie on that bed from which there is no rising. Whence shall
I find salvation from hell[2], if by death I unwillingly quit
307 this world. Go thou, without ruining thyself as I (have ruined)
myself, to the Sovereign Parakkama, do that which he orders
308 thee and live devoted to him as he shall direct thee." After
309 these words he wept more distressfully and entered the dwell-
ing of god Yama difficult of approach, as if he wished to
betake himself to a territory which lay not in the realm of
the good soldiers of the Great King Parakkama.

[1] In the Devanagala inscription, line 13/14 Parakkamabāhu mentions his war with Gajabāhu. After this name an illegible space of about seven akkharas is following, and then we read *dedchā* (instead of *dedenā ha*) *yuddha koṭa* "having made war with the two [princes] Gajabāhu and ...." It is very probable that we have to supply after *Gajabāhu* the name of *Mānābharaṇa*. See H. C. P. Bell, Report on the Kégalla District (1892), p. 74-5.

[2] There are four *apāyā* or possibilities of rebirth for the sinner — 1) in hell, 2) as animal, 3) in the world of ghosts, 4) in the world of demons.

When King Parakkamabāhu who had captivated all those of good disposition without exception, heard that King Mānābharaṇa was dead, he had the Prince Kittisirimegha fetched thence. 310
Then the great dignitaries met together and with clasped hands prayed the Ruler to celebrate the festival of the king's consecration[1]. 311
At a favourable moment and under a lucky star the Ruler (now) without rivals held the happy festival of the coronation. 312
The loud noise of the divers kinds of drums was then terrible as the raging of the ocean when lashed by the storm wind of the destruction of the world. 313
Elephants equipped with gilded armour made the royal road look as if it were traversed by lightning-flashing cloud mountains. 314
The whole town in which the colours of the horses[2] gave rise, as it were to waves, was in agitation like the ocean. 315
By the variegated umbrellas and wreaths and the rows of golden flags the heavens were hid as it were, on all sides. 316
Garments were shaken and fingers snapped[3], the inhabitants of the town sent forth the cry: Live (o King)! live! 317
Covered with arches of bananas and thickly studded with jars and wreaths the whole universe consisted of a mass of festivals[4]. 318
Songs of praise were heard hymned by many hundreds of singers and the smoke of (kindled) aloe wood filled the firmament. 319
Clad in many-coloured garments, adorned with divers ornaments[5] and bearing sundry weapons in their hands, 320
practised warriors strutted around here and there with well-rounded limbs goodly to look at with their heroic forms, like 321

[1] Cf. above 71. 19, in which the first consecration as king is described, the effect of which seems to have disappeared, since Parakkamabāhu had for a time to evacuate Rājaraṭṭha and Pulatthinagara.

[2] Pun on *turaṅga, raṅga, taraṅga.* The dark-coloured horses are like the waves, the light-coloured ones their crowns of foam.

[3] Lit.: "The shaking of clothes took place (see note to 72. 288) and finger-snapping took place".

[4] P. *nekamaṅgalaṃ* (*āsi*). If the reading *sakalan-tv-ekamaṅgalaṃ* could be reconciled with the MSS. the sense, undoubtedly good, would be: the universe was a single, vast festival.

[5] The *ābharaṇāni* "ornaments" were bestowed on them by the king for their bravery, corresponding to our medals.

322 rutting elephants. The many thousands of archers with their
bows in their hand made it look as if the army of the gods
323 trod the earth. Filled with hundreds of state chariots[1] of
gold, jewels and pearls the town looked like the starry firma-
324 ment. While the mighty King whose eye was large as a
lotus flower, thus performed a long series of marvellous things,
325 he ascended himself, adorned with a wealth of ornament, to
the golden baldachin that rested on a couple of elephants
326 covered with golden cloths, wearing on his head a diadem
sparkling with the brilliance of its jewels, like to the eastern
327 mountain when it bears the rising sun, vanquishing the
fairness of the spring by the power of his own fairness and
making moist the eyes of the women in the town by the
328 water of their tears of joy. Thus beamed on by auspicious
signs, after he had encircled the town with his right side
turned towards it, he entered like unto the thousand-eyed
(Indra) into the beautiful royal palace.

329 While thus as ruler of the middle world[2], he filled the chief and the intermediary regions of the heavens with festive glory, King Parakkamabāhu, the excellent ruler of the universe, carried out the second consecration as king in the second year (of his reign).

Here ends the seventy-second chapter, called "The Description of the festival of the Royal Consecration", in the Mahāvaṃsa, compiled for the serene joy and emotion of the pious.

[1] P. *vimāna.* I do not think that the word means "palace" here, but rather that it is equivalent to *ratha* (cf. PTS. P. D. s. v. *vimāna* with detailed explanation of the term). What is meant are the chariots taking part in the processions with their sparkling ornaments of gold and precious stones.

[2] The King is here made an equal of the four (or eight) lokapālā, the rulers of the heavenly regions of whom he appears as the central figure.

Additions and Corrections

(Ed. = edition, Tr. = translation)

37. 79 Ed. Put the whole verse between marks of suspension. It is a parenthesis.

37. 103 Ed. Put: after ratanamaṇḍapaṃ.

37. 114 Ed. Read: »nāgo rogīti nicchayaṃ«.

37. 202 Ed. We have probably to read: cātuddasiṃ pañcadasiṃ yā ca pakkhassa aṭṭhamī.

37. 206 Ed. Read: coraṃ rattiyam, uggate &c.

38. 3 Ed. Read: chattagāhakajantuno.

38. 29 Ed. Read: cuto, putto Parindo pi tatiye, tassa bhātuko &c.

38. 65 Ed. I propose to read: Akāsi paṭimāgehe Bahumaṅgalacetiye | bodhisatte ca, tatthāpi Kālaselassa satthuno || &c.

38. 68 Tr. Add in the note: It is however probable that in the Mahāvaṃsa not the Buddhist yojana but the common Indian yojana is meant which has the double length (a little more than 9 miles). See Parker, Ancient Ceylon, p. 255 f.

38. 79 Ed. Expunge the ? after nidassitaṃ and put it after samattho.

38. 88 Ed. Read: °kule instead of °kūle.

41. 33 Ed. Read: Puratthimaṃ instead of pur°.

41. 82 Ed. Read: gahetvā khipi; tīh' evaṃ aṅgulīhi sa taṃ chupi.

41. 96 Ed. Read: Uttare instead of utt°.

42. 67 Tr. Add in the note: The Giritaṭa is the present Giritalaveva, and the Gaṅgātaṭa the present Kantalai lake. Cf. the notes to 70, 286, 312.

44. 56 Ed. Read: Janapadaṃ instead of jan°.

44. 71 Ed. Read: Uttaraṃ inst. of utt°.

44. 90 Ed. Read: sakkā hantuṃ ti dārakaṃ«.

47. 66 Ed. Read on p. 89[2]: tatth' eva instead of tath' eva.

48. 66 Tr. Add in note 4, line 8 after °gehāni: (Cf. Ceylon Journal of Science I, p. 145 ff.).

49. 17 f. Ed. Read: paṭimāyo ca kārayi || pāsāde cetiye c'eva vihāre ca anappake.

49. 78 Ed. Expunge the full stop after avalokiya.

49.81 Ed. Expunge the comma after sādhukaṃ.

50.34 Ed. Read: Pāsāde Ratane sabbasovaṇṇaṃ &c.

50.48 Ed. Read: 'samo instead of samo.

51.88 Ed. Read: Kuṭṭhaka° instead of Tuṭṭhaka°.

54.57 Ed. Read: rājaṃ instead of rājā.

59. 2 Ed. Read: »Abhisekamaṅgalatthaṃ pāsādādiṃ anekakaṃ kiccaṃ &c.

59.49 Ed. Read: Sundarivhaṃ instead of Sunārivhaṃ.

61. 4 Ed. Read: 'khilā instead of khilā.

61.36 Ed. We have probably to read Ariyadesīso.

61.40 Ed. Read: saṃgāmaṃ tena rājinā.

61.53 Ed. Read: te 'khīṇatosā instead of te khīṇa°.

65. 6 Ed. Read: Paṭiladdha° instead of Patiladdha°.

66.26 Ed. Read: kumāraṃ instead of kuṃāraṃ.

66.59 Ed. I propose reading ten' ato instead of te tato.

66.80 Ed. Read: Ranamburaṃ instead of Ratamb°.

66.143 Ed. Read: °opāya? instead of °opaya°.

70.54 Ed. Read: Rājaraṭṭhaṃ instead of rāja°.

70.98 Ed. Read: Ambavanaṃ instead of Ambuv°.

70.103 Ed. Read: Janapadaṃ instead of jana°.

70.112 and 120 Ed. Read: gaṅgā° instead of Gaṅgā°.

70.181 Ed. Read: vasī karita° instead of vasīkarita°.

72.58 Ed. Read: Ārakkha° instead of ārakkha°.

72.106 Ed. Expunge the » « before and after sāvadhāranaṃ.

72.121-2 Ed. Put: at the end of v. 121 and » at the beginning of v. 122.

72.127 Ed. Expunge » before sakalārātivāhinī.

72.170 Ed. Read Kālavāpiyaṃ instead of Kāḷa°.

Genealogical Tables

(See J. Still, Index to the **Mahawansa**, p. 79 ff.; Wickremasinghe, EZ. I, p. 184, II, p. 58)

I

From Sirimeghavaṇṇa to the Chattaggāhaka

Mahāsena

1. Sirimeghavaṇṇa 37. 53 — brother? 37. 100

2. Jeṭṭhatissa II 37. 100 (son of brother?)

3. Buddhadāsa 37. 105

4. Upatissa I 37. 179 — 5. Mahānāma 37. 209

6. Sotthisena 38. 1, 2 — Saṃghā married to the 7. Chattaggāhaka 38. 3

8. Mittasena to 14. Pīṭhiya 38. 4—34

II

From Dhātusena to Kittisirimegha

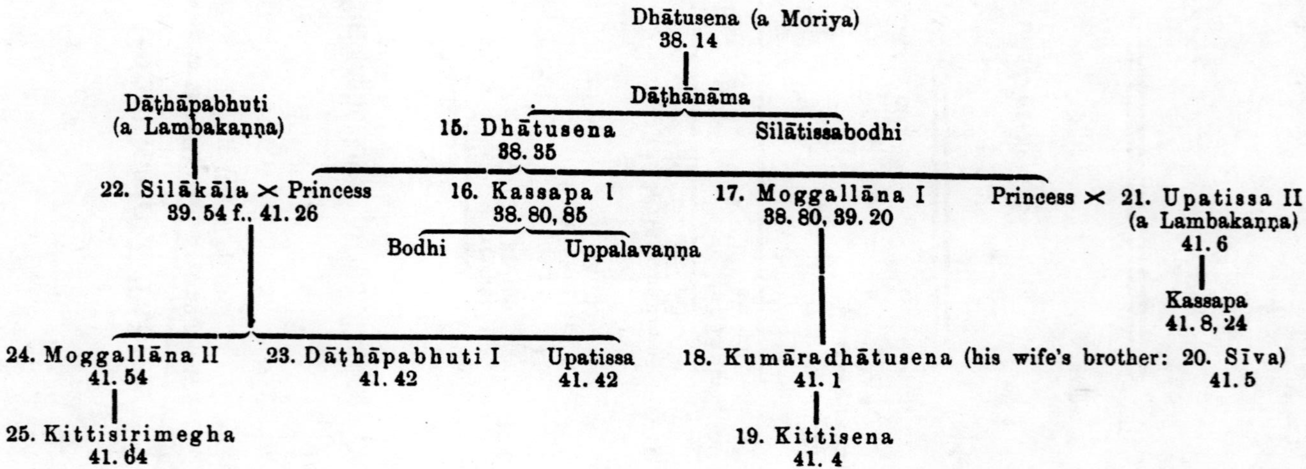

III[a]

From Mahānāga to Aggabodhi II

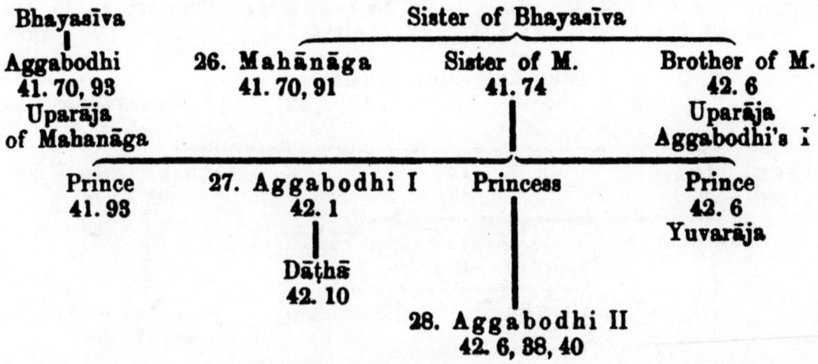

III[b]

Samghatissa and his successor

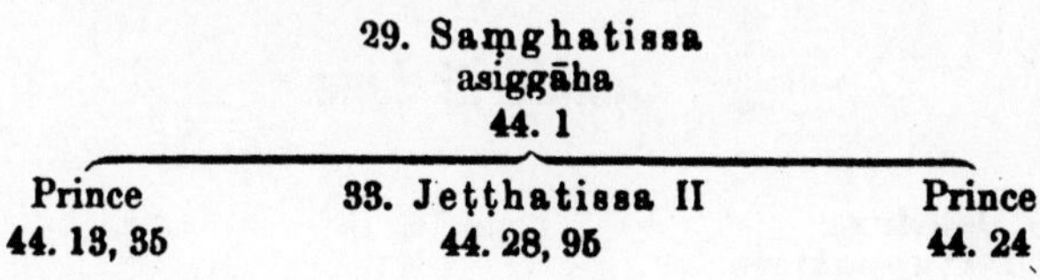

IV

From Silāmeghavaṇṇa to Udaya I

Senāpati of (29) Saṃghatissa

31. Silāmeghavaṇṇa Asiggāha[1]
44. 8, 65

Mahātissa of Rohaṇ
45. 38

32. Aggabodhi III SSB.[2]
44. 83, 118

Māna
44. 123

35. Kassapa II
44, 124, 137, 144

Princess × 36. Dappul
45. 36, 80

Mānaka? = 41. Mānavamma
45. 6 47. 1, 62

Mānavamma? = Mān
45. 52 45. 8, 1

42. Aggabodhi V
48. 1

43. Kassapa III
48. 20

44. Mahinda I ādipāda
48. 26

Princess

45. Aggabodhi VI SM.
48. 42

47. Mahinda II
48. 76

Saṃghā (2)
48. 54

46. Aggabodhi VII
48. 39, 68

Dappula (2)
48. 90, 117

48. Udaya I
49. 1

Mahinda
48. 69, 75

[1] His predecessor was 30. Moggallāna III., Senāpati of Aggabodhi II (44. 2,

[2] His successors were 33. Jeṭṭhatissa II and 34. Dāṭhopatissa I (s. III[b],

V

Collateral Line

Dāṭhāsiva
= 34. Dāṭhopatissa I
44. 88, 128

Sister of D.

Hatthadāṭha
= 37. Dāṭhopatissa II
44. 154; 45. 22

38. Aggabodhi IV SSB.[1]
46. 1

[1] His successors were 39. Datta (46. 41) and 40. Hatthadāṭha (46. 45). T
41. Mānavamma (see IV) ascends the throne.

VI

From Udaya I to Sena II

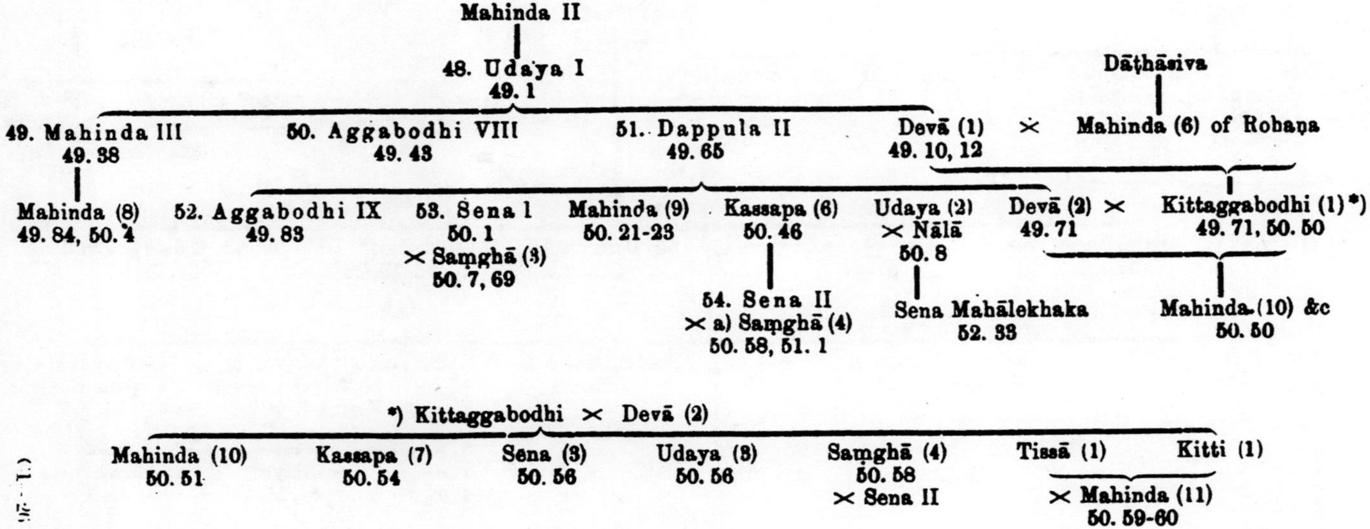

VII

From Sena II to Vikkamabahu I

(Sena I) Kassapa (6)

54. Sena II SSB. 50. 48, 51. 1 × Saṃghā (4)
Mahinda (11) 50. 59, 51. 7, 68 × a) Tissā (1), 50. 60, 51. 15; b) Kitti (1) 50. 60, 51, 16
55. Udaya II × Tissā (2) 51. 94
56. Kassapa IV × Tissā (3) 52. 1

57. Kassapa V SMV. (von a) × a) Saṃghā (5), 51. 18; b) Senā (2) 51. 98; c) Devā (3), 52. 64; d) Rājinī 52. 67
58. Dappula III 53. 1
59. Dappula IV (von b) 53. 4
Senā (2) 51. 93
Tissā (2) 51. 93

Saṃghā (5) (von a) 51. 18
Kittaggabodhi (von b) 51. 94
60. Udaya III 53. 18
61. Sena III 53. 13, 28
62. Udaya IV (?) 53. 28, 39

Mahinda (12) (von a)?) 51. 99
63. Sena IV (von a)?) 53. 39, 54. 1
Tissā (3) 52. 2
Siddhattha (von d) 52. 68
Sakkasenāpati (von c) 52. 52 × Vajirā 52. 62
64. Mahinda IV (von c) 54. 1, 7 × Kitti (2) 54. 50

65. Sena V 54. 57
Udaya 54. 58
66. Mahinda V 55. 1

67. Vikkamabāhu I (Kassapa 55. 10) 56. 1

VIII

From Vikkamabāhu I to Vijayabāhu I

Brother of Kitti — Kitti × Mahinda IV

Mahinda V

Devalā 57. 27 — Lokitā 57. 27 × Kassapa 57. 28 (55. 10) = 67. Vikkamabāhu I 56. 1

Bodhi × Buddhā
aus dem Geschlecht des Dāṭhopatissa

Lokitā 57. 41 × . . . . × Moggallāna 57. 29, 41, 42 — Loka 57. 29

Kitti = 74. Vijayabāhu I[1] — Mittā — Mahinda — Rakkhita

[1] Kings between Vikkamabāhu I and Vijayabāhu I were 68. Kitti, 69. Mahālānakitti, 70. Vikkamapaṇḍu, 71. Jagatīpāla, 72. Parakkamapaṇḍu I, 73. Loka (56. 7—57. 2).

IX

Vijayabāhu's I Family

74. Vijayabāhu I

× a) 1. Līlāvatī 59. 25

Yasodharā × Vīravamma 59. 27

2. Līlāvatī 59. 28 × Vikkamabāhu II 59. 50

Sugalā 59. 28 × 1. Sirivallabha 59. 45

× b) Tilokasundarī 59. 29

a) Subhaddā × Vīrabāhu 59. 43
b) Sumittā × Jayabāhu 59. 43
c) Lokanāthā × Kittisirimegha 59. 44
d) Ratanāvatī × 1. Mānābharaṇa 59. 44
e) Rūpavatī died 59. 45
f) Vikkamabāhu II

× a. Sundarī 59. 49 — × b. Līlāvatī 59. 50

X

Descent of Parakkamabāhu I

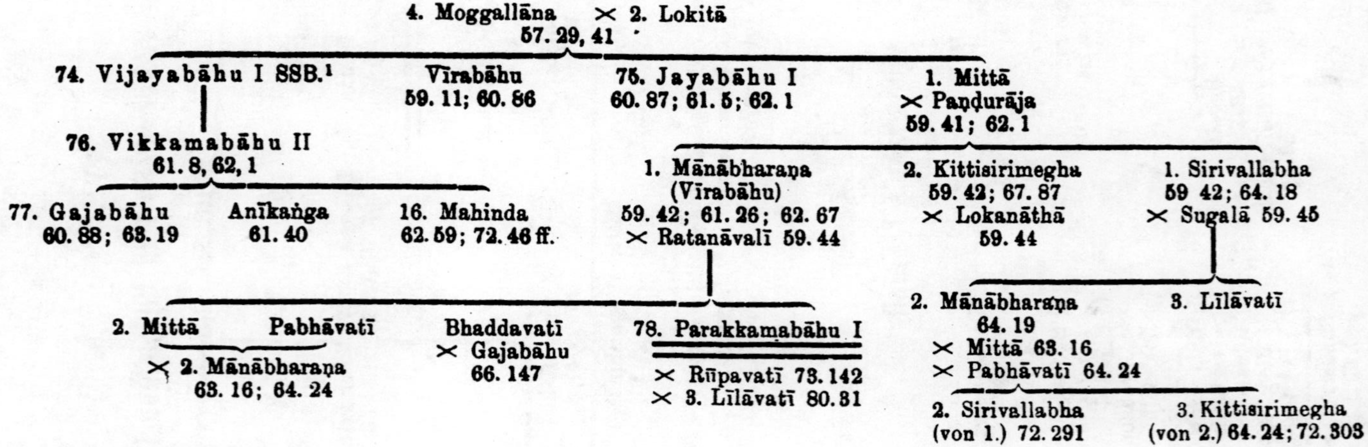

[1] See Table IX

Supplementary Notes

1) Introduction, p. XXII. Mr. A. M. Hocart, C. J. Sc. G. II, p. 34 refers to the part played by the sister's son in Ancient Germany, according to Tacitus, Germania 20: Sororum filiis idem apud avunculum qui apud patrem honor. Quidam sanctiorem artioremque hunc nexum sanguinis arbitrantur. "The sister's son is in as great honour with the uncle as with the father. Some consider this tie of blood more sacred and closer."

2) Introduction, p. XXV ff. I wish to direct the reader's attention to the inscriptions on the pillars of King Nissaṅka Malla's "Council Chamber" in Polonnaruva. They supply us with useful information as to the highest officials and the constituent members of the royal council at the time of that king. At the king's right hand there sat 1) the *mahādipāda*, 2) the *ādipādas*, 3) the *senāpati*, 4) the *adhikāras* (principle chiefs), 5) the Chief Secretary (*mahālekha*); — and on his left side 1) the *maṇḍalikas* (governors of the provinces), 2) the eighty four (chiefs of smaller districts), 3) the heads of the merchants. — The number 84 exactly corresponds to the 84 *sāmantā* appointed by Parakkamabāhu in Dakkhiṇadesa, Mhvs. 69. 16. — See H. W. Codrington, JRAS. C. Br. XXIX, Nr. 77, 1924, p. 304 ff.; the same, HC. p. 68.

3) 37. 218 (p. 22, n. 4) The Dhūmarakkha is situated on the right bank — not left bank — of the Mahaveliganga. It is, no doubt, identical with the Dimbulāgala-kanda, the so-called "Gunner's Quoin", near Mahagantota (ancient Kacchakatittha), E. of Polonnaruva. In my Transl. of the Mahāvaṃsa, p. 72, n. 1 and p. 289—90 must be corrected accordingly. H. Storey, C. A. L. R. III. 3, p. 229.

4) 53. 30. For the daily ritual in the Dalada-Maligava, Kandy, see Arthur A. Perera, C. A. L. R. VI. 2, p. 67 f.

5) For the identification of the topographical names in ch. 66 &c. I refer also to H. Storey, Parákrama Báhu the Great, C. A. L. R. VII. 1, p. 17 ff.

List of Abbreviations

A. = Aṅguttara Nikāya (ed. PTS.).
Abhp. = Abhidhānappadīpikā.
AIC. = Ed. Müller, Ancient Inscriptions of Ceylon, 1883.
Ann. Rep. = Annual Report.
ASC. = Archaeological Survey of Ceylon.
BR. = Böhtlingk und Roth, Sanskrit Wörterbuch.
C. A. L. R. = Ceylon Antiquary and Literary Register.
C. J. Sc. G. = Ceylon Journal of Science, Sect. G.
Col. Ed. = Colombo Edition of the "Mahawansa from the thirty-seventh Chapter", 1877.
D. = Dīgha Nikāya (ed. PTS.)
Dh. = Dhammapada (ed. PTS.)
DhCo. = Dhammapada Commentary (ed. PTS.)
EI. = Epigraphia Indica.
EZ. = Epigraphia Zeylanica (ed. Wickremasinghe).
HC. = H. W. Codrington, A Short History of Ceylon, 1926.
Jā. = Jātaka.
JāCo. = The Jātaka together with its Commentary, ed. Fausböll, 1877 ff.
JAs. = Journal Asiatique.
JPTS. = Journal of the Pali Text Society.
JRAS. = Journal of the Royal Asiatic Society.
JRAS. C. Br. = Journ. Roy. As. Soc., Ceylon Branch.
Kh. = Khuddaka Pāṭha, together with its Commentary, ed. Helmer Smith (PTS.), 1915.
LSI. = Linguistic Survey of India (Sir George Grierson).
M. = Majjhima Nikāya (ed. PTS.)
Mem. = Memoirs (of the ASC.)
Mhbh. = Mahābhārata.
Mhvs. = Mahāvaṃsa.
Milp. = Milindapañha ed. Trenckner, 1880.
Nett. = Nettipakaraṇa (ed. PTS.)
Nik.-s. = Nikāyasaṅgraha (ed. Wickremasinghe).
P. = Pāli.
Pieris 1 = Ceylon, the Portuguese Era, by P. E. Pieris, 2 Bde. 1913—4.
Pieris 2 = Ceylon and the Portuguese 1505—1658, by P. E. Pieris, 1920.
Pieris 3 = Ceylon and the Hollanders 1658—1796 by P. E. Pieris, 1924.
PTS. = Pali Text Society.
PTS. P. D. = The PTS.'s Pali Dictionary by Rhys Davids and Stede.
Pūjāv. = A Contribution to the History of Ceylon, extracted from the "Pūjāvaliya", 1893.
Pv. = Petavatthu (ed. PTS.)

Rājaratn. = Rájaratnákaraya or History of Ceylon, ed. Saddhananda, 1887.

Rājāv. = The Rájávaliya, ed. by B. Guṇasékara, 1899; — transl. by the same, 1900.

Rām. = Rāmāyaṇa.

S. = Saṃyutta Nikāya (ed. PTS.)

S. and B. = Sumaṅgala and Batuwantudawa, editors of Mhvs., Col. Ed. — The same, Mhvs. transl. (into Sinhalese), 1917.

Sn. = Suttanipāta (ed. PTS.)

SMV. = Silāmeghavaṇṇa.

S. P. = Sessional Papers.

SSB. = Sirisaṃghabodhi.

Thag. = Theragāthā (ed. PTS.)

Thīg. = Therīgāthā (ed. PTS.)

Vin. = Vinaya Piṭaka, ed. Oldenberg.

Vv. = Vimānavatthu (ed. PTS.)

W. = The Mahávaṇsa, part II, containing Chapters XXXIX to C, by L. C. Wijesiṇha.

ZII. = Zeitschrift für Indologie und Iranistik.

PART II

To

Mr. A. M. Hocart,

Archaeological Commissioner, Ceylon,

in sincere gratitude.

INTRODUCTION

Recent years have brought us two comprehensive works on the chronology of Ceylon: 1) JOHN M. SENAVERATNE, "The Date of Buddha's Death and Ceylon Chronology", JRAS. C. B. XXIII, No. 67 (1914), p. 141 ff. and 2) DMDZ. WICKREMASINGHE, "Ceylonese Chronology", as Introduction to vol. III of his Epigraphia Zeylanica.

Still earlier investigations dealing with a longer period are: 3) SYLVAIN LÉVI, "Les Missions de Wang Hiuen Ts'e dans l'Inde" in JAs. 1900, p. 297 ff., 401 ff., translated by JOHN M. SENAVERATNE, JRAS. C. B. XXIV, No. 68 (1915—16), p. 75 ff. (with "Notes" by the Translator p. 106 ff. and 4) E. HULTZSCH, "Contributions to Singhalese Chronology", JRAS. 1913, p. 517 ff.)[1]

I mention further 5) H. W. CODRINGTON, "A Short History of Ceylon" where on p. XIII there is a "Note on the Chronology of Ceylon" which deserves attention.

The numerous single investigations particularly those in the JRAS. C. B. will be quoted in their place. Their authors are: P. E. PIERIS, E. W. PERERA, S. DE SILVA, B. GUNASEKARA, H. C. P. BELL, E. R. AYRTON, H. W. CODRINGTON etc.

The two first named articles (S. and WICKR.) start as I did myself in the translation of the Mahāvaṃsa from FLEET's date of 483 B. C. for the Nirvana of Buddha. Even if this date is not absolutely exact — arguments are advanced for the year 487 B. C. — it is as well to retain it for the moment. Now WICKREMASINGHE, EZ. I. p. 155 ff., has proved that even in

[1] I quote the above articles as follows: 1) = S., 2) = WICKR., 3) = L., 4) = H. with the page number (in the case of 3 that of the English translation).

Ceylon itself there are traces of an era starting from 483 B. C. whereas later, almost certainly in the 7th century, 544/3 B.C. was adopted as the year of the Nirvana. Thus the most important thing is to find out the point in the chronology of Ceylon where the transition from the one era to the other takes place, where consequently we find an excess of 61 years.

SENAVERATNE (p. 143)[1] goes farthest in his assumption that the era of B. C. 483 was in use up to the close of the 15th century when a reform of the calendar took place, 544 B. C., being adopted as the year of Buddha's death, 93 instead of 61 years being erroneously added. At the same time the Śaka era (78/9 A. D.) was dated back 93 years. Later, about the 18th century, with a new reform of the calendar, the Buddha era was adjusted to the difference of 61 years. S. gets rid of the surplus number by the assumption that several of the kings' names handed down by tradition for the 15th and 16th centuries refer to the same person, that others are the names of co-regents, while many are mere inventions. Parakkamabāhu VI. is identical with Parakkamabāhu IX., Bhuvanekabāhu VI. with Bh. VII., while Parakkamabāhu VII. and VIII. never existed (p. 176—177).

SENAVERATNE defends his thesis with great acumen and extraordinary learning. But against it there is a series of synchronisms by which we can prove that the era 544/3 must be much older than S. assumes. Moreover the simultaneous alteration of the Śaka era is very unlikely. For this and other reasons SENAVERATNE's hypothesis was rejected during the discussion following his lecture on the subject. In spite of all the weakness and untrustworthiness of Sinhalese chronology, WICKREMASINGHE is nevertheless right in taking up a more conservative attitude towards its tradition.

One cause of great uncertainty also lies in the fact that in our calculations we have to rely for the most part on the

[1] See also the detailed analysis of SENAVERATNE's hypothesis by C. SCHURHAMMER in "Ceylon zur Zeit des Königs Bhuvaneka Bāhu und Franz Xavers 1539—1552" by C. SCHURHAMMER and E. A. VORETZSCH I. (1928), p. 67 ff.

figures for the reigns of the individual kings. Here we cannot rule out the possibility that many of these reigns were at least partly contemporaneous, that it is a case of simultaneous or of joint reigns. But the means for establishing this in individual cases are wanting. We have of course to do also with round numbers. When it is e. g. said that such and such a king reigned 12 years, possibly a few extra months have been thrown in. The sum total of such additions produces however, considerable inexactitude.

The main point however, is that our sources often differ more or or less in their statements regarding the length of the various reigns, that for many of the kings in the Cūlavaṃsa and other documents figures are wanting altogether or can only be obtained approximately by calculation.

Matters are better, at least in my opinion, with the single dates for certain of the more important events, especially those starting with Buddha's Nirvana. I do not deny that some of these dates may have been got at by the authors by the simple process of adding up the years of the reigns. Nevertheless I have the impression that there was a limited number of dates which rested on ancient tradition and had as their starting-point the year of Buddha's death[1]. There are already traces of something like a Buddha era in the Dīpavaṃsa and the Mahāvaṃsa, as for instance, when it is said in Dīp. 17. 78, that Devānaṃpiyatissa was crowned 236 years after Buddha's entry into Nirvana. Or again when in both chronicles (Dīp. 6. 1, Mhvs. 5. 21) there is the remark that 218 years had elapsed between the Nirvana and the coronation of Asoka.

It is possible that in later times a chronological system was constructed out of these individual dates to which the reigns of the kings were adjusted, not of course without some violence. Then a new confusion arose when at a certain time

[1] I regard also the statement in Mhvs. 33. 80 f., that the Abhayagirivihāra was founded 217 years, 10 months and 10 days after the Mahāvihāra as an ancient tradition, though it rests on a different basis. A figure so exact cannot be obtained by mere addition.

through a misunderstanding the cause of which we do not know, the Nirvana of the Buddha was dated back 61 years. At some point or other in the list of the kings this number must be allowed for. Then it is an open question — granted an ancient tradition — whether in converting these single dates into the Christian era we are to start from 483 B. C. or 544 / 3 B. C.

In the face of all this uncertainty it is advisable in our chronological investigations to rely chiefly on foreign testimony regarding the history of Ceylon. There are above all the synchronisms afforded by Chinese annals and South Indian inscriptions. Then we have the confirmatory evidence of Sinhalese inscriptions, especially those of the mediaeval and modern times. Subsidiary to these are the single dates. The skeleton framed by this "foreign testimony" is indeed meagre in the extreme and the evidence is unequally distributed. A good deal remains doubtful. The blame lies partly in the method of description of the Cūlavaṃsa which conceals so much that to us seems particularly important. What a pity, for instance, that it has nothing to say about the relations with China which would seem to have been not inconsiderable. The name of China is not even once mentioned.

I come now to the fine and careful work of Wickremasinghe. When I wrote the preface to Vol. I. of my translation of the Cūlavaṃsa in which I promised an introduction to the chronology for Vol. II., I had not then seen W.'s "Chronological Table of Ceylon Kings" (EZ. III, p. 1 ff.). Later I had doubts whether a treatment of the same subject by myself might not be superfluous. I think, however, that readers of my translation will be glad to have at hand a list of the kings with their more or less probable dates. They will also like to have a more or less comprehensive survey of the material on which our calculations rest.

One thing more. Wickr. makes no attempt at reconciling the two chronological computations of 483 B. C. and 544/3 B. C. He is apparently convinced that this is at present impossible and wishes to avoid increasing the uncertainty by a new and again uncertain chronology. In converting into the Christian era he starts as far No. 76 (Kumāradhātusena)[1] from 483 B.C. Up to No. 94 (Dappula I.) he places the two computations side by side. From No. 95 (Dāṭhopatissa I.) up to the interregnum after No. 124 (Mahinda V.) he places the figures of the first computation in brackets, thus treating them as less probable and from No. 125 (Kassapa = Vikkamabāhu I.) he follows only the era of 544/3 B. C.

Here I venture a step further. I believe namely that the change of the era falls in the earliest period of the Cūlavaṃsa, that is at the close of the 4th century A. D. Here accordingly is the period where we must allow for the excess of 61 years.

My theory stands and falls with the identity of Ts'a-li Mo-ho-nan of the Chinese annals (L. 83, 89) with King Mahānāma, No. 5 (63). Mo-ho-nan, so it is said, sent a letter, with gifts in the year 428 A. D. to the Chinese Court. This seems to contradict another notice from Chinese sources quoted by L. 75 according to which a king of Ceylon Chi-mi-kia-po-mo (that is Śrī Meghavarman) sent an embassy to the Indian King San-meon-to-lo-kiu-to (that is Samudragupta) asking permission to build a monastery at Bodh Gayā as shelter for pilgrims from Ceylon. The Sinhalese king Śrī Meghavarman is without doubt Sirimeghavaṇṇa, No. 1 (59) the first ruler of the so-called Little Dynasty. Samudragupta reigned from 326 — (about) 375 A. D. According to the traditional chronology the reign of Sirimeghavaṇṇa is reckoned from 362—389 A. D.

But the Cūlavaṃsa reckons 79—80 years from the death of Sirimeghavaṇṇa to Mahānāma's ascent of the throne which would thus occur at the earliest in 468 A. D. And in fact Wickr. 12 gives the date of 468-490 for Mahānāma's reign. But how does this agree with the other notice giving the year 428 for Mahānāma's embassy?[2]

---

[1] This — not Kumārādidhātusena — is of course the right form of the name. The *ādi* is merely periphrastic, "the Dhātusena who begins with Kumāra". See my Transl., note to 41. 35, 44. 6.

[2] I have pointed out the discrepancy Mhvs. Transl. p. XL, note 2

Wickremasinghe tries to solve the difficulty by saying: "This (i. e. the embassy) may have taken place probably when Mahānāma was a priest wielding power in Upatissa's reign." This argument is refuted by the fact that Mo-ho-nan is distinctly described as a Ts'a-li, i. e. kshatriya, as king.

The solution of the problem must be sought elsewhere. Both Chinese notices are right, but the numbers given in the Sinhalese sources for the reigns of Sirimeghavaṇṇa up to Mahānāma are wrong. Their sum total is 129 to 130 years, but they have been expanded about 60 or 61 years in order to reconcile the old era of 483 B. C. with the new one of 544/3.

It is just here indeed that the traditional dates give the impression of artificial expansion. Buddhadāsa and his two sons (Nos. 61-63) are given a reign of 92/3 years! According to the Rājāvaliya they even reigned 142 years! These are fantastic figures. Possibly my theory may throw a new light on 37. 100. Suppose we assume that Sirimeghavaṇṇa's reign after 362 A. D. was considerably shorter, that perhaps a great part of the 27/8 years allotted to it falls within the period when he was reigning along with Mahāsena or as his rival, we might perhaps follow the reading of the MSS. S. 5, 6, 7 *bhātā* (not *bhātu*) *tassa kaniṭṭhako* according to which we should translate: "his youngest brother, Jeṭṭhatissa, still a youth, hereupon raised the umbrella of dominion in Laṅkā." It is in any case only very reluctantly that I have decided to depart from the original text.

Be that as it may, if the Chinese notices and the hypothesis I have built on them are right, we must shorten the period between Mahāsena's death and that of Mahānāma by 60 to 61 years and this gives us for Mahānāma's death the year 430 or 431 A. D. Mahānāma, if we keep to the 22 years ascribed to him by tradition, would have reigned from 409 —431 A. D.

---

without seeking a solution. Cf. also J. M. Senaveratne, JRAS. C. B. xxiv, No. 68 (1915-16), p. 113.

It is impossible to determine individually how the reigns of Mahānāma's predecessors were distributed. I pointed out above that we might already begin shortening these with Sirimeghavaṇṇa. Upatissa with his 42 years may be discarded entirely, it seems to me, or at least but a very small portion of his reign be allowed to stand. He may be purely fictitious or perhaps a prince who reigned along with his father and either never came to the throne himself or if so, only for a short period. Here above all when the transition from the one era to the other had been effected, there set in those efforts to adjust the balance by manipulation of the figures.

There is one thing I should like finally to point out. If we go back for the change of the era to Sirimeghavaṇṇa and his immediate successors there is an inherent probability in this. It coincides with the transition from the Mahāvaṃsa to the Cūlavaṃsa. That we have here a significant breach in the history of Ceylon, a powerful reaction in favour of the Theravāda after a period of decline can scarcely be disputed.

LIST OF SINHALESE KINGS

I have made my own list of the kings of the Cūlavaṃsa, but have added WICKREMASINGHE'S figures in brackets. Where former lists differ from my own this has also been indicated in brackets. Thus for instance, (166. Vijayabāhu VI.) means that this king (Cūlavs. ed. II. 656 f.) is wanting in my list. — Udaya I. (Dappula II.) means that the king whom I call Udaya I. appears elsewhere as Dappula II.

ABBREVIATIONS:

M. = Mahāvaṃsa or from No. 59 onwards Cūlavaṃsa.
Rv. = Rājāvaliya (published and translated by B. GUNASEKARA.)
Pv. = Pūjāvaliya (A Contribution to the History of Ceylon, extracted from the Pūjāvaliya, Colombo 1893).
Ns. = Nikāyasaṃgrahaya (ed. WICKREMASINGHE).
Rr. = Rājaratnākaraya (ed. SADDHANANDA, Colombo 1887).
Nar. = Narendracaritāvalokanapradīpikā as quoted by WICKREMASINGHE.

Figures in italics denote that we have to do with fictitious numbers, whereas the others rest on more or less probable calculation. Figures in bold type are single traditional dates and chiefly those from non-Sinhalese sources or from inscriptions which serve to confirm the chronology of the Mahāvaṃsa.

The figures in the last column refer to the notes following the list of the kings.

	Length of reign M.	Rv.	Pv.	Date	Notes
	1. Mahāvaṃsa				
1. Vijaya	38	38	38	*483 – 445* B.C.	1
Interregnum	1	. . .	1	*445—444*	
2. Paṇḍuvāsudeva	30	32	30	*444 - 414*	
3. Abhaya	20	22	20	*414—394*	
Interregnum	17			*394—307*	
4. Paṇḍukābhaya	70	70	70		
5. Gaṇatissa)	. . .	40 — —	. . .		
6. Muṭasiva	60 — —	60 — —	60 — —	*307—247*	
7. Devānampiyatissa	40 — —	40 — —	40 — —	247—207 247	2
8. Uttiya	10 — —	?	10 — —	*207—197*	
9. Mahāsiva	10 — —	?	10 — —	*197—187*	
10. Sūratissa [1])	10 — —	10 — —	10 — —	*187—177*	
11. Sena / 12. Guttika	22 — —	22 — —	22 — —	*177—155*	
13. Asela [2])	10 — —	10 — —	10 — —	*155—145*	
15. Eḷāra	44 — —	44 — —	44 — —	*145—101*	
16. Duṭṭhagāmaṇī	24 — —	24 — —	24 — —	101—77	
16. Saddhātissa	18 — —	37 — —	18 — —	77—59	
17. Thūlathana	— 1 10	1 8 —	1 — 10	59	
18. Lañjatissa [3])	9 — 15	39 — —	9 8 15	59—50	
19. Khallāṭanāga	6 — —	. . .	6 — —	50—43	
20. Vaṭṭagāmaṇī	— 5 —	— 5 —	— 5 —	43 43	
21. Pulahattha / 22. Bāhiya / 23. Panayamāra / 24. Piḷayamāra / 25. Dāṭhika	14 7 —	14 — —	3 7 —	43—29	
(20.) Vaṭṭagāmaṇī	12 — —	12 — —	12 — —	29—17	3
26. Mahācūḷīmahātissa	14 — —	50 — —	14 — —	17—3	
27. Coranāga	12 — —	. . .	12 — —	3 B.C. — 9 A.D.	4
28. Tissa	3 — —	3 — —	3 — —	9—12 A.D.	

1) Rv. mentions two sons of Devānampiyatissa, 1) Sūratissa, 2) Upatissa, each of whom reigned 10 years. It then says that in the days of King Uttiya two usurpers seized the power and reigned 22 years.

2) As to the chronological difficulties regarding Asela see Wickr. p. 5, n. 1.

3) Rv. calls the successor of Tulnā King Lāminitissa who had slain him and reigned 39 years. Then it passes on the Vaḷagambāhu. The Pv. also calls Tul's successor Lāmāṇitis.

	Length of reign			Date	Notes
	M.	Rv.	Pv.		
29. Anulā	4 3 —	3 4 —	5 2 —	12—16 A. D.	
30. Kuṭakaṇṇatissa	22 — —	22 — —	22 — —	16—38	
31. Bhātikābhaya	28 — —	18 — —	18 — —	38—66	
32. Mahādāṭhikamahānāga	12 — —	12 — —	12 — —	67—79	
33. Āmaṇḍagāmaṇī	9 8 —	9 — —	9 8 —	79—89	
34. Kaṇirajānutissa	3 — —	. . .	3 — —	89—92	
35. Cūlābhaya	1 — -	. . .	1 — —	92—93	
36. Sīvalī	— 4 —	. . .	— 4 —	93	
37. Iḷanāga[1]	9 — —	. . .	6 — —	93—102	
38. Candamukhasiva	8 7 —	. . .	8 7 —	103—112	
39. Yasalālakatissa	7 8 —	. . .	7 8 —	112—120	
40. Subharāja	6 — —	. . .	6 — —	120—126	
41. Vasabha	44 — —	44 — —	44 — —	127—171	
42. Vaṅkanāsikatissa	3 — —	3 — —	3 — —	171—174	
43. Gajabāhugāmaṇī	22 — —	24 — —	22 — —	174—196	
44. Mahallanāga	6 — —	6 — —	6 — —	196—202	
45. Bhātikatissa	24 — —	24 — —	24 — —	203—227	
46. Kaniṭṭhatissa	18 — —	. . .	18 — —	227—245	
47. Khujjanāga[2]	2 — —	. . .	2 — —	246—248	
48. Kuñcanāga	1 — —	20 — —	1 — —	248—249	
49. Sirināga I.	19 — —	. . .	19 — —	249—268	
50. Vohārikatissa	22 — —	22 — —	22 — —	269—291	
51. Abhayanāga	8 — —	2 — —	8 — —	291—299	
52. Sirināga II.	2 — —	2 — —	2 — —	300—302	
53. Vijayakumāra	1 — —	6 — —	1 — —	302—303	
54. Saṃghatissa	4 — —	4 — —	4 — —	303—307	
55. Sirisaṃghabodhi	2 — —	?	2 — —	307—309	
56. Goṭhābhaya	13 — —	13 — —	13 — —	309—322	
57. Jeṭṭhatissa I.	10 — —	10 — —	10 — —	323—333	
58. Mahāsena	27 — —	24 — —	27 — —	334—361/2 362	5

[1]) WICKREMASINGHE is I think, wrong when he says on p. 8 that I had overlooked the fact that Iḷanāga was deposed in the first year of his reign by the Lambakaṇṇas. I inserted the three years (Mhvs. 35. 27) dominion of the Lambakaṇṇas Mhvs. Transl. p. XXXVII, last line, as "interregnum". When W. takes the round figure of 10 years for the interregnum + Iḷanāga's reign I can only approve.

[2]) According to Rv. Bhātikatissa's successors were: 1) Kuḍānā (20 years), 2) Vēratissa (22 years), 3) Abāsen (2 years). Then Sirinā (= No. 52) reigned 2 years.

	Length of reign									Date		Notes
	M.			Rv.			Pv.					
2. Cūlavaṃsa												
1. (59.) Sirimeghavaṇṇa	28c	—	—	28	—	—	28	—	—	362–409	412	6
2. (60.) Jeṭṭhatissa II.	9	—	—	10	—	—	9	—	—			7
3. (61.) Buddhadāsa	29c	—	—	80	—	—	29	—	—			
4. (62.) Upatissa I.	42	—	—	42	—	—	42	—	—			
5. (63.) Mahānāma	22	—	—	20	—	—	22	—	—	409–431	428	8
6. (64.) Sotthisena	—	—	1	—	—	1	—	—	1	431		
7. (65.) Chattagāhaka	1c	—	—	1	—	—	1	—	—	431–432		
8. (66.) Mittasena	1	—	—	6	—	—	1	—	—	432–433		
9. (67.) Paṇḍu[1]	27	—	—	. . .			27	—	—	433–460		
10. (68.) Parinda												
11. (69.) Khuddapārinda												
12. (70.) Tīritara												
13. (71.) Dāṭhiya												
14. (72.) Pīṭhiya												
15. (73.) Dhātusena[2]	18	—	—	18	—	—	18	—	—	460–478		
16. (74.) Kassapa I.[2]	18c	—	—	18	—	—	18	—	—	478–496		
17. (75.) Moggallāna I.	18c	—	—	18	—	—	18	—	—	496–513		
18. (76.) Kumāradhātusena	9c	—	—	9	—	—	9	—	—	513–522	515	9
19. (77.) Kittisena[3]	—	9	—	9	—	—	—	9	—	522		
20. (78.) Sīva I.	—	—	25	25	—	—	—	—	25	522		
21. (79.) Upatissa II.[4]	1	6	—	1	10	—	1	6	—	522–524		
22. (80.) Silākāla	13c	—	—	13	—	—	13	—	—	524–537	527	10, 11
23. (81.) Dāṭhāpabhuti	—	6	6	—	6	—	—	6	—	537		
24. (82.) Moggallāna II.	20c	—	—	20	—	—	20	—	—	537–556		
25. (83.) Kittisirimegha	—	—	19	19	—	—	19	—	—	556		

[1]) For Nos. 9—14 (67—72) Rv. has also 27 years.

[2]) Rr. has the same number of years.

[3]) I do not think that Wickr. is right when he follows Rv. in giving 9 years instead of nine months to No. 19 (77). There are other instances of the Sinhalese sources giving years instead of the months or days of the Mhvs. (No. 20, 25, 36), people being accustomed to reckon by years. We have no example of the reverse. Moreover with regard to No. 19 (77) Pv. agrees with the Mhvs. It seems to me that it is only in cases where both Pv. and Rv. together are against the Mhvs. that weight attaches to their statements. Wickr.'s reference to the reading *vassamhi* in S 5 is no help. It is so isolated in comparison with the other MSS. that it is clearly a mere slip of the scribe.

[4]) According to Nar. 2 y. 6 m.

	Length of reign M.	Length of reign Rv.	Length of reign Pv.	Date		Notes
26. (84a) Mahānāga	3c — —	3 — —	3 — —	556-559		
— (84b) Lāmāni Singānā	. . .	9 — —	9 — —	559—568		
27. (85.) Aggabodhi I.	34c — —	30 — —	34 — —	568—601		
28. (86.) Aggabodhi II.	10c — —	10 — —	10 — —	601-611	609	12
29. (87.) Saṃghatissa	. . .	— 2 —	— 2 —	611		
30. (88.) Moggallāna III.	6 — —	6 — —	6 — —	611-617		
31. (89.) Silāmeghavaṇṇa	9 — —	9 — —	9 — —	617-626		
32. (90.) Aggabodhi III. SSB.		16 — —	16 — —			
33. (91.) Jeṭṭhatissa III.	16c — —	— 5 —	— 5 —	626-641		
Aggabodhi IV.		. . .	. . .			
34. (92.) Dāṭhopatissa I.		12 — —	12 — —			
35. (93.) Kassapa II.	9 — —	9 — —	9 — —	641-650		
36. (94.) Dappula I.[1]	— — 7	10 — —	3 3 —	650		
37. (95.) Dāṭhopatissa II.	9c — —	9 — —	9 — —	650-658		13
38. (96.) Aggabodhi IV. SSB.	16c — —	16 — —	16 — —	658-674		
39. (97.) Datta[2]	2 — —	10 — —	2 — —	674-676		
40. (98.) Hatthadāṭha	— 6 —	— 6 —	— 6 —	676		
41. (99.) Mānavamma	. . .	35 — —	35 — —	676—711		
42. (100.) Aggabodhi V.	6 — —	6 — —	6 — —	711-717		
43. (101.) Kassapa III.	. . .	7 — —	7 — —	717-724	718	14
44. (102.) Mahinda I.	3 — —	3 — —	3 — —	724-727		
45 (103.) Aggabodhi VI. SMV.	40c — —	40 — —	40 — —	727-766	742/6	15
46. (104.) Aggabodhi VII.	6 — —	6 — —	6 — —	766-772		
47. (105.) Mahinda II. SMV.	20 — —	20 — —	20 — —	772-792		
48. (106.) Udaya I. (Dappula II.)	5 — —	5 — —	5 — —	792-797		
49. (107.) Mahinda III. SMV.	4 — —	7 — —	4 — —	797-801		
50. (108.) Aggabodhi VIII.	11 — —	11 — —	11 — —	801-812		
51. (109.) Dappula II. (III.)	16 — —	12 — —	16 — —	812-828		
52. (110.) Aggabodhi IX.	3 — —	. . .	3 — —	828-831		
53. (111.) Sena I. SMV.	20 — —	. . .	20 — —	831-851		
54. (112.) Sena II.	35c — —	35 — —	35 — —	851-885		
55. (113.) Udaya II. (I.)	11 — —	40 — —	11 — —	885-896		
56. (114.) Kassapa IV. SSB.	17 — —	. . .	17 — —	896-913		16
57. (115.) Kassapa V. SMV.	10c — —	6 — —	6 — —	913-923	918/9	17
58. (116.) Dappula III. (IV.)	— 7 —	— 7 —	— 7 —	923		
59. (117.) Dappula IV. (V.) SMV.	12c — —	12 — —	12 — —	923-934		

[1]) The Mhvs. does not count the three years' reign in Rohaṇa.

[2]) According to Nar. No. 39 (97) reigned 2 y. 6 m.

	Length of reign M.	Length of reign Rv.	Length of reign Pv.	Date		Notes
60. (118.) Udaya III. (II.)	3c — —	8 — —	8 — —	934–937		
61. (119.) Sena III.[1]	9c — —	9 — —	9 — —	937–945		
62. (120.) Udaya IV. (III.)	8c — —	3 — —	8 — —	945–953	**948**	18
63. (121.) Sena IV.	3 — —	3 — —	3 — —	953–956		
64. (122.) Mahinda IV. SSB.	16c — —	12 — —	16 — —	956–972	**960**	19
65. (123.) Sena V.	10c — —	10 — —	10 — —	972–981		
66. (124.) Mahinda V.	36c — —	}48 — —	48 — —	981–1029	**1017**	20
Interregnum	12 — —					
67. (125.) Vikkamabāhu I. (Kassapa)	12c — —	12 — —	12 — —	1029–1041		
68. (126.) Kitti	— — 7	. . .	. . .	1041		
69. (127.) Mahālānakitti	3c — —	3 — —	3 — —	1041–1044		
70. (128.) Vikkamapaṇḍu	1 — —	3 — —	3 — —	1044–1047	**1046**	21
71. (129.) Jagatīpāla	4 — —	1 — —	4 — —	1047–1051		
72. (130.) Parakkamapaṇḍu I	2 — —	6 — —	1 — —	1051–1053		
73 a. (131.) Loka (Lokissara)	6c — —	. . .	6 — —	1053–1059		
73 b. (132. Kassapa)[2]	— 6 —	. . .	. . .	1059		
74. (133.) Vijayabāhu I. SSB	55 — —	80 — —	54 — —	1059–1114		22
75. (134.) Jayabāhu I.	. . .	3 — —	13 — —	1114–1116		
76. (135.) Vikkamabāhu II. (I.)	21 — —	28 — —	28 — —	1116–1137		
77. (136.) Gajabāhu (II.)[3]	22 — —	. . .	. . .	1137–1153		
78. (137.) Parakkamabāhu I. SSB.	33 — —	32 — —	33 — —	1153–1186		23
79. (138.) Vijayabāhu II.	1 — —	. . .	1 — —	1186–1187		
80. (139.) Mahinda VI.	— — 5	— — 5	— — 5	1187		
81. (140.) Nissaṅkamalla	9 — —	9 — —	9 — —	1187–1196		
82. (141.) Vīrabāhu I.	— — 1	. . .	— — 1	1196		
83. (142.) Vikkamabāhu III. (II.)	— 3 —	— 3 —	— 3 —	1196		
84. (143.) Coḍagaṅga	— 9 —	— 9 —	— 9 —	1196–1197		

[1]) In Rājāv. the sequence of Nos. 59—66 (117—124) is as follows: 1. Dapuḷu 12 y. (evidently = No. 59, Dappula IV.), 2. Udā 8 y., 3. Sen 3 y., 4. Udā 3 y., 5. Sen 9 y., 6. Sen 3 y., 7. Midelsalā 12 y., 8. Salamevan 10 y. (= No. 65), 9. Mihindu 48 y. (= Mahinda V. No. 66). — Pūjāv. has 1. Dapuḷu 12 y., 2. Udā 3 y., 3. Sen 9 y., 4. Udā 8 y., 5. Sen 9 y., 6. Sen 3 y., 7. Midelsalā 16 y., 8. Salamevan 10 y., 9. Mihindu 48 y.

[2]) Having regard to Mhvs. 57. 65 and 74, it is advisable to insert the Kesadhātunāyaka Kassapa as a distinct sovereign after Loka.

[3]) Rājāv. and Pūjāv. do not mention Gajabāhu at all as king.

	Length of reign			Date		Notes
	M.	Rv.	Pv.			
85. (144.) Līlāvatī[1])	3 — —	3 — —	3 — —	1197—1200		
86. (145.) Sāhasamalla	2 — —	9 — —	2 — —	1200—1202	**1200**	24
87. (146.) Kalyāṇavatī[2])	6 — —	6 — —	6 — —	1202—1208		
88. (147.) Dhammāsoka	1 — —	6 — —	1 — —	1208—1209		
89. (148.) Anīkaṅga	— — 17	— — 17	— — 17	1209		
Līlavatī[1])	1 — —	1 — —	1 — —	1209—1210		
90. (149) Lokissara (II.)	— 9 —	— 5 —	— 5 —	1210—1211		
Līlāvatī[1])	— 7 —	— 4 —	— 7 —	1211		
91. (150.) Parakkamapaṇḍu II.	3 — —	3 — —	3 — —	1211—1214		
92. (151.) Māgha	21 — —	19 — —	21 — —	1214—1235		
93. (152.) Vijayabāhu III.	4 — —	24 — —	24 — —	1232—1236		
94. (153.) Parakkamabāhu II.	35 — —	32 — —	32 — —	1236—1271	**1236**	25
95. (154.) Vijayabāhu IV.	2 — —	. . .	. . .	1271—1273		
96. (155.) Bhuvanekabāhu I.	11 — —	. . .	. . .	1273—1284	**1283**	26
97. (156.) Parakkamabāhu III.	. . .	. . .	. . .	*1284—1291*		
98. (157.) Bhuvanekabāhu II.[3]	. . .	. . .	. . .	*1291—1302*		
99. (158.) Parakkamabāhu IV.[4])	. . .	. . .	. . .			
100. (159.) Bhuvanekabāhu III.	. . .	. . .	. . .	*1302—1346* (99–101)		
101. (160.) Vijayabāhu V.	. . .	. . .	. . .			
102 (161.) Bhuvanekabāhu IV.	. . .	. . .	. . .	1346—1353	**1350/1**	27
103. (162.) Parakkamabāhu V.	. . .	. . .	. . .	1348-1360	**1354 60**	28
104. (163.) Vikkamabāhu IV. (III.)	. . .	. . .	. . .	1347—1375	**1360/1**	29
105. (164.) Bhuvanekabāhu V.	20 — —	. . .	. . .	1360—1391	**1385**	30
106. (165.) Vīrabāhu II.	. . .	. . .	. . .	1391—1397	**1396**	31
(166. Vijayabāhu VI.)	. . .	. . .	. . .		**1405—11**	32
(167. Parakkamabāhu)	. . .	. . .	. . .			
107. (168.) Parakkamabāhu VI.	52 — —	52 — —	. . .	1410—1468		33
SSB.						
108. (169.) Jayabāhu II.	. . .	. . .	. . .	1468—1473		
109. (170.) Bhuvanekabāhu VI.	7 — —	7 — —	. . .	1473—1480	**1475**	34
110. (171.) Parakkamabāhu VII.	. . .	. . .	. . .	1480—1484		
111. (172.) Parakkamabāhu VIII.	. . .	20 — —	. . .	1484—1518		
(173. Parakkamabāhu IX.)	. . .	22 — —	. . .	1506—1528		35

1) The first time Līlāvatī reigned along with Kitti, the second time with Vikkantacamūnakka, finally alone.

2) Along with Āyasmanta Camūpati.

3) Reigned according to Rr. 24 years. According to Daḷadāsirita (Wickr.) Nos. 97 and 98 (156 and 157) reigned at times together. Wickr. reckons the sum total of their reigns at 16 years.

4) Wickr. reckons the beginning of the reign as 1303 A. D.

	Length of reign			Date	Notes
	M.	Rv.	Pv.		
112. (174.) Vijayabāhu VI. (VII.	. . .	18? – –	. . .	1509–1521	36
113. (175.) Bhuvanekabāhu VII.	. . .	21 – –	. . .	1521–1550	37
114. (175 d) Vīravikkama[1]	. . .	45? – –	. . .	1542–?	38
115. (175 b) Māyādhanu[1]	. . .	70 – –	. . .	1521–1581	39
(176. Dharmapāla)	. . .	. . .	. . .	1551–1597	
116. (177.) Rājasīha I.	. . .	. . .	. . .	1581–1593	
117. (178.) Vimaladhammasuriya I.	. . .	12 – –	. . .	1592–1604	
118. (179.) Senāratana	7 – –	25 – –	. . .	1604–1635	
119. (180.) Rājasīha II.	52 – –	. . .	. . .	1635–1687	
120. (181.) Vimaladhammasuriya II.	22 – –	. . .	. . .	1687–1707	
121. (182.) Vīraparakkamanarindasīha	33 – –	. . .	. . .	1707–1739	
122. (183.) Sirivijayarājasīha	8 – –	. . .	. . .	1739–1747	
123. (184.) Kittisirirājasīha	35c – –	. . .	. . .	1747–1782	40
124. (185.) Sirirājādhirājasīha	18 – –	. . .	. . .	1780–1798	
125. (186.) Sirivikkamarājasīha	18 – –	. . .	. . .	1798–1815	

In the middle of the 16 th century a number of princes reigned at the same time in different parts of the Island. The most eminent of these was Māyādhanu, the Māyādunne of Rv. The Vīrakkama of Mhvs. 92. 6 is probably identical with Kumāra Baṇḍāra (Rv.). In addition to these Jayavīra Baṇḍāra who wielded power in the Highlands and Rājasīha or Rayigam Baṇḍāra are mentioned as contemporaries.

Residences

Mahāvaṃsa: Nr. 1: Tambapaṇṇī. — Nr. 2, 3: Upatissagāma (10. 52). — Nr. 4—58: Anurādhapura.

Cūlavaṃsa: Nr. 1 (59)—15 (73): Anurādhapura. — Nr. 16 (74): Sīhagiri. — Nr. 17 (75)—63 (121): Anurādhapura [Pulatthinagara temporary residence of Nr. 46 (104) and Nr. 53 (111); Pulatthinagara and Rohaṇa of Nr. 65 (123)]. — Nr. 67 (125)—73 b (132): Rohaṇa. — Nr. 74 (133)—92 (151): Pulatthinagara. — Nr. 93 (152): Jambuddoṇī. — Nr. 94 (153): Jambuddoṇī (Pulatthinagara 88. 29 ff.). — Nr. 95 (154): Pulatthinagara. — Nr. 96 (155): Jambuddoṇī (Subhagiri 90. 42). — Nr. 97 (156): Pulatthinagara (90. 56). — Nr. 98 (157)—101 (160): Hatthigiripura. — Nr. 102 (161)—104 (163): Gaṅgāsiripura. — Nr. 105 (164)—113 (175) Jayavaḍḍhana. — Nr. 114 (175 d): Sirivaḍḍhana. — Nr. 115 (175 b)—116 (177): Sītāvaka. — Nr. 117 (178)—125 (186): Sirivaḍḍhana.

NOTES

1. The first traditional synchronism is that of the landing of Vijaya on the Island with the Nirvana of Buddha. Mhvs. 6. 47, Dīp. 9. 40. It makes the impression of having been purposely invented that the event might thereby have a greater significance. But it would be a mistake if for that reason we were to regard as inventions those single dates referring to later kings (Devānampiyatissa and Vaṭṭagāmaṇī). For here we start not from Vijaya but only from the Nirvana. But the reigns of the kings between Vijaya and Devānampiyatissa seem to have been manipulated in order to obtain the synchronism Vijaya-Nirvana.

2. A seemingly ancient tradition makes Devānampiyatissa a contemporary[1] of the Maurya king Asoka. There is no urgent reason for doubting the fact. According to Dīp. 17. 78, Devānampiyatissa was consecrated as king[2] 236 years (that is in the 237 th year) after the Nirvana. This figure corresponds to the sum of the years which according to Dīp. and Mhvs. had elapsed since Vijaya. If we take the date arrived at by FLEET for Buddha's death — 483 B. C. we get the year 247 6 B. C. as Devānampiyatissa's coronation year and the fact of his being a contemporary of Asoka is confirmed.

3. According to Ns., p. 10[14] Vaḷagam Abā came to the throne 439 y. 9 m. 10 d. after the Nirvana[3]. This gives us 43 B. C This agrees with the statement of Mv. 33. 80 f. as

---

[1] For further details of my transl. Mhvs., Introd. p. xxxi ff.

[2] Also in Ns., p. 2[19].

[3] Cf. also EZ. II. 205.

to the foundation of the Abhaya-vihāra[1]. According to the statement in Mhvs. the foundation took place 217 y. 10 m. 10 d. after that of the Mahāvihāra the date of which is, according to FLEET, in May 246. Therefore the Abhayagiri-vihāra was founded in March 28 B. C., after Vaṭṭagāmaṇī had had regained the kingdom.

4. According to Rv. a famine called *bämiṇi-sāya* took place under Coranāga and lasted three years. This is said to have coincided with the beginning of the Saka era 78 A. D. = 622 A. B. The statement cannot be reconciled with the other events of the chronology. It would seem that the tradition about this famine was uncertain, for it is placed by Pv. 19[3] in the reign of Vaṭṭagāmaṇī.

5. For the end of the reign of Mahāsena and therewith of the so-called Great Dynasty Rv. and Rr. agree in giving 844 y. (? Pv. 846) 9 m. 25 d. after the Nirvana. Ns. 14[10] reckons the beginning of the reign as 818 A. B., so that with a reign of 27 years the end would fall in 845 A. B. This[2] seems to me in fact one of those single dates which rest on a sure traditional basis. This is also easy to understand. The tradition was that of the Bhikkhus of the Mahāvihāra and for them the death of Mahāsena meant the end of a period of persecution and the beginning of a new period of prosperity. In Mhvs. trsl. p. xxxviii I have calculated the year of Mahāsena's death as 352 A. D. The difference between it and that of Wickr. and S. can be adjusted by assuming that the round numbers of a reign usually include some extra months.

6. I refer the reader to the Chinese account mentioned on p. V which makes Sirimeghavaṇṇa a contemporary of the Indian king Samudragupta (326–375 A. D.).

7. Fa-hian comes to Ceylon 411–412 A. D. A thera mentioned by him is perhaps identical with the Mahādhammakathin named in Mhvs. 37. 175 (cf. note to the passage) as living

---

[1] See Mhvs. transl., p. xxxiv f.

[2] Cf. also SENAVERATNE, JRAS. C. B. xxiii, No. 67 (1914), p. 216.

under Buddhadāsa (Ayrton, JRAS. 1911, p. 1142). Of course this thera may have survived Buddhadāsa, as the chronology seems to indicate.

8. For Mahānāma's reign Chinese sources furnish us with an exact date A. D. 428. See above p. V ff. For the arrival of Buddhaghosa in the reign of Mahānāma tradition furnishes us with a date which assuming 544/3 as the year of the Nirvana, yields 412/3 A. D.

9. For Kumāradhātusena's (Kumārdās) reign a Chinese notice mentioned by Tennent[1] will serve. It says: "In the year 515 on the occasion of Kumara Das raising the chatta, an envoy was despatched with tribute to China." Unfortunately Tennent does not state whether the name of the Sinhalese king is mentioned in the Chinese account. Possibly it is a deduction of his own. At any rate according to my own calculation, the year 515 would fall in the beginning of the reign of Kumāradhātusena.

10. A further Chinese notice quoted by L. (see p. 91 f.) offers difficulties. According to this, an embassy of the Sinhalese king Kia-che Kia-lo-ha-li-ya brought tribute to the Chinese Court in the y. 527 A. D. As a rule Kia-che is the transcription of the name Kassapa. But it is impossible that this could be Kassapa I. since he reigned before Kumāradhātusena (see note 9). S. Lévi has already pointed out that the second name Kia-lo-ha-li-ya might refer to Silākāla (Ambaheraṇa Salamevan). It should be noted too, that Silākāla was the son-in-law of Upatissa II. (III.) and that according to Mhvs. 41. 8 ff., this king had a son called Kassapa who was Silākāla's most dangerous rival. It might therefore be assumed that the Chinese account had confused these two persons or that the Sinhalese tradition had made out of one Kassapa Silākāla two individuals.

11. For Silākāla we have one more single date handed down in the Ns. p. 17[28]: 1088 A. B. = 544/5 A. D. Accord-

---

[1] Ceylon, 2nd ed. I, p. 596.

ing to Wickr. this date refers to the introduction of the Vetulla Canon (*dhammadhātu*)[1] which according to Ns., Rr. and Mhvs., took place in the twelfth year of the king's reign. This does not quite agree with our chronology, for according to Ns. the beginning of Silākāla's reign would fall in 532/3 A. D. (instead of 524)[2]. If we might assume an error in the tradition and read 1080 instead of 1088 A. B. there would be complete agreement.

12. According to Mhvs. 42. 44 ff., the king of Kaliṅga came to Ceylon in the reign of Aggabodhi II. and entered the Order under the guidance of the Thera Jotipāla. According to H. W. Codrington (HC. p. 35, 51) this king of Kaliṅga had been driven out by Pulakesin II. of the Cālukya dynasty who had seized the kingdom of Kaliṅga. This took place according to Jouveau-Dubreuil, 609 A. D. This year must therefore fall within the reign of Aggabodhi II.

13. According to Mhvs. 47. 33 ff., Mānavamma tries in vain to wrest the dominion over Ceylon from King Dāṭhopatissa II. He is helped in this by his friend Narasīha at whose court in Jambudīpa he had taken refuge. According to H. p. 557, this is the Pallava king Narasiṃhavarman I. who reigned 630–668 A. D. This enables us to fix an approximate date for Dāṭhopatisa II.

14. From Chinese sources (L.) we know that in the y. 718/9 a Chinese pilgrim Vajrabodhi visited Ceylon and was received with honour by King Chi-li Chi-lo. The name of the king as it is given here, may very well be an abbreviation of Siri-Silāmegha(vaṇṇa). L. suggests Mānavamma, who also had the biruda of Silāmegha. Ayrton (Ceylon Notes and Queries II, Jan. 1914, p. xxvii ff.) quite rightly objects to this for chronological reasons. But his own identification with Aggabodhi VI. also offers difficulties with my calculation as well as with that of Wickr and S. I suggest Kassapa III, No. 43 (101).

---

[1] See my transl. Cūlavs. I, note to 41. 37.

[2] According to Rr. 1088 A. B. = 852 (sic!) after the introduction of Buddha's doctrine, was the date for Silākāla's ascent of the throne.

As we know, the biruda of Silāmegha alternates with that of Sirisaṃghabodhi. Since Kassapa III. was the second predecessor of Aggabodhi VI. who was certainly called Silāmegha (Mhvs. 48. 42), he is almost sure to have had the same surname, though this may not be expressly stated. All we know of him is that he was a very pious prince (Mhvs. 48. 20 ff.).

15. There is no difficulty about the two embassies of King Chi-lo-mi-kia to the Chinese Court in the years 742 and 746. That king was Aggabodhi VI. Silāmegha, No. 45 (103).

16. Inscriptions of the 1st and 16th years (according to my calculation therefore 896, 912) of the reign of Kassapa IV., No. 56 (114) in Wickremasinghe, EZ. II. 9 ff., I. 200 ff.; H. C. P. Bell, Anurādhapura, 7th Progress Report 1891 (= S. P. xiii. 1896) p. 60.

17. According to Mhvs. 52. 70 ff., Kassapa V. undertakes with the Pāṇḍyas an expedition against the Coḷas. It is unsuccessful. There is evidently an allusion to this (H. p. 525 f.) in the Udayēndiram inscription of the 15th year of the Coḷa king Parāntaka I. = 921 2. In it he boasts of his victory over the Pāṇḍyas and over an army come from Laṅkā. In an inscription, discussed by Rai Bahadur Venkayya, of the 12th year of the same king's reign this twofold success is also mentioned.

18. Under Udaya IV. (III.) No. 62 (120), there was an incursion of the Coḷas into Ceylon who wished to seize the regalia of the Pāṇḍya king deposited there under Dappula IV. (V.) (Mhvs. 53. 9, 40 ff.). Anurādhapura was taken it is true, but the main object was not attained, as Udaya had taken the treasures to Rohaṇa for safety. According to H. 524 f. this event took place in the last year of the reign of Parāntaka I., and R. B. Venkayya has proved that it is only in his latest inscriptions of 943 4 to 947 8 that this king calls himself "Conqueror of Ceylon".

19. According to Mhvs. 54. 11 ff. the troops of the Vallabha king made an unsuccessful incursion into Ceylon under Ma-

hinda IV. No. 64 (122). CODRINGTON (HC. p. 39, 53) supposes this to be the Coḷa prince Parāntaka II. whose general was defeated in 960. This date therefore falls in the reign of No. 64 (122).

20. Of Mahinda V. No. 66 (124) it is related in Mhvs. 55. 16 that in the 36th year of his reign the Coḷas carried off him, his queen and all his treasure to India. H. 522 ff. assumes that this king was Rājendra-Coḷa who boasts of having captured the crowns of the king and of the queens of Ceylon. He first mentions the conquest of Ceylon in 1017/8 but not in the inscriptions of the foregoing year. The year 1017 is therefore that of Mahinda's capture.

21. The Coḷa king Rājādhirājadeva relates (H. 520 f.) in an inscription of the year 1046 that he had deprived 4 kings of Ceylon of their crowns: a) Vikramabāhu, b) Vikramapāṇḍya, c) Vīraśalāmegha and d) Śrīvallabhamadanarāja. This clearly refers to events related in Mhvs. 56. Here the following kings are mentioned as being at war with the Coḷas: 1) Vikkamabāhu, No. 67 (125) = a[1], 2) Kitti, 3) Mahālānakitti, 4) Vikkamapaṇḍu = b, 5) Jagatīpāla, 6) Parakkama. Of 3, 5, and 6 it is distinctly stated that they were slain in battle with the Coḷas, of 3 it is said besides that his crown fell as booty to the Damiḷas. Nos. 1 and 4 however, whose names are clearly recognizable in Rājādhirāja's inscription, ended otherwise: No. 1 died of a disease, No. 4 in combat with No. 5. Still their crowns may have been among the booty. At any rate the year 1046 falls in that period; the events may have reached their conclusion about 1050.

22. For Vijayabāhu I. No. 74 (133) to Parakkamabāhu I. No. 78 (137) I refer the reader to WICKREMASINGHE's excellent treatment of the subject in EZ. I, p. 122 ff. and II. 205 ff.

---

[1] I should now prefer to read in Mhvs. 56. 6 *Devanagaraṃ* instead of *d°* and translate "he betook himself to Devanagara (Dondra) and entered the company of the gods."

23. For Parakkamabāhu's campaign against Rāmañña (Mhvs. 76. 10 ff.) cf. H. C. P. Bell, Rep. on the Kẹgalla Dist., p. 73 ff. It took place in the 12th year of his reign. The Rāmañña prince Bhuvanāditta named in the Devanagala inscription, is identified by Bell with the king Narabaditsi-tsithu who reigned 1167—1204 (Phayre, History of Burma, p. 50, 281, 289).

24. The coronation day of Sāhasamalla ist the earliest absolutely certain date in Sinhalese history. In the Polonnaruva inscription of this king (EZ. II, p. 219 ff.) the date given for the event is Wednesday (*badā*), the 12th day of the light half of the month Binẹra (August-Sept.), after the expiration of 1743 y., 3 m. and 27 days of the Buddha era. Fleet (JRAS. 1909, p. 327, 331) has calculated the date as Wednesday, 23rd August, 1200 A. D.

25. According to the Attanagaluvaṃsa Parakkamabāhu II., No. 94 (153), came to the throne in the year 1824 after the Saṃbodhi = 1779 A. B. = 1235/6 A. D., according to S. 155 = 1296 A. D. (reckoned from 483 B. C., not from 544/3 B. C., as the year of the Nirvana).

26. According to Mhvs. 90. 43 ff. the Tooth Relic came in the reign of Bhuvanekabāhu I., No. 96 (155), into the possession of the Pāṇḍya king Kulaśekhara. This king reigned (H.) 1268—1308 A. D. Under Bhuvanekabāhu's successor Parakkamabāhu III. the relic is restored by friendly negotiation. Codrington (JRAS. C. B. xxviii, No. 72, 1919, p. 82 ff.) refers to Maqrīzi's account of a Sinhalese embassy to the Egyptian Court in the year 1283 A. D. and identifies the name of the Sinhalese king mentioned in the account with that of Bhuvanekabāhu I.

27. For Bhuvanekabāhu IV., No. 102 (161), the Laṅkātilaka inscription is important. See B. Gunasekara, JRAS. C. B. X, No. 34 (1887) p. 83 ff.; H. C. P. Bell, Kẹgalla Dist., p. 92; Wickr. 29 f. It gives Śaka 1264 = 1342 A. D. as the year of his ascent of the throne. According to Mhvs. 90. 108 (also Ns., Nar.) 1894 A. B. = 1350/1 was the 4th year of his reign,

the beginning of the reign therefore 1346/7. The difference is probably due to the fact that his appointment as yuvarāja took place in the y. 1342, this event being often reckoned as the beginning of the reign. According to CODRINGTON (HC. p. 83) No. 102 (161) reigned at least until 1353/4.

28. Cf. the preceding note also for Parakkamabāhu V., No. 103 (162). According to the Hapugastenne inscription (JRAS. C. B. XXII, No. 65, 1912, p. 362) the 11 th year of his reign was = Śaka 1281 expired = 1359/60 A. D. The first year of his reign would be accordingly Śaka 1270 = 1348/9 A. D. But at that time No. 102 (161) was reigning and his successor probably yuvarāja. In the Vegiri-devale inscription (WICKR.) Parakkamabāhu V. in 1351/2 still calls himself āpā.

29. The Vigulavatta inscription (H. C. P. BELL, Kégalla Dist., p. 78) gives Śaka 1282 = 1360/1 A. D. as the 4 th year of the reign of Vikkamabāhu IV., (III.) No. 104 (163). His reign would accordingly have begun in Śaka 1278 = 1356/7 A. D. This agrees with the Niyamgampāya inscription (WICKR. 31) which gives the 17th year of his reign as 1916 A. B. = 1373/4 A. D.

30. For Bhuvanekabāhu V., No. 105 (164), we have several dates. Cf. S. 174 f., WICKR. 33 f. The most important are: a) according to Ns. 1929 A. B. = 1385/6 A. D. was the 14 th year of his reign which makes 1371/2 that of his coronation. — b) according to Mhvs. 91. 13 (Ns. also) he is succeeded after 20 years (thus in 1391) by Vīrabāhu. — c) according to the Vegiri-devale inscription, Bh. V. made an endowment in the 30 th year of his reign. He must therefore have lived at least 10 years after 1391 and claimed the royal dignity. Mhvs. 91. 13 would not agree with this if we were to assume the reading *kāleko* (not *sāleko* with Col. Ed.); for the passage would then state that only after his (i. e. Bhuvanekabāhu's) death (*niṭṭhite kāle*) Vīrabāhu of the Alakeśvara family, seized the power.

31. Ns. 30[30] Council under the leadership of Dhammakitti 1939 A. B. expired = 1396 A. D.

32. Vijayabāhu VI., No. (166), is not mentioned in the Mhvs. The chronicle ignoring the tragic end of the Alagakkonāras,

jumps over to Parakkama VI. I refer the reader to the note to 91. 3 of my translation. Dates according to L. (JRAS. C. B. xxiv, No. 68, 1915–6, p. 96 ff.): 1405, arrival of the Chinese Tcheng-houo in Ceylon; 1409 Tcheng-houo comes again to Ceylon and carries the king (No. 166) captive to China. The king is set free again in 1411 or 1412, but murdered the night after his return.

33. For Parakkamabāhu VI., No. 107 (168), we have again several dates. The most important are the following: a) ascent of the throne according to Mhvs. 91. 15 as well as the inscription of Embekke-devale (H. C. P. Bell, Ceylon Notes and Queries, viii, Dec. 1916, p. cxxxi ff.): 1953 A. B. = 1409/10 A. D.) (according to other sources and to Wickr. 2 years or 5 years later). — b) Chinese accounts (in Tennent, Ceylon I, p. 6'0 f.), that in the year 1459 A. D. a king of Ceylon Pu-la-ko-ma Ba-zae Lacha had for the last time sent tribute to China. The king was evidently No. 107 (168). In the years 1416 and 1421 A. D. it is even related that the King of Ceylon brought the tribute in person.

34. With regard to the date for Bhuvanekabāhu VI., No. 109 (170), the Kalyani inscription of King Rāmādhipati of Pegu is important in that it mentions his embassy to King Bhuvanekabāhu, the son of Parakkamabāhu, in the Śaka year 837[1] = 2019 A. B. = 1476 A. D. Cf. Codrington, HC. p. 93, 100; Taw Sein Ko, Indian Antiquary xxii, 1893, p. 11 ff., 29 ff. &c.

35. According to the Kelaniya inscription (AIC. No. 162) Parakkamabāhu IX., No. (173), ascended the throne in 2051 A. B.[2] = 1507/8 A. D. The 12 th year of his reign fell according to the Munessaram Sannasa, in 2060 A. B., giving 1504 5 for his ascent of the throne, thus a difference of three years.

36. According to the Dondra inscription (H. C. P. Bell, Kęgalla Dist. p. 85 f.) the Śaka year 1432 = 1510 A. D. fell in the year after the 4 th year of the reign of King Vijayabāhu VI.,

---

[1] Thus according to the modern Burmese era which begins in March 639 A. D. See C. Mabel Duff, Chronology of India, p. 51.

[2] Wickr. 42 would prefer to read 2049 (*ekun panas* instead of *ek panas*) This would give 1505/6 A. D.

No. 112 (174), his ascent of the throne would fall accordingly in 1505 A. D.

37. P. E. PIERIS, The Date of Bhuvaneka Bāhu VII. (JRAS. C. B. XXII, No. 65, 1912, p. 267 ff.) comes to the conclusion that No. 113 (175) reigned 1521–1551 A. D.

38. Vīravikkama, No. 164 (175 d), came to the throne (according to Mhvs. 92. 6) 2085 A. B. = 1541/2 A. D.

39. Māyādhanu (Mayadunne), No. 115 (175 b), died according to Rājalekhana (WICKR.), Śaka 1503 = 1581/2 A. D.; Rājasīha I., No. 116 (177), according to Rv. Śaka 1514 = 1592/3 A. D.; Vimaladhammasuriya I., No. 117 (178), according to Rv. Śaka 1525 = 1603/4 A. D.; he came to the throne (Mhvs. 94. 5) 2135 A. B. = 1591/2 A. D.; Senāratana, No. 118 (179) died according to Rājalekhana (WICKR.) Śaka 1557 = 1635/6 A. D. and Rājasīha II., No. 119 (180), Śaka 1609 = 1687/8 A. D.; Vimaladhammasuriya II., No. 120 (181), Śaka 1629 = 1707/8 A. D.

40. Kittisirirājasīha, No. 123 (184), ascended the throne (Mhvs. 99. 2) 2290 A. B. = 1746/7 A. D. He died Śaka 1703 = 1781/2 A. D. He sends embassies to Siam (Mhvs. 100. 59 and 91) 2293 and 2296 A. B. = 1749/50 and 1752/3 A. D. Lastly Mhvs. 100. 282 gives 2301 A. B. = 1757/8 A. D. as the date for the consecration of the rebuilt Rajata-vihāra.

Contents of Chapters 73–101

Chapter 73

Parakkamabāhu I. begins the fulfilment of his task as ruler (v. 1-10). — Benevolence to the poor, reform and conciliation of the Order (v. 11-22). — Buildings such as alms-halls and hospitals (v. 23-39). — Medical care (v. 40-54). — Construction of the city walls (v. 55-60). — The royal palace and neighbouring buildings (v. 61-94). — Laying out of the Nandana and Dīpuyyāna gardens with their various buildings (v. 95-123). — Building of the temple of the Tooth Relic by Mahinda and of the Golden thūpa by Queen Rūpavatī (v. 124-147). — Building of streets, of three suburbs with vihāras and of fourteen city gates (v. 148-164).

Chapter 74

Restoration of Anurādhapura (v. 1-14). — Foundation of Parakkamapura, administrative measures (v. 15-21). — Rebellion in Rohaṇa (v. 22-39). — Rakkha sent to Rohaṇa (v. 40-43). — A rising of the mercenaries in Koṭṭhasāra is suppressed (v. 44-49). — Rakkha's campaign (v. 50-66). — Bhūta joins him, the two generals continue the campaign (v. 67-80). — The flank at Lokagalla secured, advance to Uddhanadvāra (v. 81-88). — Expedition against Dīghavāpi (v. 89-98). — Parakkamabāhu issues strict commands to take the sacred relics, Tooth and Alms-bowl, from the rebels. Their capture after heavy fighting at Uruvelā (v. 99-126). — Sūkarabhātu escapes from prison and flees to Rohaṇa, Mañju sent in pursuit of him (v. 127-132). — Renewed fighting with the rebels (v. 133-142). — Death of Rakkha (v. 143-152). — The rebels gather fresh courage, battles in the Guttasālā district (v. 153-157). — At the command of the King the relics are sent to Pulatthinagara; Mañju who negotiates their dispatch, secures the rear of the army by an expedition to the Dīghavāpi district (v. 158-180). — Parakkamabāhu brings the relics with great ceremony to the capital (v. 181-248).

Chapter 75

Combats in Dīghavāpi-maṇḍala (v. 1-18). — Advance of the Kañcukināyaka Rakkha along the coast by way of Gimhatittha and Mahāvālukagāma as far as Mālāvaratthalī (v. 19-68). — Expedition of the Damiḷādhikārin Rakkha starts from Doṇivagga (v. 69-97). — Decisive battles, finally at Mahāsenagāma, capture of Mahānāgahula and union with the other Rakkha (v. 98-120). — Fresh combats in Khaṇḍavagga and Mahāgāma (v. 121-140). — Feigned retreat to Pūgadaṇḍāvāṭa and decisive actions against the rebels (v. 141-148). — Mañju joined in Kumbugāma. Rakkha's troops capture Dvādasasahassaka and destroy the rebels there, Mañju's soldiers succeed in taking Queen Sugalā prisoner (v. 149-184). — Stern punishment of the guilty, clemency towards those who submit (v. 185-193). — Victorious return of the army to Pulatthinagara (v. 194-204).

Chapter 76

Risings in Rohaṇa and Mahātittha (v. 1-9). — Insolence of the ruler of Rāmañña (v. 10-35). — Parakkamabāhu determines to make war on him and prepares for the campaign (v. 36-52). — Victories in Rāmañña and conclusion of peace (v. 53-75). — Succession disputes in Madhurā, Parakkamabāhu petitioned for aid by the Paṇḍu king, sends an army under Laṅkāpura to Southern India (v. 76-85). — Landing and victorious actions with Kulasekhara's generals, occupation of Rāmissara (v. 86-101). — Restoration of the Ratanavālukacetiya in Anurādhapura by captive Damiḷas; on the completion of the work Parakkamabāhu celebrates a great festival (v. 102-120). — Continuation of the war in Southern India;

combats with Kulasekhara himself at the fortified camp of Parakkamapura opposite Rāmissara and further victorious actions (v. 121-192). — Prince Vīrapaṇḍu, the lawful heir to the throne, joins Laṅkāpura; capture of Madhurā (v. 193-219). — Fresh combats with Kulasekhara's generals which end with the taking of Semponmāri (v. 220-266). — Continuation of the campaign; Neṭṭuru the key position of the Sīhalas (v. 267-290). — Reinforcements arrive from Laṅkā under Jagadvijaya. The town of Rājinā finally taken by force from Kulasekhara, he himself escapes (v. 291-334).

Chapter 77

Kulasekhara renews the fight. Laṅkāpura subjugates several of his subordinate leaders and gains a victory at Ponaamarāvatī (v. 1-24). — Vīrapaṇḍu consecrated king in Madhurā (v. 25-31). — Continuation of the war against Kulasekhara who finally seeks refuge in the Coḷa country (v. 32-70). — Further actions culminate again in a fight for Ponaamarāvatī (v. 71-95). — Laṅkāpura sends the booty to Ceylon, Parakkamabāhu founds the village of Paṇḍuvijaya in memory of the successful campaign (v. 96-106).

Chapter 78

Second account of Parakkamabāhu's reform of the Church. Mahākassapa head of the Council (v. 1-30). — The King's ecclesiastical buildings: Jetavana (with Tivaṅka house, circular temple for the Tooth Relic etc.), Āḷāhana pariveṇa (with Laṅkātilaka, Baddhasīmāpāsāda etc.) (v. 31-55). — Fixing of the boundaries by the King (v. 56-70). — Pacchimārāma, Uttarārāma, Mahāthūpa (v. 70-78). — Vihāras in the suburbs and the Kapila-vihāra (v. 79-95). — Restoration of the buildings in Anurādhapura (v. 96-109).

Chapter 79

The laying out of gardens (v. 1-12). — Erection or restoration of thūpas and other sacred buildings in Rājaraṭṭha

(v. 13-22). — Building or restoration of reservoirs and irrigation canals (v. 23-69). — Similar works in Rohaṇa (v. 70-84). — Conclusion (v. 85-86).

Chapter 80

Vijayabāhu II. reigns piously (v. 1-14). — He is murdered by Mahinda VI. who is followed by Kittinissaṅka, famed for his pious foundations (v. 15-26). — Brief reigns of Vīrabāhu, Vikkamabāhu, Coḍagaṅga, Līlāvatī (with Kitti), Sāhasamalla, Kalyāṇavatī (with Āyasmanta) (v. 27-41). — There follow Dhammāsoka, Anīkaṅga, Līlāvatī (with Vikkantacamūnakka), Lokissara, Līlāvatī (with Parakkama) and Parakkamapaṇḍu II. (v. 42-53). — Tyrannical reign of Māgha (54-80).

Chapter 81

After a time of great confusion Vijayabāhu III. takes over the government in Jambuddoṇī (v. 1-16). — He fetches the relics of the Tooth and the Alms-bowl which had been hidden by the theras on the Kotthumala mountain and builds for them a safe sanctuary on the Billasela mountain (v. 17-39). — He has sacred texts transcribed, builds vihāras and restores decayed buildings (v. 40-63). — He carefully educates his two sons Parakkamabāhu and Bhuvanekabāhu and appoints the former as his successor (v. 64-80).

Chapter 82

Parakkamabāhu II. brings the Tooth Relic to Jambuddoṇī, builds a temple for it and makes three urns as receptacles for it (v. 1-14). — Miraculous apparition (v. 15-49). — The setting up of the relic accompanied by a great festival (v. 50-53).

Chapter 83

Benevolent reign of the King (v. 1-7). — The Damiḷas conquered and driven out (v. 8-35). — Incursion of the Jāvakas; they are defeated by the King's nephew, Vīrabāhu (v. 36-52).

Chapter 84

Restoration of property in the Island according to former conditions (v. 1-6). — Reform of the Order, invitation to foreign theras like Dhammakitti (v. 7-16). — The King builds monasteries, sees to the better training of the bhikkhus, celebrates great festivals for the Order, honours eminent theras and bestows abundant gifts on the bhikkhus (v. 17-44).

Chapter 85

Parakkamabāhu II. builds in Sirivaḍḍhana a vihāra and has the two sacred relics brought thither from Jambuddoṇī with great ceremony (v. 1-36). — Offerings to the bhikkhus and a sacrificial festival for the Buddha (v. 37-58). — Building of the Billasela-vihāra and other monasteries and restoration of decayed structures in Kalyāṇī, Hatthavanagalla, Devanagara. Veneration of a relic of Mahākassapa in Bhīmatittha (v. 59-89). — Veneration of the Tooth Relic in the Sirivijayasundara-vihāra and other meritorious works (v. 90-98). — Great kaṭhina offering and sacrificial festival (v. 99-117). — Pilgrimage to the Sumanakūṭa (v. 118-122).

Chapter 86

The King has all kinds of meritorious works performed by his minister Devapattirāja (v. 1-17) — Making of a road from Gaṅgāsiripura to Sumanakūṭa and buildings on the summit (v. 18-36). — Embellishment of the Hatthavanagalla-vihāra and road-building at Bhīmatittha (v. 37-43). — Laying out of a large cocoplantation, building of the village Mahālabujagaccha. Devapattirāja honoured by the King (v. 44-58).

Chapter 87

A threatened famine prevented by the exhibition of the Tooth Relic (v. 1-13). — The King gathers round him his five sons and his sister's son and gives them advice (v. 14-38). — With the consent of the bhikkhu community he transfers the government to his eldest son, Vijayabāhu (v. 39-74).

Chapter 88.

Vijayabāhu chooses Vīrabāhu as his intimate friend (v. 1-9). — He builds a temple for the Tooth Relic (v. 10-17) and divides the protection of the country among his brothers (v. 18-28). — Affection of the people (v. 29-42). — Vijayabāhu's buildings erected during his journeys through the country (v. 43-61). — War with Candabhānu (v. 62-76). — Buildings in Subhagiri and Anurādhapura (v. 77-89). — Restoration of Pulatthinagara (v. 90-121).

Chapter 89

Parakkamabāhu consecrated king in Pulatthinagara (v. 1-10). — Ceremonial transference of the Tooth and Bowl relics from Jambuddoṇī to the above town (v. 11-46). — Great Upasampadā ceremony in Sahassatittha (v. 47-63). — Distinction conferred on deserving bhikkhus (v. 64-71).

Chapter 90

End of Vijayabāhu IV. (v. 1-3). — Bhuvanekabāhu I. escapes from the rebel Mitta to Subhagiri (v. 4-11). — Mitta murdered in Jambuddoṇī by rebel mercenaries who immediately support the King (v. 12-30). — Establishment of his dominion and meritorious works of Bhuvanekabāhu I. (v. 31-42). — Incursion of Āriyacakkavattin who carries off the Tooth Relic to the Paṇḍu country (v. 43-47). — Parakkamabāhu III. regains the relic by negotiation (v. 48-55). — He reigns in Pulatthinagara (v. 56-58). — Bhuvanekabāhu II. reigns as pious king (v. 59-63). — Parakkamabāhu IV. builds a temple for the Tooth Relic and celebrates a festival for it (v. 64-79). — Literary activity of the King. His buildings (v. 80-104). — Bhuvanekabāhu III., Vijayabāhu V., Bhuvanekabāhu IV. (v. 105-9).

Chapter 91

Parakkamabāhu V. and Vikkamabāhu V. Alagakkonāra founds Jayavaḍḍhanakoṭṭa (v. 1-8). — Bhuvanekabāhu V., Virabāhu II. (v. 9-14). — Parakkamabāhu VI. His meritorious works (v. 15-36).

Chapter 92

Jayabāhu II., Bhuvanekabāhu VI., Paṇḍita Parakkamabāhu VII., Vīra Parakkamabāhu VIII., Vijayabāhu VI., Bhuvanekabāhu VII. (v. 1-5). — Vīravikkama (in Kandy) earns merit by offerings to the Order. Pilgrimages, festivals etc. (v. 6-31).

Chapter 93

Māyādhanu (v. 1-3). — Rājasīha I. (in Sītāvaka) is converted to Hinduism and persecutes the Buddhist priests (v. 4-17).

Chapter 94

Vimaladhammasuriya I. in Goa (v. 1-6). — He brings the Tooth Relic from the Labujagāma-vihāra to Kandy and builds a temple for it (v. 7-14). — He summons bhikkhus from Arakan and furthers the Order (v. 15-23).

Chapter 95

Senāratana saves the Tooth Relic from the Portuguese and proceeds to Mahiyaṅgaṇa where a son is born to him, with significant signs (v. 1-16). — Returning to Kandy, he divides the realm by lot among his three sons (v. 17-26).

Chapter 96

Rājasīha II. dispossesses his brothers and becomes sole king (v. 1-6). — He is distinguished by personal courage (v. 7-10). Successful fights with the Portuguese (v. 11-37). — Vigorous rule in the interior (v. 38-42).

Chapter 97

Vimaladhammasuriya II. builds a temple for the Tooth Relic and furthers the Order by the admission of monks from Arakan (v. 1-15). — Pilgrimages and other meritorious works (v. 16-22). — Narindasīha lays the Order under obligations, undertakes pilgrimages, performs other pious works and builds the new temple for the Tooth Relic (v. 23-47). — The sāmaṇera Saraṇaṃkara takes the Tooth Relic under his protection and at the instigation of the King, performs several important works (v. 48-62).

Chapter 98

Vijayarājasīha marries princesses from Madhurā who embrace Buddhism and are its devoted disciples (v. 1-20). — The King's relations with Saraṇaṃkara (v. 21-24). — Veneration of the Tooth Relic with great festivities (v. 25-57). — Sacrificial festival of lamps (v. 58-64). — The building of vihāras and the embellishment of Sirivaḍḍhana (v. 65-70). — Sermons (v. 71-79). — Banishment of the Paraṅgis, visit to the sacred places (v. 80-86). — Embassy to Ayojjhā in order to fetch bhikkhus. The King's end (v. 87-97).

Chapter 99

Kittisirirājasīha reigns piously and seeks to spread the Buddhist doctrine (v. 1-24). — Honours conferred on the bhikkhus from Rakkhaṅga and furtherance of the Order (v. 25-35), — Pilgrimage to the sacred places (v. 36-41). — Great festivities in Sirivaḍḍhana, specially in honour of the Tooth Relic (v. 42-74). — Continuation of the Mahāvaṃsa (v. 75-80). — Friendly relations of the King and his brothers who like himself, are believing Buddhists (v. 81-107). — Military embroilment with the Olandas who take Sirivaḍḍhana, but suffer a severe defeat (v. 108-139). — The Tooth Relic which had been concealed from the enemy is brought back to the town (v. 140-149). — The Olandas sue for peace (v. 150-167). — The King cares for the welfare of the Order (v. 168-182).

Chapter 100

Veneration of the Tooth Relic by the King who makes large offerings to it and celebrates festivals (v. 1-43). — Reform of the Order, embassy to Ayojjhā to King Dhammika who sends bhikkhus under the leadership of the thera Upāli to Laṅkā where they are received with great festivities (v. 44-90). — The King himself visits the monks from Sāminda in the Pupphārāma where dwellings are assigned them and instigates the holding of an Upasampadā ceremony (v. 91-96). — Furtherance of the newly established Order; the envoys who had accompanied the monks from Sāminda return thither (v. 97-135). — Dhammika again sends bhikkhus to Laṅkā. Death of Upāli (v. 136-148). — Envoys whom Kittisiri had sent to Dhammika return with rich gifts (v. 149-170). — Efficacy of the Siamese monks in Laṅkā; their return to Siam (v. 171-179). — The making of a Buddha image in Sirivaḍḍhana and ceremony of the Festival of the eyes (v. 180-200). — Rebuilding of the Gaṅgārāma and furnishing of the monastery (v. 201-215). — Foundation of a monastery in Kuṇḍasālā (v. 216-219). — Restoration of the cult on the Sumanakūṭa (v. 220-228). — Restoration of destroyed monasteries and their property, namely of the Rajata-vihāra which is described in detail (v. 229-292). — Further meritorious works of the King and of his minister Suvaṇṇagāma (v. 293-301).

Chapter 101.

Sirirājādhirājasīha reigns piously (v. 1-18). — Sirivikkamarājasīha at first a pious prince, becomes a tyrannical monster. The people rise against him and banish him to the mainland. The British take possession of the kingdom (v. 19-29).

CHAPTER LXXIII

ACCOUNT OF THE REBUILDING OF PULATTHINAGARA

Now when the Ruler Parakkama had accomplished his 1
consecration as king, he the wise one, best among those who
understand what is good (for the people), thought thus: "By 2
those kings of old who turned aside from the trouble of fur-
thering the laity and the Order — who through lust, hatred,
fear and delusion went wofully astray[1], who caused great evil 3
by the gathering of immeasurable taxes and the like — has
this people aforetime been grievously harassed. May it hence- 4
forth be happy, and may the Order of the great Sage —
long sullied by admixture with a hundred false doctrines, rent 5
asunder by the schism of the three fraternities and flooded
with numerous unscrupulous bhikkhus whose sole task is the 6
filling of their bellies — (that Order) which though five thousand
years have not yet passed, is in a state of decay, once more
attain stability. Of those people of noble birth who here and 7
there have been ruined, I would fain by placing them again
in their rightful position, become the protector in accordance
with tradition. Those in search of help I would fain support 8
by letting like a cloud overspreading the four quarters of the
earth[2], a rich rain of gifts pour continually down upon them.

[1] *Chanda, dosa, bhaya, moha* are called A. II. 18 *cattāri agatigamanāni*. Cf. *chandāgatiṃ* (*dosāgatiṃ* etc.) *gantuṃ* D. III 133[21], *chandā agatiṃ gacchati* Nett. 44[1] etc.

[2] The Buddhist cosmology recognises four chief continents. Cf. Vv. 20. 10 *catunnaṃ mahādīpānaṃ issaraṃ yo'dha kāraye*. S. V. 343[20] *catunnaṃ dīpānaṃ paṭilābho*. In contrast to these are the 2000 small dīpas by which they are surrounded (VvCo. 104[14]). In the Gal-vihāra inscription

9 All this was (for me) while with arduous struggle I sought
10 the royal dignity, the absolutely preconceived result. Now is
the time to carry out what I have wished." In consideration
of this he bestowed office on those who deserved it[1].
11 Hereupon he had the drums beaten and those in search
of help called together and he allotted them yearly a large
12 alms equal in weight to his body. Then the Ruler in order
to promote the furtherance of the Order, assembled the great
13 community dwelling in the three fraternities. Further he called
together many distinguished teachers learned in the methods
14 of discriminating between failure and non-failure, and as he
himself was the foremost among those versed in the rules of the
Order and acquainted with right and wrong, he could distin-
15 guish the genuine from the false ascetics. Further being in
virtue of his impartiality free from liking and disliking, and
as a result of his unweariedness arduously active day and
16 night, he cured like a clever, expert physician who distin-
17 guishes between curable and incurable disease, those which
were curable and set aside those which were incurable by the
method prescribed by the rules of the Order, free in his de-
18 cisions from error. From the days of King Vaṭṭagāmaṇī
Abhaya[2] the three fraternities had lost their unity, despite
19 the vast efforts made in every way by former kings down to

the Buddha is compared to a rain-cloud which pours its blessing over the four continents. These continents are: Uttarakuru, Jambudīpa, Pubbavideha and Aparagodāna (Wickremasinghe, EZ. II, p. 273, n. 3). For the Brahmanic teaching of the Dvīpas see Kirfel, Kosmographie der Inder, p. 110 ff.

[1] Verses 2—10 form one sentence. It is governed by *idāni kālo vidhātuṃ etaṃ sabbaṃ mayā sambhāvitaṃ*. What he has aspired to is: 1) with regard to the mass of the people that they should be happy (v. 4 a); 2) with regard to the Order, that it might attain stability (*yathā assa addhaniyaṃ* v. 6 d); 3) with regard to the nobility, that the king should again become their protector (v. 7 d: *pālanaṃ* must be supplemented by an *assaṃ* from *assa* in 6 d "may I be"); 4) with regard to those in want, that the king may support them (v. 8 d).

[2] For the schism in the Order at the time of this prince see Mhvs. 33. 95 ff.

the present day. They turned away in their demeanour from
one another and took delight in all kinds of strife. But the 20
all-wise Ruler who had already in past existences striven after
the purification of the Order as something which must be
attained[1], achieved its union, whereby he had to endure double 21
as much heavy toil as in his efforts for the royal dignity.
And he made the Order as uniform as milk and water so 22
that it could last in purity for five thousand years[2].

Hereupon the best of men had a square hall[3] erected in 23
the middle of the town with four entrances and several large

[1] P. *gahitabbato* is an adverbial formation from *gahitabba* = skr. *grahītavya*. It would correspond to skr. *grahītavyatas*. Cf. Whitney, Indische Grammatik § 1098.

[2] Verses 12—22 form one sentence. The principal verb in 22 c d is *akāsi* (*jinasāsanaṃ khīrodakībhūtaṃ*), subject *bhūpati* in 21 d. The gerunds *rāsikatvā* (12 c) and *saṃnipātiya* (13 d), as also *samaggaṃ katvā* (21 d) are subordinate. This last is preceded by the pret. and pres. participles: — *paṭighānunayāvajjito* (15 b), *atandito* (15 d), *samupadhārento* (16 c), *tikicchanto* and *vivajjayaṃ* (17 a b), as well as *anayāpetasaṃkappo* (17 c) and *anubhonto* (21 c). These are all of them attributes of the subject. The object of *samaggaṃ akāsi* is *nikāyattitayaṃ* with the three attributes in 19 b c d of which the first has a still closer adverbial definition in 18 and 19 a ("in spite of the great efforts" etc.); *payāsena* must be supplemented by *katena*. — The brief account of our chronicle is confirmed by the Gal-vihāra inscription of Parakkamabāhu in Polonnaruva. Cf. Ed. Müller, AIC nr. 54; Wickremasinghe, EZ. II. 256 ff. From the contents it is even possible to establish certain connections between the inscription and the account of the Cūlavs., though these are of too vague a character for us to draw far-reaching conclusions from them. Both start with the schism of the church under Vaṭṭagāmaṇī. Both speak of the intention that the Order should now be secure in its stability for 5000 years. In the Cūlavs. the king is compared to a cloud spreading itself over the four continents just as the inscription uses this comparison of Buddha. See also note to 78. 5. In chap. 78 a second and more detailed account of the reform of the church follows, Rājāvalī says (trsl. by B. Guṇasekara, p. 59) quite briefly: "he reconciled the religious differences which had existed since the reign of Vaḷagam Abā." The account in the Nikāyasaṃgraha is more detailed (p. 22 of Wickremasinghe's ed.).

[3] P. *catussāla* = skr. *catuḥśālā* denotes a square surrounded by buildings. We must imagine therefore a square court surrounded on all sides by halls open to the interior. Cf. Mhvs. 37. 15. The word occurs as the name of a particular building in Anurādhapura in Mhvs. 15. 47, 50; 35. 88.

24 rooms and instituted a great almsgiving in which everything
needful was to be had daily for many hundreds in number
25 who had kept the precepts of moral discipline[1]. And every
year the Ruler of men had given to each of them according
to his age, garments and mantles, (thus) at all times full of
26 benevolence. Thereupon he had four almshouses built in the
four districts of the town and had them erected in separate
27 divisions, and therein he placed many vessels of bronce, cushions
28 and pillows, mats, carpets and bedsteads as well as cows by
the thousand that gave sweet milk. Then near these (halls)
29 at a spot with pure water he laid down charming gardens
adorned with trees that bore abundant blossom and fruit, and
30 fair as the garden of Nandana[2]. Further generous as he was,
he set up in their neighbourhood rich provender houses
31 supplied with money and money's worth which contained all
necessities such as syrup, sugar, honey and the like. And
32 (there) he instituted for many thousands of bhikkhus from
all four regions of the earth who practised moral discipline
and other virtues, for Brahmans belonging to a mendicant
33 order, as well as for many other supplicants and poor tra-
vellers daily a great almsgiving, he the wise (prince), untiring,
unwearying, with a heart full of love.

34 Hereupon the Ruler of men, filled with pity, had another
great hall built for many hundreds of sick people, fitted for
35 their sojourn there, and had placed in it in the way above
described, a complete collection of all articles of use. There
36 also he gave to each sick person a special slave and a female
slave to prepare day and night according to need, medicines
37 and food, solid and liquid. There too he had many provender
houses built in which a quantity of medicine, money and
38 money's worth and the like were collected. To discerning
and skilful physicians who were quick at distinguishing various
(bodily) conditions and who were versed in all the text books,

[1] P. *sīlapālānaṃ* refers as W. assumes, to monks. "Age" in v. 25 (P. *yathāvuḍḍhaṃ*) means then the period of belonging to the Order.

[2] The pleasure garden of the god Indra. E. W. Hopkins, Epic Mythology, p. 141.

he gave maintenance according to their deserts, recognising 39
the merits in all of them and made them day and night
practise the medical art in the best manner. He himself on 40
the four Uposatha days in the month, having laid aside all
his ornaments and having taken upon himself the vow of the
sacred day, pure with pure upper garment, surrounded by his 41
dignitaries, was wont to visit that hall, his heart cooled with
pity[1]. With an eye that charmed by goodness he gazed at 42
the sick. And as the Ruler of men was himself versed in
medical lore[2], he the all-wise summoned the physicians ap- 43
pointed there, tested in every way their healing activities, and 44
if their medical treatment had been wrongly carried out he
met them with the right method, pointed it out to them as
the best of teachers and showed them the proper use of the 45
instruments by skilfully treating several people with his own
hand. Then he tested the favorable or unfavorable condition 46
of all the sick, let those who were rid of their illness have
garments given to them and then rejoicing in good, after he 47
had taken his reward[3] from the hands of the physicians and
given them their reward[3], he returned to his palace. By such 48
means year by year he being (himself) free from disease,
freed the sick from all their illnesses.

Yet another miracle never before seen or heard was mani- 49
fest in him who was rich in the virtue of pity rightly exercis-
ed. To that hall there came, tortured by great pain, a crow 50
suffering from an ulcer that had formed in her cheek. As if 51

[1] P. *dayāsītalamānaso.* Cf. 73. 141. The heart is hot with passion. Passion is cooled by pity. We Northerners would be more inclined to say it is "warmed".

[2] P. *āyubbede* = skr. *āyurvede.* The Ayurveda "Veda of the (Lengthening of the) Span of Life" was held to be the basis of all medical knowledge and was regarded as an *upāṅga* of the Atharvaveda. See Winternitz, Gesch. der ind. Literatur, III, p. 542; J. Jolly, Medicin, p. 12 f.

[3] Each time the expression *patti* is used. Employed of the king, it means the merit working itself out in the *kamma.* This merit is found in the healing activity of the physicians and is left by them to the king, because he is its spiritual parent. Cf. note to 42. 50. Employed of the doctors, *patti* means the payment for their services.

chained by the strong bands of his pity she sat as if with clipped wings, motionless outside the hall moaning piteously.
52 The physicians who rightly recognised her condition, caught
53 her and cured her at the Great King's command. Her disease cured, the King set her upon an elephant and having made her walk round the town, her right side towards it, he set
54 her free. Where, when and by whom was ere such exceeding great mercy even to animals seen or heard?

55 Thereupon King Parakkamabāhu, the hero, to whom all right-minded people were devoted, set about the rebuilding in grandeur and beauty of the superb city of Pulatthinagara
56 which had reached such a state that nought but its name remained, and which no longer sufficed to make manifest his
57 superlatively royal glory[1]. The Monarch now had a high chain of walls built which on all sides enclosed the fortified
58 town[2] and was larger than the town wall[3] of former kings and gleamed with its coating of lime bright as autumn clouds.
59 Then after he had built round this three walls[4] each in turn
60 smaller than the other, he laid down various streets. Then he

[1] For the following description compare above all A. M. Hocart, The Topography of Polonnaruva (ASC. Memoirs II. 1926, p. 3 ff.). H. W. Codrington is certainly right in his assumption that the description in the Cūlavaṃsa proceeds from south to north. I refer the reader at once to the second and later account of Parakkamabāhu's building activities in 78. 31 ff.

[2] By *khandāvāra* I understand here the inner walled part of the town in contrast to the open parts of the town lying around it. The "chain of walls" refers probably to the rampart of the town still recognisable, stretching for about a mile from north to south and half a mile from east to west. Within this rampart lies the „citadel" with the royal castle. See note to v. 61.

[3] The abl. *purapākāracakkato* shows that we must take the positive *mahantaṃ* in the sense of a comparative, as is often the case. The new structure was thus more extensive than the older one.

[4] The Kauṭalīya lays down that three trenches each narrower than the other, must surround the wall of a castle. The dug out soil may have served for the construction of the "small wall". See Kauṭ. 2. 3. 21 (in Jolly's ed. p. 31; in J. J. Meyer's translation p. 65[10] in that of Shamasastry, p. 57).

erected around his own palace and around his whole dwelling
a second inner wreath of walls[1] and built thereon a palace[2] 61
seven storeys high, furnished with a thousand chambers and
adorned with many hundreds of pillars painted in divers hues.
It was richly supplied with hundreds of alcoves[3] which were 62
like to the summit of the Kelāsa[4] mountain and were radiant
with manifold ornaments of climbing plants and flowers. It 63
had doors and windows of gold large and small, well divided
walls and stairs and offered conveniences for every season.
It was ever adorned with many thousands of various beds 64
which were made of gold, ivory and the like and had costly

[1] P. *anupākāramaṇḍalaṃ*, lit. a secondary circle of walls.

[2] The word for "palace", *pāsādaṃ*, first occurs in v. 70. All the verses between contain attributes of which I have made independent sentences. There is no doubt that the palace is recognisable in the ruins which are marked "palace" on the plans. It is enclosed along with a number of subsidiary buildings by a rampart (the *anupākāra* of the text) "forming an oblong of roughly 440 by 264 yards" (A. M. Hocart, l. c., p. 9). The enclosed ground is now known by the name of the "citadel", and the palace stands in the southern part of the square. Cf. for the whole H. C. P. Bell, ASC. 1911—12 (= S. P. III, 1915), p. 50 ff. When the Cūlavs. speaks of a thousand apartements and many hundreds of pillars that is of course merely the stereotyped exaggeration constantly recurring in such descriptions. At the same time there is a striking number of tiny rooms grouped round the central main part of the building in the groundfloor. There are more than fifty of them. Without doubt there were further apartments in the upper storeys. That the palace at least in its central portions consisted of one or several storeys is proved by the extraordinary strength of the walls enclosing the innermost chamber. These are more than ten feet thick. Then too a broad staircase is still standing which led from the south of this room upwards. Unfortunately our chronicle gives instead of exact figures merely the customary phrases prescribed by poetics.

[3] P. *kūṭāgāra*. Rāvaṇa's palace is also described in the Rāmāyaṇa 5. 9. 14 (Bombay ed. 1902) as *kūṭāgāraiḥ śubhāgāraiḥ sarvataḥ samalaṃkataṃ*. The commentary on the passage explains *kūṭāgāraiḥ* by *guptasvalpagṛhaiḥ*.

[4] Buildings which are high, pointed and white in colour (covered with stucco), especially stūpas (78. 77), are frequently compared to the Kelāsa mountain (cf. 68. 41 and note).

65 coverings. The height of its splendour[1] was reached in the
royal sleeping apartment which was ever immeasurably re-
66 splendent with a thick bunch of pearls[2] suspended at its four
corners, white as moonbeams and gleaming so that they
67 laughed to scorn the beauty of the divine Gaṅgā. (The sleep-
ing apartment) was adorned with a wreath of large golden
lampstands which breathed out continually the parfume of
68 flowers and incense. With the network of tiny golden bells[3]
suspended here and there and giving forth a sound like the
69 sound of the five musical instruments, the palace made known,
as it were, the rich fulness of the merits of the King. This
70 splendid palace, like to a matchless structure of Vissakamman[4],
charming and peerless, he, the first among the protectors of
the earth, built and gave it the name of Vejayanta[5].

71 For the carrying out of the ceremonies of expiation by
the Brahmans (he built) the Hemamandira and for the recitation
72 of magic incantations the charming Dhāraṇīghara[6]. For li-
stening to the birth stories of the great Sage which were
related by a teacher appointed there for the purpose, (he built)

[1] So I translate *sanāthīkataṃ uttamaṃ* (cf. skr. *sanāthīkṛ* as well as below v. 152) in v. 67 d. Verses 66 b to 67 a b contain attributes of *sirīsayanagabbhena* in 67 c, v. 65 attributes of *thūlamuttakalāpena*.

[2] In Rām. 5. 9. 17 it is said of Rāvaṇa's palace *nistulābhiśca muttābhistalenābhinirājitam*.

[3] The *kiṅkiṇi(ka)jāla* is one of the ornaments of the maṇḍapas (JāCo. I. 32[31]; DhCo. I. 274[2]) and of the pāsādas (D. II. 183[6]; Mhvs. 27. 16, 27).

[4] Skr. *Viśvakarman*, the architect of the gods, often associated and confused with Tvaṣṭar. Cf. Hopkins, Epic Mythology, p. 201. He is the builder of Varuṇa's palace (ibid. p. 118) and of the divine hall of assembly (ibid. p. 113).

[5] This is the name of Indra's palace. See 48. 136.

[6] I take *hemamandira* "golden house" and *dhāraṇīghara* „house of incantation" as the names of the buildings in question. *Santi* in a is as otherwise *santikamma*, to be understood in the technical sense of skr. *śānti*. Cf. with *parivattana* in c *parivattanamanta* JāCo. I. 200[16]. It is impossible now to say which of the present ruins correspond to the buildings mentioned. We should probably look for them in the various structures in the immediate vicinity of the palace.

the fair Maṇḍalamandira[1]. For the reception of the magic 73
water and of the magic thread given him by the yellow-robed
ascetics (he built) the Pañcasattatimandira[2]. Lastly he who 74
ever trod the path of the true doctrine, erected a sermon
house[3]. It was surrounded by an enclosure of coloured cur-
tains and adorned with costly canopies. By reason of the 75
many-hued, sweet-smelling flowers laid down here and there
as offerings it had the semblance of a single nosegay. Its 76
interior was constantly lighted by lamps with scented oil and
perfumed by incense of gum resin. It was gaily adorned with 77
many likenesses of the Victor (Buddha) in gold and the like
and was resplendent with a garland of pictures of the Omniscient
One, which were painted on stuff. When that Prince among 78
kings entered it to place with his own hand a (jewel as) eye[4]
upon the statue of the Victor, or to honour by sacrifice the 79
Tathāgata, or to listen to the unsurpassable true doctrine
— (then) was it like unto a divine hall of assembly. It was 80

[1] That is "circle house". Of course the building which was to serve for the narration of the jātakas was first erected and then an *ācariya* appointed for the purpose. Bell (ASC. 1906, p. 10ff.; cf. EZ. II. 238ff.) regards the *maṇḍalamandira* as the so-called Potgul-vehera to the south of Pulatthinagara. But I do not believe that he is right.

[2] That is "the house of the seventy-five". The reason for the name is unknown. Obviously the building was meant to serve for the holding of parittā ceremonies. Water and thread play the most important part in these, as the white thread which runs through the hands of all the participating priests starts from a vessel filled with water. At the close the foreheads of the priests are sprinkled with the water.

[3] Again verses 74 to 81 form one sentence. The attributes in 74 to 81 b precede the object *dhammāgāraṃ* in 81 c. Of these we have made independent sentences. The most important building in the neighbourhood of the palace is the "Rājamāligāva" situated to the east of it. It is an oblong structure on a terrace of three tiers. The walls of the terrace are decorated with beautifully carved reliefs. Whether indeed we may call the building a *dhammāgāra* is doubtful. It looks like a hall of audience or like a council-hall. Cf. ASC. 1905 (= S. P. XX. 1909), p. 8ff.

[4] The eyes of Buddha statues consisted frequently of precious stones (dark blue sapphires). Their insertion took place with specially solemn ceremonies.

graced by a wonderful peacock which drove people out of
81 their senses whenever screeching its peacock cry, it began
its dance together with the dancing girl who danced there
while they struck up a sweet rhythmic song[1].

82 Further in order to listen to the rhythmic songs of the
many musicians and to behold their charming dance, the
Monarch had built near the palace the Sarassatīmaṇḍapa[2].
83 It glittered in every direction with its golden pillars. It was
delightful with paintings relating to his (Parakkamabāhu's)
84 deeds. It was embellished by a wishing-tree offering all de-
sired things which sparkled with all kinds of ornaments such
85 as earrings, bracelets, necklaces and the like, which was re-
splendent with garments of linen, silk, Chinese stuff and other
86 materials, which gleamed with its golden trunk and a row of
branches, and which was adorned by a flock of numerous birds
which were painted on it.

87 Further he had the fair maṇḍapa erected which bore the name Rājavesibhujaṅga[3]. It was like unto the hall of the gods, called Sudhammā, which descended to earth, just as if

[1] The peacock was thus a mechanical toy which however existed apparently only in the imagination of the poet. "Rhythmic" is *layānvita* or in v. 82 *layopeta*. The Indians distinguish three *layāḥ* or tempi: *druta*, *madhya* and *vilambita*.

[2] "Maṇḍapa of Sarasvatī". She is the goddess of eloquence, here of the arts of the muses in general. It is impossible to identify either this building or the one following. The description is unfortunately purely formal. The fact of both buildings being described as maṇḍapas suggests something of the pavilion kind, provisional in character. Verses 82 to 86 and 87 to 91 again form each one sentence, built up in the same way as the sentence in v. 74 to 81.

[3] The name is difficult to explain. A suburb of Pulatthinagara is called thus (73. 153; 78. 79), and this name again seems to be connected with the epithet Rājavesibhujaṅgasilāmegha applied to Ilaṅkiya in 76. 192. The word *vesī* means "harlot", "prostitute". *Bhujaṅga* in addition to "snake" means the "lover of a prostitute" (BR. s. v., c). This meaning is here to be assumed in the name owing to the association with *vesī*. In the inscripton of Ihala Puliyankulam of the time of Parakkamabāhu I., dealt with by CODRINGTON (JRAS. C. B. XXX, nr. 79, p. 271), he has the surname of *ari-rāja-vesi-bhujaṅga*.

the good deeds of all people were accumulated at one spot.
It was three-storeyed, ornamented with coloured pictures, 88
surrounded by lines of fair vedikās[1], exquisite, adorned with 89
a costly chair beneath a wishing-tree which offered the singers
and other people the wished-for objects. It shimmered with its 90
manifold precious stones like the diadem, sparkling in the sun,
of that fair lady, the island of Laṅkā, whom he won by the force
of his arms[2]; and it was like unto the wreath of tresses of 91
the protector of the world of men[3]. In the same way he 92
built the fair Ekatthambha-pāsāda[4] that ended with a ma-

[1] What *vedikā* means is not easy to determine. Noteworthy is the frequency of the phrase *vedikāya parikkhitta* „surrounded by a vedikā" as for instance a bathing pond, a *pokkharaṇī* D. II. 179[7] ff. Here most probably it means a railing, since just before the same has been said of a stair case. As a staircase when it is of gold etc. has golden *thambhā* (that is railing gates) and *sūciyo* (i. c. cross-bolts), as well as an *uṇhīsa* (cornice) of silver, in the same way the vedikā of the pond has it. Cf. further VvCo. 340[5], where *kañcanavedimissaṃ* is explained by *suvaṇṇamayāya vedikāya sahitaṃ parikkhittaṃ*. A vedikā is part of a heavenly pāsāda just as the rooms, the windows, the network of bells (Mhvs. 27. 16). The lohapāsāda had a *pavāḷavedikā*, a vedikā of coral (Mhvs. 27. 26). There was a *nānāratanavedikā* round the bodhi tree (Mhvs. 30. 70). A vedikā belongs to a stūpa (Mhvs. 32. 4; 34. 41), to an image house (Mhvs. 78. 40), to a bathing-house (Mhvs. 78. 46). Cf. also note to 76. 118.

[2] I divide *nijabāhubalā* (= instr.) *aruṇe*. For it is hardly admissible to take the whole as a parallel compound to *laṅkaṅganāya*.

[3] W. regards this as referring to Śiva. The reference is suitable, since Śiva wears the crescent moon in the hair over his forehead, his tresses are therefore illumined.

[4] Lit. „one-pillar-palace". In such a one-pillar-palace, *gehe ekathūnike*, was Cittā the daughter of Paṇḍuvāsudeva confined, to prevent her coming into contact with any man. JāCo I. 441[24–25] also mentions an *ekatthambhakapāsāda* which serves as a king's dwelling. For an idea of what such a structure looked like, v. 94 a b is important where it is compared to a candelabra. One must therefore oddly enough imagine the pāsāda as something in the form of a dovecote. It should be remembered however, that the rooms both in the royal castle at Polonnaruva and in the Baddhasīmapāsāda were extremely small, not more than 8×10 ft. In Veherabendigala I saw something like a room just large enough for a man stretched at full length to lie down in.

93 kara[1] and rose aloft as if it had split open the earth. And
it was adorned with a superb golden chamber[2] that was
94 placed above on a golden column, possessed of the beauty of
a cave of gold for this lion among kings, and which glittered
like a candelabra on a golden foot.
95 Again the Ruler, the leader of earth protectors, had a
private garden laid down in a region close to the kings house.
96 As one felt that it showed by its beauty a likeness to the
(heavenly) pleasure garden Nandana, and by lavishing charm
charmed the eyes of men[3], it received the name of Nandana[4].
97 Its trees were twined about with jasmin creepers and it was
filled with the murmur of the bees drunk with enjoyment of
98 the juice of the manifold blossoms. There campaka, asoka
and tilaka trees, nāgas, punnāgas and ketakas, sal trees, pā-
99 ṭalī and nīpa trees, mangos, jambū and kadamba trees, vakulas,
coco palms, kuṭajas and bimbijālakas, mālatī, mallikā, tamāla
100 and navamālikā shrubs[5] and yet other trees bearing manifold
fruits and blossoms rejoiced the heart of the people who went
101 thither. Pleasant it was, and with the cry of the peacocks
and the gentle twitter (of the birds) it always delighted the
102 people. It was furnished with a number of ponds with be-

[1] A dolphin-like mythical animal often employed as ornament especially on balustrades of staircases.

[2] P. *jātarūpanivāsena*, with a dwelling-room, a habitation of gold.

[3] I separate thus: ... *janānaṃ nayanā* (acc. pl.) *nandanā-daṃ nandayati*. The fem. *nandanā* is found also S. I. 6[10].

[4] Verses 95 to 112 are one sentence: ... he laid down ... the private garden ... by name Nandana ..., whose trees ... and it was filled ... There follow further attributes of *gharuyyānaṃ*, partly in adjective form, partly as relative sentences (cf. *yattha* in v. 100, 109, 111; *yaṃ* in v. 110).

[5] The botanical names are in the same order 1. michelia champaka, 2. jonesia asoka, 3. unknown (Skr. *tilaka*), 4. mesua ferrea, 5. rottlera tinctoria, 6. pandanus odoratissimus, 7. shorea robusta, 8. bignonia svaveolens, 9. nauclea cadamba, 10. mangifera indica, 11. eugenia jambolana, 12. nauclea cordifolia, 13. mimusops elengi, 14. cocos nucifera. 15. wrightia antidysenterica or nericum antidysentericum, 16. momordica monadelpha, 17. jasminum grandiflorum, 18. jasminum sambac, 19. xanthochymus pictorius, 20. a variety of jasminum sambac.

autiful banks whose chief decoration were red and blue lotos flowers and which appropriated all that was the loveliest of
the lovely. It was adorned too with a large gleaming bath- 103
room[1] supported by pillars resplendent with endless rows
of figures in ivory, which was fair and like to a mountain 104
of cloud pouring forth rain by (reason of) the showers of
water which flowed constantly from the pipes of the apparatus,
and which seemed to be the crown jewel of the beauty of 105
the garden[2] and ravished the eye. The garden was (further) 106
resplendent with an extensive palace[3] adorned with many
columns of sandalwood, resembling an ornament on the earth's 107
surface, that glittered, peerless, shimmering, and with an
octagonal maṇḍapa resembling an ear ornament. It was also 108
adorned with another large, fair, charming maṇḍapa that had
the charm of a wreath of serpentine windings[4]. There in the 109
garden the Silāpokkharaṇī[5] pond continually captivated the
King who was highest among rulers of the earth, who had
attached the good without number to himself. Still more 110
delightful was the garden by (means of) the Maṅgalapokkharaṇī

[1] P. *dhārāmaṇḍapa* (v. 105) corresponds to the skr. *dhārāgṛha*. From the description it is clear that a shower bath is meant.

[2] P. *uyyānalakkhiyā*. It must be borne in mind that *lakkhī* is at the same time the name of the goddess of beauty, Lakṣmī. Thus in the picture the garden is compared with the goddess and the "palace" with an ornament of her diadem.

[3] P. *vimānena*. Writers are fond of using the term half mythically. By *v.* is understood mainly the abodes of blessed spirits which hover in the air. In JāCo. I. 328[15] a tree serves as *vimāna* for the devatā dwelling there. Save here and in the following the word occurs but rarely as a name for human habitations.

[4] Is the idea here pillars with baroque spirals such as are found on a structure of the so called quadrangle in Polonnaruva?

[5] I. e. stone pond. Having regard to the two names occurring in v. 110, I prefer to take this as a proper name. W. also understands *puṇṇapokkharaṇī* in v. 111 as such. It is quite possible. We must then join *sugandhivāripūrena* with *nandayantī* "which gladdened by the fulness of perfumed water". My translation of vv. 111, 112 was determined by the circumstance that °*pūrena* and *puṇṇa*° occur next to each other.

pond, and provided with the Nandāpokkharaṇī pond it looked
111 like the divine garden of Nandana. Yet another pond gleamed
112 there, filled with a stream of perfumed water, gladdening the
royal moon, and it was ever fair with rich beauty and splendour, furnished with the cave called Vasanta and with bathing ponds[1].

113 Again on land that resembled an island because the water
divided into two arms, the foe-subduer laid down a second
114 garden, the Dīpuyyāna[2]. There one saw the Dhavalāgāra[3]
that like to the summit of the Kelāsa, was made entirely of
115 stucco, wonder exciting. The garden was adorned with a
Vimāna which bore the name of Vijjāmaṇḍapa because it was
116 built to show forth the various branches of science. And there
too gleamed the beautiful, roomy[4] Doḷāmaṇḍapa[5] that was

[1] The *pokkharaṇīhi ca* comes in rather lamely after bathing-ponds have been already mentioned in v. 109 to 111. The question is where must the garden be looked for. In my opinion no weight can be attached to the structures in it mentioned in the text. The description is purely formal, made up according to the recipe for describing a garden. Even the enumeration of the many trees means nothing. The author is merely displaying his botanical knowledge or rather his acquaintance with literary sources like Abhp. 536 ff. Of actual facts which could be utilised little remains but that it was a *gharuyyāna* a house arden (private garden). We must look for it therefore in the immediate neighbourhood of the royal castle and I believe therefore that it filled the northern half of the citadel. Doubtless it contained pavilions and bathing arrangements. A. M. Hocart is inclined to look for the Nandana garden to the east of the palace and outside of the citadel, mainly on account of the *silāpokkharaṇī*, since a bathing pond answering this description does in fact lie under the eastern wall of the citadel.

[2] Opinion is now unanimous, I think, that the "island park" lies on the so-called "promontory" that juts out in the Topaveva west of the citadel and on which are now situated the rest house and the bungalow of the Archaeological Survey. For the ruins of the Promontory see the plan ASC. 1901 (=LIII. 1907). For the bathing-house in the Dīpuyyāna cf. EZ. II. 143.

[3] I. e. "white house", to be taken as a proper name.

[4] The meaning of *pavivīta* in unknown. Skr. *vivīta* (cf. Kauṭalīya 2. 2. 1) means a (fenced-in) pasture.

[5] I. e. "swing pavilion".

furnished with a swing hung with tiny pretty golden bells.
The garden was further resplendent with the vimāna called 117
Kīḷāmaṇḍapa[1] where the king at the head of the sport officials
connoisseurs of the merry mood[2], was wont to amuse himself.
And it was for ever embellished by the so-called Sanimaṇḍapa[3] 118
which consisted of ivory, and again by another (maṇḍapa), the
superb so-called Moramaṇḍapa[4] and also by the Ādāsamaṇḍapa[5] 119
whose walls consisted of mirrors. There too the bathing 120
pond Anantapokkharaṇī[6] with its stones whose layers resembled
the coils of (the serpent king) Ananta, continually captivated
the people. There the bathing pond Cittāpokkharaṇī[7] with 121
its gay pictures rejoiced the foe-subduer Parakkamabāhu, the
royal sage. Resplendent there was a four-storeyed, peerless 122
palace, painted with various pictures and bearing the name
Siṅgāravimāna[8]. The garden was adorned with tāla and 123
hintāla palms, was resplendent with nāga and punnāga trees
and was rich in banana, kaṇṇikāra and kaṇikāra trees[9].

[1] I. e. "play pavilion" or "games pavilion".

[2] P. *hassarasa* = skr. *hāsyarasa*. On the theory of the rasas s. note to 72. 94.

[3] The name might mean "pavilion of (the planet) Saturn". The Col. Ed. reads against the MSS. *Sānimaṇḍapa* which would mean "carpet pavilion, pavilion of the curtains".

[4] I. e. "peacock pavilion".

[5] I. e. "mirror pavilion".

[6] Ananta is here the name of the world serpent Śeṣa (see HOPKINS, Epic Mythology 23—24). It is also called Anantabhoga, and it would be possible to insert this name also here in *anantabhogasaṃkāsasaṃnivesasilā* (instead of "coils of the a"). W. seems to do this. But then it is not clearly indicated in what the comparison consists. In my opinion the steps surrounding the pond were laid somewhat in this form: ∽∽∽

[7] I. e. "picture pond".

[8] P. *vimānaṃ siṅgārasaddapubbaṃ*, lit. a vimāna in which the word *siṅgāra* (Skr. *śṛṅgāra*, "ornament, love, a particular rasa") stands in front (of the name). *Pubba* is used here instead of the customary *ādi* (note to 44. 6).

[9] The botanical names are in the same order: 1. borassus flabelliformis, 2. phoenix paludosa, 3. mesua ferrea, 4. rottlera tinctoria, 5. musa sapientum, 6. pterospernum acerifolium, 7. premna spinosa (?). — Verses

124 Now there was in the palace of the Monarch of all races
of rulers, among those belonging to the closest of his followers,
a man named Mahinda. He was a worshipper of the triad
125 of the Jewels[1], understood what was blessed and unblessed,
was wise, pure in heart, versed in the means of accomplishing
126 many meritorious actions, never went astray through lust,
hatred, fear or delusion, was never satiated with the fulness[2]
of goodness, as little as the ocean by the (streaming in of
127 the) waters. He was gifted with conscientiousness and modesty,
attacked ever with brave courage and was a discerning guar-
128 dian of moral discipline. Now this man with the favour
of the sublime Monarch who was ever a helper in all (good)
129 enterprises, caused a pāsāda to be built for the honour of
the sacred Tooth Relic which was pure by its suffusion with
the nectar of the eighty-four thousand portions of the doctrine.
130 The same (pāsāda) was embellished by a roofing and doors
and windows of gold and was resplendent with numerous
131 paintings within and without. It gleamed with canopies of
various colours like a golden mountain surrounded by a net
132 of lightning. It was resplendent with curtains which glistened
in brilliancy, and with a series of couches covered with costly
133 coverings. It was like to a dwelling of the goddess of beauty,
glorious as if all the grace found in each living being were
134 concentrated in one spot[3]. It was resplendent with its vast,
charming hall of the moon, which was wonderfully beautiful,
white as light, or as pearl ornaments, or as geese, or as snow,
135 or as a cloud. Banners were fixed on it, it was fair, with
gilded summit, bright, calling forth delight, beautiful[4].

113—123 again form one sentence which must be analysed according to note to v. 96. According to the description in this passage, the garden must have been full of buildings. That would fit the "promontory" on which there are many ruins, amongst others those of a bathing-pond.

[1] See note to 46. 17.

[2] P. *oghehi* lit. by the floods.

[3] The sentence must be construed thus: *āvāsaṃ viya Siriyā jotantaṃ sabbasmiṃ dehadhārinaṃ rāmaṇeyyakaṃ* (what is gracious = grace) *viya ekattha piṇḍitaṃ*.

[4] The verses 124 to 135 are one sentence. The subject is *Ma-*

Further the King, the sole banner of the stem of the 136
nobility, possessed a dear consort who had come forth, re-
joicing the eyes of the people, as the moon (rises) from the
ocean, from (the house of) the great king Kittisirimegha[1], 137
who loved him, the highest of rulers, as Sītā (loved) Rāma.
Amongst all the ladies of the harem, many hundreds in number, 138
she was by far his best loved. She loved the triad of the 139
jewels and beyond her own husband who was like to the King
of the gods (Indra), she cared for none even as much as grass
whoever he might be. She did what the Lord of men wished, 140
had friendly speech, was adorned with the ornament of many
virtues such as faith, discipline and the like, was skilful in 141
dance and song, possessed an intelligence (sharp) as the point
of the kusa grass, her heart was ever cooled by the practice
of the virtue of pity[2]. She, the Queen Rūpavatī, most 142
beauteous of beauteous women, the clever, the virtuous, pure in
action, the highly-famed, mindful of the doctrine of the Victor 143
which teaches of impermanency, had learned many sayings of
the great Sage and kept them in her memory, as for instance
"Short is the life of the lamentable men; the pious man should 144
live as if his head were in flames; there is no escape from

hindanāmako (v. 127 c), predicate and object are *kāresi pāsādaṃ*. Verses 124—127 contain the attributes to the subject, verses 130—134 (after an adverbial in 128, 129) the attributes to the object *pāsādaṃ*. It is to be noted that nothing is said about the spot where this temple of the Tooth Relic was built. A. M. Hocart assumes that it must have stood in the Dīpuyyāna, since the kings used to keep the sacred relic near the palace. He says (Memoirs ASC. II. 4): "Perhaps that puzzling structure called the Mausoleum, without doors or windows may be the temple in question." V. 130 seems on the other hand to contradict this. However the Tooth Relic was in Rohaṇa in the early times of Parakkama. Its recapture is first described in the following chapter. If then Mahinda's building was to serve for the keeping of it, its recapture was either actually expected or the structure belongs to the time after the close of the campaign described in Chap. 74. Cf. also 74. 198 ff.

[1] This seems to be the king of that name mentioned in 41. 65. The name of the queen is given in v. 142.

[2] Cf. above v. 41 with the note.

145 death"[1]. Thus as she knew the short-lived nature of beings
who wander about the ocean of existences, and as she knew
that there was no firm hold there that could compare with
146 meritorious works, so she was unwearied in much well-doing,
and as thereby she achieved her speedy escape from the cycle
147 (of rebirths) she built in the midst of the town a vast golden
thūpa[2], as it were a golden ship to reach the saving shore
of Nirvana.

148 Further in this beautiful town the all-wise (king) had
different kinds of streets laid down, many hundreds in number,
adorned with many thousands of dwellings of two, three and
149 more storeys and provided with various bazaars where all
wares were to be had and in which day by day there was
150 incessant traffic of elephants, horses and chariots — (streets)
which were here and there enlivened by people who were ever
indulging in great games.

151 Then he laid down in the vicinity three suburbs called
152 Rājavesībhujaṅga, Rājakulantaka and Vijita, adorned with
three three-storeyed pāsādas which possessed every excellence
153 and every beauty, and crowned by three vihāras which were
154 named Veḷuvana, Isipatana and Kusinārā[3]. But between the

[1] The strophe is taken from Saṃyutta 4. 9. 5 (= I. 108). It is worth noting that in S. the Sinhalese MSS. have in the same way as here in the Mhvs. the reading *hīḷeyyānaṃ*, whereas the parallel to the preceding strophe requires *hiḷeyya naṃ*, which seems to be the Burmese reading. There can of course be no question of our correcting the passage, since the author without doubt followed the Sinhalese tradition, though erroneous. In its proper form the translation of the quotation runs: ... "Short is the life of man, the pious man will despise it, he will live as if etc. etc."

[2] H. C. P. Bell (ASC. 1909 = VI. 1914, p. 6) has already identified this with the thūpa of the so-called Pabulu-vehera, situated within the ramparts, thus in the town itself and in its northeastern part.

[3] In the account 78. 79 ff. the three *sākhānagarā* are called 1. Rājavesībhujaṅga, 2. Sīhapura (instead of Rājakulantaka) and 3. Vijita and the vihāras built in them are given in order as Isipatana (in 1), Kusinārā (in 2) and Veḷuvana (in 3). I believe the designation *Rājakulantaka* ("end i. e. starting-point, of the dynasty") is an allusion to Sīhapura, for this was the name of the town founded by Vijaya's father Sīhabāhu (Mhvs. 6. 35) in Lāḷaraṭṭha. To identify the suburb of Vijita with the

royal palace and the three towns the monarch had built at a
distance of a gāvuta[1] from each other, charming sermon houses
and image chapels[2] and splendid vihāras adorned with rest- 155
houses for bhikkhus from all four regions of the heavens.

In the town Pulatthi(nagara) by name furnished thus with 156
all accessories and provided with every luxury, like to a garden
made beautiful by union with the joy of spring, which he 157
himself enlarged so that it was four gāvutas long and seven
gāvutas[3] broad, which bore his name — the beauteous one — 158
which possessed a splendid wreath of walls, which was re-
splendent with fair dwellings, which contained large as well as
small streets, which was an elixir for the eyes — (in this town) 159
the Lord of men who was like to Purimdada (Indra), who was
skilled in the preserving of all advantages, those not yet achieved 160
and those already achieved, had fourteen gates erected: the
superb King's Gate[4], the beautiful Lion Gate, the great Ele- 161
phant Gate, further the Indra Gate, the gate called after
Hanumant[5], the lofty Kuvera Gate, the brightly painted Caṇḍī
Gate, as well as the Rakkhasa Gate[6], the high-towering Ser- 162

town of the same name mentioned in Mhvs. 7. 45 is quite unhistorical. But it is not impossible that the suburb was named after that town. The three monasteries were called after especially sacred places: ... Veḷuvana after the park near Rājagaha which was given to Buddha by Anāthapiṇḍika; Isipatana after the park in Benares where Buddha preached his first sermon; and Kusinārā after the place where he entered Nirvana. For Veḷuvana see below note to 78. 87.

[1] Cf. 78. 91, 85. 20. According to the Kauṭalīya 2. 20 a *gāvuta* (skr. *gavyūta* or *goruta*) would be the equivalent of $^1/_4$ *yojana* (cf. note to 38. 68 and I, p. 349) that is, if the Indian yojana as is likely, is the standard of measurement, a little over two miles (according to the Buddhist *yojana* the half of that).

[2] P. *saddhammapaṭimāghare* = *saddhammaghare paṭimāghare ca.*

[3] If we reckon the *gāvuta* as over two miles then what is meant here could not possibly be the city with its ramparts alone which reached nothing like these dimensions, but the outlying open town as well.

[4] For the King's Gate, *rājadvāra*, see note to 74. 199.

[5] The monkey king, Rāma's ally in his campaign against Rāvaṇa, king of Laṅkā.

[6] For Kuvera see note to 37. 106, for the rakkhasas note to 39. 34. Caṇḍī (the same in Skr.) is a name of the goddess Durgā, wife of Śiva.

pent Gate and the resplendent Water Gate, further the Garden
163 Gate and the beautiful Māyā Gate[1], the Mahātittha Gate[2], and the splendid Gandhabba Gate[3].

164 In this manner did King Parakkamabāhu who possessed the firmness of the king of the mountains, whose intelligence was sharp as the thunderbolt, make the aforetime small town of Pulatthinagara which had suffered by many wars, splendidly adorned as the city of the Tāvatiṃsa gods.

Here ends the seventy-third chapter, called «Account of the Rebuilding of Pulatthinagara», in the Mahāvaṃsa, compiled for the serene joy and emotion of the pious.

[1] Māyā is the name of the mother of Gotama Buddha.

[2] Through this gate ran in all probability the road leading to Anurādhapura and from here to the well known port Mahātittha on the western shore of Ceylon.

[3] P. *gandhabbā* = Skr. *gandharvā*, denotes a group of semi-divine beings who are regarded as the heavenly musicians. They are the male counterpart of the *accharā*, the nymphs.

CHAPTER LXXIV

ACCOUNT OF THE FESTIVAL OF THE TOOTH RELIC

With the idea that the original capital[1] Anurādhapura 1
which had been utterly destroyed in every way by the Coḷa
army, was specially deserving of honour, since its soil was 2
hallowed while he lived[2] by the feet of the Master, distin-
guished by the wheel with its thousand spikes and its rim,
and because it was the place where the southern branch of 3
the sacred Bodhi tree (was planted) and where a doṇa[3] of
relics was preserved — (with this idea) the Lord of men be- 4
gan to take in hand its restoration. Hereupon the discerning 5
Lord of men summoned a high dignitary and instructed him
in accordance with his wishes. The latter accepted the charge 6
without disregarding it in any way, with bent head, made
obeisance with clasped hands, betook himself to Anurādhapura 7
and himself acquainted with the appropriate action, began to
carry out to the uttermost the king's command. Within the 8
compass of the capital of the former kings the skilled one
restored within a short time the large and the small walls,
the streets, the pāsādas and the gate towers. the charming 9

[1] P. *mūlarājadhānī*. The word *mūla*° has a twofold meaning, that of "original" (as for instance in *mūlabhāsā* "primitive language") and that of „first" (to which everything else goes back, as in *mūlāmacca* "first dignitary"), of "important", "pre-eminent".

[2] According to the legend the Buddha also visited the site of the future Anurādhapura during his three sojourns in Laṅkā. The picture of the wheel on the sole of the foot is one of the 32 great bodily marks of a *mahāpurisa* (see D. II. 17), who will either become a great world ruler or a Buddha.

[3] A measure of capacity used specially for corn. Skr. *droṇa*.

bathing-ponds and the delightful gardens as they had been
10 formerly; also the cetiyas of the three fraternities, the Mahā-
cetiya and the others, as well as the numerous vihāras such
11 as the Lohapāsāda and the like, as well as the pāsāda serving
him as dwelling, with its gates, bastions and towers, with its
12 royal courtyard, and embellished with a charming moon
chamber, and brought it about that the whole town furnished
13 with these and other marvellous works was as aforetime. Thus
he had the buildings set up by many former kings repaired
14 in haste by one of his dignitaries. For all wishes are fulfilled
for the wise who partake of the harvest of good deeds
accumulated in many existences.

15 Hereupon the all-wise (Prince) laid the foundations of the
town called Parakkama(pura)[1]. It was furnished with gates
16 and towers, with walls, moats, streets, pāsādas and shops and
adorned with parks which were embellished with pāsādas,
erected there for the shelter of many hundreds of bhikkhus
17 who strove after moral discipline and other virtues. It was
superb, prosperous and wealthy like Ālakamandā, the town
of the gods, and ever crowded with people.

18 Then he issued orders as to the way in which the officials
appointed over the various districts of the island of Sīhala
19 should collect without loss the taxes levied on each district
without oppressing the people in their particular territory.
20 Further in every month on the four Uposatha days, in ponds
and all other places in the island of Laṅkā for all creatures

[1] A Parakkamapura is mentioned in 72. 151. It must have been situated in Dakkhiṇadesa. If that is the town meant here, *kārāpesi* in v. 17 can only refer to its restoration and embellishment. Moreover Pulatthinagara itself bore the name of Parakkamapura. It was according to 73. 157 *attanāmaṅkita*, just as under Vijayabāhu I. it was called according to the Velakkāra inscr. (EZ. II. 246), Vijayarājapura. I consider it not improbable that verses 15 to 17 also refer to Pulatthinagara and its restoration, and that the compiler who found the two names in different sources, referred them erroneously to two different towns. What he tells us of this Parakkamapura is in any case nothing more than the usual customary phrases. Pūjāv. and Rājāv. say nothing about the founding of a town Parakkamapura.

without exception, such as game, fish and the like, living on 21
dry land and in the water he commanded safety (of life), he
who was himself threatened by no peril.

Now in the province of Rohaṇa numerous vassals after 22
the death of the Monarch Mānābharaṇa, deviated from the
right way[1]. Not knowing the character of King Parakkama, 23
and harassed in their hearts by fear they did not make their
appearance before the Sovereign. As they thought again and again 24
of their own shortcomings their terror was in course of time
redoubled. They knew in truth quite well that the great 25
courage of that lion-like King could not be surpassed by others:
all they thought of was that not a day's life would remain 26
to them once the union of the kingdom had taken place[2], but
they thought not at all of the further course (of events).
With speeches like this: "shall we ever permit a hostile army 27
even to set eyes on our country with its rivers, mountains
and ravines?" they brought all the inhabitants of the pro- 28
vince under their influence and betook themselves to the Queen-
mother Sugalā[3]. "Thy grief, o Queen, called forth by Mānā- 29
bharaṇa's death, shall not torment thy heart as it pleases.
Who then so long as we are in life, shall enter this our land 30
with its many inaccessible fastnesses?" With such like and 31
similar words they persuaded the Queen and all united, they
built at each difficult spot as far as the frontier of the 32
country, numerous fortifications, which were immovable even
by elephants, had trenches dug everywhere, placed there barri- 33

[1] P. *niggatikā*. The translation is uncertain. In Skr. *nirgati* does not occur in literature. W. "were brought to great distress . . . and had become utterly helpless." I start from the fundamental meaning "to go out of", i. e. the right way.

[2] P. *raṭṭhe saṃjātasaṃvaḍḍhe*. I believe that *saṃvaḍḍha* = Skr. *saṃvṛddha* stands here as so often, in place of the abstract, as only in that case is the proper construction of the compound possible. The union of the kingdom consists in the incorporation of Rohaṇa. The vassals fear that in such an event they will not escape justice.

[3] The consort of Sirivallabha (59. 45) and mother of the younger Mānābharaṇa.

cades of briars sharp-pointed as iron, made the roads in-
34 accessible with felled and fallen trees. Thereupon all the sol-
diers native to the province, thousands in number rebelled
35 and took up their place everyone in one of the big strong-
holds, girded for fight, well armed with offensive and defensive
36 weapons, full of violence, with strong forces[1]. The Queen
Sugalā who had not a mind capable of reflection and was
37 inclined herself by nature to evil, let the fatal words of these
people influence her. She made over to them the great pos-
38 sessions of pearls, jewels and the like over which she had
control, as well as the rich treasures belonging to the Tooth
and Alms-bowl Relics as if she were throwing them into the
39 fire, gave them office, ignorant of the right and the wrong
occasion, and began herself through them to start the revolt.
40 When the Lord of men Parakkama whose courage was
hardly to be surpassed, heard of these events he smiled gaily
41 and joyously. He summoned his general Rakkha by name,
a war-tried man, told him how matters stood exactly as he
42 had heard of them and spake to him (thus): "Arise in haste,
quench thoroughly the forest fire of the hostile army which
43 has broken out with a rain shower of arrows, appoint people
whom it is necessary to appoint, to keep the country in order
and come again quickly." Thereupon he sent him off with
strong forces.
44 Now the Sīhala and Keraḷa (mercenaries) dwelling in
Koṭṭhasāra[2] banded themselves together with the Velakkāra
45 force[3] and took counsel together: "The Lord of men has sent
forth many famous warriors together with high dignitaries to

[1] Verses 22—35 form one sentence. The subject is *sāmanta* in 22 which is again repeated by *yodhā* in 34. The predicate is *nisīdiṃsu*. All the other verbs are gerunds with which are co-ordinated participles referring to the subject, or absolute locatives.

[2] The place lies not far from Pulatthinagara in an easterly (south- or north-easterly) direction (see note to 61. 43). According to our passage, it seems to have been a garrison for mercenaries.

[3] For the Keraḷas see note to 53. 9, for the Velakkāras note to 60. 36. It is plain from our passage that the Velakkāras were a troop of (Dravidian) mercenaries.

take Rohaṇa; let us meanwhile take possession of Rājaraṭṭha."
And they all of one accord began the war. King Parakkama- 46
bāhu before whom every sovereign bowed, sent some digni- 47
taries who were heroes thither with fitting army and train.
He had those slain who deserved it, granted several villages 48
to those inhabitants living under a common selfgovernment,
had a number of other villages made into such as were de- 49
signed for the royal use[1] and free himself from fear[2] of any
kind, he made an end of fear of the foe.

But after the general Rakkha had with bowed head, pro- 50
strate, received the command of the Great King he marched,
the highly-famed hero, from Pulatthinagara, betook himself 51
to the locality named Barabbala[3] and halted there. When the 52
whole of the forces in Rohaṇa together with the inhabitants
of the province[4] received news, in accordance with the facts,
of his gradual approach, they came to the decision: "as long 53
as we are in life we shall not permit him to cross the fron-

[1] It is plain from this passage that certain villages had been assigned to the mercenaries for usufruct. In addition to the execution of their ringleaders (48 a b) they are now punished by the withdrawal of such villages which means a decrease in their revenues. Of the villages taken away some are allotted to peasant holders as communal property (*gaṇa*), others are declared royal property. I do not believe therefore, that W. is right in translating *gaṇa* by "assemblies of monks". *Gaṇa* here is rather the technical, administrative term (skr. the same, cf. BR. s. v. *gaṇa* 3). For mediaeval village constitution in Ceylon on which this passage throws a side-light, see H. W. Codrington, H C. p. 45 ff.

[2] P. *bhaya* includes the two concepts: fear (subjective) and danger (objective). Cf. above v. 21.

[3] H. W. Codrington discusses the campaigns described in 74. 50 ff. in his "Notes on Ceylon Topography in the twelfth century" II. Unfortunately the place names mentioned in verses 50—78 cannot be determined. Later details show however, that this part of the campaign took place in the districts on the right bank of the Mahaveliganga, mainly in Bintenne and the adjoining regions. Barabbala, Kaṇṭakavana, Ambalala, Sava, Divācandantabāṭava, Kiṃsukavatthu, Vaṭarakkhatthalī, Dāṭhāvaḍḍhana and Sahodara are unknown.

[4] P. *mahācamū* and *raṭṭhavāsino:* contrast beetween the regular army and the militia.

54 tier of our kingdom and enter here", and with great fury,
recking nothing of their life, they marched to the same place
55 intent on the opening of hostilities. Thereupon the general
Rakkha gave this army fearful battle, slew many soldiers,
56 broke through the trees which they had felled and flung across
the road, and with large forces reached the place called
57 Kaṇṭakavana[1]. He fought with the hostile army that had
taken up its position there by the building of a stronghold,
58 broke through the fortifications, forced an entrance and after
robbing many thousand warriors of their life, he marched
59 farther and came to the place called Ambalala. He offered
battle to the army stationed there, broke through the strong-
60 hold there and made the whole battlefield full of flesh and
blood. Then he marched from there farther, broke through
61 the strong fortification of Sava and slew many soldiers. Be-
yond this lay the forest Divācandantabāṭava hemmed in on
62 both sides of the accessible road by high mountains, and where
just at its heart the road was endangered and all traffic made
impossible by many huge trees which they had felled and
63 thrown down. In this forest from one to two gāvutas in extent
the hostile army had laid down one behind the other seven
very inaccessible fortifications whose stout gates were not to
64 be shaken even by rutting elephants. Against this army that
had firmly determined: "we shall in no case permit him to
enter as he thinks fit into any single stronghold occupied by
65 us[2]" he delivered for several months day and night terrible
66 battles and while he slaughtered many thousands of warriors
together with their leaders, the general Rakkha with large
forces took up a position on the spot[3].

[1] I. e. "Thorn wood". The part. *chindanto* is parallel with *mārento* in 55 c, *chinditvā* is subordinate to the part. *pātite*. Cf. *chinnapātitarukkhehi* in 33 c, as also *chinditvā pātitehi* (*rukkhehi*) in 62 b.

[2] I should prefer here to place the full stop after *sabbathā* and thus take this word in the *oratio recta*. For the position of *iti* see note to 37. 114.

[3] Verses 55—66 form one sentence. Subj. *Rakkhacamūnātho* in 55 a, again repeated by *camūnātho* in 66 d; pred. is *nisīdittha* in 66 c. The construction in v. 61—65 is as follows: ... "after he in the

When the hero, the Great King Parakkama, heard during 67
his sojourn in Pulatthinagara from the mouth of the mes-
sengers of Rakkha's constant battles, he gave orders to the 68
Adhikārin Bhūta who dwelt in his palace thus: "An indecisive
struggle for so long a time with these wretched rebels is
fitting neither for me nor for thee; smite in pieces according 69
to these my orders the whole of the fortifications along with
their gates, slay the whole of the numerous army and send 70
me then speedily a true report of these doings." He assigned
him numbers of soldiers and sent this man experienced in the 71
art of war, to the scene of the fight[1].

Hereupon Bhūta marched forth from superb Pulatthinagara 72
and joined with strong forces the commander-in-chief Rakkha.
Without in any way departing from the orders of the illustrious 73
Lord of men, they both had doublets of buffalo hide made
(for their men) for protection against the arrows, made the 74
great army ready for battle, offered a sharp encounter, slew
numerous warriors, many hundreds in number, broke through 75
the seven strongholds, laid down as they were one behind
the other, started from there again and came to the village
of Kiṃsukavatthuka[2]. Here too they fought a fearful, bitter 76
fight. Then after they had set out from there and had reached
Vaṭarakkhatthalī, and after they had here destroyed a hostile 77

forest D. (61 d) ... (there follow the attributes 61 d to 63 a) ... with the army (65 b), which, after it ... had set up fortifications (63 b — 64 a), was firmly determined ... had fought (65 d) ..."

[1] It is plain that Rakkha's action in the difficult ground of the Divācandantabāṭava forest had come to a standstill. Bhūta is sent to his aid. Cf. further the note to v. 90.

[2] Here one might assume the end of the sentence, since the part. *yāta* may be regarded as a finite verb. But the subject changes in the sentence. In v. 72 the sing. *so* is subject; but *yātā* must be supplemented by an *ubho* (after Bhūta's joining with Rakkha). *Mārento* which is the reading of all the MSS. (= skr. *mārayantaḥ*) must also be taken as plural. In the continuation of the sentence there is again a change of subject. At first as we see by *vattentā*, the plural (*ubho*) remains subject. Then in v. 78 it is the singular *Rakkhacamūnātho*. The preceding gerundives in verses 76—78 b are to be treated as loc. abs.

army which had approached from various directions, and there-
78 upon offered battle at the village called Dāṭhāvaḍḍhana and
had further fought an action at the village called Sahodara,
79 the general Rakkha who had large forces and train with him,
sent on many thousands of warriors of his own neighbourhood[1]
80 to do away with the hostile army at Lokagalla. Then he destroyed a vast hostile army that approached with the intention meanwhile of overwhelming the commander-in-chief (Rakkha). and retired[2].

81 The great four-membered army that had marched to Lokagalla so utterly destroyed the division there that only the
82 tidings thereof remained, took away from it all its possessions[3]

[1] I take *ṭhapetvāna* in the sense of "putting aside for a particular purpose." By the removal of a considerable part of Rakkha's troops the foe is emboldened to make fresh attacks. The operations which H. W. Codrington certainly interprets aright l. c., now become topographically intelligible. Events hitherto have taken place along a line east of the Mahaveliganga. Rakkha probably follows the main road leading from Dastota by way of Mahiyaṅgaṇa (Alut-nuvara) to Bibile. With Codrington we may look for Sahodaragāma somewhere in the region of Bibile. Here Rakkha is forced to halt, to secure in the first place his threatened right flank. The name Lokagalla without doubt corresponds to the modern Loggala. There is a small river of this name which rises on the saddle of Passara and flows northwards to the Mahaveliganga which it joins just where the river bends at right angles to the north. I am informed by Mudaliyar Wanasundara-Badulla that an old short cut led across the saddle of Passara from Buttala along the Loggala-oya to the Mahaveliganga. The rebels had reckoned with the possibility that the enemy might use this road for their advance and had occupied it. Rakkha however, advances farther east along the main road. A farther penetration southwards lays him open to the risk however, of being attacked in the flank from Loggala or cut off in the rear. Hence the expedition in this direction briefly described here.

[2] All MSS. have *palāyati.* I will not risk altering it. Moreover it makes good sense. Rakkha cannot for the moment advance. He is content to release himself from the foe who is pressing hard on him. Too much stress need not be laid upon the *māretvā* "cut up" in 80 d. It merely expresses the successful defence.

[3] W. translates: ... "Yet could they not completely cut off their great resources." He has misunderstood *acchinditvāna.* What we have to do

and betook itself then to the place where the commander-in-
chief was sojourning. The two armies joined forces, advanced 83
to Majjhimagāma[1] and here made the firm resolve: "We shall
not permit the commander-in-chief in Lokagalla to seize the 84
sacred Tooth Relic and the precious Alms-bowl Relic[2]." At 85
the village of Kaṇṭakadvāravāta[3] they fought a great battle
with the hostile army, destroyed the troops of the enemy and
then marched to Uddhanadvāra. With the hostile army which 86
after laying down fortifications, had taken up a position there
they fought a severe action, blew up the fortifications along 87
with their gates, destroyed many of the enemy and took up
a position in that village to equip army and train (anew).
Queen Sugalā took the sacred relics, the Tooth and the Alms- 88
bowl, and betook herself to Uruvelā[4].

with here is not the *a* priv. + *chind*°, out the frequently used verb *acchindati* "to take away by force" (skr. *ā* + *chid*; cf. PTS. P. D. s v.) The *dhanajātaṃ* which has been taken away consists of course of elephants, horses, chariots, arms.

[1] Now Medagama, 10 miles south of Bibile. It still lies on the highroad leading from Mahāgāma in the south to Polonnaruva. According to H. W. Codrington to the south of Medagama lately a milestone was discovered with a short inscription of Nissaṅka Malla (letter of 20th Dec. 1927).

[2] *Lokagallaṭṭhasenānāthādhikārino* cannot possibly be the subject of the principal sentence as W. assumes. That must be sought rather. in *dve senā* in 83a. There is no reason either why the generals who had fought at Loggala should be so set upon the gaining of the sacred relics. In a far greater degree was this the case with Rakkha. The idea is rather this: Parakkama's generals fear that the hostile troops which had been defeated at Lokagalla might withdraw to the main army and there insist above all on safeguarding the relics, since all was already lost in the field. This Rakkha and his followers were determined at all costs to prevent..

[3] H. W. Codrington compares this with a present Katupelella. I cannot find the name either in the Census or on the map. Sinh. *pẹḷella* means "gate" = P. *dvāra*.

[4] For Uddhanadvāra see note to 61. 16. It was situated near Monaragala, thus about 10 to 12 miles SSE. of Medagama. According to 61. 25 it was the capital of that part of Rohaṇa called Aṭṭhasahassa which was ruled by Sirivallabha. Here his widow Sugalā lived and the sacred relics were kept in her neighbourhood. Uruvelā whither she

89 But for the purpose of disposing of the hostile army in
90 Dīghavāpi[1] the Lord of men Parakkama had sent forth with
an army the Adhikārin Kitti and the Jīvitapotthakin Kitti and
yet other dignitaries with a thoroughly equipped army and
91 train[2]. They engaged the foe who coming from the direction
of Erāhuḷu[3], had taken up a position at the village called
92 Givulaba, in a terrible battle, broke through their fortifications
there, killed many enemies, started from there again and
93 reached Uddhagāma. There they laid down fortifications, carried
on war for three months and put the great army to flight.
94 With a hostile army that had erected fortifications near the
locality called Hihobu, had dug trenches and spread thorn
95 bushes, and which with massed troops had taken up a position
96 ready for combat, they then fought a terrible battle. They broke
through the whole stronghold together with the gates and
entered by force repulsing each attack with a hail of arrows[4].
97 Thereupon they advanced farther and scattered as before, a
hostile army that at a spot about a gāvuta in extent beside
98 the village of Kirindagāma had as before set up fortifications
and there taken up a position, and halted with vast forces at
the place called Dīghavāpi[5].

brought them for safety is identified with good reason by Codrington with Etimole which is situated about 5 to 6 miles south-east of Monaragala. What is curious is that Sugalā when she is forced to flee, does not put a greater distance beetwen herself respectively the relics, and the enemy.

[1] Parker (Ancient Ceylon, p. 396) was the first as far as I know, to identify this and rightly so with Mahakandiyaveva, 25 to 30 miles NE. of Bibile and about the same distance SW. of Batticaloa. The Ratemahatmaya Bibile assured me that the old name Dikveva is still well known among the people.

[2] I do not believe that the expedition is only now set going after the occupation of Uddhanadvāra by Rakkha. It is far more likely that it was begun earlier by the two Kittis, probably sent of by Parakkama at the same time with Bhūta. The author is going back in his description.

[3] Codrington is assuredly right in identifying this with the present district Eravur, NW. of Batticaloa.

[4] Lit. They made the combat one where it was difficult for anyone to come near (*durāsadaṃ*).

[5] The single localities mentioned such as Uddhagāma, Hihobu,

The Ruler of men, Parakkama, the best of far-seeing men, 99
sent to his dignitaries who were at that place, the fol-
lowing message: "Shattered[1] in combat the foe is in flight. 100
They have seized the splendid sacred relics of the Alms-bowl
and the Tooth and are fain, through fear, to cross the sea. 101
So have I heard. If this is so, then the island of Laṅkā will
be desolate. For though here on the Sīhala island various 102
jewels and pearls and the like and costly kinds of various
precious stones are found, yet of quite incomparable costliness 103
are the two sacred relics of the Lord of truth, the Tooth and
the Alms-bowl. At the cost of much valuable property and 104
by the constant amassing of well-tried and armed warriors I
have freed this superb island of Laṅkā from every oppression, 105
but all my pains would be fruitless[2]. My head adorned with 106
a costly diadem sparkling with the splendour of various precious
stones, would only be consecrated[3] by the longed-for contact 107
with the two sacred relics of the Great Master, the Tooth
and the Alms-bowl. Therefore must ye all, with the same 108
end in view, with army and train and without in any way
departing from the orders I give, conquer the hostile army 109
and speedily send me the splendid Tooth Relic and the sacred
Alms-bowl." The Adhikārin Kitti by name who was in the 110
district of Dīghavāpi, received his message with bowed head,
and with his division after assembling about him the many 111
leaders, he marched to the place which the commander-in-chief

Kirinda cannot be determined. At any rate this Kirinda is different from the place of the same name on the coast south of Tissamahārāma. Doubtless however, these events took place on a line running from north to south west of Batticaloa. Moreover the object of the whole undertaking is intelligible. By pressure on the right wing of the enemy the thrust against the main position in the centre at Uddhanadvāra was to be eased. The army columns then unite at Uddhanadvāra for the decisive blow (v. 111, 113).

[1] P. *bhinditvā* in a passive sense. See Cūlavs. ed. I, Introd. p. XV.

[2] Lit. "These by me, the island liberator, made efforts will be perfectly (*kāmaṃ* "at one's own pleasure") fruitless."

[3] P. *parittito* (lit. "purified") with reference to *uttamaṅgaṃ*, because this ("the head") is only a paraphrase for the person ("my head" = "I").

112 (Rakkha) was occupying. A vast army consisting of hostile
divisions and inhabitants of the country[1], advanced with all
113 its leaders, plentifully supplied with arms, equipped for combat,
brave, a veritable host of heroes, against the village of
114 Uddhanadvāra, full of lust for battle. "Of the enemy who
have invaded our country we shall not let a single foe escape.
115 On the road which would be the line of retreat of the foe
we shall place barricades and make the roads to an extent
116 of two to three gāvutas impassable and round about the terri-
117 tory occupied by the enemy cut off the supply of food. Then
when the whole hostile army is weakened we shall fight an
action with it in which because of our rain of arrows they
118 will have difficulty in approaching us[2], and destroy them."
So thought the army and after it had in the way above
described, put up strong barricades it took up a position,
119 keen for battle. Thereupon the Adhikārin Bhūta, the com-
mander-in-chief Rakkha and the Adhikārin called Kitti, the
120 heroes, crushers of the hostile army, after equipping their
great army on the battle-field advanced thence according to
121 orders all together and destroyed in a terrible combat a great
number of soldiers so that nought but their name remained.
They broke with large forces through the stronghold called
122 Maharīvara, marched thence farther, assembled all of them at
the place Voyalaggamu by name and war-experienced (as they
123 were) took up a position there. The hostile army which was
lying opposite in the district called Sumanagalla they destroy-
124 ed in the way described above, and after they had in a terrible
battle which was fought at the place called Badaguṇa scattered
in desperate battle the entire army of the foe which stood here
125 and had also put to flight in combat the whole army which after
laying down fortifications in the district called Uruvelā, had
126 taken up their position there, they took possession of the

[1] I read *sapattavaggikā* and believe this adjective belongs to the *mahācamū* of the following compound. We have thus again the distinction between the regular troops and the militia.

[2] Cf. above v. 96 and note.

splendid relics of the sacred Bowl and of the sacred Tooth and halted on the spot at the head of their mighty army[1].

At that time an officer of King Mānābharaṇa, the general 127
by name Sūkarabbhātudeva, the foolish one, who had been placed 128
in chains by King Parakkama, had burst his fetters and had
escaped to Rohaṇa. Then the Ruler of men summoned the 129
Adhikārin Mañju[2] and spake to him (thus): "The general
Sūkarabhātu has fled to his country, thou must come up with 130
him before he has gained a hold anywhere." Therewith
the Lord of men sent him off. He betook himself from Pu- 131
latthinagara to the place called Sāpatagamu[3]. There he fought
a great battle with the hostile army. He slew many soldiers 132
and after laying down a fortification took up a position himself there at the head of his large army.

Now[4] all the many rebels, each in his division, roused the 133
whole population of the country down to the very boys (in

[1] Herewith one object of the warlike operations has been attained. The actions described in vv. 119-126 must have taken place in a relatively limited territory SE. of the modern Monaragala. As the sequel shows, Parakkama's generals had obviously not yet advanced as far as Guttasālā (Buttala) (cf. v. 154, 156).

[2] It is remarkable that the MSS. have the form Mandin. Likewise 75. 152, 185. It is however beyond doubt that the same general is meant as the one mentioned in 74. 144, 75. 150 as Mañju.

[3] CODRINGTON identifies this with the modern Hapatgamuva. It lies about 8 miles NW. of Badulla in the Viyaluva Korale, on the right bank of the Mahaveliganga at the spot where it flows from west to east. This throws light on the whole episode. Since Sūkarabhātu has crossed the Mahaveliganga, it may be said that he has escaped to Rohana. His object was plainly to organise the rebellion in Malaya, in the rear and flank of Rakkha's troops. For that reason Parakkamabāhu is forced to send a new division against him. Mañju suppresses the movement in Malaya, Sūkarabhātu himself however, escapes, joins the rebels in position opposite Rakkha, and takes over the leadership here in the sequel (see v. 153). Mañju remains posted for the moment in order to safeguard the flank of the main army.

[4] I believe that v. 132 closes the Sūkarabhātu episode for the moment, The sequel takes place as v. 136 shows, in front of Rakkha's army. A more exact localisation is impossible, since the individual places cannot be identified. The situation only becomes clear again in v. 154.

134 open revolt). With the firm resolve, even at the sacrifice of
their life, not to give up the two relics of the Tooth and of
135 the Alms-bowl, they assembled with hostile intent, mastered
136 by insolence, at the village called Bhattasūpa. Thereupon the
commander-in-chief Rakkha, as also the Adhikārin Kitti and
137 the Adhikārin Bhūta and many other officers gave terrible
battle to the hostile army, and skilled in war as they were,
138 let not two escape by the same way. They took, in loyal
devotion to the King, the Tooth Relic and the Bowl Relic
with them, instituted a great sacrificial festival and withdrew
139 unthreatened from any quarter. Now the whole hostile army,
well equipped, having taken up arms with fury, gathered
140 together from every side[1] at the place called Demaṭavala and
141 fought a mighty, terrible and horror-rousing battle[2]. By the
(corpses of the) men slain in the terrible fight and (the mass
of) the cast-off weapons the commander (Rakkha) and the
142 other dignitaries, left (the foe) on every side not even room
to place their feet, and after taking[3] with them the splendid
relics of the sacred Bowl and of the sacred Tooth, they reached the village named Sappanārukokilla.

143 Carried off by an attack of dysentery, the commander
Rakkha now went thither in accordance with his doing — all
144 living forms are indeed transitory. The two adhikārins Mañju
and Kitti by name[4] without omitting any honour due to his

[1] Demaṭavala according to Codrington is now even the name for Okkampitiya which lies a few miles E. of Buttala. Popular tradition identifies the vihāra of Okkampitiya with the monastery where Saddhātissa found refuge after his defeat in battle by his brother Duṭṭhagāmaṇī. See Mhvs. 24. 39 ff.

[2] Verse 140 a is hopelessly corrupt. According to the somewhat highhanded emendation of S. and B., W. translates "(the whole army of the enemy) that was at Vápi".

[3] Note that the line *gahetvā pavare dāṭhāpattadhātubhadantake* is exactly the same as v. 126 a b. Nevertheless *gahetvā* in the two places must be taken in a different sense. As in this passage a śloka of 6 pādas appears in the same way as these appear elsewhere, the line may be a later addition. The intention was to stress that Rakkha took the relics along with him on all his expeditions. Cf. v. 138.

[4] One expects that along with Kitti Bhūta would be mentioned

rank, carried out the ceremonies of the dead[1]. Now that the 145
wise commander was dead and the Ruler of men tarried afar
off, they brought together with exceeding energy the whole 146
army of the Sovereign who was endowed with terrible courage,
and while these heroes allowed no possibility of any sort for 147
any kind of panic and celebrated a great festival for the two
sacred relics, they sent their report to the illustrious Ruler 148
of men and tarried yet a few days on the spot. When the 149
Sovereign Parakkama heard of these events he had erected[2]
on the spot where the commander had been burnt, a vast 150
alms-hall with four entrances, and in order to honour (the
dead) by sacrifice he sent the (following) order: "Collect for 151
those bhikkhus coming from the four regions of the heavens
and for the other bhikkhus a plentiful gift of alms." (Thus)
he (commanded), the best among the grateful, the first among
those who have attained knowledge. The two experienced 152
commanders joyfully carried out the order in fitting manner
and remained on the spot.

The rebels thought, since the commander-in-chief was dead 153
and they (themselves) had gained a leader in Sūkarabhātu,
they would meanwhile try for victory, and all gathered to- 154
gether in the district of Guttasālā[3]. When the vast, foe- 155
crushing army of King Parakkama heard that, it advanced 156
with its leaders, fighting at various places a severe action,
from all sides against the district of Guttasālā. Thereupon all 157

here. Cf. the association in v. 119, 136. Mañju is still in position (v. 166 ff.) in the N. W., in Malaya. He had thus merely to be summoned to the funeral rites.

[1] P. *petakiccāni*. According to the Brahmanical view as it is here and often expressed in ceremonial, the deceased before he is admitted to the world of the manes, becomes a *preta* a "roaming soul". The *ekoddiṣṭaśrāddha* is offered to the preta. Hillebrandt, Ritualliteratur p. 90.

[2] I am now of opinion that direct speech begins first at 150 c. The gerund *kāretvā* is, as seems clear from 149 cd, to be subordinated to the finite verb *pesesi*.

[3] Now the modern **Buttala**. See note to 51. 109. The scene of the contests and the further course of the operations is now again perfectly clear.

the rebels gave up this village and withdrew through fear to
158 the village (and) district of Mahāgāma[1]. When the Sovereign
Parakkama heard of these events he of matchless bravery sent
159 a messenger with the order: "That ye fight as chance wills
it, while dragging the relics about from village to village
160 pleaseth me not. Send ye both relics at once to me." When
161 the commanders of the army received this massage they with
the intention of sending the sacred relics, the Tooth and the
162 Bowl to Pulatthinagara, entrusted an officer with their care,
started from the village called Hintālavanagāma, and after they
163 had as before fought a terrible battle with the approaching
hostile army at Khīragāma[2] and had put it to flight on all
164 sides, they entered Khīragāma, fought here also a severe action
and cut down many. Then they marched farther from that
place, fighting at Tanagaluka, and Sukhagirigāma, at Kaṭa-
165 dorāvāda[3] and Ambagalla[4], as well as at Taṇḍulapatta like-
wise a furious action, and after bringing hither with great
pomp both relics, the Tooth and the Bowl, they sent them
166 to the Adhikārin Mañju. This (officer) had at the village
called Sākhāpatta[5] and at Lokagalla cut down many soldiers
and brought all the dwellers in (the district of) Dhanumaṇḍala[6]

[1] Now Magama, the old capital of Rohaṇa (see note to 45. 42) in the agricultural district of Tissamahārāma.

[2] Khīragāma is the place where according to 79. 71 (cf. note to the passage) a cetiya was erected to Queen Ratanāvalī who was cremated there. Codrington as he informs me by letter (20th Dec. 1927), has discovered this ṣtūpa in Badalkumbura near Alupota in the Kandukara Korale, about halfway between Buttala and Medagama. It is situated not far from the old high road. It is not impossible that we have to do in v. 162 ff. with movements of retreat in a northerly direction from Buttala, since Bhūta and Kitti were trying to get into touch with Mañju. For Hintālavanagāma see also note to 75. 7.

[3] Perhaps the same as the Kaṇṭakadvāravāta mentioned 74. 85. Thus Codrington.

[4] W. separates the compound *Kaṭadorāvādambagallake* into *Kaṭadorāvā Dambagallake* which I consider impossible.

[5] According to Codrington the same as Sāpatagamuva; certainly right. The latter form is nearer to the Sinhalese.

[6] The mention of Lokagalla now Loggala (see note to 74. 79) shows

into his power. He was stationed there, went forth to meet 167
the relics of the Tooth and the Bowl, celebrated for them
sacrificial festivals day and night, entrusted the Kammanātha 168
Añjana with the care of the relics and sent the two relics to
the Great King. Thereupon he set forth, marched to the vil- 169
lage called Bokusala and held counsel, being versed in counsel,
with all the dignitaries: "Our foes know their own country. 170
When we come near them they disperse on every side, pene-
trate then (again) into the territory that we have brought 171
into our power, in order to conquer it, and vex the people.
But would our master, the world conqueror, prize as much as 172
a blade of grass, a kingdom even if it were utterly subdued,
but by disregard of his commands, he who knows the
course of war? Therefore will we honour the command of 173
our illustrious monarch and in order that the foe may not be
able to return to the territory[1] already subdued by us, post 174
there at different places a strong force with officers, and when
thus our enemies have their roots cut off by us, we will set 175
forth to lay our heads at the foot lotus of our master." Thus
he resolved who was wise among those who understand de-
cisions. Hereupon all the dignitaries who agreed with his 176
words, set forth with the vast army, ready for battle, and 177
marched to the village of Vālivāsaragāma in a district where
many roads meet. After they had arrived there and deprived
many foes of their life, they set forth thence and built a 178
fortification at the place called Balapāsāṇa. Having posted
there the Laṅkāpura[2] Kitti and another large army consisting 179

that Mañju was still in position near the place where he had come into contact with Sūkarabhātu (74. 131 and note). From 70. 17 it is clear that Dhanumaṇḍala was a district in Malaya, approximately corresponding to the present Viyaluva division.

[1] The gen. *vasīkatassa ṭhānassa* stands instead of the loc. governed by *pavisanti*. Cf. Cūlav. ed. I, Introd. p. XVI.

[2] W. translates "Kitti and Laṅkāpura". He takes the last-named apparently for the general of this name (76. 83) often mentioned in the sequel to whom apparently 70. 218 also refers. According to the last passage this Laṅkāpura was the son of the Laṅkādhinātha Kitti.

of the four members, all the dignitaries and leaders set forth
180 at the head of the main army with large forces to subdue
from one strip of country to the other the numerous rebels
in the district called Dīghavāpi[1].
181 Meanwhile the Ruler of the kingdom, King Parakkamabāhu,
tarried in beauteous Pulatthinagara where there was no war
182 trouble. Endowed with the gifts of faith and insight and
with the effects of many meritorious works, he the first among
183 those versed in art, spent the day in pleasant pastimes. But
now when he learned that the relics were gradually drawing
nearer, he spake, his heart full of the greatest satisfaction
184 and joy: "In truth a great gain for me! Blessed is my life,
the finest fruit of my labours for the peace of the realm is
185 mine now that I may behold and reverence these two relics
of the Monarch of sages." With these and the like exclama-
186 tions he the virtuous one, went forth well bathed, beautifully
clad, well anointed and beautifully adorned at the head of
187 the festively arrayed princes and dignitaries, like to the moon
in autumn when it is surrounded by the stars, the distance
188 of a yojana to meet (the relics). At the first glimpse he who
was honoured by the pious, honoured them with all kinds of
ornaments, with the most varied kinds of precious stones and
189 pearls, with costly jewels, with all kinds of incense, with lamps
190 and sweet-smelling flowers and with many perfumes giving
expression to his reverence, as if the Enlightened One were
191 still in life. Unceasingly shedding tears of joy and with tiny
hairs bristling as if the inward rapture had burst forth,
192 beautifying his whole body, and with floods of the highest
joy making drunk his soul, as if he possessed limbs which
193 were overwhelmed by showers of the finest nectar, the stead-

[1] Mañju's plan was plainly this, to suppress the revolts which were constantly breaking out in the rear of the army stationed at Guttasālā-Buttala, in the same way as he had until now covered the flank in Dhanumaṇḍala. Hence he now marched eastwards into the Dīghavāpi district. In Mhvs. 75. 3, 4 Balapāsāṇa is likewise associated with Dīghavāpi. Verses 176—180 form one sentence in which the subject *sabbe 'maccā* (v. 176) is once more repeated by *sabbe 'maccā padhānā ca* (v. 179)

fast one, the superb one bore the splendid Tooth Relic on his head, like to the Moon-bearer[1] who bears the crescent moon
upon his head. He showed all his companions the two relics 194
while well versed in the sacred writings, he proclaimed their
glory, and after he the all-wise had had a great sacrificial 195
festival celebrated by them (his companions) the Ruler of men
had the relics laid down on the spot[2]. He who kept a watch 196
over all his senses, set up a strong guard; he commanded that
gifts of every kind should be offered, and then his heart filled 197
with the joy of faith, he returned with his dignitaries and his train to his abode like god Brahmā to the Brahma palace.

Thereupon the King had erected in the middle of the 198
town for the Tooth Relic a splendid temple of fine proportions,
like to the hall of assembly, Sudhammā[3]. From the King's 199
Gate onward[4] he had the road for the distance of a yojana
made perfectly level like the palm of the hand. Then he who 200
had his joy in the welfare of all beings, had erected everywhere triumphal arches with coloured pictures on them that
delighted the heart of the people, and beneath these outspread 201

[1] Name of Śiva who is represented with the crescent moon in the hair above his forehead.

[2] P. *tatth' eva*, i. e. just at the spot where he had raised the Tooth Relic to his head and showed it to his train. According to vv. 187, 199 it was about a yojana (that is about nine miles) from the southern door of the town. Here the relics are kept provisionally until their festive entry into the town.

[3] Skr. *sabhā sudharmā*, the hall of the god Indra. E. W. Hopkins, Epic Mythology, p. 58. It is difficult to say which building in Polonnaruva is meant by this *dāṭhādhātughara*. According to 73. 124 ff. Mahinda one of the king's followers, had built such a temple. Later on (78. 41) the circular building in Jetavanārāma is mentioned as the temple of the Tooth Relic. This one can however scarcely be meant in this passage, as it would be difficult to compare it with a *sabhā*. Probably the relics were changed about from place to place and this is reflected in a certain vagueness of the tradition.

[4] See 73. 160. As the relics were brought hither from the south we may assume that the King's Gate lay in this direction. The loc. *rājadvāramhi* in place of the abl. with *patthāya* is explained by the influence of the metre. Likewise 75. 72.

canopies[1] tied with garlands of all kinds of flowers in gaily-
202 hued succession. The pillars of the triumphal arches he decked
singly with different stuffs and the upper part he provided
203 with rows of umbrellas and whisks[2], with bunches of all kinds
of flowers, with fluttering cloths[3] and banners and other costly
204 things fit as votive offerings. The two sides of the street he
embellished with fruit-bearing trees, such as sannīras[4], banana,
205 areka and coco palms and furnished them with vases filled
with charming nosegays, with all kinds of banners and pennons,
206 with lamps and incenses and the like, and adorned the road,
capable of distinguishing the true from the false way, like the
207 street Sudassana of the lord of the thirty gods[5]. Then after he
who understood how to win good people for himself, had speedily
furnished the gate court of the temple of the Tooth Relic
208 like to (the town) Alakā[6], the Monarch had a priceless jewel
209 hollowed out and filled with sweet-smelling powder. Here the
Increaser of the realm placed the superb Tooth Relic, then
210 laid the jewel in a casket of precious stones and this again
he placed in a costly box of gold. But the Bowl Relic he
211 placed in a costly golden maṇḍapa that sparkled with the
rays of various precious stones, that was wonderful and
212 shimmering like the rainbow, that rested on four wheels, that
was indeed lovely and like to a bundle of rays of the rising
sun, on a beautifully arranged seat covered with costly carpets
213 in a sweet-smelling layer of flowers. Then he capable of
maintaining what has been won, made people of the clan of

[1] P. *vitānānaṃ patānake*, lit. "outspreadings of canopies." *Vicitravaṇṇasaṃtāne* precedes. The stretching out of the canopies is described by the three derivatives of the root *tan* (with *vi*, *pa* and *saṃ*).

[2] The whisk, *cāmara*, made of the tail of the yak, bos grunniens, belongs like the umbrella to the insignia of royalty.

[3] P. *vitānchi*. The word cannot mean "canopy" again here. The instrumentals in v. 202 d and 203 are governed by *sajjetvā*.

[4] Name of the King's cocopalm.

[5] P. *tidasindassa*. Indra or Śakra is meant. *Tridaśa* is also in Skr. a general designation for the gods. Sudarśana is in epic poetry the name of Indra's palace (E. W. Hopkins, Epic Mythology, p. 55, 141).

[6] The same as Ālakamandā (37. 106), town of the God Kuvera.

the Lambakaṇṇas with umbrellas, whisks and swords in their
hands and other people of noble families place themselves 214
round the maṇḍapa for its protection. Round about the 215
maṇḍapa he placed splendidly attired dancing girls in many
hundreds of (other) costly maṇḍapas, each of these being ac- 216
companied by people bearing lutes, flutes, drums and the like
in their hands and by bands of female musicians who were 217
like to the heavenly musicians[1], to do honour with their dance,
their song and their music (to the relics). With all kinds of 218
flowers, with incense and various perfumes he filled the town
with fragrance[2] and delighted the crowd of people. With the 219
light of many thousands of lamps he transformed the heavenly
regions and the intermediate regions into pure glory. With 220
rows of umbrellas and whisks, with rows of coloured banners
and all kinds of pennons he veiled the whole firmament. With 221
the trumpeting of elephants and the neighing of horses, with
the clatter of chariot wheels and the rattle of kettledrums;
with the enrapturing tone of all the festive shell trumpets, 222
with the roll of the great drums and the cries of victory of
the bards; with the shouts of acclamation and loud clapping 223
of hands and the jubilant cries (of the people) he filled the
regions of the heavens with noise[3]. The Monarch himself 224
arrayed with all his ornaments, mounted his favourite, beautiful
elephant[4] which was hung with coverings of gold, and sur-

[1] P. *gandhabbī*. The *gandhabbā*, skr. *gandharvāḥ* are semi-divine beings, the heavenly musicians. They are thought of as males, their feminine counterpart are the Apsaras. A feminine *gandhabbī* could only arise in the Pāli stage after the more general meaning "musician (pure and simple)" had been formed for the masculine alongside of the original meaning.

[2] P. *vāsayitvā* from the denom. *vāsay*. Likewise in Mhvs. 5. 139 "His seat after being perfumed, used to be hung up". My translation of that passage was wrong.

[3] P. *sādhukāraninādena*. By the constantly repeated cry of *sādhu* the people are accustomed to give expression to their joy and enthusiasm during festive processions. *Kārento mukharā disā*, lit.: "made the heavens talkative".

[4] P. *pavaraṃ nāgaṃ . . . subhaṃ*.

225 rounded by many dignitaries, who rode their steeds[1], he
226 went forth with great pomp[2] from the splendid town, betook
himself to the sacred Tooth Relic and to the glorious Bowl
Relic, reverenced them in worthy fashion with hands folded
227 on the brow, and while offering to them with his own hands
sweet-smelling flowers he went on his way with both relics[3].
228 Now at an unusual time a great cloud gathered spreading
herself forth[4]. With her hollow rumbling she increased the
roll of the drums and with the bright bouquet of the rainbow
229 she adorned the space of the heavens. She made lustrous
lightning quiver on all sides, an instructress for the dance
230 begun by the peacocks. Together with the dust raised by
231 the hoof-beat of the horses she made the wreath of the sun's
rays disappear and veiled the whole firmament in thick darkness.
232 When the dignitaries saw all this they thought again and
again: she will pour forth violent rain to disturb the high
233 festival, and their hearts filled with sore trouble, they betook
themselves to the all-wise Ruler and considered what was to
234 be done. But the Great King who knew the excess of his
own power and the unimaginable majesty of the great Sage,
235 spake (thus): "Be ye not troubled; here a marvellous high
festival is being celebrated that captivates the hearts of men
236 and gods, and I have set forth with unapproachable courage,
rich in merit, rich in wisdom, rich in glory, rich in fame.
237 What god, what Māra and Brahmā would be able to hinder
238 the magnificent festival taken in hand by me? Harbour therefore no fear when ye convey the two relics, but set forth on

[1] P. *vāhanārūḷha*. The word *vāhana* means it is true, not merely riding animals but vehicles of every kind, also chariots.

[2] P. *ānubhāvena mahacca* seems to be a transposition of *mahacca ānubhavena*. D. I. 49[32], M. II. 118[14] we have *mahacca rājānubhāvena*. Buddhaghosa says (Sumv. I. 148[14]) *mahācca rājānubhāvenāti, mahatā ca rājānubhāvena; mahaccā ti pi pāli, mahatiyā ti attho; liṅgavipariyāyo esa.*

[3] Verses 198 to 227 form one sentence. The principal verb is *paṭipajji*. The preceding verbs are gerunds or present participles.

[4] Lit.: A great untimely cloud came up, spreading itself out (v. 231 c d) increasing . . . decorating . . . etc. making the whole firmament veiled in a mass of darkness.

your way." With these words the discerning (prince) set forth.
Then the great cloud while filling all the ponds and rivers 239
outside the range of the festival with floods of rain, as she 240
approached the great procession, moved along before it and
rained just enough to lay the dust of the ground[1]. When all 241
the inhabitants of the town who had gathered together and
the virtuous sons of the Sage, many hundreds in number, saw
this miracle they cried: "In truth of great majesty is this 242
Ruler of men, the foe-subduer; in consequence of his high merit
he has appeared in Laṅkā. Here is merit, here is wisdom, 243
here is pious devotion[2] to the Tathāgata, here is fame and
glory and exceeding great sublimity." Proclaiming these and 244
other words of highest wonderment they filled all regions of
the heavens with loud songs of praise. While thus the Monarch 245
accomplished such a series of wondrous things as had never
been seen or heard of before, he celebrated the high festival 246
in a manner befitting his majesty, and after the wise (prince)
had had the two relics brought into the temple of the Tooth
Relic, the hero who was a single light for the whole world, 247
celebrated for seven nights long a festival of lamps.

Thus did the King Parakkamabāhu before whom monarchs 248
did obeisance, institute in pious fashion for the glorious relics
a great festival that like none other called forth joy, rejoicing,
wonder and admiration from all people who beheld it.

Here ends the seventy-fourth chapter, called "Account of the Festival of the Tooth Relic", in the Mahāvaṃsa, compiled for the serene joy and emotion of the pious.

1 *Hutvāna purato sayaṃ* must be joined "placing itself at the head". The acc. *dharā-parāga-mattaṃ* is governed by *pasamaṃ nayaṃ* (pres. part. of *neti*) lit.: bringing to rest, stilling.

2 Notice here the expression *bhatti* = skr. *bhakti* i. e. love, surrender in faith. The *bhaktimārga* as path to salvation comes in Hinduism as third after *karmamārga*, practice of the ritual, and after *jñānamārga* philosophic knowledge. The use of *bhatti* in this passage shows plainly the influence of Hindu ideas on Buddhism. What Viṣṇu is to Hinduism that Buddha is here — the object of *bhakti* (see H. Jacobi, Die Entwicklung der Gottesidee bei den Indern, p. 28). The word *bhatti* occurs again in the same sense in 85. 33 and 121 and in 93. 9, 10 in *Sivabhatti* which is contrasted with the Buddhist faith.

CHAPTER LXXV

THE CONQUEST OF ROHAṆA

1 Now all the dignitaries and leaders set forth with great
2 forces to occupy the district of Dīghavāpimaṇḍala[1]. After
fighting a great battle at the place Savanaviyala and utterly
3 destroying the stronghold there with its twelve gates, and
after fighting further at the place Gomayagāma, at Chaggāma
4 and at the stronghold Balapāsāṇa[2] a severe action and shatter-
ing the hostile army, they halted at the stronghold named
5 Balapāsāṇa with army and train. Thereupon the dignitaries
and leaders set out thence, fought a sharp combat in the
6 district of Mālavatthuka, and while fighting at various places
— at Vadhagāmakapāsāṇa, at the village called Mulutta, at
7 Senaguttagāma, at Bolagāma, at the place Vānaragāma and at
Gallambaṭṭhikagāma great battles in terrible succession, they
marched from all sides against the village of Hintālavanagāma[3].

[1] The narrative starts immediately after 74. 180 and continues the description of the operations set on foot by Mañju. Cf. *sabbe 'maccā padhānā ca mahābalapurakkhatā* (74. 179 c d) with *sabbe amaccā ca padhānā ca mahabbalā* (75. 1 a b).

[2] Balapāsāṇa is already mentioned in 74. 178. It must be assumed either that the place had in the meantime been abandoned by Kitti or that vv. 2, 3 are merely a repetition of 74. 176 ff. Codrington identifies Chaggāma with the modern Sakamam, situated near the east coast at Tirrukovil.

[3] It is, I believe, impossible to determine the places named in vv. 5, 6. But evidently the troops march in broad alignment throught the district of Dīghavāpi in a concentric direction — hence *samantato* — to Hintālavanagāma. This must be looked for according to 74 162 near Khīragāma, thus somewhat north of Buttala. In this region the troops of Kitti and Bhūta were probably standing. Thus there is evidently a plan for uniting the whole army and striking a decisive blow in the neighbourhood of Guttasālā and Mahāgāma.

With the hostile army that stood here after it had erected 8
on a space of three gāvutas[1], a strong fortification with many
entrenchments, they fought a great battle, slew numbers of 9
soldiers and took up a position on the spot, spreading fear
amongst the foe. But now the rebels all set off for Dīgha- 10
vāpimaṇḍala with the intention of (re-)taking the (already)
captured province[2]. When the dignitaries in Hintālavanagāma 11
received exact tidings of this undertaking they sent off many
soldiers. These covered in two nights a tract of ground of 12
twenty gāvutas[3], fought a great battle, cut down the foe and 13
so terrified them that they gave up trying to renew the con-
test. Then they returned victorious to their place[4]. Hereupon 14
all the dignitaries near this village having fought with the
foe — who after throwing up an entrenchment at the place 15
named Ādipādapunnāgakhaṇḍa were standing in the district
of Guttasālā — a great battle and after likewise fighting at
Corambagāma, further at the village of Mūlānagāma and at 16
Kuddālamaṇḍala a severe action, set forth from the place called 17
Hintālagāma. They fought an action at Kittirājavālukagāma,
further a terrible battle at the place called Uladā, at the 18
village named Vāluka and after fighting an action at Huyala-
gāma, they halted, slaying many enemies[5].

[1] Over six miles. See note on 73. 154.

[2] Thus the revolt breaks out again in the rear and the flank of the army. The pacification of the Dīghavāpi district had not been successful.

[3] More then 40 miles.

[4] I. e. to the headquarters at Hintālagāma.

[5] One must not be misled by the accounts of the success of single actions. It is clearly the case here of guerilla warfare. In open fight the rebels offer little resistance. But when the revolt seems to have been suppressed at one place, it at once breaks out anew in another. The accounts of "great battles" (*mahāyuddha*) and the "bitter or severe actions" (*tumula raṇa*) in which the hostile army is shattered and countless soldiers slain, are too much of a formula to lay claim in all their details to historical credence. Every encounter whether important or unimportant, is described very nearly in the same way. The capture of the relics was certainly an important moral success. But the main object of the whole enterprise, as it is alleged in 74. 40 ff. was not

19 Now to make the town Mahānāgahula which had been
inhabited by former kings, a royal capital[1] by the Great King
20 were sent forth the Damiḷādhikārin Rakkha and Rakkha the
Chief of the chamberlains, and they having equipped a great
21 army, set forth full of lust for battle. The Chief of the
chamberlains Rakkha hereupon sent off the Kesadhātu by name
22 Devarāja, who dwelt in Pañcayojana, with a great army, and
after destroying numbers of foes there, he being experienced
23 in the art of war, smote the enemy who after throwing up
many entrenchments at the village of Gimhatittha, in order
to make it the royal capital, had taken up their stand there,
so utterly that nought but the tidings of them remained.
24 Then to allow the exhausted army to recover from the combats,
the hero tarried a few days on the spot[2].

25 Thereupon the enemy gathered together and driven by
their heavy grief, they took grave counsel (together) as follows:
26 "The power of the Ruler of men Parakkama, which is like

achieved. Cf. below v. 149 ff. Parakkama's troops were unable to pass the Buttala line. The King realises that and develops an entirely new plan of campaign, an attack from the north-west, with Dakkhiṇadesa as base.

[1] A curious expression meaning about the same as "to bring into his power". For the idea must be that Parakkama now risks a direct advance against the capital of Rohaṇa. But perhaps we have to do with an old corruption of the text? Note that the pāda *tato kātuṃ rājadhāniṃ* is immediately repeated in 22 c.

[2] The military expeditions of the two Rakkhas dealt with in detail by CODRINGTON in his Notes on Ceylon Topography in the Twelfth Century, II., are quite intelligible as regards their plan and course. That of the Kañcukināyaka Rakkha is first spoken of. His task was to penetrate from Dakkhiṇadesa along the south-west and the south coast as far as Mahānāgahula situated at the mouth of the Valaveganga (cf. note to 58. 40). Before he begins the advance he secures his left flank by the expedition which starts from Pañcayojana, now Pasdun-Korale, east of Kalutara (cf. note to 57. 71). The hostilities then begin at Gimhatittha, now Gintota, a few miles west of Galle. Rakkha had apparently penetrated as far as this place from the frontier of Dakkhiṇadesa as which we may regard the Kaluganga, without encountering resistance. The rebels who were about to fortify Gimhatittha as a residence for Sugalā were evidently completely surprised.

to the fire at the destruction of the world, is hard to subdue
even by the kings in the whole of Jambudīpa. Even the Lord 27
of men Gajabāhu and the Ruler Mānābharaṇa, these two lion-
like kings, skilled in war, who prepared a great army and 28
spent much money, though they fought day and night in
divers ways, when they heard the sound of his drum of triumph 29
were scattered afar. They became as glowworms at the rising
of the sun, and since tortured by fear, they were not even 30
able to stay in their own country, they seeing no other way
of escape, sought refuge with (the god of the dead) King Yama.
Save the wilderness, there is for us no other protection. In 31
every way our land is furnished with mountain wildernesses
and the like. Therefore let us at all inaccessible places throw 32
up many entrenchments, make all the well-known highways
impassable, lay down many robbers' paths, and when then our 33
land has been made impassable let us gather ourselves together
and open battle." Herewith the rebels being all of one 34
accord, marched to the mouth of the Gālu river[1] full of
the lust of battle. When the Chief of the chamberlains 35
heard thereof, he marched thither, fought a great battle with
them and put them to flight. The army which had been 36
shattered in the battle joined from all sides with the foe who
had his position at Mahāvālukagāma[2]. The Chief of the 37
chamberlains Rakkha gave his army time to breathe; then he
marched farther in order to fight the foe at Mahāvālukagāma.
He shattered all the enemy and made the battlefield (bloody) 38
as the world of the Nāgas[3] when afflicted by the Garuḷas[3].

[1] W. is probably right in identifying the Gālunadī with the Ginganga at whose mouth at Gintota the troops of Rakkha had according to v. 24 halted. Gālu can scarcely have anything to do with the name of the town of Galle. It is a question, whether we should not keep to the MSS. reading of *gālurajjumukhadvāraṃ.*

[2] Now Veligama halfway between Galle and Dondra. It appears that the main body of the hostile army had its position at this place. When its vanguard had been beaten by Rakkha near the mouth of the Gālu river the whole army concentrated at Veligama.

[3] P. *garuḷa* is the skr. *garuḍa*. This in the singular is in the first place the name of a mythical griffin-like bird which is regarded as Viṣṇu's

39 He drove them thence as a panther many gazelles and the
40 victory gained, halted there himself with large forces. Then
the Chief of the chamberlains who was himself versed in the
consideration of advantage and disadvantage, while he sojourned
41 in Vālukagāma, reflected thus: "These foes perish of a truth
in great numbers, like moths who know not the danger of
42 the fire and are burnt therein. But when they have perished
the land will become like to a wilderness. And they know
43 not the great-heartedness of our King. From now onwards
we must grant the foes who surrender, freedom from punish-
44 ment and give them protection". Hereupon he sent to some
of the inhabitants of the province the message: "All those who
45 would preserve their lives, let them come to me." Now when
the merchants who dwelt in the port of Vālukagāma[1] to whom
46 their life and their money were dear, heard that, they came
in great numbers and (with them) other of the inhabitants
from all sides to the Chief of the chamberlains Rakkha and
47 presented themselves to him, tortured with fear. Hereupon
he sent his soldiers forth and made them several times fight
an action with the foe at different places such as Devanagara
48 and at Kammāragāma, at Mahāpanālagāma and at the village
of Mānakapiṭṭhi, at the ford called Nīlavāla and at the village
49 named Kadalīpatta[2]. He remained victor at all these places
50 and received graciously all who came to him. Now all the

steed. At the Pāli stage the word in the plural serves as designation of a whole group of such birds. They are the deadly enemies of the serpent spirits called Nāgas. See note to 41. 80.

[1] It is interesting to learn that Veligama was at that time (12th c.) a not unimportant trading-centre, thanks probably to the spacious and sheltered bay on which it lies.

[2] The progress of the Kañcukināyaka along the coast is easy to follow. Devanagara is the modern Devundara (Dondra) at the southern point of the island. Kammāragāma the village Kamburugamuva halfway between Veligama and Matara which last we recognise in Nīlavālatittha, since it lies near the mouth of the Nilvalaganga. The name Matara means "great ford". The remaining names can no longer be identified. What is striking is the sequence of the narrative, since Devanagara could only be occupied **after** the capture of Kammāragāma and Nīlavālatittha.

rebels made the resolve: "We shall not permit the all too 51
mighty army of the foe after crossing the river at the place
Mahākhetta, to fight (with us)". They set forth and them-
selves full of fury, reached the bank of the river. When the 52
Chief of the chamberlains heard of this event he sent forth
his army to march thither to fight with the foe. Thereupon 53
the best soldiers of the two parties fought a severe action in
the middle of the river. Now raged between the two armies 54
a terrible battle like to that of the gods with the Dānavas[1]
who rose from the ocean. While now the great warriors 55
stood in battle with the hostile army, they reflected thus:
"An indecisive battle with these people is the same as a defeat. 56
If not to speak of our Lord, the Chief of the chamberlains
hears such tidings, that means a great humiliation. Let us 57
therefore break in pieces the foe like small sugar canes, fling 58
them into the water of the river and make them food for the
fish and the turtle, otherwise it is we who shall still their
hunger." They fought an exceeding terrible battle like the 59
monkeys who leapt over the ocean[2] in the combat between
Rāma and Rāvaṇa. They caused the swift river to flow with 60
flesh and blood and set forth with strong forces to take Dīghāli[3].
The warriors marched thither and rooted out the host of their 61
foes as elephants a banana grove into which they have broken.

[1] The Dānavas are demon-like creatures, asuras, enemies of the Devas. This passage refers to the fight described in the Mahābhārata 1. 5. 19, in which the gods after getting hold of the amṛta conquer the demons who then withdraw below the ground and into the sea. Cf. Hopkins, Epic Mythology, p 48; H. Jacobi, Mahābhārata, p. 5.

[2] Refers to the battle described in the Rāmāyaṇa VI. 24.

[3] It is not easy to establish the locality of these battles. It is clear that Mahākhetta (v.50) and Dīghāli must be situated close together. Codrington looks for them (cf. note to 72. 63) on the Nilvalaganga north of Matara. But since Rakkha has already taken Devanagara, he must stand on the left bank of this river. We must thus assume that the rebels were trying to turn Rakkha's left flank and that he was therefore forced to give up the advance eastwards and to make a change of front northwards. The identification of Dīghāli with Dikvella is difficult to maintain, since the river is absent upon and at which the fights described must have taken place.

62 There shattered, the enemy gathered together again at the place called Suvaṇṇamalaya[1] and began the combat anew.
63 Then the Chief of the chamberlains also sent thither numbers of soldiers. There hailed down an uninterrupted rain of arrows
64 and after ascertaining through spies a passage leading through the forest, they penetrated the path pointed out by them,
65 slew many soldiers who had sought shelter in the various entrenchments and cleansed Suvaṇṇamalaya also from the briers
66 (of the rebels). Hereupon the Chief of the chamberlains who was himself on the way to Mālāvaratthalī, sent to the soldiers
67 who had marched to Suvaṇṇamalaya the (following) message: "I am on the march to the village of Mālāvaratthalī; set ye
68 forth also on the way thither." When the people heard that, they did so, and he took them all with him and betook himself to Mālāvaratthalī[2].

69 The war-skilled Damiḷādhikārin Rakkha by name, betook
70 himself at the head of a strong force to Doṇivagga[3]. When

[1] Codrington says: "Suvaṇṇamalaya is Ranmalékanda situated northwest of Kirama, or the range which includes this hill and divides West Giruva Pattu from Matara district". Kirama lies NNE. from Matara about 20 miles distant.

[2] It is clear from the passage that the march to Suvaṇṇamalaya was only the lateral expedition of a division detached from the main army. I do not believe therefore that Mālāvaratthalī should be looked for as in the line of march after Suvaṇṇamalaya. It lay rather on that followed by the Kañcukināyaka in his advance. As this was directed towards Mahānāgahula, thus in the direction of the lower course of the Valaveganga (see note to 58. 39), I should look for Mālāvaratthalī farther south, somewhere between Viraketiya and Tangalla.

[3] We may assume that the narrative here goes back somewhat in time and that the advance of the second Rakkha in Doṇivagga took place simultaneously with that of the first Rakkha in Gimhatittha or very soon after. Parakkamabāhu's plan of campaign was evidently to advance from two sides against Mahānāgahula, the capital of Rohaṇa, from the west and the north-west. Doṇivagga is the depression at Pelmadulla-Opanake, about twelve miles east of Ratnapura. The name is preserved in that of the small river Denavaka which flows through the depression. As there is considerable rice cultivation in this region it is particularly suited for the gathering of an army.

the numerous rebels heard tidings thereof, they gave true
tidings of the situation to the Laṅkāpura Rakkha who was 71
in the town called Mahānāgahuḷa and sent an urgent message
to come hither immediately. They thought: the road leading 72
from Doṇivagga to Navayojana is very difficult, therefore let
us hinder the (direct) passage into our province from there 73
at the difficult places[1], and with great fury they set about
beginning hostilities. The war-skilled Damiḷādhikārin Rakkha 74
wished now before the beginning of the war on the part of
the enemy, to strike a decisive blow[2] and in his lust for 75
fighting, sent off many soldiers and the Kesadhātu Loka and
the Saṅkhanāyaka Nātha by name and other officers. These 76
fought a great battle and won a great victory. The shattered 77
foe flung into confusion by great terrors, gathered again at
the place Guralaṭṭhakalañcha. Now the Damiḷādhikārin Rakkha 78
again sent forth his great army to take away this place also[3].

[1] The passage offers difficulties. What is now called Navadun Korale (= Navayojana; cf. note to 72. 60) is mainly the region of Pelmadulla. Formerly however, Navayojana, as Codrington points out, seems to have been of greater extent. I am inclined to think that it embraced in mediaeval-times the whole region east and south-east of Pasdun Korale, i.e. Kukul Korale, Hinidum Pattu, Moravak Korale. It was in this territory that the combats described in 72. 60—64 took place. Kālagiribhaṇḍa also mentioned there is probably only a part of Navayojana. The purport of our passage seems to me to be this: the rebels have no fear of being threatened from the west, from Navayojana, as in that case Rakkha would first have to cross the Rakvana mountains. He will, they thought, avoid this difficult line of march, but is more likely to advance along the direct road (*raṭṭhapavesana*). This would be more or less the road leading now from Madampe south-eastward to Ambalantota at the mouth of the Valaveganga. It was here at the places fit for resistance that the rebels believed the defence should be organised. We shall see in the sequel that Rakkha later on nevertheless risked the march over the mountains.

[2] P. *mukhabhaṅga*, see note to 63. 30.

[3] The name Guralaṭṭhakalañcha suggests the Atakalan Korale. With this is designated the name of the district in which Madampe lies. It is quite intelligible that Rakkha wishes to gain a footing here, in order to secure for himself access to the road leading to Mahānāgahula. The Col. Ed. reads *Garuḷaṭṭhakalañcha* as against the MSS. It is a risky thing however, to change names just in order to get a particular meaning.

79 The brave warriors arose, broke through many entrenchments,
even broke through the main fortifications which were provid-
80 ed with numerous gates and reached the place which the foe
was occupying. They took whom they could alive, sent many
81 other foes straight into the jaws of death, put to flight the
others who found no further support, and cleansed this place
82 also from the briers (of the foe). Then they returned (to
Rakkha), and he showed them befitting favours.

83 Now in order to protect the enemy whom the king's
majesty had turned to ashes, by the application of kindness,
84 even as a cloud (shelters) the forest set on fire by the glow
of the summer sun, the prudent Damiḷādhikārin returned to
85 Doṇivagga[1]. He appointed to every district that he had
captured, the appropriate people, took those who had sub-
mitted to his dominion[2] under his dominion and purged this
86 district also[3]. The enemy who after throwing up entrench-
ments, had taken up their position at Pūgadaṇḍakaāvāṭa[4],
87 renewed the fight with strong forces. The Damiḷādhikārin,
well skilled in the game of war, thereupon sent thither also
88 many soldiers with their officers. The brave warriors went
forth and with the rain of arrows which they let rain[5], with
89 the rattle of the drums and the clash of swords they were
like to the flashing march of a storm cloud that appears out

[1] The fact that Rakkha returns to Doṇivagga and that now like his namesake, (75. 41 ff.) he seeks to win over the rebels by kindness shows that he has not achieved his object. The breach planned along the main road to Mahānāgahula has not succeeded, the advance has been checked at a certain place.

[2] I should expect *vase yante* rather than *vase honte* (cf. 77. 10 and note).

[3] Probably Doṇivagga. It is to be assumed that the revolt broke out also in Rakkha's rear.

[4] The place cannot be identified with certainty. If what is meant is the place Dandava lying between Kahavatta and Opanake, the rebels had advanced very near to Rakkha's base. Later on Pūgadaṇḍāvāṭa becomes Rakkha's headquarters (cf. 75. 143).

[5] P. *vassitā* is instr. sg. for *vassitena;* in the same way *vivattanā* stands in d for *vivattanena.*

of season. Through delight in their own heroism[1] chasing
away the weariness of combat, they celebrated the goddess 90
of heroes with their drums of victory. When they thereupon
heard that numbers of the foe had built a stronghold at the 91
place called Tambagāma and had taken their stand there, the
heroes of tried valour were minded to show that nothing but
heroic action pleased them, marched by night thither and invaded 92
(the place), through the sound of their war drums challenging
the foe to fight. But when the rebels heard the clatter of the 93
drums they thought a thunderbolt had fallen on their heads
and in the greatest panic some fled while others perished. 94
But those (victors) burned down the fortification so that nought
but ashes remained and returned with strong forces to Pū- 95
gadaṇḍāvāṭa[2]. The Damiḷādhikārin Rakkha called back his
own troops and sent forth to subdue the enemy who lurked 96
here and there in their district, the four-membered army with
its officers. This army cut down at Bodhiāvāṭa, at Bhinnāla- 97
vanagāma[3] and at Atarandāmahābodhikkhandha numbers of
the enemy, fought also a night action and returned thence.

Now the Damiḷadhikārin marched at the head of strong 98
forces to the place called Sūkarālibheripāsāṇa[4]. Without 99

[1] P. *vīrarasa-assādā.* Again an allusion to the Indian rasa doctrine. See note to 72. 94.

[2] Again it is the case of a direct attack on Mahānāgahula, but which again did not lead to a break through. Tambagāma is without doubt the village of Tambagomuva lying about 8 miles ESE. of Madampe near the road leading to Ambalantota from which it is separated by the Rakvanaganga. The village gives its name to the district Tambagam Pattuva. (Census Ceylon, 1921, II, p. 490.)

[3] The Col. Ed. reads here *Hintālavanagāmake.* In the writing this form is hardly distinguishable from the form which I have adopted. In any case this Hintālavanagāma could have nothing to do with the place of that name mentioned 74. 162; 75. 7, 11, 17, which was situated at Khīragāma not far from Buttala.

[4] In this name are combined two neighbouring places, Sūkarāli and Bheripāsāṇa. The first is the present Urubokka, the second Beralapanatara. We owe these identifications to Codrington. I had them also from the principal of the Dharmasalava in Ratnapura, Urapola Ratanajoti, with whom I discussed the passages of the Mhvs. in ques-

disregarding in any way the orders of the Ruler of men
(Parakkamabāhu) he restored the people who without being
100 hostile, had hidden themselves here and there, to their district
as before. And after he had placed the proper officials in the
101 district (thus) won, he set forth at the head of a fearsome,
strong army and reached the village named Sīmātālatthalī[1].
102 Now the many rebels lurking in various places[2], summoned
103 hither the army of the inhabitants of the country. Thus in
possession of large forces, they then also summoned the Laṅkā-
pura Rakkha whom they had themselves made commander-
in-chief and who at the head of many hundreds of warriors
104 filled the world with the sound of his drums and kettledrums,

tion. The two places are only about two miles distant from one another in the Moravak Korale south of Pelmadulla-Madampe, on the other side of the Rakvana mountain range. I believe Rakkha's tactics were somewhat like this: The general has realised that a break through along the highway (now Madampe-Tambagomuva-Ambalantota) is impossible. He tries it now with an outflanking manoeuvre. With this object he crosses the mountain range to the south of Rakvana in order to attack the enemy from Moravak Korale (= Navayojana) that is just from the side where the rebels thought themselves safeguarded by the difficulty of the ground (see note to v. 73). The passage was without doubt the Bulutota pass which forms a natural saddle between the Galkanda and the Kurulukanda. It seems to me not improbable that it was already used in mediaeval times. After the crossing of the Bulutota pass Rakkha had however another parallel chain to traverse. It may be assummed that for this he made use of the deepest depression at Butkanda over which in the future the road will run which is to meet the Bulotota road from the south (Deniyaya). It is here that the footpath now runs which joins Rakvana with Deniyaya. Codrington's comparison of the Mahābodhikkhanda mentioned in v. 97, with Butkanda has now greater significance. It must be assumed that the expedition described in v. 96-97 had the character of a reconnaissance.

[1] Ratanajoti told me of a village Hintalgoda in Moravak Korale but I cannot find the name either in the list of place names in the Census (vol. II.) or on the map.

[2] Evidently as sentries on the look-out. Verses 102 and 103 show what surprise and terror the appearance of Rakkha in Moravak Korale caused among the rebels. First the militia are called out to help and then the commander-in-chief himself who according to v. 70, was at that time in Mahānāgahula.

and so advanced to Nadībhaṇḍagāma[1]. When the Damiḷādhi- 105
kārin heard of this undertaking, the prudent one summoned
his soldiers and held with them the following speech: "Here 106
shall ye now show your devotion to your Lord (the king)
and I shall be witness to your heroism. Think not: this is 107
bad ground, the foe are very dauntless, but believe without
doubting in the winning of the victory on the battlefield 108
through the majesty of our Lord and Master. But go first
and occupy the right place for the battle." Thereupon these 109
set forth with great determination and occupied full of daring,
a position near Mahāsenagāma[2] in order to fight. Now the 110
warriors on both sides flung themselves on to the battlefield.
With the sparks born of their arms as they beat against each
other, starring the whole firmament as it were by day, and 111
with the outpouring of their rain of arrows filling all regions
of the heavens, they began the battle, letting their battle-cry
sound forth. But the Damiḷādhikārin, the mighty one, won 112
the head of the Laṅkāpura Rakkha together with his heroism.
Then did the rebels melt away irretrievably as the tide of 113
the waters of the ocean when it has passed its shores[3]. The 114
battlefield there was full of crows, vultures and the like, but
the Damiḷādhikārin who had won the victory by combat held 115
high festival and surrounded by the divisions of his army,
he the highly-famed took possession of the town of Mahānāgāhula[4].

Now the Chief of the chamberlains Rakkha marched forth 116
from Mālāvaratthalī[5] and betook himself in haste to the town

[1] Codrington has recognised this in the present Obada (Sinh. *ō, oya* is always rendered by *nadī*). As Obada lies below Urubokka, about nine miles distant as the crow flies, on the river of that name in West Giruva, it proves that Rakkha in his advance followed the valley of the Urubokka-oya.

[2] We may assume that the place where the decisive battle took place was not far from Obada.

[3] The rebels dispersed as the surf of the sea disperses on the shore.

[4] In this section the MSS. give the name as *Mahānāgakula*, otherwise *-hula* or *-sula*.

[5] See above v. 68.

117 Mahānāgahula. He sought out the Damiḷādhikārin and the
latter discerning and aware of the favorable as of the un-
118 favorable occasion, took counsel with him as follows: "In
accordance with the commands of our Lord we have taken
the town of Mahānāgahula, yet still there are many foes left
119 alive. These robbed of all resources, have withdrawn to
Khaṇḍavagga. But that our soldiers just after they have
120 gained the victory, should march in haste thither pleaseth me
not. Where our Lord sets his foot there is our refuge." For
121 that reason they remained on the spot[1], and while they let
the people who without being enemies had hidden themselves
here and there, come to them and appointed each to his own
district again, they spent the time even there in the town of
122 Mahānāgahula. But the many rebels who had betaken them-
selves to Khaṇḍavagga, stirred up the inhabitants of the
123 district with the wish to renew the war. They gathered
themselves all together at the place called Khaṇḍavagga. The
124 Damiḷādhikārin thought that now was the right time for the
contest, he advanced from the town of Mahānāgahula and began
125 a fearful battle in Bakagalla[2]-Uddhavāpi. The skilful (general)
beat them all and then returned. Several of the enemy came
126 hereupon to Saṃghabhedakagāma; but the general Sūkara-
bhātudeva took his soldiers and came thirsting for the fight to

[1] The word *ettha* here is curious, especially in conjunction with *tatth' eva* in 121 c. The final words of Rakkha's speech are also obscure. Possibly we have to do with a corruption of the text. I believe that the words *tasmā ettha nisīdiya* belonged originally to the oratio recta and that after that something with which the speech ended and which made the foregoing sentence more intelligible has been lost.

[2] Codrington successfully identifies Bakagalla with the present Kog-gala (sinh. *kokā* "crane" is rendered by p. *baka* which has the same meaning) which is situated only 5 miles North of Ambalantota, that is about the same distance NE. of the ancient Mahānāgahula. This proves the fact that even the capture of the capital does not discourage the rebels. They withdraw just so far as to place the Velaveganga between themselves and the enemy and renew hostilities. The actions which follow (vv. 125—140) are only so many attempts on Mahānāgahula. Though in single skirmishes Parakkama's troops are victorious, no lasting success is achieved.

Mahāgāma[1]. Now the Damiḷādhikārin himself called his soldiers 127
together and sent them first to Saṃghabhedakagāma. The 128
brave heroes betook themselves now to the battlefield and after
they had in the fire of the majesty of the illustrious Ruler
of men destroyed numbers of the foe, they returned to the 129
town of Mahānāgahula and held there in fitting manner high
festival. But in order also to get the general (Sūkarabhātu) 130
into his power, the Damiḷādhikārin sent off the Laṅkāpura
Deva and many other soldiers to fight against him. They 131
betook themselves to the battlefield and with arrows sent un-
ceasingly covering the whole heaven and raising their thunder- 132
ing[2] battle-cry they dashed forward to the battlefield, slew the
general and shattered the foe. Then these brave warriors 133
too came to Mahāgāma[3] with the sound of their victorious
drums making joyful the Damiḷādhikārin. Thereupon an elder 134
brother of the Laṅkāpura Rakkha who had seized the leader-
ship of the army, gathered together the many foes whom 135
death had spared and marched for a combat such a rebels
fight[4], to the town of Mahānāgahula[5]. The Damiḷādhikārin 136
now also sent soldiers thither, they shattered him after slay-
ing many of the enemy. The shattered soldiers came to a 137
place called Kuravakagalla. The Damiḷādhikārin Rakkha march-
ed from the town Mahānāgahula, shattered them all and re- 138
turned. Now there came together from all sides to Mahāgāma
the Lokagalla Vikkama by name and many other foes in order 139
to fight with the Mūlapotthakin Māna. But in this fight 140

[1] For Sūkarabhātudeva see 74. 127ff. Where Saṃghabhedagāma lies is uncertain. Mahāgāma is doubtless Magama in the territory of Tissamahārāma.

[2] P. *gajjantā*. The comparison which it is impossible for us to render sufficiently exactly, is borrowed from the storm. The mass of the arrows are the cloud darkening the heavens, the battle-cry is the thunder.

[3] One expects here Mahānāgahula instead of Mahāgāma and on the other hand in v. 135 instead of Mahānāgahula rather Mahāgāma. Have we not to do here with a mistake of the compiler's?

[4] P. *corayuddhāya*, corresponding more or less to our guerilla warfare.

[5] Cf. above note to v. 133.

along with the life of the foe the Mūlapotthakin Māna by name speedily won the victory.

141 Now the Damiḷādhikārin took counsel with the dignitaries: "When we see the destruction of the foe in every single fight
142 and the panic of those fleeing hither and thither, then we think the enemy has lost the courage for renewing the war and yet one does not perceive that they are wholly rooted
143 out. Let us give up the middle of the province and when here and there hidden (rebels) have come into the middle of the province, defeat them[1]." With that the prudent one, the
144 highly-famed returned to Pūgadaṇḍāvāṭa. But the rebels who had not seen through his plan, streamed together from everywhere out of the wilderness into the middle of the province.
145 When the Damiḷādhikārin received true tidings of these events, he started thence at the head of his men, fought with the
146 numbers of foes at the village of Bodhiāvāṭaka, as well as with the foe everywhere else — at the place called Sūkarālibheri-
147 pāsāṇa and at the stronghold called Madhutthala — great battles
148 and robbed them of their life. Then he penetrated to the middle of the province, sent his army also thither in various
149 directions and rooted them out all and sundry. Hereupon he received a message which came to him from the leaders stand-

[1] In consideration of the sequel I should assume that *cajitvāna* is subordinate to the principal verb *hanissāma* rather than to the part. *nilīnesu*. Rakkha's plan is clear and proves successful. By *raṭṭhamajjha* is meant the agricultural country on the right bank of the Valaveganga with Mahānāgahula. That is it is true, in his power, but the rebels have withdrawn into the inaccessible wilderness surrounding it on all sides. In order now to entice them into the open country where he hopes to defeat them decisively, he ostensibly abandons the captured territory and withdraws to his original base near Doṇivagga. For it is here we must look vor Pūgadaṇḍāvāṭa (cf. above v. 86, 95). This explains also why in the following combats with the rebels wo are in fact taken in by Rakkha's manoeuvre, the former names Bodhiāvāṭa (v. 97) and Sūkarālibheripāsāṇa (v. 98) recur. The Madhutthala named along with them must also be situated near Sūkarāli = Urubokka. All these places are situated on the border of the *raṭṭhamajjha* into which he finally penetrates to annihilate the enemy.

ing in Huyalagāma and marched to Kumbugāma[1]. Thereupon 150
the general stationed in Huyalagāma by name Mañju, and
the two generals called Kitti and Bhūta came surrounded by 151
numbers of heroic officers, to the same place, holding high
festival of joy. The general by name Mañju[2], hereupon, 152
showing honour to the Damiḷādhikārin Rakkha, spake the
following words: "So long as the many foes which have 153
broken away from your country and are hidden in the various
inaccessible places have not got a footing, let us slay them 154
all, while the enemy who has sought refuge in the wilderness
of Aṭṭhasahassaka and the Queen Sugalā we will take captive[3]. 155
But if the many foes who sojourn in the wilderness are hard
for you to overcome, we shall send off soldiers." The Damiḷādhi- 156
kārin agreed with these words. He advanced in haste with
his army into the region of the Vananadī[4] and son came near 157
to the foe who in order to reach the mountain wilderness,
had speedily betaken themselves to Mālāvaratthalī. When they 158
heard that Rakkha was on the march[5], they withdrew, tor-

[1] We have seen above in v. 19 that the generals Mañju, Kitti and Bhūta after vain attempts to reach Mahāgāma by Guttasālā, halt at Huyalagāma. Now they try to get into touch with Rakkha. As Huyalagāma cannot have lain far from Buttala, we may look for Kumbugāma somewhere on the road leading along the southern base of the mountains. [2] Cf. note to 74. 129.

[3] Aṭṭhasahassaka (cf. note to 61. 24) is the territory east of the Valaveganga. Thus Mañju and his generals undertake the operations in eastern Rohaṇa, Rakkha those in the western part of the province.

[4] There is scarcely a doubt that with Vananadī is meant the Valaveganga. The ger. *pavessa* must be = *pavissa*. A causative form is impossible since the object belonging to it is wanting. *Saha senayā* agrees only with a *pavisati*. But perhaps we might render *vananadī-passaṃ pavessa* by: "he advanced along the V." That would make excellent sense. The rebels have evidently occupied Mahānāgahula after Rakkha's withdrawal. In order now to cut them off from communication with eastern Rohaṇa, Rakkha marches from Kumbugāma down the Vananadī. His plan succeeds. The rebels turn westward by way of Mālāvaratthalī (see note to v. 66) to the mountains of Dvādasasahassaka, the present district of Giruva (note to 61. 22).

[5] That is in further pursuit of them.

tured by fear, into the great forest and sought refuge on the
159 Mahāpabbata. The Damiḷādhikārin surrounded the mountain,
fought a great battle with them and utterly destroyed them.
160 Then after occupying Dvādasasahassaka thus set free from the
briers (of the rebels), he considered what should be done with
161 the many foes taken alive and had many hundreds of the
162 enemy impaled in villages and market-towns. Likewise round
about the village of Mahānāgahula the mighty one had num-
163 bers of the foe impaled, several too hanged on the gallows
and burnt to ashes and after taking up his abode in the vil-
164 lage of Mahānāgahula, he had under a favorable constellation
the drums of government of the illustrious Ruler of men
165 beaten in villages and market-towns. After sending a messenger
announcing these events to the Ruler of men and receiving
166 from the Great King a mark of honour, he took up his abode,
the discerning, the highly-famed (general), in that same Dvā-
dasasahassaka, pondering over the needful measures.

167 All the chief dignitaries[1] in Kumbugāma reflected (thus):
168 "From the time that we set forth to war in Rohaṇa the sol-
diers sent forth by us have here and there in great battles
169 covered the earth with the bones of the foe, and even all the
brave warriors who dwell in Jambudīpa would not be able to
170 withstand these soldiers. Why then should we henceforward
think to carry on war with the foe hidden here and there
171 through fear? Queen Sugalā is the cause of these people
172 becoming rebels and has led them into the wilderness[2]. There-
fore we must get the Queen alive into our power." With such
resolve the discerning (generals) marched from Kumbugāma
173 and came to Harītakīvāta. After they had there in various
places posted good soldiers, known as courageous people, in
174 the necessary numbers, they advanced thence fully armed to
Kaṇhavāṭa and when at the place called Vanagāma, they

[1] The narrative now deals with the operations in eastern Rohaṇa which we may imagine as taking place simultaneously with the events related in vv. 156—166.

[2] Owing to the presence of the obj. *te* the part. pres. *pavisantī* must be taken in a causative sense (see Cūlavs. ed. I, Introduction p. XIV).

caught sight of the hostile army with whom was the Queen, 175
they fought there a great (and) fearful battle. With the sound
of their drums of victory cleaving open, as it were, the earth,
they seized the Queen and all her treasures of many a kind[1]. 176
Having appointed for the guarding of the treasure the necessary
chamberlains, they brought the war game begun there to an 177
end and after covering the earth with the hands and feet and
heads of the foe and taking those alive to whom this had to 178
happen, they made the province of Rohaṇa everywhere free
from the briers (of the rebels).

Now by some kind of wile, taking with them a few sol- 179
diers, the three Phālakālas who were near the end of their
life, and the two Laṅkāpuras by name Taddhigāma and Pabbata, 180
had escaped out of the hand of the foe[2] and were in flight
tortured by fear. But the two brothers, the generals[3] and 181
the Laṅkāpura known by the name of Kaḍakkuḍa, as well as
many other officers with their soldiers, having reached Ud- 182
dhanadvāragāma[4], shattered them in a great battle and then
reached Nigrodhamāragalla[5]. Hereupon the great dignitaries 183
with their officers pursued the enemy, sent the head of the
Phālakāla to the highest dignitaries[6], captured the Laṅkāpura 184

[1] The place where the capture of Sugalā took place is not yet determined. The name Valgama or Valagama to which the P. *Vanagāma* would correspond, occurs frequently in Ceylon. A Valagama is situated in the Bintenna Pattu. It is however very doubtful if this can be the one meant.

[2] The enemies from whom Phālakāla and the others had escaped were of course the troops of Parakkamabāhu.

[3] For the *dve bhātaro daṇḍanāthā* see note to 70. 279. They are mentioned here for the last time.

[4] See note to 61. 16. Uddhanadvāragāma was the capital of eastern Rohaṇa (Aṭṭhasahassaka).

[5] Verses 179—182 form one sentence. The subjects are in v. 181. The principal verb is *upāgamuṃ* to which the gerunds *samāgantvā, pabhinditvāna* are subordinate. The accusatives in v. 180 are governed by *pabhinditvāna* as objects. As attribute they have the pres. part. *palāyante* to which *mucchitvā* and *gahetvāna* are again subordinate.

[6] That is Mañju together with Bhūta and Kitti who had not personally taken part in the pursuit of the Phālakālas.

Pabbata by name, alive and destroyed the foe so utterly that nought but the tidings of them remained[1].

185 Thereupon the clever Adhikārin Mañju[2] made the following proposal: "From the time when we began to conquer this
186 Rohaṇa we have never — apart from[3] the boundless terror-inspiring destruction of our enemies in battle through the
187 majesty of our Lord — treated the foe with sternness so as to teach the people what evil results treason to the king brings
188 about. Therefore those deserving of harshness let us treat harshly and let us be ever kind to those who deserve kindness,
189 and in this way in accord with the commands of our Lord and Master, win them over to ourselves." All agreed with
190 zeal to his proposal. They caused many foes to whom severity was due, to be brought before them, and at villages and market-
191 towns they had numbers of stakes set up on which they impaled many hundreds of the enemy. Many other foes they
192 had hanged on the gallows and burnt and showed forth in every way the majesty — hard to subdue, scarcely to be surpassed, arousing astonishment — of the Ruler of men Pa-
193 rakkamabāhu. Then while they showed due grace to those who were accessible to kindness and were worthy of being treated with kindness, they brought peace to the province, as clouds in the rainy season to a forest burnt by fire.

194 When the Ruler of men Parakkama heard tidings of these events he sent an exceeding gracious message of the following
195 content: "In the first place send hither all the dignitaries
196 taken alive and the Queen Sugalā. The burden of the whole administration there is to be given over to the Adhikārin Bhūta. Then along with the whole of the four-membered army
197 sent forth from here, preceded by the numerous bhikkhu community dwelling there, after leaving the necessary garrison
198 in the various districts, under a constellation regarded as fa-

[1] I prefer to join the two pādas *kariṃsu* as far as *sapattake* with v. 184 instead of with v. 185. *Sabbaṃ* is to be taken in an adverbial sense as emphasising *sabbathā*.

[2] See note to 74. 129.

[3] I take the ger. *hitvāna* in this sense in this passage.

vorable, the whole of the dignitaries shall assemble and present themselves before me."

The dignitaries all carried out his orders without omitting 199
anything. They marched from Rohaṇa and reached at the 200
head of their large army, Pulatthinagara. Accompanied by
the dwellers in Pulatthinagara, who played music, shouted
with joy, clapped their hands in applause, waved cloths a 201
thousandfold again and again and let their cries of victory
resound – they drew near to the superb royal palace and cleans- 202
ed their heads with the blossom dust of the foot-lotus of the 203
illustrious King of kings enthroned (there) in splendour.

Thus had this Ruler of men, pursuing the path of politi- 204
cal wisdom and of virtue, with exceeding terrible majesty[1], more powerful than a forest conflagration, of keen understanding, together with his heroes made Rohaṇa free from the briers of the foe.

Here ends the seventy-fifth chapter, called «The Conquest of Rohaṇa», in the Mahāvaṃsa, compiled for the serene joy and emotion of the pious.

[1] The word that I here translate by "majesty" is the P. *tejo*. As this has the original meaning of "glow", the comparison with the forest conflagration has also a linguistic connection. The compound must be separated thus: *dava-dahana-uggatara-atibhīma-tejo.*

Chapter LXXVI

ACCOUNT OF THE CAPTURE OF THE TOWN OF RĀJINĀ

1 While now the Monarch gifted with insight, day and night
strove unweariedly for the furtherance of the laity and of the
2 Order, there banded together in the eighth year of the reign
of the illustrious Ruler of men all the inhabitants of the pro-
3 vince of Rohaṇa and stirred up by an all too foolhardy vil-
lain[1], they revolted anew, to cruel destruction foredoomed.
4 When King Parakkamabāhu heard of these events he sent
5 once more a great army with dignitaries thither; and as he
fought at all the villages and market-towns named aforetime
6 ever renewed battles and made the enemy as fuel for the fire
of his own majesty, he shortly freed the whole province of
Rohaṇa from the briers (of the rebels).

7 In the sixteenth year of this King of kings, in the pro-
8 vince immediately bordering on Mahātittha[2] several people
dwelling in that province, who were near the end of their
life[3], stirred up a revolt and began the war which seemed to
9 them the better (lot)[4]. Thither also the (prince) gifted with
discernment, sent a four-membered army and destroyed the
foe so that they became as dust.

10 Between the countries of Laṅkā and Rāmañña[5] there had
never been a dissension since they were inhabited by people

[1] I incline to take *kenapi pāpakammena* as referring to a person, *pāpakamma* thus to be taken like the skr. *pāpakarman* (cf. BR. s. v. as a bahuvrīhi compound.

[2] See note to 48. 81.

[3] The fate to which they are doomed tempts them to the foolish revolt.

[4] Better (*vara*) than subjection to Parakkamabāhu's dominion.

[5] That is Pegu in Lower Burma.

who held the true faith. The rulers of the island of Laṅkā 11
and the monarchs of Rāmañña were both in like manner true
disciples of the Sugata[1]. Hence all former monarchs in both 12
countries in deeply-rooted trust, filled with friendly feeling[2]
were wont to send each other many costly gifts and in this 13
way for a long time to maintain intercourse without dissension.
Also with King Parakkamabāhu the Monarch of Rāmañña 14
kept up friendly relations even as former rulers who had for
a long time held firmly to him. But once upon a time the 15
deluded one hearkened to the words of slanderers, of certain
messengers who came back from our land, and deprived the 16
envoys of the Sovereign of Laṅkā who came into his own
country, of the maintenance formerly granted. Furthermore 17
he issued the order that elephants which had (hitherto) been
sold by many (traders) to foreign countries[3] were no longer
to be sold. Further with evil intent he made the restriction 18
that elephants which had formerly been sold there for a
hundred or a thousand silver nikkhalas[4] must (henceforth) be 19
sold for two or three thousand[5]. He also did away with the 20
age-old custom of presenting an elephant to every vessel in
which gifts[6] were conveyed. When he caught sight of a letter 21

[1] P. *paramasogatā*. Cf. skr. *saugata* from *sugata*, a frequent name of the Buddha which designates him as the guide on the path of salvation. R. O. Franke in his translation of the Dīghanikāya renders *sugata* by "he who completes the path".

[2] *Daḷhasaṃrūḷhavissambhā* and *sahitā* are attributes of *bhūpālā*, and the instr. *cittena hitā* (this last for *hitena*) belongs to *sahitā*.

[3] We see thus that Burma in the Middle Ages traded in elephants with foreign countries.

[4] An unknown coin. The word is without doubt connected with the P. *nikkha* or *nekkha* = skr. *niṣka* which likewise denotes a weight and a coin.

[5] VV. 18, 19 seem to be in contradiction to v. 17. I think however that in v. 17 the emphasis is to be placed on *nekattha nekehi*. It is the free trade in elephants that according to v. 17 the king makes an end of, putting in its place a royal monopoly. This is immediately followed by an enormous rise in prices.

[6] Evidently from foreign sovereigns, in the first place the king of Laṅkā with whom according to v. 13 such exchange of gifts had fre-

written on gold, addressed to himself, he under the pretext
22 that they were envoys sent to Kamboja[1], or saying something
of that kind, had the envoys of the Sovereign of Laṅkā after
taking from them all their goods and chattels, thrown into a
23 fortress in the Malaya country[2]. And although he learned
exactly how his own envoy Tapassin by name, had had every
24 distinction conferred on him by the Ruler of Laṅkā, he ne-
vertheless bereft of all political wisdom, took everything away
from the envoys of the Monarch of Laṅkā: their money, their
25 elephants and their vessels, had blocks of wood fastened to
their feet to their greatest torture, and employed them in the
26 work of sprinkling water in the prisons. When once upon a
time a prince of Jambudīpa Kassapa by name, sent costly gifts
27 along with a letter on gold, he forbade his people to land and
in an insulting manner made them take the letter back to their
28 town. One day he had the Sīhala envoys summoned to him
and declared to them: "Henceforth no vessel from the Sīhala
29 country shall be sent to my kingdom. Give us now in writ-
ing the declaration that if (messengers) from there are again
sent to us, in case we should slay the envoys who have come
30 here, no blame of any kind will attach to us[3]. If ye give
not the declaration ye shall not have permission to return
31 home." After he had made them sign this, so that in the
event of a transgression they should not return again to their
32 country[4], he took the paper from their hand. The teacher

quently taken place. The King of Rāmañña does not put an end to the intercourse but alters it in a way which shows unfriendliness.

[1] Name of Western Siam.

[2] Malaya denotes as in Ceylon and in Southern India (see 76. 195) the mountainous regions of the country.

[3] In the original direct discourse: "if ... are sent here ... in case ye slay ... no blame will attach to you".

[4] The passage is doubtful. I believe that *sa-raṭṭha-anāgamāya* is meant to express the intended result. The prince wishes by means of the signature to have the possibility of ridding himself of all undesirable people from Laṅkā. W's translation fails because it assumes *āgama* instead of *anāgama*.

Vāgissara and the scholar Dhammakitti[1] he sent off in a leaky
vessel into the open sea. Once upon a time he took from 33
the hands of the messengers the gifts and goods which the
Ruler of Laṅkā had sent in order to buy elephants, with the 34
promise that he would give them fourteen elephants and silver
money[2], but he told merely lies and gave them nothing.
Further they seized by force a princess whom the Ruler of 35
Laṅkā had sent to Kamboja land.

When King Parakkamabāhu heard of these many insults 36
committed by that (prince), he thought with the greatest in-
dignation: "Where in the whole of Jambudīpa is there a king 37
who would be capable of treating my envoys in such a manner?"
He summoned his ministers and spake: "Either the capture 38
or the slaying of the king of Arimaddana[3] must be effected."
Hereupon there spake a distinguished official of the public 39
accounts, the Damiḷādhikārin by name Ādicca, with clasped
hands — he wished himself to undertake the enterprise — to 40
the King thus: "It is not necessary to entrust[4] the chief digni-
taries with this task. If I do not stray a single step from 41
the path of thy order it will be for me, if I undertake the
task — even should I be quite alone — in very truth not diffi- 42
cult to carry out in successful fashion the commands of my
lord whose commands are hardly to be transgressed." When the 43
King heard that he was content. He placed under him the
troop leaders who were to be sent and commanded him to
depart speedily. Then the highly-famed one gave the order 44
without delay to make ready ships of various kinds, many
hundreds in number. Now all the country round about the 45

[1] These were evidently the envoys from which the written declaration had been wrung. They reached home in spite of the leaky ship, otherwise their death would without doubt have been mentioned. They escaped it as by a miracle.

[2] In the original again the or. recta: "We shall give you &c." The goods are therefore paid partly in cash partly with elephants

[3] For this capital of Burma see M. Bode, Sāsanavaṃsa, Dissertation, p. 20 and passim.

[4] P. *yojetvālaṃ* stands for *yojetu(ṃ) alaṃ*.

coast was one great workshop fully occupied with the build-
46 ing of the ships taken in hand. When within five months he
had had all the ships well built, he assembled them in haste
47 at the port of Pallavavaṅka. Then endowed with vast royal
power[1], he had provisions supplied[2] for a whole year such as
48 rice and the like and abundant weapons of war, such as armour
and the like; further gokaṇṇaka arrows[3] of iron with sharp
points, many hundred thousand in number for defence against
49 elephants, also different kinds of medicines, preserved in cow
horns for the healing of venomous wounds caused by poisoned
50 arrows, as well as all kinds of remedies for curing the poison
of infected water in the many swampy stretches of country;
51 also iron pincers for extracting arrow-heads which are difficult
to move when they have pierced deeply and the shaft has
52 broken, lastly also skilful physicians and serving women —
53 everything in complete fashion[4]. After he versed as none
other in the right measures, had made a strong force —
54 numbering many hundreds of thousands — embark, the Ruler
sent all the ships off on one day loaded with all kinds of arms
55 and filled with capable soldiers. Now when this assemblage
of ships all at the same time[5] sailed forth in the midst of
56 the ocean it looked like a swimming island. Subdued by
adverse winds some of these ships went down, some drifted
57 on to foreign shores. Numbers of trusty warriors who had
embarked in one of the vessels landed on the Crows' island[6].
58 They fought a battle there, captured several of the inhabitants

[1] P. *mahārājiddhisaṃyuto* in v. 52 d.

[2] P. *paṭipādesi* in v. 52 c.

[3] *Gokaṇṇa* in Skr. also means a particular type of arrow. The elephants (*vāraṇā*) against which they are to serve as defence (*cāraṇa*) are of course the war elephants of the enemy. The MSS. are more favorable to the form of the word *gokaṇṭaka* which might easily be a synonym for *gokaṇṇaka*.

[4] *Anūnaṃ* is associated as adverb with *paṭipādesi* and refers to everything that has gone before.

[5] So I understand the P. *samaṃ*.

[6] P. *Kākadīpa*. Perhaps the name of one of the Andaman Islands?

of the island alive, brought them then to the King of Laṅkā
and presented them to him. Warriors of great fighting strength 59
who sailed on five vessels landed on the territory of Rāmañña
in the port called Kusumi[1]. These doughty soldiers with the 60
Nagaragiri Kitti at the head, equipped with armour and weapons,
slew from their landing-place the troops belonging to the Rā- 61
mañña country, many thousands of them in terrible combat and
while they, like to rutting elephants, hewed down around many 62
coco palms and other trees and set fire to the villages, they laid
waste a great part of the kingdom. But the ship on which the 63
Damiḷādhikārin Ādicca commanded, landed in the territory (of
Rāmañña) at the port of Papphālama, and while at once the 64
people with the Damiḷādhikārin at the head, fought a grue-
some, fearful, foe-destroying battle and captured alive many 65
people living in the country, they plunged the Rāmañña king-
dom into sore confusion. Thereupon the Sīhalas with terrible 66
courage, fearful with their swords, burst into the town of
Ukkama and slew the Monarch of the Ramaṇas. When they had 67
subdued the Ramaṇas and brought their country into their
power, the great heroes[2] mounted a splendid white elephant.
They rode round the town free from all fear turning the right 68
side towards it and thereupon made known by beat of drum
the supremacy of the Sovereign of Laṅkā[3].

[1] Evidently the Kusima(tittha) frequently mentioned in the Sāsanavaṃsa.

[2] Probably Ādicca and Kitti are meant.

[3] The Burmese chronicles have nothing to say about such a catastrophe having overtaken their country. The description in the Mahāvaṃsa is without doubt very much exaggerated. The fact of a successful campaign against Rāmañña is, however, confirmed by the important inscription of Devanagala in the Kegalla district, Galboda Korale, Meda Pattuva, whose significance H. C. P. Bell was the first to recognise (Report on the Kegalla District, ASC. 1892, p. 73 ff). According to this inscription — one of Parakkamabāhu I. — the war against Aramaṇa was determined on in the 12th year of the King's reign. The reigning king of Aramaṇa at that time is called Bhuvanāditta. The inscription also mentions the town of Kusumi (cf. v. 59) and tells finally of the granting of land to Kit-Nuvaragiri (= Kittinagaragiri v. 60) evidently

69 Then overwhelmed by fear the people in the Rāmañña
land, seeing no other protection, gathered together and held
70 counsel. With the instructions: "Year by year must we from
now onwards send elephants to any amount as tribute from
71 our property — in order that the Monarch of Laṅkā may not
72 lay on us intolerable (burdens), ye must influence him[1] and
73 thereby at all times full of pity, have mercy on us all" —
they sent in haste their messengers with letters in their hand
to the bhikkhu community[2] dwelling in the island of Laṅkā.
74 Through the friendly words of the community living in the
three fraternities, the Ruler of Laṅkā was moved to kindness,
75 and while the Ramaṇas sent him yearly numbers of elephants,
they made anew with the Laṅkā Ruler who kept his treaties
faithfully, a pact of friendship.

76 Now the Paṇḍu king by name Parakkama, in the town of
Madhurā[3], when his capital was besieged by the war-loving,
77 hostile king named Kulasekhara who had come thither with
an army, had found in the territory of Jambudīpa no king
78 with whom he might have taken refuge. He sent messengers
to the Monarch of Laṅkā with the message: "O Thou with
79 whom I may take refuge, thy two feet shall be for me who

as reward for his services. The Damiḷādhikārin Ādicca is not mentioned. He appears to have died soon after the campaign, as he does not occur again in the Cūlavaṃsa.

[1] Thus I translate the phrase *anusāsaniṃ vad.*

[2] The sense of the passage in on the whole clear. The Ramaṇas try through the medium of the Church to obtain favorable terms of peace from Parakkamabāhu. The details offer difficulties. Line 71 a b is hopelessly corrupt. Since the MSS. all agree, the corruption must be traced to the archetype. The emendation tried by S. and B. is hardly successful. Three words *acchiddaṃ*, *amhākaṃ*, . . . *īdisaṃ* seem certain. Verses 71 c to 72 d if translated literally would be rendered by: "we all must be taken pity on (*dayitabbā*) by you, reverent masters (*bhadantehi*), in that ye , persuade (*vadantehi tassa anusāsaniṃ*) the King that he does not have done (to us) (*kāreti*) what is heavy to be borne."

[3] For the South Indian people called Paṇḍu and their capital of Madhurā (now Madura in the south of the province of Madras), see 50. 12 and note. V. A. Smith, Early Hist. of India, p. 336.

am a moth in the fire of the majesty of my foe, a cage of
diamond". When the sovereign of Laṅkā heard their speech,
he spake thus: "If the distress of him who has placed him- 80
self under my protection be not removed, how would my name
of Parakkamabāhu[1] be fitting? He who trusts in me is hard 81
to vanquish by a foe, be he who he may. From what foe
among the brutes is the hare in peril who has fled to the moon[2]?
General Laṅkāpura, slay Kulasekhara, establish the Paṇḍu 82
king in his realm and then return." The general by name 83
Laṅkāpura, a very courageous man, versed in the means of
war, a forest fire for the wide(-spreading) wilderness of the 84
foe, received with the words "Be it so!" the King's command
like a wreath upon his head and accompanied by many war-
skilled officers, he marched at the head of an army invincible 85
in battle and came to Mahātittha.

King Kulasekhara had (in the meantime) slain the Paṇḍu 86
king with his wife and children and captured the town Madhurā
by name. Laṅkāpura received from the Great king who had 87
heard of these events, anew the order to conquer the kingdom
and make it over to a scion of the house of Parakkama[3]. He
set forth for the port Taladilla[4] by name on the opposite
coast. He embarked his great army on many hundreds of 88

[1] The name means "arm of courage, possesed of courageous arms". Parakkamabāhu's campaign against Southern India is confirmed by Coḷa inscriptions (Inscr. of Arpakkam near Kāñcī) according to which the result for the Sīhala troops was not so brilliant as the Mhvs. would have us believe. After initial successes they were forced to retire. Cf. for further details V. A. Smith, Early History of India, p. 340; H. W. Codrington, Short History of Ceylon, p. 62, 74. To the name Kulasekhara corresponds Kulottuṅga in Indian inscriptions (EI. VII, p. 170 ff.).

[2] The Hindu thinks he sees the picture of a hare in the disk of the full moon, just as we speak of a "man in the moon". The moon is therefore called in P. *sasin* = skr. *śaśin*, from *sasa* = *śaśa* "hare".

[3] Instead of the names Laṅkāpura and Parakkama the original has pronouns.

[4] The MSS. have all *Taladilla* or *Talandilla*, in v. 92 only the first form. The Col. Ed. reads *Talabbilla* with the variant *Talavvilla*, I do not know with what authority.

ships, started off and sailed a day and a night on the back
89 of the ocean. When he caught sight of the coast, since a
hostile army was standing there, he made all his troops put
90 on their armour on board. As the ships had to lie in deep
water[1] and because with a landing just at this spot, the
91 armour of the whole army would have been wet through, he
made the troops get into hundreds of boats of small size[2].
Then when the rain of arrows from the Damiḷas standing on
92 the coast, came flying, he had shields fashioned of leather set
up in front of the people (as protection) against the arrows
and so landed in the Paṇḍu kingdom at the port called Ta-
93 laḍilla. After putting to flight the Damiḷas at the port and
capturing the harbour, he took up a position there and fought
94 with vast forces four battles. When the five officers, Vaḍa-
valattirukka-nāḍāḷvāra[3], Kuṇḍayamutta-rāyara, Villava-rāyara[4],
95 Añcukoṭṭa-nāḍāḷvāra and Narasīhadeva by name, advanced to
96 fight[5], he fought also with these, slew many Damiḷas, took
97 away their horses, put to flight the great army and occupied
Rāmissara[6]. He fought with them while he was posted there,

[1] P. *agādhe saṃnivattanabhāvato.* The meaning is this. The coast was so flat that the ships could not lie close to the shore. They had to turn (*saṃ-ni-vatt*) at some distance in deep water (*agādhe*) and embark the troops in boats (see the following note).

[2] P. *ekadoṇināvā. Doṇī* must be taken here in the sense of a particular measure of volume, otherwise *eka* would be unintelligible. Skr. *droṇī* means "boat" as also a measure of volume.

[3] According to O. Schrader (private letter 22 XII 23) *nāḍāḷvāra* is derived from the popular Dravidian *nāḍu* "land, district" and *āḷ* "man" (Canarese *āḷu* "soldier"). A Nāḍāḷvāra would thus be the leader of the troops of a particular district.

[4] *Rāyara* is a title which according to O. Schrader, corresponds to skr. *rājānaḥ.* Canarese *rāyaru.*

[5] Of the five officers four are also mentioned several times later on; (Kuṇḍayamutta, 76. 177; Villava 76. 163 ff.; Añcukoṭṭa 76. 98, 191, 239, 247, 300; Narasīhadeva, 76. 174). Only the first mentioned does not occur again. It is significant that Añcukoṭṭa occurs as a place name in 76. 235, the Nāḍāḷvāra probably taking his name from the locality. See also note to v. 180.

[6] Skr. *Rāmeśvara*, situated on a sandy island which joins the Indian mainland with Adam's Bridge, with a famous temple often described but belonging to a later period (15th to 16th cent).

five combats and after fighting nine battles[1] he fought[2] in
the tenth against the six officers Silāmegha, Naratuṅgabrahma- 98
mahārāja, Ilaṅkiya-rāyara, Añcukoṭṭa-rāyara, Phaḷudhiya-rāyara 99
by name and him called Panasiyarāja[3], as well as the five 100
officers named above who had advanced with great forces. He
bore away the victory, seized many horses[4], slew the Damiḷas 101
and penetrated from Rāmissara a distance of four gāvutas[5]
to Kundukāla which lies between the two seas. The many 102
Damiḷas who had fled through fear, took refuge in the forest;
he captured several of them and had them impaled there.
Some of these, at the command of the Ruler of Laṅkā who 103
thought to have all the cetiyas formerly destroyed by the
Damiḷas rebuilt by them, he had brought to Laṅkā and the 104
work of restoration begun on the Ratanavāluka-cetiya[6]. The 105
Sovereign of Laṅkā had the thūpa which had been destroyed
by the Damiḷas restored, and in order at the close to celebrate
the festival of the crowning ornament[7], he betook himself 106
with his ministers and the court to Anurādhapura and assembled

[1] That is besides the five combats the four mentioned in v. 93.

[2] The verb governing the accusative in vv. 99—100 is *yuddhaṃ katvā* in v. 100 c which is treated as in 38. 36, as a transitive verb.

[3] In the Col. Ed. the names *Naratuṅgabrahmamahārājavhayo* in 98 and *Panasiyarājavhayo* are changed contrary to all the MSS. into *Naratuṅgabrahmahā rāyaravhayo* and *Paṇasiyarāyaravhayo*. Apparently the editors wanted to avoid the wrong close of the verse °*rājavhayo*, but in v. 95 we have just as wrong a °*devavhayo* which is not corrected in Col. Ed. Mentioned again later are Sīlamegha(ra) 76. 238, 299; 77. 90 and Ilaṅkiya 76. 191 f. For Añcukoṭṭa see above.

[4] The organization of the Damiḷa army evidently differed materially from that of the Sīhalas in the greater number of its cavalry. In all accounts of victories gained (see already above v. 96) horses are always mentioned as the principal booty.

[5] That is about 8 miles. Kundukāla was situated on the tongue of land jutting out from the continent to the island of Rāmeśvara.

[6] Name of the Mahāthūpa in Anurādhapura corresponding to what is now known as the *Ruvanväli*. It is used here for the first time. The allied designation *Hemavālukacetiya* occurs already in 51. 82.

[7] P. *thūpikāmaha*. By *thūpikā* is understood the pointed cone resting on the cube-like structure which forms the apex or finial of the thūpa.

107 the great bhikkhu community on the island of Laṅkā. He
provided the community with the four articles of use and
when the fourteenth day[1] had arrived he had made known in
108 the town by beat of drum: "The town shall be decorated;
and provided with perfumes, flowers and other offerings shall
the people come to the place of the Mahāthūpa." After he
had then on the day of the full moon performed in right
109 manner all the old customs, he himself came as the shadows
grew longer, from the royal palace[2]. In divine beauty he was
adorned with costly ornaments, with crown, necklace[3], bracelets
110 and the like, (all) richly set with jewels. In front of him went
the ladies of the court many hundreds in number, with the
111 grace of heavenly nymphs, their bodies decorated, and there
followed him[4] numbers of distinguished officers with richly
112 decorated garments and resplendent in bright clothing. With
the mass of the elephants and horses gleaming with their
golden harness, doing reverence[5] to the cetiya with a gift of
113 lamps distributed over their bodies, and with the burden of
the mass of human beings he pressed as it were, the earth
together. With umbrellas, whisks and banners he veiled in
114 a sense the countenance of the firmament. With the sound
of the manifold instruments of music he cleft asunder the
mountain ravines, with the splendour of his majesty he comple-
115 tely bewitched the eyes of the laity[6] and with the beams of

[1] That is the full-moon day.

[2] This is the final sentence, taken up from v. 116 a b. In 116 d we have the finite verb *aṭṭhāsi* of the whole sentence beginning with v. 107 which I have split up into its component parts, translating the participles and gerunds by principal verbs.

[3] P. *mālā* means like skr. *mālā* also necklace, neck-chain.

[4] In v. 110 and 111 *purakkhato* and *anvito* are in opposition.

[5] W. seems not to have taken account of the feminine form *pūjentīhi*. It proves that the part. must be referred to *hatthiassaghaṭāhi*. It is thus the elephants and the horses not "worshippers" who wore the lamps. These were probably fastened to the bodies of the animals (*sabbaṅgadīpa*) by means of ribbons or by a framework.

[6] Of "tears of joy" there is nothing in the text; *haraṃharaṃ* is a duplication of intensity.

the golden utensils, chests, banners, vessels, fans, jars and the
like he steeped the place in radiant glory[1]. Thus on he came 116
and took his place with the splendour of the King of the gods
in the court of the cetiya. Many hundreds of bhikkhus who 117
had come hither, surrounded the cetiya, closing it round, as
it were, with a railing of coral[2]. The King then had the 118
golden point placed on the thūpa and showed the world there-
with the beauty of the Kelāsa mountain with the sun on its
summit. On this day too there reigned in the town also dur- 119
ing the night great brightness with the lamp festival of the
King and because of the point placed upon the thūpa. When 120
thus the Monarch Parakkamabāhu had celebrated the great
festival of the sacred thūpa, he betook himself again to
Pulatthinagara.

But the general (Laṅkāpura) had a strong camp called 121
Parakkamapura built at Kundukāla, and as he wished to make
it last long, he erected three high walls of stone, two thou- 122
sand, four hundred cubits long[3] and twelve gate towers, and a 123
building with a hall square[4] and three trenches in such a way
that the waters flowed from ocean to ocean[5]. While he tarried 124
in this stronghold he subdued officers like Kañcakuḍiyarāja[6]
by name, Coḷagaṅga and others. Since in this way the power 125
of the Sīhalas waxed from day to day, King Kulasekhara
sent again Sundarapaṇḍurāja[7] and Paṇḍurāja by name and 126

[1] P. *piñjaraṃ karaṃ* "making ruddy, light-coloured".

[2] P. *paralavedikāya*. Here *vedikā* has again clearly the meaning of railing. Cf. note to 73. 88. The coral colour is supplied by the reddish yellow colour of the monks' robes.

[3] As *ratana* means the same as *hattha* (see 37. 172) that is roughly about $1^1/_2$ ft. thus the wall was 3600 ft. in extent.

[4] See note to 73. 23. Here there were evidently as W. supposes, barracks for the soldiers.

[5] The fortifications were spread right across the whole of the peninsula and thus safeguarded it and the camp from the mainland. *Tathā* belongs of course to *kāretvā parikhātayaṃ* and *yathā* (*gacchanti*) refers to *tathā*.

[6] We have to read here and in v. 130 *So Kañcakuḍiya°*; *so* refers each time to Laṅkāpura. Cf. note to 76. 170,

[7] Is mentioned again 76. 174.

127 many other officers with troops to drive them thence. Laṅkā-
pura fought with them three combats, put them to flight and
128 took the village called Carukkaṭṭa. And he set out from there
and fought with these same officers as well as with the Damiḷa
129 Āḷavandapperumāḷa[1] a great battle, carried away the victory
and captured the villages by name Koḷuvura and Maruthūpa.
130 In the district Kañcakuḍiya and in the district named Koḷūru
131 the general subdued the soldiers called Maravara[2]. In the
district of Vīragaṅga the mighty (general) plundered many vil-
lages and market towns such as Kuṇappuṅallura and others,
132 and after subduing the powerful officer called Māḷava-rāyara[3]
and thousands of Damiḷas, he took up his abode there.
133 Thereupon he returned and betook himself to Parakkamapura
134 to satisfy his troops by the distribution of food and pay[4]. On
the march thither he gave battle to Āḷavanda who had his
position at the village called Vaḍali and slew him.
135 Since now the powerful king Kulasekhara — who possess-
ed the courage of a lion, whose great army was war-tried,
136 who well understood the expedients of war — although he
had sent forth his great dignitaries with big army and train
had not been able to win the victory, he himself set forth
137 to fight. Māḷava-cakkavattin, Māḷava-rāyara by name, Pa-
138 rittikkuṇḍiyāra[5] and Toṇḍamānāraya by name; Tuvarādhipati-

[1] Is mentioned again 76. 131, 145, 223, 232.

[2] This is probably the caste or rather tribe of the Marāvar living in the district of Madura (See Imperial Gazetteer of India s. v. Madura), where with the Vellālar and the Kallar (= Kallara in 76. 246) they are characteristic. They seem to be descended from the aborigines and were known in early times as fearless soldiers.

[3] Cf. below in v. 137 *Māḷava-cakkavattin* and *Māḷava-rāyara*. The first name again in 76. 235, 265, 274, 284; 77. 27, the second 76. 210, 267 f. Māḷava is the name of a tribe. See Epigraphia Indica VII, Appendix, nr. 10, 64, 409.

[4] A veiled allusion to certain difficulties with which Laṅkāpura was faced during his advance. Note too that the place Vaḍali named in v. 134 is later on again occupied by him (see v. 169) and that only after severe fighting.

[5] For Māḷava see note to 76. 132. Parittikkuṇḍiyāra is again mention-

veḷāra, Vīrapperaya-rāyara, Seṅkuṇḍiya-rāyara and Nigaḷadha-rāyara by name, Karummaḷatta-rāyara and Nakula-rāyara, 139
Puṅkoṇḍa-nāḍāḷvāra and Karamba-rāyara by name, Kuṇḍiyūru 140
and Athalayūru-nāḍāḷvāra[1] by name, Kaṅgayara, the two
Vīragaṅgas, Muva-rāyara, Aḷattūru-nāḍāḷvāra, the three Maṇṇa- 141
ya-rāyaras, Kaḷavaṇḍiya-nāḍāḷvāra and Keraḷasīhamuttara —
these and other officers, as well as those named above he 142
took with him, further the remaining troops in the province
of the Paṇḍu King Parakkama, the whole forces of his mother's 143
brothers in the two Koṅgu districts and the whole of his own
forces in the kingdom of Tiriṇaveli[2]. Also Niccavinodavāṇava- 144
rāyara[3], Paṭṭi-rāyara, Taṅkuttara-rāyara and Tompiya-rāyara
by name, Āḷavandapperūmāḷa, him called Coḷakonāra as well 145
as Tāṅgipperūmāḷa and Aḷakhiya-rāyara by name, him called 146
Mānābharaṇamahārāja, Avandiya-rāyara, Muṇayadha[4]-rāyara
by name and the Damiḷa Viṭṭāra: also these officers with vast 147
army and train he took with him and marched near to Pa-

ed in 76. 221. As regards the other names mentioned in 137—141, Toṇḍamānāraya occurs again in 76. 315, 77. 1 ff., Tuvarādhipati again in 76. 315, 77. 67; Vīrapperaya again in 76 316, 77. 6 f., Seṅkuṇḍiya 76. 221, 77. 7, 35; Nigaḷadha again 77. 16 ff.; Karummaḷatta again 76. 216; Puṅkoṇḍa again 76. 240, 273 ff., 77. 57, 92; Athalayūru again 76. 260. 77. 27; Kaṅgayara again 76. 260, 316, 77. 15; Vīragaṅga again 76. 131, 179 ff.; Muva again 76. 216; Aḷattūru again 76. 184, 214 ff., 305; Maṇṇaya again 77. 7, 35 (cf. note to 76. 220); Kaḷavaṇḍiya again 76. 267, 316, 77. 10 ff.; Keraḷasīhamuttara again 77. 7. Nakula, Karamba and Kaṇḍiyūru do not occur again.

[1] The Col. Ed. has contrary to the MSS. °*tha'aṇḍūru*.

[2] Now Tinnevelli, the district filling out the extreme south-east corner of the Indian peninsula. The correct form of the name is Tirunelvēli. See Imp. Gazetteer of India s. v.; W.'s note to the passage. The two Koṅgu districts are according to 76. 288, Teṅkoṅgu and Vaḍakoṅgu.

[3] Of the officers named here Niccavinodavāṇava occurs again in 77. 76. For Āḷavandapperūmāḷa see note to 76. 128; a Coḷakonāra is mentioned again 76. 163, 181, 188, 77. 77, 86. Tāṅgipperūmāḷa 76. 190; Muṇayadha 77. 40. The other names are only mentioned here

[4] Again the Col. Ed. changes the name, contrary to the MSS. into Mundiya.

148 rakkamapura. "Only when I shall have cut off the heads of
the Sīhalas shall this time my sacrifice to the gods in holy
149 Rāmissara take place!" Letting such lion-like cry sound
forth, he occupied a strong encampment at the village of Erukāṭṭa
150 and Iḍagaḷissara. Now in order to destroy the strong encamp-
ment of Parakkamapura, Kulasekhara sent forth a great army
from the land side and another embarked in numbers of ships
151 from the ocean. When thus the mighty force coming from dif-
ferent sides began the fight it was as if two seas overflowed their
152 shores. Laṅkāpura made his great army put on their armour,
advanced from his strong encampment and began the battle
153 with the others. But the army of the Damiḷas suffered fight-
ing in the battle (heavy loss by) sword blows and arrow shots.
154 It weakened, turned tail and withdrew to its own stronghold.
In this way it fought in the offensive three and fifty actions.
155 But when King Kulasekhara saw this disaster in every combat,
156 he himself set forth and sent out his troops to fight. Laṅkā-
pura had all the gates opened and placing his army like a
157 great mountain in front of him, he came forth. He slew in
combat numbers of Damiḷas[1], took away their horses, gained
the victory and pressed forward in pursuit as far as Kurum-
158 bāṇḍanakaḷi. While he was beginning here to build a strong
encampment[2], Kulasekhara gathered together his great army
159 which had been shattered in the fight, took also his picked
troops[3] whom he cherished as his life, marched hither himself
160 and opened fight awaking terror among the foe. With thou-
sands of fish, namely the (glittering) swords, with hundreds
of waves, namely the horses, with the mass of the waters,
namely the infantry, with the lines of surf namely the um-
161 brellas[4], with the flowing of the streams[5], namely the arrows,

[1] Of course we must read *Damiḷe 'neke.*

[2] Loc. abs. It must be supplemented by *tena.* "When by him (Laṅkāpura) was begun the building of a strong encampment."

[3] P. *sārabhūtaṃ mahāsenaṃ.* By *sāra* is meant the duramen (heart-wood) of a tree.

[4] The white umbrellas are the badges of the officers.

[5] P. *āpagānipātena.* What is meant are the streams flowing into

with the clamorous din, namely the drums, the whole battle-
field was terror-striking like the ocean. When thus the great 162
battle was fought, the Sīhalas endowed with great courage,
stilled the twitching in their arms[1]. They slew Villava-rāyara 163
by name and Coḷakonāra and the mighty officer, Yādhava[2]-
rāyara, many hundreds of soldiers and officers of the king; 164
also they wounded the horse on which King Kulasekhara was
riding. Kulasekhara with his army turned to flee in order 165
therewith to give the Sīhalas, as it were, occasion for yet
more furious sword strokes. When in fight he fled, he not 166
only surrendered his courage but also his throne, his umbrella,
his ornaments and all else. Laṅkāpura marched to the fortress 167
called Erukkāvūra where his enemy King Kulasekhara had
resided, burned it down and then after erecting a new strong- 168
hold, Laṅkāpura[3] tarried there some time. Then he set forth
and marched to Vaḍali[4]. Thence he advanced farther and 169
hereupon took Deviyāpattana by force. Then he betook him- 170
self to Siriyāvala and after completely vanquishing in bitter
combat the well-armed Khuddakañcakuṇḍa-rāyara[5] commanding 171
the stronghold named Koḷuvukkoṭṭa, he put to flight in battle
numbers of dignitaries of King Kulasekhara, captured also 172
this strong place and burned down seven and twenty large
villages in (the district) Dantika. Hereupon he fought with

the ocean.. The comparison of the combat to the raging sea is described exactly in accordance with the rules of Indian poetics.

[1] They had abundant opportunity of satisfying their thirst for fighting.

[2] The first two names occur already in 76. 94, 145, but are also mentioned again later on (Villava 76. 173, 185; a Coḷakonāra 76. 173, 181 and 188, 77. 77 and 86, also a Yādhava 76. 173, 177). Cf. note to 76. 180. Yādava is a South Indian clan name. See EI. VII. Appendix, nr. 331, 332, 334 etc.

[3] All the MSS. have here *laṅkāvidū* which should be adopted on principle in the text. W. supposes it might be a corruption of *kālavidū*. Not impossible.

[4] See above note to v. 133.

[5] The same as *Cullakañcakuṇḍa* "the small Kañcakuṇḍa" in 76. 185 ff. 217 ff. The name is most closely connected with that of the district *Kañcakuḍiya* 76. 130, this again with the proper name *Kañcakuḍiyarāja*, 76. 124.

173 the Damiḷa Paṇḍiyāṇḍāra[1] dwelling in Koḷuvukkoṭṭa who was of terrible courage, with both Coḷakonāras, with the officer
174 Yādhava-rāyara and with Villava-rāyara, with the Damiḷa Kāliṅga-rāyara with Sundarapaṇḍu-rāyara, with Narasīhadevara
175 and with Paṇḍiya-rāyara as well as with the (officers) in the village of the brāhmaṇas, shattered them and slew many
176 Damiḷas. He took (as booty) many horses and armed with troop and train, took up a position at the place named
177 Kuṇḍayaṃkoṭṭa. He brought into his power the three Damiḷa officers, Kuṇḍayamutta-rāyara, Kaḍiliya-rāyara and Yādhava-
178 rāyara and took up a position at that place, well understanding right places. Further the great hero brought into his
179 power Paṇḍiya-rāyara in the fortress of Vikkamacoḷappera
180 and the three, Paṇḍimaṇḍala-nāḍāḷvāra, Vīragaṅga-rāyara and Kaṅgakoṇḍapperayara, who were in Kāmānākkoṭṭa and advanced to Maruthukoṭṭa with the object of fighting a decisive battle[2].

[1] Only occurs here. For Coḷakonāra see note to 76. 144, for Yādhava note to 76. 163, for Villava ibidem; for Sundarapaṇḍu note to 76. 126. Kāliṅga is mentioned again 76. 214 ff., 77. 40.

[2] Verses 170-180 form one sentence. The principal verb is *pāyāsi* (180 c), subordinate to it are the gerunds in 170-172 and the gerunds and pres. part. in 175-6 as well as those in 178 and 180 a. The nominatives in 172 c—174 d, in 177 a—c and in 178 c—179 c are independent of the construction of the sentence and are summed up with *iti* (*icc-etchi* 175 a, *iti sāmante tayo* 177 c d, *icc-ete tayo* 179 d). Note how in the account of the contests in Southern India the names of the Damiḷa officers repeat themselves. Only once in this passage are Kaḍiliya, Paṇḍiyamaṇḍala and Paṇḍiyāṇḍāra mentioned, as well as Kaṅgakoṇḍapperayara, with which Kaṅgakoṇḍakalappa 77. 75 may be compared. Paṇḍiya-rāyara is mentioned twice in this passage but not otherwise, Yādhava here in v. 173 and 177, before in v. 163. In v. 163 a Coḷakonāra, a Villava and a Yādhava are mentioned as having fallen. Possibly these may often be place names as above in the case of Añcukoṭṭa (see v. 235) rather than names of persons, Villava-rāyara meaning for instance, the rāyara of Villava (see note to 77. 9). Kuṇḍayamutta and Narasīhadeva occur already in 76. 94-95, Vīragaṅga already in 76. 131, 140 and and later repeatedly (76. 181 ff.). Sundarapaṇḍu 76. 126. It is expressly stated that there are two Coḷakonāras (76. 173). It is the same below with Tondriya (181). The same with Aḷattūru-nāḍāḷvāra (184, 214) and with Vīragaṅga (140). In v. 141 three Maṇṇaya-rāyaras are mentioned.

There he gave the Colakonāra, the other Tondriya, the otncer 181
Suttāṇḍāra, the Damiḷa Vīragaṅgara, Kuttāṇḍāra and others a 182
severe combat. He robbed Tondriya of his life, took his horses 183
away from him, slew many Damiḷas and occupied besides the
fortress known by the name of Kaṅgakoṇḍāna. Then he set 184
from there, took up a position at the place named Paṇiva,
fought there with the two Aḷattūru-nāḍāḷvāras, with Pandriya-
rāyara, Villava-rāyara and Cullakañcakuṇḍa-rāyara[1] a great 185
battle, shattered them and captured Paṇivakkoṭṭa. Then he 186
turned and betook himself to Kaṅgakoṇḍāna[2] where he had
stood formerly. Hereupon he marched to Vālakkoṭṭa[3] to fight 187
there, fought there against Kaṇḍadevamāḷava-rāyara, against the
two Vīragaṅgaras and the Damiḷa Colakonāra a great battle, 188
shattered them all and slew numbers of Damiḷas, seized from 189
them many horses and captured with this fortress (Vālakkoṭṭa)
also (the fortress) Neṭṭūru[4]. He himself took up a position
there, brought Kuttāṇḍā(ra)[5], Vīragaṅga and Tāṅgipperūmāḷa 190
and the Damiḷas dependent in him, many hundreds in number,
as well as Ilaṅkiya and Añcukoṭṭa-rāyara under his influence, 191
gave them earrings and other ornaments. But on Ilaṅkiya- 192
rāyara he conferred the well-known and coveted title of Rā-
javesibhujanga-Silāmegha[6].

Meanwhile Laṅkāpura learned that the very youngest son of 193
the Paṇḍu King Parakkama, Prince Vīrapaṇḍu by name, at the 194
murder of his unhappy royal father — who had fallen with wife
and child into the power of the enemy — by some wile or other 195

[1] See above v. 170 and note.

[2] W. translates *paccāvutto* wrongly by "he proceeded to . . ." Its meaning is far rather "he returned to . . ." Cf. skr. *prati-ā-vart*. Evidently the attack on Paṇiva had not the wished-for success.

[3] The text here is very corrupt, but the name Vālakkoṭṭa is assured

[4] W. suggests, though doubtfully, Nellore. That is quite impossible Nellore lies north of Madras. The scene of the combats described lay between Ramisseram and Madhurā. Cf. v. 197.

[5] Cf. above v. 182.

[6] The gerund *datvā* in 192 b shows that the sentence here is not finished. The principal verb is *pesesi* in 196 a. For the title Rājavesibhujaṅga see note to 73. 91 c d (p. 10, n. 3).

had been saved from the hands of the foe and now, since through
fear he dared not come near, was sojourning in the province of
196 Malaya[1]. He (Laṅkāpura) sent a messenger to him: "I have here
in war again and again completely vanquished Kulasekhara
197 together with his dignitaries and am now standing, after cap-
turing a part of the realm, not far from Madhurā at a distance
198 of two or three gāvutas[2]. But my Master who had in view
the protection of thy royal father, has since the murder of
199 this Ruler by his foes, at the tidings of this, given me the
following charge: 'he has placed himself under my protection,
if now he has been slain by the hostile king, ye shall now
200 slay the latter and make over the realm of the Paṇḍu King
201 Parakkama to a scion of his house, if such there be'. There-
fore come without fear in haste hither, and take over the
dominion in thy father's kingdom." Thus ran the friendly
202 message in accord with the truth[3]. When the Prince heard
of this matter in the right manner, he betook himself to him
203 without delay. Hereupon Laṅkāpura sent a letter to Laṅkā
to the Great king with the news that the prince had arrived
204 destitute. When the Great king had attentively heard this
report, he sent joyfully many golden and silver vessels worthy
205 to eat from, as well as many gold and silver lamp-stands and
exquisite garments from his own stock, worthy to clothe
206 himself with, earrings and chains and bangles set with jewels
207 and the like as a gladdening gift. And the Prince accepted
the whole of the heart-ravishing gift reverently making obei-
sance in the direction in which the King was.

208 Hereupon Laṅkāpura fought with great might against
Kaṇḍadevamāḷava-rāyara in Muṇḍikkāra, drove him from this
209 place and brought the Damiḷas into his power in the two

[1] As in Ceylon and Pegu (76. 22) also in Southern India name for the mountainous country. Cf. the name of the **Malayālis** who live in the districts of Arcot and Salem, that is in the mountains west of Pondicherry.

[2] About four to six miles. See note to 73. 154.

[3] The words *ti vatvā saccaṃ vaco mudu* in v. 201 d refer to *dūtaṃ pesesi* in v. 96, comprehending the contents of the message.

districts Kiḷamaṅgala and Melamaṅgala[1] while he tarried there.
Then by restoring Muṇḍikkāra to Māḷava-rāyara — whose 210
heart was overwhelmed with fear and who bereft of all de-
fiance, had placed himself under his protection — he placed 211
him in his (old) position and appointed him chief of the two
districts of Maṅgala. When then Laṅkāpura, while tarrying 212
in Anivalakoṭṭa, had appointed the colonel Gokaṇṇanāṇḍa who
was in Muṇḍannānaṃkoṭṭa as chief[2], he set forth from there 213
and surprised Neṭṭūru[3]. He fought with the officers quartered
in Mānavīramadhurā, with the two Aḷattūru-nāḍāḷvāras, with 214
Kāliṅga-rāyara[4] and Kalikāla-rāyara a great battle. The 215
mighty one slew many Damiḷas, as well as Kalikāla-rāyara
and brought Madhurā into his possession. He brought here- 216
upon many Damiḷas, as well as Muvaraya and Karumbūḷatta-
rāyara[5] into his power, marched then with his troops to the 217
castle of Aḷattūru-nāḍāḷvāra, fought hard to subdue, with
Kāliṅga-rāyara and Cullakañcakuṇḍa-rāyara a great battle, 218
drove them with terrible courage from this place, and after 219
he had then burnt down many well-known villages, the great
hero betook himself again to Neṭṭūru[6]. Now there came 220
from the south hither Cullakañcakuṇḍa-rāyara, the two
Aḷattūru-nāḍāḷvāras, Mannāya-rāyara[7], further Parittikuṇḍiyāra 221

[1] Upper and Lower Maṅgala (W.).

[2] The loc. *Anivalakkoṭṭe* (cf. below note to v. 235) belongs equally to *vasaṃ* and to (*nāyakaṃ*) *katvā*. The supplementing of the word *nāyakaṃ* is to be inferred from *gokaṇṇanāṇḍanāyakaṃ* and *nāyakaṃ vidhāya* in v. 211. W. has quite a different rendering but hardly a correct one "and made him (the Māḷava-rāyara) chief of Gokaṇṇanāḍu in Muṇḍānaṇkoṇḍa."

[3] Mentioned already in v. 189, a proof that the fighting went on with alternate vicissitudes round about Madhurā.

[4] For this name see 76. 174.

[5] Cf. for these names 76. 140 and 139.

[6] Verses 208—219 form one sentence. They show how rapidly one event followed another. Neṭṭūru formed, as is shown also by verses 285-7, 294, 303 ff., henceforth a main centre for Laṅkāpura's operations.

[7] Perhaps the same as the Maṇṇaya-rāyara mentioned in 76. 141, 77. 7 and 35. For the other names in 221 – 223 see note to 76. 170 (Cullak°); n. to 76. 180, 181 (Aḷ-n), 76. 137 (Par. and Seṅk.).

and Seṅkuṇḍi-rāyara and many other war-skilled Damiḷas,
222 officers from the immediate retinue of King Kulasekhara:
223 Kāliṅga-rāyara, Tennavanappalla-rāyara and Āḷavandapperūmāḷa[1],
all people hard to vanquish who after equipping their army,
224 came to the place Pātapata by name, their heart full of fury
225 and firmly determined this time to conquer the foe. When
Laṅkāpura heard of the matter he, the expert, sent officers
226 thither with a big army and train. They marched thither,
invested the fortress from all sides, burned down a score of
227 large villages near the stronghold and after making their
report, sent a messenger to Laṅkāpura to ask if they were
228 to take the fortress or not. At such tidings Laṅkāpura once
more sent forth a great army and gave the charge to capture
229 the fortress. When now they received the command sent to
230 them, they began all of them to open a fearful fight. There
raged between the two armies a battle — hardly bearable,
awful, exasperating — like to the raging of the storm at
231 the destruction of the world. Damiḷas thousands in number
they deprived of life, besides that the Tennavanappalla-rāyara
232 from the immediate retinue of the King. When Āḷavandappe-
rūmāḷa after receiving a wound, took flight, they slew the
horse he had mounted and seized this and many other steeds,
233 and while they brought joyous laughter to the lotus counte-
nance of the goddess of fortune of heroes, the Sīhalas shatter-
234 ed with a lion's courage the army of the Damiḷas. After
Laṅkāpura had taken possession of Pātapata he later on brought
the troops standing there over to his side.
235 Laṅkāpura betook himself thereupon to Anivalakkikoṭṭa[2]
236 and subdued Mālava-cakkavattin in Añcukoṭṭa. After he had
in like manner captured Toṇḍi and Pāsa[3], he advanced to
Kurundaṅkuṇḍiya to clear the region lying northwards of the

[1] Kāliṅga above 76.173 note; Āḷavaṇḍapperūmāḷa 76.128, 232, Tennavanappalla falls in battle according to v. 231.

[2] Probably the same as above in v. 212, Anivalakkoṭṭa. The place is repeatedly mentioned below v. 276 ff. Cf. note to v. 238.

[3] The two places must have lain very near together since their names 77.81 are formed into the compound Toṇḍipāsa.

enemy. After he had there subdued Vaḷuṭṭhi-rāyara, he 237
bestowed on him as a gift of favour, a golden bracelet and
the like. Then he marched thence and betook himself to 238
Tirivekambama[1]. Here he subdued Silāmeghara, Kanasiya-
rāyara and Añcukoṭṭa-nāḍāḷvāra[2] and showed them all 239
marks of favour as before (to Vaḷuṭṭhi). Thereupon the great 240
hero whose word was to be trusted[3], sent a message to Puṅ-
koṇḍa-nāḍāḷvāra[4] in order to bring him under his influence.
But when the latter without showing himself, went to 241
Semponmāri, Laṅkāpura betook himself thither in order to
capture Semponmāri. To capture this fortress a Coḷa army 242
had once upon a time marched hither and could not take it
in spite of a four days' fight. This inaccessible stronghold 243
the Sīhalas with their lion-like courage, captured[5] without
allowing more time than half a day to pass. After they had 244
broken through two outerwalls and four gate-towers, they
penetrated like singly marching elephants[6] into the interior
of the fortress, slew there the Damiḷas, many thousands in 245
number, and conquered thus in a moment the stronghold
Semponmāri. Thereupon (came) the troop of the Kallaras, the 246
Maravaras[7], as also the Goḷihaḷas and the Kuntavaras, the army 247
of Vallakkuttāra and the troop of Ūcena, as also the mighty
army in the district of Añcukoṭṭa: these exceeding brave, hot- 248

[1] Is also mentioned in v. 266 and 276 in close connection with Kurundaṅkuṇḍiya or Anivalakki.

[2] Kanasiya is only mentioned here. For the two others see above notes to v. 95 and 99.

[3] P. *saccasaṃdho*. This is specially stressed. Evidently Laṅkāpura had guaranteed Puṅkoṇḍa's safety. Puṅkoṇḍa nevertheless does not risk presenting himself to Laṅkāpura, as he distrusts his promises.

[4] See note to 76. 137.

[5] *Duggaṃ* must be supplemented by the verb *gahesuṃ* from v. 245 c.

[6] W. "one by one like unto so many elephants." I think however, that we must take *paccekahatthino* in the same sense as 72. 248 ("solitary elephants, rogue elephants"). Cf. the note.

[7] Cf. above note to 76. 130. The troops mentioned in v. 246-7 are those belonging to particular tribes or those drawn from the men of certain districts who are capable of bearing arms.

headed forces of the Damiḷas, numbering some fifty to sixty
249 thousand, surrounded thereupon the fortress occupied by the
Sīhalas and opened at once a most embittered fight. Then
250 the Laṅkāpura Deva[1] and the Laṅkāgiri Sora opened the gate
251 by the southern tower, accompanied by their troops (and)
with a courage scarcely to be surpassed, robbed Damiḷas thou-
252 sands of them, of their life, shattered with lion-like courage
the unruly Damiḷa army come from that direction hitherward,
253 as lions a herd of elephants. From the southern door there
broke forth at this moment the general Gokaṇṇa and the
254 Kesadhātu Loka by name, slew many soldiers of the enemy
on the battlefield and shattered to the last man the hostile
255 forces which remained over from the slaughter. From the
northern tower-gate came the mighty Kesadhātu Kitti and
the officer named Jagadvijaya for which scarce any man was
256 a match. The heroes shattered in no time the Damiḷa army
257 after robbing many Damiḷa warriors of their life. Thus the
Sīhalas destroyed at once in a moment the whole forces of
258 the Damiḷas, put them to flight, captured many steeds and
found themselves — the victory gained, famous by reason of
many deeds of heroism — again together in the fortress far-
259 famed under the name of Semponmāri. Thereupon he subdued[2]
the Kuntavaras, the soldiery of the Kallaras, the army of the
260 Goḷihaḷas and the troop of the Maravaras, the army of
Vallakkuttāra and the following of Ūcena, the Athalayūru-
261 nāḍāḷvāra and Kaṅgayara[3] and their shattered army, the
dwellers in Tāḷayūrunāḍu, the army in Kalahayināḍu and the
262 dwellers of Athalayunnāḍu and those of Kākannāḍu[4]: all
these Damiḷa forces all that lay (in a line) from the village
263 of Cellāru up to the frontier of the Coḷa region he brought
264 into his power and bestowed on them favours as before. He
accepted the gifts which were brought him by the Vessas and

[1] Already mentioned in 75. 130. Cf. further 76. 310 ff.

[2] I anticipate here the finite verb *vasaṃ ānesi* occurring in v. 263 b.

[3] For these two names see note to 76. 137.

[4] The names of districts (*nāḍu*) in v. 261, 262 do not occur otherwise.

the Yavanas[1] and distinguished these people also by countless marks of favour. To Māḷava-cakkavattin who placed himself 265
under his protection he restored Semponmāri and appointed him to his (former) post. Then he set forth from there 266
and came again to Tirivekambama and starting hence he reached Kurundaṅkuṇḍi[2].

Now Kaḷavaṇḍi-nāḍāḷvāra had in battle with great forces 267
wrested Muṇḍikkāra[3] from Māḷava-rāyara. Then seeing no 268
other aid, Māḷava-rāyara approached Laṅkāpura: "be thou my protection". Laṅkāpura at once summoned his best 269
officers, the two Kesadhātus, known to the people as Kitti and Loka, and the general Gokaṇṇa and charged them as 270
their commander, to open hostilities and restore Muṇḍikkāra to Māḷava-rāyara. These betook themselves to the spot, began 271
a combat hard to withstand, drove the foe from Muṇḍikkāra, slew many Damiḷas and after they had placed Māḷava-rāyara 272
once more in his former position, they returned thence to Laṅkāpura.

Another officer, Puṅkoṇḍa-nāḍāḷvāra[4] by name, betook 273
himself to the place called Siriyavala, fought while there a 274
great battle with Māḷava-cakkavattin, put him to flight and took the village known by the name of Jayaṅkoṇḍāna and 275
immediately after that Semponmāri itself. When the hero Laṅkāpura, best of steadfast men, heard of this event, he set 276
forth himself at once from the fortress Anivalakki and advanced, in order to take Semponmāri, to Tirivekambama[5]. When 277
Puṅkoṇḍa-nāḍāḷvāra learned of this event, he left Semponmāri and betook himself from there to Siriyavala. Thereupon the hero 278

[1] P. *vessa* = skr. *vaiśya* is the name of the third caste. *Yavana* does not necessarily mean the Greeks (Ionians) but all westerns living in India, more especially those of Arabian origin. See E. R. Ayrton, Ceylon Notes and Queries, I, 1913, p. VIII.

[2] See note to 76. 238.

[3] Cf. 76. 210—211. For Kaḷavaṇḍi note to 76. 137.

[4] See above note to 76. 137.

[5] The continued recurrence of place names previously mentioned (cf. 76. 170; 76. 241, 258; 76. 212, 235; 76. 238, 266) shows again that all these contests were waged within a fairly circumscribed area.

Laṅkāpura marched to Semponmari and when now Puṅkoṇḍa-
279 nāḍāḷvāra came thither with the intent to surrender, but
without presenting himself, betook himself again to the place
Siriyavala, Laṅkāpura also marched to the village of Siriyavala
280 and began from all sides an embittered combat. Now Puṅkoṇḍa-
281 nāḍāḷvāra sent the following message: "I will submit to thee,
if safety is vouchsafed me, since I am mastered by great fear;
282 if not, I dare not come." At the tidings of this Laṅkāpura
who was himself free from fear, sent a return message with
283 the purport that he should come. At the message of the
hero Laṅkāpura whose word was to be relied on, the former
284 free of all dread, betook himself to him. Thereupon Laṅkā-
pura bestowed on him many favours, summoned also Māḷa-
285 va-cakkavattin to him, reconciled the two and after he had
placed them both in their former positions, the great hero
286 betook himself to Neṭṭūru. The two villages which had been
laid waste, Rājasihamahāḷa and Vāḷugāma by name he rebuilt
287 and after he had dammed up two tanks in Siriyavala and
two tanks also in Perumpalaya, he had the tilling of the fields
taken in hand.

288 The Ruler Kulasekhara took the troops in Tiriṇaveli[1], as
well as the troops of the two brothers of his mother in Ten-
289 koṅgu and Vaḍakoṅgu[2], and versed in the various expedients
of statecraft, such as the distribution of honours and the like,
he made deserters of many Damiḷas who had already been
290 subdued and began now, equipped with forces to march forth
to battle. When the prudent Laṅkāpura heard trustworthy
291 tidings of this he destroyed the traitorous Damiḷas root and
branch, true to the command of his Lord whose task it was
to subdue the miscreants.

292 Thereupon there came sent by the Great king to cover
his rear, the hero Jagadvijaya[3] by name whose courage ex-
293 ceeded that of the whole world, accompanied by many foot

[1] See 76. 143 with the note. [2] Cf. 77. 43.

[3] As he is already mentioned in v. 255 in the struggle for Semponmāri, it may be assumed that Laṅkāpura had sent him to Laṅkā for reinforcements.

soldiers and steeds to Anivalakki after crossing the ocean.
The far-famed Laṅkāpura likewise left Neṭṭūru and betook 294
himself to Anivalakki. He sought out the newly-arrived
(Jagadvijaya), embraced him and having conversed with him 295
in heartfelt and friendly manner, the foe-crusher returned to
Neṭṭūru. Setting forth from there, he came, having knowledge 296
of the right places, to the place known by the name of
Mundrannaddhāna and took up far-famed for his courage, his
position there. At the place called Kīḷakoṭṭa and at the place 297
by name Maṅgalama[1] he fought with the Damiḷas, slew many
soldiers, took such foes as one was obliged to seize, alive and 298
captured many horses which had been left on the battlefield.
Then he set forth from there, came to Orittiyūrutombama and 299
endowed with a surplus of invincible courage, he fought with
Puṅkoṇḍa-naḍāḷvāra, Silāmeghara and Añcukoṭṭa-nāḍāḷvāra[2] 300
a great (and) terrible battle. After cutting down many Da- 301
miḷas he betook himself to Siriyavala, burned down the two-
storeyed palace of Puṅkoṇḍa-nāḍāḷvāra who had not submitted 302
to him and marched from the place Tirikkānappera farther.
The general Jagadvijaya now advanced from Anivalakki to 303
Neṭṭūru, set forth from there and shattered, himself un- 304
approachable[3], the fortresses called Madhurammāṇavīra,
Pāttanallūru and Soraṇḍakkoṭṭa. Returned to Neṭṭūru he tarried 305
there and brought the two Aḷattūru-nāḍāḷvāras and Cullakañca-
kuṇḍa-rāyara[4] to submission. When once the hero with great 306
forces came to Pāttanallūru, he sent to Laṅkāpura the follow-
ing message: "Thou must come with greatest haste to the 307
river called Vayiga; I must needs see thee, there is some-
thing to report." When the hero Laṅkāpura received these 308
tidings, he set off with all speed thence and began the march
with large forces. The hostile army which was standing at 309

[1] Cf. below note to 77. 38.

[2] The three named here belonged to those chieftains who having submitted to Laṅkāpura (v. 280 ff., v. 238) had since deserted (v. 289).

[3] Pun on *dugge—duggamo*, the latter referring to the subject. The skr. *durgama* is an epithet of Siva.

[4] See above v. 220 and note.

310 the place called Tirippāḷuru, saddled its numerous horses, came
hither and halfway began to fight a terrible combat with the
Laṅkāpura Deva and the other heroes who were present
311 in the battle. Thereupon the heroes dispersed the great
army even as the beams of the sun spreading forth (disperse)
312 the mass of the darkness. Thus did Laṅkāpura whose bravery
was as the fire of the last day, capture in a moment
313 Tirippāḷuru and took up his abode there. The officer by name
Jagadvijaya, versed in good counsel, shattered the great army
314 of Damiḷas dwelling in Pannaṭṭānkoṭṭa, capable of starting a
battle on the battlefield, brought the fortress into his power
and halted there.

315 King Kulasekhara in his exceeding fury took Tuvarādhi-
316 pativeḷāra, as well as Toṇḍamānara, Vīrapperayara and
Nigaya-rāyara, Kaḷavaṇḍiya-nāḍāḷvāra and the other Kaṅga-
317 yara[1], made his many soldiers ready for battle and betook
318 himself, his loins girt for battle, to Rājinā. The great general
of terrible courage charged his terrible army to give battle
319 to Laṅkāpura. The hero Laṅkāpura thereupon, expert in
320 affairs, explained the affair to Jagadvijaya: "In order together
with me to put to flight the Monarch Kulasekhara, thou must
so as to attack from the one side, make thy troops ready for
321 battle and come hither with all haste." After he had sent
him a message of such purport and had at the same time
322 equipped his own strong army, he set forth from there and
fought a great battle with the Damiḷas. They were van-
323 quished, withdrew at once to Rājinā, closed the tower-gates
with the small and the great gates and the Damiḷas
now with their Monarch kept to the centre of the town.
324 Thereupon the heroes at the head, the general Gokaṇṇa, the
325 Kesadhātu named Loka and the Laṅkāpura Deva, who had
arrived at the west gate, began to tear down the walls and
326 to blow up the tower-gates. The Laṅkāpura Deva and the
general Gokaṇṇa after shattering walls and tower-gates, pene-

[1] Nigaya is mentioned again in the sequel (77. 69). As regards the other names see note to 76. 137.

trated within. But the haughty Kesadhātu, the mighty Loka 327
by name, thought: by the way the others went I go not;
he slew numbers of heroic warriors, brought down many steeds, 328
blew up the southern gate and at once penetrated within.
Thereupon Kulasekhara fled, his heart overwhelmed with fear, 329
no longer even master of the clothes he wore, by the postern
of the eastern tower-gate[1] which he had had opened, and 330
by a lucky chance he escaped out of the hands of his foes.
These all cut down numbers of soldiers of the Damiḷas, took 331
away many horses and much treasure of many a kind, and 332
shaking their garments, dancing around, clapping their hands
and rejoicing, they celebrated the festival of victory. There- 333
upon Laṅkāpura and the general Jagadvijaya entered Rājinā
along with the other heroes.

Thus thrives ever more and more the state of those who 334
have done good, who are endowed with a keen understanding,
who understand statecraft and moral discipline, whose riches
are their terrible majesty, whose manliness fails not, even as
the moon in the light half of the month (waxes) from day
to day.

Here ends the seventy-sixth chapter, called «Account of the Capture of the Town of Rājinā», in the Mahāvaṃsa, compiled for the serene joy and emotion of the pious.

[1] The loc. *gopure* stands for the gen. *gopurassa*; *pācīnadvārā gopuṛe* means the same as *pācīnagopuradvārā*.

CHAPTER LXXVII

THE CONQUEST OF THE PAṆḌU KINGDOM

1 The Monarch Kulasekhara who had fled thence through fear
found again a firm footing in Toṇḍamāna's[1] mountain fortress.
2 The forces of Vīranukkara and other (soldiers) from Kakkoḷa,
3 the forces of Madhuraddhamakkāra[2]. came to Rājinā, related
the whole story of King Kulasekhara and persuaded Laṅkā-
4 pura to betake himself at once to Madhurā. Thereupon Laṅkā-
pura and the general Jagadvijaya equipped with great luck,
5 set forth for the town of Madhurā, gave over to the Prince
Vīrapaṇḍu the dwelling of his royal father, which was his
6 birthplace, and took up their abode in the town. They had
summoned to them the three Vīrapperayaras: him called
Sirivallabha, Rājā Nārāyaṇa, and him called Parakkamapaṇḍu,
7 (further) the officer Maṇṇaya-rāyara and Seṅkuṇḍi-rāyara, the
8 other Vīrapperayara Keraḷasīhamuttara[3] and bestowed on them
ornaments and the like. To Coḷagaṅgara who had submitted,
9 they made over the supreme direction of the district Paritti-
kkuṇḍi[4] formerly administered by him, and restored him to his
10 former position. Kaḷavaṇḍiya-nāḍāḷvāra[5] came indeed with the
intention of submitting[6], but when he had entered Madhurā,

[1] Cf. above 76. 137.

[2] Evidently local troops which had voluntarily submitted to the victor.

[3] Vīrapperayara is clearly a title here. Cf. 76. 138 and 316. Of the other names Maṇṇaya is mentioned 76. 141, 77. 35, Seṅkuṇḍi 76. 138 (q. v.) and Keraḷasīhamuttara 76. 141.

[4] Coḷagaṅga(ra) is mentioned 76. 124. The place name Parittikkuṇḍi is met with in Parittikkuṇḍiyāra 76. 137 and 221.

[5] See 76. 141.

[6] P. *vase hessaṃ* as or. recta. Cf. a similar phrase 75. 85.

he thought: I fear to let myself be seen, and returned without 11
presenting himself, to his place. Thereupon Laṅkāpura march-
ed into his district to take it. The unrivalled one, equipped 12
with great power and courage, offered him battle, defeated
him and captured Aḷagvānagiri. Kaḷavaṇḍiya-nāḍāḷvāra and 13
another named Sūradeva submitted and besought the general
for (the restoration of) his district; at his request Laṅkāpura 14
handed over to him the district. Then the far-famed betook
himself to the district of Kurumba-rāyara and after he had 15
also subdued Kurumba-rāyara and likewise brought Kaṅgayara
in Niyama into his power, the hero betook himself later to 16
the place called Tirripputtūru in order to make subject to
himself also Nigaḷadha-rāyara[1].

Nigaḷadha-rāyara gathered together his own army, took 17
with him also the Coḷa officers, Akalaṅka-nāḍāḷvāra and
Kañcamba-rāyara, Malayappa-rāyara and Kiccārattarayara[2] as 18
well as their numerous troops and the many horses in their 19
possession, marched thence and began a combat hard to
withstand. But the army of the Sīhalas transformed the 20
hostile host together with steeds and infantry — stretching 21
three gāvutas wide[3] from Tirripputtūru to Ponaamarāvatī, along
the highway between the two places — into a single mass
of flesh. After it had shattered these vast forces it came to 22
Ponaamarāvatī, burned down the three-storeyed palace built
there, and after setting fire to many other houses and well- 23
filled granaries of rice, the hero (Laṅkāpura) in order to rob
the inhabitants of their fear, had the drums beaten, took the 24
people who were settled in the district under his own dominion
and returned to Madhurā[4].

[1] Of the names mentioned in vv. 13—16 those of Sūradeva and Kurumba do not otherwise occur. For Kaḷavaṇḍiya see 76. 141, for Kaṅgayara see 76. 140, for Nigaḷadha 76. 138.

[2] Akalaṅka, Mayalappa and Kiccārattarayara are mentioned again later (77. 55 ff)

[3] The front extended thus over a distance of something like six miles (cf. 73. 154 and note).

[4] The subject changes in this sentence. In the principal sentence

25 Now the Monarch (Parakkamabāhu) whose commands stand
firm, sent the order to hold the festival of the coronation for
26 Prince Vīrapaṇḍu. When Laṅkāpura heard of this command
of the King's which could not be gainsaid, he set about mak-
27 ing the preparations for the consecration. He then charged the
28 Lambakaṇṇas Māḷava-cakkavattin, Māḷava-rāyara and Athala-
yūru-nāḍāḷvāra to carry out the duties of the Lambakaṇṇas[1],
had then as one whose commands are scarcely to be evaded,
29 the drums beaten in the kingdom and gathered together all
the officers in the Paṇḍu realm at the head of their own
30 troops and adorned with all their ornaments. Then in a temple
of the deities to the north of the palace of former kings,
31 adorned with the drums of victory captured aforetime, the
highly-famed one carried out the consecration of the Prince
and made him in accord with tradition, walk round the town,
his right side turned towards it.

32 Meanwhile the Ruler Kulasekhara who had fled to the
mountain fortress of Toṇḍamāna, had brought Toṇḍamāna
33 round to his side. He took his army as well as his own
troops, and together with Anujīvisamiddha, a man of terrible
34 courage, he set forth from that hill fortress and reached the
important stronghold called Maṅgalama into which he entered.
35 With Maṇṇaya-rāyara and Seṅkuṇḍiya-rāyara who had sub-
36 mitted to the Sīhalas[2] he fought a great battle; he captured
their fortress and took up a position there. When Laṅkāpura
heard of the matter and how it had happened, he thought:
37 "Only when I shall have driven the hostile Ruler from this

(v. 24) *vīro* is the subject and *āgañchi* the finite verb. The gerunds occurring in vv. 21—23 have as subject *senā Sīhaḷādhīnā*. They are thus again treated as absolute locatives. Cūlavs. ed. I. Introd., p. XVI.

[1] We learn two things from this passage: that a Lambakaṇṇa clan existed also in Southern India and that the members of this clan performed particular functions at the festival of the king's consecration. For the three names see notes to 76. 132 and 137.

[2] Thus according to 77. 7. It must be assumed that the Toṇḍamāna named in v. 32 who figures in 76. 315 as one of Kulasekhara's followers, had submitted to the Sīhalas, but under Kulasekhara's influence had again deserted them.

place and cleansed this district so rich in mountain and forest
strongholds shall I return." He left the town of Madhurā, 38
put up a stronghold near Maṅgalaṃkoṭṭa[1] and took up his
position there. With mighty forces they fought a great battle 39
with the three brothers of the wife of Toṇḍamāna: Kallakka- 40
veḷāra, Muṇayadha-rāyara and Kāliṅga-rāyara[2], captured the 41
fortress, slew many Damiḷas and after later on taking Sīvali-
puttūru also the highly-famed ones[3] took up a position there. 42
Thereupon the hostile Monarch Kulasekhara gathered together
the troops standing in Tiriṇaveli[4], sent also to the two brothers 43
of his mother a message and took the troops in Tenkoṅgu
and Vaḍakoṅgu[5] and after the great general had brought 44
this whole army together, he gave the order to halt at the
fortress called Sāntaneri. Now Laṅkāpura and the general 45
Jagadvijaya immediately set forth on the way to take this strong-
hold. To bar the way to the enemy Kulasekhara versed in the 46
right expedients, had the great tank pierced. When the hero 47
Laṅkāpura heard tidings of this he said: "When one goes forth
to fight a decisive battle with the foe the sight of a pierced 48
tank on the way is not good." So the mighty one immediately
had it dammed up again. Thereupon he advanced with great 49
forces and courage against yonder strong fortress, fought a
bitter fight, broke quickly into it, slew him called Kallakka- 50
veḷāra and many other Damiḷas and captured numbers of horses
of the Damiḷas. Then they pressed forward into the two vil- 51
lages belonging to Toṇḍamāna, called Ṭirimalakke and Kattala,
burned down the village called Tirimalakke so that nought 52

[1] Of course the same as the fortress Maṅgalama mentioned in v. 34, and which also occurs in 76. 297.

[2] For the two last names cf. 76. 146 and 76. 174 ff. The first occurs again 77. 50.

[3] Instead of the sing. (*Laṅkāpuro* v. 36 c) the new sentence (from v. 39 a b) has the plur. What is meant are Laṇkāpura and his generals. Sīvaliputtūru is the present Srivillipatur (cf. also W.) in the Tinnevelli District not far from the borders of Travancore.

[4] See 76. 143 and 288 and notes.

[5] See 76. 288.

but its name remained, because it was there that the Paṇḍu
53 king Parakkama had been murdered[1]. Then he set forth from
there and after reaching the village Coḷakulantaka the highly-
54 famed one tarried there for some time[2]. King Kulasekhara
now took the two brothers of his mother, also the troops of
55 the twain and their many horses, further Akalaṅka-nāḍāḷvāra,
56 and Pallava-rāyara, Malayappa-rāyara, Kaṇḍamba-rāyara and
Kiccārattarayara who was endowed with great power and
courage, and with all these Coḷa officers and their numerous
57 army as also with Kaḷavaṇḍiya-nāḍāḷvāra and his troops and
58 with Puṅkoṇḍa-nāḍāḷvāra[3] at the head of his army, the mighty
one came himself to the place called Palaṅkoṭṭa and ordered
59 his great army to Paṇḍunāḍukoṭṭāna and the place called
Ūriyeri[4], this time firmly determined on the vanquishing of
60 the foe. Thereupon Laṅkāpura and the general Jagadvijaya
61 went forth from the village of Coḷakulantaka to battle. They
so planned it that the hostile army which had occupied the two
great fortresses[5], were disinclined for giving battle in the open
62 field, had then a great entrenchment made at the village of
Ūriyeri above the tank and took up a position there during
63 the night. But the hostile army which had occupied the two
fortresses, dispersed and went thither where the Ruler Ku-

[1] W.'s happy suggestion of *ettha hato* is certainly correct. I may remark that all the MSS. have *etthă gato*; *etthāgato* as read by the Col. Ed. occurs nowhere.

[2] There is a change again in number, this time from the plur. (*paviṭṭhā*) in v. 51 c to the sing. (*nisīdittha*) in 53 c.

[3] For Akalaṅka see 77. 17, for Malayappa 77. 18, for Kaḷavaṇḍiya 76. 141 and Puṅkoṇḍa 76. 139. All these names occur again later. The same with Pallava and Kaṇḍamba who have so far not been mentioned.

[4] The locatives *Paṇḍunāḍukoṭṭāne* and *Ūriyerivhaye ṭhāne* are directly dependent on *niyojesi*. The skr. *niyojayati* is also used with the locative of that to which anyone is determined or commanded. In 72. 207 we have the same as in this passage *Kyānagāme niyojetvā*. Cf. further 77. 82. It is therefore quite unnecessary to change *ṭhāne* into *ṭhātuṃ* as is done by the Col. Ed. — Palaṅkoṭṭa (see also W.) is the present Palam-kotta in the Tinnevelli District.

[5] That is Paṇḍunāḍukoṭṭāna and Ūriyeri.

lasekhara was standing. Now Laṅkāpura and the general 64
Jagadvijaya well discriminating between favorable and un-
favorable places, marched to Palaṅkoṭṭa. The heroes fought 65
a terrible battle with the hostile sovereign, slew many warriors
captured many steeds, put the Monarch Kulasekhara at once 66
to flight and took Palaṅkoṭṭa. Then they set forth from there,
came into the domain of him called Tuvarādhipativeḷāra and 67
received the horses and elephants supplied by him[1]. But when 68
they heard: the Monarch Kulasekhara has come to Madhurā[2],
they in order to drive him from this place, hereupon marched 69
to Adharaṭṭeri, subdued there Nigaya-rāyara and showed him
many marks of favour. Now when they again set forth from 70
this place the Ruler Kulasekhara smitten with fear, betook
himself to the Coḷa country. Hereupon Laṅkāpura charged 71
the dignitary by name Jagadvijaya, to take up a position at
the place called Pāttanallūru. He himself went at the head 72
of his troops to Tirikkāṇappera. But King Kulasekhara had
meanwhile by various entreaties won over the Coḷa King to 73
his side and at the command of this king he took the army
and the many horses of him called Pallava-rāyara, also 74
him called Inandapada together with Toṇḍamāna, the rāyara
called Rājarājakalappa, further Kaṅgakoṇḍakalappa-rāyara, as 75
well as the Nakāranibiḷupa-rāyara, the hero Niccavinodavāṇava- 76
rāyara, Narasīhapadmara and Seḳīrapadma-rāyara, Rājinda- 77
brahmamahārāja and Mādhava-rāyara . . . as also Coḷakonāra,
Janābrahmamahārāja and Coḷatirikka-rāyara — these troop 78
leaders in Uccaṅkuṭṭha he took with him, with these he took also 79
Niyarāya and Kappiñcimpekūla, further Mādhava-rāyara and
Kaṇḍuveṭṭi, further Koṅgamaṅgala-nāḍāḷvāra, Akalaṅka-nāḍāḷ- 80
vāra and Kaṇḍamba-rāyara, as also Kiḷamaṅgala-nāḍāḷvāra,
Visālamutta-rāyara[3] and their many horses and sent them to 81

[1] The context shows that Tuvarādhipativeḷāra (for whom see 76. 138, 315) had submitted voluntarily.

[2] The fact that Kulasekhara can dare to attack Madhurā which was formerly (see v. 38) in Laṅkāpura's hands, shows that so far he had suffered no overwhelming defeat. He even succeeds in enlisting the Coḷas in his cause.

[3] Of the numerous names mentioned here six occur earlier: Pallava

82 Toṇḍi and Pāsa[1]. When Laṅkāpura heard of the matter he was minded to so destroy them that only their name should remain. The hero ordered the general Jagadvijaya by name to Madhurā, he himself then set forth from Tirikkānappera
83 and marched to the town of Kiḷenilaya situated on the borders of Madhurā. Now the mighty Coḷa army opened the great
84 combat. For a distance of four gāvutas[2] he filled the road with corpses, he also slew many soldiers who had flung them-
85 selves into the sea and dyed the water of the ocean ruddy with the blood of the foe[3]. He took (as booty) many horses
86 and captured many Damiḷas alive — Rājindabrahmamahārāja and Nandipadmara[4], Narasīhapadmara and Coḷakonāra — and again
87 with great forces, burned to the ground Vaḍamaṇamekkuṇḍi,
88 Maṇamekkuṇḍi and Mañcakkuṇḍi. Then having laid waste by fire a strip of the Coḷa country seven gāvutas in extent[5] and
89 thus quelled the Coḷas, he returned thence, and when he came to the village called Velaṅkuṇḍi under the dominion of Nigaḷadha-rāyara[6], he sent to him the message to appear
90 before him. But as Nigaḷadha-rāyara was at that time under the sovereignty of King Kulasekhara he took the Monarch
91 Kulasekhara, as well as Silāmeghara, and Akalaṅka-nāḍāḷvāra and Kaṇḍamba-rāyara, Malayappa-rāyara and Visālamutta-

77.55, Toṇḍamāna 76.187, Niccavinodavāṇava 76.144, Coḷakonāra 76.145, Akalaṅka 77.17, Kaṇḍamba 77.55. Cf. the accompanying notes. The name Mādhava-rāyara is twice mentioned. Three occur later: Narasīhapadmara 77.86, Rājindabrahma 77.86, and Visālamutta 77.91. Cf. with Kaṅgakoṇḍakalappa, Kaṅgakoṇḍapperayara 76.180 note; with Kīḷamaṅgala-nāḍāḷvāra, the name of the district Kīḷamaṅgala in 76.209; and with Kaṇḍuveṭṭi the name of Narasīha's capital Kaṇḍuveṭhī in 47.7.

[1] P. *Toṇḍipāsaṃ*. Cf. note to 76.236.

[2] About 8 miles.

[3] The description is extraordinary. From what has gone before the battle must have taken place in the neighbourhood of Madhurā, therefore not near the sea.

[4] Nandipadmara is not mentioned in the list given in v. 73 ff.

[5] About 14 miles.

[6] For Nigaḷadha cf. 76.138, 77.16 f.

rāyara, Kaḷavaṇḍi-nāḍāḷvāra and the troops of Tiriṇaveli, and 92
Puṅkoṇḍa-nāḍāḷvāra, and with mighty forces he came to
Ponaamarāvatī[1] to fight a decisive battle. When Laṅkāpura 93
received tidings of these events he set forth with great forces
from Velaṅkuṇḍi to vanquish the hostile ruler. The hostile 94
army which advancing from five sides[2], began the battle he
shattered in a moment with fearsome courage, slew Damiḷas 95
thousands in number, took (as booty) many horses and put the
Ruler Kulasekhara to flight. Nigaḷadha-rāyara thereupon sent 96
in his terror the message: "Thou shalt have the whole of
my treasures and my many horses, and shalt pardon my of- 97
fence, but thou must by no means prepare my destruction[3]."
When Laṅkāpura heard that he sent a return message: "Thy 98
treasures and thy horses are of no use to me, fear not and 99
come in person and present thyself". When he heard that,
he came to seek out Laṅkāpura. When the latter saw him 100
he showed him favour, assigned him the province and gave
him abundant money with which to rebuild his palace which
had been burned down. Then the far-famed one started forth, 101
came to Niyama and freed the whole province from the briers
(of the enemy). He introduced into the country everywhere 102
for trade kahāpaṇas which were stamped with the name of
the Ruler Parakkama. To Prince Vīrapaṇḍu he made over 103

[1] According to 77. 20 ff., Laṅkāpura had already fought with Nigaḷadha for Ponaamarāvatī. In the list enumerated in v. 73 ff. the following of Nigaḷadha's allies are n o t mentioned: Silāmeghara (cf. note to 76. 99), Malayappa (77. 18, 55), Kaḷavaṇḍi (76. 141) and Puṅkoṇḍa (76. 139). For Tiriṇaveli see 76. 143. — Vv. 84—92 form in the original o n e sentence. The subject however, changes. The subject belonging to all the gerunds in 84-89 (up to *pahinitvāna*) is *Laṅkāpuro*, from v. 90 onwards it is *so* (*Nigaḷadha-rāyaro*). We must therefore again assume that the preceding gerunds are treated as locative absolutes (Cūlavs. ed. I. Introd., p. XVI) S. and B. try to overcome the difficulty by emendation, they change *pahinitvāna* (v. 89 c) into *pahinittha*.

[2] W. refers *āgamma* to the subject (*Laṅkāpuro*) *bhīmavikkamo* but it is really subordinate to *pavattita* in *pavattitamahāhavaṃ sattusenaṃ*.

[3] The text is corrupt. I have tried to help matters by a conjectural rendering (*vināsanaṃ*) which seems to me not quite so far-fetched as the emendations of the Col. Ed.

the government and sent with speed to Sīhala the many horses, men and elephants captured from the Coḷa country and from the Paṇḍu land[1].

104 Now King Parakkamabāhu that lion among royal princes, founded in memory of the conquest of the Paṇḍu country the
105 splendid village Paṇḍuvijaya by name, which prospered through all time. But to the Brahmans he whose joy was in giving, gave an alms.

106 Parakkamabāhu, the first in the race of rulers of the earth, whose mind was endowed with discrimination between what was statesmanlike and what was unstatesmanlike, who was an abode of every virtue, gifted with the gracious beauty of the god of love ruled a long time alone over the ocean-bounded earth.

Here ends the seventy-seventh chapter, called "The Conquest of the Paṇḍu Kingdom", in the Mahāvaṃsa, compiled for the serene joy and emotion of the pious.

[1] The narrative ends abruptly. One is faced by a series of questions which remain unanswered. What becomes of Kulasekhara? What of the great coalition of South Indian princes Coḷas and Paṇḍus described in v. 72 of whom at the most only a few individuals were conquered? Does Vīrapaṇḍu succeed in maintaining his power? Since Kulasekhara did not fall in battle he will scarcely have left his rival in peace. What is Laṅkāpura's after fate? It is curious that his return to Ceylon is never mentioned and that there is no word of the distinctions bestowed on him by Parakkamabāhu. It is pretty clear that the chronicler has concealed the failure which overtook the expedition after its initial success. The ideal figure of Parakkama which he has in mind, must not be dimmed by association with any misfortune. South Indian inscriptions relate that Laṅkāpura was defeated and that his head with those of his officers was nailed to the gates of Madhurā. In the 4 th year of Kulottuṅga Coḷa III (1181-2) Vīrapaṇḍu was driven out and the Sinhalese troops finally defeated. H. W. Codrington, HC., p. 62. See also note to 76. 80.

CHAPTER LXXVIII

THE BUILDING OF VIHĀRAS

Now after the sovereign of Laṅkā, Parakkamabāhu who 1
had received consecration as king, who was experienced in
statecraft, had thus made peaceful the land of Laṅkā, he 2
cherished, full of zeal, the wish to further the advancement
of the Order of the Master for which he had striven when
attaining the royal dignity, since it was a most excellent
merit. Since he perceived that the few loyal bhikkhus — apart 3
from the maintenance of wives and children and so forth by
the community in the villages belonging to the community, in 4
which they saw their sole duty, beyond which there was
none — did not wish to have ceremonies in common, nor even to
see one another[1], he desired even before the purification of 5

[1] The sentence is difficult. I think the meaning is this that the attitude of the few loyal bhikkhus *(susīle keci bhikkhavo)* who would not hear of intercourse and of common action with the others, shows the evil conditions existing in the Saṃgha. The *dussīlā bhikkhavo* were in the majority, the *susīlā* were isolated. As regards the construction of the sentence, I believe that *puttadārādiposanaṃ* is governed by *thapetvā* (4 a) and *ekakammādiṃ dassanaṃ pi* by *n'ākaṅkhante.* By *saṃghagāma* are meant the villages in which the men were active as *ārāmikā.* Wives and children of the *ārāmikā* were supported by the monastery and this was the only duty from which the *susīlā bhikkhavo* did not absolve themselves and the one which brought them into contact with the others. W's version according to which the priests had only thought of the feeding of their (former) wives and children I consider impossible. The text reads: *saṃghassa puttadārādiposanaṃ.* But one cannot say that the Saṃgha has children and wives. Only the individual bhikkhu has these. Thus the gen. *saṃghassa* does not belong to *puttadārādi* but to *posanaṃ.* Note too the *ādi.* This refers to sick

the Order[1], for the purpose of furthering the Order of the
Victor, to achieve unity[2] among the bhikkhus of the three
6 fraternities. Even as the Ruler of men Dhammāsoka (with)
Moggaliputtatissa, so he entrusted the Grand thera Mahā-
7 kassapa by name, with the task — an experienced man who
knew the Tipiṭaka and was exceedingly well versed in the
Vinaya, a light of the race of theras, conciliatory, long since
8 consecrated. He made the thera Ñāṇapāla in Anurādhapura
together with his pupils and the bhikkhus in the province
9 of Sapara[3] come to Pulatthinagara, further together with the
thera Moggallāna, the thera Nāgindapalliya and all the other
10 bhikkhus in the province of the Yuvarāja[4], as well as those
belonging to the three fraternities in Rohaṇa after he had
placed at their head the distinguished thera Nanda who dwelt

people and those incapable of work who must of course also be looked after in the *saṃghagāma* of the monastery.

[1] P. *ādo* is used as a preposition and governs the following accusative.

[2] An account of the church reforms of Parakkamabāhu is found already in 73. 12-22. That this should be followed by a second detailed account is probably due to the fact that the compiler of the Cūlavaṃsa had two different sources both of which he employed for his narrative. In a similar way the building activities of the king are dealt with twice over (in 73. 23 ff. and 78. 28 ff.). As regards the reform of the Order I have already referred in the note to 73. 22 to the Gal-vihāra inscription of Parakkama and to certain similarities in form between it and the account of the Cūlavs. A further similarity occurs in the second narrative (78. 2 ff.). The name of the Grand thera Mahākassapa is mentioned as spokesman in the negotiations in which capacity he is also mentioned in the inscription. Then too in both sources a parallel is drawn between King Dhammāsoka and the head of the Third Council, Moggallāna (Mhvs. 5. 228 ff.) on the one hand, and Parakkamabāhu and Mahākassapa on the other. According to the inscription, Mahākassapa was an inmate of the Udumbaragiri-vihāra, that is Dimbulāgala, now Gunner's Quoin Hill on the right bank of the Mahaveliganga about 5 miles SSE. of Mahagantota near Polonnaruva. Cf. WICKREMASINGHE, EZ. II. 184 ff.; the same, Catal. of Sinhalese Mss. in the Brit. Museum, p. XV.

[3] Apparently the present province of Sabaragamuva.

[4] That is in Dakkhiṇadesa. The bhikkhus mentioned in vv. 8-10 are not named in the inscription.

in the Selantara monastery. Hereupon the Ruler sent a summons 11
to the bhikkhus dwelling in the Mahāvihāra for (bringing
about) the mutual concord.

Since the shamelessness had passed all bounds and the 12
schism had lasted a long time, many bhikkhus would hear
nothing of conciliation. Many began departing to foreign lands, 13
others left the Order, some wished for a sitting in the secret
court of justice[1]. Hereupon one approached the great (and) 14
exceedingly difficult task: conciliation seemed as difficult as
the hurling of the Sineru[2] mountain. But the Ruler, impartial, 15
firm in his resolves and just, encouraged the bhikkhus and
with great pains persuaded them to agree. He had the single 16
points in dispute as they arose settled by the bhikkhus among
whom Mahākassapa was the oldest. He was himself present 17
as protector of the court together with those lions among
teachers who knew the three Piṭakas, and while according to 18
precept he led those bhikkhus capable of being cured to puri-
fication, he established harmony among the bhikkhus of the
Mahāvihāra. But the undisciplined he excluded from the Order, 19
and that they might not by striving after gain do harm to
the Order, he assigned them lucrative positions. After he had 20
thus with great pains purified the Mahāvihāra, he set about
bringing the bhikkhus of the Abhayagiri — who since the 21
time of Abhaya[3] had formed a separate group — as well as

[1] I have kept as much as possible to the reading of the MSS. and believe that *līnavinicchayamaṇḍala* denotes a secret judicial process in contrast to the official *dhammakamma* of the Order (see note to 39. 57). For the meaning "hidden, concealed" for *līna* cf. Mhvs. 75. 153 where however, it is combined with a loc., as well as *līnavuttika*, 47. 3, "leading a solitary, hidden life". The Col Ed. reads *icchum eke nisajjam pi na vinicchayamaṇḍale* and W. translates accordingly: "and many wished not even to sit (with their brethren) in the hall of judgement".

[2] Cf. note to 54. 43. One may compare *sinerukkhipanaṃ* with *sakkharākhipana* "the hurling of stones" (as an accomplishment, *sippa*, JaCo. I. 418[30]).

[3] Vaṭṭagāmaṇī Abhaya. The story of the separation of the monks of the Abhayagiri-vihāra from those of the Mahāvihāra is related in Mhvs. 33. 95 ff.

the inmates of the Jetavana — who had separated themselves
22 from the days of the Ruler of men Mahāsena[1], (they) who
gave out as Buddha's word the Vetulla-Piṭaka[2] and the like
which were no words of Buddha and who had turned away
23 from religious duties — into concord with the inmates of the
Mahāvihāra who were rich in all virtues, even as glass stones
24 with jewels. But as they lacked inward virtue as moral
dicipline and the like, they came even through the influence
of the Great community and of the King to no joyful ac-
25 ceptance of the Buddha teaching. And while the just King
together with people versed in the right method held the
trial, he found not a single member of the Order that had
26 kept himself unspoiled[3]. He caused many ascetics to be received
as sāmaṇeras, the undisciplined he dismissed and gave them
27 lucrative positions. While thus within a short time achieving
purification and unity, he with great pains established again
the community as it had been in Buddha's time.

28 Every year he brought the Great community to the river
bank[4], made them take up their abode in a garden there
29 while he with his dignitaries paid them respect. Then after
firmly anchoring ships in the stream he had a charming
30 maṇḍapa of beautiful proportions erected on them. Then
when he had given to the bhikkhus costly robes and all
kinds of articles of use, the wise Prince made them hold the
ceremony of admission into the Order[5].

[1] See Mhvs. 37. 32 ff.

[2] For the heretical Vetullavāda to which the Dhammarucika monks living in the Abhayagiri monastery adhered, see Mhvs. 36. 41, 110 ff. and 37. 1 ff.; Nik. s., p. 12. A. M. Hocart, Mem. ASC. I, 1924, p. 15 ff.

[3] P. *pakatatta*, lit. "with the original self (being, character)". In Vin. I. 280[12] the word means "in the original condition, restored, cured"; In JāCo. I. 236[29] it has a similar meaning to that in our passage as attribute of *bhikkhu* along with *sīlavā vipassanāya yuttapayutto*.

[4] On the bank of the Mahaveliganga.

[5] Even to-day the monks in Ceylon in order to be quite undisturbed, are fond of performing their rites in a pavilion built on piles in a sheet of water about a stone's throw from the bank.

Now for the bhikkhus increased in this manner to many 31
hundreds the King was desirous of building in goodly fashion
large vihāras, suitable for dwelling in. He (therefore) founded 32
the great monastery by name Jetavana[1], making as it were
visible to the eye the beauty of the Jetavana (in Sāvatthī[2]).
For the theras dwelling there in the sacred district, firmly 33
persevering in discipline, he built eight costly pāsādas, three
storeys high. For the thera named Sāriputta who persevered 34
firmly in discipline, he erected a vast (and) glorious pāsāda
with rooms, terraces and chambers. Also nine incomparable, 35
three-storeyed image houses (he built) furnished with all
appurtenances[3] and diversely adorned with images. For the 36
seventy-five pariveṇas (he built) as many long pāsādas with
charming figures (painted), two storeys high; (further) one 37
hundred and seventy-eight small pāsādas, thirty-four gate-towers
and two houses for books; huts, grottoes, halls and many 38
sleeping-houses with ornaments of flowers and creepers and
with figures of gods, Brahmas and the like. Creating out of 39
brick and stucco an elixir for the eyes[4] (he built) the Tivaṅka
house for the Tivaṅka image[5], shimmering with rows of figures 40

[1] What is meant here is without doubt the group of monastic buildings within the city to the north of the citadel, on the so-called Quadrangle. Cf. above all H. C. P. Bell, Rep. ASC. 1903 (= LXV, 1908), p. 6 ff., as well as A. M. Hocart, Mem. ASC. II, 1926, p. 4 ff.

[2] The monastery was like its namesake in Anurādhapura, called after the celebrated park in Sāvatthī which Anāthapiṇḍika presented to the Buddha and the Order. See Oldenberg, Buddha, p. 166; H. Kern, Manual of Indian Buddhism, p. 28.

[3] For *paṭiyatta* as substantive in the meaning of "equipment, articles of clothing or of general use", cf. Mhvs. 29. 22. The alteration by the Col. Ed. into *sattatimatte* I cannot approve of. The numeral adj. is *nava* in *navāppaṭisammate* — as is proved by all the MSS. — which S and B likewise felt obliged to alter. The Col. Ed. treats the text too arbitrarily. I believe that *paṭiyatta* here means all the ornaments and garments belonging to a Buddha image with which it is decked out on festive occasions. Cf. note to 38. 64 (towards the end) and to 38. 56.

[4] The beauty of the building acted on the eyes like an elixir (*rasāyana*). In my edition I have joined the sentence to the preceding. But I think now that it belongs to the following one.

[5] It is difficult to say what is meant by *tivaṅka* in *t-ghara* and

41 of lions, kinnaras[1], geese and the like, with many diversely perforated balustrades[2] and with railings. (Further he built) a beautiful round temple wholly of stone for the Tooth Relic[3], adorned with glorious pillars, staircases and outer walls[4] and
42 so forth. (Further the built) three sermon halls, a cetiya[5],
43 eight long cloisters and a refectory of (great) length and breadth, eighty-five fire-houses covered with bricks and one hundred and seventy-eight privies.

t-paṭimā. Mr. PARANAVITANE, the epigraphist of the ASC. (letter of 25-4-28) assumes that the term means the same as *tribhaṅga*. This is the name given in Indian Iconography to a statue with "three bends", that is in the posture in which Viṣṇu or the Nāgas are often represented. He refers to Selalihinisandesa 68, where there is a mention of Tivaṅka images in the Kelani-vihāra and believes that this passage in the Mhvs. refers to these very statues in Kelaniya. It cannot be a Buddha image which is meant in this case. It seems to me certain that the *tivaṅkaghara* of our passage refers to a building in Pulatthinagara and in the Jetavana-vihāra. But cf. note to 85. 66. The most likely seems to be the Heṭa-dāgē, an image house on the Quadrangle with three Buddha figures (cf. HOCART, l. l., p. 5) or that building known as the Thūpārāma also situated there. The first seems however, to be a work of Nissaṅka-Malla (80. 19 and note), while the other belongs to the time before Parakkamabāhu. The expression *tivaṅka* remains however in both cases inexplicable.

[1] Mythical beings represented with human bodies and heads of horses. I may remark that W. joins v. 40 to the following as description of the *dāṭhādhātughara*.

[2] P. *jālakavāṭa*, lit. net-enclosure.

[3] Without doubt the Vaṭa-dā-gē situated on the Quadrangle opposite the Heṭa-dā-gē. BELL, l. l., p. 21 ff. and Rep. ASC. 1904, p. 5 ff. HOCART, l. l., p. 4. It is a circular building consisting of two concentric terraces. On the upper terrace was a cetiya in which the relic was preserved. In an inscription on the outer stairs Nissaṅka Malla boasts that he has had the building made. It is however evidently a case of restoration. The outer staircase is indeed of later origin.

[4] I take *bhiti* "outer wall" to mean the railings leading round the terraces.

[5] There is no stūpa in the domain of the Jetavana. One must assume therefore that the terraced tower Sat-mahal-pāsāda on the Quadrangle was built as a cetiya. It could not serve as a dwelling, for it is as massive as a dagoba with nothing but a tunnel-like circular passage in the basement.

After he had thus by cleansing the Order, cleansed the 44
inward impurity of the bhikkhus, in order to cleanse the
outward impurity, that one might be able to bathe in
great heat he had eight bath-houses of stone erected, named 45
Vaṭṭanahānakoṭṭha, Guhānahānakoṭṭha, Padumanahānakoṭṭha,
Bhaddanahānakoṭṭha[1] and so forth, adorned with pillars, 46
staircases and railings. There also the Great king had many
walls built. Thus there were in Jetavana in all five hundred 47
and twenty buildings. With the distribution of abundant
articles of use, he made the community take up its abode there.

Further the Prince had built there the Āḷāhana-pariveṇa[2] 48
which had all the distinguishing marks (belonging to such a
building), being not too far away and the like, and which
was universally acknowledged as beautiful. There he built for 49
the thera a splendid pāsāda with rooms and terraces, with a
choice of various apartments, embellished by turrets, three
storeys high. Further forty long pāsādas and as many privies, 50
eight small pāsādas and six gate-towers, thirty-four fire-houses 51
and two larger outer walls, the Subhaddā-cetiya and the
Rūpavatī-cetiya[3]; besides that a charming image house of five 52
storeys for which — as it was adorned with ornaments of
flowers and creepers and with figures of gods and Brahmas 53
and embellished with buildings, with turrets, grottoes, apartments

[1] The "round bathing-house", "cave-", "lotus-b.-h." and the "bathing-house of happiness". The temple on the Quadrangle popularly known as the Thūpārāma is not mentioned among the buildings of the Jetavana, probably because it already belonged to the time before Parakkamabāhu. Hocart, l. l., p. 5.

[2] H. W. Codrington is certainly right when he says that the description in the Mhvs. proceeds from south to north. In chap. 73 the secular buildings in the citadel and its immediate neighbourhood are mentioned. In chap. 78 follow the monastic foundations joining it on the north. The Āḷāhana-pariveṇa is therefore probably the group of buildings lying outside of the city which is now popularly but wrongly called the Jetavanārāma.

[3] To the group of buildings which we assume formed the Āḷāhana-pariveṇa there belonged in fact several stūpas. The largest of these is popularly known as the Kiri-vehera. More to south lies the Rankot Dagoba. This has, however, nothing to do with the Āḷāhana-pariveṇa,

54 and halls[1] — the name of Laṅkātilaka was befitting[2]. In this (temple) he had erected a standing image which was an elixir for the eyes[3], which had the size of the living Buddha[4],
55 which (likewise) was called Laṅkātilaka. (He) also (built) the twelve-storeyed Uposatha-house which bore the name of Baddhasīmāpāsāda, which was furnished with numbers of
56 turrets, with buildings containing apartments and halls and with cells as dwelling-places[5]. To determine the boundary[6]

but is identical with the Ratanāvalī-cetiya built or completed by Nissaṅka Malla (80. 20). The Mhvs. expressly states that this King adorned it with a *suvaṇṇatthūpikā*, "with a golden pointed cone". The name Rankot means "golden point".

[1] The buildings form the immediate surroundings of the temple enriching its beauty.

[2] The name still sticks to the image house of the Āḷāhana group. It is proved besides by an inscription on the building itself in which Parakkamabāhu is named as its builder. See H. C. P. Bell, Rep. ASC. 1910—11 (= X. 1914), p. 30 ff. Lately an exact description of the plan of the building has been given by A. M. Hocart, Mem. ASC. II, 1926, p. 11 ff. This plan agrees on the whole with that of the Thūpārāma (see above note to v. 45). As regards the name of the temple, *tilaka* means "a patch of coloured stuffs worn on the forehead as ornament... or as emblem of a sect" (BR.); at the end of a compound it means "ornament of something", here therefore "ornament of the Island of Laṅkā". — The construction of the sentence is as follows: *yattha* in v. 53a stands for the loc. *yamhi* (*paṭimāgehe*) and to this then belong the locatives °*rūpini* and *sobhite* in v. 52.

[3] See above note to v. 39.

[4] According to Bell's calculation (l. l., p. 36) the statue in the Laṅkātilaka temple when intact, measured 41 ft. in height (roughly 12. 5 m.).

[5] It is generally supposed that the remains of this building are to be found in the so-called "priory" situated in the domain of Āḷāhana-pariveṇa and remarkable for its quantity of small and narrow cells (*pañjarageha* "cage"!). Cf. H. C. P. Bell, Rep. ASC. 1911—12 (= III. 1915), p. 81 ff.

[6] P. *bandhāpetuṃ tahiṃ sīmaṃ*. By *sīmā* is meant the boundary line enclosing the monastic buildings within which alone ecclesiastical acts could legally be performed. The regulations for establishing such a *sīmā* are to be found in the Vinaya, Mahāvagga 2. 6 ff. (= I. 106 ff.). Cf. with our passage Mhvs. 15. 188—194, where it is related of King

there the King betook himself, adorned with all his ornaments,
with the dignitaries and the ladies of the court, with a vast 57
army and with his train in the splendour of the King of
the gods, to the great vihāra. At the invitation of the
Great community of whom Mahākassapa was the oldest, the 58
Monarch — with the tune of songs of praise, with the sound of
musical instruments and the noise of the shouts of greeting
filling the four regions of the heavens, surrounded by many
people bearing golden and other jars and baskets and many 59
banners and umbrellas — took with great solemnity the golden 60
plough before which was harnessed the elephant of state and
went forth ploughing the furrow[1]. To remove[2] all scruples 61
regarding landmarks formerly drawn at this spot, the bhikkhu
community took up a position at different points, after pre- 62
viously by a solemn act, bound to bring full success, removing
in due order the ancient landmarks[3] and made known to the
King the landmarks along the furrow (which he ploughed).
The King drew three partial boundaries and a main boundary. 63
The boundary stones set up in the eight regions of the
heavens, east and so forth, were distant (measured) with a
staff five cubits in length[4] from the Laṅkātilaka temple forty- 64

Devānampiyatissa how he draws in person the *sīmā* of the Mahāvihāra, just as Parakkamabāhu that of the Āḷāhana-pariveṇa. The two desciptions have a considerable resemblance to each other even in the wording (cf. 78. 56-7 with 15. 189; 78. 58 with App. B, v. 6 of my edition of the old Mahāvaṃsa). This may be due either to the stereotyped character of all these descriptions or to Dhammakitti's conscious borrowing from the older work.

[1] Cf. *mahāchaṇamhi vattente . . . kasanto bhūmipo agā* with *mahatā chaṇapūjāya kasanto bhūmipo agā* in Mhvs. App. B. (to 15. 191), v. 7 c d. This comparison shows that *mahāchaṇamhi* not *mahājanamhi*, is the right reading.

[2] It was strictly forbidden to encroach on an existing boundary by a new *sīmā*. The old boundary had first to be removed by a *kammavācā* (v. 62 d), that is a solemn act of the community. Cf. note to 37. 56.

[3] I think that the two lines of v. 62 should be reversed.

[4] P. *pañcahatthāya yaṭṭhiyā*. For *hattha* see note to 37. 172. The standard of measurement had thus a length of (5 × 18 in.) roughly

four, forty-nine, thirty-eight, thirty-six, thirty-five, fifty-seven,
65 forty-five, sixty-six staves respectively. The boundary stone
set up in the southern region of the heavens was distant from
66 the Gopāla rock[1] fifty-eight staves[2], and the boundary stone
that was set up in the northern region of the heavens, was
67 fifty staves from the Vijjādhara cave[3]. These stones served
for the marking of the main boundary. At the Baddhasīmā-
pāsāda there was a fixed boundary of thirty-five staves in
68 length and breadth[4]. At the sacred space called Khaṇḍasīmā[5]
the boundary was fixed at fifteen staves in length and six
69 staves in breadth[6], and at the pāsāda of the thera the fixed
boundary was eighteen cubits in length and twenty cubits in
70 breadth[7]. This vihāra the King dedicated to the bhikkhus
along with the (necessary) articles of use.

In the same way the Ruler of men had the foundations

7½ ft. (= 2.55 m.). The distances were thus successively 330, 367½, 285, 270, 262½, 427½, 337½, 495 ft. Cf. for this A. M. Hocart, Mem. ASC. II. 1926, p. 5-7. By "main boundary" (*mahāsīmā*) is meant that enclosing the whole of the buildings belonging to the Āḷāhana-pariveṇa. Inside this there were according to 67c to 69, three smaller sections which were marked off by "sub-boundaries" or "part-boundaries" (*khaṇḍasīmā*). This distinction corresponds to the description of the fixing of the boundary of the Mahāvihāra Mhvs. 15. 193 which speaks of *nimittāni* "boundary marks" pure and simple and *sīmantaranimittāni* "inner boundary marks".

1 This is probably the rock lying between the Baddhasīmā-pāsāda and the Rankot stūpa. According to the popular idea the chasm served as an abode for those bhikkhus who wished to give themselves up to meditation.

2 Therefore 435 ft.

3 That is 375 ft. from what is now called the Gal-vehera. Cf. below note to v. 73.

4 Therefore 262½ ft. × 262½ ft.

5 Just as the main building took its name from the fixing of the main boundary (*baddhā sīmā*) so one of the sub-sections from that of the sub- or part-boundary.

6 Therefore 112½ ft. × 45 ft.

7 Thus with the cubit (*hattha*) calculated at 18 in. only about 27 ft. × about 30 ft.

laid of the Pacchimārāma[1]. Here in the pariveṇas, which 71
were twenty-two in number (there were) just as many two-
storeyed long pāsādas and twenty fire-houses, forty-one 72
two-storeyed small pāsādas as well as thirty-five privies and 73
two cloisters; one sermon hall and ten gate-buildings. He
dedicated this vihāra along with the (necessary) articles of
use also to the bhikkhus.

Likewise the Ruler of men had the Uttarārāma[2] built. By 74
breaking down the rock not far from the Great thūpa he
bringing into play every kind of skilled work, had three 75
grottoes made by expert craftsmen, namely the Vijjādhara
grotto, the cave with the image in sitting posture and the
grotto with the recumbent image.

The Ruler also had the Mahāthūpa[3] erected which bore 76
the name of the Damiḷathūpa because it had been built by

[1] The "West Monastery". Hocart (Mem. ASC. II, p. 6) supposes this building to be the unexcavated ruins adjoining the remains of the Āḷāhana-pariveṇa on the west.

[2] There can be no doubt that what is meant is the so-called Galvehera. The front of a rock rising about 30 ft. above the surrounding region is polished. It stretches from SW. to NE. gradually sloping away on either side. The rock is about 16 chains (roughly 320 m.) distant from the Great Thūpa situated farther north. Hewn out of the rock wall just about its centre, is a grotto, 26 ft. wide, 12 ft. 9 in. deep and 9 ft. 9 in. in height. The massive rock above the cave is still some 12 to 13 ft. thick. This rock ceiling is supported on two pillars on the front side of the cave. In the background of the cave there is an image of the Buddha sitting on a throne. This cave is the *Vijjādhara-guhā* of our passage. To the left of it from the spectator's point of view, there is the figure of a sitting Buddha 15 ft. high, hewn out of the solid rock. To the right, also hewn out of the solid rock, there is a colossal figure of a recumbent Buddha about 49 ft. long, at its head the upright figure of Ānanda grieving over his dying master. It is probable that both the statues of the sitting and of the recumbent Buddha were originally contained in a grotto or niche made of rock and brickwork. These were the *nisinnapaṭimālena* and the *nipanna-paṭimāguhā*. These figures now stand uncovered in the open air. For the whole matter cf. H. C. P. Bell, Rep. ASC. 1907 (= V. 1911), p. 7 ff.

[3] The "Great stūpa" evidently borrowed its name from the Mahāthūpa (Ruvanveli Dagoba) in Anurādhapura. In its present state it is

77 Damiḷas who had been brought hither after the conquest of the Paṇḍu kingdom. It had a circumference of one thousand three hundred cubits[1] and was the largest of all thūpas, like to
78 a second Kelāsa[2], and (built) without the miraculous power of arahants and without the miraculous power of the gods, alone by kingly miraculous power.

79 Also he had built in the suburb called Rājavesibhujaṅga the Isipatana-vihāra[3] which was a delight for the ascetics.
80 There (there was) one relic shrine and three three-storeyed image houses with costly images and resplendent with brightly
81 coloured painting, further a two-storeyed pāsāda whose ornaments called forth delight, two long pāsādas and four gate-
82 buildings, eight small pāsādas, a sermon house, a cloister as
83 well as eight fire-houses and six privies, a fine bathing-house wholly of stone, a boundary wall and a garden which belonged to the bhikkhu community.

84 Furthermore in the suburb of Sīhapura the Ruler (gifted)
85 with a lion's courage had the Kusinārā-vihāra erected. There (there was) a relic shrine, three image houses of three storeys,
86 six long pāsādas, a sermon hall, a cloister, sixteen small pāsādas, three gate-buildings, eleven privies and six fire-houses.

87 In the suburb called Vijita King Parakkamabāhu also

a great heap of ruins overgrown with jungle, looking like a natural hill over which run the paths of the wild elephant. The name of Damiḷathūpa has been preserved to the present day in the name Demaḷamahaseya which is however, erroneously given to another building (see note to v. 87).

[1] P. *ratana* = *hattha* = roughly 18 inches (according to Fleet, JRAS. 1912, p. 237). The circumference was therefore roughly 1950 ft. The circumference of the Mahāthūpa in Anurādhapura is 929 ft. (Parker, Ancient Ceylon, p. 286, 306), that of the Abhayagiri 1115 ft.

[2] See note to 68. 41.

[3] For the three suburbs and their monasteries cf. the earlier account in 73. 151-5. It does not quite agree with ours. If we follow it, the monasteries would be distributed thus: Rājavesibhujaṅga: Veḷuvana—Rājakulantaka (= Sīhapura): Isipatana—Vijita: Kusinārā, so far as importance can be attached to the order in which they are given.

built the Veḷuvana-vihāra[1]. Therein (there were) three three- 88
storeyed image houses with beautiful images, gleaming with
brightly coloured paintings, a thūpa and a cloister, a two- 89
storeyed pāsāda, four gate-buildings, four long pāsādas and
eight small pāsādas, one refectory and one sermon hall, further 90
seven fire-houses and twelve privies. Gāvuta on gāvuta[2] (along 91
the road) the Ruler of men had vihāras[3] erected, furnished
with charming image temples, with gate-buildings, outer
walls and sermon halls. For such bhikkhus as loved solitude 92
and had taken upon them the whole of the duties of the
ascetic, he had the Kapila-vihāra built as a good abode.
There (there was) a costly two-storeyed pāsāda, four long 93
cloisters and four long two-storeyed pāsādas, further a dwelling- 94
house of brick with diverse coloured painting and adorned
with turrets, built in honour of the sage Kapila, four small 95
pāsādas and three privies. Also these vihāras he dedicated
along with the (necessary) articles of use to the bhikkhus.

Now in order to rebuild the vihāras in Anurādhapura 96
formerly destroyed by the Damiḷas and which many kings
had not restored because it was so difficult, he sent an official 97
and completed the three thūpas aforetime destroyed by the
Damiḷas, the Ratanavāluka-thūpa[4] one hundred and twenty

[1] Some distance to the north of the Great thūpa there lies an image temple similar in plan to the Thūpārāma and the Laṅkātilaka, famous for the fresco paintings on its inner walls. I was told there that the priests frequently called this temple the Veḷuvana. If one could trust this tradition we should have a clue to the position of the Vijita suburb. See however, A. M. Hocart's objections, Mem. ASC. II. 1926, p. 6. He calls the structure "the Northern Temple". The popular name of the building is Demaḷamahaseya which however originally must have belonged to the Mahāthūpa or Damiḷathūpa. I am also inclined to regard the Potgul-vihāra situated to the south of the city, as one of the suburb monasteries of Pulatthinagara. According to an inscription discovered there (Wickremasinghe, EZ. II. 238 ff.) it was originally built by Parakkamabāhu, and it would be curious if such an important structure were not to be mentioned at all in the Mhvs. Cf. on the subject H. C. P. Bell, Rep. ASC. 1906 = XX. 1910, p. 14 ff.

[2] Cf. for this 73. 154 f. and note. [3] Lit.: Gāvuta-vihāras.

[4] = Mahāthūpa. Cf. note to 76. 104. There are four thūpas mention-

98 cubits high, the Jetavana-thūpa one hundred and forty cubits
high, the Abhayagiri-thūpa one hundred and sixty cubits high,
99 as well as the great Maricavaṭṭi-thūpa[1] eighty cubits high. These
100 were (all) overgrown with great trees, bears and panthers
dwelt there and the ground of the jungle scarce offered a
101 foothold by reason of the heaps of bricks and earth. After
having the forest hewn down and (the thūpas) built in the
proper fashion, and faced with stucco, he also cleared the
courtyard of the cetiya.

102 The Lohapāsāda destroyed by the Coḷas — which measured
in every direction one hundred cubits[2], one hundred in length
and breadth[3] and as much in height, which was adorned with
103 many hundreds of apartments, with fine turrets and with rows
of cells[4] and which had several storeys, whose embellishment
104 called forth admiration — the Ruler of men restored by raising
105 again its thousand and six hundred pillars[5]. Sixty large
pāsādas (like) the one named Sepaṇṇipuppha, as also the
106 destroyed pāsāda called Mahindasena he had renewed, also
boundary walls and numbers of pariveṇas, and after erecting
a house for alms he celebrated a great festival for the offering
107 of alms. In the ancient pariveṇas, the Thūpārāma and others,
he saw to the restoration of whatever was decayed or had

ed in the text, not three, and it looks as if the Maricavaṭṭi had been added later.

[1] Taking the four stūpas in the order of their size (cf. above note to v. 77) we have for the Abhayagiri 240 ft., for the Jetavana 210 ft., for the Mahāthūpa 180 ft. and for the Maricavaṭṭi 120 ft. According to Smither, Architectural Remains of Anurādhapura, p. 52, 47, 27 in his time the height of the three first thūpas lying in ruins was: 1) Abhayagiri (wrongly called Jetavana by Sm.) 245 ft., 2) Jetavana (by Sm. Abhayagiri) 232 ft., 3) Ruvanveli (= Mahāthūpa) 198 ft. The Maricavaṭṭi-thūpa measured then (p. 20) over 80 ft. It is now restored.

[2] = 150 ft. The surface area of the Lohapāsāda is in reality rather more than 231 × 232 ft. as is proved by the pillars still standing in the basement. P. M. Burrows, The Buried Cities of Ceylon, p. 29.

[3] So I understand *hatthasatūrukaṃ* in contrast to *uccato tattakaṃ*.

[4] P. *sīhapañjara* "lion's cage". The cells of the Baddhasīmā-pāsāda are also called *pañjara* in v. 55.

[5] That is in fact the number of the foundation pillars still standing.

fallen in. On the Cetiyagiri[1] he had sixty-four thūpas rebuilt 108
and had restored on the old buildings whatever was decayed or had fallen in.

What sensible man when he has thus realised that the 109
pure-minded, even if they live in the greatest happiness, find their supremest bliss in meritorious works — would grow weary in the works of virtue which procure every happiness in the world?

Here ends the seventy-eighth chapter, called «The Building of Vihāras», in the Mahāvaṃsa, compiled for the serene joy and emotion of the pious.

[1] The Mihintale mountain. See note to 38. 76.

Chapter LXXIX

THE LAYING OUT OF GARDENS AND THE LIKE

1 As the King wished to make all articles (of food) needed
by the townspeople easily attainable, he laid out gardens at
2 different places. He who was the delight of his subjects, laid
out the garden called Nandana which was adorned with
3 hundreds of trees bearing fruit and blossom. The King planted
coco palms, mango and bread-fruit trees, areka and Palmyra
4 palms and other trees, a hundred thousand of each kind and
laid out in this way with great pains a large garden destined
for the community, which because the name was appropriate,
5 was known generally as the Lakkhuyyāna. For the bathing
of the bhikkhus in the hot season he had two charming ponds
6 made there beneath hollow rocks. The Monarch also laid out
the Dīpuyyāna[1] resplendent in beauty which was to be glorified
7 by his own continual presence during the day; further the
Mahāmeghavanuyyāna, the Cittalatāvana, the garden called
8 Missaka and that called Rājanārāyaṇa; the garden called Laṅkā-
tilaka and the garden called Tilokanandana, that called Vā-
9 narākara and that called Nayanussava; the garden Manohara
by name and the Nimmitapura, the Jaṅghābhāra and the
10 Puṇṇavaddhana by name; the garden of the name of Saṃ-
sāraphala and that called Phārusaka, that called Sālipota and
11 that called Somanātha; the Ṭhānakoṅkaṇa and the Uttarakuru
by name, that called Bharukaccha and that called Pulacceri;
12 the gardens called Kiḷākara, Paṇḍavāvana and Rāmissara, as
well as the Sāmisaṃtosuyyāna, the Cintāmaṇuyyāna and the
Pacuruyyāna.

[1] See above 73. 96 ff. 113 ff.

In Rājaraṭṭha the King had ninety-nine new thūpas built 13
in many villages and market towns. On seventy-three relic 14
shrines the Ruler had what was decayed or fallen in
repaired and the coating renewed. He restored six thousand 15
one hundred decayed image houses and built three hundred
new image houses. He had four hundred and seventy-six 16
divers kinds of images made and ninety-one Bodhi Trees planted.
For the community hailing from the four regions of the 17
heavens he had built as an abode for them when coming and
going two hundred and thirty dwellings. He erected fifty-six 18
sermon halls, nine cloisters, as well as one hundred and forty-
four gate-buildings; one hundred and ninety-two chapels with 19
altars for flowers, sixty-seven outer walls and thirteen temples
for the gods[1]. For the bhikkhus coming from foreign lands 20
he had twelve parks (laid out) and two hundred and thirty
rest-houses[2] built. Further the Ruler saw to the restoration 21
of twenty-nine sermon halls, thirty-one grottoes and five parks; 22
likewise of fifty-one rest-houses and of seventy-nine decayed
temples to the gods.

To put away the sufferings of famine from living creatures 23
that most excellent of men had many tanks and canals made
in divers places. By damming up the Kāragaṅgā by a great 24
barrier between the hills[3] and bringing its mighty flood of
waters hither by means of a vast canal called the Ākāsagaṅgā[4], 25
the Ruler created that king of reservoirs continually filled
with water and known by the name of Parakkamasamudda[5] 26

[1] P. *devālaya*, thus sanctuaries for Hindu deities. Numerous temples to Viṣṇu and Śiva were discovered in Polonnaruva.

[2] P. *āgantukasālā* "house (or hut) for strangers".

[3] So I understand *mahatā girisetunā*. W's translation "stone wall" I consider inadmissible, since "*giri*" is always "mountain" never "stone".

[4] Skr. *Ākāśagaṅgā*, name of the Ganges river which is conceived as flowing in space until it descends to earth.

[5] The Parakkamasamudda mentioned here is different from the reservoir of the same name named in 68. 40. This as we saw (note to the passage) is situated in Dakkhiṇadesa and was formerly known as Paṇḍavāpi the corresponding name for which is now Pandaveva. The Parakkamasamudda of 79. 26, which belongs to the river system of the

in which there was an island resplendent with a superb royal
27 palace and which was like to a second ocean. He also built
the great tank Parakkamataḷāka with a sluice[1] of a hundred
28 cubits[2], and which was made fast[3] by stone construction. Further
the Ruler of men built the Mahindataṭaḷāka[4] and the Ekāhavāpi

Kūragaṅgā, is described in more detail in v. 40 ff. A canal starting from it waters the Mahāmegha park. In 79. 7 this park is named immediately after the Dīpuyyāna in Pulatthinagara among the parks laid out by Parakkamabāhu I. A sluice of the reservoir was situated according to v. 45 near the Caṇḍī gate. This name appears in 73. 161 among the gates of Pulatthinagara. One must therefore look for the Parakkamasamudda of 79. 26 at Polonnaruva and it is evidently identical with the Topaveva. This was formerly far more extensive than now and was connected with the Dumbutuluveva situated farther south. See on the whole subject A. M. Hocart CJSc. G I, p. 161. In 79. 57 a Parakkamasāgara is mentioned. As it was also connected with the Kāragaṅgā, its name is probably merely a variant of Parakkamasamudda. But in v. 28 c Parakkamasāgara is mentioned along with the Parakkamasamudda and next to a Parakkamataḷāka. It is therefore possible that there were more than two reservoirs called after the King.

[1] That *paṇālī* means the sluice or the outflow from the tank is clear from v. 42, 43. The *mātikā*, the water canals (called *äla* now in Snh.) start from the *paṇālī*. In Skr. *praṇādī* or *praṇālī* means according to BR. a "drainage canal". The term *paṇālī* is explained by the construction of the sluices of the old tanks in Ceylon, as described by Parker (Ancient Ceylon, p. 373 ff.). They consist of a walled culvert of about 2 – 4 ft. in breadth which runs across the whole dam. and is only slightly raised above the base of the dam. To this culvert there leads on the slightly sloping inner side of the dam a square shaft also walled in. This is called in Sinhalese *bisō-koṭuva*. The shaft serves for regulating the wooden apparatus (p. *āvaraṇa* "lock", see v. 69 with note) by the raising and dropping of which the culvert is wholly or partially closed or opened and thus the outflow of the water regulated or completely shut off. The shaft with the lock thus divides the culvert into an inflow and an outflow channel.

[2] Therefore about 150 ft. The number can only apply to the length of the culvert.

[3] P. *dugga.* I believe that here we must take the adjective in the meaning of "sure, fast" which has developed out of the meaning "difficult of access". In the same way the substantive *dugga* (originally "a place difficult of access") has become "a strong place", then a "fortress".

[4] A Mahindataṭa was already mentioned in 42. 29 as a work of

tank, as well as the Parakkamasāgara whose flood-escape was
walled up[1]; also small tanks at different places a thousand 29
four hundred and seventy-one (in number). At three hundred 30
tanks the Monarch had as many stone sluices built. Ancient 31
tanks which had burst he again dammed up in great number:
the great tank Maṇihīra, the Mahādāragallaka, the tank called 32
Suvaṇṇatissa and that called Dūratissa, the Kālavāpi tank and
the one Brāhmaṇaggāma by name, the tanks called Nālikera- 33
mahāthamba, Raheṛa, Giritaḷāka and Kumbhīlasobbha; the 34
Kāṇavāpi, Padīvāpi and the tank called Kaṭi, the Pattapāsāṇavāpi
and the tank called Mahaṇṇa; the tanks with the names 35
Mahānāmamatthaka, Vaḍḍhana, Mahādatta and Kāṇagāma;
the tanks Vīra, Valāhassa and Suramāna and the tanks called 36
Pāsāṇagāma and Kālavalli; the tank by name Kāhalli and 37
that called Aṅgagāma, the Hillapattakakhaṇḍa and the Madagu[2].

Aggabodhi I. If the Mahindataḷāka is identical with this, it can only have been a restoration.

[1] P. *koṭṭhabaddhanijjhara*. By *nijjhara* (originally "waterfall") are meant the flood escapes or "waste-weirs" (Parker l. l. p. 374) serving for the overflow of the water when the reservoir is too full. The weir of the Parakkamasāgara is walled in (*koṭṭhabaddha*). Note that in Skr. *koṣṭhaka* may also mean an encircling wall, and on the other hand that the corresponding Sinhalese word *koṭura* (see above v. 27 note) is also used in connection with waterworks. In Mhvs. 68. 16 *Koṭṭhabaddha* is the name of a causeway on the Jajjara-nadī.

[2] Of the tanks enumerated here six (Valāhassa, Mahādāragalla, Mahādatta, Kumbhīlasobbha, Pattapāsāṇa and Kāṇa) are mentioned in 60. 50 as having been restored by Vijayabāhu I. Cf. note to the passage. The Maṇihīra is the work of Mahāsena (Mhvs. 37. 47), likewise the Suvaṇṇatissa (Wickremasinghe, EZ. II. 28, called Rantisa in the Mediri-giriya inscr.) and the Mahādāragalla (37. 47); the Dūratissa, one of Saddhātissa (Mhvs. 33. 9); the Giritaṭāka, one of Aggabodhi II. (42. 67; cf. note to 70. 312). Rahera is frequently mentioned now as locality, now as mountain apparently situated not far from Anurādhapura, (Mhvs. 21. 5; 41. 44; 44. 7), also as an irrigation canal (41. 31). Kāṇagāma was a place in Rohaṇa (45. 43) and Hillapattakakhaṇḍa is in 72. 41 the name of a ford of the Mahaveliganga. The remaining names occur only in this passage. Of these Padīvāpi (v. 34) might be identical with the Padaviya tank in the north-east corner of the North Central Province, 40 miles from Anurādhapura. Cf. Wickremasinghe, EZ. I. 202.

38 These decayed tanks the Ruler had restored to their original
state and in the same way four hundred and sixty-seven small
39 tanks which had been destroyed. In many tanks the King
well aware of the right moment, had breaches (a total of)
one thousand three hundred and ninety-five (in number)
40 dammed up so that they were firm again. The King also
had a canal constructed, called Gambhīrā (the deep), which
started at the flood-escape called Makara of the Parakkama-
41 samudda. (He also constructed) the great canal by name
Hemavatī which branched off from the same (tank) in
42 the direction of the Mahāmeghavana; in the same way
the canal known by the name of Nīlavāhinī which started
43 from the sluice called Mālatīpuppha of the same (tank) and
the canal Salaḷavatī by name which branched off from the
44 Kiḷākaruyyāna sluice; further the great canal called Vettavatī
which took its start from the sluice known by the name of
45 Vettavatī; the canal Tuṅgabhaddā coming from the Dakkhiṇā
sluice and the canal Maṅgalagaṅgā which branched off from
the sluice called Maṅgala, as well as the canal called Campā
46 from the sluice near the Caṇḍī gate. (He built) also the
Sarasvatī (canal) which branched off from the Toyavāpi and
led to Puṇṇavaddhanavāpi and the Veṇumatī (canal) from its
47 western side; further the (canal) Yamunā which branched off
from the Puṇṇavaddhana tank to the west and the Sarabhū
48 (canal) which ran northwards; also the canal called Candabhāgā
which flowed through the centre of the Lakkhuyyāna, and
the Nammadā (canal) which branched off in the domain of the
49 Jetavana-vihāra; further the canal named Nerañjarā which
flowed from that tank in a northerly direction, and the
50 Bhagīrathī, which started from the Anotatta tank; as also
the (canal) called Āvattagaṅgā which branched off from there
to the south and the Tambapaṇṇī (canal) which flowed from
51 the Ambāla tank towards the north; the Aciravatī (canal)
which ran westwards from the Mahāvālukagaṅgā, fitted for
52 many a long year to prevent famine, and the Gomatī (canal)
which branching off from there flowed eastwards, and the
53 Malāpaharaṇī (canal) running northwards; also the canals

flowing eastwards from the Aciravatī: the Sataruddhā, Nibbindā,
Dhavalā and Sīdā; further the Kālindī canal which flowed 54
in a southerly direction from the southern overflow of the
vast Maṇihīra tank; as also the canal called Kāverī which 55
flowed from the Giritaḷāka tank to the Kaddūravaḍḍhamāna
tank, and the Somavatī canal running from the Kaddūra- 56
vaḍḍhamāna tank to the Arimaddavijayaggāma (tank). The 57
Monarch also constructed the Godāvarī canal which branched
off from the Kāragaṅgā and flowed to the Parakkamasāgara.[1]
(Lastly) the Prince had the ruined canal called Jayagaṅgā[2] 58
restored. It branched off from the Kālavāpi and flowed to
Anurādhapura. Five hundred and thirty-four small canals he 59
had constructed and three thousand three hundred which had
been destroyed he restored to what they had been before. In 60
the province of the Yuvarāja (Dakkhiṇadesa) the discerning
Sovereign had numerous works of various kinds constructed
at numbers of places. On the site of the house where he was 61

[1] The names mentioned in vv. 40—57 show how strong was the tendency to call new buildings and the like after ancient and sacred places. Mahāmeghavana and Jetavana are of course called respectively after the park and the monastery in Anurādhapura. Hemavatī is the skr. *Haimavatī*, a name of the Ganges. Sarasvatī and Yamunā are well known rivers in Northern India. Vetravatī is a tributary of the Yamunā, now called Betwa. Kālindī (v. 54) is a frequent name for the Yamunā (see BR. s. v.). Nammadā is the skr. *Narmadā*, now the Nerbudda whose valley bounds the Vindhya mountains in the south. Tuṅgabhadrā is the name of a river in the Dekkan, likewise Kāverī, Godāvarī and quite in the south in Tinnevelli, the Tāmraparṇī. The Bhagīrathī (v. 49) is the name of one of the sources of the Ganges, and the Gomatī is a left tributary of the same stream. The Aciravatī is so named after a river which flows past Sāvatthī = skr. Śrāvastī, now the Raptī. The Nerañjarā is called after the river at the sacred place where Buddha received Enlightenment (Oldenberg, Buddha, p. 129). Campā (v. 45) is the name of an old Indian town in Aṅga near the present Bhagalpur in Bengal. Candrabhāgā, Āvartakā, Veṇumatī are Indian river names (BR. s. v.). Nibbindā (v. 53) corresponds perhaps to the Nirvindhyā named in Meghadūta 28. Anotatta (v. 49) which was situated in the country of the mythical Uttarakurus was made sacred according to Vin. I. 28[2] by a visit of the Buddha.

[2] Now Yodi Ela.

born in Puṅkhagāma[1] he erected the Sūtighara-cetiya one
62 hundred and twenty cubits high. He had twenty-two relic
shrines erected, thirty-seven Bodhi Trees (planted), one hundred
63 image houses, fifteen caves, twenty-one dwellings for the
community in the four regions of the heavens and eighty-
64 seven rest-houses for strangers. He put up chapels with altars
for flowers, twenty-nine in number, seven sermon halls as well
65 as five outer walls and forty-three images of divers kinds.
66 He restored twenty-four ruined image houses. The Mahāgallaka
tank[2] and the Tālaggallaka tank, the Rājinī weir[3], the weir
67 called Telapakka, the weir on the Jajjarā[4] and the Vilattākhaṇḍa
(weir) the Monarch made fast for the flourishing of the harvest
68 in the land. Three hundred and fifty-eight damaged places
69 in tanks and the stone sluices on thirteen tanks as well as
one hundred and sixty locks[5] and small tanks which were
damaged, thirty-seven in number — these the Monarch had
repaired.

70 Also in the province of Rohaṇa the King who had delight
in meritorious works, had divers buildings erected in villages
71 and market towns. On the site of his mother's pyre in Khīra-
gāma[6] the Monarch (erected) the Ratanāvalī-cetiya, one hundred
72 and twenty cubits[7] in height. Further (he founded) sixteen

[1] See note to 61. 26. The height of the tope was roughly 180 ft.

[2] Cf. Mhvs. 68. 34 and 43.

[3] P. *nijjhara*. See note to v. 28. What is here called *nijjhara* is probably the same as *vāri(saṃ)pāta* Mhvs. 48. 148; 68. 35, 37.

[4] Probably an allusion to the great irrigation works described in Mhvs. 68. 16 ff. which needed repair. In the case of a river *nijjhara* means the dam (*setu*) built in it through which a part of the water is conducted into a lateral canal. If the river has a large volume of water, it flows over the dam and forms a "fall" like the flood-escape in a tank.

[5] P. *āvaraṇe*. I believe this is meant for the shafts and the apparatus for regulating the outflow of the water at the sluices (see note 1 to v. 27).

[6] See note to 74. 163.

[7] That is 180 ft. The size (*āyāma*) probably refers to the height. According to H. W. Codrington (letter of 1-4-28), the measurement of the tope of Badalkumbura gave a circumference of 926 ft. which would in fact give a height of about 180 ft.

relic shrines, seven Bodhi Trees and also vast Bodhi temples
and seventy Bodhi Tree terraces[1] and two-storeyed image 73
houses forty-three in number, two sermon halls and seventy-
five images, thirty-seven dwellings for the community from 74
the four regions of the heavens, forty-seven outer walls and
twenty gate-buildings; also fifty-nine rest-houses for guests, 75
four parks and three statues of the Metteyya. After the 76
Sovereign had then built five dancing-halls, he had everything
here and there which was broken down and decayed restored.
Thirty-seven thūpas, twenty-two Bodhi Tree terraces, two 77
hundred and seventy-four large image houses, one relic temple, 78
seven temples for images in recumbent posture, forty caves
and four brick houses; four long pāsādas, and six three-storeyed 79
pāsādas, twenty-nine sermon halls and three cloisters, one 80
hundred and twenty-six dwelling-houses, one hundred and
twenty-eight houses for books and four rest-houses for guests,
twenty-four temples to the gods, one hundred and three 81
tower-gates, one hundred and twenty-six outer walls
these all the Sovereign had restored. The Ruler also made 82
fast two hundred and sixteen leaking tanks belonging to the
community, like the great Uruvelā tank and the Paṇḍukolamba
tank and others, further eighteen decayed sluice locks and two 83
hundred and five ruined small tanks. On ten tanks he repaired 84
the stone sluices and here and there he had forty-four canals dug[2].

By constructing in this way beautiful vihāras, gardens, 85
tanks and the like he adorned with these numerous (works)
the whole of Laṅkā.

Thus Parakkamabāhu, the Ruler of men, by whom were 86
performed divers and numerous kinds of meritorious works,
who continually found the highest satisfaction in the teaching

[1] P. *bodhikoṭṭhake.* Here also *koṭṭhaka* (see above note to v. 28) is used in the sense of walling up. It is a usual custom to surround the sacred trees with a terrace, even if it consist merely of stones heaped together.

[2] This verse ends the first continuation of the Mahāvaṃsa ascribed to Dhammakitti. See my edition of the Cūlavaṃsa I. Introd. p. III.

of the Master, who was endowed with extraordinary energy and discernment, carried on the government for thirty-three years[1].

Here ends the seventy-ninth chapter, called «The Laying out of Gardens and the Like», in the Mahāvaṃsa, compiled for the serene joy and emotion of the pious.

[1] The same number of years in Pūjāv. and Rājaratn. Rājāv. 32 years.

CHAPTER LXXX

THE SIXTEEN KINGS

Thereupon the sister's son of this Great king, the wise 1
poet sovereign King Vijayabāhu[1], became monarch in Laṅkā.
When he had received consecration as king the prudent one 2
in his great mercy released from their misery those dwellers
in Laṅkā whom his uncle, the Sovereign Parakkama, had 3
thrown into prison and tortured with stripes or with fetters.
By restoring at different places to various people their village 4
or their field he increased the joyfulness[2] of them all. As 5

[1] In Polonnaruva there is an inscription of Vijayabāhu II. which supplements the account of our chronicle (Wickremasinghe EZ. II. 179 ff.). In it he also describes himself as sister's son of Parakkamabāhu. We know three sisters of this king, but I doubt if any of these three was the mother of Vijayabāhu II. Wickremasinghe thinks she was Bhaddavatī, the wife of Gajabāhu, who would in fact be the most likely. But in 70. 333 (cf below note to v. 31) we have the distinct statement that Gajabāhu had no son. This is not easy to get over. I am inclined to think that there was a fourth unnamed sister of Parakkamabāhu's married to a Kaliṅga prince. Then it would be intelligible (cf. below, note to v. 18) that Vijayabāhu, the son of this prince and of a sister of Parakkamabāhu, should in his turn, appoint a Kaliṅga prince as his successor, and that the latter should describe him as head of the clan. The inscription relates further that Vijayabāhu was in Siṃhapura, the capital of Kaliṅga, when Parakkama summoned him to Laṅkā. Parakkama's relations with the Kaliṅga dynasty are intelligible. He had himself Kaliṅga blood in his veins through his grandmother Tilokasundarī whom Vijayabāhu I. fetched from this dynasty to secure the continuance of his house (Mhvs. 59. 29 ff.).

[2] Vv. 3 and 4 show Parakkamabāhu in a curious light. According to this account, he was a severe if not cruel ruler, who made his subjects slave that he might gratify his love of splendour. Vijayabāhu II. grants an amnesty at his accession.

Alakā for (the god) Kubera and Amarāvatī for Sakka, so was
6 Pulatthinagara for him the royal city. He himself composed
in the Māgadha tongue a most excellent letter, sent it to the
7 monarch living in Arimaddana[1], concluded with this beloved
(prince) a friendly treaty as aforetime his great grandfather
8 Vijayabāhu[2], and (being) highly famed, to increase the joy of
the bhikkhus in the land of Laṅkā and Arimaddana, he made
9 the Order of the Buddha lustrous. As the Ruler departed
not from any precept of the political teaching of Manu, he
rejoiced the people through the four heart-winning qualities.
10 Endowed with kindness, purity and other virtues, he found
his highest satisfaction in the triad of the jewels, Buddha and
11 the like. Of most excellent character he, ever joyous in spirit,
12 provided the bhikkhus with the four articles of use. Mani-
festing great exertion, he like a wise Bodhisatta, everywhere
13 in every way interested himself in all beings. Shunning the
four wrongful paths[3] he in his great insight, practised in the
exercise of justice, towards good and evil favour and severity.
14 Thus this Monarch respected by the laity and the Order, per-
forming many meritorious works, carried on the government
for one year[4].

15 Now after a traitor, Mahinda by name, of the Kuliṅga
clan[5], who had won as his spouse a cowherd's daughter, Dī-

[1] The capital of Rāmañña (Lower Burma, Pegu). Cf. Mhvs. 76. 38. We see from this passage that the Māgadha tongue, that is Pāli, was the medium of international intercourse, in the same way as Latin in the Middle Ages.

[2] Vijayabāhu I. is called not quite correctly, the grandfather (*pitāmaha*) of Vijayabāhu II. For his relations with Rāmañña see Mhvs. 60. 5 ff.

[3] See note to 37. 108.

[4] The same length of reign in the Pūjāv. in which the King's name is given as Paṇḍitavijayabāhu. He has the same name in the Nik.-s. and Rājaratn.

[5] W. translates "Mahinda of Kaliṅga" and gives a wrong colouring to the affair. The MSS. have *Kuliṅgo* and also the Col. Ed. The clan name of the Kuliṅga occurs already in Mhvs. 19. 2. Pūjāv. calls the usurper Kilinkesdā Mihindādipāṇo (*kesdā* is *kesadhātu*). Rājaratn. and

panī by name, had treacherously slain the Monarch, (he) the 16
deluded one without gaining the consent of the generals, of
the warriors, of the indignant inhabitants of the country and 17
of the whole of the dignitaries, carried on in most evil fashion
the government in Laṅkā for five days.

After his murder the Uparāja of King Vijayabāhu, born in 18
Kaliṅga, Kittinissaṅka by name[1], became king. After he had 19
received royal consecration he had built in superb Pulatthinagara
a beautiful temple of stone for the Tooth Relic[2]. He had the 20
lofty Ratanāvalī-cetiya made firm and embellished the splendid

Nik.-s. Kilinkesdā Mihindu, and Rājāv. merely Kilinkesdā. Pūjāv. and Rājāv. like the Mhvs. give him a reign of just five days.

[1] King Nissaṅka Malla has left many and ample inscriptions. Ed. Müller has edited 15 of them in the AIC (nr. 143 ff.) Wickremasinghe 18 in all, EZ. (I. 121 ff., II. 70, 84, 91, 96, 98, 123, 125, 128, 130, 134, 137, 143, 146, 148, 153, 157, 165 ff.). Their contents are very similar. With regard to his descent we learn (for ex. in the famous Galpota inscription in Polonnaruva, EZ. II. 98 ff.) that he was born in the Kaliṅga country in the town of Siṃhapura as son of the King Jayagopa and the Queen Pārvatī. The Great king of Laṅkā the Chief of the clan (*kula-jeṭu*) — without doubt Vijayabāhu II. is meant — had summoned him thither to take over the government. He had been at first prince and viceroy and had then ascended the throne in virtue of the law of succession. This right is frequently stressed in the inscriptions and justified by his descent from Vijaya, the first king of Laṅkā. Without doubt this right was much disputed and it looks as if the bombastic style of Nissaṅka Malla's inscriptions had the object of increasing the prestige of the new Kāliṅga dynasty in Ceylon.

[2] In the inscriptions (for ex. Galpota-I., C, line 1) and the Heṭa-dā-gē portico inscr., 1. 19; EZ. II. 89 and 113) Nissaṅka Malla claims to have built the *daḷadā-geya*, which was named after him, as well as the *vaṭa-geya*. This last is evidently the so-called Vaṭa-dā-gē on the Quadrangle which was, however, in reality, a work of Parakkamabāhu I. and probably only restored by Nissaṅka Malla. See note to 78. 41. What the *daḷadā-geya* was and where it was situated is not certain. One is inclined to think first of the Heṭa-dā-gē situated opposite the Vaṭa-dā-gē. That is according to the inscriptions on the building itself, apparently a work of Nissaṅka Malla. But in spite of its traditional title, it was probably not a *dā-gē*, a "relic shrine" but an "image house". Cf. the note to 78. 39. As *dā-gē* the Sat-mahal-pāsāda might merit consideration, unless this is a work of Parakkamabāhu I. (note to 78. 42).

21 structure with a golden point[1]. After building the vihāra[2]
adorned with a hundred pāsādas which bore his name, he
made it over to the bhikkhu community and supported it.
22 The Jambukola-vihāra resplendent with walls and pillars
shimmering in gold and silver, where the floor was of red
23 lead and the bricks of the roof were of gold, the wise (Monarch)
had rebuilt and placed therein seventy-three golden statues of
24 the Master[3]. With the four-membered army the Ruler full
of pious devotion, went forth to the Samantakūṭa and performed
25 there his devotions[4], and everywhere on the island of Tamba-
paṇṇī[5] he had flower gardens and fruit gardens and numbers
26 of houses for the community laid down[6]. While in this way

[1] The tope is therefore called even to-day the Rankot-Dāgoba "Golden point dagoba". It has nothing, however, to do with the Mahāthūpa in Polonnaruva with which it is associated in the index to my edition. The Rankot lies to the south of the Āḷāhana-pariveṇa. The height is given in the Galpota inscription C, line 2 as 80 cubits (= 120 ft.). The Rankot-Dāgoba Gal-āsana inscr. (EZ. II. 134 ff.), belongs to the time at which that Dāgoba was built. The expression *bandhāpeti* "has made fast or firm" is, as a rule, employed of the restoration of old buildings.

[2] Not yet identified.

[3] The famous cave temples of Dambul are situated about 47 miles north of Kandy on the road to Anurādhapura. There is an inscription on the rock wall there of Nissaṅka Malla (Wickremasinghe, EZ. I. 121 ff.) in which at the end, he boasts of having constructed or embellished these caves and of having given them the name of *Suvarṇagiriguhā*. The 73 statues set up by the king are also mentioned in the Prītidānaka-maṇḍapa inscr. line 30 (EZ. II. 173).

[4] The inscriptions mention repeatedly the journeys of the King to the sacred places of the Island. Adam's Peak (*Samantakūṭa* = Sinh. *Samanaḷa*) is expressly mentioned in the inscription on the vestibule wall of the Heṭa-dā-gē (l. 3 EZ. II. 94).

[5] The ancient name for Ceylon, originally of that part in particular where Vijaya landed. See Mhvs. 6. 47, 7. 38 f., 41.

[6] In the inscriptions the King also boasts repeatedly of successful campaigns against the Coḷas, Pāṇḍyas and other peoples in Southern India. It is almost impossible to disentangle the historical facts from the exaggerations. In the kingdom itself he claims to have increased the prosperity of the people by lightening taxation, by the laying out of gardens and tanks and by a generous giving of alms. He claims also to have reformed the Church. The mention of the fixing of the

day by day the Ruler accumulated many a merit, he carried on the government for nine years[1] in most excellent fashion.

His son, the King known by the name of Vīrabāhu[2], 27
hereupon ruled for one night and then fell into the power of death.

Thereupon the younger brother of that same king Kitti- 28
nissaṅka, King Vikkamabāhu[3], enjoyed the royal dignity
for three months. He was slain by the Ruler Coḍagaṅga, 29
a sister's son of King Nissaṅka, who carried on the government
for nine months[4]. Thereupon the powerful general Kitti had 30
the eyes of this king put out, deposed him and had the
government carried on for three years without mishap[5] by 31
Līlāvatī, the first mahesī of the sovereign Parakkamabāhu.

gāvuta and of the setting up of milestones is interesting (Inscr. of the vestibule wall of the Heṭa-dā-gē, line 12; EZ. II. 94). Mr. H.W. Codrington has actually discovered a number of such gāvuta stones with inscriptions (letter of 1-4-28). They stand along the ancient high road (Mahāgāma-Kataragama-Buttala-Medagama-Bibile-(Mahiyaṅgaṇa).

[1] The same number in Pūjāv. and Rājāv. These and the Rājaratn. ascribe the same merit to Nissaṅka Malla as the Mhvs. The Sinhalese chronicles distinguish like the inscriptions, between the temple of the Tooth Relic and the circular building. The number of the statues set up in the Dambul-vihāra is given in the Pūjāv. as 72, in the Rājaratn. as 63.

[2] In the Galpota inscr. B, line 1-2 (EZ. II. 111) he is called the son of Nissaṅka Malla. Pūjāv. also mentions that his reign only lasted one night.

[3] Mentioned in the inscr. of the vestibule wall of the Heṭa-dā-gē line 13-14 as *āpā* "prince". Pūjāv. and Rājāv. give him the same length of reign as the Mhvs.

[4] The same in Pūjāv., In Rājāv. Coḍagaṅga is mentioned as the general who carried on the government for three years for Līlāvatī. Kitti is therefore not mentioned at all here.

[5] Pūjāv. like the Mhvs., Rājaratn. and Nik.-s. enumerates only the names Vīrabāhu, Vikkamabāhu, Coḍagaṅga, Līlāvatī without other details. Līlāvatī was the daughter of Sirivallabha and Sugalā. Coḍagaṅga (in the form of Coḷagaṅga) and Vikkamabāhu (Vikkantabāhu) are named as princes (*rājaputtā*) who lived at the court of Gajabāhu (70. 238), but were not his sons (cf. 70. 333).

32 Thereupon King Sāhasamalla of the race of Okkāka, a
lion in courage, carried on the government for two years[1].
33 Then having deposed this Monarch, the general Āyasmanta[2],
a man of almost unsurpassable courage, a supporter of his
34 royal family, prudently had the government carried on with
wise policy for six months by Kalyāṇavatī, the first mahesī
35 of Kittinissaṅka[3]. This Queen Kalyāṇavatī, who was devoted
to the Order of the Master, had a vihāra called after her,
36 built in the village Paṇṇasālaka by name, for love of the
village, and assigned it villages, fields, articles of use, slaves,
37 gardens and so forth. With her consent, the general Āyasmanta,
who administered the government in all Laṅkā, who came of
38 the Khandhāvara family, sent the Adhikārin Deva to charming
Valliggāma, had a vihāra erected there[4] and assigned to the
39 Great community. He built the pariveṇa known by his name
40 of Sarājakulavaḍḍhana[5] and caring for its support, he assigned

[1] Pūjāv. the same. In Rājāv. there is only mention of a king of the Okkāka family (without the name) who reigned 9 years. There is an inscription of Sāhasamalla in Polonnaruva with the exact date of his coming to the throne in the Buddha era (Wickremasinghe, EZ. II. 219 ff.), according to which Fleet has calculated the event as occurring on Wednesday, the 23 rd of August, 1200 A. D. (Fleet, JRAS. 1909, p. 327, 331). This is the first absolutely certain date in the history of Ceylon. See E. Hultzsch, JRAS. 1913, p. 518; Wickremasinghe, EZ. I. 123, note 4; II. 220; H. W. Codrington, HC., p. 67. 75.

[2] Pūjāv. and Rājāv. call him Elaḷu Ābō Senevirat. This is the same general who appears in inscriptions as Lak Vijayasingu Senevi Ābōnāvan Tāvurunāvan (EZ. II. 112, line 15; 226, l. 19). Wickremasinghe EZ. II. 191 shows that probably Āyasmanta is the same as the Kitti mentioned in v. 30 who calls himself in an inscription Lag Vijayasingu Kit Seniviyan and describes himself as the minister of Līlāvatī (E. Müller, AIC. Nr. 157).

[3] Kalyāṇavatī is mentioned in inscriptions of Nissaṅka Malla (for ex. EZ. II. 94, line 13 and 111, l. 2) under the form *Kalyāṇa*. A short inscription of hers is also preserved in Bopitiya (EZ. II. 190 ff.) in which she calls herself Kalyāṇavatī. Pūjāv. and Rājāv. give her a reign of 6 years.

[4] See 90. 96.

[5] That means "furtherer of his royal family". See v. 33. I am now inclined to believe that there and here we should read with W. *sarājakulavaḍḍhana* (= *svarāj*°) not *sa r*°.

it villages and fields surrounded by parks and the like and
which could scarcely be visited by a bad harvest, together
with articles of use and slaves male and female. Having 41
scrupulously separated the four castes who had become im-
pure through mixture, he bent on doing good, had a text
book compiled which had law as its subject.

Thereupon there reigned for one year[1] a royal prince 42
Dhammāsoka by name, who on coming to the throne was
aged three months. The Mahādipāda Anīkaṅga came at the 43
head of a great army from the Coḷa kingdom, slew the ruler
in Pulatthinagara, Prince Dhammāsoka, together with the 44
general Āyasmanta and reigned seventeen days[2]. But the 45
general, Vikkantacamūnakka, the villain, slew the Monarch
Anīkaṅga and had the government carried on for a year[3] by 46
the first consort of King Parakkamabāhu, Līlāvatī by name,
who had already reigned before.

Now came King Lokissara by name, who had been 47
wounded in the shoulder by a spear, with a great Damiḷa
army from the opposite shore, brought the whole of Laṅkā 48
under his sway and reigned, dwelling in Pulatthinagara, nine
months[4]. Hereupon the general Parakkama, the best among 49
men of decision, endowed with great power and courage,
belonging to the family of the Kālanāgaras, consecrated the 50
Mahesī Līlāvatī[5] who came of the dynasty of the Sun and
Moon, in the royal dignity, she who afterward shone in royal

[1] Pūjāv. the same. In Rājāv. it is expressly stated that it was Āyasmanta who raised the prince to the throne. The prince's age at his ascent of the throne is given as 5 months, the length of Āyasmanta's regency as 6 years.

[2] The same number in Pūjāv. and Rājāv.

[3] In Pūjāv. and Rājāv. the general is called Manakkā Senevi. The length of the regency is given as one year.

[4] Pūjāv. and Rājāv. 5 months.

[5] Līlāvatī thus enjoyed the royal dignity nominally at least three times (v. 30 f., 45 f., 49 f.). For inscriptions of this queen see EZ. I. 176 ff., II. 192 ff, 238 ff. The last named was found at Potgul-vehera in Polonnaruva and says that the queen had this building restored. It was one of the foundations of Parakkamabāhu I. For the general Parakkama see Dāṭhāvaṃsa v. 4.

51 splendour. When then a space of about seven months[1] had
passed for the Mahesī, there landed with a great Paṇḍu army
52 from the Paṇḍu kingdom the glorious Paṇḍu King Parakkama,
53 deposed the Queen and her general Parakkama and after he
had cleared Laṅkā from the briers (of revolt), he ruled the
realm in superb Pulatthinagara for three years[2], without
54 transgressing the political precepts of Manu. But since in
consequence of the enormously accumulated, various evil deeds
55 of the dwellers in Laṅkā, the devatās who were everywhere
entrusted with the protection of Laṅkā, failed to carry out
56 this protection, there landed a man who held to a false creed,
whose heart rejoiced in bad statesmanship, who was a forest
fire for the burning down of bushes in the forest of the good,
57 — that is of generosity and the like — who was a sun whose action
closed the rows of night lotus flowers — that is the good
doctrine — and a moon for destroying the grace of the groups
58 of the day lotuses — that is of peace — (a man) by name
Māgha, an unjust king sprung from the Kāliṅga line, in
59 whom reflection was fooled by his great delusion, landed as
leader of four and twenty thousand warriors from the Kaliṅga
60 country and conquered the island of Laṅkā. The great scorching fire — King Māgha — commanded his countless flames
of fire — his warriors — to harass the great forest — the
61 kingdom of Laṅkā[3]. While thus his great warriors oppressed
the people, boasting cruelly everywhere: "We are Keraḷa
62 warriors", they tore from the people their garments, their
ornaments and the like, corrupted the good morals of the
63 family which had been observed for ages, cut off hands and
feet and the like (of the people), destroyed many houses and
tied up cows, oxen and other (cattle) which they made their
64 own property. After they had put fetters on the wealthy
and rich people and had tortured them and taken away all

[1] The same in Pūjāv.; Rājāv. 4 months.

[2] The same in Pūjāv. and Rājāv.

[3] In verses 56-60 the compiler gives specimens of his intimacy with the rules of Indian poetics — alaṃkāra. The comparisons belong to the species *rūpaka*. Cf. Daṇḍin, Kāvyādarśa 2. 66 ff.

their possessions, they made poor people of them. They wreck- 65
ed the image houses, destroyed many cetiyas, ravaged the
vihāras and maltreated the lay brethren. They flogged the 66
children, tormented the five (groups of the) comrades of the
Order[1], made the people carry burdens and forced them to
do heavy labour. Many books known and famous they tore 67
from their cord and strewed them hither and thither. The 68
beautiful, vast, proud cetiyas like the Ratanāvalī(-cetiya)[2] and
others which embodied as it were, the glory of former pious
kings, they destroyed by overthrowing them and allowing 69
alas! many of the bodily relics, their souls[3] as it were, to
disappear. Thus the Damiḷa warriors in imitation of the 70
warriors of Māra, destroyed in the evil of their nature, the
laity and the Order. Hereupon they completely invested 71
Pulatthinagara and captured Parakkama, that man of great
might and valour. They put out the Monarch's eyes and 72
plundered all his treasures, pearls, jewels and so forth. Then 73
the leaders of the soldiers with Mānābharaṇa at the head,
consecrated the Kāliṅga Māgha to the glorious royal dignity
of Laṅkā.

Now after the Ruler Māgha had in this manner taken 74
possession of the kingdom and attained the royal dignity, he
dwelt in Pulatthinagara. The Monarch forced the people to 75
adopt a false faith and he brought great confusion into the
four sharply divided castes[4]. Villages and fields, houses and 76
gardens, slaves, cattle, buffaloes and whatever else belonged to
the Sīhalas he had delivered up to the Keraḷas. The vihāras, the 77
pariveṇas and many sanctuaries he made over to one or other
of his warriors as dwelling. The treasures which belonged to 78

[1] P. *sahadhammike*, that is the bhikkhus and bhikkhunīs, the novices, *sāmaṇerā*, of male and female sex, and the young girls who were being prepared for the profession of nuns (*sikkhamānā*).

[2] Here for the first time the now customary name (Sinh. *Ruvanväli*) is used for the Mahāthūpa in Anurādhapura.

[3] Lit. "their life" (*jīvitaṃ*).

[4] V. 41 ab must be compared with 75 c d. The "false faith" was Hinduism.

the Buddha and were the property of the holy Order he seized and thus committed a number of sins in order to go to hell.
79 In this fashion committing deeds of violence, the Ruler Māgha held sway in Laṅkā for twenty-one years[1].
80 Thus in Laṅkā this and that ruler out of great lust for power, have slain this and that lord of men, but have themselves in consequence of these deeds, attained to no good old age, and even when they had achieved the kingly dignity, they could not alas! enjoy it for long. Hence the wise man should refrain from the destruction of living beings and renounce wanton lust for power.

Here ends the eightieth chapter, called «The Sixteen Kings», in the Mahāvaṃsa, compiled for the serene joy and emotion of the pious.

[1] The same in Pūjāv. According to Rājāv. 19 years. The description of Māgha's reign in both chronicles agrees entirely with that of the Mhvs. Rājaratn. and Nik.-s. continue their enumeration of the names (cf. note to 80. 31). In the first: Sāmagalla (read Sāhasamalla), Kalyāṇavatī, Dharmāśoka, Nekaṅga, Änilīlāvatī, Lokeśvara, Līlāvatī, Paṇḍita Parākramabāhu; in the second: Sāhasamalla, Kalyāṇavaṭī, Dharmāśoka, Äniyaṅgana Līlāvatī, Lokeśvara, Līlāvatī, Parākramapāṇḍi. Then there follows in Rājaratn. the account of the tyrannical reign of the Kāliṅga Megha. Nik.-s. has the form Māgha.

CHAPTER LXXXI

THE REIGN OF ONE KING

During this alien rule[1] several virtuous people had founded 1
on divers of the most inaccessible mountains a charming town
(or) a village[2] and dwelling here and there protected the laity 2
and the Order so that they were in peace. On the summit of
the Subha mountain[3] hard to ascend by the foe, the Senāpati 3
Subha had founded a town, as Vessavaṇa the town Ālakamandā,
and dwelling here and fending off the Keraḷa devils, he protected 4
the (surrounding) country and the Order. On the summit of
the Govindamala[4] hard to reach by the rebels, the Ādipāda 5
ruler Bhuvanekabāhu by name, whose courage was known to
the world, had founded a town and by dwelling there, he 6
protected the province of Rohaṇa, the community of the
bhikkhus and the Order[5].

[1] P. *rājantara* (cf. 87. 46) formed like *desantara*. The translation "interregnum" is also permissible, since no lawful kings reigned.

[2] P. *nagaraṃ gāmaṃ*. When in the sequel the buildings on the rocks are designated as *nagarāni* the reason is probably that larger settlements arose at the foot of the rock fortresses and under the protection of these. The word *nagara* is associated with the idea of a permanent stronghold.

[3] *Subhapabbata*, now Yāpahu (= *yahapavu* = P. *yasapabbata*), an isolated rock like Sīgiri, not far from Maho. Cf. H. C. P. Bell, ASC. 1910-11 = X. 1914, p. 52 ff.; 1911-12, p. 60 ff.; F. H. Modder, JRAS. C. B. XIII, nr. 44, 1893, p. 97 ff.

[4] This form of the name is hardly right. The Col. Ed. has altered it into *Govindācala*. I should rather propose *Govindasela*, since its name to-day is *Govindahela*. The Govindahela is known by the name of "Westminster Abbey". This imposing rock rises 20 miles west of Tirukkovil, south of the village of Bovala in the Mahavedirata Korale (Census, 1921, II, p. 460). Cf. F. Lewis, JRAS. C. B. 1908, nr. 61, p. 167 ff.; 1914, nr. 67, p. 279 ff.

[5] When *bhikkhusaṃgha* and *sāsana* are named together here, the first means the persons, the second the thing, that is the doctrine and the free practice of it in the Order.

7 In the same way again the general called Saṅkha founded in the district Maṇimekhala by name, on the lofty mountain
8 Gaṅgādoṇi a superb town and while dwelling there, gave as little heed to the infamous army of the Ruler Māgha, though
9 it was but two yojanas away, as to a blade of grass and protected without fear that district and the Order.

10 Now at that time there was a king known by the name of Vijayabāhu, belonging to the line of King Saṃghabodhi[1], a
11 man of splendid courage who after he had through fear of the foe withdrawn to divers inaccessible forests and had long dwelt there, attained the dignity of a king of the Vanni[2].
12 The mighty one brought all the dignitaries of the Sīhalas
13 under his influence, marched forth with a Sīhala army and destroyed the whole of the four-membered forces of the foe which were armed for battle, as a mighty flame of fire[3]
14 (destroys) the darkness. All the Damiḷa warriors who dwelt as they pleased in the single villages and houses he drove
15 forth. After he had freed superb Māyāraṭṭha[4] from the briers (of the foe), the Ruler built on the lofty summit of the
16 Jambuddoṇi[5] mountain a splendid town with fine walls and gate-towers, resided there in happiness and carried on the government as capable monarch.

[1] Sirisaṃghabodhi I. See Mhvs. 36. 73 ff.

[2] Here the tribe of the Vanni is mentioned for the first time. The name does not occur in the older Mahāvaṃsa nor in the Cūlavaṃsa of Dhammakitti. The Vannis live to-day, but a few hundred in number, in small villages on the northern frontier of the North-Central Province. They go in for agriculture and preferably for hunting. Their origin is unknown. The surrounding inhabitants call them Veddas as a rule, and the Census of 1921 evidently includes them among these. They themselves repudiate all connection with the Veddas on whom they look down with contempt. Cf. H. Parker, The Vanniyas, The Taprobanian, Feb. 1887, p. 15 ff.; and Ancient Ceylon, p. 36 ff.

[3] P. *tejakkhandha*, synonym for *aggikkhandha*.

[4] It is noteworthy that in this second continuation of the Cūlavaṃsa the names Dakkhiṇadesa and Rājaraṭṭha vanish and are replaced by *Māyāraṭṭha* and *Patiṭṭhāraṭṭha*. Cf. note to 81. 46.

[5] Now Dambadeniya, about 18 miles south-west of Kurunegala. Cf. F. H. Modder, JRAS. C. B., XV, nr. 48, 1897, p. 23 ff.

And further: during these disturbed times all the Grand 17
theras with Vācissara at the head, had carried away from
Pulatthinagara the Almsbowl Relic and the Tooth Relic of
the Master, had gone forth, had betaken themselves to 18
Māyāraṭṭha and there on the mountain Kotthumala in a safe 19
region had buried both the relics carefully in the earth and
so preserved them[1]. Now some of these Grand theras with 20
Vācissara at the head, who sought that protection for Laṅkā
on which depended the continuance of the Order, had crossed 21
the vast ocean, despite its raging waves, had betaken themselves
to the lands of the Paṇḍus, Coḷas and other (peoples). Now 22
Vijayabāhu sending forth his great dignitaries, summoned all
these theras who were a mine of mercy[2] back from there. When 23
the Grand theras arrived he greeted them with reverence and
asked them: "Where are the two relics, the Tooth and the
Almsbowl preserved"? At their answer, "In such and such a 24
place", the Monarch's whole body was filled with a fivefold
joy[3]. Led by the crowd of the Grand theras, the Ruler set 25
forth with his army for the Kotthumala mountain. After he 26
had performed a great sacrificial festival[4] round about the
mountain, he beheld there gazing with his whole soul[5], the

[1] Pūjāv., Rājāv. and Rājaratn. agree with the Cūlavaṃsa as regards the rescue of the two relics from Pulatthinagara and the bringing of them to Māyāraṭṭha. The chronicles call the mountain Kotmalaya. The thera Vācissara is not mentioned. In our passage *khemaṭṭhānamhi* in v. 19b must be understood as appositional addition to *padesamhi*.

[2] *Ye karuṇākarā* cannot refer to Vijayabāhu, but only to *te mahāthere*.

[3] Lit. "one whose whole body was filled with . . ." The five kinds of joy are according to Childers (P. D. s. v. *pīti*) *khuddakā p.* "slight joy", *khaṇikā p.* "momentary joy", *akkantikā p.* "joy that comes like a sudden shock", *ubbegap.*, "transporting joy" (that will make you leap into the air) and *pharaṇap.*, "all-pervading joy".

[4] The King marches round the mountain with his attendants as a pilgrim walks round a holy place and has sacrificial ceremonies performed at the four cardinal points.

[5] P. *cakkhumano.* W's translation "with great delight" is too weak. We have here a formation like *hiṃsamano* Dh. 390 (DhCo. IV. 148 = *kodhamano*) "whose intention was the eye, that is gazing".

27 two relics of the Tooth and of the Almsbowl. With a heart
as full of joy as if he had found a jewel like the wheel and
the rest[1] or a great treasure, or as if he had attained Nirvana,
28 the Sovereign took unto himself the two relics and blessed
like Mandhātar[2], he bore them with great celebrations from
29 village to village, from town to town and brought them to
the beautiful city of Jambuddoṇi where the pious people began
30 a great and splendid festival. Now while the wise King day
by day celebrated a great sacrificial ceremony for the relics,
31 he thought thus: "In order that if in future time another
interregnum[3] occurs, no evil from alien enemies shall befall
32 these relics of the Sage, I will carefully provide for them a still
33 more inaccessible place, fast and sure." Thus pondering he had the
Billasela[4] (mountain) made fast on every side with walls, gate-
34 towers and the like, that save by the gods in the air, it could
not be trodden by any human foes. And on the summit of
the rock he built a superb temple for the Tooth Relic,
35 ravishing as a divine palace descended from the world of the
gods. Around this he laid out a park for the community with
36 divers pāsādas and maṇḍapas, delightful for taking an airing
when passing the day or when passing the night therein,
37 provided with lakes and bathing-ponds. In this relic temple
the wise (monarch) had the two relics, Tooth and Bowl, carefully
38 placed with great solemnity. After making over the park for
the community to the faithful theras who were charged with

[1] P. *cakkādiratanaṃ*. This refers to the seven jewels which belong to the *cakkavattin* or world ruler (cf. Childers, s. v. *ratana*); the first of these is *cakka* the wheel, as symbol of world dominion.

[2] See 37. 53 and note.

[3] Should we not read *puna* instead of *pana* in 31 b, or is *pana* used with the same meaning?

[4] Now *Beligala* (so Pūjāv., Rājāv. and Rājaratn.). This is the name of a hamlet in the Otara Pattuva of the Kegalla District and of a Korale in the same district. The Beligala Korale is mentioned in the Kaḍaim-pota (H. C. P. Bell, Report on the Kégalla District, p. 2) as well as in the Siri Laka-kaḍayuru (H. Nevill, The Taprobanian, June 1888, p. 55, 60). The rock of Beligala on which the relics were hidden resembles in isolation and steepness that of Yāpahu (cf. Bell, l. l, p. 25 ff.).

the care of the relics, he decreed a regular offering of alms.
Also he commanded that a sacrificial ceremony of surpassing 39
kind should be performed for the relics day by day in most
perfect fashion.

Now in his faith the Sovereign set about rendering helpful 40
service to the Order of the perfectly Enlightened One. If one
asks how (this was done), the account runs thus: Deeply 41
grieved in his heart that on the island of Laṅkā so many
books that dealt with the true doctrine had been destroyed
by the alien foe, the Ruler called together laymen endowed 42
with a good memory and with knowledge, pious, well instructed,
free from indolence and skilled in quick and fair writing, and 43
along with these, many other writers of books and made all these
write down in careful fashion the eighty-four thousand divisions 44
of the doctrine and made over to them in accordance with
the number of the divisions the like number of gold kahāpaṇas[1]. 45
He also performed a sacrificial festival for the doctrine and thus
heaped up a fulness of merit. The theras and the middle-aged 46
and young (bhikkhus) and also the sāmaṇeras in Tisīhala[2]
who had taken on themselves the burden of a life of discipline,
all these protectors of the teaching of the Master he gathered 47
together and made harmony where there had been discord.
And then the Monarch pondered thus: "The ceremony of 48
admission to the Order[3] is the foundation of the prosperity
of the Order. How would it be if I had it performed now in
the right way?" And joyful at heart, he endowed the whole vast 49
reunited community richly with the eight articles of necessity[4]
and made them hold for seven days the ceremony of admission 50
to the Order which was preceded by offerings and honours

[1] This account is extremely significant for the history of the tradition of the sacred texts in Ceylon. It is found also in Pūjāv., Rājāv. and Rājaratn.

[2] This expression which refers to the threefold division of the Island into Patiṭṭhāraṭṭha, Māyāraṭṭha and Rohaṇa and which frequently recurs, is used here for the first time. Cf. note to 81. 15.

[3] P. *upasampadā*.

[4] See note to 60. 71.

51 instituted by himself. After the Ruler had laid out the park
known to the world by his name of Vijayasundara and destined
52 for the community[1], he made it over to them. In his chari-
tableness the Ruler thought: "Bhikkhus and sāmaṇeras who
53 study the Tipiṭaka in faith and lead in every way the pious
life that springs from it, must never be troubled about their
54 livelihood. They shall come to the gate of my house and
receive whatever articles of use they are in need of." And
he invited them full of reverence, and gave to the many
55 bhikkhus who came to the portals of his palace excellent and
56 costly offerings, well versed in giving. Then the King ordered
further for all ascetics who had reached the rank of thera or
57 grand thera, regular maintenance[2]. Thus in doing good to
the Order the Monarch naturally honoured thereby the triad
of the jewels — Buddha and the others.

58 In Vattalagāma[3] the King had built for the bhikkhus in
a perfect manner the vihāra called after his own name
59 Vijayabāhu. In the vihāra Kalyāṇī by name, the Ruler had
the vast and splendid cetiya which had been destroyed by the
60 Damila soldiers, made fast again and a golden finial put upon it,

[1] This monastery is also mentioned in Pūjāv. and Rājaratn. as a foundation of Vijayabāhu. In Mhvs. 85. 90 it is called Sirivijayasundara. It was situated in Jambuddoṇi.

[2] In the Rājaratn. which is particularly concerned with Vijayabāhu the following strophe is quoted in praise of the generosity of the King.

Cātuddisāyātajinatrajānaṃ
āpānabhūtaṃ gharam āsi tassa
yadicchitappaccayalābhahetu
devaddumo vāsi mahānubhāvo.

"For those sons of the Victor who came from the four regions of the heavens his house became the refuge, because there they received all articles of use as they wished. Like a heavenly tree was the sublime one". The "heavenly tree" is of course, the "wishing tree" (skr. *kalpadruma*).

[3] The building of the Vijayabāhu-vihāra is also related in Pūjāv., Rājāv. and Rājaratn. The village of Vattala lies on the right bank of the Kelaniganga, a little above its mouth. Thus it is not far from the Kelani-vihāra whose restoration is also mentioned in the Sinhalese chronicles.

as well as a gate-tower on its eastern side. There too he restored 61
whatever was decayed in the image houses, the encircling wall
and the like and on all other (buildings). The King also gave 62
the order that all pāsādas, image-houses, vihāras, pariveṇas,
and likewise cetiyas, maṇḍapas, outer walls, gate-towers 63
and the like which were in Māyāraṭṭha, should be put into
the condition in which they were formerly, and that new
buildings should be erected.

Now as the King wished to accomplish himself still more for 64
the furtherance of the laity and of the Order, he reflected thus:
"At a time when I had already reached a great age and 65
youth had vanished, I gained the good fortune of the royal
dignity and have until now enjoyed it. Now after the destruction 66
of all the evil foes who still remain over after the conquest
and thereby to protect my people and after renewing the 67
structures of the destroyed and decayed vihāras to bring about
the furtherance of my people — for that I have now but a
short time." With such considerations the discerning Monarch 68
together with those people versed in the lore of signs, tested
the (bodily) signs of both of his own sons Parakkamabāhu 69
and Bhuvanekabāhu and attained this knowledge: "The signs
on Parakkamabāhu are such that he will in accordance there- 70
with accomplish through the majesty of his power the
destruction of the enemy and will unite all Laṅkā under one
umbrella, so that none shall be above him; and that he will 71
further the spotless Order of the Omniscient one; will spread his
fame over the chief and the intermediate regions of the heavens;
will receive from the most divers countries gifts as princesses for 72
his women's apartments and the like, and will be for long a
world ruler on the Island." When he realised this, with eyes 73
filled with tears of joy, he made him sit on his knee and kissed
him on the head. Then he gazed again and again full of love 74
on the younger prince, who stood near, gave them twain much
excellent advice, made them by training practised in all arts, 75
accomplishments and the like. Then the Ruler entrusted of 76
the twain his elder son to the assembled community at whose
head stood the Grand master known by the name of Saṃ- 77

gharakkhita. And again he entrusted the same (thera) with the two relics, the Tooth and the Almsbowl of the Sage,
78 as also with the whole Great community and also with the people dwelling in Laṅkā and ruled this himself in perfect fashion[1].

79 After the Sovereign had in this manner sowed the royal seed in the wide field of Laṅkā, he entered heaven after a reign of four years[2].

80 Even as this Ruler of men, Vijayabāhu, protected the entire world of the laity and the Order of the Victor, so should all future rulers of Laṅkā protect both, bestowing on them security.

Here ends the eighty-first chapter, called «The Reign of One King», in the Mahāvaṃsa, compiled for the serene joy and emotion of the pious.

[1] The meaning is that the King made Saṃgharakkhita Head of the Church and entrusted him with the education of the heir to the throne. As head of the Order Saṃgharakkhita had to look after the spiritual welfare of the people over whom the King exercised secular dominion.

[2] According to Rājāv. the King had reigned 24 years. But according to v. 65 he only came to the throne at an advanced age.

CHAPTER LXXXII

THE EXHIBITION OF THE MIRACLE OF THE TOOTH RELIC

After the death of his father King Parakkamabāhu 1
united the whole of the people who were in Tisīhala, adorned 2
the fair town and as if he were the peer of the King of the
gods, he first of all had the ceremony of the royal consecration
performed. On account of his learning he himself received 3
the famous name of Kalikāla-sāhicca-sabbaññupaṇḍita[1]. On 4
his younger brother Bhuvanekabāhu he conferred the dignity
of yuvarāja and made over to him a part of the kingdom.
With the thought: I will make the maiden Laṅkā my own, 5
to no other (shall she belong), he turned his proud spirit to
the destruction of the alien foe. He thought: in the first 6
place I will perform a sacrificial festival for the Tooth Relic
of the Sage, then will I go forth to war against the
Damiḷas, and with great pomp and ceremony he brought 7
the Tooth Relic from the Billa mountain to the splendid town
of Jambuddoṇi[2]. "I have the desire at every moment when I 8
think of it to worship the Tooth Relic with devotion at the
three periods of the day" — so thought the Ruler and had built 9
near his palace a fair and costly temple for the Tooth Relic.
In the midst of this the King had a splendid throne set up 10
and decked with a costly covering. Out of a large precious 11

[1] That is "the scholar who is entirely familiar with the literature of the Kali Age". The expression *sāhicca* "art of poetry, literary work" = skr. *sāhitya*, was until now absent from the dictionaries. The Kali Age (*kalikāla, kaliyuya*) is the last of the four ages, the one in which we are living.

[2] Thus too Pūjāv. According to Rājāv., the king had brought the relic from Jambuddoṇi to Samiddhipura.

stone the Ruler had a casket fashioned for the Tooth Relic
12 and again as receptacle for this a large, superb, costly jewel-
13 case of bright, valuable precious stones. Then for five thousand
gold nikkhas[1] he had as receptacle for this case a second
14 splendid chest fashioned, and then again for twenty-five thousand
15 silver nikkhas a third chest. Now when the King starting
with the relic temple, had adorned the town, and had devoutly
16 celebrated a great sacrificial ceremony for the Tooth Relic, he
took the Tooth in the lotus of his hand[2] and spake in the
midst of the Great community the following solemn declaration[3]:
17 "Our sublime Buddha, god of the gods, the Sage, strong in
miraculous power visited this island of Laṅkā three times,
18 and that most supreme of men went away, having sojourned
here and there and having made of sixteen prominent places
19 spots hallowed by his use[4]. Therefore it is that Laṅkā is not
under the power of kings of a false faith, but under the power
of kings of the true faith it flourishes in the right manner.
20 Aforetime also on this island the Ruler of men by name
Asela, son of the Ruler Muṭasīva, wise in statecraft, conquered
21 the Damiḷas Sena and Guttaka who carried on horse-dealing[5]

[1] P. *nikkha* or *nekkha* = ved. *niṣka*, is a weight with which the precious metals are weighed. According to Abhp. 480, 888 it seems to be equal to 5 suvaṇṇas. This would agree with the Indian reckoning which makes one niṣka (= 1 pala = 4 or ·5 suvarṇas) equal to 56.875 gr. The figures in our passage are certainly a fantastic exaggeration.

[2] A frequent *rūpaka*. Cf. Daṇḍin 66 (note to 80. 60) *pāṇipadma*.

[3] P. *saccakriyaṃ akā*. See note to 51. 56.

[4] P. *pāribhogika*. This is in the first place a term for relics which are reverenced as articles of use belonging to a saint, such as the alms-bowl of the Buddha. In contrast to these are the bodily (*sārīrika*) relics, as for instance the Tooth Relic. Here places are called *pāribhogika* because the Buddha by use (*paribhogena*), by sojourning there had hallowed them. The legend of Buddha's three visits to Laṅkā is related in Mhvs. 1. The 16 places where according to tradition he sojourned on these occasions, are given by W. in his translation p. 277, note. The most important are Mahiyaṅgaṇa, Kelaniya, Adam's Peak, the sites of the various topes in Anurādhapura, Tissamahārāma etc.

[5] P. *assanāvikaputte dve*. W. translates "sons of the horse merchant" which is also possible. But *putta* may better be taken as a mere paraphrase as in *kammāraputta* etc. Cf. on the whole Mhvs. 21. 10 ff.

by sea, and held sway while sheltering the Order of the
Victor. Then the famous Great king Duṭṭhagāmaṇī Abhaya 22
vanquished Eḷāra of the Coḷa country and protected the
laity and the Order. Again the Monarch Vaṭṭagāmaṇī 23
vanquished in combat five very cruel Damiḷa princes and
protected the laity and the Order. Then the Ruler of men, 24
Dhātusena, subdued six Damiḷa kings with their countless
great warriors, and sheltered the laity and the Order. Again 25
the great Vijayabāhu put to flight in battle the Coḷiyas and
the Damiḷas and protected the laity and the Order. Now I 26
too have the wish to vanquish the insolent Damiḷas who have
destroyed vihāras and other buildings and also the Order of
the Master and still have their abode in Patiṭṭhāraṭṭha[1], 27
the twain, King Māgha and Jayabāhu[2], and to further the
laity and the Order. That is a true word and yet more I say: 28
the highly virtuous, far-famed monarchs with the Kosala king 29
at the head, heard from the mouth of the Master while he
lived, the preaching of the doctrine and saw many a miracle
and their wishes were (thereby) fulfilled. Rulers mighty in 30
miraculous power like Dhammāsoka and the others who were
born when the fully Enlightened One no longer lived, beheld 31
divers miracles like the figure of the perfectly Enlightened
One[3] produced (in miraculous manner) and the like, and made
each his life thereby rich in fruit. But when the Guide of 32
the worlds, having fulfilled the task of a Buddha, in the
region of the Mallas, outstretched on the couch of great

[1] See note to 81. 15. The Sinhalese form of the name is Pihiṭiraṭa.

[2] It is clear that the reign of Vijayabāhu III. and the beginning of his son's reign fall within the 21 years assigned to Māgha in 80. 79. The usurper Jayabāhu has so far not been mentioned, both names are in the Pūjāv. however.

[3] What is meant are miracles such as that described in Mhvs. 31. 96 ff. As Duṭṭhagāmaṇī is about to replace the relics in the Mahāthūpa the casket in which they are contained, rises in the air, opens of itself and the relics assume the form of the Buddha and perform the miracle which was performed by the Master under Gaṇḍa's mango tree in Sāvatthī. For the so-called *yamakappāṭihāriya* see DhCo. III. p. 206 ff.

33 Nirvana, came, as regards miracles, to the five great resolves[1],
then assuredly the Exalted One came also to lesser resolves.
34 From that day to this all the relics which exist, those of the
body, as those associated with articles of use, perform through
35 the power of the Master miracles here in this our world.
When therefore the Guide of sages, coming to this and that
36 resolve, saw (in spirit) in the five thousand years' duration
of his Order, the future monarchs who take upon themselves
37 the burden of faith and of moral discipline, then I think not
that the Exalted One will not with the eye of omniscience
have seen me also among them. But if I have been seen by
38 the Incomparable One[2], if even I have been added to the
number of these great men and rulers of antiquity — loyal to
39 the faith in every respect — if I after destroying the alien foe
in terrible war, may accomplish the furtherance of the laity
40 and the Order, then may the Tooth Relic now perhaps make
manifest to me a fair miracle." After these words he became
lost in contemplation.

41 At this moment the Tooth Relic rose from the lotus of
his hand, like to the crescent moon, in the air, assumed the
42 glorious form of the Prince of the wise, diffused clusters
of rays of light sixfold in hue, illumined the whole town,
43 manifested thus a glorious miracle, enraptured the Ruler
of men, returned from the air and settled again on his hand.
44 With the shouts of applause and the songs of praise of the
great crowd of people and above all of the Great community
45 who rejoiced at the sight of the superb miracle of the relic,
the whole town was at this time everywhere full of intense
46 excitement. "This day I have gained life, this day my life
has become of worth; this day hurrah! my life has become
47 perfectly fruitful. Having by the power of my merit beheld
to-day such a miracle and having also seen the blessing

[1] For the *mahādhiṭṭhānapañcaka* see Mhvs. 17. 46 ff. In vv. 51—52 the miracle mentioned in the preceding note is foretold here. The lesser resolves refer to other miracles not included in the five great resolves, such as that expected now by the king.

[2] P. *tādinā* "of him who is so as he is and no other".

of merit richly earned by the people[1], I now have been enrolled 48
among those earlier rulers of men, famed for the fulness of
their virtues in this Order of the Sage." With these words 49
the Great king, great in insight and miraculous power, gave
forth a lion's roar in the midst of the vast assembly.

After the Ruler with the whole of his sixty-four 50
ornaments[2], such as the diadem, the bracelet and so forth
had made an offering to the Tooth Relic, he laid it carefully 51
in the jewel-casket and after placing this lustrous (casket)
in the golden chest he again placed this carefully in the fair 52
and costly chest fashioned of silver.

The Tooth Relic thus preserved in the best way in three 53
chests one within the other, he then placed in his relic temple. For seven days long he celebrated with the (offering of the) seven kinds of precious articles[3], with great wreaths and perfumes and with all kinds of food solid and liquid a great sacrificial festival.

Here ends the eighty-second chapter, called «The Exhibition of the Miracle of the Tooth Relic», in the Mahāvaṃsa, compiled for the serene joy and emotion of the pious.

[1] The blessing consists in the sight of the miracle taking place before the eyes of all and of the effects which proceed from it. The MSS. have *sambhataṃ puññasampadaṃ* and so has my edition. The Col. Ed. alters it to *°bhatā °padā*, but *°bhataṃ °padaṃ* is acc. case and depends, like *pāṭihāriyaṃ* on *disvā*. By the power of his merit the King has seen the miracle and he has also seen the blessing of the people's merit which shows itself therein that they were found worthy of the same vision as the king.

[2] Cf. for this E. W. Perera, Ceylon Notes and Queries, III. April 1914, p. XXXVI ff., where the enumeration of the regalia in the Sinhalese Thūpavaṃsa is discussed.

[3] P. *ratanehi sattahi.* The seven *ratanāni* are: *suvaṇṇa* (gold), *rajata* (silver), *muttā* (pearls), *maṇi* (precious stones like sapphire and ruby), *veḷuriya* (a semi-precious stone (?) like cat's eye), *vajira* (diamond), *pavāḷa* (coral). See Childers, s. v.

CHAPTER LXXXIII

THE STORY OF THE SUBJUGATION OF THE HOSTILE KINGS

1 Since all the inhabitants of Laṅkā had seen the effect of
the merits of the King, they lived from that time onward
2 filled with still greater reverence towards him, in fear, in joy
and in love, never were they capable of transgressing his
3 commands. All the sovereigns of the divers countries sent the
King gifts, since their hearts were inclined to admiration of
his majesty.

4 People whose heads were to be cut off he punished only
in stern fashion with dungeon and fetters[1] and then set them
5 free again. But for such people as deserved prison the Ruler to
whom pity was the highest, ordained some lighter punishment[2]
6 or other, and reprimanded them. But on people who should
have been banished from the country the Ruler who might
be likened to Manu, laid but a fine of a thousand (kahāpaṇas).
7 But on all those who deserved a fine, he looked with in-
dignation and with all sorts of words of rebuke he made of
them honest men.

8 Then all these people, the forces of the foe in Laṅkā who
abiding in forest strongholds and elsewhere, had become
9 unconquerable by his father, the hero vanquisher of foes, the
King set about subjugating by the power of his majesty and

[1] *Kārāgārabandhanamattato* cannot be joined to *parimocayi*. In this case *puna* would be quite unintelligible. It belongs far rather to *niggaṇhitvāna*.

[2] I think that *niggahaṃ katvā* as well as *niggaṇhitvāna* in v. 4 must mean a punishment and not a mere admonition. This is expressed by *ovadi* in v. 5c. But the punishment was always less severe than the guilty person had deserved. The same also in v. 6 and 7. In *niggaha-*

by the might of his loving spirit[1]. The Sīhala kings in the 10
land of the Vanni who were equipped with army and train,
he brought completely under his influence, sitting merely on his
lion's throne[2]. All the Sīhalas with their lion-like courage who 11
dwelt in Tisīhala[3], these all the Ruler of men assembled around
him and made them content. Then he dared to overthrow 12
the great Damiḷa warriors who building great fortresses, had
settled here and there in the country. Of all the Sīhalas who 13
on the field were as lions against rutting elephants — the
enemy — he sent some hither, others thither. The great 14
Sīhala warriors wherever they came, harassed the Damiḷa
warriors as the Garuḷas the Nāgas[4].

At that time the Damiḷa kings, Māghinda and Jayabāhu[5] 15
had set up fortifications in the town of Pulatthi(nagara),
famous for its wealth, in the village of Koṭṭhasāra[6], in
Gaṅgātaḷāka[7], in the village of Kākālaya[8], in the Padī district 16
and in Kurundi[9], in Mānāmatta, in Mahātittha and in the
harbour of Mannāra[10], at the landing-place of Pulacceri and 17
in Vālikagāma, in the vast Gona district and in the Gonusu
district, at Madhupādapatittha and at Sūkaratittha[11]: at these 18

vācā (v. 7 c) *niggaha* it is true, means "rebuke". That is after all the mildest punishment.

1 Thus by force or by kindness. As regards the construction of the sentence, *paripanthīnaṃ balaṃ* should probably be taken as in apposition to *sabbe vanaduggādinissite*.

2 Without recourse to force, merely by his prestige as sovereign. For the Vanni cf. note to 81. 11.

3 See note to 81. 46.

4 See note to 75. 38.

5 Cf. 82. 27.

6 Situated not far from Pulatthinagara. See note to 61. 43.

7 Now Kantalai, see note to 70. 286.

8 "Crow's Home". The name does not otherwise occur.

9 The two names appear again in 88. 64 next to each other. In the Siri Laka-kaḍayuru (The Taprobanian 1888, p. 55) they are noted among the districts of the Pihiṭi-raṭa (Patiṭṭhā-raṭṭha).

10 Now Mantai and Mannar. See notes to 48. 81 and 61. 39.

11 Of the six last localities only Madhupādapatittha is mentioned once more. It may be assumed that like the foregoing places, they were all situated in Northern Ceylon.

19 and other places, and committing all kinds of violent deeds, had
20 stayed there a long time. Their forty and four thousand
soldiers, Damiḷas and Keraḷas, who hard pressed by the spear-
21 armed Sīhala warriors, were unable to resist, came terror-
stricken to Pulatthinagara and held counsel thus as to their
22 future conduct: "King Parakkamabāhu is of high majesty
and has miraculous power. Who in the world is strong enough
23 to neglect his commands? Even the monarchs of foreign lands
24 have now come under his influence, also all the Sīhalas. Even
some of us Damiḷas are his followers. What is the use of
25 words about others? But what, what shall we people do? Now
we have all become dim like glow-worms at the rising of the
26 radiant sun. Therefore in the future it is impossible for us
to take up our abode on the Sīhala island, we will go to
27 another country." They took all their elephants and horses,
as well as their pearls and costly precious stones, the royal
28 diadems and all the beauties of the harem, all ornaments,
cloths, mantles, baskets and every kind of valuable with them
29 in their fear and began to leave the town. But owing to the
action of the King's merit they mistook the regions of the
30 heavens. They thought it was the eastern gate and marched
31 out through the western gate[2] and came to Kālavāpi where
the army of the Sīhalas had set up an entrenched camp.
32 With all their goods they had alas! also to sacrifice their life
by each giving his to the Sīhala warriors, thus carrying out
33 themselves what the King had only thought. And all the Sīhalas
taking from them their accumulated treasures, became from this
34 time onward rich people[3], as in ancient times all the dwellers

[1] Vv. 15—21 form one sentence. The construction is as follows: The 40000 soldiers of the two Damiḷa kings who after erecting fortifications in such and such places, had been settled there for a long time, came and held counsel.

[2] The mistake of the Damiḷas is, of course, nothing but a fiction of the compiler. The intention of the mercenaries was to reach the western coast with their booty and there cross to India. At Kālavāpi the Sīhalas intercepted them. Pūjāv. gives the same account of the occurence as the Cūlavs.; Rājāv. a different one.

[3] P. *sampannā* of pregnant significance in allusion to the *sampadaṃ* following in v. 34.

in Mithilā who gained the wealth which the kings a hundred
in number, had through fear flung away[1]. After thus ac- 35
complishing by his power the crushing of the alien foe, he
set himself to bring about the prosperity of all Laṅkā.

When the eleventh year of the reign of this King had 36
arrived, a king of the Jāvakas known by the name of
Candabhānu landed with a terrible Jāvaka army under the 37
treacherous pretext that they also were followers of the Buddha[2].
All these wicked Jāvaka soldiers who invaded every landing- 38
place and who with their poisoned arrows, like to terrible
snakes, without ceasing harassed the people whomever they 39
caught sight of, laid waste, raging in their fury, all Laṅkā.
Just as flashes of lightning with floods of water (visit) a place 40
destroyed by lightning with flames of fire[3], so Laṅkā which
had been harassed by Māgha and others was ravaged anew
by the Jāvakas. Then the King sent forth his sister's son, 41
the heroic Prince Vīrabāhu, with soldiers to fight the Jāvakas.
The fearful Rāhu, namely Vīrabāhu, with his terrible appearance 42
completely destroyed (the moonlight, namely) Candabhānu in
the fields of heaven, namely in the battle[4]. He placed his 43

[1] Cf. W., note to this passage. The story alluded to here is related in the Ummaggajātaka (Fausböll, Jāt. VI. 389 ff.). Through the cleverness of the Bodhisatta the inhabitants of Mithilā capture the possessions of 101 kings against whom they had been fighting. Cf. Jāt. VI. 409[24]: *tato paṭṭhāya ca kira Mithilavāsino sahiraññā jātā.* To get the proper construction in our passage the words *yathā purā* must be joined to the following and not to the preceding as is done by W., for which an *iva* or *yathā* in v. 34 would be indispensable.

[2] P. *sogatā*, followers of the Sugata, the guide to the path of salvation. The Pūjāv. also mentions Candrabhānu as the leader of the Jāvakas. According to Rājāv. his soldiers were Damiḷas.

[3] The *pāvakāsanī* and the *nīrāsanī* are contrasted. Both are devastating thunderstorms. In the one case it is the kindling flashes of lightning that cause the destruction, in the other the floods of rain causing inundations. W's translation "fury of a flood of water" and "fire and lightning" seems to me weak, as it takes *asani* at first in its derived and the second time in its original signification.

[4] A picture suggested by the name of Candabhānu ("Moonshine"). Rāhu is the demon who causes the eclipses. We have again to do with

heroic Sīhala soldiers here and there and began to open fight
44 with the Jāvaka warriors. The good Sīhala warriors, sure in
aim, the archers, shattered in pieces with their sharply pointed
45 arrows, in the battle the countless number of arrows whizzing
against them with their poisoned tips which were shot swiftly
one after the other by the Jāvaka soldiers from a machine[1].
46 Going forth to the combat like Rāma, Prince Vīrabāhu slew
47 numbers of Jāvakas, as Rāma (slew) the Rakkhasas. The
Veramba wind[2], namely Vīrabāhu, possessed of great vehemence,
shattered again and again the forest wilderness, namely the
48 Jāvaka foes. After thus putting to flight the Jāvakas in
combat, he freed the whole region of Laṅkā from the foe.
49 Hereupon he betook himself to Devanagara, worshipped there
the lotus-hued god[3] and celebrated for him a divine sacrifice.
50 He had erected there a priveṇa that was intended for the
Order; it received the name of Nandana[4], since it was the
51 delight of the people. Thereupon he turned and came to the
town Jambuddoṇi, he sought out Parakkamabāhu, and he
was overjoyed.

compounds of the *rūpaka* order (skr. *Vīrabāhur eva Rāhuḥ*). See notes to 80. 60, 82. 16. According to the Rājāv. however, it was not the sister's son but the younger brother of the King, who vanquished Candrabhānu.

[1] P. *yantamutte (bāṇe)*. Something apparently like the ancient catapult. Mhvs. 72. 251 mentions huge stones being hurled from such machines.

[2] *Veramba* is the name given to strong winds which blow in great heights (cf. PTS. P. D. s. v.). The corresponding word in Skr. is *vairambha*. A synonym for *verambavāta* is *kālavāta*.

[3] That is "the blue-coloured". Name of Viṣṇu. Cf. 85. 85 ff. Devanagara (or-pura) is the present Dondra, Sinh. Devundara. The place has been already mentioned in 60. 59 and 75. 47, but here for the first time we have a notice of the shrine of Viṣṇu celebrated in the Middle Ages. According to tradition it was built in 790 A. D. It was plundered and destroyed by the Portuguese in 1588 A. D. See P. E. Pieris, Ceylon and the Portuguese, (= P. 2) p. 109 f. It is significant that Vīrabāhu offered his sacrifice of victory in a Hindu sanctuary. At the same time however, he builds a pariveṇa for the Buddhist Order, thus putting his attitude towards their parity beyond doubt. Even to-day a Hindu *devālaya* and a Buddhist *vihāra* stand side by side in Dondra.

[4] That is "joy, delight, ecstasy"

Now after he had thus carried on divers great wars and after he had scattered the terrible crowd of all his foes, the great and mighty Sovereign Parakkamabāhu attained the fame of victory[1]. 52

Here ends the eighty-third chapter, called «The Story of the Subjugation of the Hostile Kings», in the Mahāvaṃsa, compiled for the serene joy and emotion of the pious.

[1] South Indian inscriptions give an essentially different picture of the reign of Parakkamabāhu II. from our chronicle. According to these, Ceylon was invaded by the Pāṇḍyas about the middle of the 13th century. They say that of the kings of Ceylon one was killed and another forced to pay tribute. This shows that Parakkama never united the whole island under his dominion. H. W. Codrington, HC. p. 77, 87.

CHAPTER LXXXIV

THE SERVICES RENDERED TO THE ORDER

1 Thereupon the Ruler, versed in the ordinances of Manu,
caused to be determined to what families the villages, fields,
2 houses and so forth long since seized by the alien foe, belonged
by heredity, and had them returned to their aforetime owners
3 as before. Then he caused to be determined which villages,
parks and the like were the property of the Buddha and the
Doctrine, which (were) the assigned maintenance villages (for
4 ordinary needs), which the villages belonging to the Chapters,
which the villages which were personal possessions, which
(were) the villages of the eight sanctuaries[1] and the villages
5 of the pariveṇas and had them given back. Further he appointed
the five groups of menials and the ten groups of menials
belonging to the royal household and determined their rank[2].
6 While the Ruler made all the inhabitants of Laṅkā wealthy
and possessors of fortune, he took care that the whole country
7 had abundant food. All the corrupt groups (of bhikkhus) who
since the Interregnum lived only for their own desires, following
forbidden occupations[3], with senses ever unbridled, he sought
8 out rigourously, dismissed them (from the Order) and thus
9 purified the Order of the perfectly Enlightened One. Then
the King sent many gifts to the Coḷa country[4] and caused to
be brought over to Tambapaṇṇi many respected Coḷa bhikkhus

[1] P. *aṭṭhāyatanagāmake.* It is difficult to say what is meant by this. For the explanation we must look above all to v. 17 f.

[2] See Mhvs. 67. 58 and note.

[3] Professions which are not fitting for the samaṇa are enumerated in Dīgha-Nik. I. 1. 10 (= I. p. 5). Cf. R. O. Franke, Dīgha Transl. p. 7, n. 2.

[4] The same account in Pūjāv.

who had moral discipline and were versed in the three Piṭakas 10
and so established harmony between the two Orders[1].
Then when the Ruler learned that among the many high- 11
principled bhikkhus dwelling permanently in Tambaraṭṭha[2]
there was a Grand thera, Dhammakitti[3] by name, radiant in 12
the glory of moral discipline, and that once when this thera
was on his mendicant round, a lotus flower had blossomed on 13
his path, he was filled with admiration and sent a religious
gift, incense, sandal-wood, food and the like which had been
in contact with the Tooth Relic and likewise a choice and 14
princely gift[4] to Tambaraṭṭha. He made the Grand thera 15
come to the island of Laṅkā, rejoiced again and again, as if
he had beheld[5] the Perfect One, celebrated for him a great 16
sacrificial festival and provided him who was a (worthy)
vessel for offerings and honours[6], in careful manner with an
offering of the four necessaries. Now in order to provide 17
for the protection of the Order furthered by him, the Great
king built round about his capital for the eight Grand theras 18
who dwelt in the eight sanctuaries[7] and for the discerning
theras dwelling in villages or in the wilderness of the forest,

[1] These are the Hīnayāna and the Mahāyāna. The first school had its principal seat in the Mahāvihāra, the second according to Mhvs. 78. 21 ff., in the Abhayagiri and Jetavana vihāras. Cf. also W., note to the passage. See now S. Paranavitane, Mahāyānism in Ceylon, C. J. Sc. G. II. 1, p. 35 ff.

[2] Probably a province in Southern India. Pūjāv. has instead Tambalingum. It would appear from the Rājāv. that Candrabhānu came from Tambalingum. So also H. W. Codrington, HC., p. 77.

[3] The name of Dhammakitti recurs several times. According to Wickremasinghe, Catalogue of Sinhalese MSS. in the Brit. Mus. p. 21 b, 35 b, the Dhammakitti of this passage was the compiler of the first continuation of the Mahāvaṃsa.

[4] W's translation "and other royal gifts" is incorrect. Here *dhammapābhata* and *rājapābhata* are contrasted with one another.

[5] Not as W. has it: "as if he had seen an Araha". Pūjāv. has *budun rahatan duṭurā sē*.

[6] *Pūjasakkārabhājanaṃ* belongs to *taṃ* in 16 d. For the figurative meaning of °*bhājana* cf. note to Mhvs. 44. 70.

[7] See above note to v. 4.

19 many communal monasteries, suitable for dwelling in, extensive
embellished with divers pāsādas, provided with various maṇḍapas,
20 furnished with divers bathing-ponds, adorned with cloisters which
were places of sojourn by day and by night, surrounded by
21 a series of flower parks and tree parks and granted them to
them. Further he celebrated with all articles of equipment a
22 great sacrificial festival. Thereupon the King gathered together
the Great community of the (bhikkhus) dwelling in villages and
in the wilderness of the forest and chose out all those who
strove continually for the keeping pure of moral discipline,
23 those who took upon themselves pious duties and were tried
in the leading of their life in the strictest way[1], who were
endowed with the virtues of renunciation and so forth and
24 were steadfast in the precepts for the conscientious. He built
for them on the heights of the Puṭabhatta[2] rock a forest
dwelling, assigned it to them and supported them therewith.
25 As they made of the strictest conduct a reality, he made
Laṅkā through them in his days as it were, an abode of
26 arahants. With the reflection that theras who were acquainted
with the sacred texts were rare in the Island, he had all books
27 brought from Jambudīpa, had many bhikkhus instructed in
the sacred texts, as also in all sciences, such as philosophy,
grammar and the like and thus made of them cultivated people.
28 In this manner furthering conduct and learning, the wise
(prince) honoured with such a religious sacrifice the Guide to
29 the path of salvation (Buddha). The Ruler caused his
younger royal brother, Bhuvanekabāhu by name, to be in-
30 structed, so that he was versed in the three Piṭakas. He
made him carry out the precepts for the theras and hold
lectures of instruction thereon. But to the many bhikkhus who
31 hearkened he granted in the midst of the Great community
their appointment as theras, and presenting them with all
articles of equipment, he celebrated an offering for the theras.
32 Seeking for an occasion fraught with blessing, in order to

[1] P. *lūkhappaṭipatti*, cf. v. 25. The compound is missing in the PTS. P. D.

[2] In Pūjāv. Paḷābatgal.

reach by the noble eight-fold path the saving shore from the
ocean of re-births[1], he had built in the third and sixth, then 33
again in the eleventh, twelfth and seventeenth, as also in the 34
twenty-first, twenty-seventh and thirtieth years of his reign
thus eight times, a vast hall (resting) on sixty pillars[2]. Round 35
about it he erected a great and splendid maṇḍapa. This again
he had adorned with divers coloured stuffs and made numerous 36
groups of bhikkhus abide there by turn for the purpose of
rest. Day by day full of zeal, he did them honour with a 37
great festival of gifts in his name and granted to many
sāmaṇeras admission to the Order. Then following on this, he 38
conferred on bhikkhus the highest rank, namely the dignity
of a thera, Grand thera and the like[3], and accumulating many 39
important wares[4] of great value and many beautiful articles
of equipment even to the measure of a king of elephants, 40
the Ruler first presented to those who had attained the
rank of a Grand thera, articles of equipment worthy of a king
and then allotted to all the ascetics who were theras and to 41
those who had been dismissed from the dependance on a
teacher[5], and to the others in their order, the eight articles
of equipment[6].

[1] The section v. 32 to 41 is absent in the Pūjāv. The *aṭṭhaṅgikamagga* consists of the eight members: *sammādiṭṭhi* "right insight", *sammāsaṃkappa* "right thought", *sammāvācā* "right speech", *sammākammanta* "right doing," *sammāājīva* "right gaining of livelihood", *sammāvāyāma* "right endeavour", *sammāsati* "right deliberation", *sammāsamādhi* "right spiritual concentration."

[2] The same 89. 49.

[3] W. renders *āyatanādhika* as title along with *thera* and *mahāthera* "incumbent of temple". But this seems to be contradicted by v. 40 *mahātherāyatanaṭṭhāna* "rank of a Grand thera." *Ayatana* must therefore be combined with *thera* and *mahāthera* in v. 38.

[4] P. *garubhaṇḍa* also 85. 105.

[5] P. *nissaya.* By this is understood the relation between an older bhikkhu, the *upajjhāya* and a younger, the *antevāsin.* The first has to instruct the second in all details of the monastic life and the younger must take the older as his model. He who has finished his course of instruction is *nissayamutta.*

[6] See note to 60. 71.

42 Thus the King, the best of men, celebrated every seven days the great and superb festival of the eight bestowals[1],
43 and later celebrating several times over the festival of admission into the Order, he made the Order of the Victor prosperous.
44 Thus the King by granting it in this way manifold support, caused as the moon[2] the ocean, the good Order of the Tathāgata — the king of the true doctrine — to grow in perfect fashion.

Here ends the eighty-fourth chapter, called «The Services Rendered to the Order», in the Mahāvaṃsa, compiled for the serene joy and emotion of the pious.

[1] The expression *aṭṭhopasampatti* must refer to the offering of the *aṭṭha parikkhārā* (v. 41). *Upasampatti* is not the same as *upasampadā* "admission to the Order". It is to this festival which took place later (*pacchā*) that v. 43 alludes. In 89. 50 *upasampatti* is also used in connection with the distribution of articles of use to the bhikkhus, while the celebration of the *upasampadā* takes place later (v. 63).

[2] P. *sudhākara*, skr. the same, lit. "mine of nectar". Cf. for this verse E. W. Perera, The Sinhalese and Spring Tides. in Ceylon Notes and Queries I, Oct. 1913. p. XVI.

CHAPTER LXXXV

THE PERFORMANCE OF ALL KINDS OF PIOUS WORKS

Hereupon the Ruler of men built in the splendid, incom- 1
parable, glorious town, by name Sirivaḍḍhana[1], his birthplace,
a vihāra exceeding rich and vast[2]. It was furnished with 2
pāsādas and maṇḍapas and with high walls and gate-towers,
adorned with bodhi trees, with cetiyas, with groves and image
houses, bright with all kinds of paintings[3] and embellished 3
over and over with ornaments. Then he had the stretch of 4
road from the town of Jambuddoṇi to the town of Sirivaḍḍhana
levelled in the length of half a yojana and the breadth of an
usabha[4], so that it was fair as the surface of a drum, and 5

[1] It is now generally recognized that this Sirivaḍḍhana has nothing to do with Kandy (cf. Copleston, The Identification of the Sirivaḍḍhanapura of Mahâwansa, Chap. LXXXV., JRAS. C. B. XII, Nr. 43, 1892, p. 206 ff.). It was situated according to v. 4 only half a yojana from Jambuddoṇi-Dambadeniya. All my MSS. have in v. 4 *aḍḍhayojana°*, not *aṭṭhayojana°* which must be assumed, if we adopt W's translation: "about eight yojanas". If the *yojana* of the Mhvs. is the usual Indian *yojana*, then the distance between the two towns is about 4 1/2 miles. Pūjāv., if the printed text can be relied on, has *aṭayodanak*.

[2] P. *visālavibhavaṃ* ("possessing great riches") *mahāvihāraṃ*. There is just a doubt whether we have to take the subst. as appellative or with W. as a proper name. I adopt the former and that with reference to the Pūjāv. where we have *rajamahaveherak* "one great King's Monastery". Thus we must of course read in v. 56 not *Mahā°* but *mahā°*.

[3] P. *nānākammavicitta;* cf. *cittakamma* "varied painting".

[4] In the line *dīghavitthāi ato aḍḍhayojanūsabhamatthake* the *aḍḍhayojana* refers evidently to *dīgha* and *usabha* to *vitthāra*. The first is the length, the second the breadth of the road. An *usabha* is equal to 20 *yaṭṭhi* = 140 *ratana* or *hattha*, (roughly = 18 inches), thus 210 ft. = 64 metres. The Pūjāv. gives a very detailed description of the festival of the transference of the relics to the new monastery.

caused it to be strewn throughout its length with fine white
6 sand and adorned on both sides with many flags and pennons
strung high by which the sun's rays were warded off, with
7 rows of banana stems and with numbers of filled jars which
contained decorations of flowers and were fair with their
8 bright painting. On the whole of this free tract he had erected
9 at a distance of every five cubits a royal arch and at a distance
of every ten cubits an arch of stuff as well as at a distance
of every hundred cubits[1] a large pāsāda covered with variegated
10 painting, with a high point, three-storeyed and furnished with
11 an image of the perfectly Enlightened One[2]. Then he decorated
the vihāra[3] round about the walled-in district of the monastery
12 with many and vast arches which were fair by reason of their
variety and gleamed with the grace of the arch of the King
of the gods[4], — further with white umbrellas which resembled
13 the picture of the full moon, — with banners five-fold in hue
and of divers form, which were fair as heavenly dancers who
14 dance in the court of the atmosphere — with rows of maṇḍapas
set with jewels that sparkled everywhere, which possessed the
beauty of a series of many palaces descended from the world
15 of the gods — with rows of figures of Brahma, that danced
in lines holding white umbrellas and were beautiful because
16 they were worked by a mechanism[5], — with divers-hued
mechanical figures of the gods which moved to and fro with

[1] Thus at distances of 7½, 15 and 150 ft. *Toraṇa* means the arch spanning the street on festive occasions. As to *paṭṭatoraṇa* we must think of the framework of bamboo stalks as being covered with coloured stuffs. We are not told what the *rājatoraṇa* looked like.

[2] From *tato* (end of v. 3) to v. 10 one sentence. Pred. and subj. are at the end. The King erected 1) rājatoraṇaṃ, 2) paṭṭatoranaṃ, 3) mahāpāsādaṃ on the levelled surface (*samīkatatale*) between J. and S. To the loc. *tale* belong the attributes in 5 cd and in 7 d (*alaṃkate*); to this last belong the instrs. in v. 6 and 7. In v. 8 the loc. *samīkatatale* is rendered collective by *etasmiṃ vipulokāse.*

[3] I anticipate obj. and pred. in 19 d.

[4] The rainbow is considered Indra's weapon. Stress is once more laid on the variegated colouring of the toraṇas.

[5] Lit. "beautiful by the contrivance of a machine".

hands folded before the brows, — with rows of mechanical 17
figures of horses which ran hither and thither and possessed
the grace of rows of raging waves of the sea, — with elephants 18
wearing the ornaments of elephants, which were (likewise)
mechanical figures feigning to be clouds descended to the
earth: — with all these and other votive offerings which called 19
forth ecstasy in people he embellished the vihāra. Then again 20
he made the whole of the inhabitants in Laṅkā take up their
position in a circle round the vihāra, filling the space of a
gāvuta[1] and giving forth shouts of praise, and glorified the 21
virtues of the perfectly Enlightened One. To these (he added) 22
the bhikkhus and the sāmaṇeras as also the lay brethren and
the lay sisters, bearing flowers destined as offerings for the festival
of the Buddha and (lastly) all the other men and women who 23
were acquainted with the merits of the three (sacred) objects[2],
with votive offerings in their hands, adorned with all their
ornaments. Thereupon the Monarch himself decked out in all 24
his ornaments, accompanied by his four-membered army, urged
by his faith, placed the two relics, the Tooth and the Bowl, on 25
a costly chariot, adorned with every kind of chariot ornament.
Then one by one he had displayed before him[3] divers votive
offerings, such as flags of gold and flags of silver, golden 26
vessels and silver vessels, fly-whisks of gold and fly-whisks
of silver, chests of gold as also silver chests, golden fans and 27
charming silver fans, golden bowls with lotus flowers[4] and 28
bowls of silver with lotus flowers, filled jars[5] which were 29
fashioned of gold and such as were fashioned of silver and
so on; and afterwards holding a great sacrificial festival with 30

[1] See note to 73. 154.

[2] See note to 37. 214.

[3] P. *purato pantiso* (v. 29), that is in single groups or divisions before he himself started.

[4] P. *pokkharaṇī*, i. e. "lotus-pond". We must imagine the basins in which the flowers were borne as being oblong in form like small bathing-ponds.

[5] In the *puṇṇakalasā* which are either carried or set up on festive occasions one sees now specially often the yellow-gold blossoms of the areca palm.

31 these divers (offerings)[1] ever and again to the sound of the
five musical instruments[2], he by degrees brought (the relics)
on this decked out road to the town of Sirivaḍḍhana. After
32 carefully laying them down in the midst of the vihāra in a
spacious maṇḍapa on a covered Buddha seat, he set about
33 making the various people[3] celebrate a sacrificial festival. In
the morning all people who had a true thirst[4] for meritorious
works, adorned with their ornaments, venerated the Tooth
34 Relic and the Bowl Relic in religious devotion[5], with divers
kinds of flowers, such as jasmin, campaka blossoms, the blossoms
of the ironwood tree[6] and the like, distinguished by their
colour and perfume, and which were mingled with flowers of
35 gold. They venerated them with heaps of aromatic rice which
gleamed like a collection of the long since amassed fame of
36 the Great king. They venerated them with divers kinds of
fruits, such as bananas, bread-fruit, mangoes and so forth,
which were quite ripe, fragrant, lovely in colour, perfectly
37 sweet. Then afterwards when the King himself had venerated
the two most holy relics with all kinds of votive offerings, he
38 likewise, true to the good custom, provided the bhikkhu
community carefully with food and drink, with dishes solid
and tender, with drinks that one sips and with those one
39 drinks[7]. Thereupon the Ruler, joyful in heart, distributed to
many hundreds of bhikkhus the eight articles of equipment

[1] P. *tehi tehi* (possibly *pantiso* also) belongs to the following *kārāpento mahāpūjaṃ*.

[2] The five instruments are enumerated in Abhp. 139 ff. They are *ātata*, *vitata* and *ātatavitata*, drums stretched "on the one side", "on the two sides" and "wholly with leather", *susira*, "flute, pipe", and *ghana* "cymbal".

[3] The various groups of people enumerated in v. 21—23.

[4] P. *puññasoṇḍa*. The word *soṇḍa* "drunkard" used here in a figurative sense, as also in *dhammasoṇḍatā*, Jāt. V. 482[17] (PTS. P. D. s. v.).

[5] P. *bhattiyā*, see note to 74. 243.

[6] P. *jāti*, jasminum grandiflorum, *campaka*, michelia champaca, *nāga*, mesua ferrea.

[7] *Khajjabhojjehi* is the more detailed explanation of *anna* and *leyyapeyyehi* that of *pāna* in the compound *annapānehi*.

in great abundance. After that throughout the three watches 40
of the night he had the whole space round about the vihāra
lit up with many hundreds of thousands of lamps burning
fragrant oil, with lovely festoons of numberless, tiny, camphor 41
lamps (so that it was) like to the starry firmament. The 42
Monarch instituted a sacrificial for the Buddha[1]. The festival
was ravishing by reason of the many exquisite dances and 43
songs of the dancers who on splendid stages[2] erected here
and there, performed while assuming different characters[3],
divers dances and sang various songs. The noise[4] of the 44
festival was increased by the sound of the five musical
instruments[5] which produced the illusion of the roar of the 45
great ocean of his meritorious works[6] that was so strong that
it surpassed[7] the booming of the sea, while the drums shamed
the thunder-claps of Pajjunna[8]. The feast resounded with the 46
pious voices of the preachers of the good doctrine who placing
themselves on the preachers' seats carefully spread at divers
spots by the faithful, laid hold of the beautiful fans[9] and 47
preached the good doctrine that went straight to the heart of

[1] Subj., pred. and obj. *mahīpālo buddhapūjaṃ pavattayi* stand at the close of the whole sentence in v. 51 cd. The preceding verses contain attributes to the object *buddhapūjaṃ*, namely *manoharaṃ* (v. 42-3), *vivaḍḍhitaṃ* (v. 44-5), *ghositaṃ* (v. 46-7), *maṇḍitaṃ* (v. 48-9), *pasatthaṃ* (v. 50-51).

[2] P. *raṅgamaṇḍala* = sinh. *raṅgamaḍala.*

[3] What is meant are the different parts they play. The dances are always mimic in character.

[4] The term "noise" must be supplemented from the foregoing. In the text itself there is only *vivaḍḍhitaṃ* directly related to *pūjaṃ.*

[5] See above note to v. 30-31.

[6] Very doubtful. I take *bhama* to mean "error, illusion", which is also the meaning of the skr. *bhrama.* W's translation cannot be reconciled with the text.

[7] Skr. *dūrīkaroti* can also mean "leaves behind it, surpasses".

[8] Skr. *Parjanya* the God of rain and of the storm. Cf. Jāt. I. 331[21] ff.; D. N. II. 260[25]; Mhvs. 21. 31.

[9] During solemn ceremonies the priest holds a fan in his right hand and great importance is attached to its being held in a dignified way.

48 their hearers. It was made beautiful by the jubilant cries[1] of the four retinues (of the Buddha)[2] who ever giving grateful
49 expression to their joy, went hither and thither praising unceasingly with cries of applause the merits of the three (sacred)
50 objects with the words: O Buddha! O Doctrine! O Order! Its praise was proclaimed by the elders (of the clan) of the
51 Balibhojakas[3] arrayed in all their ornaments, who taking their stand at the divers regions of the heavens after the custom of a Nandin procured[4] without ceasing the blessing of the Buddha.
52 With the thought: even in the highest heaven the Prince of the gods celebrates such a festival for the Buddha, the Ruler
53 had that same ceremony manifested here (on earth), and as former kings also, rulers of Sīhala, had in their miraculous power held even such a sacrificial festival for the Enlightened
54 One, so he showed it likewise at the present time to the dwellers in Sīhala. And so with the words addressed as it
55 were to all men: of such kind is the fruit on the wishing-creeper[5] of the pāramitās[6] of the omniscient (Buddha), he celebrated seven days long even such a great sacrificial festival
56 for the three (sacred) objects. Then in making the great

[1] P. *sādhukāra.* Cf. note to 74. 223.

[2] These are the bhikkhus and bhikkhunīs, lay brethren and lay sisters.

[3] See note to 38. 13.

[4] P. *buddhasantiṃ karontehi.* The expression *santiṃ kar* (skr. *śānti*) shows that the task of the people was to fend off all influences emanating from evil spirits which might disturb the course of the festival. *Nandividhipurassaraṃ* is in keeping with this, for in the Indian drama the *nāndin* has in the prologue to deliver the introductory prayer (*nāndī*) which is fraught with blessing. Cf. STEN KONOW, Das Indische Drama, p. 24. We can understand too why the elders of the Balibhojaka clan were entrusted with this office. The name signifies these animals, birds in particular, such as the crows that live on the *bali*, the daily sacrifice offered to the spirits. Such spirits are embodied in these birds and the sacrifice satisfies and conciliates them so that they do no harm.

[5] Also in Skr. *kalpalatā* along with *kalpavṛkṣa* etc. of the tree of Paradise on which grows everything that gives joy and delight to mankind.

[6] See note to 37. 180.

vihāra[1] the property of the community and in giving it over
to the Order, he filled himself with merit and fame. Thereupon 57
the King erected a pariveṇa that was called by his name
Parakkamabāhu, adorned with lofty pāsādas, granted the
vihāra[2] the divers objects of use suited to it, as well as 58
several rich maintenance villages, and celebrated a great sacrificial feast.

The King made his yuvarāja[3] erect in the Billasela-vihāra 59
the pariveṇa called Bhuvanekabāhu after him, embellished 60
with pāsādas, maṇḍapas and the like and then celebrated in
the town called Sirivaḍḍhana in the manner described, with 61
all votive offerings with care seven days long a great sacrificial
festival for the three (sacred) objects. But also in the splendid 62
town of Hatthigiripura[4] the King made the same (yuvarāja) erect
a vast vihāra, and after having built in his name a superb 63
pariveṇa, called Mahāmahindabāhu, he celebrated a great feast
of sacrifice and gathered thereby merit. He restored the decayed 64
five-storeyed pāsāda built long before in the splendid town
of Kalyāṇī by King Yaṭṭhālatissa[5], and in repairing what was 65
destroyed by having it coated with stucco, he made it again
as it had been originally. There too he restored in similar 66
fashion the temple of the recumbent statue of the King
of sages and the temple of the Tivaṅka image[6]. There too 67
the Ruler had the spacious, four-square courtyard of the great
cetiya laid with great stone slabs, making of it a perfectly 68

[1] See note to 85. 2.

[2] Namely the vihāra in which the Parakkamabāhu-pariveṇa was erected. *Pariveṇa* and *vihāra* are thus not used synonymously as W. thinks.

[3] That is his younger brother Bhuvanekabāhu, see 82. 4.

[4] I. e. "Elephant mountain town", now Kurunegala.

[5] He was the son of Mahānāga who was the brother of Devānampiyatissa and founder of the dynasty of Rohaṇa, whence arose in the fourth generation Duṭṭhagāmaṇī. (Mhvs. 22. 2 ff., 10 ff.). For Kalyāṇī see note to 61. 35.

[6] Cf. note to 78. 39. The images named here are the same as those mentioned in the Selalihinisandesa 68, to which Paranavitane has already called attention. According to the Ss. there were two of these.

level surface, and then he erected in front of the (cetiya) a
69 large maṇḍapa. Further the Ruler with great and religious
devotion held several times in that vihāra a sacrificial feast for
70 the Bodhi tree, the cetiya and the Enlightened One, with votive
offerings of flowers, lamps and food — magnificent, abundant,
spreading joy among the people, and acquired thereby merit.
71 Thereupon the King granted to the vihāra for the purpose
of holding a daily sacrificial festival of lamps, a large, fair,
72 delightful garden of cocopalms which he had had laid out in
his own name in the immediate neighbourhood of the vihāra.
73 Then the two-storeyed, circular relic temple in the vihāra
called Hatthavanagalla[1], erected[2] by the monarch Goṭhābhaya,
74 by name, on the spot where King Sirisaṃghabodhi gave his
75 head as gift to the poor man[3] — this temple the best of kings
had repaired and provided with a golden point and made three
76 storeys high. In the selfsame monastery he built on the spot
where the corpse of his royal father had been laid down[4] a superb
77 cetiya. There too he had erected an octagonal image house and had
78 a stone image of the Buddha set up in it. The glorious King heard
that of that son of the Enlightened One[5], the Thera Mahākassapa,
79 who had received during the lifetime of the Enlightened One —
the Guide to the path of salvation — the Master of the worlds —
his most holy garment of rags as heritage[6] and after his death
80 had taken over the spiritual kingship and protected it — (that)
of this Mahākassapa a single relic, a tooth, (existed and) in

[1] Now Attavanagalla on the small river of the same name, about 18 or 20 miles north-east of Colombo.

[2] Hatthavanagallavihāravaṃsa 9. 7 (p. 32 of the edition by Alwis). Here the building is described as *bhavanaṃ vaṭṭulaṃ*.

[3] Mhvs. 36. 91 ff. should be compared with this. The history of Sirisaṃghabodhi's end is told in greater detail in the Hatthavanagalla-vihāravaṃsa 8 (p. 25 ff. of the ed.) and embellished with many miraculous tales.

[4] Namely on the pyre. The corpses of the kings were disposed of by burning.

[5] Buddha's disciples are described as his spiritual sons.

[6] Cf. for this Saṃyutta 16. 11. 28 f. (II. 221), and the remarks to my translation of the S. N. II, p. 270 and 284.

course of time had come to Tambapaṇṇī and was now preserved 81
in the vihāra of Bhīmatittha in the province of Pañcayojana[1].
Thereupon the King in whom there sprang up religious devotion, 82
love and highest veneration towards that Thera[2], betook himself,
surrounded by his four-membered army to the great monastery 83
and after he had beheld there the splendid (relic), he celebrated
full of joy with an immeasurable quantity of beautiful kinds
of fragrant flowers and likewise with lamps and incense and 84
heaps of rice, with great care for three days a sacrificial
festival for the Tooth Relic. Then when the Monarch learned 85
that in the sacred town of Devanagara which was a mine of
meritorious works, the shrine long since erected to the lotus-
hued god — the King of the gods, had now fallen into decay, 86
he betook himself to the superb town and in rebuilding the 87
dwelling of the King of the gods like to the heavenly mansion
of the King of the gods[3], he made of it an abode of all
riches. Then the best of men had the town filled with all 88
splendours even as the beauteous city of the gods[4]. Hereupon 89
he determined to celebrate every year in the town an Āsāḷhī
festival[5] for the god.

Now the Great king betook himself to the splendid town 90
of Jambuddoṇī. Here he had built round the Sirivijayasundara- 91
vihāra[6] erected by his royal father, a high wall and gate-
towers and then had the three-storeyed relic temple restored[7]. 92

[1] Now Bentota on the coast between Colombo and Galle. For Pañcayojana see note to 57.71.

[2] That is towards Mahākassapa. W. erroneously associates *there* with "the elder who had the charge thereof".

[3] The word *devarājālaya* is twice used here. The temple of the King of the gods (Viṣṇu) in Devanagara is made as beautiful as the palace of the King of the gods (in this case Indra) in heaven.

[4] P. *devanagaraṃ viya* in allusion to its namesake, the town of Viṣṇu's shrine.

[5] P. *āsāḷhā, -ḷhī* is the name of the month June-July. The day of the full moon of this month was one of high festival even before the time of Buddha (Jāt. I. 50). Buddha was born on that day.

[6] Cf. above 81.51 where the monastery is called Vijayasundarārāma.

[7] Cf. with this 82.9 ff.

There he placed the Tooth Relic of the Great Sage on a raised
93 throne of great value and celebrated in the order described
above, for seven days a great sacrificial feast for the three
(sacred) objects which procure every conceivable blessing. With
94 the wish to have daily before his eyes a figure of the Guide
to the path of salvation, as rejoicing to the heart as the
95 figure of the living Master, the Lord of men had portrayed[1] by
numbers of specially skilled painters on a great tablet a splendid
96 Buddha figure, showing[2] the Exalted One as he took when alife
an airing in a large jewelled cloister set with divers precious
97 stones. Hereupon the King of high renown gathered together
the whole Order of the bhikkhus dwelling on the island of
98 Laṅkā as well as a multitude of people and celebrated in the
town of Sirivaḍḍhana in the manner described earlier, for
seven days a great festival for the Buddha.

99 Now when the Great king heard that unimaginable bless-
ing attaches to a kaṭhina[3] offering, he thought, joyful of
100 heart in faith: "In honour of the eighty greatly glorious
disciples[4] of him who is alone the bridge over the shoreless
terrible ocean of the circle of rebirths, who alone is the
banner of the Sakya clan[5], whose dignity is venerated by the
101 people of the whole world, the Wise, the King of the wise,
the Master, the preserver of the world, the seer, who is master
(of his senses), the kinsman of the world[6], the kinsman of

[1] P. *mahācittapaṭe . . . lekhāpesi.* Probably the picture was painted on a piece of stuff. In the Pūjāv. where the picture is also described, the expression *petikaḍa* is used, according to Clough, "piece of cloth on which an image of Buddha is painted". Mhvs. 27. 18 ff., relates that the picture after which the Lohapāsāda was built, was designed on a *paṭa.*

[2] Lit. a Buddha figure like the Exalted One walking . . . taking an airing in a cloister. The *ca* in 95 c is disturbing. Perhaps one should read *va* (= *eva*).

[3] See note to 41. 48. Parakkamabāhu's kaṭhina offering is also related in Pūjāv. and Rājāv.

[4] See note to 37. 176.

[5] Round the banner (*ketu*) the clan gathers; the word is therefore used figuratively for "leader, chief, the highest". Cf. skr. *manuvaṃsaketu*, Raghuvaṃsa 2. 33. The Buddha represents the acme of the Sakya clan.

[6] P. *lokabandhu.* So called on account of his world-embracing love.

the sun[1] — (in honour of his eighty disciples) I will give a 102
great and splendid kaṭhina offering of eighty (robes)." The wise 103
(prince) then called together the whole of the men and women
dwelling on the island of Laṅkā and made them all carry 104
out in the shortest time the whole of the work (for the making)
of (these) garments beginning with the preparation of the 105
cotton. And on one day he gave away together with all the
useful and important wares[2], the eighty kaṭhina robes. But 106
after he had prepared all this and versed in offering, had
distributed it among all the theras dwelling in Tambapaṇṇī[3],
he held for the eighty great disciples, for each one of them, 107
on the same day, eighty great sacrificial feasts. In this way 108
he often bestowed many kaṭhinas on the Great community
and increased thereby his great merit.

And the King thought several times with longing joyful 109
through faith: "I will dedicate to the Enlightened One the
royal dignity of Laṅkā." He adorned in fitting manner his 110
royal palace like the palace of the Lord of the gods and
the town like the city of the gods. Then he placed the Tooth 111
Relic of the Great Sage (Buddha) on a costly lion's seat which
he had fashioned in the royal abode, and with divers fly- 112
whisks and umbrellas, with divers jewelled crowns, with divers
ornaments and robes, with divers heaps of jewels, with divers 113
elephants and steeds, with divers infantry and chariots, with
divers beatings of drums and divers sounds of shell trumpets, 114
with divers flags and pennons, with divers rows of banana
trees, with divers bowls of milk[4], with divers trees in blossom,
with divers splendidly fragrant wreaths, with divers superb 115

[1] P. *bhānubandhu*. Because like the sun he illumines the whole world, at the same time also because (cf. W., note), the princely house of the Sakya is said to belong to the dynasty of the sun. The synonym *ādiccabandhu* is a frequent name of the Buddha. Buddhaghosa explains it in Suttanipāta 915 by *ādiccassa gottabandhu* (Helmer Smith, Paramatthajotikā, p. 562).

[2] See 84. 39 and note.

[3] See note to 80. 25.

[4] P. *khīrataṭāka*. Lit. "ponds of milk". The explanation is similar to that of *soṇṇapokkharaṇī* in 85. 28. See the note.

116 palanquins, with divers kinds of excellent rice, with divers splendid kinds of cake, with divers superb lamps, frankincense and perfumes — with all these and other votive offerings
117 worthy of a king, he celebrated with care, after assembling the Great community of the bhikkhus dwelling on the island of Laṅkā for seven days a great sacrificial feast.

118 The best of kings also betook himself with his four-membered forces to the Samantakūṭa[1], this forehead jewel of
119 the rock mountains. There he venerated the foot-print — to be venerated by gods and other beings — of the highest God
120 of gods[2], the King of truth, the Master. Round about the monarch of the mountains he granted to the extent of ten gāvutas[3] the land rich in various precious stones and thickly
121 peopled with men and women, in religious devotion to the sacred foot-print and sacrificed to it again with ornaments of jewels.

122 Thus did the discerning King who had faith in the Buddha, amass a great quantity of meritorious works as bridge for the crossing of the ocean of the circle of rebirths, or as ladder with which to reach the highest heaven.

Here ends the eighty-fifth chapter, called «The Performance of all Kinds of Pious Works», in the Mahāvaṃsa, compiled for the serene joy and emotion of the pious.

[1] The pilgrimage to Adam's Peak is mentioned in the Pūjāv.

[2] The title *devātideva* for the Buddha which already occurs in Mhvs. 1. 57, points again to a later stage of development. Cf. note to 50. 65.

[3] That is about 20 miles.

CHAPTER LXXXVI

INCITEMENT TO THE PERFORMANCE OF ALL KINDS OF PIOUS WORKS

Thereupon the King thought: "Since I now wield the royal 1
dominion over all Laṅkā, it is indeed for me a heavy burden[1]
to make pilgrimages hither and thither and to venerate 2
according to one's desire the hallowed places, to perform daily
meritorious works and to care for the welfare of the world.
But which of my dignitaries has the capacity to accumulate 3
a blessing of merit which would be equal to my aspiration
and to care (likewise) for the welfare of the world? Now 4
there is my dignitary Devappatirāja by name, a true believer
in the Buddha, the Doctrine and the Community. When he 5
striving after the dignity of a Guide to the path of salvation,
made the firm resolve[2], straightway there sprang from the three 6
eyes of a coconut planted by him three shoots. Once when
he beheld a poor man he to whom mercy was the highest,
gave him all his possessions together with children and wives 7
and uttered the wish: I will be a Buddha. Therefore when 8
he shall have heard my wish he will fulfil it." So thinking,
he had him summoned and spake to him thus: "By swamp, 9
mountain and wilderness as though created by the powerful[3],

[1] P. *bhāra*. The idea is this: the meritorious tasks which I have taken upon myself are too much for me alone. I must look round for helpers who will work with and for me with the same ideas and objects.

[2] Namely that the miracle described in 5 cd and 6 ab should be manifested as sign of the fulfilment of his wish to become one day a Buddha. Cf. 50. 65, 85. 119 and notes.

[3] P. *vasavattin*. As epithet of Māra, also in Thūpavaṃsa 65[13], with

unwelcome Māra, the road leading to the Sumana mountain[1]
10 is at many places obstructed, (made) inaccessible and causes
difficulties to the people of the eighteen provinces who make
11 a pilgrimage thither in order to accumulate blessing by
venerating the footprint of the Sage. Do thou therefore make
12 it accessible. Further: I have heard that in the vihāra called
Hatthavanagalla[2], at the spot where a Grand thera gifted
13 with miraculous powers, making through the majesty of his
merit earth and air to resound with thunder, attained the
14 dignity of an arahant, a five-storeyed pāsāda with a roofing
of golden bricks erected by King Upatissa[3], has in the course
15 of time fallen into decay, so that now nought but the pillars
16 remain. Do thou also restore this in my name. And just as
King Nissaṅka laid out a garden of fruit-trees in the Bhīma-
17 titthavihāra[4], do thou also plant in the same manner in my
name a large garden full of cocopalms and other trees". With
these words he entrusted him with each single meritorious
undertaking[5].

18 Devappatirāja agreed with "aye!" and betook himself in
the first place to Gaṅgāsiripura[6]. There he had fashioned a
19 magnificent image of Sumanadeva[7] furnished with all the fair
bodily signs and decked it out with ornaments of gold and
20 jewels. But after that he wished to visit the Samantakūṭa[8].
He took the image of the god (Sumana) along with him in

reference to the *paranimmitavasavattidevā* who are Māra's retinue and are themselves described as Māras.

[1] Name of Adam's Peak.

[2] See 85. 73 and note.

[3] We do not know which Upatissa is meant, for neither the first king of this name (37. 179 ff.) nor the second (41. 6) has such a building ascribed to him.

[4] See 85. 81 and note. There is an account of the parks laid out by Kittinissaṅka in 80. 25 (and in the Rājāv.).

[5] We must of course write *taṃtaṃpuññakriyāsu*.

[6] According to Pūjāv. = Gampala, now Gampola situated about 11 miles to the south of Kandy. Cf. 88. 48, 90. 107.

[7] The local guardian spirit of Adam's Peak. See Mhvs. 1. 33.

[8] = Sumanakūṭa. See note to 60. 64.

festive procession[1], set forth, betook himself first to the village 21
Bodhitala and began from here to build bridges. Here at the 22
mouth[2] he made a large and magnificent bridge of thirty-five
cubits, and over the Khajjotanadī one of thirty cubits, likewise
at Ullapanaggāma one of thirty-six cubits, at Ambaggāma 23
one of thirty-four cubits in length[3]. (The bridges were) very 24
strong and good so that elephants, horses, cattle and buffaloes
could pass over them. And above each single embankment of 25
the bridges he had fair houses built, adorned with lofty pillars
and the like, had invitations sent to numbers of bhikkhus, 26
gathered them together at different places, distributed among
them abundant alms and celebrated a great sacrificial festival.
He built rest-houses, finished the building of bridges, laid 27
down at the remaining places frequent stepping-stones[4], had 28
the wilderness cleared and (in this way) a great road built.
Then he betook himself to the Samantakūṭa, showed veneration
to the sacred footprint, set up in the courtyard of the cetiya 29
of the sacred footprint the image of the god (Sumana) and
erected a maṇḍapa for the holy footprint. Round about it he 30
had a wall built, and discerning as he was, had the maṇḍapa
fastened with strong chains to iron pillars in this wise to 31

[1] P. *ussavena saha.* Pūjāv. has *peraharin* "with a procession".

[2] P. *mukhadvāramhi.* The mode of expression is not quite clear. W. translates: "and nigh unto the mouth of the Khajjota river he built a bridge ... and ... across the same river". This is indeed difficult to reconcile with the original text. We have to think of these bridges as causeways between the rice fields (cf. *setubandha* in v. 25). The numbers are, taken in order, roughly 52, 45, 54, 51 ft.

[3] Devappatirāja proceeds from Gampola up the left bank of the Mahaveliganga. Ullapanaggāma is the modern Ulapana (4 m from Gampoḷa as the crow flies). Ambaggāma is the present Ambagamuva (6 m from Ulapana). The Khajjota river is called in Pūjāv. *Kaṇamädiri-hoya* (we have to read thus instead of *-haya*). Sinh. *kaṇamädiri* means "glow-worm", like the P. *khajjota.* It is curious that the farther course of the road is not described. It probably led over to the valley of the Kadalīgāma river and then ascended this valley. See note to 60. 66 and below v. 41.

[4] At marshy spots where no causeway could be built, to give firm foothold.

secure it, and then again he sacrificed for three days to the
32 sacred footprint with lamps and the like. He himself placed
on his head a lamp with fragrant oil, and venerating again
33 and again in the name of his Master the Great king and
walking round the sacred footprint with his right side towards
34 it, he spent the whole night. Hereupon he had this whole
occurrence in its true sequence from the beginning written
35 down on a lofty stone pillar and had this monument of the
glory of the Great king of kings Parakkamabāhu set up
36 with rejoicing. Thereupon he informed the King of the whole
occurrence by the mouth of a messenger and sent (the message) off, since his wishes had been completely carried out.

37 After that Devappatirāja betook himself to the Hatthavanagalla-vihāra and had erected there at great cost, in the
38 manner commanded by the King, a three-storeyed pāsāda with
a lofty point and gave it over to the Grand master[1], the wise
39 Anomadassin by name. Then he celebrated according to the
order of the Great king, an almsgiving and had a stone inscription put up.

40 Thereupon the High dignitary betook himself to the
landing-place Bhīmatittha and built at the mouth of the
41 Kālanadī a bridge of eighty-six cubits[2]. Then after building
at Kadalīsenagāma[3] a bridge of a hundred staves[4] and over
42 the river of Sālaggāma one of forty staves[4] and over the

[1] P. *mahāsāmin*. Cf. with this note to 53. 23. Anomadassin was the Superior (abbot) of the monastery.

[2] The Kālanadī is the present Kaluganga. The length of the bridge is about 129 ft., the mouth of the Kaluganga is however considerably wider than that.

[3] If Kadalīsenagāma is the same as Kadalīgāma in 60. 66, the building of the bridge was a continuation of the road to Adam's Peak. The identity of the two is however very questionable. W. suggests Kehellenava in the Kalutara District, Rayigam Korale. Pūjāv. has Kēlsēnāva.

[4] The calculation according to *yaṭṭhi* "rod, measuring rod" here is curious. According to 78. 63 (cf. the note to the passage) a *yaṭṭhi* equals 5 *hattha*. The two measurements in v. 41 would accordingly be 750 and 300 ft. respectively.

Sālapādapa swamp one of a hundred and fifty cubits[1] and in
addition to these other bridges here and there at difficult
places, and numerous parks and sermon halls, he celebrated 43
once more a great festival of almsgiving.

And again the High dignitary of the King had laid out 44
from the Bhīmatittha-vihāra as far as the landing-place (of
the Kālanadī)[2] on a space a yojana broad, a great garden of 45
cocopalms, called after Parakkamabāhu, beautifully shady and
rich in fruit. Then having all the work in the different 46
districts, such as the spinning of the cotton and so forth,
undertaken and finished in a day, the highly-famed one 47
presented the bhikkhu community with six and twenty kaṭhina
robes and celebrated therewith a great sacrificial festival.
Giving in like manner, he wandering around here and there, 48
presented the bhikkhu community once again with sixty-six
kaṭhina robes.

Then he had the whole of the vast forest called Ma- 49
hālabujagaccha[3] cleared by the roots, a fine village built there
and in its neighbourhood a large grove of jack-trees[4] planted. 50
Then he erected there in the name of the King an image
house of three storeys, surrounded by bodhi tree, cetiya, park 51
and encircling wall and celebrated a great sacrificial festival.
Having thus performed in the name of his royal Master[5] much 52
meritorious work, he informed the King of everything on
his return.

Now was the King filled with great affection for him. He 53
made the village called Mahālabujagaccha and other villages
built by him his hereditary property and granted them to 54

[1] Roughly 225 ft. W. gives the number as "fifty". He has overlooked the *sata* in *satahatthakaṃ*.

[2] Kālanadītittha, now Kalutara. Cf. 56. 12 and note. The distance between Bentota and Kalutara is 12 miles. The breadth of the plantation would be 9 miles, if the Indian yojana is meant.

[3] Pūjāv. *Mahadelgas namvū mahavanaya.* Sinh. *del* is the name of the bread-fruit tree artocarpus incisa. — P. *labuja.*

[4] Pūjāv. *kosvanayak.* Sinh. *kos* is artocarpus integrifolia. — P. *panasa.*

[5] P. *rājaññanāmato* stands here in the same sense as *mahārājassa nāmato* in v. 32 or *mahārājaniyogato* in v. 39 or *rājanāmena* in v. 51.

him. Thereupon he betook himself with him to the temple
55 of the Tooth Relic and spake thus in the midst of the
community: "This my most excellent dignitary has at all
times been true of heart to me and to the three (sacred) objects.
56 Therefore because activity for the welfare of the Buddha and
of the King was for him the highest, is he dear to me and
57 precious. Therefore will I with a gift dear to me make a
sacrifice to the Tooth Relic". And he dedicated the excellent
dignitary with wife and children to the Tooth Relic of the
Sage.

58 In such wise did the protector of the middle world from that times make that same most excellent Devappatirāja celebrate continually with many costly votive gifts, sacrificial festivals to the world-extolled Triad of the jewels.

Here ends the eighty-sixth chapter, called «The Incitement to the Performance of all Kinds of Pious Works», in the Mahāvaṃsa, compiled for the serene joy and emotion of the pious.

CHAPTER LXXXVII

THE HANDING OVER OF THE BURDEN OF DOMINION

Now once upon a time when through the influence of evil 1
planets a great heat arose in Laṅkā by which everything was
burnt up, when the corn withered and a famine was inevitable 2
and the whole of the people dwelling in Laṅkā were filled
with the greatest anxiety, the King gave orders for a splendid 3
festival to be held for the three (sacred) objects, for the cetiyas
and the bodhi trees and for the protectors Metteya and other
miracle-working highest deities[1] who were to be venerated by 4
various offerings, and even to turn the whole of Laṅkā into
one great festival[2]. After antecedent sacrificial ceremonies, he 5
gathered together the Great community of the bhikkhus, caused
them recite the Paritta[3] and bear the Tooth Relic of the 6
Great sage round the town in fitting manner, the right
side turned towards it, and made (in firm faith) the resolve:
the heavens shall rain. Thereupon great clouds gathered on 7
every side, flashing with lightning and again and again
thundering, so that it was bliss for the ears of all people, 8
and they began to rain, destroying the glowing heat, making 9

[1] For *devātideva* used here of the future Buddhas at the head of whom stands Metteya, cf. note to 85. 119.

[2] The construction is difficult. W. merely translates freely according to the sense. We must take the words *kārāpetvāna* and *mahussavaṃ* twice, first *uttamaṃ mahussavaṃ kārāpetvāna* (namely for the things and persons mentioned in 3 and 4) and then *sabbaṃ Laṅkaṃ ekaṃ mahussavaṃ kārāpetvāna.* For this last cf. idioms like *vadho ver' eko* "pure murder and bloodshed", M. II. 244[3]; *ekobhāsā disā sabbā vidhāya,* Mhvs. 74, 219, JāCo. V. 194[5] etc.

[3] See note to 46. 5.

joyful the people, driving away the famine, beautifying the
country and reviving the corn[1].
10 "By the power of the Buddha do these rain-clouds pour
11 forth such rain, making joyful our hearts. Who therefore among
gods, brahmas and men is capable of understanding how great
12 are these excellent qualities of the Buddha? But our King
also is mighty and strong in miraculous power, a king like
13 to him there has not been and there will not be." With such
words ever and again repeated, the dwellers in Laṅkā praised
the excellence of the Monarch of sages and also the excellence
of their King.
14 While in this wise the King protecting Order and laity in
15 justice and filling with precious contents his own character,
enjoyed for long the good fortune of the royal dignity, he on
one occasion summoned to him along with his sister's son, Vīra-
16 bāhu, his five capable sons — Vijayabāhu, Bhuvanekabāhu[2],
17 Tibhuvanamalla, Parakkamabāhu and Jayabāhu — and began in
18 this wise to give these six advice: "Dear ones, hearken to
my words: there are here in the world these three (kinds) of
sons: the low kind, those of like kind, those of higher kind[3].
19 Now those who know not how to enjoy at its true worth[4] the
wealth of their parents which has come to them as a family
20 heritage, but destroy it, as monkeys a wreath of flowers, and
now live without wealth — the pious ancients have called 'sons
21 of a low kind'. But those who enjoy such possessions as they
have received them in like manner as their fathers, protecting
them as a family heritage, these ye must know are the '(sons)

[1] The removal of a drought by the exhibition of the Tooth Relic is also described in the Rājāv.

[2] The two brothers Vijayabāhu and Bhuvanekabāhu are mentioned together in an inscription found in Yāpahu. H. C. P. Bell, ASC. 1911-12 = S. P. III. 1915, p. 63.

[3] Lit. "lower (similar, higher) born or become". Cf. skr. *apajāta* and *anujāta*. The three kinds are distinguished in the same way in the Itivuttaka, p. 63^{1}, 64^{6}. For *avajāta* cf. also DhCo. I. 178^{2}.

[4] P. *guṇānurodhato*. W's translation "by a virtuous life" is too weak and too general. The idea is: they are not conscious of how valuable is the heritage that has come to them, they squander it frivolously.

of like kind.' But yet another kind I name — those who 22
besides the possessions taken over as family heritage, acquire
thereto many other possessions and as prudent people enjoy 23
in happiness — these are known as the 'sons of higher kind'.
From my father I have inherited alone (the province of) 24
Māyāraṭṭha[1] but have now again conquered the two other
provinces and brought the three kingdoms completely under 25
one umbrella. All the Damiḷas who were for him invincible,
I have vanquished and all the kings of the Vanni[2] dwelling 26
here and there in mountain and wilderness I have brought
over to my side. Having spread my fame everywhere also in 27
foreign lands, I have for long held sway in just fashion. I 28
have brought hither king's daughters from Jambudīpa with
gifts and thereby made the nobles in the foreign land your
kinsmen. The heroes of the Paṇḍus and the Coḷas, the kings 29
sprung from the dynasties of the Sun and Moon, have sent
me diadems and ornaments. Also have I gathered together 30
without ceasing a mass of jewels which can be enjoyed not
only by all of you here, but even in future time by seven
generations of my descendants, even as the (god) Kubera 31
(gathered together) his nine treasures, the shell and the rest[3].
I have put down the evil-doers and protected the honest and 32
brought unanimity to the Order of the Enlightened One.
Therefore have I become for my royal father a higher born 33
son, be ye also my sons, like me, higher born sons. As in 34
days of old the sixty thousand sons of King Sagara[4] of the
race of Okkāka, built as many towns, divided all land in 35

[1] See notes to 81. 15 and 46.

[2] See note to 81. 11.

[3] The nine treasures of Kubera are, according to Apte (Skr. Eng. Dict. s. v. *navanidhi*; cf. also Amarakosha, ed. W. L. Shastri Pansikar, v. 142): 1) *mahāpadma* "great lotus flower", 2) *padma* "lotus flower", 3) *śaṅkha* "shell", 4) *makara* "dolphin", 5) *kacchapa* "tortoise", 6) *mukunda* "a particular precious stone", 7) *kunda* "jasmine", 8) *nīla* "sapphire", 9) *kharva* "dwarf". The names are also personified as names of genii who are guardians of the treasures in question. Cf. Hopkins, Epic Mythology, p. 143.

[4] For the legend of the Sāgaras, see Mahābhārata, III. 106 ff.

Jambudīpa into sixty thousand parts and held sway each for
36 himself in harmony; — further as aforetime the ten brothers,
the kings, divided Jambudīpa into ten parts and ruled in wise
37 fashion: so shall ye, my sons, divide this Laṅkā and supporting[1]
38 one another as is fitting, hold sway in able fashion, but never
expose a weakness to the enemy." In this wise he admonished
his own sons and his sister's son.

39 Hereupon he summoned the Great community in great
numbers[2] and the King asked them: "Which of these six
40 princes, my sister's son and my own sons, is worthy of the
royal crown?" When the Great community heard these words
41 of the King, they expressed themselves thus: "O Great king
thy princely sons and this thy sister's son are all capable
42 men and well instructed; they are all practised in fighting,
crushers of the alien foe and worthy of the royal crown as
43 protectors of the laity and the Order. But thy eldest son
Vijayabāhu has from childhood believed with joy in the triad
44 of the jewels. His heart was ever set on the care of infirm
bhikkhus, he was trustworthy, grateful, gifted with the merits
45 of faith and discernment. He was a support for such as had
no support, ever abounding in pity for aged people and
46 suffering creatures. Many kinsmen by marriage of the bhikkhu
community who had become enslaved during the period of
47 alien dominion[3] and many other people he freed from their
slavery by the gift to their masters of gold, precious stones
48 and other valuables. Many thieves who had committed thefts
even in the royal palace, turned to him when punishment

[1] The reading of the MSS. *yāyantā* ought not to be changed into *sāsantā*. I assume that *yāyati* has here a causative meaning "to make go, to further, to support".

[2] Not "the chief priests and the people", as W. has it. *Mahājanaṃ* is in apposition to *mahāsaṃghaṃ*. The "people" have nothing to do with the question of the succession. In the sequel it is the priesthood alone who give the answer. Cf. also v. 71.

[3] P. *rājantara.* See note to 81. 1. It is the time of the reign of Māgha (and of Jayabāhu, 82. 27, 83. 19) that is meant. W. has misunderstood the passage in translating "when he took the government into his hands".

overtook them. They gave up their anguish and their fear 49
and unharmed, without suffering the loss of a limb[1], their
lives were spared. When O King! he beheld the people who 50
went forth to each village to collect[2] the taxes due to the
King, he gave his own money, freed thus from various dues 51
all people in distress and protected them continuously, versed
in the protection of subjects. Also many of the Sīhala kings 52
of the Vanni whom thou wast desirous of subduing, sought him
out first and then only did they fearless pay their visit to thee.
›Ye must henceforth serve for ever with devotion[3] Vijayabāhu 53
who will in the future protect the continuation of our race,‹ 54
thus are the wives in the families of the dignitaries wont in
all reverence to admonish their husbands. When fathers and 55
mothers, fain to listen to the sweet infant voices of their two
year and three year old children, ask them: ›Whom do ye 56
serve?‹ they say: ›We wish to serve Vijayabāhu‹. Children 57
beaten in wrath by father and mother come to him and tell
their woe. Then Vijayabāhu makes the parents come to him, 58
exhorts them in his pity to beat their children no longer and 59
lets them have from his own storehouse the necessary food
for their various children. How canst thou O King, — even 60
as a man who gifted with seeing eyes, looks at the heavens
where the full moon stands and yet asks where is then the
full moon? — knowing as thou dost that in Vijayabāhu the 61
merits dwell which constitute the ornament of the royal dignity,
yet ask the Order? Learn then O Great king! that he 62
possesses the lucky signs to hold sway not only over Laṅkā-
dīpa but even over Jambudīpa."

After the Ruler had heard of these and his many other 63
merits from the mouth of the community, his eyes became
moist with tears of joy thereat. Full of contentment he 64
summoned to him his son Vijayabāhu, made him sit on a seat

[1] P. *aṅgahāni.*

[2] Wrongly translated by W. It is not a case of people embezzling the taxes, but of the revenue officers who wished to collect them.

[3] P. *saṃbhattā.* Cf. with this the term *bhạtti* = skr. *bhakti*, note to 74. 243.

65 (like his own) near him, and then the Great king informed
him of all that must still be carried out for the laity and
66 the Order and which had not yet been done by himself. "The
Ratanāvalī-cetiya[1] destroyed by alien foes, thou shalt restore
67 and adorn it with a golden point. Pulatthinagara, that splendid
ornament of all towns,[2] which was the ancient royal city of
68 the Sīhala sovereigns, do thou restore as it was of yore, with
high walls and gate-towers, with four gates well distributed,
69 and surrounded by a deep trench; and do thou bring thither
to the former relic temple, fair as a heavenly palace, the two
70 relics of the Tooth and the Bowl. In this royal city of former
kings I wish myself to celebrate the high festival of the royal
71 consecration. But do thou bring the whole bhikkhu community in great number[3], dwelling in the three Sīhala provinces, to Sahassatittha[4], let them there after antecedent
72 sacrifice, celebrate in the Mahāvālikagaṅgā the festival of admission to the Order and thus make the Order of the Victor
prosperous.

73 After speaking thus and otherwise of all that was to be done for the laity and the Order, he gave over the burden of government into his hands.

74 And further the King entrusted him with the five remaining sons of the royal house, and the two sacred relics of the holy Sage, the Tooth and the Bowl, as also with the host of the ascetics, with the group of all the dignitaries and also the land of Laṅkā.

Here ends the eighty-seventh chapter, called «The Handing over of the Burden of Dominion», in the Mahāvaṃsa, compiled for the serene joy and emotion of the pious.

[1] See note to 80. 68.

[2] P. *sabbapurītilaka*. The word *tilaka* ("badge of a sect") has here (as so often also skr. *tilaka*) a figurative meaning "ornament, adornment".

[3] For *bhikkhusaṃghaṃ mahājanaṃ* cf. note to v. 39.

[4] Now Dastota, a ford over the Mahaveliganga south of Polonnaruva. That the bhikkhus were fond of performing their ceremonies in a building erected in the water at some distance from the bank is well known. Dastota was at that time a spot considered especially sacred where such ceremonies were performed with great pomp, as is shown also in 89. 47 ff.

CHAPTER LXXXVIII

THE REBUILDING OF PULATTHINAGARA

Fearless in heart, King Vijayabāhu gave his consent and 1
took over the burden of the government. Now he thought: 2
"I will show my father so long as he is in life, that I am a
son of the higher kind." And he probed ever further: "Who 3
is there now fitted to be the element 'friend' among the seven
elements of government, as ruler, minister, friend and the like[1]:
trustworthy, a clever counsellor, a comrade in misfortune, who 4
speaks the truth, who is good to me?" And he realised: 5
"There is the Ādipāda Vīrabāhu, the son of my father's
sister, well-bred, adorned with virtues, skilled in all tasks.
Since the time when we played (together) in the sand till 6
to-day he has showed the highest confidence in me and in
(all) good people. He cannot bear to stand anywhere if he 7
does not see me, and I also cannot bear to take a seat without
seeing him. He is at pains even as I, to further the laity and 8
the Order, richly dowered with mental and bodily power.
Therefore is he fitted for the element friend". He summoned 9
him to him and entrusted him with the position of a devoted
friend.

[1] The *satta rajjaṅgāni* are enumerated in Abhpd. 350. They are: *sāmi* "ruler, monarch", *amacca* "minister", *sakhā* "friend", *koso* "state treasure", *duggaṃ* "fortress", *vijitaṃ* "land, kingdom" and *balaṃ* "army". In the Kauṭalīya, they are enumerated at the beginning of Book 6 as the (*sapta*) *prakṛtayaḥ*: *svāmyamātyajanapadadurgakośadaṇḍamitrāṇi*. Why J. J. Meyer in his translation should have left out *kośa* (p. 397) I cannot understand. Cf. ib. p. 399[20], as well as R. Shamasastry, Kauṭilya's Arthaśāstra, trsl., p. 319. In Subhūti's Abhidhānappadīpikāsūci a verse is quoted from Kāmandaki in which the same terms are grouped together.

10 Then he thought: "Now I must perform a meritorious
work — splendid, sublime, rejoicing the heart. I was entrusted
11 with the two relics, the Tooth and the Bowl. For these I
must now build a new temple. On the other hand, the an-
12 cient relic temple erected by my royal forefathers[1], has fallen
13 into decay. This I will restore." With this consideration, he had
fetched from all parts many groups of artists experienced in
14 every branch of art and many other workmen; and erecting
new structures doubly as fair to look at as the former build-
15 ings, he completed the whole temple of the Tooth Relic, so
that it was beauteous as a heavenly palace; placed there the
16 two relics of the Enlightened One and ordered his own guard
to institute day by day a great sacrificial festival richer than
17 aforetime, for the relics. From this time onward the King
succeeded in making the love of his royal father (for him)
increase continuously, twofold and threefold.

18 Thought the Ruler: my royal father shall have no grief
arising from the separation from his sons, and he made his
19 two younger brothers, Parakkamabāhu and Jayabāhu, dwell
20 continually near their father. Hereupon he summoned his
younger brother Tilokamalla and placed under his command
21 all the Sīhala troops quartered in the space between the town
22 of Jambuddoṇi and the southern sea and made him take up
his abode in Mahāvatthalagāma[2], to protect his royal father
23 on the south. Then he reflected: "In the north, foes coming
from the opposite coast are wont to land in Khuddavāligāma.
24 Who is so fitted to protect this side — perilous, since it is
here that fighting is wont to begin — as my brother, the Prince

[1] P. *piturājūhi.* W. translates "by the King, my father". He evidently regards *rājūhi* as a plur. maiest. I believe however, that the term applies to Vijayabāhu III. and Parakkamabāhu II. What is meant is the relic temple in the Vijayasundara-vihāra in Jambuddoṇi which is said in 85. 91-2 to have been built by Vijayabāhu III. and renewed by Parakkamabāhu II.

[2] Perhaps identical with Vattalagāma mentioned in 81. 58. The difference in the writing may possibly be explained in this way that *vattala* is the pure Sinhalese form, while *vatthala* is adapted to the Pāli.

Bhuvanekabāhu?" The Ruler summoned him therefore, made 25
over to him the great army that stood in the north and 26
commanded him to take up his abode in Sundarapabbata[1], in
order to protect his royal father from this quarter. But the 27
King himself armed, marched with Vīrabāhu hither and thither,
crushed all villains, made Laṅkā free from the briers (of the 28
enemy) and after getting his father's permission, he set forth
with the intention of restoring Pulatthinagara.

Now at this time the Great king Parakkamabāhu, as if 29
borne on the great wave of his love for his son, set about
accompanying his son, full of sympathy, travelling everywhere 30
after him, although the son did not wish it. Then the son ever 31
and again forced his father in reverent manner to return, he
himself going on his way. Then his father issued the order: 32
"All people who cherish love for my son let them accompany
him." When they heard these words of his, then all the high 33
dignitaries of the King and all the generals, all the great 34
hero warriors and all the elephant drivers, all the riders and
all the charioteers were filled with the greatest joy. "Now our 35
Bodhisatta Vijayabāhu[2] sets forth to restore the royal city of
Pulatthinagara. If he goes we shall go with him at once." Thus 36
they spake and started forth well equipped to accompany him.
When a certain number of dignitaries, soldiers and others, 37
out of laziness, were not minded to go, their wives said to
them: "Ye, our lords, may come with us or not, at any rate 38
we are going with the King who seeks the best, and we shall 39
dwell with him in the newly restored, splendid town". And
they set forth therewith on their way before them. Even 40
children deserted their fathers, if they would not go with
them and followed the King. When the King beheld the great 41
crowd of people setting forth, each deserting his village, his
house and his comfortable possessions, he persuaded them 42
again and again in his great anxiety, and induced all those

[1] The same as Subhapabbata or Subhagiri = Yāpahu.

[2] The influence again of the Mahāyāna. Cf. 50. 65, 85. 119, 86. 5. Also in Rājaratn. and Nik.-s. the King is called Bōsat Vijayabāhu.

43 whom it was right to induce, to return. Then he betook
himself with the four-membered army in the desired strength,
44 to the great and loftily situated fortress of Vātagiri[1]. After
building a splendid royal palace on the summit of this mountain,
45 surrounded by an extraordinarily high wall, he stored there
in case of need, the whole of the great treasure given over
46 to him by his royal father. Thereupon he built on the same
high rock a fine monastery for the community, invited the
47 Grand thera, the head of the Mahānettappāsāda-shrine[2], made
over to him the splendid monastery, celebrated a great sacrificial festival and established a regular offering.

48 Hereupon the King went forth to Sumanakūṭa, venerated
the footprint of the Sage (Buddha) and betook himself there-
49 after to Gaṅgāsiripura[3]. There in the ancient vihāra that bore
the name Nigamaggāmapāsāda, he saw to the restoration of
50 what was ruinous and decayed, established for the bhikkhus
dwelling there a regular almsgiving and came thereafter to
51 Sindhūravāna. Here the King erected the vihāra called Va-
ṇaggāmapāsāda and after building there in the name of his
52 royal father[4] the pariveṇa called Abhayarāja, he granted it
the various articles of equipment, villages, fields and so forth.
53 Then the Monarch betook himself to the splendid Hatthigiri-
pura[5]. While here in the great vihāra built by his princely uncle
54 (Bhuvanekabāhu), he gazed along with Prince Vīrabāhu[6] and
his army again and again at the ever to be honoured spot
55 where his corpse was laid (on the pyre), he felt anguish and
gained there again and again the inner conception of imper-

[1] Vākirigalla in the Kegalla District. Cf. note to Mhvs. 58. 31.

[2] A Mahānettapabbata is mentioned in Mhvs. 50. 74.

[3] Gampola. See 86. 18.

[4] The pariveṇa is n o t called after his father Parakkamabāhu II. Here it is the case of a *patti* (see note to 42. 50). The merit is transferred to the dead king.

[5] Kurunegala. See 85. 62 where mention is made of the building of the Vihāra by Bhuvanekabāhu, the younger brother of Parakkamabāhu II.

[6] Cf. 83. 41 ff.

manency[1]. Hereupon he erected there a splendid, three-storeyed 56
image-house and had made for it a great image of the Buddha.
Then having had further a fine statue of his uncle fashioned, 57
he set it up there adorned with all ornaments. The Ruler 58
assigned (his foundation) fine maintenance villages fitted for
their purpose, lying around the image-house, as well as numbers
of people for service, and decreed for it (the foundation) the 59
name Bhuvanekabāhu-pariveṇa, using for it the name of that
(uncle). Then after he had settled the town (Hatthigiri) densely 60
with men and women, he had it enclosed with wall, moat and
so forth. Thereafter the brave King set forth and marched 61
with the vast four-membered army to Subhagiripura[2].

At that time the Lord of men Candabhānu, formerly[3] beaten 62
after hard fighting, having collected from the countries of
the Paṇḍus and Coḷas and elsewhere many Damiḷa soldiers, 63
representing a great force, landed with his Jāvaka army in
Mahātittha. After the King had brought over to his side the 64
Sīhalas dwelling in Padī, Kurundi[4] and other districts, he
marched to Subhagiri. He set up there an armed camp and 65
sent forth messengers with the message: "I shall take Tisīhala[5];
I shall not leave it to thee. Yield up to me therefore together
with the Tooth Relic of the Sage, the Bowl Relic and the 66
royal dominion. If thou wilt not, then fight." Thereupon 67
Vijayabāhu summoned the Ruler[6] Vīrabāhu, took counsel with
him, had a strong force equipped for him and spake: "Hurrah, 68
to-day both of us shall see the strength of our arms." Then the
two set forth[7], surrounded the great army of Candabhānu on 69
all sides and fought a great battle, terrible as a combat of
Rāma. Then were the hostile warriors subdued in battle and 70

[1] P. *aniccalakkhaṇa.* This is a term drawn from the technique of *jhāna*, meditative absorption. See HEILER, Die buddistische Versenkung, p. 18 ff.

[2] I. e. Yāpahu.

[3] Cf. 83. 36 ff.

[4] See note to 83. 16.

[5] See note to 81. 46.

[6] Vīrabāhu has here and in v. 90 the title of *mahīpati*, just as Bhuvanekabāhu in v. 79 has the title of *rājan*.

[7] Note the change of subject in the case of *vatvāna* and *nikkhamitvā*.

weaponless the soldiers of the foe[1] wandered around, prayed
71 and implored, tortured by fear, were benumbed, trembled,
begged for mercy in the fight, whined and grieved full of
72 terror. In their distress certain of the foe fled to the forest,
73 others to the sea, others again to the mountains. After
Vijayabāhu had thus fought and slain many soldiers, he sent
74 the Lord of men Candabhānu flying defenceless. But the
loveliest women of his court and all the elephants and horses,
75 the swords and many other weapons, the entire treasure, the
trumpets of victory, the umbrella of victory, the drum of
victory, the banner of victory — all these he sent to his father.
76 Having in this way fought the fiery battle, conquered the
province and won the victory, he united Laṅkā under the
umbrella of his dominion.
77 Hereupon he had this town (Subhagiri) also surrounded
by a high rampart and a trench and built there a superb
78 royal palace. Having finished it, he established then in that town
a regular almsgiving for the great bhikkhu community. Then he
79 spake encouragingly to his younger brother King Bhuvaneka-
bāhu and made him take up his abode as before in Subhapabbata.
80 Now the Ruler betook himself to Anurādhapura and there
round about the Thūpārāma and all the other sacred places
81 he had the mighty forest — that was like a stronghold created
by Māra — felled and a wall erected which was as a bridge
82 over the stream of his hopes. Then after the Ruler had had
these sacred places embellished by new buildings, he celebrated
83 a great sacrificial festival. But as he wished to complete the
work of restoration on the Ratanāvalī-cetiya[2], begun but not
84 finished by his royal father, he assembled with the greatest
speed all people dwelling in the town from the places where
85 individuals sojourned, ordered numbers of skilful workmen
hither and having established for the community at whose head
86 stood the chief Thera of the Senānātha-pariveṇa[3] a regular

[1] *Veribhaṭā tadā* in 71 d takes up again the *tadā veriyodhā* in v. 70 a b.

[2] See 87. 66.

[3] This is the building erected by the general Kuṭṭhaka under Udaya II. and called in Mhvs. 51. 88, Senasenāpati-pariveṇa.

almsgiving[1], he appointed the Thera to look after the work
of restoration. Thereupon the Monarchs of the Vanni who 87
were living in Patiṭṭhāraṭṭha, sought out the Ruler, bringing
him many gifts. He (on his part) presented them with rocking 88
chairs, white umbrellas, fly-whisks and other insignia for the
great kings of the Vanni people. Therewith he made them 89
all contented, charged them to protect the town (Anurādhapura)
and betook himself from there to Pulatthinagara.

There the Monarch summoned to him the ruler Vīrabāhu: 90
"We shall embellish this town, originally the royal city, and
fill the universe with the camphor perfume of the exuberant 91
abundance of our glory." After these words he took counsel with
him and spake thereupon: "In the town called Pulatthinagara 92
there are now pāsādas, image-houses, vihāras, pariveṇas, cetiyas
and relic temples, walls, gate-towers, houses of the aḍḍhayoga 93
and of the hammiya kind[2], maṇḍapas, sermon halls, temples to
deities and other buildings. Some of these stand erect, covered 94
with grass, trees and whatever else has grown upon them.
Others have collapsed without support as the whole of their
pillars perished; others again alas! will fall, bending under 95
the weight of walls cracked from top to foot, because other
support is wanting. Some of these, through decay and old age 96
are like greybeards, and unable to stand erect, they become more
bowed from day to day. With many the joists are broken[3] and 97
their pinnacles destroyed[4], with others the roofs have decayed[5]

[1] *Niṭṭhāpeti* means here "to fix, to establish", the object *dānavaṭṭaṃ* being governed by it.

[2] I leave the two terms *aḍḍhayoga* and *hammiya* (skr. *harmya*) untranslated. Both are names for particular types of dwelling-houses which we are unable to describe further.

[3] P. *chinnatulāyaṭṭhī*. I believe that *tulāyaṭṭhi* (lit. balance-beam) means the horizontal beams, while *gopānasī* (v. 98; cf. 37. 141) means the beams of the rooftree. The construction of the compound is: "many are such in which . . . are broken off.

[4] P. *naṭṭhaviṭaṅkakā*. The original meaning of *viṭaṅka* which is omitted in the PTS. P. D. is according to Abhp. "dovecote".

[5] P. *vidhastavaḷabhī*. This is an interesting voucher for *vaḷabhi* which

98 and the bricks are broken. In others by the breakage of the
damaged rooftree the bricks of the roof have fallen and only
99 walls and pillars remain. In others again the gates have fallen
in and the hinging of the gate-posts destroyed; in others again
the steps have become loosened and the railings have fallen
100 in. Of many all that can be seen are parts still hanging
together[1] of the original foundation wall: of many not even
101 the place where they once stood is now to be seen. Of what
use are many words? This town which has lost all its glory
we shall again make glorious. The Ruler must give his consent.
102 Then later he may celebrate the royal consecration in the
splendid city." With this charge he sent a messenger to his
father.

103 When the King heard these tidings, his heart was full of
joy, and as he himself had cherished the wish to restore the
104 original royal town, he summoned the circle of the great digni-
taries from every quarter, and issuing his commands to all the
105 inhabitants of Laṅkā, he brought together the workers in iron,
106 the turners, bamboo workers[2], blacksmiths, potters, goldsmiths,
painters, porters, workmen, slaves, the caṇḍālas who understood
107 work for hire, the bricklayers, workers in stucco, carpenters
108 and the guilds of masons, and in addition to these all black-
smith's tools, such as bellows, hammers, tongs, sledge-hammers,
anvils, as well as many sharp saws, axes, hatchets, (wedges)
109 for splitting trees and for crushing stones, knives, chisels[3],
shovels, mats, baskets and so forth. All these appliances he
110 gave carefully to the people and also much money, such as

occurs in the canon (M. I. 175[16], 177[32]), only in the compound *va-ḷabhīratha* which must be translated "covered-in carriage".

[1] Thus I translate *nibandhana*. In Skr. it means figuratively at least a joint of words, a compound.

[2] In the Saṃyutta Comm. (I. 193[19] of the Siamese ed.) *veṇakule* is explained by *vilīvakule*.

[3] P. *koṭisa*. In skr. *koṭiśa* means "harrow" according to BR., but this cannot be the case here. Some kind of pointed instrument must be meant (cf. *koṭi* "point").

pearls, precious stones and the like and sent it with the people[1]
to his royal son. Thereupon in the devastated land, long
desolate, King Vijayabāhu, happy at heart, had the water 111
system — tanks, ponds, dykes, pools and the like — in 112
which the embankments had given way, and which were de-
prived of their deep water, dammed up as before, filled with 113
deep water, covered with divers lotus blossoms and stocked
with all kinds of fish. Then he had many valuable fields 114
which had always been ground on which grew every kind of
corn, newly planted, had all kinds of crops grown here and 115
there and made the whole fair land prosperous. And the Ruler 116
restored superb Pulatthinagara as it had been aforetime, sur-
rounded by a moat, deep as the sea, with a fine chain of walls
like to the Cakkavāḷa mountains[2], provided with divers vihāras, 117
surrounded by various monastic parks with divers bathing-ponds,
filled with a variety of cetiyas, sprinkled with various aḍḍha- 118
yogas[3], adorned with divers pāsādas, built over with a variety
of hammiyas[3], embellished with divers maṇḍapas, provided 119
with all sorts of temples to deities, resplendent with every
kind of gate-towers, fair with the rows of divers houses, 120
boasting a variety of streets, with four well-distributed gates,
with fine squares and road-crossings.

In this fashion the King had the town of Pulatthinagara 121
— comparable to the city of Indra[4] — restored, so that it surpassed Mithilā, subdued Kañcipurī, laughed to scorn Sāvatthī, subdued Madhurā, turned to shame Bārāṇasī, reduced Vesālī to nothing and made Campāpurī[5] tremble with her glory.

[1] P. *saha senāya. Senā* means here the staff of workers raised by the King.

[2] These are the mountains which are supposed to surround the earth which is conceived of as a disk. Cf. Skr. *cakkabāla, -vāḍa,* BR. s. v. 2; W. Kirfel, Kosmographie der Inder, p. 186.

[3] For *aḍḍhayoga* and *hammiya* see above note to v. 93.

[4] Amarāvatī, see 80. 5. The town is described in the Mahābhārata, III. 1714 ff.

[5] A series of the most famous Indian towns. 1) Mithilā, capital of the Videhas, now northern Bihār; 2) Kāñcipurī, in Southern India

Here ends the eighty-eighth chapter, called «The Restoration of Pulatthinagara», in the Mahāvaṃsa, compiled for the serene joy and emotion of the pious.

on the Coromandel Coast, one of the seven sacred towns of India. 3) Śrāvastī, capital of the Kośala country in present Nepal (T. W. Rhys Davids, Buddhist India, p. 40); 4) Madhurā, here probably the town Mathurā on the Jumna, chief locality of the Śūrasena, mentioned AN. II. 57 (BR. s. v. *madhura* 3 c); 5) Bārāṇasī, now Benares; 6) Vaiśālī, in the Videha country, in Buddhist times the chief locality of the Licchavi clan, like Sāvatthī often mentioned in the sacred Canon; 7) Campā, in the territory of the Aṅgas, now Bhāgalpur on the Ganges, Bihār. Note the sacred number seven. See also the two notes to 89. 4.

Chapter LXXXIX

DESCRIPTION OF THE FESTIVAL OF THE KING'S CONSECRATION AND OTHER FESTIVALS

The King spake: "This Pulatthinagara is now thus restored 1
as before, dowered with all that belongs to a city. This town is 2
now radiant with happiness, splendour and beauty. She has
surpassed Jetuttara and will now surpass Sāgalā. After van- 3
quishing Suṃsumāragiri, what need hath she to care for Sā-
keta? Ha! even Rājagaha she wishes to capture as it is. She 4
has destroyed Saṃkassa and now scorns Indapatta. She dares
to challenge[1] Kapilavatthu[2]. Therefore shall the King, the 5

[1] P. *saṃkhyaṃ ussahate kattuṃ*. I think that *saṃkhya* here is = skr. *saṃkhya* and means "fight" (BR. s. v. 4). The Col. Ed. reads *sakhyaṃ* and W. translates: "seeketh friendship with K." This I think is not so good, as *ussahate* has then no meaning. It looks as if the author here as also in 88. 121, by the accumulation of synonyms for the term "surpass", wishes to show his intimacy with the rules of alaṃkāra. Cf. the expressions in Daṇḍin's Kāvyādarśa 2. 62 ff. with those used in this passage.

[2] The author returns here, repeating himself, to the idea already treated in the final strophe of chap. 88. He displays his geographical knowledge which he apparently borrows from the Abhidhānappadīpikā where in v. 200 and 201 all the towns named by him are enumerated: 1) Jettutara, often mentioned in the Jātakas as the capital of the Sivi country (skr. *śibi*). Cf. FAUSBÖLL Jāt., Index; 2) Sāgalā, abode of the King Milinda (Milp. ed. TRENCKNER, p. 1); 3) Suṃsumāragiri, according to M. I. 95, II. 91; S. III. 1, IV. 116; A. II. 61 etc. a town in the country of the Bhaggas (skr. *Bharga*); 4) Sāketa, name of the town Ayodhyā (now Oudh) in the Kosala country. M. I. 149 and often otherwise in the Nikāyas and the Jātaka book; 5) Rājagaha, capital of Māgadha; 6) Saṃkassa (skr. *Sāṃkāśya*), mentioned in the Jātakas, according to JāCo. IV. 265[28] thirty yojanas from Sāvatthī, was situated

chief of kings, even as Sakka, the overlord of the gods, did
6 in the city of Sakka[1], enter this city in all his majesty to
celebrate the festival of the royal consecration." Therewith
7 he sent a messenger to his father. When the King heard
from the mouth of the messenger the uninterrupted narrative,
he rejoiced greatly and betook himself at the head of his
8 army with all the mighty pomp worthy of a king, from the
town of Jambuddoṇī to the chief capital (of the kingdom).
9 And King Vijayabāhu went the distance of a gāvuta[2] towards
him and accompanied the Great king to the royal capital.
10 For seven days he celebrated in the town the high festival
of the royal consecration and carried it out in the (right)
11 sequence to the end. But after he had made over the Northern
province[3] to Vīrabāhu and made him take up his abode in
12 the prosperous royal city, he declared: I shall bring the
relics of the Sage to this royal city, and betook himself with
his royal father to the town of Jambuddoṇī.

13 Hereupon the King gathered together a great multitude
of the inhabitants of Laṅkā and had the great highway from
14 the town of Jambuddoṇī to splendid Pulatthinagara, five yo-
janas[4] wide made level and throughout, always at a distance
15 of half a yojana, he had a costly rest-house built, gracefully
(adorned) with festive banners, rows of bananas, triumphal
16 arches and the like. Thereupon he placed the two relics of
the great Seer, Tooth and Bowl, on a high chariot which was
17 fair in its splendour as a heavenly chariot. With numerous

to the west of Kanyakubja (now Kanauj) between the Ganges and the Jumna (cf. Vin. II. 299); 7) **Indapatta** (skr. *Indraprastha*), town in the Kuru territory on the site of the present Delhi; 8) **Kapilavatthu**, capital of the Śākyas in the territory of the present Nepal, birthplace of Buddha.

[1] See note to 88. 121.

[2] About two miles.

[3] The expression is *raṭṭhaṃ uttamaṃ*, quite in the sense of Rājaraṭṭha or Patiṭṭhāraṭṭha.

[4] According to the context, this would be the whole distance from Jambuddoṇī to Pulatthinagara. But the distance is much greater, about 75 miles, as the crow flies (5 y. = 45 miles).

groups of the bhikkhu community who, paying homage, en-
circled[1] on every side the incomparable, splendid, festive chariot,
of the sacred relics, as if they were the hosts of the Brahmas 18
who surround the sacred chariot of Brahma, he set forth from
the superb city, great Jambuddoṇī. The sacrificial festival
which he arranged[2] was beautified by the people entrusted 24
with the various duties[3] who letting unceasingly their cries of
Hail! resound, went before or followed after[4] and bore with
them for the sacrificial festival umbrellas of gold and pearl, 19
golden fly-whisks, inlaid with pearl, banners of gold and pearl,
wreaths set with gold and pearl, further golden and silver 20
jars[5], fans of gold and silver, golden and silver vases, golden
and silver shells, golden and silver bowls, golden and silver 21
urns, golden and silver basins, golden and silver mirrors,
golden and silver banana trees, tiny shells of gold and silver, 22
golden and silver horses, golden and silver elephants, as well 23
as countless silver and golden lamp-stands and the rest. The
festival was surrounded by rows of elephants excellent by 25
reason of the elephant ornaments by which they were o'er-
spread[6], by rows of steeds worth seeing for the abundance of
every kind of equine ornament, by the ranks of heroic warriors 26
who with divers weapons in their hands and wearing warlike
ornament, played their war games, by the ranks of princes, 27

[1] Thus I translate *samantā sevamānehi*. This *sevamānehi* is like the attribute to *bhikkhusaṃghagaṇehi*, also to *brahmasamūhehi* and governs the acc. *rathaṃ* in 17 a as well as in 17 d.

[2] This is taken from v. 36 a *mahāpūjaṃ pavattento*. The following accusatives are attributes of *mahāpūjaṃ*: *manoharaṃ* (v. 24 d), *parisevitaṃ* (v. 27 d), *maṇḍitaṃ* (v. 28 d), *parivāritaṃ* (v. 30 d), *parighositaṃ* (v. 32 d), *pasaṃsitaṃ* (v. 34 b), *thomitaṃ* (v. 34 c) and *parisevitaṃ* (v. 35 d).

[3] P. *taṃ-taṃ-dhurā-niyuttehi* (v. 24 c). The people meant are those who have particular functions to perform at a sacrificial festival.

[4] Taken from vv. 23-24, *purato pacchato pi ca . . . gacchantehi . . . manussehi*. *Gahetvā* in v. 23 c by which the accusatives in v. 19 to 23 a b are governed, is subordinate to *gacchantehi*. The people carry their votive offerings with them in the procession.

[5] Should not the reading here be *-kumbhe pi* rather than *-kumbhehi*?

[6] Lit.: "by the outspreading (*vitthāra*) of the elephant ornaments."

28 nobles and councillors who wore festive clothing and flaunted
manifold ornament. The glory (of the festival) was enhanced
29 by the cries of people who thirsting for merit shouted O hail!
30 O hail! O hail! The festival was surrounded by serried rows
of lay sisters and lay brethren who led pure lives and who
in their zeal each for himself pressed forward bearing flowers
31 and the like as offerings. Around it raged the uproar of
sturdy palace servitors who were ever and again now here
32 now there, well beaten in fun by other sturdy palace servitors
as if they were people fighting out a mighty quarrel with one
33 another. It was filled with the songs of praise[1] of the bards
who sang festive songs, making thereto on the five instruments
34 fine music which spread abroad and charmed[2] the hearers,
also with the songs of the minstrels who again and again let
35 their praises resound. In devotion there surrounded it the
dancers and the actors who performed dances and sang songs
36 delightful to see and to hear. Thus performing by degrees
in perfect order the high sacrifice, he was wont when in mov-
37 ing along the decorated road, he came to the previously
erected rest-houses, to set up the relics in each of these, (he)
performed each time a high festival, started again from each
38 (rest-house), continued ever on his way and so brought by
degrees the relics of the Prince of the wise to the royal
capital[3].

39 Then after the King had turned the whole city into a
single great place of festival — at a favorable moment when
40 constellation, day and hour were auspicious, in the ancient,
decorated relic temple, fair as the palace of the King of the
41 gods — most splendid of all temples — he solemnly and in
careful manner placed the two relics on a costly throne em-
42 bellished by all manner of jewels. From that time onwards,

[1] Lit.: "was praised by . . . and belauded by . . ."

[2] P. *savaṇīyataraṃ*, lit. "very well worth hearing".

[3] Vv. 16-38 form one sentence. The principal verb is *ānayi* (v. 38 d with the immediately preceding gerunds). The gerunds *saṃṭhapetvā* v. 16 c and *nikkhamitvā* v. 18 c are subordinate to *pavattento mahāpūjaṃ* (along with the attributes belonging to it; cf. notes to vv. 18 and 24/19).

day by day more, with the four kinds of perfume[1], with fine,
fragrant incense, with divers kinds of blossoms of the punnāga, 43
nāga, pūga[2] and other trees, with countless camphor lamps
of precious stones giving a brilliant light, with rows of cande- 44
labra on which burned fragrant oil, with dishes full of the
finest rice prepared with sweet milk, with heaps of food 45
composed of sweet-smelling rice like to the Kelāsa[3] mountain,
with all hard and soft foods and with all that can be drunk
or sipped and other (things) the wise Prince celebrated for 46
another three months a world-rejoicing sacrificial festival for
the relics, amid the clang of the shell trumpets[4] and thus
brought (the festival) to a close.

Then spake the Ruler: "Let us perform in Sahassatittha 47
a blameless festival for admission to the Order[5]." He first sent 48
the Monarch Vīrabāhu thither. There he made him erect besides
several thousand rooms of sojourn for the community[6], a lofty 49
house of festival resting on sixty pillars[7] which gleamed with
manifold ornament and possessed arches covered with cloth[8].
Hereupon he had prepared the divers objects for the ceremony 50
of admission to the Order and all the four articles of use.
And then after the Vanni kings who in this and that province, 51
in Patiṭṭhāraṭṭha, in Rohaṇa and so forth, had collected with
great care, much rice with the divers ingredients such as fish, 52
meat and the rest, (had gathered together) great loads of
grain, sour and sweet milk, butter and so forth, also honey, 53
treacle, thickened sugar juice, raw sugar, lump sugar and the
like, as well as all things fitting for an offering to the Great

1 According to Abhp. 147, the *catujjātigandhā* are 1) *kuṅkuma* "saffron"; 2) *yavanapuppha* (?); 3) *tagara* = skr. *tagara* tabernaemontana coronaria and a fragrant powder prepared from the blossoms of the shrub; 4) *turukkha* = skr. *turuṣka* "incense".

2 Rottleria tinctoria (kamala tree), mesua ferrea (ironwood tree), areca catechu (areca palm).

3 See note to 68. 41. The tertium comparationis is the white colour.

4 Lit.: "together with the shell trumpet festival".

5 See above note to 87. 71.

6 P. *saṃghārāma*.

7 P. *saṭṭhitthambhamahālaya* as in 84. 34.

8 P. *paṭṭatoraṇa* as in 85. 9.

54 community, King Vijayabāhu betook himself thither. He
issued the invitation: "Let us take in hand the arrangement
55 of a festival for admission to the Order. Let all the Grand
theras, all the middle-aged and the youthful who have trust
56 in their hearts towards us, the lords among the ascetics not
fail to come to Sahassatittha," and (he) sent messengers
57 everywhere (with the invitation)[1]. When all the individual
groups of ascetics settled in Tambapaṇṇī heard this news, they
58 rejoiced greatly and set forth on their way from every quarter,
without allowing even the administrator of their provisions to
59 remain behind, and in haste the heroes among the ascetics
60 assembled by degrees well prepared in Sahassatittha[2]. The
King who again and again[3] surveyed Sahassatittha surrounded
61 as it was with ascetics felt a befitting[4] joy, and in abundant
measure the Ruler supplied the Great bhikkhu community as
62 was seemly, with excellent food and drink. Then celebrating
day by day here in Sahassatittha a great sacrificial festival,
63 he made those bhikkhus who were called thereto, perform
the ceremony of admission for those who were desirous of
entering the Order, and celebrated the ceremony of admission
64 to the Order for half a month. Thereupon the King granted
the rank of a Grand Master[5], the rank of a Chief Thera[6],
the rank of a Grand Thera and the rank of a Pariveṇa-Thera[7]
65 to such (bhikkhus) who because they had brought about the
prosperity of the Order, deserved to receive this or that rank.

[1] Vv. 47-56 form one sentence which opens with three loc. abs. *kārāpite* (49 a), *sajjāpitesu* (50 c) and *ānītesu* (53 c).

[2] P. *āgantvā* (with the acc. of the place) *saṃnipatiṃsu* is merely periphrastic.

[3] P. *muhuṃ*, used in the same way as the double *muhuṃ muhuṃ*. The same in Jā. V. 32[27] *kiṃ maṃ muhuṃ pekkhasi haṭṭhalomo* (*muhuṃ* being explained by the commentary as *punappuna*).

[4] P. *sulabha*. Cf. skr. *sulabha*, BR. s. v., 1 b. The joy corresponds to the great number of bhikkhus who have put in an appearance.

[5] P. *mahāsāmipada*. Cf. note to 53. 23.

[6] P. *mūla(thera)pada*. Cf. 69. 34 *mūlāmacca*.

[7] P. *theraparivenādikaṃ padaṃ* seems to mean "the rank where the word *pariveṇa* precedes *thera*."

Then having bestowed on them the eight articles of use, fair, 66
worthy of a king, to the value of a thousand (gold pieces),
and also to the other ascetics in succession, costly articles of 67
use, he sent many remaining articles of use to the bhikkhus
settled in the Paṇḍu and Coḷa countries. Then when all his 68
wishes had received fulfilment, he guided by right knowledge[1],
sent a messenger to his father and announced to him: "All 69
meritorious works which I have performed I have performed
in the name of my royal father."

Thus in granting admission to the Order to numerous 70
ascetics at the great ford of the Vālikā river called Sahassa,
in the correctly drawn[2] boundary, known as the 'throwing
up of the waters'[3], he made lustrous the nine-fold doctrine[4]
of the sublime Buddha.

After he had for a long time made over the burden of 71
government[5] to his own world-famed son, this most excellent

[1] P. *ñāṇapubbaṃgamaṃ katvā,* "placing right knowledge at the head." He was conscious that he was only his father's representative. W. uses the words in the oratio recta and translates: "What-soever merit hath been performed by me with a pure mind."

[2] P. *parisodhita,* lit. purified.

[3] P. *ukkhepasīmā,* a term difficult to explain and occurring again 94. 17 and 97. 12. It has reference to the ceremony being performed in a building erected in a lake or in a river (see above note to 87. 71). The boundary which must enclose the space set apart for ecclesiastical functions must thus be drawn in the water. In fixing it water would have to be "thrown up" (skr. *kṣip* with *ud*), just as the earth is thrown up in fixing a boundary on land. W's note gives a correct definition: "a space in a sheet of water, duly defined, for purposes of ordination and other ecclesiastical functions" But this does not explain the etymology of the expression.

[4] P. *navaṅgikaṃ sāsanaṃ.* The nine "members" (*aṅgāni*) of the holy scriptures are 1) *sutta* "discourse"; 2) *geyya,* the same with an admixture of verse; 3) *veyyākaraṇa* "exposition" without verse (chiefly the Abhidhamma); 4) *gāthā* "stanza"; 5) *udāna;* 6) *itivuttaka;* 7) *jātaka,* the well known three books belonging to the tipiṭaka; 8) *abbhutadhamma* "discourses relating to mysterious conditions"; 9) *vedalla,* title of some special suttas.

[5] P. *bhūbhāra,* lit. "burden of the earth". Cf. skr. *bhūbhartṛ* "prince, ruler".

King Parakkamabāhu who as described[1], performed through his son an abundance of meritorious works, entered heaven when he had attained his thirty-fifth year (of reign)[2].

Here ends the eighty-ninth chapter, called »Description of the Festival of the King's Consecration and Other Festivals», in the Mahāvaṃsa, compiled for the serene joy and emotion of the pious.

[1] *evaṃ evaṃ* even in this way.

[2] According to Rājāv. 32 years, Pūjāv. 33 years. The number given in the Mhvs. includes those years when Vijayabāhu carried on the government. The latter is called Bōsat Vijayabāhu by the Nik.-s. as well as by the Rājaratn.

CHAPTER XC

THE HISTORY OF THE EIGHT KINGS, OF VIJAYABĀHU AND HIS SUCCESSORS

Now in the second year of King Vijayabāhu[1] who after 1
Parakkamabāhu's death, held sway over all Laṅkā, one of his 2
generals, Mitta by name, a faithless friend[2], won over as as-
sociate a slave belonging to the immediate entourage of the
King. Out of lust for dominion the recreant made him whom 3
he had bribed by gifts, slay the Ruler at night. Now when 4
the younger brother of the King, the King Bhuvanekabāhu[3] 5
heard of this event, he left the town of Jambuddoṇī, mounted
in his fear a covered litter[4] and sped on his way to the
fortress of Subhācala[5]. But people who had received gifts 6
from the hands of the evil general Mitta, and were therefore
bound to him from the outset, nine wicked, brutal brothers 7
from the clan of the Monasīhas[6], pursued him and pitilessly
pierced the Monarch's litter so fiercely with their pointed spears 8
that everything — seat, girths and the like[7] were in tatters.

1 Rājāv. jumps from Vijayabāhu IV., passing over his immediate successors, to the history of Alakeśvara and the Chinese invasion. See note to 91. 14.

2 P. *dummitta* with reference to the general's name *mitta* "friend".

3 Rājaratn. calls him Lokekabāhu Bhuvanekabāhu, Nik.-s. Mahābhuvanaikabāhu.

4 P. *yāna*, used of every kind of conveyance. W's translation "litter" is undoubtedly right.

5 Subhācala is like its synonyms: Subhagiri, Subhapabbata, Sundarapabbata, the name for the present so-called Yāpahu.

6 See note to 38. 13.

7 P. *andolipaṭṭakādikaṃ*. The seats of these litters were evidently suspended in girths to counterbalance the shaking. Hense the expression *andoli* "swing", while *paṭṭaka* means the girths.

9 He (Bhuvanekabāhu) sprang to the ground from the litter and
betook himself in haste, unharmed, to the village of Kāla-
10 gallaka[1]. Here from a stall where elephants were tethered[2],
11 he took a specially good elephant, mounted it and having
again crossed the great Koḷabhinna river then in flood, the
King reached that selfsame Subhagiri.

12 Now the Senāpati Mitta forced his way into the town of
Jambuddoṇī, into the palace of the Great king, seated himself
13 on the splendid lion throne of the Great king, and showed him-
self, the recreant, to the whole army his person adorned with
14 the royal ornaments. But now all the dignitaries who sup-
15 ported him, came together, one following the other. They
thought: "We must under all circumstances win over by (means
of) proper pay the whole army, that part belonging to our
16 own country as well as the alien part." They began in the
first instance, to hand over their pay to the chivalrous Āriya
17 warriors[3] at the head of whom was Ṭhakuraka. But these
declared: "We have at all times been people who one felt
must be won over. Now ye must under all circumstances,
18 first of all by good pay win over the Sīhala warriors and
make them contented." And none of them now accepted the
19 pay. "Be it so", answered the others. They paid all the
Sīhaḷas their money and then called upon the Āriya to take
20 their pay. But again they refused with the words: "Our pay
21 shall be handed to us later; we shall not take it now." So
although all the ministers ever and again urgently pressed
22 them[4] to accept their pay, the well-armed[5] Āriya knights

[1] Probably Kalugallagama in the Kudagalboda Korale, NNW. from Kurunegala.

[2] P. *gajabandhaniyaṃ* is the loc. of *-dhanī* (fem. of *-dhana*).

[3] In contrast to the Sīhalas, these must be South Indian mercenaries. The reader is referred to the tribe of the Ariya mentioned in 61. 36 and 63. 15. This (not *āriya*) would be at any rate the correct form of the name according to the phonetic rules of Pāli. See also below v. 44.

[4] P. *nibandhaṃ karoti* "makes an urgent petition". Cf. VvCo. 260[16] *devī punappunaṃ nibandhaṃ karoti* "the queen urged him again and again (to fulfil her wish)."

[5] P. *sajjitā*. This is obviously meant to call attention to the

declared: "We shall say everything in the presence of the
King." They betook themselves to the King's abode and when 23
they saw the Senāpati Mitta sitting on the lion throne, they
stood for a time respectfully there. Then the warrior Ṭha- 24
kuraka who was possessed of an undaunted heart, gave his
comrades a sign, took his sharp sword and in a moment 25
swiftly struck off the Senāpati's head so that it fell to the
ground. Now when hereupon a great hubbub arose in the 26
town, all the Sīhala soldiers who were a mighty force, banded
themselves together and asked the Āriya soldiers with Ṭha- 27
kuraka at their head: "Why have ye done this evil deed?"
They replied: "It took place at the command of King Bhu- 28
vanekabāhu who abides in Subhagiri." With the words: "Be 29
it so", all the Āriya and Sīhala warriors united and brought
the King, their lord, Bhuvanekabāhu from the town of Subha- 30
giri to the town of Jambuddoṇī and with reverence conse-
crated him King.

From that time onward the King made the whole double 31
army obedient to his will by assigning them salaries and the
like, drove back all the Damiḷa foes, like Kāliṅgarāyara, 32
Coḷagaṅgadeva and the rest who had landed from the opposite
coast, as also the Vanni kings in Sīhala, Kadalīvāṭa, Āpāna, 33
Tipa, Himiyānaka and so on, and freed Laṅkā from the briers 34
of the foe. He took up his abode for several years in the
town of Jambuddoṇī, betook himself thereupon to the town 35
of Subhagiri, had built here an extensive royal city, gleaming
in the beauty, and abode there.

As he then won over all his subjects by a just policy, he 36
was a just king and a believing adherent of the Doctrine. He 37
bestowed on the skilful scribes of the sacred books abundant
money and had the whole of the Tipiṭaka copied by them, 38
had it preserved here and there in the vihāras of Laṅkā,
and thus the Lord of men caused the dissemination of the
sacred texts[1]. Several times, too, the Ruler caused the festival 39

threatening aspect of the situation. The Āriyas are fully armed throughout the negotiations.

[1] P. *pālidhamma* could also mean "the Doctrine in the Pāli tongue".

of admission to the Order — which is a festival for the world — to be so celebrated that it was radiant with the splendid
40 offerings made, and thus he brought growth and prosperity to the Order of the Sage — the Order whose sublime greatness must be reverenced by the (inhabitants of the) three
41 worlds. He celebrated daily a great sacrifice for the Tooth Relic and he provided the bhikkhu community with the four articles of equipment.

42 In this wise he wrought good, while dwelling in Subhagiri and after carrying on the government for 11 years, he entered heaven.

43 Once when (here in Laṅkā) a famine arose[1], there landed, sent with an army by the five brothers, the kings who held
44 sway in the Paṇḍu realm, a Damiḷa general known by the name of Āriyacakkavattin who though he was no Āriya[2] was
45 yet a great dignitary of great power. He laid waste the kingdom in every direction and entered the proud stronghold, the town
46 of Subhagiri. The sacred Tooth Relic[3] and all the costly treasures there he seized and returned with them to the Paṇḍu
47 kingdom. There he made over the Tooth Relic to King Kulasekhara[4] who was as the sun for the lotus blossom of the stem of the great kings of the Paṇḍus.

[1] There is a gap in the text here. Of v. 43a the MSS. have only *chātasmiṃ*, five syllables are therefore wanting. The Col. Ed. supplements *jāyamānasmim*. I should prefer *chātasmiṃ idha jātasmiṃ*, because the similarity of the first and third words would make the slip of the writer of the archetype easily intelligible.

[2] See above, note to v. 16.

[3] According to 89. 41 Vijayabāhu had deposited the Tooth and Bowl Relics in Pulatthinagara. Evidently his successor had brought them back to Subhagiri to the town built by him there, a theory supported by 90. 41. The Sinhalese kings liked to keep the palladium of the kingdom in their immediate neighbourhood. It is remarkable how in the later parts of the Mhvs. the *pattadhātu* is relegated to the background — it is only just mentioned again in 90. 72 — and how the whole religious and political interest centres in the *dāṭhādhātu*.

[4] Kulasekhara reigned 1268—1308 (H. W. Codrington, HC. p. 80). His general Āriya Cakravartin is mentioned in a South Indian inscription (No. 110 in Annual Report of Epigraphy, Southern Circle, Madras Government, 1903 according to Codrington, l. c. p. 87).

Hereupon the son of the Bodhisatta Vijayabāhu[1] and grand- 48
son of the mighty King Parakkamabāhu (II.), Parakkama- 49
bāhu by name, became king and raised aloft — as if to fend
off like a cloud the heat from the people who dwelt in 50
Laṅkā — the umbrella (of dominion), the emblem of its proud
kings — fair through the cool shade (it gave) and like to the
disk of the full moon. And he reflected: "That Tooth Relic 51
which was taken to the Paṇḍu kingdom — that relic of the
Prince of the wise, our highest protecting deity, worthy of
veneration by our race, how shall I bring it back from there?" 52
And as the Ruler saw no other means but friendly negotiation,
he set forth in the company of several able warriors, betook 53
himself to the Paṇḍu kingdom and sought out the Ruler of
the Paṇḍus. By daily conversations he inclined him favourably,
received from the hands of the King the Tooth Relic, returned 54
to the Island of Laṅkā and placed the relic in superb Pu- 55
latthinagara in the former relic temple. Then the Ruler took 56
up his abode in this city and began to carry on the govern-
ment without transgressing the precepts laid down for kings[2].
The King performed daily a festival for the Tooth Relic and 57
accumulated unweariedly a great abundance of meritorious
works. He provided the bhikkhu community with robes and 58
the other articles of use and thus having furthered the laity
and the Order, he fell under the power of death.

The son of Bhuvanekabāhu, the ruler of the town of 59
Subhagiri[3], Bhuvanekabāhu became king in Hatthigiri-

[1] See 88. 35 and note. The Mhvs. tells us nothing of the fate of the younger brothers of Bhuvanekabāhu I.: Tilokamalla, Parakkamabāhu and Jayabāhu (88. 19-20). Evidently they died before Bhuvanekabāhu.

[2] P. *rājanīti*. W's translation "laws of Manu" is too restricted.

[3] With reference to a fragmentary interpolation in three MSS. after the line 59 a b see my edition as well as W's note on p. 316. The translation would run as follows: "With the constant thought: the son of Bhuvanekabāhu, the ruler of the town of Subhagiri, the prince by name Bhuvanekabāhu, cherishes the desire for (usurping) the royal dignity at a future time, the King Parakkamabāhu ordered a barber with the help of the king's people to put out both his eyes although

60 pura[1]. The Lord of men wishing to acquire merit, rejoicing
in generosity and other good deeds, instituted permanently a
61 regular alms of food for the bhikkhu community. Every year
the King celebrated in a manner worthy of the highest kingly
power, the festival of his coronation and in conjunction with
62 that in the Jeṭṭhamūla[2] month, after an opulent sacrificial
festival, he had the ceremony of admission to the Order
performed. Thus he made the Order of the Victor shine
63 brightly. After having performed these and many other
meritorious works in manifold ways, the second[3] Bhuvaneka-
bāhu also fell a victim to impermanence.

64 His still more eminent son, Parakkamabāhu[4], wise and
dowered with courage, was (thereupon king) in the superb
65 city. With the love of faith in the three (sacred) objects, he
assembled the bhikkhus and made them perform several times
66 over the ceremony of admission to the Order. In the royal
courtyard he erected in careful fashion a temple for the Tooth
Relic, fair with its walls and pillars, painted with bright-hued
67 pictures, provided with golden spires[5], with gate posts of
68 gold, splendid, three storeys high. There he set up a canopy
69 of coloured stuffs, strips of cloth and the like. This he decorated

he was his younger brother (cousin) . . . ." The last words are unintelligible because the sentence has been left unfinished.

[1] The text here has like 99. 77 the synonym *Hatthiselapura* (Kurunegala). The Nik.-s. calls the king Vat-himi-bhuvanaikabāhu.

[2] June—July.

[3] The Col. Ed. has *dutiye* and W. translated accordingly: "in the second year of his reign." Codrington (C. A. L. R. X. 2, p. 91) emended this into *dutiyo* and this emendation is confirmed by all the MSS. known to me. Codrington, (HC. p. 82), points out quite rightly that according to the Daḷadā-sirita the King must have reigned at least 9 years. The wording of v. 61 points also to a longer reign. Rājaratn. gives the number of years reigned and the number of the coronation festivals as 24.

[4] Nik.-s. and Rājaratn. call him Paṇḍitaparākramabāhu. For *āsi* in 64 d 91. 9 with note should be compared. The ascent of the throne by Parakkamabāhu IV. took place according to the Daḷadā-sirita in the Saka year 1247 = 1325/6 A. D. (Codrington, l. c.).

[5] P. *siṅga* = skr. *śṛṅga*, BR. s. v. 1 f. Cf. 90. 90.

with garlands of gold, silver and pearl which hung down on
all sides and he attached to it a wall of silken curtains adorned 70
therewith[1]. Here (in the tent) he spread a seat, radiant with
coloured draperies, and decorated it on every side with rows 71
of golden and silver vases and with rows of candelabra of
silver, gold and precious stones. On this seat he then full of 72
reverence, placed the casket with the Tooth Relic and the
casket with the Bowl Relic. Hereupon he set about performing 75
day by day a great sacrificial festival in worthy fashion for
the relics of the Master — a festival glorious with flowers 73
and perfumes and with lamps and incense, provided with all
foods soft and solid and with all that one drinks or sips,
beautified by the reverberating[2] sound of the five musical 74
instruments, fair through the dances and songs performed by
the dancing girls and the actors, preparing delight for the
world. With villages and fields, women slaves and men slaves, 76
with elephants, cattle, buffaloes and other gifts he celebrated
a sacrificial festival for the relics. With the reflection: "What 77
the daily ceremonial was in the lifetime of the Enlightened
One, the highest guide of the whole world, that of the Tooth
Relic shall be from this day henceforth," the King composed 78
in the Sīhala tongue a work expounding this, with the title
"Ceremonial of the Tooth Relic[3]" and in keeping with it he 79
performed daily a daily ceremony for the relic[4].

[1] This is the description of a kind of tent. First its ceiling (up to 68 c) is described and then the side walls. The instrumentals in 68 d and 69 a b must belong to the gerund *alaṃkariya*, but at the same time to *sobhitaṃ* through the medium of *olambamānāhi*.

[2] P. *vijumbhamāna*, otherwise as a rule *vijambh*. Cf. skr. *jrambh*, *jṛmbhate*.

[3] P. *dāṭhādhātucāritta*, rendering of the Sinh. *daḷadāsirita*. The work — it was mentioned above, note to 90. 63 — still exists. See GEIGER, Literatur und Sprache der Singhalesen, p. 9.

[4] The passage is significant. It shows that in Ceylon just as in the temples of Egypt a daily ritual was observed wherein the relics (and the images, cf. the allusions in 38. 56, 53. 30) took the place of the living and present Buddha. See Arthur A. PERERA C. A. L. R. VI. 2, p. 67 f., and above Cūlavaṃsa I, p. 359; note 4. Cf. also below 97. 33, 101. 4.

80 To the office of royal teacher the King appointed a Grand
thera from the Coḷa country, a self-controlled man, versed in
81 various tongues and intimate with philosophic works. Ever
and again he heard from him continuously all the Jātakas,
82 learned them (by heart) and retained their contents. Then he
rendered by degrees these five hundred and fifty beautiful
83 Jātakas from the Pāli tongue into the Sīhala speech[1]. He
recited them in the midst of the Grand theras who were
84 intimate with the three Piṭakas, and after correcting them,
he had them written down and distributed throughout Laṅkā.
85 And these Jātakas he made over to a wise thera, Medhaṃkara
by name, whom he had gained for the purpose, that they
86 might be preserved in the succession of his disciples and
thereby handed down still further. Then after having built
87 for him a pariveṇa with the King's own name, he assigned him
the four villages of Purāṇagāma, Sannīrasela, Labujamaṇḍaka
88 and Moravaṅka. In the vihāra of Titthagāma[2] where the big,
89 long pāsāda forty-five cubits in size erected by the great
Vijayabāhu[3], had fallen into decay, King Parakkamabāhu
90 himself built a beautiful, long pāsāda[4] of thirty cubits in size,
two storeys high, provided with lofty spires[5], glorious with

[1] This translation of the Jātakas bears the Sinhalese title *Pansiyapanasjātaka*. See Geiger, l. c. p. 6. Probably the king was not himself the author of the Jātaka translation. But he may have started the work, and it was an act of courtesy on the part of the translators that they ascribed it to the king. Cf. Wickremasinghe, Catalogue of Sinh. Manuscr. in the Br. Mus., p. 118 ff.; Malalasekera, Pāli Literature of Ceylon, p. 127.

[2] Without doubt this is the present Totagamuva, about a mile north of Hikkaduva not far from the coast in the Galle District. Śrī-Rāhula Thera, the author of the Sāḷalihiṇi-sandesa is called after it.

[3] Vijayabāhu IV. with the epithet of Bodhisatta, thence called "The great" here.

[4] In the description of the architectural works of Parakkamabāhu I in Pulatthinagara *dīghapāsādā* and *cūlapāsādā* are constantly contrasted with each other (see 78. 36, 37, 50). We have evidently to do with particular architectural terms.

[5] See above note to v. 66.

bright-hued painting, and assigned it then to the venerable 91
Grand thera Kāyasatti who dwelt in the Vijayabāhu-pariveṇa[1].
He also granted him a village, called Sālaggāma, on the banks 92
of the river[2] forming the boundary (of the monastery), making
it a possession of the pariveṇa. In fair Titthagāma he had a 93
park laid down, provided with five thousand cocopalms. In 94
Devapura[3] he built a long temple consisting of two storeys,
provided with four pairs of gates for the image of the recumbent
lion[4]. To this temple he assigned the grove-encircled village 95
Gaṇṭhimāna by name which he proclaimed as the property of
the Buddha. In the vihāra of Valligāma[5] the Ruler erected a 96
long pāsāda, consisting of two storeys, which after his own
name, was called Parakkamabāhu(-pāsāda), and granted it the 97
(village) Sāligiri[6] by name as a large maintenance village be-
longing to the Great community. In fair Viddumagāma, not far 98
from the town of Rājagāma he had a splendid vihāra built,
connected with the Sirighanānanda-pariveṇa, with a bodhi tree 99
and an image-house and assigned it to his teacher, the Grand
thera from the Coḷa country[7]. Thereupon he founded in the 100
charming district of Māyādhanu[8] a new town with fine walls
and gate-towers. There he had a fair temple erected to 101
the gods with lofty spires and two storeys, provided with
walls and gate-towers, placed there a glorious statue of 102

[1] Cf. 81. 58.

[2] All the MSS. have *upa sīmanadītīraṃ*. *Sīmanadī* might also be the name of the river. The emendation of the Col. Ed. into *Gimhanadī* (now Ginganga; cf. 75. 22, *gimhatittha* = Gintota) is certainly tempting, but I do not venture a departure from the uniform reading of the MSS.

[3] Devapura or Devanagara = Devundara, Dondra. See 60. 59.

[4] I. e. the recumbent Buddha who is always compared to a lion at rest.

[5] See 80. 38.

[6] W. points to ***Elgiriya***, a village in the Veligama Korale, 6 miles NNE. of Veligama and 10 miles NW. of Matara.

[7] See above v. 80 f.

[8] The territory whose centre was Sītāvaka about 25 miles E. of Colombo.

the lotus-hued King of the gods (Viṣṇu) and celebrated a great sacrificial festival.

103 After performing such and other good deeds for the laity and the Order and many meritorious works, he fell under the power of death.

104 Gifted with the power of meritorious works which he had performed formerly, he after attaining worthless wealth, renounced desire and did nought but good, finding above all pleasure in doing his best[1]. Thinking of what is best for you and on universal impermanance, decide, O ye pious people, whose wealth is faith, for meritorious works[2] amongst which generosity and moral discipline have first place[3].

105 After his death Vannibhuvanekabāhu was king and
106 after his death came King Vijayabāhu. But after the death of these kings the all-wise Bhuvanekabāhu[4], the fourth, was ruler in Gaṅgāsiripura[5] situated in the charming vicinity

[1] The acc. *attattham* must be governed by *rato*. This, it is true, is otherwise construed with the loc.

[2] P. *katvā gaṇhatha* is a verbal combination witnessing to Sinhalese influence. The equivalent in Sinh. for which however, I have no example in the literature, would be *koṭagannavā*. Since *gannavā* gives a reflective sense to the verb to which it is attached, *katvā gaṇhatha* means "do for yourselves what is for your advantage".

[3] With verse 102 or 101 the second part of the Cūlavaṃsa which begins with chapter 80, comes to an end. The MSS. also indicate this. Cf. my ed. I. p. IV of the Introd., as well as the notes to the passage. If we assume that it closed originally with v. 102, which is indicated by two of the MSS., then there was added later a summarizing śloka and then a strophe in artificial metre. Exactly the same thing occurs at the close of the first part (79. 84). The addition was evidently intended to veil the break in the text and lead over to the new part.

[4] (Vanni-) Bhuvanaikabāhu, Vijayabāhu and the fourth Bhuvanaikabāhu are also mentioned by the Nik.-s. and Rājaratn., as successors of Parakkamabāhu IV. The inscription of the Laṅkātilaka-vihāra belongs to Bhuvanekabāhu IV. (see B. Gunasekara, JRAS., C. B. X, nr. 34, 1887, p. 83 ff.). He built this and the Gadaladeniya-vihāra. See note to 91. 30. The King's minister Senālaṅkādhikāra who is named in the inscr., is also mentioned in Nik.-s.

[5] Gampola, see 86. 18.

of the Mahāvālukagaṅgā — a religious man, a mine of fair vir- 107
tues. He who gives heed to tradition, let him know that in 108
the fourth year of his reign, one thousand, eight hundred and
ninety-four years had elapsed since the Nirvana of the Sage[1].
When ye have understood how in antiquity the most ex- 109
cellent men when they had experienced the time hard to
experience[2] of a Buddha, did good unweariedly without ceas-
ing, such as almsgiving and so forth, so ought ye in perfect
fashion to perform all good (deeds).

Here ends the ninetieth Chapter, called «The History of the eight Kings, of Vijayabāhu and his Successors», in the Mahāvaṃsa, compiled for the serene joy and emotion of the pious.

[1] I. e. 1350 A. D. The same in Nik.-s., but Rājaratn. has the figures 1896 = 1352 A. D. Both numbers are approximative. According to the Laṅkātilaka inscription Bhuvanekabāhu IV. ascended the throne already in 1266 of the Śaka era, i. e. 1344-5 A. D. For the whole subject see H. W. Codrington, HC. p. 83. 88.

[2] *Dullabbhanīyam atidullabha-* is merely tautological, *labbhanīya* is furthermore a spurious form, made to suit the metre.

CHAPTER XCI

HISTORY OF THE FOUR KINGS, OF PARAKKAMABĀHU AND HIS SUCCESSORS

1 Now after the death of Bhuvanekabāhu there were two
kings, Parakkamabāhu[1] and the discerning Vikkamabāhu[2].
2 There lived then at the time of Vikkamabāhu in the fair town
known by the name of Peraddoṇī[3], situated in the charming
3 neighbourhood of the Mahā(vāluka)gaṅgā, an eminent prince,
sprung from the Giri family, the discerning Alagakkonāra[4]
4 by name, adorned with majesty, faith and other virtues, full
of the desire to further the laity and the Order, of great might.
5 "The town of Kalyāṇī shines with her palaces, bodhi
trees, her superb cloisters and maṇḍapas, with walls, halls,
image temples and cetiyas, with her gorgeous shops, her
6 splendid gate-towers and arches." Now to the South of
this town Kalyāṇī which is described in such words, which

[1] According to the Hapugastenna inscr. (JRAS., C. B. XXII, nr. 65, p. 362, CODRINGTON, HC., p. 89) Parakkamabāhu V. ascended the throne simultaneously with Bhuvanekabāhu IV. in the year 1344/5. He reigned for a time (probably till 1356/7) with him and after that along with Vikkamabāhu IV. (III. according to C.).

[2] For inscrs. of the time of Vikkamabāhu IV. see BELL, Report on the Kẹgalla District, p. 78. According to the inscr. of Vigulavatta (not far from Gampola), the fourth year of the King's reign coincides with the end of the Saka year 1282 = 1360 A. D., his ascent of the throne falls therefore in 1356/7 A. D.

[3] I. e. Peradeniya not far from Kandy on the Mahaveliganga.

[4] Our chronicle makes short work of the undoubtedly eminent personality of this man. There is a good deal more about the founder of Jayavaḍḍhana in the Rājāv., the Rājaratn. and the Nik.-s. What is above all important is that Alagakkonāra succeeded in breaking the power of the Jaffna king which was then at its height. Cf. also below note to v. 9. For the Kitsirimevan inscription of Kelani and the Alagakkonāra mentioned in it see C. A. L R. I, p. 152; II, p. 149, 182.

was visited by the great Sage, in a place where pious people dwelt, who were devoted[1] to the Buddha and so forth, on the
great lake not far from the spacious village of Dārugāma[2], 7
he built the famous town of Jayavaḍḍhanakoṭṭa[3], embellished with great trains of walls, with gateways, bastions and the
like. While he dwelt in the town, the mighty one, craving 8
for meritorious works, performed many good deeds, such as
the furthering of the Order and the rest. In that town the 9
fifth Bhuvanekabāhu[4] was (king), religious, venerating with constant reverence the Buddha and the other (sacred) objects.

1 The single words in this compound are placed with great freedom. *Buddhādiyuttajanakappitasādhuṭhāne* stands evidently for *buddhādi-yutta-sādhu-jana-kappita-ṭhāne*. *Buddhādi* stands for Buddha, Dhamma and Saṃgha. *Yutta* means in the first place "joined with something", then "hanging on, adhering to something"; *kappita* means "provided with something".

2 The village is called so in the Rājaratn. Thus *Dārūrugāma*° in the Mhvs. stands instead of *uru-Dārugāma*°.

3 Later simply called Cotta by the Portuguese. The town covered what are now the eastern districts of Colombo.

4 As in 90. 64, *āsi*, thus *ahu* must be supplemented by *rājā*, or else *ahu* (*āsi*) has the more pregnant meaning "he lived, he reigned". I do not believe that the Mhvs. considers Bhuvanekabāhu to be the name under which Alagakkonāra reigned. This opinion is found only in the Rājaratn., when it says: *Alagakkōn nam mantrīśvarayāno Bhuvanekabāhu-nam mahāraja-va Gaṅgasiripura rājyaśrīya-ṭa pämiṇa devalova giyēya* "The great minister Alagakkōn by name who had become king under the name of Bhuvanekabāhu went, after enjoying in Gaṅgāsiripura the good fortune of the royal dignity, to the world of the gods." But in the Mhvs. we should, in this case, expect an *iti* or *ti nāmena* after *Bhuvanekabhujo*. The assumption that Alagakkonāra and Bhuvanekabāhu are one and the same has now been given up (cf. JRAS. C. B. XXIV, nr. 68, p. 103, note *) above all because in the Attanagalu-vihāravaṃsa it is said that the work was translated in the Śaka year 1304 (= 1382/3) in the reign of Bhuvanekabāhu, at the instigation of Alakeśvara (or Alagakkonāra). — The tradition followed by the Rājaratn. probably confuses Alagakkonāra with his son Vīra Alakeśvara who (under the name of Vijayabāhu) is said to have reigned a number of years as king, though after Vīrabāhu's death. For further particulars see E. W. Perera, Alakéswara: his Life and Times, JRAS. C. B. xviii, Nr. 55 (1904), p. 281 ff.; H. W. Codrington, HC., p. 85, 89. Cf. below, note to v. 14.

10 To the community he dispensed in abundant measure regular repasts and other alms and to achieve the furtherance of the
11 Order, he gathered the bhikkhus together, ascertained those who lived immoral lives and had them cast forth from the Order, but he showed favour to the conscientious obtained for them the precedence and so made the Order of the Victor
12 shine. For seven thousand pieces of silver he had a casket fashioned, preserved in it the Tooth Relic and sacrificed to it in lasting reverence.

13 When the time of this King — after he had held sway for twenty years[1] — had expired, a man called Vīrabāhu
14 attained the royal dignity, did likewise all (that was good) such as furthering the Order and fell under the power of the King of death[2].

[1] The 20th year of the reign of Bhuvanekabāhu V. falls in the year 1391/2 A. D., the beginning of the reign accordingly in 1372/3. It seems, however, that he reigned for some time, if only in name, together with Vīrabāhu. Cf. S. de Silva, Vijaya Báhu VI., JRAS. C. B. xxii, no. 65, p. 316 ff.; H. W. Codrington, HC. p. 89. In the inscription on the Alampundi plate (see V. Venkayya, EI. III, p. 224 ff.) King Virūpākṣa of the Vijayanagara Dynasty, boasts that he had vanquished the kings of the Tuṇḍīra, Coḷa and Pāṇḍya as well as the Siṃhala. The inscr. is dated in the Śaka year 1305 for 1307 = 1383/4.

[2] The Mhvs. passes over here a very remarkable episode in the history of Ceylon the knowledge of which we owe above all to Chinese sources. (Cf. J. M. Senaveratne according to Sylvain Lévi, JRAS. C. B. xxiv, nr. 68, p. 98 ff; further xxviii, nr. 73, p. 31 ff.) and to the Rājāv. From the different sources we gather that the son of the great Alagakkonāra, Vīra Alakeśvara, under the name of Vijayabāhu (VI.) seized the royal dignity in battle with his brother Vīrabāhu. During his reign in Jayavaḍḍhanakoṭṭa a Chinese expedition of the Emperor Yung-lo under the leadership of Tsheng-huo came to Ceylon. The Chinese came into conflict with the Sinhalese ruler who is called A-le-ko-na-r (Alagakkonāra) and took the king away with them as prisoner. The Rājāv. calls the leader of the Chinese Mahā-Cīn-Dosraja, the king taken prisoner by him, Vijayabāhu. Here then instead of the family name, the adopted name is given. Now it seems to me that by confusing this Vijayabāhu (VI) with V. IV. the above discussed gap in the Rājāv. is explained (note to 90. 1). The probability of a mistake is supported by the fact that the Rājāv. speaks of four younger brothers of King V. who are said to

Then at a later time, in the year one thousand nine 15
hundred and fifty-three after the final Nirvana of the holy
Enlightened One, came King Parakkamabāhu[1], an abode 16
of wisdom and manly virtue, a scion of the race of the Sun,
in the charming town named Jayavaḍḍhana — to the in-
comparable, sublime fortune of the royal dignity and with
faith in the three (sacred) jewels, he set about the holding of
a festival. For the tooth of the Prince of the wise the Ruler 17
built a three-storeyed, splendid pāsāda which offered a superb
sight. Then he fashioned a golden casket, fair, beautifully 18
set with the nine precious stones, and another casket in the
form of a shell, gleaming in manifold splendour and set with
the most exquisite jewels and which held the first casket; and
yet another golden casket into which he also put the second.
Finally the King who strove after salvation in the present as 19

have been murdered. Now Vijayabāhu IV. had in fact four brothers according to Mhvs. 87. 16-17. According to the Rājāv. the capture took place A. B. 1958 = 1404 A. D. For the whole see CODRINGTON HC. p. 85 f., 89. If one accepts this Vijayabāhu who is omitted in the Mhvs., as the sixth of the name in the list of the kings, then instead of Vijayabāhu VI. (92. 4) one must read Vijayabāhu VII.

[1] The Mhvs. has nothing to say about the events which preceded the reign of Parakkamabāhu VI. Cf. for this H. W. CODRINGTON, HC., p. 85 ff., 89. The date given in the Mhvs. for the beginning of the reign 1953 A. B. = 1409 A. D. is also found in the Saddharmālaṅkāraya. In another passage however in this work the date is given as 1958 A. B. = 1414 A. D. The same in the inscr. of Pepiliyana (see below, note to v. 24). It may be assumed as probable that Parakkamabāhu VI. came to the throne in 1412, remained three years in Rayigam (District Kalutara, Census of Ceylon 1921, II, p. 44) and removed in 1415 to Jayavaḍḍhana where the coronation took place. The Mhvs. has hardly anything of historical value either to tell us about the reign of Parakkamabāhu VI., except perhaps in v. 24, that his mother's name was Sunettā. It is a great pity that the compiler of the third part of the Cūlavs. restricts himself almost entirely to stereotyped descriptions of festivals for the Tooth Relic. Our knowledge of modern events is gained from quite other sources. In the first place there is the Rājāvalī, also in the version given by Valentyn (Oud en Nieuw Oost-Indien, vol. V); further Do Couto and De Barros (see D. FERGUSON, The History of Ceylon, from the Earliest Times to 1600 A. D. as related by de Barros and do Couto,

in future existences[1], made a (fourth) large, incomparably
magnificent casket which he covered with gold of the finest
lustre, and in these four superb caskets he placed the tooth.
20 Then calling to mind all the festivals in Laṅkā celebrated by
kings who were filled with pure reverence for the sacred Order
of the Enlightened One, he thought: "I too will in like manner
venerate him unweariedly with all the produce of my king-
21 dom[2]." With such reverential thoughts he celebrated in his
faith sacrificial festivals in all manner of ways for the relics
and the like. To the community he dispensed regular repasts,
22 together with the eight articles of equipment, month by
month, as well as every year sacrificial offerings and a gift
23 of kaṭhina robes for the bhikkhus in the three provinces and
a great almsgiving in pious fashion and garments every year
and thereby he, the highly famed, who longed for merit, laid
24 up merit. In memory of his mother the meritorious (King)
had erected in the Pappaṭa grove[3] in her name the Sunetra-
25 pariveṇa[4] and a monastery for the community and granted it
many villages and fields[5]. Then putting down in that selfsame
26 place an abundant alms destined for the community, to be
distributed for three days among the ascetics who had come

JRAS. C. B. xx, nr. 60 (1909), p. 1 ff.). For the reign of Parakkamabāhu VI. I refer the reader besides CODRINGTON, l. c. p. 90 ff., 99 f., to E. W. PERERA, The Age of Srí Parákrama Bábu VI., JRAS. C. B. XXII, nr. 63 (1911), p. 6 ff. For inscriptions of this king see E. MÜLLER, AIC. no. 160; H. C. P. BELL, Report on the Kégalla District, p. 81 ff.

[1] This is probably the meaning of *bhavavibhava*. Cf. below v. 36.

[2] In these last paricchedas the language is treated with extraordinary arbitrariness. The construction of the compounds and the position of the words in them is often quite contrary to rule. The translation can therefore only give the general meaning of such passages.

[3] The name is preserved in that of the Pepiliyana-vihāra not far from Colombo (Census, 1921, vol. II, p. 36). An inscription in this monastery is dated in the 39 th year of the reign of Parakkamabāhu VI. The date of his ascent of the throne is given as A. B. 1958 = 1514.

[4] Sunetrā or Sunetradevī, the wife of Vijayabāhu (VI.) who is supposed to be the father of Parakkamabāhu VI., was a Kālinga princess.

[5] *Gāmakhette* is governed by *pūjetvā* in 25 c. Thus in my edition the comma must be placed after *pūjetvā*, not after *tapassinaṃ*.

from the three provinces, he laid up in pious fashion an abundance
of merit. He had the sacred three Piṭakas together with the 27
commentaries and the ṭīkās copied and caused a summary of
the teaching of the Buddha[1] (to be made). He also granted 28
villages and the like to the scribes, that they might copy day
by day the books of the true doctrine. Whatever had fallen 29
into decay on the Mahiyaṅgaṇa-cetiya and other cetiyas every-
where he had renewed and the plaster coating repaired. In 30
the same way he had all the stucco work and so forth carried
out on the Gaṇḍālādoṇī monastery and on the Laṅkātilaka[2]
and others. While celebrating a great feast and a great 31
sacrificial festival he repeatedly had the ceremony of admission
to the Order performed. Thus the wise Lord of men having 32
taken on himself the burden of government and wrought good
for fifty and two years[3], bestowed on the bhikkhu community, 33
serving it in faith, twenty-six thousand one hundred and forty
times the three garments and other articles of equipment and 34
three thousand four hundred and thirty-two kaṭhina robes.
Piously devoted to the three (sacred) objects he who greatly 35
venerated the Order of the Victor, dispensed immeasurable
wealth and in this wise did all kinds of good.

Dowered with faith, discernment and charitableness, a superb 36
jewel of virtue, he recognizing the worthlessness of acquired
riches, performed in such wise, continually, unweariedly meri-
torious works. When ye have understood that, ye as those
who know and are striving after salvation in this existence
and in future existences[4], should also continually and in the

[1] I take *buddhassa sāsanasaṃgahaṃ akā* to mean this and refer the reader to titles of books like Abhidhammatthasaṃgaha, Paccayasaṃgaha, Saddhammasaṃgaha etc. W. gives a totally different rendering. He takes *saṃgaha* in the sense of "kindliness, protection, favour" and translates: "encouraged the religion of Buddha". It seems to me, moreover, that in vv. 27 and 28 special stress is laid on the literary activity of the King. Of course he only suggested the work.

[2] Both vihāras, Gadaladeniya and Lankatilaka are situated not far from Kandy.

[3] Rājāv. and Rājaratn. have the same.

[4] See above note to v. 19.

right way do a quantity of meritorious works[1] which bestow you many a happiness.

Here ends the ninety-first chapter, called «History of the Four Kings, of Parakkamabāhu and his Successors», in the Mahāvaṃsa, compiled for the serene joy and emotion of the pious.

[1] For *katvā gaṇhātha* cf. 90. 104 with the note.

CHAPTER XCII

HISTORY OF THE SEVEN KINGS, OF JAYABĀHU AND HIS SUCCESSORS

After his death, his grandson Jayabāhu[1] became king; 1
then Bhuvanekabāhu, after he had murdered him (Jayabāhu).
After obtaining the royal consecration, he lived seven years. 2
After his death Parakkamabāhu known on account of his
learning by the name of Paṇḍita, was king in that fair town, 3
and hereafter Vīraparakkamabāhu. On his death Vijaya- 4

[1] The kings in vv. 1—5 are numbers 168 (169) to 113 (175) of my list. Parakkamabāhu VIII. had two sons: Vijayabāhu VI. (VII.) and (Dharma)pakkamabāhu IX. Both seem to have been made co-regents by their father in the year 1509. But Parakkamabāhu IX., although he lived at least till 1528, was apparently of no great influence. He is not at all mentioned in our chronicle. — The Rājāv. makes Vīra-Parakkamabāhu, not Jayabāhu, the successor of Parakkamabāhu VI. The same name appears again however later as that of Paṇḍita-Parakkamabāhu's successor. The Rājaratn. inserts a king Vīrabāhu before Jayabāhu to whom a reign of 12 years is ascribed. The list of the kings (= Mhvs. 92. 1-5) in the Sinhalese chronicles is as follows:

Rājāv.	Vīra-Parakkamabāhu (1468–1472/3)	Rājaratn.	Vīrabāhu (12 yrs.) Jayabāhu
	Bhuvanekabāhu (VI) (7 yrs.) (1472/3—1480/1)	„	Bhuvanekabāhu
	Paṇḍita-Parakkamabāhu (VII) 1480/1—1484	„	Paṇḍita-Parakkamabāhu
	Vīra-Parakkamabāhu (VIII) (20 yrs.) ? 1484—1518	„	Vikrama-Parakkamabāhu
	Dharma-Parakkamabāhu (22 yrs.) 1509—1528		
	Vijayabāhu (VI) 1509—1521		
	Buvanekabāhu (VII) 1521—1551		Bhuvanekabāhu

bāhu was king whose adornment was his virtue, and after
5 his death Bhuvanekabāhu was king. And after these kings,
each according to his faith and his power, had achieved the
furtherance of the laity and the Order, they went thither in
accordance with their deeds.

6 Now Vīravikkama a mighty man, sprung from the line
of Sirisaṃghabodhi[1], became king in the year two thousand
and eighty-four after the final Nirvana of the Enlightened One[2].
7 Dwelling in the town of Seṅkhaṇḍasela-Sirivaḍḍhana[3], beautifi-
8 ed by the course of the Mahāvālukagaṅgā, he gladdened his
subjects by the four heart-winning qualities and undertook in
9 his faith meritorious works. The fair relic of the Prince of
the wise he brought to a piece of land charmingly situated
10 not far from his royal palace. Then he built a cetiya and

The years of the reigns are given according to CODRINGTON (HC., p. 93 ff.) Inscriptions: Bhuvanekabāhu VI.: inscr. of Dedigama, BELL, Report of Kegalla Dist., p. 83 ff.; Vijayabāhu VI., ibid. p. 85 ff. (on the Kelani inscr. and Dharma-Parakkamabāhu, ibid. p. 86); Bhuvanekabāhu VII., JRAS. C. B. XXII, no. 65, p. 267 ff. See further below, note to 95. 5. The history and chronology of Ceylon at the end of the Middle Ages suffer particularly from the fact that the island was not under one dominion but was split up into several kingdoms. Thus kings who were contemporaries are represented as succeeding one another. The kings in the above list reigned in Koṭṭe (Dharma-Parakkamabāhu perhaps in Kelani). Then in addition to these there are the dynasties of Sītāvaka and Kandy. Vīravikkama (v. 6) is according to WICKREMASINGHE (EZ. III. p. 44) probably identical with Kumāra Baṇḍāra, the son of Vijaya Baṇḍāra who reigned in Kandy at the time of Vijayabāhu VI. (VII.) and Bhuvanekabāhu VII.

[1] Mhvs. 36. 73 ff.

[2] = 1540 A. D. Rājaratn. has 2085 A. B. = 1541 A. D.

[3] I. e. Kandy. The account evidently goes back here to the rise of the kingdom of Kandy, the high country (*uḍa-raṭa*) that did its utmost to preserve its independence as against the kings in Koṭṭe and Sītāvaka until it fell under the power of Rājasīha in 1580. It is regrettable that the compiler has no interest in political questions, but considers only the relations of the kings to the Order. To judge by the number of figures contained in his narrative, it looks as if he had consulted a *puññapotthaka* (cf. Mhvs. 32. 25 ff.) i. e. a book in which the meritorious works of the king are inscribed.

near to it a two-storeyed house for the Uposatha[1] ceremony,
as well as round about the town eighty-six dwellings for the 11
community furnished with a roofing of brick and so forth,
made the bhikkhus take up their abode here and there,
granted them maintenance and heard preached the true doc-
trine of the Victor. After celebrating a magnificent sacrificial 12
festival, he hearkened in faith to fifty-five sermons of the
doctrine the preaching whereof lasted the whole night. On 13
thirty thousand leaves he had (sacred) books written down
and to the Tipiṭaka he made an offering of sixty thousand
(gold pieces). He had one hundred and eighty images made 14
of the Enlightened One and one hundred and thirty caskets
for the placing therein of relics and so laid up a store of
meritorious works. He left his town, wandered on foot[2] for 15
a day a distance of seven gāvutas[3] and venerated Mahiyaṅgaṇa 16
by celebrating with divers fragrant flowers, with lamps,
frankincense and the like, a great festival. The Ruler of men 17
betook himself also in one day to the Sumanakūṭa[4] and sacrificed
there by pouring one hundred jars of oil into a lamp fifteen
cubits in girth and five cubits high[5]. [Since his desire was fixed 18
on the highest path[6], he had the impassable road[7] put in

[1] P. *dvibhūmakaṃ uposathamālakaṃ* is curious. *Mālaka* is otherwise only an enclosed open space, a courtyard, serving for the holding of certain ceremonies. *Dvibhūmaka* as attribute of *mālaka* is unsuitable. In other instances moreover, we have only *uposathagga, uposathāgāra, uposathaghara*, showing that a house is meant. If this were not the case in our verse we might have here a structure of the type of a "double platform", E. R. Ayrton, Memoirs, ASC. I. p. 18 ff.; A. M. Hocart, ibid., p. 57 ff.; the same in Codrington, HC. p. 186.

[2] Lit. with the power of his own feet.

[3] I. e. about 14 miles. Mahiyaṅgaṇa, now Alut-nuvara, is 24 miles distant from Kandy as the crow flies. The King's pilgrimage is of course to the Mahiyaṅgaṇa-thūpa.

[4] Adam's Peak cannot be reached in one day from Kandy.

[5] The meaning of the passage is clear, but the language incorrect. The circumference of the bowl into which the oil was poured, would be about 22 ft. the height about 7 ft.

[6] I. e. on the road leading to the highest perfection, to salvation, the path of good works.

[7] Of course the road up to Adam's Peak.

order and provided, for the convenience of the (pilgrims) going
19 to and fro, with seven hundred and eighty stone steps. After
the Ruler had in this and other ways performed many meritorious works, he thought to hold the ceremony of admission
20 to the Order.] The wise (Prince) had many dwellings put
up on the bank of the river. Thither he brought the bhikkhus
21 dwelling in the three provinces and instituted a great festival.
Then after specially inviting from among those bhikkhus a
body of thirty-five bhikkhus with the Grand thera Dhammakitti at the head, he made them celebrate a great festival
22 and grant admission to the Order to three hundred and fifty-five able sons of good family whom he had himself chosen
23 out. The King heard that in the town of Pāṭaliputta[1] (in
days of yore), the Ruler of men Mahāsena had fed daily a
24 community of one thousand bhikkhus, but unsatisfied even
with this magnificent effort, he had thought of giving alms
25 by the cultivation of a piece of land[2]. He had surrendered
the bliss of the royal dignity, betaken himself to the northern
town of Madhurā[3], there laboured and with the grain produced,
26 had in faith made an offering of alms. When[4] he heard this
the wise (Prince) who had joy in a pure gift of alms, cultivated a rice field with his own bodily powers and instituted
with the grain produced, in blameless fashion, an offering of
27 alms. With faith in the three (sacred) objects he presented

[1] Capital of the Maurya dynasty, now Patna in the province of Bihār on the Ganges.

[2] P. *vatthusuddhiṃ kāritvāna*, lit. "after he had carried out the cleansing of a piece of ground." Field cultivation is considered the purest and noblest work. An offering of that which has been acquired by such work, an offering of field products is therefore characterized as *suddhadāna* (v. 26).

[3] The town Madhurā or Mathurā on the Yamunā (Jumna), to distinguish it from the South Indian Madhurā (51. 33 etc.) is called the "Northern Madhurā".

[4] Vv. 23—26 are one sentence; *dinnadānaṃ* in v. 26 is a object directly governed by *sutvāna*. The preceding verses with *Mahāseno* as subject are however, so constructed as if it were *dānaṃ adāsīti sutvāna*. The author fails in the construction.

an offering of two thousand one hundred and eighty-two
garments. Spending five hundred and eighty-seven thousand 28
pieces of money, the King had meritorious works performed
therewith. Sixty and two elephants and horses and four 29
hundred and fifty head of cattle and buffaloes did the Ruler
of men offer in sacrifice. Striving thus and in many other 30
ways after good, he performed many meritorious works and
made himself a pathway to heaven.

Thus he performed in faith, steadfast, rejoicing in the 31
welfare of others, after discerning the worthlessness of acquired corporeal existence and other (possessions), in pious manner many meritorious works which bring many a happiness. If ye then have discerned this, as people who have great fear of the terrible evil of the cycle of rebirths, then must ye, remembering what is of true worth, relinquish all desire for corporeal existence and the like (possessions) and strive unweariedly after meritorious works.

Here ends the ninety-second chapter, called «History of the Seven Kings, of Jayabāhu and his Successors», in the Mahāvaṃsa, compiled for the serene joy and emotion of the pious.

CHAPTER XCIII

HISTORY OF THE TWO KINGS, OF MĀYĀDHANU AND OF HIS SUCCESSOR

1 At his death there resided in the province bordering on
the sea-coast, in the fair and renowned Jayavaḍḍhanakoṭṭa
2 (and elsewhere) here and there kings sprung from the race
of the Sun. Amongst these there was one, the illustrious Ruler
3 of men, Māyādhanu[1] by name. His son was the mighty
Rājasīha by name. He went forth, fought here and there

[1] It is characteristic of the attitude of the author of this part of the Cūlavaṃsa and of his indifference to the significant events happening in the plains, that the Portuguese are not yet mentioned. They landed in 1505 or 1506 (cf. D. Ferguson, The Discovery of Ceylon by the Portuguese in 1506, JRAS. C. B. XIX, No. 59 (1907), p. 284 ff.) and had their chief seat in Colombo, in the fort which they had built there. It is just as characteristic that a man of the importance of Māyādhanu (Māyādunne) is dismissed with the mention of his name. He was the youngest brother of Bhuvanekabāhu VII., and at the division of the kingdom in A. D. 1521, had received the region between the coast land and the mountains with Sītāvaka as capital. Sītāvaka is the present Avisavella about 26 miles east of Colombo, situated on a left tributary of the Kelaniganga. In a series of severe and fluctuating struggles with his brother and his successor, as well as with the Portuguese, for the supreme dominion in Ceylon, Māyādunne maintained himself successfully till his death in 1581. Dharmapāla (1550--1597) the feeble successor of Bhuvanekabāhu VII. who was completely dependent on the Portuguese, adopting Christianity (about 1557) in order to maintain himself with their help — is not even mentioned in the Mahāvaṃsa. As a historical source our chronicle is now hardly of any value at all. Of native sources there is only the Rājāvalī left and it has many defects. Our main information now comes from the Portuguese accounts, above all João Ribeiro, Fatalidade historica, Lissabon 1836 (translated into English by P. E. Pieris under the title "The Historic Tragedy of Ceilão", Colombo

and won the victory. The victor, the great fool, even slew 4
his own father[1] and brought the royal dignity into his power,
the deluded one. In the town of Sītāvaka the King known 5
by the name of Rājasīha, for a time did good, devoted in faith
to the Order. But one day the King, after he had brought 6
a gift of alms, asked the Grand theras full of anxiety: "How
can I undo the crime of my father's murder?" Then the wise 7
theras expounded him the doctrine[2], but could not win over
the wicked mind of this fool. They spake: "To undo the 8
committed crime is impossible". Full of fury like some terrible
poisonous snake which has been struck by a stick, he asked 9
the adherents of Siva[3]. The answer they gave him that it

1925, 3rd ed.) and Fernão de Queiroz, Conquista temporal e spiritual de Ceylão, Colombo, Government Press, 1916. These sources have been utilized by P. E. Pieris. Taking up the work begun by D. Ferguson (cf. above, as well as note to 91. 15), Pieris published in the JRAS. XXII, No. 65, p. 267 ff., first the important article "The Date of Bhuvanekabāhu VII.", the result of which was a complete transformation of the chronology of Ceylon in the 16th century. Then there appeared "Ceylon, the Portuguese Era" in 2 vols. Colombo, 1913-14 and "Ceylon and the Portuguese 1505-1658", Ceylon, 1920. (Cf. with this S. G. Perera, the 'Conquista de Ceylão' by Fernão de Queyroz, S. J. in C. A. L. R. II, p. 158 ff.; 263 ff.; H. W. Codrington, HC., p. 94 ff.). Then for a part of the 16th century there are the lately published Portuguese archives: "*Ceylon in the time of King Bhuvanekabāhu and Franz Xavers* 1539-1552", published and annotated by G. Schurhammer and E. A. Vorretsch, 2 vols. Leipzig, 1928. Again "*Ceylon and Portugal*", pt. I., Kings and Christians 1539-1552, from the original documents at Lisbon, by P. E. Pieris and M. A. H. Fitzler. Schurhammer's Introduction to the first volume of the work mentioned above, gives a complete bibliography, a sketch of the history of the Island 1539-1552 from the Portuguese documents and a detailed analysis of the narratives hitherto existing.

[1] Whether Rājasīha who was a magnificent general and had distinguished himself at the age of 11 by his bravery, was really his father's murderer, may be doubted. Cf. note below to v. 9.

[2] I now prefer to read *tassa dhammaṃ* instead of *tass' adhammaṃ*.

[3] The motives alleged here for Rājasīha's conversion to Hinduism scarcely accord with the facts. The real reason for it was that the Buddhist priesthood who had always been favoured by him and his father Māyādunne, actually joined a conspiracy got up against him by

was possible, he received like ambrosia, smeared his body with
10 ashes and adopted the religion of Siva. He annihilated the
Order of the Victor, slew the community of the bhikkhus,
11 burned the sacred books, destroyed the monasteries and thus
barred his way to heaven. Become a (dead) tree-trunk in the
12 cycle of rebirths, he adopted a false faith. He placed miscreant
ascetics of false faith on the Sumanakūṭa to take for them-
13 selves all the profit accruing therefrom. In this way the
impious fool as he did not know what he should accept and
accepted what he should not have accepted, brought great evil
upon himself.

14 At that time through fear of the King, bhikkhus left the
Order; those among them who were swayed by fear of the
cycle of rebirths, went hither and tither.

15 Harming the welfare of the whole laity and of the stainless
Order of the Buddha, he carried on the government only in
16 virtue of merit formerly acquired. Dowered with sovereign
might, the criminal brought the whole island of Laṅkā into
his power and carried on the government[1].

17 Thus this monarch, equipped with royal might, manifested
his sovereign power; but after heaping up every kind of crime,
he fell under the dominion of Māra. When one thus perceives
the misfortune that meets one who through sinful and false
belief has become the victim of delusion, one should in fear,
free from all inclination to carelessness, bring about much
blessing.

Here ends the ninety-third chapter, called «History of the Two Kings, of Māyādhanu and of his Successor», in the Mahāvaṃsa, compiled for the serene joy and emotion of the pious.

the Portuguese. To justify their treacherous conduct, these clerics may also have invented the murder of Rājasīha. Cf. Pieris 2, p. 94. See also W. F. Guṇawardhana, Raja Siṃha I., Parricide and Centenarian, JRAS. C. B. xviii, Nr. 56 (1905), p. 382 ff.

[1] The year of his death is given by the Rājāv. as 1514 of the Śaka era = 1592/3 A. D. How great was the admiration of the people for this "last great king of the Sinhalese race" is shown by the fact that even to-day he receives divine honours under the name of Ganegoda Deviyo. Pieris 2., p. 114.

CHAPTER XCIV

HISTORY OF KING VIMALADHAMMASURIYA

In the days of this King a scion of the Sun Dynasty in 1
Gaṅgāsiripura had betaken himself to the harbour of Kolamba[1].
As he did not receive permission to remain there, he went to 2
the province of Gova. After he had dwelt here a long time,
he slew a mighty and famous chieftain by name Gajabāhu[2]. 3
After the victory he received distinctions of many kinds, and
because in his prudence he understood the favorable moment, 4
returned to Laṅkā. The mighty one brought the troops of
the five districts of the highland country over to his side
and after the death of (Rājasīha) the slayer of his father,[3] 5
when the year two thousand, one hundred and thirty-five
from the nirvana of the Master[4] had arrived, he (the prince), 6
full of faith, mighty by reason of his merit, became king
under the name of Vimaladhammasuriya, highly famed, in
the town of Sirivaḍḍhana.

[1] Konappu, later Vimaladhammasuriya was a son of Virasundara who belonged to the royal house. Vīrasundara was partisan of Rājasīha, but was slain by him for having conspired against him. His son fled to Colombo (*Kolambatittha*) to the puppet king Dhammapāla. Later he was banished to Goa (*Govaraṭṭha*) where he succeeded in gaining the confidence of the Portuguese. PIERIS 2, p. 92 f., 112; CODRINGTON, HC., p. 105.

[2] It was the case of a duel with a pugnacious officer. The episode is related also in the Rājāv. (p. 92 of B. GUṆASEKARA's translation). Konappu's success may have drawn the attention of the Portuguese to him.

[3] Rājasīha is called *pitughāta* here not on account of the murder of his father Māyādhanu, but on account of that of Vīrasundara.

[4] A. B. 2135 = 1591 A. D. The date is right.

7 He surrounded the whole of the vast city with a massive
8 wall on the heights of which he had placed at intervals eighteen
tower structures. Then to ward off the foe, he posted sentries,
9 freed the whole kingdom of Laṅkā from all oppression and
after he had raised a princess of equal birth to the rank of
10 first mahesī and had received his consecration as King, this
famous (prince) who in his faith desired meritorious works,
11 set about furthering the laity and the Order. The Ruler of
men reflected where the tooth of the Enlightened One could
be, and when he heard it was in the Labujagāma-vihāra[1], he
12 rejoiced greatly. He had the Tooth Relic which had been
brought to Labujagāma in the province of Saparagamu[2] fetched
13 (thence) and in order to venerate it day by day in his own
fair town and to dedicate a ritual to it, the wise (prince) had
14 a two-storeyed, superb relic temple erected on an exquisitely
beautiful piece of ground in the neighbourhood of the royal
palace. Here he placed the tooth and in lasting devotion
brought offerings to it.

15 As there were no bhikkhus in the island of Laṅkā on whom
the ceremony of admission to the Order had been performed[3], the
King sent officials to the country of Rakkhaṅga, invited
16 Nandicakka and other bhikkhus, had them brought to the is-
land of Laṅkā, made them take up their abode in the noble
city of Sirivaḍḍhana and cared for them in reverent manner.
17 Then in the Mahāvālukagaṅgā, at the landing-place called
Gaṇṭhamba, within a boundary drawn in the water[4], he had

[1] I. e. Delgamuva, not far from Kuruvita, north of Ratnapura. The relic was preserved before that in Kotte. Cf. 91. 17 ff. Why it was taken from there to the monastery in Delgamuva is not known. Probably the idea was to save it from the Portuguese.

[2] Now Sabaragamuva. The province which stretches in front of the south-western slopes of the central mountains, bounded on the West by the West province and on the South by the South province.

[3] The cause of this decay of the Buddhist Church was in all probability due to the hostile attitude of Rājasīha towards it. Rakkhaṅga is the name of a district in Lower Burma, now Arakan. Cf. for this Pieris 2, p. 141.

[4] P. *udakukkhepasīmāyaṃ*. For this term see note to 89. 70.

a fine building erected and thither in the year two thousand, 18
one hundred and forty after the nirvana of the Victor[1], he
led the bhikkhus, had the ceremony of admission to the Order 19
performed in this Great bhikkhu community on many of the
sons of good family and thus protected the Order of the
Enlightened One. And he also made many sons of good birth 20
submit themselves to the ceremony of renunciation of the world
and provided them also abundantly with the four articles of
use, and after he had in this and many other ways, striving 21
after good, performed many meritorious works, he cleared him-
self a pathway to heaven. Later the selfsame wise King 22
made his younger brother[2] who had gone through the cere-
mony of renunciation of the world and (as member) was in
the Order of the Buddha, leave the Order, entrusted him with
the burden of the government and then passed away in ac-
cordance with his deeds[3].

In this wise the Monarch equipped with kingly power, 23
after performing many meritorious works, adorning the
Order of the Victor, made manifest a blameless sovereign

[1] 2140 A. B. = 1596 A. D.

[2] Senāratana was Vimaladhammasuriya's cousin. We know however (see note to 63. 51) that cousins who are brother's sons call themselves brothers.

[3] Rājāv. gives as the year of his death 1525 of the Śaka era = 1603/4 A. D. Of the mighty events which took place during the reign of Vimaladhammasuriya I. the Mahāvaṃsa says not a word. The whole period was filled with wars against the Portuguese and their protegé Dharmapāla which were carried on both sides with the greatest bitterness and even cruelty. In A. D. 1594 the Sinhalese destroyed a Portuguese force which had advanced to Kandy. Three years later Dharmapāla died after reigning nominally in Kotte 47 years. In his will he left his kingdom to the King of Portugal. The Portuguese solemnly took possession of the lowlands in the name of their sovereign. The kingdom of Kandy maintained its independence. During the reign of Vimaladhammasuriya the Sinhalese came for the first time into contact with the Dutch through the embassy under *Joris van Spilbergen* which coming from the east coast of the Island in 1602, visited the court of Kandy. For the whole subject cf. PIERIS 2, p. 112-165; CODRINGTON, HC., p. 105 ff.

power[1]. And yet such a discerning man whose highest good was religion[2], fell under the power of Māra: when one has once realised the permanent condition of misery and of all other (suffering), one must find his joy in unwearied striving.

Here ends the ninety-fourth chapter, called «History of King Vimaladhammasuriya», in the Mahāvaṃsa, compiled for the serene joy and emotion of the pious.

[1] The first two lines of the strophe resemble in wording the final strophe of 93.

[2] The sing. *caturo saddhādhano tādiso* must be referred to *mahipo*; *iti* is, as so often, placed within the sentence, instead of behind *tādiso*.

CHAPTER XCV

HISTORY OF KING SENĀRATANA

After Senāratana by name had received consecration as 1
king, dowered with meritorious works, such as generosity and
the rest and at all times full of reverence, he inclined his 2
subjects to him by the four heart-winning qualities. He
celebrated a festival for the Tooth Relic and a great alms-
giving. The mahesī of the (late) king who had been his elder 3
brother[1] he made his own first mahesī and dwelt in that same
town (of Sirivaḍḍhana).

At that time merchants in the seaport of Kolamba who 4
had sojourned there a long time, had become puffed up with
pride[2]. They were, all of them, the so-called Paraṅgi[3], he- 5
retical evil-doers, cruel and brutal. They spread themselves
over several fair provinces, laid waste fields and gardens, 6
burned down houses and villages, destroyed the noble families
and in this wise brought ruin on Sīhala. They broke into 7
the towns, into the relic shrines and monasteries, destroyed
the image houses, Bodhi trees, Buddha statues and so on, did 8
great harm to the laity and the Order, built at various places

[1] The wife of Vimaladhammasuriya I. (see note to 94. 22) Dona Catherina, who was considered the rightful heiress to the kingdom of Kandy. Vimala had married her to give his reign a semblance of legitimacy. Pieris, 2, p. 125.

[2] P. *ussannaka*. W. "they waxed very strong", which is of course also possible.

[3] I. e. Franks, designation of the Portuguese who are mentioned here for the first time at a period when their power was declining. What is said in the sequel about the Portuguese agrees with what we know about Azavedo's procedure.

9 forts[1] and carried on war[2] unceasingly. King Senāratana
brought the Tooth Relic to a safe place in the province
called Pañcasata[3], almost impassable owing to forests, moun-
10 tains and rivers, made people dwell there who were entrusted
with the preservation of the relic and thus protected the Tooth
11 Relic well, showing it the usual reverence. Then he left the
city (Sirivaḍḍhana). Movable goods, the sons of the former
12 king and the admirable Mahesī, excellent by wealth and virtue,
who was pregnant, he took carefully with him in a litter[4]
13 and betook himself to Mahiyaṅgaṇa[5]. While he sojourned in
this town the Queen bore under a particularly favorable con-
14 stellation, a splendid son[6], dowered with brilliant marks. At
that time the leader of the foe saw at night a terror-stirring
dream. From the east[7], from that town (Mahiyaṅgaṇa) there
15 came a spark of the size of a glow-worm. Growing ever bigger
it came to the centre of Kolamba, waxed here to unmeasured
16 size and burned up everything at once. On that day in con-
sequence of its splendour, the enemy who had penetrated to
Sirivaḍḍhana, took flight with the haste of those who are
17 threatened with peril. The Ruler of men guarded his son

[1] P. *balakoṭṭake bandhitvā*. Cf. the name of the town Jayavaḍḍhanakoṭṭa (91. 7), called Kotte for short.

[2] P. *yujjhamānā ṭhitā*, a periphrastic formation corresponding to the Sinh. combination of the present gerund in *min* with the verb *siṭinavā*. See Geiger, Literatur und Sprache der Singhalesen § 63a. The root *ṭhā* expresses a continuous state.

[3] I. e. Pansiyapattu or Dumbara, NE. of Kandy.

[4] P. *yoggena*, no doubt rightly explained by W.

[5] In the year 1611 A. D. the Portuguese general de Azavedo advanced as far as Kandy. He found the town deserted and placing a garrison in Balane to secure the entrance to the mountains, he returned to Colombo. This is connected no doubt with what is related in v. 11-12. The date of the prince's birth must have been 1612 (see next note).

[6] This is the son of Senāratana and Dona Catherina, the widow of his predecessor. He was called Mahā-Āsthāna and later as king called himself Rājasīha. His stepbrothers Kumārasīha and Vijayapāla were the Queen's sons by her first marriage. See below v. 22.

[7] P. *puratthimadisābhāgā*. Wrongly translated "from the western side" by W.

who grew by degrees like another moon, and the other (sons)
with the greatest care, and when he saw that the right time 18
had come, he took all his possessions and returned to the city
of Sirivaḍḍhana. When his sons, namely the sons of the former 19
king and his own son, were grown up he, because his heart
clung to them in love, was minded to divide amongst them 20
his mountain-girt provinces, had (their names) properly written
on three leaves, laid the leaves near the Tooth Relic[1], led the 21
princes thither and made them take their choice. Then when 22
the Ruler beheld the leaves which fell in this wise: to the
eldest Kumārasīha the province Ūva, to Vijayapāla the pro-
vince Mātula and to the youngest Rājasīha the five highland 23
provinces[2] — he when he saw that the lot with the five highland 24
provinces had fallen to his own son, rejoiced greatly and he
said: "He hath great merit."

The Ruler of men thus gave over the divers provinces to 25
his sons. Then, giving alms and performing other meritorious
works according to his capacity, for the furthering of the
people and the Order, he lived (yet) seven years[3].

The Ruler who out of love had divided the provinces 26
among his own and his other sons in order to protect Laṅkā
and this our Order was doomed then to inevitable death.

Here ends the ninety-fifth chapter, called «History of King Senāratana», in the Mahāvaṃsa, compiled for the serene joy and emotion of the pious.

[1] The lottery becomes in this way a sacred action, an oracle. The division of the Kandy kingdom took place in 1628.

[2] P. *uddha pañca raṭṭhakā*. These are districts lying round about Kandy, the most important parts of the kingdom with the capital. Uva embraces the eastern, Matale the northern districts. It should be noted that the form *Mātula* for Matale is only found in the latest part of the Cūlavaṃsa (96. 4, 98. 65); in 66. 71 we have Mahātila.

[3] The year of his death is therefore 1635 A. D. The Rājāv. gives 1555 of the Saka era = 1633/4 A. D. One must assume that from 1628 to 1635 Rājasīha was reigning along with his father. Kumārasīha had died before Senāratana, as is pointed out by the Rājāv. The struggles with the Portuguese lasted with fluctuating success throughout Senāratana's reign. Of importance are the negotiations of the Sinhalese King with the Dutch which began in the year 1612. For a time (in 1620) the Danes tried to get a footing on the island. For the whole subject see Pieris, 2, p. 171-221; Codrington, l. c., p. 109 ff.

CHAPTER XCVI

HISTORY OF KING RĀJASĪHA

1 Now while these Rulers of men, sojourning in different
places, enjoyed for a short time the pleasures of the royal
2 dignity in harmony, they carried on war against the Paraṅgis
and gained here and there victories[1]. But then they quarrelled
3 among themselves, the three brothers, the Lords of men. One
of them, the renowned **Rājasīha** by name, dispossessed the
4 older brothers and made them his vassals. After one (Kumāra-
sīha) had been put to death by poison, the other (Vijayapāla
who dwelt) in Mātula, mounted a chariot, and started off with
one man whom he took with him and betook himself after
5 crossing the frontier of the province, abroad[2]. But the other,
Rājasīha[3], a man whose commands were not lightly to be

[1] In the year 1630 A. D. the princes won a brilliant victory at Randenivela in lower Uva over the Portuguese who had occupied Badulla and had plundered and set fire to the town. The Portuguese general, Constantino de Sa y Noronha fell himself in the battle. Four years later (1634) Kumārasīha was removed by poison, and to this time belong the first disagreements between Vijayapāla and Rājasīha. There must however, have been a reconciliation, for Vijayapāla took part in the battle of Gannoruva in 1938 and the victory of the Sinhalese was largely owing to him. The Portuguese under the leadership of their captain-general Diogo de Mello had occupied and destroyed Kandy, but they evacuated the town and on their retreat were surrounded and annihilated. See below note on v. 22. The successes in war of the Sinhalese against the Portuguese are glorified in the poems Kostantinuhaṭanē and Mahahaṭanē. See A. de Silva, JRAS. C. B. xxiv, No. 68 (1915-16), p. 56.

[2] For Vijayapāla's tragic fate according to Portuguese documents, see P. E. Pieris, The Prince Vijayapāla of Ceylon, 1634—1654, Colombo 1928.

[3] Or perhaps "the second (*aparo*) Rājasīha".

slighted, difficult to attack, hard to vanquish, of a lion-like
courage, took possession of the kingdom as it had at the 6
beginning belonged to his father; as if he had been created
by gods, pious in the faith, for the furthering of laity and
Order, he was mighty, dowered with the bravery of war-
skilled heroes.

Once upon a time indulging in youthful sports, he went 7
a-riding with a companion who had mounted an other horse,
himself on horseback. At a given sign, the horse ran along 8
the street, but sank in a marshy place. Determined and
courageous, the powerful (prince) sprang aloft, swung himself 9
on to the horse of his next companion throwing off its rider
and rode on his saddle further. At the dangerous ford of the 10
Gaṅgā, which is called Suvaṇṇatthambha[1], he sprang from the
rock on this side and reached the rock on the opposite bank.

After manifesting in this and in many other ways, his 11
strength, the greatly renowned (prince) cherished the wish to
care for the furtherance of laity and Order. He prepared every 12
kind of implement of war and the rest, took in order to open
the fight, the battle-equipped Sīhalas and set forth under a 13
favorable constellation, at a happy moment from the town of
Sirivaḍḍhana with elephants, steeds and princely retinue, with 14
great warriors and so on, with great dignitaries and so on,
with foot soldiers who bore bows, swords, spears and other
weapons, in front the music with drums, kettledrums and 15
other instruments. In order to acquire merit by the giving
of alms and the like, the King took also the sons of Buddha[2]
with him, marched hither and thither, made the sound of the 16
war drums resound like the terrible clash of thunder and
fearless began the fight. At first he fought a great battle 17
with the foe in the five highland provinces[3], slew many of

[1] Now Ranten-tota, ford over the Mahaveliganga.

[2] I. e. bhikkhus.

[3] P. *pañcuddharaṭṭhagehe.* Here we have another example of the influence of the Sinhalese language. *-gehe* is equivalent to the Sinh. *-gē*, the genitive suffix, and is used as postposition with local meaning. As to the beginnings of such forms in an inscription of the 10th century see Wickremasinghe, EZ. I. 182.

18 the miscreants and drove the powerful wretched enemies from
every place; breaking down their strongholds, the Ruler of
19 men remained victorious. The foes fled, looking on every side
(for safety), tortured with fear, flung themselves from the
20 mountain precipices, sprang into the mountain gorges and were
scattered as cotton in the wind, when he rushed into the
battle-field like a terrible lion that has broken into a herd
21 of elephants[1]. After fighting again and again in different
places with the foe and killing and putting to flight numbers
22 of people on the side of the enemy, he conquered several
provinces, freed them from oppression, destroyed the strong-
holds and so manifested his great power[2].

23 There were however, many of the enemy who tortured by
fear, had hidden themselves and escaped. They stayed for a
24 time in the fortresses at the various places near to the sea,
then these heretical villains began again and again to plunder
25 the different provinces. When Rājasīha whose commands were
not lightly to be slighted, heard thereof, he betook himself
26 to Dīghavāpi[3] which lies to the East. While he, experienced
in all the statecraft taught by Manu, sojourned there, he
27 received news of the Olandas[4]. He thought that good, sent

[1] The language of the passage is in the form in which the MSS. have it and as I have adopted it in my edition, absolutely incorrect. It is however very doubtful whether we are justified in altering it, as the fault may lie with the author. The Col. Ed. alters *migarājā va nibbhayo* into *-rāje va nibbhaye.* I should nevertheless prefer to keep these words and to read *sampatto* in v. 20a instead of *sampatte,* which may be influenced by *yūthamhi.*

[2] There can be no doubt that the preceding verses refer to the victories of the Sinhalese arms mentioned in the note to v. 2. But the events are described in quite general terms.

[3] For the district Dīghavāpi see 74. 89 and note.

[4] Vimaladhammasuriya I. had already been in touch with the Dutch (see note to 94. 22). Under Rājasīha II. Dutch envoys already appeared in 1937, and the King on his part sent three of his own people to Admiral Westerwold, who lay with his vessels at Goa, to blockade it. Dutch vessels appeared at Batticaloa where a Portuguese garrison lay, and the united forces of the Sinhalese and the Dutch forced the Portuguese to surrender the fort (18th May, 1938). A treaty was made with

two dignitaries to their fair land, had a number of people
fetched from there in many ships and when these arrived in 28
the rich, prosperous, thickly populated coast lands near Dīgha-
vāpi, he showed them favour. As he wished to display to them 29
the military forces of his Laṅkā, he sent them the command
to look quietly on. Then he began the fight with the foe 30
stationed near, slew a great mass of the foe and captured the
stronghold. The Ruler of men made over the place to the 31
inhabitants of Olanda and showed them many other favours
and made everyone contented.

From this time onward the Ruler of Laṅkā began at the 32
head of both armies[1], to carry on war by land and water on
every side. He destroyed the fortresses situated at different 33
places and protected by massive stone walls, slew the enemy,
erected in the whole of Laṅkā strongholds garrisoned by strong 34
forces and after absolutely annihilating the foe who had ra-
vaged so long (in Laṅkā) and freeing (the country) from their 35
oppression, he in order to ward off the enemy, charged the
inhabitants of Olanda with the protection of Laṅkā in the
places situated on the sea. After arranging that these were 36
to appear before him every year with presents of divers kinds,
the Ruler of men returned, like Vajirapāṇi[2] when he had 37
conquered in the battle against the Asuras, with his retinue
to his town (of Sirivaḍḍhana)[3].

Westerwold which was ratified in Batavia whither Rājasīha sent two envoys. It enabled the Dutch to gain a firm footing on the island. These are the events to which vv. 25 ff. refer. The narrative describes in one-sided fashion — not surprising in chroniclers — the achievements of the Sinhalese. That they alone conquered Batticaloa is not in accordance with the facts. The chief merit belongs to the Dutch guns. PIERIS 2, p. 227 ff.; CODRINGTON, HC., p. 117 ff.

[1] That is the Sinhalese and the Dutch.

[2] Name of Indra: "who carries the thunderbolt (*vajira*) in his hand."

[3] Here again in the Mhvs. only the one-sided Sinhalese standpoint is given. In diplomacy the Dutch were without doubt superior to King Rājasīha, while on the other hand, he was a very unreliable ally for them. Rājasīha's reign was not so void of friction after the treaty with the Dutch as one might assume from our chronicle. It was disturbed

38 Now while the Ruler of men, Rājasīha, dwelt here in safety,
the wise (prince) sought out in fitting manner those people who
were worthy of a position and granted them various positions
39 such as that of senāpati and the like. Villages, fields and so
on, everything that had belonged to the Buddha and the
gods, in accordance with tradition, the Ruler of men gave
40 back as it had been formerly. He brought kings' daughters
hither from the town of Madhurā, and after holding sway
41 powerfully for fifty and two years[1], the mighty Monarch
Rājasīha, who had guarded as his own eye in the best way
the Order of the royal Sage of the line of the Sun and the
laity, he the best of men went over to the king of death.
42 Thus this exceeding mighty King, the ruler, who under-
stood how to annihilate hostile forces, was yet unable with
his strength and his other qualities to gain the mastery over
death. When the discerning have grasped from the first, at
the very beginning this superiority of Māra, they must with
great zeal continually do meritorious works, such as alms-
giving and the rest.

Here ends the ninety-sixth chapter, called «History of King Rājasīha», in the Mahāvaṃsa, compiled for the serene joy and emotion of the pious.

internally by risings, as in 1641 by that plotted by Vijayapāla. The struggles between the Portuguese and the Dutch went on, the luck being sometimes on the one side sometimes on the other. Finally the Dutch triumphed. With the capture of Colombo (A. D. 1656) the fate of the Portuguese dominion was sealed. Immediately after that there was a breach between Rājasīha and the Dutch. The conflicts of the years which follow were multiplied for Rājasīha by inward strife. Lasting peace was not achieved, in spite of a peace favorable to the Sinhalese being signed in the year A. D. 1677, until the death of the King ten years later. Pieris 2, p. 228-290; Pieris 3, p. 1-35; Codrington, HC., p. 118 ff., 133 ff.

[1] From A. D. 1635 (death of Senāratana) till A. D. 1687. Rājāv. makes the mistake of giving 1614 of the Śaka era = 1692/3 A. D. as that of Rājasīha's death.

CHAPTER XCVII

HISTORY OF THE TWO KINGS, OF VIMALADHAMMA AND HIS SUCCESSOR

Now his son Vimaladhammasuriya became king whose 1
ornament was his faith and other virtues, who was a friend
of the three jewels. As his first mahesī he took the daughter 2
of the mahesī in the town of Madhurā who had been fetched
thence, gladdened his subjects by the four heart-winning
qualities and protected uninterruptedly in peace and justice 3
the realm of Laṅkā as a lord of men whose ornament was
his virtue.

Having attained his consecration as king, the King in pious 4
faith in the doctrine of the Victor, prepared in divers ways every-
thing needful for a sacrificial festival for the Tooth Relic. In 5
honour of the Tooth of the Prince of the wise he erected a
fair, three-storeyed pāsāda, resplendent with all kinds of
(artistic) work, and for the sum of five and twenty thousand 6
silver pieces he had a reliquary made which he covered with
gold and ornamented with the nine precious stones. In this 7
great reliquary that resembled a cetiya of precious stones, he
laid the Tooth of the Victor.

As the Ruler thought to hold the festival of admission to 8
the Order, he prepared fair garments and other articles of
use, five hundred of each kind, made everything over with 9
gifts and the like, together with a royal letter to prudent
officials. These he sent to the country of Rakkhaṅga and 10
invited[1] the bhikkhu community with the thera Santāna at

[1] The embassy to Rakkhaṅga (= Arakan, see note to 94. 15) took place in the year A. D. 1697. The Dutch supplied the vessels for conveying the monks from Burma to Ceylon, which contributed not a little

11 the head. Thus he brought thirty-three bhikkhus to the
beautiful town of Sirivaḍḍhana, made them amid tokens of
12 respect, take up their abode there and provided them with
the four necessaries. Then after he had erected in the right
way, as formerly, a building at the landing-place of the
13 Gaṅgā, within a boundary drawn in the water, he brought
the bhikkhu community thither, had the ceremony of ad-
mission performed on thirty-three sons of good family and
14 so helped the Order of the Victor to attain new glory. Then
full of faith he had one hundred and twenty sons of good
15 family appointed to the position of sāmaṇeras, provided them
abundantly with the four necessaries, had them instructed in
the true doctrine and thus laid up a store of merit.

16 Thinking of the great merit that lies in the use of the
feet[1], he betook himself to the Sumanakūṭa and celebrating
17 with jewels, pearls and the rest, with offerings of gold and
precious stones and with divers stuffs and so forth, a great
festival, he tarried there seven days.

18 He sheltered with a great umbrella of silver the foot-print
of the Sage which was stamped on the Sumanakūṭa and ce-
lebrated a great festival.

19 Day after day he listened to (the sermon of the) doctrine
and since even on days which were not uposatha days, he
20 kept the ordained fasts, he did much good. In this and many
other ways, longing for good, he day and night unweariedly
21 did much good. The King having thus cared for the welfare
of the laity and the Order, fell under the power of death
after a reign of twenty and two years[2].

to the friendly relations established between them and the court of Kandy. The ceremony of the *upasampadā* took place again (*pure viya*) at Gaṇṭhambatittha (Getamba). The description in v. 8 ff. has a great resemblance also in the wording to that describing analogous circumstances under Vimaladhammasuriya I. (94. 15 ff.). Compare for instance, v. 12 c d with 94. 17 c d, v. 15 a b with 94. 20 c d.

[1] I. e. the merit of the pilgrimages. See 92. 15 ff. where the pilgrimages of Vīravikkama to Mahiyaṅgaṇa and to Adam's Peak are described.

[2] Vimaladhammasuriya II. reigned from A. D. 1687-1707. He was

Generous in all that is good, as in the giving of alms and 22
the like, with great wisdom, full of devotion he helped the
excellent teaching of the excellent King of the wise, the one
and only guide of the world, to attain glory. Help ye, there-
fore also evermore and unweariedly the excellent doctrine to
attain glory.

Thereupon his son Sirivīraparakkamanarindasīha be- 23
came king. This King who was an abode of discernment and
manly virtues, in order to protect the royal dignity in Laṅkā, 24
fetched princesses from the town of Madhurā and made them
first mahesīs. He performed meritorious works such as the 25
giving of alms and the like, celebrated daily a festival for the
Tooth Relic and thus laid up a store of merit. He showed 26
care for the bhikkhus who had been admitted to the Order
during his father's life, had many sons of good family submitted
in faith to the ceremony of world-renunciation and thus
furthered the Order. In order to venerate the Mahiyaṅgaṇa- 27
cetiya that was erected already in the lifetime of the Buddha,
the mighty King betook himself thither, sacrificed to the cetiya 28
with all kinds of coloured stuffs and while celebrating a sa-
crificial festival with silver and golden flowers, abundantly 29
with divers fragrant blossoms of the kind that grow on land
and in water[1], with food solid and soft, he laid up much merit.

At the head of a great army he went forth twice to the 30
same Mahiyaṅgaṇa and celebrated a great sacrificial festival.
Twice the Lord of men went in faith to Sumanakūṭa, sacrificed 31

extraordinarily pacific compared with his predecessor. Although at first he had again and again to remonstrate with the Dutch about the non-fulfilment of obligations to which they had pledged themselves in the treaty of 1677 (see CODRINGTON, HC., p. 135; PIERIS 3, p. 46 f.) and although the Dutch managed to put the King off, there was no war during this whole period.

[1] The compiler must have had something of the sort in his mind. But I am doubtful if we should simply change *-jātake bahuṃ* into *-jākehi ca*, as does the Col. Ed. It might be better to assume an obscure expression on the part of the author. His knowledge of Pāli was by no means excellent. It is also hard to imagine that the second reading, if it did stand there originally, could have been corrupted into the first.

32 there and so laid up a store of merit. At the head of a great
retinue he left the great city, went forth to the great (city)
33 Anurādhapura and celebrated a great sacrificial festival. He
had a robe made the size of the robe of the Deliverer[1] and
sacrificed to the Tooth of the Deliverer in divers ways with
34 articles befitting the sacrifice. Not far from the capital[2], on
the fair bank cliff of the Gaṅgā, the Lord of men laid out
35 in a great cocopalm plantation a suburb by name Kuṇḍasālā
and dwelt there[3]. And there at that self-same spot he had
dwelling huts put up in fitting manner and made sāmaṇeras
take up their abode in them. He performed day by day many
36 good works like the giving of alms and the rest, had books
copied and when he saw that the temple which his royal
37 father had erected in the capital for the Tooth Relic, had
fallen into decay, his heart was grieved. The Lord of men
38 had the beautiful (temple) rebuilt, two-storeyed, splendid; he
provided it with a portal resplendent with all kinds of bril-
liant ornaments, made it so that with its stucco coating it
39 resembled a mountain of silver, provided it with a graceful
roof and had thirty-two jātakas depicted in coloured painting[4]
on the two walls of the courtyard: the Vidhurajātaka[5], the
40 Guttila- and Ummaggajātaka; the Dadhivāhana-, Mahākaṇha-,
Sutanu- and Chaddantajātaka, the Dhammaddhaja-, Dhamma-
41 pāla- and Mahājanakajātaka; the Padamāṇava-[6], Dhamma-
soṇḍa-, Mahānāradakassapa-, Mahāpaduma-, Telapatta- and
42 Cullapadumajātaka; the Sattubhatta-, Aṇḍabhūta-, Campeyya-

[1] P. *sugata*, lit. "he who has gone well" who has gone ahead on the path to deliverance. R. O. Franke translated the word by "Pfadvollender" the "path finisher" or "path accomplisher".

[2] P. *mūlapura*. Sirivaḍḍhana (Kandy) is meant. The Gaṅgā is, as often, the Mahaveliganga.

[3] Kundasale about four miles E. S. E. of Kandy, situated on the Mahaveliganga. The popular name for the King was Kundasala after this place which was his favorite residence.

[4] I am anticipating the words *ime dvattiṃsajātake vicittacittakammena kārāpetvāna* in v. 44 d, 45 a.

[5] The Vidhurapaṇḍitajātaka, no. 545 of the Fausböll edition.

[6] Padakusalamāṇavajātaka, no. 432 of Fausböll.

and Sasajātaka, the Visayha-, Kusa-, Sutasoma-[1], Sivi- and 43
Temajātaka[2]; the Culladhanuddhara-[3] and the Saccaṃkiraka- 44
jātaka, the Dummedhajātaka and the Kāliṅgabodhijātaka;
the Sīlavajātaka[4] and the Maṇḍavyajātaka[5], as well as the
Vessantarajātaka. While thus having these thirty-two jātakas 45
faultlessly represented in coloured painting, the Lord of men
laid up an immeasurable store of merit.

In the midst of the town he had erected round the great 46
Bodhi tree, the cetiyas and the temple of Nāthasura[6] — en-
closing them on all sides — a fine wall of stone, massive, 47
lofty, brilliant in its coating of stucco, like to a necklace of
pearls adorning the necks of the ladies of the town and created
thereby for himself an abundance of renown.

Among the sāmaṇeras who lived at his own time (was one) 48
who was dowered with the virtue of a moral life, who ever
rejoiced in unweariedness, in the many works of elucidation 49
and in the words of the Enlightened One, a poet, one learned
in the scriptures, ready of speech, teacher of a host of disciples,
renowned, who devoted his life to his own and to others' weal, 50
who shone like the moon in the heaven of the Order in Laṅkā.
For this sāmaṇera, Saraṇaṃkara by name, who was an abode 51
of faith and of knowledge, rejoicing in unweariedness, the
Ruler — distinguishing him again and again by honours 52
spiritual and secular — had a reliquary made one and a
half cubits high for preserving the relic of the King of the 53
wise, the Enlightened One, the highest Protector of the world.
He covered it with gold, set it with 700 jewels and made
over the shimmering casket to the sāmaṇera together with 54

[1] There are two jātakas of this name, the Mahā- and Cullasutasomajātaka, no. 537 and 525 of Fausböll.

[2] Temiya- or Mūgapakkhajātaka, no. 538 of Fausböll.

[3] Culladhanuggahajātaka, no. 374 of Fausböll.

[4] Sīlavanāgajātaka, no. 72 of Fausböll.

[5] Apparently the Kaṇhadīpāyanajātaka in which the ascetic Maṇḍavya plays the chief part. No. 444 of Fausböll.

[6] Like Nāthadeva (100. 248) the name of Viṣṇu as the protecting deity (*nātha*) of the island.

the relic as well as many books about the true doctrine and
55 so distinguished him. The Lord of men granted him clothing
and other necessaries as well as numerous people for service
and honoured him thus with secular gifts.
56 To procure a long existence for the true doctrine, the Lord
of men invited (that same) Saraṇaṃkara in befitting manner
57 and had composed by this discerning sāmaṇera who strove
after pure enlightenment, that work on the true doctrine
entitled the Sāratthasaṃgaha, furnished with eleven thousand
sections[1], further a commentary in the tongue of Laṅkā on
58 the Mahābodhivaṃsa[2], as well as a commentary on the work
Bhesajjamañjūsā[3] which was composed at the time when the
former King Parakkamabāhu held sway in the town of
59 Jambuddoṇī[4] by that discerning thera, assiduous in well-doing
who was head of the (bhikkhus) dwelling in the Pañcapari-
60 veṇa[5], with the wish that thus those who have devoted them-
61 selves to the spiritual life should be spared illness. After the
wise (prince) had performed these and many other meritorious
works and had carried on the government for thirty and three
years, he fell into the power of death[6].

[1] P. *gantha.* The meaning "section" is uncertain. In no case are we justified in referring to Wilson, as does W., according to whom the skr. *grantha* denotes a distinct number of syllables (32), because Wilson is speaking of a metre, which however W. himself admits.

[2] For this see Geiger, Pāli, p. 25, no. 29. 2; Malalasekera, Pāli Literature of Ceylon, p. 156 ff. Whether by Saranaṃkara's "commentary" (*atthavaṇṇanā*) the Eḷu-Bodhivaṃsa is meant seems doubtful.

[3] "Medicine-chest". Probably a collection of recipes of the character of the Indian Bhaiṣajyaratnāvalī (Jolly, Medicin, p. 2).

[4] Parakkamabāhu II. is meant.

[5] A monastery called Pañcapáriveṇamūla is mentioned 67. 61. One could also translate: "of the bhikkhus living in the five pariveṇas".

[6] The Chronicle concerns itself solely with the king's relation to the Church and is fulsome in its praise of his merits. It does not mention a single word about the conspiracy which nearly cost him his life. As little does it mention the very unsatisfactory conditions existing for the most part in the territories occupied by the Dutch nor the conflicts, arising out of questions of commercial policy, between the people of

After the King had attained the highest bliss on the island of Laṅkā, he left behind his kinsfolk, his friends and his life, and went to that state where all that is left behind. When ye have grasped that, ye remembering the truth of the oral admonitions of the highest Sage, should practise meritorious doing that surpasses all else, that brings the bliss of deliverance, that grants the bliss of the world of the gods. 62

Here ends the ninety-seventh chapter, called «History of the Two Kings, of Vimaladhamma and his Successor», in the Mahāvaṃsa, compiled for the serene joy and emotion of the pious.

Kandy and the foreigners. Like his predecessor Narindasīha he kept the peace. At any rate the Dutch understood by occasional gifts to keep him in good humour. Pieris 3, p. 52—65.

CHAPTER XCVIII

HISTORY OF SIRIVIJAYARĀJASĪHA

1 After Narindasīha's death the younger brother[1] of the
Mahesī of this king[2] became king, adorned with the ornament
2 of virtue. Known by the name of Sirivijayarājasīha, he
was after the attainment of his consecration as king, piously
3 attached to the Triad of the jewels. He was diligent in
hearkening to the sermon of the doctrine, unwearied, discerning, ever full of zeal intent on intercourse with pious and
4 good people. To establish his own dynasty he fetched princesses from the town of Madhurā and made them his chief
5 mahesīs. He won over the people in Laṅkā in the best manner
possible by the four heart-winning qualities and took up his
6 abode in the fair town (Sirivaḍḍhana). The Mahesīs of the
King, too, gave up the false faith to which they had been
long attached, and adopted in the best manner possible the
7 true faith which confers immortality. They heard the incomparable, true doctrine of the Buddha, the highest Protector
of the world and thus adored with constant devotion the
8 Buddha and the other (sacred) objects. In their faith they

[1] In *kaniṭṭhabhūta* I see the influence of the Sinhalese on the Pāli of the chronicler, *vū* being added in Sinhalese at the end of attributive adjectives.

[2] According to 97. 24 (cf. 98. 4!), Narindasīha's Mahesī was a princess from Madhurā. With the ascent of the throne by her brother a foreign dynasty is thus introduced into Laṅkā. The series of Sinhalese kings ends with Narindasīha. The succession of Vijayarājasīha meanwhile, was not undisputed. A strong party at court supported the claims of Unambuva, a son of Narindasīha's by a concubine. It seems however, that he voluntarily renounced the throne. Later on he lived safe and sound at the court of Kandy.

worshipped the Tooth Relic day by day with sacrifice, with
jasmine and other blossoms and with all kinds of flower
festivals, with sweet betel mixed with camphor and other 9
things, with lamps with fragrant oil, with sweet-smelling
sandal wood and so forth, with divers kinds of fragrant in- 10
cense, with sugar and honey and with other drugs, with gar-
ments, ornaments and so on, with silver and golden bowls 11
which were abundantly filled with all that one can chew, eat,
sip, drink and taste, with curtains, carpets and the like, with 12
many articles of use and with costly robes — and thus and
otherwise laid up a store of merit. They kept constantly 13
the five moral commandments[1] and the uposatha vows even
on days that were not uposathas, diligent in hearing the
(sermon of the) true doctrine. Even as the yak cows (protect 14
their tails)[2], so they preserved the memory of the Buddha
and the other (sacred objects)[3]. They worked for their per-
fection, had sacred books copied. They strove after the bless- 15
ing that lies in generosity. They understood to perfection
the regular offering of food and other (occasional) distribution
of food to wandering or sick (bhikkhus). They were not 16
attached to acquired wealth but dispensed (it in) continual
feeding and the like. They made young people renounce the
world, showed them favour of many kinds. They had good in- 17
struction given in the knowledge of the sacred scriptures and
of pious duties and by dispensing always what was desired
they were like to a wishing-tree. Kind beyond measure and 18
very full of pity they thought of all people in Laṅkā as a
mother of her children, and were merciful and mines of virtue.
They had images and reliquaries fashioned in the best manner 19

[1] P. *pañcasīlaṃ*. Cf. with this Mhvs. trsl. 1. 62.

[2] Cf. with this passage Buddhavaṃsa 2. 124 f. *yathāpi camarī vālaṃ kismici paṭivilaggitaṃ | upeti maraṇaṃ tattha na vikopeti vāḷadhiṃ || tatheva catūsu bhūmīsu sīlāni paripūriya | parirakkha sabbadā sīlaṃ camarī viya vāḷadhiṃ* ||— an allusion to the legend that the yaks would rather die than have any harm happen to their greatest ornament, their tail.

[3] There are six different *anussatiyo* — *Buddha-*, *dhamma-*, *saṃgha-*, *sīla-*, *cāga-* and *devatā-anussati.*

possible and always fearing every sin and ever rejoicing over
20 every meritorious deed, adorned with the ornament of such
and many other virtues, they were highly regarded in the
21 whole island of Laṅkā. The King had dwelling-places erected
here and there and made the sāmaṇeras take up their abode
22 in them and pious as he was, he showed them full of zeal,
much favour with garments and other necessaries, heard the
23 splendid true doctrine from these sāmaṇeras and revered
(especially) the sāmaṇera Saraṇaṃkara by name who strong
in faith dwelt in the Uposathārāma, who was a mine of virtues.
24 He invited him and had a commentary on the four bhāṇavāras[1]
made by him in the language of Laṅkā and thus protected
the knowledge of the sacred scriptures.

25 Since the Lord of men had heard from foolish people out-
side (of the Buddhist Order) that great evil would befall if
26 he were to place the relic in a new relic temple, he gave
orders that this should be done by other people[2] and betook
himself thence to another town. While he sojourned there
27 the dignitaries assembled and together with the caretakers[3]
and other people, they tried with all their might to open the
28 reliquary. But although they tried the whole night long they
did not succeed. The dignitaries went thither and told the
29 matter to the Great king. When the King heard that, he
came in haste to the splendid town and after the Ruler had
reverently made offerings with all kinds of fragrant flowers,
30 with lamps, incense and the like and shown his reverence,

[1] For purposes of recitation the whole of the Tipiṭaka is divided into *bhāṇavāras*, sections of equal length. There are said to be 2547 of these (Childers, s. v.). It seems to me, however, as if the word in our passage is used instead of *nikāya*. The commentary would then have embraced Dīgha-, Majjhima-, Saṃyutta- and Aṅguttara-Nikāya.

[2] The passage is wrongly rendered by W. *Aññaṃ puraṃ* is not governed by *kātuṃ* in 26 b, it belongs to *gantvā*, but *kātuṃ* must be supplemented by the object ("it") from the preceding.

[3] *Vattakārakā* (meaning literally "fulfilling the duty or the task") refers I believe, to the guardians who were appointed just at that time, to look after the shrines and see that they were kept in proper condition. See Pieris 3, p. 70.

he took hold of the lock and at once opened the reliquary
without difficulty. Then after opening one after the other the 31
caskets inside it, he beheld the Tooth of the Enlightened One.
"It is accomplished, with success" uttering these joyful words, 32
he assembled the inhabitants of the town, prepared a great
feast and celebrated a great sacrificial festival. As he gazed 33
on the wonderful (relic) the Monarch was transported with
joy and enthusiasm. As offerings he presented an elephant
and a horse, jewels, pearls and the like, took the sacred Tooth 34
of the Prince of the wise in the lotus of his hand, showed
it forth and so caused all to rejoice in perfect fashion. The 35
relic temple built in the time of former kings he furnished
with all kinds of stuffs interwoven with gold, lit lamps with 36
divers-smelling oils, had filled jars placed about, and then in
this gaily decorated temple, like to a heavenly temple, he 37
placed on a silver throne the Tooth of the Prince of the wise.
He arranged a great festival, made a sacrifice to the relic and 38
after cleansing the whole town in a worthy manner and
strewing it with sand he placed during this festival of the 39
Tooth Relic, round about the temple, within in the court and
without on the terrace, further in the royal court and in all 40
the streets on either side with lofty poles placed upright, an
unbroken series of festive arches, bound thereon banana stalks 41
and adorned them fair with areca and coconut blossoms and
other flowers. With the brightly hued, gleaming and shimmer- 42
ing streamers tied bunch-wise to the points of the poles, the sky
above the town looked pleasant as if it were filled with flights of 43
cranes. Here and there he placed in due order filled jars and 44
in the maṇḍapas in a circle in front of the temple terrace he
fastened canopies shimmering with silver and golden and other
embroideries, hung thereabout brightly gleaming curtains, 45
spread there in fair fashion carpets resplendent with many a 46
work of art and also strewed around the five kinds of flowers,
lāja and the like[1]. Then after the Ruler had put the whole 47

[1] P. *lājapañcamakaṃ*, lit. "that in which *lāja* is the fifth". See for this PTS. P. D. s. v. *lāja*. This is the name for the blossom of the

city in order so that it looked as if the former kings of Laṅkā
were celebrating a festival with the thought that in like
48 fashion the King of the gods makes a feast in the city of
the gods[1], he himself with royal ornaments adorned, gathered
49 together in that town the sāmaṇeras who dwelt in Laṅkā,
further the lay brethren and lay sisters, all the inhabitants
of the town and the people who dwelt outside in the provinces.
50 Out of mercy towards them[2] the Ruler of the earth for whom
pity was the highest, flung himself on the ground in most
51 humble posture[3] and so worshipped the Tooth of the Prince
of the wise. Then the King took it in the lotus of his hand
52 and his heart filled with the highest joy, he left the relic
temple. With silver umbrellas, with a golden casket, with
53 row upon row of fair fly whisks, with manifold offerings of
flowers, consisting of silver, golden and other blooms, with
54 divers jewels and pearls, with robes, ornaments and many other
sacrificial articles, with the fivefold music[4] he celebrated a
great sacrificial festival, like to a stream flowing on uninter-
55 ruptedly. Then the King, the Ruler of Laṅkā betook himself

dalbergia arborea. W's version is quite different (note to the passage). He takes *lāja* in the sense of "roasted rice" and remarks "Paddy when roasted bursts and the grain inside the husk expands in the shape of a beautiful white flower. These are used on public occasions and festivals as a mark of respect, for showing the ground whereon a shrine is taken or on which a high person walks over."

[1] The style is extremely stilted. Literally the passage should be translated thus: "showing the town in such a way that one would be obliged to soy: in such wise did the former princes of Laṅkā celebrate a festival, whereby they thought: thus doth the King of the gods etc. etc." The idea is this: the King has adorned the city as magnificently as the kings of yore were wont to do on like occasions, and the splendour they displayed was due to the fact that they imitated divine models.

[2] He will not rob the people of the purifying spectacle of the sacred relic.

[3] P. *pañcapatiṭṭhitaṅgo*, lit. with a body in which five (parts of the body) lie fast. Childers thus explains the term: "to prostrate oneself before a superior so completely that the forehead, elbows, waist, knees and feet rest on the ground."

[4] See note to 85.30.

to the maṇḍapa outside (in front of the temple) which was adorned with divers bright ornament and standing here, dis-
played the sacred Tooth. Having thus given the greatest joy 56
to the mighty multitude gathered round, he brought the Tooth
Relic back to its place. Thus by bringing full contentment 57
to all as if by the sight of the Buddha in person, he laid up
a store of much good.

Now after the Lord of men had offered abundantly with 58
all kinds of ornament, such as gold, jewels, pearls and the
like, with sacrificial offerings like elephants, horses, slaves 59
male and female, with flowers like jasmine, campaka[1] and
other blossoms, with fragrant sandal wood and the like, he 60
bethought himself of the great blessing inherent in a sacrifice
of lamps. Hence the Lord of men issued the command that
in their own town and in the cetiyas in the divers provinces
on one and the same day[2], people should make an offering 61
of lamps, and in that selfsame night he gathered together the
people and celebrated a sacrifice of lamps with seven hundred 62
and ninety thousand, six hundred lamps. Thus with burning 63
lamps the Ruler of Laṅkā made the land of Laṅkā like to
the star-strewn firmament. With an offering of three hundred[3] 64
thirty and three thousand, eight hundred flowers he laid up
a store of merit.

This King rich in virtue who found joy in causing images 65
of the Buddha to be made, had erected in Ālokalena[4] and other
vihāras in the province of Mātula, as well as here and there
in the rock temples of the various (other) provinces, Buddha 66
statues in life-size, in recumbent, standing and sitting posture
and new cetiyas which bring happiness to living creatures,
and he had many decayed image houses restored and increased 67
thereby showing favour to the people, the quantity of his merit.

[1] Michelia champaka; Sinh. *sapu-mal.*

[2] The words *ekāhe va* must be taken in the oratio recta.

[3] For *koṭi* which here probably means 100,000, see PTS. P. D. s. v. In has the general meaning of an extremely high number.

[4] Now the Alu-vihāra not far from Matale situated in the cleft of a mighty primeval landslide.

68 In the town of Sirivaḍḍhana the Lord of men did away
with the royal palace and many other buildings that had
69 been founded formerly but had meanwhile fallen into decay.
In place of these the Lord of men built new houses which
70 excelled by reason of their mason work and the like, made
fine gates[1] and erected a magnificent gate-building furnished
with iron gateways, adorned with ornaments[2] of divers form
and consisting of two storeys.

71 While he resided in this town, he full of zeal when listen-
ing to the sermon of the doctrine, had maṇḍapas erected
72 within the royal courtyard. He furnished them completely
with coloured arches and the like, put up canopies, spread
73 seats, brought then with great ceremony[3] many preachers of
the true doctrine thither, made them be seated and lay hold
74 of their white fans. Then he hearkened to the good, heart-
penetrating doctrine as it was preached by them along with
enlightening explanation and the like, and filled with pious
75 joy the Ruler honoured it with gold and silver, with lamps,
incense and the like, with divers coloured stuffs, (in short)
76 with sacrificial articles of every kind, the Monarch himself in
common with the dignitaries and the troops and so on many
occasions laid up a store of abundant good.

77 Now when the King heard through the true doctrine that
spiritual offerings[4] are a great thing, he intent on the wel-
78 fare of the people dwelling in the various provinces, had
dwellings and sermon halls erected here and there in places
79 fitted for the assembling of a great multitude of people. Then
the Lord of men sent to the various places numerous preachers
of the doctrine and others, had the people gathered together
and the true doctrine preached to them and in this way he
offered a spiritual offering.

[1] One is tempted here to join *cārudvārāni yojetvā* with the following *ayodvārasamāyutaṃ*, but for its giving a scarcely tolerable tautology.

[2] P. *laṭākamma*, lit. "creeper work".

[3] P. *mahussavena*, not as W. translates "with much trouble". That would be *mahussāhena*.

[4] P. *dhammadāna*, every kind of religious instruction. The opposite is *āmisadāna* "secular offering" (food, clothing etc.).

The infamous Paraṅgis, the infidels, the impious ones who 80
at the time of King Rājasīha had still remained behind in
the town and now dwelling here and there, rich in cunning, 81
endeavoured by gifts of money and the like to get their creed
adopted by others, led a life without reverence for the doctrine 82
(of the Buddha). When the King heard thereof he became
vehemently indignant, issued commands to his dignitaries, had 83
their houses and their books destroyed and banished from the
country those who did not give up their faith[1].

On the Sumanakūṭa made sacred by the footprint of the 84
Enlightened One the Ruler celebrated a sacrifice of lamps and
all other festivals. In Anurādhapura, in Mahiyaṅgaṇa and in 85
other places he likewise celebrated a great sacrificial festival.
To east and west (of the town) where water made the road 86
impassable, he had stone bridges put up for the comfort of
those coming and going.

When the Monarch realised that the Order of the Victor 87
was declining because a bhikkhu community was not to be
had in Laṅkā he was greatly moved. As he was minded to 88
invite a bhikkhu community, he considered in every possible
way where the Order of the Sage could possibly still exist.
Then he heard from the Olandas[2] the welcome news that the 89
Order still existed in various countries, in Pegu, Rakkhaṅga,

[1] The King's measures are thus directed against the Roman Catholic Church and against the Portuguese still settled in the country. For the Catholic mission in Ceylon at the time of the Dutch settlement and its ultimate suppression see Pieris 3, p. 70 f.

[2] The only passage where Vijayarājasīha's relations with the Dutch are noted. If in spite of the friction caused by trade, these relations led to no open rupture, this was largely due to the easy going and at times really feeble policy of the Dutch. Their forbearance was met by increased claims on the part of the court of Kandy. An embassy to Pegu was first sent off in the year 1740. The Dutch Company placed a vessel at its disposal which was however wrecked off the coast of Pegu. A second embassy seems to have gone to Siam in 1741. Envoys of the Sinhalese king came also in 1746 to Siam and succeeded in persuading a number of bhikkhus to undertake the journey to Ceylon. Vijayarājasīha however, died 1747 before their arrival. See Codrington, HC. p. 139 f. and especially p. 154; Pieris 3, p. 71 ff.

90 Sāminda[1]. Now in order to test the condition of the Order
of the Sage in these various countries, the King had letters
91 carefully written in the sacred language[2], gave them over to
ministers and other dignitaries and sent these forth singly.
When the Lord of men heard the news that in the kingdom
92 of Ayojjhā[3] the Order existed in all its purity and in the best
condition, in order to bring from that same country sons of
93 the Victor to Laṅkā, he sent dignitaries thither to whom he
gave a writing together with many gifts and sacrificial implements.
94 For the placing therein of the Tooth of the Prince of the
wise the Monarch had a fair, golden reliquary made one and
a half cubits high and encrusted with costly jewels and pearls.
95 But before it was finished his merit was exhausted[4] after he
had reigned eight years.
96 This prince who was adorned with the ornament of faith
and of many other virtues, who was at pains to purify to the
utmost the splendid Order of the Buddha, that best of men after
he had done much good, went finally thither to Namuci[5].
97 In this wise did the King of Laṅkā whose joy was in the
welfare of others, who worked for his own and others' salvation,
carry on the government, as best among the best, the Ruler
of men who loved virtue. Ye who wish for your prosperity
in this world and for abundant happiness in the world beyond
must therefore wholly give up indolence and do a multitude of
meritorious works which will bring you many a happiness.

Here ends the ninety-eighth chapter, called «History of Sirivijayarājasīha», in the Mahāvaṃsa, compiled for the serene joy and emotion of the pious.

[1] Name of Siam.

[2] P. *mūlabhāsā* "fundamental or main language", i. e. Pāli.

[3] Ayodhyā, now Ayuthya, name of the old capital of Siam, north of Bangkok, situated on the banks of the Menam. Cf. J. DAHLMANN, Indische Fahrten (1927) I. 111 ff.

[4] The *puñña* in virtue of which he had attained the royal dignity. For "reigned" the original has *ṭhito* "lived (as king)".

[5] Skr. *namuci* is the name of one of the demons slain by Indra. In Pāli Namuci is a designation of Māra (S. I. 67[10]; A. II. 15[20]) specially of Kilesamāra (Jāt. V. 455[10]), in our passage of the god of death.

CHAPTER XCIX

ACCOUNT OF THE KING'S CONSECRATION AND OF OTHER FESTIVALS

After the passing of this Monarch dowered with splendid 1
virtues, his brother-in-law[1] became king of kings. Gifted with physical beauty (he was) a delight to the eyes of the people, filling the whole superb island of Laṅkā with splendour, a prince of glorious grace.

When in the island of Laṅkā the year two thousand, two 2
hundred and ninety since the nirvana of the Enlightened One
had come[2] this Ruler of men whose joy was the welfare of 3
Laṅkā, comforted his subjects who were afflicted by their parting from the Great king. This whole people racked by 4
suffering, like to the darkness (which sets in) when the sun
after it has illumined the whole world, goes down — the far- 5
famed King made free from grief, like to the (newly) rising
sun which illumines the whole world (afresh) and having taken 6
over the royal dignity of Laṅkā, he made everyone joyful to
the utmost. After attaining his consecration as king, the
Lord of men who was devoted in faith to the Triad of the 7
jewels, Buddha and the others, strove unweariedly after merit.
The highly famed one had the whole town (of Sirivaḍḍhana) 8
cleansed and decorated with stuffs, triumphal arches and the
like. Then he gathered together the whole of the inhabitants
of Laṅkā completely in the fair, glorious town and moving 9
along with royal magnificence, the Great king whose merit

[1] The brother of Vijayarājasīha's Mahesī who according to 98. 4, came from Madhurā. He had come to the court of Kandy with his sister and with his father Narenappa Nayaker.

[2] = A. D. 1746. The right year for Vijayarājasīha's death is 1747.

was now having its effect[1], marched round the town, his right side turned towards it, thus making known that the realm of
10 Laṅkā bereft of its king had again a king. The Lord of men dowered with abundant merit, resided in Sirivaḍḍhana.
11 The virtuous one had (already aforetime) made the firm resolve[2] to shelter the Order of the Sage and now under the name of Kittisirirājasīha he ruled gloriously this our Laṅkā. Enjoying the good fortune of the royal dignity of Laṅkā, full of discernment, recognizing that his wealth consisted in faith, he mindful of what things are of worth and of what things are worthless, prepared in piety a festival.
12 for the three sacred objects, Buddha and so forth[3]. He gave up evil friends and enjoyed intercourse with the learned people; he passed his time with the good and hearkened to
13 the incomparable doctrine. Pious and wise as he was, the Lord of men distinguished between what should be done and what should not be done. What should not be done he avoided,
14 but to that which should be done he held fast. By the four heart-winning qualities he made all people well disposed to
15 him and he was worthy of the praise of the learned. Hearing that reward lies in a spiritual offering[4] and success in the hearkening to the true doctrine and merit in the copying of works of the true doctrine, as also in sacrificial festivals for
16 the doctrine he thought: that which is in accordance with the true doctrine[5] must be done. He had maṇḍapas erected in

[1] For *puññodaya* — here used as an adjective — see note to 37. 139.

[2] P. *paṇidhayo katvāgato*. I regard *katvāgato* again as a compound verb formed under the influence of the Sinhalese, of the type *geṇenavā*: *geṇāvā*. The King had already made the resolve in a former existence. The effect in the present of his meritorious *kamma* is that he becomes king of Laṅkā (P. *patvāna Laṅkaṃ imaṃ*), and he can now carry out his resolve.

[3] V. 6c to the close of v. 11 is a single sentence. The construction is however, quite inorganic and it is impossible to translate the sentence as a whole. It is the same with the following.

[4] See note to 98. 77.

[5] P. *saddhammato* must be understood adverbially. Cf. skr. *dharmatas* "according to law or rule, lawfully."

many places for sermons, made canopies therein of stuff of 17
varied colours, furnished them in every possible way with
arches and other ornaments, lit lamps and spread seats, brought 18
thither with worthy service and honour preachers of the true 19
doctrine, invited them full of reverence, made them sit down
on the well prepared seats, made these preachers recite parts 20
of the true doctrine and listened with devotion the whole
night long to many suttantas, such as the Dhammacakka
Suttanta[1] and others. Since he recognized the worthlessness 21
of body, life and wealth as worthlessness and the worth of
listening to the true doctrine as worth, he was pious and 22
joyful and celebrated in common with the dignitaries and the
troops, a great festival with articles of sacrifice of every kind.
For the welfare and blessing of the multitudes dwelling within 23
and without the town the Lord of men repeatedly had spiritual 24
offerings offered and thus performed a meritorious work consisting in spiritual offerings.

Full of reverence towards the bhikkhu community[2] who 25
had come from Rakkhaṅga, towards the bhikkhus of Laṅkā
and towards the many sāmaṇeras, who had renounced the
world, the Lord of men showed them favour with offerings 26
of robes and other necessaries and had the Paritta and other
salutary texts recited by them. Thus on many occasions he 27
furthered the true doctrine, made offerings of necessaries and
so increased the store of his merit.

At a cost of nine thousand, six hundred (kahāpaṇas) he 28
in his piety had a magnificent golden book made. On its 29
golden leaves he had many Suttantas inscribed such as the

[1] What is meant is the story of the Buddha's first sermon in Bārāṇasī to the *pañcavaggiyā bhikkhū*, the companions of his earlier period of asceticism. The account is given in the Vinaya, Mahāvagga I. 6. 10 ff. (= I. 8 ff.). Cf. S. V. 420 ff.

[2] Bhikkhus from Rakkhaṅga had come to Ceylon under Vimaladhammasuriya I. (94. 15) and under the second king of this name (97. 10). Kittisiri had some brought from Siam. This is narrated as a kind of appendix in 100. 54 ff. In all probability the Siamese monks are to be considered as included in this passage.

30 Dhammacakka Sutta and others and had these recited by preachers of the true doctrine the whole night long. Honouring them with many articles, he listened repeatedly to the
31 incomparable doctrine. The Lord of men called scribes together, made them copy out in one day the Dīgha-Nikāya[1], showed
32 them much favour and then had the sacred text preached the whole night long in the right manner. He celebrated a great
33 sacrificial festival, listened to (texts) and recited himself. In his piety he had the Saṃyutta-Nikāya and many other books
34 copied and gave the scribes money. People who had renounced the world and inhabitants of houses[2] had other sacred books carefully copied and when these were shown to him he was
35 highly pleased, showed them with money and other gifts much favour and thus in his pious zeal took a share in the merit of other dwellers in Laṅkā.

36 Yearning for merit the Lord of men betook himself with his retinue to superb Anurādhapura. Here the King sacrificed
37 to the Bodhi tree and the sacred cetiyas with elephants, and horses, with gold, silver and the like, and thus in divers ways
38 laid up a store of pious works. Then too in royal splendour the highly-famed Lord of men visited the Mahiyaṅgaṇa-cetiya and the superb Nakhā-cetiya and reverenced them by the celebration of a great festival and so laid up a store of merit.
39 In order to honour with sacrifices the beautiful cetiyas and vihāras erected by the Lord of men Parakkama in superb Pu-
40 latthinagara, the highly famed King rich in faith, betook himself thither with a great retinue and sacrificed to them in
41 the right way. Endowed with faith and other virtues the King also honoured the Rajata-vihāra[3] and brought together a store of merit.

42 After a sacrificial festival for the lotus-hued patron god and other deities such as was popularly recognized as bring-

[1] P. *dīghāgamaṃ*; *āgama* is synonym for *nikāya*. The same in 33 *saṃyuttāgama*.

[2] P. *pabbajitā* and *gahaṭṭhā*, i. e. priests and laymen. The sentence in 34-35 is linguistically quite incorrect.

[3] Now Ridi-vihāra, north of Kurunegala.

ing luck even in the days of former sovereigns of Laṅkā[1],
he had for the purpose of a military display[2], the whole town 43
without exception put in order like the city of the gods. He
gathered together all the inhabitants of Laṅkā and in the town 44
he had the people from the individual provinces separated and
made them dwell in different places, provided with standards. 45
Then he had the symbols[3] in the temples of the gods placed
on the back of an elephant. He had the elephant surrounded[4] 46
by divers beaters of the drum and the tambourine and by
crowds of dancers[5], by various groups of elephants and divers
groups of horses, by people wearing the Brahman dress of 47
various stuffs and with (divers) ornaments, by people carrying
divers umbrellas and divers fly-whisks; by various groups of 48
women and various groups of dignitaries, by people carrying
divers shields and divers swords, by such as carried divers 49
spears and various symbols[6], by such as carried various stuffs

[1] Something of this sort must have been in the mind of the chronicler when he wrote this passage with its absolutely confused style. *Maṅgala-saṃmataṃ* must be taken as attribute to *pūjā* contained in the compound which follows (42 c d). The Col. Ed. tries at least to smoothe away the difficulties by reading instead of the *°bhūpālā* of the MSS. *°bhūpā va*. I fear this amounts to a correction of the author.

[2] P. *senaṅgadassanatthāya*. W. does not give the full sense of this expression. That a military tournament is meant is clear from verses 44-45 a b. The assembled people are divided according to the individual local contingents of which the army is made up. Each contingent has its special flag. The army thus forms the main element in the festive procession.

[3] P. *devaṭṭhāna-āvudhāni*. Skr. *āyudha* means besides "weapon", "implement" in general. W. translates quite correctly "the emblems of the gods that were in the temples".

[4] Anticipates *hatthiṃ parivāriya* in v. 51.

[5] The compound is not in the least clear. *Maddalakehi* at the end seems to be an adjective form; *saṃkiṇṇa* might be used substantively as is often the case with the past part = "accumlation". The wearisome repetition of *nānā* in the sequel is probably meant to express the endlessness of the procession. The same occurs in 85. 112 ff. and 88. 117 ff. The words *soṇṇa* and *rūpiya* are repeated in the same way in 85. 26 ff. and 89. 19 ff.

[6] Here again *āvudha* is used. I should prefer here to take the word

50 and various banners; by people who had come from various
regions and who understood the different tongues; by such as
were practised in the various arts and by divers artisans —
51 with such and many other people he had the elephant sur-
rounded, ordering them to go immediately in front or behind.
52 Thereupon the King set forth, like to the Prince of the gods,
with great (and) royal splendour and marched round the whole
town, his right side turned towards it. Finally[1] they all
arrived again and entered (the town) according to their rank[2].
53 When our King of kings[3], dowered with faith, wisdom
and other virtues, was wont every year to hold the Āsāḷhi[4]
54 festival, he was minded beforehand to celebrate a sacrificial
festival for the Buddha. He had a canopy fastened on the
55 back of the royal elephant beautifully ornamented with gold
embroidery. Then he had the elephant whose tusk was as
56 the bright moon[5], decorated with ornaments and then sur-
rounded by (other) elephants whose riders held in their hand
silver umbrellas and fly-whisks[6] and flowers of every kind, by

in the same sense as in v. 45, as "weapons" are already mentioned in the foregoing.

[1] P. *niṭṭhite* used as adverb, as also in v. 58.

[2] This verse is a good example of the utter neglect of style where the subject *so rājā* (*nikkhamitvā, katvā*) in the same verse is followed by the plural predicate *pavisanti*.

[3] P. *amhākaṃ rājarājānaṃ*. The expression "our King" is particularly noteworthy. In the whole of the Mahāvaṃsa it occurs only here under Kittisirirājajasīha (cf. also v. 133 and 163, as well as 100. 228) and seems to prove that our section was composed under this king and during his lifetime, cf. v. 76 ff. and note to 100. 300. The construction of the sentence is again quite confused. The subject stands in the acc.; *-guṇādayo* which I regard as a transposition of *-ādiguṇo*, is changed by the Col. Ed. into *-guṇodayo*. But does this help us much? The sentence remains in disorder.

[4] The āsāḷha month corresponds to June-July. The festival held in this month brings in the rainy season. H. Kern, Manual of Indian Buddhism, p. 100.

[5] P. *subbha-candi-radaṃ*. I separate the compound thus, *candi* seeming to me to stand for skr. *candra* or *candrin*. The explanation is however, uncertain.

[6] The acc. *rajatacchattacāmare* is governed by *gāhaka* in the follow-

people having in their hand articles of sacrifice and wearing
garlands of flowers, by people with various banners and pennons 57
and by such as wore divers garments, by various royal digni-
taries and by people come hither from various regions. Finally 58
the Lord of men placed the splendid sparkling casket of
gold in which the bodily relic[1] of the Buddha was contained 59
carefully under the canopy and by the strewing of flowers
let a rain of flowers rain (upon it). With the shouts of the 60
cries of "Hail"!, with the sound of the shell trumpets and
the cymbals and with the rattle of the various drums celebrat-
ing high festival[2], good and pious people their hearts filled 61
with astonishment and admiration, with hands folded before
the brow, paid lasting reverence (to the relic). But the Lord 62
of men had the Tooth Relic reverenced with all kinds of
particularly costly sacrificial gifts by people who bore lamps
on poles and who were festively attired. Then placing at the 63
head the relic which holds the first place among all things
worthy of reverence by gods, demons and men, he ordered 64
all the rest, such as gods[3] and men to follow behind. He
himself in royal splendour to the strains of hymns of praise
which promised happiness, set forth in all the majesty of a
Great king, with great magnificence showing men how even 65
thus the King of the gods in the city of the gods is wont
to celebrate high festival for the relics.

Dowered with faith and many other virtues, devoted to 66
the Buddha, his Doctrine and his Order, collected, mindful of
what is worth and of what is worthless, ever performing
meritorious works, such as almsgiving and the like; distinguish- 67
ed by splendid virtues, piety, wisdom, mercy, shining over the

ing compound. Thus we have again to do with a compound resolved into its component parts (= *rajatacchattacāmarapuppphagāhakaārūḷhahatthīhi*).

[1] Not "relics" (W.); it is only a case of the Tooth Relic.

[2] I am inclined to think that *kārento* which might be the direct equivalent of the skr. *kārayantas*, belongs to the following *janā pūjenti*.

[3] By *surā* are meant the figures of deities or divine symbols which are carried in processions.

island, with faith in the Enlightened One, living according to the good doctrine of the Sage, dowered with the ten powers[1], ever giving alms and performing other meritorious works unweariedly and full of zeal, mindful of what is worth and of what is worthless, he ever acted in this way for the welfare of all men.

68 With great ceremony he instituted day by day a great
festival for the Tooth Relic, reverential towards the triad of
69 the jewels. His own community which had been received into
the Order in his own time, he provided in pious reverence
70 from his own property with the four articles of use. Devoted
in piety to the true doctrine he listened again and again to
(the preaching of the) doctrine and accumulated in pious re-
71 verence numerous meritorious works. He furthered as during
the lifetime of the Buddha the Order of the Victor and in-
72 creased the happiness of the people dwelling in Laṅkā. When
he heard of the doings of former kings, of Parakkamabāhu
and others, he recognized it as right and imitated their doings.
73 He learned the duties of a king, was filled with reverence for
kingly duties, shunned the (four) false paths, schooled himself
in the four heart-winning qualities, showed his brothers and
74 others all favour by befitting action, made them contented
and won their hearts by caring for them in the right way.

75 In this manner the Sovereign of Laṅkā, the Lord of men,
whose joy was in the welfare of others sheltered in the best
way, ever unweariedly the Order of the Master as likewise
the laity, and when he learned the history of the many rulers
of men who had formerly been kings in Laṅkā, he mused on
their deeds and made the resolve: "I also will fulfil the duties
76 of a king." In making this resolve he thought of the work,
entitled Mahāvaṃsa[2], in which the ancient history of the
kings of the great dynasty as of those of the lesser dynasty
77 is narrated in the form of verses, from Mahāsammata to (the

[1] See PTS. P. D. s. v. *bala.*

[2] For this passage see my edition of the Cūlavaṃsa, I, Introduction p. IV-V.

kings of) Hattiselapura[1]. And the King of Laṅkā caused an 78
examination to be made in due order of this book existing on
the island of Laṅkā and of the same chronicle of the kings
of Laṅkā brought from the Sāminda country — of these two 79
books separately — and when he heard that the Mahāvaṃsa 80
was deficient, he also caused the unknown history of the kings
of the latter time — beginning with Parakkamabāhu up to the
kings of the present time — to be written down and to be
continued (thus) the royal chronicle.

Thus while he neither transgressed the commandments (laid 81
down) for a king nor the precepts of religion, the Lord of
men carried on the royal government in justice and peace. In 82
accordance with the duties of a king he daily did good, such
as almsgiving and the like, mindful of the sublime religion,
practising the four heart-winning things, practising generosity 83
and friendly speech and care for the welfare of others, and con-
stant in condescension. To show the world that he respected 84
his royal brothers[2] as himself he assigned the two uparājas
vehicles and retinue and every kind of distinction, made them 85
thus completely contented and thus showed forth in the best
way the fourfold heart-winning qualities. These two who 86
in this wise attained distinction, celebrated each for himself
a great festival for the Tooth Relic. They had books copied

[1] I. e. Kurunegala. According to this passage the chronicle came down to the time of Parakkamabāhu IV., who resided in Kurunegala. The MSS. confirm this where after 90. 102 a new section begins. The mode of expression in this passage (v. 80) is only in so far inexact as the reign of Parakkamabāhu IV. does not begin the new part but stands at the close of the old. That the Siamese Mahāvaṃsa goes further than the original Mahāvaṃsa of Mahānāma is not expressly stated. The Mahānāyaka of the Malvatu-vihāra in Kandy, Tibbatuvava, was entrusted by the King with the task of comparing the two chronicles and of completing the Sinhalese Mahāvaṃsa (cf. P. E. Pieris, 3, p. 142). In all probability, therefore, he was the author of chapters 90. 104 to 100 of the Mahāvaṃsa.

[2] The King had two brothers of whom the one was brought with him and his sister to Ceylon by their father Narenappa Nayaker (Pieris 3, p. 78) while the youngest was born there.

87 and gave the scribes money. They invited the bhikkhu com-
munity and each for himself continually gave them alms, such
88 as constant maintenance and the like. By listening to the
pious doctrine they learned to distinguish between what should
be done and what should be left undone, abhorred sinful
89 actions and were full of zeal for meritorious deeds. By testing
they discovered the ablest, most skilful and most pious sāmaṇeras;
and to these sāmaṇeras they presented as gift the eightfold
necessaries[1], so that they were worthy of a king, had the
90 ceremony of admission to the Order performed for them and
took care that they were rightly instructed in the precepts of
monastic discipline and in the suttantas. Then they had
dwellings erected which was a great blessing[2] (for themselves),
91 made the monks dwell therein caring for them meanwhile in
worthy fashion full of reverence. They considered in every
92 way what should be done for the laity and the Order, developed
in accordance with the intentions of the King, kindness to-
wards the good and sternness towards the bad, according to
93 their deserts, strove in this wise and with other means after
good and acted according to the intentions of the King as
good friends of the laity and of the Order.

94 Many former kings for the sake of gaining the royal
dignity or for other reasons did not look on each other as
95 brothers or otherwise (as friends), but fought one another and
as a result of their discord their subjects were even so minded.
But these three (brothers) who had yet attained such royal
96 power, shunned all discord and showed no weaknesses. They
dwelt together in one town and were ever friendly with one
97 another as their own shadows. Thus there was never the least
enmity among them on account of the royal dignity and they
developed the virtues of the Bodhisatta in the Sīlavajātaka[3].

[1] See note to 60. 71.

[2] On account of the merit, the *puñña*, inherent in such performances.

[3] Cf. Mahāsīlavajātaka (Nr. 51), Fausböll I. 261 ff. The point of the comparison lies in the fact that the Bodhisatta as King Mahāsīlava of Benares, although his position was threatened by the Kosala king, undertakes no deed of violence in order to preserve his kingdom.

The Licchavis too of Visālā carried on the government in 98
harmony and without discord and won thereby the victory[1].
Rulers of men of little discernment, infatuated by the beauty 99
of the maiden Laṅkā, did what they ought not to have done
and fell in consequence into much misfortune. But rulers of 100
great discernment, made happy by the beauty of the maiden
Laṅkā, did what they ought and were thereby happy and
famous. As rulers of this kind have these three Lords of men 101
held fast to harmony, and I say: that was wonderful.

When the Great king, rich in virtue, saw his brother to 102
whom he had granted the umbrella and other distinctions
enter (in pomp) with royal retinue, he rejoiced, gazed at him 103
again and again and realized thus in himself the unique,
sublimest spiritual perfection[2].

As the highest in the dynasties of the princes of the earth, 104
as supporting pillars of the Order, possessed of immeasurable
virtue, living according to the pious doctrine, shunning to
follow the path of evil, associating with pious friends, desirous
of reaching the road to the salutary path of delivrance — thus 105
these Rulers dowered with pious virtue, who saw in faith their
highest good, did honour with sacrifice in piety to the Tooth
of the blessed Enlightened One and to the Doctrine and the
Order, accumulated abundant merit assuring the fullest sal-
vation and piously sheltered the Order of the Sage and this
stainless Laṅkā. For ever (therefore) shall one honour this 106
Ruler of Laṅkā, distinguished by virtue, who ever remembers
the fulness of valuable qualities of the Sage, the sole Lord
protector of the world, having piously accepted them in his
heart, and who then further remembers[3] his sublime doctrine
and his Order[4].

[1] Visālā, name for Vesālī (note to 37. 80). Our verse alludes to the fact that the Licchavis were able to maintain themselves against the advancing Kosalas while the Sakiyas succumbed to them. Rhys Davids, Buddhist India, p. 259—60.

[2] P. *bhāvayī* .. *brahmabhāvanaṃ ekakaṃ*. W. translates freely "only turned his mind to contemplate the virtue of benevolence to all men."

[3] I translate *anussarantaṃ* thus in contrast to the preceding *sarantaṃ*, the former being a necessary corollary of the latter.

[4] *Dhammagaṇaṃ* is a dvandva compound and *gaṇa* = *saṃgha*.

107 Thus this Monarch dowered with great royal power, the great King of kings, protected the Order of the Sage and this stainless Laṅkā in pious fashion; making men of all countries contented and dispensing to them great happiness he made gods and men beam with joy, discerning, strong in merit, miraculous power and dominion.

108 While the highly famed Great king, dowered with great power, resided in the great town and protected the laity and
109 the Order, the powerful Olandas, sea merchants who had been entrusted with the protection of Laṅkā at the time of King Rājasīha[1], fulfilled the task of envoys to the kings who ruled
110 in Laṅkā. Every year they were wont to bring with great reverence and great ceremony as gifts and lay before the King
111 various stuffs, made in different countries, along with many other articles, fitted for the use of a king, which they had
112 carefully chosen out. In consequence of former actions of the inhabitants of Laṅkā or in consequence of their neglect of the deities and so forth who were entrusted with the care of
113 the laity and the Order, they were now angered in the highest degree and in every way cruelly tortured the inhabi-
114 tants of Laṅkā[2]. When the highly famed Great king heard of these events he thought this was not as it should be, and
115 sent dignitaries forth. The dignitaries set forth with the people living in Laṅkā, fought a fearful battle with the Olanda
116 people, destroyed the foe, burned down his strongholds and terrified him in every possible way.

117 Now when the enemy were thus tortured by fear a cruel treacherous man[3] placed himself at their head, low-minded,

[1] Rājasīha II. Cf. 96. 35.

[2] The meaning is this: The inhabitants of Laṅkā have obviously failed in their duty to the deities who like Viṣṇu are the protectors of the country; they have neglected their worship. To punish them the offended deities rouse the wrath of the Dutch for the oppression and injury of the people of Laṅkā in every possible way.

[3] Baron van Eck is meant here. He succeeded Schreuder as governor of Ceylon in 1762. The word *khīṇāyu* is an allusion to the fact that van Eck died suddenly, immediately after the unfortunate campaign against Kandy. Cf. v. 135.

a villain, the end of whose life was near, and with a great 118
following consisting of Jāvakas and many other people he
laid waste in every (possible) way the various provinces and
villages, the vihāras and the temples of the gods, the bridges,
rest-houses and the like. The dignitaries charged by the Ruler 119
of Laṅkā fought here and there in every way with their war-
skilled troops, but although they defeated the foe in various 120
places, the enemy were not to be warded off, and they ad-
vanced against the town. The war-equipped high dignitaries 121
hindered the foe on the way by every means, took up a
frontal position against them and checked their gradual ad-
vance. The discerning Great king, the Ruler of Laṅkā, who 122
understood the conditions of the time, thought: it is impossible
to stop the advance of the foe who are like a forest fire, and
he entrusted the two uparājas with the sacred Tooth Relic, 123
the Mahesī, his sister and all valuable treasures, to watch
over them well and sent them to a province which was 124
scarcely passable owing to mountains, forests and difficult
roads. Thereupon the hostile hosts like cruel armies of yakkhas, 125
forced their way into the town and destroyed the sacred
books and everything else. Surrounded by his great digni- 126
taries like the senāpati and others, and by war-skilled heroes
who knew the right occasions from the wrong, the Great 127
king took up a position at the head of his great army here
and there in the suburbs situated not far from the capital,
and invested the town on every side. The people dwelling 128
in Laṅkā who had remained true to the teaching of the Buddha
adopted the plans of the King and cut down here and there
many of those who had gone over to the enemy, whomever 129
they caught sight of, but the envoys of the King and the
other officials and the community of the bhikkhus they took
under their protection. The bold warriors gifted with heroism 130
who were on the King's side played the war game, and as their
aim was the protection of the Order of the Victor, they fought 131
surrounded by their warlike men in every way with the enemy
who were posted at various positions on the road, put them 132
to flight, began then to fight also with those who lay in the

133 town and repeatedly caused them great losses[1]. I think it
was no wonder that men adopted the plans of our King: the
134 deities did the same. Hence after a short time the greatly
deluded leader of the enemy was smitten with fear, horror
and delusion which came over him owing to the might of the
135 gods and owing to the power of the merit (of the King). He
left the fair town, fled without prestige and landed in the
136 fire of death. Victims of the power of infatuation all the
hostile armies who had advanced, were helpless and shelterless,
137 and came to a bad end. Some were visited by illness, some
tortured by hunger and disease, some were slain in fight,
some had lost themselves in mountain and wilderness: thus
were the miserable people on the enemy's side destroyed.
138 "Protected in such wise by gods, men and others", one said,
"this Monarch is certainly of great power: he is rich in
139 merit. Who in the world will be able to neglect the com-
mands of so mighty a king who is so rich in merit[2]?"

[1] Verses 130—132 describe the guerilla tactics employed by the Sinhalese. The attacks are directed first against the communications in the rear, the positions in the line of march. The troops in Kandy are thereby isolated and so exposed to attack.

[2] The whole section vv. 108-139 (cf. vv. 159 ff. and note) is perhaps historically the most valuable part of the latest Cūlavaṃsa. It refers to the military events of the year 1765 (see H. W. Codrington, HC., p. 142 f.; P. E. Pieris, 3, p. 118 ff.). The causes of the conflict again lay in the sphere of trade policy. The King wanted to secure his share in the areca and elephant trade, and to compel the Dutch to yield this he harmed and hindered the business of the Dutch Company in every possible way, particularly in their export of cinnamon which was for them specially important. At first the Dutch sought to keep the peace by weak surrender. It was not until 1763 under the Governor van Eck that they decided on warlike measures. Their first venture in this year was a failure. Two years later the Dutch troops entered Kandy, but suffered so under the perpetual attacks of the Sinhalese that they were soon obliged to evacuate the town and withdraw with the severest losses to Colombo. Three facts are passed over by the chronicle in silence: 1) There was a conspiracy in 1761 against Kittisiri, important so far as it was obviously the work of the nationalistic circles at Court and was directed against the Dravidian dynasty. 2) At the beginning of the hostilities the King started negotiations with the

When after the hosts of the enemy had been done away 140
with, the Great king no longer beheld a hostile army, the
Ruler had the fair town cleansed as formerly and in fitting 141
manner the temple of the Tooth Relic and the other sanc-
tuaries specially beautifully decorated. He was filled with 142
pure reverence towards the sublime doctrine of the Enlightened
One, meditated ever on the sublime words of the Enlightened
One, was filled with remembrance of the virtues of the sons
of the Enlightened One and ever reverenced the Tooth of the
Royal Enlightened One. The Ruler of men who in such wise 143
was completely devoted to the three sacred objects, could not
bear the pain accruing to him from his separation from the
Tooth Relic. So the Great king, strong in faith, betook him-
self[1] with his retinue to the most impassable part of the
province, and when there he caught sight of the reliquary, 144
he reverenced it piously, his heart full of astonishment and
admiration. He bent his head to the ground, worshipped (the 145
relic) with his head, greeted reverently the community of the
bhikkhus and so chased away his pain. Filled with good 146
comfort, he raised the casket with the relic to his head, held
a great feast and celebrating with the sound of the cries of 147
"Hail"! and the fivefold musical instruments a great cere-
monial festival, he entered into his town. Then when the 148
people of Laṅkā saw the Ruler with the relic, they rejoiced
greatly and sent forth their cries of "Hail!". He brought 149
the relic into the former Tooth temple and instituted all the
former festive customs in increased measure.

The Saṃgharāja[2] and many other sons of the Buddha in 150

British, which however, led to nothing. The British emissary to the Court of Kandy was Pybus. 3) A famine in his own country caused by the neglect of agriculture during the war forced Kittisiri in 1766 to make a peace treaty with the Dutch very unfavourable to himself. By this treaty he made over to the Dutch the whole coastal district of the island, so that the kingdom of Kandy was completely cut off from the outer world and absolutely dependent on the good will of the Company.

[1] One expects of course a *gantvā* to govern the acc. *mahāduggaṃ raṭṭhaṃ*.

[2] This was the Saraṇaṃkara mentioned in 97. 51 and 98. 23. The

all the monasteries of the town who saw that the danger of
151 the cycle of rebirths is far greater than the danger of the
foe, had not given up the monastic life but had departed
152 with books, relics and articles of use, and dwelling outside
of the country had protected the Order. The King of kings
153 brought them all speedily back to the town, had the mo-
nasteries in the town cleansed and made the bhikkhus take
up their abode in them. Then he sought out from among
those who were charged to school themselves in the study of
the scriptures and in the carrying out of the commandments,
154 the appropriate preachers, invited them and listened ever and
again to the Rājovāda[1] and other portions of the sacred
scriptures.

155 The many Olanda people who had been our foes thought
156 of the custom of the country. They all came together, took
counsel with one another and said: "to capture the whole of
Laṅkā is impossible." After they had finally realised this
157 they consulted ever and again: "The people here who rebelled
against the King, the ruler of Laṅkā have gone to perdition;
158 it will be the same with us. It is fitting therefore, that we
dwell here in the town with humility, love and reverence
159 towards the sovereign of Laṅkā." Together with gifts for
the King they took full of reverence the beautiful, empty
160 silver reliquary which had been carried away by the great
fool and which sparkled like a cetiya, as well as the golden
161 canopy[2]. They thought: we shall seek pardon for the wrong

title of *saṃgharāja* borne by the head of the whole priesthood but which had fallen into disuse since the 15th century, had been conferred on him by Kittisiri in 1750. P. E. Pieris 3, p. 76.

[1] I. e. "Admonishing of the King" Perhaps this is the same as the Rājavagga of Aṅguttara, III. 147 ff.

[2] When the Dutch under van Eck advanced on Kandy the Sinhalese secured the Tooth Relic (v. 123 f.), but the *karaṇḍaka*, in which it was preserved and the *sivikā* ereeted over it in the temple fell into the hands of the enemy. Van Eck took them with him on his retreat to Colombo. His successor however, J. W. Falck, returned these highly sacred objects. The result of this prudent and conciliatory policy was

committed by our countrymen and shall from now onwards live (in peace), betook themselves to the Ruler, praised him,
showed him reverence and spake many friendly words. The 162
King, the sovereign of Laṅkā, pardoned them their great
wrong and showed them distinction in every way. In this 163
wise by friendly negotiations our King achieved with them
firm and lasting[1] friendly relations. The Olanda people also 164
became thoroughly reconciled with the King of Laṅkā and were wont every year to present him along with valuable gifts, the products of various countries, with a royal letter
which had been handed to them. But the Ruler had the 165
sacred casket which had fallen into the hands of the infidels,
covered with gold and silver and set with jewels. After having 166
thus made its beauty like to that of the sun[2] he had the Tooth Relic placed therein and reverenced it as the King of the gods.

Thus was the pride of the wicked hosts of the infidel foe 167
destroyed. Ha, (so great was) the power of the merit of the pious, believing Ruler of the Sīhalas. Thinking of this astonishing, wonderful thing, people should devote themselves full of reverence to the virtue of the true faith which is incomparable, praised by the good, splendid.

Since at that time there was not a single bhikkhu on the 168
fair island of Laṅkā, he had after taking over the burden of
government, residing in Sirivaḍḍhana, made many sāmaṇeras 169
and as many sons of good family go through the ceremony of renunciation of the world and of admission to the Order.
Of these bhikkhus some were preachers of the doctrine and 170
acquainted with the precepts of monastic discipline, some led
a life of contemplation or that of hermits. After he had thus 171
ordained so many hundreds of bhikkhus dowered with this and other virtues[3] he beautified the whole of Laṅkā (formerly)

that the beleaguered garrison left behind in Kandy and reduced to sore straits, was granted a free passage.

[1] P. *thiraṃ katvāna* must, I think, be referred to *mettibhāvaṃ*.

[2] P. *sataraṃsi*, the "hundred-rayed", name of the sun.

[3] Pāda a is of course defective. We expect *evamādiguṇayutte*. But

172 bereft of bhikkhus. Day by day he performed meritorious
works, invited the community and dispensed to it daily food
and food for the sick, mindful of the welfare of the bhikkhu
community.

173 For bhikkhus and sāmaṇeras there were two kinds of disease,
such as had to do with the body and such as affected the
mind. To cure mental disease the best of men had the Vinaya
174 texts and the Suttantas preached. After he had had the bhikkhus
instructed in the Vinaya and the Suttantas which are the cause
of the removal of desire and other diseases among mental
175 diseases, the Ruler — when suffering arises through bodily
disease it is difficult for the bhikkhus to school themselves
in the study of the scriptures and in the carrying out of the
176 commandments[1] — to calm disease like fever[2] and the like
for this reason invited the community. He appointed for them
177 two physicians, well schooled in the medical art, and nurses.
To these he granted villages and fields and facilities in the
178 way of garments, ornaments and the like, and as price for
medicines he gave them yearly a hundred (money pieces) from
179 the royal treasury. In the various monasteries the Ruler asked
after the health or ill-health of the sāmaṇeras and the bhikkhus
and gave them the requisite care.

180 In this wise also the King of kings dispensed gain for the
community. "Of all gains[3] the gain of health is the highest
181 and best", thus the Buddha taught and therefore even he also
dispensed[4] it. He furthered in the best way the Order of
the Enlightened One by making it lustrous.

emendation is inadmissible. The fault is the author's, the MSS. are not to blame.

[1] V. 175 is a kind of parenthesis. In correct language the sentence would be accompanied by an *iti* or *iti cintiya* as a reflection of the King's. Cf. note to 100. 52.

[2] W. is probably right in connecting *jara* here with skr. *jvara* (not P. *jarā* "age").

[3] Note that *lābha* means a gain or advantage of an external kind.

[4] *Apūjayi* is here used as synonym for *dāpayi* in 180 b.

Formerly the rulers of Laṅkā, the best of most excellent men, the supports of the Order, removed the infidelity of the hosts of the foe and then bore the burden of the royal dignity. When the King heard thereof and himself compassed in spirit the doctrine revealing itself to him and fraught with immeasurable blessing, he performed continually meritorious works, unweariedly, a support of the Order[1]. 182

Here ends the ninety-ninth chapter, called »Account of the King's Consecration and of Other Festivals», in the Mahāvaṃsa, compiled for the serene joy and emotion of the pious.

[1] The panegyric character of many strophes occurring in this chapter of the chronicle seems again to prove that it was composed when the king Kittisirirājasīha was alive. The poet flatters him with the conventional phrases.

CHAPTER C

THE HISTORY OF KITTISIRIRĀJASĪHA

1 The highly famed Lord of men[1] honoured the Tooth Relic
with constant reverence even as (a world ruler) his wheel[2]
and worshipped it in every way sacrificing[3] with all kinds of
flowers, such as sumana, campaka, punnāga, nāga, kaṇikāra,
2 ketakī[4], white and blue lotus flowers and the like, as well
as with perfumes of every sort, such as sandal and aloe wood;
3 with divers kinds of fragrant incense, with sugar, honey and
so forth and with delicious remedies like betel nut, camphor
4 and betel leaves; with various prepared dishes such as sweet
food, rice and cake, with golden bananas and rose-apples,
with bread fruits, mangoes and phārusa fruits[5], with date
5 plums[6], oranges[7] and sweet muṇḍakas, with yellow and green

[1] I anticipate the subject *mahāyaso* (v. 8c) and *janindo* (v. 12a). The sentence goes on to v. 22 in which the first finite verb appears. Various gerunds occur before this and the subject "the King" is repeated several times.

[2] P. *cakka.* This is the first of the seven jewels (*ratanāni*) peculiar to the *rājā cakkavattī*, the world-ruling king (cf. for this D. II. 172 ff., III. 61 ff.; M. III. 172; PTS. PD. s. v. *ratana*), a marvellous chariot that carries him victoriously over all countries.

[3] I anticipate *pūjetvā* in v. 8.

[4] The botanical names are successively: 1) jasminum grandiflorum, 2) michelia champaka, 3) rottleria tinctoria, 4) mesua ferrea, 5) pterospermum acerifolium, 6) pandanus odoratissimus.

[5] Cf. also Mhvs. 89. 43 and note.

[6] P. *timbarūsaka* a kind of diospyros. The fruit called *timbaru* is compared in Ja. VI. 457[1] to the youthful female breast. We do not know what the *phārusa* is.

[7] P. *nāraṅga* = skr. *nāraṅga* which is borrowed from the Persian *nārang*. *Muṇḍaka* again is unknown.

coconuts, with ripe pomegranates, with dates, grapes and various 6
other fruits, with many fine roots[1] and sprouts of every kind.
With such and other offerings, with the five kinds of musical 7
instruments, with many of the things taken over from former
kings and with new thereto he worshipped the Tooth Relic 8
day by day, thereby intent on merit, increasing the store of
his meritorious works. With gold and silver, with fair precious 9
stones and pearls, with countless, brightly embroidered,
gleaming stuffs; with canopies, curtains and robes, with many 10
articles of use and manifold ornaments, with many elephants 11
and steeds, as well as with cattle and buffaloes, with many
slaves male and female and with numerous villages and fields
he sacrificed full of zeal to the Tooth of the Enlightened One 12
and when the Prince of men beheld it he was filled with pious
joy. He was minded to have the golden casket completed 13
which had been begun under former kings but had never
been finished. After a splendid, jewel-encrusted[2] casket had 14
been made for two thousand suvaṇṇas and seven nikkhas[3],
the Lord of men ever intent on meritorious action, had a 15
costly, splendid, magnificent, large diamond placed on the point;
one hundred and sixty-eight beautiful, costly, splendid (smaller) 16
diamonds, well worth seeing, and one hundred and seventy-
one topazes[4] he had put on it, further he had it set with 17
five hundred and eighty-five blue sapphires and four thousand 18
eight hundred and eighty rubies, also he had it set with seven 19
hundred and seventy-eight pearls, and when the costly casket

[1] P. *sādhukandehi*. The word *kanda* „root" (skr. the same) is missing in Childers and also in the PTS. P. D.

[2] P. *maṇivaṇṇa*. The word *vaṇṇa* does not mean "colour" here, but "beauty, ornament", as is often the case.

[3] *Suvaṇṇa* as well as *nikkha*, as also skr. *suvarṇa* and *niṣka* denote a weight and a coin. The *nikkha* is = 15 *suvaṇṇa* (PTS P. D. s. v.).

[4] P. *puppharāgamaṇiratane*. It is true that *puppharāga* by itself means "topaz" (= skr. *puṣparāga*). What is expressed however, is the fundamental meaning "flower coloured". Thus we have in the same way *nīlamaṇi* "blue gem" (17 d) for "sapphire" and *rattamaṇiratana* "red gem" (18 c d) for "ruby".

20 was finished he had two further caskets made in which to
place it and had these also set with costly splendid, beautiful
21 jewels. The Ruler of men had the casket made by the famous
22 King Vimaladhammasuriya[1] overlaid with gold. Then the
Ruler of men, celebrating a great festival, placed the Tooth
23 of the Sage in these same (caskets). Full of pious joy the
Ruler dedicated a large village, Akarabhaṇḍa by name, to the
Tooth of the Prince of the wise.

24 At the festival of the relic the Ruler in his mercy thought
25 to show the Tooth Relic to the inhabitants of Laṅkā. After
the Ruler had had the whole town of Sirivaḍḍhana carefully
cleansed and decorated throughout with arches of many-
26 coloured stuffs, with rows of arches of banana leaves, with
bunches of coco blossoms and with all kinds of flags and
27 pennons, he gathered together in the town all the people of
Laṅkā. The Ruler of men himself, adorned with all the royal
28 ornaments, like the King of the gods, betook himself after
he had previously celebrated many great sacrifices of all kinds,
to the temple of the Tooth Relic, sacrificed to it in every
29 possible way, worshipped it, he the Ruler by throwing himself
in humble posture[2] to the earth out of reverence for the
30 Tooth Relic of the King of the wise. Then he took the
golden lotus flower together with the Tooth in the lotus of
31 his hand and went forth from the temple with it. With sa-
crificial ceremonies, celebrated[3] with silver umbrellas and fly-
whisks of yak tails[4], with golden and silver flowers, with the
32 five kinds of flowers, lāja[5] and so forth, with many jewels
and pearls, with gold and silver, with various coloured stuffs

[1] In Mhvs. 94. 11 ff. it is related that he brought the Tooth Relic from Labujagāma to Kandy. Nothing is said in the passage about the making of a *karaṇḍa*.

[2] Cf. 98. 50 and note.

[3] P. *kāriyamānapūjāsu* in v. 34 c.

[4] P. *camarīcāmarehi*. The fem. *camarī* is also employed in Skr. (BR. s. v. *camara*). See above 98. 14, as well as Jāt. IV. 256 *camarinaṅguṭṭha*.

[5] Cf. 98. 46 and note.

and many kinds of ornaments, with divers fragrant flowers, 33
with many lamps and incense, and amid the sound of the five
musical instruments, the shell trumpets, the cymbals and the
rest, and amid the noise of the many thousandfold cries of 34
Hail! — it was like foam-crowned billows[1] — the highly 35
famed King marched in procession like a world ruler in his
chariot[2]. In the superb, beautiful maṇḍapa, decorated with 36
all kinds of brightly embroidered cloths, like a heavenly
maṇḍapa stood the King, the Ruler of men, like the King of 37
the gods at the head of the company of the gods, and then
the King showing the multitude of the people the sacred
beautiful Tooth of the Prince of the wise, right hard to attain
in hundreds of thousands of world ages, filled them all with 38
bliss, heaped up a store of merit and laid (the relic) again
in the casket.

In this wise, feeling every kind of bliss, as at the sight 39
of the living Buddha, the multitude also increased the store
of their merits.

Intent on good, he repeatedly exhibited the Tooth Relic 40
in the same way and so stored up much good. Of villages 41
and fields devoted by former kings of Laṅkā to the Tooth
Relic he took not away the very least. Day by day holding 42
a great sacrificial festival in joyful faith, he dedicated many
elephants and horses and in the same way bulls and buffaloes,
as well as a prosperous, populous village by name Rajakatthala, 43
and another large village by name Muttāpabbata[3] and gained
thereby for himself the value of meritorious works.

He was mindful of the purity of the Order. Amongst the 44
bhikkhus who were formerly present on the splendid island
of Laṅkā, and amongst all the sāmaṇeras who had undergone

[1] P. *kallolamāliṇī va* stands quite independently of the construction of the sentence, as a kind of parenthesis. It refers to the whole procession.

[2] See note to 100. 1, Note 2.

[3] There is a village Radagoda in the Kandy District, Medapalata Korale, a village Mutugala in the Kurunegala District, Udukaha Korale West (Census 1921, II, p. 60, 328).

the ceremony of world renunciation, were some who had fear
45 of evil, respected the true doctrine, living in good moral
discipline, in pure fashion. Others cherished evil, were of
46 bad moral living, followed false doctrine, took pleasure in the
maintaining of women and children and in domestic duties
and devoted themselves to unseemly professions such as astro-
logy, medical activity[1] and the like.
47 When the Ruler heard tidings of such unprincipled
(bhikkhus) he sought out[2] with care from among the pious
48 (bhikkhus) who were on the side of the high principled, the
respected sāmaṇera, named Saraṇaṃkara, who led a pure life,
dwelt in the wilderness, took pains for the furthering of the
Order of the Victor, was careful of moral discipline, virtuous,
49 well instructed, experienced in the interpretation of the words
50 of the Enlightened One. With the reflection that this was the
right thing to do, the Ruler with his support, ordered accord-
ing to precept, an investigation, took strong measures against
51 them and had them seriously admonished that from now on-
wards those who had renounced the world should for ever avoid
unseemly task, like astrology, medical activity and the like and
52 should foster[3] the study of the words of the Buddha. As the
King was minded to further the Order which had fallen into
53 decay, he strengthened the influence of the high principled,
54 and in many ways gave the Order support. The Ruler was
appalled at the thought that with the lack of bhikkhus on
whom the ceremony of admission to the Order had been per-
55 formed, the pure Order of the Victor should perish on the

[1] That is the activity of the *kapurāla*, the sorceror or devil-priest whose help is sought in cases of illness and for warding off the harmful influence of the planetary deities.

[2] P. *sammā vijānitvā* cannot belong to *pavattiṃ*, as W. seems to think, but must govern the following accusatives. For Saraṇaṃkara cf. above 97. 51, 60; 98. 23; as well as note to 99. 150. The Saṃgharāja died in the year 1778.

[3] The construction of the sentence is quite wrong. It would be right if instead of *rakkhituṃ* in 52 b we had *rakkhantūti* whereby vv. 51 and 52 a b would be characterized as oratio recta.

whole island, and with the reflection: if a Ruler like myself
carries on the government in the island of Laṅkā, then the 56
Order of the Victor ought not to perish, — further with the
reflection: the furtherance of the Order which was not at-
tained in the time of former rulers in spite of their sending 57
hither and thither for bhikkhus, this will I now bring to pass,
the Ruler of men, the Monarch, rich in merit, since he de- 58
sired a long continuance of the Order of the great Seer, when 59
the year two thousand two hundred and ninety-three after
the final nirvana of the Prince of the wise[1] had come — sent
messengers to whom he gave besides gifts of many kinds and 60
many sacrificial articles, a splendid royal letter, to the superb
town of Ayojjhā[2], to fetch hither sons of the Buddha. In 61
this wise the Ruler of Laṅkā who was minded to purify the
Order of Buddha, began the furtherance of the Order of the
Prince among victors.

The dignitaries took the royal letter and the rest and 62
started with great ceremony and with great zeal on their way.
With the Olanda people who were entrusted with the pro- 63
tection of Laṅkā, they embarked and sailed to the land of
Sāminda. When the town of Ayojjhā was reached the Ruler 64
of men in that country accepted the royal letter and the rest,
as was the custom. In best fashion the prudent one showed 65
the dignitaries the honour befitting them and took note of
the excellent royal letter. When the Ruler of men Dhammika 66
by name, who striving after the dignity of a Buddha, fulfilled
the ten pāramīs[3] and took the Order under his protection,

[1] = 1749 A. D. . What is meant is the time of the close of the embassies to Siam which had already begun under Kittisiri's predecessor Vijayarājasīha. We have an interesting account of these embassies by a member: "An Account of Kirti Sri's Embassy to Siam in 1672 Saka, 1750 A. D., published by P. E. Pieris in JRAS. C. B. xviii, nr. 54, 1903, p. 17 ff. I see no reason to doubt the genuine character of the document. The relations established by the coming of the bhikkhus from Siam are potent in their influence even to-day. The Siamese sect is the wealthiest and the most influential in the island of Ceylon. For the vicissitudes experienced by these embassies see Pieris 3, p. 71, 73, 75 ff.

[2] See note to 98. 91. [3] See for this note to 37. 180.

67 heard the news of the decline of the Order of the Victor in
Laṅkā, and of the other (evils) he was most deeply moved.
68 The Ruler thought: "I will be a helper in order to achieve
there the furtherance of the Order of the Enlightened One."
69 He summoned the Saṃgharāja in the Sāminda country and
many other well instructed Grand theras, versed in the doctrine
and acquainted with the rules of the Order, who had for a
70 long time renounced the world, who were capable of carrying
out the business of the Order and took counsel with them
71 carefully about the matter. He called together a Chapter
consisting of a group of ten (bhikkhus), an abode of virtues,
easily satisfied and content, dowered with the virtues of a life
of piety and discipline, and besides the Thera Upāli as head.
72 These the Ruler who was well inclined to the Great king on
the island of Laṅkā — like to King Vessantara[1] — sent[2] to
73 Laṅkā, to the splendid relic temple of the Victor and (with
them) books on the doctrine and on monastic discipline which
74 did not exist in the island of Laṅkā, further a golden image
(of the Buddha) and a superb golden book, a magnificent royal
letter, gifts of various kinds and dignitaries of the King of
75 Ayojjhā (as envoys)[3]. The great vessel[4] which after the golden
image and the other gifts had been put in order, was sent off
came without disaster over the sea[5] rich in perils, hiding many
76 a disaster, to the fair, splendid island of Laṅkā and reached
77 the harbour of Tikoṇamāla[6]. When the Great king, the Ruler
of Laṅkā had tidings of this, he had all the inhabitants of

[1] The last human incarnation of the Bodhisatta; cf. Vessantarajātaka (Nr. 547; VI. 479 ff. in Fausböll's edition).

[2] All the accusatives in vv. 71-74 are governed by *apesesi*, to those in v. 71 must be added the gerund *nimantayitvāna*. The gifts, among them the golden image, are enumerated in the narrative quoted above (note to v. 59). The number of the theras with Upāli at their head, is however given as twenty-one, with eight sāmaṇeras in addition.

[3] Three in number according to the narrative.

[4] The subject *nāvā* in 75 c is repeated with *mahānāvā* in 76 d. The language in the whole section is extremely careless.

[5] P. *gambhīre*, used substantively and supplemented by *samudde*.

[6] I. e. Trincomalee.

the town of Sirivaḍḍhana called together. In joyful faith the 78
Ruler of men celebrated a great feast. From the sea as far
as superb Sirivaḍḍhanapura he had the road put in order and 79
rest-houses[1] erected at various places. Then the Ruler sent forth
the Mahāsenāpati and other dignitaries and made them fetch 80
in the right order the golden image and the sacred books,
the bhikkhu community and everything else. When with great 81
pomp and great ceremony they making their way had reached
the vicinity of the Mahāvālukagaṅgā which comes down from 82
the Sumanakūṭa, the Ruler of the town Sirivaḍḍhana, the Ruler 83
of men desirous of gaining the reward accruing from the festive
reception of the three sacred objects[2], the highly famed Great
king intent on merit, went forth with the army in piety to meet 84
them with elephants, steeds and so forth. He showed reverence
to the august Grand thera and to the others and at the same 85
time greeted the great community. Having exchanged with
them in the best way possible the customary speeches of wel-
come, he came with the three sacred objects at the head, to 86
his town. In the fair Puppharāma[3], in a graceful brick-roofed
building erected by him, in this decorated monastery he made 87
the august community of monks take up their abode. Then
he provided them in fitting manner with the necessaries and 88
charged officials to enquire day by day after their health or
ill-health. The Ruler of men accepted the splendid royal letter 89
sent by the King of Ayojjhā and he made the royal envoys who 90
had arrived and the other officials take up their abode in a
fitting place and showed them all the distinction to which they
were entitled. In the year two thousand two hundred and 91
ninety-six after the final nirvana of the Enlightened One[4],

[1] P. *ārāme*, thus buildings which were specially intended for the sojourn of the monks.

[2] In the train of the envoys from Siam there were 1) a golden figure of the Buddha (*Buddha*), 2) sacred books (*dhamma*) and 3) the bhikkhus with Upāli at the head (*saṃgha*).

[3] "Flower monastery" the now so-called Malvatu-vihāra situated immediately on the lake of Kandy.

[4] = 1752 A. D.

92 in the month Āsāḷha[1] when it was full moon, the all-powerful
93 Great king, dowered with vast royal power, betook himself
to the monastery. He had seats carefully spread in the middle
94 of the fine Uposatha house contained therein. Then he invited
the Grand thera Upāli, dowered with the quality of a life
led in moral discipline, experienced in all clever methods, who
95 had his pleasure in the welfare of all beings, and second to
him the Thera Āriyamuni[2] together with the (rest of the)
community and bade them be seated. Then with the cele-
96 bration of a great festival the Ruler of men, the Ruler of
Laṅkā, made these perform on the most distinguished of the
sāmaṇeras of Laṅkā the ceremony of admission to the Order.
97 From that time onwards he was wont to fetch hither
sāmaṇeras and others who were versed in the linguistic text-
books on the sacred scriptures, and have performed on them
98 the ceremony of admission to the Order. In the same way
he sought out rightly all those who were worthy of the
ceremony of world renunciation and of admission to the sublime
99 Order of the Enlightened One and had the ceremony of world
renunciation and of admission performed on them according to
precept. Among the bhikkhu communities who thus had become
100 numerous in Laṅkā, he again sought out those bhikkhus who
were full of lasting zeal in preserving the study of the sacred
scriptures and of the rules of monastic life and who were
101 qualified for and worthy of the position of a teacher, and
charged them to take instruction from the brethren of the
Order who had come from Ayojjhā. Now among those high
principled bhikkhus who carried out the commands of the
102 Victor, there was one who[3] had long been at pains to make

[1] The month June-July.

[2] In the narrative (p. 34) quoted above (note to v. 59) the Grand thera Āriyamuni is mentioned as second to Upāli.

[3] All the relative sentences beginning with *yo* in vv. 102-107 refer to *taṃ* in v. 107 c. This part of the long-winded sentence is but loosely connected with the preceding which ends with *niyojiya*. If we might alter *niyojiya* into *niyojayi* and put a full stop after it, the construction of the sentence would be all right.

lustrous the Order of the Sage which for a long time had
been on the verge of ruin in Laṅkā, — who in accordance 103
with his insight, as far as possible untiringly, day and night,
made lustrous the sacred scriptures of the Prince of the wise
and his rules for monastic life — who also instructed as dis- 104
ciples many others in the sacred scriptures and the rules for
monastic life and thus in worthy manner brought splendour
to the Order, — who striving for his own salvation and that 105
of others, with the wish to obtain long continuance for the
Order of the Sage, ever took pleasure in a pure life, — who 106
as regards virtue, discipline and devotion to duty was as a
mirror for all the sons of the Victor in Laṅkā who were intent
on their salvation, — who during the time that he was a 107
sāmaṇera was called Saraṇaṃkara: this son of the Victor living
in pious discipline now that he had been admitted to the 108
Order, he (the King) invested with the dignity of a Saṃ-
gharāja[1]. Amongst the bhikkhus who had joined him, he
sought out in both monasteries[2] such as were skilled and well
versed in the carrying out of the duties of the Order of the 109
Master and assigned them positions of rank. Explaining to
them: ye all who live out the doctrine of the Victor, should 110
act in harmony, day and night unweariedly, in accordance with
the rule of the Order and according to the sacred scriptures,
the Ruler showed them much favour and in this wise made 111
the Order lustrous so that it should continue for long in Laṅkā.

The royal envoys too, arrived from the Sāminda country, 112
and the others sought out the King, handing over to him the
royal letter and the other gifts. The Great king, the Ruler 113
of Laṅkā, accepted everything, and after the Monarch had
made a close inspection of the superb royal document he highly 114
pleased, had favours conferred on them. Now the Ruler who
for his own good, the good of others and the good of the
Order, had again and again performed meritorious works, who 115

[1] See above note to 99. 150 and to 100. 69.

[2] In the Malvatu and the Asgiriya-vihāras in Kandy, which are the seats of the two mahānāyakas, the heads of the Church of Ceylon.

was devoted to the true doctrine, a light of the Order, greatly
116 wise was wont to visit the monastery and to test in every
way in the midst of the community, the means for long continuance of the Order. As he wished to make lustrous the
117 Order, he invited in fitting manner the Grand thera Upāli
and listened with believing heart from the Dīgha-Nikāya, the
118 Saṃyutta-Nikāya, the Saddhammasaṃgaha and from various
other books, the (sections on the) tenfold royal duties and the
119 four heart-winning qualities. To faith awakened, of deep
discernment, he thus learned to distinguish between what ought
and what ought not to be done, between what is meritorious
action and what is sin, what is blameworthy and what is not
120 blameworthy, and he left undone all things which should not
be done, which are sinful and blameworthy, and strove as
best he could after the things which ought to be done and
121 are not blameworthy. Almsgiving and other meritorious works
he performed day by day, and after he had had the whole
122 town decorated as formerly he full of reverence invited the
dignitaries who had come from Ayojjhā and all the people of
Laṅkā, the Grand thera (Upāli) with the other bhikkhus (from
123 Sāminda) as well as the bhikkhus from Laṅkā, the sāmaṇeras
and all the others, and celebrating as formerly with royal
124 ornaments and all kinds of other sacrificial gifts a great festival
he exhibited the Tooth Relic for the salvation, blessing and
happiness of them all.

125 Since the royal envoys wished to do reverence to the
Mahiyaṅgaṇa-cetiya and the other cetiya places, he sent them
126 in the company of Laṅkā officials, to the various places, let
them as they desired, perform their devotions and sent them
127 home after showing them to the utmost befitting favours. In
the same way giving them sacrificial articles and appointing
officials (charged with their care), he enabled the bhikkhu
128 community with Upāli at the head, to visit the sixteen sacred
places[1] in Laṅkā, Mahiyangaṇa and so forth, as well as the

[1] According to W. these were: 1) Mahiyaṅgaṇa, 2) Nāgadīpa, 3) Kalyāṇī, 4) Samantakūṭa, 5) Divāguhā, 6) Dīghavāpi, 7) Mutiyaṅgaṇa

cetiyas in Sirivaḍḍhana and other towns. Then he had sacred 129
boundaries[1] fixed, and intent on the good of the bhikkhus,
Uposatha houses and dwellings erected here and there. Devoted 130
in faith to the bhikkhu community he had in three years
monasteries founded and made bhikkhu communities take up
their abode in them. In the periods of the rainy season[2] he 131
provided the fitting maintenance, listened to the sermon of
the true doctrine and kept the uposatha fasts. When the 132
bhikkhus were presented[3] with the various necessaries he gave
them in addition to the otherwise customary robes[4], kaṭhina
robes[5]. In the course of these three years he had the cere- 133
mony of admission to the Order performed on seven hundred
persons in the august community, and for three thousand sons 134
of good families he caused the granting of the ceremony of
world renunciation as sāmaṇeras for the good of mankind.

For the good of the world the King, the Ruler of men, 135
effected the furtherance of the Order: for that reason must
all gracious Brahmas, Suras and Asuras grant the Monarch
happiness and long life!

In the year that bears the name of Sūkara the Ruler of 136
men Dhammika the sage, who had helped so much to further
the Order in Laṅkā, since he strove after the dignity of a
Buddha, sent once more from the town Ayojjhā a group of 137

(in Badulla), 8) Tissamahāvihāra (Tissamahārāma in Mahāgāma, Rohaṇa) 9) the Bodhi tree, 10) Maricavaṭṭi-cetiya, 11) Ratanavāluka (Mahāthūpa), 12) Thūpārāma, 13) Abhayagiri, 14) Jetavana, 15) Selacetiya (9 to 15 in Anurādhapura), 16) Kājaragāma (Rohaṇa).

[1] P. *kāretvā baddhasīmāyo*, lit. "he had fixed boundaries made". The expression *simaṃ bandh* is used for the fixing of the territorial boundaries of a monastery which was carried out with particular ceremonies (Mhvs. 15. 131 ff.; 78. 61 ff).

[2] P. *antovassesu*. That is the rainy period lasting three or four months which the bhikkhu along with his companions, must spend in a settled abode (in the monastery).

[3] P. *pavāritesu*. What is meant is the Pavāraṇā ceremony held at the end of the rainy season.

[4] P. *parivāracīvarehi*. *Parivāra* here has the sense of "ingredient accessories" (PTS. P. D. s. v.).

[5] See note to 41. 48.

more than ten priests with two theras at the head — the Grand thera Visuddhācariya[1], who was an abode for the virtue of a life lived in discipline, whose ornament were faith and
138 the other virtues, who was a mine of virtue, and the capable,
139 learned second thera Varañāṇamuni — to Laṅkā for the further-
140 ance of the Order in Laṅkā. When this community arrived the highly famed King of Laṅkā accompanied them as for-
141 merly with great honours into the town, made them take up their abode in the Pupphārāma and dispensed to them daily regular food and everything else as formerly.

142 After accumulating a store of merit the distinguished Thera Upāli who during these three years unweariedly day and night
143 had done all that was to be done for the furtherance of the Order, was severely troubled by a disease of the nose which
144 befel him. The Sīhala Ruler had the best medical treatment given to the incomparable Grand thera (thus) seized by ill-
145 ness. Again and again the highly famed King went to the monastery, visited the Grand thera and when he learned, his
146 heart deeply moved, that the disease was incurable he celebrated with sacrificial objects of every kind, a sacrificial festival for the Buddha and ascribed the merit of it[2] to him (the
147 Grand thera). When the Thera was dead the Ruler of men had the corpse with great ceremonial laid in a covering of
148 fine stuff, had many sacrificial ceremonies performed, the corpse brought to the pyre and the prescribed rites carried out and thus accumulated merit.

149 The King was aware of how helpful the Ruler of men, Dhammika, the sovereign of the Sāminda country, had been in the furtherance of the Order of the King of the wise in Laṅkā, by twice sending a pious bhikkhu community and by
150 bringing about the presence of many hundreds of bhikkhus, whereas formerly there had not been a single bhikkhu on the

[1] As regards the word *mahāvisuddhācariyattheraṃ* we must I think, join the *mahā* with *theraṃ* in order to get the counterpart to *anutheraṃ* in 138 b.

[2] For *pattidāna* see note to 42. 50. In this case the *patti* is transferred to a dying man, not one already dead.

island of Laṅkā and by sending books of every kind which 151
were lacking. He thought: "To a man like that who has 152
given me so much help I will also pay in befitting manner 153
fitting honours." He ordered ministers forth to whom he
gave a model of the Tooth of the Sage fashioned out of a
costly jewel and many varied gifts such as a likeness of the 154
Victor, a shell curved towards the right[1] and other things,
and also a splendid, specially artistic royal letter, and sent 155
with them the bhikkhu community who wished to return to
their own country (Sāminda). With great reverence all the 156
dignitaries received this and journeyed forth to the country
of Sāminda. When they arrived[2] there King Dhammika was 157
joyful in heart. He gazed to his hearts content at the likeness
of the Tooth of the Sage and at the rest, and full of joy as 158
if he had (himself) received the Tooth of the Enlightened One,
he celebrated day by day a great festival. Then when he
heard and had taken note of the many words expressed in 159
the royal letter: the transference[3] of the merit of the further-
ance of the Order and so forth, he put glad confidence in the
King of Laṅkā. He gave over (to the envoys) many books 160
which were not in Laṅkā, a beautiful likeness of the sacred
footprint[4], as sacrificial gifts for the Tooth of the Victor golden 161
canopies and umbrellas and all kinds of beautiful and splendid
presents, suitable for the royal use, as well as a royal letter 162
in which expression was given to the share in all merits as
his own admission to the Order[5] and the like, wherein the

[1] Such shells are very rare and precious. Their possessor is supposed to be exceedingly lucky. Shells of this kind are mentioned among the gifts exchanged between King Devānaṃpiyatissa and King Asoka (Mhvs. 11. 22, 30).

[2] The acc. pl. *saṃpatte* is governed by *apesesi* in v. 163 c. Vv. 156-163 certainly form a most clumsy sentence.

[3] This refers to what is related in v. 146.

[4] Cf. with this the note to v. 254.

[5] I assume that *attūpasaṃpadā* means that Dhammika belonged himself, if only for a time, to the Order, as is customary even to-day in the royal family of Siam. With this he had acquired great merit a part of which was to accrue to Kittisirirājasīha.

163 reasons for the friendly relations between the two kings found
expression, and sent all that to fair, holy Laṅkā.
164 All this the highly famed King of Laṅkā accepted. When
he beheld the books of the good doctrine and the gifts like
165 the footprint of the Sage, he rejoiced greatly and paid great
honour to the gifts. He celebrated a great festival and showed
166 them to all the people. Then when he had looked at the
royal letter and taken note of the many words expressed in
it, such as the transference of merit and the like, also the
167 friendly relations mentioned, the Ruler of the Sīhalas was
filled with the highest bliss by satisfaction at the transferred
168 merit[1]. He thought: "The reward accruing from the meritorious
works like furtherance of the Order I have experienced in this
169 life, what shall one say of that which may be perfectly en-
joyed in a future existence?" In this wise the Ruler believed
170 firmly in the three sacred things. The Ruler of Laṅkā betook
himself to the monastery and heard the sermon of the true
doctrine preached by the Grand theras who had arrived the
171 second time. He charged those bhikkhus who had been ad-
mitted into the Order by the chapter of monks who had arrived
first, to take instruction from the bhikkhu chapter at whose
172 head Visuddhācariya[2] stood, and had the ceremony of admission
to the Order performed in proper fashion by those theras on
numerous sons of good family.
173 Of the bhikkhus in Laṅkā some whose ornament was
their virtue, learned with the Grand Thera by name Visuddhā-
174 cariya, absorption which is the way to nirvana; others learned
175 with the second Thera Varañāṇamuni the content of the doc-
trine and monastic rules, as well as linguistic knowledge. Thus
the King pledged the bhikkhus of Laṅkā to the study of the
176 sacred scriptures and to the practice of moral discipline and
so sheltered the Order of the Enlightened One. And the
177 bhikkhus of Laṅkā were zealous and discerning. Received into

[1] P. *pattānumodanena* stands as is shown by the preceding verse, for *patti-anum°*.

[2] See above v. 136 ff.

the branch of those ascetics who are without wants, who have taken upon themselves a life of discipline, unwearied, never indolent, they made of the doctrine of the Victor a reality,
zealous by day and night, absorbed in difficult texts; and the 178
King showed them honour by the dispensing of dwellings and
the like. The chapter of bhikkhus which had come the second 179
time and wished to return to their own country he sent away
with Olanda merchants. On a firmly fixed rock situated on 180
a beautiful spot not too far to the east of the town of Siri-
vaḍḍhana he had hewn out by skilful workers, masons and 181
others a splendid standing image of the Victor nine cubits[1]
high and he had the radiant, shining stone image overlaid 182
with gold plates so that it resembled the living Sage. Round 183
about this Buddha statue he had erected a lofty, massive,
beautiful stone wall and superb stone pillars placed and a 184
splendid, beautiful two-storeyed temple built fair to look at,
as well as a roomy court, outer walls, maṇḍapas and so forth 185
set up in the best way. Then he put thereon canopies and
curtains of all kinds of coloured stuffs. Round about he placed 186
arches one after another and provided them in every way
with much ornament. Here and there he set up various flags 187
and pennons and on the day of the sacrificial festival of the
eyes[2] he lit a row of lamps, placed filled jars (about) and 188
carried out in blameless fashion the various customs prescribed
for festivals. To the people who supplied the coloured paint- 189
ings, he dispensed abundantly robes, ornaments and the like
and satisfied their wishes in every way. Then he made the 190
splendid loud clang of the musical instruments, like shell
trumpets, kettledrums and so forth resound, like the roar of
the wide sea, and under a good constellation, at a good hour, 191
on a good day determined as favourable he put in the eyes
and celebrated a great festival. Numerous silver bowls and 192
many silver vessels, costly necessaries and valuable monks'

[1] I. e. 13—14 ft.

[2] What is meant is the putting in of the eyes in the Buddha statue which always took place with quite special ceremonies.

193 robes, banners, white umbrellas, shields, fly-whisks and fans —
194 all these and other fair objects of sacrifice the Ruler offered,
mindful of the reward accruing from a sacrifice to the Buddha,
with the thought that it was as if it took place in the pre-
195 sence of the still living Prince of the wise, with a heart full
of the joy of faith, intent on merit. Many and manifold foods
196 also such as sweet dishes, rice, solid dishes and others, sugar,
honey, betel, lime, camphor and so forth, also remedies and
197 perfumes of every kind like sandal[1] and the like, beautiful
flowers, like jasmine, campaka blossoms and others — all these
198 and other objects of sacrifice he offered in pious fashion. The
makers of the Buddha image and the other people he rejoiced
by an offering of many animate and inanimate things, elephants,
199 cattle, buffaloes and so forth. If one reckons the sums spent
in the making of the Buddha statue and the other offerings
200 on the occasion of this vihāra festival according to their
money value, the result was sixteen thousand one hundred
and fifty (kahāpaṇas).

201 The large, beautiful vihāra, well worth seeing, which is
known as Gaṅgārāma because it was built on a fair spot near
202 the Mahāvālukagaṅgā was founded by the King under the
203 name of Rājamahāvihāra. This vihāra, thus superbly furnished
with glory and splendour, was also destroyed by the enemy[2]
204 who had penetrated into the town. The King had it in the
best way restored to its original condition, and just as he had
205 held a solemn ceremony at the former eye festival, so (now)
he held another eye festival. After the Ruler of men had
dispensed in great abundance to the painters and so forth
206 garments, ornaments and other articles and had sacrificed
with many sacrificial gifts, he erected near by a fair monastery

[1] I think *sāragandha* should be taken in this sense like the corresponding skr. word.

[2] Thus we learn here that all these festivities described in the foregoing took place before the capture of Kandy by van Eck in 1765, that on this occasion the Gaṅgārāma founded by the King, was also destroyed, but as related in the following, restored after the destruction of the Dutch expedition, when the change of name possibly took place

for the community and made a chapter of bhikkhus who 207
devoted themselves with lasting zeal to the study and the fulfilment of moral duties, take up their abode there, providing 208
them in every way with what was necessary. Then by holding in the way described formerly, full of reverence for the
Triad of the jewels, a sacrificial festival for the Buddha, and 209
at the same time sacrificing to the chapter of the bhikkhus, he increased the fulness of merit for himself and the laity.

Now in order that this beautiful fair vihāra, worthy to 210
be seen, that was erected in this manner, and all the numerous
sacrificial ceremonies inaugurated there and the many meri- 211
torious works such as the offerings to the community – should be continued for a long time in the right way, the Ruler
determined a village situated near the vihāra by name Arup- 212
pala, and many other villages and fields, and gardens also,
as well as the large, populous village by name Udakagāma[1] 213
in the district of Māyādhanu and granted them (to the mo-
nastery). And the King confirmed this in perpetuity by 214
having an inscription graven on the beautiful mountain (in the stone).

In this way the King of kings dowered with splendid 215
virtues, since he realised the worthlessness of acquired wealth, in his piety had sacrificial festivals celebrated for the Buddha and sacrificial festivals for the community of the excellent sons of the Victor and so performed perpetually all valuable, meritorious works[2]. Therefore should ye all also perpetually perform without wearying, meritorious works.

In the fair, splendid suburb by name Kuṇḍasālā, the Ruler 216
of men had erected in a charming garden a vihāra fair to
look on, supplied in the best way possible with outer walls 217
and maṇḍapas, and brought thither relics and images of the

[1] Now Diyagama. Three villages of this name might be the one in question: 1) Diyagama in the Kalutara District, Vaddubadda; 2) Diyagama in the Magul Otota Korale, Kurunegala; 3) Diyagama in Deyaladahamuna Pattuva, Kegalla (Census 1921, II, p. 48, 282, 514).

[2] Lit. "the full value of meritorious action" (*sāraṃ* in contrast to *asāraṃ* in a).

218 Sage. Then he dedicated (to the vihāra) the garden that was adorned with bread-fruit trees, mango trees, cocopalms and other fruit trees, as well as many fields and villages and people
219 for the service of the monastery, and celebrated, intent on merit, day by day all sacrificial ceremonies, such as offerings of food and the like.

220 The wicked king known by the name of Rājasīha in the town of Sītāvaka[1] who had committed parricide and destroyed the Order of the Victor, as he could not distinguish what it
221 was right to do, had adopted a false faith, was devoted to the adherents of the false faith and ordered them to take for themselves the income accruing from the worship of the sacred
222 footprint of the Enlightened One on the Sumanakūṭa. From that time onwards the adherents of the false faith destroyed
223 everything there. When the highly famed Great king heard of these things he realised, reverently devoted to the En-
224 lightened One, that this was unseemly. He commanded the adherents of the false faith from now onwards not to do so, and charged the sons of the Buddha to carry out in the right
225 way the many sacrificial ceremonies which should be performed there. He dedicated the flourishing, populous, large village
226 named Kuṭṭāpiṭi to the sacred footprint and to shield it from the heat of the sun, he erected above it a maṇḍapa with cur-
227 tains, adorned with an umbrella on the point, fastened it with iron chains and accumulated much good by the celebration of sacrificial ceremonies. But the income accruing therefrom he assigned to the Order.

228 In this manner did our happy, sublime[2] Sīhala Ruler in the knowledge that what that deluded king had done, because he knew not the virtues of the sublime Sage — was unseemly, put away all the wrong and by entrusting the spotless bhikkhu community of the sublime sons of the Buddha therewith, he

[1] Cf. for this 93. 3 ff. especially v. 12. Line 220 a agrees in wording with the line 93. 5 a.

[2] Note that in this strophe the word *pavara* occurs in each of the four lines.

celebrated a ceremonial festival for the Buddha which granted sublime immortality.

The Majjhavela-vihāra[1] built by the ruler, King Vaṭṭa- 229
gāmaṇī, which had fallen into decay, and the cetiya belonging 230
to the vihāra he had rebuilt in the finest way and granted
it the village called Siṅgatthala[2] that had been long separated
from it. Day by day he celebrated there in the right way a 231
sacrificial ceremony and so smoothed the road to heaven which
he would have to tread in the future.

To the Dutiyasela-vihāra[3] the Ruler of men granted the 232
village by name Ratanadoṇi[4], having learnt from the record
of a stone inscription that it had formerly belonged to it but 233
had been severed from it, and he the highly famed, intent on
merit, celebrated a sacrificial festival.

For the restoration of the Majjhapalli-vihāra[5] the Ruler 234
conferred distinction on the bhikkhu Saṃgharakkhita in pious
fashion. He caused a great recumbent image (of the Buddha) 235
to be made and finally he had a great festival celebrated there
and the festival of the eyes held. In order also to perform 236
the (customary) sacrificial ceremonies he dedicated the village
called Mālāgāma[6] (to the monastery) and had a sacrificial
festival celebrated daily according to rule. To the sāmaṇera 237
called Siddhattha the Ruler granted the large Rajata-vihāra[7]
erected by King Duṭṭhagāmaṇī when inspired[8] by the wish 238

[1] W.: Medavela-vihāra.

[2] Probably Singagoda, Kinigoda Korale, Kegalla District (Census 1921, II, p. 514).

[3] W.: Devanagala-vihāra.

[4] Perhaps Ruvandeniya, Galboda Korale, Kegalla District (Census 1921, II, p. 520).

[5] W.: Meddepola-vihāra.

[6] The Census 1921, II, p. 298, 368 mentions a village Malagamuva and another Malgomuva. Both are situated in the Kurunegala District, the first in the Galboda Egoda Korale, the second in the Medapattu Korale East. The latter seems to be meant here.

[7] See note to 99. 41.

[8] P. *patthetvā āyatena* is a composite verb formed after the Sinhalese model (*geṇenavā, geṇāvā*).

for the august position of a chief disciple of Metteya[1], the
239 King of the wise. After the Ruler of Laṅkā had caused the
ceremony of admission to the Order to be performed on him,
he granted this bhikkhu and all the sons of the Victor dwell-
ing in the Uposathārāma rank and showed them favour in
240 every way. Then in order to restore this vihāra which had
long been in the state of a ruined house, the Ruler of men
241 in Laṅkā assigned it divers artisans, painters and others, as
well as much fine gold wherewith to gild the Buddha images,
242 and all handiwork and so forth. That prince among ascetics
— Siddhattha — accepted all this and removed in the best
243 possible way everything that had been destroyed by age. He
had a lofty, massive stone wall and a fine plaster floor built
244 in the house, and outside a maṇḍapa, as well as (a picture)
the figure of the Buddha in combat with Māra above on the
rock face. Then when he had caused creeper work of flowers
245 to be applied in the best manner possible and had caused a
vast image of the recumbent Buddha to be fashioned out of
good bricks, lime and clay and also many sitting and standing
246 images of the Victor, he had represented in the best way
possible in painting on the beautiful inner wall, enlightened
247 ones like Muhuttamuni[2], a thousand in number. And at the
foot of the vast statue of the recumbent Buddha he had placed
248 one after the other beautiful images, that of the Buddha's
constant servant and protector of the true doctrine[3] — Ānanda,
that of the Bodhisatta Metteya, that of the sublime patron
249 deity (Viṣṇu), and that of King Gāmaṇī. He overlaid the five
250 great images of the Buddha with gold, and when he had thus
in every possible way finished the works which were to be

[1] Metteya is the future Buddha. Each Buddha has two pre-eminent disciples ascribed to him (*aggasāvakā*). Those of the historical Buddha were Sāriputta and Moggallāna.

[2] I do not know who is meant here. W. omits the name in his translation.

[3] *Saddhammarakkhino* refers to Ānanda. It is he who according to Vin. II. 287, was questioned as to the *dhamma*, by Mahākassapa at the first Council

made in the inside (of the shrine), he had pourtrayed also
outside on the wall a series of glorious figures of gods and
Brahma figures with flowers in their hands, which looked as 251
if they had appeared for worship. Then too he caused a great,
beautiful triumphal arch to be made, well worth seeing, further 252
two lion figures on either side of the portal and in the empty
interstices of the wall figures of demons. Also he had pictures 253
pourtrayed in coloured painting of the sixteen holy places[1],
Mahiyaṅgaṇa and the others, further of the famous foot-print 254
on the Saccabaddha mountain[2], of the ten pāramīs[3], of the
three forms of (right) action[4], as well as of many jātakas in
which subjects like the five great renunciations[5] are treated
of. In the maṇḍapa he had all kinds of figures introduced, 255
series of lions, series of elephants, series of geese and creeper
work of flowers. In the delightful cave above in the same rock 256
he built a vast image house, well worth seeing, splendid, beauti-
ful with many sculptures fashioned to perfection and so forth. 257
There he had a beautiful, vast, life-like sitting Buddha made —
splendid was this figure and fair to look at — and on either 258
side well fashioned, upright standing statues of the Bodhisatta 259
Metteyya and of the lotus-hued god[6]. He also caused many
other figures to be set up: figures of sages, figures of many 260
hundreds of the perfect[7], the four and twenty Buddhas, the

[1] See note to 100. 128.

[2] This is a sacred mountain in Siam, called Saccabandhana in the narrative (p. 31) mentioned above (Note to 100. 59). There was a footprint of the Buddha on it which had come there miraculously. King Dhammika had sent a model of this footprint along with other gifts to the King of Laṅkā.

[3] See note to 37. 180.

[4] P. *tidhā cariyaṃ*. The three forms are *lokatthacariyā*, *ñātatthacariyā* and *buddhicariyā* "action for the advantage of the world, for the advantage of one's kinsfolk and for one's (own) enlightenment." See DhCo. III. 441[10].

[5] P. *pañcamahāpariccāgā*. The surrender of the five precious possessions, the wife, the children, the royal dignity, life, limbs. DhCo. l. c. Childers, PD. s. v. *pariccāga*.

[6] See note to 83. 49.

[7] P. *asekkha* "he who no longer undergoes training", synonymous with *arahant*.

261 whole of the Bodhi trees in the same number, the four and
twenty intimations[1], the sixteen holy places, fair forms of
spiritual beings and others, the five great Councils[2] and yet
262 divers other beautiful pictures well worth seeing. Then he
263 brought thither relics of the Sage and had a cetiya erected,
adorned with a golden finial. In the image house itself he
264 had placed on the lofty vaulted[3] ceiling a sitting figure of
the Sage surrounded by his five hundred followers, Sāriputta
265 at the head. In the court he had walls and maṇḍapas erected
at different places, as well as several gate-buildings and here
266 and there stairs and other fine buildings, partly the restoration
of much that had suffered by age, partly also many new
(buildings).

267 All these fine structures the King dedicated (to the mo-
268 nastery) at the festival of the eyes by dignitaries whom he
had sent[4], and in addition clothing, ornaments and much else.
He had rows of various triumphal arches without gaps put
269 up, placed on them the necessary ornament, gave orders for
270 the sacred ceremonies and while celebrating in worthy fashion
a great rite, he carried out the festival of the eyes under a
lucky star and at a favourable hour.

[1] Each of the 24 Buddhas who according to the legend, precede the historical Buddha — they are enumerated Mhvs. 1. 5 ff. — has his special sacred tree under which he attains enlightenment. To each in a former existence on a particular occasion, a Buddha gives the intimation (*vyākaraṇa*) that he too shall in time attain the dignity of a Buddha.

[2] The Mahāvaṃsa 3, 4 and 5. 268 ff. gives an account of the three first Councils (*dhammasaṃgīti*) in Rājagaha, Vesālī and Pāṭaliputta. Of the two other Councils the one is the Church reform under Parakkamabāhu I (Mhvs. 78. 1 ff), the other perhaps that under Parakkamabāhu II (Mhvs. 84. 7 ff.). We get an idea of what the representation of such a council might have looked like from a fresco from Qyzil near Kutscha (Central Asia) the subject of which is the first Council. See A. von Le Coq and E. Waldschmidt, Die buddhistische Spätantike in Mittelasien VI. p. 79 und Tafel 14.

[3] P. *uddhaṃ pabbhāra-m-uttame*. Very likely a picture on the ceiling.

[4] The construction of the sentence is quite irregular. It seems to me, however, that *pesite 'macce* is acc. pl. which like the preceding accusatives is made to depend on *datvāna*.

From that time onwards there came hither many in-
habitants of the whole kingdom from all quarters, like the 271
sea when it overflows the land. When all the people who
had gathered there beheld the many golden and other works 272
of art which had been carried out, there their hearts were
filled with joy, as if they saw the Enlightened One at the
miracle of the double appearances[1]. In joyful and high spirits 273
they celebrated amid cries of Hail! a great festival and thus
paved their way to Heaven. At that festival he invited the 274
bhikkhu community of the vihāra, had seats prepared in the
inner room of the vihāra, made bhikkhus who were preach- 275
ers of the true doctrine sit down thereon, and had the
Mahāmaṅgalasutta[2] and other sacred texts worth hearing re- 276
cited by them and thus celebrated in worthy manner a sacri-
ficial festival of the doctrine[3]. All the people who saw and 277
heard this, in that they at one and the same time beheld the
Enlightened One[4] and heard the true doctrine, were filled 278
daily in every possible way with the highest joy and ecstasy,
as if by a sermon of the living Sage. Thus he made manifest 279
both: the beauty of his form and the charm of his sermon.

Outside in the court he placed pillars of stone, erected a
maṇḍapa, spread seats therein and after establishing the great 280
multitudes gathered round the maṇḍapa in the five major and
other commandments relating to moral discipline, he made 281
them listen daily to abundant texts. Full of reverence he[5]
also invited the preachers of the doctrine to preach the doctrine
repeatedly during the three watches of the night.

[1] The *yamakaṃ pāṭiheraṃ* is often mentioned, as is the case in the ancient Mahāvaṃsa (See my translation, note to 17. 44; cf. DhCo. III, p. 199 ff.; Samantapāsādikā, ed. Takakusu I, p. 88 ff).

[2] In the Suttanipāta, Cūlavagga, Sutta 4 (ed. by Dines Andersen and Helmer Smith, p. 46).

[3] P. *dhammapūjā*. The *dhamma* itself is the *pūjāvatthu*, the "object of sacrifice", because the sacred texts are recited.

[4] I. e. the images of the Buddha in the Rajata-vihāra.

[5] The subject from v. 274 onwards is throughout the King. W. quite unnecessarily takes Siddhattha (see v. 238) as the subject of *nimantiya* in 281 b.

282 In the year two thousand three hundred and one after the
final nirvana of the Enlightened One[1] he had the vihāra called
283 Rajata restored and the great festival celebrated. He then
thought of repairing the splendid cetiya erected on a clear,
284 fine large slab of rock to the south of the vihāra but which
was so dilapidated that it resembled a heap of dust. Therefore
he had fetched from all quarters lime, bricks, stones and so
285 forth. Hereupon he had a fine, square throne built of stone
in the best possible manner whereon he placed a relic of the
286 sublime Enlightened One. At the restoration of the cetiya,
he erected on a neighbouring, particularly beautiful piece
of land for the community whom he invited thither in
287 fitting manner for the purpose, setting up a marked out
boundary, a monastery with an Uposatha house and other
288 (buildings) provided with a brick roof and so forth. On the
land round about he laid out beautifully a large park adorned
with divers blossoming trees, with divers blossoming creepers,
289 with divers fruit trees and the like, and where there were
many bathing-ponds. And full of zeal as he was, he piously
made the sons of the Victor dwell there and devote themselves
to study and religious exercises.

290 In such wise was the place restored by royal power, vi-
sited (in days of yore) by great saints and honoured by the
291 former rulers of Laṅkā. When the highly famed King heard
thereof he fixed the boundary of the vihāra solemnly in the
292 same way (as before), performed there all the solemn cere-
monies, arranged in still more abundant measure (than before)
for an almsgiving to the community and the like and laid up
293 a store of merit. Near the Dohaḷa mountain[2] adorned with
rows of trees like pūga, punnāga, nāga[3] and others, resound-
294 ing with the sweet twitter of all kinds of birds, provided
with cool, spotless white stone slabs, enlivened with herds of
295 divers animals, there was in the fair monastery situated there

[1] I. e. 1757 A. D.

[2] Mentioned in 44. 56. See note to the passage.

[3] For the tree names cf. 73. 98, 74. 204, 79. 3.

which bore the name of Sūkara[1], an image house of the Victor, erected by a dignitary who was charged therewith by the King. There the councillor Suvaṇṇagāma setting up 296
stone pillars, built an Uposatha house and dedicated it to the sons of the Sage. He also had supplies of wood collected 297
for pillars and the like and numerous dwellings built there. To the bhikkhus to whom dwellings had been assigned there, 298
the Lord of men devoted many villages, fields and so on for the provision of what was necessary. After that Ruler of men 299
had caused all this to be brought about he kindly dedicated it to that prince of ascetics, Dhammarakkhita.

After the Ruler of men had in such wise stored up divers 300
kinds of merit he passed in the thirty-fifth year of his reign from this world thither in accordance with his deeds.

When one reflects on the worthlessness of wealth and of the 301
life of the flesh one utterly rejects the yearning thereafter. Ye also, revering the Triad of the sacred things, ought to perform good works such as spiritual exertions and the like[2].

Here ends the hundredth chapter, called «The History of Kittisirirājasīha», in the Mahāvaṃsa, compiled for the serene joy and emotion of the pious.

[1] The Col. Ed. reads *sūkarāvāṭanāmamhi* instead of the *sūkaravhayanāmamhi* of my MSS. W. gives Varávaḷa as the modern name of the monastery.

[2] The whole of the hundredth chapter has the character of a supplement to chapter 99 and treats especially of the services of the King to the Church. It repeatedly alludes to events which have been touched upon in the foregoing (cf. 98. 91 with the note to 100. 59, also the note to 100. 203). I have already pointed out (note to 99. 53) that Tibbotuvave's contribution to the Cūlavaṃsa (see note to 99. 76) which deals with the reign of Kittisirirājasīha is composed in praise of this king and completed during his lifetime. This is the case too with the greater part of the hundredth chapter. Here too in v. 228 we meet with the expression *amhākaṃ Sīhalindo* and the benediction in v. 135 sounds as if it were addressed to a living person. At the end however Kittisiri's death is mentioned. The last part of the hundredth chapter must thus have been added later, whether by Tibbotuvave himself or by another author. The break cannot be fixed with certainty, it might possibly be at v. 228.

CHAPTER CI

SUPPLEMENT[1]

1 On his death, his younger brother Sirirājādhirājasīha[2]
2 received consecration as king in Laṅkā. After attaining his
consecration as king, he devoted himself with pious joy to
the Triad of the Jewels, zealous in listening to the true doc-
3 trine, unwearied, discerning. The Ruler of men continued, as
formerly without abatement that furtherance of the laity and
4 the Order which his brother had carried out. The highly famed
offered meat and drink and so on as before to the sublime Tooth
5 Relic without depriving it of anything. He commanded that
the regular almsgiving which had been established for the
sons of the Victor should be given to them in the order in-
6 troduced by the (former) king. The bhikkhus who with the Thera
Upāli at their head had arrived from Sāminda, came to the
7 town of Sirivaḍḍhana. Here those bhikkhus who had come from
there, with the Thera Upāli at their head, established a sacred
boundary to the south of the town in the so-called Kusumā-
8 rāma[3], according to the ñattidutiya process[4]. When he saw

[1] Chapter 101 of the Mhvs. has been composed and added to their edition of the chronicle (1877) by H. SUMANGALA and BATUWANTUDAWA. See MALALASEKERA, Pali Literature, p. 142. No MS. however of those which I could examine, reaches beyond v. 292 of ch. 100, and I do not know on which authority the vv. 100. 293—301 are based.

[2] Reigned 1780-1798 (cf. v. 18). It was during the reign of Rājādhirājasīha that the capitulation of Colombo took place (15 th Feb., 1796) and with that the passing of the dominion from the Dutch to the British. Cf. PIERIS 3, p. 142 ff.; CODRINGTON, HC., p. 133 ff.

[3] Synonym for Pupphārāma 100. 86, 141, now the Malvatu-vihāra.

[4] This is a particular form of a *saṃghakamma* or ecclesiastical act. See Vin II. 89^{3} and 91^{37} (= Cullav. 4. 14 2 and 11).

that the Uposatha house built formerly by King Kittisiri, was
decayed, the Ruler of men who was intent on merit, first of 9
all raised the ground on all sides and then by the adding of 10
still more stones he put up the walls inside the boundary.
He put up stone pillars and so built the Uposatha house 11
which the Ruler made over[1] to the community from the four
regions of the heavens.

The King was acquainted with various literary works, works 12
in Pāli and Sanskrit, he rejoiced in the continuous giving of
alms, was in form like the god of love[2]. As expert in the 13
text books relating to language he made a poem in the Sīhala
tongue out of the Asadisajātaka[3] and had it written down.
With a heart full of faith he reverenced[4] the Tooth Relic in 14
faith with a hundred thousand lamps which he had lit in a
single night. Hearing of the great merits of a kaṭhina offer- 15
ing over all gifts of alms, he every year presented kaṭhina[5]
robes to the community. He had an image of the Aṅgirasa[6] 16
made in bronze in the proportions of the King and since he
strove after the dignity of a Buddha, he erected in the 17
monastery called Gaṅgārāma which was held to be pious, a
graceful cetiya well worth seeing.

[1] The description of the building is obscure. V. 9 seems to refer to the securing of the whole base, v. 10 to the laying down of a walled terrace and v. 11 a b to the building of the house itself.

[2] P. *makaraddhaja* = skr. *makaradhvaja* "whose badge is the makara, the dolphin".

[3] Jātaka nr. 181 in Fausböll II. p. 86 ff.

[4] I believe that here we should read *sammānesi* instead of *samānesi* as the meaning of the latter can hardly be harmonized with *dāṭhādhātuṃ*. The instr. *dīpasatasahassena* would also not fall within the construction of the sentence. We must, it is true, put up with a slight disturbance of the metre, when reading *sammānesi*.

[5] See note to 44. 48.

[6] Aṅgiras in the Rigveda is the designation of "beings half gods half men who act as intermediaries between the two, as sons of Heaven, as ancestors of men, as those who impart to mankind the gifts of the gods" (Grassmann). The expression *aṅgirasa* is already used of Buddha, Therag. 1252 (quoted S. I. 196). Cf. also A. III, 239^{25}; Jā. V. 141^{1}.

18 After the Ruler had accumulated these and other merits
he passed after an eighteen years' reign from this world in
accordance with his deeds.
19 The sister's son of Rājādhirājasīha, the Lord of men,
Sirivikkamarājasīha[1], the discerning ruler of the country
20 hearkened to the doctrine preached by the Victor. The Ruler
found pleasure therein and sacrificed to the sacred Tooth Relic
21 jewels, pearls and other (valuables) and many villages and
fields. To the community whose head is the Buddha, he
22 dispensed often delicious foods and so strove after eternal
happiness. These and other merits the Ruler accumulated.
23 But as he indulged in intercourse with impious people he
changed (for the worse). He had the chief councillors, the
24 great dignitaries and many other officials gathered together
and destroyed his subjects like a devil. He had the people,
25 many hundreds in number, brought to different spots and had
them impaled, merciless as death. Much wealth that had
26 come to the people by inheritance, the King had confiscated
like a thief that robs villages. And because the Ruler com-
27 mitted in this way many evil deeds the Sīhalas and the in-
habitants of the town of Colombo[2] rebelled. They all came
28 hither, captured the criminal king alive when the eighteenth
year after his consecration had passed, and brought him to
29 the opposite coast[3]. After they had brought the King, the
torturer of his people, to the opposite coast the Ingirīsi by
name seized the whole kingdom.

End of the Mahāvaṃsa

May there be prosperity!

[1] Reigned 1798-1815. For the rise of the British power in Ceylon during the reign of this king and for the reign itself see CODRINGTON, HC. p. 155 ff., where also on p. 169 f., 182 there is a list of the bibliography of the subject.

[2] This means the British.

[3] I. e. To the Indian mainland.

B The Oldest Part of the Cūlavaṃsa

See Cūlavaṃsa trsl. I, p. 351 – 358.

C The Later Parts of the Cūlavaṃsa

I

From Kittinissaṅka to Codagaṅga

Kāliṅga Prince

81. Kittinissaṅka = Nissaṅkamalla | 83. Vikkamabāhu III. | daughter

82. Vīrabāhu I. (son of 81) | 84. Coḍagaṅga (son of the daughter)

II

From Vijayabāhu III. to Parakkamabāhu IV.

93. Vijayabāhu III.

94. Parakkamabāhu II. | Bhuvanekabāhu 81. 68 | daughter

95. Vijayabāhu IV. 90. 1 | 96. Bhuvanekabāhu I.[1] 90. 4 | Vīrabāhu 83. 41, 87. 15

97. Parakkamabāhu III. 90. 49 | 98. Bhuvanekabāhu II. 90. 59

99. Parakkamabāhu IV. 90. 64

[1]) Other sons of Parakkamabāhu II. are Tilokamalla, Parakkamabāhu and Jayabāhu (87. 16 f.)

III

The family of Alagakkonāra

A

Alagakonnāra = Alakeśvara 91. 3 — Arthanāyaka — daughter

Alagakonnāra = Alakeśvara 91. 3
- Kumāra Alakeśvara

daughter
- Vīra Alakeśvara (Vījayabāhu VI.) cf. 91. 14 note
- Vīrabāhu = 106. Vīrabāhu II. 91. 13

IV

From Parakkamabāhu VIII. to Rājasīha I.

111. Parakkamabāhu VIII.
- (Parakkamabāhu IX.)
- 112. Vijayabāhu VI. (VII.)
  - 113. Bhuvanekabāhu VII.
    - daughter
      - (Dharmapāla)
  - Rājasīha = Rayigam baṇḍāra
  - 115. Māyādhanu
    - 116. Rājasīha I.

V

From Vimaladhammasuriya I. to Narindasīha

Vīrasundara
- 117. Vimaladhammasuriya I.
  - Kumārasīha 95. 22
  - Vijitapāla 95. 22

brother
- 118. Senāratana
  - 119. Rājasīha II. 95. 23, 96. 3
    - 120. Vimaladhammasuriya II.
      - 121. Narindasīha 97. 23

VI

From Vijayarājasīha to Vikkamarājasīha

122. Vijayarājasīha brother-in-law of 121

123. Kittisirirājasīha brother-in-law of 122

124. Rājādhirājasīha brother of 123

Sister of 124
- 125. Vikkamarājasīha

Indices

The indices refer not only to the Cūlavaṃsa but also to my edition and translation of the old Mahāvaṃsa so that the whole chronicle is comprised within. The abbreviations are: M. ed. = The Mahāvaṃsa, edited by W. G., PTS. 1908. — M. tr. = The Mahāvaṃsa, translated by W. G., PTS. 1912. — C. ed. I = Cūlavaṃsa, being the more recent part of the Mahāvaṃsa, vol. I, PTS. 1925. — C. ed. II = the same, vol. II, PTS. 1927. — C. tr. I = Cūlavaṃsa &c., translated by W. G., vol. I, PTS. 1929. — C. tr. II = the same, vol. II, PTS. 1930.

I. List of words

akkhaṇavedhin **72**. 245
akkhamālā **46**. 17; **57**. 6
akkhi "axle" **38**. 94
agati **37**. 108; **99**. 73, 104
aggikapalla **60**. 70
añña — saka **47**. 10, 14
aṭṭhamūlavihārā **61**. 59
aṭṭhāyatanāni **84**. 4, 18
aḍḍhayoga **88**. 93, 118
adhikārin **66**. 66; **70**. 278
anālaya **42**. 42; **46**. 4
anuyyāna **68**. 58
anussati **98**. 14
annapāsana **62**. 53
antaraṅgadhura **69**. 32
apāya **72**. 306
appamaññā **39**. 18
abhiññā **4**. 12; **52**. 38
abhisamaya **1**. 32; **12**. 27
amaramantar **42**. 3; **52**. 38
arahant (M. tr. p. 292) **1**. 14
āgāmiya **44**. 148
ājira **35**. 3
ādi (in proper names) **44**. 6, 122; **46**. 1; **48**. 50; **91**. 2; **98**. 2
ādipāda **53**. 13
āyubbeda **73**. 42
ārāmika **37**. 63
ālinda **35**. 3
āḷambara **69**. 20
āvaraṇa **79**. (27,) 69
āvudha **99**. 45

iti (in the oratio recta) **37**. 114; **44**. 16, 90; **45**. 20; **48**. 30, 116; **74**. 64; **77**. 99; **94**. 23
itthāgāra **59**. 33
iriyāpatha **3**. 25

udakukkhepasīmā **89**. 70; **94**. 17; **97**. 12

upacāra **60**. 82
upanayana **64**. 13
upanissaya 5. 45, 172
upasampatti **84**. 42; **89**. 50
upāya **66**. 143
upāyā (the four) **58**. 3
upāsana **24**. 1; **51**. 100
uposatha (M. tr. p. 296) **37**. 201
ubbāhikā **4**. 46 f.

eka- **61**. 13
ekatthambhakapāsāda **73**. 92
eḷakatthambha **60**. 11

odakantika **72**. 238

kaṅkuṭṭhaka **32**. 6
kañcuka **48**. 140
kaṇṇavedha **62**. 53
katamaṅgala **35**. 111
kapparukkha **51**. 124
kappiyakāraka **37**. 173
kamāgata **69**. 30
kalanda **37**. 204
kavāṭaka **35**. 25
kiṅkiṇijāla **73**. 68
kumbhaṇḍaka **12**. 20
kulambaṇa **36**. 26
kusalodaya **71**. 24
kūṭāgāra **73**. 62
ketu **85**. 100
koṭisa **88**. 109
koṭṭhaka **1**. 56
koṭṭhabaddhanijjhara **79**. 28

khaggalatā **72**. 102
khaṇḍa **66**. 108
khandhāvāra **73**. 57
khīṇāsava (M. tr. p. 292) **3**. 9

gaṇa **51**. 52; **74**. 48
gaṇasaṃgaṇikā **60**. 17
gati **37**. 51; **72**. 286
gantha **97**. 56
gandhabbī **74**. 216
gabbhaparihāra **62**. 36
gamiyabhatta **51**. 61
garubhaṇḍāni **84**. 39; **85**. 105
gāvuta **65**. 4; **73**. 157
girisetu **79**. 24
guṇā (the five) **26**. 26
gokaṇṇa **70**. 36
gopura **60**. 12

cakkhumana **81**. 26
caṇḍa **72**. 252
caturaṅgin **70**. 217
catussālā **73**. 23
cumbaṭa **24**. 31
celukkhepa **72**. 288
corayuddha **75**. 135

chidda **66**. 63

jaṭila 1. 16
jara **99**. 176
jātakamma **62**. 45
jālakavāṭa **78**. 40
jeṭṭhāpacāyaka **41**. 9

tapassin, tapovana **41**. 99
tādin **15**. 62
tālāvacara **17**. 7
tikkhaggapada **66**. 87

ticīvara **41**. 29
tilaka **87**. 67
tivaṅka **78**. 39; **85**. 66
tulāyaṭṭhi **88**. 97

thūpikā **76**. 105, 118

daṇḍissara **52**. 3; **53**. 30; **60**. 22
dūrīkaroti **85**. 44
deḍḍubha **37**. 132
doṇī **76**. 91
dosā (the five) **26**. 26

dhanajāta **58**. 8
dhammakamma **39**. 57
dhammadāna **98**. 77; **99**. 15
dhammadhātu **41**. 37
dhammapābhata **84**. 14
dhammasaṃgaha, -saṃgīti **3**. 17; **4**. 63
°dhātuka **57**. 69
dhātugabbha **60**. 56; **68**. 28

nandana **63**. 38; **73**. 29
nandin **85**. 50
nāḍāḷvāra **76**. 94
nāḍu **76**. 261-2
nāmakaraṇa **62**. 52
nāyaka **62**. 56
nikkhala **76**. 18
niggatika **74**. 22
nijavaḍḍhita **67**. 90
nijjhara **79**. 28, 66
niṭṭhite **99**. 52, 58
nidāna **37**. 133
nibandha **90**. 21
niyatti **48**. 108
niyojeti **72**. 207; **77**. 59, 82
nirodha **35**. 104
nisseṇigaha **39**. 3
nīta **67**. 96
nettika **60**. 14

pakatatta **78**. 25
paccayā (the four) **37**. 76
paccekabatthin **72**. 248; **76**. 244
pañcapatiṭṭhitaṅga **98**. 50; **100**. 29
paṭiccakamma **5**. 264
paṭipatti **20**. 30
paṭiyatta **78**. 35
paṭivedha **20**. 30
paṇālī **79**. 27
paṇīkata **72**. 91
paṇḍupalāsa **45**. 5
pattanikkujjana **45**. 31
patti **42**. 50; **44**. 109; **52**. 69; **73**. 47; **100**. 146, 159
patthaṇḍila **60**. 3
padakkhiṇaṃ karoti **37**. 196
parikkhārā (the eight) **60**. 71
paricchedа **42**. 39
paribhoga **51**. 20
parivattana **73**. 71
pariveṇa **37**. 63 (M. tr. p. 294 is misleading)
parisā (the four) **70**. 106
pavivīta **73**. 116
pavivekin **71**. 27
paveṇigāma **60**. 75
pākasāsana **72**. 186
pāṭava **72**. 103
pāṭihāriyapakkha **37**. 202
pādajāla **38**. 64; **52**. 65; **53**. 50

pādamūlaka **66**. 66
pāpuratthaṛaṇāni **54**. 24
pāpena (pāpakammena) **52**. 77; **53**. 8, 40
pāmaṅga **11**. 28
pāramitā (the ten) **37**. 180
pāsāda **37**. 59; **72**. 244
piṭṭhito karoti **70**. 314
piṭṭhipāsāṇa **68**. 27
pīṭhasappin **49**. 19
pīti (five kinds of) **81**. 24
puññakiriyā (the ten) **37**. 180
puññodaya **37**. 139; **53**. 23
pupphādhāna **30**. 51
pubba (= ādi) **73**. 122
pubbakāra **64**. 15
puratthā **38**. 110
pessiya **67**. 58; **84**. 5

pharati **72**. 251

balipaṭṭa **57**. 7
bāhuja **59**. 12
bodhikoṭṭhaka **79**. 72
bodhighara **38**. 43

bhatti **74**. 243; **85**. 33; **93**. 9
bhaya **74**. 49
bhava **4**. 66
bhavavibhava **91**. 19.
°bhājana **44**. 70; **84**. 16.
bhāṇavāra **98**. 21
bhānubandhu **85**. 101
bhāva **66**. 39, 42
bhūmi **64**. 41

makara **73**. 92
maṅgalikāni (the eight) **27**. 37
maṇḍapa **37**. 103
marumba **29**. 8
mahacca **74**. 225
mahārukkha **72**. 11
mātulā **57**. 28
mukha **70**. 156, 217
°mukha **50** 53
mukhabhaṅga **63**. 30
muttacāgin **60**. 81
muddhavedī **32**. 5
muhuṃ **89**. 60
mūla° **74**. 1
mūlaghaccaṃ **58**. 56
medavaṇṇapāsāṇa **1**. 39

yaṭṭhimadhukā **32**. 46
yathācāraṃ **60**. 1
yavana **76**. 264
yogga **42**. 8; **44**. 84; **70**. 207; **95**. 12
yojana **38**. 68; cf. C. I tr. p. 319

raṅgabhūmi **31**. 82
raṅgamaṇḍala **85**. 42
raṭṭha **57**. 71
ratanavāluka **76**. 104
randha **70**. 212
rasa **72**. 94
rājadhammā (the ten) **37**. 107
rājapābhata **84**. 14
rājavesibhujaṅga **73**. 91
rājinī **50**. 58
rāyara **76**. 94

laya **73**. 79
lājapañcamaka **98**. 46
līna **78**. 13
lekha **49**. 21

vaṭaṃsa **11**. 28
vaḍḍhita **67**. 52
vaḍḍheti **50**. 66
vattakāraka **98**. 27
vattati **54**. 59
vaḷabhi **88**. 97
vasavattin **86**. 9
vassabāra **23**. 74
vātaroga **56**. 5
vātābādha **37**. 141
vāripāta **48**. 148; **68** 35; (**79**. 66, 67)
vāseti **74**. 218
vāha **68**. 30
vāhana **74**. 225
vāhinī **72**. 255, 295
vijumbhati **90**. 74
viṭaṅka **88**. 97
vidhunita **67**. 96
vibhutta **71**. 24
vimāna **72**. 323; **73**. 107
vilivakāraka **88**. 105
visodheti **38**. 53
vedaṅga **62**. 33
vedikā **27**. 16; **73** 88; **76**. 117. Cf. M. tr. p. 296
vessa **76**. 264
vopanāmika **67**. 45
vyādha **69**. 20

saṃrambha **72**. 18
saṃkhata, saṃkhāra **4**. 66
saṃkhya **89**. 4
saṃgaha **91**. 27
saṃgahavatthūni (the four) **37**. 108; (**41**. 56)
saccakiriyā **18**. 39; **25**. 16; (**51**. 56;) **70**. 209; **82**. 16
satthavaṭṭi **37**. 150
satthāgama **67**. 88
sanāthīkata **73**. 67
santi **73**. 71; **85**. 50
saṃdhibheda **70**. 168
sannīra **39**. 16; **74**. 201
samaṇī **59**. 21
samattha with gen. **48**. 20
samavutti **42**. 3
samāpatti **5**. 123
samī **72**. 9
saraṇa **1**. 32, 62
sahavaḍḍhita **67**. 52
sahoḍha **23**. 11; **35**. 11
sādhukāra **74**. 223; **85**. 48
sāpadānaṃ **37**. 203
sābhimata **61**. 50
sāmaṇera **39**. 48
sāragandha **100**. 196
sāhicca **82**. 3
sikhāmaha **63**. 5
sivikāsotthisālā **10**. 102
su° before a finite verb **50**. 27
sugaṇṭhika **49**. 34
sudhākara **84**. 44
sūri **60**. 19
sekha **3**. 24
sogata **76**. 11; **83**. 37
soṇḍa **85**. 33
sotāpatti, -panna **1**. 33; (**12**. 21)

hammiya 88. 93, 118
haraṃharaṃ 76. 114
haṣsa 66. 56; 73. 117
hemavaḍḍha 38. 63
homa 62. 33

II. Names of Persons

Ajātasattu and successors 4. 1 ff.
Alagakkonāra 91. 3, 9 N.
Aḷattūru 76. 180 N., 184, 214
Asoka (Dhammāsoka) 5. 19 ff., 11. 18; 38. 44 &c.
Āriyamuni 100. 95
Udaya I. 49. 1, 45
Upāli 100. 71, 94, 117, 142
Okkāka 2. 11 f., 45. 38; 80. 32; 87. 34
Kālāsoka 4. 31, 63; 5. 14
Kuṭṭhaka 51. 88
Kumāradāsa (and Kālidāsa) 41. 1
Kulasekhara 76. 76, 80 N. — 90. 47
Kuvaṇṇā 7. 11 ff.
Koṭalla 64. 3; 70. 56
Gokaṇṇa 63. 34; 66. 35
Caṇḍavajji 5. 120 ff.
Cāṇakka 5. 16; 64. 45
Cittā 9. 1, 13 ff.
Coḷakonāra 76. 145, 173, 180 N., 181
Tondriya 76. 180 N., 181
Dāsaka 5. 105 ff.
Dīghasanda(na) 15. 212; 38. 16
Duyyodhana 64. 43
Dussanta 64. 44
Dhammakitti 84. 11
Dhammāsoka see Asoka
Dhammika 100. 66, 136 &c.
Nandā 5. 15 ff.; 64. 45
Narasīha 47. 4, 7 N.
Nālā 50. 9
Nigrodha 5. 37 ff.
Patañjali 37. 217
Panāda see Mahāpanāda
Parakkamacamūnātha 80. 49, 52
Bimbisāra 2. 25 ff.
Buddhaghosa 37. 215 ff., 224
Bhaddaji 31. 7 ff.
Mandhātar 2. 2; 37. 53; 81. 28
Mahākassapa 3. 4; 5. 1; 78. 6
Mahādhammakathin 37. 175
Mahānāma 39. 42
Mahāpanāda 2. 4; 31. 8; 37. 62; 51. 9
Mahāsaṃmata 2. 1, 23; 47. 2; 99. 77
Māna, Mānavamma 57. 4, 14, 25
Moggaliputta 5. 95 ff.; 78. 6
Rāma 64. 42; 68. 20; 73. 137; 75. 59; 83. 46; 88. 69
Rāvaṇa 64. 42; 75. 59
Vajiragga, Viduragga 51. 105; 53. 46
Varañāṇamuni 100. 138, 174
Visuddhācariya 100. 137, 171, 173

Vihāradevī **22**. 12, 20, 29; **24**. 53
Sagararājino **87**. 34
Samaṇī **59**. 21
Saraṇaṃkara **97**. 51, 60; **98**. 23; **99**. 150 N.; **100**. 49, 107
Siggava **5**. 99, 120 ff.
Sirisaṃghabodhi **36**, 73 ff.; **81**. 10; **85**. 73; **92**. 6. — **44**. 83; **46**. 1; **59**. 10
Silāmeghavaṇṇa **44**. 83 N.
Sītā **73**. 137.
Sunettā **91**. 24
Soṇaka **5**. 104
Hanumant **73**. 161

III. List of Passages

1. 4. — **3**. 6, 7. — **4**. 30, 45, 51, 62. — **5**. 23, 61, 145, 216, 227, 262. — **7**. 56 ff. — **9**. 8, 17, 23. — **11**. 2, 5. — **12**. 16, 55. — **13**. 18, 19. — **15**. 27 f., 59. — **17**. 41. — **19**. 10, 28. — **20**. 22, 30, 37. — **21**. 4 ff. — **22**. 17, 53, 67, 68. — **23**. 11, 24, 37 f. — **24**. 35, 48, 56. — **25**. 89, 93. — **26**. 23-5. — **27**. 46. — **28**. 28. — **29**. 2, 58. — **30**. 25, 42-50. — **31**. 21, 26, 43, 53, 124. — **32**. 34. — **33**. 4, 42, 51, 98, 103. — **34**. 27, 36. — **35**. 13, 116-8. — **36**. 26, 31, 102, 116, 124. — **37**. 35, 66 ff., 91, 100, 101, 114, 116, 129, 138, 159, 171, 184, 185 f., 200. — **38**, 3, 8, **9**, 21, 29, 35, 59, 60, 94, 96, 98, 110. — **39**. 6, 14, 17, 23, 26, 27, 34, 42, 52, 53, 59. — **41**. 9, 44, 66, 71, 73, 82, 89, 99, 103. — **42**. 1, 15-6, 26, 28, 62, 66, 69. — **44**. 7, 13, 21, 38, 44, 56, 69, 87, 88, 90, 106, 119, 123, 151. — **45**. 30, 54, 56, 70, 75., — **46**. 1, 32, 33. — **47**. 2-3, 10, 40, 45. — **48**. 8, 20, 25, 29, 54, 61, 72, 79, 94, 101, 104. — **49**. 1, 2, 3, 9, 18, 23, 24, 27, 47, 52, 58, 61, 62, 74, 81, 83, 86, 93. — **50**. 9, 27, 34, 52, 53, 58, 73, 74. — **51**. 20, 56-7, 98. — **52**. 4, 12, 19, 22, 26, 29, 31, 32, 43, 46, 80. — **53**. 7, 44. — **54**. 9, 57, 59-60, 62, 68, 70-1. — **55**. 16, 20. — **56**. 16. — **57**. 8, 9, 33. — **58**. 15, 45, 56. — **59**. 1, 2, 22, 32, 49. — **60**. 14, 26, 30, 44, 84. — **61**. 31, 36, 40, 53, 72. — **62**. 10, 13, 65. — **63**. 12-5. — **64**. 3, 19, 22, 28, 40, 41-7, 53. — **66**. 7, 12, 25, 47, 53, 56, 59, 62, 63, 66, 72, 78, 85, 86, 104, 109, 115, 116, 143-5, 150. — **67**. 21, 44, 45, 46, 61, 65. — **68**. 1-2, 25, 31. — **69**. 20. — **70**. 20, 42-4, 85, 92, 127, 128, 145,

181, 208, 289, 290, 292, 321. — **71**. 10, 13-5, 32. — **72**. 18, 28, 43, 58, 80, 91, 95, 101-2, 104, 106-7, 113, 122-8, 139, 140, 141-7, 152, 188, 205-14, 209, 211, 227-8, 236, 258, 318. — **73**. 2-10, 12-22, 41, 57, 74-81, 95-112, 111, 124-35, 133. — **74**. 22-35, 26, 55-66, 56, 64, 72-8, 79, 80, 82, 83, 96, 100, 105, 107, 129, 140, 142, 150, 165, 173, 178, 198-227, 199, 225, 228-31, 240. — **75**. 19, 85, 88, 97, 120, 134-5, 143, 156, 179-82. — **76**. 3, 8, 12, 18-9, 29, 31, 40, 55, 70-2, 87, 90, 98, 100, 112, 124, 130, 186, 192, 208-19, 212. — **77**. 20-4, 52, 58, 84-5, 97. — **78**. 2-4, 13, 52-4, 60, 62, 102. — **79**. 27. — **80**. 15, 33, 39. — **81**. 2, 6, 19, 22, 26. — **82**. 21, 33, 47. — **83**. 4, 5-7, 8-9, 15-21, 33-4, 40. — **84**. 14, 15, 38, 40. — **85**. 1, 3-10, 4, 38, 42-51, 45, 82. — **86**. 17, 22. — **87**. 4, 19, 37, 39, 46, 50. — **88**. 11, 86, 100. — **89**. 4, 16-38, 20, 47-56, 68. — **90**. 43, 46, 63, 68, 92, 104, 109. — **91**. 9, 25, 27. — **92**. 23-6. — **94**. 23. — **95**. 4, 14. — **96**. 5, 19-20. — **97**. 29. — **98**. 14, 24, 26, 47-8, 61, 69, 73. — **99**. 6-11, 11, 16, 43, 45, 46, 53, 55, 56, 60, 63, 104, 113, 163, 171, 175, 181. — **100**. 1, 35, 48, 52, 71-4, 75, 102-7, 129, 137, 157, 162, 167, 215, 248, 268, 281, 295. — **101**. 14.

IV. The Chronicle

1) Composition (Cf. C. ed. I, p. I ff.): **37**. 51; **38**. 59. — **79**. 84. — **90**. 102; **99**. 76 ff. — the author of the last portion contemporary with Kittisirirājasīha **99**. 53, 133, 163; **100**. 228. — — **2) Sources**: Different sources: **7**. 43-5 and **9**. 9-11; **73**. 12 ff. and **78**. 6 ff. — a new source? (the Rohaṇa chronicle) **22**. 1; **45**. 37; **57**. 3; — (**47**. 1; **81**. 40). — puññapotthakāni **32**. 25; traces of p: dry numbers or lists of names **20**. 17-28; **24**. 12, 47; **26**. 25; **27**. 47; **32**. 26 ff.; **38**. 45 ff.; **60**. 48 ff.; **79**. 62 ff.; **82**. 12 ff.; **92**. 10-29; **100**. 14, 200; absence of a record **37**. 46. — annals kept at court **59**. 7 ff. — — **3) Chronological dates**: **4**. 1, 8; 5. 21 f., 280; **20**. 1 ff., 32, 49; **41**. 27; **42**. 44; **44**. 144, 153; **47**. 15; **52**. 78; **53**. 44; **55**. 22; **58**. 41; **60**. 5; **80**. 32; **90**. 108; **91**. 15;

92. 6; **94.** 5, 18; **99.** 2; **100.** 59, 91, 282. — — **4) Style and language** (cf. C. ed. I, p. XIV ff.). Alaṃkāra: **18.** 14, 68; **52.** 42; **58.** 15; **60.** 44; **70.** 292; **72.** 51, 102, 144, 209, 255 f., 314, 323, 326; **76.** 160 f., 233, 311 f.; **80.** 56 ff., 60; **82.** 5, 16, 41, 44 ff.; **83.** 13, 25, 38, 40, 42; **85.** 12 ff., 35, 44 ff.; **88.** 91, 121; **89.** 2 ff.; **90.** 34, 47, 49; **96.** 20; **99.** 4, 122; **100.** 30, 34 &c. — Puns: **1.** 13, 25; **5.** 256; **9.** 29; **14.** 43; **15.** 27; **17.** 8 f.; **26.** 6; **31.** 56; **33.** 65; **37.** 115; **50.** 65, 83; **51.** 108; **67.** 92; **72.** 295, 315; **85.** 87 f.; **90,** 2 &c. Metrical licenses: **37,** 135 a b, 138 a b; **62.** 49 c d; **65.** 11 c d; **66.** 44 a b; **67.** 44 c d. See also C. ed. I, p. XI ff. — Irregular grammatical forms. See also C. ed. I, p. XIV ff.: **44.** 11, 31, 44; **47.** 55; **50.** 10; **62.** 60; **70.** 262; **75.** 26; **90.** 109. — Loc. inst. of gen. **38.** 115. — Causative inst. of the simple root and the contrary: **48.** 102; **70.** 287; **75.** 156 &c.; **47.** 18; **48.** 61; **75.** 171 &c. — Simple verbe inst. of passive and the contrary: **44.** 26; **50.** 18; **51.** 54; **76.** 330 &c.; **70.** 208. — Gerund inst. of Loc. abs.: **39.** 26; **48.** 79 N.; **77.** 24 N.; **88.** 67 ff. — Irregular compounds: **39.** 59; **91.** 6, 20'; **99.** 46. — Irregular construction of sentences: **41.** 103; **49.** 58; **72.** 128, 249; **92.** 17, 23–26; **96.** 19–20; **99.** 6 ff., 42 ff.; **100.** 51 f. — Influence of the metre **74.** 199; **75.** 72. — Influence of Sinhalese **70.** 85; **90.** 104; **91.** 36; **95,** 8; **96.** 17; **98.** 1. — **5) Literary references.** Indian epic literature **64.** 42 ff.; **66.** 143; cf. II, s. vv. Duyyodhana, Dussanta, Rāma. āyurveda **73.** 42; nīti literature **48.** 80, 96; **55.** 7; **64.** 3; **66.** 130 ff. (142); **70.** 56; **73.** 59; yuddhaṇṇava **70.** 56; the rasa theory **66.** 56; **72.** 94, 265; **73.** 117; **75.** 89. — Canonical Pali literature: Quotation of a Buddha-word **73.** 143; **99.** 180 f. — Dhammasaṃgīti, -saṃgaha **3.** 17; **5.** 276. — Tipiṭaka and Aṭṭhakathā: **5.** 84, 275; **27.** 44; **33.** 100; **37.** 223; **41.** 58; **60.** 6; **84.** 9, 29; **90.** 37, 83; **91.** 27. — 84000 sections: **5.** 78 (cf. **5.** 173 ff.); **33.** 12. — Navaṅgika sāsana **89.** 70. — Vinaya, dhamma, suttanta: **3.** 30, 34; **5.** 150 f.; **20.** 56; **54.** 34; **99.** 90, 170, 173 f. — Nikāyā (the four) **33.** 72; **99.** 31, 33; **100.** 117. — Saccasaṃyutta **14.** 58. — Abhidhamma: **5.** 150; **37.** 221; **44.** 109; **51.** 79; **52.** 49 f. — Paritta texts: **37.** 226; **51.** 80;

99. 26. — Single suttantas: 5. 68; **12**. 26, 29, 31, 34, 39, 41, 51; **14**. 22, 39, 63; **15**. 4, 176, 178, 186, 195, 197, 199; **16**. 3; **37**. 191, 195; **51**. 79; **99**. 20, 29, 154; **100**. 275. — Single jātakas: 5. 264; **12**. 37; **35**. 30; **64**. 41; **83**. 33 f.; **97**. 39-45; **99**. 97; **100**. 74, 254. — Peta-, Vimānavatthu: **14**. 58. — Dhammasaṅgaṇi: **37**. 225; **52**. 50; **60**. 17. — Cittayamaka 5. 146. Kathāvatthu 5. 278. — Younger Pāli literature: **37**. 93, 225, 236; **39**. 49, 56; **91**. 27; **97**. 57, 59; **100**. 118. — Sinhalese literature **37**. 228, 233; **90**. 78, 83; **98**. 24. — **6) External confirmation or correction of the chronicle** (cf. M. tr., p. XV ff.). a) Sinhalese books. Sirimeghavaṇṇa to Mahānāga: **37**. 92, 105, 178, 208, 247; **38**. 1, 8, 10, 45, 50, 112; **39**. 58; **41**. 1-5, 6, 26, 27, 37, 53, 63, 91, 102. — Aggabodhi I. to Dāṭhopatissa II: **42**. 13, 15, 39, 40, 67, 68; **44**. 1, 22, 63, 65, 82, 117, 144, 153; **45**. 16, 35, 80. — Aggabodhi IV. to Aggabodhi IX: **46**. 39, 44, 46; **47**. 1, 66; **48**. 19, 25, 38, 67, 74; **49**. 37, 39, 42, 64, 82, 92. — Sena I. to Loka: **50**. 1, 85; **51**. 1, 26, 89, 134; **52**. 36, 81; **53**. 1, 4, 12, 27, 38, 51; **54**. 1, 56, 72; **55**. 33; **56**. 6, 9, 12, 14, 16; **57**. 1. — Vijayabāhu I. to Parakkamabāhu I: **60**. 91; **62**. 1; **63**. 18, 19; **79**. 86. — Vijayabāhu II. to Māgha: **80**. 14, 15, 26, 29, 30, 32, 33, 34, 42, 44, 45, 48, 51, 53, 79. — Vijayabāhu III. to Vijayabāhu IV.: **8**[illegible]. 19, 44, 51, 56, 58, 79; **82**. 7; **83**. 30-1, 37, 42; **84**. 9, 24; **85**. 1-4, 95, 99, 118; **86**. 49-50; **87**. 9; **88**. 35; **89**. 71; **90**. 1. — Bhuvanekabāhu I. to Rājasīha II: **90**. 4, 59, 63, 64, 105-6, 108; **91**. 3, 32; **92**. 1; **93**. 16; **94**. 2-3, 22; **95**. 25; **96**. 40. — b) Ceylon inscriptions: **37**. 53; **39**. 11. — **42**. 3 ff.; **44**. 98. — **46**. 20, 29; **48**. 24. — **50**. 9, 45, 68, 70; **51**. 12, 26, 74, 88, 90, 105, 134; **52**. 1, 11, 13, 17, 33, 45, 58; **53**. 4, 13; **54**. 1, 7, 35, 48. — **58**. 1, 56, 59; **59**. 49; **60**. 5, 16, 21, 36, 66, 91; **63**. 19; **72**. 300; **73**. 20, 87; **76**. 68; **78**. 5, 6 ff. — **80**. 1, 18, 19, 20, 23, 24, 25, 27, 28, 32, 33, 34, 50. — **87**. 16; **90**. 108; **91**. 1, 3, 16, 24; **92**. 1. — c) South Indian inscriptions: Kassapa V: **52**. 98. Dappula IV: **53**. 9. Udaya IV: **53**. 44. Mahinda V: **55**. 22. Parakkamabāhu I.: **76**. 80; **77**. 103. Parakkamabāhu II.:

83. 52. Bhuvanekabāhu I.: **90.** 47. BhuvanekabāhuV. **91.** 13. — d) Chinese Annals: Sirimeghavaṇṇa &c.: **37.** 53, 175. Kassapa I.; **39.** 27. Aggabodhi VI: **48.** 42. (Vijayabāhu VI.): **91.** 14.

V. The World

A. Cosmology. 1. Three worlds, hell and heaven: **4.** 38; **34.** 14; **37.** 178; **44.** 117; **60.** 91; **72.** 306; **90.** 40; **92.** 30; **94.** 21. — The moon and the tides **84.** 44. — Regions of the heavens: **28.** 13, 16, 18, 20, 36, 39; **31.** 86; **63.** 51; **72.** 300, 329; **74.** 150; **95.** 15; **96.** 25. — 2. The earth: The dīpas **73.** 8. — Meru (Sineru) **31.** 53; **37.** 79; **42.** 2; **54.** 43; **78.** 24. — Cakkavāḷa mountains **88.** 116. — Udayācala **72.** 326. — Uttara Kuru **1.** 18; **30.** 58; **51.** 50. — 3. Destruction of the world **70.** 253; **72.** 93, 313; **75.** 26; **83.** 47. — — **B) Geography and Ethnography.** **I. India.** a) Geographical Names:

Anotatta-lake **1.** 18. Aparantaka **12.** 34.
Ayojjhā **56.** 13. Avanti **4.** 17.
Ujjenī 5. 39; **13.** 8, 10 (Dakkhiṇagiri-v. **13.** 5; **29.** 35).
Uttaramadhurā **88.** 121; **92.** 25. Uruvelā **1.** 12, 16 f., 43.
Kañcīpura **88.** 121. Kaṇḍuveṭhi **47.** 7.
Kapilavatthu **2.** 15; **89.** 4. Kasmīra **12.** 9; **29.** 37.
Kāsipura see Bārāṇasī.
Kusāvatī **2.** 6. Kusinārā **3.** 2.
Kusumapura see Pāṭaliputta.
Kelāsa **32.** 53; **68.** 1; **73.** 62 &c.; **89.** 45 (Kelāsa-v. **29.** 43).
Kosambī 4. 17 (Ghositārāma **29.** 34).
Gaṅgā 5. 253; 8. 23; **11.** 30 &c.
Gandhāra **12.** 9. Giribbaja 5. 114. Gova **94.** 1-2.
Campāpurī **88.** 121. Jetuttara **89.** 2.
Tambaraṭṭha **84.** 11. Tāmalittī **11.** 23 N., 38; **19.** 6.
Tiriṇaveli **76.** 143, 288. Neṭṭūru **76.** 189.
Payāga **31.** 6. Palaṅkoṭṭa **77.** 58. Pallavabhoga **29.** 38.
Pāṭaliputta (Kusumapura, Pupphapura) **4.** 31; **5.** 39, 120; **11.** 24; **17.** 10; **18.** 8, 68; **92.** 23 (Asokārāma **5.** 80, 163, 174; **29.** 36).

Pāvā **4**. 17.
Pupphapura see Pāṭaliputta.
Bārāṇasī (Kāsipura) **1**. 14; **41**. 37; **88**. 121 (Isipatana-v. **29**. 31).
Bodhimaṇḍa **29**. 41; **37**. 215; **39**. 47.
Madda **8**. 7.
Madhurā (dakkhiṇā M.) **7**. 49, 51; **50**. 12 N.; **76**. 76; **96**. 40; **97**. 2, 24; **98**. 4 (cf. also Uttaramadhurā).
Malaya **76**. 195. Mahāraṭṭha **12**. 37.
Mahisamaṇḍala **12**. 29.
Mithilā **2**. 6; **83**. 34; **88**. 121.
Rājagaha **2**. 6; **29**. 30; **89**. 3 (Veluvana-v. **15**. 17).
Rāmissara **76**. 97. Lāḷaraṭṭha **6**. 5, 36; **7**. 3.
Vaṅga **6**. 1. Vanavāsa **12**. 31; **29**. 42.
Viñjhāṭavī **19**. 6; **29**. 40.
Visālā, Vesālī **4**. 9, 22; **88**. 121; **99**. 98 (Mahāvana-v. **4**. 12; **29**. 33).
Saṃkassa **89**. 4. Sāketa **89**. 3. Sāgala **89**. 2.
Sāvatthī **88**. 121 (Jetavana-v. **1**. 44; **29**. 32).
Sīvalīputtūru **77**. 41.
Sīhapura **6**. 35; **59**. 46.
Suṃsumāragiri **89**. 3. Soreyya **4**. 21. Himavant **12**. 41.

b) Names of tribes or castes.

Ariyā **61**. 36; **63**. 15. Āriyā **90**. 16 ff.
Kaṇṇāṭā **55**. 12. Kallarā **76**. 246.
Kāliṅgā **6**. 1; **37**. 92; **42**. 44 &c.
Kāsī **5**. 114. Keraḷā **53**. 9. Koḷiyā **31**. 18.
Coḷā **21**. 13; **36**. 112; **52**. 70 &c.
Damiḷā **1**. 41; **21**. 10 &c.; **38**. 11 f. &c.
Paṇḍū **7**. 50, 69; **50**. 12; **76**. 76 &c.
Maravarā **76**. 130, 246, 259. Yādhavā **76**. 163.
Yonā, Yavanā **10**. 90; **12**. 34, 39; **76**. 264.
Licchavī **99**. 98. Vaṅgā **6**. 1. Vajjī **4**. 9 ff.
Vallabhā **47**. 15, 18, 24; **54**. 12 ff.
Sakyā **2**. 15 ff.; **8**. 18.

2. Farther India

a) Geographical names, names of tribes

Ayojjhā **98.** 91; **100.** 60. Arimaddana **76.** 38.
Kamboja **76.** 21. Kākadīpa **76.** 57.
Kusumitittha **76.** 59.
Jāvakā **83.** 36 ff.; **88.** 63; **99.** 118.
Pegu **98.** 89. Malaya **76.** 22.
Rakkhaṅga **94.** 15; **97.** 10; **98.** 89; **99.** 25.
Rāmañña **58.** 8; **60.** 5; **76.** 10–69.
Sāmindavisaya **99.** 78; **100.** 63 &c.

3. Ceylon

a) Physical character, climate &c.

The ocean: **22.** 49, 85; **41.** 79; **57.** 5; **71.** 18; **72.** 255; **85.** 44 f.; **88.** 20. — Wilderness, swamps, forests, rocks: **33.** 48; **39.** 2; **61.** 46; **66.** 51; **68.** 10; **70.** 2 ff., 84; **81.** 3, 5, 33; **86.** 9; **87.** 26; **95.** 9. — Irregular rain: **21.** 27; **70.** 208. — Drought and famine: **32.** 29; **36.** 20, 74; **37.** 189; **87.** 1 ff.; **90.** 43. — Wind, thunderstorms: **57.** 56; **72.** 3; **74.** 228 ff.; **87.** 7 ff. — Earthquake (as a miracle): **5.** 259 ff.; **15.** 26, 194; **17.** 55; **18.** 50; **19.** 47; **29.** 62; **31.** 110.

b) Products of the island (or imported)

1. Minerals:

Jewels (maṇi, three kinds **11.** 22) **28.** 18, 40; **61.** 6, 56; **62.** 32; **64.** 32; **68.** 12; **72.** 326; **97.** 53; **98.** 33, 95; **99.** 165; **100.** 16 ff.; and precious stones (ratana, seven or nine kinds **27.** 37; **91.** 18; **97.** 7) **11.** 8 f., 16; **22.** 60; **31.** 60; **34.** 73; **66.** 44; **69.** 33; **89.** 41; **90.** 71; **97.** 17. — Beryl (veḷuriya) **11.** 16; diamond (vajira) **100.** 15; ruby (kuruvinda, rattamaṇi, lohitaṅka) **28.** 19; **100.** 18; **11.** 16; sapphire (indanīla, uppala, nīlamaṇi) **11.** 16; **28.** 19; **100.** 17; topaz (pupphărāga) **100.** 17. — Pearls (eight kinds **11.** 14) **11.** 16, 22; **28.** 36; **34,** 47 f.; **61.** 6, 56; **62.** 32; **64.** 32; **70.** 92; **89.** 19; **97.** 47; **98.** 33, 95;

100. 19. — Gold **11**. 31; **22**. 64; **27**. 33; **28**. 14; **29**. 57; **33**. 11; **61**. 57; **66**. 139; **68**. 12; **89**. 19 ff.; **91**. 18; **97**. 17, 53; **98**. 44, 75, 94; **99**. 54, 165; **100**. 30, 72, 75, 241. — Silver **27**. 27, 33; **28**. 20, 33; **29**. 57; **89**. 20 ff.; **90**. 71; **97**. 18; **98**. 44, 75; **99**. 55, 165. — Copper (loha, tambaloha) **23**, 87; **27**. 42; **28**. 16; **31**. 85; **36**. 31. — Iron (ayo) **23**. 87; **98**. 69. — Rock-crystal (phaḷika) **27**. 36; **29**. 9. — Medavaṇṇapāsāṇa **1**. 39; **30**. 57, 59; **31**. 121. — Yellow orpiment (haritāla) **34**. 52. — Cinnabar (kuruvinda?) **29**. 8. — kaṅkuṭṭha, kind of earth **32**, 6. — Red arsenic (manosilā) **15**. 80, 114, 149; **29**. 12; **34**. 52. — Vermilion (hiṅguli) **27**. 18. — Corals (pavāḷa) **27**. 26, 31; **28**, 37 f. &c. — Shells (saṅkhā) **71**. 25; s. dakkhiṇāvaṭṭa **11**. 22, 30; **100**. 154.

2. Trees and shrubs; fruits, flowers

Akkha (terminalia belerica) **32**. 29. amba (mangifera indica) **14**. 17 ff.; **15**. 38; **22**. 4 f.; **79**. 3, 85; **100**. 4, 218. asana (terminalia alata tomentosa) **23**. 87. asoka (jonesia asoka) **73**. 98. ādāri-creeper **17**. 31. āmalaka (emblica officinalis) **5**. 26; **11**. 31; **28**. 36; **54**. 23. udumbara (ficus glomerata) **15**. 112; **23**. 87. kaṇ(ṇ)ikāra (pterospermum acerifolium) **73**. 123; **100**. 1. kadalī (musa sapientum) **M**. ed. p. 331, v. 5; **70**. 211; **72**. 318; **73**. 123; **75**. 61; **85**. 36, 114; **98**. 41; **100**. 30. kadamba (nauclea cadamba) **73**. 98. kadambapupphā **17**. 31; 19. 73, 75; 25. 48; **33**. 85; **35**. 104, 116. kapittha (feronia elephantum) 29. 11. kamuka (areca palm) **98**. **41**. kuṭaja (wrightia antidysenterica) **73**. 99. ketaka (pandanus odoratissimus) **33**. 50; **73**. 98; 100. 1. khajjūra (phoenix silvestris) **100**. 6. kharapatta (tectona grandis) **32**. 5. campaka (michelia champaca) **73**. 98; **98**. 59; 100. 1, 197. jambū (eugenia jambu) 36. 71 ff.; **73**. 98; 100. 4. tamāla (xanthochymus pictorius) **73**. 99. tāla (palmyra palm) **10**. 59; **23**. 46, 59; **73**. 123; 79. 3. timbarūsaka (the tinduka tree) **100**. 5. tilaka (?) **73**. 98. dāḍima (pomegranate) **100**. 5. nāga (iron-wood tree) **73**. 98, 123; **85**. 34; **89**. 43; **100**. 1, 293. nāraṅga (orange) **100**. 5. nālikera (cocopalm) **23**. 59; **61**. 65; **73**. 99; **74**. 204; **79**. 3; **86**.

5, 17, 45; **97**. 34; **98**. 41; **100**. 5, 218 (the shell **57**. 8). nigrodha (ficus indica) **10**. 35 f., 89; **15**. 147. nīpa (nauclea cadamba) **73**. 98. panasa (artocarpus integrifolia) **28**. 23; **79**. 3; **85**. 36; **86**. 50; **100**. 4, 218. picula (tamarix indica) **15**. 28. punnāga (rottleria tinctoria) **73**. 98, 123; **89**. 43; **100**. 1, 293. pūga (areca palm) **36**. 47; **79**. 3; **100**. 3, 293. phāruṣa (?) **100**. 4. bodhirukkha (ficus religiosa) see VIII, C, 3. madhu, -ūka (bassia latifolia) **34**. 56; **44**. 18; **83**. 18. muṇḍaka (?) **100**. 5. muddikā (grape) **100**. 6. rambhā (musa sapientum) **100**. 4. rājāyatana (buchanania latifolia) **1**. 52, 54, 67 f. labuja (artocarpus incisa) **90**. 87; **94**. 11 f. vakula (mimusops elengi) **73**. 99. vaṭa (ficus indica) **6**. 16. sattapaṇṇa (alstonia scholaris) **30**. 47. sannīra (king coconut tree) **74**. 204; **100**. 5, 26. sāla (shorea robusta) **3**. 2; **5**. 161; **73**. 98. sirīsa (acacia sirissa) **15**. 78. harītaka (terminalia chebula) **5**. 26; **11**. 31. hintāla (kind of palm tree) **73**. 123. Bamboo (veḷu) **11**. 10; **70**. 213. sugar-cane, sugar, molasses **34**. 62; **35**. 92; **61**. 53; **89**. 53; **100**. 196. sandal-wood **11**. 28; **58**. 9; **61**. 57; **100**. 2, 196. aloe (agaru) **61**. 57; **100**. 2. betel (tambūla) **35**. 62; **54**. 22, 46; **100**. 3, 196. garlic (lasuna) **54**. 22 f. pepper (marica, pipphalī) **25**. 114; **54**. 23. ginger (siṅgivera) **28**. 21; **54**. 23. saffron (piyaṅgu) **24**. 25. camphor (kappūra) **58**. 9; **61**. 57; **69**. 24; **89**. 43; **100**. 3, 196. liquorice (yaṭṭhimadhuka) **32**. 46. — Bean (māsa) **23**. 51. sesam (tila) **29**. 12; **34**. 56. — Cotton **57**. 56; **72**. 3; **86**. 46. — Lāja **98**. 46; **100**. 31. pāṭali (bignonia suaveolens) **73**. 98. gaṇṭhipuppha **30**. 59. jasmin **15**. 27; **29**. 61; **30**. 27; **73**. 99; **98**. 8; **100**. 1. lotus **19**. 18; **22**. 45, 53; **34**. 47, 53 f.; **73**. 102; **88**. 113; **100**. 1, 30 (the stalk: muḷāli **7**. 12).

3. Animals

Elephant, wild or domesticated **7**. 56; **18**. 28; **23**. 8, 47, 49; **29**. 4; **37**. 112; **41**. 23, 47 ff.; **47**. 9; **51**. 37, 43, 112 f.; **61**. 6; **70**. 219, 229, 265; **72**. 3, 88, 155, 314, 325; **76**. 48, 70; **89**. 22; **96**. 20; **99**. 46 and passim. young el.s. **62**. 22, 25. rutting el.s. **66**. 150; **72**. 321; **74**. 63; **83**. 13. solitary el.s. **72**. 248; **76**. 244. catching wild el.s. **72**. 105. el.-trainer and driver

22. 63; **88**. 34. hatthisālā **14**. 62; **15**. 1. āḷhaka **19**. 73; **35**. 24. sivigeha "canopy on an el.'s back" **99**. 55, 59. el.-trade **76**. 17-34. white el.s **62**. 21. six-tusked race **22**. 61. maṅgalahatthī see below V, B, 3. (danta "ivory" **27**. 32, 35; **37**. 100 ff.) — Horse **7**. 56; **70**. 127, 265; **72**. 315; **74**. 221; **76**. 112; **85**. 113; **88**. 34, 74; **92**. 29; **99**. 46 &c. h. s among the Damiḷas **76**. 100. horse dealing (sindhu-h.) **21**. 10; **23**. 71; **31**. 38. — Buffalo, wild or domesticated **23**. 79; **67**. 2; **86**. 24; **90**. 76; **92**. 29 (māhisa camma **25**. 36). lion, not indigenous **6**. 5; **27**. 30; **60**. 40; **66**. 90, 104; **67**. 6, 48; **70**. 24, 141, 219; **72**. 3, 68, 88, 108, 152, 155, 221; **83**. 13; **96**. 5 (migarājā **96**. 20). tiger, not indigenous **27**. 30. panther **75**. 39. bear **5**. 31; **67**. 41. boar **10**. 4; **23**. 66; **54**. 32; **67**. 44; **83**. 18. elk (gokaṇṇa) **14**. 3; **23**. 66; **70**. 36. deer or antelope (miga, hariṇa) **5**. 154 f.; **23**. 66; **54**. 32; **66**. 90; **67**. 48; **72**. 68; **75**. 39. monkey **54**. 32; **68**. 20; **87**. 20. hare 23. 65. mouse **5**. 30. cow **90**. 76; **92**. 29. bullock (usabha) **60**. 74. dog **28**. 9, 41; **36**. 44; **54**. 32; **60**. 74 (bitch: soṇī **7**. 9). yak-cow, not indigenous (camarī) **98**. 14; **100**. 31. — Vulture **75**. 114. crane **98**. 43. peacock **57**. 7; **73**. 101; **74**. 229. crow **60**. 74; **75**. 114. parrot **5**. 29. cuckoo **73**. 101. goose **30**. 65; **35**. 97; **73**. 134. kalanda **37**. 204. karavīka **5**. 32. (birds in cages **70**. 292; **72**. 209). — Glow-worm **75**. 29; **83**. 25; **86**. 22. bee **5**. 31; **34**. 52; **73**. 97. moth (paṭaṅga) **75**. 41. — Crocodile **70**. 4. iguana **28**. 9 f. tortoise **75**. 58. — Fish **75**. 58; **88**. 113. — Snakes (nāga) **5**. 161; **37**. 112 ff. (sappa) **21**. 19. (deḍḍubha) **37**. 132. (ghoravisa) **93**. 8.

c) Geographical and ethnographical names

1. Names of the Island

Sīhala, Laṅkā passim. — Prehistoric names **15**. 59, 93, 127. — Tambapaṇṇī **7**. 41; **80**. 25; **85**. 106; **89**. 57. — Tisīhala **81**. 46; **82**. 1; **87**. 25, 71; **88**. 65.

2. Names of provinces (raṭṭha) and districts (maṇḍala) (18 provinces: **86**. 11)

Aṭṭhasahassaka **61**. 24; **75**. 154
Ambavana **66**. 85; **69**. 9
Āḷisāra **60**. 14; **70**. 106
Uttararaṭṭha **70**. 92
Ūvaraṭṭha (see Hūva) **95**. 22
Erāhuḷa **74**. 91
Kantakapeṭaka **69**. 9
Kalyāṇī **1**. 63, 74; **22**. 12 ff.; **61**. 35
Kālagiribhaṇḍa **72**. 62
Kirinda **74**. 97
Kurundī **83**. 16; **88**. 64
Giribā **69**. 9
Girimaṇḍala **51**. 111
Guttasālā **61**. 12; **74**. 154
Janapada **44**. 56; **66**. 110
Tabbā **69**. 9
Dakkhiṇadesa **38**. 24; **41**. 35; **42**. 8 &c.
Dīghavāpi **74**. 89, 180; **75**. 1; **96**. 25
Dīghāli **72**. 63; **75**. 60
Dumbara **70**. 8
Dvādasasahassaka **61**. 22; **75**. 156 N.
Dhanumaṇḍala **74**. 166
Navayojanaraṭṭha **72**. 61; **75**. 72
Nāgadīpa **1**. 47; **20**. 25; **42**. 62
Nilagallaka **70**. 14
Pañcayojanaraṭṭha **57**. 71; **72**. 57; **75**. 21; **85**. 81
Pañcasataraṭṭha **95**. 9
Pañcuddharaṭṭha **94**. 4; **95**. 23 f.; **96**. 17
Patiṭṭhāraṭṭha **55**. 22 N.; **81**. 15 N.; **88**. 87
Padī **83**. 16; **88**. 64
Pillaviṭṭhi **69**. 8
Puratthimadesa **41**. 33
Buddhagāmaraṭṭha **69**. 9
Bodhigāmavararaṭṭha **69**. 9
Majjhimavagga **70**. 20
Malaya **7**. 68; **24**. 7; **25**. 5; **41**. 10 &c.
Mahākhetta **72**. 63; **75**. 50
Mahātila **66**. 71
Mahāthala **48**. 3
Mahāraṭṭha **72**. 141, 163, 190
Māyāraṭṭha **81**. 15; **87**. 24
Merukandara **41**. 19; **70**. 282
Moravāpi **69**. 8
Ratanākararaṭṭha **42**. 18; **69**. 31
Rattakararaṭṭha **68**. 23
Rājaraṭṭha **52**. 4; **55**. 22; **61**. 30
Rohaṇa **22**. 6, 8; **35**. 27 f.; **38**. 12 &c.
Laṅkāgiri **70**. 88
Lokagalla **74**. 79
Sapara(gamu) **78**. 8; **94**. 12
Sūrambavana **70**. 87
Hūvaraṭṭha (see Ūva) **60**. 66

3. Towns and villages

Aṅgamu **70**. 130
Anurādhapura **10**. 76, 106 and passim
Antaraviṭṭhi **60**. 68; **61**. 46
Ambaggāma **86**. 23

Ambavana **66**. 85
Āḷigāma **70**. 112
Uddhanadvāra **61**. 16
Upatissagāma **7**. 44
Ullapanaggāma **86**. 23
Kadalīgāma **60**. 66
Kadalīnivāta **44**. 6; **48**. 50
Kammāragāma **75**. 47
Kalahanagara **10**. 42
Kalyāṇī **72**. 151
Kājaragāma **19**. 54; **45**. 45
Kālagallaka **90**. 9
Kālagiribhaṇḍa **72**. 62
Kālatittha **56**. 12; **86**. 44
Kuṇḍasālā **97**. 34
Kumbugāma **75**. 149
Koṭṭa see Jayavaḍḍhanakoṭṭa
Koṭṭhasāra **61**. 43; **74**. 44
Konduruva **72**. 231
Kolamba(tittha) **94**. 1; **95**. 4, 15
Kolambahālaka **25**. 80; **33**. 42
Khīragāma **74**. 163; **79**. 71
Gaṅgāsiripura **86**. 18; **88**. 48
Gimhatittha **75**. 22
Gilīmalaya **60**. 65
Guttasālā **24**. 17; **51**. 109
Jayavaḍḍhanakoṭṭa **91**. 7
Jambukola (= Dambul) **70**. 72; **72**. 136
Jambukola (harbour) **11**. 23; **18**. 7
Jambuddoṇī **81**. 29; **85**. 4
Tambagāma **75**. 90
Taḷātthala **70**. 107
Titthagāma **90**. 88
Tilagulla **58**. 43
Demaṭavala **74**. 139
Devanagara **56**. 6; **60**. 59; **75**. 47
Doṇivagga **75**. 69
Dvāramaṇḍala **10**. 1; **23**. 23
Dhanapiṭṭhi **46**. 41
Dhanuvillika **70**. 15
Nandigāma **25**. 14; **38**. 14
Nālandā **70**. 167
Nīlavālatittha **75**. 48
Parakkamapura **72**. 151; **74**. 15
Puṅkhagāma **61**. 26
Pulatthinagara **44**. 122; **46**. 34 and passim (three suburbs of P. **73**. 151 ff.; **78**. 79 ff.).
Perādoṇī **91**. 2
Bakagalla **75**. 124
Badalatthala,-lī **58**. 43; **66**. 43 N.
Buddhagāma **58**. 43; **66**. 19.
Bubbula **70**. 99
Bodhigāmavara **66**. 78
Bhīmatittha **85**. 81; **86**. 40
Maṅgalabegāma **67**. 52
Majjhimagāma **74**. 83
Maṇḍagalla **58**. 43
Māṇḍagāma **45**. 47
Mannāra **61**. 39
Mallavāḷāna **70**. 61
Mahāgalla **44**. 3
Mahāgāma **22**. 8; **45**. 42
Mahātittha **7**. 58; **48**. 81; **51**. 28
Mahānāgahula **58**. 39; **60**. 90
Mahāvālukagāma **75**. 36, 45
Mālāvaratthalī **75**. 68, 157
Muttākara **70**. 63
Rakkhapāsāṇa **57**. 67
Ratanagāma **42**. 18
Rāmucchuvallika **70**. 11, 14 N.

Labujagāma 94. 12
Lābugāma 10. 72
Vattalagāma 81. 58
Vālikākhetta 70. 62
Vikkamapura 72. 147
Vijitapura 7. 45; 25. 19 ff.
Saṃkha(nātha)tthalī 63. 43; 64. 22
Saraggāma 66. 71
Sarogāma 71. 18
Sahodara 74. 78, 79 N.
Sākhāpatta 74. 166
Sāligiri 90. 97
Sāpatagamu 74. 131, 166 N.
Siriyāla 66. 20
Sirivaḍḍhana(near Jambuddoṇī) 85. 1
Sirivaḍḍhana = Kandy 92. 7; 94. 6, 16
Sītāvaka 93. 2 N., 5
Sīmātālatthalī 75. 101
Sīhagiri 39. 2 ff.
Suvaṇṇamalaya 75. 62
Sūkarālibheripāsāṇa 75. 98
Seṅkhaṇḍaselasirivaḍḍhana 92. 7
Hatthigiripura, -selapura 85. 62; 99. 77
Hintālavanagāma 74. 162; 75. 7
Huyalagāma 75. 149

4. Mountains
(p. = pabbata, g. = giri)

Ariṭṭha-p. 10. 64; 44. 86
Kāsa-p. 10. 27; 25. 50
Gopāla-rock 78. 65
Govindamala(-sela) 81. 5
Cetiya-p. 16. 4; 17. 23; 38. 75 &c.
Doḷa-p. 10. 44 (cf. M. tr., p. 289)
Dohaḷa-p. 44. 56; 100. 294
Dhūmarakkha-p. 10. 46; 37. 213 (cf. C. tr. I, p. 359, 3)
Pañjali-p. 32. 14
Paluṭṭha-p. 58. 18
Pācīnatissa-p. 41. 14; 44. 14
Billasela 81. 33
Mārapabbata 48. 129
Missaka-p. 13. 14, 20; 17. 23
Laṅkā-p. 66. 80
Vāta-g. 58. 31; 88. 43
Samantakūṭa, Sumanak. 1. 33, 77; 7. 67; 60. 64; 92. 17; 97. 16 ff.
Siridevinaga 66. 19
Sīlakūṭa (Missaka) 13. 20
Subhakūṭa (Missaka) 15. 131
Subha-p., Sundara-p. 81. 3; 88. 26, 61 ff.
Sumanakūṭa see Samantakūṭa
Soṇṇa-g. 34. 4.

5. Rivers, fords
(g. = gaṅgā, n. = nadī)

Kacchakatittha 10. 58; 23. 17; 37. 213 N.
Kaṇha-n. 53. 20
Kadamba-n. 7. 43; 15. 10; 41. 61
Karinda-n. 32. 14
Kāla-n. 86. 40, 44
Kālavāpi-n. 70. 126 f.
Kumbhīlavāna-n. 68. 32
Gaṅgā see Mahāvāluka-g.
Gambhīra-n. 7. 44; 28. 7

Gālu-n. **75**. 34
Gāḷha-g. **48**. 132
Gokaṇṇa see Mahāvālukag.
Goṇa-n. **35**. 13, 113
Jajjara-n. **68**. 16; **79**. 67
Mahā-n. **51**. 121
Mahārukkhatittha **72**. 11
Mahāvāluka-g. (Gaṅgā) **10**. 44, 47; **21**. 7; **38**. 12; **71**. 17 &c. (Gokaṇṇa **41**. 79; **71**. 18)
Mālāgāmatittha **72**. 50
Yakkhasūkaratittha **72**. 21
Vana-n. **75**. 156
Saṅkhavaḍḍhamānaka-n. **68**. 32
Sahassatittha **87**. 71
Indian river-names conferred on Ceylonese canals **79**. 57 N.

6. Tanks (v. = vāpi)

Abhaya-v. **10**. 84
Ambāla-v. **68**. 49 N.
Karaviṭṭhavilatta-v. **68**. 49 N.
Kāla-v. **38**. 42 &c.
Kirā-v. **68**. 49 N.
Gaṅgātaṭāka **70**. 286
Giritaṭāka **70**. 312; **72**. 149
Giribā-v. **68**. 49 N.
Giriyā-v. **68**. 49 N.
Tintiṇigāmaka-v. **68**. 49 N.
Tilagullaka-v. **68**. 49 N.
Tissa-v. **20**. 20 &c.; **70**. 149
Dīgha-v. **1**. 78; **74**. 89 &c.
Dūratissa-v. **33**. 9; **49**. 8; **79**. 32
Nāgasoṇḍi **42**. 28 (**14**. 36; **16**. 6)
Paṇḍa-v. **60**. 48; **68**. 39
Padī-v. **79**. 34
Parakkama-samudda, -sāgara **68**. 40; **79**. 26, 28, 40
Buddhagāmakanijjhara **68**. 49 N.
Maṇihīra-v. **37**. 47; **42**. 34
Maṇḍika-v. **68**. 49 N.
Mahākirāla-v. **68**. 49 N.
Mahāgalla-v. **44**. 3
Mahindataṭa-v. **42**. 29; **79**. 28
Mora-v. **69**. 8; **72**. 177
Rattamālakaṇḍa-v. **37**. 48
Vāsā-v. **68**. 49 N.
Suvaṇṇatissa-v. **79**. 32
Sūkaraggāma-v. **68**. 49 N.

Monasteries and Monastic buildings

(vih. = vihāra, pariv. = pariveṇa, c. = cetiya; A. = Anurādhapura, P. = Pulatthinagara, M. = Mahāgāma)

Abhayagiri-vih. in A. (different names) **33**. 81 ff.; **35**. 120; **37**. 59; **52**. 13; **78**. 21. — **37**. 97, 123; **44**. 96; **53**. 33. — **41**. 96; 50. 79. — **42**. 28, 63; **50**. 26. — **48**. 135
Ambatthala-c. **13**. 20; **37**. 69
Ākāsa-c. **22**. 26
Āḷāhana-pariv. **78**. 48
Āloka-lena **98**. 65
Issarasamaṇa-vih. **19**. 61; **20**. 14; **39**. 10
Uttarārāma in P. **78**. 73
Udumbaragiri-vih. **78**. 5 N.
Kantaka-c. **16**. 12

Kappūra-pariv. in A. **45**. 29; **46**. 21
Kalyāṇi-c. and -vih. **1**. 75; **81**. 59
Kassapagiri-vih. **44**. 98
Kālavāpi-vih. **38**. 50 N.
Kūṭatissa-vih. **51**. 74
Gaṇḍālādoṇi-vih. **91**. 30
Ganthākara-pariv. **37**. 243; **52**. 57
Catuvihārā in A. **53**. 37; **54**. 5
Candagiri-vih. in M. **60**. 61
Cittalapabbata-vih. **22**. 23; **24**. 9; **45**. 59
Cūlagalla-vih. **35**. 13; **42**. 49
Cetiyapabbata-vih. **19**. 62; **20**. 17
Cetiyas of Mahinda and Saṃghamittā in A. **20**. 44, 53; **38**. 58
Jambukola-vih. **20**. 25; **60**. 60
Jambukolaḷena **60**. 60; **80**. 23
Jetavana-vih. in A. (**37**. 59 N.) **37**. 33, (65); **41**. 40; **78**. 21 &c. — in P. **78**. 32 ff.
Jotivana-vih. **37**. 65, **52**. 59 = Jetavana in A.
Tissa(mahā)-vih. in M. **20**. 25; **22**. 23; **45**. 59
Tissārāma **52**. 24
Thūpārāma in A. **1**. 82; **17**. 30 &c.; **37**. 207 &c. — in P. or M. **60**. 56
Dakkhiṇa-vih. in A. **33**. 88; **42**. 14; **44**. 140
Dakkhiṇāgiri-vih. **33**. 7; **38**. 50 N.; **42**. 27; **52**. 60
Dappulapabbata-vih. **49**. 1 N., 30; **50**. 80
Dāṭhaggabodhi-pariv. in M. **45**. 42
Dāṭhādhātughara in A. **37**. 95. — in P. **73**. 128 ff.; **74**. 198; **78**. 41; **87**. 69; **89**. 40; **90**. 55. — in Jambuddoṇī **81**. 34; **82**. 9; **85**. 91; **88**. 12 ff. — in Subhagiri **90**. 46 N. — in Hatthigiripura **90**. 66 f. — in Kotte **91**. 17. — in Kandy **94**. 14; **97**. 5, 37; **98**. 35; **99**. 141
Dīghasanda-pariv. **15**. 212; **38**. 16
Devanagara-vih. **60**. 63 N.
Nāga-vih. **22**. 9; **45**. 58
Nipannapaṭimāguhā, Nisinnapaṭimālena in P. **78**. 75
Pacchimārāma in P. **78**. 70
Paṭhama-c. in A. **14**. 45; **19**. 61; **38**. 9
Paṇḍavāpi-vih. **60**. 63 N.
Pappaṭa-vih. **91**. 24
Pupphārāma **100**. 86, 141.
Baddhasīmāpāsāda, uposathahouse in P. **78**. 55 ff.
Billasela-vih. **85**. 59
Bhaṇḍika-pariv. **52**. 58
Bhīmatittha-vih. **85**. 81; **86**. 16
Macchatittha-vih. **48**. 24
Maṇihīra-vih. **37**. 40
Maṇḍalagiri-vih. **46**. 29; **60**. 63 N.; **71**. 3
Madhutthala-vih. **60**. 63 N.

Mayūra-pariv. (Mora-) in A. **37**. 172; **38**. 52
Maricavaṭṭi-vih. in A. **26**. 8 ff.; **44**. 149 &c.
Mahāthūpa in A. (different names) **15**. 51; **28**. 3 ff.; **42**. 32; **76**. 108 &c. — **20**. 19; **33**. 21. — **15**. 167; **51**. 82. — **80**. 68
Mahāpariv. in A. **42**. 26; **48**. 65
Mahāpāli in A. **20**. 23; **37**. 181. — in M. **45**. 42
Mahā-vih. in A. **15**. 8 ff., 214; **37**. 4 ff., 54 &c.
Mahiyaṅgaṇa-c. and -vih. **1**. 24, 42; **25**. 7; **36**. 34, 58; **51**. 74; **92**. 16 &c.
Māṭambiya **46**. 19
Yaṭṭhālāya-vih. in M. **22**. 7
Rajatalena-vih. **28**. 20 N., **35**. 4; **99**. 41; **100**. 237 ff.
Ratanapāsāda in A. **36**. 7; **48**. 135 &c.
Ratanāvalī-c. in P. **80**. 20 (**78**. 51 N.). — in Khīragāma **79**. 71
Rohaṇa-vih. **45**. 54
Laṅkātilaka in P. **78**. 53 f. — near Kandy **91**. 30
Lohapāsāda in A. **27**. 20 ff.; **37**. 59 &c.
Vijjādhara-cave in P. **78**. 66, 74
Veḷuvana-vih. **42**. 43; **44**. 29
Vessagiri-vih. near A. **20**. 15, 20; **39**. 11 N.
Silā-c. in A. **1**. 82
Silāsobbhakaṇḍaka-c. in A. **33**. 87
Sotthiyākara-vih. in A. **37**. 82, 84
Hatthavanagalla-vih. **85**. 73 ff.; **86**. 12, 37

Names of tribes &c.

Pulindā **7**. 68
Vannī **81**. 11; **83**. 10 &c.
Sīhalā passim
Clan names in C. **19**. 2 N.; **38**. 13 N.
(Paraṅgī **95**. 5; **98**. 80)
(Olandā **96**. 26; **98**. 89; **99**. 109)

VI. King and Kingdom

A. The king and the royal family

Cf. C. tr. I, Introd. p. XV ff.

1. The king (rājā, mahārāja, mahīpati, narapati &c. &c. passim). a. Sun- and Moon-dynasty **62**. 5; **63**. 11; **72**. 121; **87**. 29; **91**. 16; **93**. 2; **94**. 1; **96**. 41. Mahāsammata as ancestor **2**. 1, 23; **47**. 2; **99**. 77. Okkāka **2**. 11 f.; **45**. 38; **80**. 32. — b. Bodily marks of a king **22**. 59; **48**. 114; **57**. 49; **59**. 34 ff.; **62**. 46 ff.; **87**. 62. cakkavattin **100**. 35. — c. Abhiseka (molimaṅgala) **7**. 46 ff., 72; **9**. 29; **10**. 78; **36**. 123; **56**. 3 f.; **59**. 2, 8; **67**. 16; **72**. 312 ff.; **87**. 70; **89**. 5 ff.; **90**. 61; **94**. 10. abh. performed twice **11**. 7 and 40 f.; **71**. 19 ff. and **72**. 311 ff. — d. The king assumes a new name **36**. 98; **44**. 128; **45**. 22; **58**. 1; **94**. 6. the biruda Sirisaṃghabodhi **44**. 83; **46**. 1; **54**. 72; **59**. 10.

2. The queen (rājinī **24**. 13 &c.). a. mahesī **7**. 47; **8**. 28; **10**. 37, 78; **22**. 7, 12, 22; **33**. 36; **37**. 211; **46**. 27; **51**. 6, 86; **55**. 8, 16; **56**. 15; **62**. 19 ff.; **97**. 2; **98**. 1; **99**. 123. two mahesīs **33**. 45-7; **59**. 25, 30; **64**. 24; (**97**. 24; **98**. 4). — devī **22**. 3; **33**. 47; **34**. 86; **35**. 21; **36**. 42, 50; **48**. 113; **55**. 10; **63**. 4, 6; **64**. 24. aggamahesī **54**. 10; **70**. 33; **94**. 9; **97**. 2, 24; **98**. 4. — b. Political marriages **7**. 52 ff.; **51**. 15 ff., 92 f.; **54**. 9 f.; 59. 27 ff., 40 ff.; **63**. 6 ff.; **87**. 28; **97**. 24; **98**. 4.

3. The princes (rājaputta **5**. 194; **7**. 10 &c.) a. Education **64**. 3. — b. Ādipāda **41**. 34; **49**. 3; **50**. 8, 25, 46 f.; **51**. 94, 126; **52**. 4, 8, 42; **53**. 1, 4, 13, 19, 28, 39; **54**. 1, 11; **55**. 11; **57**. 4, 61; **59**. 12; **60**. 88; **61**. 2 ff. mahādipādā **44**. 136; **50**. 10, 44; **51**. 1; **58**. 7; **67**. 91. — c. Yuvarāja **42**. 6; **44**. 123, 137; **50**. 6, 21, 31; **51**. 13, 15, 18, 53 ff.; **52**. 1 f., 6, 37, 42; **53**. 1, 4, 13, 19, 28, 39; 54. 1, 7, 58; **58**. 1; 59. 7; **61**. 3; **63**. 42; **67**. 26; **85**. 59. — uparāja 5. 154; **6**. 38; **9**. 12, 14; **14**. 56; **22**. 2 ff.; **41**. 93; **42**. 6; **44**. 84, 119, 124; **46**. 24; **50**. 58 f.; **51**. 7, 12, 94; **53**. 1, 4, 13, 39; 59. 11; **60**. 40, 80, 86 f. two

uparājas **99**. 85, 124. — d. Malayarāja, -rāyara **41**. 35; **42**. 6; **44**. 53; **46**. 29; **52**. 68; **53**. 36; **69**. 6; **70**. 62, 155. Cf. C. tr. I, p. XV—XX, XXIV.

4. The princesses (rājadhītā, rājakaññā **5**. 194; **7**. 59 &c.) a. rājinī as tittle **49**. 3; **50**. 58; **54**. 11, 63; **59**. 41; **60**. 84; **62**. 1.

5. The bhāgineyya **1**. 45; **5**. 169; **11**. 20; **16**. 9; **18**, 2; **48**. 90; **49**. 71; **61**. 4 N.; **62**. 60; **83**. 41; **87**. 38, 41; **88**. 5.

6. Right of succession **33**. 1–4, 20; **49**. 65, 84; **50**. 44; **52**. 37; **54**. 1; **60**. 87; **61**. 4; **62**. 59; **63**. 22; **80**. 27, 28; **90**. 1, 4, 49, 59. Cf. C. tr. I, p. XX–XXIV.

B. Attributes of royalty; royal life

1. Residence (rājadhānī) **61**. 25; **74**. 1; **88**. 103; **90**. 35. palace (pāsāda, rājageha, -ghara, -mandira) **9**. 11; **10**. 74; **12**. 46; **35**. 63; **66**. 127; **68**. 42; **70**. 237, 312; **73**. 70; **92**. 9; **98**. 68. rājadvāra **14**. 60; **22**. 15; **25**. 105; **35**. 53, 63. rājaṅgaṇa **5**. 47; **72**. 214; **90**. 66. royal throne (pallaṅka, āsana, sīhāsana) **25**. 98; **27**. 32 ff.; **31**. 76 f., 88; **35**. 52, 54; **76**. 166; **85**. 111; **90**. 13, 23; **100**. 285. — 2. Royal insignia and ornaments (rājasādhana, -bhaṇḍāni, -bhūsaṇa, -ābharaṇa) **11**. 28; **35**. 102; **39**. 28; **41**. 20; **46**. 38; **48**. 89; **50**. 51; **55**. 16 f.; **56**. 10; **71**. 28; **74**. 224; **76**. 166; **82**. 50; **90**. 13 (crown **11**. 28; **44**. 145; **71**. 28; **72**. 326. cūḷāmaṇi **33**. 46. ekāvalī **44**. 127; **46**. 17. (seta)chatta **11**. 28; **17**. 7; **19**. 59; **31**. 39, 78; **33**. 40; **35**. 15, 69; **44**. 19 f.; **55**. 1; **64**. 33; **69**. 4. cāmara **76**. 113; **85**. 26; **89**. 19; **99**. 47, 55; **100**. 193. vālavījanī **11**. 28; **31**. 78; **39**. 53. maṇitālavaṇṭa **31**. 78). royal order **15**. 188; **24**. 58; **25**. 67; **31**. 32, 114; **58**. 2, 57; **76**. 68 &c. royal treasure bhaṇḍāgāra) **69**. 27; **70**. 265. — 3. State elephant **14**. 61; **17**. 6; **19**. 72 ff.; **34**. 86; **35**. 20 f.; **78**. 60 &c. state horse **22**. 52; **34**. 86. state carriage **31**. 38; **72**. 323. — 4. The harem (orodha, itthāgāra, antepura) **14**. 46; **15**. 189; **17**. 63; **59**. 33; **60**. 85; **70**. 266; **88**. 74 (dancing girls **29**. 24). the king's retinue (parivāra, balattha, sevakā &c.) **31**. 112; **35**. 52;

38. 22; **67**. 15; **70**. 254; **72**. 118 ff.; **83**. 24; **88**. 33 f.; **89**. 31 f. (satta rajjaṅgāni **88**. 3. rājakammāni **69**. 22. rājakammikā **62**. 34. paricārakā **63**. 53. pañca and dasa pessiyavaggā **7**. 56; **67**. 58; **84**. 5). — 5. Funeral rites, cremation of the members of the r. family **24**. 14; **25**. 72 f.; **32**. 58, 79 f.; **34**. 34; **36**. 121; **61**. 9; **67**. 89; **85**. 76.

C. Politics

1. Nīti, rājanīti (naya, sippa) **10**. 23; **48**. 80, 96; **55**. 3; **58**. 1; **64**. 3; **70**. 56; **90**. 56; **99**. 81. Manunīti **80**. 9, 53; **83**. 6; **84**. 2; **96**. 26. dhamma, dasa rājadhammā (dasa puññakriyā) **7**. 74; **37**. 107, 180; **52**. 43; **70**. 31; **97**. 3; **99**. 73, 75, 81 f.; **100**. 118. saṃgahavatthūni (the four) **37**. 108; **52**. 43; **92**. 8; **95**. 2; **97**. 2; **99**. 14, 73, 83; **100**. 118. — Support of poor subjects **52**. 3; **53**. 30; **60**. 22, 74, 77 f.; **62**. 32. of poets **60**. 75, 79. — 2. Distinctions conferred upon officials **61**. 19; **68**. 5; **69**. 30; **70**. 19, 277 ff.; **96**. 38. — Relations to foreign sovereigns **11**. 18 ff., 27 ff.; 58. 8; 60. 5 f., 24 ff.; **62**. 54; **67**. 95; **76**. 11 ff.; **80**. 6 ff.; **87**. 29; **88**. 87 f.; **98**. 89 ff.; **99**. 109 ff., 164; **100**. 63 ff., 151 ff. honours paid to foreign ambassadors **7**. 70; **11**. 25 f. &c. — Treaties **71**. 1 ff. — Organised espionage **66**. 130 ff.; **67**. 19. — Foes of the King, rebels. corā **36**. 21, 80 f., 91; **37**. 18; **59**. 4. dāmarikā **61**. 71; **74**. 34 ff.; **75**. 10, 34 ff.; **76**. 3.

D. Brahmanism at court

1. Brahmans supported by the king **48**. 23; **51**. 65 ff.; **77**. 105. brahmanical rites observed at court **62**. 33, 45 ff.; **63**. 5; **64**. 13 ff. the purohita **10**. 79; **11**. 26; **34**. 24; **62**. 28, 33, 46 (dija **11**. 20, vippaseṭṭha **67**. 29). care for Hindu temples **79**. 19, 22, 81; **85**. 85 ff.

E. The king and the Buddhist order

1. Bhikkhus as advisers of the king **42**. 22; **57**. 38 f.; **87**. 39 ff., 62 ff.; as mediators in conflicts of the royal family

24. 50 ff.; **51**. 14; **52**. 9; **53**. 25 ff.; **70**. 328 ff. political influence of the clergy **33**. 17 ff.; 60. 87; **61**. 1; **76**. 73 ff. — Bh.s accompany the king in the field **25**. 3; **96**. 15. — 2. Princes educated by bh.s **81**. 76 f. members of the royal family enter the order **15**. 18 ff.; **17**. 57 f.; 18. 5; **34**. 28 f., 35; **84**. 29; **94**. 22. conversion to Buddhism of foreign mahesīs **98**. 6 ff. — 3. Kings cause sermons to be held or hearken to them **32**. 44; **41**. 58; **54**. 34 ff.; **60**. 8; **62**. 31; **92**. 11 f.; **98**. 73 ff.; **99**. 15 ff., 20, 30 ff., 88; **100**. 116 ff., 275, 280 f. they recite holy texts **52**. 48 ff.; **54**. 4; **60**. 17. — 4. K.s or princes cause holy texts to be copied **45**. 3; **60**. 22; **81**. 40 ff.; **90**. 37 f.; **91**. 27; **92**. 13; **97**. 36; **99**. 86. payment of the scribes **91**. 28; **99**. 33. — Literary works composed at the k.'s instigation **54**. 35; **97**. 56 f., 59; **90**. 78 f., 82 f.; **98**. 24. sacred books fetched from abroad **84**. 26; **100**. 73. bhikkhus fetched from abroad to Ceylon **60**. 5 f.; **84**. 9, 11 ff.; **94**. 15 f.; **97**. 10 f.; **98**. 89 ff.; **100**. 58 ff., 136 ff. — The king cares for the accomplishments of the clergy **84**. 26 f.; **98**. 16 f.; **99**. 173 ff.; **100**. 101 ff. — 5. Clerical acts, particularly the pabbajjā and upasampadā ceremonies, performed at the k.'s instigation **60**. 7; **78**. 30; **81**. 49 f.; 84. 37, 43; **87**. 72; **89**. 47; **90**. 39, 62, 65; **91**. 31; **92**. 19, 21 ff.; **94**. 20; **97**. 8, 13, 26; **98**. 16; **99**. 168 ff.; **100**. 94 ff., 133 f., 172. purification of the order and church-reform caused by the k. **5**. 236 ff.; **36**. 41, 111 ff.; **39**. 57; **44**. 46, 76; **51**. 64; **52**. 44; **73**. 2 ff.; **78**. 2 ff.; **84**. 7 ff.; **91**. 11; **100**. 44 ff. the k. determines a sīmā **15**. 184 ff.; **78**. 56 ff. — 6. Dedication to the church or to a sanctuary of the kingdom, the regalia &c. **18**. 36; **19**. 31; **31**. 90, 92, 111 f.; **32**. 36; 39. 31; **42**. 61; **82**. 50; **85**. 109 ff.; **86**. 57. donations equal to the bodily weight **51**. 128; **60**. 21; **73**. 11. the k. grants titles to the bh.'s **84**. 31, 38; **89**. 64 ff.; **100**. 239. — 7. Conflicts with the bh.'s **44**. 74 ff.; **53**. 14 ff.; **93**. 6 ff., 10. — Persecution of the christians **98**. 80 ff.

F. Administration of the kingdom

1. Officials and titles (cf. C. tr. I, p. XXV ff. and p. 359, 2). chatta mark of distinction for officials **70**. 85, 122. — General expressions: adhikārin **66**. 66; **70**. 278, 297 f.; **72**. 21, 37, 75. 122, 123, 138, 160, 207, 232, 265. adhinātha **70**. 216, 278. antaraṅgadhura **69**. 32, 35. amacca **4**. 37; **5**, 35, 239 &c.; **58**. 30; **66**. 72 &c. (mahāmacca **16**. 10; **61**. 1; **72**. 96, 129 &c.; mahāmatta **72**. 70, 181; mūlāmacca **69**. 34). maṇḍalika, maṇḍalanāyaka **46**. 31; **51**. 109, 122; **54**. 8; **69**. 5; **70**. 242, 246. mantin **66**. 113; **89**. 27. saciva **66**. 67; **67**. 90; **68**. 7, 18; **70**. 83, 324. sāmanta (**58**. 20); **61**. 63; **66**. 142; **69**. 5, 16; **70**. 9, 57, 129, 136, 179, 189, 242, 246, 314; **72**. 16 ff., 50, 54, 78, 82, 165. — Special designations: asiggāha **39**. 54; **42**. 42; **44**. 1, 43, 54, 58 ff.; **66**. 29. ādipotthakin (bhaṇḍārap°, bhaṇḍāgārādhikārin) **69**. 27; **72**. 27, 160, 182, 196, 207. kañcukin (-nāyaka) **63**. 53; **69**. 26; **70**. 44; **72**. 58; **75**. 176. kammanātha (°nāyaka) **72**. 58, 206. gaṇaka (°amacca) **11**. 20; **69**. 30; **76**. 39. chattaggāha (-nāyaka) **38**. 3; **59**. 16; **66**. 29; **70**. 60; **72**. 68. jīvitapotthakin **70**. 174, 318; **72**. 161; **74**. 90. daṇḍanātha, °nāyaka °adhināyaka) **11**. 26; **70**. 5, 8, 15, 19, 64, 68, 124, 279; **72**. 36, 65, 162, 222. dovārika **35**. 51. dhammagehakanātha **59**. 16. nagaraguttika **10**. 81. bhaṇḍārapotthakin, bhaṇḍāgārādhikārin see ādipotthakin. mahālekha **52**. 33; **72**. 1, 161, 166, 170, 182, 206. mūlapotthakin **75**. 139 f. lekhaka **66**. 155. sabhāpati (kuṭhārasabhānāyaka) **67**. 61, 64, 70, 80. seṭṭhinātha **59**. 16. senāpati (senāni, °adhināyaka, camūpati, dhajinīpati &c.) **11**. 25; **15**. 212; **35**. 59; **50**. 82; **51**. 30, 40, 88; **52**. 16, 28; **53**. 43 ff.; **54**. 13 ff., 58 ff.; **55**. 2; **56**. 7; **64**. 9 ff., 22; **65**. 13 ff., 27 ff.; **66**. 2 ff.; **67**. 82; **70**. 123, 129 ff., 153 ff., 285; **72**. 45, 49, 76, 122 f., 137 f.; **90**. 12; **96**. 38 (sakkasenāpati **52**. 52, 61 ff., 72 ff.; **54**. 53. andhasenāpati **41**. 87). — Titles: kesadhātu **57**. 65 ff.; **72**. 2, 5, 7, 107; **76**. 253 ff., 324 ff. &c. (cf. C. ed. II, p. 601, col. 2); (-nāyaka **70**. 68, 279). jitagiri **72**. 25. damiḷādhikārin **75**. 20 ff., 69 ff.; **76**. 39. nagaragiri, °galla **66**. 35, 62; **70**. 68, 89, 146, 199, 318; **72**. 107; **76**. 60. nīlagiri 70. 137, 140.

māragiri **72**. 11, 164, 174. laṅkāgiri **72**. 27, 124 f.; **76**. 250. laṅkādhikārin **70**. 278, 283, 306, 316. laṅkādhināyaka (°nātha &c) **70**. 24, 95 ff.; 123, 174, 205, 220. laṅkāpura **72**. 39, 222; **75**. 70; **76**. 250, 324, 326. lokagalla **72**. 222. saṅkha(ka)nāyaka **70**. 278; 72. 31, 41; **75**. 75.

2. Administration of justice. The k. the highest judge **21**. 14. alleviation of punishment **36**. 80 f.; **83**. 4 ff.; **87**. 48 f. amnesty **34**. 84; **62**. 42; **80**. 2 ff. — Law-books **49**. 20; **80**. 41. — Crimes: high treason **35**. 10; **36**. 21, 91; **87**. 48(?). robbery **61**. 67. indebtedness **36**. 39. — Forensic procedure **35**. 10; **37**. 38; **78**. 13. — Punishment: hiṃsāmutto vohāro **36**. 28. fine **83**. 6. prison **35**. 22; **54**. 31; **62**. 42; **70**. 238, 264; **83**. 4. mutilation, capital punishment **35**. 11, 36, 43; **36**. 121; **59**. 22; **60**. 42 ff.; **75**. 160 ff., 190 ff., **83**. 4; **87**. 49.

3. Internal administration. Book-keeping at court **66**. 155; **69**. 27. – Taxes **61**. 53, 70; **68**. 54; **73**. 3; **74**. 18 f.; **87**. 50. alleviation of taxes **36**. 26. the gāmabhojaka **61**. 73. — The village community **10**. 103; **23**. 4; **38**. 38; **55**. 31; **60**. 75; **74**. 48 f.; **84**. 3 ff.; **86**. 53. — Administration organised by Parakkamabāhu I. **69**. 27 ff.; **74**. 48 f.

G. Army and war

1. The soldiers (bhaṭā **39**. 20; **58**. 20 &c.; yodhā **22**. 44; **69**. 7 &c.; sūrā **69**. 36; **99**. 119 &c; vīrā **72**. 248 &c.) Enrolling of soldiers **10**. 24. soldier's pay **90**. 15, 18 f., 20. — Four-membered army **18**. 29; **25**. 81; **70**. 217, 226; **71**. 18 &c. balavāhana **15**. 189; **17**. 28; 25. 1, 57; **70**. 23, 69 &c. war elephants **25**. 26 ff., 81; **41**. 23; **50**. 21 ff.; 70. 229; **76**. 48 &c. chariot warriors **25**. 81 (rathin **88**. 34; rathesabha **15**. 189; sārathi **14**. 42). cavalry **25**. 81 (numerous in the Damiḷa armies **76**. 100, 298, 331). infantry (patti) **25**. 81. — Mercenaries (āyudhīya **61**. 69; āyudhajīvin **66**. 67): Sīhalā **55**. 12; **61**. 69; **74**. 44: **90**. 17 ff. Damiḷā, Keraḷā, Kaṇṇāṭā **45**. 11; **55**. 5, 12; **69**. 18; **70**. 230; **74**. 44. the Velakkārā **60**. 36; **63**. 24, 29; **74**. 44. villages granted to the mercenaries for maintenance **74**. 48. — Militia **67**. 70; **70**. 82, 187, 260; **72**.

127; **74**. 52, 112; **75**. 102; **99**. 42 ff. (among the Damiḷas **76**. 130, 246 f., 259 ff.). vyādhā, kirātā, corā as soldiers **69**. 20; **70**. 285; **72**. 208. — Officers (sāmanta see F 1). an umbrella their badge **66**. 49; **70**. 122; **76**. 160; **88**. 75. a palanquin their conveyance **70**. 85, 122; **72**. 100. — Trumpets **25**. 65; **65**. 27; **66**. 32; **72**. 119; **74**. 222; **85**. 113; **88**. 75; **89**. 46. drums **69**. 20; **70**. 227; **74**. 222; **75**. 104; **76**. 161; **85**. 114; **88**. 75; **96**. 15 f.; **99**. 46. flags **70**. 225; **85**. 113; **88**. 75. a relic as field-badge **25**. 1; **26**. 9. — 2. Weapons (āyudha, āv° **7**. 36; **69**. 7, 38; **99**. 49 &c.; five kinds **7**. 16; **41**. 48; **70**. 229). Bow and arrows **6**. 29; **7**. 19; **25**. 89 ff., 99; **33**. 63, 65; **35**. 31; **55**. 6; **57**. 43; **66**. 27; **70**. 114; **72**. 134, 246, 250; **74**. 96, 117; **83**. 44; **96**. 14. poisoned arrows **76**. 49; **83**. 38, 45. gokaṇṇa arrows **76**. 48. archers **25**. 82; **69**. 19; **70**. 116; **72**. 244, 322. — Sword: asi **10**. 59 ff.; **22**. 44, 53; **66**. 108; **72**. 84. khagga **25**. 63, 89; **30**. 93; **31**. 79; **64**. 4; **66**. 24, 31, 49; **72**. 102; **88**. 74 &c. tharu **24**. 1; **69**. 22. (royal swords **72**. 102–4). — Dagger: churikā **55**. 6, 17; **69**. 24. asiputtaka **41**. 24. nikkaraṇī **44**. 112. — Spear: kunta **25**. 1; **26**. 9; **36**. 47; **96**. 14; **99**. 49. satti, sattha **69**. 20; **70**. 116; **90**. 7. tomara **24**. 35; **70**. 116. salla **70**. 307. — Lasso **7**. 20; **10**. 55. — Club **23**. 58; **69**. 17. — catapults **72**. 251; **83**. 44. — Armour (kavaca) **69**. 7, 38. shield **25**. 58, 62 ff.; **67**. 42; **99**. 48. doublet of buffalo hide **74**. 73. — 3. The war (yuddha **1**. 63; **38**. 36 &c.) Preparation of war **68**. 7, 38, 52; **69**. 28, 33, 38; **70**. 1, 57. yuddhopakaraṇāni **69**. 5, 14, 17, 34; **70**. 1; **96**. 12. — Review of troops **99**. 42 ff. sham-fights **89**. 26, 31 f. manoevers **69**. 36. — Four methods of war **58**. 3. guerilla warfare (corayuddha) **75**. 18 N., 135. ambush **66**. 75 f. stratagem **25**. 56. — Battle (yuddha, saṃgāma, raṇa &c. **24**. 19; **70**. 246; **72**. 5, 17; **96**. 17 &c.). single combat of the commanders **25**. 67 ff., 83 ff.; **41**. 47 ff.; **60**. 30 ff. victory and defeat (jaya and parājaya, -bhava **70**. 78 f., 180, 225, 246; **71**. 16 &c.). celebration of victory **76**. 332. ābharaṇaṃ as distinction of victorious officers **72**. 320. officers of the defeated foe beheaded **70**. 122. — Naval battles **70**. 63 ff., 91; **96**. 32. — Field entrenchments **10**. 46; **25**. 20;

37. 19; **38**. 36; **70**. 61, 72, 93, 100, 130 ff., 161, 163 ff.; **72**. 232 ff., 258; **74**. 32 ff., 62, 86 f., 94; **76**. 121 ff. &c. fortresses **81**. 1 ff.; **88**. 43, 60, 77; **96**. 22, 34; **99**. 116; defence, besiege, capture, plundering of fortresses **25**. 21 ff.; **51**. 34; **58**. 55 f.; **70**. 235 f., 251 ff., 288 ff.; **72**. 209 ff., 250 ff.; **76**. 244 f., 324 ff.

VII. The people

A. Clans, castes, guilds.

1. Clan-names **19**. 2; **35**. 16 ff.; **38**. 13; **39**. 44; **41**. 69; **42**. 30; **66**. 35; **69**. 13; **74**. 213; **80**. 15; **85**. 51; **90**. 7; **91**. 3 (Moriyā and Lambakaṇṇā in India **5**. 17; **77**. 27 f.) — Castes (vaṇṇā **72**. 145) and guilds **7**. 57; **19**. 1, 3; **69**. 24; **80**. 41, 75. seṭṭhin **11**. 26; **19**. 2, 67; **59**. 16. khattiya, rājañña **3**. 3; **7**. 47; **17**. 63; **19**. 54, 66; **87**. 28; **89**. 27. brāhmaṇa, dvija, vippa **3**. 3; **9**. 2; **10**. 20, 102; **19**. 2; **33**. 37 ff.; **34**. 24; **35**. 18; **37**. 41; **62**. 33, 46; **64**. 16; **66**. 132; **67**. 94. vessa **3**. 3; **20**. 15; **76**. 264. sudda **3**. 3. — Kulīna: hīna **61**. 50, 52, 62, 68; **66**. 153. kulaputta **72**. 304; **92**. 22; **97**. 13 f., 26; **99**. 169; **100**. 134, 172; kulitthī **60**. 78; kulavaṃsa **95**. 6; kulapati **23**. 19. — Slaves (dāsa, dāsī) **9**. 4, 15, 19, 22, 24; **27**. 12; **61**. 68; **70**. 202; **88**. 106; **90**. 2 (shaving of the head **6**. 42. redemption of slaves **87**. 46). outcasts (caṇḍāla) **5**. 57; **10**. 91 ff.; **33**. 2; **35**. 18; **66**. 132; **88**. 106.

2. Single professions (kammakāra **61**. 68; **69**. 21; **99**. 50; pesakāra, pessiya **7**. 56; **30**. 6; sippika, -in **34**. 73; **66**. 139; **88**. 13, 85. list of craftsmen **88**. 105-7. (wandering craftsmen **66**. 139). payment of the craftsmen **27**. 22 f.; **30**. 14, 18 f.; **88**. 110; of artists **100**. 198 f. farmer and herdsman: kasikamma **69**. 37; **76**. 287; gopa(ka), gopāla **9**. 22; **10**. 13, 17; **19**. 2. smith: kammāra **68**. 25; **88**. 105; lohakāra **68**. 25; soṇṇakāra **18**. 24; **66**. 139; **68**. 25. goldsmith's works **98**. 94; **100**. 30, 72. barber &c: nhāpita, nhāpaka, kappaka **29**. 20; **34**. 84; **69**. 26; **70**. 44. bricklayer: (iṭṭhaka)vaḍḍhaki **30**. 5, 8, 30; **35**. 101, 109 f.; **37**. 27; **88**. 106. mason: silākoṭṭaka **68**. 25. wood-carrier: dārubhatika **34**. 22. writer: lekhaka

37. 26; **66**. 155; **99**. 33. merchant: vāṇija **5**. 49; **7**. 24; **28**. 21 ff.; **75**. 45; **95**. 4; **99**. 109 (wandering traders **66**. 134). hunter: luddaka, vyādha **28**. 9, 41; **67**. 19; **70**. 35, 44. fisherman: bālisika, kevaṭṭa **22**. 62; **28**. 37.

B. Settlement

1. Village: gāma, passim. fence of briers round a v. **66**. 87 (gāmika "villager" **23**. 66; **67**. 70; jānapada **29**. 22). — small town: nigama (negama **70**. 254). — town: nagara, pura, purī **87**. 67 (nāgara **4**. 5, 15; **14**. 59; **17**. 63; **79**. 1 &c.; pora **29**. 22). – 2. Description of a town **10**. 84 ff.; **73**. 55 ff.; **88**. 92 ff., 116 ff.; **91**. 5. four districts of a t. **73**. 26. streets: vīthi **34**. 76; **73**. 59. houses: geha, ghara, āgāra (special kinds: aḍḍhayoga, hammiya **88**. 93, 118). houses of more than one storeys: pāsāda **88**. 92; **91**. 5 &c. (cf. VII, C, 12 e). halls: sālā, catussālā **15**. 47, 50; **35**. 88; **37**. 15; **73**. 23; **76**. 123. alms-houses: dānasālā **54**. 30; **73**. 26. hospitals: vejjasālā (**37**. 182;) **49**. 18, 19; **52**. 25, 57; **54**. 31, 53; **73**. 34. dispensaries: bhesajjageha **52**. 27. lying-in hospitals: sivikāsotthisālā **10**. 102; sūtighara **79**. 61. shops: āpaṇa **5**. 52; **23**. 29; **34**. 76; **91**. 5. gardens, parks (uyyāna), bathing-ponds (pokkharaṇī), bath-houses (nhānakoṭṭhaka): **15**. 2, 7, 8, 30, 202, 207; **35**. 97, 98; **37**. 33; **68**. 57 f.; **73**. 95–123; **78**. 45 ff.; **79**. 1 ff.; **100**. 288 f. jantāghara **15**. 31. — 3. Fortification of the city **60**. 2 f.; **73**. 57 ff.; **94**. 7 f. wall and trench (pākāra, parikhā) **25**. 8; **35**. 96; **60**. 3; **70**. 236; **91**. 5, 7. gate-towers, bastions &c. (gopura, dvāraṭṭāla, dvārakoṭṭha, patthaṇḍila, toraṇa, khandhāvāra) **51**. 34; **60**. 3; **70**. 116, 190; **91**. 5, 7; **96**. 30; **98**. 70. gates (four) **34**. 79; **35**. 97. fourteen gates of Pulatthinagara **73**. 160 ff. — 4. Suburbs (of P.) **73**. 151 ff.; **78**. 79 ff.

C. Domestic and social life

1. The family. Terms of kinship **7**. 65; **9**. 16, 24, 26 f.; **10**. 7, 29, 73 f., 82; **11**. 20; **48**. 51, 82; **51**. 24; **52**. 11; **57**. 28; **59**. 28; **61**. 1; **62**. 2; **63**. 38, 40, 51, 53; **64**. 33; **67**. 16; **69**. 23; **70**. 266; **93**. 3; **99**. 1, 123. three kinds of sons **87**. 18 ff. —

Marriage (pariṇaya) **72**. 91. marriage-outfit of a bride **7**. 55 ff.; **87**. 28. brides from India **7**. 50 ff.; **87**. 28; **96**. 40. allusion to the buying of brides **72**. 91. master of the house (kuṭumbika) **23**. 61, 90; **24**. 25. fire kept in the house **10**. 14. — Pregnancy **22**. 42 ff.; **62**. 36. child-birth, birth-rites **9**. 21; **62**. 45. childhood **87**. 55 ff.; **88**. 6 (wet nurse **35**. 20). domestic ceremonies **22**. 65, 74; **62**. 53; **63**. 5; **64**. 13. — Death and funeral **74**. 144 f.

2. Food and drink **7**. 24; **10**. 3; **14**. 55; **22**. 44, 70; **24**. 56; **29**. 28; **30**. 37, 39; **32**. 30, 39 f., 45, 49; **34**. 55 f., 62; **35**. 65, 67, 92 f.; **36**. 69, 100; **54**. 22 f.; **70**. 211; **73**. 36; **85**. 38; **89**. 44 ff., 51 ff.; **100**. 4, 195 f. — morning meal **25**. 114. pod-pepper and other spice **25**. 114; **26**. 16; **28**. 21; **54**. 22 f. — Intoxicating drinks (surā) **25**. 32; **54**. 70 f. — Betel chewing **35**. 62; **54**. 22; **100**. 3, 196.

3. Dress (vattha **11**. 29; **29**. 28; **35**. 65; **36**. 53 &c.) and ornaments (ābharaṇa **7**. 27 &c.). Stuffs **58**. 9; **70**. 109; **73**. 84; **90**. 70. — Turban **11**. 28; **23**. 38; **32**. 78; **35**. 53 (hair-knot **66**. 103). mantle **35**. 102; **60**. 70; **66**. 103, 109. shoes (pāduka, upāhanā) **11**. 28; **30**. 14, 39. — Ornaments, unguents, perfumes (sugandha **89**. 42) 7. 55; **11**. 28; **25**. 91; **32**. 29; **34**. 52; **66**. 44 f., 134; **70**. 108) **73**. 84; **76**. 206, 237; **85**. 41, 116; **89**. 19; **97**. 47. añjana **11**. 29; **34**. 52. incense **89**. 42.

4. Articles of personal use (tools &c.). Umbrella (ātapatta, chatta) **76**. 113; **89**, 19; **99**. 47, 55 (cf. VI, B, 2). fan **11**. 28; **31**. 78; **76**. 115; **85**. 27, 46; **89**. 20; **100**. 193. napkin **11**. 29. twigs for cleansing the teeth 5. 25. — Knife (vāsī) **28**. 24 f. hammer, axe and other tools **29**. 3; 88. 108 f. — Pottery, vessels: kalasa **74**. 205; **85**. 28. kumbha **89**. 20; **90**. 71. ācāmakumbhī **27**. 40. ghaṭa **29**. 57 ff.; **76**. 112, 115; **85**. 26; **92**. 17. thāla, thālī **89**. 21, 44; paṭiggāha **89**. 21. pātī **30**. 12. bhājana **11**. 31; **22**. 5, 64 (fig. **44**. 70; **84**. 16). bhiṅkāra **11**. 28; **76**. 115; **89**. 20. saraka **32**. 55. — Spoon **27**. 40. basket (piṭaka, puṭa) **36**. 93; **88**. 109. water-strainer **36**. 92.

5. Household-furniture. Bed: mañcaka **24**. 40; **27**. 39; **54**. 31; sayana, seyyā **22**. 83 ff.; **23**. 39; **25**. 102; **31**. 107 f.;

62. 23, 24 &c. chair, pīṭha: **27**. 39; pallaṅka **27**. 32 ff.; **31**. 76 f. sivikā **11**. 31; **32**. 7. — Carpet, mat **14**. 51; **25**. 102; **27**. 35; **34**. 54; **73**. 64; **88**. 109; **90**. 70; 98. 46. — Lamp **25**. 101; **31**. 80; **33**. 6; **34**. 55, 77; **74**. 205; **85**. 40 f.; **89**. 43 f.; **90**. 71; **92**. 17; **99**. 62. lamp-stand **76**. 205; **89**. 23. — Mirror: ādāsa: **100**. 106; dappaṇa **89**. 21. — Charcoal-pan **60**. 70. bell **21**. 15. mill-stone (nisada) **23**. 6; **28**. 40; **30**. 9. chest (mañjūsā) **30**. 60. — parissāvana **36**. 92.

6. Measures and weights, time, money. Measures of length: yojana (cf. M. tr. p. 297, Nr. 34) **1**. 21; **5**. 23, 179, 262; **6**. 13, 35; **18**. 29; **20**. 12; **23**. 22, 26; **28**. 7, 13 ff.; **38**. 68 (note is incorrect; cf. C. tr. I, p. 349), **85**. 4; **86**. 44; **89**. 14. gāvuta **65**. 4; **73**. 154; **74**. 63; **76**. 197; **89**. 9. usabha **22**. 42; **23**. 88; **25**. 43; **85**. 4. hattha **1**. 41; **18**. 27; **25**. 43; **70**. 128; **78**. 63, 69. ratana **15**. 167; **30**. 58, 63; **72**. 235; **78**. 77; **92**. 17. vidatthi **28**. 14. aṅgula, -li **18**. 27; **28**. 14; **30**. 59. porisa **72**. 235. yaṭṭhi **78**. 63; **86**. 41. bāṇapāta **72**. 239. dhanu **35**. 31. tāla **17**. 43. — Square measures: ammaṇa **38**. 77. karīsa **10**. 30; **28**. 13; **35**. 83, 86. — measures of capacity: ammaṇa **30**. 7 ff. doṇa **15**. 167; **31**. 18; **74**. 3. nāḷī **30**. 37; **32**. 45. — weights: nikkha(la) **76**. 18; **82**. 13 f.; **100**. 14. — — Time: year (vassa, saṃvacchara passim, hāyana **41**. 3; **44**. 153 &c.). months (māsa **3**. 16; **5**. 279; **25**. 8 &c.). names of months **1**. 12, 19, 46, 73; **3**. 2; **11**. 37, 40, 42; **12**. 2; **13**. 14, 18; **16**. 2, 14; **17**. 1, 17; **18**. 7, 61 f., 64; **19**. 9; **20**. 33; **29**. 1, 14, 63; **31**. 109; **39**. 37; **41**. 80; **85**. 89; **90**. 62; **100**. 91. sukka-, kālapakkha **18**. 61 f., 64; **19**. 9; **20**. 33; **29**. 14; **31**. 109. day (divasa passim, vāsara **62**. 10, 32; **70**. 263 &c.). yāma **25**. 105; **85**. 40. — — Money: kahāpaṇa **4**. 13; **21**. 26; **25**. 100; **30**. 14, 18; **53**. 29, 32 f.; **77**. 102; **81**. 45. gold coins **27**. 21; **48**. 7; **81**. 45; **100**. 14. silver coins **91**. 12; **97**. 6. sums of money in numbers only (to be supplied by kahāpaṇa) **6**. 24 f.; **7**. 61; **10**. 18, 24; **23**. 36 ff.; **26**. 22; **34**. 87; **35**. 64, 72; **89**. 66; **92**. 13.

7. Traffic and trade. Roads: maggānumagga **67**. 20. — footpaths **70**. 4; **72**. 240. high-roads (mahāmagga) in C. **25**. 6 ff.; **50**. 37; **58**. 41; **73**. 163; **74**. 83; **89**. 13 f. cause-

ways and bridges **70**. 127 f.; **86**. 21 ff.; **98**. 86; **99**. 118. resthouses **60**. 66; **89**. 15; **99**. 118. mile-stones **80**. 25 N. — Means of conveyance: yāna, vāhana **10**. 31 ff.; **58**. 21; **61**. 6; **99**. 84. carriage (ratha) **7**. 56; **14**. 42; **15**. 189; **31**. 38; **33**. 46; **70**. 127; **89**. 16. cart (sakaṭa) **28**. 21 ff.; **30**. 6; **34**. 46. litter **70**. 85, 122; **72**. 100; **90**. 5, 8; **95**. 12; (? **15**. 189; **25**. 1, 57; **70**. 23, 69). — Trade: (merchant see VII, A, 2). navigation and ocean-trade **6**, 43; **7**. 51, 58; **8**. 11; **11**. 23, 38; **18**. 7 f.; **19**. 4, 17, 70; **23**. 24; **35**. 26 f.; **58**. 9; **69**. 33; **100**. 63 ff., 75 ff. harbours in C. Mahātittha **7**. 58; **25**. 79; **48**. 81; **51**. 28; **60**. 34; **88**. 63 &c. Jambukola **11**. 23, 38; **18**. 7; **19**. 23 ff. Uruvelapaṭṭana **28**. 36. Mattikāvāṭatittha **60**. 34. Mannāra **61**. 39; **83**. 16. Vālukagāma **75**. 45. Pallavavaṅka **76**. 46. Pulacceri **83**. 17 (?). Bhīmatittha **86**. 40. Kolambatittha **94**. 1. Tikoṇamālatittha **100**. 76. in India: Tāmalittī **11**. 38; **19**. 6. — Articles of trade: horses from India (sindhava) **21**. 10; **23**. 71; **31**. 38. elephants from Birma **76**. 17-34. jewels **69**. 33. spice **28**. 21; **54**. 46; **58**. 9. stuffs **58**. 9.

8. Rural life. Agriculture (kasikamma) **69**. 37. its intrinsic value **92**. 24 ff. clearing of the jungle **23**. 51; **68**. 30. — Irrigation works **68**. 16 ff., 32 ff.; **79**. 27 ff.; **88**. 111 ff. mātikā "canal" **61**. 65; **68**. 24, 33; **79**. 25 ff., 40 ff. (nettika **60**. 14). vāpiṃ (see V, C, c, 6) gaṇh, kar, bandh **10**. 88; **23**. 92 f.; **35**. 120; **36**. 3; **37**. 46; **38**. 42; **42**. 34; **51**. 73; **79**. 69. structure of a tank: dam (bandhana, setu, setubandha) **42**. 34; **68**. 17, 23, 26, 28. paṇālī "outflow running through the dam, sluice" **79**. 27, 30, 42 ff., 68. āvaraṇa "lock" **60**. 52; **61**. 65; **79**. 27 N., 69. koṭṭhabaddha "square hole (for the lock)" **68**. 16; **79**. 27 N., 28. weir (vāripāta) **48**. 148; **68**. 35, 37, 40. flood-escape (nijjhara) **68**. 33, 50; **79**. 28, 66. — raising of the water by means of machines **34**. 45. subterranean canals **35**. 98. — Fields **23**. 51; **68**. 30, 52 ff.; **88**. 114 f.; **92**. 26. produce of the fields **23**. 51; **34**. 3; **68**. 31; **92**. 26. corn (dhañña) **68**. 7, 38; **70**. 1. sowing and harvest **10**. 31; **24**. 58; **34**. 3. barn **68** 31. — coco-plantation **90**. 93. sugar-mill **34**. 41; **61**. 53. — Herdsman

9. 22; **10.** 13, 17; **19.** 2. assagopa **39.** 1: hatthipaka **88.** 34. cattle (goṇā) **35.** 42. domestic animals: elephant, cow, buffalo, dog, see V, C, 3, b, 3.

9. Education of the people, literary life. Education: wandering schoolmasters **66.** 138. art of writing, letters **7.** 51, 57; **8.** 7; **22.** 15; **23.** 25, 33, 35; **33.** 40; **66.** 36; **67.** 55, 58; **76.** 30; **98.** 90; **100.** 64, 158. lekhaka **99.** 33. royal inscriptions and sannas **28.** 2; **33.** 50; **54.** 28; **86.** 34 f., 39; **100.** 214. — Appreciation of books, their destruction and restitution **52.** 50; **80.** 67; **81.** 41 ff.; **99.** 125. See also V, E, 4. — Knowledge of languages and dialects **66.** 130; **69.** 22; **90.** 80. Pāli as ecclesiastical language **98.** 90. grammar **64.** 3. philosophy **90.** 80. — Poetry: kāveyya **42.** 13; **64.** 3. poets in C. **42.** 13; **60.** 75. See V, E, 4.

10. Sport and amusement. Sport (kīḷā **66.** 111): hunting **5.** 154; **10.** 2; **14.** 1, 4; **70.** 32 ff.; **72.** 263 (bow and javelin, the hunter's weapons **14.** 4; **70.** 41). capture of wild elephants **72.** 105. art of fencing **24.** 1; **64.** 4; **69.** 22. pugilistic contest **63.** 30; **75.** 75. riding on horseback or on elephant **22.** 56; **23.** 72 ff.; **24.** 1; **62.** 6; **64.** 4; **69.** 22; **88.** 34; **95.** 7 ff. Archery (dhanusippa **57.** 43) **23.** 86 ff.; **24**, 1; **69.** 19; **72.** 243, 245; **83.** 45. plays in water **26.** 7, 10; **70.** 31. — Music and dance: music (turiyavādita **34.** 60; tālāvacara **17.** 7). song (gītā) **34.** 79; **72.** 94. dance (nacca) **34.** 60, 79; **85.** 43. musicians **30.** 91; **69.** 24; **72.** 94, 264. singers **72.** 264; **85.** 43. dancers and dancing girls **10.** 87; **29.** 24; **32.** 78; **74.** 217; **85.** 43. wandering musicians **66.** 132 f.; bards and minstrels **74.** 222; **89.** 34. musical instruments, turiya (five kinds **73.** 68; **85.** 30, 45; **89.** 33) **29.** 25; **76.** 114. lute **30.** 75; **31.** 82; **72.** 264; **74.** 216. trumpet **74.** 222; **99.** 60; **100.** 33, 190. flute **72.** 264; **74.** 216. cymbal **99.** 60; **100.** 33, 190. drums: bheri **74.** 221; **96.** 15; **99.** 46; maddala **96.** 15; **99.** 46; mudiṅga **74.** 216; kāhala **74.** 222. — rasa-theory **66.** 56; **72.** 94, 265; **73.** 117; **75.** 89. laya **73.** 79. — dance and music at festival occasions **34.** 60, 79; **74.** 215–7; **85.** 42 f.; **89.** 33 ff.; **90.** 74; **99.** 46. d. and m. as amusement of ladies and princes and at court **25.** 99, 102; **29.** 24; **64.** 4;

69. 22; **70**. 31; **73**. 141. — Public amusements: samajjā **34**. 79 (cf. E. Hardy, Album Kern, p. 61 ff.). Āsāḷha-feast **85**. 89; **99**. 53. vasanta-kīḷā **64**. 17. — stage for mimics (raṅgabhūmi) **31**. 82. puppet-plays **66**. 133. snake-charmers **66**. 131. mendicant artists **52**. 30; **53**. 30. — festival processions **31**. 36 ff.; **37**. 77 ff.; **38**. 77; **52**. 53 ff.; **72**. 313 ff.; **74**. 224 ff.; **76**. 108 ff.; **89**. 16 ff.; **99**. 45 ff., 53 ff. decoration of the streets **19**. 38; **34**. 76 f.; **37**. 74 ff.; **62**. 43; **74**. 199 ff.; **85**. 4 ff.; **89**. 14 f.; **98**. 40 ff.; **99**. 7 f., 43; **100**. 25 ff. illumination **34**. 80. donations distributed to the people at festival occasions **29**. 20 f., 27 f.

11. Medicine. Physicians and medical art **32**. 38; **73**. 16 f., 39; **99**. 176 f.; **100**. 144. wandering quacks **66**. 137. kings as physicians **37**. 112–50; **73**. 34–54. gynecology **37**. 140. veterinary science **25**. 34; **37**. 112 ff., 128; **73**. 50 ff. medical books **97**. 59. — Diseases **15**. 60, 63; **35**. 66; **36**. 82 ff.; **37**. 141; **52**. 25, 77; **56**. 5; **99**. 176. cripples **37**. 148. poisoning **66**. 131, 138. chirurgical instruments **37**. 150; **76**. 51. bleeding **37**. 128. medicaments: bhesajja 5. 224; **22**. 30; **32**. 38; **76**. 49 f. &c. honey and ghee 5. 49 ff., 215. — Hospitals and dispensaries see VII, B, 2.

12. Art: architecture, plastic and graphic art. Architecture. a. building material (dabba) **25**. 39; **37**. 25, 29: paṃsu **30**. 6 f. mattikā **11**. 29; **29**. 5; **30**. 21. cuṇṇa **88**. 106; **100**. 284. sudhā **25**. 29; **29**. 8; **32**. 1; **34**. 46; **68**. 27; **91**. 29 f.; **97**. 38, 47. iṭṭhakā **25**. 29; **28**. 5, 7 ff.; **30** 15 f.; **35**. 85; **88**. 98, 106; **92**. 10; **100**. 87, 284 (tambalohiṭṭhakā **27**. 42). giñjaka **88**. 97. silā **25**. 29; **33**. 23, 25; **35**. 118; **36**. 102; **68**. 25; **88**. 107; **97**. 47; **98**. 86; **100**. 284, 296. medavaṇṇapāsāṇā **30**. 57; **31**. 119, 121. — b. Workmen: vaḍḍhaki see VII, A, 2; **88**. 106 f..— c. Various buildings: ekaṭṭhūṇikageha, ekatthambhapāsāda **9**. 3; **73**. 92. pāsāda, aḍḍhayoga, hammiya see VII, B, 2. — d. Elements of a house: ājira **35**. 3. ālinda **35**. 3; **98**. 44. dvāra **73**. 63; **88**. 99. kavāṭa **35**. 25; **73**. 63. bhitti **73**. 63; **88**. 98. thambha **27**. 30; **36**. 102; **60**. 11; **78**. 41; **88**. 98; **100**. 296 f. sopāna **34**. 44; **73**. 63; **78**. 41; **88**. 99. vedikā **27**. 16, 26; **73**. 88; **88**. 99.

gabbha **27**. 15, 28; **73**. 61. kūṭāgāra **27**. 15, 26; **73**. 62; **78**. 38, 49, 55. viṭaṅka **88**. 97. sīhapañjara **27**. 16, 28. chadana (**72**. 211); **97**. 39. valabhi **88**. 97 (tulāyaṭṭhi **88**. 97; gopānasī **37**. 141; **88**. 98). — e. Pāsāda (dīgha-, cūlap° **78**. 36 f., 50; **90**. 90): pākāra **27**. 41. kūṭāgāra, gabbhasālāghara, pañjarageha **78**. 55. dvārakoṭṭhaka **27**. 41. gopura **60**. 12. pāsādatala **25**. 98, 105; **28**. 3. thūpikā **31**. 13; **73**. 135. siṅga **90**. 66, 90. underground tunnel **55**. 7. — Thūpa, cetiya (M. tr., p. 295, Nr. 26). a tree as cetiya **1**. 67. thūpa "tomb" **20**. 53; **37**. 44. cetiya "tomb" **20**. 44; **25**. 73. cetiya = thūpa **29**. 15; **30**. 57; **86**. 51 &c. dhātugabbha = thūpa **60**. 56; **68**. 28; **79**. 14. silāmaya th° **35**. 118. model of a th° **30**. 11 ff. — erection of a th° **30**. 15 ff. mantling of a ruined th° (kañcuka) **1**. 42; **33**. 23, 25; **35**. 85, 121; **36**. 12. — parts of a th°: foundation **29**. 2–12 (maṅgaliṭṭhakā **29**. 15, 46–63). moonstone **31**. 61. toraṇa **38**. 10. vālikaṅgaṇa, -mariyādā, cetiyaṅgaṇa **33**. 31; **34**. 70; **37**. 60. hatthipākāra, -vedī **33**. 5; **38**. 10; **39**. 30; **41**. 95. pupphādhāna **30**. 51, 56; **33**. 22. pādavedikā **34**. 41; **35**. 2. dhātugabbha **30**. 57 ff., 62 ff; **34**. 49. sudhākamma **32**. 1; **33**. 5; **34**. 46. the "tee": caturassacaya **31**. 124; muddhavedī **32**. 5; soṇṇathūpa **100**. 263. vedikā on the tee **34**. 39; **35**. 2. figures of sun and moon on the tee **36**. 66. thūpikā **44**. 133; **76**. 105; **80**. 20; **87**. 66. chatta **33**. 5; **35**. 2; **36**. 24, 65; **38**. 54; **44**. 133. vajiracumbaṭa **36**. 66; **38**. 74; **41**. 95. — Maṇḍapa, provisional pavillon, erected for various purposes: as a chapel **100**. 227; for a sermon **98**. 71 ff.; **100**. 279; in connection with a pāsāda **14**. 47; **27**. 29 ff.; **36**. 99, or with a temple **100**. 185, 217, 243. ratanam° **27**. 29; **37**. 103. silām° **36**. 102. thambhā, chatta and vedikā of a m° **27**. 30 f.; **100**. 226. — f. Ornamentation of the buildings (the object itself or its representation in relief or in fresco-painting): pupphapuṇṇaghaṭā **30**. 90; **32**. 4. strings of pearls **27**. 31; **30**. 66 f., or of bells **27**. 16, 27; **30**. 66; **73**. 68. ratanapadumāni **27**. 34; **30**. 68. — Figures (pantī "rows") of animals **27**. 30, 37; **30**. 65; **100**. 255, or of deities **27**. 30; **30**. 74 ff.; **89** ff., 92, or of sun, moon and stars **27**. 33; **30**. 68; **36**. 66; or of sacred symbols **27**. 37; **30**. 65, 92;

36. 103. agghiyapantī **30**. 92. pañcaṅgulikapantī **32**. 4. — Pupphalatā **30**. 65; **73**. 62; **100**. 244, 255. vijjullatā **30**. 96. rūpalatākamma **98**. 70. — Painted representations of the sixteen sacred places **100**. 253, 261, or of jātakas **30**. 88; **97**. 39–45, or of scenes from the life of the Buddhas **30**. 78 ff.; **100**. 261 ff.

b. Plastic art. Statues of the Buddha **35**. 89; **38**. 65, 86; **39**. 6, 7, 40; **45**. 61; **49**. 14, 44; **51**. 76; **52**. 65; **53**. 49; **78**. 74 f.; **79**. 78; **85**. 10, 66; **88**. 56; **90**. 94; **92**. 14; **98**. 66; **100**. 154, 235, 257. golden or gilded images **30**. 72; **48**. 137; **49**. 77; **50**. 34, 66; **51**. 23, 48 f.; **55**. 20; **61**. 57; **100**. 72, 75, 249. stone images **36**. 104, 128; **37**. 14; **38**. 61; **42**. 18; **44**. 68; **51**. 77; **52**. 12; **53**. 50; **85**. 77; **100**. 181. bronze images **36**. 31; **37**. 31. images made of stucco **100**. 245. — Buddhist iconography **38**. 62–4 with N.; **45**. 61; **52**. 26, 65; **53**. 50; **73**. 78; **98**. 66. — Statues of Metteyya and of other bodhisattas **38**. 68; **45**. 62; **51**. 77; **79**. 75; **100**. 248, 259; of Ānanda, Sāriputta, Moggallāna **39**. 53; **51**. 80; **100**. 248; of Mahinda and of his companions **37**. 68, 79, 87; **38**. 58; of princes **39**. 52; **88**. 57; **100**. 249. — Images of gods **30**. 73 ff.; **86**. 19; **90**. 102; **100**. 248, 259. tivaṅka images **78**. 39; **85**. 66. — Figures of animals **39**. 52; **100**. 252.

c. Graphic art (cf. the notice in a) Paintings on stuff **27**. 18. a picture of the Buddha **85**. 94 ff. — Mural paintings **78**. 35 ff., 40, 52, 88; **90**. 66, 90; **100**. 244, 247 ff., 250 ff., 260 ff.

d. Special arts. Ivory work **37**. 100 ff. — mosaic **51**. 69. — figures moved by mechanism **85**. 15 ff.

VIII. Hindu religion and popular belief

A. Hindu gods (deva **18**. 51; **32**. 63 f.; **51**. 108; **70**. 223; **96**. 39 &c. amara **99**. 107. sura **72**. 322; **100**. 135. — 1. Hindu cult in C. **45**. 55; **48**. 143; **73**. 71; **83**. 49; **90**. 101 f. veda and vedaṅga **5**. 107, 143; **10**. 20; **62**. 33; **64**. 16. the brāhmaṇa caste see VII, 1. brahmanical ceremonies **62**. 33, 45, 52 f. bhatti **74**. 243; **85**. 33, 70, 82, 121; **93**. 9. Hinduism forcibly introduced **80**. 75; **83**. 9 ff. Hindu temples (devālaya, -ṭhāna) **37**. 40; **79**. 19, 22, 81; **88**. 93, 119; **99**. 45. — 2. Groups of gods: tāvatiṃsā, tettiṃsā and their heaven **27**. 18; **30**. 44, 89; **31**. 79. tusita gods and their heaven **32**. 72 ff.; **33**. 13. dvattiṃsā kumāriyo **30**. 89; **31**. 80. brahma gods **18**. 51; **85**. 15; **87**. 11. planetary gods (gaha) **87**. 1. — 3. the three great gods: Brahmā **30**. 74; **74**. 197, 237; **89**. 17 (the brahma world **5**. 139; **19**. 45; **31**. 11). Viṣṇu (nāthasura &c.) **7**. 5; **83**. 49; **85**. 85 ff.; **90**. 102; **97**. 46; **99**. 42; **100**. 248. (Lakkhī **72**. 101. Āsāḷhi festival **85**. 89). Śiva **73**. 91; **74**. 193; **93**. 9 f. (Caṇḍī **73**. 161). — 4. Other gods: Indra (Sakka, Devinda, Vāsava, Sujampati, Pākasāsana, Sahassakkha, Nārāyaṇa, Vajirapāṇi) **15**. 185; **17**. 13; **21**. 31; **28**. 6; **30**. 74; **31**. 34, 78; **37**. 151; **39**. 23; **47**. 25; **51**. 108; **62**. 11; **65**. 19; **72**. 59, 168, 186, 265, 299, 328; **74**. 206; **85**. 12; **96**. 37. his residence, his palace, his hall of justice, his garden **15**. 185; **73**. 70, 87; **74**. 198, 206; **80**. 5; **88**. 121; **89**. 5, 40. his trumpet **30**. 74. his bow **85**. 12. Kuvera (Vessavaṇa) **10**. 89; **27**. 29. his residence Ālakā **37**. 106; **39**. 5; **74**. 207; **80**. 5. his treasures **87**. 31. Skanda **45**. 45, 55; **57**. 7. Vissakamman **18**. 24; **28**. 6 ff.; **30**. 11; **31**. 34, 76; **73**. 69. Pajjunna **21**. 31; **85**. 44 (devo vassati **21**. 32; **36**. 77). Soma **62**. 5; **63**. 14. Bṛhaspati **42**. 3; **52**. 38. Sarasvatī **73**. 86. Yama **72**. 249, 309; **75**. 30. Māra **30**. 75; **31**. 85; **41**, 48; **66**. 99; **74**. 237; **80**. 70; **86**. 9; **88**. 81; **93**. 17; **96**. 42. Namuci **98**. 96. the four lokapālā (mahārājā) **30**. 89; **31**. 79; **72**. 59. minor gods **30**. 75; **31**. 78, 82. — 5. Demigods, nymphs &c. Kandappa **77**. 106. kumbhaṇḍā **12**. 20. gandhabbā **12**. 20; **73**. 163. accharā **25**. 102; **27**. 13. nāgā (bhujagā &c.) and garuḍā (supaṇṇā) **1**. 84; **5**. 28; **12**. 9 ff.; **14**. 40; **19**. 3, 19 ff.; **31**. 19, 27 ff., 46 ff.; **50**. 27; **75**. 38; **83**. 14. Nāga king Aravāla **12**. 9, 15, 19. Kālanāga **5**. 87; **30**. 75; **31**. 27, 46, 83. Mahānāga **41**. 77 ff. Ananta **73**. 120. Nāgas original inhabitants of C. **1**. 45 ff., 63 ff., 71 ff.; **19**. 35. — 6. Demons. asurā **1**. 84; **51**. 39; **72**. 299; **96**. 37; **99**. 63. dānavā **75**. 54. kiṃnarā (-riyo) **5**. 212; **78**. 40. rakkhasā (-siyo) **12**. 45 ff.; **15**. 60; **39**. 34; **54**. 66; **72**. 70; **83**. 46. yakkhā (-iṇiyo) **9**. 23; **10**. 84 f.; **12**. 20 f.; **18**. 52; **19**. 3; **31**. 81; **36**. 82 ff.; **50**. 36; **55**. 21; **99**. 125. y.s in bodily shape **10**. 104; **14**. 7. twenty-eight y.-chiefs **30**. 90; **31**. 81. the y. Kālavela **10**. 84; **37**. 44. y.s original inhabitants of C. **1**. 20 ff.; **7**. 9, 11, 30 ff.; **63**. 12. pretā and bhūtā **10**. 104; **74**. 145. — demons in animal shape **7**. 9; **10**. 53 ff.; **14**. 3, or changing their shape **7**. 26, or producing animal beings **10**. 4. — Rāhu **83**. 42.

B. Popular belief. 1. Spirits, local or tutelar deities (devatā, deva, devaputta, maru) **5**. 27; **8**. 13, 25; **15**. 67, 81, 135, 165; **19**. 19; **20**. 41; **22**. 19, 80; **23**. 10; **27**. 30; **30**. 15, 50, 99; **31**. 56, 83 f., 93; **32**. 63; **37**. 238; **42**. 54; **57**. 32, 38; **70**. 210; **80**. 55; **99**. 112, 133. tree spirits **1**. 52; **5**. 42; **10**. 89. mountain deities **14**. 3 (Sumanadeva **1**. 33; **86**. 19). gnomes **14**. 38. chattamhi devatā **28**. 6. devatās in animal shape **28**. 9. vyādhideva **10**. 89. devapalli **57**. 38. offerings to the d.s (bali) **15**. 67, 135; **36**. 89. — 2. Magic art and witchcraft. Incantations, charms **41**. 80 ff.; **51**. 81; **52**. 80; **57**. 6 ff.; **66**. 138. magic water and thread **7**. 9; **73**. 73. rag-trees **49**. 27. magic remedies **46**. 37. fending of the influence of evil spirits (santi) **85**. 50. — Rainfall effected by charm **37**. 189 ff.; **87**. 1 ff. — Oracle, soothsaying, signs (nimitta) and their interpretation **6**. 2; **8**. 10, 14; **14**. 53; **22**. 46 f., 68; **35**. 66; **39**. 22; **57**. 38 f., 53; **62**. 38 ff.; **66**. 132; **67**. 29 f., 32; **77**. 48; Brahmans as soothsayers **9**. 2. casting lots **95**. 20 ff. — Dreams and their interpretation **62**. 12 ff., 21 ff.; **66**. 47 ff.; **95**. 14 f. — Bodily marks and their interpretation **5**. 45; **22**. 59; **35**. 109; **48**. 114; **57**. 49; **59**. 34 ff.; **62**. 46 ff.; **81**. 68 f.;

87. 62. — Astrology **35**. 71; **57**. 48; **100**. 46, 51. auspicious and inauspicious constellations **19**. 47; **29**. 1; **31**. 109; **62**. 37, 55; **63**. 47; **67**. 31, 62, 91; **70**. 240; **71**. 28; **89**. 39; **96**. 13; **100**. 191.

IX. Buddhism

Buddha, dhamma, saṃgha (vatthuttaya, ratanattaya) **5**. 81; **12**. 28; **13**. 13; **21**. 8; **23**. 13; **26**. 23 f.; **64**. 15; **87**. 43; **90**. 65; **91**. 6, 9, 16; **92**. 27; **97**. 1; **98**. 2; **99**. 11; **100**. 169, 301.

A. Buddha. 1. Bodily and mental qualities of a B. **3**. 1, 6; **5**. 91; **17**. 46; **18**. 22; **54**. 29; **74**. 2; **85**. 54; **99**. 67. former B.s **1**. 5 ff.; **15**. 34 ff.; **27**. 11; **39**. 51. future B.s. **32**. 73; **37**. 242; **38**. 68; **51**. 77 f.; **52**. 47; **80**. 12; **87**. 3; **100**. 237. paccekabuddha **1**. 55; **5**. 50. — 2. Gotama B.: in former existences **42**. 5. his life **1**. 12 ff.; **2**. 22; **3**. 1 ff.; **35**. 31; **51**. 10; **73**. 162; **74**. 3. miracles performed by the B. **17**. 44; **82**. 29; **100**. 272. his visits to C. **1**. 19 ff.; **15**. 160 ff.; **74**. 2. his disciples **3**. 4 ff., 9 ff.; **37**. 176; **39**. 53; **51**. 80; **85**. 78 ff., 107. the five great resolves **17**. 46 ff.; **18**. 22; **82**. 33. titles of the B. **1**. 57; **82**. 17; **85**. 100 f.; **90**. 51.

B. Dhamma. 1. puñña, apuñña; kamma **32**. 22 f.; **37**. 51; **93**. 15, 17; **94**. 21 f.; **95**. 24 et passim. saṃsāra **22**. 34 ff.; **30**. 44; **32**. 21, 81 ff.; **37**. 152; **93**. 11, 14; **100**. 237 &c. three bhavas **4**. 66. gati, agati **37**. 51 N., 108; **80**. 13. patti **42**. 50 N.; **44**. 107; **52**. 69; **100**. 146, 159. — 2. The eightfold path **12**. 42; **84**. 32. compassion with living beings **35**. 6; **49**. 36; **52**. 15, 28; **54**. 32; **60**. 74; **74**. 20 f. — 2. Influence of Mahāyānism (cf. PARANAVITANE, Mahāyānism in Ceylon, C. J. Sc. G. II, p. 35 ff.) **1**. 57; **50**. 65; **80**. 12; **82**. 17; **85**. 119; **86**. 5–7; **87**. 3; **90**. 51. kings as bodhisattas **36**. 90; **88**. 35; **90**. 48; **100**. 136.

C. Samgha passim (cātuddisa s° **32**. 34; **45**. 54; **73**. 155; **79**. 17. gaṇa "chapter" **60**. 17; **89**. 18, 57; = saṃgha **99**. 66, 106). 1. Organisation of the order: pabbajjā, upasampadā (see V, E, 5; M. tr., p. 294, 296) **5**. 129 ff.; **12**. 30 ff.;

14. 31 f.; **37**. 210, 223; **57**. 19; **81**. 49 f.; **84**. 37, 43; **87**. 72; **89**. 47 ff. &c. shaving of the head **5**. 46; **16**. 11. the yellow robe **5**. 229; **14**. 13; **18**. 10. cripples not admitted **57**. 19. pabbajjā of nuns **15**. 19 ff. — pañca sahadhammikā **80**. 66: sāmaṇera **13**. 4; **22**. 25; **31**. 119 &c.; **99**. 25, 89, 169, 173; **100**. 44, 96 f., 238. bhikkhu passim (samaṇa **14**. 8; **26**. 21; **30**. 37; **33**. 93; **66**. 144; **67**. 94; **97**. 14. yati **37**. 175; **53**. 15; **57**. 19; **89**. 58 ff.). — thera, mahāthera **37**. 218; **89**. 64 et passim. ayyaka **45**. 69. yatissara **67**. 61, 80. — bhikkhunī **5**. 198 ff., 208; **19**. 68, 78 ff.; **26**. 15 &c. therī **19**. 65, 77. — nissaya **36**. 112. upajjhāya (antevāsin) **5**. 69, 206, 208. ācariya (sāvaka) **5**. 70, 208. — the bhaṇḍāgārika **89**. 58. — bhikkhus living in villages or in the wilderness **52**. 19, 22; **53**. 14 ff.; **54**. 20; **57**. 32; **84**. 18, 22; **99**. 170. tapodhana, tapassin **53**. 14 ff.; **54**. 20; **89**. 57; **91**. 25. wandering bhikkhus **98**. 15. — retirement from the order **93**. 14 f. occupations not allowed to bh.s **84**. 7; **100**. 45 f. kulasaṃsagga **33**. 95. — exclusion **5**. 270 ff.; **37**. 39; **94**. 22. cremation of dead bh.s **20**. 34 ff., 43 f., 47, 53; **100**. 148. — titles granted to bh.s: sāmin (mahās°, sāsanas° &c.) **52**. 20; **53**. 23; **81**. 76; **86**. 38; **89**. 64. saṃghathera **4**. 56; **37**. 45. saṃgharāja **100**. 69, 108. rājaguru **90**. 81.

2. Necessaries of a bh: catupaccayā **3**. 14; **5**. 196; **22**. 24; **33**. 94; **37**. 76 N.; **51**. 122; **60**. 10, 15, 69; **84**. 16; **89**. 50; **90**. 41; **94**. 20; **97**. 11; **98**. 22; **99**. 26. aṭṭha parikkhārā (sāmaṇakā p°) **4**. 26 N.; **20**. 24; **26**. 21; **30**. 37, 39; **54**. 25; **60**. 71; **84**. 21, 39, 41; **85**. 39; **88**. 52; **89**. 66 f.; **91**. 21, 33; **97**. 8; **99**. 89. ticīvara, chacīvara **33**. 26; **34**. 7, 84; **35**. 77; **36**. 40, 110, 131; **41**. 29; **91**. 23, 33; **100**. 132. patta **14**. 52; **24**. 26 ff.; **35**. 7. parissāvana **35**. 74. dhammakaraka **22**. 68. akkhamālā **46**. 17; **57**. 6.

3. The vihāra. Four vihāras **53**. 37; **54**. 5, 33, 54. aṭṭha mūlavihārā **61**. 59. aṭṭhāyatanāni **84**. 4, 18. assama **72**. 145. bhikkhunupassaya **18**. 11 f.; **20**. 21; **37**. 43 &c. ārāma **10**. 101; **15**. 185; **19**. 41; **24**. 13 (cf. **22**. 23); **29**. 32 &c. — sīmā **14**. 32; **15**. 183 ff.; **78**. 56 ff.; **100**. 129, 287, 291. sīmāsamugghāṭa **37**. 36 f., 56. pākāra **36**. 8, 37; **78**. 51, 91; **100**. 217, 265 &c.

— Component parts of a v. (**49**. 32; **60**. 11 ff.; **78**. 32 ff., 49 ff., 70 ff., 79 ff.; **79**. 13 ff., 62 ff.; **84**. 18 ff.; **85**. 2 f.; **86**. 50 f.; **100**. 240 ff., 282 ff.): mālaka **15**. 29, 36 ff.; **16**. 15; **32**. 58 &c. bodhi tree **34**. 31; **37**. 91; **48**. 5; **49**. 15; **68**. 28; **79**. 16, 62, 72; **85**. 2, 70; **86**. 51; **90**. 99. the bodhi tree of Bo-gaya **15**. 22; **17**. 17, 47 ff.; **18**. 34 f., 42; **19**. 43, 56; **20**. 4 ff.; **37**. 246. the bodhi tree in the Mahāvihāra, Anurādhapura **17**. 30, 40; **18**. 4 ff.; **19**. 1 ff.; **20**. 1; **23**. 28; **28**. 1; **34**. 58 ff.; **36**. 52, 103, 126; **37**. 85; **38**. 55, 57, 67, 69; **41**. 29, 32, 94; **42**. 66; **44**. 45, 65; **48**. 70, 124; **51**. 78; **52**. 11, 24. its eight saplings **19**. 60–2. the b. trees of former Buddhas **15**. 78, 112, 147. — pāsāṇa-vedī, silā-v° round a bodhi tree **36**. 52, 103; **37**. 91; **42**. 19; bodhikoṭṭhaka **79**. 72. dvāratoraṇa **36**. 103, 126. bodhighara **15**. 205; **37**. 15, 31; **38**. 43, 69; **41**. 65; **42**. 19, 66; **48**. 70; **49**. 15. 74; **51**. 54; **53**. 10; **60**. 62; **79**. 72. — thūpa or cetiya (see VII, C, 12, e) **17**. 37 ff.; **26**. 8 ff.; **29**. 1 ff.; **78**. 51 &c. thūpaghara, cetiya° **31**. 60; **35**. 87, 90 f.; **36**. 9, 106; **48**. 66. — Single buildings: dwelling house for the priests (pāsāda, āvāsa &c.) **27**. 9 ff.; **36**. 11; **60**. 11, 57; **78**. 33 ff., 49 ff., 67, 81 f.; **90**. 96; **92**. 11; **100**. 297. guhā, lena **3**. 19; **16**. 12; **20**. 16; **78**. 38, 66, 74 f. pariveṇa **15**. 204, 206 ff.; **35**. 57, 88; **36**. 8, 10; **57**. 20; **78**. 36, 71. relic temple **37**. 15; **46**. 29; **78**. 41; **85**. 75; **90**. 66 ff.; **94**. 14; **97**. 36 ff.; **98**. 25, 35. image house (paṭimāgeha &c.) **35**. 89; **37**, 15, 183; **60**. 83; **68**. 28; **78**. 53 ff., 85 ff.; **85**. 77; **86**. 50; **88**. 56; **90**. 99; **98**. 67; **100**. 295. dhammasālā **78**. 42, 73; **79**. 21; **98**. 78 (dhammāsana, therāsana **3**. 22, 35; **44**. 115; **85**. 46). uposathaghara, -āgāra **15**. 37; **34**. 30; **35**. 85; **36**. 16, 107; **37**. 201; **51**. 70; **78**. 56; **92**. 10; **100**. 93, 287. padhānaghara &c. **36**. 105; **37**. 232; **39**. 58; **42**. 46; **44**. 119; **46**. 11. aggisālā **78**. 43, 51, 71, 86. potthakālaya **78**. 37. dānasālā **37**. 182; **74**. 150. āgantukasālā **79**. 20, 22, 63, 80. bhattasālā, bhojanasālā **15**. 205; **20**. 23; **36**. 12; **78**. 42 (bhattanāvā **37**. 181 N.; **42**. 67). salākagga **15**. 205; **36**. 74; **49**. 32. caṅkamana **15**. 208; **78**. 42. nahānakoṭṭhaka **78**. 45 f., 83. vaccakuṭi **78**. 43, 50, 86. — Servants and officials in a v. (ārāmika &c.) **37**. 63, 173; **46**. 14, 28; **52**. 26; **57**. 21; **78**. 4 N.; **88**. 58; **97**. 55; **98**. 27; **100**. 218. dāsā **46**. 10, 20; **80**. 36, 40; **100**. 11.

4. Duties of the bhikkhus, vihāra-life. Dasasīlaṃ **18.** 10. — Scholarly studies **90.** 80; **100.** 178. tepiṭaka **5.** 84, 275; **27.** 44; **78.** 7. — Performing of ecclesiastical acts: dhammakamma **39.** 57 (cf. VI, E, 5); kammavācā **5.** 207. — Recitation of sacred texts **3.** 33, 36; **41.** 58 f. gaṇasajjhāya **31.** 86; **32.** 11, 63; **34.** 49. preaching of the doctrine (dhammadāna **98.** 77 ff.; **99.** 15, 24): dhammadesanā, -desaka, -kathika &c. **14.** 22, 58; **15.** 4 &c.; **32.** 45; **35.** 92; **60.** 20; **85.** 46 f.; **98.** 73, 79; **99.** 18 f., 170; **100.** 275 (maṇḍapas erected for the preachers **98.** 72; **99.** 16. seats prepared for the pr.s **4.** 51; **99.** 18. fans in the hands of the pr.s **85.** 46; **98.** 73). — kulūpaka, -ga **30.** 40; **56.** 116. — Ceremonies performed by the bh.s: vassa, antovassa **1.** 14; **3.** 15; **16.** 8; **17.** 1; **18.** 2; **100.** 131. uposatha **5.** 235, 273; **13.** 14, 18; **29.** 63; **32.** 41; **35.** 76; **36.** 16; **51.** 83; **53.** 29; **74.** 20; **100.** 131 (pāṭihariyapakkha **37.** 202) (cf. IX, C, 3: uposathaghara). pavāraṇā **5.** 235, 280; **17.** 1; **20.** 24; **34.** 62; **37.** 90; **100.** 132. kaṭhina **44.** 48; **85.** 99 ff.; **86.** 46 ff.; **91.** 34; **100.** 132. paritta **46.** 5; **51.** 80; **52.** 80; **62.** 31; **87.** 5; **99.** 26. — Ceremonies performed in buildings erected in water (udakukkhepasīmā) **78.** 28 ff.; **87.** 71; **89.** 47, 70; **94.** 17; **97.** 12. — Higher attainments. upanissaya (marks of future holiness) **5.** 45, 172, 194. padhāna **36.** 105; **42.** 46 (cf. IX, C, 3: padhānaghara). kammaṭṭhāna **5.** 148. meditation, trance (jhāna) **5.** 123, 220; **15.** 209; **23.** 63; **35.** 104; **88.** 55. vipassanā, -ssaka **5.** 152; **19.** 16; **99.** 170; **100.** 174. — The path of salvation (sotāpatti &c.) **13.** 17; **15.** 18; **23.** 61; **27.** 44; **29.** 68; **31.** 101. anāsava, khīṇāsava **5.** 112; **20.** 54 f.; **28.** 24; **29.** 6. arahant, -hatta **1.** 14; **5.** 46, 172, 214; **14.** 14, 33; **16.** 11, 17; **19.** 46, 65 f.; **23.** 63; **25.** 104; **26.** 5; **29.** 68 f.; **31.** 95, 100; **84.** 25; **86.** 13. tādin **34.** 49. iddhi **1.** 37; **5.** 174; **12.** 15; **13.** 19; **14.** 14; **30.** 99; **32.** 15. abhiññā **4.** 12; **5.** 152, 275; **13.** 4; **14.** 14; **22.** 34; **52.** 38. — Theras as soothsayers **15.** 169 ff. miracles performed by th.s **5.** 258 ff.; **12.** 10 f., 49 f.; **13.** 19; **14.** 35; **15.** 38 ff.; **31.** 85; **32.** 15. nirvana of th.s **5.** 219, 226 f.; **20.** 33.

5. Cult. Inauguration of a monastic building **26.** 14 ff.; **36.** 130. music and dance at festival occasions **5.** 181; **34.** 60.

Vesākha-festival **1**. 12; **32**. 35; **34**. 59; **35**. 100; **36**. 40, 109, 130; **44**. 46; **51**. 84. āsāḷha-festival **99**. 53. abhiseka (nettapūjā, nettamaha, akkhipūjā) **5**. 94; **38**. 58: **39**. 7; **100**. 187, 191, 204 f., 235, 267. Cf. EZ. II, p. 254. — traces of a temple ritual: the Buddha-image or a relic of the B. is treated as the living master (buddhupaṭṭhāna **34**. 61) **38**. 64; **52**. 26; **53**. 30; **78**. 35; **90**. 77 ff.; **97**. 33; **100**. 182. — Relic-cult (sārīrikā dhātuyo **17**. 12; **80**. 69; **99**. 58. paribhogikā dh. **55**. 17; **82**. 18, 34): dāṭhādhātu **17**. 14; **37**. 92 ff.; **38**. 8, 70 f.; **42**. 33; **44**. 45; **51**. 22; **54**. 5, 45; **57**. 22; **60**. 16; **61**. 56, 61; **64**. 30; **70**. 266, 310; **72**. 304; **73**. 128; **74**. 38, 84, 88, 103, 126, 142, 147, 165, 167, 183 ff., 193, 198 ff., 226, 246; **81**. 17 ff., 26 ff., 33 f., 77; **82**. 6 ff., 40 ff.; **84**. 13; **85**. 25, 33, 92, 111; **86**. 54 ff.; **87**. 5, 69, 74; **88**. 10, 15, 65; **89**. 16–46; **90**. 41, 46 f., 54 f., 67, 72, 77; **91**. 12, 19; **92**. 9; **94**. 11 ff.; **95**. 2, 9 ff., 21; **97**. 4 ff., 25, 52; **98**. 8, 25, 37 ff., 94; **99**. 58, 63, 68, 86, 105, 123, 141, 143 ff., 166; **100**. 1 ff., 12, 22 ff., 40 ff., 124 (an image of the d. **100**. 153, 157). pattadhātu **17**. 12; **20**. 13; **33**. 48, 55; **37**. 192; **61**. 56, 61; **64**. 30; **70**. 266, 310; **72**. 304; **74**. 38, 84, 88, 103, 126, 142, 147, 165, 167, 188 ff., 210, 226; **81**. 17 ff., 77; **85**. 25, 33; **87**. 69, 74; **88**. 10, 66; **89**. 16–46; **90**. 72. dakkhiṇakkhakadhātu **17**. 14, 20, 24, 37 ff., 50; **37**. 207 N.; **42**. 53 ff.; **64**. 30. kesadhātu **39**. 49 ff.; **44**. 45; **50**. 71; **54**. 41; **64**. 30. gīvaṭṭhidhātu **20**. 19; **64**. 30. — the relics of the Mahāthūpa **17**. 51; **31**. 16 ff., 45 ff. relics of theras **20**. 44; **85**. 80. — Miracles performed by relics **17**. 25 ff., 43, 51 f.; **31**. 97 ff.; **82**. 41 ff. — Reliquaries (caṅgoṭa, karaṇḍaka) **31**. 77, 87 f.; **50**. 71; **76**. 115; **85**. 27; **89**. 21; **90**. 72; **91**. 18 f.; **92**. 14; **97**. 6, 53 f.; **98**. 27 ff., 94; **99**. 160, 165; **100**. 13 ff. — Relic feasts **88**. 16; **90**. 41, 57, 75; **95**. 2; **97**. 25; **99**. 68; **100**. 8 &c.

6. History of the Saṃgha. The three councils **3**. 5 ff.; **4**. 9 ff.; **5**. 228 ff. Buddhist sects **5**. 1 ff. (cf. M. tr., p. 276 ff.). theravāda, ācariyavāda **5**. 2; **37**. 227; **52**. 46; **54**. 46 f. &c. vibhajjavāda **5**. 271 f. mahāsaṃghikā **5**. 4; **59**. 68. — Schisms in C. **33**. 95 ff.; **37**. 2 ff. — church-reforms see VI, E, 5. — tayo nikāyā **41**. 97 and N.; **44**. 131; **45**. 16; **46**. 16; **48**. 73; **51**. 14,

64, 133; **52**. 10, 12, 35, 80; **54**. 4, 27; **55**. 20; **60**. 10, 13, 56; **70**. 181, 328; **73**. 5, 12, 20; **76**. 74; **78**. 5, 10. dve nikāyā **46**. 15. dhammārucikā **5**. 13; **38**. 75; **52**. 17 f. vetullavāda **36**. 41, 111; **42**. 35; **78**. 22. sāgalikā **5**. 13; **39**. 41; **42**. 43; **52**. 7. dhammadhātu **41**. 37–40. sassataditthi **5**. 269. ubhayasāsana (= hīna- and mahāyāna) **84**. 10 (cf. IX, B, 2). — Ascetic groups of bh.s in C: paṃsukūlino **47**. 66; **48**. 4; **49**. 80; **50**. 63, 76; **51**. 52; **52**. 21, 27; **53**. 25, 48; **54**. 18, 24, 25; **61**. 59. lābhavāsino **54**. 27; **60**. 68, 72. vantajīvakā **60**. 69. tapovanavāsino **41**. 99 N.; **52**. 22; **53**. 14 ff.; **54**. 20. — Bhikkhus in the Cola and Paṇḍu country **36**. 112 ff.; **89**. 67; **90**. 80. foreign bh.s fetched to C. **60**. 5 f.; **84**. 9, 11 ff.; **94**. 15; **97**. 10; **98**. 89 ff.; **100**. 58 ff., 122 ff. — Persecution of the order by Rājasīha I. **93**. 10 ff.; **100**. 220 ff. by the Paraṅgis **95**. 7 ff. by the Olandas **99**. 112 ff., 125. — Non-buddhist sects: titthiyā **5**. 74. jaṭilā **1**. 16. nigaṇṭhā **10**. 97 ff.; **33**. 43, 79; **39**. 20. paribbājakā **7**. 6; **8**. 11; **10**. 101. tāpasā **7**. 11; **66**. 135 f. ājīvakā **10**. 102.

7. The laity (upāsaka, -sikā **89**. 30). ariyā: puthujjanā **5**. 113. conversions **1**. 32, 33; **12**. 19 ff., 27 ff.; **14**. 23, 40, 58, 64; **19**. 46. saraṇa, sīla **1**. 32, 62; **14**. 23, 40; **22**. 69; **25**. 110; **35**. 75; **36**. 73; **54**. 29; **98**. 13; **100**. 280. uposatha vows **17**. 6; **35**. 76; **37**. 202 f.; **39**. 18; **48**. 10; **60**. 21; **97**. 19; **98**. 13; **100**. 131. padakkhiṇaṃ kar **18**. 36; **29**. 48; **31**. 94; **37**. 196; **72**. 328. — Sacrificial offerings to the community or to a sanctuary: pūjā, dāna **17**. 62; **32**. 35; **34**. 57, 59; **35**. 74 f.; **44**. 46; **54**. 37, 39; **64**. 15; **70**. 193 ff.; **85**. 26, 70, 112–6; **89**. 19 ff.; **90**. 73 ff.; **97**. 29 ff.; **98**. 52 ff., 58 ff., 76; **100**. 211, 225 &c. pūjopakaraṇāni **70**. 193 f., 198; **98**. 93 (saṅkha **70**. 194; **100**. 190. pañcaturiyāni **70**. 194; **98**. 54; **100**. 7, 33, 190. setacchatta &c. **70**. 194; **98**. 52; **99**. 55; **100**. 31, 193. dhajapatākā **70**. 194; **99**. 57; **100**. 187. puṇṇaghaṭā **29**. 48; **30**. 90; **32**. 4; **98**. 36; **100**. 188. Cf. also VI, C, 9). pūjāvatthūni **97**. 33; **98**. 54, 75; **99**. 22, 56; **100**. 124, 146, 197, 205 f. (food, garments, carpets &c. **30**. 36 f.; **31**. 113; **32**. 35, 39; **33**. 72; **34**. 62; **35**. 77 ff., 92 ff.; **36**. 100, 131; **51**. 61; **85**. 116; **90**. 73; **92**. 27; **97**. 29; **98**. 10 f., 15; **99**. 26; **100**. 10, 195, 205 &c.

Cf. catupaccayā, aṭṭhaparikkhārā, ticīvara, chacīvara in IX, C, 2; kaṭhina in **IX**, C, 4. salākabhatta (cf. salākagga IX, C, 3); **27**. 11; **34**. 64; **48**. 73. — medicaments **22**. 30, 37; **60**. 70; **98**. 10; **100**. 3, 196. — flowers, perfumes, incense **15**. 27 f.; **22**. 30, 37; **30**. 27; **85**. 70, 83; **90**. 73; **92**. 16; **97**. 29; **98**. 8 ff., 64, 75; **99**. 56; **100**. 3, 33, 197. — valuables, gold, jewels &c. **17**. 62; **36**. 125 f.; **61**. 56; **85**. 121; **97**. 28; **98**. 11, 33, 53; **99**. 37; **100**. 9, 31 f. — elephants, horses, cattle, buffalos **90**. 76; **92**. 29; **98**. 33; **99**. 37; **100**. 42. — slaves, male and female **46**. 10, 20; **80**. 36, 40; **90**. 76; **100**. 11. — lamps and oil **32**. 41; **92**. 16 f.; **98**. 75; **100**. 33. lamp-feasts, illuminations **32**. 37; **35**. 79; **76**. 119; **85**. 40 f., 70 f., 84, 116; **86**. 31; **98**. 60 ff., 84). — Festival processions in honour of a sanctuary see VII, C, 10. Covering of a thūpa with costly stuffs **33**. 10 f.; **34**. 42, 46 ff., 74; **44**. 44; **54**. 37, 42. — Donations of land, tanks and fields **34**. **63**; **35**. 83, 117 f., 120; **36**. 3; **85**. 120 f.; **88**. 52; **90**. 76 &c. maintenance villages (bhogagāma) **46**. 14 f.; **49**. 21, 26 ff.; **52**. 46; **53**. 31; **60**. 66 ff., 72 f.; **61**. 54; **84**. 3 ff.; **85**. 58; **90**. 87, 97 &c. — Ceremonies connected with donations **15**. 25; **26**. 18; **27**. 46. — Pilgrimages **66**. 136; **80**. 24; **85**. 118; **86**. 1, 9 ff.; **88**. 48; **92**. 15–8; **97**. 16, 27 ff.; **99**. 36 ff.; **100**. 125 ff. the sixteen sacred places in C. **1**. 77 ff.; **100**. 128, 253. the sacred foot-print on the summit of the Samanakūṭa **1**. 77; **60**. 64; **85**. 118 ff.; **86**. 10, 28 ff.; **88**. 48; **97**. 18; **98**. 84; **100**. 221 ff. the same in Siam **100**. 160, 253.

Additions and Corrections

I. Mahāvaṃsa ed.

2. 11. Put; after Okkākā, and read pavuttā instead of paputtā.

4. 30 d. Read: taṃpakkhagābhiṃ.

5. 169. Put comma insteed of full stop at the end of the verse.

5. 170. Read: tassa tassa and put full stop after nāmato. Pāda c begins Yācitvā.

19. 3 c. Read: seṇīnaṃ.

19. 70 d. Read: vidū.

23. 11 c. Read: sahoḍhaṃ.

33. 8 c. Read: Velaṅgaviṭṭhikaṃ.

35. 11 a. Read: sahoḍhe.

35. 13 a. Read: Goṇakanadītīre.

35. 113 a. Read: Goṇanadiyā.

36. 7 c. Read: Ratanapāsādaṃ (proper noun).

37. 45 b. Expunge the comma after so.

p. **337**, col. 2, line 30. Read Kukkuṭārāmo, a monastery in I. 5. 122; in C. **37.** 15.

p. **339**, col. 2, line 10. Add Goṇakanadī **35.** 13, 113.

p. **344**, col. 1, line 29. Add **14. 44** after Paṭhamo thūpo.

p. **349**, col. 1, line 20. Add Ratanapāsādo, a building in A. 36. 7.

p. **350**, col. 1, line 25. Add Vattaniya, a monastery in I. **29.** 40.

p. **350**, col. 1, line 44. Read: a monastery in I. (instead of C.).

p. **353**, col. 2. Expunge the last article Honakanadī.

p. **356**, line 19. Read: sahoḍhaṃ gaṇhāti cf. skr. sahoḍha.

II. Cūlavaṃsa ed. I

37. 79. Put the whole verse between marks of suspension. It is a parenthesis.

37. 103. Put: after ratanamaṇḍapaṃ.

37. 114 d. Read: »nāgo rogīti nicchayaṃ.«

37. 202 a b. We have probably to read: cātuddasiṃ pañcadasiṃ yā ca pakkhassa aṭṭhamī.

37. 206 b. Read: coraṃ rattiyaṃ, uggate &c.

38. 3 b. Read: chattagāhakajantuno.

38. 29 c d. Read: cuto, putto Parindo pi, tatiye tassa bhātuko &c.

38. 60 d. Read: attanā instead of attano.

38. 65. I propose to read: Akāsi paṭimāgehe Bahumaṅgalacetiye | bodhisatte ca, tatthāpi Kālaselassa satthuno &c.

38. 77 b. Read: kaṃsalohajaṃ.

38. 79 c d. Read: ko hi nāma samattho? ti mukhamattaṃ nidassitaṃ.

38. 88 c. Read: rājakule.

41. 82 c d. Read: gahetvā khipi; tīh' evaṃ aṅgulīhi sa taṃ chupi.

41. 89 b. Expunge the comma after vasaṃ.

41. 96 b. Read: Uttare instead of uttare.

44. 51 b. Add the note: °vihārakaṃ all MSS. and Ed.

44. 56 b. Read Janapadaṃ (it is proper noun).

44. 90 b. Read: sakkā hantuṃ ti dārakaṃ«.

44. 123 c. Read: 'parajjhitvā.

47. 66. Read p. 89[2]: tatth' eva.

48. 20 d. We have probably to read: pubbavuttito instead of -no.

49. 17 d—18. Read: paṭimāyo ca kārayi || pāsāde cetiye c' eva &c. with full stop after anappake.

49. 78 d. Expunge the full stop after avalokiya.

49. 81 b. Expunge the comma after sādhukaṃ.

50. 34 a b. Read: Pāsāde Ratane sabbasovaṇṇaṃ satthubimbakaṃ.

50. 48 d. Read: 'samo instead of samo.

51. 88 d. Read: Kuṭṭhaka° instead of Tuṭṭhaka°.
54. 57 a. Read: taṃ rājaṃ.
56. 6 c. Read: Devanagaraṃ (it is proper noun).
59. 2 a. Read: »Abhisekamaṅgalatthaṃ pāsādādiṃ &c.
59. 49 b. Read: Sundarivhaṃ.
61. 4 d. Read: 'khilā instead of khilā.
61. 36 a. We have probably to read: Ariyadesīso.
61. 51 c, Note. Read: thā instead of ṭhā.
61. 53 d. Read: 'khīṇatosā instead of khīṇa°.
65. 6 c. Read: Paṭiladdha°.
66. 26 c. Read: kumāraṃ.
66. 56 a. Perhaps we should read: Nānāhassarasaññussa.
66. 59 d. I propose to read ten' ato instead of te tato.
66. 80 d. Read: Ranamburaṃ.
66. 143 a. Read: °opāya° instead of °opaya°.
70. 54 a. Read: Rājaraṭṭhaṃ (it is proper noun).
70. 98 d. Read: Ambavanaṃ instead of Ambu°.
70. 103 a. Read: Janapadaṃ.
70. 112 d. Read: gaṅgāpasse instead of Gaṅgā°.
70. 120 a. Read: gaṅgājalaṃ instead of Gaṅgā°.
70. 181 c. Read: vasī karitasaṃdhāno.
72. 58 a. Read: Ārakkha° instead of ārakkha°.
72. 106 d. Expunge »« before and after sāvadhāranaṃ.
72. 121-2. Put: at the end of v. 121 and » before Billavhayamhi.
72. 127 b. Expunge » before sakalārātivāhinī.
72. 170 d. Read: Kālavāpiyaṃ.

III. Cūlavaṃsa ed. II

Introd. p. III, l. 6. Read: anxious.
73. 96 cd. Read: nayanā nandanādaṃ.
73. 145 d. Expunge the comma after natthitaṃ.
74. 46 a. Read: Rājaraṭṭhaṃ.
74. 64 d. Read: na dassāmāti sabbathā« &c.
74. 149 c. Expunge » before yasmiṃ.
74. 150 c. Put » before cātuddisikadīnānaṃ.

74. 206 d. Read: maggāmaggavicakkhaṇo.
75. 24 b. Read: yuddhakilantakaṃ.
76. 124 c. Read: So Kañcakuḍiya°.
76. 130 a. Read: So Kañcakuḍiya°.
76. 157 a. Read: Damiḷe neke.
76. 190 b. Read: °pperūmāḷaṃ.
76. 192–3. Read: vissutaṃ ‖ etth' antare &c.
76. 223 a. Read: °pperūmāḷo.
76. 232 a. Read: °pperūmāḷe.
76. 316 a. Read: Vīrapperayaraṃ.
77. 52 b. Read: jhāpetvā.
78. 38 d. Put; at the end of the verse.
78. 39 b. Expunge; after akkhirasāyanaṃ.
80. 33 d. Read: Sarājakulavaḍḍhano.
80. 37 c. Read: Khandhāvara°.
80. 39 b. Read: Sarājakulavaḍḍhanaṃ.
82. 37 a b. Read: passanto › bhagavā ñāṇacakkhunā tesu maṃ pi ca &c.
85. 56 a. Read: mahāvihāraṃ, not Mahā°.
86. 17 d. Read: taṃtaṃpuññakriyāsu.
86. 18 b. Read: Gaṅgāsiripuraṃ.
88. 22 b. Read: dakkhiṇasmiṃ disantare.
90. 82 b. Expunge the comma after tadanantaraṃ.
91. 24 d. Read: Sunettapariveṇakaṃ.
91. 25 c d. Put comma after pūjetvā and expunge it after tapassinaṃ.
93. 7 a. Read: tassa dhammaṃ instead of tass' adhammaṃ.
97. 18 a. Read: °kūṭācala°.
98. 61 a. Expunge « after karontū and insert it after ekāhe va.
98. 95 d. Expunge the full stop after ṭhito.
99. 29 d. Expunge the comma after so.
99. 80 d. Read: yāv' etarahi.
99. 89 d. Read: parikkhārāni.
99. 107 b. Read: Laṅkaṃ.
100. 15 d. Put comma after narādhipo.
100. 16 b. Expunge the comma after varaṃ.

100. 44 a. Insert; after so.

101. 14 c. Read: saṃmānesi.

p. **601**, col. 1, ult. Read: **73**. 62, 114; **78**. 77; **89**. 45.

p. **609**, col. 2, Devanagara. Add: **56**. 6.

p. **612**, col. 1, line 29. Add: Pajjunna, the Hindu rain-god **85**. 44.

p. **612**, col. 2, line 13. Add: Paṇḍiyāṇḍāra, a D. chief **76**. 173.

p. **613**, col. 2, line 12. Expunge 18 and insert **88**. 18 on the following line after **87**. 16.

p. **620**, col. 1, Mahāvālukagaṅgā. Add: **78**. 28.

p. **623**, col. 2, line 4 from below: Ratanāvalicetiya. Add: **80**. 20; a thūpa in Khīragāma **79**. 71.

p. **624**, col. 1. Expunge the article Rājakulavaḍḍhana.

p. **624**, col. 1, Rājaraṭṭha. Add: **74**. 46.

p. **630**, col. 1. After Sarassatīmaṇḍapa insert the article Sarājakulavaḍḍhana, a pariveṇa built by Āyasmanta **80**. 39 (cf. **80**. 33).

p. **632**, col. 2. Add after Sudhammā the article: Sunetrapariveṇa, a monastic building erected by Parakkamabāhu VI. **91**. 24.

p. **632**, col. 2. Expunge the article Sunārī and add after Sundarapabbata: Sundarī, a Kāliṅga princess **59**. 49.

p. **642**, line 31. Add: **tithimā*, s. m., the moon **95**. 17. — Cf. skr. *tithipraṇī*.

p. **644**, line 4. Add: +*dhani*, s. m. sound, noise **99**. 60. — skr. *dhvani*, Ch., Abhp. 128.

p. **650**, line 19. Add: **rakkhin*, adj., protecting, guarding; *saddhamma*° **100**. 248. — skr. *rakṣin*.

p. **652**, line 5. Add: +*vipphuliṅga*, s. n. a spark of fire **72**. 84; **75**. 110; **95**. 14. — skr. *visphuliṅga*, Ch., Abhp. 35.

p. **654**, line 27. Add: **sāhicca*, s. n. art of poetry **82**. 3. — skr. *sāhitya*.

p. **657**. To make agree this list of kings with that in C. tr. II, Introduction expunge the separate numbers 90 and 92 of Līlāvatī's second and third reign, and then read 90 instead of 91, and 91, 92, 93 &c. up to 125 instead of 93, 94 &c. up to 127.

IV. Mahāvaṃsa, tr.

Introd. p. XXXVI ff. WICKREMASINGHE's Chronological Table of Ceylon kings in EZ. III, p. 4 ff. differs somewhat from my list of kings. As nr. 5 he adds after Paṇḍukābhaya the name of Gaṇatissa which does not occur in the Mhvs., and therefore nrs. 6–28 in W.'s list correspond to 5–27 of my list. Instead of nrs. 28–32 WICKR. has only nr. 29 Anulā, omitting the names of the paramours of this queen. Nrs. 30–58 correspond to 33–61 of my list. In Cūlavaṃsa trsl. II, Introduction I accepted WICKR.'s table.

2. 11. Translate the verse thus: and sixteen even unto Okkāka. These (kings) who are mentioned in groups reigned in due order, each one in his capital — and add the note: We must with the Ṭīkā read *pavuttā* instead of *paputtā*.

5. 69. The note 4 on page 31 is indeed misleading (WICKREMASINGHE EZ. II, p. 276). Read thus: *Upajjhāyassa*. Every novice on his entrance into the order chooses an *upajjhāya* "spiritual preceptor" and an *ācariya* "teacher". The former instructs him in the rules of the monkish life, the latter in the study of the holy scriptures. In his relation to the upajjhāya the novice is called *saddhivihārika*, and *antevāsika* in his relation to the ācariya.

5. 139. Read: after it had been perfumed, instead of for better care thereof.

7. 43. Page 58, note 3 read Malvatu-oya inst. of Malvaṭṭe-oya.

9. 23. Read Citta instead of Cittā.

10. 53. The note 1 on page 72 is wrong. Read thus: According to v. 62 foll. not far from the Kacchakatittha (see note to v. 58), on the right bank of the Mahaveliganga. The Dhūmarakkhapabbata is also mentioned Mah. 37. 213. It is identical with the Dimbulāgala (anciently Udumbaragiri, cf. Cūlav. tr. II, p. 102, note to 78. 5), the so-called "Gunner's Quoin". H. STOREY, Ceylon Antiquary and Literary Register III, p. 229).

10. 90. To Yonas add the note: See E. R. AYRTON, Ceylon Notes and Queries I, Oct. 1913, p. VIII.

11. 10 ff. As to *yaṭṭhi* Professor N. Law (letter of 3 rd April 1930) calls my attention to skr. *yaṣṭi* in the meaning "necklace", occurring in the Kauṭalīya Arthaśāstra 2. 11. 29 (p. 76 of Shama Sastry's edition). Accordingly we should translate thus:

(10) At the foot of the Chāta mountain there appeared[1]) three cane-like necklaces of the size of a chariot whip. (11) Of them one was a creeper-necklace of bright silver: on this might be seen brilliant delightful creepers of golden colour[2]). (12) One was a flower-necklace[3]): on this again might be seen flowers of many kinds, of manifold colours, in full bloom. (13) At last, one was a bird-necklace[4]) whereon might be seen numbers of birds and beasts of various colours, as if they were living.

Notes: [1]) P. *jata*. — [2]) Perhaps *suvaṇṇapaṇṇā* "with golden leaves". — [3]) P. *kusumayaṭṭhi*, commonly called *puṣpahāra*, a string made of golden flowers. — [4]) I. e. a necklace formed by a string of birds made of gold and other precious metals. Cf. also the description of the various necklaces in the Kauṭalīya 1. 1.

11. 22. Here we should translate: Those three kinds of precious stones and the three chariot-like[1]) necklaces &c. — with Note [1]): Refers to *rathapatodena samānā parimāṇato* in v. 10.

11. 26. Read: the rank of general, instead of the rank of staff-bearer — and add the note: In *daṇḍanāyaka* the word *daṇḍa* means "army", and *nāyaka* "leader". Cf. Cūlav. tr. I, p. XXVI.

15. 4 (p. 96, N. 2). The note should run thus: I. e. "the discourse of the fool and the wise man" = Majjhima, Nr. 129 (III. 163).

15. 38 (p. 100, l. 12). Read mango-fruit instead of mango-tree.

17. 31 (p. 118, l. 25–6). Read: was covered with kadamba-puppha- and ādāri-creepers — and add in note 3 after This creeper: (skr. *kadambapuṣpā*; the name seems to prove that the flowers of this creeper remind those of the kadamba-tree).

19. 73, 75 (p. 134, l. 11 and 17). Read Kadambapuppha-thicket.

22. 7. Expungê in note 3 the words: Tradition seems &c., and add: Cf. on Yatahalena H. C. P. Bell, Kégalla-District, p. 35–6.

24. 22 (p. 165, N. 5). The note should run thus: According to local tradition the battle took place near Yudagannava 1½ miles NNW. of Buttala. The spot is marked by a thūpa (now in ruins).

24. 39. To came to a vihāra (p. 167, l. 18) add the note: According to popular tradition this vihāra was that of Okkampitiya, about five miles East of Buttala.

25. 48 (p. 173, l. 28). Read: surrounded by a kadambapuppha-thicket.

25. 99 (p. 177, l. 16). Read: sitting on the throne, instead of in the royal chamber.

30. 84 (p. 206, note 2). Add: Cf. Suttanipāta 976 foll.

32. 40 (p. 224, N. 2). *Jāla-pūva* means "net-cake". I was told in Ceylon that even now cakes of a peculiar shape are prepared there for which such a denomination would be befitting.

33. 43 (p. 232, l. 6) Read: 'The great black Sīhala is fleeing'.

33. 85 (p. 235, l. 22). Read: concealed herself in a kadamba-puppha-thicket.

35. 104 (p. 254, l. 6). Read: in a kadambapuppha-thicket.

35. 116 (p. 255, l. 2). Read: on the place of the kadamba-puppha-thicket.

36. 6. Add to note 1, p. 256: In Sinhalese inscriptions he is called Maḷu Tissa. See H. C. P. Bell, ASC. 1896, p. 47–8.

p. **274**, l. 12. Read: Sum. I, p. 258 ff.

p. **288**, l. 12. Read: south-east of Anurādhapura, instead of south-west of A.

p. **289**, l. 31—290, l. 2. (See above note on 10. 53). The passage should be corrected thus: Its position is shown clearly by Mah. 10. 53, 57, 58. We must look for it on the right bank of the Mahaveliganga, not far from the Kacchaka-ford. It is the Dimbulāgala rook, the so-called "Gunner's Quoin", as Mr. H. Storey has shown.

V. Cūlavaṃsa, tr. I

Introd. p. XXII, l. 7. To *bhāgineyya* add the note: Mr. A. M. Hocart, C. J. Sc. II, p. 34, refers to the part played by the sister's son in Ancient Germany, according to Tacitus, Germania 20: Sororum filiis idem apud avunculum qui apud patrem honor. Quidam sanctiorem artioremque hunc nexum sanguinis arbitrantur. "The sister's son is in as great honour with the uncle as with the father. Some consider this tie of blood more sacred and closer."

Introd. p. XXV, line 9. Add the note: The inscriptions of King Nissaṅka Malla's "Council Chamber" in Polonnaruva supply us with useful information as to the highest officials and the constituent members of the royal council at the time of that king. At the king's right hand there sat 1) the *mahādipāda* (p. XVIII), 2) the *ādipādas* (p. XVI), 3) the *senāpati* (p. XXVI), 4) the *adhikārins* (p. XXV), 5) the Chief secretary (*mahālekha*, p. XXVIII); — and on his left side 1) the Governors of the provinces (*maṇḍalika*, p. XXV f.), 2) the eighty-four chiefs of smaller districts (*sāmanta*, p. XXV), 3) the heads of the merchants (*seṭṭhin*). The number 84 exactly corresponds to the 84 *sāmanta* appointed by Parakkamabāhu in Dakkhiṇadesa (Mhvs. 69. 16). See H. W. Codrington, JRAS. C. Br. XXIX, Nr. 77, 1924, p. 304 ff.; the same, HC. p. 68.

37. 175 (p. 16, N. 5). The identification of Mahādhammakathin with *Ta-mo-kiu-ti* is doubtful as *-kiu-ti* would correspond to a *-gutta* rather than to a *-kathiṇ*.

P. 17, 18, 19, 20 top. Read Upatissa I. instead of Upatissa II.

37. 213 (p. 22, N. 4). Read: right bank, instead of left bank.

38. 68 (p. 36, N. 4). Add at the end of the note: It is however probable that in the Mahāvaṃsa not the Buddhist *yojana*, but the common Indian *yojana* is meant which has the double length. See Parker, Ancient Ceylon, p. 255 f.

P. 52, top. Read Upatissa II. instead of Upatissa III.

41. 89 (p. 60, N. 5). Add at the end of the note: But we may also take *vasaṃ* as part. pres. and assume that the sentence extends to v. 92 with *pāhesi* as finite verb.

42. 67 (p. 73, N. 2). Add in the note: Cf. note to 70. 286 and 312.

48. 66 (p. 116, N. 4). Add in line 8 of the note after °*gehāni*: (Cf. C. J. Sc. G. I, p. 145 ff.).

56. 6. The translation should run thus: he thought it not the time to carry on war and came suddenly into the company of the gods when he just had visited (the town of) Devanagara.

59. 7. The translation is not precise enough. It should run thus: After the wise (prince), that best of men, had held the position of a yuvarāja seventeen years he caused (this number of years) to be written down (in the annals). — Add the note: *Sattarasavassāni* refers as adverbiale to *yuvarājapadaṃ sito santo* and is at the same time object of *likhāpayi*.

60. 64 (p. 220, N. 2). On line 13 of the note read thus: The Jambukola-vihāra is the monastery erected by Devānampiyatissa at the landing place Jambukola (Mhvs. 20. 25) and Jambukolalena the Dambul monastery 26 miles N. of Matale with its celebrated rock temple.

VI. Cūlavaṃsa, tr. II

74. 151. My translation of the verse is wrong. It is based on a reading cātuddisikaādīnaṃ, but the cātuddisikadīnānaṃ of the MSS. is quite correct and we must translate: "Collect for the poor (bhikkhus) from the four regions of the heavens a plentiful gift of alms."

81. 67 (p. 141, l. 17). Read: after that, instead of for that.